Constitutional challenge:
1) ND Doctrine
2) Legislative Veto
3) Appointment & Removal
4) Separation of Powers

Statute

Judication

mal ~ APA §§ 554-57

aration of Functions
hibition of Ex Parte
ontacts
mpartial Decision making
ndings & Reasons

Agency
Action

Informal: Statute
rules & Procedure
Due Process:
① Liberty or Property
Interest?
② Process due?

Rule Making

Formal
APA § 554-57

Informal
§ 553 of APA

Hybrid
⇓
Statute

Unless:

Rulemaking

Judicial Review → Limits

1) Procedural Defects
2) Contrary to Law
3) Arbitrary & capricious
4) Unsupported by substantial
   Evidence

1) Precluded by
   Statute
2) Committed to
   Agency discretion
   by law

1) Standing (who?)
2) When?
   - Finality
   - Exaustion
   - Ripeness

West's Law School
Advisory Board

STATE AND FEDERAL ADMINISTRATIVE LAW

Second Edition

By

Michael Asimow
Professor of Law
University of California, Los Angeles

Arthur Earl Bonfield
John Murray Professor of Law
University of Iowa

and

Ronald M. Levin
Professor of Law
Washington University

AMERICAN CASEBOOK SERIES®

WEST
GROUP

ST. PAUL, MINN., 1998

American Casebook Series and West Group are trademarks registered in the U.S. Patent and Trademark Office.

COPYRIGHT © 1989 WEST PUBLISHING CO.
COPYRIGHT © 1998 By WEST GROUP
                    610 Opperman Drive
                    P.O. Box 64526
                    St. Paul, MN 55164–0526
                    1–800–328–9352

Library of Congress Cataloging-in-Publication Data

Asimow, Michael.
    State and federal administrative law / by Michael Asimow, Arthur
Earl Bonfield, and Ronald M. Levin. — 2nd ed.
      p.   cm. — (American casebook series)
    Authors' names appear in reverse order on previous ed.
    ISBN 0–314–07206–3 (hard)
    1. Administrative law—United States—Cases. 2. Administrative
law—United States—States—Cases. I. Bonfield, Arthur Earl.
II. Levin, Ronald M., 1950–   . III. Title. IV. Series.
KF5402.A4B66   1998
342.73'06—dc21   98–28102
                                          CIP

ISBN 0–314–07206–3

2nd Reprint — 2004

To

Bobbi, Courtney, Dan, Hillary, Ian, and Paul

and

Doris and Lauren

and

Anne Carol

*

Preface to the Second Edition

This edition carries forward the basic conception of the first edition: integrated treatment of state and federal administrative law, a straight-procedure orientation, and reliance on problems to bring the subject out of the clouds.

The basic conception of the first edition was the brainchild of Arthur Bonfield. Professor Bonfield did not participate in this edition. His name remains on the book in recognition of his many contributions that we have carried forward to this edition. Of course, Professor Bonfield may not agree with everything we have said or suggested in this edition. Ronald Levin has replaced Professor Bonfield as co-editor of the casebook with Michael Asimow. Naturally, Levin brings his own perspectives to the problems addressed in this book.

Although some of the material has been reorganized, the emphasis, structure and approach of this edition are largely the same as in the first edition. The authors are gratified at the reception given to the first edition, and also grateful for suggestions made by some of its users.

We have tried to edit the materials in such a manner that the book can be used in a variety of ways. Some instructors teach it front to back, while other, including one of the authors, teach some of the external control chapters near the back of the book first. One of the authors teaches the course almost entirely through the problems, starting each discussion with the relevant problem and using the cases and text as resources to discuss that problem.

We also know of instructors who, despite the special emphasis of this book, have used the first edition to teach a basically federal law course. They report satisfaction with that approach. But we do invite teachers to draw liberally on the state law material, to the extent their individual tastes may dictate. We believe it offers perspectives that are frequently interesting and frequently illuminating.

MICHAEL ASIMOW
RONALD M. LEVIN

May, 1998

*

Preface to the First Edition

There are many other administrative law coursebooks already on the market. What new contribution could another book possibly make?

This book is different from the other books in at least one major respect. That difference is immediately apparent from the name of the book: STATE AND FEDERAL ADMINISTRATIVE LAW. All of the other books concentrate primarily or exclusively on federal law. They either ignore state administrative law entirely or mention it only in a superficial way. This book, on the other hand, has committed itself to take state administrative law as seriously as federal law and to treat both as an integrated whole.

We believe that students will benefit from a sustained exposure to state administrative law and to continuing comparisons between state and federal law. As further explained in § 1.3, we see two important advantages from an integrated study of state and federal administrative law.

First, there is much to be learned from a study of state law that cannot be learned from a study of federal law alone. State and federal law often differ; and the circumstances surrounding state and federal administrative processes often differ. These differences add a dimension to the study of administrative law that cannot be understood or evaluated by studying either state or federal law or their respective administrative processes separately. The reason for this is that a comparative state-federal approach to the study of our subject suggests problems or solutions to problems in the administrative process that are not otherwise apparent.

Second, most law students will deal with state administrative agencies in their practice more frequently than with federal agencies. The reason for this is that the largest *number* of licensing problems, public contract problems, business regulatory problems, and benefit problems faced by individuals and entities in this country are a product of state or local agency action rather than federal agency action. As a result, for most students there is a clear professional advantage to a study of state law as well as federal law.

In another respect this book is more traditional. It is a book about administrative procedure. Unlike some other books in the field, it does not attempt to combine administrative procedure with a study of one or more regulated industries. Instead, the goal of this book is to teach the administrative process: adjudication, rulemaking, political controls of agency action, freedom of information, and judicial review. The substantive law that agencies apply is left for other courses such as environmental law, labor law, unfair trade practices, or the like.

The straight-procedure approach utilized in this book is based on our belief that the processes of all agencies have enough in common to make the study of administrative law meaningful. This approach makes it possible to organize the course much more clearly and to use all available classroom hours for study of traditional administrative process subject.

Of course, the disadvantage of the straight-procedure approach is that students may sometimes feel that the course is too theoretical, that it appears to jump around between cases that describe wildly dissimilar agencies and functions, and that it does not adequately take account of the important relationship between procedure and substantive law.

To offset this disadvantage, our book makes extensive use of problems and questions. For the most part, the problems are practical and professionally-oriented. They take the student into the law office or into an agency where he or she must deal with a client with a particular problem in a specific context. Problems can help to bring the subject down to earth, root it in real experience, and demonstrate the important relationship between substantive law and procedure. A substantial number of questions used in this book seek also to accomplish the same result: they raise issues calculated to ensure that procedures are considered in relation to specific contexts as well as in relation to general principles.

In this book we have attempted to accomplish three other major objectives. First, we have attempted to induce our readers to engage in a "cost-benefit" examination of the procedures used by agencies. We discuss this function more fully in § 1.6. Consequently, we have tried, throughout this book, to articulate clearly the values that administrative procedure issues place in conflict. For example, in administrative law there is frequently a struggle between such worthy values as efficiency and effectiveness of agency operation and the adequate protection of private interests. We cannot satisfy all of the demands of private parties for exhaustive procedures to protect their interests and also satisfy all of the demands of agencies for authority to act swiftly and economically so as to implement effectively and efficiently public policies mandated by the legislature. When values of this kind conflict, we have tried to force them to the surface, and to be as explicit as possible about the costs and benefits of particular procedures.

Another major theme that pervades this book is the political accountability of agencies. Throughout the book we ask whether particular procedural requirements or substantive limits imposed on agencies are likely to ensure that the agencies are responsive to the wishes of the body politic and whether there are more effective and efficient means by which to accomplish that result. We also devote a substantial portion of the book to the examination of legislative and executive techniques for checking agency action. On this subject, particularly, the states can teach some lessons to the federal government.

Finally, this book seeks to examine the mechanics of the rulemaking process in some detail and, therefore, devotes proportionately more space to that subject than do other coursebooks. This reflects our conviction

that rules and the rulemaking process have become much more important during the last twenty five years than they were previously, and that
there have been many recent state and federal developments in the
mechanics of the rulemaking process that deserve careful examination in
a current course on administrative law.

Cases and other quoted materials used in the book have been heavily
edited in the interest of concise presentation. We have indicated dele-
tions from the text of these materials by using three dots, but we have
cut out citations and footnotes without any notation. In order to save
space we have also refrained from using parallel citations to the many
state cases used in this book, citing them only by reference to the widely
available regional reporters.

ARTHUR EARL BONFIELD
MICHAEL ASIMOW

December, 1988

*

Acknowledgments

Second editions are easier to produce than first editions, but we have needed, and are grateful for, the help of a number of people in preparing this revision. In particular, we thank Mrs. Jane Bettlach for her prompt and proficient secretarial assistance and law students Lara Burnazian and Laura Harper for their research assistance. We also thank our professional colleagues Bob Brown, Jeffrey Lubbers, Jim Rossi and John Rogers for their thoughtful suggestions.

Finally, we want to thank the following publishers, authors, and journals, for their generous permission to reprint excerpts from their copyrighted publications indicated below:

(1) ABA Journal: The Lawyer's Magazine, published by the American Bar Association: Cooper, "Administrative Law: The 'Substantial Evidence' Rule," 44 A.B.A.J. 945 (1958).

(2) Administrative Law Review, published by the Section of Administrative Law and Regulatory Practice (formerly the Section of Administrative Law), American Bar Association: Minow, "Letter to President Kennedy," 15 Administrative Law Review 146 (1963); O'Reilly, "Regaining a Confidence: Protection of Business Confidential Data Through Reform of the Freedom of Information Act," 34 Administrative Law Review 263 (1982); Rochvarg, "State Adoption of Federal Law--Legislative Abdication or Reasoned Policymaking," 36 Administrative Law Review 277 (1984); The Section of Administrative Law, "Restatement of Scope-of-Review Doctrine," 38 Administrative Law Review 235 (1986); Breyer, "Judicial Review of Questions of Law and Policy," 38 Administrative Law Review 363 (1986); Perritt, "Negotiated Rulemaking and Administrative Law," 38 Administrative Law Review 471 (1986); Bonfield, "Chairman's Message," 40 Administrative Law Review iii (Winter 1988); Simeone, "The Function, Flexibility, and Future of United States Judges of the Executive Department," 44 Administrative Law Review 159 (1992); Pierce, "Seven Ways to Deossify Agency Rulemaking," 47 Administrative Law Review 59 (1995); Shapiro, "Agency Priority Setting and the Review of Existing Agency Rules," 48 Administrative Law Review 370 (1996). Reprinted by permission. Copyright 1963, 1982, 1984, 1986, 1988, 1992, 1995, 1996, American Bar Association.

(3) American Enterprise Institute, publisher of Regulation: Scalia, "Two Wrongs Make a Right: The Judicialization of Standardless Rulemaking," Regulation 38 (July-Aug. 1977); Scalia, "A Note on the Benzene Case," Regulation 27 (July-Aug. 1980); Scalia, "The Freedom of Information Act Has No Clothes," Regulation 15 (Mar.-Apr. 1982). Copyright 1977, 1980, 1982, The American Enterprise Institute. Reprinted with permission.

(4) Arkansas Law Review: Shane, "Political Accountability in a System of Checks and Balances: The Case of Presidential Review of Rulemaking," 48 Arkansas Law Review 161 (1995).

(5) Columbia Law Review: Golin, Note, "Solving the Problem of Gender and Racial Bias in Administrative Adjudication," 95 Columbia Law Review 1532 (1995). This article originally appeared at 95 Colum. L. Rev. 1532 (1995). Reprinted by permission.

(6) Cornell Law Review and Fred B. Rothman & Co.: Fuchs, "The Hearing Officer Problem," 40 Cornell L.Q. 281 (1955). Copyright 1955 by Cornell University. All rights reserved.

(7) Kenneth C. Davis, ADMINISTRATIVE LAW TREATISE (2d ed. 1979).

(8) Duke Law Journal: McGarity, "Some Thoughts on Deossifying the Rulemaking Process," 41 Duke Law Journal 1385 (1992).

(9) Environmental Law: Funk, "When Smoke Gets In Your Eyes: Regulatory Negotiation and the Public Interest--EPA's Woodstove Standards," 18 Environmental Law 55 (1987).

(10) Harvard Law Review: Gellhorn, "Adverse Publicity by Administrative Agencies," 86 Harvard Law Review 1380 (1973); Stewart, "The Reformation of American Administrative Law," 88 Harvard Law Review 1667 (1975). Copyright 1973, 1975, The Harvard Law Review Association.

(11) Legal Times: Taylor, "Repeal the Independent Counsel Law," Legal Times, May 20, 1996, at 25. Reprinted with permission of *Legal Times,* 1730 M St., N.W., Suite 802, Washington, D.C. 20036. Phone: 202-457-0686. Copyright, 1996.

(12) Little Brown & Co.: L. Jaffe, JUDICIAL CONTROL OF ADMINISTRATIVE ACTION (1965); A. Bonfield, STATE ADMINISTRATIVE RULE MAKING (1986).

(13) Northwestern University Law Review: Shepard, "Fierce Compromise: The Administrative Procedure Act Emerges from New Deal Politics," 90 Northwestern University Law Review 1557 (1996). Reprinted by special permission of Northwestern University School of Law, *Northwestern University Law Review*, vol. 90, 1996.

(14) Russell Sage Foundation: J. Handler, THE CONDITIONS OF DISCRETION (1986). Reprinted from THE CONDITIONS OF DISCRETION, by Joel Handler, copyright 1986, The Russell Sage Foundation. Used with permission of the Russell Sage Foundation.

(15) University of Chicago Law Review: Davis, "A New Approach to Delegation," 36 University of Chicago Law Review 713 (1969); Pildes & Sunstein, "Reinventing the Regulatory State," 62 University of Chicago Law Review 1 (1995).

(16) University of Michigan Press: G. Robinson, AMERICAN BUREAUCRACY: PUBLIC CHOICE AND PUBLIC LAW (1991). Copyright © by the University of Michigan 1991.

(17) University of Pennsylvania Law Review and Fred B. Rothman & Co.: Robinson, "The Making of Administrative Policy: Another Look at Rulemaking and Adjudication and Administrative Procedure Reform," 118 University of Pennsylvania Law Review 485 (1970).

(18) Temple Law Review: Devlin, "Toward a State Constitutional Analysis of Allocation of Powers: Legislators and Legislative Appointees Performing Administrative Functions," 66 Temple Law Review 1205 (1993).

(19) Virginia Law Review and Fred B. Rothman & Co.: Bonfield, "The Federal APA and State Administrative Law," 72 Virginia Law Review 297 (1986).

(20) Wisconsin Law Review: Sargentich, "The Reform of the American Administrative Process: The Contemporary Debate," Wisconsin Law Review 385 (1984). Copyright 1984, University of Wisconsin.

(21) Yale Law Journal and Fred B. Rothman & Co.: Handler, "Discretion in Social Welfare: The Uneasy Position in the Rule of Law," 92 Yale Law Journal 1279 (1983). Reprinted by permission of The Yale Law Journal Company and Fred B. Rothman & Co. from the Yale Law Journal, Vol. 92, p. 1270.

(22) Yale University Press: J. Mashaw, BUREAUCRATIC JUSTICE (1983); J. Mashaw, GREED, CHAOS, AND GOVERNANCE (1997). Copyright 1983, 1997, Yale University Press, reprinted with permission.

*

Summary of Contents

Page

PREFACE TO SECOND EDITION --- v
PREFACE TO FIRST EDITION --- vii
ACKNOWLEDGMENTS -- xi
TABLE OF CASES -- xxvii

Chapter 1. Introduction --- 1
§ 1.1 Administrative Agencies and Administrative Law ------------- 1
§ 1.2 Reasons for Studying Administrative Law--------------------- 2
§ 1.3 State and Federal Administrative Law ----------------------- 2
§ 1.4 Administrative Procedure Acts------------------------------- 3
§ 1.5 A Snapshot of the Administrative Process------------------- 5
§ 1.6 Costs and Benefits of Administrative Procedure and Proce-
           dural Reform -- 10
§ 1.7 Agency Legitimacy and Administrative Law ------------------ 11
§ 1.8 Problem--- 16

PART I. AGENCY PROCEDURES

Chapter 2. The Constitutional Right to a Hearing ------------- 18
§ 2.1 Hearings and Welfare Termination: Due Process and Mass
           Justice-- 20
§ 2.2 Interests Protected by Due Process: Liberty and Property-- 33
§ 2.3 Timing of Trial–Type Hearings ----------------------------- 51
§ 2.4 Elements of a Hearing -------------------------------------- 64
§ 2.5 The Rulemaking–Adjudication Distinction ------------------- 73

**Chapter 3. Administrative Adjudication: Fundamental
        Problems** --- 83
§ 3.1 Statutory Rights to an Adjudicatory Hearing--------------- 83
§ 3.2 Limiting the Issues to Which Hearing Rights Apply --------- 100
§ 3.3 The Conflict Between Institutional and Judicialized Deci-
           sion–Making--- 109
§ 3.4 Administrative Judges and Decisional Independence --------- 149

Chapter 4. The Process of Administrative Adjudication ----- 163
§ 4.1 The Pre–Hearing Phase: Notice, Investigation and Discov-
           ery -- 163
§ 4.2 The Hearing Phase-- 182
§ 4.3 The Decision Phase: Finding Facts and Stating Reasons ----- 196

Page

§ 4.4   Effect of Decision: Res Judicata, Stare Decisis, Equitable
        Estoppel --- 202

Chapter 5.   Rulemaking Procedures ------------------------------- **218**
§ 5.1   Introduction: The Importance of Rulemaking ------------------ 218
§ 5.2   Definition of "Rule" -- 223
§ 5.3   Initiating Rulemaking Proceedings --------------------------- 235
§ 5.4   Public Participation -- 244
§ 5.5   Procedural Regularity in Rulemaking ------------------------- 262
§ 5.6   Findings and Reasons -- 286
§ 5.7   Issuance and Publication ------------------------------------ 294
§ 5.8   Regulatory Analysis --- 304
§ 5.9   Negotiated Rulemaking --------------------------------------- 314

Chapter 6.   Rules as Part of the Agency Policymaking Process ----- **323**
§ 6.1   Exemptions From Rulemaking Procedure ------------------------ 323
§ 6.2   Required Rulemaking --- 358
§ 6.3   Rulemaking Petitions and Agency Agenda–Setting -------------- 378
§ 6.4   Waivers of Rules -- 386

PART II.   NONJUDICIAL CONTROL OF AGENCY ACTION

**Chapter 7.   Control of Agencies by the Political Branches
            of Government** --- **396**
§ 7.1   Introduction -- 396
§ 7.2   Delegation of Legislative Power to Agencies ----------------- 397
§ 7.3   Narrowly Defining an Agency's Authority to Avoid Consti-
        tutional Questions --- 419
§ 7.4   Delegation of Adjudicatory Power to Agencies ---------------- 428
§ 7.5   Rationale for Legislative and Executive Review of Agency
        Action --- 439
§ 7.6   Legislative Controls -- 440
§ 7.7   Executive Control: Personnel Decisions ---------------------- 464
§ 7.8   Executive Oversight --- 492

Chapter 8.   Freedom of Information and Other Open Government Laws - **507**
§ 8.1   Freedom of Information -------------------------------------- 507
§ 8.2   The Sunshine and Advisory Committee Acts -------------------- 525

PART III.   JUDICIAL REVIEW

Chapter 9.   Scope of Judicial Review ---------------------------- **534**
§ 9.1   Scope of Review of Agency Findings of Basic Fact ------------ 535
§ 9.2   Scope of Review of Issues of Legal Interpretation ----------- 557
§ 9.3   Scope of Review of Application of Law to Facts -------------- 571
§ 9.4   Judicial Review of Discretionary Determinations in Adjudi-
        cation --- 578

Page

§ 9.5   Judicial Review of Discretionary Decisions in Rulemaking --   592

Chapter 10.   Remedies and Reviewability of Agency Decisions -- **611**
§ 10.1   Judicial Remedies -- 612
§ 10.2   Damage Actions as a Form of Judicial Review ------------------ 621
§ 10.3   Recovery of Fees -- 627
§ 10.4   Preclusion of Judicial Review ------------------------------------ 632
§ 10.5   Commitment to Agency Discretion -------------------------------- 638

Chapter 11.   Standing to Seek Judicial Review and the Timing of Judicial Review ------------------------------------ **647**
§ 11.1   Standing to Seek Review -- 647
§ 11.2   Timing of Judicial Review -- 667

INDEX --- 781

*

Table of Contents

Page

PREFACE TO SECOND EDITION -- v
PREFACE TO FIRST EDITION -- vii
ACKNOWLEDGMENTS -- xi
TABLE OF CASES -- xxvii

Chapter 1. Introduction -- 1
§ 1.1 Administrative Agencies and Administrative Law ------------- 1
§ 1.2 Reasons for Studying Administrative Law ---------------------- 2
§ 1.3 State and Federal Administrative Law ----------------------- 2
§ 1.4 Administrative Procedure Acts -------------------------------- 3
§ 1.5 A Snapshot of the Administrative Process ------------------- 5
§ 1.6 Costs and Benefits of Administrative Procedure and Proce-
        dural Reform --- 10
§ 1.7 Agency Legitimacy and Administrative Law --------------------- 11
§ 1.8 Problem --- 16

PART I. AGENCY PROCEDURES

Chapter 2. The Constitutional Right to a Hearing ------------- 18
§ 2.1 Hearings and Welfare Termination: Due Process and Mass
        Justice -- 20
        Goldberg v. Kelly -- 22
        Notes and Questions --- 29
§ 2.2 Interests Protected by Due Process: Liberty and Property -- 33
        § 2.2.1 "Liberty" and "Property" According to *Roth* ------- 33
                 Board of Regents v. Roth ----------------------------- 33
                 Notes and Questions ---------------------------------- 38
        § 2.2.2 Defining "Property" ------------------------------------ 42
                 Cleveland Board of Education v. Loudermill ---------- 42
                 Notes and Questions ---------------------------------- 44
        § 2.2.3 Defining "Liberty" ----------------------------------- 46
                 Sandin v. Conner ------------------------------------ 47
                 Notes and Questions ---------------------------------- 50
§ 2.3 Timing of Trial–Type Hearings ------------------------------ 51
        Mathews v. Eldridge -- 52
        Notes and Questions -- 61
§ 2.4 Elements of a Hearing --------------------------------------- 64
        Ingraham v. Wright -- 64
        Notes and Questions -- 68
§ 2.5 The Rulemaking–Adjudication Distinction -------------------- 73
        Londoner v. Denver -- 73

Page

§ 2.5   The Rulemaking–Adjudication Distinction—Continued
         Bi–Metallic Investment Co. v. State Board of Equalization   75
         Notes and Questions   76
         Cunningham v. Department of Civil Service   78
         Notes and Questions   80

Chapter 3. Administrative Adjudication: Fundamental
Problems **83**
§ 3.1   Statutory Rights to an Adjudicatory Hearing......................   83
         § 3.1.1   Federal Law—Right to a Hearing Under the APA   84
                   City of West Chicago v. NRC................................   85
                   Notes and Questions...   89
         § 3.1.2   Rights to a Hearing Under State Law   93
                   Sugarloaf Citizens Ass'n v. Northeast Maryland Waste
                       Disposal Authority.......................................   94
                   Metsch v. University of Florida   95
                   Notes and Questions...   97
§ 3.2   Limiting the Issues to Which Hearing Rights Apply   100
         Heckler v. Campbell   100
         Notes and Questions   104
§ 3.3   The Conflict Between Institutional and Judicialized Deci-
         sion–Making...   109
         § 3.3.1   Personal Responsibility of Decisionmakers   110
                   Morgan v. United States   110
                   Notes and Questions...   112
         § 3.3.2   Separation of Functions and Internal Agency
                   Communications..   117
                   Walker v. City of Berkeley..................................   118
                   Notes and Questions...   119
         § 3.3.3   Bias: Personal Interest, Prejudgment, Personal
                   Animus   123
                   Andrews v. Agricultural Labor Relations Board   123
                   Notes and Questions...   128
         § 3.3.4   Ex Parte Contacts..   132
                   Professional Air Traffic Controllers Organization (PAT-
                       CO) v. Federal Labor Relations Authority (FLRA)   132
                   Notes and Questions...   139
         § 3.3.5   Agency Adjudication and Legislative Pressure.......   142
                   Pillsbury Co. v. FTC..   142
                   Notes and Questions...   146
§ 3.4   Administrative Judges and Decisional Independence   149
         § 3.4.1   Selection and Appointment of ALJS   151
                   Acus, the Federal Administrative Judiciary   151
         § 3.4.2   Bias of Administrative Law Judges........................   153
                   Elaine Golin, Note, "Solving the Problem of Gender
                       and Racial Bias in Administrative Adjudication"   153
                   Grant v. Shalala..   154
         § 3.4.3   ALJS: The Central Panel Issue   158
                   Joseph J. Simeone, "The Function, Flexibility, and
                       Future of United States Judges of the Executive De-
                       partment"   158
                   Paul Verkuil, et.al., The Federal Administrative Judi-
                       ciary..   159

Page

§ 3.4   Administrative Judges and Decisional Independence—Continued

       § 3.4.4   ALJS: The Administrative Court Issue 160
               Newton Minow Letter to President Kennedy 160
               Paul Verkuil, et. al. The Federal Administrative Judiciary 161

Chapter 4.   The Process of Administrative Adjudication **163**

§ 4.1   The Pre–Hearing Phase: Notice, Investigation and Discovery 163

       § 4.1.1   Notice and Parties to Adjudication 163
               Block v. Ambach 163
               Notes and Questions 165

       § 4.1.2   Investigation and Discovery: An Agency's Power to Obtain Information 170
               Craib v. Bulmash 170
               Notes and Questions 174

       § 4.1.3   Alternative Dispute Resolution in Administrative Adjudication 180

§ 4.2   The Hearing Phase 182

       § 4.2.1   Evidence at the Hearing 182
               Reguero v. Teacher Standards and Practices Commission 182
               Notes and Questions 185

       § 4.2.2   Official Notice 189
               Franz v. Board of Medical Quality Assurance 189
               Notes and Questions 192

§ 4.3   The Decision Phase: Finding Facts and Stating Reasons 196
       In the Matter of Ciba–Geigy Corp. 196
       Notes and Questions 198

§ 4.4   Effect of Decision: Res Judicata, Stare Decisis, Equitable Estoppel 202

       § 4.4.1   Res Judicata and Collateral Estoppel 203
               University of Tennessee v. Elliott 203
               Notes and Questions 205

       § 4.4.2   Consistent Decisionmaking: Stare Decisis 208
               United Automobile Workers of America v. NLRB 208
               Notes and Questions 209

       § 4.4.3   Estoppel 210
               Foote's Dixie Dandy, Inc. v. McHenry 211
               Notes and Questions 212

Chapter 5.   Rulemaking Procedures **218**

§ 5.1   Introduction: The Importance of Rulemaking 218
       Notes and Questions 221

§ 5.2   Definition of "Rule" 223

       § 5.2.1   Generality and Particularity 223
               Acus, A Guide to Federal Agency Rulemaking 223
               Notes and Questions 224

       § 5.2.2   Prospectivity and Retroactivity 229
               Bowen v. Georgetown University Hospital 230
               Notes and Questions 232

§ 5.3   Initiating Rulemaking Proceedings 235
       Chocolate Manufacturers Ass'n v. Block 235
       Notes and Questions 238

Page

§ 5.4 Public Participation -------- 244
  § 5.4.1 Informal Rulemaking ------------------------------- 245
    Notes and Questions ------------- 245
  § 5.4.2 Formal Rulemaking ------------------------------- 247
    United States v. Florida East Coast Railway Co. --------- 247
    Notes and Questions ------------- 250
  § 5.4.3 Hybrid Rulemaking and the Limits on Judicial Supervision of Administrative Procedure -------- 253
    Vermont Yankee Nuclear Power Corp. v. Natural Resources Defense Council, Inc. [NRDC] ------------------- 254
    Notes and Questions ------------- 258
§ 5.5 Procedural Regularity in Rulemaking ------------------ 262
  § 5.5.1 Role of Agency Heads ------------------------- 262
  § 5.5.2 Ex Parte Communications and Political Influence in Rulemaking ------------------------------- 264
    Home Box Office, Inc. v. FCC ------------------ 264
    Sierra Club v. Costle ------------------------------- 267
    Notes and Questions ------------- 272
  § 5.5.3 Bias and Prejudgment ------------------------- 279
    Association of National Advertisers, Inc. v. Federal Trade Commission ------------------------------- 279
    Notes and Questions ------------- 284
§ 5.6 Findings and Reasons ------------------------------- 286
  California Hotel & Motel Ass'n v. Industrial Welfare Comm'n ------ 286
  Notes and Questions ------------------------------- 290
§ 5.7 Issuance and Publication ------------------------------- 294
  Nguyen v. United States ------------------------------- 296
  Notes and Questions ------------------------------- 300
§ 5.8 Regulatory Analysis ------------------------------- 304
  Executive Order 12866 Regulatory Planning and Review ----------- 304
  Notes and Questions ------------------------------- 306
§ 5.9 Negotiated Rulemaking ------------------------------- 314
  Acus, A Guide to Federal Agency Rulemaking ------------------- 314
  William Funk, "When Smoke Gets in Your Eyes: Regulatory Negotiation and the Public Interest—EPA's Woodstove Standards" ------------------------------- 316
  Notes and Questions ------------------------------- 319

Chapter 6. Rules as Part of the Agency Policymaking Process ------------------------------- **323**
§ 6.1 Exemptions From Rulemaking Procedure ---------------- 323
  § 6.1.1 Good Cause Exemptions ------------------------- 323
    Notes and Questions ------------- 324
  § 6.1.2 Exempted Subject Matter ------------------------- 329
    Notes and Questions ------------- 329
  § 6.1.3 Procedural Rules ------------------------------- 332
    United States Department of Labor v. Kast Metals Corp. --- 332
    Notes and Questions ------------- 335
  § 6.1.4 Nonlegislative Rules ------------------------------- 336
    § 6.1.4a Legislative and nonlegislative rules ------ 336
    § 6.1.4b Policy statements ------------------------- 338
      Mada–Luna v. Fitzpatrick ------------------- 338
      Notes and Questions ------------------------- 341

Page

§ 6.1 Exemptions From Rulemaking Procedure—Continued
§ 6.1.4c Interpretive rules -------------------------- 347
Hoctor v. United States Department of Agriculture ------------------------- 347
Notes and Questions ---------------------- 352
§ 6.2 Required Rulemaking ------------------------------------- 358
§ 6.2.1 Federal Law ------------------------------- 358
NLRB v. Wyman–Gordon Co. ----------------------- 358
NLRB v. Bell Aerospace Co. ------------------------ 363
Notes and Questions ------------------------------- 365
§ 6.2.2 State Law ----------------------------------- 369
Megdal v. Oregon State Board of Dental Examiners ------ 370
Notes and Questions ------------------------------- 373
§ 6.3 Rulemaking Petitions and Agency Agenda–Setting ------------ 378
WWHT, Inc. v. FCC ---------------------------------- 379
Notes and Questions ------------------------------------ 381
§ 6.4 Waivers of Rules -------------------------------------- 386
WAIT Radio v. FCC ----------------------------------- 386
Notes and Questions ---------------------------------- 389

PART II. NONJUDICIAL CONTROL OF AGENCY ACTION

Chapter 7. Control of Agencies by the Political Branches of Government --- **396**
§ 7.1 Introduction -- 396
§ 7.2 Delegation of Legislative Power to Agencies -------------------- 397
§ 7.2.1 The Nondelegation Doctrine and Federal Agencies --- 397
§ 7.2.1a From *Field* to the New Deal -------------- 398
§ 7.2.1b From the New Deal to the Present ------ 401
§ 7.2.1c Revival of the Delegation Doctrine------- 402
Amalgamated Meat Cutters and Butcher Workmen v. Connally ----------------------- 402
Industrial Union Department, AFL–CIO v. American Petroleum Institute -------------- 404
Notes and Questions ----------------------------- 408
§ 7.2.2 The Non–Delegation Doctrine and State Agencies 413
Thygesen v. Callahan ------------------------------- 414
Notes and Questions ------------------------------- 416
§ 7.3 Narrowly Defining an Agency's Authority to Avoid Constitutional Questions -------------------------------------- 419
Kent v. Dulles --- 420
Notes and Questions ------------------------------------ 421
Boreali v. Axelrod -------------------------------------- 422
Notes and Questions ------------------------------------ 426
§ 7.4 Delegation of Adjudicatory Power to Agencies -------------- 428
§ 7.4.1 Generally------------------------------------- 428
Commodity Futures Trading Commission v. Schor ------ 429
Notes and Questions ------------------------------------ 432
§ 7.4.2 Delegation of Authority to Penalize or Fine -------- 435
McHugh v. Santa Monica Rent Control Bd. --------------- 435
Notes and Questions -------------------------------------- 437

Page

§ 7.5　Rationale for Legislative and Executive Review of Agency
　　　　Action... 439
　　　　Arthur Earl Bonfield, State Administrative Rule Making 439
§ 7.6　Legislative Controls... 440
　　　　§ 7.6.1　The Legislative Veto... 440
　　　　　　　　Immigration and Naturalization Service [INS] v. Cha-
　　　　　　　　　dha 441
　　　　　　　　Notes and Questions.. 451
　　　　§ 7.6.2　Alternatives to the Legislative Veto 456
　　　　§ 7.6.3　Other Legislative Controls 461
§ 7.7　Executive Control: Personnel Decisions 464
　　　　§ 7.7.1　Appointment of Officers...................................... 464
　　　　　　　　Buckley v. Valeo... 464
　　　　　　　　Notes and Questions.. 467
　　　　§ 7.7.2　Removal of Officers 473
　　　　　　　　§ 7.7.2a　The Rise of the Independent Agency ... 473
　　　　　　　　　　　　Humphrey's Executor v. United States 475
　　　　　　　　　　　　Notes and Questions 476
　　　　　　　　§ 7.7.2b　Removal Issues in the Modern Era 478
　　　　　　　　　　　　Morrison v. Olson.............................. 478
　　　　　　　　　　　　Notes and Questions 487
§ 7.8　Executive Oversight 492
　　　　Executive Order 12866 Regulatory Planning and Review 493
　　　　Notes and Questions 495

**Chapter 8.　Freedom of Information and Other Open Gov-
　　　　ernment Laws**.. **507**
§ 8.1　Freedom of Information 507
　　　　§ 8.1.1　Protecting Deliberation: § 552(b)(5) 510
　　　　　　　　NLRB v. Sears, Roebuck & Co. 510
　　　　　　　　Notes and Questions.. 516
　　　　§ 8.1.2　Confidential Private Information: § 552(b)(4) 519
　　　　　　　　Chrysler Corp. v. Brown.................................. 519
　　　　　　　　Notes and Questions.. 523
§ 8.2　The Sunshine and Advisory Committee Acts 525
　　　　§ 8.2.1　Sunshine Acts 525
　　　　§ 8.2.2　Federal Advisory Committee Act (FACA) 529

PART III.　JUDICIAL REVIEW

Chapter 9.　Scope of Judicial Review **534**
§ 9.1　Scope of Review of Agency Findings of Basic Fact 535
　　　　§ 9.1.1　The Substantial Evidence and Clearly Erroneous
　　　　　　　　Tests.. 536
　　　　　　　　Universal Camera Corp. v. NLRB 536
　　　　　　　　DeFries v. Association of Owners, 999 Wilder............. 541
　　　　　　　　Notes and Questions.. 545
　　　　§ 9.1.2　Independent Judgment and De Novo Review 550
　　　　　　　　§ 9.1.2a　Federal Decisions 550
　　　　　　　　§ 9.1.2b　State Decisions 553
　　　　　　　　　　　　Frink v. Prod.................................. 555
　　　　　　　　　　　　Notes and Questions 557

Page

§ 9.2 Scope of Review of Issues of Legal Interpretation 557
 Connecticut State Medical Society v. Connecticut Board of Exam-
  iners in Podiatry 558
 Chevron U.S.A., Inc. v. Natural Resources Defense Council 560
 Notes and Questions 563
§ 9.3 Scope of Review of Application of Law to Facts 571
 McPherson v. Employment Division 571
 Notes and Questions 575
§ 9.4 Judicial Review of Discretionary Determinations in Adjudi-
  cation 578
 Salameda v. Immigration and Naturalization Service 579
 Notes and Questions 585
§ 9.5 Judicial Review of Discretionary Decisions in Rulemaking .. 592
 Motor Vehicle Manufacturers Ass'n v. State Farm Mutual Automo-
  bile Ins. Co. 592
 Borden, Inc. v. Commissioner of Public Health 599
 Notes and Questions 602

Chapter 10. Remedies and Reviewability of Agency Deci-
  sions **611**
§ 10.1 Judicial Remedies 612
  § 10.1.1 Judicial Jurisdiction 612
  § 10.1.2 Cause of Action and Remedy 617
    § 10.1.2a Injunction and Declaratory Judgment .. 617
    § 10.1.2b Mandamus 618
    § 10.1.2c Certiorari 620
    § 10.1.2d Other Writs 621
§ 10.2 Damage Actions as a Form of Judicial Review 621
  § 10.2.1 Tort Liability of Government 622
    § 10.2.1a The Federal Tort Claims Act 622
    § 10.2.1b State and Local Government Liability .. 623
  § 10.2.2 Tort Liability of Officials 624
    § 10.2.2a Bases of Liability 624
    § 10.2.2b Immunity From Liability 625
§ 10.3 Recovery of Fees 627
 Notes and Questions 627
§ 10.4 Preclusion of Judicial Review 632
 Bowen v. Michigan Academy of Family Physicians 632
 Notes and Questions 635
§ 10.5 Commitment to Agency Discretion 638
 Heckler v. Chaney 638
 Notes and Questions 643

Chapter 11. Standing to Seek Judicial Review and the
  Timing of Judicial Review **647**
§ 11.1 Standing to Seek Review 647
  § 11.1.1 Standing to Seek Review in the Federal Courts:
    Historical Introduction 648
  § 11.1.2 Injury in Fact and Zone of Interest Tests 649
    Association of Data Processing Service Orgs. v. Camp ... 649
    Notes and Questions 652

Page

§ 11.1 Standing to Seek Review—Continued
   § 11.1.3 Imminent Injury, Causation, Remediability—The
             Public Action -- 655
             Lujan v. Defenders of Wildlife -------------------- 655
             Notes and Questions ------------------------------ 662
§ 11.2 Timing of Judicial Review ------------------------------- 667
   § 11.2.1 Introduction --- 667
   § 11.2.2 The Final Order Rule -------------------------------- 669
             FTC v. Standard Oil Co. of California ------------ 669
             Notes and Questions ------------------------------ 672
   § 11.2.3 Ripeness -- 675
             Abbott Laboratories v. Gardner ------------------ 675
             Notes and Questions ------------------------------ 680
   § 11.2.4 Exhaustion of Administrative Remedies ------------- 686
             McCarthy v. Madigan ----------------------------- 686
             New Jersey Civil Service Ass'n (NJCSA) v. State -- 691
             Notes and Questions ------------------------------ 693
   § 11.2.5 Primary Jurisdiction ------------------------------- 699
             Farmers Insurance Exchange v. Superior Court ---- 699
             Notes and Questions ------------------------------ 703

App.
A.   United States Constitution (Selected Provisions) ----------- 707
B.   Federal Administrative Procedure Act United States Code,
      Title 5 -- 710
C.   Model State Administrative Procedure Act (1981) ------------ 728

INDEX --- 781

Table of Cases

The principal cases are in bold type. Cases cited or discussed in the text
are roman type. References are to pages. Cases cited in principal
cases and within other quoted materials are not included.

Abbott Laboratories v. Gardner, 675,
678, 679, 680, 681, 682, 683, 684, 685,
686
Action For Children's Television v. F. C. C.,
275
Action on Smoking and Health v. C.A.B.,
324, 325
Adamo Wrecking Co. v. United States, 637
Adams v. Board of Review of Indus. Com'n,
199
Adams v. Walker, 490
Adams Fruit Co., Inc. v. Barrett, 567
Advocates for Highway and Auto Safety v.
Federal Highway Admin., 327, 394
Agosto v. Immigration and Naturalization
Service, 551
Air Courier Conference of America v. Amer-
ican Postal Workers Union AFL–CIO,
653, 654
Air Line Pilots Ass'n, Intern. v. Department
of Transp., 108
Air Transport Ass'n of America v. C.A.B.,
243
Air Transport Ass'n of America v. Depart-
ment of Transp., 335
A.L.A. Schechter Poultry Corporation v.
United States, 400, 401, 402, 428
Alaska, State of v. United States Dept. of
Transp., 355
Alexander v. State By and Through Allain,
472
A.L.I.V.E. Voluntary, State v., 453
Allentown Mack Sales and Service, Inc. v.
N.L.R.B., 535, 549, 589
Altenheim German Home v. Turnock, 72
Aluli v. Lewin, 375
Alyeska Pipeline Service Co. v. Wilderness
Society, 628
Amalgamated Meat Cutters and Butch-
er Workmen of North America,
AFL–CIO v. Connally, 402, 408, 409
Amalgamated Transit Union v. Skinner,
222

American Academy of Pediatrics v. Heckler,
329, 336
American Ass'n of Exporters and Import-
ers–Textile and Apparel Group v. United
States, 331
American Bankers Life Assur. Co. of Flori-
da v. Division of Consumer Counsel, Of-
fice of Atty. Gen., 241
American Bus Ass'n v. United States, 344
American Cetacean Soc. v. Baldrige, 620
American Federation of Government Emp.,
AFL–CIO v. Block, 324
American Federation of Labor and Con-
gress of Industrial Organizations v. Un-
employment Ins. Appeals Bd., 438
American Horse Protection Ass'n, Inc. v.
Lyng, 386, 645
American Hosp. Ass'n v. Bowen, 335, 343
American Hosp. Ass'n v. N.L.R.B., 105, 366
American Min. Congress v. Marshall, 243
American Min. Congress v. Mine Safety &
Health Admin., 352, 354
American Min. Congress v. USEPA, 292
American School of Magnetic Healing v.
McAnnulty, 617, 619
American Textile Mfrs. Institute, Inc. v.
Donovan, 309, 408
American Trading Transp. Co., Inc. v. Unit-
ed States, 91
Anaconda Co. v. Ruckelshaus, 81
Anaya, State ex rel. Duran v., 490
Anderson, Matter of, 585
Andrade v. Lauer, 697
Andresen v. Maryland, 176
Andrews v. Agricultural Labor Rela-
tions Bd., 123, 128, 130
Anne Arundel County, Md. v. United States
E.P.A., 242
Appalachian Power Co. v. E.P.A., 325
Appeal of (see name of party)
Ardestani v. I.N.S., 630
Arlington Heights, Village of v. Metropoli-
tan Housing Development Corp., 664
Ashbacker Radio Corp. v. F.C.C., 91

Askew v. Cross Key Waterways, 417
Associated Fisheries of Maine, Inc. v. Daley, 312
Associated Indem. Corp. v. Shea, 552
Association of American Physicians and Surgeons, Inc. v. Clinton, 531
Association of Data Processing Service Organizations, Inc. v. Board of Governors of Federal Reserve System, 607
Association of Data Processing Service Organizations, Inc. v. Camp, 649, 652, 654
Association of Nat. Advertisers, Inc. v. F. T. C., 252, **279,** 284
Association of Pacific Fisheries v. E.P.A., 590
Atascadero State Hosp. v. Scanlon, 624
Atchison, T. & S.F. Ry. Co. v. Scarlett, 337
Atlas Roofing Co., Inc. v. Occupational Safety and Health Review Com'n, 434, 435, 438
Auer v. Robbins, 378, 645
Aulenback, Inc. v. Federal Highway Admin., 683
Automotive Parts & Accessories Ass'n v. Boyd, 291
Aylett v. Secretary of Housing and Urban Development, 548

Bagdonas v. Department of Treasury, 201
Bailey v. Richardson, 38, 39
Baker v. Cameron, 576, 577, 578
Baker v. F.A.A., 390
Balsam v. Department of Health and Rehabilitative Services, 227
Baltimore Gas and Elec. Co. v. Natural Resources Defense Council, Inc., 260, 606
Barker, State ex rel. v. Manchin, 460
Barlow v. Collins, 651
Barr v. Matteo, 626
Barry v. Barchi, 45, 61
Barry & Barry, Inc. v. State Dept. of Motor Vehicles, 417
Bates v. Sponberg, 117
Bekiaris v. Board of Ed. of City of Modesto, 553
Bell Aerospace Co. Div. of Textron Inc. v. N.L.R.B., 366, 367, 368, 369
Bellis v. United States, 176
Bennett v. Spear, 654, 655, 672, 674
Bennett, State ex rel. Schneider v., 472
Berkovitz by Berkovitz v. United States, 622, 623
Bessemer Mt., Matter of, 375
Better Government Ass'n v. Department of State, 682, 685, 686
Bi-Metallic Inv. Co. v. State Bd. of Equalization, 75, 76, 77, 78, 100, 226
Bio-Medical Applications of Clearwater, Inc. v. Department of Health and Rehabilitative Services, Office of Community Medical Facilities, 91
Bishop v. Wood, 44

Bivens v. Six Unknown Named Agents of Federal Bureau of Narcotics, 625, 626, 686
Bixby v. Pierno, 554, 557
Blanding v. Sports & Health Club, Inc., 550
Blank v. Department of Corrections, 461
Block v. Ambach, 163, 165, 166, 167
Block v. Community Nutrition Institute, 654
Board of Curators of University of Missouri v. Horowitz, 71, 337
Board of Regents of State Colleges v. Roth, 33, 39, 40, 41, 42, 45, 46, 50, 61
Board of Regents of University of Washington v. E.P.A., 276
Bone, State ex rel. Wallace v., 471
Book v. State Office Bldg. Commission, 472
Borden, Inc. v. Commissioner of Public Health, 590, **599,** 602, 605, 606, 608, 609
Boreali v. Axelrod, 422, 426, 438
Bose Corp. v. Consumers Union of United States, Inc., 553
Bowen v. Georgetown University Hosp., 230, 233, 234, 235
Bowen v. Michigan Academy of Family Physicians, 632, 635, 636, 645
Bowen v. Yuckert, 105
Bowsher v. Synar, 455, 456, 473, 489, 490
Bradford Central School Dist. v. Ambach, 655
Brocal Corp. v. Pennsylvania Dept. of Transp., 241
Brock v. Cathedral Bluffs Shale Oil Co., 344
Broom, State v., 438
Brown v. Secretary of Health and Human Services, 645
Brown Exp., Inc. v. United States, 335, 344
Buckley v. Valeo, 464, 467, 470
Burlington, City of v. Dague, 629
Buttrey v. United States, 93
Butz v. Economou, 121, 625
Butz v. Glover Livestock Commission Co., Inc., 587, 626

Califano v. Sanders, 615
California, Dept. of Educ., State of v. Bennett, 698
California Hotel and Motel Ass'n v. Industrial Welfare Commission, 286, 290, 293
Camp v. Pitts, 116, 201, 590
Carolina Power and Light Co. v. United States Dept. of Labor, 672
Carsten v. Psychology Examining Committee of Bd. of Medical Quality Assur., 655
Carter v. Carter Coal Co., 417
Casey v. O'Bannon, 73
Castillo-Villagra v. I.N.S., 193, 194
CBS Inc. v. Comptroller of the Treasury, 375
Celebrezze, State ex rel. v. National Lime & Stone Co., 564
Charles A. Field Delivery Service, Inc., Matter of, 210

Checkosky v. S.E.C., 606

Chemical Mfrs. Ass'n v. Natural Resources Defense Council, Inc., 392

Chemical Waste Management, Inc. v. United States E.P.A., 90, 250, 567

Chevron, U.S.A., Inc. v. Natural Resources Defense Council, Inc., 90, 353, 534, 558, **560,** 564, 565, 566, 567, 568, 569, 570, 576, 579, 586, 587, 605

Chicago, City of v. International College of Surgeons, 615, 616

Chiles v. Children A, B, C, D, E, and F, 419

Chocolate Mfrs. Ass'n of United States v. Block, 235, 240, 241, 259

Chrysler Corp. v. Brown, 353, 510, **519,** 523, 524

Cinderella Career & Finishing Schools, Inc. v. F. T. C., 129, 284

Citizens Ass'n of Georgetown v. Zoning Commission of Dist. of Columbia, 275

Citizens to Preserve Overton Park, Inc. v. Volpe, 115, 116, 200, 201, 227, 260, 579, 586, 587, 588, 589, 591, 643, 644

City of (see name of city)

Civil Aeronautics Bd. v. Hermann, 175

Clardy v. Levi, 92

Clark–Cowlitz Joint Operating Agency v. F.E.R.C., 367

Clarke v. Securities Industry Ass'n, 653, 654

Cleveland Bd. of Educ. v. Loudermill, 42, 44, 45, 46, 62, 72

Clonlara, Inc. v. State Bd. of Educ., 358

Clowes v. Terminix Intern., Inc., 549

Cohen v. Ambach, 194

Coleman v. Miller, 666

Commodity Futures Trading Com'n v. Schor, 429, 433

Common Cause v. Nuclear Regulatory Commission, 526, 529

Common Cause of California v. Board of Sup'rs of Los Angeles County, 663

Commonwealth of (see name of commonwealth)

Community Action Research Group v. Iowa State Commerce Commission, 382

Community Nutrition Institute v. Young, 345, 355

Connecticut Bankers Ass'n v. Board of Governors of Federal Reserve System, 108

Connecticut Light and Power Co. v. Nuclear Regulatory Commission, 239, 242

Connecticut State Medical Soc. v. Connecticut Bd. of Examiners in Podiatry, 558, 563, 564, 565, 569

Consumer Federation of America and Public Citizen v. United States Dept. of Health & Human Services, 293

Consumers Union of United States, Inc. v. F. T. C., 452

Convalescent Center of Bloomfield, Inc. v. Department of Income Maintenance, 207

Corn Products Co. v. Food and Drug Administration, 251

Cort v. Ash, 705

Couch v. United States, 176

Council of Southern Mountains, Inc. v. Donovan, 326

County Council for Montgomery County v. Investors Funding Corp., 438

Cox Enterprises, Inc. v. Board of Trustees of Austin Independent School Dist., 528

Craib v. Bulmash, 170, 174, 176, 177

Critical Mass Energy Project v. Nuclear Regulatory Com'n, 523

Cronin v. United States Dept. of Agriculture, 685

Crow v. Industrial Commission, 114

Crowell v. Benson, 428, 429, 432, 433, 551, 552, 553, 554

Crowley Caribbean Transport, Inc. v. Pena, 645

Cull, People v., 301

Cunningham v. Department of Civil Service, 78, 80, 100, 226

Cuomo v. United States Nuclear Regulatory Com'n, 685

Cusano v. Dunn, 91

Czerkies v. United States Dept. of Labor, 638

Dalton v. Specter, 512 U.S. 1247, p. 643

Dalton v. Specter, 511 U.S. 462, p. 673

Daniels v. Williams, 69

Darby v. Cisneros, 696

Davis v. Scherer, 626

Davis & Randall, Inc. v. United States, 195

D. C. Federation of Civic Associations v. Volpe, 147, 148

DCP Farms v. Yeutter, 148

DeFries v. Association of Owners, 999 Wilder, 535, 541, 547

Degge v. Hitchcock, 621

Dental Soc. of State v. Carey, 662

Department of Defense v. Federal Labor Relations Authority, 525

DeRieux v. Five Smiths, Inc., 326

Dickson v. Secretary of Defense, 391

Director, Office of Workers' Compensation Programs, Dept. of Labor v. Greenwich Collieries, 187

Director, Office of Workers' Compensation Programs, Dept. of Labor v. Newport News Shipbuilding and Dry Dock Co., 655

District of Columbia v. Train, 240

District of Columbia Common Cause v. District of Columbia, 666

District of Columbia Hosp. Ass'n v. Barry, 290

Doe, United States v., 177

Dole v. Service Employees Union, AFL–CIO, Local 280, 175

Dunlop v. Bachowski, 200, 642

Duquesne Light Co. v. E.P.A., 325

Duran, State ex rel. v. Anaya, 490

Dyna–Med, Inc. v. Fair Employment and Housing Com'n, 439

Eagle–Picher Industries, Inc. v. United States E.P.A., 686
Edelman v. Jordan, 624
Edison Elec. Institute v. USEPA, 645
Edmond v. United States, 468
Edwards, State ex rel. McLeod v., 472
Elizondo v. State, Dept. of Revenue, Motor Vehicle Division, 373
Enourato v. New Jersey Bldg. Authority, 454, 455
Environmental Defense Fund v. Thomas, 501
Environmental Defense Fund, Inc. v. Hardin, 673
Environmental Defense Fund, Inc. v. Ruckelshaus (EDF II), 673
Erika, Inc., United States v., 635
Estep v. United States, 433, 536
Ethyl Corp. v. Environmental Protection Agency, 254, 260
Ettinger v. Board of Medical Quality Assur., Dept. of Consumer Affairs, 188
Excelsior Underwear, Inc., 358, 359, 365
Ex parte (see name of party)

Fajardo v. Morgan, 576
Farmers Ins. Exchange v. Superior Court (People), 699, 703, 704, 705
Farrar v. Hobby, 629
F.C.C. v. Allentown Broadcasting Corp., 547
F.C.C. v. ITT World Communications, Inc., 528
F.C.C. v. Sanders Bros. Radio Station, 648, 649
F. C. C. v. WNCN Listeners Guild, 106, 389
Federal Deposit Ins. Corp. v. Mallen, 61
Federal Election Com'n v. NRA Political Victory Fund, 491
Federal Power Commission v. Hope Natural Gas Co., 551
Federal Power Commission v. Texaco, Inc., 105, 106
Federal Radio Commission v. Nelson Bros. Bond & Mortg. Co. (Station WIBO), 399
Federal Trade Commission v. Gratz, 399
Fertilizer Institute v. United States E.P.A., 354
Field v. Clark, 398, 400
First Sav. & Loan Ass'n of Borger v. Vandygriff, 139, 141
Fitzgerald v. Hampton, 188
Flagstaff Broadcasting Foundation v. F.C.C., 210, 345
Flast v. Cohen, 666
Florida Audubon Soc. v. Bentsen, 665
Florida East Coast Ry. Co., United States v., 76, 89, **247,** 250, 251, 252, 253
Florida Power & Light Co. v. Lorion, 116
Florida Power & Light Co. v. United States, 239
Fogle v. H & G Restaurant, Inc., 284

Foote's Dixie Dandy, Inc. v. McHenry, 211, 212, 214, 215
Ford Motor Co. v. F. T. C., 367, 368
Foundation on Economic Trends v. Heckler, 16
Fox v. Wisconsin Dept. of Health and Social Services, 664
Franklin v. Massachusetts, 673
Franz v. Board of Medical Quality Assur., 189, 193, 194, 195
Freytag v. Commissioner, 469
Friedman v. Rogers, 129
Frink v. Prod, 555, 557
F.T.C. v. American Nat. Cellular, Inc., 478
F. T. C. v. Cinderella Career & Finishing Schools, Inc., 130, 179
F.T.C. v. Standard Oil Co., 355 U.S. 396, p. 549
F. T. C. v. Standard Oil Co. of California, 449 U.S. 232, p. **669**
Functional Music, Inc. v. F.C.C., 684

Garces v. Department of Registration and Ed., 418
Gavrilovic, United States v., 327, 328
General Assembly of State of N. J. v. Byrne, 454
General Dynamics Corp., United States v., 705
General Elec. Co. v. Gilbert, 352
General Elec. Co. v. United States E.P.A., 215, 216
General Motors Corp. v. Ruckelshaus, 353
Gestuvo v. District Director of United States Immigration and Naturalization Service, 212, 214
Gibson v. Berryhill, 128
Giffin v. Chronister, 697
Gilbert v. Homar, 62
Goldberg v. Kelly, 19, 20, **22,** 29, 31, 33, 39, 51, 61, 64, 68, 70, 72, 120, 122, 196
Goldsmith v. United States Board of Tax Appeals, 39, 42
Gonzalez–Rivera v. I.N.S., 178
Goss v. Lopez, 46, 68, 69, 72
Grand Jury Subpoena Duces Tecum Dated Oct. 29, 1992, In re, 177
Grant v. Shalala, 154
Greate Bay Hotel & Casino v. Tose, 706
Greene v. Babbitt, 92
Greer v. Illinois Housing Development Authority, 654
Greer v. State, 472
Grein v. Board of Educ. of School Dist. of Fremont, Dodge County, 529
Grier v. Kizer, 227
Grimaud, United States v., 438
Guardian Federal Sav. and Loan Ass'n v. Federal Sav. and Loan Ins. Corp., 378
Guentchev v. I.N.S., 202
Gumbhir v. Kansas State Bd. of Pharmacy, 418

Hannah v. Larche, 51

Hardin v. Kentucky Utilities Co., 648

Harlow v. Fitzgerald, 626

Harris v. Mechanicville Central School Dist., 592

Hawaii Helicopter Operators Ass'n v. F.A.A., 325

Hechler, State ex rel. Meadows v., 461

Heckler v. Campbell, 100, 104, 105, 106, 337, 390

Heckler v. Chaney, 638, 643, 644, 645

Heckler v. Community Health Services of Crawford County, Inc., 214

Heckler v. Day, 674

Heckler v. Lopez, 206

Her Majesty the Queen in Right of Ontario v. United States E.P.A., 683

Hewitt v. Helms, 47, 50, 72

Hibbing Taconite Co., Matter of, 375

High Horizons Development Co. v. State, Dept. of Transp., 82

Hillman v. Northern Wasco County People's Utility Dist., 418

Hoctor v. United States Dept. of Agriculture, 347, 353, 354, 356

Hodel v. Virginia Surface Min. and Reclamation Ass'n, Inc., 61

Hoke v. Brinlaw Mfg. Co., 188

Holmes v. New York City Housing Authority, 373

Home Box Office, Inc. v. F. C. C., 264, 272, 273, 274, 275, 276

Hopkins Dodge, Inc., United States v., 368

Horn v. Ventura County, 82, 167

Hornsby v. Allen, 373

Horsehead Resource Development Co., Inc. v. Browner, 240

Hortonville Joint School Dist. No. 1 v. Hortonville Educ. Ass'n, 129, 130

Hot Spot, Inc., In re, 166

Hovey Concrete Products Co., State ex rel. v. Mechem, 434

Hudson v. Palmer, 69

Hudson v. United States, 207

Hughes v. Rowe, 628

Humphrey's Ex'r v. United States, 475, 476, 477, 478, 489, 491

Hunt v. Washington State Apple Advertising Com'n, 662

Huntington, Town of v. New York State Div. of Human Rights, 675

I.C.C. v. Brotherhood of Locomotive Engineers, 643, 674

Idaho Farm Bureau Federation v. Babbitt, 243

IMS, P.C. v. Alvarez, 590

Independent Guard Ass'n of Nevada, Local No. 1 v. O'Leary on Behalf of United States Dept. of Energy, 331, 332

Independent United States Tanker Owners Committee v. Dole, 291

Independent United States Tanker Owners Committee v. Lewis, 91

Indian Towing Co. v. United States, 623

Industrial Com'n of Ohio, State ex rel. Jeffrey Min. Machinery Div., Dresser Industries, Inc. v., 536

Industrial Safety Equipment Ass'n, Inc. v. E.P.A., 227

Industrial Union Dept., AFL–CIO v. American Petroleum Institute, 402, 404, 408, 411, 426, 606

Ingraham v. Wright, 64, 68, 69

In re (see name of party)

I.N.S. v. Chadha, 441, 452, 453, 455, 456, 457, 487, 489

I.N.S. v. Lopez–Mendoza, 178

International Broth. of Teamsters v. Pena, 331

International Chemical Workers Union, In re, 384

International Harvester Co. v. Bowling, 131

International Harvester Co. v. Ruckelshaus, 254

Interstate Commerce Commission v. Brimson, 174, 439

Iowa Citizen/Labor Energy Coalition, Inc. v. Iowa State Commerce Com'n, 241

Iron Workers Local No. 67 v. Hart, 438

Irval Realty Inc. v. Board of Public Utility Com'rs, 508

Issuance of a Permit by Dept. of Environmental Protection to Ciba–Geigy Corp., Matter of, 196, 199, 200

Jackson v. Concord Co., 438

Jackson County Public Hospital v. Public Employment Relations Bd., 549

Janis, United States v., 178

Jeffrey Min. Machinery Div., Dresser Industries, Inc., State ex rel. v. Industrial Com'n of Ohio, 536

JEM Broadcasting Co., Inc. v. F.C.C., 336, 684, 685

Jenkins v. McKeithen, 51

J.F. Ahern Co. v. Wisconsin State Bldg. Com'n, 472

Johnston v. Department of Professional Regulation, Bd. of Medical Examiners, 548

Joseph v. United States Civil Service Commission, 330, 331

Ju Toy, United States v., 551

J.W. Hampton, Jr., & Co. v. United States, 399

Kalaris v. Donovan, 491

KCST–TV, Inc. v. F.C.C., 390

Keating v. Office of Thrift Supervision, 176

Keim v. United States, 491

Kelly v. United States Dept. of Interior, 327

Kendall v. United States ex rel. Stokes, 496, 501, 619

Kent v. Dulles, 420, 421, 426, 427

Kent Corp. v. N.L.R.B., 517

Kentucky v. Graham, 624

Kentucky, Dept. of Banking and Securities, Commonwealth of v. Brown, 623

Kincaid, State ex rel. v. Parsons, 227
Koniag, Inc., Village of Uyak v. Andrus, 169
Kraft v. Jacka, 202

Lam v. Bureau of Sec. and Investigative Services, 166
Landgraf v. United StatesI Film Products, 233
Larson v. Domestic & Foreign Commerce Corp., 615
L. A. Tucker Truck Lines, Inc., United States v., 697
Lechmere, Inc. v. N.L.R.B., 567
Legislative Research Com'n By and Through Prather v. Brown, 459
Lentz v. McMahon, 217
Levin v. Murawski, 175, 176
Liberty Homes, Inc. v. Department of Industry, Labor and Human Relations, 608
Lincoln v. Vigil, 346, 643
Lindahl v. Office of Personnel Management, 638
Local No. 290, Plumbers and Pipefitters v. Oregon Dept. of Environmental Quality, 662
Londoner v. Denver, 73, 76, 77
Lopez v. Heckler, 725 F.2d 1489, p. 206
Lopez v. Heckler, 713 F.2d 1432, p. 206
Lopez v. Henry Phipps Plaza South, Inc., 64
Louisiana Environmental Action Network v. Browner, 685
Lujan v. Defenders of Wildlife, 655, 663, 665
Lujan v. National Wildlife Federation, 653
Lunding v. Walker, 491
Lyness v. State Bd. of Medicine, 120, 122

Mada–Luna v. Fitzpatrick, 338, 343, 344, 345, 347
Mahoney v. Shinpoch, 284, 285
Malek–Marzban v. Immigration and Naturalization Service, 330
Manchin, State ex rel. Barker v., 460
Marbury v. Madison, 619
Marcello v. Bonds, 92
Market St. Ry. Co. v. Railroad Commission of State of Cal., 194
Markgraf, United States v., 646
Marshall v. Barlow's, Inc., 172, 177, 332
Marshall v. Jerrico, Inc., 128
Martin v. Occupational Safety and Health Review Com'n, 566
Martin, State ex rel. v. Melott, 473
Martinez v. Department of Industry, Labor and Human Relations, 458, 459
Mason v. Thetford School Bd., 637
Massachusetts State Pharmaceutical Ass'n v. Rate Setting Com'n, 263, 275
Massieu v. Reno, 697
Mathews v. Eldridge, 52, 61, 62, 64, 68, 70, 71, 72, 81, 92, 188, 674, 697
Matlovich v. Secretary of the Air Force, 391
Matter of (see name of party)
Matthews v. Weinberg, 377

Mazza v. Cavicchia, 114
McAvoy v. H. B. Sherman Co., 637
McCain v. Employment Division, 578
McCarthy v. Industrial Commission, 194, 195
McCarthy v. Madigan, 686, 693, 694, 696, 697
McDonald v. Watt, 366
McFaddin v. Jackson, 419
McGee v. United States, 698
McHugh v. Santa Monica Rent Control Bd. (Smith), 435, 438, 439
McIntire v. Wood, 619
McLeod, State ex rel. v. Edwards, 472
McLouth Steel Products Corp. v. Thomas, 343, 345
McNary v. Haitian Refugee Center, Inc., 636
McPherson v. Employment Division, 571, 576, 577, 578
Mead v. Arnell, 453, 460
Meadows, State ex rel. v. Hechler, 461
Mechem, State ex rel. Hovey Concrete Products Co. v., 434
Megdal v. Oregon State Bd. of Dental Examiners, 370, 373, 374, 375
Meier v. American Maize–Products Co., Inc., 241
Melott, State ex rel. Martin v., 473
Melton v. Rowe, 326
Memphis Light, Gas and Water Division v. Craft, 45
Mendoza, United States v., 205, 206
Mendoza–Lopez, United States v., 637
Mercy Hospitals of Sacramento, Inc., 365
Meritor Sav. Bank, FSB v. Vinson, 233
Methodist Hospitals of Dallas v. Texas Indus. Acc. Bd., 311
Metromedia, Inc. v. Director, Div. of Taxation, 375
Metropolitan Washington Airports Authority v. Citizens for Abatement of Aircraft Noise, Inc., 455, 456, 472
Metsch v. University of Florida, 93, 95, 98
Meyer v. Nebraska, 40, 50
Michigan, State of v. Thomas, 311
Mid–American Waste Systems, Inc. v. City of Gary, Ind., 69, 70
Milford v. Gilb, 517
Miller v. Fenton, 553
Miller v. Horton, 625
Miller v. Johnson, 567
Minnesota Public Utilities Com'n's Initiation of Summary Investigation, In re, 142
Mississippi Power & Light Co. v. Mississippi ex rel. Moore, 567
Missouri Coalition for Environment v. Joint Committee on Administrative Rules, 453
Missouri Health Facilities Review Committee v. Administrative Hearing Com'n of Missouri, 655
Missouri Hosp. Ass'n v. Air Conservation Com'n, 310

Missouri Power & Light Co., State ex rel. v. Riley, 637

Mistretta v. United States, 411, 490

Moberg v. Independent School Dist. No. 281, 527

Montana Air Chapter No. 29, Ass'n of Civilian Technicians, Inc. v. Federal Labor Relations Authority, 645

Moore v. East Cleveland, Ohio, 40

Morgan v. United States (Morgan II), 304 U.S. 1, pp. 113, 251

Morgan v. United States (Morgan I), 298 U.S. 468, pp. **110,** 112, 113, 114, 115, 116, 117, 251, 262, 263

Morgan (Morgan IV), United States v., 115, 116, 140, 141, 155, 263

Morrison v. Olson, 467, 468, **478,** 487, 489, 490

Morrison v. University of Oregon Health Sciences Center, 94

Mortensen v. Pyramid Sav. & Loan Ass'n of Milwaukee, 654

Morton v. Ruiz, 300, 369

Moser v. United States, 215

Motor Vehicle Mfrs. Ass'n of United States, Inc. v. State Farm Mut. Auto. Ins. Co., 260, 579, **592,** 602, 603, 606, 607, 609, 645, 680

Mt. Healthy City School Dist. Bd. of Educ. v. Doyle, 623

Muskopf v. Corning Hospital Dist., 623

Myers v. Bethlehem Shipbuilding Corp., 695

Myers v. United States, 472, 474, 475, 476, 491, 501

National Ass'n for Advancement of Colored People v. Federal Power Commission, 381

National Automatic Laundry and Cleaning Council v. Shultz, 682

National Black Media Coalition v. F.C.C., 240

National Communications Ass'n, Inc. v. American Tel. and Tel. Co., 704

National Congress of Hispanic Am. Citizens v. Usery, 384

National Credit Union Admin. v. First Nat. Bank & Trust Co., 652, 653, 654

National Family Planning and Reproductive Health Ass'n, Inc. v. Sullivan, 354

National Lime Ass'n v. Environmental Protection Agency, 260

National Lime & Stone Co., State ex rel. Celebrezze v., 564

National Nutritional Foods Ass'n v. Food and Drug Administration, United States Dept. of Health, Ed. and Welfare, 263

National Petroleum Refiners Ass'n v. F. T. C., 222, 223

National Small Shipments Traffic Conference, Inc. v. I.C.C., 263

National Velour Corp. v. Durfee, 434

New Jersey Civil Service Ass'n v. State, 691, 695, 696

New Jersey, Dept. of Environmental Protection, State of v. USEPA, 327

New York v. Burger, 177

New York City Dept. of Environmental Protection v. New York City Civil Service Com'n, 637, 638

New York City Employees' Retirement System v. S.E.C., 355

New York, State of v. Lyng, 301

New York, State of v. Reilly, 506

Neyland v. Board of Educ. of Town of Redding, 637

Ng Fung Ho v. White, 551, 553

Nguyen v. United States, 296, 300, 301

Nielsen Lithographing Co. v. N.L.R.B., 207

Nixon v. Administrator of General Services, 487

Nixon v. Fitzgerald, 626

Nixon, United States v., 337, 518, 519

N.L.R.B. v. Bell Aerospace Co. Div. of Textron, Inc., 363

N.L.R.B. v. Donnelly Garment Co., 129

N.L.R.B. v. Hearst Publications, 576

N.L.R.B. v. Mackay Radio & Telegraph Co., 114

N. L. R. B. v. Sears, Roebuck & Co., 507, **510,** 516, 517, 518

N.L.R.B. v. St. Francis Hosp. of Lynwood, 365

N.L.R.B. v. Universal Camera Corp., 190 F.2d 429, p. 547

N.L.R.B. v. Universal Camera Corp., 179 F.2d 749, p. 547

N. L. R. B. v. Wyman–Gordon Co., 358, 365, 366, 375

Nor–Am Agr. Products, Inc. v. Hardin, 673

North American Cold Storage Co. v. Chicago, 61

Northeast Ohio Regional Sewer Dist. v. Shank, 311

Northern Arapahoe Tribe v. Hodel, 325

Northern Pipeline Const. Co. v. Marathon Pipe Line Co., 428, 432, 433, 552

Northside Sanitary Landfill, Inc. v. Thomas, 292

Northwestern Bell Telephone Co., Inc. v. Stofferahn, 286

Office of Personnel Management v. Richmond, 212, 215

Ohio, State of v. United States Dept. of the Interior, 570

Ohio Valley Water Co. v. Ben Avon Borough, 550, 551, 552, 553, 554

Ojai Unified School Dist. v. Jackson, 553

Oklahoma City, City of v. State ex rel. Oklahoma Dept. of Labor, 418, 419

Oklahoma Press Pub. Co. v. Walling, 174, 176

Olabanji v. I.N.S., 187

1616 Second Ave. Restaurant, Inc. v. New York State Liquor Authority, 132

One Tract of Real Property, United States v., 64

On–Line Financial Services, Inc. v. Department of Human Rights, 695
Opinion of the Justices, In re, 179 A. 344, p. 434
Opinion of the Justices, 431 A.2d 783, p. 459
Opinion of the Justices, 309 N.E.2d 476, p. 470

Pacific Gas & Elec. Co. v. Federal Power Commission, 344, 345
Pacific Legal Foundation v. California Coastal Com'n, 682
Pacific States Box & Basket Co. v. White, 602
Panama Refining Co. v. Ryan, 400, 401, 402, 428
Panhandle Producers & Royalty Owners Ass'n v. Economic Regulatory Admin., 345
Paralyzed Veterans of America v. D.C. Arena L.P., 353, 355
Parcell v. State, 470, 471, 472
Parratt v. Taylor, 69
Parsons, State ex rel. Kincaid v., 227
Parsons v. United States, 491
Partain v. Maddox, 491
Patsy v. Florida Board of Regents, 698
Paul v. Davis, 50, 51, 69
Payne, United States v., 207
Pell v. Board of Ed. of Union Free School Dist. No. 1 of Towns of Scarsdale and Mamaroneck, Westchester County, 592
Pennsylvania v. Delaware Valley Citizens' Council for Clean Air, 629
Pennsylvania Indus. Chemical Corp., United States v., 215
Pennsylvania State Bd. of Pharmacy v. Cohen, 373
Pension Ben. Guar. Corp. v. LTV Corp., 91, 199, 260, 261, 566, 587
People v. ____(see opposing party)
Peralta Community College Dist. v. Fair Employment and Housing Com'n (Brown), 438
Perry v. Sindermann, 39, 41, 42, 44
Petroleum Information Corp. v. United States Dept. of Interior, 516
Pfaff v. United States Dept. of Housing and Urban Development, 366
Pieper Elec., Inc. v. Labor and Industry Review Com'n, 548
Pierce v. Underwood, 631
Pievsky v. Ridge, 492
Pillsbury Co. v. F. T. C., 142, 146, 147, 148
Playboy Enterprises, Inc. v. Meese, 627
Pollack v. Simonson, 91
Portela–Gonzalez v. Secretary of the Navy, 693
Portland Audubon Soc. v. Endangered Species Committee, 90, 140
Portland Cement Ass'n v. Ruckelshaus, 242, 243, 259
Powderly v. Schweiker, 301

Process Gas Consumers Group v. Consumer Energy Council of America, 452
Professional Air Traffic Controllers Organization v. Federal Labor Relations Authority, 132, 139, 141, 146
Public Citizen v. United States Dept. of Justice, 531
Public Citizen v. Young, 309
Public Citizen Health Research Group v. Tyson, 610
Public Citizen, Inc. v. F.A.A., 292
Public Service Co. of New Hampshire, Appeal of, 142

Rafeedie v. I.N.S., 697
Railroad Commission of Tex. v. Rowan & Nichols Oil Co., 311 U.S. 570, p. 551
Railroad Commission of Texas v. Rowan & Nichols Oil Co., 310 U.S. 573, p. 551
Raines v. Byrd, 666, 667
Ramos v. Texas Tech University, 98
Rauenhorst v. United States Department of Transp., Federal Highway Admin., 394
Realty Group, Inc. v. Department of Revenue, 356
Redwood Village Partnership v. Graham, 626
Reguero v. Teacher Standards and Practices Com'n, 182, 185
Reich v. Great Lakes Indian Fish and Wildlife Com'n, 174
Reiter v. Cooper, 704
Reno v. Catholic Social Services, Inc., 683
Retail, Wholesale and Dept. Store Union, AFL–CIO v. N. L. R. B., 234, 367
Rhoa–Zamora v. I.N.S., 193
Richard v. Commissioner of Income Maintenance, 240
Richardson v. Perales, 186
Richmond Tenants Organization, Inc. v. Kemp, 64
Riley, State ex rel. Missouri Power & Light Co. v., 637
Riverbend Farms, Inc. v. Madigan, 328
River Park, Inc. v. City of Highland Park, 82
Riverside, City of v. Rivera, 629
Rodway v. United States Dept. of Agriculture, 292, 330
Roe v. Wade, 40
Rollins Environmental Services, Inc., Matter of, 131
Rosenthal v. Hartnett, 439
Rowell v. Andrus, 302
R.R. Donnelley & Sons Co. v. F.T.C., 675
Rust v. Sullivan, 354, 421, 567
Ryan v. New York Telephone Co., 205
Rybachek v. United States E.P.A., 243

Safe Bldgs. Alliance v. E.P.A., 321
Salameda v. I.N.S., 579, 585, 587, 588, 592
Saleeby v. State Bar of California, 41
Salk v. Weinraub, 637

Sandin v. Conner, 47, 50, 72

Sangamon Val. Television Corp. v. United States, 275

San Luis Obispo Mothers for Peace v. United States Nuclear Regulatory Com'n, 116

Save a Valuable Environment (SAVE) v. City of Bothell, 130

Scheuer v. Rhodes, 625

Schluraff v. Rzymek, 491, 492

Schneider, State ex rel. v. Bennett, 472

Schweiker v. Chilicky, 625

Scott, People v., 177

Seacoast Anti–Pollution League v. Costle, 89, 250

Sealed Case, In re, 518

S.E.C. v. Blinder, Robinson & Co., Inc., 491

S.E.C. v. Jerry T. O'Brien, Inc., 175

S.E.C. v. Lavin, 176

Securities and Exchange Commission v. Chenery Corp., 201, 293, 588

Sehlmeyer v. Department of General Services (Stempf), 175

Sepulveda v. Block, 326

Serrano v. Priest, 628

Service v. Dulles, 337

Shalala v. Guernsey Memorial Hosp., 354

Shapiro v. United States, 177

Shaughnessy v. Pedreiro, 635

Shell Oil Co. v. E.P.A., 244

Shell Oil Co. v. Federal Power Commission, 251

Sherman v. Board of Regents of University of State of N. Y., 578

Ship Creek Hydraulic Syndicate v. State of Alaska, 200

Shurtleff v. United States, 491

Shuttlesworth v. Birmingham, Ala., 408, 409

Siegert v. Gilley, 51

Sierra Club v. Costle, 140, 267, 272, 273, 274, 275, 276, 277, 278, 291, 498, 501, 503

Sierra Club v. Morton, 663

Sims, People v., 207

Small Refiner Lead Phase–Down Task Force v. USEPA, 312

Smiley v. Citibank (South Dakota), N.A., 234

Smith v. National Transp. Safety Bd., 508

Soglin v. Kauffman, 373

Solite Corp. v. United States E.P.A., 243

Sotelo–Aquije v. Slattery, 631

Southwestern Bell Telephone Co. v. Oklahoma Corp. Com'n, 142

Spilotro v. State, ex rel. Nevada Gaming Com'n, 202

Spradlin v. Arkansas Ethics Com'n, 471

Springer v. Government of Philippine Islands, 470

State v. _____ (see opposing party)

State Bd. of Registration for Healing Arts v. Finch, 161

State ex rel. v. _____ (see opposing party and relator)

State Farm Mut. Auto. Ins. Co. v. Dole, 681

State of (see name of state)

State Through Bd. of Ethics for Elected Officials v. Green, 471

Stauffer Chemical Co., United States v., 205

Steadman v. S. E. C., 187

Steel Co. v. Citizens for a Better Environment, 664

Stewart v. Smith, 331

St. Joseph Stock Yards Co. v. United States, 550, 551, 552, 553, 554

Stoller v. Commodity Futures Trading Com'n, 366

Storer Broadcasting Co., United States v., 105, 106

Straka, State v., 226

Sugarloaf Citizens Ass'n v. Northeast Maryland Waste Disposal Authority, 93, **94,** 97, 98, 99

Sullivan v. Zebley, 105

Sun–Brite Car Wash, Inc. v. Board of Zoning and Appeals of Town of North Hempstead, 654

Sutton, United States v., 324

Swick v. City of Chicago, 46

Syncor Intern. Corp. v. Shalala, 355

Tennessee Elec. Power Co. v. Tennessee Val. Authority, 648, 649

Tenney v. Brandhove, 626

Tew v. City of Topeka Police and Fire Civil Service Com'n, 337

Texas Boll Weevil Eradication Foundation, Inc. v. Lewellen, 417

Texas Food Industry Ass'n v. United States Dept. of Agriculture, 630

13th Regional Corp. v. United States Dept. of Interior, 619

Thunder Basin Coal Co. v. Reich, 683, 684

Thygesen v. Callahan, 414, 416

Tidewater Marine Western, Inc. v. Bradshaw, 357

Times Mirror Co. v. Superior Court (State), 516

Tite v. State Tax Commission, 438

Todd & Co., Inc. v. S.E.C., 417

Toilet Goods Ass'n, Inc. v. Gardner, 678, 679, 680, 682, 685

Town of (see name of town)

Trans–Pacific Freight Conference of Japan/Korea v. Federal Maritime Commission, 291

Trebesch v. Employment Div., 374

Trident Seafoods Corp., United States v., 216

Trust & Inv. Advisers, Inc. v. Hogsett, 131

Tull v. United States, 435

Tumey v. State of Ohio, 128

Unger v. National Residents Matching Program, 45, 69, 70

United Auto. Workers of America v. N.L.R.B., 208, 209, 210

United Church of Christ v. F. C. C., 167, 168, 649

United Food and Commercial Workers Intern. Union, AFL–CIO, Local No. 150–A v. N.L.R.B., 367

United States v. ———— (see opposing party)

United States Dept. of Labor v. Kast Metals Corp., 332, 335, 336, 344

United States Gypsum Co., United States v., 535

United States Lines, Inc. v. Federal Maritime Commission, 91

United States Telephone Ass'n v. F.C.C., 347

United Steelworkers of America, AFL–CIO–CLC v. Schuylkill Metals Corp., 240

United Technologies Corp. v. United States E.P.A., 353

Universal Camera Corp. v. N.L.R.B., 535, 536, 545, 547, 548, 549, 557

University of Kansas Faculty, Matter of, 115

University of Tennessee v. Elliott, 203, 205

Upton v. S.E.C., 216

USA Group Loan Services, Inc. v. Riley, 320

Uzwij v. Robins, 699

Vail v. Board of Educ. of Paris Union School Dist. No. 95, 46

Valmonte v. Bane, 51

Vandygriff v. First Sav. and Loan Ass'n of Borger, 139

Van Harken v. City of Chicago, 71, 72, 439

Veg–Mix, Inc. v. United States Dept. of Agriculture, 107

Vermont Yankee Nuclear Power Corp. v. Natural Resources Defense Council, Inc., 91, 199, 200, **254,** 258, 259, 260, 261, 275, 291, 344, 603, 606

Vietnam Veterans of America v. Secretary of the Navy, 337

Village of (see name of village)

Vitarelli v. Seaton, 337

Volvo GM Heavy Truck Corp. v. United States Dept. of Labor, 696

WAIT Radio v. F. C. C., 459 F.2d 1203, p. 389

WAIT Radio v. F. C. C., 418 F.2d 1153, p. **386,** 390

Walker v. City of Berkeley, 118, 119, 120, 122

Wallace, State ex rel. v. Bone, 471

Walter v. Torres, 626

Walters v. Radiation Survivors, 32, 70, 71, 72

Ward v. Keenan, 695

Ward v. Village of Monroeville, Ohio, 128

Warren v. Marion County, 417

Warren v. United States, 553

Warth v. Seldin, 664

Washington Ass'n for Television and Children v. F.C.C., 698

Washington Research Project, Inc. v. Department of Health, Ed. and Welfare, 525

Watergate II Apartments v. Buffalo Sewer Authority, 695

Watson v. Pennsylvania Turnpike Commission, 491, 492

Waukegan, City of v. Pollution Control Bd., 438

Webster v. Doe, 636, 643, 644

Weeks v. Personnel Bd. of Review of Town of North Kingstown, 553

Weinberger v. Hynson, Westcott & Dunning, Inc., 106, 107

West Chicago, Ill., City of v. United States Nuclear Regulatory Com'n, 85, 89, 90, 92, 97, 98, 107, 250

Western States Petroleum Ass'n v. E.P.A., 628

Western States Petroleum Ass'n v. Superior Court (Air Resources Bd.), 591

Whispering Pines Mobile Home Park, Ltd. v. City of Scotts Valley (Dickerman), 195

White v. Roughton, 373

Wiener v. United States, 476, 477, 489, 491

Wilcox v. People ex rel. Lipe, 490, 491

Wilderness Soc. v. Morton, 627

Williamson v. Lee Optical of Okl., 40

Wisconsin v. Constantineau, 50

Wisconsin Elec. Power Co. v. Costle, 382

Withrow v. Larkin, 119, 120, 122

Wittler v. Baumgartner, 472

Wolff v. McDonnell, 47, 50

Wong Wing v. United States, 437

Wong Yang Sung v. McGrath, 92

Woodby v. Immigration and Naturalization Service, 188

Wright v. Central Du Page Hospital Ass'n, 434

Wright v. Plaza Ford, 439

WWHT, Inc. v. F. C. C., 379, 381, 382

Yakus v. United States, 401, 402, 403, 636, 637

Yellow Freight System, Inc., United States v., 705

Yerardi's Moody Street Restaurant and Lounge, Inc. v. Board of Selectmen of Randolph, 621

Yesler Terrace Community Council v. Cisneros, 226, 227

Young, Ex parte, 624

Youngstown Sheet & Tube Co. v. Sawyer, 496, 497, 501

Zablocki v. Redhail, 40

Zinermon v. Burch, 69

STATE AND FEDERAL ADMINISTRATIVE LAW

Second Edition

*

Chapter 1

INTRODUCTION

§ 1.1 ADMINISTRATIVE AGENCIES AND ADMINISTRATIVE LAW

Administrative agencies are units of government other than the legislature and the courts. Agencies typically have legal power to affect the rights or duties of individuals or entities outside the government. Agencies administer or execute law under powers delegated to them by statutes. There are thousands of agencies at all levels of government—federal, state, and local.

Administrative agencies may be headed by a single official or by several officials, and may be called a department, commission, board or another name. Most agencies are part of the executive branch of government but others are independent of the executive. While the heads of most agencies are appointed by the chief executive, in the states some agency heads are directly elected.

Agencies vary in size from units with no full time officials or employees and minuscule budgets to units with many thousands of employees and budgets in the billions of dollars. Some agencies make millions of determinations each year (such as Medicare and social security decisions) while others make only a handful of determinations. Agencies are specialists. Some specialize in a particular problem wherever it occurs, like labor-management relations or consumer protection, while others specialize in problems arising in particular industries, like transportation or securities.

Many agencies are *regulatory* in the sense that they enforce a mandatory scheme of prohibitions or obligations, such as environmental protection. Other agencies are *benefactory,* meaning that they disburse benefits such as social security. To carry out these diverse missions, agencies are authorized by statute to investigate, to prosecute, to make law, to adjudicate, to license, and to perform various other functions.

Administrative law deals with the legal principles common to all administrative agencies, including the procedures that agencies use to

1

carry out their functions and the rules relating to judicial review of agency actions. Administrative law also defines the role of the courts, the legislature, and the chief executive, vis-à-vis agencies. It does not deal with the *substantive* law enforced by agencies. Substantive issues relating to taxation, labor relations, welfare, or environmental law, for instance, are covered in courses on those particular subjects.

A course in administrative law, therefore, has much in common with a course on civil procedure. It cuts across many substantive law areas and assumes that administrative agencies have enough in common to be worth studying. In short, administrative law is a course in procedural law rather than a course in substantive law.

§ 1.2 REASONS FOR STUDYING ADMINISTRATIVE LAW

The reasons for studying administrative law are compelling. Our society may fairly be characterized as an administrative state. Agency administered law regulates or affects almost all aspects of our lives on a daily basis. Consequently, virtually every lawyer routinely encounters state and federal administrative agencies and administrative law problems.

If you are doing real estate work, you will have to deal with agencies administering the local zoning and land use planning laws as well as environmental laws and building and safety laws. If you practice tax, immigration, or labor law, you will be in intimate contact with administrative bureaucracies at every stage of your practice. A general business lawyer deals with many different agencies—agencies that license occupations and professions, regulate the issuance of securities, enforce antidiscrimination laws, administer consumer protection laws, oversee environmental protection laws, and apply safety in the workplace laws. If you represent hospitals or banks, you have to deal with a maze of regulatory agencies. If you represent clients receiving social security or welfare payments or involved in government contracting or seeking government grants, you will have to deal with the agencies administering those programs. The handling of a driver's license problem requires you to deal with an agency.

Every time this happens, you will, of course, have to know the applicable substantive law; but you will also have to know about administrative procedure and judicial review of agency action. For all these reasons, a knowledge of administrative law is as essential as a knowledge of civil procedure.

§ 1.3 STATE AND FEDERAL ADMINISTRATIVE LAW

This administrative law coursebook differs from other such books. Other coursebooks use predominantly federal materials to introduce students to the subject. In contrast, this book constantly compares state and federal materials.

State administrative law is important in its own right. In a recent case which dealt with the question of whether a federal court rather than an Idaho state court should decide a dispute involving claims by an Indian tribe to submerged lands, the U. S. Supreme Court said:

> It is a principal concern of the court system in any State to define and maintain a proper balance between the State's courts on one hand, and its officials and administrative agencies on the other. This is of vital concern to States. As the Idaho State Attorney General has explained, "everywhere a citizen turns—to apply for a life-sustaining public benefit, to obtain a license, to respond to a complaint—it is [administrative law] that governs the way in which their contact with state government will be carried out." In the states there is an ongoing process by which state courts and state agencies work to elaborate an administrative law designed to reflect the State's own rules and traditions concerning the respective scope of judicial review and administrative discretion. *Idaho v. Coeur d'Alene Tribe*, 117 S.Ct. 2028, 2037 (1997)

Aside from the intrinsic importance of the subject, one reason to study state law along with federal law is that there are many differences between them. As a result, a comparison of state and federal law can stimulate insights into problems and solutions in the administrative process that cannot be obtained from federal materials alone.

A second reason to study state administrative materials is to better prepare yourself to deal with the realities of law practice. Most citizens and lawyers confront state and local agencies much more often than federal agencies. Knowledge of state and local administrative practice is, therefore, essential to prepare for the kind of law practice you will actually encounter. In addition, you probably have already had personal opportunities to deal with state and local government agencies. Therefore, a study of state law examples may be more meaningful than a study confined wholly to more remote federal law examples.

§ 1.4 ADMINISTRATIVE PROCEDURE ACTS

The principal sources of administrative law are federal and state constitutions, statutes, and judge-made common law. Of special importance are administrative procedure acts (APAs). The federal government and most of the states have general and comprehensive APAs. *We will be considering state and federal APA provisions in virtually every class.* APAs are *general,* meaning that they apply to all or most agencies rather than to just one or a few. And they are *comprehensive,* meaning that they deal with the the main problems in administrative law: public access to agency information, agency rulemaking procedure, agency adjudication procedure, and judicial review.

Some people opposed the enactment of general and comprehensive APAs. Because there are enormous differences between agencies, the opponents of the APA concept believed that each agency should have its own procedural statute. However, others believed that the benefits of a single statutory procedural code binding on all agencies were substantial, and that a *minimum* code that dealt only with *general and fundamental principles* rather than with details was both desirable and feasible. Once the federal APA was adopted, most states followed suit. *See* Arthur E. Bonfield, "The Federal APA and State Administrative Law," 72 Va. L.Rev. 297, 303–308 (1986).

Here is some background on the federal Act:

The landmark [federal APA] was the bill of rights for the new regulatory state. Enacted in 1946, the APA established the fundamental relationship between regulatory agencies and those whom they regulate-between government, on the one hand, and private citizens, business, and the economy, on the other hand. The balance that the APA struck between promoting individuals' rights and maintaining agencies' policy-making flexibility has continued in force, with only minor modifications, until the present. The APA's impact has been large. It has provided agencies with broad freedom, limited only by relatively weak procedural requirements and judicial review, to create and implement policies in the many areas that agencies touch: from aviation to the environment, from labor relations to the securities markets. The APA permitted the growth of the modern regulatory state.

The APA and its history are central to the United States' economic and political development. In the 1930s and 1940s when the APA was debated, much in the United States was uncertain. Many believed that communism was a real possibility, as were fascism and dictatorship. Many supporters of the New Deal favored a form of government in which expert bureaucrats would influence even the details of the economy, with little recourse for the people and businesses that felt the impacts of the bureaucrats' commands. To New Dealers, this was efficiency. To the New Deal's opponents, this was dictatorial central planning. The battle over the APA helped to resolve the conflict between bureaucratic efficiency and the rule of law, and permitted the continued growth of government regulation. The APA expressed the nation's decision to permit extensive government, but to avoid dictatorship and central planning. The decision has shaped the nation for fifty years.

Since the time of the APA's adoption, and even before, some commentators have suggested that the APA was universally beloved legislation.... This widely held perception of the APA's history is inaccurate. The APA's development was not primarily a search for administrative truth and efficiency. Nor was it a theoretically centered debate on appropriate roles for government and governed. Instead, the fight over the APA was a pitched political battle for the life of the New Deal. The more than a decade of political combat that preceded the adoption of the APA was one of the major political struggles in the war between supporters and opponents of the New Deal. Republicans and Southern Democrats sought to crush New Deal programs by means of administrative controls on agencies....

The APA that finally emerged in 1946 did not represent a unanimous social consensus about the proper balance between individual rights and agency powers. The APA was a hard-fought compromise that left many legislators and interest groups far from completely satisfied. Congressional support for the bill was unanimous only because many legislators recognized that, although the bill was imperfect, it was better than no bill. The APA passed only with much grumbling.

George B. Shepherd, "Fierce Compromise: The Administrative Procedure Act Emerges from New Deal Politics," 90 Nw.U.L.Rev. 1557, 1558–60 (1996).

Most state APAs were enacted between 1955 and 1980, although California led the way in 1945. The state acts usually apply to most or all agencies of the state but they do not cover local administrative agencies. The APAs of more than half of the states are based in whole or in part on the 1961 Model State APA (MSAPA). *See* 15 U.L.A. 137 (1990). In 1981 the Commissioners on Uniform State Laws adopted an entirely new MSAPA. A number of states have already adopted some of the provisions of the 1981 MSAPA.

§ 1.5   A SNAPSHOT OF THE ADMINISTRATIVE PROCESS

Suppose that the state legislature has been deluged with complaints about unfair practices in the automobile insurance industry. It is not sure exactly how to solve the problem, so it enacts a rather vaguely worded statute prohibiting unfair and discriminatory automobile insurance practices. This statute, of course, is not self-enforcing. So the legislature creates an agency called the Automobile Insurance Commission (AIC) to enforce it, and authorizes the AIC to engage in a variety of activities to secure that result. According to statute, the AIC will have a director (or perhaps several agency heads), a staff, and a budget.

What techniques are available to the AIC in carrying out this mission?

i. *Research and publicity.* One relatively uncontroversial function that the AIC will be authorized to perform is to find out what the problems are and what solutions are available. For this purpose it may simply serve as a central clearing house for information on the subject of automobile insurance. On the other hand, the AIC may find that it needs more information so it may commission research by its staff or by outside consultants.

AIC might also decide to publicize the results of its findings. For example, it might publish a directory of automobile insurance premiums or a study of consumer complaints against insurance companies. Publicity of this kind can be an important aid to consumers in making their own economic decisions and thus can help the free market work more efficiently.

ii. *Rulemaking.* We have assumed the legislature was not certain of the precise scope of the automobile insurance problem or how it should be solved. Often, a statute of this sort can be enacted only by a compromise between proponents and opponents which resolves very few of the hard issues. Instead, the responsibility for solving those issues is passed to an agency. The political process, which was not completed in the legislature, will then resume in the agency when it takes up these issues.

The agency enabling act will probably authorize it to adopt rules which set forth automobile insurance practices that are allowed and forbidden. (Incidentally, the words "rule" and "regulation" mean the same thing and will be used interchangeably in this book). For instance, suppose AIC believes that it is unfair for insurers to charge different premiums to consumers with different ZIP codes. It will first study the problem. Then it will propose, and later adopt, rules prohibiting such conduct. Broadly speaking, rules are agency statements of *general* applicability and *future* effect that implement, interpret, or prescribe law or policy.

In practical effect, agency rules are just like statutes because they determine legal rights and duties. The state APA undoubtedly will require AIC to furnish advance notice to the public of its intention to adopt these rules, allow the public to comment on the proposals, consider and respond to those comments, explain the rules, publish them, and allow a grace period before they become effective.

Administrative rules are a very important part of the legal landscape today. There are rules relating to taxation, safety in the workplace, welfare benefits, air and water pollution, social security and Medicare benefits, automobile safety, civil rights, and much, much more. Next time you're in the law library, look at the many bookshelves containing the Code of Federal Regulations (C.F.R.). While the official United States Code is contained in perhaps two dozen volumes, C.F.R. comprises hundreds of volumes. And those volumes contain only *federal* regulations—the published rules of your state and city agencies fill many more volumes and probably also surpass in size the state statutes and city ordinances. In addition to these published rules, agencies issue many documents called guidelines, interpretations, manuals, bulletins, circulars, or policy statements, to guide the public and their own staff in interpreting the law and in determining how agency discretion will be exercised. These documents are still considered rules but tend not to be legally binding and can be adopted with lesser formalities or even no formalities at all.

iii. *Licensing.* A license authorizes an individual or entity to engage in a specified activity. The statute creating AIC might authorize it to license insurance companies or insurance brokers. The AIC will issue rules specifying the qualifications for obtaining a license (financial qualifications, education, experience, an exam etc.) and rules specifying what licensees may and may not do. It will also issue rules providing when and how licenses may be revoked or suspended.

Licensing schemes can be beneficial. They help to assure that consumers are served only by properly qualified entities or professionals. But such schemes also have costs. They are a barrier to entry, often requiring licensees to have more education, experience or financial resources than are really needed. In that case, licensing tends to decrease competition and increase prices without compensating public benefit. A regulated industry may have "captured" an agency so that the agency power is turned against the interests of the public rather than the regulated industry. For these reasons, we suggest close scrutiny when analyzing the desirability of licensing schemes.

Permits are a form of license. An agency may be authorized to require a permit before specified action may occur. If AIC adopted a permit system, for example, an automobile insurance company might be required to secure permission from that agency before changing its rates or changing the terms of its policies. Permits are often required before a power plant may be built, before a new bank may be opened, and before new drugs or pesticides may be sold.

Permit systems are sometimes necessary, as in the case of an extremely dangerous activity like building a nuclear power plant or selling a new drug. However, they are costly to administer, usually entail long delays, may be harmful to the competitive system (which requires competitors to respond promptly to market conditions), and may in practice allow an administrator to substitute his or her wisdom for that of the market. And note that a staff member who must make a decision to grant a permit is likely to be conservative and cautious; that might mean that some products are never approved. For example, many drugs are available in Europe but not in the United States, because our system of regulation is more restrictive. The wisdom of this result is, of course, debatable.

A less drastic approach is sometimes referred to as a clearance system. Under that approach, an agency requires certain steps to be taken by the regulated party before that party may proceed with a specified type of action. If the agency does nothing, the party may proceed. Thus the agency must take affirmative steps to stop the project. One important example of a clearance system concerns environmental impact statements; a builder might be required to file such a statement before taking action that could be detrimental to the environment. Or a corporation may be required to file disclosure documents and issue a prospectus before selling securities. Under the clearance approach, AIC might require automobile insurance companies to notify AIC before changing the rates or the terms of their policies.

iv. *Investigation and law enforcement.* An agency needs to ensure that those subject to the statute and rules actually follow them. The agency must keep in touch with regulated parties to make sure that they understand their responsibilities. It must be prepared to receive complaints from the public and needs a staff to investigate those complaints. To effectively enforce the law, an agency must have formal investigatory powers to subpoena documents, inspect premises, and obtain routine reports from regulated parties. If agency staff believes it has uncovered a law violation, the agency must be able to initiate enforcement action against the offender because statutes and rules will not enforce themselves, and members of the public often do not have the resources, the will, or the information to do so. For practical purposes, therefore, an agency functions much like a police department *and* a prosecuting office.

v. *Adjudication.* An adjudication is an agency determination of *particular* applicability that affects the legal rights or duties of a specified person based upon his or her individual circumstances. For example, AIC might adjudicate whether the license of a particular insurance company or broker should be suspended or revoked because of a violation of AIC rules.

The AIC might also be empowered to resolve disputes between consumers and insurance companies over questions of coverage, rates, or unjust cancellation. In other words, agencies are sometimes authorized to decide private-party disputes that would ordinarily be decided in the courts. An important example is workers' compensation; agencies administering compensation schemes resolve disputes between employers and employees over injuries on the job.

State and federal APAs prescribe the procedures that agencies must follow when engaging in adjudication. In addition, the due process clauses of state and federal constitutions impose significant constraints on agency adjudication. As a result, AIC will typically be required to afford the parties involved in adjudication a trial-type hearing of some sort. That hearing will normally be conducted by a person called a presiding officer, a hearing officer, or an administrative law judge (the names of these administrative judges vary among different agencies and different states). The administrative judge's decision usually may be appealed to the agency head. This part of administrative law may seem familiar because it is not unlike civil procedure. But the differences between courts and adjudicating agencies are profound.

An agency is usually (though not always) a party to the dispute it is adjudicating. A court, on the other hand, is an uninvolved arbiter. In addition, because an agency specializes in its particular regulatory process, it acquires experience and technical expertise. Judges, on the other hand, are usually generalists, not specialists. Finally, an agency makes the rules, investigates violations, prosecutes cases, and adjudicates cases; a court only adjudicates cases and therefore is not subject to conflicts between potentially inconsistent functions. All of these factors raise serious problems in assuring fair and impartial agency adjudication.

vi. *Ratemaking.* Suppose the legislature wants to regulate auto insurance rates. As a practical matter, it cannot set the rates itself, because the process is extremely time-consuming and the rates require constant adjustment as market conditions change. Therefore, it will have to delegate the ratemaking power to AIC.

Administrative price fixing is a common technique, particularly in situations of natural monopoly (local phones, gas, electricity, cable TV) or when market failures of one sort or another are thought to prevent the market from functioning properly. In the recent past we have partially or completely abandoned government price fixing of transportation (trucking, airlines, busses, railroads, pipelines) and financial services (banking, stock brokerage). Increasingly, utility services are being deregulated. In some places, rent control persists although it also seems to be fading away.

In order to fix prices on either an industry-wide or a company-specific basis, AIC must observe appropriate procedures. Depending on whether the rates are industry-wide or company-specific, the appropriate process may look more like rulemaking or adjudication. Either way, the process will be a lengthy one since the rates can be set only after detailed economic information is collected and analyzed and a fair rate of return is determined. In any case, one may question whether rate fixing is needed or even useful in a competitive market like automobile insurance.

vii. *Judicial review.* Judicial review of administrative action occurs very frequently. Unlike other countries (such as France), in this country there is no specialized administrative court. The same judges resolve private disputes and review agency action. Broadly speaking, courts review final agency action (both rules and adjudication) for errors of law and for reasonableness in finding facts or exercising discretion. A typical challenge to agency action may include allegations that it was procedurally improper, that it was unconstitutional or inconsistent with applicable substantive law, that it was unsupported factually, or that it was arbitrary.

Inevitably, if AIC adopts rules that either consumers or the insurance industry do not like, the procedural and substantive validity of the rules will be challenged in court. Similarly, if AIC revokes a license, the licensee will probably seek judicial review. In short, judicial review is a fundamental and extremely common element of our administrative process.

viii. *Legislative and executive review.* In addition to judicial review, both the legislative and executive branches of government scrutinize the actions of agencies. The legislature engages in oversight, investigating agency action and amending agency enabling statutes when it deems that desirable. In some states, the legislature has other powers to control agencies such as a power to delay or even veto agency rules or other actions. The legislature can also influence agency action by increasing or decreasing the agency's budget or defunding it altogether.

The chief executive (the governor in our example) will appoint the head or heads of AIC. Especially because the field of auto insurance is politically sensitive, members of the governor's staff will keep track of AIC's activities. The governor may have the authority to remove the AIC agency heads for any reason. However, if AIC is an "independent" agency, the governor can remove the heads only for good cause. A statute may also give the chief executive authority to delay or veto agency rules. And the governor has substantial control over AIC's budget; he or she can request budget increases or decreases and, in many states, has a line item veto which can be used to decrease the agency's current spending.

The above snapshot of the administrative process is meant only to convey a general idea of what agencies do and how they are controlled. In fact, the administrative process is very diverse. Each agency, for good reasons, has its own way of doing business. As a result, when a client has a problem with a particular agency, you have to consult not only general principles of administrative law but also that agency's enabling act, its substantive and procedural rules, and the administrative and judicial precedents relating to the regulatory scheme in question.

§ 1.6 COSTS AND BENEFITS OF ADMINISTRATIVE PROCEDURE AND PROCEDURAL REFORM

To determine whether a particular legal requirement relating to the administrative process makes sense, you must first consider the principal objectives of sound agency administration. Agencies should act lawfully, be responsive to the wishes of the public, make accurate and sound determinations, and treat affected persons fairly. Agencies should also act in an efficient, effective, and economical manner. Sometimes these objectives conflict with each other—for example, extra procedures to assure accurate and fair results may cause unacceptable delays or be very expensive.

Thus each procedural requirement calls for a comparison of its costs and benefits. First, determine the benefits of the requirement by asking whether it is likely to achieve one or more of the objectives mentioned in the previous paragraph. Second, estimate the costs of that requirement by asking about the extent to which it interferes with one or more of those objectives. Finally, try to determine whether the benefits of the particular requirement outweigh its costs. And be sure to consider possible alternatives to the requirement that might achieve the objectives sought at a lesser cost.

Of course, this cost-benefit approach is not intended to be rigorously scientific. It is value laden at every turn and must be resolved by an exercise of judgment. While empirical data may be helpful, such data cannot finally resolve the inquiry. The defensibility of the cost-benefit judgment depends on the quality of the arguments marshalled in its support rather than on the basis of any equation seeking to reduce disparate costs, benefits, and values, to a single common denominator, so that they may be mechanically compared.

An issue that pervades the subject of administrative law concerns agency discretion. Agencies always have a range of permissible options they can choose in resolving a particular problem by rulemaking or adjudication. This range of choice is called "discretion." One of the great tasks of administrative law is to find the optimum degree to which agency discretion should be constrained by the legislature, the courts, or by the agency itself. Unfettered discretion gives agencies maximum flexibility to deal with unforeseen or changing problems, but it also allows them to act in irresponsible or arbitrary ways. Fettered discretion denies agencies flexibility in dealing with unforeseen or changing problems and limits their opportunities to act in irresponsible or arbitrary ways.

Another underlying administrative law problem relates to the essential nature of bureaucracies. The question is whether legal requirements can prevent a bureaucracy that is created to advance the public interest from becoming captured by the groups it is intended to regulate, from taking action primarily to serve the self interest of the bureaucracy rather than the interests of the public, or from becoming rigid, wasteful, ineffective, and generally counter-productive.

Critics of the administrative process claim it suffers from many ills. They complain that the process is often unresponsive to the public will, slow and cumbersome, ineffective and inefficient, and unfair to private interests. Critics of the administrative process often advance deregulation as the solution to these problems. However, when deregulation is not feasible, such problems can often be alleviated through procedural reform.

State, federal, and local legislative bodies, and the agencies themselves, constantly tinker with the administrative process. Congress is perpetually involved in considering administrative procedure reform although, surprisingly, the basic outlines of the federal APA have remained unchanged since its enactment in 1946. Until recently, the Administrative Conference of the United States (cited throughout this book as ACUS) generated many proposals for reform, but unfortunately ACUS was defunded by Congress in 1995. At the state level, the National Conference of Commissioners on Uniform State Laws have proposed a series of Model APAs, most recently in 1981, and are in the process of proposing legislation concerning the independence of administrative judges.

§ 1.7 AGENCY LEGITIMACY AND ADMINISTRATIVE LAW

As discussed in the previous subsection, the administrative process should be lawful and fair and produce accurate results at acceptable cost.

In addition, the process must strive for *legitimacy*. In this context, legitimacy means that the exercise of power by administrative agencies is recognized by regulated parties and the community at large as politically acceptable.

In most cases federal and state constitutions do not even mention administrative agencies and agency heads are not elected (with a few exceptions at the state level). As a result, the legitimacy of the exercise of power by administrative agencies has constantly been questioned. Many people simply don't accept the idea that administrative agencies should be permitted to exercise legal power. Theorists have long struggled with the legitimacy problem. *See generally* Richard B. Stewart, "The Reformation of American Administrative Law," 88 Harv.L.Rev. 1667 (1975), for an excellent treatment of legitimacy theories.

Recently, public choice scholars have further attacked the legitimacy of the administrative process, on the theory that agencies mostly carry out special-interest deals previously brokered in the legislature. Some scholars argue that most delegations of authority to administrative agencies are objectionable. *See* Peter Aranson et. al., "A Theory of Legislative Delegation," 68 Cornell L.Rev. 1 (1983).

> Public choice theorists insist that we jettison our vision of governance as a benign input/output machine for the definition and effectuation of the public interest. In its place, governmental action is explained in terms of self-interested political bargaining in the pursuit of individual or group material interests. The black box of macropolitics and bureaucratic decisionmaking has been pried open to reveal copious opportunities for "rent-seeking" behavior both by the people's representatives and by the "experts" in charge of public programs. . . .

> Rather than effectuating the public good while maintaining liberty and democratic control, public institutional arrangements are virtually all explained as devices to facilitate private gain at public expense. On this view, broad delegations of power and limitations on executive control structure politics in the interest of "iron triangles" of self-aggrandizing representatives, bureaucrats, and interest groups. Judicial review cements the gains from private deals for the use of public power, and agency processes are designed primarily to permit "capture" by the already advantaged. Pursuit of the "public interest" as a guide to understanding the structure and behavior of public institutions is thus replaced root and branch by hypotheses featuring pursuit of private material gain.

Jerry L. Mashaw, GREED, CHAOS, AND GOVERNANCE: USING PUBLIC CHOICE TO IMPROVE PUBLIC LAW 118–19 (1997). Mashaw, however, believes that the public choice critique is overdrawn. He finds that it often fails to explain what legislatures or agencies actually have done, *id.* at 32–37, and he argues that broad delegations to agencies are more likely to enhance the public welfare than narrow ones. *Id.* at 131–57. We return to the debate about delegation of power in § 7.2.

Given these attacks on the legitimacy of the administrative process, what theories can be advanced in support of its legitimacy? Until the 1930's, the general view was that agency power was legitimate because agencies serve as a *transmission belt* for implementing specific statutes. In this view, the politically responsible legislature has already answered the major policy questions; unelected agencies just fill in the details.

According to the transmission belt model, the role of administrative law is to protect private liberty and property interests. Courts should, therefore, compel agencies to follow fair procedures and should make sure that agencies have stayed within statutory bounds. However, as indicated in § 7.2, most legislative delegations provide agencies with great discretion that is unfettered by specific statutory language. Consequently, the "transmission belt" model fails to provide an adequate legitimating theory.

In the 1930's the New Deal arose out of the economic chaos of the Great Depression. The New Deal spawned numerous agencies operating under broad delegations of power. These epochal events gave rise to a new theory of administrative law which prevailed under the 1970's. Agencies were expected to solve the nation's economic and social problems on the basis of their special *expertise*. The use of technical expertise would ensure that agency actions were consistent with the specific wishes of the elected legislature. Under this approach, agencies should be allowed to function as teams of experts and administrative law should protect agency action from unwarranted judicial or executive intrusion. Today, our faith in expertise has declined, since it is evident that many of the problems to be solved by agencies are primarily political rather than technocratic. Consequently, the expertise model has fallen from favor.

The *pluralist* or *interest representation* model views the activities of unelected agencies as legitimate to the extent agencies engage in a fair political process. This model suggests that all special interests should be represented in the administrative process; a desirable outcome reconciles the claims of these interests in a way that best reflects their political influences. Judicial review assures that everyone who should be at the table has been invited. In this model, therefore, the role of administrative law is to insure that agencies use a process that approximates the political process.

However, there are a number of serious problems with this approach, including the difficulty of making agency officials abide by legislative compromises with which they may disagree. As Stewart points out:

> In many fields of administration, the widespread effects of governmental decisions or the need for swift, decisive action may render formal schemes of representation for all affected interests intolerably burdensome. Even where these imperatives are absent, the case for interest representation may be doubtful if we are to give weight to policy outcomes as well as to processes of decision. A measure of

deregulation seems eminently desirable in many sectors, yet interest groups that have become formally enmeshed in agency administration are unlikely to call for the agency's abolition. In other areas, it would be desirable for agencies to adopt policies designed to maximize allocational efficiency, but such policies are unlikely to emerge from a formalized process of bargaining among affected interests that will generate pressures for compromise and an "equitable" division of burdens and benefits. 88 Harv.L.Rev. at 1804–05.

Still another approach to the legitimacy issue has emerged recently. Under the *civic republican* model, the role of government is to encourage a *deliberative* process in which the views of all citizens are respected in pursuit of the common good. Civic republicans reject the pluralist notion that the role of government is simply to broker deals according to the political influence of interest groups. Under the civic republican model, the agency rulemaking process promotes deliberation because the notice and comment system invites all citizens to participate and articulate their own values. Civic republicans like the fact that agency heads, who are more insulated from politics than elected representatives, make the final calls and must explain their decisions. That explanation must include a discussion of alternatives that were proposed by commentators but rejected by the agency. We discuss the obligation to explain agency decisions in §§ 4.3 and 5.6. See generally Mark Seidenfeld, "A Civic Republican Justification for the Bureaucratic State," 105 Harv.L.Rev. 1512 (1992).

Under the civic republican view, broad delegations to administrative agencies are good. The role of administrative law should be to facilitate the deliberative process, minimize political influences over the administrative process, and assure that agency decisions are well explained and rational in light of the information available to the agency.

But not everyone is convinced by the civic republican argument.

I think that the civic republicans are naive in believing that answers to intensely disputed policy questions can be arrived at through deliberative exercises in which all interests are equally represented. I am skeptical of the suggestion that true equality of citizen participation in the political arena can be achieved in the face of huge disparities of wealth in the private sector. Public participation in environmental rulemaking, for example, requires expertise in a vast array of scientific and engineering disciplines and effective representation by legal counsel. While large companies and trade associations have the resources to participate effectively in such exercises, local [and even national] environmental groups do not.... In the end, the public must rely primarily on the regulatory agencies to provide the statutory protections. Therefore, the deliberative advantages of any hurdles that the civic republicans would place in the way of expeditious rulemaking by way of procedural, analytical, and judicial oversight requirements must be measured against the reductions in the protections that the agencies can effectively provide.

Thomas O. McGarity, "The Courts and the Ossification of Rulemaking: A Response to Professor Seidenfeld," 75 Tex.L.Rev. 525, 531–32 (1997).

Lacking a comprehensive theory that provides legitimacy for agency exercise of political power, scholars may turn to *procedural regularity* as well as the system of *checks and balances*. The procedural regularity idea holds that agency rulemaking is a legitimate exercise of power because agencies must employ APA notice and comment procedures. This form of procedure guarantees a measure of direct democratic participation in the process. In recent years, as we will see in Chapter 5, the simple APA provisions on rulemaking process have been vastly elaborated; APA procedure now provides quite substantial opportunities for private interests to influence the result.

The checks and balances idea emphasizes that agency power is subject to a variety of important controls that helps to ensure both legality and political responsiveness. Judicial review (especially so-called "hard look" review discussed in § 9.5) functions as a very real check on agency discretion. Legislative controls include intrusive legislative oversight hearings, cutting an agency's budget, various forms of legislative veto (especially at the state level), and passing amendatory legislation. In addition, the executive branch is likely to impose a variety of controls on agency rulemaking up to and including removal of the agency heads. Legislative and executive controls on agency action are discussed in Chapter 7. However, legislative and executive branch controls and imposition of sanctions on agencies involve extensive and costly monitoring of agency activity. As a result they are not very effective in preventing abuse of power by agencies except in rare cases.

There is a link between the procedural regularity theory and the checks and balances theory. One way to view administrative procedure is that it serves to facilitate the exercise of judicial, legislative and executive political controls. The notice, comment, and explanation requirements of the APA build a record suitable for searching judicial review. Moreover, special interest groups that were instrumental in securing the passage of legislation remain intensely interested in agency rulemaking under that legislation. The APA notice and comment procedure alerts these groups to the possibility that an agency might deviate from the compromises that led to the legislation in question. As a result, these interested groups can use the APA comment procedure to change the agency's course before it is too late. Moreover, once alerted to the problem, these groups are likely to seek legislative or executive assistance to bring the agency back to the correct path. This "fire alarm" theory is most closely associated with public choice theorists Matthew McCubbins, Roger Noll, and Barry Weingast (a trio often referred to as McNollgast). *See, e.g.*, "Administrative Procedures as Instruments of Political Control," 3 J.L.Econ. & Org. 243 (1987). These authors distinguish fire alarm oversight from "police patrol" oversight, in which a legislature goes out to uncover problems on its own.

§ 1.8 PROBLEM

You are a member of the staff of a state legislator who is the chair of the Technology Subcommittee. You have been meeting with representatives of several companies engaged in genetic engineering research and the production of genetically engineered products. In particular, one of the companies wants to begin testing a manufactured virus that it claims will lower the freezing point of unpicked oranges and thus preserve the oranges from deadly frosts.

Assume that at present there is no state or federal regulation of bio-engineered products (unless they are foods or drugs). The technology obviously is dangerous and there is a lot of community resistance to the proposed tests because of concern that the virus might spread and cause all sorts of environmental problems. Yet the benefit to mankind, and to the manufacturing companies, of a successful product would be enormous.

Is this an area in which there should be regulation? Should there be a new agency to deal with the problem? What powers should the agency have?

See Christine C. Vito, Comment, "State Biotechnology Oversight: The Juncture of Technology, Law and Public Policy," 45 Maine L.Rev. 329 (1993); *Foundation on Economic Trends v. Heckler,* 756 F.2d 143 (D.C.Cir.1985).

Part I

AGENCY PROCEDURES

In this Part we examine the procedures used by agencies in the performance of their functions affecting private rights. Consequently, the primary focus of this Part is on agency *adjudication,* the administrative process for determining the legal rights of specified individuals based on their particular circumstances, and on *rulemaking*, the administrative process for making legal determinations of general applicability. A consideration of the agency procedures utilized in these processes involves an examination of constitutional, statutory, and common law requirements.

Chapter 2

THE CONSTITUTIONAL RIGHT
TO A HEARING

———————

The Fifth Amendment to the Constitution, which applies to the federal government, provides that no person shall "be deprived of life, liberty, or property, without due process of law." Section 1 of the Fourteenth Amendment, which applies to state government, contains similar language. State constitutions also provide for due process and may provide greater (but not lesser) protection than the federal Constitution.

You are familiar with the *judicial* procedures required before the state imposes a criminal sanction or a civil remedy. However, a vast number of governmental decisions that have a negative impact on individuals are not administered through courts (although courts usually can *review* these decisions). This chapter is about the extent to which government agencies must provide "process" when they take such decisions. Here are some examples of the sort of decisions which involve the vital interests of literally millions of people every year:

i. *Benefit decisions.* An agency refuses to grant, or it reduces or terminates, social security old age or disability payments, welfare benefits, or food stamps.

ii. *Access to services.* A state educational institution suspends or expels a student, asserting poor academic performance or violation of rules. A municipal utility cuts off a customer, claiming nonpayment of bills.

iii. *Licenses.* An agency suspends a driver's license, or it prevents a lawyer or doctor from practicing his or her profession.

iv. *Jobs or contracts.* Government fires an employee or it terminates a contract.

v. *Taxes.* An agency asserts that a taxpayer owes more in taxes than the taxpayer believes is correct.

vi. *Institutional decisions.* A prisoner is denied parole or placed in solitary confinement because of alleged violation of prison rules.

If such disputes are not resolved informally (as most of them are), an adversely affected person is often entitled by a statute or by the constitution to a fair hearing at which an impartial decision-maker adjudicates the conflict.

This chapter is intended to introduce several themes which recur throughout the book. These are:

i. *Administrative law matters.* The availability of some type of hearing is extremely important to persons who believe they are victims of wrong decisions taken by a clumsy and insensitive bureaucracy. If such persons have a right to hearing, they can seize government's attention and get the dispute settled by an impartial decision-maker.

ii. *Administrative procedure is costly.* Take welfare hearings—the subject considered next. Giving people hearings before cutting them off the rolls costs welfare agencies money and reduces the funds available for helping poor people. It delays the removal of unqualified people from the welfare rolls and encourages people to appeal just to delay the termination of their payments. Hearings take up a lot of time and energy which case-workers could spend helping their clients. Are these costs always worth it?

iii. *Administrative law is about discretion.* A person has "discretion" when he or she can legally choose between several alternatives. Government frequently has a vast discretion in discharging administrative functions. Much of administrative law can be viewed as a study of the rules and institutions which limit that discretion. In this chapter, we consider whether a hearing is a good way to limit and structure an agency's discretionary power over individuals.

iv. *Issues of administrative law involve fundamental value conflicts.* Your position will be determined largely by your own philosophical and political viewpoint, but a study of administrative law can inform these positions. Some of the conflicts that this chapter illuminates are: Should non-traditional forms of property and liberty (like welfare benefits or a student's interest in staying in school) receive as much procedural protection as we give to traditional kinds of property or liberty? Where should the line be drawn between full procedural protection and conflicting administrative interests, like the need to operate efficiently or to conserve scarce budgetary resources? How much of the limited resources of the courts should be invested in judicial review of administrative decisions? Is traditional adversary judicialized procedure the best way to protect people's interests against detrimental administrative action?

The chapter opens with an important and dramatic administrative law decision. The majority and dissenting opinions in *Goldberg v. Kelly* illuminate these value conflicts with stirring rhetoric in a setting of immense practical importance: the conflict between an individual and a state welfare bureaucracy. Much of the material which follows in this chapter is a reaction to Justice Brennan's opinion in *Goldberg*—largely a retreat from it. Did Justice Brennan have his priorities straight in *Goldberg*? Or did he promise more than our government can deliver?

§ 2.1 HEARINGS AND WELFARE TERMINATION: DUE PROCESS AND MASS JUSTICE

Before turning to the *Goldberg* decision, we supply some background about welfare. Aid for Families with Dependent Children (AFDC) is one of many federal, state and local need-based welfare programs, including Supplemental Security Income (SSI), Medicaid, food stamps, general relief, rent supplements and many others.

AFDC was fundamentally altered and renamed Temporary Assistance for Needy Families (TANF) by welfare reform legislation enacted in 1996. Under TANF, welfare is no longer an "entitlement," and the states are permitted to design their own programs. These changes to the welfare system may cast doubt on the underlying theories and arguments set forth by Justice Brennan in the *Goldberg* decision.

Because *Goldberg* deals with procedural rights of AFDC recipients, we provide some background here on AFDC as it existed until 1996. Established in 1935, AFDC furnishes federal money to the states; the states provide additional funds, set their own level of benefits, and administer the program (within the constraints of federal law). In 1994, there were over 14 million recipients of AFDC, receiving close to 26 billion dollars per year. The great majority of recipients live in single-parent households, usually headed by females with one or more children. An additional 6.3 million people receive SSI, a federal program intended for disabled or aged people in need. Millions of others are enrolled in other need-based programs such as food stamps or general assistance.

Qualification for AFDC is based on need, and the welfare bureaucracy must constantly assess and reassess the need of vast numbers of people. Although welfare varies from state to state, even in the most generous states a family must be nearly destitute before it qualifies for aid. In contrast to prior years, the determination of need and resources is based on relatively routinized standards, allowing for little judgment on the part of the caseworker and little consideration of a recipient family's special circumstances.

Welfare may be denied, reduced, or terminated for various reasons, such as a failure to meet the needs standard because of a change in resources. In addition, welfare can be terminated if a qualified parent does not cooperate in obtaining support from an absent parent, a parent fails to meet work or community service requirements, or other rule violations are detected. *Goldberg v. Kelly,* which follows, addresses the question of what sort of appeal procedure must be provided when the recipient does not agree with the welfare department's decision to terminate benefits.

For flavor, here is Professor Joel Handler's sketch of the welfare system:

> Volume [of recipients] is a brutal fact of the welfare state ... vast numbers of people in our society, as presently organized, will need financial and other assistance. This is especially true for the client group on which we focus: female-headed households. Volume is the cardinal enemy of discretion, professional judgment, individualization; heavy caseloads force routinization....

> Values and attitudes toward the poor are varied, long-standing, and greatly affect how the poor are treated. Society has always distinguished between the deserving and undeserving poor, those whose poverty is blameless and those who are blameworthy. In a prior age, the blind, the halt, and the lame were in the former category; those who could work but failed were in the latter. Today, the aged and the disabled have joined the former, but the nonaged— the childless adults, and the female-headed households—are still the undeserving. It is not only the failure of work that draws the community's hostility; fueling the furies are race, sex, and various forms of deviant behavior and life style.

> .... Programs for the undeserving are very different [from Social Security]. They are state and local, discretionary, decentralized, and subject to a great many moralistic and punitive practices....

> The final cause of the ills of public assistance programs is the distribution of wealth and power. One can never forget that the people we are talking about are extremely dependent. They are ill-prepared to effectively participate in public programs, and, in particular, to understand the procedural systems designed to secure benefits and rights for them. The bureaucracy has control over the information, the resources, the staying power, the power of retaliation; workers, even if well-meaning, are pressed for time, short of money, and, in all honesty, feel that they know what is best for the clients....

> Two additional comments: the utter chaos that one witnesses in the public assistance offices—the crowds, the waiting, the shouting, the maze of cubicles, the forms, the fear and resignation of the applicants, and the anger and frustration of the workers; second, that by forcing public assistance recipients to supplement their welfare grants by resorting to General Assistance and private charity—where available—the recipients are now confronting the most discretionary, moralistic public and private programs, in which there are virtually no legal protections.

"Discretion in Social Welfare: The Uneasy Position of the Rule of Law," 92 Yale L.J. 1270, 1271–74 (1983).

GOLDBERG v. KELLY

397 U.S. 254 (1970).

BRENNAN, J.:

The question for decision is whether a State that terminates public assistance payments to a particular recipient without affording him the opportunity for an evidentiary hearing prior to termination denies the recipient procedural due process in violation of the Due Process Clause of the Fourteenth Amendment.

[Recipients of the federally-assisted Aid to Families with Dependent Children (AFDC) or New York's general relief program sued in federal District Court. They alleged that New York state and city officials administering these programs terminated their aid without prior notice and hearing, thereby denying them due process of law.

The various plaintiffs complained that they had been dropped from the rolls for illegal or incorrect reasons. One plaintiff was terminated because she refused to cooperate with the city in suing her estranged husband; she contended that the cooperation requirement did not apply to her case. Another was dropped because he refused to accept counseling for drug addiction; he claimed he did not use drugs. A third was dropped for a factually erroneous reason; she fainted from lack of food while waiting at the welfare office to which her files had been transferred. Later she and her children were forced to go to the emergency room because of eating spoiled food donated by a neighbor. Her aid was reinstated after the suit was filed. Brief for Appellees, 83–84]

[Under recently adopted procedural rules] a caseworker who has doubts about the recipient's continued eligibility must first discuss them with the recipient. If the caseworker concludes that the recipient is no longer eligible, he recommends termination of aid to a unit supervisor. If the latter concurs, he sends the recipient a letter stating the reasons for proposing to terminate aid and notifying him that within seven days he may request that a higher official review the record, and may support the request with a written statement prepared personally or with the aid of an attorney or other person. If the reviewing official affirms the determination of ineligibility, aid is stopped immediately and the recipient is informed by letter of the reasons for the action. Appellees' challenge to this procedure emphasizes the absence of any provisions for the personal appearance of the recipient before the reviewing official, for oral presentation of evidence, and for confrontation and cross-examination of adverse witnesses. However, the letter does inform the recipient that he may request a post-termination "fair hearing." This is a proceeding before an independent state hearing officer at which the recipient may appear personally, offer oral evidence, confront and cross-examine the witnesses against him, and have a record made of the hearing. If the recipient prevails at the "fair hearing" he is paid all funds erroneously withheld. A recipient whose aid is not restored by a "fair hearing" decision may have judicial review. . . .

I

The constitutional issue to be decided, therefore, is the narrow one whether the Due Process Clause requires that the recipient be afforded an evidentiary hearing *before* the termination of benefits. The District Court held that only a pre-termination evidentiary hearing would satisfy the constitutional command, and rejected the argument of the state and city officials that the combination of the post-termination "fair hearing" with the informal pre-termination review disposed of all due process claims. The court said: "While post-termination review is relevant, there is one overpowering fact which controls here. By hypothesis, a welfare recipient is destitute, without funds or assets.... Suffice it to say that to cut off a welfare recipient in the face of ... brutal need without a prior hearing of some sort is unconscionable, unless overwhelming considerations justify it." The court rejected the argument that the need to protect the public's tax revenues supplied the requisite "overwhelming consideration." "Against the justified desire to protect public funds must be weighed the individual's overpowering need in this unique situation not to be wrongfully deprived of assistance.... While the problem of additional expense must be kept in mind, it does not justify denying a hearing meeting the ordinary standards of due process. Under all the circumstances, we hold that due process requires an adequate hearing before termination of welfare benefits, and the fact that there is a later constitutionally fair proceeding does not alter the result." ....

Appellant does not contend that procedural due process is not applicable to the termination of welfare benefits. Such benefits are a matter of statutory entitlement for persons qualified to receive them.[8] Their termination involves state action that adjudicates important rights. The constitutional challenge cannot be answered by an argument that public assistance benefits are a "privilege" and not a "right." Relevant constitutional restraints apply as much to the withdrawal of public assistance benefits as to disqualification for unemployment compensation, ... or to discharge from public employment.... The extent to which procedural due process must be afforded the recipient is influenced by the extent to which he may be "condemned to suffer grievous loss," Joint Anti–Fascist Refugee Committee v. McGrath, 341 U.S. 123

---

8. It may be realistic today to regard welfare entitlements as more like "property" than a "gratuity." Much of the existing wealth in this country takes the form of rights that do not fall within traditional common-law concepts of property. It has been aptly noted that "[s]ociety today is built around entitlement. The automobile dealer has his franchise, the doctor and lawyer their professional licenses, the worker his union membership, contract, and pension rights, the executive his contract and stock options; all are devices to aid security and independence. Many of the most important of these entitlements now flow from government: subsidies to farmers and businessmen, routes for airlines and channels for television stations; long term contracts for defense, space, and education; social security pensions for individuals. Such sources of security, whether private or public, are no longer regarded as luxuries or gratuities; to the recipients they are essentials, fully deserved, and in no sense a form of charity. It is only the poor whose entitlements, although recognized by public policy, have not been effectively enforced." Reich, Individual Rights and Social Welfare: The Emerging Legal Issues, 74 Yale L.J. 1245, 1255 (1965). See also Reich, The New Property, 73 Yale L.J. 733 (1964).

(1951) (Frankfurter, J., concurring), and depends upon whether the recipient's interest in avoiding that loss outweighs the governmental interest in summary adjudication. Accordingly, as we said in Cafeteria & Restaurant Workers Union v. McElroy, 367 U.S. 886 (1961), "consideration of what procedures due process may require under any given set of circumstances must begin with a determination of the precise nature of the government function involved as well as of the private interest that has been affected by governmental action."

It is true, of course, that some governmental benefits may be administratively terminated without affording the recipient a pre-termination evidentiary hearing.[10] But we agree with the District Court that when welfare is discontinued, only a pre-termination evidentiary hearing provides the recipient with procedural due process.

For qualified recipients, welfare provides the means to obtain essential food, clothing, housing, and medical care. Thus the crucial factor in this context—a factor not present in the case of the black-listed government contractor, the discharged government employee, the taxpayer denied a tax exemption, or virtually anyone else whose governmental entitlements are ended—is that termination of aid pending resolution of a controversy over eligibility may deprive an *eligible* recipient of the very means by which to live while he waits. Since he lacks independent resources, his situation becomes immediately desperate. His need to concentrate upon finding the means for daily subsistence, in turn, adversely affects his ability to seek redress from the welfare bureaucracy.

Moreover, important governmental interests are promoted by affording recipients a pre-termination evidentiary hearing. From its founding the Nation's basic commitment has been to foster the dignity and well-being of all persons within its borders. . . . Welfare, by meeting the basic demands of subsistence, can help bring within the reach of the poor the same opportunities that are available to others to participate meaningfully in the life of the community. At the same time, welfare guards against the societal malaise that may flow from a widespread sense of unjustified frustration and insecurity. Public assistance, then, is not mere charity, but a means to "promote the general Welfare, and secure the Blessings of Liberty to ourselves and our Posterity." The same governmental interests that counsel the provision of welfare, counsel as well its uninterrupted provision to those eligible to receive it; pre-termination evidentiary hearings are indispensable to that end.

---

10. One Court of Appeals has stated: "In a wide variety of situations, it has long been recognized that where harm to the public is threatened, and the private interest infringed is reasonably deemed to be of less importance, an official body can take summary action pending a later hearing." R.A. Holman & Co. v. SEC, 299 F.2d 127 (1962) (suspension of exemption from stock registration requirement). See also, for example, Ewing v. Mytinger & Casselberry, Inc., 339 U.S. 594 (1950) (seizure of misla- beled vitamin product); North American Cold Storage Co. v. Chicago, 211 U.S. 306 (1908) (seizure of food not fit for human use); . . . In Cafeteria & Restaurant Workers Union v. McElroy, supra, summary dismissal of a public employee was upheld because "[i]n [its] proprietary military capacity, the Federal Government . . . has traditionally exercised unfettered control," and because the case involved the Government's "dispatch of its own internal affairs."

Appellant does not challenge the force of these considerations but argues that they are outweighed by countervailing governmental interests in conserving fiscal and administrative resources. These interests, the argument goes, justify the delay of any evidentiary hearing until after discontinuance of the grants. Summary adjudication protects the public fisc by stopping payments promptly upon discovery of reason to believe that a recipient is no longer eligible. Since most terminations are accepted without challenge, summary adjudication also conserves both the fisc and administrative time and energy by reducing the number of evidentiary hearings actually held.

We agree with the District Court, however, that these governmental interests are not overriding in the welfare context. The requirement of a prior hearing doubtless involves some greater expense, and the benefits paid to ineligible recipients pending decision at the hearing probably cannot be recouped, since these recipients are likely to be judgment-proof. But the State is not without weapons to minimize these increased costs. Much of the drain on fiscal and administrative resources can be reduced by developing procedures for prompt pre-termination hearings and by skillful use of personnel and facilities. Indeed, the very provision for a post-termination evidentiary hearing in New York's Home Relief program is itself cogent evidence that the State recognizes the primacy of the public interest in correct eligibility determinations and therefore in the provision of procedural safeguards. Thus, the interest of the eligible recipient in uninterrupted receipt of public assistance, coupled with the State's interest that his payments not be erroneously terminated, clearly outweighs the State's competing concern to prevent any increase in its fiscal and administrative burdens. . . .

II

We also agree with the District Court, however, that the pre-termination hearing need not take the form of a judicial or quasi-judicial trial. We bear in mind that the statutory "fair hearing" will provide the recipient with a full administrative review.[14] Accordingly, the pre-termination hearing has one function only: to produce an initial determination of the validity of the welfare department's grounds for discontinuance of payments in order to protect a recipient against an erroneous termination of his benefits. Thus, a complete record and a comprehensive opinion, which would serve primarily to facilitate judicial review and to guide future decisions, need not be provided at the pre-termination stage. We recognize, too, that both welfare authorities and recipients have an interest in relatively speedy resolution of questions of eligibility, that they are used to dealing with one another informally, and that some welfare departments have very burdensome caseloads. These considerations justify the limitation of the pre-termination hearing to minimum procedural safeguards, adapted to the particular characteristics of wel-

---

14. Due process does not, of course, require two hearings. If, for example, a State simply wishes to continue benefits until af- ter a "fair" hearing there will be no need for a preliminary hearing.

fare recipients, and to the limited nature of the controversies to be resolved. We wish to add that we, no less than the dissenters, recognize the importance of not imposing upon the States or the Federal Government in this developing field of law any procedural requirements beyond those demanded by rudimentary due process. . . .

The hearing must be "at a meaningful time and in a meaningful manner." In the present context these principles require that a recipient have timely and adequate notice detailing the reasons for a proposed termination, and an effective opportunity to defend by confronting any adverse witnesses and by presenting his own arguments and evidence orally. These rights are important in cases such as those before us, where recipients have challenged proposed terminations as resting on incorrect or misleading factual premises or on misapplication of rules or policies to the facts of particular cases.[15]

We are not prepared to say that the seven-day notice currently provided by New York City is constitutionally insufficient per se, although there may be cases where fairness would require that a longer time be given. Nor do we see any constitutional deficiency in the content or form of the notice. New York employs both a letter and a personal conference with a caseworker to inform a recipient of the precise questions raised about his continued eligibility. Evidently the recipient is told the legal and factual bases for the Department's doubts. This combination is probably the most effective method of communicating with recipients.

The city's procedures presently do not permit recipients to appear personally with or without counsel before the official who finally determines continued eligibility. Thus a recipient is not permitted to present evidence to that official orally, or to confront or cross-examine adverse witnesses. These omissions are fatal to the constitutional adequacy of the procedures.

The opportunity to be heard must be tailored to the capacities and circumstances of those who are to be heard. It is not enough that a welfare recipient may present his position to the decisionmaker in writing or secondhand through his caseworker. Written submissions are an unrealistic option for most recipients, who lack the educational attainment necessary to write effectively and who cannot obtain professional assistance. Moreover, written submissions do not afford the flexibility of oral presentations; they do not permit the recipient to mold his argument to the issues the decisionmaker appears to regard as important. Particularly where credibility and veracity are at issue, as they must be in many termination proceedings, written submissions are a wholly unsatisfactory basis for decision. The secondhand presentation to the decisionmaker by the caseworker has its own deficiencies; since the

---

15. This case presents no question requiring our determination whether due process requires only an opportunity for written submission, or an opportunity both for written submission and oral argument, where there are no factual issues in dispute or where the application of the rule of law is not intertwined with factual issues.

caseworker usually gathers the facts upon which the charge of ineligibility rests, the presentation of the recipient's side of the controversy cannot safely be left to him. Therefore a recipient must be allowed to state his position orally. Informal procedures will suffice; in this context due process does not require a particular order of proof or mode of offering evidence.

In almost every setting where important decisions turn on questions of fact, due process requires an opportunity to confront and cross-examine adverse witnesses.... Welfare recipients must therefore be given an opportunity to confront and cross-examine the witnesses relied on by the department.

"The right to be heard would be, in many cases, of little avail if it did not comprehend the right to be heard by counsel." We do not say that counsel must be provided at the pre-termination hearing, but only that the recipient must be allowed to retain an attorney if he so desires. Counsel can help delineate the issues, present the factual contentions in an orderly manner, conduct cross-examination, and generally safeguard the interests of the recipient. We do not anticipate that this assistance will unduly prolong or otherwise encumber the hearing.... Finally, the decisionmaker's conclusion as to a recipient's eligibility must rest solely on the legal rules and evidence adduced at the hearing. To demonstrate compliance with this elementary requirement, the decisionmaker should state the reasons for his determination and indicate the evidence he relied on, though his statement need not amount to a full opinion or even formal findings of fact and conclusions of law. And, of course, an impartial decisionmaker is essential. We agree with the District Court that prior involvement in some aspects of a case will not necessarily bar a welfare official from acting as a decisionmaker. He should not, however, have participated in making the determination under review.

Affirmed.

Mr. Justice Black, dissenting....

The Court [today] relies upon the Fourteenth Amendment and in effect says that failure of the government to pay a promised charitable instalment to an individual deprives that individual of *his own property,* in violation of the Due Process Clause of the Fourteenth Amendment. It somewhat strains credulity to say that the government's promise of charity to an individual is property belonging to that individual when the government denies that the individual is honestly entitled to receive such a payment.

I would have little, if any, objection to the majority's decision in this case if it were written as the report of the House Committee on Education and Labor, but as an opinion ostensibly resting on the language of the Constitution I find it woefully deficient. Once the verbiage is pared away it is obvious that this Court today adopts the views of the District Court "that to cut off a welfare recipient in the face of ... 'brutal need' without a prior hearing of some sort is unconscionable," and therefore, says the Court, unconstitutional. The majority reaches this result by a process of weighing "the recipient's interest in avoiding" the termination of welfare benefits against "the governmental interest in summary adjudication." Today's balancing act requires a "pre-termination evidentiary hearing," yet there is nothing that indicates what tomorrow's balance will be. Although the majority attempts to bolster its decision with limited quotations from prior cases, it is obvious that today's result does not depend on the language of the Constitution itself or the principles of other decisions, but solely on the collective judgment of the majority as to what would be a fair and humane procedure in this case. . . .

The Court apparently feels that this decision will benefit the poor and needy. In my judgment the eventual result will be just the opposite. While today's decision requires only an administrative, evidentiary hearing, the inevitable logic of the approach taken will lead to constitutionally imposed, time-consuming delays of a full adversary process of administrative and judicial review. In the next case the welfare recipients are bound to argue that cutting off benefits before judicial review of the agency's decision is also a denial of due process. Since, by hypothesis, termination of aid at that point may still "deprive an *eligible* recipient of the very means by which to live while he waits," I would be surprised if the weighing process did not compel the conclusion that termination without full judicial review would be unconscionable. After all, at each step, as the majority seems to feel, the issue is only one of weighing the government's pocketbook against the actual survival of the recipient, and surely that balance must always tip in favor of the individual. Similarly today's decision requires only the opportunity to have the benefit of counsel at the administrative hearing, but it is difficult to believe that the same reasoning process would not require the appointment of counsel, for otherwise the right to counsel is a meaningless one since these people are too poor to hire their own advocates. Thus the end result of today's decision may well be that the government, once it decides to give welfare benefits, cannot reverse that decision until the recipient has had the benefits of full administrative and judicial review, including, of course, the opportunity to present his case to this Court. Since this process will usually entail a delay of several years, the inevitable result of such a constitutionally imposed burden will be that the government will not put a claimant on the rolls initially until it has made an exhaustive investigation to determine his eligibility. While this Court will perhaps have insured that no needy person will be taken off the rolls without a full "due process" proceeding, it will also have insured that many will never get on the rolls, or at least that they will remain destitute during the lengthy proceedings followed to determine initial eligibility.

For the foregoing reasons I dissent from the Court's holding. The operation of a welfare state is a new experiment for our Nation. For this reason, among others, I feel that new experiments in carrying out a welfare program should not be frozen into our constitutional structure.

They should be left, as are other legislative determinations, to the Congress and the legislatures that the people elect to make our laws.

Mr. Chief Justice Burger, with whom Mr. Justice Black joins, dissenting. . . .

The Court's action today seems another manifestation of the now familiar constitutionalizing syndrome: once some presumed flaw is observed, the Court then eagerly accepts the invitation to find a constitutionally "rooted" remedy. If no provision is explicit on the point, it is then seen as "implicit" or commanded by the vague and nebulous concept of "fairness." . . . .

I would wait until more is known about the problems before fashioning solutions in the rigidity of a constitutional holding.

By allowing the administrators to deal with these problems we leave room for adjustments if, for example, it is found that a particular hearing process is too costly. The history of the complexity of the administrative process followed by judicial review as we have seen it for the past 30 years should suggest the possibility that new layers of procedural protection may become an intolerable drain on the very funds earmarked for food, clothing, and other living essentials.[3]

Aside from the administrative morass that today's decision could well create, the Court should also be cognizant of the legal precedent it may be setting. The majority holding raises intriguing possibilities concerning the right to a hearing at other stages in the welfare process which affect the total sum of assistance, even though the action taken might fall short of complete termination. For example, does the Court's holding embrace welfare reductions or denial of increases as opposed to terminations, or decisions concerning initial applications or requests for special assistance? The Court supplies no distinguishable considerations and leaves these crucial questions unanswered.

[Stewart, J., also dissented].

Notes and Questions

1. *The Goldberg decision.* Because just about everything that follows in this chapter is a reaction to *Goldberg*, be clear on the issues determined:

    i. The right to a continued flow of welfare benefits is an interest which is protected by procedural due process. What analysis did the Court employ to come to that conclusion? Will that analysis furnish predictable results in future cases?

    ii. The demands of procedural due process are flexible and contextual rather than rigid and noncontextual. Application of that concept requires a balancing of interests in light of the particular circumstances. Is a court competent to make such judgments?

---

3. We are told, for example, that Los Angeles County alone employs 12,500 welfare workers to process grants to 500,000 people under various welfare programs. The record does not reveal how many more employees will be required to give this newly discovered "due process" to every welfare recipient whose payments are terminated for fraud or other factors of ineligibility or those whose initial applications are denied.

iii. Due process requires a hearing *before* welfare benefits are terminated. A post-termination hearing is not sufficient. Why did the Court require a hearing before the benefits stop? Must hearings always occur before the government deprives an individual of liberty or property?

iv. A pre-termination hearing must include specified ingredients. What are those ingredients and how do they differ from those required in a post-termination hearing? Did the Court hold that this combination of ingredients must be provided in every situation in which a person's property is adversely affected by government action?

Justice Black predicted that judicial review of a pre-termination decision would also become a requisite; however, it still remains unclear precisely when a statute can constitutionally preclude judicial review of administrative determinations. *See* § 10.4.

2. *The purposes of due process.* In thinking about the due process issues presented in this chapter, a good starting point is to ask what interests might be served by trial-type hearings. Due process decisions, and commentators on those decisions, have claimed many possible advantages for such hearings. Evaluate each of the following propositions in the context of welfare.

i. A trial-type hearing serves a *dignitary* function. It treats the individual as important, worthy of careful consideration, not just a cog in a giant machine. It affirms the value of fair procedure *for its own sake*.

ii. A trial-type hearing helps the individual *to understand and accept* a negative government decision. Therefore it tends to enhance people's satisfaction with government and to diminish their desire to resist or undermine it.

iii. A trial-type hearing is a good way to reach an *accurate* decision—to find out exactly what happened and to apply law and policy correctly. Therefore, it protects individuals against factually or legally erroneous decisions by agencies.

iv. Hearings create a system of agency precedents which decision-makers follow in later cases. This helps to assure that agency decisions are *consistent* with each other—that persons in like circumstances are treated alike.

v. A right to a trial-type hearing serves an *empowerment* function. Demanding a hearing is a good way for recipients to *seize the attention* of a bureaucratic institution and to prevent their problems from being ignored or slipping through the cracks. On a practical level, having a right to demand a time-consuming hearing helps a person to negotiate a settlement.

vi. If people have a right to a trial-type hearing before an impartial decision-maker, officials are more likely to act *seriously and reflectively*. Or, to examine the other side of the coin, will the bother of having to hold a hearing deter officials from acting boldly and decisively?

vii. A trial-type hearing is a good way to help government exercise *discretion* wisely. Decision-makers usually have some latitude (such as whether a prisoner who engages in fighting should be punished and, if so, how and for how long). We call this latitude *discretion* and recognize that discretionary decisions are sometimes unwise.

viii. The use of trial-type hearings may *serve the purposes* of the substantive programs in which they occur. For instance, in the welfare context, hearings may help assure that the right people get benefits. Hearings may also help identify recurring problems and thus improve the system. For example, they may suggest that a problem might better be solved by adopting a rule or a guideline, rather than continued resolution on a case-by-case basis.

ix. A trial-type hearing facilitates *judicial review* because it produces a decision based exclusively on a record made at the hearing and results in a written decision. Thus a reviewing court can focus on precisely what the agency did and why.

Are you persuaded that trial-type hearings really have some or all of these advantages? What are the *disadvantages* that should be set off against these advantages?

3. *In the wake of Goldberg. Goldberg* triggered a massive increase in the number of AFDC hearings. The decision occurred in March, 1970. In 1969, The New York Department of Social Services employed 11 hearing officers and a support staff of 20. In 1989, the Department employed 105 hearing officers and a support staff of 141. In 1969, 1300 appellants sought hearings and one thousand decisions resulted. In 1989, more than 150,000 hearings were requested and 77,000 decisions were issued. In 1969, hearing officers held an average of 5 hearings a week and drafted decisions in long hand. In 1989, hearing officers face calendars of 28 to 35 scheduled hearings daily and draft decisions on a statewide computer system which can print and issue a decision in Albany the same day. See Cesar A. Perales, "The Fair Hearings Process: Guardian of the Social Service System," 56 Brook.L.Rev. 889, 891 (1990).

About 90% of welfare recipients represent themselves in welfare hearings. Still, the hearings appear to produce results: in 1989 in New York, 80% of the issues decided in hearings were decided in favor of appellants. Perales, *supra*, at 892.

Do these figures tend to confirm the empirical predictions of Justice Brennan or those of Justice Black and Chief Justice Burger? Do they suggest that many recipients asked for hearings solely to keep their checks coming a little longer?

4. *Consequences of Goldberg.* Considering the consequences likely to flow from the decision, was *Goldberg* an unambiguous victory for persons who are or may be in the future dependent on welfare? In practice, where is the money to pay for the hearings likely to come from? Who are likely to be the primary beneficiaries of the decision? How would welfare officials be likely to deal with the consequences of the decision?

5. *Adversariness and mass justice.* The fundamental question raised by *Goldberg* is whether adversary trial-type hearings are the best way, or even a

good way, to protect the rights of people who depend on government for benefits. This problem is addressed in *Walters v. Radiation Survivors*, § 2.4 N.4. Compare these views:

> [Compared to the pressures on welfare administrators to cut costs] virtually no pressure ... is ordinarily exerted on behalf of the welfare client. It is in this context that the lawyer who represents the impoverished client introduces a new element. By fighting for his client, by carrying the issue involved in his client's cause into the judicial or quasi-judicial process, the lawyer not only creates the possibility of reversing an improper interpretation of law which may affect others in comparable straits but increases the administrator's potential for effecting humane policy.

Edward V. Sparer, "The Role of the Welfare Client's Lawyer," 12 U.C.L.A.L.Rev. 361, 375 (1965).

> [R]eliance on the complaining client is virtually fatal. In order for the due process system to be invoked, the following conditions have to be met: clients have to be aware that an injury has occurred; they have to think that the agency is at fault; they have to be aware of the existence of a remedy; they have to have the resources with which to pursue that remedy; and finally, they have to make a calculation that the benefits of pursuing the remedy outweigh its costs. Two things must be noted about these conditions. All of them have to be satisfied if the due process procedures are to be utilized; if there is a failure in any one of them, then the process will not be used. And, each and every one of the conditions is a difficult hurdle to negotiate for the average person dealing with a large-scale public organization....

> The final step in the process of invoking due process is to calculate whether the benefits of pursuing the remedy outweigh the costs ... [such as] the time and energy of the complainant and the costs of seeking help. Another cost deals with the relationship between the victim and the harmdoer. [Asserting one's right to due process is a hostile act.] This is particularly so if the claim is made in a formal setting such as a court or administrative hearing with professional advocacy help ... For some types of decisions, there is no relationship to speak of and the potential benefits of claiming will outweigh the costs ... In many other situations there are continuing relationships and considerable potential for at least the fear, if not the fact, of retaliation

> .... [I]t was found that 90% of all welfare documents required an eighth grade reading level. Yet the mean level of education for the aged poor is 7.5 years; and more than 20% of the SSI non-participants had less than five years of schooling, the amount considered to be functionally literate. More than 20 percent were foreign born, so that English as a second language might be a problem.

> .... People approach these programs, then, in a vulnerable personal situation, and are confronted with ambiguous information. At this point, they face a hostile government bureaucracy—waiting rooms, offices, receptionists, officials, paper, forms, questions....

Joel Handler, THE CONDITIONS OF DISCRETION 22–32 (1986).*

§ 2.2 INTERESTS PROTECTED BY DUE PROCESS: LIBERTY AND PROPERTY

The balance of this chapter discusses the means by which courts have limited the procedural requirements imposed by due process. The first approach, addressed in this section, entirely excludes certain interests from the categories of "liberty" and "property." The second approach is to describe due process requirements as variable rather than fixed and dependent on the particular context in which they arise. That technique will be addressed in §§ 2.3 and 2.4. The third approach is to identify the action in question as generalized, not individualized. Due process does not apply to generalized government action such as rule-making. That approach is discussed in § 2.5.

The language of the Fifth and Fourteenth amendments is clear: to be entitled to procedural due process, a person must be deprived by government of "liberty" or "property." The application of those abstract terms to particular cases has proved to be difficult. Recall how the Court dealt with the issue of whether a continued flow of welfare payments is an interest protected by due process in *Goldberg*.

§ 2.2.1 "LIBERTY" AND "PROPERTY" ACCORDING TO *ROTH*

In *Board of Regents v. Roth*, which follows, the Court reconceptualized the terms "liberty" and "property." Is the approach taken in the *Roth* case more theoretically satisfactory than the approach used in *Goldberg?* Is it easier to apply to actual cases?

BOARD OF REGENTS v. ROTH
408 U.S. 564 (1972).

Stewart, J.

In 1968 the respondent, David Roth, was hired for his first teaching job as assistant professor of political science at Wisconsin State University–Oshkosh. He was hired for a fixed term of one academic year. The notice of his faculty appointment specified that his employment would begin on September 1, 1968, and would end on June 30, 1969. The respondent completed that term. But he was informed that he would not be rehired for the next academic year.

The respondent had no tenure rights to continued employment. Under Wisconsin statutory law a state university teacher can acquire tenure as a "permanent" employee only after four years of year-to-year employment. Having acquired tenure, a teacher is entitled to continued

* © The Russell Sage Foundation, 1986.   Foundation.
Used with permission of the Russell Sage

employment "during efficiency and good behavior." A relatively new teacher without tenure, however, is under Wisconsin law entitled to nothing beyond his one-year appointment. There are no statutory or administrative standards defining eligibility for re-employment. State law thus clearly leaves the decision whether to rehire a nontenured teacher for another year to the unfettered discretion of university officials.

The procedural protection afforded a Wisconsin State University teacher before he is separated from the University corresponds to his job security. As a matter of statutory law, a tenured teacher cannot be "discharged except for cause upon written charges" and pursuant to certain procedures. A nontenured teacher, similarly, is protected to some extent *during* his one-year term. Rules promulgated by the Board of Regents provide that a nontenured teacher "dismissed" before the end of the year may have some opportunity for review of the "dismissal." But the Rules provide no real protection for a nontenured teacher who simply is not re-employed for the next year. He must be informed by February 1 "concerning retention or non-retention for the ensuing year." But "no reason for non-retention need be given. No review or appeal is provided in such case."

In conformance with these Rules, the President of Wisconsin State University–Oshkosh informed the respondent before February 1, 1969, that he would not be rehired for the 1969–1970 academic year. He gave the respondent no reason for the decision and no opportunity to challenge it at any sort of hearing.

The respondent then brought this action in Federal District Court alleging that the decision not to rehire him for the next year infringed his Fourteenth Amendment rights. He attacked the decision both in substance and procedure. First, he alleged that the true reason for the decision was to punish him for certain statements critical of the University administration, and that it therefore violated his right to freedom of speech. Second, he alleged that the failure of University officials to give him notice of any reason for nonretention and an opportunity for a hearing violated his right to procedural due process of law.

The District Court granted summary judgment for the respondent on the procedural issue, ordering the University officials to provide him with reasons and a hearing. The Court of Appeals, with one judge dissenting, affirmed this partial summary judgment. The only question presented to us at this stage in the case is whether the respondent had a constitutional right to a statement of reasons and a hearing on the University's decision not to rehire him for another year. We hold that he did not.

I

The requirements of procedural due process apply only to the deprivation of interests encompassed by the Fourteenth Amendment's protection of liberty and property. When protected interests are implicated, the right to some kind of prior hearing is paramount.[7] But the range of interests protected by procedural due process is not infinite.

The District Court decided that procedural due process guarantees apply in this case by assessing and balancing the weights of the particular interests involved. It concluded that the respondent's interest in re-employment at Wisconsin State University–Oshkosh outweighed the University's interest in denying him re-employment summarily. Undeniably, the respondent's re-employment prospects were of major concern to him—concern that we surely cannot say was insignificant. And a weighing process has long been a part of any determination of the *form* of hearing required in particular situations by procedural due process. But, to determine whether due process requirements apply in the first place, we must look not to the "weight" but to the *nature* of the interest at stake. We must look to see if the interest is within the Fourteenth Amendment's protection of liberty and property.

"Liberty" and "property" are broad and majestic terms. They are among the "[g]reat [constitutional] concepts ... purposely left to gather meaning from experience...." For that reason, the Court has fully and finally rejected the wooden distinction between "rights" and "privileges" that once seemed to govern the applicability of procedural due process rights. The Court has also made clear that the property interests protected by procedural due process extend well beyond actual ownership of real estate, chattels, or money. By the same token, the Court has required due process protection for deprivations of liberty beyond the sort of formal constraints imposed by the criminal process.

Yet, while the Court has eschewed rigid or formalistic limitations on the protection of procedural due process, it has at the same time observed certain boundaries. For the words "liberty" and "property" in the Due Process Clause of the Fourteenth Amendment must be given some meaning....

II

"While this court has not attempted to define with exactness the liberty ... guaranteed [by the Fourteenth Amendment], the term has received much consideration and some of the included things have been definitely stated. Without doubt, it denotes not merely freedom from bodily restraint but also the right of the individual to contract, to engage in any of the common occupations of life, to acquire useful knowledge, to marry, establish a home and bring up children, to worship God according to the dictates of his own conscience, and generally to enjoy those privileges long recognized ... as essential to the orderly pursuit of happiness by free men." *Meyer v. Nebraska*, 262 U.S. 390, 399. In a Constitution for a free people, there can be no doubt that the meaning of "liberty" must be broad indeed.

---

7. Before a person is deprived of a protected interest, he must be afforded opportunity for some kind of a hearing, "except for extraordinary situations where some valid governmental interest is at stake that justifies postponing the hearing until after the event." ...

There might be cases in which a State refused to re-employ a person under such circumstances that interests in liberty would be implicated. But this is not such a case.

The State, in declining to rehire the respondent, did not make any charge against him that might seriously damage his standing and associations in his community. It did not base the nonrenewal of his contract on a charge, for example, that he had been guilty of dishonesty, or immorality. Had it done so, this would be a different case. For "[w]here a person's good name, reputation, honor, or integrity is at stake because of what the government is doing to him, notice and an opportunity to be heard are essential." *Wisconsin v. Constantineau*, 400 U.S. 433, 437. In such a case, due process would accord an opportunity to refute the charge before University officials.[12] In the present case, however, there is no suggestion whatever that the respondent's "good name, reputation, honor, or integrity" is at stake.

Similarly, there is no suggestion that the State, in declining to re-employ the respondent, imposed on him a stigma or other disability that foreclosed his freedom to take advantage of other employment opportunities. The State, for example, did not invoke any regulations to bar the respondent from all other public employment in state universities. Had it done so, this, again, would be a different case. For "[t]o be deprived not only of present government employment but of future opportunity for it certainly is no small injury. . . ." The Court has held, for example, that a State, in regulating eligibility for a type of professional employment, cannot foreclose a range of opportunities "in a manner . . . that contravene[s] . . . Due Process," and, specifically, in a manner that denies the right to a full prior hearing. *Willner v. Committee on Character*, 373 U.S. 96 [bar admission]. In the present case, however, this principle does not come into play.[13]

To be sure, the respondent has alleged that the nonrenewal of his contract was based on his exercise of his right to freedom of speech. But this allegation is not now before us. The District Court stayed proceedings on this issue, and the respondent has yet to prove that the decision not to rehire him was, in fact, based on his free speech activities.

---

12. The purpose of such notice and hearing is to provide the person an opportunity to clear his name. Once a person has cleared his name at a hearing, his employer, of course, may remain free to deny him future employment for other reasons.

13. The District Court made an *assumption* "that non-retention by one university or college creates concrete and practical difficulties for a professor in his subsequent academic career." And the Court of Appeals based its affirmance of the summary judgment largely on the premise that "the substantial adverse effect non-retention is likely to have upon the career interests of an individual professor" amounts to a limitation on future employment opportunities sufficient to invoke procedural due process guarantees. But even assuming, *arguendo*, that such a "substantial adverse effect" under these circumstances would constitute a state-imposed restriction on liberty, the record contains no support for these assumptions. There is no suggestion of how nonretention might affect the respondent's future employment prospects. Mere proof, for example, that his record of nonretention in one job, taken alone, might make him somewhat less attractive to some other employers would hardly establish the kind of foreclosure of opportunities amounting to a deprivation of "liberty."

Hence, on the record before us, all that clearly appears is that the respondent was not rehired for one year at one university. It stretches the concept too far to suggest that a person is deprived of "liberty" when he simply is not rehired in one job but remains as free as before to seek another.

III

The Fourteenth Amendment's procedural protection of property is a safeguard of the security of interests that a person has already acquired in specific benefits. These interests—property interests—may take many forms.

Thus, the Court has held that a person receiving welfare benefits under statutory and administrative standards defining eligibility for them has an interest in continued receipt of those benefits that is safeguarded by procedural due process. *Goldberg v. Kelly.*[15] Similarly, in the area of public employment, the Court has held that a public college professor dismissed from an office held under tenure provisions, and college professors and staff members dismissed during the terms of their contracts have interests in continued employment that are safeguarded by due process. . . .

Certain attributes of "property" interests protected by procedural due process emerge from these decisions. To have a property interest in a benefit, a person clearly must have more than an abstract need or desire for it. He must have more than a unilateral expectation of it. He must, instead, have a legitimate claim of entitlement to it. It is a purpose of the ancient institution of property to protect those claims upon which people rely in their daily lives, reliance that must not be arbitrarily undermined. It is a purpose of the constitutional right to a hearing to provide an opportunity for a person to vindicate those claims.

Property interests, of course, are not created by the Constitution. Rather, they are created and their dimensions are defined by existing rules or understandings that stem from an independent source such as state law—rules or understandings that secure certain benefits and that support claims of entitlement to those benefits. Thus, the welfare recipients in *Goldberg v. Kelly* had a claim of entitlement to welfare payments that was grounded in the statute defining eligibility for them. The recipients had not yet shown that they were, in fact, within the statutory

---

15. *Goldsmith v. Board of Tax Appeals*, 270 U.S. 117 (1926), is a related case. There the petitioner was a lawyer who had been refused admission to practice before the Board of Tax Appeals. The Board had "published rules for admission of persons entitled to practice before it, by which attorneys . . . duly qualified under the law of any state or the District, are made eligible. . . . The rules further provide that the Board may in its discretion deny admission to any applicant, or suspend or disbar any person after admission." The Board denied admission to the petitioner under its discretionary power, without a prior hearing and a statement of the reasons for the denial. Although this court disposed of the case on other grounds, it stated . . . that the existence of the Board's eligibility rules gave the petitioner an interest and claim to practice before the Board to which procedural due process requirements applied. It said that the Board's discretionary power "must be construed to mean the exercise of a discretion to be exercised after fair investigation, with such a notice, hearing and opportunity to answer for the applicant as would constitute due process."

terms of eligibility. But we held that they had a right to a hearing at which they might attempt to do so.

Just as the welfare recipients' "property" interest in welfare payments was created and defined by statutory terms, so the respondent's "property" interest in employment at Wisconsin State University–Oshkosh was created and defined by the terms of his appointment. Those terms secured his interest in employment up to June 30, 1969. But the important fact in this case is that they specifically provided that the respondent's employment was to terminate on June 30. They did not provide for contract renewal absent "sufficient cause." Indeed, they made no provision for renewal whatsoever.

Thus, the terms of the respondent's appointment secured absolutely no interest in re-employment for the next year. They supported absolutely no possible claim of entitlement to re-employment. Nor, significantly, was there any state statute or University rule or policy that secured his interest in re-employment or that created any legitimate claim to it. In these circumstances, the respondent surely had an abstract concern in being rehired, but he did not have a *property* interest sufficient to require the University authorities to give him a hearing when they declined to renew his contract of employment.

IV

Our analysis of the respondent's constitutional rights in this case in no way indicates a view that an opportunity for a hearing or a statement of reasons for nonretention would, or would not, be appropriate or wise in public colleges and universities. For it is a written Constitution that we apply. Our role is confined to interpretation of that Constitution.

We must conclude that the summary judgment for the respondent should not have been granted, since the respondent has not shown that he was deprived of liberty or property protected by the Fourteenth Amendment. The judgment of the Court of Appeals, accordingly, is reversed and the case is remanded for further proceedings consistent with this opinion.

[DOUGLAS, J. dissented, arguing that Roth was entitled to a hearing because he alleged that the dismissal was based upon expression protected by the first amendment. Also dissenting, MARSHALL, J. contended that due process requires a statement of reasons and, if need be, a hearing whenever the government denies an individual a job. He argued that the job is "property" and that "liberty" protects the right to work.]

Notes and Questions

1. *The right-privilege doctrine.* A government job was once considered a "privilege" and not a "right," meaning that a deprivation of the job triggered no right to procedural due process. The leading case was *Bailey v. Richardson,* 182 F.2d 46 (D.C.Cir.1950), *aff'd by equally divided court,* 341 U.S. 918 (1951). Clearly reflecting the cold war attitudes of the time, *Bailey* is a landmark of the McCarthy era.

Ms. Bailey was dismissed from her "non-sensitive" job in the U.S. Employment Service on the asserted basis that reasonable grounds existed for the belief that she was disloyal. She received a hearing but was not allowed to confront the unnamed FBI informants who stated that there was reason to believe she was a member of the Communist Party. She denied this under oath, affirmed her loyalty to the United States, and placed a great deal of evidence of her loyalty on record. The Court of Appeals held that a government job is not property and that a dismissal for disloyalty is not an infringement of liberty, despite its stigmatic effect. Consequently, the government need not provide any procedure at all, much less confrontation of informants.

In addition to government jobs, many other relationships between private parties and government were treated as "privileges." Among them were licenses to do the sort of business that the state could prohibit entirely (like selling liquor), subsidies, welfare benefits, and the ability to contract with the government. The theory of the right-privilege distinction was that since government did not have to give a person a job, a license, or a contract, due process did not apply to the withdrawal of these benefits.

Goldberg v. Kelly was a critical turning point on the road to discarding the right-privilege distinction. In a footnote in *Roth* (not reproduced in the text), the Court referred to *Bailey* and said: "The basis of this holding has been thoroughly undermined in the ensuing years . . . [T]his Court now has rejected the concept that constitutional rights turn upon whether a governmental benefit is characterized as a 'right' or a 'privilege.' " 408 U.S. at 571, n.9.

But is the right-privilege distinction really dead? Is the distinction between tenured and untenured government jobs in *Roth* a modern counterpart to the right-privilege distinction? What is wrong with the right-privilege distinction as a basis for applying the requirements of procedural due process?

2. *Definition of "property."* Procedural due process has always protected a person's interest in traditional forms of property (such as the right to own and use goods). Justice Stewart's definition of property breaks new ground. Under *Roth,* the right to receive welfare benefits is a statutory "entitlement" and thus property. Similarly, *Perry,* discussed in N.7, held that a professor's right under implied contract to keep his job is "property." Would you have defined these sorts of interests as "property" before you knew about the *Roth* decision? Can you sell these interests or transfer them to another as you can with traditional property?

Stewart makes clear that the existence of a property right depends upon some *entitlement* created and defined by an *independent source*. The source might be a state or federal statute or even a regulation (see *Goldsmith* cited in n.15 of *Goldberg*). This "positivist" approach to identifying property has profound consequences. If a property right wholly depends upon an entitlement created by an independent source of law, the state can modify or eliminate the right by modifying or repealing its positive law source.

3. *What is "liberty"?* Did *Roth* define "liberty" in a positive law or a natural law mold? Why did the refusal to rehire Roth not deprive him of liberty? Is a "liberty" interest something identified in state law? Or is

"liberty" something that everyone has without regard to whether the state provided it?

Stewart relied upon the open-ended natural law analysis of *Meyer v. Nebraska* in sketching the contours of liberty. *Meyer* was a 1923 decision which declared invalid a Nebraska law prohibiting the teaching of foreign languages to young children. Note that *Meyer* was a *substantive* due process case, not a *procedural* one. The state law was invalid, not because of the procedures which Nebraska used, but because it "materially" interfered "with the calling of modern language teachers, with the opportunities of pupils to acquire knowledge, and with the power of parents to control the education of their own." *Roth* establishes that this definition of "liberty" applies to *both* procedural and substantive due process.

Elements of substantive due process survive in cases which require a compelling state interest in order to interfere with people's "fundamental" interests such as control over their bodies or their family relations. *See, e.g., Roe v. Wade,* 410 U.S. 113 (1973) (right to abortion); *Moore v. East Cleveland,* 431 U.S. 494 (1977) (right of closely related family members to live together); *Zablocki v. Redhail,* 434 U.S. 374 (1978) (right to marry).

In the economic area, there is little left of substantive due process (or of its close counterpart, substantive equal protection). The courts will accept any rational justification for statutes that limit economic rights. *See, e.g., Williamson v. Lee Optical Inc.,* 348 U.S. 483 (1955) (imagining reasons why state law regulating optometry might be rational). However, it remains true that a wholly irrational decision is substantively invalid under the due process or equal protection clauses.

This chapter concerns *procedural,* not *substantive* due process. Although remnants of substantive due process still exist, as explained in the preceding paragraphs and in the next text note, economic rights receive far more protection under procedural due process than under substantive due process.

4. *Free speech rights.* Roth argued that he lost his job because the University disapproved of constitutionally protected speeches. However, the majority believed that issue was not before the Court and thus did not reach it. Because "liberty" includes first amendment rights, government invades liberty if it refuses to rehire an employee because of disagreement with his political speeches. The decision remands to the trial court to decide whether Roth was discharged in violation of his first amendment rights. Why is this claim to be resolved in the federal district court rather than in an administrative hearing?

Roth's claim was plausible. Of 442 non-tenured teachers, only four were not renewed. Roth had been involved in demonstrations against the Vietnam War and had caustically criticized the university administration. Roth ultimately prevailed on his first amendment claim in the district court. He was awarded $6746 in damages; by that time he had another teaching job at Purdue. Chronicle of Higher Education, Nov. 26, 1973.

5. *Discretion and due process.* The Court held that Wisconsin infringed no liberty or property rights so Roth was entitled to no process. Nevertheless, the effect of a non-renewal decision upon the career of a young professor is quite drastic—often academically terminal. Do you think that

there should be a right to a hearing whenever government exercises discretionary power in a way which drastically and negatively affects a person's life? Is a hearing *more important* when the government exercises discretionary power than when it applies a non-discretionary standard? If so, should federal courts adopt the California approach discussed in the next note?

6. *State constitutional law.* Although the California constitution uses the same language as the federal, the California Supreme Court has rejected the *Roth* approach. It holds that a discretionary standard can trigger due process protection.

Saleeby v. State Bar, 702 P.2d 525 (Cal.1985), involved a claim by a defrauded client for reimbursement from the state's Client Security Fund. By statute, "any payments from the fund shall be discretionary and shall be subject to such regulation and conditions as the [State Bar] shall prescribe." The Bar denied payment from the Fund to Saleeby. It declined to provide a hearing or any statement of reasons for its decision. After summarizing *Roth*, the court said:

> California has expanded upon the federal analytical base by focusing on the administrative process itself. . . . [D]ue process safeguards required for protection of an individual's statutory interests must be analyzed in the context of the principle that *freedom from arbitrary adjudicative procedures* is a substantive element of one's liberty.
>
> No firm rule can be established to ascertain what protections are necessary in a particular situation. Rather the relief to be afforded depends upon balancing the various interests involved. Generally, the dictates of due process necessitate considering (1) the private interest that will be affected by the official action, (2) the risk of an erroneous deprivation of such interest through the procedures used, and the probable value, if any, of additional or substitute procedural safeguards, (3) *the dignitary interest in informing individuals of the nature, grounds, and consequences of the action and in enabling them to present their side of the story before a responsible governmental official*, and (4) the governmental interest, including the function involved and the fiscal and administrative burdens that the additional or substitute procedural requirement would entail. . . . [emphasis added]

The court held that Saleeby had a right to be heard and to respond (orally or in writing) to the Bar's determination and the Bar must issue sufficient findings to afford judicial review.

Is the *Saleeby* approach better than the *Roth* approach in achieving the purposes of due process discussed in § 2.1? What is the "dignitary interest" to which the court refers and how does a hearing vindicate that interest? Will courts encounter difficulties in administering the *Saleeby* approach?

7. *De facto tenure. Perry v. Sindermann,* 408 U.S. 593 (1972), decided the same day as *Roth,* was factually similar but with one vital difference: Sindermann was not protected by a formal tenure system but he alleged a right to reemployment based on *implied contract.* The contract arose from guidelines on which he had relied during his ten-year teaching career and on the practices of the institution. The Court held that an entitlement could be based on implied as well as express contract, since implied contract rights

are protected in state courts. Does *Perry* mean that the government must grant a hearing any time it breaches a contract? We return to this question in § 2.2.2 N.5.

8. *Deprivation.* Note that the Constitution requires due process only if a person is "deprived" of life, liberty, or property. Is there a constitutional distinction between being "deprived" of what you already have and being "denied" something which you want but do not yet have?

Language in *Roth* suggests that this distinction may be important. Stewart wrote: "The Fourteenth Amendment's procedural protection of property is a safeguard of the security of interests that a person has *already acquired* in specific benefits ... [emphasis added]" Contrast this with *Goldsmith v. Board of Tax Appeals,* cited approvingly in n.15 of *Roth,* which holds that due process must be provided in connection with an application for admission to practice before the Board of Tax Appeals. But the Court has yet to rule definitively on this issue.

§ 2.2.2 DEFINING "PROPERTY"

The *Roth* case held that a tenured professor's job or the continued flow of welfare benefits is "property" while an untenured professor's job is not. According to *Roth,* property interests are created and limited by positive law such as state statutes. Does it follow that a statute that creates "property" can also prescribe the procedure for taking it away?

CLEVELAND BOARD OF EDUCATION v. LOUDERMILL
470 U.S. 532 (1985).

[Respondents worked for cities in Ohio. One was a security guard, the other a bus mechanic. By law, they could be discharged only for cause. They were discharged without any opportunity to respond to the charges against them prior to the discharge. One was discharged for lying on his employment application, one failed an eye examination. Ohio law provided no pre-termination hearing, only for a post-termination hearing and judicial review. The post-termination hearing occurred about nine months after the discharge.]

WHITE, J.:

.... Respondents' federal constitutional claim depends on their having had a property right in continued employment. *Board of Regents v. Roth.* If they did, the State could not deprive them of this property without due process.

Property interests are not created by the Constitution, "they are created and their dimensions are defined by existing rules or understandings that stem from an independent source such as state law...." *Roth.* The Ohio statute plainly creates such an interest. Respondents were "classified civil service employees," entitled to retain their positions "during good behavior and efficient service," who could not be dismissed "except ... for ... misfeasance, malfeasance, or nonfeasance in office." The statute plainly supports the conclusion, reached by both lower courts, that respondents possessed property rights in continued employment. . . .

The Parma Board argues, however, that the property right is defined by, and conditioned on, the legislature's choice of procedures for its deprivation. The Board stresses that in addition to specifying the grounds for termination, the statute sets out procedures by which termination may take place. The procedures were adhered to in these cases. According to petitioner, "[t]o require additional procedures would in effect expand the scope of the property interest itself."

This argument, which was accepted by the District Court, has its genesis in the plurality opinion in *Arnett v. Kennedy*, 416 U.S. 134 (1974). *Arnett* involved a challenge by a former federal employee to the procedures by which he was dismissed. The plurality reasoned that where the legislation conferring the substantive right also sets out the procedural mechanism for enforcing that right, the two cannot be separated:

> "The employee's statutorily defined right is not a guarantee against removal without cause in the abstract, but such a guarantee as enforced by the procedures which Congress has designated for the determination of cause.

> ". . . [W]here the grant of a substantive right is inextricably intertwined with the limitations on the procedures which are to be employed in determining that right, a litigant in the position of appellee must take the bitter with the sweet."

This view garnered three votes in *Arnett,* but was specifically rejected by the other six Justices. Since then, this theory has at times seemed to gather some additional support. More recently, however, the Court has clearly rejected it. . . . In light of these holdings, it is settled that the "bitter with the sweet" approach misconceives the constitutional guarantee. If a clearer holding is needed, we provide it today. The point is straightforward: the Due Process Clause provides that certain substantive rights—life, liberty, and property—cannot be deprived except pursuant to constitutionally adequate procedures. The categories of substance and procedure are distinct. Were the rule otherwise, the Clause would be reduced to a mere tautology. "Property" cannot be defined by the procedures provided for its deprivation any more than can life or liberty. The right to due process "is conferred, not by legislative grace, but by constitutional guarantee. While the legislature may elect not to confer a property interest in [public] employment, it may not constitutionally authorize the deprivation of such an interest, once conferred, without appropriate procedural safeguards."

In short, once it is determined that the Due Process Clause applies, "the question remains what process is due." The answer to that question is not to be found in the Ohio statute. . . .

[The Court found that Ohio's pre-termination procedures did not provide due process. See § 2.3 N.4.]

REHNQUIST, C.J., dissenting.

.... We ought to recognize the totality of the State's definition of the property right in question, and not merely seize upon one of several paragraphs in a unitary statute to proclaim that in that paragraph the State has inexorably conferred upon a civil service employee something which it is powerless under the United States Constitution to qualify in the next paragraph of the statute. This practice ignores our duty under *Roth* to rely on state law as the source of property interests for purposes of applying the Due Process Clause of the Fourteenth Amendment. While it does not impose a federal definition of property, the Court departs from the full breadth of the holding in *Roth* by its selective choice from among the sentences the Ohio legislature chooses to use in establishing and qualifying a right....

Notes and Questions

1. *The bitter with the sweet.* Since "property" does not exist in the abstract but arises only from statute, contract, or other interest protected by law, what is wrong with Rehnquist's contention that the state should be allowed to create the procedural as well as the substantive contours of property interests? In other words, why shouldn't the property-holder take "the bitter with the sweet"?

In the portion of the opinion discussed in § 2.3 N.3, the Court held that a written, rather than oral, pretermination proceeding is sufficient protection for a discharged employee if a full hearing is provided after the discharge. Was this determination a factor in persuading the majority justices to reject the "bitter with the sweet" approach?

2. *Consequences of Loudermill.* Do decisions like *Perry v. Sindermann* (§ 2.2.1 N.7) and *Loudermill* go too far in rigidifying public employment so that government must choose between a spoils system and a tenure system which is highly protective of employee job security? Will government be willing or able, practically speaking, to fire incompetent employees if they have entitlements to their jobs protected by due process?

Will these cases encourage government to contract out to private employers such traditional governmental tasks as trash collection, recreation area maintenance, public transportation and the like? Since job security is purely a matter of employer-employee bargaining in the private sector, the private sector may be able to furnish such services more efficiently than government.

3. *Jobs as property—Bishop v. Wood.* How can you tell whether a government job is "property"? Many jobholders have much less protection than a fully tenured college professor but more protection than Mr. Roth. For example, in *Bishop v. Wood,* 426 U.S. 341 (1976), a policeman was classified as a "permanent employee." The ordinance provided that "if a permanent employee fails to perform work up to the standard of the classification held, or continues to be negligent, inefficient, or unfit to perform his duties, he may be dismissed by the City manager. Any discharged employee shall be given written notice of his discharge setting forth

the effective date and reasons for his discharge if he shall request such a notice." No North Carolina cases had interpreted this ordinance.

The federal trial judge "who of course sits in North Carolina and practiced law there for many years" concluded that the policeman "held his position at the will and pleasure of the city." The Supreme Court deferred to this construction and held that the job was not "property." Should this sort of determination be left to a case-by-case analysis by trial courts, or should there be a uniform rule that always treats a "permanent" job as property?

4. *The new property—beyond Roth.* Besides certain jobs and welfare benefits, what other relationships between persons and government are *entitlements*? Among the most important are *licenses* to do what cannot be done without governmental permission (for example, to drive a car or practice medicine). *See e.g. Barry v. Barchi,* 443 U.S. 55 (1979) (suspension of horse trainer's license). Equally important is the right to public *services* such as education. *See e.g. Memphis Light, Gas and Water Div. v. Craft,* 436 U.S. 1 (1978) (right to continued service from municipal utility).

5. *Contracts with government.* Assume an individual makes a contract with state or local government and the government threatens to breach the contract. In addition to normal rights under state law for breach of contract, can the victim of breach argue that government has deprived him of "property"? If so, does the government violate due process by failing to provide notice and a hearing before it breached? If the government violated due process when it breached the contract without providing a hearing, it might be liable for violation of federal civil rights statutes in addition to its normal liability for breach.

The positivist approach of *Roth* and *Loudermill* might support such a conclusion, since, by definition, a contract creates a legitimate claim of entitlement under state law. But it is unclear whether every breach of contract by government deprives the private party of property. Somehow, a city's threatened breach of a contract to buy $500 worth of paper clips from a private vendor does not feel like a constitutional case.

After all, state contract law seldom allows for specific performance of contracts; damages are the normal remedy for breach in all but exceptional cases. But if breach must be litigated in a prior administrative hearing, the hearing officer could order the government not to breach—the equivalent of specific performance. In effect, treating contracts rights as property prevents the state from committing what contract theorists call "efficient breach" (i.e. the situation in which the saving to the state from breaching exceeds the amount of damages it will have to pay). Besides, this approach would transfer a vast number of routine contract disputes from state to federal courts and transform them from contract cases to civil rights cases.

In *Unger v. National Residents Matching Program,* 928 F.2d 1392 (3d Cir.1991), Unger alleged that Temple University Medical School breached a contract to admit her into a dermatology residency. Since Temple provided no prior hearing before reneging on the agreement, she sued it for damages under 42 U.S.C. § 1983 (which allows federal court actions for damages if state or local government violates a plaintiff's constitutional rights).

The court ruled that only a few types of government contracts are protected by due process—those involving extreme dependence (like welfare benefits) or those in which the contract itself allows the state to terminate only for cause (as in *Roth* or *Loudermill*). The residency program in question met neither criteria. Unger was required to pursue her rights under state law.

However, there is another approach to the contract rights issue. Perhaps a garden variety contract right is "property," but due process is satisfied by normal state law contract remedies (which, of course, occur after the breach and are usually limited to damages). We consider this possibility further in § 2.4.

6. *Due process and de minimis deprivations. Goss v. Lopez,* 419 U.S. 565, 576 (1975), held that "as long as a property deprivation is not *de minimis,* its gravity is irrelevant to the question whether account must be taken of the Due Process Clause.... " The length and severity of deprivation, while another factor to weigh in determining the appropriate form of hearing, "is not decisive of the basic right to a hearing of some kind." Thus a "10–day suspension from school is not *de minimis* in our view and may not be imposed in complete disregard of the Due Process Clause." We discuss the *form* that such a hearing should take in §§ 2.3 and 2.4.

What sort of deprivation of property would be *de minimis*? See *Swick v. City of Chicago,* 11 F.3d 85 (7th Cir.1993). The court held that placing a police officer on paid sick leave, so that he could not wear a badge or carry a gun or arrest people, is a *de minimis* deprivation. "Otherwise we shall be hearing appeals next in cases in which the public employer reneged on a promise to give the employee an office with a view, or a second secretary, or leave to coach a Little League team."

7. *Problem.* Seaside High School hires part-time athletic coaches to work not more than 20 hours per week. Coaching contracts provide that if a coach's work is satisfactory and the coach's services are needed for the next academic year, the contract will be renewed. If a contract is not renewed because of unsatisfactory service, the principal must explain the basis of the decision in writing.

Rex, the principal of Seaside High, hired Doris to coach girls' tennis for the spring semester. The contract called for compensation of $400 per month for four months. Rex's daughter, Ann, was on the team. Ann and Doris did not get along very well and Ann, because of poor attitude, was not allowed to play in several important matches. However, Seaside's team was undefeated, and most of the girls were pleased with Doris.

Rex declined to renew Doris' contract for the following academic year, even though a coach was needed. He stated no reasons and refused to discuss the matter with Doris. What are Doris' rights? *See Vail v. Board of Educ.,* 706 F.2d 1435 (7th Cir.1983), *aff'd by equally divided Court,* 466 U.S. 377 (1984).

§ 2.2.3 DEFINING "LIBERTY"

After *Board of Regents v. Roth,* the Court encountered difficulty in deciding whether particular administrative decisions deprived persons of "liberty." For example, does a person sentenced to prison have any "liberty" left?

SANDIN v. CONNER

515 U.S. 472 (1995).

REHNQUIST, C.J.:

[Conner is serving a sentence of 30 years to life in a Hawaii prison. As punishment for resisting a strip search, he was sentenced to 30 days in segregation (e.g. solitary confinement). Although Conner was given a hearing by the Adjustment Committee, he was not permitted to present witnesses during the hearing. The Ninth Circuit held that there was a disputed question of fact as to whether Conner had been deprived of liberty without due process. The court held that a liberty interest was involved because:

i) Conner was being disciplined for misconduct under *Wolff v. McDonnell*, 418 U.S. 539 (1974); and

ii) the prison regulations concerning misconduct contained non-discretionary standards that the committee had to follow. *Hewitt v. Helms*, 459 U.S. 460 (1983).]

Our due process analysis begins with *Wolff*. There, Nebraska inmates challenged the decision of prison officials to revoke good time credits without adequate procedures.... We held that the Due Process Clause itself does not create a liberty interest in credit for good behavior, but that the statutory provision created a liberty interest in a "shortened prison sentence" which resulted from good time credits ... The Court characterized this liberty interest as one of "real substance" and articulated minimum procedures necessary to reach a "mutual accommodation between institutional needs and objectives and the provisions of the Constitution...."

[Later] the Court embarked on a different approach to defining state-created liberty interests ... focusing on whether state action was mandatory or discretionary ... *Hewitt*, in evaluating the claims of inmates who had been confined to administrative segregation, first rejected the inmates' claim of a right to remain in the general population as protected by the Due Process Clause ... The Clause standing alone confers no liberty interest in freedom from state action taken within the sentence imposed. It then concluded that the transfer to less amenable quarters for nonpunitive reasons was "ordinarily contemplated by a prison sentence." Examination of the possibility that the State had created a liberty interest by virtue of its prison regulations followed. Instead of looking to whether the State created an interest of "real substance" comparable to the good time credit scheme of *Wolff*, the Court asked whether the State had gone beyond issuing mere procedural guidelines and had used "language of an unmistakably mandatory character" such that the incursion on liberty would not occur "absent specified substantive predicates." Finding such mandatory directives in the regulations before it, the Court decided that the State had created a protected liberty interest. It nevertheless held that the full panoply of procedures conferred in *Wolff* were unnecessary to safeguard the inmates' interest and, if imposed, would undermine the prison's management objectives.

As this methodology took hold, no longer did inmates need to rely on a showing that they had suffered a "grievous loss" of liberty retained even after sentenced to terms of imprisonment. For the Court had ceased to examine the "nature" of the interest with respect to interests allegedly created by the state. *Board of Regents of State Colleges v. Roth* ... In a series of cases since *Hewitt*, the Court has wrestled with the language of intricate, often rather routine prison guidelines to determine whether mandatory language and substantive predicates created an enforceable expectation that the state would produce a particular outcome with respect to the prisoner's conditions of confinement....

By shifting the focus of the liberty interest inquiry to one based on the language of a particular regulation, and not the nature of the deprivation, the Court encouraged prisoners to comb regulations in search of mandatory language on which to base entitlements to various state-conferred privileges. Courts have, in response, and not altogether illogically, drawn negative inferences from mandatory language in the text of prison regulations. The Court of Appeals' approach in this case is typical: it inferred from the mandatory directive that a finding of guilt "shall" be imposed under certain conditions the conclusion that the absence of such conditions prevents a finding of guilt ...

Hewitt has produced at least two undesirable effects. First, it creates disincentives for States to codify prison management procedures in the interest of uniform treatment. Prison administrators need be concerned with the safety of the staff and inmate population. Ensuring that welfare often leads prison administrators to curb the discretion of staff on the front line who daily encounter prisoners hostile to the authoritarian structure of the prison environment. Such guidelines are not set forth solely to benefit the prisoner. They also aspire to instruct subordinate employees how to exercise discretion vested by the State in the warden, and to confine the authority of prison personnel in order to avoid widely different treatment of similar incidents. The approach embraced by *Hewitt* discourages this desirable development: States may avoid creation of "liberty" interests by having scarcely any regulations, or by conferring standardless discretion on correctional personnel.

Second, the *Hewitt* approach has led to the involvement of federal courts in the day-to-day management of prisons, often squandering judicial resources with little offsetting benefit to anyone. In so doing, it has run counter to the view expressed in several of our cases that federal courts ought to afford appropriate deference and flexibility to state officials trying to manage a volatile environment. Such flexibility is especially warranted in the fine-tuning of the ordinary incidents of prison life, a common subject of prisoner claims since *Hewitt*.

In light of the above discussion, we believe that the search for a negative implication from mandatory language in prisoner regulations has strayed from the real concerns undergirding the liberty protected by the Due Process Clause. The time has come to return to the due process principles we believe were correctly established and applied in *Wolff* . . . Following *Wolff*, we recognize that States may under certain circumstances create liberty interests which are protected by the Due Process Clause. But these interests will be generally limited to freedom from restraint which, while not exceeding the sentence in such an unexpected manner as to give rise to protection by the Due Process Clause of its own force, see, e.g., *Vitek v. Jones*, 445 U.S. 480 (1980) (transfer to mental hospital), and *Washington v. Harper*, 494 U.S. at 210 (1990) (involuntary administration of psychotropic drugs), nonetheless imposes atypical and significant hardship on the inmate in relation to the ordinary incidents of prison life.

Conner asserts, incorrectly, that any state action taken for a punitive reason encroaches upon a liberty interest under the Due Process Clause even in the absence of any state regulation. [The Court distinguishes *Bell v. Wolfish*, 441 U.S. 520 (1979) (concerning punishment of pretrial detainees) and *Ingraham v. Wright*, § 2.4 (concerning corporal punishment of students).]

The punishment of incarcerated prisoners . . . serves different aims than those found invalid in *Bell* and *Ingraham*. The process does not impose retribution in lieu of a valid conviction, nor does it maintain physical control over free citizens forced by law to subject themselves to state control over the educational mission. It effectuates prison management and prisoner rehabilitative goals. Admittedly, prisoners do not shed all constitutional rights at the prison gate, *Wolff* . . . [but] discipline by prison officials in response to a wide range of misconduct falls within the expected parameters of the sentence imposed by a court of law. . . . We hold that Conner's discipline in segregated confinement did not present the type of atypical, significant deprivation in which a state might conceivably create a liberty interest . . .

Nor does Conner's situation present a case where the State's action will inevitably affect the duration of his sentence. Nothing in Hawaii's code requires the parole board to deny parole in the face of a misconduct record or to grant parole in its absence even though misconduct is by regulation a relevant consideration. The decision to release a prisoner rests on a myriad of considerations. And, the prisoner is afforded procedural protection at his parole hearing in order to explain the circumstances behind his misconduct record. The chance that a finding of misconduct will alter the balance is simply too attenuated to invoke the procedural guarantees of the Due Process Clause. . . .

We hold, therefore, that neither the Hawaii prison regulation in question, nor the Due Process Clause itself, afforded Conner a protected liberty interest that would entitle him to the procedural protections set forth in *Wolff*. The regime to which he was subjected as a result of the misconduct hearing was within the range of confinement to be normally expected for one serving an indeterminate term of 30 years to life.[11]

The judgment of the Court of Appeals is accordingly reversed.

[Justices Ginsburg, Breyer, Stevens, and Souter dissented.]

Notes and Questions

1. *How much liberty does a prisoner retain?* Prior to *Sandin*, numerous Supreme Court cases, and hundreds of lower court cases, struggled with the issue of when, if ever, a prisoner retains a liberty interest protectible by procedural due process. *Sandin* swept away much of this body of law.

Many pre-*Sandin* cases, such as *Hewitt v. Helms*, found that prison regulations confer liberty interests if they constrain the prison officials' discretion. Recall and compare the distinction between tenured and non-tenured professors drawn by *Roth*. This "positivist" approach to defining liberty of prisoners was rejected in *Sandin*. What reasons does the Court give for overturning the *Hewitt* approach? Are these reasons persuasive? Do these reasons cast any doubt on *Roth*?

Recall that *Roth* seemed to define "liberty" in "natural law" terms, by relying on the *Meyer v. Nebraska* definition. *Wolff* followed this approach by suggesting that a prisoner is deprived of liberty if subjected to discipline for misconduct. This "natural law" approach to defining liberty of prisoners was also rejected in *Sandin*. Are the Court's reasons for doing so persuasive?

After *Sandin,* does a prisoner retain *any* constitutional rights? See note 11 of the opinion. Any rights to procedural due process?

2. *Stigma as deprivation of liberty.* Recall that the Court held that Mr. Roth had not been stigmatized by the University. The state "did not base the nonrenewal of his contract on a charge, for example, that he had been guilty of dishonesty, or immorality. Had it done so, this would be a different case. For '[w]here a person's good name, reputation, honor, or integrity is at stake because of what the government is doing to him, notice and an opportunity to be heard are essential.' *Wisconsin v. Constantineau,* 400 U.S. 433 ..." The *Constantineau* case held that a person was entitled to a prior hearing before the state posted his name as a "public drunkard."

In later decisions, however, the Court has held that state imposition of a stigma, by itself, is not an invasion of liberty so that no prior hearing is required. In *Paul v. Davis,* 424 U.S. 693 (1976), the police circulated a flyer bearing Davis' photo and labelling him as an "active shoplifter." The Court held that Davis was not entitled to a hearing. The police might have defamed him but had not deprived him of liberty.

The Court distinguished the *Roth* dictum by holding that liberty might be invaded by the imposition of a stigma *plus some other change of right or status recognized by state law*—such as discharge from a job. Similarly, it distinguished *Constantineau* because a "public drunkard" could not pur-

---

11. Prisoners such as Conner, of course, retain other protection from arbitrary state action even within the expected conditions of confinement. They may invoke the First and Eighth Amendments and the Equal Protection Clause of the Fourteenth Amendment where appropriate, and may draw upon internal prison grievance procedures and state judicial review where available.

chase alcoholic beverages. Thus that case also met the "stigma-plus" test. In this fashion *Paul* converted reputational "liberty" protected by due process from a natural law to a positivist conception.

In dissent, Justice Brennan argued that, under the majority view, the state could convene a commission to conduct ex parte trials of individuals so long as the only official judgment was a public condemnation and branding of the person as a Communist, traitor, murderer or any other mark that "merely" carries social opprobrium.

3. *Investigatory hearings.* Brennan's dissenting comments in *Paul* raise the question of whether due process applies to administrative investigations which may result in conclusions that are harmful to the persons investigated. In *Hannah v. Larche,* 363 U.S. 420 (1960), the Court held that voting registrars summoned to testify before the Civil Rights Commission had no right to cross-examine their accusers, since the proceedings of the Commission were purely investigatory. The Commission was seeking information in order to advise Congress and the executive branch about civil rights problems. It could not issue orders or impose any sanctions. However, in a later case, the Court limited *Hannah.* It held that due process did apply to state investigative proceedings that sought to uncover and publicize criminal activity by unions and brand individuals as criminals. *Jenkins v. McKeithen,* 395 U.S. 411 (1969). Under these cases and the majority view in *Paul v. Davis,* was Brennan's assessment correct?

4. *Problem.* The Madison Social Welfare Department (MSWD) maintains a hotline to receive information about child abuse. A Madison statute requires that the names of all persons suspected of child abuse should be placed on a registry maintained by MSWD. Any employer engaged in education of children or child care must consult the registry before hiring a new employee. Any such employer who hires a person whose name appears on the list must notify MSWD in writing.

The statute provides that MSWD must notify any person whose name is placed on the list. Such person can write to MSWD and show cause why his or her name should be removed from the list.

Anna slapped her child in the face because she suspected him of stealing from her wallet. A neighbor who observed the incident phoned the hotline. Based on this information, Anna's name was added to the child abuse list. Anna sent a letter to MSWD asking that her name be removed, but MSWD declined to do so. Anna has recently completed a course in school counseling and hopes to get a job with her local school district.

Anna sues MSWD in federal court, arguing that she has been deprived of due process. How should the court rule? See *Valmonte v. Bane,* 18 F.3d 992 (2d Cir.1994). Compare *Siegert v. Gilley,* 500 U.S. 226 (1991).

§ 2.3　TIMING OF TRIAL–TYPE HEARINGS

Even if government action has worked a deprivation of liberty or property, the question remains: what process is due? *Goldberg* determined that a trial-type hearing must be held *before* termination of benefits. The timing question is often critical, because a hearing after the event may do little to repair the damage caused by an administrative error. Yet a requirement that a hearing be held before benefits, employment, or some other entitlement can be terminated may impose substantial financial and programmatic costs upon an agency.

Mathews v. Eldridge asks whether trial-type hearings must be provided *before* termination of benefits to *disabled* persons under Title II of the Social Security Act. The complex state-federal system which adjudicates disability claims is described in the *Mathews* opinion. Some additional background on the disability program is helpful in evaluating the decision.

> The Social Security Administration (SSA) operates the largest system of administrative adjudication in the Western world. It makes well over 3 million determinations per year on claims for benefits under the Old–Age, Survivors, Disability, and Health Insurance (OASDHI) programs. The portion of the Social Security system considered here, the disability program, is itself massive. Since 1974, initial claims for disability benefits ... have averaged nearly 1,250,-000 annually [now 3,500,000 annually].

> There are perhaps 5,600 state agency personnel (supported by 5,000 more) whose sole function is to adjudicate disability claims. Over 625 federal administrative law judges [now 1020] hear administrative appeals from state agency denials. This total of more than 6,000 adjudicators approaches the size of the combined judicial systems of the state and federal governments of the United States. And the claims that these officials adjudicate are not small. The average, present, discounted value of the stream of income from a successful disability application is over $30,000 [now $90,000]. Disability claims, on the average, thus have a value three times that required by statute for the pursuit of many civil actions in federal district courts. More than 4.3 million disabled workers and their dependents draw annual benefits, which in fiscal year 1982 totaled $21.2 billion. When the Medicaid and Medicare payments for which these beneficiaries are automatically eligible are included, the total figure is $32.4 billion. By any measure the system is massive.

Jerry L. Mashaw, BUREAUCRATIC JUSTICE 18–19 (1983).

MATHEWS v. ELDRIDGE
424 U.S. 319 (1976).

POWELL, J.:

The issue in this case is whether the Due Process Clause of the Fifth Amendment requires that prior to the termination of Social Security disability benefit payments the recipient be afforded an opportunity for an evidentiary hearing.... Respondent Eldridge was first awarded benefits in June 1968. In March 1972, he received a questionnaire from the state agency charged with monitoring his medical condition. Eldridge completed the questionnaire, indicating that his condition had not improved and identifying the medical sources, including physicians, from whom he had received treatment recently. The state agency then obtained reports from his physician and a psychiatric consultant. After considering these reports and other information in his file the agency informed Eldridge by letter that it had made a tentative determination that his disability had ceased in May 1972. The letter included a statement of reasons for the proposed termination of benefits, and advised Eldridge that he might request reasonable time in which to obtain and submit additional information pertaining to his condition.

In his written response, Eldridge disputed one characterization of his medical condition and indicated that the agency already had enough evidence to establish his disability. The state agency then made its final determination that he had ceased to be disabled in May 1972. This determination was accepted by the Social Security Administration (SSA), which notified Eldridge in July that his benefits would terminate after that month. The notification also advised him of his right to seek reconsideration by the state agency of this initial determination within six months.

Instead of requesting reconsideration Eldridge commenced this action challenging the constitutional validity of the administrative procedures established by the Secretary of Health, Education, and Welfare for assessing whether there exists a continuing disability. He sought an immediate reinstatement of benefits pending a hearing on the issue of his disability. . . . In support of his contention that due process requires a pretermination hearing, Eldridge relied exclusively upon this Court's decision in *Goldberg v. Kelly*. . . .

A

Procedural due process imposes constraints on governmental decisions which deprive individuals of "liberty" or "property" interests within the meaning of the Due Process Clause of the Fifth or Fourteenth Amendment. The Secretary does not contend that procedural due process is inapplicable to terminations of Social Security disability benefits. He recognizes . . . that the interest of an individual in continued receipt of these benefits is a statutorily created "property" interest protected by the Fifth Amendment. Rather, the Secretary contends that the existing administrative procedures, detailed below, provide all the process that is constitutionally due before a recipient can be deprived of that interest.

This Court consistently has held that some form of hearing is required before an individual is finally deprived of a property interest. The "right to be heard before being condemned to suffer grievous loss of any kind, even though it may not involve the stigma and hardships of a criminal conviction, is a principle basic to our society." The fundamental requirement of due process is the opportunity to be heard "at a meaningful time and in a meaningful manner."

In recent years this Court increasingly has had occasion to consider the extent to which due process requires an evidentiary hearing prior to the deprivation of some type of property interest even if such a hearing is provided thereafter. In only one case, *Goldberg v. Kelly,* has the Court held that a hearing closely approximating a judicial trial is necessary. In other cases requiring some type of pretermination hearing as a matter of constitutional right the Court has spoken sparingly about the requisite procedures. . . .

These decisions underscore the truism that "[d]ue process, unlike some legal rules, is not a technical conception with a fixed content unrelated to time, place and circumstances." "[D]ue process is flexible and calls for such procedural protections as the particular situation demands."

Accordingly, resolution of the issue whether the administrative procedures provided here are constitutionally sufficient requires analysis of the governmental and private interests that are affected. More precisely, our prior decisions indicate that identification of the specific dictates of due process generally requires consideration of three distinct factors: First, the private interest that will be affected by the official action; second, the risk of an erroneous deprivation of such interest through the procedures used, and the probable value, if any, of additional or substitute procedural safeguards; and finally, the Government's interest, including the function involved and the fiscal and administrative burdens that the additional or substitute procedural requirement would entail.

We turn first to a description of the procedures for the termination of Social Security disability benefits and thereafter consider the factors bearing upon the constitutional adequacy of these procedures.

B

The disability insurance program is administered jointly by state and federal agencies. State agencies make the initial determination whether a disability exists, when it began, and when it ceased. . . . In order to establish initial and continued entitlement to disability benefits a worker must demonstrate that he is unable

> to engage in any substantial gainful activity by reason of any medically determinable physical or mental impairment which can be expected to result in death or which has lasted or can be expected to last for a continuous period of not less than 12 months. . . .

To satisfy this test the worker bears a continuing burden of showing, by means of "medically acceptable clinical and laboratory diagnostic techniques," that he has a physical or mental impairment of such severity that

> "he is not only unable to do his previous work but cannot, considering his age, education, and work experience, engage in any other kind of substantial gainful work which exists in the national economy, regardless of whether such work exists in the immediate area in which he lives, or whether a specific job vacancy exists for him, or whether he would be hired if he applied for work."

.... The continuing-eligibility investigation is made by a state agency acting through a "team" consisting of a physician and a nonmedical person trained in disability evaluation. The agency periodically communicates with the disabled worker, usually by mail—in which case he is sent a detailed questionnaire—or by telephone, and requests information concerning his present condition, including current medical restrictions and sources of treatment, and any additional information that he considers relevant to his continued entitlement to benefits. Information regarding the recipient's current condition is also obtained from his sources of medical treatment.

If there is a conflict between the information provided by the beneficiary and that obtained from medical sources such as his physician, or between two sources of treatment, the agency may arrange for an examination by an independent consulting physician. Whenever the agency's tentative assessment of the beneficiary's condition differs from his own assessment, the beneficiary is informed that benefits may be terminated, provided a summary of the evidence upon which the proposed determination to terminate is based, and afforded an opportunity to review the medical reports and other evidence in his case file. He also may respond in writing and submit additional evidence. The state agency then makes its final determination, which is reviewed by an examiner in the SSA Bureau of Disability Insurance. If, as is usually the case, the SSA accepts the agency determination it notifies the recipient in writing, informing him of the reasons for the decision, and of his right to seek *de novo* reconsideration by the state agency. Upon acceptance by the SSA, benefits are terminated effective two months after the month in which medical recovery is found to have occurred.

If the recipient seeks reconsideration by the state agency and the determination is adverse, the SSA reviews the reconsideration determination and notifies the recipient of the decision. He then has a right to an evidentiary hearing before an SSA administrative law judge.

The hearing is nonadversary, and the SSA is not represented by counsel. As at all prior and subsequent stages of the administrative process, however, the claimant may be represented by counsel or other spokesmen. If this hearing results in an adverse decision, the claimant is entitled to request discretionary review by the SSA Appeals Council, and finally may obtain judicial review.[21]

Should it be determined at any point after termination of benefits, that the claimant's disability extended beyond the date of cessation initially established, the worker is entitled to retroactive payments.... If, on the other hand, a beneficiary receives any payments to which he is later determined not to be entitled, the statute authorizes the Secretary to attempt to recoup these funds in specified circumstances.

21. Unlike all prior levels of review, which are *de novo,* the district court is required to treat findings of fact as conclusive if supported by substantial evidence.

C

Despite the elaborate character of the administrative procedures provided by the Secretary, the courts below held them to be constitutionally inadequate, concluding that due process requires an evidentiary hearing prior to termination. In light of the private and governmental interests at stake here and the nature of the existing procedures, we think this was error.

Since a recipient whose benefits are terminated is awarded full retroactive relief if he ultimately prevails, his sole interest is in the uninterrupted receipt of this source of income pending final administrative decision on his claim. His potential injury is thus similar in nature to that of the welfare recipient in *Goldberg* . . . .

Only in *Goldberg* has the Court held that due process requires an evidentiary hearing prior to a temporary deprivation. It was emphasized there that welfare assistance is given to persons on the very margin of subsistence:

> "The crucial factor in this context—a factor not present in the case of . . . virtually anyone else whose governmental entitlements are ended—is that termination of aid pending resolution of a controversy over eligibility may deprive an *eligible* recipient of the very means by which to live while he waits."

Eligibility for disability benefits, in contrast, is not based upon financial need. Indeed, it is wholly unrelated to the worker's income or support from many other sources, such as earnings of other family members, workmen's compensation awards, tort claims awards, savings, private insurance, public or private pensions, veterans' benefits, food stamps, public assistance, or the "many other important programs, both public and private, which contain provisions for disability payments affecting a substantial portion of the work force. . . . "

As *Goldberg* illustrates, the degree of potential deprivation that may be created by a particular decision is a factor to be considered in assessing the validity of any administrative decisionmaking process. The potential deprivation here is generally likely to be less than in *Goldberg,* although the degree of difference can be overstated. As the District Court emphasized, to remain eligible for benefits a recipient must be "unable to engage in substantial gainful activity." Thus, in contrast to the discharged federal employee in *Arnett,* there is little possibility that the terminated recipient will be able to find even temporary employment to ameliorate the interim loss.

. . . [T]he possible length of wrongful deprivation of . . . benefits [also] is an important factor in assessing the impact of official action on the private interests. The Secretary concedes that the delay between a request for a hearing before an administrative law judge and a decision on the claim is currently between 10 and 11 months. Since a terminated recipient must first obtain a reconsideration decision as a prerequisite to invoking his right to an evidentiary hearing, the delay between the actual cutoff of benefits and final decision after a hearing exceeds one year.

In view of the torpidity of this administrative review process and the typically modest resources of the family unit of the physically disabled worker,[26] the hardship imposed upon the erroneously terminated disability recipient may be significant. Still, the disabled worker's need is likely to be less than that of a welfare recipient. In addition to the possibility of access to private resources, other forms of government assistance will become available where the termination of disability benefits places a worker or his family below the subsistence level.[27]

In view of these potential sources of temporary income, there is less reason here than in *Goldberg* to depart from the ordinary principle, established by our decisions, that something less than an evidentiary hearing is sufficient prior to adverse administrative action.

D

An additional factor to be considered here is the fairness and reliability of the existing pretermination procedures, and the probable value, if any, of additional procedural safeguards. Central to the evaluation of any administrative process is the nature of the relevant inquiry. In order to remain eligible for benefits the disabled worker must demonstrate by means of "medically acceptable clinical and laboratory diagnostic techniques" that he is unable "to engage in any substantial gainful activity by reason of any *medically determinable* physical or mental impairment . . ." In short, a medical assessment of the worker's physical or mental condition is required. This is a more sharply focused and easily documented decision than the typical determination of welfare entitlement. In the latter case, a wide variety of information may be deemed relevant, and issues of witness credibility and veracity often are critical to the decisionmaking process. *Goldberg* noted that in such circumstances "written submissions are a wholly unsatisfactory basis for decision."

By contrast, the decision whether to discontinue disability benefits will turn, in most cases, upon "routine, standard, and unbiased medical

---

26. *Amici* cite statistics compiled by the Secretary which indicate that in 1965 the mean income of the family unit of a disabled worker was $3,803, while the median income for the unit was $2,836. The mean liquid assets—*i.e.,* cash, stocks, bonds—of these family units was $4,862; the median was $940. These statistics do not take into account the family unit's nonliquid assets—*i.e.,* automobile, real estate, and the like.

27. *Amici* emphasize that because an identical definition of disability is employed in both the Title II Social Security Program and in the companion welfare system for the disabled, Supplemental Security Income (SSI), the terminated disability-benefits recipient will be ineligible for the SSI Pro-

gram. There exist, however, state and local welfare programs which may supplement the worker's income. In addition, the worker's household unit can qualify for food stamps if it meets the financial need requirements. Finally, in 1974, 480,000 of the approximately 2,000,000 disabled workers receiving Social Security benefits also received SSI benefits. Since financial need is a criterion for eligibility under the SSI program, those disabled workers who are most in need will in the majority of cases be receiving SSI benefits when disability insurance aid is terminated. And, under the SSI program, a pretermination evidentiary hearing is provided, if requested.

reports by physician specialists" concerning a subject whom they have personally examined.[28] In *Richardson v. Perales,* 402 U.S. 389, 404 (1971), the Court recognized the "reliability and probative worth of written medical reports," emphasizing that while there may be "professional disagreement with the medical conclusions" the "specter of questionable credibility and veracity is not present." To be sure, credibility and veracity may be a factor in the ultimate disability assessment in some cases. But procedural due process rules are shaped by the risk of error inherent in the truthfinding process as applied to the generality of cases, not the rare exceptions. The potential value of an evidentiary hearing, or even oral presentation to the decisionmaker, is substantially less in this context than in *Goldberg.*

The decision in *Goldberg* also was based on the Court's conclusion that written submissions were an inadequate substitute for oral presentation because they did not provide an effective means for the recipient to communicate his case to the decisionmaker. Written submissions were viewed as an unrealistic option, for most recipients lacked the "educational attainment necessary to write effectively" and could not afford professional assistance. In addition, such submissions would not provide the "flexibility of oral presentations" or "permit the recipient to mold his argument to the issues the decision maker appears to regard as important." In the context of the disability-benefits-entitlement assessment the administrative procedures under review here fully answer these objections.

The detailed questionnaire which the state agency periodically sends the recipient identifies with particularity the information relevant to the entitlement decision, and the recipient is invited to obtain assistance from the local SSA office in completing the questionnaire. More important, the information critical to the entitlement decision usually is derived from medical sources, such as the treating physician. Such sources are likely to be able to communicate more effectively through written documents than are welfare recipients or the lay witnesses supporting their cause. The conclusions of physicians often are supported by X–rays and the results of clinical or laboratory tests, information typically more amenable to written than to oral presentation.

A further safeguard against mistake is the policy of allowing the disability recipient's representative full access to all information relied upon by the state agency. In addition, prior to the cutoff of benefits the

28. The decision is not purely a question of the accuracy of a medical diagnosis since the ultimate issue which the state agency must resolve is whether in light of the particular worker's "age, education, and work experience" he cannot "engage in any ... substantial gainful work which exists in the national economy".... Yet information concerning each of these worker characteristics is amenable to effective written presentation. The value of an evidentiary hearing, or even a limited oral presentation, to an accurate presentation of those factors to the decisionmaker does not appear substantial. Similarly, resolution of the inquiry as to the types of employment opportunities that exist in the national economy for a physically impaired worker with a particular set of skills would not necessarily be advanced by an evidentiary hearing. The statistical information relevant to this judgment is more amenable to written than to oral presentation.

agency informs the recipient of its tentative assessment, the reasons therefor, and provides a summary of the evidence that it considers most relevant. Opportunity is then afforded the recipient to submit additional evidence or arguments, enabling him to challenge directly the accuracy of information in his file as well as the correctness of the agency's tentative conclusions. These procedures, again as contrasted with those before the Court in *Goldberg,* enable the recipient to "mold" his argument to respond to the precise issues which the decisionmaker regards as crucial.

Despite these carefully structured procedures, *amici* point to the significant reversal rate for appealed cases as clear evidence that the current process is inadequate. Depending upon the base selected and the line of analysis followed, the relevant reversal rates urged by the contending parties vary from a high of 58.6% for appealed reconsideration decisions to an overall reversal rate of only 3.3%. Bare statistics rarely provide a satisfactory measure of the fairness of a decisionmaking process. Their adequacy is especially suspect here since the administrative review system is operated on an open-file basis. A recipient may always submit new evidence, and such submissions may result in additional medical examinations. Such fresh examinations were held in approximately 30% to 40% of the appealed cases, in fiscal 1973, either at the reconsideration or evidentiary hearing stage of the administrative process. In this context, the value of reversal rate statistics as one means of evaluating the adequacy of the pretermination process is diminished. Thus, although we view such information as relevant, it is certainly not controlling in this case.

E

In striking the appropriate due process balance the final factor to be assessed is the public interest. This includes the administrative burden and other societal costs that would be associated with requiring, as a matter of constitutional right, an evidentiary hearing upon demand in all cases prior to the termination of disability benefits. The most visible burden would be the incremental cost resulting from the increased number of hearings and the expense of providing benefits to ineligible recipients pending decision. No one can predict the extent of the increase, but the fact that full benefits would continue until after such hearings would assure the exhaustion in most cases of this attractive option. Nor would the theoretical right of the Secretary to recover undeserved benefits result, as a practical matter, in any substantial offset to the added outlay of public funds. The parties submit widely varying estimates of the probable additional financial cost. We only need say that experience with the constitutionalizing of government procedures suggests that the ultimate additional cost in terms of money and administrative burden would not be insubstantial.

Financial cost alone is not a controlling weight in determining whether due process requires a particular procedural safeguard prior to some administrative decision. But the Government's interest, and hence that of the public, in conserving scarce fiscal and administrative re-sources is a factor that must be weighed. At some point the benefit of an additional safeguard to the individual affected by the administrative action and to society in terms of increased assurance that the action is just, may be outweighed by the cost. Significantly, the cost of protecting those whom the preliminary administrative process has identified as likely to be found undeserving may in the end come out of the pockets of the deserving since resources available for any particular program of social welfare are not unlimited.

But more is implicated in cases of this type than ad hoc weighing of fiscal and administrative burdens against the interests of a particular category of claimants. The ultimate balance involves a determination as to when, under our constitutional system, judicial-type procedures must be imposed upon administrative action to assure fairness. We reiterate the wise admonishment of Mr. Justice Frankfurter that differences in the origin and function of administrative agencies "preclude wholesale transplantation of the rules of procedure, trial and review which have evolved from the history and experience of courts." The judicial model of an evidentiary hearing is neither a required, nor even the most effective, method of decisionmaking in all circumstances. The essence of due process is the requirement that "a person in jeopardy of serious loss [be given] notice of the case against him and opportunity to meet it." All that is necessary is that the procedures be tailored, in light of the decision to be made, to "the capacities and circumstances of those who are to be heard," *Goldberg v. Kelly,* to insure that they are given a meaningful opportunity to present their case. In assessing what process is due in this case, substantial weight must be given to the good-faith judgments of the individuals charged by Congress with the administra-tion of social welfare programs that the procedures they have provided assure fair consideration of the entitlement claims of individuals. This is especially so where, as here, the prescribed procedures not only provide the claimant with an effective process for asserting his claim prior to any administrative action, but also assure a right to an evidentiary hearing, as well as to subsequent judicial review, before the denial of his claim becomes final.

We conclude that an evidentiary hearing is not required prior to the termination of disability benefits and that the present administrative procedures fully comport with due process.

The judgment of the Court of Appeals is *Reversed.*

[Brennan and Marshall, JJ. dissented. They observed:].... The Court's consideration that a discontinuance of disability benefits may cause the recipient to suffer only a limited deprivation is no argument. It is speculative.... Indeed in the present case, it is indicated that because disability benefits were terminated, there was a foreclosure on the Eldridge home and the family's furniture was repossessed, forcing El-dridge, his wife and children to sleep in one bed....

Notes and Questions

1. *Dispensing with prior hearings in emergencies.* The courts have long recognized that in case of emergency the state could deprive an individual of liberty or property without a prior hearing, even if a later remedy is inadequate. *See* note 10 in *Goldberg.* The classic case is *North American Cold Storage Co. v. Chicago,* 211 U.S. 306 (1908), in which the Court upheld a state law providing for the destruction without prior hearing of food held in cold storage which the authorities, after inspection, believed to be rotting and creating a menace to public health. The Court stated that an adequate remedy is provided by a tort action in which the authorities who destroyed the food would have to prove that the food was unfit. However, under present law the officials are likely to be immune from liability; in some states the city may be liable, but plaintiff would have a difficult burden of proof. *See* § 10.2.

In more recent cases involving the exigency problem, the Supreme Court has allowed an agency to act first and provide a hearing later. "An important government interest, accompanied by a substantial assurance that the deprivation is not baseless or unwarranted, may in limited cases demanding prompt action justify postponing the opportunity to be heard until after the initial deprivation." *FDIC v. Mallen,* 486 U.S. 230 (1988) (suspension of banking executive under indictment for felony involving dishonesty).

For example, a mine safety agency closed a mine because an inspection determined that it posed dangers to the health or safety of the public or significant and imminent environmental harm. A hearing on the propriety of the closure was available promptly thereafter. *Hodel v. Virginia Surface Mining Ass'n,* 452 U.S. 264 (1981). Similarly, a state racing board acted properly when it summarily suspended the license of a horse trainer after a drug test showed one of his horses to have been drugged. Here, too, a prompt post-suspension hearing was available. *Barry v. Barchi,* 443 U.S. 55 (1979).

In these cases, did the need for summary action to protect public health, welfare, or safety outweigh the need of the private party for a prior hearing? Can any of these cases be justified on the basis that a neutral test, inspection, or audit that triggered the summary action is an adequate substitute for a pre-deprivation trial-type hearing?

Prior to *Mathews,* it was generally held that, absent exigent circumstances, due process required governments to provide a hearing *prior* to depriving a person of liberty or property. *Mathews* permitted an agency to take action determining property or liberty interests prior to an evidentiary hearing in order to save the government money, not because of any emergency. This was a new departure.

2. *Timing and the new property.* The balancing equation laid out in *Mathews* (rather than the more rigid approach taken in *Goldberg*) is the analytical format now used to determine both the *timing* of constitutionally required hearings as well as to determine the *elements* of the hearing. How did Justice Powell distinguish *Goldberg* from *Mathews* on the timing issue? Are his arguments persuasive? Are his factual assumptions well supported?

3. *Timing and employment decisions.* While *Roth* indicated that a *prior* hearing must be provided before an employee is discharged from a tenured

government job, later cases have been more cautious. In recognition of government's interest in immediate removal of an employee to which it objects, the Court has accepted abbreviated pre-termination procedures designed to insure only that the government has probable cause for its decision—not that the decision was right. However, a full-fledged trial-type hearing must be provided promptly after removal.

In *Cleveland Board of Education v. Loudermill*, § 2.2.2, the Court held that pre-termination procedure serves as an "initial check against mistaken decisions—essentially, a determination of whether there are reasonable grounds to believe that the charges against the employee are true and support the proposed action." This means that an employee must receive oral or written notice of the charges against him, an explanation of the employer's evidence (although it is not clear how detailed this must be), and an opportunity to present his side of the story—orally or in writing.

How useful is the *Loudermill* pre-termination procedure? Even the most unbiased of hearing officers might lean in the direction of going forward with the discharge and allowing the employee's explanation to be evaluated in a post-termination hearing.

4. *How long is too long?* How long can a post-termination hearing be delayed? The government clearly has an incentive to stall; it is tempting to let the backlog grow rather than invest scarce resources in shrinking the backlog. After all, the longer a hearing is delayed, the fewer hearings must be held since many petitioners will get discouraged, move away, or get other jobs. Yet it is difficult for a court to say exactly how long is too long.

In *Mathews*, the Court tolerated a delay of well over one year in providing disability benefits. In fact, because of the multiple layers of review and an increasing backlog, there is often a delay of several years between the time benefits are cut off or an initial application is denied and the time a hearing is granted. In *Loudermill*, the Court noted that a delay in the post-termination hearing could itself be a constitutional violation, but held that Loudermill's wait of about nine months was not unreasonable.

5. *Suspension or discharge?* In many cases, an agency has the option to suspend a public employee with pay rather than fire him or her outright. A trial-type hearing must be provided after the suspension at which the employee may challenge the propriety of such action.

In *Gilbert v. Homar*, 117 S.Ct. 1807 (1997), the Supreme Court ruled that due process allows the suspension of a tenured campus policeman without a prior hearing and *without pay*. In this case, the policeman had been arrested and criminally charged for drug offenses. Applying *Mathews* balancing, the Court gave little weight to the policeman's private interest in receiving an uninterrupted flow of paychecks for the relatively brief period until a post-suspension hearing was provided. On the other hand, the state has a substantial interest in immediately suspending employees in positions of public trust who are charged with felonies; and "government does not have to give an employee charged with a felony a paid leave at taxpayer expense."

Finally, the risk of erroneous deprivation was low. If a pre-suspension hearing were required, by analogy to *Loudermill*, the only issue would be whether there were reasonable grounds for the suspension. In this case, the criminal charges against the policeman were independently verifiable and provided a reasonable basis for the action. Even if the college president had discretion whether or not to suspend the policeman, that discretion could be invoked at the post-suspension hearing—which might benefit the employee since by then the deciding officials would have more information about the arrest and charges.

In licensing cases, a state often finds that exigent circumstances require that a professional license be immediately suspended. For example, public safety might require that a medical licensing board immediately suspend a physician's license rather than allow the physician to continue practicing until a hearing is provided. Under § 14(c) of the 1961 MSAPA (on which most state APAs are based), "If the agency finds that the public health, safety, or welfare imperatively requires emergency action, and incorporates a finding to that effect in its order, summary suspension of a license may be ordered pending proceedings for revocation or other action. These proceedings shall be promptly instituted and determined." *See also* 1981 MSAPA § 4–501 (providing for emergency adjudicative procedures) and federal APA § 558(c). The latter provision requires in many cases that an agency give the licensee an opportunity to achieve compliance before suspending or revoking a license.

6. *Problem.* Elm City constructed and operated Elm Grove, a large apartment project for low income residents. The relevant statute recites that the problem of low income housing is critical and that poor people have a right to decent housing.

Muriel Miller and her four teenaged children are tenants in Elm Grove. Muriel's sole source of income is AFDC and food stamps. When she moved in on January 1, she signed a one-year lease which stated that the lease could be renewed only by agreement between Elm Grove and the tenant. It also stated that tenants could be evicted at any time if they failed to follow the rules of Elm Grove. The rules required that tenants refrain from using or dealing illegal drugs or disturbing other tenants. The lease provided that tenants must vacate their apartment within 10 days of receiving an eviction notice. It also stated that Elm Grove would furnish a hearing within two weeks after the apartment is vacated due to eviction if the tenants believe they violated no rules.

Muriel received a notice of eviction on April 19 which stated that occupants of her apartment had violated the rules by using or dealing drugs on Elm Grove's property. The notice furnished no specific details. It ordered her to move out by April 29 and informed her that a hearing would be held on May 6 if she requested one.

Muriel seeks an injunction in federal district court against her eviction, denying that she or her family had violated the rules and arguing that she has been denied procedural due process. Should the injunction be granted?

Assume Elm Grove loses this case. Could Elm Grove regain the right to discharge tenants without a prior hearing if it replaced the existing one-year leases as they expired with month-to-month tenancies?

See Richmond Tenants Org. v. Kemp, 956 F.2d 1300 (4th Cir.1992); *Lopez v. Henry Phipps Plaza South, Inc.*, 498 F.2d 937 (2d Cir.1974); *U. S. v. One Tract of Real Property*, 803 F.Supp. 1080 (E.D.N.C.1992).

§ 2.4 ELEMENTS OF A HEARING

Courts employ the balancing formula of *Mathews v. Eldridge* to determine *what process* is due as well as *when* it is due. Recall the list in *Goldberg* of the precise elements of a due process hearing. Does a *Goldberg* pre-termination hearing differ in any substantial way from a normal civil trial before a judge? From a *post*-termination welfare hearing? The post-*Mathews* cases are less rigid than *Goldberg* and in many situations call for less elaborate process or none at all.

INGRAHAM v. WRIGHT
430 U.S. 651 (1977).

POWELL, J.

This case presents questions concerning the use of corporal punishment in public schools: First, whether the paddling of students as a means of maintaining school discipline constitutes cruel and unusual punishment in violation of the Eighth Amendment; and, second, to the extent that paddling is constitutionally permissible, whether the Due Process Clause of the Fourteenth Amendment requires prior notice and an opportunity to be heard. [The plaintiffs were eighth and ninth grade students who were subject to disciplinary paddling at their Florida junior high school. The punishment consisted of paddling the student on the buttocks with a flat wooden paddle measuring less than two feet long, three to four inches wide, and about one-half inch thick.

One plaintiff testified that because he was slow to respond to his teacher's instructions, he was subjected to more than 20 licks with a paddle while being held over a table in the principal's office. The paddling was so severe that he suffered a hematoma requiring medical attention and keeping him out of school for several days. The second plaintiff was paddled several times for minor infractions. On two occasions he was struck on his arms, once depriving him of the full use of his arm for a week.

The lower court rejected both the cruel and unusual punishment and due process claims. The Supreme Court held that corporal punishment was not cruel and unusual in light of the long history of its use and the common law rule that teachers could impose reasonable but not excessive force to discipline a child. The Court then turned to the due process claim.]

The Fourteenth Amendment prohibits any state deprivation of life, liberty, or property without due process of law. Application of this prohibition requires the familiar two-stage analysis: We must first ask whether the asserted individual interests are encompassed within the

Fourteenth Amendment's protection of "life, liberty or property"; if protected interests are implicated, we then must decide what procedures constitute "due process of law." Following that analysis here, we find that corporal punishment in public schools implicates a constitutionally protected liberty interest, but we hold that the traditional common-law remedies are fully adequate to afford due process.

A

. . . . The Due Process Clause of the Fifth Amendment, later incorporated into the Fourteenth, was intended to give Americans at least the protection against governmental power that they had enjoyed as Englishmen against the power of the Crown. The liberty preserved from deprivation without due process included the right "generally to enjoy those privileges long recognized at common law as essential to the orderly pursuit of happiness by free men." *Meyer v. Nebraska*. . . . Among the historic liberties so protected was a right to be free from, and to obtain judicial relief for, unjustified intrusions on personal security. . . . It is fundamental that the state cannot hold and physically punish an individual except in accordance with due process of law.

This constitutionally protected liberty interest is at stake in this case. There is, of course, a de minimis level of imposition with which the Constitution is not concerned. But at least where school authorities, acting under color of state law, deliberately decide to punish a child for misconduct by restraining the child and inflicting appreciable physical pain, we hold that Fourteenth Amendment liberty interests are implicated.

B

"[The] question remains what process is due." Were it not for the common-law privilege permitting teachers to inflict reasonable corporal punishment on children in their care, and the availability of the traditional remedies for abuse, the case for requiring advance procedural safeguards would be strong indeed. But here we deal with a punishment—paddling—within that tradition, and the question is whether the common-law remedies are adequate to afford due process. . . . Whether in this case the common-law remedies for excessive corporal punishment constitute due process of law must turn on an analysis of the competing interests at stake, viewed against the background of "history, reason, [and] the past course of decisions." The analysis requires consideration of three distinct factors. . . . *Mathews v. Eldridge.*

1

Because it is rooted in history, the child's liberty interest in avoiding corporal punishment while in the care of public school authorities is subject to historical limitations. Under the common law, an invasion of personal security gave rise to a right to recover damages in a subsequent judicial proceeding. But the right of recovery was qualified by the concept of justification. Thus, there could be no recovery against a teacher who gave only "moderate correction" to a child. . . . Under that longstanding accommodation of interests, there can be no deprivation of substantive rights as long as disciplinary corporal punishment is within the limits of the common-law privilege.

This is not to say that the child's interest in procedural safeguards is insubstantial. The school disciplinary process is not "a totally accurate, unerring process, never mistaken and never unfair. . . . " In any deliberate infliction of corporal punishment on a child who is restrained for that purpose, there is some risk that the intrusion on the child's liberty will be unjustified and therefore unlawful. In these circumstances the child has a strong interest in procedural safeguards that minimize the risk of wrongful punishment and provide for the resolution of disputed questions of justification. We turn now to a consideration of the safeguards that are available under applicable Florida law.

2

. . . . Florida has preserved the traditional judicial proceedings for determining whether the punishment was justified. If the punishment inflicted is later found to have been excessive—not reasonably believed at the time to be necessary for the child's discipline or training—the school authorities inflicting it may be held liable in damages to the child and, if malice is shown, they may be subject to criminal penalties. . . .

Although students have testified in this case to specific instances of abuse, there is every reason to believe that such mistreatment is an aberration. The uncontradicted evidence suggests that corporal punishment in the Dade County schools was, "[w]ith the exception of a few cases . . . unremarkable in physical severity." Moreover, because paddlings are usually inflicted in response to conduct directly observed by teachers in their presence, the risk that a child will be paddled without cause is typically insignificant. . . . In those cases where severe punishment is contemplated, the available civil and criminal sanctions for abuse—considered in light of the openness of the school environment— afford significant protection against unjustified corporal punishment. Teachers and school authorities are unlikely to inflict corporal punishment unnecessarily or excessively when a possible consequence of doing so is the institution of civil or criminal proceedings against them.[46]

It still may be argued, of course, that the child's liberty interest would be better protected if the common-law remedies were supplemented by the administrative safeguards of prior notice and a hearing. We

---

46. The low incidence of abuse, and the availability of established judicial remedies in the event of abuse, distinguish this case from *Goss v. Lopez,* 419 U.S. 565 (1975). The Ohio law struck down in *Goss* provided for suspensions from public school of up to 10 days without "any written procedure applicable to suspensions." Although Ohio law provided generally for administrative review, the Court assumed that the short suspensions would not be stayed pending review, with the result that the review pro-ceeding could serve neither a deterrent nor a remedial function. In these circumstances, the Court held the law authorizing suspensions unconstitutional for failure to require "that there be at least an informal give-and-take between student and disciplinarian, preferably prior to the suspension. . . . " The subsequent civil and criminal proceedings available in this case may be viewed as affording substantially greater protection to the child than the informal conference mandated by *Goss.*

have found frequently that some kind of prior hearing is necessary to guard against arbitrary impositions on interests protected by the Fourteenth. But where the State has preserved what "has always been the law of the land," the case for administrative safeguards is significantly less compelling. . . .

3

But even if the need for advance procedural safeguards were clear, the question would remain whether the incremental benefit could justify the cost. Acceptance of petitioners' claims would work a transformation in the law governing corporal punishment in Florida and most other States. Given the impracticability of formulating a rule of procedural due process that varies with the severity of the particular imposition, the prior hearing petitioners seek would have to precede any paddling, however moderate or trivial.

Such a universal constitutional requirement would significantly burden the use of corporal punishment as a disciplinary measure. Hearings—even informal hearings—require time, personnel, and a diversion of attention from normal school pursuits. School authorities may well choose to abandon corporal punishment rather than incur the burdens of complying with the procedural requirements. Teachers, properly concerned with maintaining authority in the classroom, may well prefer to rely on other disciplinary measures—which they may view as less effective—rather than confront the possible disruption that prior notice and a hearing may entail. Paradoxically, such an alteration of disciplinary policy is most likely to occur in the ordinary case where the contemplated punishment is well within the common-law privilege.

Elimination or curtailment of corporal punishment would be welcomed by many as a societal advance. But when such a policy choice may result from this Court's determination of an asserted right to due process, rather than from the normal processes of community debate and legislative action, the societal costs cannot be dismissed as insubstantial.[52] We are reviewing here a legislative judgment, rooted in history and reaffirmed in the laws of many States, that corporal punishment serves important educational interests. This judgment must be viewed in light of the disciplinary problems commonplace in the schools. . . .

"At some point the benefit of an additional safeguard to the individual affected . . . and to society in terms of increased assurance that the action is just, may be outweighed by the cost." *Mathews v. Eldridge*. We think that point has been reached in this case. In view of the low incidence of abuse, the openness of our schools, and the common-law safeguards that already exist, the risk of error that may result in

---

52. "It may be true that procedural regularity in disciplinary proceedings promotes a sense of institutional rapport and open communication, a perception of fair treatment, and provides the offender and his fellow students a showcase of democracy at work. But . . . [r]espect for democratic institutions will equally dissipate if they are thought too ineffectual to provide their students an environment of order in which the educational process may go forward. . . . " J. Harvie Wilkinson, *Goss v. Lopez*: The Supreme Court as School Superintendent, 1975 Sup. Ct. Rev. 25, 71–72.

violation of a schoolchild's substantive rights can only be regarded as minimal. Imposing additional administrative safeguards as a constitutional requirement might reduce that risk marginally, but would also entail a significant intrusion into an area of primary educational responsibility. We conclude that the Due Process Clause does not require notice and a hearing prior to the imposition of corporal punishment in the public schools, as that practice is authorized and limited by the common law.

AFFIRMED

[WHITE, J., joined by BRENNAN, MARSHALL, and STEVENS, JJ., dissented. He argued that traditional tort remedies do nothing to prevent punishment based on mistaken facts, so long as the punishment was reasonable from the disciplinarian's point of view. More important, the lawsuit occurs after the punishment has been finally imposed; the infliction of physical pain cannot be undone. "There is every reason to require, as the court did in *Goss*, a few minutes of 'informal give-and-take between student and disciplinarian' as a 'meaningful hedge' against the erroneous infliction of irreparable injury."]

Notes and Questions

1. *Due process at school.* Based on *Mathews* balancing, the Court decided in *Ingraham* that state common law tort remedies provide the *only* process due to high school students deprived of liberty by the infliction of corporal punishment.

Can *Ingraham* be distinguished from *Goss v. Lopez*? *Goss*, which preceded *Mathews* by one year and is discussed in § 2.2.3, held that a disciplinary suspension of high school students for ten days or less deprived them of property (because state law created an entitlement to public education) and of liberty (because the suspensions "could seriously damage the students' standing with fellow pupils and teachers as well as interfere with later opportunities for higher education and employment").

However, the court called for a proceeding markedly different from the adversary trial-type hearing mandated by *Goldberg*. It required only "*some* kind of notice and . . . *some* kind of hearing." The student must receive "oral or written notice of the charges against him and, if he denies them, an explanation of the evidence the authorities have and an opportunity to present his side of the story." The discussion with the student could occur minutes after the alleged misconduct occurs and, except in the case of exigent circumstances, it should occur before the student is removed from school.

In *Goss,* the Court indicated that a student did not have the right "to secure counsel, to confront and cross-examine witnesses supporting the charge, or to call his own witnesses to verify his version of the incident."

> Brief disciplinary suspensions are almost countless. To impose in each such case even truncated trial-type procedures might well overwhelm administrative facilities in many places and, by diverting resources, cost more than it would save in educational effectiveness. Moreover, further formalizing the suspension process and escalating its formality and

adversary nature may not only make it too costly as a regular disciplinary tool but also destroy its effectiveness as part of the teaching process.

Essentially, the "hearing" required in *Goss* is really just a conversation between the student and the disciplinarian. *Goss* is an important precedent in deciding what sort of procedure is required in cases of minor deprivations of liberty or property.

Why did the *Ingraham* court not require at least *Goss* procedure before a teacher paddles a student?

2. *Tort remedies as a form of due process. Ingraham* was the first of a number of cases in which the Court held that due process is satisfied by state tort law remedies.

In *Parratt v. Taylor,* 451 U.S. 527 (1981), prison officials negligently lost a prisoner's hobby kit worth $23. The Court did not hold that a $23 loss was a *de minimis* deprivation of property; instead, it decided that the availability of a state tort action after such a "random and unauthorized" deprivation of property satisfied the requirements of due process. After all, how could the state provide a hearing prior to the deprivation in a case like *Parratt?*

The same reasoning applies to an *intentional* destruction of a prisoner's property by a prison guard on a vendetta against the prisoner. *Hudson v. Palmer,* 468 U.S. 517 (1984). Later, overruling *Parratt* on a different issue, the Court held that a merely *negligent* deprivation of property is not a due process violation at all. *Daniels v. Williams,* 474 U.S. 327 (1986).

However, if a pre-deprivation hearing is feasible, the *Parratt* rule does not apply. See *Zinermon v. Burch,* 494 U.S. 113 (1990), in which Burch was admitted to a mental hospital and held for five months without informed consent in violation of state law. The hospital claimed that this deprivation of liberty was "random and unauthorized" under *Parratt,* so that Burch was limited to his state law tort remedy. In a 5–4 decision, the Court disagreed. It is predictable that admittees to mental hospitals will be incapable of giving informed consent to their institutionalization and it is perfectly possible to provide a pre-deprivation hearing procedure to prevent this from happening.

Recall *Paul v. Davis,* § 2.2.3 N. 2, holding that a state-imposed stigma did not deprive the plaintiff of liberty. Would a better explanation for *Paul* be that the imposition of a stigma did deprive the individual of liberty, but that state defamation remedies provided all the process that was due? In a dissent in *Ingraham* not quoted in the text, Justice Stevens made exactly this argument.

3. *State contract remedies as due process.* Recall the issue, discussed in § 2.2.2 N.5, of whether government must provide a prior hearing before it fails to perform a contract. The *Unger* decision indicated that a private party's contract right should not be treated as "property" for due process purposes.

Mid–American Waste Systems, Inc. v. City of Gary, 49 F.3d 286 (7th Cir.1995), takes a different approach. It involved an alleged breach by Gary of Mid–American's lease of a trash landfill. Gary claimed the lease was terminable at will, but Mid–American claimed that the lease ran until the site was filled up. The court treated Mid–American's contract rights as property. However, it held that due process does not require an administrative hearing when the dispute concerns the interpretation of a contract; state court adjudication provides all the process that is due.

Which approach to the contract rights problem best serves the purposes of due process—*Unger* or *Mid–American*? Or should government be required to provide notice and an opportunity for an administrative hearing *before* it decides not to perform a contract?

4. *The right to counsel in administrative hearings.* In *Walters v. National Ass'n of Radiation Survivors*, 473 U.S. 305 (1985), the Court considered a statute, first enacted in 1862, that limits an attorney's fee to $10 in a veteran's benefit case. As a practical matter, this statute prevents veterans from retaining counsel at the informal benefits hearings conducted by the VA. However, the various veterans' organizations such as the American Legion provide non-lawyer claims agents free of charge to assist claimants. Claimants represented by these lay advocates have about the same success rate as those represented by attorneys.

The Court noted that it had never decided whether *applicants* for government benefits (as distinguished from persons whose benefits are *terminated*) are entitled to due process, but it assumed for purposes of this case that they are. *See* § 2.2.1 N.8. Using *Mathews* balancing, the Court upheld the statute, refusing to follow in this case the dictum in *Goldberg* that a welfare claimant must be allowed to retain an attorney. Instead, the Court honored Congress' desire that veterans not have to divide their award with attorneys. It also paid considerable deference to the government's interest in keeping VA hearings as informal and non-adversarial as possible. The introduction of lawyers would not further this goal.

The availability of lay representatives suggests that adding lawyers to the system would be unlikely to reduce the likelihood of error. The plaintiffs argued that lay representatives might be adequate in routine cases but were not competent to deal with relatively rare but highly complex cases such as exposure to radiation or Agent Orange. However, the Court was unconvinced.

> In applying this [*Mathews*] test we must keep in mind, in addition to the deference owed to Congress, the fact that the very nature of the due process inquiry indicates that the fundamental fairness of a particular procedure does not turn on the result obtained in any individual case; rather, "procedural due process rules are shaped by the risk of error inherent in the truth-finding process as applied to the generality of cases, not the rare exceptions."

However, Justice Rehnquist's opinion was joined by only three justices. Two concurring judges agreed that there was no absolute right to retain counsel in all VA cases. These justices suggested that there might be a "special circumstances" rule. Under that approach, due process would require that individuals presenting complex cases be permitted to retain attorneys. Three justices dissented.

5. *Academic decisionmaking.* Suppose a state community college asserts that a student should be expelled for cheating and sets the case for an informal trial-type hearing. If an APA is applicable, the student will have a right to retained counsel at the hearing. *See* APA § 555(b); 1981 MSAPA

§ 4–203(b). Suppose further that no APA is applicable and the college's regulation prevents an attorney from taking part in the hearing (although the student is allowed to bring an attorney along to give advice during the hearing).

The student asserts that this regulation violates due process. Does *Walters* establish that agencies can always structure their hearings to exclude retained counsel or limit counsel's participation? Or can the case be distinguished? What are the costs and benefits of a right to retained counsel in college disciplinary proceedings? *See* Mark S. Blaskey, "University Students' Right to Retain Counsel at Disciplinary Proceedings," 24 Cal. W.L.Rev. 65 (1988).

A student dismissed for *academic* rather than disciplinary reasons is entitled to much less process—perhaps none at all. In *Board of Curators, Univ. of Mo. v. Horowitz,* 435 U.S. 78 (1978), the Court stated:

> The decision to dismiss respondent . . . rested on the academic judgment of school officials that she did not have the necessary clinical ability to perform adequately as a medical doctor. . . . Such [an academic] judgment is by its nature more subjective and evaluative than the typical factual questions presented in the average disciplinary decision. Like the decision of an individual professor as to the proper grade for a student in his course, the determination whether to dismiss a student for academic reasons requires an expert evaluation of cumulative information and is not readily adapted to the procedural tools of judicial or administrative decision-making.

Under these circumstances the Court was reluctant to "formalize" the educational process and to "further enlarge the judicial presence in the academic community and thereby risk deterioration of many beneficial aspects of the faculty-student relationship."

6. *Confrontation.* When a person is entitled to a trial-type hearing, is there *always* a right to confront and cross-examine one's accuser? In *Van Harken v. City of Chicago,* 103 F.3d 1346 (7th Cir.1997), the City decriminalized its system of adjudicating parking ticket disputes. Parking cases, carrying a maximum fine of $100, are heard by private lawyers serving as part-time hearing officers. The police officer who wrote the ticket is not expected to participate in the hearing other than through the ticket itself, which is treated as an affidavit. The hearing officer can choose to subpoena the officer in unusual cases and is also expected to conduct a "searching" cross-examination of the alleged violator.

Reducing the *Mathews* balancing to a straightforward cost-benefit analysis, the court upheld this procedure. Requiring officers to appear at the hearings, the court calculated, would cost the city 134,000 police hours per year—the equivalent of 67 full-time officers. And that is simply the monetary cost; if a case must be dismissed because the officer fails to show up (which occurred frequently when parking violations were handled through the criminal system), the dismissal would undermine the deterrent effect of parking laws and deprive the city of revenue to which it was entitled.

On the benefit side of requiring confrontation, the court figured the average fine was about $55. Suppose the probability of an erroneous determination is 5% and an officer's presence at the hearing would cut that probability to 2.5%. "Then the average saving to the innocent respondent from this additional procedural safeguard would be only $1.38 ($55 x .025)— a trivial amount."

Is *Van Harken* a correct application of *Mathews*? Or should confrontation and cross-examination of one's accuser be provided regardless of its costs and benefits?

7. *Paper hearings.* In a number of situations, the Court has held that due process does not demand an auditory proceeding—the "hearing" can be on paper. For example, *Hewitt v. Helms* (which was overruled on a different issue in *Sandin v. Conner,* discussed in § 2.2.3) concerned the process owed to a prisoner placed in administrative segregation. Applying a *Mathews* balancing analysis, the Court required only an informal, nonadversary review of the information supporting the decision, including whatever written statement the prisoner wished to submit, within a reasonable time after he was placed in segregation. The Court refused even to provide a right to an oral conference, of the sort required by *Goss*, finding that the issues to be resolved were based on "purely subjective evaluations and predictions of future behavior" and on "intuitive judgments" rather than on specific facts. As a result, an auditory trial-type hearing would not be particularly helpful.

If there are no factual issues to be resolved, an agency has discretion to dispense with an oral hearing. For example, in *Altenheim German Home v. Turnock*, 902 F.2d 582 (7th Cir.1990), the court made clear that a licensed hospital has no right to a pre-or post-termination hearing unless there is some disputed issue of material fact. Otherwise, the agency can dispense with "a full evidentiary hearing, with live witnesses and cross-examination and all the rest of the procedural hoopla treasured by Anglo American lawyers...."

What if the only issue to be resolved is how the decisionmaker will exercise discretion—must there be an oral hearing? In *Loudermill*, Justice White wrote: "Even where the facts are clear, the appropriateness or necessity of the discharge may not be; in such cases, the only meaningful opportunity to invoke the discretion of the decisionmaker is likely to be before the termination takes effect." 470 U.S. at 543. Is White's approach consistent with *Hewitt*?

8. *Adversary systems.* One fundamental issue posed by *Walters* is whether due process means a trial-type hearing. *Goldberg v. Kelly* was the high-water mark for that point of view. *Goss* opened the way for allowing informal meetings to substitute for trial-type hearings. And *Walters* establishes that Congress can choose a sharply different model for disbursing government benefits: an informal, investigatory meeting without lawyers. In light of these cases, could Congress, in a future new round of welfare reform, restructure the AFDC system to provide a non-adversary system of dispute resolution? Could a state provide for a non-adversary system for revocation of a physician's license to practice?

9. *Problem.* Madison would like to find a way to cut the cost of hearings in AFDC cases. In addition, it would like to make the process more convenient and pleasant for all concerned, including recipients and social workers who often have to sit around all day waiting for their hearing to be

called. It therefore has proposed new procedural regulations providing that hearings may be conducted by telephone conference call in cases where the welfare department wishes to decrease or to terminate benefits.

You work for a legal service office which frequently provides assistance to welfare claimants. You have been asked to submit comments about these proposed regulations. *See Casey v. O'Bannon*, 536 F.Supp. 350 (E.D.Pa. 1982); Neil Fox, Note, "Telephonic Hearings in Welfare Appeals," 1984 U.Ill.L.For. 445.

§ 2.5   THE RULEMAKING–ADJUDICATION DISTINCTION

This chapter concludes by introducing a fundamental distinction in administrative law. The distinction is between government action that affects identifiable persons on the basis of facts peculiar to each of them and government action directed in a uniform way against a class of persons. The first kind of action is called "adjudication;" an example is a welfare agency's decision to terminate a person's benefits because that person's income is too high to qualify for welfare. Procedural due process applies to this decision. The second kind of action is called "rulemaking;" an example is the establishment of a standard for determination of the income of welfare recipients. Procedural due process does not apply to this decision.

The terms "adjudication" and "rulemaking" are useful and are frequently employed in this book. Federal and state APAs rely on the distinction between rulemaking and adjudication, but do not define them precisely in accordance with the traditional usage employed here.

Our exploration of the distinction begins with two old Supreme Court cases, both of which concerned Denver property tax disputes. Upon this unlikely foundation, much of the structure of procedural due process has been erected. Later this book returns to the rulemaking/adjudication distinction and raises the issue of whether an agency has unrestricted power to choose between them. *See* § 6.2.

LONDONER v. DENVER
210 U.S. 373 (1908).

[A Denver ordinance allowed the city council, on recommendation of the board of public works, to establish a special assessment district for the purpose of paving streets. After the paving was completed, the total cost of the job had to be apportioned among the individual property owners in the assessment district. The ordinance provided that the council's determination was binding on the Denver courts.

The board recommended an apportionment to the council. Objecting owners were permitted to file written complaints with the council. The council considered the complaints and enacted an ordinance assessing each owner an amount the council believed to be appropriate. Nowhere in the process were complainants granted an opportunity for an oral hearing.

Londoner filed a lengthy complaint with the council, making every conceivable objection. One of his objections was that individual parcels in the district, including his property, were assessed arbitrarily because those with equal assessments had not benefited equally from the paving. Nevertheless, the council's ordinance stated that "no complaint or objection had been filed or made against the apportionment of said assessment."]

MOODY, J.:

.... The first step in the assessment proceedings was by the certificate of the board of public works of the cost of the improvement and a preliminary apportionment of it. The last step was the enactment of the assessment ordinance. From beginning to end of the proceedings the landowners, although allowed to formulate and file complaints and objections, were not afforded an opportunity to be heard upon them. Upon these facts was there a denial by the State of the due process of law guaranteed by the Fourteenth Amendment to the Constitution of the United States?

In the assessment, apportionment and collection of taxes upon property within their jurisdiction the Constitution of the United States imposes few restrictions upon the States. In the enforcement of such restrictions as the Constitution does impose this court has regarded substance and not form. But where the legislature of a State, instead of fixing the tax itself, commits to some subordinate body the duty of determining whether, in what amount, and upon whom it shall be levied, and of making the assessment and apportionment, due process of law requires that at some stage of the proceedings before the tax becomes irrevocably fixed, the taxpayer shall have an opportunity to be heard, of which he must have notice, either personal, by publication, or by a law fixing the time and place of the hearing. It must be remembered that the law of Colorado denies the landowner the right to object in the courts to the assessment, upon the ground that the objections are cognizable only by the [city council].

If it is enough that, under such circumstances, an opportunity is given to submit in writing all objections to and complaints of the tax to the [council], then there was a hearing afforded in the case at bar. But we think that something more than that, even in proceedings for taxation, is required by due process of law. Many requirements essential in strictly judicial proceedings may be dispensed with in proceedings of this nature. But even here a hearing, in its very essence, demands that he who is entitled to it shall have the right to support his allegations by argument however brief, and, if need be, by proof, however informal. It is apparent that such a hearing was denied to [Londoner].... The assessment was therefore void, and [Londoner was] entitled to a decree discharging [his land] from a lien on account of it.

THE CHIEF JUSTICE and JUSTICE HOLMES dissent.

BI–METALLIC INVESTMENT CO. v. STATE BOARD OF EQUALIZATION

239 U.S. 441 (1915).

HOLMES, J.:

This is a suit to enjoin the State Board of Equalization and the Colorado Tax Commission from putting in force and the defendant Pitcher, as assessor of Denver, from obeying, an order of the boards, increasing the valuation of all taxable property in Denver 40 per cent. . . .

The plaintiff is the owner of real estate in Denver, and brings the case here on the ground that it was given no opportunity to be heard, and that therefore its property will be taken without due process of law. . . .

For the purposes of decision we assume that the constitutional question is presented in the baldest way—that neither the plaintiff nor the assessor of Denver, who presents a brief on the plaintiff's side, nor any representative of the city and county, was given an opportunity to be heard. . . . On this assumption it is obvious that injustice may be suffered if some property in the county already has been valued at its full worth. But if certain property has been valued at a rate different from that generally prevailing in the county, the owner has had his opportunity to protest and appeal as usual in our system of taxation so that it must be assumed that the property owners in the county all stand alike. The question, then, is whether all individuals have a constitutional right to be heard before a matter can be decided in which all are equally concerned—here, for instance, before a superior board decides that the local taxing officers have adopted a system of undervaluation throughout a county, as notoriously often has been the case . . .

Where a rule of conduct applies to more than a few people, it is impracticable that everyone should have a direct voice in its adoption. The Constitution does not require all public acts to be done in town meeting or an assembly of the whole. General statutes within the state power are passed that affect the person or property of individuals, sometimes to the point of ruin, without giving them a chance to be heard. Their rights are protected in the only way that they can be in a complex society, by their power, immediate or remote, over those who make the rule. If the result in this case had been reached, as it might have been, by the state's doubling the rate of taxation, no one would suggest that the 14th Amendment was violated unless every person affected had been allowed an opportunity to raise his voice against it before the body intrusted by the state Constitution with the power. In considering this case in this court we must assume that the proper state machinery has been used, and the question is whether, if the state Constitution had declared that Denver had been undervalued as compared with the rest of the state, and had decreed that for the current year the valuation should be 40 per cent higher, the objection now urged could prevail. It appears to us that to put the question is to answer it. There must be a limit to individual argument in such matters if government is to go on. In *Londoner v. Denver* a local board had to determine "whether, in what amount, and upon whom" a tax for paving a street should be levied for special benefits. A relatively small number of persons was concerned, who were exceptionally affected, in each case upon individual grounds, and it was held that they had a right to a hearing. But that decision is far from reaching a general determination dealing only with the principle upon which all the assessments in a county had been laid.

Judgment affirmed.

Notes and Questions

1. *An oral hearing.* Londoner was entitled to a trial-type hearing ("the right to support his allegations by argument however brief, and, if need be, by proof, however informal"). He had already been allowed to complain in writing but that was not enough. If the case came up today, do you think that a trial-type hearing would be required?

2. *Londoner and Bi–Metallic.* Mr. Londoner gets a hearing; Bi–Metallic Investment Co. does not. Both are protesting higher property taxes. What's the difference?

A modern restatement of the *Londoner–Bi–Metallic* distinction occurs in *United States v. Florida East Coast Ry. Co.,* 410 U.S. 224, 244–46 (1973), a case considered in detail in § 5.4. *Florida East Coast* involved regulations that raised the rates that railroads must pay for the use of freight cars owned by other railroads. The issue was whether a trial-type proceeding was required or whether notice and written comment procedures would suffice. The Court observed:

> The basic distinction between rulemaking and adjudication is illustrated by this Court's treatment of two related cases under the Due Process Clause of the Fourteenth Amendment. In *Londoner v. Denver* ... the Court held that due process had not been accorded a landowner who objected to the amount assessed against his land as its share of the benefit resulting from the paving of a street ... But in the later case of *Bi–Metallic Investment Co.* ... the Court held that no hearing at all was constitutionally required prior to a decision by state tax officers in Colorado to increase the valuation of all taxable property by a substantial percentage. The Court distinguished *Londoner* by stating that there a small number of persons "were exceptionally affected, in each case upon individual grounds.... "

> Later decisions have continued to observe the distinction adverted to in *Bi–Metallic Investment Co., supra.* In *Ohio Bell Telephone Co. v. Public Utilities Commission,* 301 U.S. 292, 304–05 (1937), the Court noted the fact that the administrative proceeding there involved was designed to require the utility to refund previously collected rate charges. The Court held that in such a proceeding the agency could not, consistently with due process, act on the basis of undisclosed evidence

which was never made a part of the record before the agency. The case is thus more akin to *Interstate Commerce Commission v. Louisville & Nashville R. Co.*, 227 U.S. 88 (1913), holding that due process applied to a decision by the ICC that a specific railroad rate was unreasonable than it is to this case.... While the line dividing them may not always be a bright one, these decisions represent a recognized distinction in administrative law between proceedings for the purpose of promulgating policy-type rules or standards, on the one hand, and proceedings designed to adjudicate disputed facts in particular cases on the other.

Here the incentive payments proposed by the Commission ... were applicable across the board to all ... railroads ... No effort was made to single out any particular railroad for special consideration based on its own peculiar circumstances.... Though the Commission obviously relied on factual inferences as a basis for its order ... [these] factual inferences were used in the formulation of a basically legislative-type judgment, for prospective application only, rather than in adjudicating a particular set of disputed facts.

3. *Legislative and adjudicative facts.* In the preceding excerpt, how does Justice Rehnquist distinguish *Londoner* and *Bi–Metallic?* Compare Rehnquist's distinction with that of Davis:

The crucial difference between the two cases is that in *Londoner* specific facts about the particular property were disputed, but in *Bi–Metallic* no such specific facts were disputed, for the problem was the broad and general problem involving all taxpayers of Denver. The principle emerging from the two cases may be that a dispute about facts that have to be found on "individual grounds" [which Davis calls "adjudicative facts"] must be resolved through trial procedure, but a dispute on a question of policy need not be resolved through trial procedure even if the decision is made in part on the basis of broad and general facts of the kind that contribute to the determination of a question of policy [which Davis calls "legislative facts"]....

Adjudicative facts usually answer the questions of who did what, where, when, how, why, with what motive or intent; adjudicative facts are roughly the kind of facts that go to a jury in a jury case. Legislative facts do not usually concern the immediate parties but are the general facts which help the tribunal decide questions of law and policy and discretion....

[Adjudicative facts] are intrinsically the kind of facts that ordinarily ought not to be determined without giving the parties a chance to know and to meet any evidence that may be unfavorable to them, that is, without providing the parties an opportunity for trial. The reason is that the parties know more about the facts concerning themselves and their activities than anyone else is likely to know, and the parties are therefore in an especially good position to rebut or explain evidence that bears upon adjudicative facts. Because the parties may often have little or nothing to contribute to the development of legislative facts, the method of trial often is not required for the determination of disputed issues about legislative facts.

2 Kenneth Culp Davis, ADMINISTRATIVE LAW TREATISE 412–13 (2d ed.1979).

Do you agree with Davis that there is "often" no constitutional right to trial-type procedure in an adjudication where the only dispute concerns legislative facts or the exercise of discretion? Is the distinction between legislative and adjudicative facts clear enough for easy application by agencies and courts?

4. *Rulemaking hearings.* Justice Holmes argued in *Bi–Metallic* that no hearing would be required if the state constitution or the state legislature had doubled Denver's tax rate. Therefore, it followed that there was no right to a hearing when the same action was taken by the State Board of Equalization. Does this really follow? Should any type of procedure be constitutionally required in *Bi-Metallic*?

CUNNINGHAM v. DEPARTMENT OF CIVIL SERVICE
350 A.2d 58 (N.J.1975).

SCHREIBER, J.:

[Cunningham and Schonwald were demoted from their jobs as Directors of Design (DOD) of the Department of Transportation (DOT) when the job position was abolished. Later DOT created a new job called Director of Employee and Management Service (DEMS). By statute, Cunningham and Schonwald were entitled to priority for DEMS if it was "comparable" to their old job—DOD. By a letter to the Commissioner of Transportation, they asserted that they were entitled to a preemptive right to DEMS, but DOT ruled that DOD and DEMS were not comparable and denied the application. It also denied the applicants a hearing on the comparability issue. The issue here is whether they are entitled to a hearing.]

The right to a hearing before a governmental agency, whose proposed action will affect the rights, duties, powers or privileges of, and is directed at, a specific person, has long been imbedded in our jurisprudence ... Entitlement to the hearing may be ascribable to federal and state constitutional guarantees of due process or to the indispensability of fundamental procedural fairness.

As the administrative agency became a more widely utilized forum for governmental action, it was also recognized that, in the absence of a specific statutory or constitutional requirement, hearings before administrative agencies might not be feasible or desirable. The impracticability of holding hearings where a class or large number of persons may be affected is obvious. *Bi-Metallic Investment Co. . . .* Furthermore, since the legislature was not required to hold hearings and legislative matters usually involve substantial numbers, it was resolved that where the agency's action constituted 'purely a legislative function' a hearing was not required. Need for a hearing was to be ascertained by determining whether the administrative agency was acting in a legislative or a quasi-judicial capacity.

Finding that a certain activity is quasi-judicial or legislative presupposes an ability to recognize a judicial or legislative power, an ability which may well be lacking. Glasser has referred to the distinction as a 'treacherous' one. Classification of the type of the proceeding as the determinant may also beg the question of the need for a hearing. The same types of factual controversy and particularized effect on a person which decree a hearing may well exist in both legislative and quasi-judicial administrative agency proceedings. Illustrative of the point is public utility rate making. Rate making is generally considered legislative in nature. Yet there can be no doubt that a public utility whose rates were being fixed and challenged would be entitled to notice and hearing.[53]

The problem has also been approached by asking whether the agency is obligated to consider the evidence and apply the law to the facts as found. An affirmative response has been held to determine that the agency's function is quasi-judicial and accordingly a hearing is required ... The crucial questions are whether the fact finding involves a certain person or persons whose rights will be directly affected, and whether the subject matter at issue is susceptible to the receipt of evidence. The nature of the factual inquiries may be dispositive or assist in the disposition of the issue. A question posed in terms of general policy may clearly fall in the 'no hearing' category. Facts involved in resolution of a question of that type have sometimes been designated as legislative [citing to Davis' distinction between adjudicative and legislative facts].

Where the administrative agency is acting in a general capacity, such as rulemaking, so that the direct effect of its factual conclusions will be imposed on a class or group, as distinguished from some specific person or persons, then it may well be that such a hearing is not required. For example, no hearing would be required where the Department of Internal Revenue was prescribing standards for those who desired to practice before it, though one would be needed to deprive some individual of that right....

Contested factual issues which may be presented in an evidential manner in proceedings which are targeted at a person satisfy the first prerequisite for a hearing. In such cases adjudicative, as opposed to legislative, facts will usually be at issue. The second prerequisite is that the party affected by the administrative action have a safeguarded interest. Particularized property rights or other special interests must exist ... see *Board of Regents v. Roth* ....

Measured against these standards, a hearing is mandated in this case. The individual special interest or property right exists. Obviously,

---

53. Davis has commented: "More harmful than helpful is the proposition to which the courts often give lip service that hearings are required for judicial functions but not for legislative functions, especially when whole proceedings are characterized as judicial or legislative. The proposition is often unsound even when a function is clearly either legislative or judicial, and the proposition often causes confusion in that no one knows how to classify many functions."

Cunningham and Schonwald, by virtue of their status on the special reemployment list, may be entitled to the position. Disturbance of the relationship of a civil service employee and the governmental employer by discharge is conditioned upon demands of procedural due process. The right to promotion by virtue of a statutory seniority list entails a vital element in the employer-employee relationship sufficiently akin to removal to warrant a finding of special interest.

Furthermore, there are seemingly contested adjudicative factual issues. Under the statute the problem which must be resolved is whether the functions, duties and responsibilities of [DEMS] are the same or comparable to those previously carried out by the plaintiffs. It is not, as plaintiffs contend, whether their individual qualifications satisfy those of DEMS. The positions must be compared—not the qualifications of the individuals for the job. The Commission insists that the only pertinent facts are the specifications of the two jobs. But this may not be so. Although on the face of it the central theme as reflected in the specifications of DOD appears to be highway design engineering, and that of DEMS is general and supervisory skills, a large number of the duties described in the specifications are similar or identical. What duties has the temporary DEMS appointee actually been performing? Are these comparable to those performed by the petitioners as DOD? Is the authority of both positions similar? Are the responsibilities of each comparable? The petitioners should be given an opportunity to demonstrate that material differences are nonexistent. . . .

Petitioners should be permitted to make an offer of proof to the Commission buttressed by appropriate affidavits to reflect genuine issues as to any material facts. If petitioners have no such proof, then the need for a plenary type hearing does not exist. In that event, petitioners should be given the opportunity to present argument orally or in writing that on the basis of the specifications the positions are similar and comparable.

If an evidentiary hearing is required, it appears appropriate to follow the guidelines of the Administrative Procedure Act in 'contested' cases. . . . The judgment is reversed and the matter remanded to the Civil Service Commission for further proceedings in accordance with this opinion.

SULLIVAN and CLIFFORD, JJ. dissent. . . .

Notes and Questions

1. *Adjudicative v. legislative facts.* Davis' legislative-adjudicative fact distinction is often cited and relied on. Whether Cunningham or Schonwald is qualified for DEMS would clearly be a question of adjudicative fact. But what about the factual questions involving the comparability of DOD and DEMS—are they legislative or adjudicative facts? And did the result in this case turn on the difference?

2. *Rules applicable to single entity.* Suppose in *Cunningham* that DOT had adopted a rule that DOD and DEMS were not comparable. DOT was

well aware that the only private individuals who were interested (or would ever be interested) in the question were Cunningham and Schonwald. This hypothetical exemplifies a line of cases in which an agency adopts a rule that appears to have general applicability but in reality regulates the conduct of only a single entity (in this case, two). Moreover, it is unlikely that any other entities will ever become subject to the rule. Is the entity entitled to due process?

Compare *Anaconda Co. v. Ruckelshaus*, 482 F.2d 1301 (10th Cir.1973). The EPA proposed a rule concerning sulfur oxide emissions in Deer Lodge County, Montana. Anaconda was the only entity that generated such emissions. Because the rule was general in form, the court held that due process was inapplicable. "The fact that Anaconda alone is involved is not conclusive on the question as to whether the hearing should be adjudicatory, for there are many other interested parties and groups who are affected and are entitled to be heard."

However, the court also indicated that even if due process were required, it had been provided. Since the EPA had given Anaconda an opportunity to appear at a public meeting and submit documents and information, "we perceive no violation of Anaconda's right to procedural due process.... Unending procedure could be produced by an adjudicatory hearing. This could bring about unending delay which would not only impede but completely stifle congressional policy...."

Professor Schwartz criticizes *Anaconda* and maintains that if a facially general pronouncement is *individual in impact*, the affected person or persons should be given a judicial-type hearing. Bernard Schwartz, ADMINISTRATIVE LAW § 5.8 at 241 (3d ed. 1991). Do you agree?

3. *Application of the APA*. Note the final paragraph of the opinion—if due process requires a hearing, the hearing requirements of the New Jersey APA become applicable. In light of cases like *Mathews v. Eldridge*, this dictum might not be followed today. Most APA's provide only for a single, rather formal mode of trial-type hearings, but the requirements of due process are flexible and contextual. We return to the issue of whether the APA should apply to hearings required by due process in § 3.1.

4. *Problem*. A major political issue in Elm City is whether rapid development of residential neighborhoods with high rise apartments and shopping centers should be slowed down. A newly elected city council is considering a proposed comprehensive zoning ordinance for the city. The ordinance would provide that no new development (other than single-family dwellings) could occur in large areas of the city, including the Brentwood neighborhood. Ben, who owns an empty lot in Brentwood, seeks to cross-examine the city planner at a hearing before the Council while the proposed ordinance is pending. He wishes to show that the ordinance is far too restrictive of development and that the ambiance of Brentwood can be preserved if small shopping centers are permitted. Must the council provide him an opportunity to conduct such an examination?

Assume the council adopted the ordinance. Later, Ben asks the council to amend the ordinance to allow the construction of a small shopping center on his lot. According to statute, such an amendment should be granted in cases of "unusual hardship." He argues that he could make five times as much on his investment if he could build a shopping center. Moreover, it would be a great convenience for the neighborhood because there is no nearby shopping. Finally, he makes the same arguments that he made earlier in opposing the citywide ordinance. The council is proposing to deny the request. Is Ben entitled to a trial-type hearing?

Assume instead that the council is proposing to grant the request. Mary, Ben's neighbor, is outraged at the extra noise and traffic that a shopping center would bring to Brentwood. Is Mary entitled to a trial-type hearing? *See Horn v. County of Ventura*, 596 P.2d 1134 (Cal.1979); *High Horizons Dev. Co. v. N. J. Dep't of Transportation*, 575 A.2d 1360, 1367–68 (N.J.1990); *River Park, Inc. v. City of Highland Park*, 23 F.3d 164 (7th Cir.1994).

Chapter 3

ADMINISTRATIVE ADJUDICATION: FUNDAMENTAL PROBLEMS

Chapter 2 examined the constitutional right to a trial-type hearing. This chapter continues that theme, but now the source of the right to a hearing is statutory rather than constitutional. In many situations, the rights overlap: both due process and state or federal APAs require agencies to provide an opportunity for a trial-type hearing. However, the ingredients of the hearings required by due process and by statute are not the same: the statutory procedure is likely to be more formal than the proceeding required by due process. In many cases, there is no overlap: a statute may require a hearing even though due process does not or (particularly at the local level) due process may require a hearing even though statutes do not.

This chapter addresses some fundamental problems concerning agency hearings required by statute: When does a statute require an agency to hold a hearing? What is the relationship between statutory and constitutionally required hearings? Can an agency adjudicate a case impartially when it first made the rules and then investigated and prosecuted the very case it is about to decide? When is an agency decisionmaker disabled by bias or by having received off-the-record communications?

Chapter 4 takes up many practical problems of agency adjudication. It begins with investigation and discovery arising in the pre-hearing phase, continues with the hearing itself, and concludes with the principles relating to an agency's final decision.

§ 3.1 STATUTORY RIGHTS TO AN ADJUDICATORY HEARING

Administrative procedure statutes have taken two radically different approaches. The federal APA and the 1961 MSAPA (on which most state APAs are based) do not require adjudicative hearings. They lay out ground rules for formal hearings, but agencies need not use those procedures except where an *external source* (such as *another* statute or the state or federal constitution) requires a hearing. Such adjudication is called "formal adjudication." If no external source requires a hearing, the agency is usually free to choose its own dispute resolution procedure. Such adjudication is called "informal adjudication."

In contrast, the APAs of a number of states and the 1981 MSAPA do not leave it to an external source to decide whether a hearing is required. Instead, these APAs themselves prescribe when hearings should occur. They also provide for different hearing models of varying formality.

§ 3.1.1 FEDERAL LAW—RIGHT TO A HEARING UNDER THE APA

Read APA § 554(a). It applies only to "adjudication required by statute to be determined on the record after opportunity for an agency hearing ..." When a federal statute calls for an agency hearing that is "on the record," these are code words signaling that Congress intends that the formal adjudication sections of the APA come into play.

The mere fact that a "record" is maintained at a hearing (meaning that everything said is transcribed and typed up) does not mean the hearing is "on the record" for purposes of deciding whether the APA formal adjudication provisions apply. The phrase "on the record" really means "on the exclusive record," which in turn means that the trier of fact is not allowed to consider any evidence except that which has been admitted at the hearing. See APA § 556(e). However, many hearings that are not required to be conducted as APA formal adjudicatory hearings do in fact respect the "exclusive record" requirement. So in the end, the words "on the record" in § 554(a) really don't mean anything except to signal the intent of Congress that the APA should apply.

In APA formal adjudication:

· an agency must separate its prosecuting and adjudicating functions (§ 554(d)) and no party can engage in ex parte contact with decision-makers (§ 557(d));

· an agency must allow such cross-examination at the hearing as "may be required for a full and true disclosure of the facts" (§ 556(d));

· if the private party wins and the agency's position was not substantially justified, the private party is entitled to recover attorney fees under the Equal Access to Justice Act (discussed in § 10.3); and

· the hearing must be conducted by an administrative law judge (ALJ) who is hired and assigned to particular cases according to strict standards (§§ 3105, 7521, discussed in § 3.4).

But what happens if Congress merely provides for a "hearing" or a "public hearing" without using the code words "on the record"? Did it intend to require APA formal adjudication? Or did it intend to permit the agency to use "informal adjudication"—which means any procedures the agency finds expedient? That is the subject of the *West Chicago* case that follows.

CITY OF WEST CHICAGO v. NRC

701 F.2d 632 (7th Cir.1983).

[The Nuclear Regulatory Commission (NRC) is a multi-member federal agency that is responsible for licensing and regulation of the nuclear industry. In addition to licensing nuclear power plants, the NRC is responsible for licensing and regulating facilities that manufacture, process or store radioactive materials.

Kerr–McGee Corp. (KM) operated a thorium milling plant in West Chicago (City) from 1967 to 1973. KM had an NRC "source material" license allowing it to process and store thorium ore. Five million cubic feet of contaminated radioactive waste material still remain at the plant site. The method of decommissioning the site is in dispute and was considered in several earlier NRC proceedings.

KM's current application (for Amendment 3) seeks permission to demolish six buildings and to receive and store on-site additional contaminated material. City challenges an NRC order granting the license amendment.]

Cummings, J.:

... The Atomic Energy Act of 1954 (AEA), § 189(a), 42 U.S.C. § 2239(a), clearly requires NRC to grant a "hearing" if requested in any proceeding under this chapter, for the granting, suspending, revoking, or amending of any license or construction permit....[2] The parties in this case are arguing about the kind of "hearing" the NRC is required to conduct when issuing an amendment to a source materials license. The City argues that NRC must hold a formal, adversarial, trial-type hearing as provided by NRC regulations.... We shall refer to the hearing process outlined in those sections [of the regulations] as a "formal hearing." NRC and intervenor KM argue that the NRC may hold an informal hearing in which it requests and considers written materials without providing for traditional trial-type procedures such as oral testimony and cross-examination. We shall refer to this kind of hearing

2. § 189(a). Hearings and judicial review:

  (a) In any proceeding under this chapter, for the granting, suspending, revoking, or amending of any license or construction permit, or application to transfer control, and in any proceeding for the issuance or modification of rules and regulations dealing with the activities of licensees, ... the Commission shall grant a hearing upon the request of any person whose interest may be affected by the proceeding, and shall admit any such person as a party to such proceeding. The Commission shall hold a hearing after thirty days' notice and publication once in the Federal Register, on each application under section 2133 or 2134(b) of this title for a construction permit for a facility, and on any application under section 2134(c) of this title for a construction permit for a testing facility.

[Sections 2133 and 2134 concern licenses for nuclear reactors.]

as an "informal hearing." In the circumstances of this case, we find that an informal hearing suffices. . . .

2.   NRC Did Not Violate the Atomic Energy Act

Our inquiry cannot end with a finding that the NRC acted in conformance with its own regulations, for we must determine whether those regulations as interpreted violate the governing statute. If the AEA requires a formal hearing in the case of a materials license amendment, then the NRC must provide one, despite its interpretation of the regulations.

The City claims that a materials licensing hearing under Section 189(a) of the AEA must be in accordance with Section 5 of the Administrative Procedure Act (APA), 5 U.S.C. § 554. Section 554 does not by its terms dictate the type of hearing to which a party is entitled; rather it triggers the formal hearing provisions of Sections 556 and 557 of the APA if the adjudication in question is required by the agency's governing statute to be "determined on the record after opportunity for an agency hearing." . . . . The City argues that Section 189(a) of the AEA triggers the formal hearing provisions of the APA because it provides that the "Commission shall grant a hearing upon the request of any person whose interest may be affected by the proceeding, and shall admit any such person as a party to such proceeding."

Although Section 554 specifies that the governing statute must satisfy the "on the record" requirement, those three magic words need not appear for a court to determine that formal hearings are required. . . . However, even the City agrees that in the absence of these magic words, Congress must clearly indicate its intent to trigger the formal, on-the-record hearing provisions of the APA. We find no such clear intention in the legislative history of the AEA, and therefore conclude that formal hearings are not statutorily required for amendments to materials licenses . . .

While Section 181 of the AEA made the provisions of the APA applicable to all agency actions, it did not specify the "on the record" requirement necessary to trigger Section 554 of the APA. Thus despite the fact that the statute required the Commission to grant a hearing to any materially interested party, there is no indication that Congress meant the hearing to be a formal one. . . .

The [NRC historically held] formal hearings in all contested reactor cases, as well as in materials licensing cases. However, based on the threadbare legislative history concerning materials licenses, we are unable to conclude that the [NRC's] procedures were mandated by statute. Even if the legislative history indicates that formal procedures are required by statute in reactor licensing cases under the second, third, and fourth sentences of Section 189(a), we do not accept the City's argument that this by necessity indicates that all hearings under the first sentence must be formal as well. While the first sentence of Section 189(a) speaks in terms of "any license or construction permit," it does so in the context of a statute that distinguishes between the licensing of nuclear materials and reactor facilities.... In this case, we have no difficulty ascribing different meanings to the word "hearing" even though it appears in succeeding sentences of the same statutory section.

The City argues that under the APA, agency action is classified either as rule-making or adjudication, and since licensing is adjudication, NRC is obliged to provide a formal hearing in this case. The "on the record" requirement of APA Section 554, according to the City has been relevant primarily in cases involving rulemaking, not adjudication. *United States v. Florida East Coast Ry. Co..*, 410 U.S. 224 (1973).

In adjudication, the City claims the absence of the "on the record" requirement is not decisive. For example, Section 402 of the Federal Water Pollution Control Act (FWPCA), which provides for a public hearing, has been held by three courts including this one to require a formal hearing pursuant to Section 554. *Seacoast Anti–Pollution League v. Costle*, 572 F.2d 872 (1st Cir.), cert. den. 439 U.S. 824 (1978). The First Circuit relied principally on the adjudicative nature of the decision at issue—issuance of a permit to allow discharge of a pollutant—finding that primarily the rights of the particular applicant would be affected, and that resolution of the issues required specific factual findings by the EPA Administrator.

The court also mentioned the judicial review provision of Section 509 of the FWPCA, which provides for review of a determination required under the FWPCA to be made "on the record."... Unlike the "on the record" requirement of Section 509 of the FWPCA, there is no indication even in the judicial review section of the AEA, the governing statute, that Congress intended to require formal hearings under the APA.

Thus even in adjudication, the "on the record" requirement is significant at least as an indication of congressional intent. We agree with the courts and commentators who recognize that adjudication may be either informal or formal. Formal adjudications are those required by statute to be conducted through on-the-record proceedings. Informal adjudications constitute a residual category including "all agency actions that are not rulemaking and that need not be conducted through 'on the record' hearings."[11]

... Despite the fact that licensing is adjudication under the APA, there is no evidence that Congress intended to require formal hearings for all Section 189(a) activities. In light of the above analysis, we conclude that NRC did not violate the AEA when it denied the City's request for a formal hearing.[12]

11. Of course, if a formal adjudicatory hearing is mandated by the due process clause, the absence of the "on the record" requirement will not preclude application of the APA. *Wong Yang Sung v. McGrath*, 339 U.S. 33 (1950).

12. Because we hold that the AEA does not require a formal hearing in this case, we need not address the NRC contention that no hearing is required in the absence of a disputed issue of material fact even when the governing statute by its terms requires an "on the record" hearing. This apparently is the rule in the D.C. Circuit....

3. NRC HEARING PROCEDURES SATISFY THE REQUIREMENTS OF DUE PROCESS

The City argues that the NRC proceedings deprived it of liberty or property interests without due process of law. Yet generalized health, safety and environmental concerns do not constitute liberty or property subject to due process protection. Although the City claims that it has presented "specific documented concerns" to the NRC in its petitions, such "concerns" do not, without more, require due process protection.

Even if we were to find a protected liberty or property interest in this case, we would hold that Commission procedures constituted sufficient process. The City received a meaningful opportunity to submit statements and data explaining why the amendment should not be granted....

By pressing its request for a formal evidentiary hearing, the City has indicated its belief that written comments and documentation provide an inadequate opportunity to air its concerns. However, we are given no hint by the City of concerns other than the six listed in its November 13 submission to the Commission. Of those six, only two present factual issues, the resolution of which will in large part be based on technical or scientific data that will not necessarily be made more reliable through an oral presentation. Cf. *Mathews v. Eldridge*. In addition, as in a motion for summary judgment, it appears that both the City and KM essentially agreed on the facts but contested their interpretation, thus alleviating the need for an oral hearing.

We find that NRC correctly applied the *Mathews v. Eldridge* analysis in its order. The private interest that would be affected by official action in this case is a generalized one; in fact the health, safety and environmental interests of the City appear to be more "public" than "private...." Taking into account the technical, scientific nature of the issues, the absence of credibility questions, and the apparent lack of controverted issues of material fact, the additional value of an oral hearing in this case is minimal. Finally, convening a formal hearing involves a great deal of expense, both for the agency and the parties. According to NRC,

> A three-member licensing board or administrative law judge must be appointed, and with that come all the accouterments that make the proceeding more costly in terms of the time and materials expended: *e.g.*, participation in a pre-hearing conference, preparation of transcripts, discovery, submission of pre-filed testimony, a trial-type hearing at which witnesses are presented and cross-examined, and the preparation of findings of fact and conclusions of law.

NRC concluded, and we concur, that in this particular case, the Commission procedures afforded the City all the process that was constitutionally necessary....

The orders under review are affirmed.

Notes and Questions

1. *The real world.* Why did West Chicago want an adjudicatory hearing? Why did the NRC want to avoid holding a hearing?

Many agencies besides NRC have sought to circumvent APA adjudication procedures. In addition to the desire to avoid the formalities itemized near the end of the opinion, agencies wish to avoid having to use ALJs as presiding officers. For example, the present ALJ selection process gives an artificial edge to veterans, and agencies believe the selection system impairs their ability to select ALJs with needed technical competence. Moreover, agencies are not allowed to conduct appraisals of the performance of their ALJs. If NRC is required to use ALJs, it must hire some of these relatively high-paid professionals and it cannot assign them to any task other than judging.

These problems can be avoided if the agency is allowed to select its own presiding officer to hear the case. That person can be any agency staff member who has not previously been involved in the dispute. But it can only do so if the APA is inapplicable. See discussion of this issue in § 3.4.1.

2. *Adjudication required by statute.* When a statute calls for a "hearing," but does not use the magic words "on the record," does the statute trigger § 554(a) of the APA?

In cases of *rulemaking*, the Supreme Court held that formal procedures are not triggered by a requirement that the ICC act "after hearing." Congress must use the words "on the record" or their equivalent. *United States v. Florida East Coast Ry. Co.*, 410 U.S. 224 (1973), discussed on this issue in § 5.4.2.

However, in cases of *adjudication*, several decisions prior to *West Chicago* required formal adjudicatory procedures under statutes (like § 189(a) of the Atomic Energy Act) that call only for a "hearing" or a "public hearing." For example, see *Seacoast Anti–Pollution League* discussed in *West Chicago*. *Seacoast* involved a determination by the Environmental Protection Agency of whether to issue a license to a nuclear reactor to discharge hot water into the sea; among the factual issues was the effect of the discharge on sea life.

According to *Seacoast* and similar cases, Congress is presumed to intend formal adjudicatory procedures in a statute governing adjudication when it uses the word "hearing." *Seacoast* relied in part on the *Attorney General's Manual on the Administrative Procedure Act* (1947), a respected interpretive guide that the Justice Department published shortly after the APA was enacted. The Manual states:

> [A] statutory provision that rules be issued after a hearing, without more, should not be construed as requiring agency action "on the record," but rather as merely requiring an opportunity for the expression of views. That conclusion [is] based on the legislative nature of rule making ... No such rationale applies to administrative adjudication. In fact, it is assumed that where a statute specifically provides for administrative adjudication (such as the suspension or revocation of a license) after opportunity for an agency hearing, such specific requirement for a

hearing ordinarily implies the further requirement of decision in accordance with evidence adduced at the hearing.

Id. at 42–43. How satisfactorily did *West Chicago* distinguish these authorities? *Should* formal adjudicatory procedures be required in materials licensing cases before the NRC? How about cases of nuclear reactor licensing?

Suppose that agency regulations (but not a statute) call for a "hearing on the record." Should that trigger full APA formal adjudication?

3. *Deferring to the agency's choice—Chemical Waste. Chemical Waste Management, Inc. v. EPA,* 873 F.2d 1477 (D.C.Cir.1989), took a different tack from either *West Chicago* or *Seacoast.* The statute required EPA to "conduct a public hearing" before taking various actions relating to violation of hazardous waste management rules. Under EPA regulations, only an informal hearing was required to impose a "corrective order" on waste storage facilities that were in violation of the rules.

The court in *Chemical Waste* pointed out that the statute calling for a "public hearing" was ambiguous. Under *Chevron, U.S.A. v. Natural Resources Defense Council,* 467 U.S. 837 (1984), a reviewing court should defer to reasonable agency interpretations of ambiguous statutes. Consequently, the court deferred to EPA's regulation. We discuss *Chevron* in detail in § 9.2. Needless to say, the *Chemical Waste* approach encourages agencies to adopt procedural regulations that opt out of APA formal adjudication.

4. *Implications of "on the record."* In *Portland Audubon Society v. Endangered Species Committee,* 984 F.2d 1534 (9th Cir.1993), which is discussed further in § 3.2.4 N.4, the court held that the APA's formal adjudication provisions applied to proceedings of the Endangered Species Committee (or "God Squad"), which is empowered to grant exemptions from the Endangered Species Act. Under that Act, a hearing is held initially before an ALJ, conforming to §§ 554, 555, and 556 of the APA; the ALJ's decision is appealable to the Committee, whose proceedings are not *expressly* made subject to § 557. Three Cabinet Secretaries, three other federal agency heads, and a state representative sit on the Committee.

The statute directed the Committee to make its determination "on the record, based on the report of the Secretary [of the Interior], the record of the hearing held [before the ALJ,] and on such other testimony or evidence as it may receive." The court held: "Wherever the outer bounds of the 'after opportunity for an agency hearing' requirement [in APA § 554(a)] may lie, we hold that where, as here, a statute provides that an adjudication be determined at least in part *based on* an agency hearing, that requirement is fulfilled." As a result of the court's holding, the Committee was required to respect the APA's ban on ex parte contacts, APA § 557(d), by refraining from consulting with outsiders, including the White House.

5. *Informal adjudication. West Chicago* holds that NRC initial licensing (except perhaps for nuclear reactor cases) can be conducted as "informal," not "formal" adjudication. Aside from §§ 558 and 555, the federal APA requires no specific procedures in cases of informal adjudication. Yet § 189 does require NRC to provide a "hearing."

Did NRC provide a "hearing" before granting KM the license amendment? Does the requirement of a "hearing" in § 189 mean anything? See

United States Lines, Inc. v. FMC, 584 F.2d 519 (D.C.Cir.1978) ("hearing" includes limits on ex parte contacts with decision-maker). Shouldn't Congress provide for some rudimentary procedures in case of informal adjudication?

Suppose a court believes that an agency's procedures for informal adjudication are not fair to private parties. Yet neither the APA nor due process is applicable, and the court cannot fall back on any other statute or regulation to provide the necessary protection. Can the court mandate additional procedures as a matter of administrative common law?

In order to facilitate judicial review, some courts have required a system of notice, comment, and explanation, like that required in informal rulemaking, before an agency completes informal adjudication. *American Trading Transp. Co. v. United States*, 841 F.2d 421, 424–25 (D.C.Cir.1988); *Independent U.S. Tanker Owners Committee v. Lewis*, 690 F.2d 908, 922–26 (D.C.Cir.1982).

In rulemaking cases, the Supreme Court has made it clear that courts lack power to create extra-statutory procedure except in unusual situations. In the *Vermont Yankee* case, § 5.4.3, the Court declared that courts could not go beyond the rulemaking procedures set forth in the APA. Later, the Court extended the *Vermont Yankee* principle to adjudication. As a result, if the procedures for a particular adjudication are not prescribed by the APA or due process or some other source of law, the agency decides what procedure to provide—not the courts. *Pension Benefit Guaranty Corp. v. LTV Corp.*, 496 U.S. 633 (1990). The *PBGC* case casts serious doubt on the correctness of the D.C. Circuit cases cited in the preceding paragraph.

Note, however, the major difference between rulemaking and adjudication. In the case of informal rulemaking, the APA provides a series of adequate protections for the public. But in the case of informal adjudication, the APA provides virtually no protections at all.

6. *Comparative hearings.* In many situations, several applicants compete for a single mutually exclusive license. For example, two radio stations cannot occupy the same frequency or neither could be heard. Thus if one application for the frequency is approved, a second application for the same frequency must be rejected. Giving the second applicant a hearing after granting the first application would be meaningless. In this situation, the Supreme Court held that both applicants must be considered together in a single comparative hearing or else the second applicant's statutory right to a hearing would be "an empty thing." *Ashbacker Radio Corp. v. FCC*, 326 U.S. 327 (1945).

The *Ashbacker* principle has frequently been applied in situations where, for economic or policy reasons, only one of several applications can be approved, even though it was physically possible for both applicants to operate. See, e.g., *Bio-Medical Applications of Clearwater, Inc. v. Department of Health*, 370 So.2d 19 (Fla.App.1979) (certificates of need for hospital facilities); *Pollack v. Simonson*, 350 F.2d 740 (D.C.Cir.1965) (liquor stores within 300 feet of each other). But see *Cusano v. Dunn*, 74 A.2d 477 (Conn.1950) (reaching opposite conclusion on competing liquor licenses).

7. *Constitutionally required hearings. West Chicago* holds that the license amendment did not invade the City's liberty or property interests. (Do you agree?) Even if the City were entitled to due process, the court held that due process had been provided. (Do you agree?)

If the Seventh Circuit *had* believed that due process required a trial-type hearing, the case of *Wong Yang Sung v. McGrath*, 339 U.S. 33 (1950), would have become relevant, as the court recognized in its note 11. *Wong* was a deportation case. The statute did not require the Immigration Service (INS) to provide any kind of hearing. However, due process requires a hearing before a person can be deported. The Court held that APA formal adjudication applied to deportation hearings, because the words "required by statute" in § 554(a) were intended to include *hearings required by the constitution as well as hearings required by statute.* The Court refused to "attribute to Congress a purpose to be less scrupulous about the fairness of a hearing necessitated by the Constitution than one granted as a matter of expediency." Congress swiftly overturned the narrow holding of *Wong* and made clear that the APA was not to apply to deportation cases. See *Marcello v. Bonds*, 349 U.S. 302 (1955) (upholding this statute). The legislation did not, however, foreclose the Court from applying the *Wong* principle of construction in other regulatory contexts.

However, in recent decades the courts have often ignored or evaded the *Wong Yang Sung* gloss on the APA. *See* Robert E. Zahler, Note, "The Requirement of Formal Adjudication under Section 5 of the Administrative Procedure Act," 12 Harv.J. on Legis. 194, 218–41 (1975). A good example is *Clardy v. Levi*, 545 F.2d 1241 (9th Cir.1976), which declined to apply APA formal adjudication to federal prison disciplinary cases, even though due process then required a hearing in such cases.

A more recent example is *Greene v. Babbitt*, 64 F.3d 1266 (9th Cir.1995), which involved a decision by the Secretary of the Interior that the Samish were not a recognized Indian tribe. As a result, various Samish Indians lost welfare benefits provided only to members of recognized tribes. The court held that due process entitled the tribe to a trial-type hearing and that this hearing should conform to the APA formal adjudication procedures. The court could easily have justified the latter holding by citing *Wong Yang Sung*, but that case was not even mentioned. Instead the court merely concluded on the basis of the *Mathews v. Eldridge* balancing test that the APA procedures furnished an appropriate model for the Secretary to use.

Does the modern eclipse of *Wong Yang Sung* make sense? Note that, as *Greene* illustrates, a court that does *not* apply *Wong Yang Sung* where due process requires a hearing would presumably determine the necessary elements of that hearing using the *Mathews* test. Is it reasonable for the courts to assume, as *Wong Yang Sung* did, that whenever due process requires a trial type hearing, Congress would probably want all the components of an APA formal hearing to come into play? *See* William Funk, "Close Enough for Government Work?—Using Informal Procedures for Imposing Administrative Penalties," 24 Seton Hall L.Rev. 1, 12–15 (1993).

8. *Problem.* Mel wished to dredge and fill a swampy area on his farm which now is useless for farming and is a breeding ground for mosquitoes. Once this wetland is filled, the area would be suitable for building homes.

Under section 404 of the federal Clean Water Act, Mel must obtain a dredging permit from the Army Corps of Engineers. The statute provides that the Corps may issue permits, after "notice and opportunity for public hearings," for the discharge of dredged or fill material into navigable waters.

Ed (the Corps' District Engineer) provided public notice of Mel's application. Ed received letters from a local environmental group charging that the project would increase the risk of downstream flooding and would destroy wildlife breeding habitats. Mel argued that the project would decrease the risk of flooding, would not destroy any breeding habitats, and would assist in mosquito control. He submitted letters from community leaders and from an environmental engineer in support of his position.

Ed visited Mel's farm. He also conducted informal meetings with Mel and with several opponents of the application. He did not take any notes of what was said at these meetings. Mel was not present at the meeting with the opponents. Based on the file, the informal conferences, and the site visit, Ed denied the application, writing a one-paragraph explanation of this decision. Mel requested a formal hearing under the APA or at least an oral argument. Acting in accordance with established Corps of Engineers procedural guidelines, Ed refused to provide any further procedures.

To what additional procedure, if any, is Mel entitled? See *Buttrey v. United States*, 690 F.2d 1170, 1174–83 (5th Cir.1982).

§ 3.1.2   RIGHTS TO A HEARING UNDER STATE LAW

Most state APAs follow the 1961 MSAPA and the federal act by requiring an external source to trigger the adjudicatory procedures spelled out by the APA. The 1961 MSAPA defines a "contested case," to which its formal adjudication provisions apply, as a "proceeding, including but not restricted to ratemaking and licensing, in which the legal rights, duties or privileges of a party are required *by law* to be determined by an agency after an opportunity for hearing." 1961 MSAPA § 1(2) (emphasis added). The *Sugarloaf Citizens* case involves the Maryland version of this provision.

Like the federal APA, the 1961 MSAPA provides for only one type of hearing—a full, formal, trial-type proceeding. But if the dispute in question is not a "contested case," the 1961 MSAPA, like the federal APA, provides for virtually no procedures at all.

A number of recent state statutes and the 1981 MSAPA take an entirely different tack from the federal APA and the 1961 MSAPA. First, these statutes provide an *inclusive* definition of adjudication. With only narrow exceptions, all adjudicatory decisions are covered by the acts, regardless of whether an external source requires a hearing. Second, these statutes create several distinct classes of agency adjudication, each subject to procedural requirements specially tailored to the circumstances. The Florida statute, applied in the *Metsch* case, uses an inclusive definition of adjudication.

Some state statutes strike a compromise between the 1961 and 1981 MSAPA approaches. They define "contested case" to include any agency discretionary decision to suspend or revoke a right or privilege or to refuse to renew or issue a license, regardless of whether any other law requires a hearing. See, e.g., *Morrison v. University of Oregon Health Sciences Ctr.*, 685 P.2d 439 (Or.App.1984). In *Morrison*, the dismissal of a dental student for "lack of adequate clinical performance" triggered rights to a formal hearing because the dismissal was a discretionary revocation of a privilege.

SUGARLOAF CITIZENS ASS'N v. NORTHEAST MARYLAND WASTE DISPOSAL AUTHORITY

594 A.2d 1115 (Md.1991).

[Sugarloaf Citizens Ass'n seeks to prevent construction of a solid waste incinerator proposed by Northeast Maryland Waste Disposal Authority. Under the Prevention of Significant Deterioration (PSD) scheme in the federal Clean Air Act, several permits are needed before the incinerator can be built. The issue is whether the Maryland Department of the Environment (MDE) must hold a "contested case" hearing before granting the permit applications.]

ELDRIDGE, J.

. . . . A "contested case" is defined by the APA as follows:

"(c) Contested case.—'Contested case' means a proceeding before an agency to determine:

(1) a right, duty, statutory entitlement, or privilege of a person that is required by law to be determined only after an opportunity for an agency hearing; or

(2) the grant, denial, renewal, revocation, suspension, or amendment of a license that is required by law to be determined only after an opportunity for an agency hearing."

Under the terms of the APA, when a proceeding meets the definition of a "contested case," the agency is required to provide certain trial type procedures during the course of the proceeding. It is well established, however, that the APA itself does not grant a right to a hearing. That right must come from another source such as a statute, a regulation, or due process principles. Moreover, the statute or regulation which grants the right to a hearing may negate the fact that the hearing is to be a "contested case" or "adjudicatory" hearing. . . .

[The court held that the first required permit, a PSD permit, could be granted without an adjudicatory hearing, because it is merely preliminary. But it held that a contested case hearing must be furnished before issuance of a construction permit. Section 2–404 of the Environment Article requires that, before granting a construction permit, MED "shall (1) give public notice of the intended issuance of the permit; and (2) provide an opportunity for a public hearing in the county in which the proposed source will be located."]

.... [W]here a statute such as § 2–404 of the Environment Article requires an opportunity for an agency hearing prior to the issuance of a construction permit, the question whether such hearing is a "contested case" hearing ordinarily depends upon applying the definition of "contested case" in the APA to the agency activity, and not upon whether § 2–404 uses language indicating that the hearing is "adjudicatory." Otherwise, the definition of contested case in the APA would be superfluous ...

The position of the defendants seems to be that the definition of "contested case" in the APA should be ignored, and that the sole issue is whether an application for a construction permit under § 2–404 of the Environment Article is "legislative-type" action or "adjudicatory" action. A similar argument was flatly rejected by [an earlier case]....

[The same result occurs even if the APA was not applicable. Distinguishing an earlier case, the court noted:] Unlike the comprehensive rezoning involved in the *Woodward & Lothrop* case, a proceeding under § 2–404 of the Environment Article involves an application for a permit by a specific person or entity to construct a particular facility at a specified location. At issue may be the effect on air quality of that facility at that location. In the *Woodward & Lothrop* case ... the Court pointed out that "the difference between adjudicative and legislative facts is not easily drawn.... " The Court, quoting from Professor Davis's treatise, went on: "legislative facts do not usually concern the immediate parties but are general facts which help the tribunal decide questions of law and policy and discretion. The difference, broadly speaking, involves whether the decision is to be made on individual or general grounds." Under these general principles, a proceeding under § 2–404 would be "adjudicative" and not "legislative ..."

METSCH v. UNIVERSITY OF FLORIDA

550 So.2d 1149 (Fla.Dist.Ct.App.1989).

PER CURIAM:

Benjamin Metsch appeals from an order of the University of Florida denying his request for an administrative hearing following his unsuccessful application for admission to the University of Florida College of Law. We affirm.

Metsch, while a student at Columbia University, applied for admission to the fall 1989 entering class of the University of Florida College of Law. Metsch was denied automatic admission based upon a computer projection of his law school grades derived from his undergraduate grade point average and his Law School Admissions Test score. Metsch was then placed in the "hold" category, and his application was reviewed by the Faculty Admissions Committee. In April, 1989, Metsch received a letter from the University informing him that he had not been admitted. The following month, Metsch wrote to the law school and requested a statement of the reasons for the denial of his application, reconsideration of his application, and a hearing pursuant to section 120.57(1), Florida Statutes (1987). In his request for a hearing, Metsch alleged that his "substantial interests" had been determined by the University, a state agency. The University reconsidered his application and, by letter, affirmed and explained the denial of admission,[14] described the admissions process and suggested that he reapply for admission to the spring 1990 semester. On May 10, 1989, the University's Interim President denied Metsch's request for an administrative hearing. Metsch appeals that denial.

The formal hearing provisions of the Florida Administrative Procedure Act, section 120.57(1), "apply in all proceedings in which the substantial interests of a party are determined by an agency, unless such proceedings are exempt pursuant to subsection (5)." The exemption section 120.57(5) states that "this section does not apply to any proceeding in which the substantial interests of a student are determined by the State University System.... " Metsch argues that his substantial interests were determined by the University's denial of his application for admission and that because he was not a "student" in the State University System, subsection (5) does not apply to him. We find both arguments without merit.

The second district has established a test for ascertaining whether a substantial interest has been determined: "[W]e believe that before one can be considered to have a substantial interest in the outcome of the proceeding he must show 1) that he will suffer injury in fact which is of immediate sufficiency to entitle him to a section 120.57 hearing, and 2) that his substantial injury is of a type or nature which the proceeding is designed to protect ... "

In his request for an administrative hearing, Metsch alleged no injury and specified no interest other than his "sincere desire to study law at the University of Florida College of Law and to become a practicing member of The Florida Bar."[15]

Obviously Metsch has an interest, as that term is ordinarily used, in admission to the University's College of Law; however, his "sincere desire to study law" at that institution does not rise to the level of a "substantial interest" within the meaning of section 120.57(1). In our view, Metsch's interest can best be described as a hope or a " 'unilateral expectation' of admittance." *Ramos v. Texas Tech Univ.*, 441 F.Supp.

14. The letter stated in part that out of 900 files placed in the hold category only 163 candidates received offers of admission based on the Admission Committee's evaluation of "the application, all academic transcripts, personal statement, evaluative letters, and any other data present in the file." The Admissions Committee concluded that "[t]here were too many candidates who, in the judgment of the Committee, presented a more competitive file and ranking higher than yours."

15. Metsch's request for a statement of reasons for the denial of his application for admission as well as statements made by his counsel during oral argument reveal a nascent claim against the University for reverse discrimination. If that is indeed the "substantial injury" he claims to have suffered he may bring a claim in state or federal court for violation of his civil rights.

1050, 1054 (N.D.Tex.1977) (applicant for admission to graduate program had no liberty or property interest in being admitted), aff'd, 566 F.2d 573 (5th Cir.1978).[16] See also *Beheshtitabar v. Florida State University*, 432 So. 2d 166 (Fla. 1st DCA 1983) (student requesting readmission to doctoral program in economics at Florida State University did not have substantial interest in readmission determination and was thus not entitled to an administrative hearing pursuant to section 120.57(1)). If such hopes and aspirations were deemed substantial interests, all unsuccessful applicants for admission to a state university would be entitled to a formal hearing upon the denial of their applications. While this scenario is not the basis for our denial of Metsch's claim, we cannot ignore the repercussions that would flow from granting the relief which he seeks.

Even if the University's action determined Metsch's substantial interests, section 120.57(5) exempts from formal administrative proceedings "any proceeding in which the substantial interests of a student are determined by the State University System." Metsch's argument that this section does not preclude granting him an administrative hearing flies in the face of reason. Under his interpretation of this section, students, including those students who are also applicants, are not entitled to formal administrative hearings while applicants who are not students are entitled to such proceedings upon denial of their applications. This skewed interpretation ascribes greater rights to those who clearly have lesser interests. We will not read the Florida Administrative Procedure Act to allow such a result.

AFFIRMED.

Notes and Questions

1. *The result in Sugarloaf.* As the *Sugarloaf* decision explains, the net cast by the Maryland APA is much broader than that cast by the federal APA. A contested case hearing must be provided if a hearing is required by a *regulation or by the constitution*, as well as by a statute. Moreover, the fact that the statute called for a "public hearing" was sufficient to trigger the APA. How would *West Chicago* have been decided under the Maryland APA?

Under the Maryland APA, subsection (c)(2) defined various licensing decisions as "contested cases." Did this provision, which is not found in the 1961 APA, add anything to subsection (c)(1)? Would the neighbors protesting the project have been able to initiate a hearing if only (c)(1) were on the books?

A "contested case" hearing under the Maryland Act and the 1961 APA is a full-fledged trial-type hearing with cross-examination of witnesses. Is that kind of hearing the best way to settle the sort of issues involved in the *Sugarloaf* case? The issues in *Sugarloaf* are discussed in Edward A. Tomlin-

---

16. We recognize that Metsch, unlike the plaintiff in Ramos, raises no claims here regarding any deprivation of due process but travels instead on a claim under the Florida Administrative Procedure Act. However, *Ramos* is illustrate of the issues here.

son, "The Maryland Administrative Procedure Act: Forty Years Old in 1997," 56 Md.L.Rev. 196, 240–71 (1997).

2. *Federal and state.* Note that, unlike the Maryland APA described in *Sugarloaf*, the Florida APA provides for a hearing whenever the "substantial interests" of a person are determined by an agency, regardless of whether a hearing is required by any other statute. This is an example of the "inclusive" approach to defining adjudication. If the Florida statute applied instead of the federal APA, would a hearing be required in *West Chicago*, § 3.1.1?

3. *The result in Metsch.* Do you agree that the Law School's decision rejecting Metsch did not determine "substantial interests"? Didn't Metsch think they were substantial?

The court relied on *Ramos* which held that a rejected applicant for a university program was not deprived of due process and so had no right to a hearing. Is that decision in point in applying the Florida statute?

The court seems on stronger ground in its alternative holding—that Metsch falls under the exception for "any proceeding in which the substantial interests of a student are determined by the State University System." Surely, as the court says, the legislators would not have wanted to give greater rights to an applicant for admission than to a present student who is being excluded.

4. *Florida and 1981 MSAPA.* Suppose the 1981 MSAPA were applicable in *Metsch*. The Law School's decision not to admit Metsch seems to be an "order," since it determines that he cannot receive a particular government benefit that he wants—admission to the Law School. See § 1–102(5). Under § 4–101(a), "an agency shall conduct an adjudicative proceeding as the process for formulating and issuing an order ..." Therefore, if 1981 MSAPA had been applicable, the Law School would be required to provide an adjudicative proceeding.

5. *Formal hearings for disappointed law school applicants?* The judges who decided *Metsch* were concerned that "all unsuccessful applicants for admission to a state university would be entitled to a formal hearing upon the denial of their applications ... [W]e cannot ignore the repercussions that would flow from granting the relief which he seeks."

This is a serious concern—one can imagine the Law School swamped by the need to hold thousands of trial-type hearings each year. But was this concern valid? Very few rejected applicants will ask for any sort of review of the decision. Moreover, Florida law provides for "informal proceedings" where a case does not present a "disputed issue of material fact." In an informal proceeding, an agency is required only

  · to give a person notice of its decision together with a summary of the grounds for the decision;

  · to give the person an opportunity at a convenient time and place to present to the agency written or oral evidence in opposition to its action, or a written statement challenging the grounds which it chose to justify its action; and

  · if the person's objections are overruled, a written explanation within 7 days. § 120(2)(a).

Did Metsch's case present a "disputed issue of material fact"? If not, would providing an informal proceeding for anybody who wanted one really be a major problem for the law school?

6. *Conference, emergency and summary procedure.* The 1981 MSAPA expanded on the Florida model by providing for different and less formal types of adjudication procedure for different types of disputes. Thus it avoids the all-or-nothing structure of the federal APA and the 1961 MSAPA.

a. *Conference adjudicative hearing.* A conference hearing, under §§ 4–401 to 4–403, is a "peeled down" procedure intended for disputes in which there is no disputed issue of material fact or in which there are disputed issues but the stakes are relatively low. Under conference procedure, an impartial presiding officer dispenses with witness testimony and with cross-examination. Only the parties may testify, present written exhibits, and offer comments on the issues. Conference procedure must be authorized by an agency rule.

b. *Emergency adjudicative proceeding.* Emergency procedure, under § 4–501, applies where there is an immediate danger to public health, safety, or welfare, requiring immediate action. The agency must give notice to persons who must comply with the order and render a brief statement of findings and reasons for its action. After taking the action, it must complete any proceedings that would have been required absent an emergency. What due process case does this remind you of?

c. *Summary adjudicative proceedings.* Summary procedure applies when the stakes are extremely low—for example a monetary amount of $100 or less or a warning or other verbal sanction without continuing impact against a prisoner, student, public employee, or licensee. It also applies to a denial of an application for admission to an educational institution.

Summary procedure must be authorized by an agency rule. It consists of an opportunity to tell one's side of the story to a presiding officer (who can be any agency employee). The officer renders a brief decision (which can be oral except in cases involving a monetary matter). Generally, a party can appeal to the presiding officer's superior. What due process case does summary procedure remind you of?

7. *Comparing APAs.* The 1981 MSAPA (and Florida's APA) take a radically different approach from the 1961 MSAPA and the federal APA.

Assume your state (like most states) adopted the 1961 MSAPA many years ago. Would you recommend to the legislature that it shift to the 1981 MSAPA approach? Is the Oregon approach (mentioned in the paragraph before *Sugarloaf*) a good compromise? One of the authors of this book changed his position on these questions. See Michael Asimow, "Toward a New California Administrative Procedure Act: Adjudication Fundamentals," 39 UCLA L. Rev. 1067, 1081–94 (1992) (urging the 1981 MSAPA approach); Michael Asimow, "The Influence of the Federal Administrative Procedure Act on California's New Administrative Procedure Act," 32 Tulsa L. J. 297, 307–312 (1996) (1981 MSAPA approach is overinclusive).

In making that determination, consider the extent to which each statute:

· adequately protects the interests of private parties;

· is easy to understand and apply to particular situations;

· tailors procedures to the importance of the matters at stake;

· promotes the cause of efficient and economic government administration; and

· is sufficiently flexible to deal with unforeseen or unusual circumstances.

8. *Problem*. Our client Ralph is an employee of Library engaged in classifying new books. His employment contract provides that he cannot be discharged except for good cause. Library's rules for employees prohibit smoking anywhere in the building. The rules also provide for disciplinary sanctions in case of rule violations. A supervisor has discretion as to which sanctions should be applied, if any. For a first offense, a supervisor can place a warning letter in an employee's file and can also suspend the employee for a period not to exceed five days.

Martha, Ralph's supervisor, believes that Ralph was smoking at his desk. Ralph denies this (he says the cigarette butts in his trash can were left by a friend who stopped by to visit him). He claims that another employee who hates him told Martha that he had been smoking. Even if he did it, he wants to persuade Martha not to put a letter in his file or suspend him.

Assume that Library is operated by

i) a county which is not subject to any administrative procedure act,

(ii) a state which has adopted the 1981 MSAPA, or

(iii) the federal government.

Is Ralph entitled to a hearing and, if so, of what sort? What do you advise him to do now?

§ 3.2 LIMITING THE ISSUES TO WHICH HEARING RIGHTS APPLY

A recurring theme in this book is the interplay between agency adjudication and rulemaking. Section 2.5 explored the applicability of due process to non-individualized proceedings. Recall *Bi–Metallic* and *Cunningham*. This section considers the related issue of whether an agency must provide an adjudicatory hearing prescribed by statute on an issue if the agency has already addressed that issue in a rule. A few other devices by which an agency can narrow the issues that are subject to hearing rights are also discussed. Section 6.2 will return to the rulemaking/adjudication relationship, taking up in detail the circumstances in which rulemaking should, or must, displace adjudication as a tool of regulation.

HECKLER v. CAMPBELL
461 U.S. 458 (1983).

POWELL, J.

The issue is whether the Secretary of Health and Human Services may rely on published medical-vocational guidelines to determine a claimant's right to Social Security disability benefits.

The Social Security Act defines "disability" in terms of the effect a physical or mental impairment has on a person's ability to function in the workplace. It provides disability benefits only to persons who are unable "to engage in any substantial gainful activity by reason of any medically determinable physical or mental impairment." 42 U.S.C. § 423(d)(1)(A). And it specifies that a person must "not only [be] unable to do his previous work but [must be unable], considering his age, education, and work experience, [to] engage in any other kind of substantial gainful work which exists in the national economy, regardless of whether such work exists in the immediate area in which he lives, or whether a specific job vacancy exists for him, or whether he would be hired if he applied for work." 42 U.S.C. § 423(d)(2)(A).

In 1978, the Secretary of Health and Human Services promulgated regulations implementing this definition. The regulations recognize that certain impairments are so severe that they prevent a person from pursuing any gainful work. A claimant who establishes that he suffers from one of these impairments will be considered disabled without further inquiry. If a claimant suffers from a less severe impairment, the Secretary must determine whether the claimant retains the ability to perform either his former work or some less demanding employment. If a claimant can pursue his former occupation, he is not entitled to disability benefits. If he cannot, the Secretary must determine whether the claimant retains the capacity to pursue less demanding work.

The regulations divide this last inquiry into two stages. First, the Secretary must assess each claimant's present job qualifications. The regulations direct the Secretary to consider the factors Congress has identified as relevant: physical ability, age, education, and work experience. Second, she must consider whether jobs exist in the national economy that a person having the claimant's qualifications could perform.

Prior to 1978, the Secretary relied on vocational experts to establish the existence of suitable jobs in the national economy. After a claimant's limitations and abilities had been determined at a hearing, a vocational expert ordinarily would testify whether work existed that the claimant could perform. Although this testimony often was based on standardized guides, vocational experts frequently were criticized for their inconsistent treatment of similarly situated claimants. To improve both the uniformity and efficiency[2] of this determination, the Secretary promulgated medical-vocational guidelines as part of the 1978 regulations.

These guidelines relieve the Secretary of the need to rely on vocational experts by establishing through rulemaking the types and numbers of jobs that exist in the national economy. They consist of a matrix of the four factors identified by Congress—physical ability, age, edu-

---

2. The Social Security hearing system is "probably the largest adjudicative agency in the western world." J. Mashaw et al., Social Security Hearings and Appeals, p. xi (1978). Approximately 2.3 million claims for disability benefits were filed in fiscal year 1981. More than a quarter of a million of these claims require a hearing before an Administrative Law Judge. The need for efficiency is self-evident.

cation, and work experience—and set forth rules that identify whether jobs requiring specific combinations of these factors exist in significant numbers in the national economy.[4] Where a claimant's qualifications correspond to the job requirements identified by a rule,[5] the guidelines direct a conclusion as to whether work exists that the claimant could perform. If such work exists, the claimant is not considered disabled.

In 1979, Carmen Campbell applied for disability benefits because a back condition and hypertension prevented her from continuing her work as a hotel maid. After her application was denied, she requested a hearing *de novo* before an Administrative Law Judge. He determined that her back problem was not severe enough to find her disabled without further inquiry, and accordingly considered whether she retained the ability to perform either her past work or some less strenuous job. He concluded that even though Campbell's back condition prevented her from returning to her work as a maid, she retained the physical capacity to do light work. In accordance with the regulations, he found that Campbell was 52 years old, that her previous employment consisted of unskilled jobs, and that she had a limited education. He noted that Campbell, who had been born in Panama, experienced difficulty in speaking and writing English. She was able, however, to understand and read English fairly well. Relying on [line 202.10 of] the medical-vocational guidelines [described in n.4], the Administrative Law Judge found that a significant number of jobs existed that a person of Campbell's qualifications could perform. Accordingly, he concluded that she was not disabled.

This determination was upheld by both the Social Security Appeals Council, and the District Court for the Eastern District of New York. The Court of Appeals for the Second Circuit reversed.... The court noted ... that it

> has consistently required that "the Secretary identify specific alternative occupations available in the national economy that would be suitable for the claimant" and that "these jobs be supported by 'a job description clarifying the nature of the job, [and] demonstrating that the job does not require' exertion or skills not possessed by the claimant."

The court found that the medical-vocational guidelines did not provide the specific evidence that it previously had required. It explained that in the absence of such a showing, "the claimant is deprived of any real

4. For example, Rule 202.10 provides that a significant number of jobs exist for a person who can perform light work, is closely approaching advanced age, has a limited education but who is literate and can communicate in English, and whose previous work has been unskilled.

5. The regulations recognize that the rules only describe "major functional and vocational patterns." If an individual's capabilities are not described accurately by a rule, the regulations make clear that the individual's particular limitations must be considered. Additionally, the regulations declare that the administrative law judge will not apply the age categories "mechanically in a borderline situation," and recognize that some claimants may possess limitations that are not factored into the guidelines....

chance to present evidence showing that she cannot in fact perform the types of jobs that are administratively noticed by the guidelines." The court concluded that because the Secretary had failed to introduce evidence that specific alternative jobs existed, the determination that Campbell was not disabled was not supported by substantial evidence.

... The court's requirement that additional evidence be introduced on this issue prevents the Secretary from putting the guidelines to their intended use and implicitly calls their validity into question. Accordingly, we think the decision below requires us to consider whether the Secretary may rely on medical-vocational guidelines in appropriate cases.

The Social Security Act directs the Secretary to "adopt reasonable and proper rules and regulations to regulate and provide for the nature and extent of the proofs and evidence and the method of taking and furnishing the same" in disability cases. 42 U.S.C. § 405(a).... Where, as here, the statute expressly entrusts the Secretary with the responsibility for implementing a provision by regulation, our review is limited to determining whether the regulations promulgated exceeded the Secretary's statutory authority and whether they are arbitrary and capricious.

We do not think that the Secretary's reliance on medical-vocational guidelines is inconsistent with the Social Security Act. It is true that the statutory scheme contemplates that disability hearings will be individualized determinations based on evidence adduced at a hearing. See 42 U.S.C. § 423(d)(2)(A) (specifying consideration of each individual's condition); 42 U.S.C. § 405(b) (1976 ed., Supp. V) (disability determination to be based on evidence adduced at hearing). But this does not bar the Secretary from relying on rulemaking to resolve certain classes of issues. The Court has recognized that even where an agency's enabling statute expressly requires it to hold a hearing, the agency may rely on its rulemaking authority to determine issues that do not require case-by-case consideration. See *FPC v. Texaco Inc.*, 377 U.S. 33, 41–44 (1964); *United States v. Storer Broadcasting Co.*, 351 U.S. 192, 205 (1956). A contrary holding would require the agency continually to relitigate issues that may be established fairly and efficiently in a single rulemaking proceeding.

The Secretary's decision to rely on medical-vocational guidelines is consistent with *Texaco* and *Storer*. As noted above, in determining whether a claimant can perform less strenuous work, the Secretary must make two determinations. She must assess each claimant's individual abilities and then determine whether jobs exist that a person having the claimant's qualifications could perform. The first inquiry involves a determination of historic facts, and the regulations properly require the Secretary to make these findings on the basis of evidence adduced at a hearing. We note that the regulations afford claimants ample opportunity both to present evidence relating to their own abilities and to offer evidence that the guidelines do not apply to them.[11] The second inquiry

---

11. Both *FPC v. Texaco Inc.*, 377 U.S. 33, 40 (1964), and *United States v. Storer*   *Broadcasting Co.*, 351 U.S. 192, 205 (1956), were careful to note that the statutory

requires the Secretary to determine an issue that is not unique to each claimant—the types and numbers of jobs that exist in the national economy. This type of general factual issue may be resolved as fairly through rulemaking as by introducing the testimony of vocational experts at each disability hearing. See *American Airlines, Inc. v. CAB*, 359 F.2d 624, 633 (1966) (en banc).

As the Secretary has argued, the use of published guidelines brings with it a uniformity that previously had been perceived as lacking. To require the Secretary to relitigate the existence of jobs in the national economy at each hearing would hinder needlessly an already overburdened agency. We conclude that the Secretary's use of medical-vocational guidelines does not conflict with the statute, nor can we say on the record before us that they are arbitrary and capricious.

We now consider Campbell's argument that the Court of Appeals properly required the Secretary to specify alternative available jobs. [That holding] appears to be based on a principle of administrative law—that when an agency takes official or administrative notice of facts, a litigant must be given an adequate opportunity to respond. See 5 U.S.C. § 556(e).

This principle is inapplicable, however, when the agency has promulgated valid regulations. Its purpose is to provide a procedural safeguard: to ensure the accuracy of the facts of which an agency takes notice. But when the accuracy of those facts already has been tested fairly during rulemaking, the rulemaking proceeding itself provides sufficient procedural protection.

. . . Accordingly, the judgment of the Court of Appeals is reversed.

[BRENNAN and MARSHALL, JJ., wrote separately on other issues.]

Notes and Questions

1. *Foreclosure of hearing rights through rulemaking.* The Court holds in *Campbell* that an agency can use rulemaking to resolve an issue and thereby displace an individual's statutory right to an evidentiary hearing on that issue. In this regard, the effect of a rule differs from the effect of administrative or official notice, which is also mentioned in *Campbell*. When an agency uses official notice (a device similar to judicial notice), it can streamline its own burden of proof, but the opposing party has the right to offer a rebuttal. *See* § 4.2.2. A valid rule, on the other hand, is conclusive.

The Court justifies this foreclosure of hearing rights by saying, in part, that the rulemaking proceeding itself offered sufficient procedural protection. Does that make sense? How likely is it that Campbell would have participated in that proceeding?

scheme at issue allowed an individual applicant to show that the rule promulgated should not be applied to him. The regulations here provide a claimant with equal or greater protection since they state that an Administrative Law Judge will not apply the rules contained in the guidelines when they fail to describe a claimant's particular limitations. See n. 5, *supra*.

2. *Issues suitable for rulemaking.* The Court in *Campbell* says that the Secretary may use rulemaking to resolve "certain classes of issues"—ones "that do not require case-by-case determination." In the case of the medical-vocational guidelines (which were also commonly known as the "grid regulations"), why were the issues suitable for rulemaking?

Campbell suggests that one factor justifying the use of rulemaking was that the question of what jobs were available in the national economy for various categories of workers was "not unique to each claimant." Claimants like Ms. Campbell were not deprived of any right to present evidence "relating to their own abilities." However, in a followup case, *Bowen v. Yuckert,* 482 U.S. 137 (1987), the Court upheld another section of the grid regulations that made determinations that pertained directly to characteristics of the individual applicant. This "severity" rule provided that if an impairment were found to be "not severe," meaning that it did "not significantly limit [the applicant's] physical or mental ability to do basic work activities," the applicant's claim for benefits would automatically be dismissed. Three Justices dissented, believing that this bright-line rule was invalid because the language of § 423(d)(2)(A) of the Social Security Act, quoted in *Campbell,* required the Secretary to "consider" the applicant's "age, education, and work experience" in *every* case.

The Secretary's winning streak ended in *Sullivan v. Zebley,* 493 U.S. 521 (1990). There the Court struck down a third rule, under which a child would be deemed eligible for benefits only if he or she had one of 182 medical conditions listed in the rule. The statute provided for benefits to all children suffering from impairments of "comparable severity" to those which would entitle an adult to benefits, and the Court believed that the Secretary's rule would inevitably deny benefits to some children who met that statutory standard. Taken together, do these cases give any meaning to the concept of issues "that do not require case-by-case determination"?

3. *Presumptions. Campbell* is typical of a large number of cases in which Congress has both conferred rulemaking power on an agency and conferred a right to individualized consideration or an evidentiary hearing on private persons. In any given situation, one of these statutes must supersede the other. Recently, the Court has endorsed a presumption that the rulemaking provision will prevail. In *American Hospital Ass'n v. NLRB,* 499 U.S. 606 (1991), the Court heard a challenge to the first substantive rule issued by the NLRB since 1935. The rule defined an employee unit appropriate for collective bargaining in acute care hospitals. It was challenged by the American Hospital Association on the ground that "the National Labor Relations Act required the Board to make a separate bargaining unit determination 'in each case' and therefore prohibits the Board from using general rules to define bargaining units." In rejecting this challenge to the rule, the Court cited *Campbell,* as well as the *Storer* and *Texaco* cases mentioned therein. It said that those cases "confirm that, even if a statutory scheme requires individualized determinations, the decisionmaker has the authority to rely on rulemaking to resolve certain issues of general applicability *unless Congress clearly expresses an intent to withhold that authority.*" *Id.* at 612 (emphasis added). A similar presumption applies to the related question of whether a given statute should be construed as empowering an agency to issue rules at all. *See* § 5.1 N.2.

4. *Safety valves.* In both the *Storer* and *Texaco* cases, the Court pointed out that the regulations at issue there permitted affected persons to seek a waiver of the rules if they could show adequate reasons to justify one. These decisions have been read to imply that a waiver or "safety valve" provision is important, or perhaps critical, to the validity of rules that foreclose hearing rights. Notice that in footnote 11 of *Campbell* the Court observes that, although the grid regulations do not allow an applicant for disability benefits to request a waiver, they provide "equal or greater protection" because an ALJ is not supposed to apply them "when they fail to describe a claimant's particular limitations." Is the latter safeguard an adequate substitute for a waiver opportunity?

In *FCC v. WNCN Listeners Guild,* 450 U.S. 582 (1981), the Court upheld the Commission's rule that radio stations' changes in format would *never* be considered during license renewal proceedings. The FCC had said that decisions about format should be "regulated" exclusively by the market. The dissenting Justices argued that the rule was invalid, in part because it did not allow for exceptional treatment of unusual cases (such as where a specialized listening audience would otherwise lose access to a distinctive format such as classical music). The majority disagreed and said that its prior cases "did not hold that the Commission may never adopt a rule that lacks a waiver provision." *Id.* at 601 n.44.

Of course, even if an agency has not said in advance that it will consider waiver requests, it may simply not bother to enforce a rule in special circumstances. However, an explicit and structured provision in a rule inviting affected persons to request waivers is better calculated to ensure a reasoned decision and equal treatment to potential waiver applicants. Yet such provisions can trigger a flood of requests for special treatment; the benefits of using rules instead of case-by-case adjudication can be dissipated.

Should rules affecting across-the-board conduct always contain a provision allowing regulated persons to request a waiver? We return to this issue in § 6.4.

5. *Summary judgment.* A related situation in which an agency can limit the effective reach of a right to be heard involves "administrative summary judgment." An agency can use this device to deny a hearing, otherwise required by statute and the APA, when there are no disputed issues of material fact. This is like a summary judgment in civil litigation. *See* Fed.Rul.Civ.Proc. 56.

The Supreme Court upheld administrative summary judgment in *Weinberger v. Hynson, Westcott & Dunning, Inc.,* 412 U.S. 609 (1973), a case arising out of a massive examination of thousands of existing drugs by the FDA to ascertain whether they were effective for their claimed uses. This process (triggered by a 1962 statute) began with an examination by panels set up by the National Academy of Sciences (NAS). The statute required FDA to withdraw the licenses for such drugs unless their effectiveness was established by "adequate and well-controlled investigations" and it provided for a hearing in case of withdrawal.

FDA regulations spelled out very strict standards for what studies would be acceptable in proving the effectiveness of drugs. For example, anecdotal evidence by physicians was barred. The regulations also provided that a request for hearing must include the studies on which the applicant relied. The request for a hearing would be dismissed when it clearly appeared from the application that there was no "genuine and substantial issue of fact." This would occur if the manufacturer could not introduce any evidence of scientific studies as required by the regulations.

The Supreme Court upheld these regulations. NAS panels had evaluated 16,500 claims made on behalf of 4000 drugs. Seventy percent of these claims were found not to be supported by substantial evidence of effectiveness. The Court said:

> We cannot impute to Congress, nor does due process demand, a hearing when it appears conclusively from the applicant's 'pleadings' that the application cannot succeed ... If FDA were required automatically to hold a hearing for each product whose efficacy was questioned ... even though many hearings would be an exercise in futility, we have no doubt that it could not fulfill its statutory mandate to remove from the market all those drugs which do not meet the effectiveness requirements of the Act.

The Court emphasized, however, that the summary judgment procedure was reserved for situations in which it was clear that no material fact issues were presented. Indeed, the Court went on to hold that summary judgment should not have been granted in the *Hynson* proceeding itself, since there were genuine issues of fact presented about the effectiveness of Lutrexin, the drug in question. Moreover, the Court's approval of summary judgment related to those portions of the regulations that were "precise;" the Court warned that, where the regulations called for "the exercise of discretion or subjective judgment [by the FDA], ... it might not be proper to deny a hearing." 421 U.S. at 621 n.17.

Hynson was of great practical importance to the FDA. Had the agency been forced to provide a full-fledged adjudicatory hearing before withdrawing any drug license, removal of all the ineffective drugs from the market might have taken many decades. For example, Lutrexin was not ultimately withdrawn from the market until 1976—fourteen years after enactment of the 1962 amendments.

The 1981 MSAPA contains the functional equivalent of a summary judgment procedure: If an agency has adopted an appropriate implementing rule, it can use the *conference adjudicative hearing* model, a streamlined version of the formal adjudicative hearing, to resolve a matter as to which there is no disputed issue of material fact. § 4–401(1). If, in a case initiated under that model, a party shows the presiding officer that material facts are in dispute after all, the proceeding can be "converted" to a formal adjudicative hearing. § 4–403.

6. *Showing a material fact issue.* Even in the absence of a formal summary judgment procedure, a court might allow an agency to refrain from holding a hearing if the party who wants the hearing cannot show what would be accomplished there. "Common sense suggests the futility of hearings where there is no factual dispute of substance." *Veg-Mix, Inc. v. United States Department of Agriculture,* 832 F.2d 601, 607 (D.C.Cir.1987). Remember that in footnote 12 of *West Chicago,* the court noted the D.C. Circuit's case law to this effect but did not decide whether to follow it.

In *Connecticut Bankers Ass'n v. Board of Governors,* 627 F.2d 245, 251 (D.C.Cir.1980), the D.C. Circuit offered some guidance as to the threshold showing that it expects a party requesting an evidentiary hearing to make:

> Where a contest exists with respect to a material fact, the Board must conduct a full evidentiary hearing on that issue. Moreover, the burden of making the requisite showing to trigger the hearing requirement is not great.... "A petitioner need not make detailed factual allegations in order to meet the requirement that he raise 'issues of material fact.'" Nonetheless, a [party] does not become entitled to an evidentiary hearing merely on request, or on a bald or conclusory allegation that such a dispute exists. The [party] must make a minimal showing that material facts are in dispute, thereby demonstrating that "an 'inquiry in depth' is appropriate."

> ... Evidentiary hearings consume time, energy, and resources of the Board and parties alike, apart from the possibility of undue intrusion on and harassment of [opposing parties]. The Board is not to be burdened with a hearing requirement where a [person seeking it] has not given reason to believe a hearing would be worthwhile.

As an example, in *Air Line Pilots Ass'n v. Department of Transportation,* 791 F.2d 172, 179 (D.C.Cir.1986), the Civil Aeronautics Board approved a holding company's request to take over an airline. The pilots' union asked that this approval be conditioned on the inclusion of labor protective provisions in the merger agreement. Such conditions had been routinely incorporated into similar agreements in the past, but the Board used this case to announce a new policy: labor protective provisions would be required only if necessary to prevent nationwide labor strife. The union submitted "a single affidavit of one of its members suggesting that Board approval of [this] acquisition could cause other carriers to undertake similar transactions and thereby spark widespread labor unrest in the industry." The Board denied the union's request and refused to hold a hearing on this issue, deeming the union's claims "speculative and unsubstantiated." The court held that the Board had reasonably found an absence of a material factual dispute, so no hearing was required.

Do cases like *Connecticut Bankers* and *Air Line Pilots* create too much temptation for agencies to dismiss potentially legitimate claims without even scheduling a hearing? Should the Board at least have held a hearing to allow the union to argue for retaining the earlier, pro-labor policy?

7. *Problem.* Madison has adopted the 1981 MSAPA. Three months ago, Madison's Medical Board adopted a rule providing that no graduate of a foreign medical school (except one located in the United Kingdom or Canada) can be licensed to practice medicine in Madison. Prior to adopting this rule, the Board had always decided applications for licenses by foreign medical school graduates on a case-by-case basis.

Our client Kate attended three years of medical school at Madison University. The fourth year of medical school is all clinical; she spent the year at a hospital in Madison. However, as the result of an unfortunate personal encounter with an administrator at Madison University Medical School, she transferred to Caribbean University Medical School in the Dominican Republic for the fourth and last year of medical school. She took no courses at Caribbean; it merely awarded her a diploma based on her three years of course work at Madison University and her clinical work at the Madison hospital.

The Board refuses to grant Kate a license or even hold a hearing, stating that there are no exceptions to its rule. What do you suggest we do now?

§ 3.3 THE CONFLICT BETWEEN IN-STITUTIONAL AND JUDICIAL-IZED DECISION–MAKING

Students of the administrative process have identified two conflicting models of adjudicative decision-making. Oversimplified statements of the two models follow:

The *judicial* model suggests that an adjudicative decision by an agency is like a decision by a judge. Therefore, the administrative process should resemble judicial process as closely as possible. The administrative judge should personally listen to the evidence and argument, have no preconceptions about the case, receive no information about the case except through on-the-record submissions, and be completely independent of investigators and prosecutors. Adherents of the judicial model argue that *fairness* and *acceptability* to private litigants should be primary goals of the agency adjudication process.

The *institutional* model views an agency as if it were a single unit with the mission of implementing a specific regulatory scheme. The entire staff should be considered as members of a decisionmaking team and all should be available for off-the-record consultation. This theory holds that adjudication is a policymaking technique, along with rulemaking, advice-giving, and publicity. Each adjudicated case should promote the regulatory scheme and further agency policy. Adherents of the institutional model stress *accuracy* and *efficiency* as the dominant values to be pursued. As one commentator noted:

> The "institutional method" ... involves "the cooperative effort of a number of officers with the agency head," bringing to bear the "cumulative efforts of specialized officers" and producing "a series of automatic internal checks" by each officer upon the data and ideas the others contribute ... The safeguards to persons who have interests at stake ... lie in the professional training and responsibility of the officers involved, in cross-checking among them, and in the responsibility of the agency heads who coordinate the entire operation, decide finally upon the result, and must answer for all that transpires.
>
> Outside of government, the preponderance of human affairs calling for more than individual action is conducted by a consultative method, with or without professional participation. Business decisions are reached, human ailments are diagnosed, and club and church problems are settled in this manner.... In government too, foreign policy, military affairs, and the management of public enter-

prises and property go forward in the same way. Often vital interests of people are at stake in what transpires ... yet it is rarely suggested that the "hearing" of interested persons be attempted in connection with such matters, or, if it is, that more than an interview be accorded. Arguably, the same considerations as account for the acceptance of "institutional" methods in these contexts should point to their possible use in licensing, rate fixing, and kindred operations—for which, indeed, they were thought to suffice until relatively recently.

Ralph F. Fuchs, "The Hearing Officer Problem—Symptom and Symbol," 40 Cornell L.Q. 281, 289–90 (1955). © 1955 by Cornell University. All rights reserved.

The administrative process strikes many compromises between these two polar models, sacrificing the virtues of one of them to secure the virtues of the other. This sub-chapter and the next one address a number of problems on the borderline between judicial and institutional decisionmaking: personal responsibility of decision-makers, separation of functions, ex parte contacts, bias, and independence of the administrative law judge. As you read this material, try to analyze it as a set of tradeoffs between judicial and institutional methods of adjudication.

§ 3.3.1 PERSONAL RESPONSIBILITY OF DECISIONMAKERS

In a judicial model, the judge hears all of the evidence and argument and makes a decision based on that input. In an institutional model, one or more persons might hear the evidence and argument but someone else might make the decision. Needless to say, this makes lawyers uneasy.

During the 1930's and 1940's, in the first of four *Morgan* cases, the Supreme Court indicated a strong preference for the judicial model. The *Morgan* cases arose out of a ratemaking proceeding begun by the Secretary of Agriculture in 1930. The Secretary fixed the maximum rates of commission which all of the many livestock agents working in a single stockyard in Kansas City could charge.

The applicable statute required a "full hearing." The ratemaking case could be considered rulemaking, rather than adjudication, since there were many regulated parties. However, because of the "full hearing" statute, it became formal rulemaking. Probably, due process did not apply since there were many regulated parties, all affected in the same way. Yet in the *Morgan* cases, the Court seems to speak in constitutional terms.

MORGAN v. UNITED STATES
298 U.S. 468 (1936).

[The first *Morgan* case arose on a motion to dismiss. Plaintiff alleged that a hearing examiner took evidence but did not file a report. The Acting Secretary of Agriculture heard oral argument. The parties filed briefs. The Secretary of Agriculture made the final decision. The plaintiffs asserted that the Secretary had not heard or read any of the evidence or argument or read the briefs. Instead, he rubber-stamped a decision made by someone else. Thus, the Court assumed that the Agriculture Department had used a purely institutional approach to making the rates.

The Court noted that responsibility for making the final decision might have been delegated to the Acting Secretary who heard the argument, but it had not been. The Secretary, who had not heard the case, took responsibility for the final decision.]

Hughes, C. J.:

There must be a full hearing. There must be evidence adequate to support pertinent and necessary findings of fact. Nothing can be treated as evidence which is not introduced as such. . . .

Facts and circumstances which ought to be considered must not be excluded. Facts and circumstances must not be considered which should not legally influence the conclusion. Findings based on the evidence must embrace the basic facts which are needed to sustain the order. . . .

A proceeding of this sort, requiring the taking and weighing of evidence, determinations of fact based upon the consideration of the evidence, and the making of an order supported by such findings, has a quality resembling that of a judicial proceeding. Hence it is frequently described as a proceeding of a quasi-judicial character. The requirement of a "full hearing" has obvious reference to the tradition of judicial proceedings in which evidence is received and weighed by the trier of the facts. The "hearing" is designed to afford the safeguard that the one who decides shall be bound in good conscience to consider the evidence, to be guided by that alone, and to reach his conclusion uninfluenced by extraneous considerations which in other fields might have play in determining purely executive action. The "hearing" is the hearing of evidence and argument. If the one who determines the facts which underlie the order has not considered evidence or argument, it is manifest that the hearing has not been given.

There is thus no basis for the contention that the authority conferred by Section 310 of the Packers and Stockyards Act is given to the Department of Agriculture, as a department in the administrative sense, so that one official may examine evidence, and another official who has not considered the evidence may make the findings and order. In such a view, it would be possible, for example, for one official to hear the evidence and argument and arrive at certain conclusions of fact, and another official who had not heard or considered either evidence or argument to overrule those conclusions and for reasons of policy to announce entirely different ones. It is no answer to say that the question for the court is whether the evidence supports the findings and the findings support the order. For the weight ascribed by the law to the findings—their conclusiveness when made within the sphere of the authority conferred—rests upon the assumption that the officer who makes the findings has addressed himself to the evidence and upon that evidence has conscientiously reached the conclusions which he deems it to justify. That duty cannot be performed by one who has not considered evidence or argument. It is not an impersonal obligation. It is a duty akin to that of a judge. The one who decides must hear.

This necessary rule does not preclude practicable administrative procedure in obtaining the aid of assistants in the department. Assistants may prosecute inquiries. Evidence may be taken by an examiner. Evidence thus taken may be sifted and analyzed by competent subordinates. Argument may be oral or written. The requirements are not technical. But there must be a hearing in a substantial sense. And to give the substance of a hearing, which is for the purpose of making determinations upon evidence, the officer who makes the determinations must consider and appraise the evidence which justifies them. That duty undoubtedly may be an onerous one, but the performance of it in a substantial manner is inseparable from the exercise of the important authority conferred....

Notes and Questions

1. *"The one who decides must hear."* The first *Morgan* case strikes a powerful blow for the *judicial*, rather than the *institutional* method. Like a judge, an administrator who takes the responsibility for decision must personally have heard the case.

The broadest language of the decision cannot be taken literally. The Secretary was not required to actually "hear" the case or even read all of the evidence. The last paragraph makes clear that an examiner may take the evidence and the evidence "can be sifted and analyzed by competent subordinates." However, the person making the decision "must consider and appraise the evidence" which justifies it. Why does the Court require the official taking final responsibility for an adjudicative decision to "consider and appraise the evidence"?

2. *Getting around Morgan I.* Although the *Morgan I* principle seems reasonable, it is unrealistic if it is read broadly. The Secretary of Agriculture is not like a judge. He has a vast number of administrative and regulatory duties, concerning every aspect of American agriculture, many of them extremely important to the public. He sits as a member of the President's cabinet and must constantly deal with Congress. If he is required to familiarize himself with the voluminous and technical records in all of the ratemaking cases before him, he would have time for little else. Yet this duty is far less important than his other responsibilities. The same thing is true of most federal and many state and local agencies.

In light of that reality, how can an agency comply with *Morgan I?* Consider these options:

i. As suggested by Hughes, an agency head can delegate the power to make final decisions to someone else. In fact, the Department of Agriculture has now done exactly that; a "judicial officer" makes the final decision in all cases in which a trial-type hearing is required. However, there are two problems:

First, such delegation is not always legally permissible. Second, adjudication is sometimes a vehicle for making new law and policy. Realistically, this function cannot be carried out by staff below the level of the agency head or heads.

ii.   The person who conducts the hearing and hears the evidence could decide the case. That decision would become final unless the agency head decides to consider an appeal. The agency head need not examine the record in order to decline to hear an appeal and thus to adopt the hearing officer's decision. Under this approach, the agency head would have to personally consider appeals in only a few significant, precedent-making situations.

iii.   The decision of the hearing officer could be subject to appeal to an intermediate review board within the agency. The agency head would have discretion to consider appeals from the intermediate review board.

iv.   The agency head might consider only a highly condensed summary of the evidence and arguments in a case that is prepared by law clerks or other employees. The head would then decide the case solely on the basis of information contained in that summary.

Notice how each of these approaches departs from a pure judicial model and approaches an institutional model. For a survey and comparison of the different approaches to the problem of appeals within the agency, see Russell L. Weaver, "Appellate Review in Executive Departments and Agencies," 48 Admin.L.Rev. 251 (1996).

3.   *Intermediate reports.* Suppose that a case is heard by a hearing officer but that the agency head makes the final decision. Two issues arise: i) must the hearing officer prepare a recommended decision? ii) if there is a recommended decision, must it be disclosed so that litigants can object to it?

Statutes generally require the hearing officer to prepare a report in order to focus the issues for the benefit of both the parties and the ultimate decisionmaker and require that it be made available to the parties and that they be given an opportunity to object to it before a final decision. *See* § 557(b), (c) of the Federal Act and 1981 MSAPA § 4–215(c), (h).

What happens, however, if no statutes are applicable? The second *Morgan* case concerns the failure of the hearing examiner to prepare a recommended decision. The examiner simply submitted the lengthy record to the Secretary of Agriculture. In the absence of any pleadings or recommendations by the examiner, the issues remained unfocussed and the industry was unable to brief or argue them effectively. This problem was magnified because advocates within the Department prepared recommended findings and discussed them with the Secretary. Such advocacy raises an issue of separation of functions, which is discussed in § 3.3.2.

The Court implied that due process (or at least a statutory "full hearing") requires the preparation of an intermediate report: "Those who are brought into contest with the Government in a quasi-judicial proceeding aimed at the control of their activities are entitled to be fairly advised of what the Government proposes and to be heard upon its proposals before it issues its final command." *Morgan v. United States*, 304 U.S. 1, 18–19. A later case made clear that due process does not require an intermediate report in the absence of a showing of substantial prejudice from the failure to prepare one. *See NLRB v. Mackay Radio & Telegraph Co.,* 304 U.S. 333, 350–51 (1938).

Should due process always require preparation of an intermediate report, at least where questions of credibility must be resolved? *See Crow v. Industrial Comm'n,* 140 P.2d 321, 326 (Utah 1943) (Wolfe, C.J. concurring): "What is required to satisfy the demands of due process, that is, of a full or fair hearing, is that he who observes the witness and listens to the evidence must transmit his observations or conclusions to those others who ... are to decide ..."

4. *The right to object to an intermediate report.* If the hearing examiner prepares a recommended decision, do the parties have a right to see and object to it in the absence of a statutory requirement? *Mazza v. Cavicchia,* 105 A.2d 545 (N.J.1954) involved the revocation of a liquor license on the ground that the licensee had permitted "lewd and immoral activity on the premises." A hearing officer (called a "hearer") submitted proposed findings and recommendations to the Alcoholic Beverages Director, but the licensee was not permitted to see the report. The New Jersey Supreme Court held that due process was violated:

> The hearer may have drawn some erroneous conclusions in his report, or he may even have made some factual blunders. Such mistakes are not uncommon in both judicial and administrative proceedings; indeed, the whole process of judicial review in both fields is designed to guard against them. But if a party has no knowledge of the secret report or access to it, how is he to protect himself? .... That is why it is a fundamental principle of all adjudication, judicial and administrative alike, that the mind of the decider should not be swayed by materials which are not communicated to both parties and which they are not given an opportunity to controvert. In the instant case the hearer can be characterized as a "witness" giving his evidence to the judge behind the back of the appellant, who has no way of knowing what has been reported to the judge.... Such conduct not only constitutes a violation of the principle of the exclusiveness of the record in deciding controversies, but it shocks one's sense of fair play on which our fundamental concepts of procedure are based....

105 A.2d at 555. Thus *Mazza* comes down strongly on the side of the judicial, rather than the institutional method of decision. And all would agree that it is a good idea to allow the parties to see the intermediate report. But is this required by due process?

Is the hearer really a witness "giving his evidence to the judge behind the back of the appellant"? Did the agency procedure in *Mazza* violate the principle that the decision must be based exclusively on the record? If so, is a party constitutionally entitled to see and object to a memo from a law clerk to a judge that summarizes the record and the applicable law and makes recommendations? Compare the last paragraph of *Morgan I,* which allows competent subordinates to sift and analyze the evidence.

5. *Morgan I in practice.* Because of the practical difficulties that would arise from taking *Morgan I* too seriously, most cases brush aside claims that the decision-maker was insufficiently familiar with the record. An occasional case does find a violation. For example, the Kansas Court of Appeals said:

Because an administrative decision must be based on evidence and not conjecture, on those occasions when the deciding authority chooses not to adopt the findings and recommendations of its hearing officer, it must examine the record independently. In the absence of evidence to the contrary, it will be presumed that the deciding officials have so considered the record.... Here, however, it appears that the three board members who considered the matter were not conversant with the record to the extent required of an informed decision. All three indicated in answers to interrogatories that they had read only "portions" of the transcripts, and only one had read "some" of the exhibits. The duty of the deciding officer to consider and appraise the evidence may on occasion be an onerous one, but its performance in a substantial manner is inseparable from the exercise of the authority conferred.

Matter of University of Kansas Faculty, 581 P.2d 817, 823 (Kan.App.1978). How much of a record or of the briefs must a decisionmaker read to understand a case sufficiently to decide it on the merits?

6. *Proving a violation of Morgan I.* In the *Kansas Faculty* case, the court noted the presumption that deciding officials have complied with legal requirements, such as familiarizing themselves with the record. The presumption of regularity is rebuttable, but how can it be rebutted? In the *Kansas Faculty* case, the board members responded to interrogatories about their decision-making process.

However, it is usually not possible to subject decision-makers (or their staff or law clerks) to discovery or trial about how they made a decision. In fact, such a trial occurred at one point in the *Morgan* saga. In the fourth *Morgan* case, the Court stated:

[T]he district court authorized the market agencies to take the deposition of the Secretary. The Secretary ... was questioned at length regarding the process by which he reached the conclusions of his order, including the manner and extent of his study of the record and his consultation with subordinates ... [T]he short of the business is that the Secretary should never have been subjected to this examination. The proceeding before the Secretary "has a quality resembling that of a judicial proceeding" [citing *Morgan I*]. Such an examination of a judge would be destructive of judicial responsibility. Just as a judge cannot be subjected to such a scrutiny ... so the integrity of the administrative process must be equally respected ... It will bear repeating that although the administrative process has had a different development and pursues somewhat different ways from those of courts, they are to be deemed collaborative instrumentalities of justice and the appropriate independence of each should be respected by the other.

United States v. Morgan, 313 U.S. 409 (1941).

The admonition of *Morgan IV* has generally been respected by both state and federal courts. According to the prevailing test, inquiry into mental processes must be avoided absent "a strong showing of bad faith or improper behavior." *Citizens to Preserve Overton Park, Inc. v. Volpe,* 401 U.S. 402, 420 (1971). Thus in a case in which petitioners sought to examine the transcript of a closed meeting, the D. C. Circuit wrote:

Apparently unable to point to any independent evidence of improper conduct by the [Nuclear Regulatory] Commission, petitioners simply assert that the transcripts alone are sufficient to establish the requisite bad faith and improper conduct on the part of the Commission. We reject this approach. Petitioners must make the requisite showing *before* we will look at the transcripts. We will not examine the transcripts to determine if we may examine the transcripts.

There may be cases where a court is warranted in examining the deliberative proceedings of the agency. But such cases must be the rare exception if agencies are to engage in uninhibited and frank discussions during their deliberations. Were courts regularly to review the transcripts of agency deliberative proceedings, the discussions would be conducted with judicial scrutiny in mind. Such agency proceedings would then be useless both to the agency and to the courts. We think the analogy to the deliberative processes of a court is an apt one. Without the assurance of secrecy, the court could not fully perform its function.

San Luis Obispo Mothers for Peace v. NRC, 789 F.2d 26, 44–45 (D.C. Cir.1986). As a result, counsel can only rarely raise a plausible *Morgan I* contention. The courts generally rely on the presumption of regularity and take every opportunity to explain how such consideration might have occurred, despite evidence to the contrary.

The Supreme Court approved an exception to *Morgan IV* in *Citizens to Preserve Overton Park*, *supra*, an important case discussed in § 9.4. In *Overton Park,* the Secretary of Transportation approved a highway project in apparent violation of a statute precluding the building of roads through parks. He made no findings to explain his decision. Over a strong dissent, the Court approved a remand to the federal district court to obtain an explanation for the Secretary's decision. Note that the Court in *Overton Park* was concerned with *substantive* review—whether the Secretary's decision was rational—not with review of *procedural* issues such as whether the Secretary was sufficiently familiar with the record. Even as to review for rationality, it is unlikely that this aspect of the *Overton Park* decision will be followed.

First, *Overton Park* applies only if an agency fails to explain the decision. If the agency does furnish some explanation, the court should review the case based on that explanation. If the explanation is unsatisfactory, the court should remand to the agency for a new one. *Camp v. Pitts,* 411 U.S. 138 (1973).

Second, if an agency fails to explain its action, most cases indicate that the court should remand the case to the agency to provide an explanation rather than to conduct a trial to find out how the decision was made. *Florida Power & Light Co. v. Lorion*, 470 U.S. 729, 744 (1985): "If the court simply cannot evaluate the challenged action on the basis of the record before it, the proper course, except in rare circumstances, is to remand to the agency for additional investigation or explanation."

7. *The exclusive record for decision.* In *Morgan I*, Hughes stated: "[A hearing] is designed to afford the safeguard that the one who decides shall be

bound in good conscience to consider the evidence, to be guided by that alone . . ."

A due process and APA fundamental is that the record made at a hearing is the exclusive basis for decision. The decisionmaker cannot rely on factual information which is not in the record. *See* APA § 556(e); 1981 MSAPA § 4–221(b), (c). *See*, however, § 4.2.3, on the question of when the decisionmaker can take official notice of information that is not in the record.

8. *Oral argument.* The 1946 MSAPA required agency members personally to consider the whole record. Sec. 11 of the 1961 MSAPA omitted this provision but required agency heads to allow a party to examine a proposed decision and to present briefs *and oral argument* to the officials who made the final decision (unless a majority of them had heard the case or read the record). Under the 1981 MSAPA, however, parties must have an opportunity to file briefs upon an appeal to the agency heads but oral argument and preparation of a transcript are optional. § 4–216(e), (f). *See also* Federal APA § 557(b), (c).

If agency heads must listen to oral argument, they will become familiar with the issues in the case, thus helping to insure compliance with *Morgan I.* Should 1981 MSAPA have required agency heads to hear oral argument?

9. *Problem.* The Mountain School District wished to discharge Rex, a tenured junior high school teacher, for drunkenness. No APA is applicable. Under the district's usual procedures, a review committee (consisting of educators) conducted a three-hour hearing from noon to 3 PM. At the hearing, Rex denied that his drinking problem affected his teaching; he claimed he was always sober at school. The hearing was tape recorded.

At 6 PM the same day, the review committee issued a brief written decision, recommending that the School Board not discharge Ralph. The decision stated that Rex had a drinking problem but that it had not affected his teaching. The decision was not furnished to Rex.

Two hours later, at 8 PM, the Mountain School Board decided to fire Rex, finding that he was drunk or hung over at school on many occasions. It provided no opportunity for oral argument or the filing of briefs. The meeting of the Board was over by 9 PM. Should this decision be reversed? *See Bates v. Sponberg,* 547 F.2d 325 (6th Cir.1976).

§ 3.3.2 SEPARATION OF FUNCTIONS AND INTERNAL AGEN-CY COMMUNICATIONS

Many people have criticized the administrative process because a single agency makes the rules, investigates violations, prosecutes cases, and then decides those very cases. It seems that the agency acts as a legislator, investigator, prosecutor, judge and jury.

Nevertheless, the combination within a single body of all these functions is a hallmark of the administrative process and constitutional challenges to that combination have been unsuccessful. The functions are combined primarily for reasons of efficiency and effectiveness. Of course, these functions could be split up between different bodies. Then a different set of problems arises. *See* §§ 3.4.3 and 3.4.4.

When a single agency has combined functions, the issue shifts to whether a *single individual* within the agency can play an adversary role in the case (as investigator, prosecutor, or advocate), then serve an adjudicatory role (as administrative judge, agency head, or adviser to either of them) in the same case. For example, suppose that A both investigates a case and then serves as the administrative judge in the same case. Even though A tries to judge the case fairly, A may consciously or unconsciously rely on evidence that is not introduced at the hearing or may be predisposed to decide in favor of her own prior efforts.

To meet objections of this kind, most agencies are structured to achieve an internal separation of functions. Persons engaged in *adversary* conduct on the agency's behalf cannot serve as an administrative decisionmaker or furnish off-the-record advice to the decisionmakers or supervise persons engaged in decisionmaking. This chapter discusses provisions in state and federal APAs that require internal separation of functions.

As background to this material, try to imagine purely judicial and institutional models of separation of functions. The criminal law completely separates its functions: it is unthinkable that a prosecutor could advise a judge, off-the-record, about how to decide the case. Judge and prosecutor are not part of the same team. At the opposite extreme, the president of a corporation, deciding whether to produce a new product, is perfectly free to gather evidence, make the case for one side, and to seek confidential advice from anybody in the firm—no holds barred. That is a pure institutional model.

WALKER v. CITY OF BERKELEY
951 F.2d 182 (9th Cir.1991).

Goodwin, J.:

[Walker had been terminated from her job with the City. She believed that this decision was unjustified, and also that the assistant city manager who had conducted her pretermination hearing had been biased against her. She] appealed her discharge to the City's Personnel Board. The Personnel Board conducted evidentiary hearings and found that Walker had been discharged without cause. This decision was relayed to the City Manager, who was responsible for the final administrative decision on Walker's termination.

Meanwhile, Walker filed this action in the district court [alleging that she had been deprived of procedural due process at the pretermination hearing], and a staff attorney from the City Attorney's office was assigned to defend the City. The staff attorney filed a motion in federal court to dismiss this action while, at the same time, she was preparing her recommendation for the City Manager on the Personnel Board's termination decision.

A few days after filing her motion in federal court, the staff attorney recommended to the city manager that the Personnel Board's decision be rejected and that Walker's termination be approved. Walker contends that the City denied her due process when it caused the same staff attorney to function both as the City's attorney in the federal court case and as the decisionmaker in Walker's post-termination hearing. We agree.

The special verdict form correctly asked the jury to decide whether the City Manager, the nominal decisionmaker, had made an independent decision on Walker's termination. The jury decided that he had not. This finding necessarily pointed to the staff attorney as the actual decision-maker. . . .

In *Withrow v. Larkin*, 421 U.S. 35 (1975), the Court said: "That the combination of investigative and adjudicative functions does not, without more, constitute a due process violation, does not, of course, preclude a court from determining from the special facts and circumstances present in the case before it that the risk of unfairness is intolerably high . . ."

Due process can permit the same administrative body to investigate and adjudicate a case. *Withrow* . . . . The *Withrow* Court noted, however, that in that case, different persons had performed the investigative and decisionmaking functions. . . . By contrast, in . . . the instant case, the fatal defect was in allowing the same person to serve both as decision-maker and as advocate for the party that benefited from the decision.

In the instant case, both of the cases that the staff attorney handled involved the same parties and the same underlying issue—Walker's challenge to her termination. The staff attorney had to know that her decision on the merits as an administrator could play a major role in the outcome of the pending federal suit, in which she was representing the City. The staff attorney was able to establish an administrative decision in the City's favor, which was then introduced as evidence in the federal wrongful termination trial. . . .

The City relies on *Vanelli v. Reynolds School District No. 7*, 667 F.2d 773 (9th Cir.1982), in which we held that a school board's partic-ipation in an initial termination decision did not render the board impermissibly biased when it conducted the subsequent termination hearing. *Vanelli* involved whether an administrative body could rehear its own initial decision, a process that we analogized to the situation that exists when a judge or administrator rehears his own decision after reversal and remand. Here, by contrast, the question raised is whether the same person can serve as both administrative decisionmaker and as advocate in a federal court proceeding involving the same parties and the same underlying issue. *Vanelli* is irrelevant to this question . . .

REVERSED AND REMANDED.

Notes and Questions

1. *Due process and combination of functions.* In *Withrow*, which is quoted in *Walker*, the Supreme Court held that due process was not violated because a state agency first investigated Dr. Larkin, then conducted an

adjudicatory hearing to determine whether his license should be revoked. The Court stated:

> That is not to say that there is nothing to the argument that those who have investigated should not then adjudicate. The issue is substantial, it is not new, and legislators and others concerned with the operations of administrative agencies have given much attention to whether and to what extent distinctive administrative functions should be performed by the same persons. No single answer has been reached. Indeed, the growth, variety, and complexity of the administrative processes have made any one solution highly unlikely. Within the Federal Government itself, Congress has addressed the issue in several different ways, providing for varying degrees of separation from complete separation of functions to virtually none at all. For the generality of agencies, Congress has been content with § 5 of the Administrative Procedure Act, 5 U.S.C. § 554(d), which provides that no employee engaged in investigating or prosecuting may also participate or advise in the adjudicating function, but which also expressly exempts from this prohibition "the agency or a member or members of the body comprising the agency."

> It is not surprising, therefore, to find that "[t]he case law, both federal and state, generally rejects the idea that the combination [of] judging [and] investigating functions is a denial of due process. . . . "

In light of *Withrow*, why did the court find that due process was violated in *Walker*? In *Walker*, the court assumed that the staff attorney was the City's decisionmaker. Would the case have come out differently if the Court had assumed that the City Manager made the final decision after receiving advice from the staff attorney?

Recall the very end of *Goldberg v. Kelly:* "And, of course, an impartial decision maker is essential. We agree with the District Court that prior involvement in some aspects of a case will not necessarily bar a welfare official from acting as a decision maker. He should not, however, have participated in making the determination under review." Is that language consistent with *Withrow*?

2. *Pennsylvania view.* With *Withrow*, compare *Lyness v. State Bd. of Medicine*, 605 A.2d 1204 (Pa.1992). In *Lyness*, 8 of the 11 members of the Medical Board met by emergency conference call, heard a presentation by the Board's prosecutor, and voted to allow the prosecutor to cite Lyness for sexually molesting patients. Later a hearing examiner heard the case and recommended suspension of Lyness' license. Three years later, the full Board affirmed the examiner's fact findings but changed to penalty to license revocation. The Board's vote was 6 in favor, 1 abstention (3 members were absent). Of the 7 members present, 3 (including the abstainer who presided at the hearing) had participated in the conference call.

The court held that the due process clause of the state constitution allowed it to grant greater procedural protection than *Withrow* granted under the federal constitution. Thus it held that due process prohibits agency heads from exercising the functions of both prosecution and decision. In the future, a wall of division must be erected within the agency so that the persons who make the ultimate adjudicatory decisions are not involved in the prosecution decision.

A dissenter argued that it makes sense to repose the decision to prosecute in the agency heads rather than in the agency prosecutors. Allowing the heads to make the decision to prosecute is a valuable protection against prosecutorial zeal. "The majority obviously finds the Board short of professional ability and personal integrity, a shortage they think best supplied by prosecutors."

A provision in the 1981 MSAPA is squarely contrary to *Lyness*. See § 4–214(c).

3. *Statutory solutions to the problem of combination of functions.* APA § 554(d) covers separation of functions. Look at the language which begins *after* § 554(d)(2): "An employee or agent engaged in the performance of investigative or prosecuting functions ..." and runs to the end of (C). Also concentrate on 1981 MSAPA § 4–214(a) and (c). *See generally* Michael Asimow, "When the Curtain Falls: Separation of Functions in the Federal Administrative Agencies," 81 Colum.L.Rev. 759, 761–79 (1981).

These provisions divide agency employees into three groups in each case:

· adversaries (that is, investigators and prosecutors)

· adjudicators (meaning both the ALJ who hears the case and the agency heads who make the final decision)

· everyone else.

APA § 554(d) and 1981 MSAPA § 4–214(a) prohibit staff members in the first group (adversaries) from serving as adjudicators or from advising the adjudicators off the record. But staff members in the third group ("everyone else") can furnish off-record advice to the adjudicators. This is explicit in 1981 MSAPA § 4–213(b). Note that a staff member could be an adversary in one case and serve as an adjudicator or furnish advice to an adjudicator in a different (but similar) case.

Why do these statutes allow non-adversary staff members to give off-record advice to agency adjudicators? After all, nobody outside the agency is permitted to make such contacts with agency adjudicators. See material on ex parte contact in § 3.3.4.

4. *Additional separation of functions provisions.* Note APA § 554(d)(1), providing that an ALJ may not "consult a person or party on a fact in issue, unless on notice and opportunity for all parties to participate ..." Interpreting this language, the Supreme Court said: "Nor may a hearing examiner consult any person or party, *including other agency officials*, concerning a fact at issue in the hearing, unless on notice and opportunity for all parties to participate." *Butz v. Economou*, 438 U.S. 478, 514 (1978) (emphasis added). Note the definitions of "person" and "party" in APA § 551(2) and (3). Do you agree that "party" includes the agency that is bringing the case and employs the ALJ?

Thus § 554(d)(1) disables the ALJ (but not other agency decisionmakers, such as intermediate review boards or agency heads) from receiving ex parte advice *on factual issues* from any agency staff member (whether or not they have been adversaries in the case). But it does not appear to prohibit the ALJ from receiving advice on *law or policy* from agency staff members. And as far as agency heads are concerned, staff advice on factual matters must relate to evaluation of the evidence in the record, not introduction of new factual material. Introducing new facts would violate the exclusive record principle. See 1981 MSAPA 4–215(d), last sentence.

Note also APA § 554(d)(2), providing that an ALJ may not be *supervised* by a person engaged in performing adversary functions for the agency. Thus ALJs must be part of a separate unit within an agency, supervised only by someone who does not engage in investigation, prosecution, or advocacy. This provision is designed to prevent "command influence," since an ALJ should not have to worry that a decision against the agency would jeopardize the ALJ's career.

5. *Exceptions to separation of functions.* Congress exempted initial licensing and ratemaking proceedings from separation of functions. § 554(d)(A), (B). Why? The 1981 MSAPA contains no comparable exceptions.

Congress also excepted "the agency" and "members of the body comprising the agency" from separation of functions. This looks strange at first: to whom would the APA apply if not to the agency? In this context, however, "agency" refers only to persons in whom power is formally vested—that is, agency *heads* such as cabinet secretaries and commissioners, as opposed to their subordinates. What is the rationale for this "agency heads" exception in § 554(d)(C)? Recall that the latter exception is referred to in the *Withrow* excerpt in N.1. Again, 1981 MSAPA § 4–214 has no "agency head" exception.

The precise meaning of the (C) exception has yet to be clarified by case law. The Attorney General's Memorandum on the APA explained the exception as follows: "Thus, if a member of the Interstate Commerce Commission actively participates in or directs the investigation of an adjudicatory case, he will not be precluded from participating with his colleagues in the decision of that case." *Id.* at 58.

Therefore, the (C) exception appears to allow agency heads to *personally* engage in conflicting functions. However, it does not appear to permit agency staff adversaries—that is, staff members who have personally participated in prosecution or investigation in the particular case—to advise any decisionmaker, including the agency heads.

Again, the Attorney General's Memorandum on the APA 56 (1947) explains: ". . . on 'agency review' the agency heads, as well as the hearing examiner, will be precluded from consulting or obtaining advice from any officer or employee [who] has participated in the investigation or prosecution."

6. *The principle of necessity.* Under the "principle of necessity," a biased or otherwise disqualified judge can decide a case if there is no legally possible substitute decisionmaker. It is better, in other words, that a possibly unfair decision be made than that no decision be made at all (and a wrongdoer go unpunished or the public unprotected). Does the principle of necessity help to distinguish *Walker* and *Goldberg v. Kelly* from *Withrow v. Larkin*? Did *Lyness* overlook the principle of necessity?

7. *Problem.* The Water Resources Agency (WRA) of the State of Madison grants permits to discharge pollutants into navigable waters. In the event a permittee violates the permit, WRA can revoke or suspend the

permit and assess monetary penalties. In cases of dispute about sanctions, WRA appoints a hearing officer (usually a WRA attorney) who conducts a trial-type hearing; the hearing officer recommends a decision to the three WRA agency heads who make the final decision.

In 1995, Ralph, a WRA attorney responded to citizen complaints about smelly discharges into Sylvan Creek by Bergman Chemicals. Together with a WRA chemist, Ralph determined that Bergman was discharging different toxic chemicals into the stream than allowed by its permit. He therefore recommended that the permit be revoked, which would require the plant to be shut down. In 1996, Ralph became one of the three heads of WRA.

Ted is an WRA attorney who frequently prosecutes waste discharge cases but was not previously involved in the Bergman matter. Ted was designated to hear the Bergman Chemical case. Ted recommended that Bergman's permit should not be revoked because the violation was accidental. Instead, Bergman should pay a $200 fine.

The case then went before the agency heads. Ralph refused to disqualify himself from considering this matter. Ralph and the other agency heads read the record and decided to revoke Bergman's permit, finding that the violation was intentional and flagrant.

Should a court reverse this decision under either due process or the 1981 MSAPA? Should the result be different if Ralph did not become an agency head but gave confidential advice to the agency heads at the time they made their decision? Would the result differ if WRA was a federal agency and the APA formal adjudication requirements applied to its hearings?

§ 3.3.3 BIAS: PERSONAL INTEREST, PREJUDGMENT, PERSONAL ANIMUS

The previous section considered one kind of bias: a person engaged as a prosecutor, investigator, or advocate may find it difficult to take off the adversary hat and put on an adjudicating hat. This section considers additional problems of decisionmaker impartiality: an adjudicator is disqualified if tainted by personal animus (that is, prejudice or hostility toward a party), prejudgment of the issues, or a personal stake in the decision. As in the previous section, the fundamental question is whether an administrative adjudicator (ALJ or agency head) must be as impartial as a judge.

ANDREWS v. AGRICULTURAL LABOR RELATIONS BOARD
623 P.2d 151 (Cal.1981).

[States, rather than the federal government, regulate labor relations in the agricultural sector. California's Agricultural Labor Relations Board (ALRB) resembles the federal National Labor Relations Board (NLRB). Like the NLRB, it supervises elections in which workers decide whether they want to be represented by a union. It also adjudicates unfair labor practice cases against both employers and unions.

ALRB's general counsel filed a complaint against Andrews alleging unfair labor practices. The charges arose out of a contested election that was lost by the United Farm Workers (UFW). The Board appointed Armando Menocal as a temporary Administrative Law Officer (ALO) to hear the case. Menocal was an attorney in private practice with Public Advocates, a San Francisco public interest law firm. Counsel for Andrews moved to disqualify Menocal on the ground of bias because he and Public Advocates work on employment discrimination cases on behalf of Mexican–Americans. Menocal refused to disqualify himself. He found against Andrews. The ALRB affirmed the decision, declaring that it had made an independent review of the entire record.]

Mosk, J.:

Petitioners imply that a ground for bias was the ALO's practice of law with a firm which in the past had represented individual farm workers in a suit against the Secretary of Labor and which engaged in employment discrimination suits on behalf of Mexican–Americans. From this, it appears we are to infer that the ALO has some philosophical or political inclination that would make it impossible for him to conduct hearings impartially. Even if the nature of a lawyer's practice could be taken as evidence of his political or social outlook,[3] such evidence, as will appear, is irrelevant to prove bias. Therefore, rather than review the nature of the cases in which the ALO or his firm has participated or attempt to identify what viewpoints those cases might possibly suggest, we will simply reaffirm the general principles that make doing so unnecessary.

The right to an impartial trier of fact is not synonymous with the claimed right to a trier completely indifferent to the general subject matter of the claim before him. . . . The word bias refers "to the mental attitude or disposition of the judge towards a party to the litigation, and not to any views that he may entertain regarding the subject matter involved." In an administrative context, Professor Davis has written that "Bias in the sense of crystallized point of view about issues of law or policy is almost universally deemed no ground for disqualification." This long established, practical rule is merely a recognition of the fact that anyone acting in a judicial role will have attitudes and preconceptions toward some of the legal and social issues that may come before him.

Petitioners revive the same discarded stereotype of bias relative to disqualifying a judicial officer that Judge Jerome Frank addressed many years ago: "Democracy must, indeed, fail unless our courts try cases fairly, and there can be no fair trial before a judge lacking in impartiality and disinterestedness. If, however, 'bias' and 'partiality' be defined to mean the total absence of preconceptions in the mind of the judge, then no one has ever had a fair trial and no one ever will. The human mind,

---

3. Amici assert persuasively that imputing the values of a client to a lawyer is an improper exercise inevitably fraught with dangers of erroneous conclusions. That view is consistent with the American Bar Association Code of Professional Responsibility, E.C. 2–27, which urges every lawyer to accept representation of "unpopular clients and causes . . . [r]egardless of his personal feelings. . . ."

even at infancy, is no blank piece of paper. We are born with predispositions; and the process of education, formal and informal, creates attitudes in all men which affect them in judging situations, attitudes which preceded reasoning in particular instances and which, therefore, by definition, are prejudices. . . . Interests, points of view, preferences, are the essence of living. Only death yields complete dispassionateness, for such dispassionateness signifies utter indifference. . . . ''

Therefore, even if the viewpoint attributed to an ALO could be inferred from the nature of his legal practice or his clients—which we do not concede—that would be no ground for disqualification. A trier of fact with expressed political or legal views cannot be disqualified on that basis alone even in controversial cases. The more politically or socially sensitive a matter, the more likely it is that the ALO, like most intelligent citizens, will have at some time reached an opinion on the issue. This is an unavoidable feature of a legal system dependent on human beings rather than robots for dispute resolution.

Even assuming, arguendo, the political or legal views of an ALO could result in an appearance of bias, we cannot hold, as requested by petitioners, that a mere appearance of bias is a ground for the disqualification of a judicial officer. . . . Appearance, after all, is generally in the eye of the beholder. . . .

Thus, our courts have never required the disqualification of a judge unless the moving party has been able to demonstrate concretely the actual existence of bias.[5] We cannot now exchange this established principle for one as vague, unmanageable and laden with potential mischief as an ''appearance of bias'' standard, despite our deep concern for the objective and impartial discharge of all judicial duties in this state.

The foregoing considerations, of course, are equally applicable to the disqualification of a judicial officer in the administrative system. Indeed, the appearance of bias standard may be particularly untenable in certain administrative settings. For example, in an unfair labor practice proceeding the Board is the ultimate factfinder, not the ALO. We therefore fail to see how a mere subjective belief in the ALO's appearance of bias, as distinguished from actual bias, can prejudice either party when the Board is responsible for making factual determinations, upon an independent review of the record. In the case at bar the Board declared it did undertake such an independent review of the entire record.

Appellants further contend that the temporary status of the ALO herein should be recognized as a factor in the disqualification analysis because of his increased susceptibility to bias due to the potential influences of a continuing legal practice. However, we know of no case,

---

5. Of course, there are some situations in which the probability of likelihood of the existence of actual bias is so great that disqualification of a judicial officer is required to preserve the integrity of the legal system, even without proof that the judicial officer is actually biased towards a party. (See e.g., *Tumey v. Ohio* (1927) 273 U.S. 510, in which a judge was disqualified because of his financial stake in the outcome.)

nor have we been cited to any, that stands for the proposition that a pro tempore judicial officer is peculiarly vulnerable to a disqualification challenge because he is engaged in the practice of law before and after his temporary public service.[6] . . . .

Petitioners finally contend that bias appears on the face of the ALO's findings and recommended decision. However, because this contention rests on an erroneous legal foundation, there is no need for us to examine the substance of his report.

It is first asserted that bias may be shown by the fact that some of a hearing officer's findings are not supported by substantial evidence . . . "If the fact finder has allegedly credited unsubstantial evidence while disregarding utterly irrefutable evidence, the issue before a reviewing court should not be whether the fact finder was biased, but whether his findings of fact are supported by substantial evidence on the whole record . . ."

There is no reason to explore the heart and mind of the ALO when effective relief is readily available if the reviewing court concludes a finding is unsupported by substantial evidence. To hold otherwise would encourage a losing party to raise the specter of bias indiscriminately, whenever he could demonstrate that one finding of fact in a large administrative record was not sufficiently supported. We decline to cast that cloud of uncertainty over adjudicative proceedings.

But, petitioners assert, that bias may be established where the record shows the hearing officer uniformly believed evidence introduced by the union and uniformly disbelieved evidence produced by the employer . . . Numerous and continuous rulings against a litigant, even when erroneous, form no ground for a charge of bias or prejudice. This rule is tenable in both a judicial and an administrative context. To fulfill his duty, an ALO must make choices when conflicting evidence is offered; thus, his reliance on certain witnesses and rejection of others cannot be evidence of bias no matter how consistently the ALO rejects or doubts the testimony produced by one of the adversaries. . . .

It follows that the ALO did not err in refusing to disqualify himself.

NEWMAN, J., Concurring—. . . .

The final paragraph of the 20–page Court of Appeal opinion in this case reads: "Although the ALO could not perceive the justification of petitioners' position, it seems patently clear to us that an attorney, employed by Public Advocates, Inc. in 1975 or 1976, would be perceived as biased against employers generally in disputes against unskilled low paid Spanish-surnamed workers, asserting a community of interests and that he would particularly appear to be biased against an agricultural

---

6. . . . Under the Code of Judicial Conduct, a judge, being under a duty to regulate his extrajudicial activities so as to minimize the risk of conflict with his judicial duties, is not allowed to practice law. However . . . the code specifically exempts judges pro tempore from [this rule].

employer in a dispute with the UFW." . . . . My views are outlined briefly in these final paragraphs of [a] letter to this court . . .

[T]here is a very troubling aspect of the *Andrews* decision below which requires a sensitive, careful and decisive review by this court . . . The court below said that it seemed clear that Menocal "would be perceived as biased against employers generally in disputes against unskilled low paid *Spanish-surnamed* workers." . . . It is incumbent upon this Court to ensure that there is no hint of law in this state that an individual cannot serve as a decision-maker in a case involving a class of litigants on one side or the other who share a cultural or racial or sexual identity with the decision-maker or his/her clients. . . .

CLARK, J.—I dissent.

The appearance of bias—those circumstances leading a reasonable person to doubt the impartiality of the trier of fact—is not only a sufficient but a compelling ground for disqualification. Disqualification on the basis that a quasi-judicial officer appears biased is essential to the health and stability of the adjudicative process for two fundamental reasons. 1. The litigant's due process right to a fair hearing is protected. 2. Public confidence in the integrity of our system of justice is sustained. . . .

By requiring the near impossible—a showing of actual bias—before a quasi-judicial official must disqualify himself, the majority fail to protect due process and public confidence concerns. The "actual bias" standard protects only against the most egregious and flagrant instances of bias. Only in truly rare cases will such blatant displays of bias be openly disclosed. Bias, unlike other deprivations of due process which may be clearly determined on the record, is generally an invisible influence and for that reason must be particularly guarded against. . . . [I]s it not better to err on the side of justice rather than to impose the risk that in an instance of actual but unprovable bias the prejudiced party will be without remedy? . . . .

The majority agree that the nature of the ALO's law practice is irrelevant to prove bias, because bias refers to a mental attitude towards a party and not to political or social viewpoints regarding subject matter. However, when an ALO's law firm consistently represents the same limited class of clients, it may be reasonably concluded the ALO is programmed not only to a particular viewpoint on legal and social issues but also to a bias in favor of the particular class he represents and, correspondingly, to a predisposition against those classes generally cast in an opposing role. Bias against a class of which a party is a member is sufficient grounds for disqualification.

The majority argue that because the ALRB may itself engage in factfinding upon its independent review of the record, there exists an adequate remedy when it appears an ALO has been biased. However, after substantial investment of money and other resources in conducting a hearing and producing a decision, the ALRB is naturally reluctant to overturn such decision for any reason other than clear error on the record. Moreover, subtle but nonetheless unfair findings and other influences attributable to a biased ALO cannot be effectively recognized, established or challenged on an administrative record ... The writ should be granted and the decision set aside.

RICHARDSON, J., concurred.

Notes and Questions

1. *Personal interest.* One well established ground for disqualification of an adjudicator is personal interest—that the decisionmaker or her family has a personal (usually a financial) stake in the decision. A personal interest creates such a serious risk of bias that the decisionmaker is automatically disqualified, whether actually biased or not. *See Tumey v. Ohio,* cited in note 5 of *Andrews.* In *Tumey*, a judge received his compensation out of the fines he levied on defendants.

Tumey was extended in *Ward v. Village of Monroeville,* 409 U.S. 57 (1972), which disqualified a small town mayor from serving as a traffic court judge. The fines went into the city treasury, not the mayor's pocket. However, the fines were a significant part of the town's budget; the more fines the mayor collected as traffic judge, the less taxes he would have to levy on his constituents. On the other hand, the Court distinguished these two cases in *Marshall v. Jerrico, Inc.,* 446 U.S. 238 (1980). That decision upheld a statute under which sums collected as civil penalties for violation of the child labor laws were returned to the Employment Standards Administration of the Labor Department as reimbursement for its enforcement costs. The Court said that the official who had decided to seek penalties, an ESA assistant regional administrator, was acting in a prosecutorial rather than judicial capacity; an adjudicative hearing would be held before an administrative law judge who was independent of ESA. (Is that distinction persuasive?)

Could a bias for interest argument have been leveled against Menocal in *Andrews,* either with respect to future business he might gain or lose in his private practice because of his decision or because of the likelihood of his being rehired by ALRB as a temporary ALO in future cases?

2. *Professional bias.* What if the decision-makers *by profession* have a pecuniary interest? The Supreme Court disqualified an entire licensing agency for this reason. By law, a state optometry agency was composed solely of *independent* optometrists. The agency determined that optometrists would lose their licenses if they work for corporate employers. The Court upheld a lower court's finding that the board members had a personal pecuniary interest in limiting entry into the field to independent optometrists like themselves and keeping corporate chain stores out. *Gibson v. Berryhill,* 411 U.S. 564 (1973). *Gibson* is striking in that it ignores the rule of necessity: the agency could not take action against corporate optometry, even if that prohibition was otherwise desirable and no other agency had authority to act.

Later, the Court backed away from *Gibson*. It ruled that an optometry board consisting of a *majority* of independent optometrists was not invalid for all purposes. A bias for interest claim must be based on a particularized analysis of the facts presented. Outside a disciplinary context, due process constraints are weaker. *Friedman v. Rogers,* 440 U.S. 1, 18–19 (1979).

3. *Prejudgment or animus.* Actual bias may be of two kinds: i) prejudgment of the individualized facts of a case or ii) animus (prejudice) against a particular litigant (or a class which includes that litigant). If a decisionmaker's statements indicate that either kind of bias is present, due process requires that the decisionmaker be disqualified.

Does the fact that Menocal ruled for the union on every point, believed all of its witnesses and disbelieved all of the grower's witnesses, establish that he was biased in the union's favor?

Frequently a decisionmaker will be exposed to the facts of a case in the course of carrying out a regular agency function; later the decisionmaker must make the final decision in the case. A court is unlikely to find that statements about the case made when the decisionmaker is "in role" evidence the kind of prejudgment that would violate due process. Thus, for example, an ALJ who decides a case against a party is not disqualified from deciding it again after remand by the agency. *NLRB v. Donnelly Garment Co.,* 330 U.S. 219 (1947).

Similarly, a school board that conducts negotiations with a striking teachers' union is not disqualified from discharging teachers who participated in the illegal strike. *Hortonville Joint School District v. Hortonville Education Ass'n,* 426 U.S. 482 (1976). In *Hortonville,* the Court said: "Mere familiarity with the facts of a case gained by an agency in the performance of its statutory role does not, however, disqualify a decisionmaker ..."

Most of the prejudgment cases arise from unguarded statements "out of role" that suggest that a decisionmaker's mind has been made up. For example, in *Cinderella Career and Finishing Schools, Inc. v. FTC,* 425 F.2d 583 (D.C.Cir.1970), the agency ordered a charm school to cease and desist from various deceptive claims in its advertising.

The Commission's ALJ dismissed the charges. While the Commission was considering whether to adopt the ALJ's decision, FTC Chair Paul Rand Dixon gave a speech to newspaper publishers, criticizing them for irresponsibility in accepting advertisements. As examples, he asked: "What about carrying ads that offer college educations in five weeks ... or becoming an airline's hostess by attending a charm school?" He added that "advertising managers are savvy enough to smell deception when the odor is strong enough." The court held that Dixon's participation violated due process because the speech indicated he had prejudged the facts in the *Cinderella* case.

> Conduct such as this may have the effect of entrenching a Commissioner in a position which he has publicly stated, making it difficult, if not impossible, for him to reach a different conclusion in the event he deems it necessary to do so after consideration of the record.... The test for disqualification has been succinctly stated as being whether 'a disinterested observer may conclude that [the agency] has in some measure adjudged the facts as well as the law of a particular case in advance of hearing it'....

The rather harsh tone of the *Cinderella* decision was influenced by the fact that the courts had twice reversed FTC decisions because of comments made by Dixon in another speech and in a Senate committee report he had written before he joined the FTC. The court concluded:

It is appalling to witness such insensitivity to the requirements of due process; it is even more remarkable to find ourselves once again confronted with a situation in which Mr. Dixon, pouncing on the most convenient victim, has determined either to distort the holdings in the cited cases beyond all reasonable interpretation or to ignore them altogether.

There is an important difference between prejudgment of individualized facts relating to a private party and prejudgments about law, policy, or legislative facts. In *Hortonville*, the Court said: "Nor is a decisionmaker disqualified simply because he has taken a position even in public, on a policy issue related to the dispute, in the absence of a showing that he is not 'capable of judging a particular controversy fairly on the basis of its own circumstances ...'"

If it could be shown that Menocal was philosophically committed to the rights of California farm workers (who are overwhelmingly of Hispanic origin), should he be disqualified from judging in the *Andrews* case? What if Menocal had strong opinions about how the Agricultural Labor Relations Act should be interpreted?

4. *The appearance of bias.* The *Andrews* majority ruled that an appearance of bias (without proof of actual bias) does not violate due process. But the appearance of bias standard is often used for the disqualification of federal or state judges. Compare 28 U.S.C. § 455(a): "Any ... judge ... of the United States shall disqualify himself in any proceeding in which his impartiality might reasonably be questioned."

See 1981 MSAPA 4–202(b): a presiding officer "is subject to disqualification for bias, prejudice, interest, or other cause provided in this Act or for which a judge is or may be disqualified." Thus the MSAPA opts for a judicial approach, not an institutional approach.

The argument for an institutional approach is that agency decisionmakers, unlike judges, are responsible for carrying out a regulatory statute. As the previous section on separation of functions noted, they wear multiple hats. They may litigate against the same parties over and over, thus gaining considerable factual knowledge. They often have strong views on law and policy. They supervise prosecutors and investigators. They must defend their agency in public. A judicial "appearance of bias" standard creates many uncertainties when applied to administrative adjudicators.

In Washington, the courts use an appearance of bias standard to disqualify administrative decisionmakers, especially in local land use or environmental cases. Unfortunately, this vague standard has produced an unending stream of close cases. See, e.g., *Save a Valuable Environment v. City of Bothell*, 576 P.2d 401 (Wash.1978) (members of zoning board must be disqualified because they were active in Chamber of Commerce which supported application).

5. *Raising the bias issue.* Federal APA § 556(b) sets forth the procedure for challenging an ALJ for bias. It does not explain how to challenge the impartiality of an agency member. 1981 MSAPA § 4–202(b)–(f) explains the procedure for challenging a "presiding officer" for bias. The term "presiding officer" covers both the administrative judge and the agency heads who hear appeals. § 4–216(d).

Notice especially § 4–202(e) and (f). What is the effect of these provisions on the "rule of necessity"? Suppose that an agency is headed by a single person who is biased against a litigant before the agency. Should that person decide the case because of the rule of necessity, or is there a way around the problem? *See International Harvester Co. v. Bowling,* 391 N.E.2d 168 (Ill.App.1979); *Matter of Rollins Environmental Services, Inc.,* 481 So.2d 113 (La.1985). Both cases apply statutes allowing the governor to replace an agency head who is disqualified for bias.

In light of the difficulty of proving actual bias, should private parties be entitled to a peremptory challenge of administrative judges? Pro tempore judges? Some states permit parties one peremptory challenge of a judge in each case. And federal law permits a party to file an affidavit challenging a judge on the basis of bias. If the affidavit alleges facts that would be sufficient to establish bias, and is accompanied by a certificate of counsel stating that it is made in good faith, the judge is disqualified without further ado. But this can be done only once in each case. 28 U.S.C. § 144.

6. *Problem—financial interest.* The Madison Medical Board imposes disciplinary sanctions against physicians. By statute, it is required to charge licensees against whom it imposes discipline the entire cost of investigating and prosecuting the case. The Board keeps any funds collected and such funds make up 85% of the Board's total budget.

After a hearing, the Board suspended Dr. Smith's license for one year because he overprescribed habit-forming prescription drugs. It also charged him $78,000 (the cost of investigating and prosecuting his case). On review, Dr. Smith argued that the Board is biased against him. How should the court resolve this claim? *See Trust & Investment Advisers, Inc. v. Hogsett,* 43 F.3d 290, 296–97 (7th Cir.1994).

7. *Problem—prejudgment.* Joe's Bar is located near the campus of Madison University. It has a reputation for serving liquor to underaged patrons. The Madison Alcoholic Beverage Board (MABB) has investigated Joe's Bar on several occasions but never found sufficient evidence that liquor law violations have occurred.

"The Madison Enquirer" is a local television investigative show that did a program on teenage drinking. Irene, the Enquirer's investigative reporter, interviewed Paul, the chair of MABB. She asked him about Joe's Bar. Paul replied: "We have had a tough time finding evidence that Joe's serves kids under 21, but we think it's happening. They're very clever about not getting caught. We are employing innovative investigative techniques to prove by substantial evidence that they've done it. We're hoping for a breakthrough soon."

One week later, MABB issued a complaint against Joe's Bar for serving minors. MABB's ALJ revoked the license of Joe's Bar and the three MABB agency heads unanimously affirmed the decision. It rejected a motion that Paul should be recused. Should the decision be reversed and, if so, should the court order that the case against Joe's be dismissed? *See 1616 Second Ave. Restaurant v. New York State Liquor Authority*, 550 N.E.2d 910 (N.Y. 1990).

§ 3.3.4   EX PARTE CONTACTS

This section addresses additional conflicts between the judicial and institutional models. Judges have only one responsibility—to decide cases. In contrast, an agency is a law enforcement and regulatory body, with substantial responsibilities for rulemaking, research, investigation, and prosecution. An agency must also be acutely sensitive to prevailing political winds, because it derives its authority and budget from and is accountable to the legislative and executive branches. These responsibilities require a constant flow of communication between agency personnel and regulated parties, members of the public, legislators, and high-level executive officials. Inevitably, some of this communication touches on matters which the agency is adjudicating.

A word of clarification: this section concerns communications between agency decisionmakers and persons who are *outside the agency*. The section on separation of functions, § 3.3.2, concerned communications between decisionmakers and advisers *inside the agency*. Viewed together, the ex parte contact rule and the separation of functions rule prohibit off-record communications to agency decisionmakers from outsiders *and* from agency adversaries, but these rules permit off-record communications to decisionmakers from staff advisers if such advisers have not played adversary roles.

PROFESSIONAL AIR TRAFFIC CONTROLLERS ORGANIZATION (PATCO) v. FEDERAL LABOR RELATIONS AUTHORITY (FLRA)

685 F.2d 547 (D.C.Cir.1982).

[The members of PATCO engaged in an illegal strike against the government. Under § 7120(f) of the Civil Service Reform Act, the FLRA "shall revoke the exclusive recognition status" of a union which calls such a strike (in effect, putting the union out of business). After a hearing, the FLRA's ALJ revoked PATCO's exclusive recognition status. This decision was unanimously affirmed by the three FLRA agency heads (members Applewhaite, Frazier, and Haughton).

This case concerns certain contacts between the agency heads and others while the PATCO case was before FLRA. Concerned by the possible impropriety, the Court of Appeals ordered the FLRA to conduct a hearing with the aid of a specially appointed ALJ from another agency (John Vittone), to determine the extent and effect of these contacts.

The contacts discussed in the excerpted portion of the opinion are as follows:

(i) Secretary of Transportation Andrew Lewis phoned member Frazier. He said he was not calling about the substance of the PATCO case but wanted to tell Frazier that no meaningful efforts to settle the strike were underway. He stated that he would appreciate expeditious handling of the appeal from the ALJ decision to the FLRA agency heads. Lewis also called Applewhaite with the same message and Applewhaite told him that a written motion to expedite the appeal had to be filed. Later, such a motion was filed and FLRA shortened the filing period.

(ii) Albert Shanker, head of the American Federation of Teachers, and a long-time friend of Applewhaite's, met Applewhaite for dinner. Shanker urged Applewhaite not to revoke PATCO's exclusive recognition status.

EDWARDS, J. wrote the panel opinion. ROBINSON, J. concurred, expressing much stronger condemnation of the incidents.]

C. *Applicable Legal Standards*

1. *The Statutory Prohibition of Ex Parte Contacts and the FLRA Rules*

The Civil Service Reform Act requires that FLRA unfair labor practice hearings, to the extent practicable, be conducted in accordance with the provisions of the Administrative Procedure Act. Since FLRA unfair labor practice hearings are formal adjudications within the meaning of the APA, *see* 5 U.S.C. § 551(7), section 557(d) governs ex parte communications.

Section 557(d) was enacted by Congress as part of the Government in the Sunshine Act (1976). The section prohibits ex parte communications "relevant to the merits of the proceeding" between an "interested person" and an agency decisionmaker. . . .

Three features of the prohibition on ex parte communications in agency adjudications are particularly relevant to the contacts here at issue. First, by its terms, section 557(d) applies only to ex parte communications to or from an "interested person." Congress did not intend, however, that the prohibition on ex parte communications would therefore have only a limited application. . . .

Second, the Government in the Sunshine Act defines an "ex parte communication" as "an oral or written communication not on the public record to which reasonable prior notice to all parties is not given, but . . . not includ[ing] requests for status reports on any matter or proceeding. . . . " APA § 551(14). Requests for status reports are thus allowed under the statute, even when directed to an agency decisionmaker rather than to another agency employee. Nevertheless, the legislative history of the Act cautions:

> A request for a status report or a background discussion may in effect amount to an indirect or subtle effort to influence the substantive outcome of the proceedings. The judgment will have to be made whether a particular communication could affect the agency's

decision on the merits. In doubtful cases the agency official should treat the communication as ex parte so as to protect the integrity of the decision making process.

Third, and in direct contrast to status reports, section 557(d) explicitly prohibits communications "relevant to the merits of the proceeding." The congressional reports state that the phrase should "be construed broadly and ... include more than the phrase 'fact in issue' currently used in [section 554(d)(1) of] the Administrative Procedure Act." While the phrase must be interpreted to effectuate the dual purposes of the Government in the Sunshine Act, *i.e.*, of giving notice of improper contacts and of providing all interested parties an opportunity to respond to illegal communications, the scope of this provision is not unlimited. Congress explicitly noted that the statute does not prohibit procedural inquiries, or other communications "not relevant to the merits."

In sum, Congress sought to establish common-sense guidelines to govern ex parte contacts in administrative hearings, rather than rigidly defined and woodenly applied rules. The disclosure of ex parte communications serves two distinct interests. Disclosure is important in its own right to prevent the appearance of impropriety from secret communications in a proceeding that is required to be decided on the record. Disclosure is also important as an instrument of fair decisionmaking; only if a party knows the arguments presented to a decisionmaker can the party respond effectively and ensure that its position is fairly considered. When these interests of openness and opportunity for response are threatened by an ex parte communication, the communication must be disclosed. It matters not whether the communication comes from someone other than a formal party or if the communication is clothed in the guise of a procedural inquiry. If, however, the communication is truly not relevant to the merits of an adjudication and, therefore, does not threaten the interests of openness and effective response, disclosure is unnecessary. Congress did not intend to erect meaningless procedural barriers to effective agency action. It is thus with these interests in mind that the statutory prohibition on ex parte communications must be applied.

2. *Remedies for Ex Parte Communications*

Section 557(d) contains two possible administrative remedies for improper ex parte communications. The first is disclosure of the communication and its content. The second requires the violating party to "show cause why his claim or interest in the proceeding should not be dismissed, denied, disregarded, or otherwise adversely affected on account of [the] violation." Congress did not intend, however, that an agency would require a party to "show cause" after every violation or that an agency would dismiss a party's interest more than rarely. Indeed, the statutory language clearly states that a party's interest in the proceeding may be adversely affected only "to the extent consistent with the interests of justice and the policy of the underlying statutes."[30]

The Government in the Sunshine Act contains no specific provisions for judicial remedy of improper ex parte communications. However, we may infer from approving citations in the House and Senate Reports that Congress did not intend to alter the existing case law regarding ex parte communications and the legal effect of such contacts on agency decisions.

Under the case law in this Circuit improper ex parte communications, even when undisclosed during agency proceedings, do not necessarily void an agency decision. Rather, agency proceedings that have been blemished by ex parte communications have been held to be *voidable*.

In enforcing this standard, a court must consider whether, as a result of improper ex parte communications, the agency's decisionmaking process was irrevocably tainted so as to make the ultimate judgment of the agency unfair, either to an innocent party or to the public interest that the agency was obliged to protect.[32] In making this determination, a number of considerations may be relevant: the gravity of the ex parte communications; whether the contacts may have influenced the agency's ultimate decision; whether the party making the improper contacts benefited from the agency's ultimate decision; whether the contents of the communications were unknown to opposing parties, who therefore had no opportunity to respond; and whether vacation of the agency's decision and remand for new proceedings would serve a useful purpose. Since the principal concerns of the court are the integrity of the process and the fairness of the result, mechanical rules have little place in a judicial decision whether to vacate a voidable agency proceeding. Instead, any such decision must of necessity be an exercise of equitable discretion.

---

30. By way of example, the Senate Report suggested that:

> [T]he interests of justice might dictate that a claimant for an old age benefit not lose his claim even if he violates the ex parte rules. On the other hand, where two parties have applied for a license and the applications are of relatively equal merit, an agency may rule against a party who approached an agency head in an ex parte manner in an effort to win approval of his license.

The legislative history also notes that the dismissal provisions of §§ 556(d) and 557(d)(1)(D) supplement, rather than replace, an agency's authority to censure or dismiss an official who engages in illegal ex parte communications and to prohibit an attorney who violates § 557(d) from practicing before the agency.

32. We have also considered the effect of ex parte communications on the availability of meaningful judicial review. Where facts and arguments "vital to the agency decision" are only communicated to the agency off the record, the court may at worst be kept in the dark about the agency's actual reasons for its decision. *United States Lines v. FMC*, 584 F.2d 519, 541 (D.C.Cir.1978). At best, the basis for the agency's action may be disclosed for the first time on review. If the off-the-record communications regard critical facts, the court will be particularly ill-equipped to resolve in the first instance any controversy between the parties. *See id.* at 542. Thus, effective judicial review may be hampered if ex parte communications prevent adversarial decision of factual issues by the agency....

D. Analysis of the Alleged Ex Parte Communications with FLRA Members

... After extensive review of the ... troubling incidents we believe that they provide insufficient reason to vacate the FLRA Decision or to remand this case for further proceedings before the Authority....

Secretary Lewis' Telephone Calls to Members Frazier and Applewhaite

Transportation Secretary Lewis was undoubtedly an "interested person" within the meaning of section 557(d) and the FLRA Rules when he called Members Frazier and Applewhaite on August 13. Secretary Lewis' call clearly would have been an improper ex parte communication if he had sought to discuss the merits of the PATCO case. The Secretary explicitly avoided the merits, however, and mentioned only his view on the possibility of settlement and his desire for a speedy decision. On this basis, Solicitor Freehling and Member Frazier concluded the call was not improper.

We are less certain that Secretary Lewis' call was permissible. Although Secretary Lewis did not in fact discuss the merits of the case, even a procedural inquiry may be a subtle effort to influence an agency decision. We do not doubt that Member Frazier and Solicitor Freehling concluded in good faith that the communications were not improper, but it would have been preferable for them to heed Congress' warning, to assume that close cases like these are improper, and to report them on the public record.

We need not decide, however, whether Secretary Lewis' contacts were in fact improper. Even if they were, the contacts did not taint the proceedings or prejudice PATCO. Secretary Lewis' central concern in his conversations with Member Frazier and Member Applewhaite was that the case be handled expeditiously. Member Applewhaite explicitly told Secretary Lewis that if he wanted the case handled more quickly than the normal course of FLRA business, then the FAA would have to file a written request. If, as A.L.J. Vittone found likely, Member Applewhaite's comments led to the FAA's Motion to Modify Time Limits, *that was exactly the desired result.* Once the FAA filed a motion, PATCO filed its own responsive motions, and the FLRA was able to decide the timing issue based on the pleadings before it....

Finally, PATCO cannot claim that it was prejudiced. The failure of the Authority to notice Secretary Lewis' calls on the public record did not deprive PATCO of an opportunity to comment: PATCO filed responsive motions. (Surely PATCO cannot argue that fairness requires two opportunities to respond rather than one.) Nor has PATCO suggested how it was ultimately injured by the six-day change in the time for filing exceptions. In these circumstances we conclude that Secretary Lewis' telephone calls do not void the FLRA Decision.

Member Applewhaite's Dinner with Albert Shanker

Of course, the most troublesome ex parte communication in this case occurred during the September 21 dinner meeting between Member

Applewhaite and American Federation of Teachers President Albert Shanker—the "well-known labor leader" mentioned in Assistant Attorney General McGrath's affidavit. . . .

At the outset, we are faced with the question whether Mr. Shanker was an "interested person" to the proceeding under section 557(d). Mr. Shanker argues that he was not. He suggests that his only connection with the unfair labor practice case was his membership on the Executive Council of the AFL–CIO which, unbeknownst to him, had participated as amicus curiae in the oral argument of the PATCO case before the FLRA. This relationship to the proceeding, Mr. Shanker contends, is too tenuous to qualify him as an "interested person" forbidden to make ex parte communications to the Authority Members.

As noted above, Congress did not intend such a narrow construction of the term "interested person." . . .

The House and Senate Reports agreed that the term covers "any individual or other person with an interest in the agency proceeding that is greater than the general interest the public as a whole may have. The interest need not be monetary, nor need a person be a party to, or intervenor in, the agency proceeding. . . . "

We believe that Mr. Shanker falls within the intended scope of the term "interested person." Mr. Shanker was (and is) the President of a major public-sector labor union. As such, he has a special and well-known interest in the union movement and the developing law of labor relations in the public sector. The PATCO strike, of course, was the subject of extensive media coverage and public comment. Some union leaders undoubtedly felt that the hard line taken against PATCO by the Administration might have an adverse effect on other unions, both in the federal and in state and local government sectors. Mr. Shanker apparently shared this concern. . . .

Even if we were to adopt Mr. Shanker's position that he was not an interested person, we are astonished at his claim that he did nothing wrong. Mr. Shanker frankly concedes that he "desired to have dinner with Member Applewhaite because he felt strongly about the PATCO case and he wished to communicate directly to Member Applewhaite sentiments he had previously expressed in public." While we appreciate Mr. Shanker's forthright admission, we must wonder whether it is a product of candor or a failure to comprehend that his conduct was improper. In case any doubt still lingers, we take the opportunity to make one thing clear: *It is simply unacceptable behavior for any person directly to attempt to influence the decision of a judicial officer in a pending case outside of the formal, public proceedings.* This is true for the general public, for "interested persons," and for the formal parties to the case. This rule applies to administrative adjudications as well as to cases in Article III courts.

We think it a mockery of justice to even suggest that judges or other decisionmakers may be properly approached on the merits of a case during the pendency of an adjudication. Administrative and judicial adjudications are viable only so long as the integrity of the decisionmaking processes remains inviolate. There would be no way to protect the sanctity of adjudicatory processes if we were to condone direct attempts to influence decisionmakers through ex parte contacts.

We do not hold, however, that Member Applewhaite committed an impropriety when he accepted Mr. Shanker's dinner invitation. Member Applewhaite and Mr. Shanker were professional and social friends. We recognize, of course, that a judge "must have neighbors, friends and acquaintances, business and social relations, and be a part of his day and generation." Similarly, Member Applewhaite was not required to renounce his friendships, either personal or professional, when he was appointed to the FLRA. When Mr. Shanker called Member Applewhaite on September 21, Member Applewhaite was unaware of Mr. Shanker's purpose in arranging the dinner. He therefore had no reason to reject the invitation.

The majority of the dinner conversation was unrelated to the PATCO case. Only in the last fifteen minutes of the dinner did the discussion become relevant to the PATCO dispute, apparently when Mr. Shanker raised the topic of local approaches to public employee strikes in New York and Pennsylvania. At this point, and as the conversation turned to the discipline appropriate for a striking union like PATCO, Member Applewhaite should have promptly terminated the discussion. Had Mr. Shanker persisted in discussing his views of the PATCO case, Member Applewhaite should have informed him in no uncertain terms that such behavior was inappropriate. Unfortunately, he did not do so. . . .

We do not believe that it is necessary to vacate the FLRA Decision and remand the case. First, while Mr. Shanker's purpose and conduct were improper, and while Member Applewhaite should not have entertained Mr. Shanker's views on the desirability of decertifying a striking union, no threats or promises were made. Though plainly inappropriate, the ex parte communication was limited to a ten or fifteen minute discussion, often couched in general terms, of the appropriate discipline for a striking public employee union. This behavior falls short of the "corrupt tampering with the adjudicatory process" found by this court in *WKAT, Inc. v. FCC,* 296 F.2d 375.

Second, A.L.J. Vittone found that the Applewhaite/Shanker dinner had no effect on the ultimate decision of Member Applewhaite or of the FLRA as a whole in the PATCO case. None of the parties have disputed this finding. Indeed, even Member Frazier, who initiated the FBI investigation of the dinner, testified that "in his opinion the Shanker–Applewhaite dinner did not have an effect on Member Applewhaite's ultimate decision in the PATCO case."

Third, no party benefited from the improper contact. The ultimate decision was adverse to PATCO, the party whose interests were most closely aligned with Mr. Shanker's position. The final decision also rejected the position taken by the AFL–CIO as amicus curiae and by Mr. Shanker in his dinner conversation with Member Applewhaite. . . .

Notes and Questions

1. *State law.* One of the few ex parte contact cases arising under state law concerned 1961 MSAPA § 13. This section is similar to 1981 MSAPA § 4–213 and prohibits ex parte contacts in a "contested case." It concerned contact between an applicant for a savings and loan charter and the Texas Savings and Loan Commissioner. The Commissioner turned down the application in August. During September, the organizers met with him ex parte and furnished new economic information. In October, the organizers then filed a new application that the Commissioner granted.

An existing S & L challenged the decision. The lower court reversed the Commissioner's decision. It held that the communications concerned a "contested case" because the first and second application proceedings were "just one ongoing application." Therefore it rejected the argument that the communications were proper because no application was pending at the time they occurred. *First Sav. & Loan Ass'n v. Vandygriff,* 605 S.W.2d 740 (Tex.Civ.App.1980). The court also denied that the error had been cured when the contact was disclosed at the outset of the second hearing: "an opportunity to controvert ex parte evidence afforded weeks or months after its communication to the decision maker is far less effective than timely cross-examination following the admission of evidence."

The Texas Supreme Court reversed the decision, because there was no "contested case" at the time the communications occurred. *Vandygriff v. First Savings & Loan Ass'n,* 617 S.W.2d 669 (Tex.1981). The first application had been dismissed and the second had not yet been filed. It also held there was no prejudice to opponents of the application, because the ex parte communications were fully disclosed at the second hearing and there was opportunity to present contrary evidence. How would this case have been decided under the federal APA? *See* § 557(d)(1)(E). Under 1981 MSAPA, especially § 4–213(c) and (d)?

2. *Lewis' calls to Frazier and Applewhaite.* Did these calls violate APA § 557(d)? Consider the definition of "ex parte communication" in § 551(14). The FLRA's rules permit ex parte contacts concerning settlement. 5 C.F.R. § 2414.6(b), (d). Why is a conversation concerning settlement not a violation of § 557(d)? Could an inquiry about the status of a case or a comment about settlement be a prohibited ex parte communication? See Judge Edwards' comments in part C.1. of the *PATCO* opinion.

3. *Dinner with Shanker.* Judge Edwards indicates that Shanker's conduct was deplorable and that Applewhaite erred badly by failing to terminate the discussion when it turned to the *PATCO* matter. In his concurring opinion, Judge Robinson indicated that it was inappropriate for Applewhaite to even have dinner with Shanker. Do you agree? Is it likely that Shanker's views came as a surprise to Applewhaite? Should Applewhaite be removed from office?

Do you agree that Shanker is an "interested person"? If you had run into Applewhaite (an old friend of your father's) at the airport and made the same statements that Shanker did, would you have violated § 557(d)?

4. *The President as an interested person*. In *Portland Audubon Society v. Endangered Species Committee*, 984 F.2d 1534 (9th Cir.1993), the court considered ex parte communications by the White House staff to the Endangered Species Committee, popularly known as the "God Squad." The God Squad was a 7–person group (consisting of cabinet secretaries and other high political officials) that was charged with deciding whether to make exceptions to the Endangered Species Act. The God Squad decided to allow timber cutting that would jeopardize the northern spotted owl. The court decided that the APA adjudication provisions applied to God Squad proceedings. *See* § 3.1.1 N.4. It then turned to whether the President and his staff were "interested persons" who are "outside the agency" as those terms are used in § 557(d)(1)(A):

We believe the President's position at the center of the Executive Branch renders him, ex officio, an "interested person" for the purposes of APA § 557(d)(1). As the head of government and chief executive officer, the President necessarily has an interest in every agency proceeding. No ex parte communication is more likely to influence an agency than one from the President or a member of his staff. No communication from any other person is more likely to deprive the parties and the public of their right to effective participation in a key governmental decision at a most crucial time. The essential purposes of the statutory provision compel the conclusion that the President and his staff are "interested persons" within the meaning of § 557(d)(1)....

[T]he Endangered Species Act explicitly vests discretion to make exemption decisions in the Committee and does not contemplate that the President or the White House will become involved in Committee deliberations. The President and his aides are not a part of the Committee decision-making process. They are "outside the agency" for the purposes of the ex parte communications ban.

This case should be compared to *Sierra Club v. Costle*, which upholds the right of the President and the White House staff to engage in ex parte communication *in rulemaking*. *Sierra Club* is discussed in § 5.5.2. The Court in *Portland Audubon* distinguished *Sierra Club*, stating that entirely different norms apply in adjudication.

5. *Remedies for ex parte contact*. What should FLRA have done about the violations of § 557(d) and its own ex parte rules? See § 557(d)(1)(C); 1981 MSAPA § 4–213(e). What additional action could FLRA have taken? See § 557(d)(1)(D) and the fourth sentence of § 556(d); 1981 MSAPA § 4–213(g).

The Court of Appeals was obviously troubled by what it should do aside from laying harsh criticism on all concerned. Certainly, the hearing before ALJ Vittone must have been a humbling experience. Ordinarily, it is improper to "probe the mind" of agency decisionmakers about how they made their decision. *Morgan IV*, discussed in § 3.3.1. However, in cases of alleged ex parte contacts, the agency staff and decisionmakers must submit to a grueling inquiry into exactly who said what to whom. *Portland Audubon* had a similar outcome—the court remanded for an evidentiary hearing before an ALJ about the conversations in question. Following receipt of the

ALJ's decision, the Court of Appeals would decide whether to vacate the God Squad's decision.

Should the Court have remanded the *PATCO* case for a new FLRA decision, even though it concluded that the ex parte contacts were not prejudicial to any party? In the *Vandygriff* case, discussed in N.1, the lower court remanded the case for a new hearing despite a failure by plaintiff to prove that the Commissioner was persuaded by the ex parte information. Instead the court presumed that such harm occurred—a presumption preferable to probing the mind of the Commissioner in violation of the *Morgan IV* principle.

Moreover, the court said that the impropriety was not cured by subsequent disclosure at the second licensing hearing; the opposing party was at a severe disadvantage because it had no effective way to controvert the ex parte evidence until weeks or months after it had been communicated. The Texas Supreme Court disagreed; it said the opportunity to rebut the communications at the second hearing was sufficient and that the Commissioner was presumed to have performed his duties in compliance with the law.

6. *Who can you talk to?* Notice that § 557(d) prohibits ex parte communications between outsiders and *advisers to decisionmakers.* Thus Shanker's communication would have been equally inappropriate if directed to Applewhaite's attorney-adviser. See also 1981 MSAPA § 4–213(b). And observe also that § 557(d) goes into effect no later than the time a proceeding is noticed for hearing (or, if the outsider knows that it will be noticed, at the time he acquires such knowledge). § 557(d)(1)(E).

There is a clear conflict between the APA provisions that prohibit ex parte contacts and the goals of i) encouraging free communication between the regulated industry and regulatory agencies and ii) making available the largest possible pool of advisers from within the agency for decisionmakers to call on in difficult cases.

For example, suppose Secretary of Transportation Lewis wants to discuss the *PATCO* case with Max. Max is an FLRA attorney who is very experienced in dealing with the problem of public employee strikes. Both Max and Lewis think that Max would be prosecuting the *PATCO* case. Such a conversation (between an agency prosecutor and a person who favors the prosecution) seems entirely appropriate.

Suppose that, after the discussion between Lewis and Max occurs, someone other than Max is selected to prosecute the case. When the time for decision arrives, Member Applewhaite wants to call upon Max for advice. Would Max be disqualified from giving advice because of his earlier and innocent ex parte contact with Lewis? Alternatively, if Max serves as an adviser, would Lewis' ex parte communication violate § 557(d) and therefore must it be placed on the record under § 557(d)(1)(C)? Should it also trigger sanctions against the government under § 557(d)(1)(D) and § 556(d)?

7. *Problem.* The Madison Public Utilities Commission (PUC) sets the rate that telephone companies can charge for intrastate calls. No statute prescribes the procedure for PUC ratemaking. Madison has adopted the 1981 MSAPA. The PUC conducts adjudicatory hearings before an ALJ to set the rates; then the five agency heads make the final decision. These proceedings

determine such issues as whether a phone companies' costs are reasonable and necessary (so that the rates will reimburse the company for those costs). Consumer groups participate extensively in these hearings. The hearings may go on for months or even years.

Madison Telephone Co. (MTC) has applied to the PUC to raise its base telephone rate from $15 to $19 per month. One issue is whether the rates should cover MTC's costs to clean up toxic wastes that it buried in the ground. Consumer groups claims that these costs should be borne by the company's shareholders rather than the ratepayers.

The five commissioners of the PUC are willing to listen to ex parte presentations by any party to a rate case. Several consumers who had not previously participated in the case paid a visit to Commissioner Smith and gave her a one-hour presentation on why the cleanup costs should not be part of the rate base. Ultimately, the Commission voted 3–2 in favor of the consumer group's position; Smith was in the majority.

Should a reviewing court set aside this decision—and, if so, what should it order on remand? Would the analysis be different if MTC had made the ex parte contact, the Commission voted in its favor, and consumer groups sought judicial review? Would the analysis be different if the members of the PUC were elected officials, as they are in some states? What if the PUC were a federal agency covered by the federal APA?

See *Southwestern Bell Telephone Co. v. Okla. Corp. Comm'n,* 873 P.2d 1001 (Okla.1994); *In re Public Serv. Co.,* 454 A.2d 435 (N.H.1982); *In re Minnesota PUC,* 417 N.W.2d 274, (Minn.Ct.App.1987).

§ 3.3.5 AGENCY ADJUDICATION AND LEGISLATIVE PRESSURE

PILLSBURY CO. v. FTC
354 F.2d 952 (5th Cir.1966).

TUTTLE, C. J.:

This is a petition by the Pillsbury Company to review and set aside an order of the Federal Trade Commission (FTC) requiring Pillsbury to divest itself of the assets of Ballard & Ballard Company and of Duff's Baking Mix Division of American Home Products Corporation which the FTC found it had acquired [in 1951 and 1952] in violation of § 7 of the Clayton Act. . . .

[The issue is whether Pillsbury was deprived of due process by reason of improper interference by Congressional committees with the decisional process of the FTC while the Pillsbury case was pending before it. In 1953, an FTC hearing examiner dismissed the case against Pillsbury, but the Commission reversed this decision and ordered the examiner to proceed. In its interlocutory opinion, the FTC rejected an argument that where a company having a substantial share of the market acquires a competitor, no further proof need be introduced. This is known as the "per se" rule. Instead, the Commission determined that it was necessary to hear evidence about whether the acquisitions would cause a "substantial lessening of competition." This is known as the "rule of reason" approach. The case then resumed before the hearing examiner and evidence was received for the next several years. The examiner filed an initial decision in 1959 that the acquisitions violated § 7; the FTC decision largely following it was entered in 1960. This case seeks review of the 1960 decision.

During May and June, 1955, hearings were held before the antitrust subcommittees of the House and Senate Judiciary Committees. FTC Chairman Howrey and several of the members of his staff appeared including Earl Kintner, who was then General Counsel and later became FTC Chairman. Kintner wrote the 1960 opinion. Also present was Robert Secrest who was a Commissioner in both 1955 and 1960 and Joseph Sheehy who was Director of Litigation. Sheehy's assistant, William Kern, was also a Commissioner in 1960. Thus, of the four commissioners who participated in the 1960 decision, Secrest and Kintner were exposed to whatever interference was embodied in the hearings and Kern was indirectly affected. Of the remaining two commissioners in 1960, Mills did not participate and Anderson had no apparent connection with the 1955 hearings.]

When Chairman Howrey appeared before the Senate subcommittee on June 1, 1955, he met a barrage of questioning by the members of the committee challenging his view of the requirements of § 7 and the application of the per se doctrine announced by the Supreme Court.... [Several] members of the committee challenged the correctness of his and the Commission's position [that the rule of reason should be employed rather than the per se rule] ...

[The court quotes the Senate hearing extensively. This is a sample of two of the exchanges:]

Senator Kefauver: "This [the Pillsbury case] illustrates what I have been talking about, Mr Howrey. I think Congress expected that where there was manifestly a lessening of competition, under the amended Clayton Act a merger should not take place.

Now, here in the Southeast, a section of the country, there is a lessening of competition because one firm had 20 and something percent and the other had 20 and something percent. It would seem to me by applying the rule of reason and running the record up to 9,000 pages with more to come, and bringing in every possible economic factor, this, that, and the other, that the Federal Trade Commission is rather taking over the prerogative of congressional intent."

Mr. Howrey: "I would not think so, Senator. I think a careful study of the legislative history of amended section 7 requires the law-enforcement agency, and the quasi-judicial agency, to examine the market facts...."

[Mr. Howrey]: "Well, I think the question you are asking about the Pillsbury decision is a much greater challenge to judicial processes, because I am sitting as a quasi-judicial officer in that case. That is a much greater challenge to judicial processes than anything I did by participating in this committee of the Attorney General" [Howrey had participated in an Attorney General's committee that studied the antitrust laws].

[Senator Kefauver]: "Maybe you should not have answered my questions."

[Mr. Howrey]: "I think I will disqualify myself in the Pillsbury case for the rest of the case because of the inquiry which you have made about my mental processes in it.

"But let me answer your other question, and I think I should because I do not think I can sit in a quasi-judicial capacity and—I think you have delved too deeply into the quasi-judicial mind in the Pillsbury matter.... "

We conclude that the proceedings just outlined constituted an improper intrusion into the adjudicatory processes of the Commission and were of such a damaging character as to have required at least some of the members in addition to the chairman to disqualify themselves....

In view of the inordinate lapse of time in this proceeding, brought to undo what was done by mergers completed in 1951, we are naturally loathe to frustrate the proceedings at this late date. However, common justice to a litigant requires that we invalidate the order entered by a quasi-judicial tribunal that was importuned by members of the United States Senate, however innocent they intended their conduct to be, to arrive at the ultimate conclusion which they did reach.

As early as 1776 it was clear that ours was destined to be a government of laws and not of men. In their complaint against the abuses of the British crown, the framers of the Declaration of Independence included the statement that: "He has made Judges dependent on his Will alone, for the tenure of their offices, and the amount and payment of their salaries." Although our Founding Fathers attempted to lay this question to rest on the federal level through Article III, Section 1 of the United States Constitution, the emergence of administrative tribunals as the "fourth branch" of our federal government has revived the problem. Consequently, the federal judicial function, to the extent that it is exercised by administrative bodies, has not been able to make a clean break with the implicit influence inherent in Congressional control over tenure and salary.

But, as we all know, the problem is not as simple as this, since the arsenal of tools with which an administrative agency implements its broad statutory mandates also includes legislative rule-making power. It is this latter power which sets regulatory agencies apart from courts of law and results in their functions being labelled "quasi-judicial" and "quasi-legislative."

We are sensible of the fact that, pursuant to its quasi-legislative function, it frequently becomes necessary for a commission to set forth policy statements or interpretative rules (to be distinguished from strict "legislative" rules) in order to inform interested parties of its official position on various matters. This is as it should be.

At times similar statements of official position are elicited in Congressional hearings. In this context, the agencies are sometimes called to task for failing to adhere to the "intent of Congress" in supplying meaning to the often broad statutory standards from which the agencies derive their authority.... Although such investigatory methods raise serious policy questions as to the de facto "independence" of the federal regulatory agencies, it seems doubtful that they raise any constitutional issues. However, when such an investigation focuses directly and substantially upon the mental decisional processes of a Commission *in a case which is pending before it*, Congress is no longer intervening in the agency's *legislative* function, but rather, in its *judicial* function. At this latter point, we become concerned with the right of private litigants to a fair trial and, equally important, with their right to the appearance of impartiality, which cannot be maintained unless those who exercise the judicial function are free from powerful external influences....

To subject an administrator to a searching examination as to how and why he reached his decision in a case still pending before him, and to criticize him for reaching the "wrong" decision, as the Senate subcommittee did in this case, sacrifices the appearance of impartiality—the *sine qua non* of American judicial justice—in favor of some short-run notions regarding the Congressional intent underlying an amendment to a statute, unfettered administration of which was committed by Congress to the Federal Trade Commission.

It may be argued that such officials as members of the Federal Trade Commission are sufficiently aware of the realities of governmental, not to say "political," life as to be able to withstand such questioning as we have outlined here. However, this court is not so "sophisticated" that it can shrug off such a procedural due process claim merely because the officials involved should be able to discount what is said and to disregard the force of the intrusion into the adjudicatory process. We conclude that we can preserve the rights of the litigants in a case such as this without having any adverse effect upon the legitimate exercise of the investigative power of Congress. What we do is to preserve the integrity of the judicial aspect of the administrative process.

We are fully aware of the reluctance expressed by the Supreme Court to disqualify the members of the Federal Trade Commission for bias or prejudice (a somewhat different basis than that urged here) in *FTC v. Cement Institute*, 333 U.S. 683. There the Court seems to have placed its decision largely on the grounds of necessity. The Court said, "This complaint could not have been acted upon by the Commission or by any other government agency," since "Congress has provided for no such contingency [as disqualification]. It has not directed that the Commission disqualify itself under any circumstances ..." The quoted language would be equally applicable here if the alternative to affirming the order were a judgment prohibiting consideration and decision by the Commission for all time. Such is not the case. . . .

[W]e are convinced that the Commission is not permanently disqualified to decide this case. We are convinced that the passage of time, coupled with the changes in personnel on the Commission, sufficiently insulate the present members from any outward [sic] effect from what occurred in 1955.

It is extremely unfortunate that this complaint, seeking divestiture by Pillsbury of two other companies acquired by it, has taken this long to reach the present stage of the litigation. It commenced as a pioneer case under the new amendment to the law. However, in the meantime much law has been written as to the quantity and quality of proof needed under a Section 7 complaint while it has been pending. . . .

We conclude that the order appealed from must be vacated and the case remanded to the Commission. The Commission as now constituted can then determine what steps should then appropriately be taken in view of both the lapse of time and the present state of the case law applying Section 7.

VACATED AND REMANDED.

Notes and Questions

1. *The Pillsbury reasoning.* Whether the 1955 hearings actually influenced the FTC's 1960 decision has been doubted:

> In particular, (1) five years elapsed between the oversight hearing and the challenged decision; (2) the chairman had already disqualified himself, and the commissioners who joined in the final agency order (and whose "appearance of impartiality" was in question) had not spoken or been questioned at the oversight hearing; (3) the FTC had already spoken on the antitrust issue that the senators raised, and this issue was not even in controversy in the FTC decision after remand; and, most important, (4) the FTC did not adopt the senators' view at all, but instead adhered to the same position on the "per se" issue that it had taken originally.

Ronald M. Levin, "Congressional Ethics and Constituent Advocacy in an Age of Mistrust," 95 Mich.L.Rev. 1, 40 n.153 (1996). In this light, was the court justified in vacating the decision?

On remand in *Pillsbury,* the Commission quickly dismissed the case, declaring that the record (now fourteen years old) was too stale, and the effects of the merger were too entrenched, to make divestiture a realistic possibility.

2. *Pillsbury and the APA.* In 1976, ten years after *Pillsbury*, Congress added § 557(d) to the APA. The legislative history of that section indicates that the term "interested persons" includes members of Congress. Had it been applicable in 1966, how would § 557(d) apply to *Pillsbury*? Does *PATCO* suggest a different remedy from the one the *Pillsbury* court ordered?

3. *Congressional oversight.* Regardless of whether the court's decision was something of a windfall for the Pillsbury Company, the limits on

congressional behavior that the *Pillsbury* case sets forth are widely accepted. But should they be? The case involved a conflict between the norms of judicialized adjudication and the need for Congressional oversight. Since agencies often set policy through the adjudicatory process, Congress needs to be able to conduct oversight of such policymaking. Does the *Pillsbury* rule prevent it from doing so? We consider the oversight function further in § 7.6.3.

4. *Informal adjudication.* To what types of proceedings does *Pillsbury* apply? In *D.C. Federation of Civic Ass'ns v. Volpe*, 459 F.2d 1231 (D.C.Cir. 1971), members of Congress put pressure on the Secretary of Transportation to approve construction of a new bridge over the Potomac River. Representative Natcher, the chairman of a House appropriations subcommittee, publicly threatened that the Department would not get funding to build the D.C. subway until the bridge project was under way. Soon afterwards, the Secretary did approve the bridge.

The court said that the *Pillsbury* doctrine was inapposite to this situation, because that decision applied only to proceedings that were "judicial or quasi-judicial." The Secretary's decision did not fit that description, because he "was not required to base it solely on a formal record established at a public hearing." In other words, the *D.C. Federation* case held that the *Pillsbury* rule is limited, more or less, to decisions reached in formal adjudication.

Nevertheless, the court continued, even in informal adjudication there are some limits on legislative intervention. The court said that, under the governing statute, the Secretary's decisions were to be based on engineering and conservation considerations, not the wishes of congressmen. Thus, if the Secretary had relied on congressional pressure in approving the bridge, his decision was arbitrary and capricious. (See § 9.4.) The court was divided as to whether the decision under review had in fact been influenced by such pressure, but a majority did agree that on remand "the Secretary must make new determinations based strictly on the merits and completely without regard to any considerations not made relevant by Congress in the applicable statutes."

D.C. Federation is a leading case, but it has been criticized. According to Professor Pierce:

> *D.C. Federation* is hard to explain in a democracy in which two politically accountable branches of government share the power to make policy. . . . Our nation would be ungovernable in the absence of constant policy compromises between the executive and legislative branches. . . . [A]ny agency policymaker who took seriously the D.C. Circuit's admonition to ignore the policy views of legislators would be rendered ineffective in a matter of months.

Pierce argues that the court should have held that the Secretary could lawfully take account of Natcher's pressure, because the transportation legislation did not *expressly* prohibit such consideration. Richard J. Pierce, Jr., "Political Control Versus Impermissible Bias in Agency Decisionmaking: Lessons from *Chevron* and *Mistretta*," 57 U.Chi.L.Rev. 481, 496–98 (1990). Is this a valid criticism?

5. *Preliminary investigations. D. C. Federation* suggests a more nuanced approach to the problem of congressional pressure than does *Pillsbury*. In light of the possible conflict between *Pillsbury* and legitimate congressional oversight, other cases have been even more cautious about challenging legislative intervention in the administrative process.

A good example is *DCP Farms v. Yeutter*, 957 F.2d 1183 (5th Cir.1992). This case involved federal crop subsidies, which are limited to $50,000 per person. DCP Farms split itself up into 51 trusts to avoid this limitation. After a county committee approved subsidy payments to each trust, the Agriculture Department (USDA) began reviewing the case.

Congressman Huckaby, chairman of the relevant subcommittee, wrote USDA Secretary Yeutter that the DCP Farms arrangement violated the letter and spirit of the law; urged a careful review of this and similar cases; and threatened that he would introduce legislation to amend the law to outlaw any payments to trusts unless DCP were disqualified. USDA responded that it would take a very aggressive enforcement position toward the farms. DCP Farms did not exhaust the judicial process available within USDA for appealing such matters and sued for declaratory relief.

The court denied relief. It held *Pillsbury* was not applicable, because, when Huckaby wrote his letter, the DCP Farms matter had not yet reached the point of quasi-judicial proceedings. It would not reach that stage until the hearing, the court said. Moreover, erecting a barrier to such communications would infringe too far on Congressional oversight of administrative agencies. Huckaby's communication was part of a larger policy debate, not just a dispute about DCP Farms. The key point was that Huckaby's letter concerned a relevant issue (whether trusts can be used to avoid the $50,000 per person limit), rather than an extraneous issue as in *D.C. Federation*.

Do you agree with the court that Huckaby was free to engage in ex parte contacts until the actual hearing? Consider APA § 557(d)(1)(E). Was the threat to seek changes in the law if USDA did not submit really a "relevant issue" in the case? More generally, is the *DCP Farms* case too permissive in allowing Congressional interference with pending cases? Or was this a legitimate exercise of the oversight function? For one view, see Levin, *supra*, at 51, 57–59.

6. *Legislative casework.* Legislators often receive requests for assistance from their constituents who are embroiled in controversies with agencies. Congressional offices handle literally millions of such cases every year. Typically, the member's staff will call or write to the agency and ask about the status of the matter. These requests are often given priority treatment by agency staff. Sometimes, members seek to influence the outcome of the matter. In extreme cases, interference with pending agency adjudication can raise serious ethical issues for legislators.

Could such requests be treated as ex parte contacts that would violate state or federal APAs? In drafting APA § 557(d), Congress was anxious to protect its right to make status inquiries, which explains the specific reference to them in APA § 551(14). There is no comparable exception in 1981 MSAPA § 4–213.

Senator Dirksen once said: "I have been calling agencies for 25 years . . . Are we to be put on the carpet because we represent our constituents, make inquiries, and find out what the status of matters is, and so serve our constituents? . . . I know these people, they are good, reliable operators; they are good solid citizens. I just want to know what the status of the matter is." 105 Cong.Rec. 14057 (1959).

Is legislative casework, such as status inquiries, a form of undesirable tampering with the adjudicative process? Or is it a desirable form of democracy in action? The policy issues are reviewed in Levin, *supra*, at 16–32.

7. *Problem*. In order to open a new hospital in Madison, it is necessary to first receive permission from the Madison Hospital Agency (MHA). The statute directs MHA to consider the current and future need for additional facilities in the area before granting permission.

Midway Corp. sought to open a new hospital in Oak City called Midway Hospital, but its application was opposed by the existing hospital—Oak City General. Investors in Midway thought that there was need for an additional hospital, since Oak City General is often full and the area has been increasing in population owing to some new factories. After Midway filed its application with MHA, MHA conducted an economic study that lasted ten months. After concluding the study, the staff proposed to grant the application on the ground that there was a need for a new hospital in the area. MHA provided Midway and Oak General with an extensive hearing, following which the Director of MHA reversed the staff decision and rejected the application.

Two days after Midway filed its application, ten Madison legislators wrote to the Director, urging her to reject Midway's application. The letter stated Oak City could not support two hospitals and that if Midway were built, both Midway and Oak City General would fail. The letter concluded: "If MHA grants the Midway application, we would have to review the question of whether MHA should continue to exist. As you know, we will have to make budget cuts next year and MHA would be a prime candidate for defunding." The legislators did not send a copy of this letter to Midway, but the Director forwarded a copy to Midway immediately after she received it.

On judicial review of the MHA decision, what should the court do? Assume 1981 MSAPA is applicable.

§ 3.4 ADMINISTRATIVE JUDGES AND DECISIONAL INDEPENDENCE

In both federal and state agency adjudication, a single hearing officer normally makes the initial agency decision. The head or heads of the agency make the final agency decision. There has been a longstanding controversy about whether to view an administrative hearing officer as a real judge, with the independent status we associate with judges, or as one important member of the agency's team. Answering this question brings us back to the fundamental and now familiar conflict between the judicial and institutional models of adjudication.

At the federal level, there is a distinction between administrative law judges (ALJs) and administrative judges (AJs). ALJs hear cases of *formal adjudication* governed by the APA. Although ALJs work for the agency for which they decide cases, their independence is safeguarded by an elaborate web of statutory protections. These statutes relate to hiring of ALJs, their duties and assignment to cases, separation of functions within the agency, and the evaluation, compensation, and discharge of ALJs. The result of these protections is that agencies that employ ALJs have little control over them.

Many federal administrative cases are not covered by the APA. In many instances, these *informal adjudications* are conducted in just as formal a *manner* as "formal adjudications" described by the ALJ. The difference is that the cases are heard by AJs whose independence is not protected by statute. Because agencies dislike the statutory constraints on their use of ALJs, many of them induced Congress to take them out of the APA adjudication provisions altogether.

Most states follow the federal model: administrative judges work for the agencies for which they decide cases. However, more than twenty states and several large cities have adopted a *central panel* model. Under a central panel, judges are not employed by agencies that are parties to pending cases. Instead the judges work for a separate agency consisting entirely of judges. The judges are assigned as needed to agencies that wish to conduct hearings. Central panel judges normally write proposed, not final, decisions; the agency heads still make the final decisions.

Generally, states that have adopted the central panel model do not apply it to every state agency. Thus there is a patchwork—some agencies employ their own judges while others must use central panel judges. Sections 4–202(a) and 4–301 of 1981 MSAPA adopt the central panel approach. States are offered a choice of adopting § 4–202(a) with or without the bracketed language. What is the significance of adopting the bracketed material? Legislation to adopt a federal central panel (often called an ALJ Corps) has been introduced in every session of Congress, but has never come close to passage.

The following materials all relate to the issue of decisional independence for administrative judges. Please consider these materials in light of four questions:

(i) Should there be any changes in the system by which federal ALJs are appointed and evaluated?

(ii) You are an aide to a state legislator who is chair of a committee in charge of administrative procedures. Recently charges have been made that some administrative judges have engaged in gender or racial discrimination in their proposed decisions. What, if anything, should the legislature do about it?

(iii) Your boss's committee is considering whether to adopt the 1981 MSAPA. Agencies in your state now employ their own administrative judges. Should you recommend to your boss that the state adopt §§ 4–202(a) and 4–301 and, if so, with or without the bracketed language in § 4–202(a)?

(iv) Another item on your boss' agenda concerns casino gambling which the legislature is about to authorize. She thinks that gambling should be regulated by a new agency called the Gaming Board. The Board will have three agency heads. It will adopt regulations and issue casino licenses. The Board will have power to revoke or suspend licenses or exclude casino managers with criminal records or ties to organized crime.

Two problems: a) assuming the state adopts a central panel system, (as discussed in question (iii), should that system apply to the judges who will decide cases for the Gaming Board? b) who should make the final agency decision in Gaming Board cases—the heads of the Board or an independent administrative court? Or should these cases go straight from an administrative judge to judicial review without any stop in between?

§ 3.4.1 SELECTION AND APPOINTMENT OF ALJS

ACUS, THE FEDERAL ADMINISTRATIVE JUDICIARY

Recommendation No. 92–7.
57 Fed.Reg. 61759 (1992).

[The federal APA provided for "hearing examiners," now redesignated as "ALJs." Examiners were to be] impartial factfinders, with substantive expertise in the subjects relevant to the adjudications over which they preside, who would be insulated from the investigatory and prosecutorial efforts of employing agencies through protections concerning hiring, salary, and tenure, as well as separation-of-functions requirements. The decisions of such impartial factfinders were made subject to broad review by agency heads to ensure that the accountable appointee at the top of each agency has control over the policymaking for which the agency has responsibility.

The need for impartial factfinders in administrative adjudications is evident. To ensure the acceptability of the process, some degree of adjudicator independence is necessary in those adjudications involving some kind of hearing. The legitimacy of an adjudicatory process also depends on the consistency of its results and its efficiency. . . .

While the number of ALJs in the Federal government has leveled off in the last decade, and has actually decreased outside of the Social Security Administration, some agencies have been making increased use of AJs [meaning hearing officers who preside at adjudicatory hearings not governed by the APA]. The amount of functional independence accorded to AJs varies with the particular agency and type of adjudication; however, AJs generally lack the statutory protections guaranteed to ALJs. . . . The movement away from the uniformity of qualifications, procedures, and protections of independence that derives from using ALJs in appropriate adjudications is unfortunate. . . . This movement away from ALJs toward AJs has been fueled by perceptions among agency management of difficulties in selecting and managing ALJs. . . .

Use of ALJs and AJs

There is no apparent rationale undergirding current congressional or agency decisions on the use of ALJs or non-ALJs in particular types of cases. . . . The uniform structure established by the APA for on-the-record hearings and for qualifications of presiding officers serves to provide a consistency that helps furnish legitimacy and acceptance of agency adjudication. . . . The Conference, therefore, recommends that Congress consider the conversion of AJ positions to ALJ positions in certain contexts. . . .

One critical factor is the nature of the interest being adjudicated. The separation of functions mandated by the APA, as well as the selection criteria designed to ensure the highest quality adjudicators, are of particular value in situations where the most important interests are at stake. [Hearings that might involve substantial impact on personal liberties or freedom, or those that might result in sanctions with a substantial economic effect or those involving discrimination under civil rights laws] represent categories of proceedings that may call for ALJ use. . . .

ALJ Selection

. . . OPM [Office of Personnel Management] develops the criteria for selection, accepts applications for the register of eligibles, and rates the applicants. . . . The scores from this process determine an applicant's rank on the register of eligibles. . . . OPM rates and ranks eligibles on a scale from 70 to 100, and when an agency seeks to fill a vacancy, OPM certifies the top three names on the register to that agency [the so-called "rule of three"].

The Veterans' Preference Act . . . is applicable to selection of ALJs . . . Veterans are awarded an extra 5 points, and disabled veterans are awarded an extra 10 points in their scores. These extra points have had an extremely large impact, given the small range in unadjusted scores. In addition, under current law, agencies may not pass over a veteran to hire a nonveteran with the same or lower score on the certificate. As a consequence, application of the veterans' preference has almost always been determinative in the ALJ selection system. . . .

[T]he application of veterans' preference to the ALJ selection process has had a materially negative effect on the potential quality of the federal administrative judiciary primarily because it has effectively prevented agencies from being able to hire representative numbers of qualified women candidates as ALJs. There is also some evidence that application of the veterans' preference may have adversely affected the hiring of racial minorities. . . . [T]he Conference recommends that Congress abolish veterans' preference in the particular and limited context of ALJ selection. . . .

[In addition, the Conference recommends replacing the rule-of-three by allowing agencies to choose any applicant whose rankings placed them in the top 50% of all applicants.] . . . [T]he Conference is attempting to balance two factors. The Conference recognizes the agencies' strong interest in having a substantially larger pool of qualified candidates from which to select ALJs who meet their varying criteria and needs. It also recognizes the importance of ensuring that such a pool is highly qualified, as measured by a uniform objective rating system. . . .

ALJ Evaluation and Discipline

At present, ALJs, virtually alone among Federal employees, are statutorily exempt from any performance appraisal. Although agencies may seek removal or discipline of ALJs "for good cause" by initiating a formal proceeding at the Merit Systems Protection Board (MSPB), the Board has applied standards that have strictly limited the contexts in which such actions may successfully be taken against an ALJ. For example, agency actions premised on low productivity have never been successful before the Board. . . .

The Conference . . . recommends that a system of review of ALJ performance be developed. Chief ALJs would be given the responsibility to coordinate development of case processing guidelines . . . These guidelines, which would address issues such as ALJ productivity . . . would be one of the bases upon which Chief ALJs would conduct regular . . . performance reviews. Judicial comportment and demeanor would be another basis for review. Another factor on the list of bases for performance review, which list is not intended to be exclusive, would be the existence of a clear disregard of, or pattern of nonadherence to, properly articulated and disseminated rules, procedures, precedents and other agency policy . . .

Recently, attention has been focused on allegations of prejudice against certain classes of litigants by some ALJs. While there is no known evidence that such a problem is widespread, the Conference's view is that it is important to have a mechanism for handling complaints or allegations relating to ALJ misconduct, including allegations of bias or prejudice . . .

§ 3.4.2　BIAS OF ADMINISTRATIVE LAW JUDGES

ELAINE GOLIN, NOTE, "SOLVING THE PROBLEM OF GENDER AND RACIAL BIAS IN ADMINISTRATIVE ADJUDICATION"
95 Colum.L.Rev. 1532, 1544–47 (1995).

Recent studies have found convincing evidence of gender and racial bias in some benefits hearings conducted by ALJs. The Ninth Circuit Gender Bias Task Force's (Task Force) work on administrative hearings indicates that many claimants and their representatives view gender bias as a major problem. A statistical analysis of benefits hearings, done by the General Accounting Office (GAO), reveals a racial disparity in the outcome of hearings that cannot be explained by any other objective factor. In addition, while no empirical research has been done, anecdotal evidence suggests that members of ethnic groups and non-English speaking claimants may face a cultural bias in some ALJ hearings. Finally, the current demographics of the ALJ corps, which are shaped by the use of a veterans' preference in hiring, make ALJs vulnerable to suspicions of bias.

. . . In 1991, in response to a congressional request, the GAO investigated racial differences in benefit allowance rates for applicants to SSA disability programs. The purpose of the study was to discover why, over the past thirty years, "blacks have consistently been allowed benefits at lower rates than whites, with the magnitude of the difference ranging between 4 and 13 percentage points." . . .

[A]t the appeals level, where ALJs preside over in-person hearings, the racial difference was larger than at any other level, and "for the most part, this difference was unexplainable by demographic factors, or severity and type of impairment." Overall, ALJs allowed benefits to 55% of appealing black claimants under the DI program, while allowing benefits to 66% of white appellants. In some age groups and at higher education levels, the disparity was even more striking; for example, among claimants with more than a twelfth-grade education (the highest level tracked), there was a 17% racial difference in favor of whites in the DI program and a 19% racial difference in the SSI program. . . .

GRANT v. SHALALA
989 F.2d 1332 (3d Cir.1993).

ALITO, J.:

[Lois Grant applied for Social Security disability benefits, alleging that she could not perform any substantial gainful employment because of an injury to her knee, as well as pain, depression, and other conditions stemming from that injury. ALJ Russell Rowell heard Grant's case but he ruled she was not entitled to benefits. He ruled that she could perform sedentary work and that her complaints of pain were not credible. He relied on what he termed a "secondary gain"—her benefits would exceed her income prior to the injury (after taking taxes into account).

Grant sought judicial review in the federal district court. She amended her complaint to convert it to a class action, consisting of claimants whose cases had been or would be assigned to ALJ Rowell. She sought a declaratory judgment that Rowell was biased against disability claimants and this would deprive plaintiffs of a fair hearing. She also sought an injunction requiring that all claims that Rowell had rejected be reheard before other ALJs as well as prohibiting the Secretary of

Health and Human Services from assigning him to any other disability cases. The District Court permitted Grant to conduct extensive discovery in support of her claims.

Meanwhile the Chair of the Social Security Appeals Council conducted an investigation into the allegations against Rowell. A panel that studied 212 of his cases concluded that Rowell was not biased against disability claimants generally nor toward anyone based on race, ethnicity, or socio-economic status. The Chair found that Rowell had generally acted in a professional manner toward claimants but did criticize him for employing irregular language in 70 cases, including frequent emphasis on "secondary gain."

The Third Circuit ruled that the District Court had erred in allowing discovery. It held that § 205(g) of the Act was dispositive. It states that "the findings of the Secretary as to any fact, if supported by substantial evidence, shall be conclusive ..." As a result, the district court could review Social Security cases only on the basis of the administrative record, not on the basis of a new record created in a de novo trial. It reversed for a second reason:]

Section 205(g)'s restriction of district court fact-finding is not an empty technical requirement but instead serves a vital role in safeguarding the integrity of the administrative process. In the present context, Section 205(g) protects against discovery and court proceedings that could seriously undermine the independence of Social Security ALJs.

As the Supreme Court observed in *Butz v. Economou*, 438 U.S. 478, 513 (1978), there was considerable concern prior to the passage of the APA that "persons hearing administrative cases at the trial level could not exercise independent judgment." Therefore, "the process of agency adjudication is currently structured so as to assure that the [ALJ] exercises his independent judgment on the evidence before him, free from pressures by the parties or other officials within the agency." Relying in part on this structure, the Supreme Court concluded that the role of the modern federal ALJ is " 'functionally comparable' to that of a judge."

Availability of the type of discovery and trial that the plaintiffs sought in this case would undermine this vital independence.... It has long been recognized that attempts to probe the thought and decision making processes of judges and administrators are generally improper. In [*Morgan IV*, discussed in § 3.3.1] the Supreme Court observed that questioning a judge or administrator about the process by which a decision had been reached would undermine the judicial or administrative process....

In this case, the plaintiffs, through discovery, have already delved deeply into ALJ Rowell's decision making processes, work habits, and private communications. For example, they deposed an opinion-writer who assisted ALJ Rowell in writing opinions for five years, and they plainly intended to rely heavily on her evidence. During her deposition, under questioning by plaintiffs' counsel, she gave evidence concerning, among other things, ALJ Rowell's instructions concerning opinions that she was assigned to draft, his use of "stock" language in opinions, differences between his work procedures and views and those of other ALJs, the length of his opinions and the number of revisions he made, her evaluation of aspects of his work, his consultation of law books, his familiarity with and views about particular rules of law, whether she thought his opinions were principled or result-oriented, how often she disagreed with his decisions, whether she believed that his decisions discriminated against certain groups, how he viewed his role as a Social Security ALJ, whether he ever uttered racial or ethnic epithets, complaints about him from typists and secretaries, how he evaluated certain types of evidence, the number of hours he worked, his views regarding particular physicians in the area, his views regarding alcoholism and obesity, and many other matters....

Such efforts to probe the mind of an ALJ, if allowed, would pose a substantial threat to the administrative process. Every ALJ would work under the threat of being subjected to such treatment if his or her pattern of decisions displeased any administrative litigant or group with the resources to put together a suit charging bias. Every ALJ would know that his or her staff members could be deposed and questioned in detail about the ALJ's decision making and thought processes, that co-workers could be subpoenaed and questioned about social conversations, that the ALJ's notes and papers could be ordered produced in discovery, and that any evidence gathered by these means could be used, in essence, to put the ALJ on trial in district court to determine if he or she should be barred from performing the core functions of his or her office. This would seriously interfere with the ability of many ALJs to decide the cases that come before them based solely on the evidence and the law.

We fully recognize that bias on the part of ALJs may undermine the fairness of the administrative process. ...The type of district court trial and fact-finding that the plaintiffs sought in this case, however, are not necessary in order to safeguard the impartiality of Social Security disability adjudications. Other procedures that pose far less threat to the integrity of the administrative process are readily available.

As previously noted, the Social Security Administration has promulgated regulations prohibiting an administrative law judge from conducting a disability hearing "if he or she is prejudiced or partial with respect to any party or has any interest in the matter pending for decision." The regulations allow a claimant to seek the disqualification of an ALJ. If the ALJ refuses to step aside, the claimant can pursue an administrative appeal and subsequently obtain judicial review. This procedure is analogous to the procedure for seeking disqualification of a federal district court judge.

Furthermore, in the present case the Social Security Administration responded to the allegations against ALJ Rowell by convening a special panel and conducting an extensive analysis of a statistically significant, random sample of his disability decisions. The special panel wrote a lengthy report setting out its findings, and while it did not find any evidence of bias, the panel criticized certain practices that it detected. The acting Chair of the Appeals Council then reviewed this report and accepted its essential conclusions. The Secretary acknowledges that the plaintiffs may seek judicial review of these findings and that the district court, if it finds them insufficient, may remand the matter to the Secretary for further proceedings. We, of course, express no view regarding the correctness of the administrative findings or the adequacy of the special panel's inquiry, but we are convinced that the plaintiffs' right to an impartial administrative determination can be fully protected through the process of judicial review of the Secretary's determination.

REVERSED AND REMANDED.

HIGGINBOTHAM, J., dissenting:

. . . The Supreme Court may have described ALJs as functionally comparable to judges, but the court never held that ALJs *are* federal judges. The independence guaranteed to Article III judges is rooted in the separation of powers doctrine embodied in the Constitution of the United States. By contrast, the independence afforded to ALJs, whatever its contours may be, is not rooted in the constitution, but rather is a function of the need for administrative efficiency, the recognition of administrative expertise, and the need to build an adequate administrative record for judicial review. . . .

Accordingly, the independence enjoyed by ALJs is not without bounds. For one thing, the need for administrative efficiency is not necessarily controlling in actions where plaintiffs challenge the very legality of the agency's policy or practice. For another thing, the recognition of administrative expertise, and the need to build an adequate administrative record for judicial review, are not applicable when, as in the present case, plaintiffs do not seek to have the court review the very area in which the agency is deemed to be expert.

This is of course amply demonstrated by the facts of the present case. The Social Security Administration simply does not have any expertise in reviewing claims of general bias. Granted the agency has in place regulations to determine claims of individual bias. But those regulations are obviously not designed to handle claims of general bias. The Secretary in fact acknowledged that the existing regulations were not adequate in reviewing claims of general bias. If they were, the Secretary would have relied on them rather than instituting an "ad hoc" method in reviewing plaintiffs' claim in this case. Moreover, the ad hoc procedure set up by the Secretary is unlikely to produce an adequate record for judicial review. For example in the case of the Secretary's examination of allegations of bias on the part of ALJ Rowell, the ad hoc procedure was not established by regulation or statute; it lacked any procedural rules; it lacked discovery mechanisms; and they were no parties and no assignment of burden of proof. In short, the agency does not have the expertise in dealing with claims of general bias, and there is no reason to believe that the ad hoc procedure it has devised will produce an adequate record for judicial review.

Of course, I am convinced that the majority of ALJs perform the duties of their office consistent with the statute they are charged to execute and in compliance with the constitution. But I cannot accept the majority's position that the exercise of independent review by the district courts on the question of general bias by ALJs will have a deleterious effect on the administrative process. If anything, such an independent review can only strengthen public confidence in the administrative process. And, an administrative process which enjoys public confidence will in the end function more efficiently. . . .

§ 3.4.3 ALJS: THE CENTRAL PANEL ISSUE

JOSEPH J. SIMEONE, "THE FUNCTION, FLEXIBIL-ITY, AND FUTURE OF UNITED STATES JUDGES OF THE EXECUTIVE DEPARTMENT"
44 Admin.L.Rev. 159 (1992).

[Simeone, a Social Security Administration ALJ, favors enactment of federal legislation that would establish an ALJ Corps—a central panel of federal ALJs.]

[T]he proposed legislation's foremost value lies in the removal of the present system of such judges being associated with the particular agency and subject to its supervision, and the possibility of control. A unified corps by which judges are assigned to particular cases instead of being assigned by the particular department or agency would have the beneficent effect of removing the incongruous status and the public perception that such judges have an agency bias in favor of their controlling authority.

Second, a unified corps would be much more efficient than the present system. Under the present system, the management of administrative judges are assigned to and divided among numerous agencies so that some are overloaded and overworked while others are not so busy. The establishment of a unified corps would enable the administrative law judges to dispose of cases more uniformly.

[O]ne of the chief criticisms . . . is that a corps will decrease the expertise that such judges possess to determine cases within a particular agency . . . This criticism is, in reality, a myth. . . . It is true that judges ensconced in a particular agency acquire an experience and expertise in a particular field and are better able to understand the issues involved and make an intelligent and just decision. But being a judge who is a generalist rather than an "expert" in a particular field far outweighs the status of being an "expert" in a particular narrow field of law. A judge is a "judge." Federal and state judges are generalist judges. A federal or state judge hears all types of cases. . . .

Except, perhaps, for such specialized areas as the Nuclear Regulatory Commission or the Federal Energy Regulatory Commission, any judge of the executive department who has gone through the crucible of the examinations established by OPM is able and competent to hear any case within the federal administrative process, whether it relates to labor, immigration, social security, SEC, or the Coast Guard. . . .

PAUL VERKUIL, ET.AL., THE FEDERAL ADMINISTRATIVE JUDICIARY

Administrative Conference of the United States 169–72 (1992).

. . . The choice presented [by the proposal for a federal ALJ Corps] is between continuation of the original model of administrative law and adoption of a new model that renders administrative adjudication virtually indistinguishable from judicial adjudication.

Congress originally assigned adjudication of some types of disputes to Article I agencies rather than to Article III courts to further several goals: (1) to take advantage of specialized expertise; (2) to provide a less formal and less expensive means of resolving some types of disputes; (3) to attain a higher degree of interdecisional consistency in adjudicating disputes that arise in administering national regulatory and benefit programs; and, (4) to allow agencies to control the policy components of administrative adjudications. Adoption of the Corps proposal would represent an abandonment of each of those goals in favor of an administrative adjudication system designed to replicate the Article III courts. . . .

We do not view that as a virtue, however. It would entail abandonment of the traditional goal of providing a less formal and less expensive means of resolving specialized classes of disputes with the government. Over time, the cost of administrative adjudication would move ever closer to the cost of judicial adjudication. The potential for increased costs attributable to adoption of the formal, judicial model of adjudication is enormous. Use of the judicial model of adjudication to resolve tort disputes creates a situation in which the dispute resolution process costs approximately fifty per cent of the total amount of money awarded as compensation. By contrast, the Social Security Administration spends only 3.7 per cent of its budget on administrative adjudication. Some of this enormous difference in cost is attributable to the somewhat different issues to be resolved in tort cases versus disability cases, but a substantial proportion of the difference is attributable to the greater procedural and evidentiary formality of judicial adjudication.

Proponents of the ALJ Corps are also candid in their rejection of the value of specialized expertise that is among the principal justifications for assigning adjudicatory functions to agencies rather than to Article III judges. . . . Rejection of specialized expertise as a justification for administrative adjudication would have major implications. Converting all ALJs (and potentially [AJs]) into generalist judges would impose major costs on the agency adjudicatory system in the form of lost expertise.

ALJs preside in more than one hundred different types of adjudicatory disputes at scores of different agencies. AJs preside in another nearly one hundred different types of adjudicatory disputes at scores of other agencies. Each of the hundreds of regulatory and benefit programs in which ALJs participate are different and each is extremely complicated. A typical regulatory or benefit system can be understood only by mastering hundreds of pages of statutes and regulations, thousands of pages of judicial opinions, tens of thousands of pages of agency guidelines and decisions, and the principles of one or more disciplines other than law. . . .

§ 3.4.4 ALJS: THE ADMINISTRATIVE COURT ISSUE

NEWTON MINOW
LETTER TO PRESIDENT KENNEDY
15 Admin.L.Rev. 146 (1963).

[On resigning as chair of the FCC, Newton Minow suggested that the adjudicatory functions of the FCC (and presumably of the other federal regulatory agencies) be transferred to an independent administrative court. He also suggested that the multi-member FCC be replaced by a single administrator.]

There are several advantages to assigning the hearing functions now exercised by the Commission to a new administrative court patterned, for example, after the Tax Court.

First, it is clearly desirable to separate the prosecutory function from the function of judging. An agency should not be called upon to investigate fully whether a violation has occurred, to become steeped in all kinds of investigative reports upon which it determines that a hearing is necessary, and then to judge the merits of the case. . . .

Second, the establishment of the administrative court would greatly improve the decisional process itself . . . FCC Commissioners cannot spend several weeks analyzing the record of a case and drafting their own opinions . . . [Instead] the Commissioners determine the case largely upon the basis of the staff analysis and oral argument and adopt an institutional decision prepared by the staff. This may be a necessary process but it is clearly not an optimum one. [Under an administrative court structure] the decision-maker is wholly familiar with the record and pleadings and actually drafts his own opinion.

Finally, the administrative court will lead to better formulation of standards. Not only will the administrator be required to lay down definitive and clear policies, if the administrative court is to follow them, but the court could be expected to apply these policies in a meaningful manner which would build up a body of meaningful precedents. . . .

There is, however, one argument which does have some validity. It may be difficult, in practice, to confine the policy-making function to the administrator. The administrative court, in deciding particular cases, may find itself called upon to make policy or may take action which in the administrator's view is inconsistent with the policies he has established. In a division of responsibility such as this, there is always the possibility of some degree of friction between the administrator and the court. . . .

My purpose here has not been to present a detailed blueprint but rather to advance the principle of separation of regulatory and hearing functions, in the hope that as more voices declare for the principle, a serious study of it will be undertaken. I do not believe it is possible to be a good judge on Monday and Tuesday, a good legislator on Wednesday and Thursday, and a good administrator on Friday.

PAUL VERKUIL, ET. AL. THE FEDERAL ADMINISTRATIVE JUDICIARY
Administrative Conference of the United States 168–69 (1992).

The adjudicatory function can be placed in an institution that is independent of the agency that makes and enforces rules and policies. This institutional structure can increase the extent to which adjudicatory decisionmaking is insulated from potential sources of agency bias. Congress has chosen this institutional structure in three significant contexts—mine safety and health, occupational safety and health, and transportation safety. In each case, one agency makes all rules and enforcement decisions, while a second independent agency makes all adjudicatory decisions. . . . Various groups have urged general adoption of this institutional structure for all agency adjudication for decades.

The Administrative Conference conducted a study of this alternative in 1986. The study was unable to detect any improvement in adjudicatory decisionmaking attributable to the use of the independent adjudicating agency. It was able to document clear and significant costs and inefficiencies, however, attributable to lack of policy coordination, a high level of institutional conflict, frequent litigation between the two agencies, turf battles, and ambiguity with respect to the authority and responsibilities of the two agencies. . . .

———

Missouri and Maine have adopted administrative court structures. In Missouri, if the Administrative Hearing Commission (AHC) finds that disciplinary action is warranted in a licensing case, it can recommend but not decide on the appropriate punishment (revocation, suspension, reprimand, etc.). Unless both the licensee and the agency agree with the AHC's recommendation, the case is returned to the licensing agency for another hearing to determine punishment. In other licensing cases, however, as well as tax and certain health care cases, the AHC renders *final* adjudicatory decisions.

Thus, in *State Board of Registration for the Healing Arts v. Finch,* 514 S.W.2d 608 (Mo.Ct.App.1974), a California doctor served ten years in prison for murdering his wife, and then relocated to a town in Missouri. The Board denied his application for a medical license on the ground that it was "not suitable or appropriate to the best interests of the people of the State of Missouri to paradoxically permit an individual who has brutally murdered his wife to reenter the practice of medicine—a profession which peculiarly and uniquely is dedicated to the prolongation of human life." The AHC reversed, finding "overwhelming evidence" of rehabilitation on the basis of a psychiatric report and numerous character testimonials from local residents. A divided court affirmed the AHC. It conceded that evaluation of Dr. Finch's character would have been within the Board's discretion in past years, but the creation of the AHC had changed the situation. Rejecting the argument that the AHC's role was merely to find facts, the court said it was "inconceivable that the legislature intended any separation of the exercise of discretion from the determination of facts which are necessarily preliminary to and decisive of how that discretion is to be exercised." For a favorable evaluation of the AHC, *see* Frederick Davis, "Judicialization of Administrative Law: The Trial–Type Hearing and the Changing Status of the Hearing Officer," 1977 Duke L.J. 389, 402–08.

South Carolina's structure may be unique. That state strips agency heads in most cases of their ability to make policy through adjudication. South Carolina has a central panel of ALJs and, in most cases, the ALJ makes the final decision at the agency level. The next step is judicial review. In cases involving multi-member boards, either the private party or the staff can appeal an ALJ decision to the agency heads. However, the agency heads can reverse the ALJ's decision only on the same grounds that a reviewing court could use. In other words, the agency heads could not reverse the ALJ for reasons of disagreement about policy and are sharply limited in their ability to reverse because of disagreement about fact questions. S.C. Code §§ 1–23–380B, 610 (1996 Supp.). *See* William B. Swent, Survey, "South Carolina's ALJ: Central Panel, Administrative Court, or a Little of Both?," 48 S.C.L.Rev. 1 (1996) (praising the plan for efficiency and enhanced public acceptability).

Chapter 4

THE PROCESS OF ADMINISTRATIVE ADJUDICATION

The previous chapter explored some fundamental and enduring problems of administrative adjudication. This chapter assumes that the formal adjudication process of state or federal APAs is applicable. It explores the elements of adjudication in chronological order, starting with the pre-hearing phase and exploring issues such as notice, parties, discovery and intervention. It continues with the hearing itself and the decisional process. It concludes with some constraints on the decision (such as res judicata or stare decisis). Thus this chapter might be likened to a civil procedure course—except that we consider procedure before an agency rather than in court.

§ 4.1 THE PRE–HEARING PHASE: NOTICE, INVESTIGATION AND DISCOVERY

§ 4.1.1 NOTICE AND PARTIES TO ADJUDICATION

BLOCK v. AMBACH
537 N.E.2d 181 (N.Y.1989).

Alexander, J.:

[Petitioner Ackerman was a licensed psychiatrist who co-founded and directed the Association for Counseling and Therapy (ACT). His license was revoked because of his alleged fraud, gross negligence, and incompetence in the practice of medicine. The charges were based on Ackerman's having induced] two of his patients (A and B) to engage in sexual intercourse with him, to engage in lewd conduct, and to use inappropriate drugs during time periods covering 26 months, 78 months, 46 months and 53 months.

Thirty-five witnesses, including A, B and a third complainant, D, testified before a Hearing Panel of the State Board for Professional Medical Conduct. At this hearing, which continued over a period of some six years, petitioner denied that A, B and D were his patients or that he had engaged in sexual activity with any of them. Instead, he claimed that the group sessions he led were merely gatherings of people engaged in the discussion of a variety of topics and did not involve any form of psychotherapy treatment.

The Panel found, inter alia, that A and B were petitioner's patients; that petitioner had conducted private sessions with A "on or about the year 1973," and "on numerous occasions" instigated and participated in sexual activities involving that patient; that he had sexual relations with her on a particular day when petitioner's wife was engaged in a radio broadcast; and that A had sexual intercourse and oral sex with petitioner "on approximately 25 occasions." With only minor exceptions, the Panel sustained the charges against petitioner and recommended permanent revocation of his license and a $25,000 fine ... [The Regents Review Committee upheld the Panel's determination. Petitioner Block's case presented similar issues.]

On these appeals, petitioners argue that the administrative determinations must be annulled ... because the statement of charges in each case failed to adequately specify the dates of their alleged misconduct and therefore violated due process. They argue that the standard of specificity constitutionally required of criminal indictments should be applied in these administrative proceedings ...

Ackerman similarly argues that the charges against him cannot be sustained because he was deprived of due process in that the charges spanned a period of more than six years without indicating any specific dates of the alleged misconduct, and, moreover, no witness was able to testify as to any specific dates on which any of the alleged acts took place. He contends that he was thus deprived of the ability to assert an alibi defense or to produce contrary evidence ...

It is axiomatic that due process precludes the deprivation of a person's substantial rights in an administrative proceeding because of uncharged misconduct and it necessarily follows, therefore, that a respondent in such a proceeding is entitled to fair notice of the charges against him or her so that he or she may prepare and present an adequate defense and thereby have an opportunity to be heard ... The State APA requires that a statement of administrative charges contain "a short and plain statement of the matters asserted."

It does not follow, however, that the due process requirements for the specificity of an indictment in a criminal proceeding are to be imported and fully applied in administrative proceedings. Unlike the provisions of the ... APA, the Criminal Procedure Law requires that "[an] indictment must contain ... [a] statement in each count that the offense charged therein was committed on, or on or about, a designated date, or during a designated period of time ... "

[T]he consequences of a criminal proceeding are palpably more grave and justify a requirement of greater specificity. Moreover, criminal indictments must also be sufficiently specific to allow the accused, if convicted, to assert the defense of double jeopardy in subsequent prosecutions for the same conduct. Because administrative proceedings entail neither the dire consequences of criminal prosecutions nor the considerations of double jeopardy, there is generally no need to import the strict requirements of the criminal law and criminal trials into administrative proceedings. We hold, therefore, that in the administrative forum, the charges need only be reasonably specific, in light of all the relevant circumstances, to apprise the party whose rights are being determined of the charges against him for the preparation of an adequate defense.

In the circumstances of these administrative proceedings therefore, we reject petitioners' contentions that the general time periods alleged in the administrative charges against them violate due process ... Much of the misconduct charged in both *Block* and *Ackerman* was capable of being committed through either a single act or multiple acts and therefore may properly be characterized as continuing offenses ...

Furthermore, the other relevant circumstances in each case indicate that the general time periods alleged afforded both petitioners reasonable notice of the charges against them and enabled them to prepare and present adequate defenses.... Petitioner admitted conducting the group sessions during which much of the misconduct was alleged to have occurred and never sought to interpose an alibi defense for any particular incident. Instead, he denied the allegations of improper conduct and also contended that he could not be subject to discipline because the complainants were not his patients. Petitioner advanced these defenses at a comprehensive hearing which lasted over six years and entailed the testimony of 35 witnesses. In these circumstances, we cannot say that he was denied due process.

Notes and Questions

1. *Six years?* The *Block* opinion is unclear as to whether Ackerman was allowed to continue practicing during the incredibly long six-year period occupied by the Panel's hearing process, not to mention the additional years consumed by an administrative appeal and litigation through three levels of the New York courts.

As discussed in § 2.3, a licensing agency normally has power to suspend a licensee from practice during the pendency of the hearing process if the licensee poses a threat to the public, but this authority is often not utilized. As discussed in § 11.2.3 N.7, courts have authority to stay administrative action pending judicial review. This authority is often utilized. Hence, it is possible that Ackerman went right on practicing right up until the 1989 decision of the New York Court of Appeals.

2. *Statute of limitations.* Ackerman's misconduct occurred between 1969 and 1975. Suppose the Board didn't start proceedings against him until 1985. Should there be any statute of limitations in this type of case? Undoubtedly criminal charges or tort actions against Ackerman would be barred by limitations after ten years, but licensing statutes often do not include statutes of limitation.

Sexual misconduct like that in *Block* often is not discovered by authorities until many years after the events in question. Yet the cases often involve credibility conflicts. The time lapse can pose substantial problems for the licensee's defense, because by then memories are fuzzy, witnesses have vanished or died, and it is difficult to disprove the charges.

Absent a statute of limitations, a court might overturn administrative action on the basis of laches if a licensee can show that the delay was unreasonable and caused prejudice. Unreasonable delay could be shown if the agency failed to take action within a reasonable time after obtaining the necessary information. Prejudice could be shown if the delay caused witnesses to be unavailable or otherwise made the defense more difficult. *See Lam v. Bureau of Security and Investigative Services*, 40 Cal.Rptr.2d 137 (Cal.App.1995).

3. *Notice.* Proper notice is required by due process and by all APAs. See APA § 554(b); 1981 MSAPA § 4–206(c). Generally, though, neither APAs nor due process requires notice of specific details such as the dates on which misconduct occurred. Why did Ackerman claim that the notice should have included the dates? Why did the Medical Board not give notice of the dates?

Block indicates that the strict requirements of notice in criminal cases do not apply to licensing cases. Do you agree that "administrative proceedings entail neither the dire consequences of criminal prosecutions nor the considerations of double jeopardy"? Few criminal cases involve a sanction more dire than revocation of a physician's license and a $25,000 fine. And even though double jeopardy protection does not apply to civil cases, res judicata does apply. See § 4.4.1.

While administrative complaints need not meet the specificity requirements of the criminal law, they must provide sufficient detail to allow a respondent to prepare for the hearing. See, e.g., *In re Hot Spot, Inc..*, 546 A.2d 799 (Vt.1988), which involved suspension of the liquor license of Vinny's Hot Spot for serving intoxicated patrons and for allowing intoxicated persons to loiter on the premises. The notice stated that the bar sold liquor to A who was drunk. The investigator's report, to which the licensee had access, stated that Vinny's had allowed "a person or persons under the influence of liquor to loiter" on the premises.

At the hearing, the investigator testified that the bar allowed X, who was drunk, to buy drinks for Y. The Board suspended the license because i) Vinny had sold liquor to X who was drunk and ii) Vinny had allowed X to loiter on the premises. The penalty was based on both offenses. The court held that the notice was inadequate with respect to the first offense, but not the second. As to the second offense, the investigator's report gave Vinny's sufficient warning that a loitering charge would be pursued. However, neither the notice nor the report gave warning that the Board would punish Vinny's for selling liquor to X. The court stated:

> Notice of all alleged violations prior to an administrative proceeding is more than technical surplusage. It is necessary to enable one charged to prepare an adequate defense to all charges. Adequate notice of one violation will not cure insufficient notice of another.

Does this decision violate the rule of prejudicial error? See 1981 MSAPA § 5–116(c)(7). Was there some way to provide Vinny's with fair notice without making the Liquor Authority start the case all over again with a new notice?

4. *Forcing a hearing.* Suppose that after investigating the charges against Ackerman, the Medical Board in *Block* decided not to take any action. Can A, the victim of Ackerman's misconduct, force the Board to hold a hearing? This might be referred to as a right of private prosecution or a right of initiation. Aside from wanting personal vindication or wanting to protect other innocent victims, why would A seek a private prosecution? Why would Ackerman and the Medical Board resist a private prosecution?

The same issue arises frequently in licensing and land use cases. An agency might grant an application for a license or a zoning variance without a hearing. Can persons who want the application to be denied force the agency to hold a hearing? For example, Bob might seek a zoning variance to build a guest house in the yard that he could rent out. Carmen, a neighbor of Bob's, opposes the application because she wants the neighborhood to remain entirely occupied by one family per lot. The zoning board denies Carmen a hearing and grants Bob's application.

Generally third parties like A (the victim in *Block*) or Carmen (the disgruntled neighbor) do not have power to initiate hearings absent some statutory or constitutional authority providing such a power. However, statutes that provide a right of initiation are not uncommon. For example, statutes frequently entitle community members who object to a liquor license application or a land use application to require the granting agency to hold a hearing before granting the application. And the Communications Act provision discussed in *United Church of Christ* in N.5 confers initiation rights on consumers. Consider 1981 MSAPA §§ 4–101 to 4–103 and 1–102(5). Would those sections entitle either A or Carmen to compel the agency to hold a hearing?

Some authority suggests that Carmen might be constitutionally entitled to a hearing with respect to Bob's zoning application. See *Horn v. County of Ventura*, 596 P.2d 1134 (Cal. 1979), holding that "Carmen," an adjoining landowner, has a constitutional right to notice and hearing with respect to "Bob's" proposal to divide his property into four parcels for development. The Court held that decisions involving specific parcels of land were adjudicatory, not legislative, and thus deprived Carmen of property within the meaning of due process.

5. *Intervention.* Suppose now that the Board decides to charge Ackerman with violations of the Medical Practice Act. A feels that the Board's attorneys are doing a poor job and wishes to intervene in the proceeding by becoming a party. Why would A want to intervene? Is there some way short of intervention by which A could make her position known? See APA § 555(b) (third sentence); 1981 MSAPA § 4–211(3).

Why would Ackerman and the Board resist intervention? See Richard A. Manso, Comment, "Licensing of Nuclear Power Plants: Abuse of the Intervention Right," 21 U.S.F.L.Rev. 121 (1986). According to the Comment, in one nuclear licensing case, intervenors filed 1600 allegations—all of which were ultimately rejected. Intervention greatly prolonged the licensing process, and the delays caused serious increases in cost of the power plant.

On intervention in an administrative adjudication, see 1981 MSAPA § 4–209. Does § 4–209(a) provide for a right to intervene? What is the difference between § 4–209(a) and (b)? What is the significance of § 4–209(c)?

Federal cases involving the right to be an intervenor in an adjudicative proceeding sometimes link this issue to a different one: standing to seek judicial review, an issue discussed in § 11.1. In *United Church of Christ (UCC) v. FCC,* 359 F.2d 994 (D.C.Cir.1966), the issue was whether TV watchers have a right to initiate and to participate in FCC licensing proceedings. Thus the case involves both the issue of whether a person can force a hearing to occur and whether a person can intervene in an ongoing proceeding.

The Communications Act provided that any "party in interest" could file a petition to deny a license application. Station WLBT, in Jackson, Mississippi, applied for renewal of its license. On behalf of blacks who lived in Jackson and watched the station, UCC asserted that it was a "party in interest" entitled to file a petition to deny the application and to be a party at the hearing. UCC charged that WLBT engaged in racist programming and gross violations of the fairness doctrine. The FCC refused to allow UCC to be a party because it then allowed only economic competitors of existing stations to be parties, not listeners or viewers.

The Court held that TV viewers were "parties in interest" who had the right to petition for denial of a license, participate or intervene in a licensing hearing, and seek judicial review of an unfavorable FCC decision. Treating the right to participate at the administrative level as equivalent to standing to seek judicial review, the court said:

> Since the concept of standing is a practical and functional one designed to insure that only those with a genuine and legitimate interest can participate in a proceeding, we can see no reason to exclude those with such an obvious and acute concern as the listening audience. This much seems essential to insure that the holders of broadcasting licenses be responsive to the needs of the audience, without which the broadcaster could not exist . . .

> The theory that the Commission can always effectively represent the listener interests in a renewal proceeding without the aid and participation of legitimate listener representatives fulfilling the role of private attorneys general is one of those assumptions we collectively try to work with so long as they are reasonably adequate. When it becomes clear, as it does to us now, that it is no longer a valid assumption which stands up under the realities of actual experience, neither we nor the Commission can continue to rely on it . . .

> We cannot believe that the Congressional mandate of public participation . . . was meant to be limited to writing letters to the Commission, to inspection of records, to the Commission's grace in considering listener claims, or to mere non-participating appearance at hearings. We cannot fail to note that the long history of complaints against WLBT

beginning in 1955 had left the Commission virtually unmoved in the subsequent renewal proceedings, and it seems not unlikely that the 1964 renewal application might well have been routinely granted except for the determined and sustained efforts of Appellants at no small expense to themselves. Such beneficial contribution as these Appellants ... can make must not be left to the grace of the Commission. ...

In order to safeguard the public interest in broadcasting, therefore, we hold that some "audience participation" must be allowed in license renewal proceedings. We recognize this will create problems for the Commission but it does not necessarily follow that "hosts" of protestors must be granted standing to challenge a renewal application or that the Commission need allow the administrative processes to be obstructed or overwhelmed by captious or purely obstructive protests. The Commission can avoid such results by developing appropriate regulations by statutory rulemaking. Although it denied Appellants standing, it employed *ad hoc* criteria in determining that these Appellants were responsible spokesmen for representative groups having significant roots in the listening community. These criteria can afford a basis for developing formalized standards to regulate and limit public intervention to spokesmen who can be helpful. ...

The fears of regulatory agencies that their processes will be inundated by expansion of standing criteria are rarely borne out. Always a restraining factor is the expense of participation in the administrative process, an economic reality which will operate to limit the number of those who will seek participation; legal and related expenses of administrative proceedings are such that even those with large economic interests find the cost burdensome. Moreover, the listening public seeking intervention in a license renewal proceeding cannot attract lawyers to represent their cause by the prospect of lucrative contingent fees, as can be done, for example, in rate cases ...

The issues of standing to seek judicial review and intervention in an administrative proceeding need not be linked. For example, a party who *lacks* standing to seek judicial review need not be *excluded* from administrative proceedings, for standing to sue depends on more restrictive criteria than standing to be a party in administrative proceedings. *Koniag, Inc. v. Andrus,* 580 F.2d 601 (D.C.Cir.1978) (party can be both "interested" and "aggrieved" for intervention purposes, even though lacking standing to sue because its claim was too speculative).

6. *Problem.* You are general counsel of a state agency (the Coastal Commission) which grants permits for the development of beachfront property. Without such a permit, owners of beachfront property cannot build on their property or even make changes to existing buildings.

The agency heads are concerned that a large number of persons sometimes ask to be parties to permitting hearings. These are persons who do not live near the beach but are interested in securing access to the beach for the general public or in preventing building projects at the beach. Until now, the Commission allowed anyone who applied to be a party. The result is that a few hearings became quite complicated. Each party wanted to put on its own witnesses, introduce its own documentary and economic analyses, and cross-examine the witnesses of other parties.

What steps are suggested by 1981 MSAPA § 4–209(c)? Or should you tell your bosses that public participation is good and they should not seek to limit it?

§ 4.1.2 INVESTIGATION AND DISCOVERY: AN AGENCY'S POWER TO OBTAIN INFORMATION

In order to enforce the law, an agency must secure massive amounts of information about the industry it regulates. The information is needed for a variety of tasks, such as rulemaking, preparation of legislative proposals, or investigating possible violations of the law.

Most of the needed information is supplied voluntarily in periodic reports or in response to requests for information. Occasionally, the agency must compel disclosure of information to find out whether the law is being violated or to obtain evidence for an enforcement proceeding. It does so through a *subpoena duces tecum*. Such subpoenas are frequently called "civil investigative demands" or CIDs. An agency may also engage in *physical inspections* of homes or businesses. With respect to agency investigations, read APA § 555(c) and (d); 1981 MSAPA § 4–210. Notice the key point: agencies need a statutory basis other than the APA in order to compel the production of information. It is not an inherent power.

CRAIB v. BULMASH
777 P.2d 1120 (Calif.1989).

Eagleson, J.:

[Craib, the Labor Commissioner, is investigating Bulmash's alleged failure to pay minimum wages to persons employed to care for his sister Serena. Craib served a subpoena on Bulmash directing him to appear at the Santa Barbara office and produce records showing the names, addresses, and wages of all persons who cared for Serena for the last three years. The statute *requires* all employers to maintain these records. Bulmash failed to appear so Craib filed a petition in court seeking to enforce the subpoena. The lower court quashed the subpoena on both Fourth and Fifth Amendment grounds.]

A. Fourth Amendment

The Commissioner essentially concedes that the instant subpoena fails to comply with literal Fourth Amendment requirements for a criminal warrant … He insists, however, that judicial enforcement of the subpoena is constitutionally permissible under a standard which is less exacting than that required for a search in a criminal prosecution. Based on a recent line of cases by the United States Supreme Court, we agree.

As Bulmash suggests, it was once assumed that the compulsory production of records was a "search and seizure" in the literal Fourth

Amendment sense and that subpoenas, like warrants, were enforceable only if issued pursuant to a formal "complaint" or at least upon probable cause to suspect "a specific breach of the law." However, it is now clear that such a restrictive view of the administrative process is not constitutionally compelled. As regulatory schemes have become increasingly important in enforcing laws designed to protect the public's health and welfare, reliance on "probable cause" as a means of restraining agency subpoena power has all but disappeared.

The Commissioner correctly argues that the leading case is *Oklahoma Press Pub. Co. v. Walling*, 327 U.S. 186 (1946). There, the Supreme Court rejected a Fourth Amendment challenge to judicial orders enforcing administrative subpoenas for payroll and sales records. The subpoenas were issued by the federal wage and hour administrator to determine whether certain publishing corporations were covered under, and had violated, the Fair Labor Standards Act of 1938 (FLSA). At the outset, the court observed that "no question of actual search and seizure" is raised where the agency has not sought "to enter [the subpoenaed parties'] premises against their will, to search them, or to seize or examine their books, records or papers without their assent, otherwise than pursuant to orders of court authorized by law and made after adequate opportunity to present objections ..." The court further questioned whether the Fourth Amendment applied at all to the subpoenas at bar, noting that corporate records historically had been subject to the government's "broad visitorial power."

Accordingly, *Oklahoma Press* articulated a test which applied Fourth Amendment requirements only by analogy. The notion that a subpoena could be enforced only where a specific charge or complaint is pending was explicitly rejected. Instead, said the court, the investigation need only be for "a lawfully authorized purpose, within the power of [the legislative body] to command." In addition, the requirement of " 'probable cause, supported by oath or affirmation,' literally applicable in the case of a warrant," is satisfied as long as the subpoenaed documents are "relevant" to the inquiry. "Beyond this the requirement of reasonableness, including particularity in 'describing the place to be searched, and the persons or things to be seized,' also literally applicable to warrants, comes down to specification of the documents to be produced adequate, but not excessive, for the purposes of the relevant inquiry." In a later case, the court emphasized that, while the subpoena may be issued and served by the agency, the subpoenaed party must have the opportunity for judicial review before suffering any penalties for refusing to comply. . . .

[W]e apply the same test of "reasonableness" here. The instant record reveals no official action beyond issuance and service of the subpena. The subpoena itself does not authorize actual entry or immediate inspection, but merely requests future production of specific records at the Commissioner's office in another city. Thus, Bulmash cannot insist upon a showing of probable cause.

To the extent Bulmash properly challenges the breadth and relevance of the subpoena, these claims are not well taken. There is no dispute, of course, that the Commissioner is entitled to investigate the type of alleged wage-order violations at issue here and that such investigations are within the power of the Legislature to command. The instant subpoena described the targeted records with particularity, and sought only those records which the Commissioner could minimally expect would be available in light of pertinent record keeping requirements. Bulmash does not suggest, nor do we find, that these requirements facially impose an unreasonable burden on employers subject to their terms. . . .

Bulmash nonetheless relies on cases upholding a form of "warrant" requirement for administrative inspections of residential and commercial property. See, e.g., *Marshall v. Barlow's, Inc..* 436 U.S. 307 (1978). Even in these cases, however, the "probable cause" necessary for an administrative warrant is less stringent than that required in criminal cases. And [the *Barlow's* test] turned upon the effort of the government inspectors to make "nonconsensual entries into areas not open to the public. [Where] no such entry is made . . . the enforceability of [an] administrative subpoena duces tecum . . . is governed, not by our decision in *Barlow's* but rather by our decision in *Oklahoma Press.*" Hence, Bulmash's reliance on inspection cases is misplaced.

Finally, Bulmash seeks to distinguish the cases cited by the Commissioner on grounds that they all involve corporate records. He suggests that the rules developed for administrative subpoenas were based in part on the state's traditional "visitorial power" over corporations. Hence, he reasons, these cases do not alter the criminal probable cause standard where, as here, "private household records" of an "individual" are involved. . . .

We decline to limit *Oklahoma Press* in the manner urged by Bulmash. The documents contain information presumably accumulated in the ordinary course of business, and uniformly requested of employers. . . . It would be anomalous to prevent the Division from enforcing lawful wage and hour provisions through use of its authorized subpoena power solely because the employer possessing such records is an "individual," rather than a corporation or large business. . . . In any event, we agree with the Commissioner that no Fourth Amendment "privacy" claim can be asserted against an administrative subpoena limited to the production of records which the subpoenaed party is required to maintain, for the express purpose of agency inspection, under lawful statutes or regulations. . . .

B. FIFTH AMENDMENT

Bulmash argues that, since the instant records could facially disclose noncompliance with wage and hour laws, the Fifth Amendment is a complete defense to court-ordered compliance with the subpoena. He insists that all prerequisites for asserting the privilege are present, i.e., he is an individual who has been statutorily compelled to make incriminating statements[14] which the Division could conceivably use as a basis for imposing civil and/or criminal penalties. . . .

The Commissioner counters that the privilege simply does not apply where, as here, the subpoenaed records are required to be kept pursuant to this kind of lawful regulatory scheme. He relies on a line of cases beginning with *Shapiro v. United States*, 335 U.S. 1 (1948). [Shapiro involved a prosecution for violation of price control laws. The government subpoenaed business records which the law compelled Shapiro to maintain] The Court rejected a Fifth Amendment claim for records which are required to be kept in order to enforce regulatory schemes.

Shapiro was limited by *Marchetti v. United States*, 390 U.S. 39 (1968). In *Marchetti*, a statute required gamblers to maintain business records; the court held that the Fifth Amendment applied to these records because they were directed to a selective group inherently suspect of criminal activities. *Shapiro*, which involved an essentially noncriminal and regulatory area of inquiry, was distinguishable.]

The same approach leads us to reject Bulmash's Fifth Amendment challenge to judicial enforcement of the Commissioner's subpoena. As contemplated by *Shapiro*, the information [demanded here] is the "appropriate" subject of a lawful regulatory scheme. The reporting law is obviously intended to encourage voluntary compliance with minimum labor standards designed for the mutual benefit of employees and employers. Such standards are enforced, not with an aim to punish, but to "ensure employees are not required or permitted to work under substandard unlawful conditions, and to protect employers who comply with the law from those who attempt to gain competitive advantage at the expense of their workers. . . . "

The judgment of the Court of Appeal is reversed.

Mosk, J., dissenting:

. . . I cannot join the [majority] in importing the questionable federal required-records exception into our state constitutional privilege against self-incrimination. Once again, the majority have construed the state constitutional privilege against self-incrimination narrowly and begrudgingly, treating it as a historic relic to be, at most, merely tolerated. I dissent because the fundamental protections afforded by the California Declaration of Rights are more than mere antiquities which can be readily discarded in favor of the more limited protections provided by

---

14. It is well settled that a person can assert the privilege only to prevent "being incriminated by his own compelled testimonial communications." The contents of subpoenaed business records which have been *voluntarily* prepared are not privileged, because they were not made under compulsion. *United States v. Doe*, 465 U.S. 605 (1984). . . .

Bulmash also insists that producing the records under compulsion of the subpoena constitutes an incriminating, testimonial, and privileged act . . . because it "tacitly concedes" that the papers exist; that the subpoenaed party possesses them; and that they are authentic. However [Doe] made clear that the court was not referring to statutorily "required records . . ." And no high court case specifically addressing required records has distinguished between their *contents* and the *act* of production for purposes of determining whether the privilege applies.

federal authority.... [I]t is incontrovertible that the California Constitution is, and always has been, a document of independent force which is the first line of protection for the individual against the excesses of state officials.

... In an effort to safeguard this fundamental privilege, we have traditionally resolved the conflict between the state's desire to obtain information and the individual's right to be free from self-incrimination by providing the individual with use immunity for any self-incriminating statements made in a civil or administrative proceeding. Such an accommodation is eminently reasonable in this case, and Bulmash should be ordered to comply with the subpoena only if he is assured that the People will not use the material he is requested to produce as evidence against him in any subsequent criminal prosecution. Use immunity would protect Bulmash's privilege against self-incrimination without impairing the Labor Commissioner's effective enforcement of the Labor Code. ...

The defendant in a criminal trial "has an absolute, unqualified right to compel the State to investigate its own case, find its own witnesses ... and convince a jury through its own resources." Rather than creating exceptions to that basic right, I believe that if Bulmash is to be prosecuted for violations of the Labor Code the Labor Commissioner should obtain evidence of his crime through the time-honored method of independent investigation. I therefore dissent. BROUSSARD, J., concurs. [KAUFMAN, J., also dissented in a separate opinion.]

Notes and Questions

1. *Judicial enforcement.* Note that Craib was required to go to court to enforce the subpoena. In *ICC v. Brimson,* 154 U.S. 447 (1894), the Court indicated that an agency could not be given power to enforce its own subpoenas. It is unclear whether this decision would be followed today. Congress has abided by the *Brimson* decision and assumed that judicial enforcement is needed. However, it might be a significant time-saver if agencies could enforce their own subpoenas rather than having to go to court.

2. *Defenses to subpoena enforcement.* In subpoena enforcement proceedings, a person can raise all appropriate defenses. However, those defenses are limited. Like virtually all recent federal cases, *Craib* defers to agency demands for information. Many such demands are extremely burdensome and intrusive. Cases from the late 1940's like *Oklahoma Press* have long since removed the roadblocks. These cases make clear that such demands are almost always "reasonable" under the Fourth Amendment. The analogy is to a grand jury subpoena, not to a search warrant. Older decisions which condemned agency "fishing expeditions" are no longer followed.

Nevertheless, a few defenses to a subpoena can still be raised: the face of the subpoena might disclose that the information sought concerns a type of matter over which the agency has no jurisdiction and thus no power to investigate. *See Reich v. Great Lakes Indian Fish and Wildlife Comm'n,* 4 F.3d 490 (7th Cir.1993) (it can be determined from the face of subpoena that defendant is not subject to statute). The agency might have violated a procedural requirement in its statute or rules with respect to the issuance of subpoenas.

Finally, a trial court might find a request too vague and indefinite or unreasonably broad or burdensome. However, these kinds of claims are difficult to sustain. *See, e.g., CAB v. Hermann*, 353 U.S. 322 (1957), upholding a subpoena for all the books, records and documents of an airline and its stockholders for a period of 38 months. The only solace to the company was that inspection could take place at its place of business so that the records did not have to be copied or moved.

In addition, a court may refuse to enforce a subpoena because the subject of the demand sustains the burden of showing that the agency is acting in bad faith for an improper purpose and thus abusing the court's process. Thus it might be found that the agency is trying to harass the demandee or put pressure on him to settle some collateral dispute. Similarly, a subpoena might be quashed to protect first amendment associational interests. *Dole v. Service Employees Union*, 950 F.2d 1456 (9th Cir.1991) (protecting confidential material in union's minutes not needed for administrative case).

An agency is not required to give notice to the person investigated when it subpoenas materials from a third party—even though it will be too late for the person investigated to raise any of these defenses once the third party turns over the material. *SEC v. Jerry T. O'Brien, Inc.*, 467 U.S. 735 (1984).

California refuses to follow this case. In *Sehlmeyer v. Dep't of General Services*, 21 Cal.Rptr.2d 840 (Cal.App.1993), A complained to the Board of Psychology about B who was a licensed therapist. B then served subpoenas on 17 of A's former psychotherapists and physicians. The court held that A had a right to be notified of the subpoenas and to claim that the information was privileged or otherwise protected from disclosure. This right was based on California's constitutional right of privacy.

3. *State law and investigative subpoenas.* To the authorities discussed in the previous note, compare *Levin v. Murawski*, 449 N.E.2d 730 (N.Y. 1983), involving an investigative subpoena to a physician for specific patient records issued by the New York Medical Board. The Board stated simply that it had received complaints from patients about the doctor. The Court of Appeals held that the Board must meet a minimum threshold foundation before a court can enforce the subpoena. The foundation would resemble the requirement of probable cause in obtaining a search warrant and furnish at least some assurance of the complainants' reliability. Said the court:

> It is ancient law that no agency of government may conduct an unlimited and general inquisition into the affairs of persons within its jurisdiction solely on the prospect of possible violations of law being discovered, especially with respect to subpoenas duces tecum ... There must be authority, relevancy, and some basis for inquisitorial action.

The three dissenters in the *Levin* case argued that this requirement would frustrate disciplinary investigations of physicians (which the legislature had been trying to streamline and strengthen). Who is correct? Which authority is more in line with current attitudes about bureaucracy and privacy—carte blanche decisions like *Craib v. Bulmash* and *Oklahoma Press* or more restrictive decisions like *Levin?*

4. *Privileges.* The attorney-client privilege and the work product privilege apply to agency investigations. So does the marital communications privilege. *SEC v. Lavin,* 111 F.3d 921 (D.C.Cir.1997). States may recognize additional privileges. *See* 1981 MSAPA § 4–212(a) (which requires agencies to adhere to all privileges recognized in court).

A person who is the subject of administrative investigation (federal, state or local) may assert the Fifth Amendment privilege against self incrimination in order to withhold documents or refuse to testify. However, more often than not, the Fifth Amendment privilege is not applicable.

i. In a criminal case, a defendant can refuse to take the stand. In an administrative case, a witness cannot refuse to take the stand and be sworn (but may assert the privilege to refuse to answer specific questions). In a criminal case, the fact finder cannot draw adverse inferences against the defendant because of a claim of privilege; an agency is permitted to draw an adverse inference. *See* Paul E. Rosenthal, Note, "Speak Now: The Accused Student's Right to Remain Silent in Public University Disciplinary Proceedings," 97 Colum.L.Rev. 1241 (1997).

ii. Suppose an administrative proceeding and a criminal case are pending at the same time. For example, the same act might lead to disbarment of an attorney and to conviction of a felony. The attorney would try to defer disbarment proceedings until the criminal case is completed, because he might wish to testify in the administrative case but to rely on his privilege in the criminal case.

A court has discretion to delay the administrative matter but the attorney has no absolute right to a delay. *See Keating v. Office of Thrift Supervision,* 45 F.3d 322 (9th Cir.1995), which balances the interests of the agency, the public, and the courts, and refuses to grant a stay.

iii. If authorized by statute, the agency can offer immunity and thus compel disclosure. *See* 18 U.S.C. § 6002(2) (federal agency can compel testimony by granting use immunity to person who refuses to testify or provide other information).

iv. The privilege does not apply to corporations, partnerships or unincorporated entities like unions. Thus the custodian of an entity's records must disclose them and cannot claim any personal privilege relating to the entity's records—even if the materials might incriminate him or her. *Bellis v. United States,* 417 U.S. 85 (1974) (partnership records).

v. The privilege can be asserted only if the person fearing incrimination (or his attorney, assuming the attorney-client privilege applies) is in possession of the documents subpoenaed. *Couch v. United States,* 409 U.S. 322 (1973) (taxpayer cannot assert privilege with respect to papers in possession of accountant).

vi. The privilege does not apply to materials seized under a valid search warrant because the person from whom the documents are seized is not compelled to admit anything about them. *Andresen v. Maryland,* 427 U.S. 463 (1976).

vii. The privilege applies only to testimony that is produced by state compulsion. As a result, the contents of private papers are not privileged, because they were prepared voluntarily rather than in response to compulsion. *See United States v. Doe,* 465 U.S. 605 (1984) (business records); *In re Grand Jury Subpoena,* 1 F.3d 87 (2d Cir.1993) (personal papers). However, the privilege can be asserted if the *act* of producing the papers would be incriminatory (because it would admit that the papers existed or were authentic or that the demandee possessed them). See note 14 in *Craib.*

viii. The privilege is inapplicable to the production of records if a statute requires those records to be prepared and maintained. *See Shapiro v. United States,* 335 U.S. 1 (1948), which is discussed in *Craib.* If *Shapiro* applies, the documents must be produced even if the act of producing them might be incriminating. Again, see note 14 in *Craib.*

This note is intended only to alert you to the existence of common-law and constitutional privileges in administrative investigation; this major subject in constitutional and evidence law cannot be treated in detail here.

5. *Physical searches.* When an agency physically inspects or searches a home or business, it must ordinarily secure a search warrant. *Marshall v. Barlow's, Inc.,* which is discussed in *Craib,* holds that a warrant is required before OSHA can inspect business premises to see whether employee safety rules are being complied with.

To obtain an administrative search warrant, the inspector need not establish probable cause to believe that a violation has occurred. It is sufficient if the choice of the particular employer to be inspected was based on reasonable and neutral standards, such as a statistical sampling technique approved by the agency. The warrant can be obtained ex parte (i.e. without notice to the employer). Although the warrant requirement is easy to satisfy, at least it tends to prevent an inspection that is motivated by harassment or other improper purposes.

However, the *Barlow's* rule does not apply to certain pervasively regulated businesses like liquor or gun dealers since they have a reduced expectation of privacy. This principle was extended to permit unannounced warrantless inspections of auto dismantlers. *New York v. Burger,* 482 U.S. 691 (1987). New York law required junk yards and dismantlers to be licensed, to keep records of purchases and sales, and to submit to periodic unannounced inspections. Of course, the reason for searching junkyards is to find stolen parts so that the licensees can be prosecuted for theft.

According to *Burger,* four criteria must be met to justify warrantless administrative inspections: (i) There must be a substantial government interest in regulating the business, (ii) unannounced inspections must be necessary to further the regulatory scheme, (iii) the statute must advise the owner of the periodic inspection program, and (iv) searches must be limited in time, place and scope. The New York law met all of these criteria.

However, the New York Court of Appeals refused to follow *Burger* under the state constitution. *People v. Scott,* 593 N.E.2d 1328, 1339–46 (1992). Taking the same tack advocated by Justice Mosk's dissent in *Craib,* the *Scott* majority held that a warrant was required to inspect the premises of automobile dismantlers because "the search is undertaken solely to uncover evidence of criminality and the underlying regulatory scheme is in reality designed simply to give the police an expedient means of enforcing penal sanctions." The Court noted:

> The dissent's reliance on the "staggering" statistics [of] automobile theft in New York and the economic burdens such crime imposes are hardly a persuasive ground for relaxing [the State constitution's] proscription against unreasonable searches and seizures. The alarming increase of unlicensed weapons on our urban streets and the catastrophic rise in the use of crack cocaine and heroin are also matters of pressing social concern, but few would seriously argue that those unfortunate facets of urban life justify routine searches of pedestrians on the street.... Indeed the writs of assistance [which were general warrants in colonial times authorizing officials to search any residential or commercial premises and which induced the framers to adopt the Fourth Amendment] were themselves a response of the colonial government to an unprecedented wave of criminal smuggling....

> Our responsibility in the judicial branch is not to respond to these temporary crises or to shape the law so as to advance the goals of law enforcement, but rather to stand as a fixed citadel for constitutional rights. ...

6. *The exclusionary rule in administrative law.* Evidence that was illegally seized in violation of the Fourth Amendment is probably admissible in administrative proceedings even if it could not be admitted in a criminal proceeding because of the exclusionary rule. *See INS v. Lopez–Mendoza,* 468 U.S. 1032 (1984) (deportation proceeding); *United States v. Janis,* 428 U.S. 433 (1976) (evidence obtained by unlawful state search admissible in federal civil tax case).

However, some courts believe that evidence must be excluded in administrative proceedings if the manner in which it was obtained constituted egregious violations of the Fourth Amendment or other liberties. *See Gonzalez–Rivera v. INS,* 22 F.3d 1441 (9th Cir.1994) (deportation case—car stopped solely because passengers were of hispanic origin).

7. *Publicity.* Agencies frequently issue press releases to inform the public about a pending investigation, issuance of a complaint, or the conclusion of an adjudication.

> Adverse publicity ... imposes a deprivation on private ... firms without the due processes of law normally associated with government action encroaching upon property or persons.... But usually no protection other than the common sense and good will of the administrator prevents unreasonable use of coercive publicity. Furthermore, judicial review cannot undo the widespread effects of erroneous adverse agency publicity. The result is that the person or industry named may be irretrievably injured by inaccurate, excessive, or premature publicity. Second, agencies sometimes use adverse publicity as an unauthorized sanction ...

Ernest Gellhorn, "Adverse Publicity By Administrative Agencies," 86 Harv.L.Rev. 1380, 1419–21 (1973). Gellhorn recommends that agencies adopt published rules of policy and procedure concerning publicity of agency action. The rules should balance the need for adequately serving the public interest and the need for adequately protecting persons affected by adverse publicity. In particular, publicity should be issued only if there is a significant risk that the public health or safety may be impaired or substantial economic harm may occur unless the public is immediately notified. *See* ACUS Recommendation 73–1, 38 Fed.Reg. 16839 (1973).

FTC v. Cinderella Career & Finishing Schools, Inc., 404 F.2d 1308 (D.C.Cir.1968), held that the FTC could issue press releases announcing the filing of a complaint because consumers are entitled to know the identity of those who prey upon them. The court also held that a press release announcing that the FTC had "reason to believe" that Cinderella had violated the law did not evidence bias or prejudgment. In a concurring opinion, however, Judge Robinson argued that an agency should not automatically issue adverse publicity. It should balance the damage to private industry against protection of the public.

8. *Discovery*. Once an adjudication has formally commenced (through filing of a complaint or similar document), both the agency and the private party may seek information in the hands of the other or a third party. The 1981 MSAPA appears to provide that the normal civil rules of discovery apply to administrative proceedings. § 4–210(a). However, depositions and interrogatories are rarely employed in administrative proceedings. Usually discovery consists of disclosure of the contents of an agency's files or witness lists or subpoenas duces tecum. In addition, the agency can issue subpoenas requiring witnesses to attend the hearing.

The right to issuance of post-complaint subpoenas is narrower than an agency's right to investigate (discussed above). An ALJ may refuse to issue a post-complaint subpoena (either to the agency staff or to the private party) if the information sought would not be relevant to the charges in the complaint (as distinguished from relevant to a much broader investigation) or would be unduly burdensome. *See* APA § 555(d). Compare the bracketed and unbracketed versions of 1981 MSAPA § 4–210(a).

9. *Problem*. In Madison, it is a crime for an insurance company to engage in "deceptive or manipulative insurance practices." The Madison Insurance Commission (MIC) is headed by an elected official, currently Gloria—who is vigorously pro-consumer. MIC has power to order any insurance company doing business in Madison to cease and desist from the practice of refusing to pay justified claims. It also has power to order the refund of premiums to persons who were denied payment of proper claims.

Under the Insurance Code, MIC has power to investigate any matter relating to insurance. It can issue a civil investigative demand (CID) calling for the production of documents, the answering of written questions, or the testimony of witnesses, if it has reason to believe that any law relating to insurance is being violated. If a CID is not complied with, the state Attorney General can seek an order from the Superior Court requiring compliance. Disregard of such an order is punishable as civil contempt. If the Court orders compliance, the demandee must pay the attorneys' fees incurred by the Attorney General.

Your client, Security First Insurance Co., is a large business employing 2700 persons. Its home office is in Madison but it sells insurance in several other states through branch offices. It specializes in selling health insurance to elderly people to cover items not covered by Medicare. The MIC staff believes that Security has a pattern of refusing to pay clearly proper claims. Security denies any managerial policy which encourages such tactics or that its record is any worse than that of other companies.

Bill, a vice president of Security, has received a CID ordering him to appear in three weeks and bring with him all files and other documents relating to health insurance on persons over the age of 55 years in effect for the years 1994–1997. In addition, he was ordered to appear three weeks later to give sworn testimony. Bill says there is a record of hostility between him and Gloria. Bill particularly fears adverse publicity; MIC often issues press releases when it begins an investigation but it has not yet done so.

Bill is distressed by the breadth of the CID. Literally millions of pieces of paper are covered; it would fill sixty large trucks. There is no staff available to gather them (they are stored in several places and mixed with material on insured persons under 55 and with other kinds of insurance). Some of the older documents are on microfiche and thus difficult to read and easily lost. Many of the records involve currently insured persons and are needed for business. Moreover, management does not trust MIC to take proper care of the documents while they are inspected and copied. Many of the policies cover residents of other states. MIC believes that it has jurisdiction over non-resident insured persons because Security's home office is in Madison. Security disagrees. What is your strategy?

§ 4.1.3   ALTERNATIVE DISPUTE RESOLUTION IN ADMINIS-TRATIVE ADJUDICATION

It is widely perceived that litigation has become too slow, too adversarial, too costly, and too formal. As a result, there has been an explosion of interest in alternative dispute resolution (or ADR). Using ADR techniques, the disputants can resolve the problem without fighting it out in the courtroom. Unlike litigation, ADR can be quick, non-adversarial, cheap, and informal. Frequently, ADR can settle a dispute creatively in a way that benefits both parties; litigation, on the other hand, is often a zero sum game in which one party is a big winner and the other a big loser.

As a result, it is now common for litigants to resort to voluntary ADR to avoid or settle disputes before they enter the litigation system or before they go to trial. Numerous state and federal statutes require litigants to resort to ADR before they are permitted to try a case.

Essentially, ADR consists of the following broad classifications:

· *Negotiation.* In negotiation, the litigants and their lawyers get together to work out the problem without the assistance of advisers.

· *Mediation.* In mediation, a third party mediator helps the litigants work out the problem. However, the mediator has no authority to impose a solution. Mediation is often referred to as conciliation or facilitation. There are numerous refinements on the mediation model, such as a mini-trial in which counsel actually conduct a mock trial of the case and the parties then try to settle it.

· *Arbitration.* In arbitration, a third party arbitrator has authority to impose a solution. If the arbitration is binding, the arbitrator's decision ends the case (courts have extremely limited authority to overturn arbitral decisions). If the arbitration is non-binding, either side can reject the decision and proceed to litigation. However, there are usually risks attached to this decision (such as the requirement that a party who rejects a non-binding arbitration decision, then fails to do better in litigation, must pay the other party's attorney's fees).

A powerful movement is now underway to expand the use of ADR in administrative adjudication. This is ironic since administrative adjudication was invented as a form of ADR—to get disputes out of the courts and into agencies which were seen as specialized, inexpensive, and informal dispute resolvers. Today, it is clear that administrative adjudication all too often is slow, costly, adversarial, and formalized. As a result, there is a great opportunity to apply ADR techniques in administrative law.

In 1990 Congress amended the APA to require agencies to explore and utilize ADR in all agency functions, including adjudication and rulemaking. The 1990 Act contained a "sunset provision," but in 1996 Congress permanently authorized administrative ADR. P. L. 104–320. As to adjudication, the Administrative Dispute Resolution Act is a giant step in the direction of changing the culture of administrative law in the direction of using ADR. We explore negotiated rulemaking in § 5.9.

First, note APA §§ 556(c)(6), (7), (8), each of which was added by the ADR Act of 1990. In addition, Congress adopted 5 U.S.C. §§ 571–83. These sections authorize and encourage (but do not require) agencies to use the whole range of ADR techniques up to and including arbitration. These procedures are voluntary so that neither agencies nor regulated parties can be compelled to utilize them. The statute also suggests that there are situations in which ADR is not appropriate, such as when a matter must be authoritatively resolved in order to create a precedent. § 572(b).

ADR provisions are finding their way into state APAs as well. In 1995, the California APA was amended to authorize an agency, with the consent of all parties, to refer any adjudicative proceeding for resolution through mediation by a neutral mediator or binding or non-binding arbitration by a neutral arbitrator. The section also provides for confidentiality of any communications made in the course of ADR. Calif. Gov't Code §§ 11,420.10 to .30. See generally Brian D. Shannon, "The Administrative Procedure and Texas Register Act and ADR: A New Twist for Administrative Procedure in Texas?" 42 Baylor L. Rev. 705, 713–28 (1990).

Problem. Review the Problem about the dispute between the Madison Insurance Commission and Security First Insurance Co. in § 4.1.2. N.9. The dispute over production of documents can be resolved in court. The underlying dispute about Security's failure to pay claims can be resolved through a hearing before an administrative judge followed by a decision of the agency head; no doubt, the agency head's decision will be subjected to judicial review. Thus final resolution of the underlying dispute is years away. Until then, assuming MIC is right, consumers will remain subject to abusive claims practices. Security will find it difficult to engage in business planning and capital raising because of the uncertainty created by the ongoing dispute. Security will be subjected to massive unfavorable publicity. Insured persons whose claims were denied will be encouraged to sue the company for bad faith. Hundreds of thousands of dollars will be spent by both sides on attorneys' and experts' fees.

Is ADR appropriate for the dispute about production of documents or for the underlying dispute? If so, what techniques of ADR should be employed?

§ 4.2 THE HEARING PHASE

This subsection addresses issues that arise during the actual process of formal adjudication. That process closely resembles a judicial trial. The parties introduce documentary evidence, call and examine witnesses, cross-examine the witnesses called by their adversaries, make oral arguments, and submit briefs. See § 556(d) of the federal act; 1981 MSAPA § 4–211(2).

§ 4.2.1 EVIDENCE AT THE HEARING

REGUERO v. TEACHER STANDARDS AND PRACTICES COMMISSION
822 P.2d 1171 (Ore.1991).

Unis, J.:

[Petitioner Reguero applied to reinstate his teaching license, but Oregon's Teacher Standards and Practices Commission (TSPC) denied the application because of his sexual misconduct toward sixth-grade pupils Michelle and Leasa.] Neither Michelle nor Leasa testified. To support its allegations, TSPC introduced hearsay testimony by [Minette, a school counselor, Castner, a deputy district attorney, and Costelow, a police officer, each of whom had interviewed Michelle and Leasa.] According to this testimony, petitioner had touched Michelle's breast on one occasion and her buttocks on another occasion. TSPC also introduced hearsay and multiple hearsay testimony that petitioner had kept Leasa after school in September, locked her in the classroom, touched her "on the breast and in the vaginal area," and lowered his trousers . . .

Petitioner presented countervailing evidence. He admitted touching Michelle's breast, but said that the contact was inadvertent. With respect to Leasa's complaint of a sexual assault, he contended that she had fabricated the story to punish him for telling the school counselor that Michelle, who was her friend, was involved with prostitution and drugs. A school employee testified that she had overheard Michelle say,

"I'm gonna get [petitioner]." Two teachers testified that the doors of the classrooms could not be locked from the inside. A teacher's aide testified that she was usually present in petitioner's classroom after school and had never seen him alone with Leasa ...

We now consider whether TSPC's findings about sexual contact with Michelle and Leasa are supported by substantial evidence. Petitioner's primary claim is that TSPC may not rely entirely on hearsay that would not be admissible in a civil or criminal trial to support findings that petitioner had sexual contact with the students, when TSPC did not show that they were unavailable to testify. Petitioner asserts that such hearsay, in such circumstances, does not constitute substantial evidence. He urges us to adopt the "residuum rule," at least in cases where direct evidence is available.

A. RESIDUUM RULE

The New York Court of Appeals created the residuum rule in *Carroll v. Knickerbocker Ice Co..*, 113 N.E. 507 (1916). In that case, the court set aside a workers' compensation award that was based solely on a deceased worker's statements that he had been injured on the job. The relevant statute provided that "common law or statutory rules of evidence" were not binding on the agency that administered workers' compensation. The court interpreted that statute to mean that, although the agency could "accept any evidence that is offered, still in the end there must be a residuum of legal evidence to support the claim before an award can be made." The residuum rule requires that an administrative agency's findings be supported by some evidence that would be admissible in a civil or criminal trial ...

Some jurisdictions retain the residuum rule. Courts that adopt the rule do so in an effort to ensure reliability of evidence and cross-examination of witnesses. But legal scholars have severely criticized the rule and those rationales for it. [For example,] McCormick reasons that courts concerned about cross-examination fail to consider that

> much "legal" evidence within the hearsay exceptions is equally untested. Yet the latter is accepted even in jury trials because of its probable reliability. Consequently the residuum rule's mechanical prohibition against uncorroborated hearsay is unsound. Its sound objectives can be secured through the sensitivity of the hearings officers and the wise application of the substantial evidence test which measures the quantity and quality of the supporting evidence regardless of its category or label.

Because of its flaws, many courts that once applied the residuum rule have now abandoned it ... The Oregon statutes governing evidence in administrative hearings reject the assumption that hearsay evidence is categorically so unreliable that it cannot be substantial. Hearsay evidence is as admissible ... as any other evidence as long as it meets the statutory test of reliability.[20]

20. Oregon Rev.Stat. § 183.450(1) provides: "Irrelevant, immaterial or unduly repetitious evidence shall be excluded, but erroneous rulings on evidence shall not pre-

ORS 183.482(8)(c) provides that "substantial evidence exists to support a finding of fact when the record, viewed as a whole, would permit a reasonable person to make that finding." That statute makes no provision for weighing some classes of evidence in the record more heavily as classes than other classes of evidence in the record—for example, weighing exhibits more heavily than testimony, or non-hearsay testimony more heavily than hearsay—as a matter of law ... [T]he legislature could not have intended that a certain type of evidence, although reliable enough to be admissible under ORS 183.450(1), is categorically incapable of being substantial enough to permit a reasonable person to find in accordance with it under ORS 183.482(8)(c). Accordingly, we reject the residuum rule and [hold] that hearsay evidence alone, even if inadmissible in a civil or criminal trial, is not incapable of being "substantial evidence."

B. SUBSTANTIALITY

Our inquiry does not end there, however. In rejecting the residuum rule, we reject any categorical method of determining substantiality. While our task is not to substitute our judgment for that of the agency, we must decide whether the finding of substantiality is reasonable in the light of countervailing as well as supporting evidence.

[As proponent of the sexual misconduct charge] ... TSPC had the burden of presenting substantial evidence to support its allegations that petitioner was guilty of sexual misconduct.

The "substantial evidence" inquiry necessarily is case specific. Davis suggests, and we agree, that in assessing the substantiality of the evidence or lack of it, variable circumstances may be considered, such as: the alternative to relying on the hearsay evidence; the importance of the facts sought to be proved by the hearsay statements to the outcome of the proceeding and considerations of economy; the state of the supporting or opposing evidence, if any; the degree of lack of efficacy of cross-examination with respect to the particular hearsay statements; and the consequences of the decision either way. "When the alternative to relying on hearsay is to get the better evidence that is readily available, refusing to rely on the hearsay is appropriate." In this case, there was a convenient and apparently inexpensive alternative to relying on the challenged hearsay. Michelle [and] Leasa were readily available to be called as witnesses. No reason was given why they did not testify[22] ... TSPC had the authority to issue subpoenas to require the students to

clude agency action on the record unless shown to have substantially prejudiced the rights of a party. All other evidence of a type commonly relied upon by reasonably prudent persons in conduct of their serious affairs shall be admissible. Agencies shall give effect to the rules of privilege recognized by law. Objections to evidentiary offers may be made and shall be noted in the record. Any part of the evidence may be received in written form."

22. While the dissent suggests that the petitioner had the opportunity to subpoena the students to testify, it was not the petitioner's burden to do so. Petitioner, therefore, should not be faulted for forcing TSPC to carry its burden.

testify at the hearing. It is beyond question that the students' direct testimony is better evidence than their hearsay statements.

The importance of the facts asserted in the hearsay statements to the outcome of this proceeding is likewise indisputable. TSPC's findings of fact, conclusions of law, opinion, and order were based entirely on hearsay, particularly the hearsay testimony of Castner, Minette, and Costelow. Moreover, Castner, Minette, and Costelow were permitted to express their opinion, based on that hearsay, multiple hearsay, gossip, and rumors, that Michelle and Leasa were telling the truth ... We hold that TSPC's decision in this case was not based on substantial evidence ... We reverse the decision of the Court of Appeals and the modified order of TSPC and remand this case to TSPC for further consideration.

PETERSON, J. concurring: ... I would state this rule: Where the claim and the finding involve conduct that would constitute a crime, hearsay evidence alone is insufficient to establish the conduct ...

GRABER, J. dissenting: ... [T]he majority's disposition of the case ... analyzes the substantiality of the evidence incorrectly. The majority has—contrary to its proper role and its protestations—conducted its own fact-finding. A proper evaluation of the agency's fact-finding would lead to an affirmance ...

Notes and Questions

1. *Admission of evidence.* Separate two issues here: what evidence should be admitted? and to what extent should an agency be able to rely *exclusively* on evidence that would not be admissible in court?

As to the first issue, read APA § 556(d) (second and third sentences and last sentence); 1981 MSAPA §§ 4–212(a), (d), and (e) and 4–215(d). Oregon Rev. Stat. § 183.450(1), quoted in note 20 of *Reguero*, is similar to the MSAPA sections.

Assume that a state has adopted an Evidence Code, which codifies the rules of evidence in civil or criminal trials. The Code might, for example, prohibit a witness (other than an expert witness) from giving an opinion. If that state has also adopted 1981 MSAPA § 4–212(a), would an administrative judge be required to follow the Evidence Code's provision on opinions? Suppose the same rule is part of the state's common law of evidence?

The records in administrative cases typically contain many items of evidence that would be excluded from a judicial record. While the AJ should exclude "irrelevant, immaterial, or unduly repetitious evidence," the reality is that most oral or written evidence which a party seeks to introduce is routinely admitted. Although hearsay evidence is excluded in judicial trials (unless covered by one of the many hearsay exceptions), it is admissible in administrative cases, as illustrated by *Reguero*. 1981 MSAPA § 4–212(a) is explicit on this point and APA § 556(d) has long been interpreted to permit the admission of hearsay. Why is hearsay admitted in administrative cases but excluded in civil and criminal cases?

Some statutes require particular agencies to observe judicial standards of evidence. See, e.g. 29 U.S.C. § 160(b) (NLRB adjudications shall, "so far as practicable," be conducted in accordance with the Federal Rules of Evidence). Other agencies, such as OSHA, have adopted judicial evidence rules by regulation. 29 C.F.R. § 2200.72. The Administrative Conference has criticized such statutes and regulations. ACUS Recommendation 86–2, 51 Fed.Reg. 25642 (1986). Why?

2. *The residuum rule.* Since hearsay (and other evidence barred from judicial proceedings) is generally admitted in administrative proceedings, the second question becomes important: can an agency rely *exclusively* on evidence that would not be admissible in court? The "residuum rule" provides that findings cannot be based exclusively on hearsay evidence; the findings must be supported by some evidence admissible in civil cases although that evidence by itself need not be substantial enough to support the findings.

APA § 556(d) (third sentence) and 1981 MSAPA § 4–215(d) can be interpreted to reject the residuum rule. However, a majority of the states still adhere to the residuum rule. If you sat on the Oregon Supreme Court, would you agree with Justice Unis or Justice Peterson on this issue? Note that Peterson would preserve the residuum rule only in cases where the finding involves conduct that would constitute a crime. Why does Peterson want to limit the residuum rule to such cases?

The residuum rule is not followed in the federal courts. *Richardson v. Perales,* 402 U.S. 389 (1971), reviewed a decision by Social Security rejecting a claim for disability benefits. The ALJ, affirmed by the Appeals Council, held that Perales (who complained of disabling back pain) was in fact not disabled. The only evidence in support of this determination was a series of written evaluations by various doctors appointed by Social Security to examine Perales.

The court of appeals held that substantial evidence did not support the decision because the written and unsworn medical evidence was hearsay. The Supreme Court reversed, holding that the reports could be substantial evidence for a decision. Although Perales had not cross-examined the doctors who wrote the reports, it was his own fault—his counsel had failed to subpoena them. Even in cases where this factor is not present, federal courts do not follow the residuum rule.

3. *Hearsay and substantial evidence.* The Oregon court reviewed TSPC's findings of fact under the "substantial evidence" standard. That standard is by far the most common approach in both state and federal courts for judicial review of agency findings of fact. We explore the substantial evidence test in detail in § 9.1.1. As the court noted, "substantial evidence exists to support a finding of fact when the record, viewed as a whole, would permit a reasonable person to make that finding."

Often, the record will include evidence that would allow a reasonable person to make findings either way. In that case, the court is supposed to affirm the decision, even though the judges might have gone the other way if they had heard the case themselves. The substantial evidence test requires a court to be quite deferential toward an agency's findings of fact, but still permits the court to overturn such findings if it feels an injustice has been done.

If we assume that hearsay is admissible, and we reject the residuum rule, was the evidence presented by Minette, Castner, and Costelow sufficient to satisfy a "reasonable person" that Reguero had engaged in misconduct with Michelle and Leasa? The dissenting judge thought so.

Is the hearsay evidence used in this case the type of evidence "commonly relied upon by reasonably prudent persons in conduct of their serious affairs"? (That is the test in the Oregon statute quoted in note 20—and see the almost identical language in 1981 MSAPA § 4–215(d).) Would *you* rely on it if you had to decide whether to hire Reguero in your private school?

If reasonably prudent people would rely on this evidence, why did the majority reverse? Clearly, it was suspicious of a case based entirely on hearsay, especially considering the high stakes involved, and it must have suspected that a serious injustice might have occurred. Do you agree that TSPC, rather than Reguero, should be required to subpoena Michelle and Leasa?

4. *Hearsay and confrontation.* Could Reguero have argued that the use of hearsay evidence against him violated his due process right to confront his accusers? In *Olabanji v. INS*, 973 F.2d 1232 (5th Cir.1992), the INS ordered Olabanji to be deported because it found that his marriage to Raines (a U. S. citizen) was a sham. It relied on an affidavit by Seeber who had interviewed Raines. The court held that this procedure violated due process, since the INS could have subpoenaed Raines to testify at the hearing and be subject to cross examination, but had not done so. The INS could rely on Seeber's affidavit only if it could show that, despite reasonable efforts, it could not have secured Raines' presence.

5. *Burden of proof.* Evidence law distinguishes between the burden of producing evidence and the burden of persuasion. The burden of producing evidence allocates to one party the obligation to come forward with evidence on a particular point. The burden of persuasion indicates how strong a party's evidence on an issue must be to avoid losing on that issue. *See* APA § 556(d) (first sentence), which allocates the burden of proof to the "proponent of an order." The words "burden of proof" in this section refer to the burden of persuasion, not the burden of producing evidence. *Director, Office of Workers' Comp. v. Greenwich Collieries*, 512 U.S. 267 (1994) (agency rule that allows applicant to receive benefits if the evidence of the applicant and the employer are of equal strength violates § 556(d)).

In general, the proponent must discharge its burden of persuasion by a "preponderance of the evidence" (i.e., 51%). *See Steadman v. SEC,* 450 U.S. 91 (1981). *Steadman* was a case in which the SEC had imposed disciplinary sanctions on a broker for securities fraud. Construing the *third* sentence of APA § 556(d), the Court held that the preponderance test applies to APA formal adjudications, except where Congress dictates otherwise. Thus the SEC did not have to satisfy the common law "clear and convincing" test that is ordinarily used in contract cases in which the defense of fraud is raised.

In some situations, however, the applicable burden of persuasion is heavier than the usual preponderance standard. For example, in a criminal case, the prosecution must prove guilt "beyond a reasonable doubt." In some administrative cases, the courts have found room to manipulate burdens of persuasion in order to achieve a desired result or provide a high degree of protection against error. For example, in *Woodby v. INS*, 385 U.S. 276 (1966), the Court reviewed a deportation order. By statute, APA procedures do not apply to such proceedings. Thus the Court felt free to require the government to prove its case by "clear, unequivocal and convincing evidence." Similarly, in *Ettinger v. Board of Medical Quality Assurance*, 185 Cal.Rptr. 601 (Cal.App.1982), the court held that a state agency seeking to revoke a physician's license had to prove its case by "clear and convincing proof to a reasonable certainty."

Because Reguero applied for renewal of his certificate, he had the burden to establish all the elements required by the statute for renewal. However, since TSPC raised the sexual misconduct argument as an affirmative defense, it had the burden to establish that claim.

Considering the personal and professional harm done to someone like Reguero by an administrative finding that he engaged in sexual misconduct toward sixth-grade girls, should a court require proof of TSPC's allegations by more than a preponderance of the evidence?

6. *Responsibility of judge to bring out evidence.* In judicial trials, the responsibility for producing evidence falls on the parties. Judges aren't required to ask witnesses questions that counsel fail to ask. In administrative law, however, the rule is different. Administrative judges are expected to take an active role in developing the record. This is especially important when one of the parties is not represented by counsel. In a vast number of cases, such as social security, unemployment compensation, welfare, government personnel, or small business licensing, parties usually represent themselves. In such situations, the administrative judge may commit reversible error by failing to help the unrepresented party establish his or her case.

For example, in an unemployment compensation case, the court said: "Especially in the case of an uncounseled claimant, the Commission's responsibility involves asking the right questions. We do not think it is appropriate for the Commission to disqualify a *pro se* claimant from receiving benefits because she failed to produce evidence of facts that case law from other states says she must establish when the appeals referee never even asked her the relevant questions." *Hoke v. Brinlaw Mfg. Co.*, 327 S.E.2d 254, 258 (N.C.App.1985).

7. *Closed or open hearing.* Probably Reguero, as well as Michelle, Leasa and their parents, would prefer that the hearing be closed to the public and the media. MSAPA § 4–211(6) would require an open hearing. Should an administrative judge have discretion to close a hearing relating to sexual misconduct toward young girls?

If an agency wants to close a hearing, does an individual have a right to an open hearing? In *Fitzgerald v. Hampton*, 467 F.2d 755 (D.C.Cir.1972), a federal employee claimed that the Air Force fired him because he was a "whistleblower" (he disclosed information about cost overruns on defense contracts). The Air Force claimed he was fired because of a staff reduction caused by budget cuts. The agency wished to close the hearing, but the court held that the employee had a due process right to an open hearing. However, the case precedes the variable due process era of *Mathews v. Eldridge*.

§ 4.2.2　OFFICIAL NOTICE

A court is permitted to take *judicial* notice—i.e. treat as proven—various facts and propositions which are very likely to be true. This is a great time-saver. For example, under a typical state evidence code, a court takes judicial notice of matters "of such common knowledge ... that they cannot reasonably be the subject of dispute" or "that are not reasonably subject to dispute and are capable of immediate and accurate determination by resort to sources of reasonably indisputable accuracy." Calif.Evid.Code § 452(g), (h). However, the court must first afford each party reasonable opportunity to present information relevant to the propriety of taking judicial notice and the tenor of the matter to be noticed. Id. § 455(a).

Agencies are permitted to take *official* notice of matters which could be the subject of *judicial* notice—and they can also go further and notice matters which a court could not. Compare federal APA § 556(e) and 1981 MSAPA § 4–212(f) to the California Evidence Code provisions quoted above. Because so much can be the subject of official notice—much of it being the personal knowledge of the fact-finders—it is important that parties have a fair opportunity to "contest and rebut the facts or material so noticed."

There remain several fundamental problems: (i) agency fact-finders (both administrative judges and agency heads) are often experts in the subject matter in dispute. They should and must use that expertise in making factual judgments. *See* 1981 MSAPA § 4–215(d) (last sentence). When they do so, have they taken official notice? If so, they must first notify the parties and afford them an opportunity to rebut the agency's conclusion. Or is the use of expertise in making judgments different from taking official notice?

(ii) Agency fact finders sometimes make policy when they decide cases. Necessarily, they must rely on broad factual propositions concerning the nature of the problem to be solved and the effect of proposed solutions. When they do so, have they taken official notice? Must they notify the parties and afford an opportunity for rebuttal before they rely on broad factual propositions relevant to policymaking?

FRANZ v. BOARD OF MEDICAL QUALITY ASSURANCE
642 P.2d 792 (Cal.1982).

[The Board suspended Dr. Franz's license to practice medicine for one year and placed him on ten years' probation after finding him guilty of gross negligence, dishonesty, and falsifying a medical document. The trial court sustained the Board but the Supreme Court reversed on several of the gross negligence charges, holding that substantial evidence did not support the decision.

Wollweber was Dr. Franz's patient. Franz was a general practitioner, not a surgeon. After deciding that Wollweber needed surgery to repair a perforated ulcer, Franz scheduled surgery at Anaheim Doctors' Hospital where he had staff privileges. Anaheim had no intensive care unit (ICU). Because of Wollweber's poor state of health, complications were expected. Franz asked Dr. Olivet, the chief of surgery at Anaheim, to recommend a surgeon. Olivet recommended Dr. Ali. Wollweber signed a consent form that listed Olivet and Franz but not Ali as his surgeons. As the result of various blunders in surgery and in post-operative care, Wollweber suffered a "duodenal blowout" and died ten days after the surgery.]

NEWMAN, J.:

The agency and the [lower] court found that Franz' choice of Anaheim was gross negligence because Wollweber was a high-risk patient, Anaheim had no adequate ICU, and Franz made the choice—without regard to his patient's needs—in order to obtain surgical privileges he did not have elsewhere. They also ruled that he committed gross negligence by scheduling surgery before selecting the surgeon. He contends that those findings lack substantial evidence because the Board offered no expert testimony that acts of that kind demonstrate "the want of even scant care or an extreme departure from the ordinary standard of conduct," the definition of gross negligence.

The Board answers that any gap in the record was filled by the panel's expertise in medical matters. Because two of the panel's three members were doctors, the Board urges, it could apply special knowledge in assessing gross negligence by a doctor and needed no expert testimony on the pertinent medical standards. Moreover, as we have seen, four of the seven members of the Division that adopted the panel's decision also were doctors. On mandamus review, the Board argues, courts must defer to this off-the-record agency expertise.

The argument lacks merit. California law provides for judicial review of agency decisions to revoke or suspend medical licenses. Whatever the expertise of certain members of the panel and the Division, we cannot impute similar knowledge to a reviewing judge untrained in medical matters. Yet the trial court is confined to the record of the agency hearing, except in certain cases when evidence was improperly excluded or not previously available with due diligence. Therefore the agency record must provide as complete a basis for judicial review as due diligence makes feasible. It must include any technical matter necessary to enable a lay judge to determine whether the agency's decision has adequate support.

To rule that the agency record must be complete enough to allow judicial review of technical questions imposes no unreasonable burden on the administrative process. The Board did introduce "medical standards" testimony as to most of the gross negligence findings in this case, and inclusion of that kind of testimony appears routine in discipline matters.

We do not, of course, hold that agency adjudicators may not apply their expert opinions to decide issues of legislative fact. (See 3 Davis,

Administrative Law Treatise (2d ed. 1980) § 15.2, p. 138.[6]) A unique efficiency of many agencies is the professional competence they bring to matters delegated to them by the Legislature. We think an agency factfinder may, for example, reject uncontradicted opinion testimony that his own expertise renders unpersuasive. (See *McCarthy v. Industrial Commission*, 215 N.W. 824 (Wis.1927)).

A fortiori, the same expertise may govern even when the record contains no opinion evidence at all.

Yet due process requires, when in an adjudication an agency intends to rely on members' expertise to resolve legislative-fact issues, that it notify the parties and provide an opportunity for rebuttal.

The California Administrative Procedure Act requires notice and opportunity to rebut whenever an agency intends to take "official notice ... of any generally accepted technical or scientific matter within the agency's special field, [or] of any fact which may be judicially noticed by the courts of this State." (Gov.Code, § 11515; see Evid.Code, § 450 et seq.)[7]

The agency's notification must be complete and specific enough to give an effective opportunity for rebuttal. It must also help build a record adequate for judicial review. If it meets those requirements we can see no prejudice to the parties.[8]

We cannot accept the premise of *Brennan v. State Bd. of Medical Examiners*, 225 P.2d 11 (Cal.App.1950) that it is improper "for the board to decide ... questions [of violation of professional standards] upon the basis of the opinions held by the several members of the board," and that "*[n]either the board* nor the court could render a just decision except in reliance upon expert testimony." As *Brennan* notes, fairness is satisfied when a party "[is] apprised of the evidence against him so that he may have an opportunity to refute, test and explain it, ..."

Some questions concerning medical negligence require no expertise. Technical knowledge is not requisite to conclude that complications from a simple injection, a surgical clamp left in the patient's body, or a

---

6. Davis explains the long-recognized distinction between "legislative" and "adjudicative" facts. The latter are "facts concerning immediate parties" and what happened to them; the former are facts "utilized for informing a court's [or agency's] legislative judgment on questions of law and policy." (Id., § 15.1, p. 135.) Community standards of medical practice, and whether particular type of conduct departs grossly from those standards, are "legislative" facts. They inform the agency's judgment about what constitutes a violation of the Medical Practice Act.

7. Section 11515 provides: "In reaching a decision official notice may be taken, either before or after submission of a case for decision, of any generally accepted technical or scientific matter within the agency's spe-

cial field, and of any fact which may be judicially noticed by the courts of this State. Parties present at the hearing shall be informed of the matters to be noticed, and those matters shall be noted in the record, referred to therein, or appended thereto. Any such party shall be given a reasonable opportunity on request to refute the officially noticed matters by evidence or by written or oral presentation of authority, the manner of such refutation to be determined by the agency."

8. Arguably the notification should include a brief statement explaining the opinion held by the adjudicative body, the reasons for the opinion, and the members' qualifications to hold it.

shoulder injury from an appendectomy indicate negligence. Common sense is enough to make that evaluation. Only where the professional significance of underlying facts seems beyond lay comprehension must the basis for the technical findings be shown and an opportunity for rebuttal given.... No expertise is necessary to conclude that Franz' choice of Anaheim for Wollweber's operation was an extreme departure from the acceptable standard of medical care in that county. Accordingly there was no need for the panel to give notice of its own opinion or allow an opportunity for rebuttal. The trial court could resolve the issue on the record presented.

The same is not true, though, of the court's finding that scheduling surgery before choosing a surgeon was grossly negligent. Passaro did testify that the surgeon is responsible for independent diagnosis and evaluation of the need for an operation. Moreover, the Board's brief on appeal explains why premature scheduling involves the vice of interfering with the surgeon's independent role.

However, Ali apparently was retained the same day as surgery was scheduled or within a day or two afterward. There is no evidence he could not have cancelled the operation had he found it unnecessary after independent examination. There was no expert testimony that Franz' conduct in this instance was an extreme departure from community medical standards. Common knowledge does not supply the link between premature scheduling and independent surgical evaluation. The record does not disclose the basis of either the panel's or the Division's expert opinion on the issue, and Franz had no opportunity to refute that opinion. Hence the record was inadequate for a trial court finding that the scheduling of surgery before a surgeon was selected constituted gross negligence. The finding cannot be sustained....

If an agency has imposed a single discipline for multiple charges, some of which are found not sustained by evidence, and if there is "real doubt" whether the same action would have been taken on proper findings, the matter will be returned to the agency for redetermination of penalty.

The findings held improper in this opinion imply serious dereliction of a doctor's duty to his patient. We cannot say they had no influence in setting the discipline. On the other hand, major charges have been sustained and some discipline clearly is warranted. Franz should not practice free of restrictions while the penalty is being reconsidered. The conditions imposed by the stay order therefore should apply in the interim.

The judgment is reversed and the superior court is directed to issue a peremptory writ of mandate requiring the Board to reconsider petitioner Franz' discipline in light of our conclusions....

Notes and Questions

1. *Taking official notice.* In a medical malpractice case in court, a plaintiff would be required to offer expert testimony about medical standards

in the community (and defendant's departure from those standards) unless the negligence would be obvious even to a lay jury. In contrast, *Franz* states that a medical licensing board consisting of physicians is not required to summon experts and hear their testimony before disciplining a licensee for malpractice. Is there any justification for this difference?

Does it make any difference to Franz whether the Board proves that Franz was grossly negligent by calling expert witnesses to establish the standards or by taking official notice of medical standards in the community?

Suppose the California Supreme Court had affirmed the Board and Franz had appealed to the U.S. Supreme Court. Would that Court have reversed the Board's decision?

2. *Rebutting officially noticed evidence.* Normally a party is entitled to an opportunity to rebut facts that the agency seeks to establish by taking official notice. Why did the Court uphold the Board's finding that Franz's choice of Anaheim Hospital was gross negligence, even though Franz had no opportunity to rebut the finding?

In many instances, the first time a party learns that an administrative judge or the agency heads plan to take official notice of a fact is when the party reads the decision. In such situations, how can the party rebut the noticed fact? Generally, the agency should offer the party an opportunity to move that the record be reopened for further proceedings at which a rebuttal opportunity is provided.

The issue of official notice has been raised in numerous cases involving petitions to the Immigration and Naturalization Service by refugees seeking asylum because of a well-founded fear of persecution if they return to their home countries. In *Castillo–Villagra v. INS,* 972 F.2d 1017 (9th Cir.1992), the INS denied Castillo–Villagra refugee status and ordered him deported to Nicaragua. In his decision, the immigration judge took official notice of the following facts: i) Violeta Chamorro had been elected president of Nicaragua, ii) her non-Sandinista coalition had gained a majority in Parliament, iii) the Sandinistas had been ousted from power, and iv) Castillo–Villagra's family had nothing more to fear from the Sandinistas.

The court held that the first two facts were both legislative and non-disputable; consequently, the agency need not provide an opportunity for rebuttal. However, the third fact was legislative but disputable. The fourth fact was adjudicative and disputable. As a result, the court held that the agency should have warned Castillo–Villagra that it intended to take notice of the third and fourth facts and offered him an opportunity to respond.

Most cases hold that the opportunity to rebut officially noticed facts can occur in the form of a motion to reopen the proceedings for further evidence. *Castillo–Villagra* disagreed, because of concern that the applicant might be deported before the motion was granted. On this point, most decisions disagree. *See, e.g., Rhoa–Zamora v. INS,* 971 F.2d 26 (7th Cir.1992), which involved exactly the same officially noticed facts as *Castillo–Villagra* but which ruled that the issue could properly be raised through a motion to reopen.

3. *Legislative facts.* Both *Franz* and *Castillo-Villagra* make reference to the distinction between legislative and adjudicative facts. What is the relevance of this distinction in deciding issues relating to official notice?

Suppose that in a medical licensing case, the Board decides that, in this and future cases, it will suspend for at least one year the license of any physician who is found to have prescribed a "controlled substance" (such as amphetamines) in amounts which exceed medical needs. This decision is based on the determination that no lesser sanction would provide an adequate deterrent to doctors who are abusing their prescription-writing privileges. Must the Board allow an opportunity for rebuttal of this determination? See *Market St. Ry. Co. v. Railroad Comm'n,* 324 U.S. 548 (1945) (prediction that lowering fares would increase the number of passengers carried—no requirement that railroad have opportunity to rebut this conclusion).

4. *Official notice or evaluation of the evidence?* When the Board decided that Franz had been grossly negligent, was it (i) taking official notice of a crucial fact, as the court assumed, or (ii) was it using its experience to draw conclusions from the evidence?

When an agency relies on background knowledge and experience to evaluate evidence, it is not taking official notice of anything and need not specially notify the parties and afford an opportunity to contest the evaluation. *See* the last sentence of 1981 MSAPA § 4–215(d). However, the distinction between taking official notice and evaluating evidence is often difficult to draw. One way to read *Franz* is that it requires that the agency provide an opportunity for rebuttal in both situations.

For a similar decision, see *Cohen v. Ambach,* 490 N.Y.S.2d 908 (N.Y.A.D. 1985), involving a regulation that chiropractors could not solicit business through advertising that "is not in the public interest." Cohen sent out a newsletter entitled "Health Facts." On finding that this material was not in the public interest, the agency suspended her license. However, no witnesses testified that the newsletter was false or misleading or that it was contrary to the public interest. The court said:

> When the panel concluded, on the bare record, that petitioner violated the Department's regulation after employing their individual expertise to analyze the publication, they denied petitioner her right to an adjudicatory hearing ... While the hearing panel could properly use its expertise to analyze and interpret evidence before it, it could not use such expertise to substitute for evidence.... Finally, in relying on their expertise to analyze petitioner's publication without the benefit of any expert testimony, the members of the panel were essentially relying on material outside the record. [The court quoted the official notice provision in the state APA.] Here, no such notice [that the agency intended to take official notice] was given.

Often an agency uses its expertise to evaluate the testimony of expert witnesses. Suppose that Franz offers expert testimony that it was not gross negligence to perform ulcer surgery in a hospital without an ICU, even if complications were expected. Without introducing any contrary testimony, the Board holds that it was gross negligence. Is this reversible error? *See* the dictum in *Franz* citing *McCarthy v. Industrial Commission.*

With *Franz and McCarthy,* compare *Davis & Randall, Inc. v. United States,* 219 F.Supp. 673 (W.D.N.Y.1963), an opinion of a three-judge court written by Judge Friendly of the Second Circuit. In *Davis & Randall,* the ICC had rejected the testimony of an expert who predicted that a trucker would make a profit if it charged a certain rate. The ICC substituted its own view that the rate would not be profitable. Friendly wrote:

> Without wishing to be held to the letter, we suggest that a rejection of unopposed testimony by a qualified and disinterested expert on a matter susceptible of reasonably precise measurement, without the agency's developing its objections at a hearing, ought to be upheld only when the agency's uncommunicated criticisms appear to the reviewing court to be both so compelling and so deeply held that the court can be fairly sure the agency would not have been affected by anything the witness could have said had he known of them, *and* the court would have been bound to affirm, despite the expert's hypothetical rebuttal, out of deference to the agency's judgment on so technical a matter.

5. *Problem.* An Elm City ordinance establishes rent control and provides that rents must "provide a fair return on the owner's investment." An elected three-person Rent Control Board can order rent increases or decreases. The Board is required to follow 1981 MSAPA.

Your client Red sought a rent increase for an apartment house he owned. At a hearing conducted before the full Board, Red testified that the cost of the building, with all improvements, was $2,000,000. His books and records were introduced into evidence to prove this figure. Max, a tenant in the building, testified that he knew Gloria, Red's mother, and Gloria had recently told Max that Red had told her that he actually had only $1,400,000 invested in the building and had falsified his records. Red denied that he had ever had any such conversation with Gloria and affirmed the accuracy of his records.

Red presented the testimony of Beth, an expert appraiser, that 12% per year would be a reasonable rate of return on investment. This figure was based on an analysis of the risks of the business and of sale prices of similar buildings. Beth was not cross examined and there was no other testimony on rate of return.

The Board found that Red's investment was $1,400,000 (based on Max's testimony). It also determined that a reasonable rate of return would be 9% per year. The Board simply noted that it did not agree with Beth's analysis and it was basing its conclusion on its experience in rent control. It noted that the building was probably appreciating in value and that 9% was more than Red could get from investing in a long-term bank account. It was also the figure the Board had been using in all of its rent control cases. As a result of these findings, the Board ordered a 15% cut in rents rather than an increase.

On judicial review, should this decision be upheld? *See Whispering Pines Mobile Home Park, Ltd. v. City of Scotts Valley,* 225 Cal.Rptr. 364 (Cal.App. 1986).

§ 4.3 THE DECISION PHASE: FINDING FACTS AND STATING REASONS

Fundamental to any system of adjudicatory procedure is a requirement that the decisionmaker state findings of fact and reasons for the decision. Recall the elements of a constitutionally required adjudicative hearing in *Goldberg v. Kelly* ("the decision maker should state the reasons for his determination and indicate the evidence he relied on, though his statement need not amount to a full opinion or even formal findings of fact and conclusions of law"). All APAs include such requirements. *See* § 556(c) of the federal act and the more exacting requirements in 1981 MSAPA § 4–215(c). Indeed, § 555(e) requires a statement of reasons in certain cases of informal adjudication—one of the very few federal act provisions applicable to informal adjudication.

Can a reviewing court require an agency to make findings and provide reasons in an adjudication if no statute calls for them? And what should a reviewing court do when it is dissatisfied with an agency's statement of findings and reasons (or the absence thereof)?

IN THE MATTER OF CIBA–GEIGY CORP.
576 A.2d 784 (N.J.1990).

STEIN, J.:

This case primarily concerns the validity of the administrative procedures followed by the New Jersey Department of Environmental Protection (DEP) in renewing a permit that authorized Ciba–Geigy to discharge an average of 5.9 million gallons per day of chemically-treated effluent into the Atlantic Ocean ... The Federal Clean Water Act prohibits the discharge of any pollutant into the nation's waters without a permit ... Two communities near the point of discharge ... as well as an environmental-protection group and several concerned citizens, appealed the DEP decision....

Although administrative agencies generally act either through rulemaking or adjudication, DEP's permitting process does not fit precisely into either category. Rulemaking is a legislative-type function that usually involves policy judgments of widespread application within the agency's regulatory sphere. Rulemaking may also "originate with and involve a specific party," and in that context the agency would tailor its procedure in order to "account for the individualized effect of its proposed action." An adjudicatory procedure is typically a contested proceeding that may require a trial-type hearing and thus resembles judicial action because it determines the rights of specific individuals or a limited group of individuals.

Agencies acting in an adjudicative capacity review evidence, make findings of fact, and exercise discretion in applying the law to those facts. Although DEP did not conduct a trial-type hearing in considering Ciba–

Geigy's permit-renewal application, the agency reviewed extensive documentation submitted by both Ciba–Geigy and interested members of the public. Those documents included the application for a draft permit and its accompanying fact sheet as well as evidence offered during the public-comment period. Thus, the permit-renewal process encompassed the presentation of evidentiary-type facts to the agency.

The agency's decision to grant or deny renewal undoubtedly "requir[ed] the exercise of a discretion or judgment judicial in nature." Moreover, the agency's final determination constitutes an "administrative adjudication" which affords a permittee the opportunity to contest that decision at a hearing. Under those circumstances, the ... renewal process is best classified as a quasi-judicial procedure possessing some, but not all, of the elements of a traditional adjudicatory proceeding.

Fact-finding is a basic requirement imposed on agencies that act in a quasi-judicial capacity:

> It is axiomatic in this State by this time that an administrative agency acting quasi-judicially must set forth basic findings of fact, supported by the evidence and supporting the ultimate conclusions and final determination, for the salutary purpose of informing the interested parties and any reviewing tribunal of the basis on which the final decision was reached so that it may be readily determined whether the result is sufficiently and soundly grounded or derives from arbitrary, capricious or extra-legal considerations.

An agency must engage in fact-finding to the extent required by statute or regulation, and provide notice of those facts to all interested parties. This requirement is "far from a technicality and is a matter of substance." In addition, fact-finding ensures that agencies act within the scope of their delegated authority, and also facilitates appellate review:

> [N]o matter how great a deference the court is obliged to accord the administrative determination which it is being called upon to review, it has no capacity to review at all unless there is some kind of reasonable factual record developed by the administrative agency and the agency has stated its reasons grounded in that record for its action.

When an agency's decision is not accompanied by the necessary findings of fact, the usual remedy is to remand the matter to the agency to correct the deficiency ...

The record reveals that DEP satisfied various statutory and regulatory requirements in its review of Ciba–Geigy's application. The agency solicited, responded to, and considered written comments submitted by elected officials, environmental groups, and concerned citizens before making a determination concerning the final permit. In addition DEP held a public hearing and made available extensive documentation and information concerning the proposed discharge. The ... permit contained discharge limitations and monitoring requirements ... and required Ciba Geigy, among other things, to maintain the discharge pipeline and to monitor ocean water at beaches near the points of discharge. Interested parties and members of the public appear to have been well informed about most significant aspects of Ciba–Geigy's renewal application . . .

[The court held that DEP failed to make necessary findings under the federal EPA's Ocean Discharge Criteria regulations (ODC) which prohibit granting a permit that would cause unreasonable degradation of the marine environment, based on 10 factors] The agency never determined whether, based on the factors . . . the discharge would cause an unreasonable degradation of the marine environment. The impediment to judicial review is that there is nothing in the . . . record that indicates how DEP concluded that Ciba–Geigy's permit complied with the ODC. To that extent the agency's proceedings were insufficiently specific to enable the reviewing court to evaluate its decision. That deficiency must be addressed in any subsequent proceedings concerning the renewal of a permit . . .

Second, the record did not indicate clearly how the permit comported with New Jersey's antidegradation policy [in the state's water quality regulations]. If, for example, a discharge seeks to reduce the quality of waters below the level "necessary to support the designated uses, including but not limited to, propagation of fish, shellfish, and wildlife and recreation in and on the water," DEP must find that the diminution in water quality advances "important economic or social development in the area in which the waters are located." Any such finding should include an adequate description of the economic or societal interest that is advanced . . .

Notes and Questions

1. *Rulemaking or adjudication.* Although the court determined that DEP's water pollution permit process was adjudication, the procedure it employed resembled rulemaking. There was no trial-type hearing, only a public legislative-type hearing and an exchange of documents. Is this an appropriate choice of procedure for resolving the questions of law, fact and policy that were raised by Ciba–Geigy's application?

Either Ciba–Geigy or an opponent of the application could have triggered a trial-type hearing under the New Jersey APA, because the statute defined a determination to grant a discharge permit as a "contested case." See N.J.S.A. § 58:10A–7(d), (e), (f). However, opponents that wish to trigger a hearing must file an extensive petition for intervention and deposit an amount of money equal to the permit fee. It is unclear why the towns and groups opposing the permit did not request a hearing; perhaps it would have been too costly.

Courts in most states would have dismissed the appeal because of the petitioner's failure to have exhausted administrative remedies. However, New Jersey is quite lenient in its exhaustion requirement. It does not require exhaustion when an appeal raises solely questions of law. See § 11.2.4.

2. *Legal authority.* What was the legal basis for imposition of the requirement that the agency make findings in *Ciba-Geigy*? Due process? The New Jersey APA? The EPA's ODC regulations or New Jersey's water quality regulations? Administrative common law? *See* Sidney A. Shapiro & Richard E. Levy, "Heightened Scrutiny of the Fourth Branch: Separation of Powers and the Requirement of Adequate Reasons for Agency Decisions," 1987 Duke L.J. 387 (requirement of findings and reasons is common law technique to promote rational administrative decisionmaking and facilitate judicial review).

Federal courts are precluded from imposing procedural rules on agencies as a matter of administrative common law. *Vermont Yankee Nuclear Power Corp. v. NRDC,* § 5.4.3; *Pension Benefit Guaranty Corp. v. LTV Corp.,* §§ 3.1.1 N.5 and 5.4.3 N.5. *Vermont Yankee* held that a court could not impose rulemaking procedures requirements beyond those specified in the APA, in order to improve decisionmaking or facilitate judicial review; *LTV* said the same for adjudication procedures. If *Ciba-Geigy* had been a federal case, would it be vulnerable to criticism under *Vermont Yankee*?

3. *Rationale for requiring findings and reasons.* What are the rationales stated by the court for requiring DEP to make findings and state reasons in *Ciba-Geigy*? Are these reasons convincing? How would findings and reasons have helped the towns and others protesting Ciba–Geigy's application? Was the court trying to send a message to DEP? What message? If DEP staff members write up a statement of findings and reasons, will they have any difficulty getting the New Jersey courts to uphold the permit?

4. *Link between facts and law.* In *Ciba-Geigy* would the court have been satisfied if the DEP had recited the basic facts concerning the permit and then concluded that the permit satisfied the ODC regulations and the state anti-degradation policy?

In *Adams v. Board of Review,* 821 P.2d 1 (Utah Ct.App.1991), the issue was whether a telemarketer's neck and back injuries resulted from repetitive use of the phone at work or from non-occupational causes. There was a large body of conflicting medical evidence. The Workers' Compensation Commission summarized the evidence and found that "the preponderance of medical evidence in this case establishes that the applicant's various listed symptoms are not related to her work as a telemarketer at Unicorp." Reversing the decision because of lack of "subsidiary findings," the court said:

> The Commission's conclusion that Adams failed to prove causation, without supporting findings, is arbitrary. Administrative bodies may not rely upon findings that contain only ultimate conclusions. Given the numerous legal and factual questions regarding causation in this case, the Commission's solitary finding that Adams failed to prove causation does not give the parties any real indication as to the bases for its decision and the steps taken to reach it, nor does it give a reviewing court anything to review.

> While the purported "findings of fact" written by the ALJ contain an informative summary of the evidence presented, such a rehearsal of contradictory evidence does not constitute findings of fact. [A finding of fact] must indicate what the ALJ determines in fact occurred, not merely what the contradictory evidence indicates might have occurred

... Since we cannot even determine why the Commission found there was no causation shown, we clearly cannot assume that the Commission actually made any of the possible subsidiary findings.

5. *Explanation and discretion.* A requirement that an agency state findings and reasons is particularly valuable when the agency adjudicative action in question is highly political and involves broad discretionary standards, as in *Ciba-Geigy.* See 1981 MSAPA § 4–215(c). This is especially true since the agency is not subject to the discipline of a formal, evidentiary hearing.

If courts impose a requirement that the decision-makers explain their action, it is more likely that the decision will be carefully considered and thus less likely that discretion will be abused or exercised solely to appease powerful political forces. Judicial review of such decisions tends to be quite deferential (see § 9.4), but it would be meaningless without a contemporaneous agency explanation of the decision.

Courts sometimes interpret an underlying statute to require an explanation. The leading federal case is *Dunlop v. Bachowski,* 421 U.S. 560 (1975). *Dunlop* involved a statute allowing the Secretary of Labor to sue in District Court to set aside a union election tainted by fraud.

The Secretary refused to bring suit to set aside a particular election. The Court held his action judicially reviewable and interpreted the underlying statute to require the Secretary to state reasons for his refusal and the essential facts on which the decision was based. Such a statement would permit intelligent judicial review, would inform a complaining union member why his request had been denied, and would promote careful consideration. The Secretary had furnished a brief letter to the complainant; the Court stated that the letter might satisfy APA § 555(e) but not the more exacting requirement of explanation that it had discovered in the statute.

A good example of such judicial creativity at the state level is *Ship Creek Hydraulic Syndicate v. State of Alaska,* 685 P.2d 715 (Alaska 1984). The statute required the state to balance public good and private harm when it seized land to build a highway. The court held that the state must prepare a "decisional document" before doing so. The document would contain fact findings and an explanation of how the balance had been struck. The court implied the requirement into the underlying statute and also seemed to require it as a matter of common law since such a document was needed to facilitate judicial review. It held that the rationale of *Vermont Yankee* did not preclude it from doing so.

However, in *Citizens to Preserve Overton Park, Inc. v. Volpe,* 401 U.S. 402 (1971), the Court declined to imply a requirement of an explanation into a statute. (This important case is further discussed in §§ 9.4 and 10.5.) Pursuant to statute, the Secretary of Transportation granted funds to build an interstate highway through Overton Park in Memphis. The statute provided that a road should not be built through a park unless there is no feasible and prudent alternative. The Secretary did not explain why there was no such alternative and the Supreme Court held that no such explanation was required by the statute.

But without any explanation or administrative record, how could the Court review the Secretary's decision? The Supreme Court remanded the case to the District Court to conduct a de novo trial at which the decision would be reviewed on the full record that was before the agency when it made the decision. At the trial, the court could require the Secretary to provide an explanation if that were necessary. Two justices dissented on this latter point. They believed that the case should first be remanded to the Secretary to provide the necessary explanation. Later cases generally follow the route suggested by the dissenters. They require a remand to the decisionmaker to supply an explanation, rather than a trial at which that explanation is adduced. *See Camp v. Pitts,* 411 U.S. 138 (1973). This issue is further discussed in § 9.4.

6. *Post hoc rationalizations.* Could DEP provide the missing findings and reasons in its brief before the New Jersey Supreme Court? *Overton Park* and many other cases hold that if an agency has failed to make findings or to state reasons, the deficiency cannot be repaired by post-hoc rationalizations. This rule is regarded as a corollary of the fundamental principle that "a reviewing court, in dealing with a determination or judgment that an administrative agency alone is authorized to make, must judge the propriety of such action solely by the grounds invoked by the agency. If those grounds are inadequate or improper, the court is powerless to affirm the administrative action by substituting what it considers to be a more adequate or proper basis." *SEC v. Chenery Corp.,* 332 U.S. 194, 196 (1947).

However, does the resistance to post hoc rationalizations make sense? Agency lawyers represent the agency. At the time of judicial review, why shouldn't they be allowed to consult with the agency heads and supply any findings or reasons missing in the agency decision, so long as the findings or reasons are supported by the administrative record? Is remand to the agency a meaningless ritual, since those same agency lawyers will probably just compose the missing findings and reasons for the agency head to sign?

In *Bagdonas v. Dep't of Treasury,* 93 F.3d 422 (7th Cir.1996), the Bureau of Alcohol, Tobacco and Firearms (BATF) had power to allow a person previously convicted of a gun crime to possess firearms if it found that the applicant will not be likely to act in a manner dangerous to the public safety. After an extensive investigation, BATF turned down Bagdonas' application but furnished no explanation. Its letter simply said: "We regret to advise you that we are not presently satisfied that the above statutory requirements for granting restoration have been met."

BATF submitted a detailed affidavit to the district court that explained its reasons for denying the application. The affidavit was filed by the official who had authority to act on the application. Rather than remand to the agency, the court ruled that the affidavit could be considered as an explanation of the agency's decision which the court then upheld, although it must be "viewed critically." The court continued: "Despite our disapproval of the agency's initial handling of this matter—and with the expectation that we shall not see a similar performance again—we must conclude that" the decision was not arbitrary and capricious.

Does the *Bagdonas* decision violate the rule against post hoc rationalization? The rule in *Camp v. Pitts*?

7. *Findings at every level?* In a typical administrative adjudication, an administrative judge conducts the hearing and renders a proposed decision that contains findings of fact and conclusions of law. The matter is then considered by the agency heads. More often than not, the agency heads summarily affirm the proposed decision. The agency heads are not required to explain their decision to accept the judge's decision. One set of findings and conclusions is all that either due process or APAs require. See *Guentchev v. INS*, 77 F.3d 1036 (7th Cir.1996), which states:

> To adopt someone else's reasoned explanation *is* to give reasons.... Writing imposes mental discipline, but we lack any principled ground to declare that members of the Board must use words different from those the immigration judge selected.... The point is that an appellate tribunal is entitled to adopt the opinion of its predecessor; the form of words it chooses to do so is irrelevant.

8. *Problem.* A statute permits the Nevada Gaming Board, in its discretion, to exclude from the premises of all casinos a person who has an "unsavory reputation which would adversely affect public confidence in the gaming industry." The Gaming Board has never adopted any rules which clarify this statute but has entered about a dozen exclusion orders.

Sally, who lives in Pennsylvania, enjoys gambling and often visits Nevada casinos. After conducting a hearing, the Board entered an order excluding Sally from all Nevada casinos. Evidence presented at the hearing indicated that Sally had a long-term romantic relationship with Max. Max is generally considered to be an important figure in organized crime in Pennsylvania. Neither Max nor Sally has ever been convicted of a crime. At the hearing both Max and Sally denied any connection with organized crime. However, there was evidence that Sally often carried messages and did other chores for the members of Max's crime "family."

The Board's only finding was that Sally had an unsavory reputation which would adversely affect public confidence that the gaming industry is free from corruptive elements. On judicial review, should the Board's order be reversed if a) no APA applies? b) 1981 MSAPA applies? *See Spilotro v. State ex rel. Nevada Gaming Comm'n,* 661 P.2d 467 (Nev.1983); *Kraft v. Jacka,* 872 F.2d 862 (9th Cir.1989).

§ 4.4   EFFECT OF DECISION: RES JUDICATA, STARE DECISIS, EQUITABLE ESTOPPEL

This subchapter considers a range of problems which center on the subsequent effect of an agency adjudicatory decision.

First, it addresses the preclusive effect of a decision upon later adjudication—the doctrines of res judicata and collateral estoppel. Should these familiar principles operate differently in the administrative than in the judicial context? Next, it takes up stare decisis—the extent to which an agency should or must follow its own prior decision. Should an agency be more free than a court to reconsider its precedents? Finally, it considers the extent to which an agency is bound to respect reliance interests created by its actions—whether those actions are adjudicatory or arise out of other agency functions such as advice-giving. Should an agency be bound by the doctrines of equitable estoppel and apparent authority?

§ 4.4.1 RES JUDICATA AND COLLATERAL ESTOPPEL

Under the rule of res judicata (sometimes called "claim preclusion"), a valid and final personal judgment is conclusive of a claim. If the judgment is for the plaintiff, the claim is extinguished and merged in the judgment; if the judgment is for the defendant, plaintiff is barred from reasserting the claim. RESTATEMENT OF JUDGMENTS 2d § 17.

Under the related doctrine of collateral estoppel (or "issue preclusion"), when an issue of fact or law is actually litigated and determined by a valid and final judgment, and the determination is essential to the judgment, the determination is conclusive in a subsequent action between the parties, *even on a different claim.* Id. § 27. In administrative law, collateral estoppel arises more frequently than res judicata, because, as in *University of Tennessee v. Elliott*, which follows, the second case concerns a different "claim" but depends upon a matter determined in the first case.

If a person lacked a full and fair opportunity to litigate the issue in the first action, or other circumstances justify affording an opportunity to relitigate the issue, collateral estoppel would be improper. RESTATEMENT § 29. In recent years, collateral estoppel has frequently been applied despite a lack of mutuality: i.e. a person precluded from relitigating an issue against the opposing party is also precluded from doing so against a third person.

UNIVERSITY OF TENNESSEE v. ELLIOTT
478 U.S. 788 (1986).

WHITE, J.:

[In 1981, the University of Tennessee informed respondent Elliott, who is black, that he would be discharged for misconduct. The University stated ten separate grounds. Elliott requested a hearing under the state APA. He also filed an action in federal court alleging that his discharge was racially motivated and violated both Title VII of the Civil Rights Act of 1964 and also 42 U.S.C. § 1983 (the Reconstruction era statute providing a right to sue state officials for constitutional violations).

The administrative hearing lasted five months and involved more than 100 witnesses and 150 exhibits. It generated over 5000 pages of transcript. Elliott denied the misconduct charges and contended that the discharge was motivated by racial prejudice. An administrative assistant to the University's Vice President for Agriculture, "presid[ing] as an Administrative Law Judge (ALJ)," found that the University had proved some of the charges, and he also found that the charges were not racially motivated. He recommended that Elliott be transferred to a new assignment with different supervisors. The University's Vice President for Agriculture affirmed the ALJ's ruling. Elliott did not seek judicial review in the Tennessee courts but instead pursued his action in federal court. The University moved to dismiss because it argued that the ALJ ruling was entitled to preclusive effect.]

[As to Elliott's Title VII claim, the statute provided that] the Equal Employment Opportunity Commission (EEOC), in investigating discrimination charges, must give "substantial weight to final findings and orders made by State or local authorities in proceedings commenced under State or local [employment discrimination] law ..." [I]t would make little sense for Congress to write such a provision if state agency findings were entitled to preclusive effect in Title VII actions in federal court....

[As to Elliott's § 1983 claim], we see no reason to suppose that Congress, in enacting the Reconstruction civil rights statutes, wished to foreclose the adaptation of traditional principles of preclusion to such subsequent developments as the burgeoning use of administrative adjudication in the 20th century.

We have previously recognized that it is sound policy to apply principles of issue preclusion to the factfinding of administrative bodies acting in a judicial capacity. In a unanimous decision in *United States v. Utah Construction & Mining Co.*, 384 U.S. 394 (1966), we held that the factfinding of the Advisory Board of Contract Appeals was binding in a subsequent action in the Court of Claims involving a contract dispute between the same parties. We explained:

> ... the result we reach is harmonious with general principles of collateral estoppel. Occasionally courts have used language to the effect that *res judicata* principles do not apply to administrative proceedings, but such language is certainly too broad ... When an administrative agency is acting in a judicial capacity and resolves disputed issues of fact properly before it which the parties have had an adequate opportunity to litigate, the courts have not hesitated to apply *res judicata* to enforce repose.

Thus, *Utah Construction* teaches that giving preclusive effect to administrative factfinding serves the value underlying general principles of collateral estoppel: enforcing repose. This value, which encompasses both the parties' interest in avoiding the cost and vexation of repetitive litigation and the public's interest in conserving judicial resources is equally implicated whether factfinding is done by a federal or state agency.

Having federal courts give preclusive effect to the factfinding of state administrative tribunals also serves the value of federalism.... Perhaps the major purpose of the Full Faith and Credit Clause is to act as a nationally unifying force, and this purpose is served by giving preclusive effect to state administrative factfinding rather than leaving the courts of a second forum, state or federal, free to reach conflicting results. Accordingly, we hold that when a state agency "acting in a judicial capacity ... resolves disputed issues of fact properly before it which the parties have had an adequate opportunity to litigate," *Utah Construction & Mining Co.*, federal courts must give the agency's fact-finding the same preclusive effect to which it would be entitled in the State's courts ...

[STEVENS, J.,. joined by BRENNAN and BLACKMUN, JJ., dissented. Stevens argued that collateral estoppel principles should not apply so as to foreclose access to federal courts under § 1983.]

Notes and Questions

1. *Res judicata and collateral estoppel in administrative law.* In *Elliott* the Court holds that an unreviewed state administrative decision has preclusive effect on a § 1983 action in federal court but not on a Title VII action in federal court. Why the difference?

Many states also apply res judicata and collateral estoppel to administrative adjudications. See, e.g., *Ryan v. New York Telephone Co.*, 467 N.E.2d 487 (N.Y.Ct.App.1984). In that case, Ryan was fired for theft of company property. He sought unemployment compensation benefits but they were denied because, after a hearing at which he chose to appear with a union representative, the Labor Department upheld the theft charge. Later criminal proceedings were dismissed "in the interests of justice." Ryan sued the company for false arrest, wrongful discharge, and slander. The court held that collateral estoppel applied. The issues resolved in the administrative proceeding were dispositive of his tort claims and he had a full and fair opportunity to litigate them before the agency. It was his choice to appear without counsel.

What effect does a case like *Ryan* have on unemployment compensation hearings?

2. *Preclusion against the government.* In *United States v. Stauffer Chemical Co.*, 464 U.S. 165 (1984), the Court held that the federal government could be barred from relitigating a *legal* issue it had lost in an action involving the same party. Stauffer had won a Tenth Circuit decision that it could exclude certain inspectors from its plant. The identical issue arose in the Sixth Circuit where Stauffer had another plant. The government was precluded from relitigating the issue in the Sixth Circuit (which had not previously decided the issue).

However, *non-mutual* collateral estoppel does not lie against the federal government. *United States v. Mendoza*, 464 U.S. 154 (1984). In *Mendoza*, an earlier *trial court* decision (in the Ninth Circuit) held that certain Philippine nationals were entitled to U.S. citizenship. The government did not appeal. The present case (which also arose in the Ninth Circuit) involved the same issue but with different plaintiffs. They argued that the government was precluded from relitigating the issue.

The Court held that non-mutual collateral estoppel is not applicable against the United States (although it would be applicable against private parties). The government should be allowed (or even encouraged) to relitigate the issue, in hope of creating a conflict between the circuits, so that the issue might "percolate" to the Supreme Court. Also, the Court was concerned with the realities of government litigation: the U.S. should not be forced to appeal every case it loses in a trial court, no matter how unimportant, in order to guard against preclusion in later (and perhaps far more important) litigation. Moreover, a new administration should be able to change the policy of a prior one (which had decided to accept a defeat and not appeal).

Should the government be less vulnerable to collateral estoppel than other litigants? *See* Note, "Collateral Estoppel and Non–Acquiescence: Precluding Government Relitigation," 99 Harv.L.Rev. 847 (1986).

3. *Non–Acquiescence.* The federal government argues that it can freely relitigate an issue, despite having lost an *appellate* decision on the identical point in the *same circuit* against a different party. This is referred to as intracircuit non-acquiescence. Despite *Mendoza*, the courts have rejected the practice of intracircuit non-acquiescence. *See, e.g., Lopez v. Heckler,* 713 F.2d 1432 (9th Cir.1983) (preliminary injunction granted); 464 U.S. 879 (1983) (5–4 vote to stay the injunction); 725 F.2d 1489 (9th Cir.1984) (narrower injunction issued).

The background of the *Lopez* case was a policy of the Department of Health and Human Services (HHS). HHS terminated large numbers of persons receiving federal disability payments without any new evidence that their conditions had improved. Earlier Ninth Circuit cases had held that this was improper. But HHS went right on terminating recipients, even though they lived in the Ninth Circuit. As a result the recipients (mostly poor and quite sick) had to go to the expense of litigating the issue; because of the prior cases, they were certain to win—if they could survive long enough. In *Lopez* (a class action brought by persons whose benefits had been terminated), the court affirmed a preliminary injunction against HHS' non-acquiescence policy.

A concurring opinion said:

> The Secretary's ill-advised policy of refusing to obey the decisional law of this circuit is akin to the repudiated pre-Civil War doctrine of nullification whereby rebellious states refused to recognize certain federal laws within their boundaries. The Secretary's non-acquiescence not only scoffs at the law of this circuit, but flouts some very important principles basic to our American system of government—the rule of law, the doctrine of separation of powers embedded in the constitution, and the tenet of judicial supremacy laid down in *Marbury v. Madison* ... The government expects its citizens to abide by the law—no less is expected of those charged with the duty to faithfully administer the law.

713 F.2d at 1441. The first *Lopez* decision preceded *Mendoza;* the second *Lopez* opinion said that *Mendoza* was not applicable. 725 F.2d at 1497, n. 5. Can you distinguish *Lopez* from *Mendoza*?

Should the government *ever* be allowed to practice intracircuit non-acquiescence? Suppose, for example, that an agency lost case A before the 2d Circuit. It then wins cases B, C, and D, which presented the identical issue, in the 3d, 4th, and 5th Circuits. It can be argued that the government should be allowed to non-acquiesce in case A in order that the issue could again be presented to the 2d Circuit in case E. Case E would allow the 2d Circuit to decide whether to overrule case A in light of the contrary decisions in cases B, C, and D. *See* Samuel Estreicher & Richard L. Revesz, "Nonacquiescence by Federal Administrative Agencies," 98 Yale L.J. 679, 743–53 (1989).

In many situations, an agency cannot predict which circuit a decision will be appealed to, because a party can appeal in any circuit where it transacts business. Large corporations do business in every circuit. Suppose, for example, that the 2d Circuit has previously reversed the agency on a certain point. The agency need not change its position, even though a respondent can choose any circuit to appeal to, including the 2d. Otherwise, an adverse decision in any one circuit would become the law everywhere. However, the agency is expected to deal forthrightly with the conflict between its view and the 2d Circuit's view, not sweep it under the rug. *Nielsen Lithographing Co. v. NLRB*, 854 F.2d 1063 (7th Cir.1988). To avoid this problem, should venue statutes be changed so that a party could appeal only to the circuit where its principal place of business is located?

4. *Criminal cases.* Suppose a welfare recipient is criminally prosecuted for welfare fraud. She is convicted. In a later case before the welfare agency, the state attempts to recoup the illegal payments. Can she relitigate the issue of whether she was entitled to the payments?

Suppose she was acquitted in the criminal case. Can the state relitigate the issue of whether she was entitled to the payments?

Suppose the state's action before the agency to recoup the overpayments precedes the criminal case. The recipient wins before the agency. Can the prosecution relitigate the issue in the criminal case? *See United States v. Payne*, 2 F.3d 706, 707–10 (6th Cir.1993) (yes); *People v. Sims*, 651 P.2d 321 (Cal.1982) (no).

Suppose the recipient loses the administrative case. Can she relitigate the issue in the subsequent criminal case?

Suppose an employer is criminally convicted for violating workplace safety laws. An agency then seeks to collect civil money penalties for the same offense. Should the agency be barred by the constitutional prohibition against double jeopardy? Generally speaking, no, because double jeopardy applies only to successive *criminal* prosecutions, and administrative fines, although punitive in some respects, are not inherently a criminal sanction. *Hudson v. United States*, 118 S.Ct. 488 (1997).

5. *Full and fair opportunity to litigate.* Suppose Joe loses Case A before agency X. Under federal law, agency X decisions are not judicially reviewable. The same issue arises in Case B before agency Y. Can Joe relitigate the issue in Case B? *See Convalescent Center of Bloomfield Inc. v. Dep't of Income Maintenance*, 544 A.2d 604 (Conn.1988) (yes—absence of judicial review deprived Joe of full and fair opportunity to litigate the issue).

6. *Problem.* The Monroe Corporations Commission (MCC) licenses stockbrokers. It can impose penalties (such as license revocation) against brokers who engage in misconduct (such as insider trading).

Your client, Jed, is a stock broker in Monroe. MCC suspects that Jed used inside information about Z Corp. mergers to make large profits for himself and for clients. Jed denies that he engaged in insider trading (he says he received no tips and instead developed the information by his own shrewd analysis).

Jed has very large potential liability in civil litigation that might be brought in federal court under SEC rules by persons who sold Z Corp. while Jed and his clients were buying it.

MCC has told you that they are willing to negotiate a one-year suspension of Jed's license. Jed wants to fight the case before MCC. Do you advise him to take the deal? *See* Edmund H. Kerr & Robert J. Stillman, "Collateral Estoppel Implications of SEC Adjudications," 42 Bus.Law. 441 (1987).

§ 4.4.2   CONSISTENT DECISIONMAKING: STARE DECISIS

Under the principle of stare decisis, courts generally follow their own precedents and lower courts must adhere to precedents established by higher courts. Stare decisis assures a reasonable degree of consistency and predictability in the law; by minimizing litigation it also serves the purpose of judicial economy. Yet courts occasionally reconsider and depart from prior precedents; they do not always admit they are doing so. Do the reasons for stare decisis apply with equal force to agency adjudicatory decisions? Greater or less force? To all agency decisions?

UNITED AUTOMOBILE WORKERS OF AMERICA v. NLRB

802 F.2d 969 (7th Cir.1986).

[A collective bargaining agreement provided that National Lock Co. would "discuss" any relocation of its plant with the Union. Applicable labor law provides that a company must negotiate a plant relocation with the union if it is motivated by concern over labor costs. However, this statutory protection can be waived. The Board held that the agreement to "discuss" relocation was a waiver of the Union's right to "negotiate" over the issue. Prior Board decisions hold that a waiver of a statutory right must be clear and unmistakable. The Board did not discuss or cite any of those prior decisions in this case.]

POSNER, J.:

We grant that despite the strong judicial endorsement of the rule, the Board—which knows more about the dynamics of collective bargaining than the courts—might be able to dilute or abandon it, since the rule is a nonobvious gloss on the statute. And there [is] evidence that a desire to abandon or dilute, rather than mere oversight, does indeed lie behind the Board's failure to mention the rule.... [T]he administrative law judge had relied heavily on the presumption against inferring the waiver of a statutory right and the union had argued the presumption vigorously throughout the case. So the Board could not just have forgotten about the rule; and if it didn't mention the rule just because it did not want to weaken the force of its opinion, this would be the equivalent of wanting to dilute or abandon the rule ...

All this is rather bootless conjecture, though. For it makes no difference what the Board may have had in mind but failed to express;

an administrative agency is not allowed to change direction without some explanation of what it is doing and why. This general principle of administrative law . . . is applicable to adjudication as well as to explicit "notice and comment" rulemaking. The fact that the Board has such broad discretion in deciding which route to follow, *NLRB v. Bell Aerospace Co.,* [§ 6.2.1,] shows that the Board cannot be allowed to escape the obligation of justifying changes in its policies merely by following the common law route; the fact that common law rulemaking is retroactive buttresses this conclusion. So while not bound by *stare decisis,* the Board can jettison its precedents only if it has "adequately explicated the basis of its [new] interpretation."

. . . Forcing an administrative agency to 'fess up to its changes of position may seem productive merely of paper shuffling, and also inconsistent with the genius of the common law, which allows new doctrines to be created implicitly and even surreptitiously by judges who deny all the while that they are changing the law. Yet agencies often are forced to explicate decisions that judges and juries, not to mention legislative and executive branch officials, are allowed to make without explanation. The reason may be that agencies unlike courts are not constrained to make policy by the common law route, but can use explicit rulemaking procedures. Indeed, agencies are often criticized (none more so than the Labor Board) for not making greater use of their rulemaking powers. . . .

Another consideration may be that independent agencies, such as the Labor Board, in combining legislative, executive, and judicial functions, seem somehow to elude the constitutional system of checks and balances. But these agencies are checked by other organs of government (as a legislature with executive and judicial functions, or an executive with legislative and judicial functions, would not be), even if they lack internal checks and balances—and the Administrative Procedure Act creates some. Moreover, the rule that the agency must explain its about-faces is not limited to the independent agencies; it extends to administrative agencies within the executive branch . . .

The decision reversing the administrative law judge does not contain a reasoned analysis of the law and the evidence, and we therefore set aside the decision and return the case to the Board.

Notes and Questions

1. *UAW and waiver.* Why do you think the NLRB failed to " 'fess up' to its changes in position"? And if courts can and often do avoid unwelcome prior precedents by ignoring them or confining them "to their facts," why can't an agency do so?

Is it a waste of time for a court to reverse an agency decision which makes an unexplained shift in position even though the decision is otherwise legally correct (i.e. both the old and the new positions are consistent with the underlying statute) and supported by substantial evidence? Isn't the agency likely to reach the same result over again, this time with the necessary explanation?

The *UAW* case observes that agencies can change course through rulemaking as well as through case-by-case adjudication, although traditionally the NLRB has eschewed rulemaking (see § 6.2). Is the requirement that an agency identify and justify a change in position more important in adjudication than in rulemaking? Or less important?

2. *Traditional rule.* Traditionally agencies were considered to be free of the constraints of consistency; if a second decision was itself consistent with statute, it was upheld. See Frank Cooper, STATE ADMINISTRATIVE LAW 530–34 (1965). The recognition that agencies must explain and justify changes in position is a relatively recent development which is followed by both state and federal courts. See, e.g., *Matter of Charles A. Field Delivery Serv., Inc.,* 488 N.E.2d 1223 (N.Y.Ct.App.1985). What accounts for the traditional rule? What accounts for the change?

3. *Refusal to depart from precedent.* Suppose a party attacks an existing precedent as irrational. Is the agency required to reconsider the precedent and explain why it has decided to stay the course? Or can it just cite existing precedents without explanation? *See Flagstaff Broadcasting Foundation v. FCC,* 979 F.2d 1566 (D.C.Cir.1992). In that case, the FCC brushed aside Flagstaff's argument that the agency should abandon its criterion favoring "integration of ownership and management" in deciding which applicant for a broadcasting frequency is best qualified. That criterion disqualified Flagstaff, because its owners and directors (five women of color devoted to community activism) did not plan to manage the station on a day-to-day basis.

> The FCC denies that its decision was improper, and argues that it was merely applying established policy—an action that does not require an elaborate explanation or justification ... An agency's action will be set aside by a reviewing court whenever the agency fails to provide a reasoned basis for its decision ... This principle applies to all agency action, regardless of whether it involves established policy or the application of brand-new rules of interpretation ... Conclusory statements of binding precedent and policy will not suffice ...

Does the *Flagstaff* rule place an unduly heavy burden on agencies?

§ 4.4.3 ESTOPPEL

The principle of equitable estoppel has been applied countless times in nearly every area of law. Under that principle, if A's statement or conduct reasonably induces B's detrimental reliance, A will not be permitted to act inconsistently with its statement or conduct. Under another commonly applied private law rule, a principal is bound by the actions of its agent under either actual or apparent authority. Apparent authority arises if the principal has caused third parties reasonably to believe that the agent has authority to act—even if the agent has no such authority.

Should the government be bound by equitable estoppel and apparent authority when the action of its agent misleads a person to his detriment?

FOOTE'S DIXIE DANDY, INC. v. McHENRY
607 S.W.2d 323 (Ark.1980).

[Employers pay a tax to support the system of unemployment compensation for employees. Foote's operated two grocery stores (Hamburg and Crossett) within a single corporation. In 1971, it separately incorporated the Crossett store. Foote's had a good unemployment record which resulted in a low tax. If Foote's had filed a request for a transfer of that record, the new corporation would also have a low tax rate.

In 1971, Foote's CPA asked Yates, a field auditor for the Employment Security Division, about the new corporation's employment tax status. Foote's had always dealt exclusively with Yates about such questions. Yates said to do nothing special. In 1976, Yates retired. A new auditor discovered that the required request for transfer had not been filed in 1971. As a result, the state assessed $20,000 in additional taxes for the 1971–76 period.]

The State's claim is simply that it cannot be estopped regardless of the facts. Its position is based on a series of cases which announce the principle that the State cannot be estopped by the actions of its agent ... We abandon the principle stated in those cases that the state can *never* be estopped by the actions of its agents. Estoppel is not a defense that should be readily available against the state, but neither is it a defense that should never be available. Estoppel of the state is a principle of law recognized in more and more jurisdictions [including Alabama, California, New York, and Pennsylvania] ...

Estoppel is governed by fairness, as the court said in *United States v. Lazy FC Ranch,* 481 F.2d 985 (9th Cir.1973): "We think the estoppel doctrine is applicable to the United States where justice and fair play require it ..."

In *Gestuvo v. Immigration and Naturalization Service,* 337 F.Supp. 1093 (C.D.Cal.1971), the court recognized estoppel when certain essential elements were present. As the court stated:

Four elements are necessary: (1) the party to be estopped must know the facts; (2) he must intend that his conduct shall be acted on or must so act that the party asserting the estoppel had a right to believe it is so intended; (3) the latter must be ignorant of the true facts; and (4) he must rely on the former's conduct to his injury.

In explaining the application of estoppel, the court, in *Gestuvo,* continued: "[T]he requirements of morals and justice demand that our administrative agencies be accountable for their mistakes. Detrimental reliance on their misrepresentations or mere unconscientiousness should create an estoppel, at least in cases where no serious damage to national policy would result ..."

The decisions of the federal and state courts favoring estoppel of the government are closely aligned with the abandonment of the doctrine of sovereign immunity ... Arkansas has not abandoned the doctrine of sovereign immunity which is in our constitution ...

Estoppel will protect the citizen only to the extent that he relied upon actions or statements by an agent. In the present case there was good faith reliance by Foote's C.P.A. on the advice of the Employment Security Division's field agent. There was no reason for the C.P.A. to question the agent's credibility since he had dealt with him frequently on Employment Security Division matters and no problems had arisen. Fairness has to be a two edged sword. People who deal with the state must be fair and the same principle should apply to the state. Justice Holmes made the remark many years ago that "Men must turn square corners when they deal with the government." Years later, two commentators added the logical corollary to Holmes' remark: "It is hard to see why the government should not be held to a like standard of rectangular rectitude when dealing with its citizens." We agree with both ideas.

We are satisfied that all the circumstances of this case warrant applying the doctrine of equitable estoppel. The facts are that *only* a form was not filed which would have been routinely approved if it had been filed; that there was not a scintilla of evidence of bad faith; and that an important agent of the State of Arkansas, clothed with considerable authority, had told Foote's that it did not have to file any further documentation....

Because the State was entitled to rely upon a principle of law that we now abandon, it should be allowed to offer proof as to whether its auditor Yates did in fact make the statements attributed to him. Therefore, the cause is remanded for the sole purpose of permitting the State the opportunity of calling Yates as a witness on this fact issue. If Yates agrees that he did so advise the C.P.A., then the chancellor will enter a decree for the appellant; if Yates disagrees, or if it appears the facts are in dispute, the chancellor will make a finding and enter a decree consistent with this opinion.

Reversed and remanded.

Notes and Questions

1. *Federal law.* The *Foote's* case gives the impression that federal cases support its holding that the government can be estopped. While there are numerous lower court cases like *Georgia–Pacific* or *Gestuvo,* the Supreme Court has never accepted an estoppel claim and has rejected them on numerous occasions. The *Foote's* case ignores these Supreme Court decisions, including several that decline to estop the government in tax cases.

In *Office of Personnel Management v. Richmond,* 496 U.S. 414 (1990), a Navy personnel officer advised Richmond (orally and in writing) that he could safely take an extra job without jeopardizing his Navy retirement benefits. The advice was erroneous; Congress had changed the law. Accordingly, Richmond's benefits were cut off for six months. He sued to recover them on the basis of estoppel, but the Court rejected his claim. The Court implied that it is unlikely to uphold a claim for estoppel against the government in any circumstances, but it did not totally slam the door.

From our earliest cases [dating to 1813] we have recognized that equitable estoppel will not lie against the Government as against private litigants.... Despite the clarity of these earlier decisions, dicta in our more recent cases have suggested the possibility that there might be some situation in which estoppel against the Government could be appropriate.... Our own opinions have continued to mention the possibility, in the course of rejecting estoppel arguments, that some type of "affirmative misconduct" might give rise to estoppel against the Government....

The language in our decisions has spawned numerous claims for equitable estoppel in the lower courts.... The extraordinary number of such dispositions in this single area of the law provides a good indication that our approach to these cases has provided inadequate guidance for the federal courts and served only to invite and prolong needless litigation.

The Solicitor General proposes to remedy the present confusion in this area of the law with ... "a flat rule that estoppel may not in any circumstances run against the Government." The Government bases its broad rule first upon the doctrine of sovereign immunity, [asserting] that the courts are without jurisdiction to entertain a suit to compel the Government to act contrary to a statute, no matter what the context or circumstances. The Government advances as a second basis for this rule the doctrine of separation of powers: ... to recognize estoppel based on the misrepresentations of Executive Branch officials would give those misrepresentations the force of law, and thereby invade the legislative province reserved to Congress....

We have recognized before that the "arguments the Government advances for the rule are substantial." And we agree that this case should be decided under a clearer form of analysis than "we will know an estoppel when we see one." But it remains true that we need not embrace a rule that no estoppel will lie against the Government in any case in order to decide this case. We leave for another day whether an estoppel claim could ever succeed against the Government. A narrower ground of decision is sufficient to address the type of suit presented here [namely that in no circumstances can estoppel require the payment of money from the Treasury contrary to statutory appropriation. The Court derived this proposition from the Appropriations Clause of the Constitution, Art. I, § 9, cl.7: "No Money shall be drawn from the Treasury, but in Consequence of Appropriations made by Law."]....

Respondent would have us ignore these obstacles on the ground that estoppel against the Government would have beneficial effects ... [His] attempts to justify estoppel on grounds of public policy are suspect on their own terms. Even short of collusion by individual officers or improper Executive attempts to frustrate legislative policy, acceptance of estoppel claims for Government funds could have pernicious effects. It ignores reality to expect that the Government will be able to "secure perfect performance from its hundreds of thousands of employees scattered throughout the continent." To open the door to estoppel claims would only invite endless litigation over both real and imagined claims of misinformation by disgruntled citizens, imposing an unpredictable drain on the public fisc. Even if most claims were rejected in the end, the burden of defending such estoppel claims would itself be substantial.

Also questionable is the suggestion that if the Government is not bound by its agents' statements, then citizens will not trust them, and will instead seek private advice from lawyers, accountants, and others, creating wasteful expenses. Although mistakes occur, we may assume with confidence that Government agents attempt conscientious performance of their duties, and in most cases provide free and valuable information to those who seek advice about Government programs. A rule of estoppel might create not more reliable advice, but less advice. The natural consequence of a rule that made the Government liable for the statements of its agents would be a decision to cut back and impose strict controls upon Government provision of information in order to limit liability. Not only would valuable informational programs be lost to the public, but the greatest impact of this loss would fall on those of limited means, who can least afford the alternative of private advice. The inevitable fact of occasional individual hardship cannot undermine the interest of the citizenry as a whole in the ready availability of Government information.

2. *Rationale.* With *Richmond*, compare these views:

It is no longer realistic or just, if it ever was, to hold every person dealing with the government to knowledge of everything in the statute books and the Federal Register. As a matter of practice, most agencies consider themselves bound by erroneous advice.... Thus it may well be that the legal doctrines to the contrary serve no useful purpose. It no longer seems credible that the government will be ruined by a judicious application of estoppel.... The application of estoppel hardly means the repeal of a statute; it would simply preclude the retroactive correction as to particular individuals of a particular mistake, spreading the loss over all the taxpayers rather than the unfortunate individuals who relied to their detriment upon a governmental error or misrepresentation.

Michael Asimow, ADVICE TO THE PUBLIC FROM FEDERAL ADMINISTRATIVE AGENCIES 60–61 (1973). Do you agree? Why is the Supreme Court so reluctant to accept claims of estoppel against the government? Why are the courts of many states (such as Arkansas) willing to go the other way? Is there any difference between claims that would estop an agency from enforcing a statute and claims that would estop an agency from enforcing its own rule or case law?

3. *Prerequisites for estoppel.* What must be shown to justify estoppel, if it is to be available at all? The *Gestuvo* criteria quoted in *Foote's* are not the only possible ones, as the Supreme Court made clear in *Heckler v. Community Health Services,* 467 U.S. 51 (1984). That case involved a charitable clinic, CHS, that used federal job training money to fund its home visits to Medicare patients. CHS was orally advised on several occasions by Travelers Insurance (a private company which handled claims for the government) that its use of these funds would not reduce its Medicare reimbursements. In

reliance on that advice, the clinic increased its spending for home visits. Later the Department of Health and Human Services, explaining that Travelers' advice had been mistaken, sought to recover the excess reimbursements it had paid to CHS.

In its opinion the Court assumed for the sake of argument that the government could be bound by estoppel if the facts were strong enough. It held, however, that the basic elements of estoppel were absent here. Estoppel requires reasonable reliance. It had not been reasonable for CHS to rely on oral (as opposed to written) advice; indeed, the clinic should have obtained advice from the agency itself, not from an intermediary like Travelers. Moreover, the clinic's showing of detrimental reliance was insufficient—it was only being asked to repay government reimbursement funds that it should never have received in the first place. Thus, CHS had not suffered the loss of a legal right or any adverse change in status. Is this reasoning persuasive? Does it cast doubt on the holding in *Foote's*?

4. *Advice-giving.* Every government agency furnishes advice to the public on how to comply with the agency's law. Every day agencies advise taxpayers about whether a transaction is taxable, whether an issuance of stock must be registered, whether an alien might jeopardize her immigration status by leaving the country, or whether action taken by a professional licensee might jeopardize the license.

Advice-giving is an extraordinarily valuable service to the public (and, since it diminishes inadvertent violations of law, to the agency as well). The advice is usually correct and, when it is incorrect, the government often protects reliance interests created by the mistake even though in many cases it is not legally required to do so.

According to *Richmond,* if the government could be estopped by mistaken advice, agencies would be deterred from giving such advice. If that happened, the public as a whole might be worse off even though some individuals who had detrimentally relied on the advice would be better off. Do you agree with the prediction in *Richmond?*

5. *By any other name....* Federal law is not quite as indifferent to reliance interests as its estoppel case law seems to indicate. Occasionally, without invoking the language of estoppel, federal courts have found ways to protect people who have been misled by government. *See Moser v. United States,* 341 U.S. 41 (1951) (holding that a Swiss national had not knowingly and intentionally waived his right to apply for American citizenship, where official advice had assured him he could claim exemption from military service without penalty); *United States v. Pennsylvania Industrial Chemical Corp.,* 411 U.S. 655 (1973) (citing incorrect advice by government agents as a factor that supported defendant's claim that it had lacked "fair warning" of a criminal prohibition). Analogous doctrines will be encountered later in this book, including the principle that an agency may not promulgate retroactive rules without express congressional authority, § 5.2.2, and the principle that an agency's unforeseeable departure from its case law precedents can constitute arbitrary and capricious action, §§ 4.4.2 and 6.2.1 N.4.

A related recent development in this area is exemplified by *General Electric Co. v. EPA,* 53 F.3d 1324 (D.C.Cir.1995). In effect, that case extends *Pennsylvania Industrial* by holding, as a matter of due process, that an agency must give fair notice to a regulated party of what conduct it prohibits or requires before it can invoke sanctions against that party. "Fair notice" could mean publishing an interpretation of an ambiguous rule or otherwise informing the party of the agency's view before the regulation is enforced against the party. In the *GE* case, a complex and ambiguous EPA regulation concerned permissible methods of disposing of PCBs. GE disposed of PCBs in a manner that represented a reasonable interpretation of the regulation. The EPA read the regulation differently and sought a $25,000 penalty from GE. The court held that, although EPA's reading was reasonable, and the court would defer to it on the merits, EPA had failed to give GE fair warning of its approach. Consequently, it could not collect a penalty. For similar holdings, see *Upton v. SEC,* 75 F.3d 92 (2d Cir.1996) (SEC rules regulating broker-dealers); *United States v. Trident Seafoods Corp.,* 60 F.3d 556 (9th Cir.1995) (Clean Air Act).

Do cases like *GE,* which afford a defense based on *inadequate* notice of a government interpretation, necessarily imply that action based on *mistaken* government advice will also be protected? Do these recent developments suggest that the federal courts' resistance to estoppel may soon become irrelevant?

6. *Declaratory orders.* Declaratory orders are the administrative equivalent of judicial declaratory judgments. Declaratory orders normally apply the law to stipulated facts. Unlike an agency advice letter, a declaratory order is an administrative adjudication that binds all parties, including the agency itself. A party can rely on a declaratory order without concern about the nebulous doctrine of equitable estoppel against the government. Also, a party who disagrees with an agency's declaratory decision can seek judicial review of it. When, if ever, would you suggest that a client seek a declaratory order?

Both the federal act and the 1981 MSAPA authorize agencies to issue declaratory orders. *See* federal APA § 554(e), 1981 MSAPA § 2–103. The acts of many states are based on § 8 of 1961 MSAPA which provides: "Each agency shall provide by rule for the filing and prompt disposition of petitions for declaratory rulings as to the applicability of any statutory provision or rule of the agency. Rulings disposing of petitions have the same status as agency orders or decisions in contested cases."

Under the MSAPA provision, is an agency required to issue a declaratory order to anybody who requests one? If so, an agency might have to set aside various high priority tasks, such as rulemaking or law enforcement, in order to deal with a steady flow of declaratory order requests. How can an agency protect itself from being required to issue declaratory orders that it does not wish to issue?

7. *Problem.* Under a Madison welfare program resembling the old federal AFDC program, Ann and her two children received benefit checks for two years. Welfare Department regulations provide that female applicants for benefits must name a child's father and furnish assistance to the Department in tracking him down. When Ann applied for welfare, she told Courtney, her social worker, that she was afraid of the father, who had battered her and the children, and she did not wish to name him. Courtney said that was no problem and approved the application. This was incorrect;

Courtney had no discretion to waive the requirement of naming the father. Ann has now withdrawn from the welfare program and is supporting her children without government assistance.

An official audit has revealed the error. By statute, the Department is empowered to recover any welfare overpayments. The Department has demanded that Ann repay $14,000. It intends to garnish her paychecks until the full amount is recovered. Does Ann have any defense? *Cf. Lentz v. McMahon*, 777 P.2d 83 (Cal.1989).

Chapter 5

RULEMAKING PROCEDURES

Statutes and case law divide the administrative process into two principal processes, each governed by separate procedures. The first resembles the judicial process and is called "adjudication." Its product is an "order." Adjudication was the subject of the prior three chapters. The second process resembles the legislative process and is called "rulemaking." Its product is a "rule." (Recall § 2.5, which traced the constitutional roots of the rulemaking-adjudication distinction.) Rulemaking is the subject of this and the next chapter.

§ 5.1 INTRODUCTION: THE IMPORTANCE OF RULEMAKING

In 1978, while he was still a professor of administrative law, the future Justice Scalia wrote that "perhaps the most notable development in federal government administration during the past two decades" had been "the constant and accelerating flight away from individualized, adjudicatory proceedings to generalized disposition through rulemaking." Antonin Scalia, "Vermont Yankee: The APA, the D.C. Circuit, and the Supreme Court," 1978 Sup.Ct.Rev. 345, 376. "The increased use of rulemaking," he continued, "has changed the whole structure of administrative law...." *Id.* A similar trend has occurred in the states. There, too, courts and agencies have had to confront questions about the extent to which they should adhere, during rulemaking proceedings, to traditional norms of administrative law that developed in an adjudication context. Much of the material in this chapter explores the federal and state governments' responses to that problem.

Part of the explanation for the spread of rulemaking during the past generation was that agencies, courts, and legislatures have come to understand that, in many situations at least, rulemaking has definite advantages over adjudication as a tool for agency lawmaking and policymaking. To generalize broadly, those advantages include the following:

a. Participation by all affected parties: In adjudication, only those persons who are parties to a particular dispute normally have a right to participate in the proceeding to resolve it. Yet the decision in such a proceeding can serve as precedent for similar cases involving different parties, and they may find it difficult to persuade the agency to distinguish or overrule the prior case. In contrast, anyone who wishes to do so can participate in rulemaking. Notice is given to all concerned and anyone can submit comments.

b. Appropriate procedure: When an agency makes new law or policy, the procedures of rulemaking (which resemble legislation) are superior to those of adjudication (which resemble trials). Trials and trial records are good for establishing individualized facts but not particularly suitable for determining broad questions of legislative fact and for ventilating important issues of policy. Moreover, at least in formal adjudication, the law relating to official notice, separation of functions, and internal and external communications with decisionmakers, may insulate the decisionmakers from important factual and policy data needed to make new agency law or policy. In contrast, the procedures of rulemaking have been designed for the precise purpose of exploring issues of law, policy, and legislative fact.

c. Retroactivity: When an agency adopts a new principle in an adjudication, the agency usually has broad (but not unlimited) authority to apply it retroactively to the parties to the proceeding. As a result, the agency may upset important reliance interests. Rules, in contrast, will normally apply prospectively only, thus providing fair warning to those whose conduct is affected.

d. Uniformity: Agency law made by rule addresses classes of persons, and all persons falling within any such class will become subject to its terms at the same time and in the same way. The same is not true of agency law made in the course of adjudication, because an agency precedent technically binds only the specific parties to that adjudication, leaving other similarly situated persons free of any binding order. In addition, lawmaking by adjudication—often driven by the unique facts of individual cases—can tempt agencies to draw distinctions between otherwise similarly situated individuals on the basis of differences that may not be significant enough to justify those distinctions.

e. Political input: Lawmaking is a highly political process. Rulemaking provides a regularized opportunity for politically active persons and groups to participate in the process and to mobilize political pressures for or against a proposed agency policy. The procedures utilized in adjudication are unsuited for the making of essentially political decisions.

f. Agency agenda setting: When agencies make law through adjudications, their agenda is controlled by the happenstance of whatever cases come before them. As a result, they may be forced to spend time on relatively trivial problems and fail to address more important ones. Even if the agency has discretion to choose which cases to bring, the facts of a given case may not shape up as the agency had anticipated. When an agency decides to make law through rulemaking, it has more control over its own agenda, so that it can attack higher priority problems first. In rulemaking, the agency also avoids becoming distracted by the particular facts of each case or the particular problems of litigants; it can focus directly on the central policy issue.

g. Agency efficiency: Although rulemaking can be time consuming, it at least gives the agency the opportunity to settle an issue in a single proceeding, instead of litigating the same issue in numerous proceedings in order to accomplish that result.

h. Difficulty of research: It is easier for affected persons to locate and research applicable law issued in the form of rules than agency case law. This is so because rules are published and, therefore, are widely available, while agency case law is often unpublished and available for inspection only at agency offices. Indeed, even when case precedents can be found, it is often difficult to distill agency law from them. Agency cases are often inconsistent, and they may contain dicta of uncertain authority. Cases that make new law often do not clearly say they are doing so. But when law is set forth in rules, it is easier to ascertain and understand.

i. Oversight: For the reasons just stated, it is far easier for the executive and legislative branches to exercise oversight over the merits and legality of agency-made law when the law is made through rulemaking rather than adjudication. In addition, federal law, as well as that of most states, provides formal schemes for the legislative and executive review of rules; these schemes may be entirely circumvented if agencies make law through adjudication, because there are no comparable formal schemes for the legislative and executive review of agency law embodied in individual cases.

Nevertheless, there are some advantages to adjudication. For example:

a. Flexibility: Rules are often over-or under-inclusive; and they may operate inflexibly because they usually do not take into account individual differences in the circumstances of those subject to their terms. On the other hand, adjudication allows a response that is tailored to the special facts of each case, thereby allowing maximum flexibility and avoiding over-or under-inclusiveness.

b. Abstraction: Adjudication requires the agency to make its law on a step by step basis in concrete situations in which it can observe the actual operation of that law. Rulemaking requires the agency to create a principle divorced from the specific facts of a particular case. Because it operates abstractly, therefore, rulemaking may produce cruder, less sensitive law than adjudication does.

c. The new and unexpected: A case-by-case approach may be better where the agency is not yet in a position to make generally applicable law, due to lack of sufficient expertise or because the distinctions in the area are likely to be so numerous or complex that they resist generalized treatment in a rule.

Moreover, especially in the case of newer statutes, an agency may discover a pattern of harmful behavior that has already occurred and which should be addressed through enforcement action. If the problem was unanticipated, the agency could not have adopted a prospective rule to deal with it. Only retroactively effective adjudication can solve the problem.

d. Residual adjudication: Regardless of how many rules an agency makes, it can never dispense entirely with adjudication. There will always be ambiguities in rules that need to be answered in individual cases, thereby inevitably creating new precedents.

For a more extensive catalog of the advantages and disadvantages of rulemaking and adjudication, *see* Arthur Earl Bonfield, "State Administrative Policy Formulation and the Choice of Lawmaking Methodology," 42 Admin.L.Rev. 121, 122–33 (1990).

Notes and Questions

1. *Rulemaking "ossification."* Professor McGarity offers a pessimistic appraisal of the value of rulemaking to regulators under current conditions:

> As the "rulemaking era" dawned in the early 1970s, agencies agreed that informal rulemaking under section 553 of the Administrative Procedure Act (APA) offered an ideal vehicle for making regulatory policy. Professor Kenneth Culp Davis captured the prevailing sentiment only somewhat hyperbolically when he called informal rulemaking "one of the greatest inventions of modern government." Twenty years later, the bloom is off the rose. Although informal rulemaking is still an exceedingly effective tool for eliciting public participation in administrative policymaking, it has not evolved into the flexible and efficient process that its early supporters originally envisioned. During the last fifteen years the rulemaking process has become increasingly rigid and burdensome. An assortment of analytical requirements have been imposed on the simple rulemaking model, and evolving judicial doctrines have obliged agencies to take greater pains to ensure that the technical bases for rules are capable of withstanding judicial scrutiny. Professor E. Donald Elliott, former General Counsel of the Environmental Protection Agency, refers to this troublesome phenomenon as the "ossification" of the rulemaking process, and many observers from across the political spectrum agree with him that it is one of the most serious problems currently facing regulatory agencies.

> . . . The informal rulemaking process of the 1990s is so heavily laden with additional procedures, analytical requirements, and external review mechanisms that its superiority to case-by-case adjudication is not as apparent now as it was before it came into heavy use. Perhaps of even more concern to regulatees and the general public is recent evidence that agencies are beginning to seek out alternative, less participatory regulatory vehicles to circumvent the increasingly stiff and formalized structures of the informal rulemaking process.

Thomas O. McGarity, "Some Thoughts on 'Deossifying' the Rulemaking Process," 41 Duke L.J. 1385, 1385–86 (1992). For a similar diagnosis, see

Richard J. Pierce, "Seven Ways to Deossify Agency Rulemaking," 47 Admin.L.Rev. 59 (1995).

The precise dimensions of the ossification problem are not entirely clear. As Pierce notes, "[o]ssification has been identified as a problem only with respect to major rules predicated on assumptions concerning complicated factual and scientific relationships. Agencies continue to issue hundreds of rules annually in other contexts expeditiously and at a relatively low cost." *Id.* at 62. Nevertheless, ossification has become a prominent and widely discussed theme in current administrative law scholarship. Many of the doctrines that will be examined in this chapter can be evaluated in light of this critique.

2. *Rulemaking authority.* Because of the recognized advantages of rulemaking in the administrative process, agencies' enabling statutes are normally written to allow them to exercise broad rulemaking power in appropriate cases. Usually the statutory language eliminates any controversy as to whether an agency has authority to make policy decisions through rulemaking. And when that authority is questioned, courts will almost always presume that the agency at least has the option to proceed through rulemaking.

A leading case is *National Petroleum Refiners Ass'n v. FTC,* 482 F.2d 672 (D.C.Cir.1973), which upheld the FTC's rule requiring gas stations to post octane ratings. For five decades the Commission had used the rulemaking provision of the FTC Act for housekeeping and procedural matters only; in developing substantive trade regulation policies, it had always relied exclusively on case-by-case adjudication. Nevertheless, the court of appeals held that the statutory provision in question empowered the FTC to adopt substantive rules that would have the force of law. In reaching this conclusion, the court emphasized the enormous advantages of rulemaking over case-by-case adjudication in implementing a program of consumer protection.

Although *National Petroleum Refiners* has long been regarded as a leading case, the same court reached a contrasting result in *Amalgamated Transit Union v. Skinner,* 894 F.2d 1362 (D.C.Cir.1990). That case involved a challenge to the validity of rules issued by the Urban Mass Transportation Authority (UMTA) that required recipients of federal mass transit funds to implement a drug testing program. The section of the statute that governed federal intervention into safety matters such as antidrug programs set out a protocol for such intervention: the Secretary was to "investigate" hazardous conditions in transit systems; could "require the local public body ... to submit a plan for correcting or eliminating such conditions;" and could withhold funds until the plan was approved and implemented.

The court thought that this protocol mandated a case-by-case approach: "The dialogue between UMTA and its grantees to solve ... safety hazards was carefully designed to take place in a manner which requires UMTA to react to local plans.... It was not designed to proceed via national, impersonal rulemaking procedures which produced a federally mandated solution that might or might not be responsive to concerns at the local level." *Id.* at 1369. The court said that this section, with its emphasis on federalism and local autonomy, contrasted with other sections in which UMTA did have express rulemaking authority. Should this case be read as a retrenchment of the court's position in *National Petroleum Refiners,* or is it explainable on some narrower basis?

3. *Problem.* Auto insurance companies in the state of Madison typically rate customers by the ZIP Code in which they reside. Insurance in some neighborhoods is much more expensive, and much less available, than in other neighborhoods. The Madison Insurance Commission has authority to deal with "unfair insurance practices." It has power to adopt binding rules, but has never used that power. It also has power to enter cease-and desist orders on a case by case basis, a power it has often used. If it finds that an "unfair insurance practice" has occurred, it can order refunds of premiums or provide other appropriate relief to consumers.

You are the law clerk for one of the commissioners. At this morning's meeting between the commissioners and the enforcement staff, the staff presented data it has gathered on the practices of Ranchers Insurance Co. Ranchers is one of the larger auto insurance companies in Madison and it utilizes ZIP Code pricing. The staff seeks authorization to issue an administrative complaint against Ranchers in the hopes that this will produce a good test case on ZIP Code pricing.

What is your advice to your boss? What considerations would support his voting to authorize issuance of the complaint in this case? What considerations suggest that he should insist that the Commission commence a rulemaking proceeding to deal with the ZIP Code pricing problem? What other facts might be relevant to his decision?

§ 5.2 DEFINITION OF "RULE"

§ 5.2.1 GENERALITY AND PARTICULARITY

All APAs define the term "rule" to which their rulemaking procedures apply. Read § 551(4) of the federal APA and consider the following analysis.

ACUS, A GUIDE TO FEDERAL AGENCY RULEMAKING
39–41 (2d ed.1991).

Standing alone, the APA's definition of "rule" may not be too helpful. For example, an agency order directing Company X to cease and desist from engaging in a certain unlawful practice would fall within the literal terms of this definition. Yet, it is reasonably clear [according to the Attorney General's Manual on the APA] that a proceeding leading to the issuance of a cease-and-desist order ordinarily is adjudication and not rulemaking.

The definition of "adjudication" sheds little additional light, for "adjudication" is defined as the agency process for formulating an "order," and "order" is defined as "a final disposition whether affirmative, negative, injunctive, or declaratory in form, of an agency in a matter other than rule making but including licensing." Thus, the APA's definitional structure is largely circular, since the definition of adjudication is residual.

To understand the thrust of the APA's distinction between rulemaking and adjudication, one must turn to the discussion in the Attorney General's Manual on the APA:

> [T]he entire Act is based upon a dichotomy between rule making and adjudication. Examination of the legislative history of the definitions and of the differences in the required procedures for rule making and for adjudication discloses highly practical concepts of rule making and adjudication. Rule making is agency action which regulates the future conduct of either groups of persons or a single person; it is essentially legislative in nature, not only because it operates in the future but also because it is primarily concerned with policy considerations. The object of the rule making proceeding is the implementation or prescription of law or policy for the future, rather than the evaluation of a respondent's past conduct. Typically, the issues relate not to the evidentiary facts, as to which the veracity and demeanor of witnesses would often be important, but rather to the policy-making conclusions to be drawn from the facts. . . .

Given the breadth of the definitions of "rulemaking" and "adjudication" in the APA, it is not surprising that some confusion exists with respect to the proper classification of certain agency proceedings.

The inclusion of agency statements of "particular applicability" in the APA's definition of rule probably creates the most difficulty, for most people think of rules as addressed to general situations and adjudication as addressed to particular situations. While it is true that the great majority of rules have some general application, and adjudication is nearly always particularized in its immediate application, the drafters of the APA wished certain actions of a particular nature, such as the setting of future rates or the approval of corporate reorganizations, to be carried out under the relatively flexible procedures governing rulemaking. Consequently, the words "or particular" were included in the definition.[8]

Courts have upheld classification of agency action as a "rule" even though it applied to the activities of a single entity. Probably no great change would occur if the words "or particular" were deleted from the definition of rule in section 551 of the APA. . . .

Notes and Questions

1. *The "or particular" language.* The curious draftsmanship of § 551(4) once led then-Professor Scalia to remark that "it is generally

---

8. In 1970, the American Bar Association recommended revising the definition of "rule" to delete the words "or particular." The Administrative Conference endorsed the ABA proposal with the understanding that "[a] matter may be considered of 'general applicability' even though it is directly applicable to a class which consists of only one or a few persons if the class is open in the sense that in the future the number of members of the class may be increased."

acknowledged that the only responsible judicial attitude toward this central APA definition is one of benign disregard." Antonin Scalia, *"Vermont Yankee*: The APA, the D.C. Circuit, and the Supreme Court," 1978 Sup.Ct. Rev. 345, 383. The words "or particular" were added to the definition of "rule" at a late stage in the drafting of the APA. As the ACUS excerpt suggests, the change occurred because many administrative lawyers of that era thought of individualized ratemaking (that is, agency proceedings to set rates to be charged by a named public utility) as rulemaking. Such proceedings, although of "particular applicability," were viewed as rulemaking because the same function had historically been performed by legislatures prior to the rise of modern administrative agencies. One consequence of calling these matters "rulemaking" is they are thereby exempted from the APA's separation of functions provisions, which apply only to adjudications. Does this background make the wording of § 551(4) more defensible?

Although § 551(4) defines ratemaking as rulemaking for all purposes, many federal enabling acts require a hearing on the record before ratemaking of particular applicability. This triggers the process of "formal rulemaking," discussed in § 5.4.2, in which the agency must observe most, though not all, of the same requirements as in APA formal adjudication. *See* APA §§ 551(4), 553(c). Would due process permit individualized ratemaking for a telephone company or a cable television franchise without a hearing? Without a trial-type hearing?

2. *State law definitions.* Read the definition of "rule" in 1981 MSAPA § 1–102(10). This definition is similar to § 1(7) of the 1961 MSAPA, which defines a "rule" as "each agency statement of general applicability that implements, interprets, or prescribes law or policy, or describes the organization, procedure, or practice requirements of any agency. The term includes the amendment or repeal of a prior rule . . . . "

The phrase "the whole or a part of an agency statement of *general applicability*" is probably the most important part of the definition of "rule" in 1981 MSAPA § 1–102(10). Every statement implementing, interpreting, or prescribing law or policy that is directed at a class of persons is a rule under this definition. In contrast, an "order" in § 1–102(5) of 1981 MSAPA is "agency action of *particular applicability* that determines the legal rights, duties, privileges, immunities or other legal interests of one or more specific persons."

Under 1981 MSAPA, if a ratemaking or licensing determination is addressed to a named party, such as a particular utility or a particular licensee, it is an "order" subject to the adjudication provisions of the statute. On the other hand, ratemaking and licensing actions of general applicability, that is, addressed to all members of a described class of providers or licensees, are "rules" under the statute. The 1961 MSAPA treated ratemaking and licensing similarly. *See* 1961 MSAPA § 1(2), (7).

A few state APAs define the term "rule" more narrowly than the APA provisions just described. For example, the Washington APA definition enumerates several categories of statements that constitute rules, and the state courts have held the list to be exclusive. Therefore, certain pronouncements of general applicability that implement law or policy have been held not to be rules, even if they would have been rules under the federal definition. *See* Wash.Rev.Code § 34.05.010(15) (1995); *State v. Straka*, 810 P.2d 888, 893 (Wash.1991) (holding that definition of "rule" did not include a set of procedures approved by the state toxicologist for evaluating and maintaining breath testing machines for use in prosecutions for driving while intoxicated).

3. *Other criteria.* Review the *Bi-Metallic* and *Cunningham* cases in § 2.5. In the due process context, as in the APA context, courts often cite a variety of factors, in addition to the general-particular dichotomy, as they try to distinguish rulemaking from adjudication. Some examples: A rule is usually, or perhaps always, prospective, but an order will often be retroactive (this test is the subject of § 5.2.2). A rule usually requires a further proceeding (an adjudication) to make it concretely effective against a particular individual, while an order needs no further proceeding to make it effective. A rule is usually directed at and binds a described class that may open to admit new members, while an order is directed at and binds only those who were parties to the adjudicative proceeding. A rule ordinarily is based on findings of fact that are legislative or general in nature and is often based on predictions about the future; an adjudication is ordinarily based, at least in part, on facts specific to the parties and on findings of past events. Finally, in close cases a court might determine whether a particular proceeding is rulemaking or adjudication by asking whether rulemaking or adjudication procedures are most appropriate for its efficient, effective, and fair operation.

4. *Benefits of rulemaking label.* In the due process context, the private litigant normally would prefer to characterize the challenged action as an order rather than a rule, because the *Bi-Metallic* doctrine militates against due process rights in rulemaking. In the context of an APA, however, the private party may well prefer for a court to label the challenged action a rule. As you will recall from § 3.1, the federal APA and many state APAs specify few procedures for informal adjudication. Thus, when the private party has no hope of qualifying for *formal* (trial-type) adjudication, he or she may gain more procedural rights if the proceeding is deemed to be rulemaking than if it is deemed to be an adjudication.

For example, in *Yesler Terrace Community Council v. Cisneros*, 37 F.3d 442, 448–49 (9th Cir.1994), the Department of Housing and Urban Development (HUD) determined that the State of Washington's eviction procedure provided tenants with various procedural protections. This determination allowed local public housing authorities to dispense with an informal grievance procedure that would otherwise have been available to tenants in the projects who were facing eviction because of suspected drug dealing. The issue was whether HUD's determination was rulemaking (which would make APA notice and comment procedure applicable) or informal adjudication (subject to no procedural requirements).

The court held that the determination was rulemaking. After quoting the APA definitions of "rule" and "order," the court said:

> Two principal characteristics distinguish rulemaking from adjudication. First, adjudications resolve disputes among specific individuals in specific cases, whereas rulemaking affects the rights of broad classes of unspecified individuals [quoting the passage in *Florida East Coast Ry.*

reprinted in § 2.5]. Second, because adjudications involve concrete disputes, they have an immediate effect on specific individuals (those involved in the dispute). Rulemaking, in contrast, is prospective, and has a definitive effect on individuals only after the rule subsequently is applied . . .

Here HUD's determination that Washington's state-court eviction procedures met HUD's due process requirements has all the hallmarks of a rule. HUD's determination had no immediate, concrete effect on anyone, but merely permitted [local public housing authorities] to evict tenants in the future without providing them with informal grievance hearings. At the same time, the determination affected the rights of a broad category of individuals not yet identified. Before the decision was made, all public housing tenants in Washington had a statutory right to a pre-eviction grievance hearing. After the decision, no public housing tenant accused of certain criminal activity had such a right. We conclude that HUD's determination was a rule.

Do you agree with the court's argument that the HUD determination had "no immediate, concrete effect on anyone" and was therefore rulemaking? Indeed, couldn't it be argued that HUD's decision applied general standards to a single entity—the Washington state court system—and was therefore an adjudication? Is *Yesler* any different from a situation in which a federal agency grants a state permission to build a highway in a certain location? The highway will indirectly affect millions of citizens, but the Supreme Court has declared that this sort of decision is not rulemaking. *Citizens to Preserve Overton Park, Inc. v. Volpe*, 401 U.S. 402, 414 (1971).

5. *Legislative and nonlegislative rules.* Most of the rules discussed so far in this chapter are "legislative rules." Legislative rules are rules issued by an agency pursuant to an express or implied grant of authority to issue rules with the binding force of law. Nonlegislative rules, often called interpretive rules or statements of policy, are agency rules that do not have the force of law because they are not based upon any delegated authority to issue such rules. *See* 1 Kenneth Culp Davis & Richard J. Pierce, Jr., ADMINISTRATIVE LAW TREATISE §§ 6.2, 6.3 (3d ed.1994). The distinction between legislative and nonlegislative rules is explored in § 6.1.4. But both types fall within the definition of "rule," because even a nonlegislative rule is "designed to implement, interpret or prescribe law or policy," as provided in the federal APA (and in similar language in the MSAPAs). Thus, the term "rule" has been held to include such pronouncements as a notice to prisoners banning all smoking in a jail which was not legally binding on the prisoners, *State ex rel. Kincaid v. Parsons*, 447 S.E.2d 543 (W.Va.1994); a temporary moratorium on processing applications to build new health care facilities, *Balsam v. Department of Health & Rehab. Services*, 452 So.2d 976 (Fla.App.1984); and an in-house random sampling methodology used to audit physicians' claims for reimbursement in a health care program, *Grier v. Kizer*, 268 Cal.Rptr. 244, 253 (Cal.App.1990).

On the other hand, in *Industrial Safety Equipment Ass'n v. EPA*, 837 F.2d 1115 (D.C.Cir.1988), the court held that a "Guide to Respiratory Protection for the Asbestos Abatement Industry," published by the Environmental Protection Agency and the National Institute for Occupational Safety and Health, was not a rule and therefore was not subject to judicial review. The guide explained that one important method of minimizing workers' exposure to asbestos is the use of respirators. "Air purifying" respirators filter asbestos particles out of the air; "supplied-air" respirators contain their own air supply. The guide listed the thirteen respirators that NIOSH had certified under its regulations, but declared that, as a matter of public health policy, NIOSH and EPA recommended only two of them—the "supplied-air" kind. Manufacturers of the other eleven respirators filed suit. They contended that the guide was a rule because it had in effect decertified their devices, yet had not been promulgated according to rulemaking procedures. The court disagreed. The guide was simply an educational publication that did not "implement, interpret, or prescribe law or policy" within the meaning of the APA. The guide had, after all, made clear that all thirteen devices were perfectly lawful. Do you agree with the court's conclusion?

6. *Criticisms of the rulemaking-adjudication dichotomy.* Some scholars have argued that the distinction between rules and orders is too rigid and should be replaced by more flexible systems of procedural requirements. Professor Robinson notes:

> . . . the present approach of the APA and the individual regulatory statutes fosters a general tendency to adopt doctrinal distinctions which are not conducive to a pragmatic use of either rulemaking or adjudicative techniques. Moreover, the arbitrary distinction between modes of proceeding does not provide useful criteria for determining what are the appropriate procedures in any particular kind of case.

Glen O. Robinson, "The Making of Administrative Policy: Another Look at Rulemaking and Adjudication and Administrative Procedure Reform," 118 U.Pa.L.Rev. 485, 536–38 (1970). Professor (now Dean) Cass gives a few examples to support Robinson's critique of the metaphors that compare rulemaking with what legislatures do and adjudication with what courts do: Society expects the National Labor Relations Board to carry out its adjudicative functions in a much more political manner than would be legitimate for a court. Conversely, rulemaking by technically specialized agencies like the Occupational Safety and Health Administration is supposed to rest on far more rigorous scientific investigation than anyone could expect from a legislature. Ronald A. Cass, "Models of Administrative Action," 72 Va.L.Rev. 363, 396–97 (1986).

What might be the alternative to the rulemaking-adjudication dichotomy? Professor Davis would identify the appropriate procedures for each type of agency task and require agencies to follow those procedures whenever they perform that task—whether they do so in rulemaking or in adjudication. He believes that either in rulemaking or in adjudication, the following are appropriate:

> (1) procedure of briefs and arguments to resolve nonfactual issues of law or policy, (2) procedure of notice and comment for making new law or new policy on a nonfactual basis, (3) procedure of notice and comment for resolving issues of broad legislative fact, (4) trial procedure to find most disputed adjudicative facts, and, especially, (5) nonuse of trial procedure to perform functions other than finding adjudicative facts (or, rarely, specific legislative facts).

3 Kenneth Culp Davis, ADMINISTRATIVE LAW TREATISE § 14.4 at 23 (2d ed. 1980). For other suggestions that the rule-order distinction should be replaced, see Cass, *supra*; Paul R. Verkuil, "The Emerging Concept of Administrative Procedure," 78 Colum.L.Rev. 258, 322 (1978).

Despite criticisms of the rulemaking-adjudication dichotomy as a basis for assigning procedures to govern agency action, and alternative proposals for more functional procedural schemes, the dichotomy has survived as a major feature of contemporary administrative law. The drafters of the recent MSAPA, for instance, calculatedly chose to perpetuate the rule-order dichotomy contained in the federal act and the many state acts. They believed that the alternative of

> [c]hoosing procedures based on a distinction between legislative facts and adjudicative facts could involve substantial costs. The conclusion that trial-type procedures may only be desirable for the determination of adjudicative facts does not solve the more difficult question of how to identify such facts.... [E]stablished procedures for broad, fairly clearly defined classes of agency activities such as rulemaking and adjudication normally enable administrators to ascertain easily and accurately the method by which they should proceed when they perform their duties. Without this facility, the costs of deciding which procedures to use in any particular circumstances, including the costs of invalidating the agency decision because the wrong procedures were employed by competent administrators acting in good faith, will be excessive.
>
> Consequently, as long as the procedures used as a result of the rule-order dichotomy *generally* provide a good fit between their specific requirements and the precise function performed and are normally fair, that dichotomy seems defensible.

Arthur Earl Bonfield, "The Federal APA and State Administrative Law," 72 Va.L.Rev. 297, 311 (1986).

Although the rule-order distinction has survived, the criticisms raised by scholars are relevant to controversies regarding the manner in which agencies should implement each of those models. One specific criticism has been that trial-type procedures are too elaborate for some factual disputes that arise in adjudication—particularly when the issue is one of legislative fact or even adjudicative facts that turn on expert testimony rather than perception or credibility. Has the law adequately responded to that concern? Conversely, some have argued that the relatively spare APA procedures for rulemaking ought in certain circumstances to be supplemented by requirements that agencies find facts through methods resembling those commonly used in adjudication. Some of the law's responses to that line of argument are examined in § 5.4.

§ 5.2.2　PROSPECTIVITY AND RETROACTIVITY

Rules normally establish law or policy for the future, while orders generally concern past events and have retroactive effect. The federal APA and those of many states explicitly define rules as having "future effect." APA § 551(4). Note, however, that both § 1(7) of the 1961 MSAPA and § 1–102(10) of the 1981 MSAPA omit the "future effect" language from the definition of "rule." Can a rule have retroactive effect? What do we mean by retroactive effect? And when is retroactivity good policy?

BOWEN v. GEORGETOWN UNIVERSITY HOSPITAL
488 U.S. 204 (1988).

[In 1981 the Department of Health and Human Services (HHS) adopted a rule that revised the formula for calculating its reimbursements to hospitals for the services they rendered to Medicare beneficiaries. A group of hospitals, including Georgetown, challenged the rule in a district court, which invalidated the rule because it had been adopted without notice and comment procedure. HHS then readopted the rule in 1984, using proper procedures. The 1984 rule was retroactive, in that it purported to allow HHS to recoup from the hospitals the amounts that the agency would have saved if the 1981 rule had never been set aside (in Georgetown's case, this came to two million dollars).

In holding the retroactive effect of the 1984 rule to be invalid, KENNEDY, J., stated for the Court:]

Retroactivity is not favored in the law. Thus, congressional enactments and administrative rules will not be construed to have retroactive effect unless their language requires this result. By the same principle, a statutory grant of legislative rulemaking authority will not, as a general matter, be understood to encompass the power to promulgate retroactive rules unless that power is conveyed by Congress in express terms. Even where some substantial justification for retroactive rulemaking is presented, courts should be reluctant to find such authority absent an express statutory grant.

The Secretary contends that the Medicare Act provides the necessary authority to promulgate retroactive cost-limit rules in the unusual circumstances of this case. [The Court rejected this argument, finding that the Medicare Act did not provide authority for retroactive regulations, only for retroactivity in case-by-case adjudication.]

The Secretary nonetheless suggests that, whatever the limits on his power to promulgate retroactive regulations in the normal course of events, judicial invalidation of a prospective rule [like the 1981 HHS rule] is a unique occurrence that creates a heightened need, and thus a justification, for retroactive curative rulemaking. The Secretary warns that congressional intent and important administrative goals may be frustrated unless an invalidated rule can be cured of its defect and made applicable to past time periods. The argument is further advanced that the countervailing reliance interests are less compelling than in the usual case of retroactive rulemaking, because the original, invalidated rule provided at least some notice to the individuals and entities subject to its provisions.

Whatever weight the Secretary's contentions might have in other contexts, they need not be addressed here. The case before us is resolved by the particular statutory scheme in question. Our interpretation of the

Medicare Act compels the conclusion that the Secretary has no authority to promulgate retroactive cost-limit rules. . . .

JUSTICE SCALIA, concurring.

I agree with the Court [but write separately in order to add] that the APA independently confirms the judgment we have reached.

The first part of the APA's definition of "rule" states that a rule "means the whole or a part of an agency statement of general or particular applicability *and future effect* designed to implement, interpret, or prescribe law or policy or describing the organization, procedure, or practice requirements of an agency. . . . " 5 U.S.C. § 551(4) (emphasis added).

The only plausible reading of the italicized phrase is that rules have legal consequences only for the future. It could not possibly mean that merely *some* of their legal consequences must be for the future, though they may also have legal consequences for the past, since that description would not enable rules to be distinguished from "orders," *see* 5 U.S.C. § 551(6), and would thus destroy the entire dichotomy upon which the most significant portions of the APA are based. (Adjudication—the process for formulating orders, *see* § 551(7)—has future as well as past legal consequences, since the principles announced in an adjudication cannot be departed from in future adjudications without reason.)

Nor could "future effect" in this definition mean merely *"taking effect in the future,"* that is, having a future effective date even though, once effective, altering the law applied in the past. That reading, urged by the [Government], produces a definition of "rule" that is meaningless, since obviously *all* agency statements have "future effect" in the sense that they do not take effect until after they are made. . . . Thus this reading, like the other one, causes § 551(4) to fail in its central objective, which is to distinguish rules from orders. All orders have "future effect" in the sense that they are not effective until promulgated. In short, there is really no alternative except the obvious meaning, that a rule is a statement that has legal consequences only for the future. . . .

[Although a rule cannot be retroactive, in the sense of making illegal past conduct which was formerly legal, a rule can legitimately affect past transactions.] That is not retroactivity in the sense at issue here, i.e., in the sense of altering the *past* legal consequences of past actions. Rather, it is what has been characterized as "secondary" retroactivity. A rule with exclusively future effect (taxation of future trust income) can unquestionably *affect* past transactions (rendering the previously established trusts less desirable in the future), but it does not for that reason cease to be a rule under the APA. . . .

A rule that has unreasonable secondary retroactivity—for example, altering future regulation in a manner that makes worthless substantial past investment incurred in reliance upon the prior rule—may for that reason be "arbitrary" or "capricious," and thus invalid. . . . It is erroneous, however, to extend this "reasonableness" inquiry to purported rules that not merely affect past transactions but change what was the law in the past. . . .

This case cannot be disposed of, as the [Government] suggests, by simply noting that retroactive rulemaking is similar to retroactive legislation, and that the latter has long been upheld against constitutional attack where reasonable. The issue here is not constitutionality, but rather whether there is any good reason to doubt that the APA means what it says. For purposes of resolving that question, it does not at all follow that, since Congress itself possesses the power retroactively to change its laws, it must have meant agencies to possess the power retroactively to change their regulations. Retroactive legislation has always been looked upon with disfavor, and even its constitutionality has been conditioned upon a rationality requirement beyond that applied to other legislation. It is entirely unsurprising, therefore, that even though Congress wields such a power itself, it has been unwilling to confer it upon the agencies. Given the traditional attitude towards retroactive legislation, the regime established by the APA is an entirely reasonable one: Where quasi-legislative action is required, an agency cannot act with retroactive effect without some special congressional authorization. That is what the APA says, and there is no reason to think Congress did not mean it.

The dire consequences that the [Government] predicts will ensue from reading the APA as it is written . . . are not credible. . . . It is important to note that the retroactivity limitation applies *only* to rulemaking. Thus, where legal consequences hinge upon the interpretation of statutory requirements, and where no pre-existing interpretive rule construing those requirements is in effect, nothing prevents the agency from acting retroactively through adjudication. Moreover, if and when an agency believes that the extraordinary step of retroactive rulemaking is crucial, all it need do is persuade Congress of that fact to obtain the necessary *ad hoc* authorization. It may even be that implicit authorization of particular retroactive rulemaking can be found in existing legislation. If, for example, a statute prescribes a deadline by which particular rules must be in effect, and if the agency misses that deadline, the statute may be interpreted to authorize a reasonable retroactive rule despite the limitation of the APA.

. . . I might add that even if I felt free to construct my own model of desirable administrative procedure, I would assuredly not sanction "curative" retroactivity. I fully agree with the District of Columbia Circuit that acceptance of the Secretary's position would "make a mockery . . . of the APA," since "agencies would be free to violate the rulemaking requirements of the APA with impunity if, upon invalidation of a rule, they were free to 'reissue' that rule on a retroactive basis." . . .

Notes and Questions

1. *Literalism.* Justice Scalia was not always so insistent on reading § 551(4) literally. *See* § 5.2.1 N.1. In this instance, however, he argues that

"future effect" has to be given its literal meaning because, otherwise, nothing in § 551(4) would distinguish rules from orders. Is his argument persuasive?

As mentioned earlier, the 1961 and 1981 MSAPAs do not contain the "future effect" language found in § 551(4) of the federal APA. Under Scalia's approach, should the *Georgetown* case be decided differently under state law?

2. *Consequences of the Scalia view.* If, as Justice Scalia maintained, the Secretary's action was not a "rule" within the meaning of the federal APA, what was it? *See* § 551(6). Assuming (as is the case) that no statute required the Secretary to make his decision using formal proceedings, what procedures does the APA prescribe in such circumstances?

In the past, courts have freely given retroactive effect to *interpretive* rules, in which an agency states what it thinks existing law means but does not purport to change the law. *See, e.g., Meritor Savings Bank, FSB v. Vinson*, 477 U.S. 57 (1986) (relying on 1980 EEOC sexual harassment guidelines in assessing legality of events occurring between 1974 and 1977). Is this allowable under Scalia's view?

3. *The majority's canons.* The majority articulates two canons or presumptions of statutory interpretation. First, there is a presumption that statutes and rules do not apply retroactively. The Court reaffirmed this teaching of *Georgetown* in *Landgraf v. USI Film Products*, 511 U.S. 244 (1994). The Court explained:

> Elementary considerations of fairness dictate that individuals should have an opportunity to know what the law is and to conform their conduct accordingly; settled expectations should not be lightly disrupted. For that reason, the 'principle that the legal effect of conduct should ordinarily be assessed under the law that existed when the conduct took place has timeless and universal appeal.' In a free, dynamic society, creativity in both commercial and artistic endeavors is fostered by a rule of law that gives people confidence about the legal consequences of their actions. . . .
>
> Since the early days of this Court, we have declined to give retroactive effect to statutes burdening private rights unless Congress had made clear its intent. . . . The presumption against statutory retroactivity has consistently been explained by reference to the unfairness of imposing new burdens on persons after the fact.

Id. at 265–66, 270.

Second (and of more immediate relevance to the actual controversy in *Georgetown*), an agency may not, "as a general matter," issue retroactive legislative rules unless Congress expressly authorizes retroactivity. Under what circumstances might the Court be expected to hold that the principles it applies "as a general matter" are not controlling?

Consider the following hypotheticals: (1) HHS decides that it has been paying rural physicians too little reimbursement (relative to other physicians) during the past five years, so it promulgates a rule purporting to declare them eligible for refunds with respect to services rendered during those years. Should the *Georgetown* presumption render the rule invalid? (2)

Hospitals use a certain billing practice because an HHS regulation states that it is proper. Later the courts strike down the HHS rule and declare the practice illegal. The Secretary then issues a second regulation stating that, because hospitals could reasonably have relied on the first regulation while it was in effect, they may not be held liable for their conduct during that period. Under *Georgetown*, is the second regulation fatally retroactive? *Cf.* Carl A. Auerbach, "Administrative Rulemaking in Minnesota," 63 Minn. L.Rev. 151, 157 (1979).

4. *Reasonableness limitations.* Apart from the principle of the *Georgetown* case, the law has other doctrines that protect citizens against retroactive agency action in various circumstances. For example, when an agency imposes retroactive liability through an adjudicative order, courts review the decision for "reasonableness" or abuse of discretion. Essentially, they apply a balancing test that weighs the possible unfairness of retroactive application against the statutory interest in applying a new case law principle to the situation at hand. *See Retail, Wholesale and Dept. Store Clerks Union v. NLRB*, 466 F.2d 380, 390 (D.C.Cir.1972), discussed in detail in § 6.2.1. N.4. In fact, the district court in *Georgetown* had struck down the Secretary's Medicare regulation by applying the reasonableness test of *Retail Union*. Justice Scalia's concurring opinion says that this test should be used to determine the validity of rules that involve "secondary retroactivity." Presumably the same test would also apply to any rule that involves "true" retroactivity but is issued under express statutory authority as *Georgetown* requires.

Would the Court have been better advised to rely exclusively on the reasonableness test to handle possibly unfair retroactivity in rulemaking, instead of adopting its strict presumption? Professor Luneburg argues that retroactive rules are frequently necessary and that there is no basis for the presumption in the *Georgetown* case that retroactive regulations are invalid unless authority is "conveyed by Congress in express terms." *See* William V. Luneburg, "Retroactivity and Administrative Rulemaking," 1991 Duke L.J. 106.

5. *Second thoughts.* The Court may already be retreating somewhat from the stance it took in *Georgetown*. In *Smiley v. Citibank (South Dakota), N.A.*, 517 U.S. 735 (1996), the issue was whether California could apply its law of contractual unconscionability to credit card late-payment fees charged by a South Dakota bank to California borrowers. The case turned on whether late-payment fees are "interest," since a federal statute provides that the law of the state where the bank is located determines the legality of interest charges.

The Supreme Court upheld a regulation by the Comptroller of the Currency (a federal banking authority) defining "interest" to include credit card late-payment fees. The borrower complained that the regulation was invalid under *Georgetown* because it had retroactive effect; it was applied to a late payment fee imposed before the regulation was adopted. In a footnote to his opinion for the Court, Justice Scalia responded:

> There might be substance to this point if the regulation replaced a prior agency interpretation—which, as we have discussed, it did not. Where, however, a court is addressing transactions that occurred at a time when

there was no clear agency guidance, it would be absurd to ignore the agency's current authoritative pronouncement of what the statute means.

Is this footnote consistent with the Court's previous analysis in *Georgetown*? With Justice Scalia's previous concurring opinion?

§ 5.3　INITIATING RULEMAKING PROCEEDINGS

CHOCOLATE MANUFACTURERS ASS'N v. BLOCK
755 F.2d 1098 (4th Cir.1985).

SPROUSE, J.:

Chocolate Manufacturers Association (CMA) appeals from the decision of the district court denying it relief from a rule promulgated by the Food and Nutrition Service (FNS) of the United States Department of Agriculture (USDA or Department). CMA protests that part of the rule that prohibits the use of chocolate flavored milk in the federally funded Special Supplemental Food Program for Women, Infants and Children (WIC Program). Holding that the Department's proposed rulemaking did not provide adequate notice that the elimination of flavored milk would be considered in the rulemaking procedure, we reverse.

... The WIC Program was established by Congress in 1972 to assist pregnant, postpartum, and breastfeeding women, infants and young children from families with inadequate income whose physical and mental health is in danger because of inadequate nutrition or health care. Under the program, the Department designs food packages reflecting the different nutritional needs of women, infants, and children and provides cash grants to state or local agencies, which distribute cash or vouchers to qualifying individuals in accordance with Departmental regulations as to the type and quantity of food.

In 1978 Congress, in extending the WIC Program through fiscal year 1982, [stated]:

> The Secretary shall prescribe by regulation supplemental foods to be made available in the program under this section. To the degree possible, the Secretary shall assure that the fat, sugar, and salt content of the prescribed foods is appropriate.

To comply with this statutory redefinition ... the Department in November 1979 published for comment the proposed rule at issue in this case. Along with the proposed rule, the Department published a preamble discussing the general purpose of the rule and acknowledging the congressional directive that the Department design food packages containing the requisite nutritional value and appropriate levels of fat, sugar, and salt. Discussing the issue of sugar at length, it noted, for example, that continued inclusion of high sugar cereals may be "contrary to nutrition education principles and may lead to unsound eating practices." It also noted that high sugar foods are more expensive than foods with lower sugar content, and that allowing them would be "inconsistent with the goal of teaching participants economical food buying patterns."

The rule proposed a maximum sugar content specifically for authorized cereals. The preamble also contained a discussion of the sugar content in juice, but the Department did not propose to reduce the allowable amount of sugar in juice because of technical problems involved in any reduction. Neither the rule nor the preamble discussed sugar in relation to flavoring in milk. Under the proposed rule, the food packages for women and children without special dietary needs included milk that could be "flavored or unflavored."

The notice allowed sixty days for comment and specifically invited comment on the entire scope of the proposed rules: "The public is invited to submit written comments in favor of or in objection to the proposed regulations or to make recommendations for alternatives not considered in the proposed regulations." Over 1,000 comments were received from state and local agencies, congressional offices, interest groups, and WIC Program participants and others. Seventy-eight commenters, mostly local WIC administrators, recommended that the agency delete flavored milk from the list of approved supplemental foods.

In promulgating the final rule, the Department, responding to these public comments, deleted flavored milk from the list, explaining:

> In the previous regulations, women and children were allowed to receive flavored or unflavored milk. No change in this provision was proposed by the Department. However, 78 commenters requested the deletion of flavored milk from the food packages since flavored milk has a higher sugar content than unflavored milk. They indicated that providing flavored milk contradicts nutrition education and the Department's proposal to limit sugar in the food packages. Furthermore, flavored milk is more expensive than unflavored milk. The Department agrees with these concerns.... Therefore, to reinforce nutrition education, for consistency with the Department's philosophy about sugar in the food packages, and to maintain food package costs at economic levels, the Department is deleting flavored milk from the food packages for women and children. Although the deletion of flavored milk was not proposed, the comments and the Department's policy on sugar validate this change....

On this appeal, CMA contends ... that the Department did not provide notice that the disallowance of flavored milk would be considered.... The Department responds ... by arguing that its notice advised the public of its general concern about high sugar content in the proposed food packages and that this should have alerted potentially interested commenters that it would consider eliminating any food with high sugar content. It also argues in effect that the inclusion of flavored milk in the proposed rule carried with it the implication that both inclusion and exclusion would be considered in the rulemaking process....

[The APA, § 553(b)] requires that the notice in the Federal Register of a proposed rulemaking contain "either the terms or substance of the proposed rule or a description of the subjects and issues involved." The purpose of the notice-and-comment procedure is both "to allow the agency to benefit from the experience and input of the parties who file comments ... and to see to it that the agency maintains a flexible and open-minded attitude towards its own rules." The notice-and-comment procedure encourages public participation in the administrative process and educates the agency, thereby helping to ensure informed agency decisionmaking....

There is no question that an agency may promulgate a final rule that differs in some particulars from its proposal. Otherwise the agency "can learn from the comments on its proposals only at the peril of starting a new procedural round of commentary." An agency, however, does not have carte blanche to establish a rule contrary to its original proposal simply because it receives suggestions to alter it during the comment period. An interested party must have been alerted by the notice to the possibility of the changes eventually adopted from the comments. Although an agency, in its notice of proposed rulemaking, need not identify precisely every potential regulatory change, the notice must be sufficiently descriptive to provide interested parties with a fair opportunity to comment and to participate in the rulemaking....

The test devised by the First Circuit for determining adequacy of notice of a change in a proposed rule occurring after comments appears to us to be sound: notice is adequate if the changes in the original plan "are in character with the original scheme," and the final rule is a "logical outgrowth" of the notice and comments already given. Other circuits also have adopted some form of the "logical outgrowth" test. Stated differently, if the final rule materially alters the issues involved in the rulemaking or ... "substantially departs from the terms or substance of the proposed rule," the notice is inadequate.

There can be no doubt that the final rule in the instant case was the "outgrowth" of the original rule proposed by the agency, but the question of whether the change in it was in character with the original scheme and whether it was a "logical outgrowth" is not easy to answer. In resolving this difficult issue, we recognize that, although helpful, verbal formulations are not omnipotent talismans, and we agree that in the final analysis each case "must turn on how well the notice that the agency gave serves the policies underlying the notice requirement." Under either view, we do not feel that CMA was fairly treated or that the administrative rulemaking process was well served by the drastic alteration of the rule without an opportunity for CMA to be heard ....

Chocolate flavored milk has been a permissible part of the WIC Program diet since its inception and there have been no proposals for its removal until the present controversy.

The Department sponsored commendable information-gathering proceedings prior to publishing its proposed rule.... The National Advisory Council on Maternal, Infant, and Fetal Nutrition provided information and advice. Regional council meetings were open to the public and held in diverse areas of the country. Department of Agriculture personnel attended a number of regional, state, and local meetings and gathered opinions concerning possible changes in the food packages. The agency also gathered a food package advisory panel of experts seeking their recommendations. Food packages were designed based on the information and advice gleaned from these sources. In all of these activities setting out and discussing food packages, including the proposed rule and its preamble, the Department never suggested that flavored milk be removed from the WIC Program.

At the time the proposed rulemaking was published, neither CMA nor the public in general could have had any indication from the history of either the WIC Program or any other food distribution programs that flavored milk was not part of the acceptable diet for women and children without special dietary needs. The discussion in the preamble to the proposed rule was very detailed and identified specific foods which the agency was examining for excess sugar. This specificity, together with total silence concerning any suggestion of eliminating flavored milk, strongly indicated that flavored milk was not at issue. The proposed rule positively and unqualifiedly approved the continued use of flavored milk. Under the specific circumstances of this case, it cannot be said that the ultimate changes in the proposed rule were in character with the original scheme or a logical outgrowth of the notice. We can well accept that, in general, an approval of a practice in a proposed rule may properly alert interested parties that the practice may be disapproved in the final rule in the event of adverse comments. The total effect of the history of the use of flavored milk, the preamble discussion, and the proposed rule, however, could have led interested persons only to conclude that a change in flavored milk would not be considered. Although ultimately their comments may well have been futile, CMA and other interested persons at least should have had the opportunity to make them. We believe that there was insufficient notice that the deletion of flavored milk from the WIC Program would be considered if adverse comments were received, and, therefore, that affected parties did not receive a fair opportunity to contribute to the administrative rulemaking process....

The judgment of the district court is therefore reversed, and the case is remanded to the administrative agency with instructions to reopen the comment period and thereby afford interested parties a fair opportunity to comment on the proposed changes in the rule.

Notes and Questions

1. *Formulation of proposed rules.* Note the steps that USDA took to obtain input from the public even before it published its proposed rule. These steps were not unusual. Although proposed rules are sometimes formulated entirely on the basis of intra-agency consultations, administra-

tive judgment, and expertness, practice varies widely. Often agencies will publish informational notices (commonly called "advance notices of proposed rulemaking") indicating a subject with respect to which they are contemplating future rulemaking and soliciting public comment thereon. At other times, in formulating the text of proposed rules, agencies incorporate prior efforts of the private sector by relying upon standards originally created and adopted by trade associations or other private standard-setting organizations. Some agencies also consult standing advisory committees or potentially affected individuals or organizations prior to the formulation of particular proposed rules. The Federal Advisory Committee Act is discussed in § 8.2.2.

The decision about whether to solicit comment prior to the rulemaking proposal is usually entirely within the agency's discretion. *See, e.g.,* 1981 MSAPA § 3–101 (providing that agency "may" publish an advance bulletin or set up a committee to advise it). However, a presidential executive order requires federal agencies to publish a semi-annual list, called the Unified Regulatory Agenda, identifying all regulations under development and providing detailed information about upcoming "significant" regulatory actions (usually rules that will have an annual effect on the economy of at least $100 million). Exec. Order 12,866, § 4(b)–(c), 58 Fed.Reg. 51735 (1993).

2. *Reasonable time.* If a federal agency publishes notice of a proposed rule in the *Federal Register* on May 1 and adopts the rule on May 5, has it violated the federal APA? How should an agency or a court determine what is a reasonable time for public comment on a proposed rule? In *Connecticut Light and Power Co. v. NRC,* 673 F.2d 525 (D.C.Cir.1982), the court found that a 30 day period was not unreasonable in light of the industry's familiarity with the issue involved, but warned that no period shorter than 30 days would have been allowable. Nevertheless, the court upheld a 15 day period in *Florida Power & Light Co. v. United States,* 846 F.2d 765, 772 (D.C.Cir.1988). The court noted that the agency had been facing a 90 day statutory reporting requirement and an additional 45 day statutory deadline for issuance of the final rule. Furthermore, the agency had received 61 comments on its proposed rule, the comments had demonstrably affected the contents of the final rule, and no additional criticisms beyond those originally contained in the comments had been raised subsequently.

The Administrative Conference proposed that the APA be amended to provide for a comment period of "no fewer than thirty days," subject to the agency's right, which exists under current law, to shorten or eliminate the comment period if it could establish "good cause." ACUS Recommendation 93–4, 59 Fed. Reg. 4670, 4674 (1994). The good cause exemption is discussed in § 6.1.1. In practice agencies often allow much longer than thirty days for comments in complex rulemaking proceedings. Moreover, they frequently extend the time period in response to requests from members of the public that more time is needed to prepare comments.

3. *Detail required.* How informative must a rulemaking notice be? Section 553(b)(3) says that "either the terms or substance of the proposed rule or a description of the subjects and issues involved" must be disclosed, and many state APAs contain parallel language. Suppose a welfare department announces that it is revising its eligibility regulations. The published notice does not specify the anticipated changes but says that anyone may

obtain a free copy of the new provisions on request. Is the notice valid? *Compare Richard v. Commissioner of Income Maintenance*, 573 A.2d 712 (Conn.1990) (upholding such a notice), *with* Melanie B. Abbott, "Notice of Rulemaking in Connecticut Administrative Law: What Remains After *Richard?*," 13 Bridgeport L. Rev. 1 (1992) (criticizing this result). Should states follow the lead of 1981 MSAPA § 3–103(a)(3) and require, in most instances, that the text of the proposed rule be published?

4. *The logical outgrowth test.* The issue addressed in *Chocolate Mfrs.* is one of the most frequently litigated issues in court challenges to agency rules. Is the case correctly decided? Compare *United Steelworkers of America v. Schuylkill Metals Corp.*, 828 F.2d 314 (5th Cir.1987). In that case, OSHA proposed a rule under which employers would be required to transfer workers whose health was at risk because of their having been exposed to airborne lead. OSHA asked for comments as to whether workers should be entitled to Medical Removal Protection (MRP) benefits "that would maintain the rate of pay, seniority and other rights of an employee" in this situation. The notice did not propose or specify any particular MRP benefit. Ultimately, OSHA adopted a rule that required employers to maintain the earnings of transferred workers for eighteen months (including overtime and bonuses that the employee would have earned if not transferred)—even if the employee actually worked fewer hours or was laid off. Rejecting a § 553(b) challenge, the court concluded that the notice "more than adequately sufficed to apprise fairly an interested party that there was an issue regarding the breadth of MRP benefits." The court added that one party (the Steelworkers Union) had commented on the precise issue of what earnings protection should be afforded, and that other parties had submitted extensive, but general, comments favoring broad MRP benefits. Is the decision consistent with the *Chocolate Mfrs.* case?

5. *Logical outgrowth of what?* Observe that at one point the court in *Chocolate Mfrs.* phrased its test as "whether the final rule is a 'logical outgrowth' of the notice and comments already given." Can comments from interested persons put the public on constructive notice of a possible change in a proposed rule, as *Schuylkill* suggests? For a similar holding, see *District of Columbia v. Train*, 521 F.2d 971, 997 (D.C.Cir.1975). Yet one can also find statements in the case law that "notice necessarily must come—if at all— from the agency." *Horsehead Resource Devel. Co. v. Browner*, 16 F.3d 1246 (D.C.Cir.1994); *National Black Media Coalition v. FCC*, 791 F.2d 1016 (2d Cir.1986). Which is the better side of this argument?

6. *State provisions.* Read § 3–107 of the 1981 MSAPA. Is this provision creating a "substantially different" test more helpful or desirable than the "logical outgrowth test" developed by the federal courts under the federal APA? What are the differences, if any, between the two tests? In one jurisdiction that had adopted the § 3–107 criteria, one observer claimed that environmental rulemaking boards "have been reluctant to preliminarily adopt a rule and put it out for public comment until they believe that the language has been finalized. Once public comment has been received, the boards have been reluctant to make changes in response to such comments because changes may constitute a 'substantial difference.' " Marcia J. Oddi, "Environmental Rulemaking in Indiana: The Impact of the Substantial Difference Requirement on Public Input," 24 Ind.L.Rev. 845, 860 (1991).

Apparently after a setback for the state in court, the Indiana legislature enacted a "logical outgrowth" test. *See Meier v. American Maize–Prods. Co.*, 645 N.E.2d 662 (Ind.App.1995). Is the MSAPA test inherently stricter, or was the Indiana experience just a reflection of the manner in which it was applied? Does Oddi's observation also militate against the Fourth Circuit's application of the "logical outgrowth" test in *Chocolate Mfrs.*?

Other states' responses to the issue of variance between proposed and final rules span a wide spectrum. Some states apply a "logical outgrowth" test leniently, rejecting allegations of unfair notice. *Iowa Citizen/Labor Energy Coalition v. Iowa State Commerce Comm'n*, 335 N.W.2d 178, 181 (Iowa 1983); *American Bankers Life Assur. Co. v. Division of Consumer Counsel*, 263 S.E.2d 867, 875–76 (Va.1980). On the other hand, some jurisdictions require an agency to offer a new round of comment whenever it wishes to adopt a rule that differs "substantively" from the rule originally proposed. *See* Md. Code Ann., State Gov't § 10–113(a) (1993); *cf.* 5 Ill. Comp. Stat. Ann. 100/5–40(c) (1993). Would you expect the latter approach to prove impractical, because it will result in an endless series of rulemaking notices, further delaying the issuance of rules or subtly inducing agencies to resist even desirable changes in the text of proposed rules? Or is that approach desirable as the only effective way by which the public can have a fair chance to protect itself against unwise or unwanted rules?

In *Brocal Corp. v. Pennsylvania Dep't of Transportation*, 528 A.2d 114, 119–20 (Pa.1987), the agency adopted a schedule for reimbursement of transit companies participating in a "shared ride" program for senior citizens. Among the differences between the proposed rules and the final rules were these: uniform, industry-wide limits on reimbursement replaced a system in which limits would be set individually for each carrier; special rates were set for trips to or from Philadelphia or Pittsburgh; and limits involving non-ambulatory passengers were increased by 33%.

The court held, 4–3, that the agency was not required to solicit comments before making these changes. The Pennsylvania Documents Law provides that a final rule "may contain such modifications to the proposed text ... as do not enlarge its original purpose." The court said: "Appellants argue that the term 'enlarge the purpose' ... should be construed to include fundamental changes in methodologies. When, as here, a statute's words are clear and unambiguous, the plain language should not be disregarded under the pretext of pursuing its spirit. Purpose refers to the reason for enacting legislation, not the particular course or scheme chosen to achieve that end." Here, "[t]he method for calculating reimbursement limits was changed, not the reason for creating limits."

The court said that the Pennsylvania provision was based on the federal APA and that its holding was consistent with interpretations of the federal APA that require "additional notice [only] when the changes are significant and do not grow out of the rulemaking process." In a footnote the court observed that if the legislature had wished to provide more expansive notice, it could have chosen language such as that in the MSAPA. Is the court's reasoning persuasive?

7. *Information that forms basis of rule.* Should the notice of rulemaking be required to include scientific data or methodology upon which the

agency relied in formulating its proposal? The D.C. Circuit gave an affirmative answer in the leading case of *Portland Cement Ass'n v. Ruckelshaus*, 486 F.2d 375, 377–78, 392–94 (D.C.Cir.1973):

> We find a critical defect in the decision-making process ... in the initial inability of petitioners to obtain—in timely fashion—the test results and procedures used on existing plants which formed a partial basis for the emission control level adopted.... It is not consonant with the purpose of a rule-making proceeding to promulgate rules on the basis of inadequate data, or on data that, [to a] critical degree, is known only to the agency....
>
> In order that rule-making proceedings to determine standards be conducted in orderly fashion, information should generally be disclosed as to the basis of a proposed rule at the time of issuance. If this is not feasible, as in case of statutory time constraints, information that is material to the subject at hand should be disclosed as it becomes available.

Similarly, in *Connecticut Light and Power Co. v. NRC*, 673 F.2d 525, 530–31 (D.C.Cir.1982), the court said, in referring to the NRC's failure to disclose technical studies about fire prevention in nuclear power plants:

> The purpose of the comment period is to allow interested members of the public to communicate information, concerns, and criticisms to the agency during the rule making process. If the notice of proposed rule making fails to provide an accurate picture of the reasoning that has led the agency to the proposed rule, interested parties will not be able to comment meaningfully upon the agency's proposals. As a result, the agency may operate with a one-sided or mistaken picture of the issues at stake in a rule making. In order to allow for useful criticism, it is especially important for the agency to identify and make available technical studies and data that it has employed in reaching the decisions to propose particular rules. To allow an agency to play hunt the peanut with technical information, hiding or disguising the information that it employs, is to condone a practice in which the agency treats what should be a genuine interchange as mere bureaucratic sport. An agency commits serious procedural error when it fails to reveal portions of the technical basis for a proposed rule in time to allow for meaningful commentary.

The principle of *Portland Cement* remains alive and well in the D.C. Circuit. *Anne Arundel County v. USEPA*, 963 F.2d 412 (D.C.Cir.1992). Another court has suggested some limits:

> It is true that nine documents (in a record containing hundreds of documents) were not exposed to adversarial comment because they became part of the record after the close of the comment period. These documents consist of background information and data as well as several internal memoranda. There is nothing to indicate that the Secretary actually relied on any of these documents in promulgating the rule or that the data they contain was critical to the formulation of the rule.... Petitioner has failed to grasp the distinction between the notice of proposed rulemaking and the rulemaking record. It is the former to which the statutory right of comment applies, not the latter.

American Mining Congress v. Marshall, 671 F.2d 1251, 1261–62 (10th Cir.1982). This quotation raises the issue of whether the principle of *Portland Cement* has an adequate basis in the language of § 553. Has it? Is the principle desirable? Should it be sufficient if the agency simply describes the factual basis for its proposed rule in the notice of proposed rulemaking, or must the agency be required to disclose all of the specific information upon which it relies to support that proposal?

8. *Subsequent additions to the record.* The disclosures contemplated by *Portland Cement* are not normally incorporated into the notice of proposed rulemaking itself. Rather, they are frequently placed in a publicly available file, the "rulemaking record," where private interests may examine them and decide whether to submit critical comments. (Section 3–112 of the 1981 MSAPA provides for a rulemaking record, and established practice at the federal level does, too. For more on the nature and functions of the rulemaking record, see § 9.4 N.7.) But what if the agency (or another private interest) adds significant new material to the rulemaking record after the close of the comment period, and members of the public are given no additional opportunity to comment on the new material? In *Rybachek v. EPA*, 904 F.2d 1276, 1286 (9th Cir.1990), the EPA added 6000 pages to the rulemaking record in response to comments made during that period. The court held that the addition of these materials after the close of the comment period did not entitle the public to an opportunity to comment upon them. The court stated:

> Nothing prohibits the Agency from adding supporting documentation for a final rule in response to public comments. In fact, adhering to the [plaintiff's] view might result in the EPA's never being able to issue a final rule capable of standing up to review: every time the Agency responded to public comments, such as those in this rulemaking, it would trigger a new comment period. Thus, either the comment period would continue in a never-ending circle, or, if the EPA chose not to respond to the last set of public comments, any final rule could be struck down for lack of support in the record.

See also Solite Corp. v. USEPA, 952 F.2d 473 (D.C.Cir.1991) ("supplementary" data may be added to record if no prejudice is shown).

However, in *Idaho Farm Bureau Fed'n v. Babbitt*, 58 F.3d 1392, 1401 (9th Cir.1995), the court distinguished *Rybachek* and overturned a rule that added the spring snail to the list of endangered species. The agency added a U.S. Geologic Service report to the record after the comment period closed and relied heavily on the report in its explanation for the final rule. The report was more than a response to comments and did not merely supplement or confirm existing data. Instead, it provided the only scientific information about the reason for decline in the springs where the snails live. Moreover, the plaintiffs questioned the accuracy of the report, and the court said that the public should have had an opportunity to do so.

9. *Causation questions.* In alleging a violation of § 553(b), should a challenger be required to explain why the lack of disclosure was prejudicial? In *Air Transport Ass'n v. CAB*, 732 F.2d 219, 224 (D.C.Cir.1984), the agency relied on staff studies that had been placed in the public docket at the end of the comment period, but the court upheld the rule against procedural

challenge, in part because the petitioner "does not explain what it would have said had it been given earlier access to the staff studies. . . . 'It is . . . incumbent upon a petitioner objecting to the agency's late submission of documents to indicate with "reasonable specificity" what portions of the documents it objects to and how it might have responded if given the opportunity.'" However, in *Shell Oil Co. v. EPA*, 950 F.2d 741 (D.C.Cir. 1991), the court held that the challenger's obligation to show prejudice did not apply to a violation of the "logical outgrowth" principle; it is up to the agency to show that comments on the changes it made between the proposed and final rules would have been useless. Is this distinction persuasive? *Shell Oil* is an dramatic example of the potency of the "logical outgrowth" doctrine, because the court used that test as the basis for invalidating eleven-year-old rules that had served as a cornerstone of EPA's regulation of hazardous waste facilities.

10. *Problem.* Biologists at High Tech Corp. have developed a genetically engineered bacteria that, they hope, will lower the freezing point of citrus fruit, thus protecting the fruit from frost damage. The biologists now wish to test the bacteria on orange trees. However, considerable opposition to the tests has developed; many people are concerned that the bacteria, once released into the environment, might have dangerous effects. A few published scientific studies lend support to these apprehensions.

The State Health Department published proposed rules relating to tests of genetically engineered organisms. The proposed rules would have allowed such tests upon twenty days' notice, if an environmental impact statement were filed at the time of notice disclosing to the public all information relevant to the test that was in the possession of the individual or organization conducting the test. On behalf of her client, High Tech Corp., Marie filed a comment on the proposed regulation approving its contents.

The final rules prohibited all tests of genetically engineered organisms outside the laboratory. Marie discovered that Health Department scientists produced several extensive analyses of the problem during the comment period. These reports, which partially overlapped but went beyond the published scientific literature, opposed any open-air testing. The reports were never disclosed to persons commenting on the proposed rule but were relied upon by the agency in adopting the final rule.

What are the prospects for judicial challenge of the final rules under the federal APA and the 1981 MSAPA?

§ 5.4 PUBLIC PARTICIPATION

The federal APA provides for two kinds of rulemaking—"formal" and "informal." *Formal rulemaking* involves an opportunity for a trial-type hearing, including the right to present evidence, conduct cross-examination, and submit rebuttal evidence, conducted according to most of the adjudication provisions of the federal act. Formal rulemaking procedures are spelled out in §§ 556 and 557, but these provisions come into play only "[w]hen rules are required by statute to be made on the record after opportunity for an agency hearing." APA § 553(c). *Informal rulemaking,* often called notice and comment rulemaking, is governed by far less rigorous procedural requirements. As seen in § 5.3, the process usually revolves around an exchange of documents—a so-called "paper hearing." Informal rulemaking is the norm; formal rulemaking the exception. State APAs, in contrast, explicitly recognize only one type of rulemaking—informal rulemaking of the notice and comment variety.

To further complicate the federal picture, Congress has departed from the two APA models in the enabling acts of certain agencies. It has created statutory schemes that resemble the basic notice and comment process, but include additional or alternate procedural requirements that are designed to broaden opportunities for public participation. These intermediate models are often called *hybrid rulemaking.* The informal, formal, and hybrid varieties of rulemaking are the subject of this section.

§ 5.4.1   INFORMAL RULEMAKING

Notes and Questions

1. *Written or oral comment.* In informal rulemaking under the federal APA, the agency is free to limit public participation to written submissions unless the agency determines otherwise or some other species of law requires more. Nevertheless, federal agencies frequently exercise their discretion to conduct oral hearings on proposed rules.

The typical state APA follows 1961 MSAPA § 3(a)(2) and requires an opportunity to make written submissions to the agency concerning a proposed rule and also, if properly demanded, an opportunity for an "oral hearing." An oral hearing is construed to be an argument or legislative style hearing rather than a trial-type hearing. It must be demanded by 25 persons, a government subdivision, another agency, or an association with 25 or more members. Section 3–104(b)(1) of the 1981 MSAPA contains a similar provision.

Consider the following justification for some kind of oral proceedings in rulemaking:

> It must be admitted that in some situations oral presentations will be more effective than written submissions to communicate to an agency relevant information or arguments, and also to enable the agency to resolve any questions it may have through the oral questioning process. In some situations, oral presentations in rule making may be more effective simply because they are delivered in person, they allow a direct and instantaneous interplay of information and argument between members of the public and the agency, and they are better than written presentations to express depth of feeling or emotion. In addition, oral proceedings may be more effective than proceedings limited entirely to written submissions for provoking broad-based public opposition to a proposed rule. Oral presentations are also likely to be more effective than written submissions for persons who lack the ability to engage in effective written communication.

Arthur Earl Bonfield, STATE ADMINISTRATIVE RULE MAKING 194 (1986).

In addition, an opportunity for members of the public to make oral submissions in rulemaking may ensure greater public satisfaction with the process. An opportunity to submit only written comment may seem less effective and very remote, and thus may engender little personal satisfaction in the individual submitting such comments. One commentator noted that "[u]nless the individual commenting is filing views as part of an organization known to have significant strength before the agency, the filing of a [written] comment is much akin to dropping a feather into the Grand Canyon and trying to hear the impact." Jerre S. Williams, "Securing Fairness and Regularity in Administrative Proceedings," 29 Admin.L.Rev. 1, 16 (1977). On the other hand, an opportunity for oral communication in rulemaking may enhance the communicator's sense of meaningful participation in a significant way.

Given these potential benefits from oral proceedings in rulemaking, what considerations might make an agency reluctant to allow them? Are the MSAPA provisions that allow persons outside the agency to trigger mandatory oral hearings in rulemaking too limited—or, perhaps, not limited enough?

2. *Underwriting participation in rulemaking.* One of the major functions of rulemaking procedures is to ensure that agency rules are consistent with the political will of the community at large. Another is to ensure that agency rulemakers possess all of the information necessary to make technically sound rules. These objectives can be successfully achieved, however, only if all affected interests have a realistic opportunity to participate in the rulemaking process. The fact is that they do not. Despite the opportunities for public participation created by rulemaking procedures, some sectors of our society are unable to use them because they lack the necessary economic, educational, or organizational resources. Even though it costs less to participate in a rulemaking proceeding as opposed to an adjudicatory proceeding, it still takes significant resources for a particular interest group to monitor and to participate fully in the rulemaking process.

One problem created by the practical inability of the poor to participate in rulemaking proceedings affecting them has been characterized as follows: "An agency promulgating rules affecting the poor cannot assume that it automatically knows what is best for such people. Government administrators are usually persons with middle-class backgrounds, experiences, and associations; therefore, they tend to have middle-class viewpoints, orientations, and understandings." Arthur Earl Bonfield, "Representation For the Poor In Federal Rulemaking," 67 Mich.L.Rev. 511 (1969). Following up on this study, the Administrative Conference once urged the creation of an independent People's Counsel, financed with federal funds and authorized to represent the interests of the poor in federal agency rulemaking that would substantially affect their interests. *See* ACUS Recommendation 68–5, "Representation of the Poor in Agency Rulemaking of Direct Consequence to Them," 38 Fed.Reg. 19782 (1973).

An alternative method of using public resources to facilitate expression of the views of groups that have limited resources of their own is the payment of legal fees to underwrite private representation of those groups in particular rulemaking proceedings. Agencies experimented with this device during the 1970's, but these experiments disappeared with the advent of the

Reagan administration and have not been revived. *See* Carl Tobias, "Great Expectations and Mismatched Compensation: Government Sponsored Public Participation in Proceedings of the Consumer Product Safety Commission," 64 Wash.U.L.Q. 1101 (1986). Currently, a prevailing party can sometimes obtain an award of attorneys' fees for participation in agency adjudicatory proceedings or judicial review, but generally not in rulemaking. *See* § 10.3.

Are expenditures of public funds through these mechanisms desirable? How would you explain the fact that these measures have not flourished?

§ 5.4.2 FORMAL RULEMAKING

Procedures for so-called "formal" rulemaking are set forth in §§ 556 and 557 of the federal APA. Those sections require trial-type hearings, including the right to present evidence, cross-examine witnesses, and submit rebuttal evidence. In formal rulemaking, the record made before the agency in that proceeding is the exclusive basis for agency action. Ex parte communications, as defined by § 557(d), are prohibited; however, the separation of functions provisions of § 554(d) are inapplicable. Since the rights of private parties are much more detailed and extensive in formal rulemaking than in informal or even hybrid rulemaking, it is important to identify the circumstances in which formal rulemaking applies. Those circumstances are specified in § 553(c), which states that "[w]hen rules are required by statute to be made on the record after opportunity for an agency hearing, sections 556 and 557 of this title" are applicable. The following case construes this language.

UNITED STATES v. FLORIDA EAST COAST RAILWAY CO.
410 U.S. 224 (1973).

[In order to alleviate a nationwide shortage of railroad boxcars used for shipping freight, the Interstate Commerce Commission (ICC) adopted rules that increased the daily charge that a railroad must pay another railroad for the use of the latter's freight cars during peak use periods. Apparently the previous charges were so low that they encouraged railroads to keep the cars owned by other railroads. This, in turn, caused underinvestment in freight cars and resulted in a chronic shortage. The ICC had been directed by statute to increase the charge in order to create an incentive for railroads to return the cars quickly or to purchase their own cars.

The ICC refused to grant protesting railroads a trial-type hearing. Two lower courts held that this refusal violated §§ 556 and 557 of the APA, which in their view applied to this case by virtue of § 553(c). The railroads also argued that the agency's refusal violated § 1(14)(a) of the Interstate Commerce Act, which provides that the ICC "after hearing" can establish rules with respect to car service.]

REHNQUIST, J.: . . .

II. APPLICABILITY OF ADMINISTRATIVE PROCEDURE ACT

In *United States v. Allegheny–Ludlum Steel Corp.,* [406 U.S. 742 (1972)], we held that the language of § 1(14)(a) of the Interstate Commerce Act authorizing the Commission to act "after hearing" was not the equivalent of a requirement that a rule be made "on the record after opportunity for an agency hearing" as the latter term is used in § 553(c) of the Administrative Procedure Act. Since the 1966 amendment to § 1(14)(a), under which the Commission was here proceeding, does not by its terms add to the hearing requirement contained in the earlier language, the same result should obtain here unless that amendment contains language that is tantamount to such a requirement. Appellees contend that such language is found in the provisions of that Act requiring that:

> "[T]he Commission shall give consideration to the national level of ownership of such type of freight car and to other factors affecting the adequacy of the national freight car supply, and shall, on the basis of such consideration, determine whether compensation should be computed.... "

While this language is undoubtedly a mandate to the Commission to consider the factors there set forth in reaching any conclusion as to imposition of per diem incentive charges, it adds to the hearing requirements of the section neither expressly nor by implication. We know of no reason to think that an administrative agency in reaching a decision cannot accord consideration to factors such as those set forth in the 1966 amendment by means other than a trial-type hearing or the presentation of oral argument by the affected parties. Congress by that amendment specified necessary components of the ultimate decision, but it did not specify the method by which the Commission should acquire information about those components.

Both of the district courts that reviewed this order of the Commission concluded that its proceedings were governed by the stricter requirements of §§ 556 and 557 of the Administrative Procedure Act, rather than by the provisions of § 553 alone.... Insofar as this conclusion is grounded on a belief that the language "after hearing" of § 1(14)(a), without more, would trigger the applicability of §§ 556 and 557, it ... is contrary to our decision in *Allegheny-Ludlum*. [One] District Court observed that it was "rather hard to believe that the last sentence of § 553(c) was directed only to the few legislative sports where the words 'on the record' or their equivalent had found their way into the statute book." This is, however, the language which Congress used, and since there are statutes on the books that do use these very words, adherence to that language cannot be said to render the provision nugatory or ineffectual. We recognized in *Allegheny-Ludlum* that the actual words "on the record" and "after ... hearing" used in § 553 were not words of art, and that other statutory language having the same meaning could trigger the provisions of §§ 556 and 557 in rulemaking proceedings. But we adhere to our conclusion, expressed in that case, that the phrase "after hearing" in § 1(14)(a) of the Interstate Commerce Act does not have such an effect.

III. "Hearing" Requirement of § 1(14)(a) of the Interstate Commerce Act

Inextricably intertwined with the hearing requirement of the Administrative Procedure Act in this case is the meaning to be given to the language "after hearing" in § 1(14)(a) of the Interstate Commerce Act. Appellees ... contend that the Commission procedure here fell short of that mandated by the "hearing" requirement of § 1(14)(a), even though it may have satisfied § 553 of the Administrative Procedure Act. The Administrative Procedure Act states that none of its provisions "limit or repeal additional requirements imposed by statute or otherwise recognized by law." 5 U.S.C. § 559. Thus, even though the Commission was not required [in this rulemaking] to comply with §§ 556 and 557 of that Act, it was required to accord the "hearing" specified in § 1(14)(a) of the Interstate Commerce Act....

The term "hearing" in its legal context undoubtedly has a host of meanings. Its meaning undoubtedly will vary, depending on whether it is used in the context of a rulemaking-type proceeding or in the context of a proceeding devoted to the adjudication of particular disputed facts. It is by no means apparent what the drafters of ... the first part of § 1(14)(a) of the Interstate Commerce Act, meant by the term.... What is apparent, though, is that the term was used in granting authority to the Commission to make rules and regulations of a prospective nature.... [C]onfronted with a grant of substantive authority made after the Administrative Procedure Act was enacted, we think that reference to that Act, in which Congress devoted itself exclusively to questions such as the nature and scope of hearings, is a satisfactory basis for determining what is meant by the term "hearing" used in another statute. Turning to that Act, we are convinced that the term "hearing" as used therein does not necessarily embrace either the right to present evidence orally and to cross-examine opposing witnesses, or the right to present oral argument to the agency's decisionmaker....

We think this treatment of the term "hearing" in the Administrative Procedure Act affords a sufficient basis for concluding that the requirement of a "hearing" contained in § 1(14)(a), in a situation where the Commission was acting under the 1966 statutory rulemaking authority that Congress had conferred upon it, did not by its own force require the Commission either to hear oral testimony, to permit cross-examination of Commission witnesses, or to hear oral argument. Here, the Commission promulgated a tentative draft of an order, and accorded all interested parties 60 days in which to file statements of position, submissions of evidence, and other relevant observations. The parties had fair notice of exactly what the Commission proposed to do, and were given an opportunity to comment, to object, or to make some other form of written submission. The final order of the Commission indicates that it gave consideration to the statements of the two appellees here. Given the "open-ended" nature of the proceedings, and the Commission's announced willingness to consider proposals for modification after operating experience had been acquired, we think the hearing requirement of § 1(14)(a) of the Act was met.

. . . Although appellees have asserted no claim of constitutional deprivation in this proceeding, some of the cases they rely upon expressly speak in constitutional terms. . . . [The Court's constitutional analysis is excerpted in § 2.5.]

The Commission's procedure satisfied both the provisions of § 1(14)(a) of the Interstate Commerce Act and of the Administrative Procedure Act, and were not inconsistent with prior decisions of this Court. We, therefore, reverse the judgment of the District Court. . . .

[DOUGLAS and STEWART, JJ., dissented.]

Notes and Questions

1. *The trigger for formal rulemaking.* According to the *Florida East Coast* case, when a statute authorizes rulemaking of general applicability, it does not require an agency to go beyond the informal procedures of § 553 unless the statute explicitly provides that the rule be made after a hearing on the record, or uses language very similar to that. In effect, the Court adopted a strong presumption against the invocation of APA formal rulemaking.

If this presumption is justifiable, the Court certainly chose an unpropitious legal context in which to announce it. According to Professor Nathanson:

> Whatever may be the wisdom of [the Court's] result, it flies in the face of a consistent interpretation by the ICC and the courts [going back at least to 1911] that all rate orders of the Commission are to be made after hearings on an administrative record and are to be reviewed on that record when challenged in a court of competent jurisdiction. . . . If there is any well-established point of reference for the section 553(c) phrase "required to be made on the record after opportunity for agency hearing," it would seem to be the ratemaking provisions of the Interstate Commerce Act as consistently interpreted by both the Commission and the Supreme Court prior to *Florida East Coast.*

Nathaniel L. Nathanson, "Probing the Mind of the Administrator: Hearing Variations and Standards of Judicial Review Under the Administrative Procedure Act and Other Federal Statutes," 75 Colum.L.Rev. 721, 732–33 (1975). Did the Court err? Or was *Florida East Coast* different in some way from a typical ratemaking case?

2. *The rulemaking-adjudication distinction.* Recall the cases in § 3.1.1, involving the issue of whether a statute calling for a "hearing" triggered trial-type procedures under the federal APA in the context of *adjudication*. *City of West Chicago* basically followed *Florida East Coast*, but other cases took different approaches: *Seacoast Anti–Pollution League* applied a presumption *in favor of* formal proceedings, and *Chemical Waste Management* found the agency's choice reasonable and deferred to it. The *Florida East Coast* presumption *against* formal proceedings differs from both of the latter cases. In the adjudication context, should the courts get in line behind *Florida East Coast*, or is there adequate justification for this disparity in the

judiciary's methods of reading statutes that call in general terms for a "hearing"?

3. *Statutory "hearing" requirements in rulemaking.* Notice that *Florida East Coast* holds not only that the ICC proceeding was not governed by §§ 556 and 557 of the APA, but also that the "hearing" mandate of the Interstate Commerce Act gave the railroads no broader right to be heard than they would have possessed under the APA alone. In that connection, compare this case with *Morgan I* and *Morgan II* in § 3.3.1. Recall that the *Morgan* cases, calling for trial-type, judicial methods, were based on a statute requiring a "full hearing" before an agency set the rates that brokers could charge. Like *Florida East Coast*, the *Morgan* cases involved setting a rate for an entire industry group on a classwide basis. Are these cases reconcilable?

4. *The merits of mandatory trial-type rulemaking proceedings.* Studies of agencies' experiences with formal rulemaking have resulted in harsh criticisms of their utility. One reason for opposition to trial-type hearings in rulemaking is their perceived inefficiency. The classic example is a Food and Drug Administration formal rulemaking to decide whether peanut butter should be required to have 87 or 90 percent peanuts. The proceeding began in 1959 and ended in 1968, generating 7,736 pages of transcript. *Corn Products Co. v. FDA*, 427 F.2d 511 (3d Cir.1970).

In upholding the Federal Power Commission's use of notice and comment procedures rather than trial-type procedures to issue a rule fixing a nationwide rate for natural gas sales, a United States Court of Appeals stated:

> Were the Commission to have allowed all interested parties to submit oral testimony and conduct oral cross-examination on an undertaking so massive and novel as setting a national rate for new gas, the proceeding would have taken years, and the Commission's power to effectively regulate the industry would have been destroyed.

Shell Oil Co. v. FPC, 520 F.2d 1061, 1076 (5th Cir.1975).

A second concern is that the use of trial-type hearings in rulemaking has been found to obstruct agency action and frustrate agency regulatory goals. Professor Hamilton noted in a report to the Administrative Conference:

> [T]he primary impact of ... [trial-type] procedural requirements [in rule making] is often not, as one might otherwise have expected, the testing of agency assumptions by cross-examination, or the testing of agency conclusions by courts on the basis of substantial evidence of record. Rather these procedures either cause the abandonment of the program, ... the development of techniques to reach the same regulatory goal but without a hearing, ... or the promulgation of noncontroversial regulations by a process of negotiation and compromise.... In practice, therefore, the principal effect of imposing [formal requirements on] rulemaking ... has often been the dilution of the regulatory process rather than the protection of persons from arbitrary action.

Robert W. Hamilton, "Procedures for the Adoption of Rules of General Applicability: The Need for Procedural Innovation in Administrative Rulemaking," 60 Cal.L.Rev. 1276, 1312–13 (1972).

A third reason for the opposition to trial-type proceedings in rulemaking is a belief that they are unsuitable for determining most issues presented in rulemaking proceedings. Trial-type procedures, which include the right to present evidence, cross-examine witnesses, and present rebuttal evidence, are usually considered to be most helpful in settling disputed facts of a specific nature about particular persons and circumstances. Rulemaking procedures, on the other hand, are designed to formulate general policy. The formation of such policy may be based in part on general legislative facts, but only rarely on specific facts, and in the end is based upon value judgments. Thus, it is argued, the *desirability* of a certain policy cannot be proven through trial-type procedures—although, admittedly, the resolution of some subsidiary specific factual premises of such a policy may sometimes be aided by their use.

Against the background of these appraisals, the Administrative Conference issued a strong warning in 1972 about trial-type procedure in rulemaking:

[1]   In future grants of rulemaking authority to administrative agencies, Congress ordinarily should not impose mandatory procedural requirements other than those required by 5 U.S.C. § 553, except that when it has special reason to do so, it may appropriately require opportunity for oral argument ... or trial-type hearings on issues of specific fact.

[2]   Congress should never require trial-type procedures for resolving questions of policy or of broad or general fact. Ordinarily it should not require such procedures for making rules of general applicability, except that it may sometimes appropriately require such procedures for resolving issues of specific fact....

[3]   Each agency should decide in the light of the circumstances of particular proceedings whether or not to provide procedural protections going beyond those of section 553, such as opportunity for oral argument, ... opportunity for parties to comment on each other's written or oral submissions, a public-meeting type of hearing, or trial-type hearing for issues of specific fact.

ACUS Recommendation 72–5, 38 Fed.Reg. 19782 (1973). Notice that the ACUS recommendation did not rule out requiring trial-type proceedings on "issues of specific fact." The recommendation did not define that term. A year later the Chairman of ACUS (Antonin Scalia) explained that issues of specific fact were "factual issues which, although not adjudicative, nevertheless justify exploration in a trial-type format—because they are sufficiently narrow in focus and sufficiently material to the outcome of the proceeding to make it reasonable and useful for the agency to resort to trial-type procedure to resolve them." (Quoted in *Association of National Advertisers v. FTC*, 627 F.2d 1151, 1164 (D.C.Cir.1979).) Does this qualification in the ACUS recommendation strike you as a workable and appropriate guideline for identifying situations in which trial-type hearings should be mandated? Would it have justified requiring formal procedure in *Florida East Coast*?

5. *State law.* The 1981 MSAPA does not require any trial-type procedures in rulemaking except "[t]o the extent another statute *expressly* requires a particular class of rulemaking to be conducted pursuant to the

adjudicative procedures provided in Article IV, Section 4–101(b)." 1981 MSAPA § 3–104 Comment. It does, however, permit agencies to provide such procedures in their discretion, where they find them to be useful and feasible. How, if at all, does this approach differ from federal law as reflected in *Florida East Coast*?

6. *Problem.* Mercy Hospital Corp. owns and has operated for almost 100 years a non-profit hospital that has provided free services to poor people in Jefferson County. The directors have decided to convert to a publicly-held for-profit corporation operating a profit-making hospital. After this conversion takes place, Mercy Hospital will offer no free services to the poor.

By statute, a conversion of a corporation from non-profit to profit status must be approved by the Department of Corporations (DOC). Such approval can be granted only on terms that are "fair, just and equitable" to the public. A statute provides that DOC must provide a "fair hearing" in such cases.

Rhoda, the head of DOC, ruled that no oral testimony or cross-examination would be permitted in connection with Mercy's application. Evidence could be submitted only in writing. Any interested person was invited to submit evidence. Jay, the director of Jefferson Fund for the Homeless (JFH), submitted a letter stating that the conversion should be approved only if Mercy was required to contribute $50,000,000 to charities serving the poor in Jefferson County. The letter argued that Mercy was presently worth well in excess of that sum and it would be unjust and inequitable to allow that value to pass into private hands.

Rhoda denied Mercy's request that it be allowed to cross-examine Jay. Should the request be granted if DOC is subject to i) the federal APA, ii) the 1981 MSAPA, iii) no APA?

§ 5.4.3 HYBRID RULEMAKING AND THE LIMITS ON JUDICIAL SUPERVISION OF ADMINISTRATIVE PROCEDURE

As noted earlier, Congress has enacted a variety of "hybrid rulemaking" statutes. These statutes instruct specific agencies to make rules using procedures that are somewhat more elaborate than APA informal rulemaking:

> Although the [federal] APA does not contain an oral hearing requirement for informal rulemaking, a number of laws enacted in the 1970s contain requirements that the agency hold a "public hearing" or provide interested persons "an opportunity for the oral presentation of data, views, or arguments" in rulemaking. Statutes calling for a legislative-type hearing include the Occupational Safety and Health Act (1970); the Consumer Product Safety Act (1972); the Safe Drinking Water Act (1974); the Energy Policy and Conservation Act (1975); the Clean Water Act (1977); the Federal Mine Safety and Health Amendment Act (1977); and the Endangered Species Act Amendments (1978).
>
> A few of these hybrid rulemaking statutes require not only a legislative-type hearing, but also an opportunity for interested persons to question or cross-examine opposing witnesses. These include

the Magnuson–Moss Warranty—Federal Trade Commission Improvements Act (1975); the Securities Acts Amendments (1976); and the Toxic Substances Control Act (1976)....

The enactment of statutes requiring an oral hearing likely reflected the growing complexity of the issues involved in informal rulemaking, the perceived need to probe the accuracy of public comments on these issues, and the strong belief among legislators in the value of oral communication between regulators and the regulated.

ACUS, A GUIDE TO FEDERAL AGENCY RULEMAKING 197–98 (2d ed.1991).

At around the same time as these legislative developments, reviewing courts occasionally held that specific agency rulemaking proceedings had been conducted improperly because of an agency's failure to permit procedural devices that would supplement the usual notice and comment procedures. Because of their wide potential applicability, these court decisions were studied closely by the administrative law bar.

The advent of hybrid rulemaking led to a debate within the Court of Appeals for the District of Columbia Circuit over the issue of whether procedure rather than substance should be emphasized in judicial review of rulemaking. For example, in *International Harvester Co. v. Ruckelshaus*, 478 F.2d 615, 652 (D.C.Cir.1973), Judge David Bazelon suggested that the courts should not "scrutinize the technical merits of each decision" but should "establish a decision-making process which assures a reasoned decision.... " The debate came to a head in *Ethyl Corp. v. EPA*, 541 F.2d 1 (D.C.Cir.1976). In a concurring opinion Judge Bazelon again warned: "Because substantive review of mathematical and scientific evidence by technically illiterate judges is dangerously unreliable, ... we will do more to improve administrative decision-making by concentrating our efforts on strengthening administrative procedures." Another concurrence, by Judge Leventhal, replied: "Our obligation [of substantive review] is not to be jettisoned because our initial technical understanding may be meagre when compared to our initial grasp of FCC or freedom of speech questions.... Better no judicial review at all than a charade that gives the imprimatur without the substance of judicial confirmation that the agency is not acting unreasonably." Ultimately, the Supreme Court resolved this argument in an unusually definitive opinion.

VERMONT YANKEE NUCLEAR POWER CORP. v. NATURAL RESOURCES DEFENSE COUNCIL, INC. [NRDC]
435 U.S. 519 (1978).

[The Atomic Energy Commission (AEC, now the Nuclear Regulatory Commission) has regulatory authority over nuclear energy. Before a utility can start constructing a nuclear power plant, it must obtain a construction permit from the AEC. Applications for construction permits undergo extensive safety and environmental review by the AEC staff and a public adjudicatory hearing occurs before the permit can be granted.

At issue in Vermont Yankee's application was the environmental effect of the disposal and storage of highly toxic nuclear waste produced by operating the plant. Because this is a recurring issue, the AEC conducted a rulemaking proceeding to determine how the nuclear waste storage issue should be resolved in each licensing proceeding. The objective was to settle the issue so it would not have to be relitigated in every single license application.

The proposed and final AEC rule specified numerical values for the environmental impact of waste disposal; these values would be part of an overall cost-benefit analysis of whether the permit should be granted. The practical effect of the values assigned would be that the AEC would essentially ignore the waste disposal problem. This approach was based on the AEC's determination that in the future methods of storage of nuclear waste would be developed that would render the wastes non-hazardous.

The only support in the record for this conclusion was a 20–page report by Dr. Pittman of the AEC staff. NRDC and others sought to cross-examine Dr. Pittman, but the AEC refused to allow cross-examination. On appeal, the D.C. Circuit reversed in an opinion by Judge Bazelon. According to the court of appeals, Pittman's report had offered "conclusory reassurances" but little detailed backup on precisely how the wastes could be safely handled in the future.]

REHNQUIST, J.:

In 1946, Congress enacted the Administrative Procedure Act, which as we have noted elsewhere was not only "a new, basic and comprehensive regulation of procedures in many agencies," *Wong Yang Sung v. McGrath*, 339 U.S. 33 (1950), but was also a legislative enactment which settled "long-continued and hard-fought contentions, and enacts a formula upon which opposing social and political forces have come to rest." *Id.* Section 553 dealing with rulemaking, requires in subsection (b) that "notice of proposed rule making shall be published in the Federal Register," . . . describes the contents of that notice, and goes on to require in subsection (c) that after the notice the agency "shall give interested persons an opportunity to participate in the rule making through submission of written data, views, or arguments with or without opportunity for oral presentation. After consideration of the relevant matter presented, the agency shall incorporate in the rules adopted a concise general statement of their basis and purpose." Interpreting this provision of the Act in *United States v. Allegheny–Ludlum Steel Corp.*, 406 U.S. 742 (1972), and *United States v. Florida East Coast R. Co.*, 410 U.S. 224 (1973), we held that generally speaking this section of the Act established the maximum procedural requirements which Congress was willing to have the courts impose upon agencies in conducting rulemaking procedures. Agencies are free to grant additional procedural rights in the exercise of their discretion, but reviewing courts are generally not free to impose them if the agencies have not chosen to grant them. [This is not to say necessarily that there are no circumstances which would ever justify a court in overturning agency action because of a failure to employ procedures beyond those required by the statute. But such circumstances, if they exist, are extremely rare. . . .]

Respondents appealed from both the Commission's adoption of the rule [dealing with the environmental effects of the uranium fuel cycle] and its decision to grant Vermont Yankee's license [to operate a nuclear power plant] to the Court of Appeals for the District of Columbia Circuit. . . .

With respect to the challenge of Vermont Yankee's license, the court [of appeals] first [held] that in the absence of effective rulemaking proceedings, the Commission must deal with the environmental impact of fuel reprocessing and disposal in individual licensing proceedings. . . . The court then examined the rulemaking proceedings and, despite the fact that it appeared that the agency employed all the procedures required by 5 U.S.C. § 553 and more, the court determined the proceedings to be inadequate and overturned the rule. Accordingly, the Commission's determination with respect to Vermont Yankee's license was also remanded for further proceedings. . . .

After a thorough examination of the opinion itself, we conclude that . . . the majority of the Court of Appeals struck down the rule because of the perceived inadequacies of the procedures employed in the rulemaking proceedings. . . . The court conceded that absent extraordinary circumstances it is improper for a reviewing court to prescribe the procedural format an agency must follow, but it likewise clearly thought it entirely appropriate to "scrutinize the record as a whole to insure that genuine opportunities to participate in a meaningful way were provided. . . . " The court also refrained from actually ordering the agency to follow any specific procedures, . . . but there is little doubt in our minds that the ineluctable mandate of the court's decision is that the procedures afforded during the hearings were inadequate. . . .

In prior opinions we have intimated that even in a rulemaking proceeding when an agency is making a " 'quasi-judicial' determination by which a very small number of persons are exceptionally affected, in each case upon individual grounds," in some circumstances additional procedures may be required in order to afford the aggrieved individuals due process. *Florida East Coast R. Co.*, quoting from *Bi–Metallic Investment Co.* [§ 2.5]. It might also be true, although we do not think the issue is presented in this case and accordingly do not decide it, that a totally unjustified departure from well-settled agency procedures of long standing might require judicial correction.

But this much is absolutely clear. Absent constitutional constraints or extremely compelling circumstances the "administrative agencies 'should be free to fashion their own rules of procedure and to pursue methods of inquiry capable of permitting them to discharge their multitudinous duties.' " ... Respondent NRDC argues that ... 5 U.S.C. § 553 ... merely establishes lower procedural bounds and that a court may routinely require more than the minimum when an agency's proposed rule addresses complex or technical factual issues or "Issues of Great Public Import.... " We have, however, previously shown that our decisions reject this view. We also think the legislative history ... does not bear out its contention.... In short, all of this leaves little doubt that Congress intended that the discretion of the *agencies* and not that of the courts be exercised in determining when extra procedural devices should be employed.

There are compelling reasons for construing [§ 553] in this manner. In the first place, if courts continually review agency proceedings to determine whether the agency employed procedures which were, in the court's opinion, perfectly tailored to reach what the court perceives to be the "best" or "correct" result, judicial review would be totally unpredictable. And the agencies, operating under this vague injunction to employ the "best" procedures and facing the threat of reversal if they did not, would undoubtedly adopt full adjudicatory procedures in every instance. Not only would this totally disrupt the statutory scheme, through which Congress enacted "a formula upon which opposing social and political forces have come to rest," but all the inherent advantages of informal rulemaking would be totally lost.

Secondly, it is obvious that the court in these cases reviewed the agency's choice of procedures on the basis of the record actually produced at the hearing, and not on the basis of the information available to the agency when it made the decision to structure the proceedings in a certain way. This sort of Monday morning quarterbacking not only encourages but almost compels the agency to conduct all rulemaking proceedings with the full panoply of procedural devices normally associated only with adjudicatory hearings.

Finally, and perhaps most importantly, this sort of review fundamentally misconceives the nature of the standard for judicial review of an agency rule. The court below uncritically assumed that additional procedures will automatically result in a more adequate record because it will give interested parties more of an opportunity to participate in and contribute to the proceedings. But informal rulemaking need not be based solely on the transcript of a hearing held before an agency. Indeed, the agency need not even hold a formal hearing. Thus, the adequacy of the "record" in this type of proceeding is not correlated directly to the type of procedural devices employed, but rather turns on whether the agency has followed the statutory mandate of the Administrative Procedure Act or other relevant statutes. If the agency is compelled to support the rule which it ultimately adopts with the type of record produced only after a full adjudicatory hearing, it simply will have no choice but to conduct a full adjudicatory hearing prior to promulgating every rule. In sum, this sort of unwarranted judicial examination of perceived procedural shortcomings of a rulemaking proceeding can do nothing but seriously interfere with that process prescribed by Congress.

In short, nothing in the APA, ... the circumstances of this case, the nature of the issues being considered, past agency practice, or the statutory mandate under which the Commission operates permitted the court to review and overturn the rulemaking proceeding on the basis of the procedural devices employed (or not employed) by the Commission so long as the Commission employed at least the statutory *minima*, a matter about which there is no doubt in this case.

There remains, of course, the question of whether the challenged rule finds sufficient justification in the administrative proceedings that it should be upheld by the reviewing court. Judge Tamm, concurring in the result reached by the majority of the Court of Appeals, thought that it did not. There are also intimations in the majority opinion which suggest that the judges who joined it likewise may have thought the administrative proceedings an insufficient basis upon which to predicate the rule in question. We accordingly remand so that the Court of Appeals may review the rule as the Administrative Procedure Act provides. We have made it abundantly clear before that when there is a contemporaneous explanation of the agency decision, the validity of that action must "stand or fall on the propriety of that finding, judged, of course, by the appropriate standard of review. If that finding is not sustainable on the administrative record made, then the Comptroller's decision must be vacated and the matter remanded to him for further consideration." *Camp v. Pitts*, 411 U.S. 138, 143 (1973). The court should engage in this kind of review and not stray beyond the judicial province to explore the procedural format [beyond that required by the APA] or to impose upon the agency its own notion of which procedures are "best" or most likely to further some vague, undefined public good. . . .

Reversed and remanded.

Notes and Questions

1. *Responses to Vermont Yankee.* If the main objective of the Supreme Court's unanimous, strongly worded opinion was to send a message to the lower courts, it has been quite successful. In subsequent years, the courts have been careful to avoid imposing procedural requirements on agencies in rulemaking without at least purporting to find support in statutory or other provisions of law. Few, if any, cases have even professed to find one of the "extremely rare" circumstances that the Court said might justify an exception to the general ban on judicially created rulemaking procedures in addition to those of § 553. Whether the courts have adhered to the "spirit" of *Vermont Yankee* in their performance of the functions that the Court did allow them to exercise is, however, less clear, as subsequent notes in this section will discuss.

Meanwhile, scholarly opinion about *Vermont Yankee* has been divided. *See* Cooley B. Howarth, Jr., "Informal Agency Rulemaking and the Courts: A Theory for Procedural Review," 61 Wash.U.L.Q. 891, 913–25 (1984) (surveying commentators' views). Professor Davis contends that *Vermont Yankee* was wrong to forbid courts from creating common law rulemaking requirements to supplement those provided in APA § 553. He argues that the

Supreme Court improperly ignored APA § 559, which provides that this Act does "not limit or repeal additional requirements imposed by statute or otherwise *recognized by law*." (Emphasis added). Section 559 makes clear, Davis says, that the APA imposes only minimum, not maximum, procedural requirements. In his view, court-created administrative common law is necessary to ensure an acceptable administrative law system. *See* Kenneth Culp Davis, "Administrative Common Law and the *Vermont Yankee* Opinion," 1980 Utah L.Rev. 3. Professor Byse, on the other hand, has commended the Court for recognizing that the judiciary must respect the procedural decisions mandated by Congress, and that agencies, not courts, are in the best position to evaluate the efficacy of their factfinding procedures. Clark Byse, "*Vermont Yankee* and the Evolution of Administrative Procedure: A Somewhat Different View," 91 Harv.L.Rev. 1823 (1978). Which view is more persuasive?

2. *Hybrid rulemaking statutes after Vermont Yankee.* The Supreme Court's opinion in *Vermont Yankee* also effectively marked the demise of congressional legislation imposing trial-type procedural formalities in rulemaking. The 1970s statutes described at the beginning of this section find no counterparts in recent federal legislation.

One possible explanation for this change in congressional behavior—in addition to the *Vermont Yankee* case itself—is that empirical studies of the actual operation of hybrid rulemaking have raised serious doubts about its effectiveness. After a detailed study by Professor Barry B. Boyer of the FTC's experience with a statutory rulemaking scheme that included an express right to conduct cross-examination and present rebuttal evidence on disputed issues of fact, the Administrative Conference concluded that there was "compelling evidence" that trial-type hearing procedure "is not an effective means of controlling an agency's discretion in its exercise of a broad delegation of legislative power which has not acquired, in law, specific meaning." ACUS Recommendation 80–1, 45 Fed.Reg. 46772 (1980). *But see* William D. Dixon, "Rulemaking and the Myth of Cross–Examination," 34 Admin.L.Rev. 389 (1982) (a more positive assessment by the FTC's chief presiding officer).

Similarly, Professor (now Judge) Stephen Williams conducted a study of several cases in which appellate courts had invalidated a rule because of an agency's failure to allow more procedural opportunities than § 553 prescribed. Williams looked at what actually happened after each of these cases returned to the agency on remand. He found that most of the litigants that had won a right to cross-examination abandoned it or used it only as a bargaining chip. In the only case in which challengers actually engaged in cross-examination on remand, they derived little benefit from it. Stephen F. Williams, "Hybrid Rulemaking under the Administrative Procedure Act: A Legal and Empirical Analysis," 42 U.Chi.L.Rev. 401, 436–45 (1975).

3. *Vermont Yankee and judicial interpretations of § 553.* To what extent does *Vermont Yankee* undermine or call into question judicial interpretations of the notice and comment provisions of the federal APA, such as the logical outgrowth doctrine or the duty to disclose scientific information underlying a proposed rule? Reconsider the *Chocolate Manufacturers* and *Portland Cement* cases discussed in § 5.3.

4. *Substantive review after Vermont Yankee.* What does the Supreme Court's opinion imply about judicial review of the substance of agency rules? On remand in the *Vermont Yankee* litigation itself, the D.C. Circuit revisited the NRC's waste disposal rule and struck it down again, this time on the theory that the rule was arbitrary and capricious. Again the Supreme Court reversed the court of appeals. *Baltimore Gas & Elec. Co. v. NRDC,* 462 U.S. 87 (1983). The Court found that the agency had carefully balanced environmental and economic factors, and added that a court must give great deference to an agency's predictions, within the area of its expertise, at the frontiers of science. *See* § 9.5 N.3. Yet the Court did not condemn intensive judicial review of rules on their merits in the same strong terms as it had used to dress down the D.C. Circuit in *Vermont Yankee*; and only a few months later, the Court strongly reaffirmed "hard look" review in the *Motor Vehicle* case, reprinted at § 9.5. It seems, therefore, that—in terms of the *Ethyl* debate mentioned at the beginning of this section—the Supreme Court has rejected the "Bazelon" position, and the "Leventhal" position has prevailed.

Yet, might a court's power to hold an agency rule arbitrary and capricious serve as an indirect means of controlling the agency's procedural choices, which *Vermont Yankee* supposedly forbids? The Court commented on this possibility in *Pension Benefit Guaranty Corp. (PBGC) v. LTV, Corp.,* 496 U.S. 633 (1990). The Court recognized that in the leading case of *Citizens to Preserve Overton Park, Inc. v. Volpe,* 401 U.S. 402 (1971), it had authorized a district court to remand that case to the agency for a fuller explanation of the agency's reasoning at the time of the administrative action. The Court said in *PBGC*:

> [A]lthough one initially might feel that there is some tension between *Vermont Yankee* and *Overton Park*, the cases are not necessarily inconsistent. *Vermont Yankee* stands for the general proposition that courts are not free to impose upon agencies specific procedural requirements that have no basis in the APA. At most, *Overton Park* suggests that § 706(2)(A) of the APA, which directs a court to ensure that an agency action is not arbitrary and capricious ..., imposes a general "procedural" requirement of sorts by mandating that an agency take whatever steps it needs to provide an explanation that will enable the court to evaluate the agency's rationale at the time of decision.

At times, the "steps" that courts exhort agencies to take in order to facilitate judicial review do seem to carry rather strong implications for the agencies' procedural choices. In *National Lime Ass'n v. EPA,* 627 F.2d 416, 452–53 (D.C.Cir.1980), the court described its standard of review for EPA rulemaking as evincing

> a concern that variables be accounted for, that the representativeness of test conditions [be] ascertained, that the validity of tests be assured and the statistical significance of results determined, ... coupled with a requirement that assumptions be revealed, that the rejection of alternate theories or abandonment of alternate courses of action be explained and that the rationale for the ultimate decision be set forth in a manner which permits the public to exercise its statutory prerogative of com-

ment and the courts to exercise their statutory responsibility upon review.

Doesn't this sort of statement amount to a serious subversion of the principle of agency autonomy that the Court was trying to preserve in *Vermont Yankee*? Isn't even *PBGC* something of a retreat from that principle?

5. *Vermont Yankee in adjudication.* The principal case dealt with informal rulemaking; should its teachings also apply to informal adjudication? In *PBGC v. LTV,* the PBGC (an agency that regulates pension systems) ordered a company to resume responsibility for billions of dollars' worth of pension obligations to its employees, notwithstanding the company's resort to bankruptcy proceedings. The court of appeals held that the agency's highly informal procedures had been inadequate, because PBGC had "neither apprised LTV of the material on which it was to base its decision, [given] LTV an adequate opportunity to offer contrary evidence, proceeded in accordance with ascertainable standards, ... nor provided [LTV] a statement showing its reasoning in applying those standards." In reversing the decision of the court of appeals and sustaining the agency procedures used in this case, the Supreme Court stated:

> [T]o support its ruling, the court focused on "fundamental fairness" to LTV.... But the court did not point to any provision in [the agency's enabling act] or the APA which gives LTV the procedural rights the court identified. Thus, the court's holding runs afoul of *Vermont Yankee....*
>
> ... The determination in this case ... was lawfully made by informal adjudication, the minimal requirements for which are set forth in § 555 of the APA, and do not include such elements. A failure to provide them where the Due Process Clause itself does not require them (which has not been asserted here) is therefore not unlawful.

The Court did not explain why it believed that the principles of *Vermont Yankee*, developed in the context of informal rulemaking, should also apply to informal adjudication. Was this extension justified? Examine the text of § 555 of the APA, on which the Court relied. Does it appear to play the same role in structuring informal adjudication as § 553 does in structuring informal rulemaking?

6. *Problem.* Most agencies in the state of Monroe have established home pages on the World Wide Web to publicize their activities and create better lines of communication with the public. They routinely make notices of proposed rulemaking available at their Web sites (in addition to the traditional notices published in the Monroe Register, which is similar to the Federal Register). By clicking on links available at these sites, members of the public can send e-mail messages to express their thoughts on proposed rules. Agencies in Monroe that use the Internet in this fashion, in combination with traditional methods of inviting comment, receive far more public input in their rulemaking proceedings than they did before the advent of the Web.

However, the Monroe Occupational Safety Agency (MOSA) has resisted this trend. The Agency does maintain a Web page for informational purposes, but it does not invite or accept e-mail messages on its proposed rules. In the opinion of Eileen, the head of MOSA, anyone who really cares about a rule proposal pending at her agency ought to be willing to send a "real" letter about it.

MOSA recently promulgated an "ergonomics" rule to protect workers against repetitive motion injuries in the workplace, such as may occur from overuse of a computer keyboard. Charles is an employer who has just received a citation for failing to comply with the rule, and he wants to fight back with a protest against MOSA's policy of accepting comments on proposed rules only through "snail mail." In a court challenge to the rule, he states that he learned about this proposal through an Internet discussion group and would have commented on it through e-mail had that option been available. What are Charles' prospects for winning this case, if Monroe has adopted (a) an administrative procedure act similar to the federal APA, or (b) the 1981 MSAPA?

§ 5.5   PROCEDURAL REGULARITY IN RULEMAKING

This section focuses on the process of decision in rulemaking proceedings and on objections that interested persons outside the agency might lodge against those proceedings. It considers ex parte contacts by outsiders with the agency, bias of the agency heads, and a requirement that the agency head be personally familiar with the record before deciding. Section 3.3 focused on similar problems as they arise in *adjudication*. Solutions to these problems require tradeoffs between judicial and institutional approaches to decisionmaking—that is, between the procedural norms of the courtroom and the distinctive needs of a bureaucratic organization. One of the dominant themes of this section will be the extent to which these tradeoffs should be revised when the context changes from adjudication to rulemaking.

§ 5.5.1   ROLE OF AGENCY HEADS

Recall the discussion of *Morgan I*, § 3.3.1. That case obligates the person who takes responsibility for an agency decision to have at least some personal familiarity with the record. In *Morgan I* the Court described the proceedings as "quasi-judicial," but they actually involved ratesetting for fifty market agencies on a classwide basis. Today we would describe those proceedings as formal rulemaking. But should the *Morgan I* principle apply with equal force to *informal* rulemaking?

The federal APA and both the 1961 and 1981 MSAPAs specifically provide that agency decisionmakers must actually consider the written and oral submissions received in the course of the rulemaking proceeding. *See* federal APA § 553(c); 1961 MSAPA § 3(a)(2); 1981 MSAPA § 3–106(c). However, this requirement does not necessarily mean that the agency head must personally preside at an oral proceeding or personally read all written submissions. In practice, it is seldom feasible for an agency head to perform these functions personally, although in the end it is the agency head who must personally make the determination whether to adopt proposed rules and in what form.

Section 3–104(b)(3) of the 1981 MSAPA explicitly provides that others may preside at oral rulemaking proceedings and prepare summaries for subsequent personal consideration by the agency head. Both the federal APA and state APAs have been construed in the same manner. An agency head need not read all (or even any) of the written submissions, transcripts and summaries, but must understand their contents so that he or she can make an informed decision. *See Massachusetts State Pharmaceutical Ass'n v. Rate Setting Comm'n*, 438 N.E.2d 1072, 1078 (Mass.1982). In *National Small Shipments Traffic Conf. v. ICC,* 725 F.2d 1442, 1450–51 (D.C.Cir.1984), the court said that commissioners may rely on summaries of the record prepared by their staff. "At some point, however, staff-prepared synopses may so distort the record that an agency decisionmaking body can no longer rely on them in meeting its obligations under the law ... to accord 'consideration' to relevant comments submitted for the record by interested parties." Thus, if staff members systematically suppressed all comments on one side of a question, the agency decisionmakers would need to take independent steps to familiarize themselves with those comments.

Should state agency heads be expected to be more personally involved in such proceedings than federal agency heads? Such personal participation on the part of agency heads has been a tradition in the states to a far greater extent than in the federal government. *See* Arthur Earl Bonfield, STATE ADMINISTRATIVE RULE MAKING 229 (1986).

However, persons who wish to challenge a rule are usually not free to examine an agency head in court to ascertain whether he or she understood the record assembled during the rulemaking proceeding. Recall *Morgan IV,* discussed in § 3.3.1 N.6, holding that such examination is normally improper. Because of this principle, violations of *Morgan I* are in most cases impossible to prove, even where they occur.

Problem. Thirteen days after a new Commissioner of the Food and Drug Administration took office, he signed and issued voluminous regulations setting standards for special dietary foods. During those thirteen days he had also signed fourteen other final regulations, thirteen proposed regulations, and six other notices. Manufacturers of dietary foods sought to take a deposition of the new Commissioner to determine whether he had in fact given sufficient consideration to their 1000 pages of formal exceptions. The record also contained 20,000 additional letters, not to mention 32,000 pages of testimony and thousands of pages of exhibits, reflecting hearings lasting almost two years. The petitioners argued that the objective circumstances raised enough doubt about whether he had actually given sufficient consideration to their views to warrant the unusual step of discovery directed to that issue. What result? *See National Nutritional Foods Ass'n v. FDA*, 491 F.2d 1141 (2d Cir.1974).

§ 5.5.2 EX PARTE COMMUNICATIONS AND POLITICAL IN-FLUENCE IN RULEMAKING

During the course of every rulemaking proceeding, an agency acquires a voluminous amount of material concerning the proposed rule. The compilation of this material is known as the rulemaking record. The record serves three basic functions: it aids public participation, it provides materials helpful to the agency in making a decision, and it facilitates judicial review of the agency decision. Although the rulemaking record serves these important functions, the federal APA, the 1961 MSAPA and the many state acts based on that Model Act, are silent with respect to the creation and maintenance of any official agency record in rulemaking. Section 3–112(b) of the 1981 MSAPA, on the other hand, provides for a rulemaking record and specifies the materials it must include.

To what extent may persons outside an agency engage in off-the-record, ex parte communications with an agency about a proposed rule? In *formal* rulemaking the answer is clear. Since such rulemaking must be conducted according to the requirements of §§ 556–57 of the federal APA, ex parte communications are forbidden in that kind of rulemaking, and if they nevertheless occur the agency must disclose their substance on the public record. *See* APA § 557(d). On the other hand, in *informal* rulemaking, the assumption for many years was that the federal APA neither banned ex parte communications nor required the inclusion of such communications in the agency rulemaking record. It was early noted that the APA does not

> require the formulation of rules upon the exclusive basis of any "record" made in informal rulemaking proceedings.... Accordingly ... an agency is free to formulate rules [in informal notice and comment rulemaking] upon the basis of materials in its files and the knowledge and experience of the agency, in addition to the materials adduced in public rulemaking proceedings.

U.S. Dept. of Justice, ATTORNEY GENERAL'S MANUAL ON THE ADMINISTRATIVE PROCEDURE ACT 31–32 (1947).

HOME BOX OFFICE, INC. v. FCC
567 F.2d 9 (D.C.Cir.1977).

Before WRIGHT and MacKINNON, CIRCUIT JUDGES, and WEIGEL, DISTRICT JUDGE.

PER CURIAM:

[This case involved a challenge to FCC rules that would have limited the types of programming and advertising that could appear on pay cable channels and subscription television. For example, sports events and feature films on those outlets would have been sharply restricted. The purpose of the rules was to prevent subscription television and cable operators from outbidding regular broadcasters for the right to present these popular shows. The Commission hoped the rules would protect the economic viability of regular broadcast stations, so that the owners of those stations would continue to be able to produce public service programs and serve viewers who could only afford to watch "free" television.]

It is apparently uncontested that a number of participants before the Commission sought out individual commissioners or Commission employees for the purpose of discussing *ex parte* and in confidence the merits of the rules under review here. In fact, the Commission itself solicited such communications in its notices of proposed rulemaking....

... It is important to note that many contacts occurred in the crucial period between the close of oral argument ... and the adoption of the *First Report and Order* ... when the rulemaking record should have been closed while the Commission was deciding what rules to promulgate. The information submitted to this court by the Commission indicates that during this period broadcast interests met some 18 times with Commission personnel, cable interests some nine times, motion picture and sports interests five times each, and "public interest" intervenors not at all.

Although it is impossible to draw any firm conclusions about the effect of *ex parte* presentations upon the ultimate shape of the pay cable rules, the evidence is certainly consistent with often-voiced claims of undue industry influence over Commission proceedings, and we are particularly concerned that the final shaping of the rules we are reviewing here may have been by compromise among the contending industry forces, rather than by exercise of the independent discretion in the public interest the Communications Act vests in individual commissioners....

Even the possibility that there is here one administrative record for the public and this court and another for the Commission and those "in the know" is intolerable. Whatever the law may have been in the past, there can now be no doubt that implicit in the decision to treat the promulgation of rules as a "final" event in an ongoing process of administration is an assumption that an act of reasoned judgment has occurred, an assumption which further contemplates the existence of a body of material—documents, comments, transcripts, and statements in various forms declaring agency expertise or policy—with reference to which such judgment was exercised. Against this material, "the full administrative record that was before [an agency official] at the time he made his decision," *Citizens to Preserve Overton Park, Inc. v. Volpe, supra*, 401 U.S. at 420, it is the obligation of this court to test the actions of the Commission for arbitrariness or inconsistency with delegated authority. Yet here agency secrecy stands between us and fulfillment of our obligation. As a practical matter, *Overton Park's* mandate means that the public record must reflect what representations were made to an agency so that relevant information supporting or refuting those representations may be brought to the attention of the reviewing courts by persons participating in agency proceedings. This course is obviously foreclosed if communications are made to the agency in secret and the agency itself does not disclose the information presented. Moreover, where, as here, an agency justifies its actions by reference only to information in the public file while failing to disclose the substance of other relevant information that has been presented to it, a reviewing court cannot presume that the agency has acted properly, *Citizens to Preserve Overton Park, Inc. v. Volpe, supra,* at 415, 419–420, but must treat the agency's justifications as a fictional account of the actual decisionmaking process and must perforce find its actions arbitrary.

The failure of the public record in this proceeding to disclose all the information made available to the Commission is not the only inadequacy we find here. Even if the Commission had disclosed to this court the substance of what was said to it *ex parte,* it would still be difficult to judge the truth of what the Commission asserted it knew about the television industry because we would not have the benefit of an adversarial discussion among the parties. The importance of such discussion to the proper functioning of the agency decisionmaking and judicial review processes is evident in our cases. We have insisted, for example, that information in agency files or consultants' reports which the agency has identified as relevant to the proceeding be disclosed to the parties for adversarial comment. Similarly, we have required agencies to set out their thinking in notices of proposed rulemaking. This requirement not only allows adversarial critique of the agency but is perhaps one of the few ways that the public may be apprised of what the agency thinks it knows in its capacity as a repository of expert opinion. From a functional standpoint, we see no difference between assertions of fact and expert opinion tendered by the public, as here, and that generated internally in an agency: each may be biased, inaccurate, or incomplete—failings which adversary comment may illuminate. Indeed, the potential for bias in private presentations in rulemakings which resolve "conflicting private claims to a valuable privilege," *Sangamon Valley Television Corp. v. United States,* 269 F.2d 221, 224, seems to us greater than in cases where we have reversed agencies for failure to disclose internal studies.

. . .

Equally important is the inconsistency of secrecy with fundamental notions of fairness implicit in due process and with the ideal of reasoned decisionmaking on the merits which undergirds all of our administrative law. Certainly any ambivalence about [this inconsistency] has been removed by recent congressional and presidential actions. In the Government in the Sunshine Act, for example, Congress has declared it to be "the policy of the United States that the public is entitled to the fullest practicable information regarding the decisionmaking processes of the Federal Government," and has taken steps to guard against ex parte contacts in formal agency proceedings. . . .

From what has been said above, it should be clear that information gathered *ex parte* from the public which becomes relevant to a rulemaking will have to be disclosed at some time. On the other hand, we recognize that informal contacts between agencies and the public are the "bread and butter" of the process of administration and are completely appropriate so long as they do not frustrate judicial review or raise serious questions of fairness. Reconciliation of these considerations in a manner which will reduce procedural uncertainty leads us to conclude that communications which are received prior to issuance of a formal notice of rulemaking do not, in general, have to be put in a public file. Of course, if the information contained in such a communication forms the basis for agency action, then, under well established principles, that information must be disclosed to the public in some form. Once a notice of proposed rulemaking has been issued, however, any agency official or employee who is or may reasonably be expected to be involved in the decisional process of the rulemaking proceeding, should "refus[e] to discuss matters relating to the disposition of a [rulemaking proceeding] with any interested private party, or an attorney or agent for any such party, prior to the [agency's] decision. . . . "If *ex parte* contacts nonetheless occur, we think that any written document or a summary of any oral communication must be placed in the public file established for each rulemaking docket immediately after the communication is received so that interested parties may comment thereon. . . .

[Concurring opinions by MacKinnon, J., and Weigel, J., are omitted.]

SIERRA CLUB v. COSTLE
657 F.2d 298 (D.C.Cir.1981).

[The Environmental Protection Agency (EPA) adopted a regulation governing the emissions of sulfur dioxide by new coal-fired electric generators. In part, the rulemaking involved a struggle between Western states that produce low sulfur coal and Eastern states that produce high sulfur coal. Extremely high stakes were involved. On this appeal, one issue raised by the Environmental Defense Fund (EDF) was whether the rule was invalid because of an "ex parte blitz" that began after the close of the comment period. The "blitz" included meetings between the agency and private persons, executive branch officials, and elected officials. According to EDF, the agency had been on the verge of adopting stricter limits on sulfur dioxide emissions, but it backed down because of these meetings, in which the White House tried to influence EPA to adopt a less costly solution, and representatives of Eastern coal interests, including the National Coal Association and Senator Robert Byrd of West Virginia, sought a standard that would be more acceptable to their interests.

After spending about sixty pages discussing and rejecting substantive attacks on the rule, the court turned to the post-comment period meetings held with individuals outside of the EPA. The court's opinion was written by Wald, J.:]

[The rule was issued under the authority of the 1977 Amendments to the Clean Air Act, which] required the agency to establish a "rulemaking docket" for each proposed rule which would form the basis of the record for judicial review. The docket must contain, *inter alia*, "[a]ll documents ... which become available after the proposed rule has been published and which the Administrator [of EPA] determines are of central relevance to the rulemaking. . . . "

. . . Oral face-to-face discussions are not prohibited anywhere, anytime, in the [Clean Air] Act. The absence of such prohibition may have arisen from the nature of the informal rulemaking procedures Congress had in mind. Where agency action resembles judicial action, where it involves formal rulemaking, adjudication, or quasi-adjudication among "conflicting private claims to a valuable privilege," the insulation of the decisionmaker from ex parte contacts is justified by basic notions of due process to the parties involved. But where agency action involves informal rulemaking of a policymaking sort, the concept of ex parte contacts is of more questionable utility.

Under our system of government, the very legitimacy of general policymaking performed by unelected administrators depends in no small part upon the openness, accessibility, and amenability of these officials to the needs and ideas of the public from whom their ultimate authority derives, and upon whom their commands must fall. As judges we are insulated from these pressures because of the nature of the judicial process in which we participate; but we must refrain from the easy temptation to look askance at all face-to-face lobbying efforts, regardless of the forum in which they occur, merely because we see them as inappropriate in the judicial context. Furthermore, the importance to effective regulation of continuing contact with a regulated industry, other affected groups, and the public cannot be underestimated. Informal contacts may enable the agency to win needed support for its program, reduce future enforcement requirements by helping those regulated to anticipate and shape their plans for the future, and spur the provision of information which the agency needs. The possibility of course exists that in permitting ex parte communications with rulemakers we create the danger of "one administrative record for the public and this court and another for the Commission." *Home Box Office*. Under the Clean Air Act procedures, however, "[t]he promulgated rule may not be based (in part or whole) on any information or data which has not been placed in the docket. . . . "Thus EPA must justify its rulemaking solely on the basis of the record it compiles and makes public.

Regardless of this court's views on the need to restrict all post-comment contacts in the informal rulemaking context, however, it is clear to us that Congress has decided not to do so in the statute which controls this case. As we have previously noted:

> Where Congress wanted to prohibit *ex parte* contacts it clearly did so. Thus [the] APA ... forbids *ex parte* contacts when an "adjudication" is underway. . . .

> If Congress wanted to forbid or limit *ex parte* contact in every case of informal rulemaking, it certainly had a perfect opportunity of

doing so when it enacted the Government in the Sunshine Act [in 1976, adding § 557(d) to the APA].

That it did not extend the ex parte contact provisions of the amended section 557 to section 553—even though such an extension was urged upon it during the hearing—is a sound indication that Congress still does not favor a per se prohibition or even a "logging" requirement in all such proceedings.

Lacking a statutory basis for its position, EDF would have us extend our decision in *Home Box Office, Inc. v. FCC* to cover all meetings with individuals outside EPA during the post-comment period. Later decisions of this court, however, have declined to apply *Home Box Office* to informal rulemaking of the general policymaking sort involved here, and there is no precedent for applying it to the procedures found in the Clean Air Act Amendments of 1977.

It still can be argued, however, that if oral communications are to be freely permitted after the close of the comment period, then at least some adequate summary of them must be made in order to preserve the integrity of the rulemaking docket, which under the [Clean Air Act] must be the sole repository of material upon which EPA intends to rely. The statute does not require the docketing of all post-comment period conversations and meetings, but we believe that a fair inference can be drawn that in some instances such docketing may be needed in order to give practical effect to section 307(d)(4)(B)(i) [of that Act,] which provides that all *documents* "of central relevance to the rulemaking" shall be placed in the docket as soon as possible after their availability. This is so because unless *oral* communications of central relevance to the rulemaking are also docketed in some fashion or other, information central to the justification of the rule could be obtained without ever appearing on the docket, simply by communicating it by voice rather than by pen, thereby frustrating the command of section 307 that the final rule not be "based (in part or whole) on any information or data which has not been placed in the docket. . . . "

EDF is understandably wary of a rule which permits the agency to decide for itself when oral communications are of such central relevance that a docket entry for them is required. Yet the statute itself vests EPA with discretion to decide whether "documents" are of central relevance and therefore must be placed in the docket; surely EPA can be given no less discretion in docketing oral communications, concerning which the statute has no explicit requirements whatsoever. Furthermore, this court has already recognized that the relative significance of various communications to the outcome of the rule is a factor in determining whether their disclosure is required. A judicially imposed blanket requirement that all post-comment period oral communications be docketed would, on the other hand, contravene our limited powers of review, would stifle desirable experimentation in the area by Congress and the agencies, and is unnecessary for achieving the goal of an established, procedure-defined docket, *viz.*, to enable reviewing courts to fully evaluate the stated justification given by the agency for its final rule.

Turning to the particular oral communications in this case, we find that only two of the nine contested meetings were undocketed by EPA. [One was an informational briefing by EPA to Senate aides, which was not the sort of meeting that would require docketing. The other was a meeting with President Carter and other high-ranking White House officials. The court thus turned to the distinctive issues presented by intra-executive branch meetings:]

We have already held that a blanket prohibition against meetings during the post-comment period with individuals outside EPA is unwarranted, and this perforce applies to meetings with White House officials. . . .

[I]t is hard to believe Congress was unaware that intra-executive meetings and oral comments would occur throughout the rulemaking process. We assume, therefore, that unless expressly forbidden by Congress, such intra-executive contacts may take place, both during and after the public comment period; the only real issue is whether they must be noted and summarized in the docket. The court recognizes the basic need of the President and his White House staff to monitor the consistency of executive agency regulations with Administration policy. He and his White House advisers surely must be briefed fully and frequently about rules in the making, and their contributions to policymaking considered. The executive power under our Constitution, after all, is not shared—it rests exclusively with the President. . . . To ensure the President's control and supervision over the Executive Branch, the Constitution—and its judicial gloss—vests him with the powers of appointment and removal, the power to demand written opinions from executive officers, and the right to invoke executive privilege to protect consultative privacy. In the particular case of EPA, Presidential authority is clear since it has never been considered an "independent agency," but always part of the Executive Branch.

The authority of the President to control and supervise executive policymaking is derived from the Constitution; the desirability of such control is demonstrable from the practical realities of administrative rulemaking. Regulations such as those involved here demand a careful weighing of cost, environmental, and energy considerations. They also have broad implications for national economic policy. Our form of government simply could not function effectively or rationally if key executive policymakers were isolated from each other and from the Chief Executive. Single mission agencies do not always have the answers to complex regulatory problems. An over-worked administrator exposed on a 24–hour basis to a dedicated but zealous staff needs to know the arguments and ideas of policymakers in other agencies as well as in the White House.

We recognize, however, that there may be instances where the docketing of conversations between the President or his staff and other

Executive Branch officers or rulemakers may be necessary to ensure due process. This may be true, for example, where such conversations directly concern the outcome of adjudications or quasi-adjudicatory proceedings; there is no inherent executive power to control the rights of individuals in such settings. Docketing may also be necessary in some circumstances where a statute like this one *specifically requires* that essential "information or data" upon which a rule is based be docketed. But in the absence of any further Congressional requirements, we hold that it was not unlawful in this case for EPA not to docket a face-to-face policy session involving the President and EPA officials during the post-comment period, since EPA makes no effort to base the rule on any "information or data" arising from that meeting. Where the President himself is directly involved in oral communications with Executive Branch officials, Article II considerations—combined with the strictures of *Vermont Yankee*—require that courts tread with extraordinary caution in mandating disclosure beyond that already required by statute.

The purposes of full-record review which underlie the need for disclosing ex parte conversations in some settings do not require that courts know the details of every White House contact, including a Presidential one, in this informal rulemaking setting. After all, any rule issued here with or without White House assistance must have the requisite *factual support* in the rulemaking record, and under this particular statute the Administrator may not base the rule in whole or in part on any *"information or data"* which is not in the record, no matter what the source. The courts will monitor all this, but they need not be omniscient to perform their role effectively. Of course, it is always possible that undisclosed Presidential prodding may direct an outcome that *is* factually based on the record, but different from the outcome that would have obtained in the absence of Presidential involvement. In such a case, it would be true that the political process did affect the outcome in a way the courts could not police. But we do not believe that Congress intended that the courts convert informal rulemaking into a rarified technocratic process, unaffected by political considerations or the presence of Presidential power. In sum, we find that the existence of intra-Executive Branch meetings during the post-comment period, and the failure to docket one such meeting involving the President, violated neither the procedures mandated by the Clean Air Act nor due process.

Finally, EDF challenges the rulemaking on the basis of alleged Congressional pressure, citing principally two meetings with Senator Byrd. EDF asserts that under the controlling case law the political interference demonstrated in this case represents a separate and independent ground for invalidating this rulemaking. . . .

D.C. Federation [*v. Volpe*, 459 F.2d 1231 (D.C.Cir.1971), discussed in § 3.3.5 N.4,] requires that two conditions be met before an administrative rulemaking may be overturned simply on the grounds of Congressional pressure. First, the content of the pressure upon the Secretary is designed to force him to decide upon factors not made relevant by

Congress in the applicable statute.... Second, the Secretary's determination must be affected by those extraneous considerations.

In the case before us, there is no persuasive evidence that either criterion is satisfied. Senator Byrd requested a meeting in order to express "strongly" his already well-known views that the SO_2 standards' impact on coal reserves was a matter of concern to him. ... Americans rightly expect their elected representatives to voice their grievances and preferences concerning the administration of the laws. We believe it entirely proper for Congressional representatives vigorously to represent the interests of their constituents before administrative agencies engaged in informal, general policy rulemaking, so long as individual Congressmen do not frustrate the intent of Congress as a whole as expressed in statute, nor undermine applicable rules of procedure. Where Congressmen keep their comments focused on the substance of the proposed rule—and we have no substantial evidence to cause us to believe Senator Byrd did not do so here[539]—administrative agencies are expected to balance Congressional pressure with the pressures emanating from all other sources. To hold otherwise would deprive the agencies of legitimate sources of information and call into question the validity of nearly every controversial rulemaking.

Notes and Questions

1. *Contrasting views.* Obviously *Home Box Office* and *Sierra Club* present diametrically opposing views on the subject of ex parte communications in informal rulemaking. Which perspective is more persuasive?

Consider the reasoning of *Home Box Office*. There Judge Wright (generally known to be the author of the court's per curiam opinion) emphasized the reviewing court's interest in conducting effective review of the merits of the FCC rule. Is a prohibition on ex parte contacts in rulemaking necessary in order to enable courts to review the "full administrative record," as he suggests? Does *Sierra Club* effectively answer this point?

The court in *Home Box Office* seemed to be particularly concerned that the rulemaking record on judicial review will not reflect an agency's actual basis of decision unless it contains all ex parte communications to the agency. Was the court correct to say that, under the circumstances of this case, it "cannot presume that the agency has acted properly"? Is the court's concern limited to the problem of ex parte communications or is it a problem inherent in all administrative decisionmaking processes? Professor Nathanson responds:

---

539. The only hint we are provided that extraneous "threats" were made comes from a newspaper article which states, in part:

> The ceiling decision came after two weeks of what one Senate source called "hardball arm-twisting" by Byrd and other coal state Senators. Byrd summoned [EPA Administrator] Costle and White House adviser Stuart Eizenstat *strongly hinting* that the Administration needs his sup-

port on strategic arms limitation treaty (SALT) and the windfall profits tax, according to Senate and Administration sources.

The Washington Post, May 5, 1979, at A–1 (emphasis supplied). We do not believe that a single newspaper account of strong "hint[s]" represents substantial evidence of extraneous pressure significant enough to warrant a finding of unlawful congressional interference.

So far as judicial review is concerned, if the formulation given is an appropriate one under the governing statute, that should be sufficient to sustain the administrative action. It might be that administrative action was also motivated by some other policy considerations which could not be so easily articulated or which had no relation to the acknowledged purposes of the statute or the agency. Such ulterior purposes might or might not be suggested by disclosure of ex parte communications. Even so it is hard to see why the existence of such ulterior motives should be the proper concern of a reviewing court, any more than it would be if the court were reviewing the reasonableness of legislation.

Nathaniel L. Nathanson, "Report to the Select Committee on Ex Parte Communications in Informal Rulemaking Proceedings," 30 Admin.L.Rev. 377, 395 (1978). Do you agree with Nathanson?

Thirdly, *Home Box Office* relied on considerations of "fundamental fairness." Such fairness concerns are well recognized in the context of formal adjudication; why are they of "questionable utility" in informal rulemaking, as the court in *Sierra Club* asserts? Because ex parte contacts in informal rulemaking are not unfair at all? Or merely because any such unfairness is outweighed by beneficial aspects of ex parte contacts, or is beyond the authority of the courts to rectify?

2. *Political rulemaking.* Note that *Sierra Club* rests on an assumption that politics has a large role to play in rulemaking. For an even blunter endorsement of a political, rather than judicial or technocratic, model of the rulemaking process, consider Professor (now Justice) Scalia's reaction to the court's reasoning in *Home Box Office.* He urged that oral ex parte communications be allowed in rulemaking and that they be excluded from the official agency rulemaking record:

> It is unquestionably true that the regulated industries have had—to use the censorious phrase adopted by the *Home Box Office* case— "undue" influence in the rulemaking decisions of their governing agencies. The court might have added that Ralph Nader, Common Cause, and the Sierra Club have also had "undue" influence—in the sense that their positions, like those of the proximately affected industries, have been given greater weight than positions espoused by, let us say, private citizens such as you and me. The rulemaking process has assuredly not been an open forum producing an ultimate decision which values each presentation on the basis of its intrinsic intellectual worth, with no regard to the *political power* of its proponent.... This process of accommodating public desires, including the ardent support or vehement opposition of interest groups most proximately affected, is an essential part of the democratic process, however untidy and unanalytic it may be.... An agency will be operating politically blind if it is not permitted to have frank and informal discussions with members of Congress and the vitally concerned interest groups; and it will often be unable to fashion a politically acceptable (and therefore enduring) resolution of regulatory problems without some process of negotiation off the record.

Antonin Scalia, "Two Wrongs Make a Right: The Judicialization of Standardless Rulemaking," Regulation, July–Aug. 1977, at 38, 40–41.

Scalia concluded that a prohibition of ex parte communications would increase the likelihood that agency rulemaking would be politically unacceptable to the legislature and the people. This, in turn, would lead to three undesirable consequences. First, since it will be more difficult for an agency to gauge the political acceptability of its rules, the legislature will be required to intervene into agency rulemaking to avoid an increased number of unacceptable rules. Second, this increased need for intervention will generate tension between the agencies and Congress, making it increasingly difficult for them to get along on a day-to-day basis. Third, substantial and unnecessary costs would be imposed on regulated persons and agencies when rules turn out in the end to be politically unacceptable and, therefore, are reversed by action of the legislature.

Does Scalia—or for that matter *Sierra Club*—press the political model of rulemaking too far? Consider the analysis of Professor Glen Robinson, who was a member of the FCC when it decided *Home Box Office*, and who now views that case's position with ambivalence:

In support of allowing ex parte contacts is the argument from participation: ex parte contacts promote such participation by lessening the burdens thereof. ... Burdening information flows with the formality of notice to other parties and incorporation of information into an official record ... may be enough to discourage valuable communications with interested persons.

Moreover, informal communications can facilitate a real dialogue on policy issues. ... Confronted with often prodigious quantities of information in the form of briefs and written comments, the decision makers find themselves searching for some way to get to the heart of the matter. ... Ex parte communications between officials and outside parties is a way of checking staff-provided information and interpretation. It is a means of avoiding the problem of "staff capture," which is one of the most frustrating problems confronting higher echelon agency officials.

However, if the foregoing considerations argue against restrictions on ex parte contacts, they do so equivocally. ... When interested persons are able to present their facts and arguments to individual agency members and staff off the record, there is no check on the reliability of information presented to the decisionmakers. This raises obvious questions of fairness, as well as substantive problems of effectiveness and efficiency. ... Regulatory policymakers are often forced to place great reliance on oral briefing and discussion because of the massive quantities of paper confronting them. However, this produces a situation where even the most carefully produced commentary of one party can be negated by the offhand comments of another. Informal exchanges reinforce the natural disposition of busy agency officials to define data as the plural of anecdote. ...

As to the point that ex parte communications help to promote a real dialogue among the parties, which, inter alia, facilitates compromise and negotiated settlement, it must be asked whether this is the proper aim of agency rule making. ... Bargaining may or may not be the appropriate means for resolving disputes (it depends on the nature of the interests at stake), but in no circumstance is it appropriate without rules that prevent public policy decisions turning on who was able to contact whom, when, and so forth. This is the whole point of having a structured rule-making process.... [T]he notion that agencies are constrained by legal standards and formal processes, if it means anything, must mean that the administrative process is constrained by tighter standards of regularity and objectivity [than mere assessment of the intensity of the leading protagonists' preferences]. ... If what we are looking for is some set of constraints on the process that will help to ensure reasonably principled judgments by administrative decision makers, then it is necessary to set some formal boundaries on the kind of influences that are appropriate. The rule of law demands no less.

Glen O. Robinson, AMERICAN BUREAUCRACY: PUBLIC CHOICE AND PUBLIC LAW 144–49 (1991). For a fuller discussion, see Ernest Gellhorn & Glen O. Robinson, "Rulemaking 'Due Process': An Inconclusive Dialogue," 48 U.Chi.L.Rev. 201 (1981).

3. *Switching off HBO.* As *Sierra Club* notes, the *Home Box Office* case met with strong criticism almost from the moment it was decided. Soon other panels of the same court began questioning it and trying to narrow its reach. *See, e.g., Action for Children's Television v. FCC,* 564 F.2d 458 (D.C.Cir.1977). No doubt the decision in *Vermont Yankee* the following year also raised doubts about the permissibility of the court's holding. In any event, ever since the announcement of the *Sierra Club* opinion, judicial efforts to purge ex parte communications from informal rulemaking have essentially vanished from the case law. Nor have state courts shown any inclination to embrace the broad principles of *Home Box Office* in ordinary notice and comment rulemaking. *See, e.g., Massachusetts State Pharmaceutical Ass'n v. Rate Setting Comm'n,* 438 N.E.2d 1072 (Mass.1982); *Citizens Ass'n of Georgetown v. Zoning Comm'n,* 392 A.2d 1027 (D.C.1978).

Notice, however, that *Sierra Club* did indicate that ex parte contacts may be restricted where agency action involves "quasi-adjudication among 'conflicting private claims to a valuable privilege.' " That phrase was drawn from *Sangamon Valley Television Corp. v. United States,* 269 F.2d 221 (D.C.Cir.1959), which was also cited in *Home Box Office. Sangamon* was an FCC proceeding that involved the allocation of television channels between two communities. A Channel 2 slot on the VHF spectrum would be assigned to either the St. Louis market or the Springfield, Illinois, market. The other market would get a less profitable UHF frequency. Strictly speaking, this was a rulemaking proceeding, because the allocation of slots was to be permanent and thus could affect an indefinite number of licensees in the two cities over time. In the short run, however, two existing broadcasters in St. Louis and Springfield knew that one of them would be the main immediate beneficiary of the FCC's decision. The Commission decided to assign Channel 2 to St. Louis, but when the court learned that the St. Louis broadcaster had engaged in extensive ex parte lobbying of FCC commissioners (including visiting them in their offices, taking them to lunch, and sending them turkeys at Christmas), it invalidated the FCC's decision, stating that "basic fairness requires such a proceeding to be carried on in the open." In light of *Vermont Yankee,* should the court in *Sierra Club* have declared that the *Sangamon* holding was no longer viable?

4. *Written summary of ex parte communications.* Relying upon a specific provision in the Clean Air Act, the *Sierra Club* case requires a summary in the agency rulemaking record of oral and written ex parte communications if EPA finds them to be "of central relevance to the rulemaking." This obligation stops short of the *Home Box Office* requirement that *all* ex parte contacts during a rulemaking proceeding must be summarized for the record. Could a court impose the *Sierra Club* obligation in ordinary § 553 rulemaking, in the absence of a similar statute? *See Board of Regents of Univ. of Wash. v. EPA*, 86 F.3d 1214 (D.C.Cir.1996).

In any event, some agencies have imposed such restrictions upon themselves. *See* ACUS, A GUIDE TO FEDERAL AGENCY RULEMAKING 230–32 (2d ed.1991). For example, EPA now requires that the public record of its rulemaking proceedings (not just those under the Clean Air Act) must include ex parte written comments, as well as summaries of "significant new factual data or information likely to affect the final decision received during a meeting." Regulations of the Federal Emergency Management Agency similarly require disclosure of summaries of outside communications with "significant information and argument respecting the merits of the proposed rule." *Id.*

Contrast the approach of the 1981 MSAPA. It requires all *written* materials received or considered by an agency to be included in the record; but it does not prohibit *oral* ex parte communications, nor does it require any disclosure of them in the rulemaking record. MSAPA § 3–112(b)(3). The drafters of that Act specifically considered, but rejected, a proposal requiring agencies to summarize in writing, and include in the agency rulemaking record, all factual material relevant to the merits of a proposed rule received during oral ex parte communications. The reporter of that Act explained the rejection of this proposal as follows:

> First, it would be almost impossible to enforce such a requirement. That is so because it would be virtually impossible to demonstrate, in any situation, that factual matter relevant to the technical merits of a rule, rather than opinion or political information, was the substance of an oral ex parte conversation whose content was omitted from the agency rule-making record. Nevertheless, the possibility of success, no matter how remote, and the facial legitimacy of attempts to demonstrate a violation of such a requirement, may induce, and will facilitate, lawsuits whose only purpose is to delay the rule-making process....

> Second, it would be very difficult for agencies and courts to draw a clear line between factual information relevant to the technical merits of a proposed rule contained in oral ex parte communications, which must be reduced to writing and included in the agency rule-making record, and material of an opinion or political nature not relevant to the technical merits of a proposal, which therefore need not be included in the agency rule-making record. Finally, it is unlikely that significant or dispositive factual information relevant to the technical merits of a proposed rule will often be communicated to an agency through *oral* ex parte communications.... Even if opposing parties initially discover agency reliance on such information ... only in the required reasons statement issued at the time the rule [is] adopted, they ... can petition

the agency ... for a reconsideration of its action, and include in that petition material rebutting the previously unknown factual data on which the agency relied. In addition, all of that rebuttal material will be in the record before the court when it judicially reviews the substantive validity of the rule.

Arthur Earl Bonfield, STATE ADMINISTRATIVE RULE MAKING 340–41 (1986). Are the EPA and FEMA policies too strict? Or is the MSAPA too lenient?

5. *Executive branch intervention in rulemaking.* Presidents (and governors) frequently have an intense interest in pending agency rulemaking proceedings, because such rules may either obstruct or promote their own political agendas. For example, the President may be concerned that a rule would be too costly to business, or that it may not do enough to protect the public. Did the court in *Sierra Club* hold the President to a more lenient standard than other interested persons? Is a double standard justified?

In *Sierra Club*, the court cited ACUS Recommendation 80–6, "Intragovernmental Communications in Informal Rulemaking Proceedings," 45 Fed. Reg. 86407 (1980), which recommended that rulemaking agencies "should be free to receive written or oral policy advice at any time from the President, advisers to the President, the Executive office of the President, or other administrative bodies," without any duty of disclosure except to the extent these communications "contain material factual information (as distinct from indications of governmental policy) pertaining to or affecting a proposed rule." However, eight members of ACUS filed a separate statement, stating in part:

> We oppose this recommendation because we believe that Executive Branch agencies should be encouraged to disclose, not withhold, all of the factors which may have influenced their decisions in informal rulemaking. The public's right to know the reasons for a decision far outweighs agency decisionmakers' rights to secrecy. ...

> This recommendation extends beyond the President and his closest advisors and allows all Executive Branch agencies to involve themselves secretly in informal rulemaking. In our view agencies should be encouraged to provide their views during the public comment period so that the public might respond, or at least be aware of the views expressed. The recommendation actually encourages Executive Branch agencies as well as the White House to wait until the public record is closed before making their views known. ...

> In all likelihood this recommendation will expose agency heads to increased political pressures [based on] considerations other than those made relevant by the statutes which the particular rulemaking implements. Moreover, the courts will be unable to serve as a check upon consideration of statutorily irrelevant factors since they cannot review that which is not disclosed.

Who had the better of this argument? *See generally* Paul L. Verkuil, "Jawboning Administrative Agencies: Ex Parte Contacts by the White House," 80 Colum.L.Rev. 943 (1980).

Since 1981 Presidents have entrusted the Office of Information and Regulatory Affairs (OIRA), a subdivision of the Office of Management and Budget (OMB), with a supervisory role over agency rulemaking. Political and policy factors, as well as purely technical factors, may influence OIRA in its performance of this role. In a subsequent recommendation, ACUS proposed that "official written policy guidance" from OIRA to rulemaking agencies should be disclosed when a proposed or final rule is published, but oral communications need not be. ACUS Recommendation 88–9, 54 Fed.Reg. 5207 (1989). We consider the issues raised by this recommendation in § 7.8 N.7. This later recommendation did not, however, apply to ad hoc intervention in rulemaking by the President personally.

6. *Congressional intervention in rulemaking.* The language in *Sierra Club* endorsing congressional advocacy of constituents' interests before administrative agencies has been frequently quoted. Following out its logic, suppose an agency generally requires disclosure of ex parte contacts in rulemaking (either under a specific statute like the Clean Air Act or under agency regulations). Should members of Congress be required to submit their comments for the record during the comment period just like any other interested person? Or should they be exempted from disclosure under the same circumstances as those in which intra-executive contacts would be exempted pursuant to the ACUS recommendation discussed in the preceding note?

Notice footnote 539 of *Sierra Club*, discussing the allegation that Senator Byrd (who at the time was Senate Majority Leader) had offered to trade his support for the SALT treaty for concessions on the sulfur dioxide rule. Was the petitioners' problem that they did not have enough proof, or that the senator's conduct would not have warranted invalidation of the rule even if it had been proved?

7. *Problem.* The Madison Transportation Department (MTD) is responsible for planning the development of public transit systems in the state. Recently the department had to determine the route for an extension of the Monroe City subway system from one of its existing stations to a nearby airport. The most controversial question was whether the new line should run along the east side or the west side of Van Buren Park. Fillmore University lies along most of the eastern edge of the park, and it hoped for a subway stop on the east side for the convenience of its students and faculty. Tyler Corp., an office equipment company, has a headquarters building on the west side of the park. It favored the western route, with a stop benefiting its customers and employees. Either route would also run directly past a few small businesses and residences.

MTD commenced a notice and comment rulemaking proceeding to decide the route question. The lengthiest comments were submitted by the university and the company, each promoting its preferred route on the basis of factors such as the number of passengers who would use the new line, cost of construction, prospects for commercial development near the new station, etc. After receiving these and other written submissions, MTD held a town-meeting style public hearing about the route question. Sixty days later the department announced that it had chosen the western route.

Soon afterwards, press accounts described how lobbyists from the Tyler company had visited the state capitol after the comment period and met with department officials to urge selection of the western route. Reportedly they assured MTD that Tyler was planning a huge expansion of its operations at its facility in Monroe City, although for competitive reasons these plans had not been spelled out in Tyler's public statement. Fillmore wants to know whether it has any grounds for legal challenge because of Tyler's ex parte contacts. Assume that the department will not contest the truth of the press stories, but that no statutes or regulations purport to prohibit, or require disclosure of, oral ex parte communications during the department's rulemaking proceedings.

§ 5.5.3   BIAS AND PREJUDGMENT

Recall the material in § 3.2.3 on the various forms of bias that disqualify an adjudicatory decisionmaker. Which, if any, of those forms should disqualify a rulemaker? What would be the statutory or constitutional basis for such disqualification?

ASSOCIATION OF NATIONAL ADVERTISERS, INC. v. FEDERAL TRADE COMMISSION

627 F.2d 1151 (D.C.Cir.1979).

[In 1978, the FTC issued a notice of proposed rulemaking that suggested restrictions regarding television advertising directed toward children. The rule would have banned televised advertising for any product that is directed to children too young to understand the selling purpose of the ad. It also would have banned ads for sugared food products directed to children. Several trade associations sued to prohibit Michael Pertschuk, Chairman of the FTC, from participating in the proceeding.

Before the issuance of the notice, Pertschuk had written and spoken extensively in a variety of settings about children's television. In one speech, he referred to the "moral myopia of children's television advertising" and declared that "advertisers seize on the child's trust and exploit it as a weakness for their gain." He went on to ask: "Shouldn't society apply the law's strictures against commercial exploitation of children, and the law's solicitude for the health of children to ads that threaten to cause imminent harm—harm which ranges from increasing tooth decay and malnutrition to injecting unconscionable stress into the parent-child relationship?" He said in a letter: "Setting legal theory aside, the truth is that we've been drawn into this issue because of the conviction ... that one of the evils flowing from the unfairness of children's advertising is the resulting distortion of children's perceptions of nutritional values." In an interview with *Newsweek*, he said: "Commercialization of children has crept up on us without scrutiny or action. It is a major, serious problem. I am committed to taking action." The plaintiffs produced many other quotations from Pertschuk to similar effect.]

TAMM, J: . . .

The district court, citing this court's decision in *Cinderella Career & Finishing Schools, Inc. v. FTC*, 425 F.2d 583 (D.C.Cir.1970) [discussed at § 3.3.3 N.3], found that Chairman Pertschuk had prejudged issues involved in the rulemaking and ordered him disqualified. We hold that the *Cinderella* standard is not applicable to the Commission's rulemaking proceeding. An agency member may be disqualified from such a proceeding only when there is a clear and convincing showing that he has an unalterably closed mind on matters critical to the disposition of the rulemaking. Because we find that the appellees have failed to demonstrate the requisite prejudgment, the order of the district court is reversed. . . .

In *Cinderella,* we held that the standard for disqualifying an administrator in an adjudicatory proceeding because of prejudgment is whether "a disinterested observer may conclude that [the decisionmaker] has in some measure adjudged the facts as well as the law of a particular case in advance of hearing it." . . .

The district court in the case now before us held that "the standard of conduct delineated in *Cinderella*" governs agency decisionmakers participating in a section 18 proceeding. Section 18 [of the FTC Act, added by the Magnuson–Moss Warranty—Federal Trade Commission Improvement Act of 1974,] authorizes the Commission to promulgate rules designed to "define with specificity acts or practices which are unfair or deceptive." . . . The district court ruled that a section 18 proceeding, notwithstanding the appellation rulemaking, "is neither wholly legislative nor wholly adjudicative." According to the district court, the "adjudicative aspects" of the proceeding render *Cinderella* applicable.

The appellees . . . emphasize two allegedly "adjudicatory aspects" of a section 18 proceeding: (1) interested persons are entitled [by statute] to limited cross-examination of those who testify to disputed issues of material fact, and (2) [according to statute] a reviewing court must set aside any rule not supported by substantial evidence in the rulemaking record taken as a whole.

The district court's characterization of section 18 rulemaking as a . . . quasi-adjudicative proceeding ignores the clear scheme of the APA. Administrative action pursuant to the APA is either adjudication or rulemaking. The two processes differ fundamentally in purpose and focus. . . .

. . . Congress has, in [section 18] and elsewhere, enacted specific statutory rulemaking provisions that require more procedures than those of section 553 but less than the full procedures required under sections 556 and 557. The presence of procedures not mandated by section 553, however, does not, as the appellees urge, convert rulemaking into quasi-adjudication. The appellees err by focusing on the details of administrative process rather than the nature of administrative action.

[T]he Commission's children's advertising inquiry is designed to determine whether certain acts or practices will, in the future, be considered to contravene the FTC Act. The proceeding is not adjudication or quasi-adjudication. It is a clear exercise of the Commission's rulemaking authority.

The appellees also argue that we must apply *Cinderella* because it involves a factual prejudgment similar to the one now before us. In *Cinderella*, Chairman Dixon made statements that reflected prejudgment that Cinderella Career & Finishing Schools, Inc. had engaged in certain acts. In this case, the appellees accuse Chairman Pertschuk of prejudging issues of material fact in the children's television proceeding. We find that the appellees' argument belies a misunderstanding of the factual basis of rules.

The factual predicate of a rulemaking decision substantially differs in nature and in use from the factual predicate of an adjudicatory decision. The factual predicate of adjudication depends on ascertainment of [adjudicative facts, whereas rulemaking turns on ascertainment of legislative facts] . . . .

. . . As we already have noted, legislative facts adduced in rulemaking partake of agency expertise, prediction, and risk assessment. In *Cinderella*, the court was able to cleave fact from law in deciding whether Chairman Dixon had prejudged particular factual issues. In the rulemaking context, however, the factual component of the policy decision is not easily assessed in terms of an empirically verifiable condition. Rulemaking involves the kind of issues "where a month of experience will be worth a year of hearings."

The legitimate functions of a policymaker, unlike an adjudicator, demand interchange and discussion about important issues. We must not impose judicial roles upon administrators when they perform functions very different from those of judges. . . . [38]

The *Cinderella* view of a neutral and detached adjudicator is simply an inapposite role model for an administrator who must translate broad statutory commands into concrete social policies. If an agency official is to be effective he must engage in debate and discussion about the policy matters before him. As this court has recognized before, "informal contacts between agencies and the public are the 'bread and butter' of the process of administration." . . .

Section 18 outlines a process by which the Commission must form a preliminary view on a proposed rule, must hear comment from concerned parties, and in some cases, must hold trial-type proceedings before deciding whether to promulgate a rule. There is no doubt that the

---

38. . . . As one commentator has observed in a slightly different context:

Agencies are created to maintain or to restructure certain areas of private activity in light of expressed statutory policies. Thus, unlike courts, agencies should be positive actors, not passive adjudicators.

. . . [A]n agency should not apologize for being predisposed to implementing the goals that Congress has set for it. To call such an attitude "bias" . . . misses this central point.

Pedersen, *The Decline of Separation of Functions in Regulatory Agencies*, 64 Va. L.Rev. 991, 994 (1978).

purpose of section 18 would be frustrated if a Commission member had reached an irrevocable decision on whether a rule should be issued prior to the Commission's final action. At the same time, the Commission could not exercise its broad policymaking power under section 18 if administrators were unable to discuss the wisdom of various regulatory positions. That discussion necessarily involves the broad, general characterizations of reality that we label legislative fact.

Accordingly, a Commissioner should be disqualified only when there has been a clear and convincing showing that the agency member has an unalterably closed mind on matters critical to the disposition of the proceeding. The "clear and convincing" test is necessary to rebut the presumption of administrative regularity. The "unalterably closed mind" test is necessary to permit rulemakers to carry out their proper policy-based functions while disqualifying those unable to consider meaningfully a section 18 hearing.

Chairman Pertschuk's remarks, considered as a whole, represent discussion, and perhaps advocacy, of the legal theory that might support exercise of the Commission's jurisdiction over children's advertising. The mere discussion of policy or advocacy on a legal question, however, is not sufficient to disqualify an administrator. To present legal and policy arguments, Pertschuk not unnaturally employed the factual assumptions that underlie the rationale for Commission action. The simple fact that the Chairman explored issues based on legal and factual assumptions, however, did not necessarily bind him to them forever. Rather, he remained free, both in theory and in reality, to change his mind upon consideration of the presentations made by those who would be affected.

In outlining his legal theory of "unfairness," Pertschuk suggested that children might be harmed by overconsumption of sugared products and that they might not be able to comprehend the purpose of advertising. Insofar as these conclusions are ones of fact, they are certainly of legislative facts. . . .

The appellees have a right to a fair and open proceeding; that right includes access to an impartial decisionmaker. Impartial, however, does not mean uninformed, unthinking, or inarticulate. The requirements of due process clearly recognize the necessity for rulemakers to formulate policy in a manner similar to legislative action. The standard enunciated today will protect the purposes of a section 18 [rulemaking] proceeding, and, in so doing, will guarantee the appellees a fair hearing. . . .

Reversed.

LEVENTHAL, J., concurring:

I concur in Judge Tamm's opinion for the court. . . . The application of [the disqualification] test must take into account important differences in function and functioning between the agencies and court systems. . . . In the case of agency rulemaking, . . . the decision-making officials are appointed precisely to implement statutory programs, and with the expectation that they have a personal disposition to enforce them vigilantly and effectively. . . .

One can hypothesize beginning an adjudicatory proceeding with an open mind, indeed a blank mind, a tabula rasa devoid of any previous knowledge of the matter. In sharp contrast, one cannot even conceive of an agency conducting a rulemaking proceeding unless it had delved into the subject sufficiently to become concerned that there was an evil or abuse that required regulatory response. It would be the height of absurdity, even a kind of abuse of administrative process, for an agency to embroil interested parties in a rulemaking proceeding, without some initial concern that there was an abuse that needed remedying, a concern that would be set forth in the accompanying statement of the purpose of the proposed rule. . . .

MacKinnon, J., dissenting: . . .

In my opinion the "unalterably closed mind", where it exists, in many cases is practically impossible to prove, imposes too high a barrier to the public's obtaining fair decisionmakers and is a higher standard than the Supreme Court has applied in its recent decisions. I would require any Federal Trade Commissioner to recuse himself, or failing that to be disqualified, upon a showing by a preponderance of the evidence that he could not participate fairly in the formulation of the rule because of substantial bias or prejudgment with respect to any critical fact that must be resolved in such formulation.

Also, in my view the majority opinion places too much reliance on the strict rulemaking/adjudication dichotomy, applied in earlier cases under the Administrative Procedure Act. The Magnuson–Moss Act creates a rulemaking procedure that combines elements of *both* rulemaking and adjudication, as those functions are exercised under the Administrative Procedure Act, and this blending of the two procedures makes it impossible to look at Magnuson–Moss rulemaking as anything but a combination of the two. . . .

It is true that legislators are not required to make findings of fact to support their legislation and that they cannot be disqualified by any court for bias, but there are other safeguards in the legislative process that compensate for the absence of such safeguards as are expressly imposed or implicit in the administrative process. First of all, legislators are *elected* by the voters of their district, and those in the House are elected for a relatively short term—only two years. They can be turned out very quickly if any bias they disclose offends their constituents. Secondly, there is a protection in the sheer size of Congress—535 members of the House and Senate—that implicitly diffuses bias and guarantees that impermissible bias of individual members will not control. There is safety in numbers and a biased Congressman soon loses influence among the other members, if he ever acquired any. Also, the two house system and the Presidential veto are tremendous guarantees that legislation will not be the result of individual bias or even the impermissible bias of one house. . . .

I would not restrict members of a regulatory commission in their public discussion of policy issues, and there is nothing in the requirement that rules should be promulgated after fair hearings by unbiased Commissioners that would prohibit administrators from discussing "the wisdom of various regulatory positions." The office of the Commissioner contemplates some such activity but that does not justify their overstepping ordinary bounds of reasonableness to become loud advocates and spend three months haranguing the public with their prejudgment on basic factual issues that they must eventually decide. [W]hen a decisionmaker, who must rise above partisanship, descends to vigorous and consistent advocacy over a substantial period of time and commits himself in the public mind, he jeopardizes his ability to make fair determinations and in extreme cases, such as we have here, he should be disqualified from subsequently posing as a fair decisionmaker on the subject of his advocacy.

Notes and Questions

1. *The "unalterably closed mind" standard.* Is the disqualification test articulated in *ANA* desirable? The court argues that an agency head needs to "discuss" policy options with various constituencies. Even accepting that proposition, shouldn't the courts disqualify officials who become advocates for anticipated regulations, as Pertschuk obviously did? For comprehensive analyses of the *ANA* issue, see Ernest Gellhorn & Glen O. Robinson, "Rulemaking 'Due Process': An Inconclusive Dialogue," 48 U.Chi.L.Rev. 201 (1981); Alfred S. Neely, IV, "The Duty to Act Fairly: An Alternative to the 'Unalterably Closed Mind' Standard for Disqualification of Administrators in Rulemaking," 16 New Eng.L.Rev. 733 (1981); Peter L. Strauss, "Disqualification of Decisional Officials in Rulemaking," 80 Colum.L.Rev. 990 (1980).

2. *Formalized rulemaking.* Did the court properly discount the significance of the hybrid rulemaking procedures that Congress had adopted in the Magnuson–Moss Act? Would the court also apply the *ANA* test in a situation in which Congress had mandated *formal* rulemaking under APA §§ 556–57?

3. *ANA and adjudication.* One of the plaintiffs in this case was the Kellogg Company. Suppose that, instead of launching a rulemaking proceeding, the FTC had filed an administrative complaint against Kellogg, seeking a cease and desist order that would prohibit the company from running the same sorts of advertisements that were under attack in *ANA*. Also suppose that Pertschuk had made exactly the same public pronouncements as in the real case, but that neither he nor the Commission contended that Kellogg's ads or products were materially different from those of any other cereal manufacturer. The Commission was simply using the Kellogg proceeding as a test case. Should Pertschuk have been disqualified from participating in the hypothetical case? If so, why? Should the *Cinderella* test be understood as applying only to prejudgments of adjudicative facts?

4. *State cases.* The *ANA* standard has found some acceptance in state courts. *See, e.g., Fogle v. H & G Restaurant, Inc.,* 654 A.2d 449, 459–60 (Md.1995) (refusing disqualification). Consider, however, *Mahoney v. Shinpoch,* 732 P.2d 510 (Wash.1987). The state of Washington, like other states, provides public assistance payments, known as SSP, to needy blind, elderly,

and disabled persons who also receive such benefits from the federal Social Security Administration. The federal agency distributes both sets of benefits in a single check. In 1983 Congress passed an increase in federal benefits, but allowed states to reduce their SSP benefits to offset the increase. The Washington legislature adopted a budget contemplating the use of this option, and on October 18, 1985, the Department of Social and Health Services (DSHS) commenced rulemaking proceedings to implement that intention. A hearing on that proposed rule was scheduled to be held on November 26. On November 7, nineteen days before the scheduled hearing, DSHS wrote a letter to the Social Security Administration indicating that "the state is opting to revise the SSP per the Social Security Amendments of 1983," and the federal agency notified SSP recipients that their benefits would reflect DSHS's intended reduction.

The court concluded that the DSHS letter demonstrated that the agency had made its decision before it had considered public comment on the proposed rule and, therefore, that the rule violated the state APA (similar to 1961 MSAPA § 3(a)(2)). The court wrote:

> DSHS asks us to view its November 7 directive to the Social Security Administration as merely a preliminary signalling of an intention. . . . Looking at the letter in a light most favorable to DSHS, we nevertheless must conclude that the agency had already fixed on its decision. The letter contains no conditional or qualifying language, such as "the state is considering revising the SSP" or "the state *may* revise the SSP." . . .

> Full consideration of public comment prior to agency action is both a statutory and constitutional imperative. . . . The APA contains no harmless error provision permitting an agency not to consider public comment even when the public comment proves unpersuasive; rulemaking conducted without substantial compliance with APA requirements is per se invalid.

Is this case inconsistent with *ANA*? Or is the question in *Mahoney* actually somewhat different from that in *ANA*?

5. *Problem.* Until recently, Madison engaged in extensive regulation of oil pipelines within the state. Pursuant to legislation, the Madison Public Utilities Commission is considering deregulation of the oil pipeline industry. Sludge Pipeline Co. sought to disqualify Henry, an elected member of the PUC, from participating in all present and future phases of rulemaking directed at oil pipeline deregulation.

In the two years before the attempted disqualification, Henry had become a zealous and active opponent of deregulation legislation, expressing his views in speeches, press releases, and testimony to legislative committees. His unfavorable opinion of Sludge, a proponent of the legislation, also was clear. He referred to Sludge personnel as "jackals in lambskins" and the deregulation bill as "the biggest premeditated robbery since Jesse James rode the plains, except he had more ethics. He only stole from the rich!" One press release said that Sludge was "lying to the public" and that deregulation was "nothing more than a hoax and a planned rip-off of the public."

The trial court disqualified Henry from consideration of the pending rulemaking proceeding and all future deregulation rulemaking proceedings. The case is now on appeal to the Madison Supreme Court. Should Henry have been disqualified at all? If so, should the court order his removal from (a) the pending deregulation rulemaking, (b) any future rulemaking proceedings in which Sludge participates; or (c) all future MPUC proceedings in which Sludge is a party? Or should the court hold that, in any given future case, Sludge will have to move to disqualify Henry, and the court will have to decide the disqualification issue anew at that time? *See Northwestern Bell Telephone Co., Inc. v. Stofferahn*, 461 N.W.2d 129 (S.D.1990).

§ 5.6 FINDINGS AND REASONS

CALIFORNIA HOTEL & MOTEL ASS'N v. INDUSTRIAL WELFARE COMM'N
599 P.2d 31 (Cal.1979).

[The Commission adopted Order 5–76, a rule raising wages and fixing hours and working conditions in the "public housekeeping industry" (hotel employees). The Commission had jurisdiction over fifteen industries; it had exempted seven of these—including the manufacturing, mercantile, transportation, and motion picture industries—from its regulations on hours and days of work. The Association appealed, relying on Labor Code § 1177, which provided: "Each order [rule] of the commission shall include a statement as to the basis upon which the order is predicated, and shall be concurred in by a majority of the commissioners." The court remanded the rule in a per curiam opinion.]

An effective statement of basis fulfills several functions. First, the statement satisfies the legislative mandate of section 1177. Second, the statement facilitates meaningful judicial review of agency action.... Third, the exposition requirement subjects the agency, its decisionmaking processes, and its decisions to more informed scrutiny by the Legislature, the regulated public, lobbying and public interest groups, the media, and the citizenry at large. Fourth, requiring an administrative agency to articulate publicly its reasons for adopting a particular order, rule, regulation, or policy induces agency action that is reasonable, rather than arbitrary, capricious, or lacking in evidentiary support. Fifth, by publicizing the policies, considerations and facts that the agency finds significant, the agency introduces an element of predictability into the administrative process. This enables the regulated public to anticipate agency action and to shape its conduct accordingly. Sixth, requiring an agency to publicly justify its orders, rules, regulations, and policies stimulates public confidence in agency action by promoting both the reality and the appearance of rational decisionmaking in government....

A central function of a statement of basis is to facilitate judicial review of agency action. ... A reviewing court will ask three questions [when it reviews a rule]: first, did the agency act within the scope of its delegated authority; second, did the agency employ fair procedures; and third, was the agency action reasonable. Under the third inquiry, a reviewing court will ... uphold the agency action unless the action is arbitrary, capricious, or lacking in evidentiary support. A court must ensure that an agency has adequately considered all relevant factors, and has demonstrated a rational connection between those factors, the choice made, and the purposes of the enabling statute. . . .

In light of these considerations, we define the standard to evaluate the statement of basis required by section 1177. . . . A statement of basis will necessarily vary depending on the material supporting an order and the terms of the order. The statement should reflect the factual, legal, and policy foundations for the action taken. The statement of basis must show that the order adopted is reasonably supported by the material gathered by or presented to the commission—through its own investigations, the wage board proceedings, and the public hearings—and is reasonably related to the purposes of the enabling statute. The statement of basis is not the equivalent of the findings of fact that a court may be required to make. A statement of basis is an explanation of how and why the commission did what it did. If terms of the order turn on factual issues, the statement must demonstrate reasonable support in the administrative record for the factual determinations. If, on the other hand, the terms of the order turn on policy choices, an assessment of risks or alternatives, or predictions of economic or social consequences, the statement of basis must show how the commission resolved conflicting interests and how that resolution led to the order chosen. If an order differentiates among classes of industries, employers, or employees, the statement of basis must show that the distinctions drawn are reasonably supported by the administrative record and are reasonably related to the purposes of the enabling statute. A statement meeting these standards will facilitate review by the judiciary, the Legislature, and the regulated public by presenting a reasoned response to or resolution of the salient comments, criticisms, issues, and alternatives developed during the commission's proceedings.

The "To Whom It May Concern" provision of Order 5–76 does not satisfy this standard. The provision is simply a recitation of the commission's authority and of the procedures outlined in sections 1171 through 1204. This purported statement of basis does not fulfill any of the functions of an effective statement outlined above.

The commission argues that even if the "To Whom It May Concern" provision does not satisfy the statement of basis requirement of section 1177, the document entitled "Statement of Findings" included in the administrative record does satisfy section 1177. The commission adopted the Statement of Findings and Order 5–76 at the same meeting. The Statement of Findings does not satisfy the statement of basis requirement for several reasons.

First, section 1177 states that each order shall include a statement of basis. Sections 1182 and 1183 require that an order be published and mailed to employers. Order 5–76 does not include or even mention the Statement of Findings, and the statement was not published or mailed to employers. The statement simply remained in the administrative record. The Statement of Findings therefore does not satisfy the requirements of sections 1177, 1182, and 1183.

Second, the Statement of Findings does not address salient comments and alternatives presented during the public hearings on proposed Order 5–76. For example, the commission exempted a number of industries from its regulations covering hours and days of work, because the commission concluded that collective bargaining agreements "adequately" protected employees in those industries. However, the commission did not exempt the public housekeeping industry from coverage, even though the association presented evidence that collective bargaining in the industry was "adequate" rather than "weak." The commission did not explain how it distinguished adequate from inadequate collective bargaining agreements. The commission did not explain why it exempted other industries, but not the public housekeeping industry. Similarly, the commission reduced the workweek in the public housekeeping industry from 48 to 40 hours, without responding to the association's argument that the industry practice of having a longer workweek benefited both employers and employees because of the peak-load demand for employment peculiar to the industry. The Statement of Findings thus does not satisfy the standard of an adequate statement of basis under section 1177 outlined above.

In conclusion, the commission failed to include an adequate statement of basis in Order 5–76 as required by sections 1177, 1182, and 1184. Order 5–76 is therefore invalid as promulgated. However, the order has been in effect since 1976. The minimum wage order is of critical importance to significant numbers of employees. Those employees bear no responsibility for the deficiencies of Order 5–76. This court has inherent power to make an order appropriate to preserve the status quo pending correction of deficiencies. Order 5–76 is to remain operative pending further proceedings to be taken promptly by the commission.

The judgment is reversed with directions to issue a writ of mandate to compel the commission to take further action in a manner consistent with this opinion within 120 days of the finality of the opinion.

NEWMAN, J.—I dissent. I believe that experienced observers of how government agencies work will be astonished to learn that, when a statute requires a statement "as to the basis" on which rules are predicated, administrative rulemaking in California is now to be encumbered as [described in the majority opinion]. . . .

That much-too-detailed set of instructions to agency rulemakers should be contrasted with this introductory paragraph in § 6.01–2 of Davis, Administrative Law of the Seventies (1976): "The [Federal] Administrative Procedure Act provides in § 553 that the agency, after receiving written comments, 'shall incorporate in the rules adopted a concise general statement of their basis and purposes.' The APA does not require a statement of findings of fact. See Att'y Gen. Manual on the APA 32 (1947): 'Except as required by statutes providing for "formal" rule making procedure, findings of fact and conclusions of law are not necessary. Nor is there required an elaborate analysis of the rules or of the considerations upon which the rules were issued. Rather, the statement is intended to advise the public of the general basis and purpose of the rules.' " . . .

By no means is the To–Whom–It–May–Concern provision of Order 5–76 a model or prototype statement. It hardly merits inclusion in any formbook. In my view, though, its arguable defects have not caused prejudicial error. (Cf. Gov.Code, § 11440 ("any regulation . . . *may* be declared to be invalid for a *substantial* failure to comply"). (Italics added.) The following observations by Kenneth Culp Davis seem to me to evidence more insight as to overall fairness in governing than does the majority ("By the Court") opinion here: "[A] statement that 'findings' and 'reasons' are required for informal rulemaking would be inaccurate, for such a statement would be an oversimplification. The focus of discerning judges is not on such words as "findings' and 'reasons' but is on the total picture in each case of the reasonableness of the support for the rules in the rulemaking record and the adequacy of the agency's explanation for its determination. In most cases in which the question has been important, the adequacy of the explanation is mixed in with other facets of the challenge of the rules, so that *a focus on the explanation, without taking into account the interrelated complexities, is somewhat artificial.*"

Christian, J., concurring. . . .

It is not clear what the dissent means when it asserts that "experienced observers of how government agencies work will be astonished to learn" that this court has adopted this standard. Presumably, experienced observers of how agencies work will be familiar with developments in administrative law over the last decade. For example, students of administrative law will be familiar with the long line of cases from the federal appellate courts interpreting [federal APA] section 553(c) which contains a statement of basis requirement similar to the requirement of Labor Code section 1177. . . .

The standard adopted in the majority opinion represents a distillation of the standards articulated in these cases and commentaries. Students of administrative law familiar with these materials will not be astonished to learn that the California Supreme Court has adopted a position in line with the contemporary trend of authority.

. . . The dissent apparently is under the impression that the quoted paragraph [from Administrative Law of the Seventies] reflects Professor Davis' views on the current law pertaining to statement of basis under the federal APA. This impression is incorrect. Professor Davis quoted the Attorney General's manual merely to indicate the state of the law *in 1947.* Professor Davis then goes on to demonstrate how much the law regarding findings, reasons, statements of basis and purpose, and an agency's response to comments has evolved since then, particularly over the last 10 years. ... Perhaps the dissent is advocating that this court revert to administrative law of the 1940s. This may astonish experienced observers of how government agencies and courts work.

Notes and Questions

1. *Merits of a reasons requirement.* Are the policies identified in *California Hotel* as supporting a reasons requirement persuasive? Not everyone thinks so. Some state APAs permit agencies to issue rules without any written explanation at all. *See, e.g., District of Columbia Hospital Ass'n v. Barry*, 498 A.2d 216 (D.C.App.1985) (stating that the absence of such a requirement in the District of Columbia reflects "a deliberate policy choice" by legislative authorities). Professor Frohnmayer cites Utah as another example and defends the position of states that have made this choice:

> The rational-technical model [of rulemaking, implicit in the "reasons" requirement,] ignores the usual environment of state administrative decisionmaking. The typical state agency is not rich in staff depth. The two commodities in shortest supply in the typical state agency are likely to be political courage and executive time. The stock of each can be rapidly depleted by the burdens of this requirement. ...
>
> Furthermore, the exercise of expert judgment—and that is often the essence of a discretionary rulemaking policy choice—is often a mixture of experience, values and refined intuition. Considerations leading to the act of policy judgment may not be as easily reducible to a set of "reasons" as the 1981 MSAPA model assumes. These problems are compounded in circumstances typically encountered in state government. The agency decision may genuinely be collegial. [M]ulti-member citizen boards [may act] after hearing or reviewing hundreds of considerations from the affected public favoring or opposing a course of action. To expect the members of a body to reduce their reasoning, or to psychoanalyze that of their colleagues, into a conclusively binding set of reasons, ignores group psychology, risks extension of the decisionmaking process indefinitely, and maximizes the possibility that decisions will be based on the lowest common policy denominator. ...

Dave Frohnmayer, "National Trends in Court Review of Agency Action: Some Reflections on the Model State Administrative Procedure Act and New Utah Administrative Procedure Act," 3 BYU J.Pub.L. 1, 11–12 (1989). How persuasive is this analysis? On the facts of the *California Hotel* case, would you agree with the court that the Industrial Labor Commission's rule deserved to be remanded for want of a proper explanation?

2. *"Concise and general"?* The question of whether a state should require an explanatory statement at all is closely related to the question of how broadly existing requirements should be construed. Clearly the court in *California Hotel* read § 1177 more expansively than its words would demand. The federal courts have taken a similar path. Although Justice Newman's dissent reflects what is probably an accurate understanding of the originally intended meaning of the "concise general statement ... of basis and purpose" language of federal APA § 553(c), Justice Christian's concurrence correctly recognizes that the federal courts have applied that provision

in a much more stringent manner than its drafters anticipated. As the court in *Automotive Parts & Accessories Ass'n v. Boyd*, 407 F.2d 330, 338 (D.C.Cir. 1968), stated:

> [I]t is appropriate for us to ... caution against an overly literal reading of the statutory terms 'concise' and 'general.' These adjectives must be accommodated to the realities of judicial scrutiny, which do not contemplate that the court itself will, by a laborious examination of the record, formulate in the first instance the significant issues faced by the agency and articulate the rationale of their resolution. We do not expect the agency to discuss every item of fact or opinion included in the submissions made to it in informal rule making. We do expect that, if the judicial review which Congress has thought it important to provide is to be meaningful, the "concise general statement of ... basis and purpose" mandated by Section [553] will enable us to see what major issues of policy were ventilated by the informal proceedings and why the agency reacted to them as it did.

One tangible measure of the evolution of statements of basis and purpose in federal regulation comes from *Sierra Club v. Costle*, 657 F.2d 298 (D.C.Cir.1981), excerpted in § 5.5.2. The rule involved in that case and its accompanying statement filled 43 pages in the Federal Register. (The record in that case contained over 2520 submissions, including almost 1400 rule-making comments.) *Id.* at 314 n.22.

The *Auto Parts* gloss on § 553(c) tends to blur the contrast between the wording of that provision and the more detailed requirements that Congress has imposed on agencies engaged in *formal* proceedings (either rulemaking or adjudication). *See* APA § 557(c)(A). Why *shouldn't* the APA be read literally and as originally intended? Does *Auto Parts* violate the letter, or at least the spirit, of *Vermont Yankee*?

3. *"Major issues of policy."* The court in *Auto Parts* says that only "major issues of policy" need be addressed in a statement of basis and purpose. That phrase is not self-defining, of course. In practice, federal courts tend to equate the question of whether a statement of basis and purpose was adequate with the question of whether the agency's explanation is sufficient to prevent the rule from being held arbitrary and capricious on the merits. *See, e.g., Independent U.S. Tanker Owners Comm. v. Dole*, 809 F.2d 847 (D.C.Cir.1987); *Trans-Pacific Freight Conf. v. Federal Maritime Comm'n*, 650 F.2d 1235, 1249–50 (D.C.Cir.1980).

A practical difficulty that agencies face when they try to comply with the dictates of *Auto Parts* is that an agency cannot always anticipate what issues a court will consider important. The unpredictability of this criterion gives the agency an incentive to plan for the "worst case" scenario. Thus, although the *Auto Parts* opinion, as quoted above, says that only "major issues of policy" need be addressed, some scholars argue that, in reality, the federal courts' approach to judicial review forces agencies to discuss their rules in extravagant detail, with debilitating effects on the overall rulemaking process. We treat this controversy in greater depth in § 9.5.

4. *Responses to comments.* Modern federal cases have declared that an agency must explain how and why it reacted to important comments it

received during the course of the rulemaking proceeding. As the court stated in *Rodway v. USDA,* 514 F.2d 809, 817 (D.C.Cir.1975):

> The basis and purpose statement is not intended to be an abstract explanation addressed to imaginary complaints. Rather, its purpose is, at least in part, to respond in a reasoned manner to the comments received, to explain how the agency resolved any significant problems raised by the comments, and to show how that resolution led the agency to the ultimate rule. ... The basis and purpose statement is inextricably intertwined with the receipt of comments.

However, this does not mean that an agency must respond to every argument it receives—only to arguments that are significant and material. *See American Mining Cong. v. USEPA,* 907 F.2d 1179, 1188 (D.C.Cir.1990) (test is whether the comment, if true, would require a change in the rule). Comments that are speculative, or that do not show why or how they are relevant to the proceeding, need not be considered or answered. *See Public Citizen v. FAA,* 988 F.2d 186 (D.C.Cir.1993) (unsupported speculation); *Northside Sanitary Landfill, Inc. v. Thomas,* 849 F.2d 1516 (D.C.Cir.1988) (relevance of 420 pages of submitted documents was facially unclear and petitioner did not specifically explain their relevance).

5. *Legislative specification.* Should an obligation to respond to comments be codified explicitly in an administrative procedure act? Section 3–110(a) of the 1981 MSAPA has been criticized for omitting a requirement that the explanatory statement contain all of "the arguments for and against the rule considered by the agency," as well as the agency's "reasons for rejecting the arguments against adoption of the rule." That language did appear in an earlier draft of the 1981 Model Act, as prepared by its reporter. Similar language also appears in § 3(a)(2) of the 1961 Model State APA and in the acts of many states. Nevertheless, the Commissioners purposely deleted this language when they adopted the new Model Act. The reporter believes the Commissioners erred:

> The omitted [language is] very desirable for a number of reasons. Most importantly, forcing an agency to articulate all of the arguments raised in the proceeding for and against the rule would effectively require the agency to structure its consideration of the rule in a useful manner. This requirement would also help assure that the agency in fact considers all submissions made to it in that rule-making proceeding.... So, too, the requirement that the agency formally and clearly articulate all of the grounds for overruling the arguments made against a rule will force the agency to do that which it is supposed to do in any event: directly confront all objections to a proposed rule and determine whether they are sufficient to prevent its adoption. Requiring the agency to articulate in the concise statement the precise reasons why it rejected those arguments against the proposed rule will also facilitate public and judicial scrutiny of the rationality of the agency's action.

Arthur Earl Bonfield, "Rule Making Under the 1981 Model State Administrative Procedure Act: An Opportunity Well Used," 35 Admin.L.Rev. 77, 92 (1983). Professor Rosenblum disagrees:

> Such language would probably be harmless, but it is also needless. ... Any "concise explanatory statement" in conjunction with issuance of a

rule would be likely to contain a summary of arguments pro and con. To impose as a formal requirement, however, the stricture that reasons why arguments against the rule were rejected must be explained as a precondition to sustaining the rule's validity, would allocate inordinate decisional weight and power to the rule's opponents when it comes to judicial review. The possibility that an otherwise well-framed and reasoned rule could be invalidated because the agency failed formally to counter arguments, however specious or outlandish, advanced against it would allow rationality and common sense to be overcome by inanity or intransigence.

Victor G. Rosenblum, "Book Review," 39 Admin.L.Rev. 525, 527–28 (1987). Who has the better of this argument? Does Rosenblum's analysis suggest that the *California Hotel* opinion's rather detailed guidelines for a statement of basis were misguided, as Justice Newman's dissent maintained?

6. *Explanations on request.* One way in which a state can reduce the burdensomeness of a "reasons" requirement is to impose that obligation only where a member of the public asks for an explanation of the rule. Section 3(a)(2) of the 1961 MSAPA (incorporated in the acts of many states) requires the issuance of an explanatory statement only if the agency is "requested to do so by an interested person either prior to adoption or within 30 days thereafter." Contrast this approach to federal APA § 553(c) or § 3–110(a) of the 1981 MSAPA, both of which require agencies to provide an explanatory statement in *all* cases, not only if requested. Is that a preferable approach?

7. *Post hoc rationalizations.* Aside from the mandate of APA § 553(c), a federal agency has a further reason to make sure that its statement of basis and purpose contains a full account of its justifications for adopting a rule: If the rule is challenged in court as arbitrary and capricious, the court normally will use the agency's contemporaneously stated reasoning as the sole basis for resolving the challenge. This is the *Chenery* doctrine, which we saw in the adjudication context. *See* § 4.3 N.6. "Post hoc rationalizations" for agency action are strongly disfavored. To be sure, courts have sometimes accepted belated explanations from an agency if they "merely illuminate reasons obscured but implicit in the administrative record." But when the subsequent explanation, instead of "simply providing additional background information about the agency's basic rationale," propounds an "entirely new theory" to support the regulation, it will be rejected. *Consumer Fed'n of America v. U.S. Dep't of HHS,* 83 F.3d 1497, 1507 (D.C.Cir.1996).

Section 3–110(b) of the 1981 MSAPA codifies a version of the *Chenery* doctrine. It provides that "[o]nly the reasons contained in the concise explanatory statement may be used by any party as justifications for the adoption of the rule in any proceeding in which its validity is at issue." The language of this provision refers only to the arguments of *parties*. Should it be read to bar a court from deciding, on its own motion, to uphold a rule for reasons not articulated by the agency?

8. *Problem.* All attorneys in Madison are required to belong to the State Bar, which has statutory rulemaking power. The Bar proposed a rule that every attorney must either devote 36 hours per year to pro bono work or pay $2000 per year for the purposes of financing free legal services for the

poor. The Bar received scores of written comments both favoring and opposing the proposal. The final rule made the pro bono standard voluntary and deleted the requirement of payment. The statement accompanying the rule said: "Attorneys owe an obligation to the public to assist clients who cannot pay for services. This rule is designed to encourage attorneys to meet that obligation. Given the administrative difficulties inherent in our previous proposal, this is the right step to take now."

On judicial review, the Bar argued that one of the problems with a mandatory pro bono standard would have been the difficulty of defining what qualifies as pro bono service.

Should the court remand the rule for a better explanation? Assume, alternatively, that Madison's explanation requirements are based on those of the 1961 MSAPA, the 1981 MSAPA, the federal APA, or the Utah APA (discussed in N.1 of this section). Would any of your answers differ if the idea of mandatory pro bono service had not been raised by the Bar initially, but rather had been suggested in numerous rulemaking comments stemming from a grassroots movement led by the Madison Public Defenders Association? Finally, should the court take into account the explanation offered by the Bar at the time of judicial review?

§ 5.7   ISSUANCE AND PUBLICATION

Publication of agency rules is important, because it facilitates easy public access to their contents. That access allows affected parties to ascertain the relevant law and to adjust their conduct accordingly. Limited availability of agency rules creates a risk that individuals may be adversely affected by rules that were not only unknown to them, but that could not have been easily discovered. Because most people obey rules they know about, publication of rules also facilitates compliance with the law, thereby reducing the enforcement workload of agencies. Furthermore, the publication of rules communicates to the general public the standards by which agencies must operate, and the standards by which agencies may be measured. Publication of rules therefore helps to ensure that agencies as well as regulated parties follow the law. For all of these reasons, rules are required to be published and normally are not effective until a specified period after their publication.

Publication requirements for federal agency rules are contained in APA § 552(a)(1). These requirements, in approximately their present form, were added to the APA in 1967 as part of the Freedom of Information Act (FOIA), and some writers treat them as part of FOIA. (The main provisions of FOIA are discussed in § 8.1.)

In addition to meeting the publication requirements of the APA, federal agencies must also abide by the Federal Register Act (FRA), 44 U.S.C. §§ 1501–1511. The FRA requires the *Federal Register* to be published each federal working day. That publication includes all rules of "general applicability and legal effect" and notices of proposed rulemaking. In addition, FRA requires the publication of a complete codification of all documents having "general applicability and legal effect" that were published in the *Federal Register*. This publication is entitled the *Code of Federal Regulations* (C.F.R.) and consists of 50 titles that are arranged by subject matter similar to the U.S.Code. It is kept up to date by a process of continuous revision.

The story of the FRA's origins provides a dramatic illustration of why it is needed. The Act was a byproduct of litigation over the validity of the Petroleum Code, one of the codes of "fair competition" established during the Depression under the National Recovery Act (NRA):

> [T]here had not been devised, prior to NRA, any required, authorized, or even standard method of publishing administrative rules or decisions. It is true that Executive Orders (and codes were to be issued as such) were filed with the Secretary of State and published each year with the statutes at large. But it was not uncommon for the White House to retain orders which it preferred to keep from public view. And the Executive Orders embodying the codes were not (in many instances) even at the White House but here and there in the desk drawers of NRA officials! Such was the case with the Petroleum Code, held invalid in *Panama Refining Co. v. Ryan* [293 U.S. 388 (1935), also discussed in § 7.2.1a]. The industry used an unofficial copy. . . . The Petroleum Code had been amended. When the brief [in *Panama Refining*] came to be written it occurred to the brief writer to examine the originals (which were found with some difficulty). He discovered the sickening fact that by reason of a mistaken use of terms—the Code had been amended out of existence. . . . The President immediately supplied the missing provisions, thus making true the state of facts which had been assumed by all persons and all courts to have existed. Nevertheless the Supreme Court refused to treat the Code as properly before it. Those who heard and participated in the argument were struck by the almost gleeful eagerness with which the Court probed into the unsavory story (though it had previously been completely advised). A valuable consequence was the Federal Register Act [the same year].

Louis L. Jaffe, JUDICIAL CONTROL OF ADMINISTRATIVE ACTION 61–62 (1965).

On the state level, § 2–101 of the 1981 MSAPA requires (with certain exceptions) the periodic publication and indexing of proposed and recently adopted state agency rules in a frequently issued publication similar to the *Federal Register,* as well as the compilation and indexing of such rules in a publication similar to the C.F.R. Today, the overwhelming number of states have both types of publications. A survey completed in early 1983 revealed that published administrative rules compilations are available in thirty-three states, and codification projects were underway in at least five other states. *See* Henry P. Tseng & Donald B. Pedersen, "Acquisition of Administrative Rules and Regulations—Update 1983," 35 Admin.L.Rev. 349 (1983). Some states have lagged behind, however, such as Oklahoma, where codification did not occur until 1992. *See* Phyllis E. Bernard, "From 'Good Ol' Boys' to 'Good Young Law': The Significance of the Oklahoma Administrative Code," 18 Okla. City U.L.Rev. 267 (1993).

A general principle at both the federal and state level is that, absent good cause, a final rule does not become effective immediately upon publication or filing. Section 553(d) of the federal APA states that a final agency rule becomes effective no sooner than 30 days following publication of that final rule in the *Federal Register;* § 4(b) of the 1961 MSAPA, which has been adopted in many states, provides that a rule will become effective 20 days after its filing; and § 3–115(a) of the 1981 MSAPA states that a rule will become effective 30 days after the latest of its filing, publication, and indexing.

An important function of the delayed effectiveness provision is "to afford persons affected a reasonable time to prepare for the effective date of a rule or rules or to take any other action which the issuance of rules may prompt." U.S. Dept. of Justice, ATTORNEY GENERAL'S MANUAL ON THE ADMINISTRATIVE PROCEDURE ACT 36 (1947) (quoting from congressional reports). The delay has also proved to be of value to agencies, because it gives them time to detect and correct purely technical errors or omissions in newly adopted rules or to revise the rules in light of public reaction and unanticipated enforcement problems that surface during the pre-effective period.

NGUYEN v. UNITED STATES
824 F.2d 697 (9th Cir.1987).

Sneed, J.:

Appellee Nguyen is a retail grocer in Portland, Oregon, who was authorized to participate in the Food Stamp Program (the Program) in 1977. Retailers may not accept food stamps in exchange for non-food items. If they do so, the [Food and Nutrition Service (FNS), part of the Department of Agriculture,] can in certain circumstances penalize them with disqualification from the Program or with civil penalties.

In 1979 and again in 1980, the FNS wrote Nguyen warning him about possible violations being committed in his store. In 1981, the FNS sent undercover agents to Nguyen's store, where on six occasions they were permitted to buy conspicuous and sometimes expensive non-food items with food stamps. The salespeople specifically involved were Nguyen's sister-in-law, a store clerk, and a stock man.

Under the regulations then in effect, a previously warned retailer who maintained a "policy" of accepting food stamps for such improper items could be disqualified from the program for one year. Less severe penalties applied to violations resulting from mere carelessness or poor supervision. The FNS notified Nguyen of the violations found during the investigation and gave him an opportunity to respond. After full administrative review, the FNS imposed the stricter penalty. The FNS review officer relied in his decision in part on FNS Instruction 744–9 (the

Instruction), which is not published in Federal Register. Section III(B)(1) of the Instruction provides that as "a general rule," violations are attributable to a store's policy when at least four improper sales have been made by the owner, his close relatives, persons who run the store, or two or more clerks.

Nguyen sought review of the agency decision in district court. [He contended] that reliance on the unpublished Instruction was improper under the Freedom of Information Act (FOIA), 5 U.S.C. § 552(a)(1).... The district court ... granted summary judgment for Nguyen, ... striking down his one-year disqualification. The government appeals....

1. INTRODUCTION

The FOIA contains two provisions pertinent here. First, it requires agencies to publish in the Federal Register all "statements of general policy and interpretations of general applicability." 5 U.S.C. § 552(a)(1)(D). Second, it provides that no one may "be adversely affected" by "a matter required to be published ... and not so published." *Id.* § 552(a)(1). The Instruction here, as we have said, was never published, and Nguyen contends that these provisions invalidate his one-year disqualification. We disagree.

This circuit's precedents firmly establish that a claimant in Nguyen's position cannot succeed under § 552(a)(1) unless the unpublished material at issue affected his "substantive rights." *See, e.g.,* ... *Powderly v. Schweiker*, 704 F.2d 1092, 1098 (9th Cir.1983); ... Our earlier cases employed this substantive rights test in applying the first of the two § 552(a)(1) provisions: *i.e.,* to determine whether the agency directive had to be published. *See Powderly*, 704 F.2d at 1098.... More recently, we have used the test in construing the second provision: *i.e.,* to determine whether the directive, even if it should have been published, "adversely affected" the claimant. Thus, we must first decide whether to apply the substantive rights test to the publication requirement or to the adverse effect requirement.

2. SUBSTANTIVE RIGHTS AND THE PUBLICATION REQUIREMENT

We believe the later cases offer the best approach to this "most troublesome" problem. 1 K. Davis, *Administrative Law Treatise* § 5:10 at 341 (2d ed. 1978).

Neither the language nor the legislative history of the publication requirement suggests any connection to individuals' substantive rights. Only the phrases "of *general* applicability" and "of *general* policy" qualify which interpretations and policy-statements must be published. 5 U.S.C. § 552(a)(1)(D). Congress inserted these qualifiers where it previously had the phrase "not ... addressed to and served upon named persons." *See* S.Rep. No. 813, 89th Cong., 1st Sess. 6 (1965). The Senate characterized this change as a "technical" one, *id.*, suggesting that it considered the phrases equivalent. In an earlier version of the FOIA, Congress distinguished rules of general applicability from those that were particularized in scope, offering rates as an example of the latter. S. Rep. No. 1219, 88th Cong., 2d Sess. 4 (1964). The legislative history thus indicates a rather obvious definition of "general": that which is neither directed at specified persons nor limited to particular situations.[5]

Unquestionably, the Instruction here contained an interpretation of "general" applicability or at the very least a statement of "general" FNS policy. Therefore it ought to have been published under § 552(a)(1)(D). But this does not end the matter: § 552(a)(1) offers no relief to Nguyen unless the Instruction "adversely affected" him. On this point, the "substantive rights" test is directly apposite. The question before us, then, is whether the Instruction affected Nguyen's "substantive rights."

3. Meaning of the Substantive Rights Test

The meaning of the substantive rights test is not something that springs lightly from the page. [To] say exactly which rules "affect substantive rights"—in this context as in many others—is a problem that tends to invite over-generalization and abstraction. Our best approach is to proceed in a manner that reflects the purposes underlying the publication rule: avoidance of arbitrary agency decisionmaking and guidance for the legitimate expectations of the regulated public. In doing this, we find that three major factors should be considered in determining whether agency action affects individuals' substantive rights. Each has been considered in prior cases.

First, we have said that an unpublished interpretation affects substantive rights when it changes existing rules, policy or practice. Where an agency changes the governing rules and then applies its new policy without warning, the affected public may be unfairly and arbitrarily surprised. In this way we recognize that administrative agencies "make law" and ensure that they do so within the limits fixed by Congress.

Second, courts should consider whether the interpretation deviates from the plain meaning of the statute or regulation at issue. An agency cannot expect the public to divine its rules or interpretations. If, however, an instruction merely restates the plain meaning of statutory or regulatory terms, there will be no appearance of arbitrary decisionmak-

---

5. Moreover, linking the substantive rights test to the publication requirement, rather than to the adverse effect requirement, creates an inconsistency between 5 U.S.C. § 552 (the FOIA) and 5 U.S.C. § 553 (part of the Administrative Procedure Act (APA)). The APA exempts "interpretative rules [and] general statements of policy" from its notice-and-comment requirements. 5 U.S.C. § 553(b)(A). This court has defined such rules and policy statements as those not involving substantive rights. Thus, to define the FOIA's "statements of general policy or interpretations of general applicability" as those which *do* involve substantive rights would be to ascribe opposite meanings to essentially the same words. The logical conclusion is rather that those

non-substantive agency instructions exempted from the APA's notice-and-comment procedures are nonetheless subject to the FOIA's publication requirement.

This view is also consistent with 5 U.S.C. § 552(a)(2), which provides that agencies must make available for inspection "those statements of policy and interpretations that have been adopted by the agency and are not published in the Federal Register." This provision has sometimes been thought to conflict with § 552(a)(1)(D). Its meaning, however, is straightforward in light of the foregoing: it applies to those interpretations and policy statements directed to *particular* parties or circumstances.

ing and prior publication is much less important. "Lawmaking" by an administrative agency cannot mislead. One must know the law. However, to restate the law after having either not stated it or misstated it previously neither confers nor withdraws substantive rights. . . .

Finally, we have said that an agency rule is substantive if it is of binding force and narrowly limits administrative discretion. The public's need to know of agency interpretations is greatest when the interpretation will be *conclusive* in the agency's ultimate decision. When an agency produces a "field-level instructional guide" simply to assist its own employees in administering a regulation, it has not made law affecting substantive rights. In brief, notice must be given both to make and to change such "law." Of course, the line between judicially proper "law" made by an administrative agency and an agency interpretation that merely *recommends* guidelines or inferences for agency officials is not a bright one. Lawmaking and administration occupy different ends of a spectrum in which one softly merges into the other. Rules of thumb to guide officials, however, occupy a position on the administration side of that spectrum.

4. APPLICATION OF THE TEST TO THIS CASE

Applying these three factors to the case at hand, we conclude that Instruction 744–9 did not adversely affect Nguyen's substantive rights.

First of all, the district court specifically found that the Instruction made no change in past agency practices, and Nguyen does not contend that he was relying on any prior agency interpretations of what would constitute his store's "policy." Second, as to whether the Instruction merely restated the plain meaning of the term "policy," we agree with Nguyen that the ordinary store owner could not have anticipated that the FNS would specify four violations (or two or eight for that matter) perpetrated by the owner's family, a manager, or more than one clerk, as evidencing the operating policy of the store. However, the FNS had twice warned Nguyen that any further improper sales in his store could lead to disqualification, so even this factor does not lie entirely in his favor.

The third factor, as already suggested, tips the balance to the government's position. The Instruction's interpretation of store policy describes a *"general rule"* of persuasive, rather than conclusive, force. It is a guideline, an instruction on how to administer the law. It is worded in terms of considerations that *"may"* be used in the final determination of the appropriate penalty for Program violations. [T]he Instruction requires examination of evidence extenuating the violations, and . . . firmly directs the agency reviewer to make case-by-case determinations rather than mechanically applying per se rules. Thus section III(B)(1), of which Nguyen complains, operates essentially not to determine rights but to trigger further agency scrutiny.

We are thus convinced that the interpretation of the word "policy" contained in the Instruction did not "adversely affect" Nguyen's substantive rights within the meaning of the FOIA. . . . *Cf. Linoz v. Heckler,* 800 F.2d 871, 874, 877–78 & n. 11 (9th Cir.1986) (hearing officer's *exclusive reliance* on provisions of unpublished government claims manual that were *binding* in benefit determinations, that *changed* existing policy, and that *created exception to published regulation* violated the FOIA) (alternative holding)....

To be sure, the FNS's ultimate decision "adversely affected" Nguyen. That deprivation resulted from enforcement by the proper agency of the law promulgated by Congress. In its enforcement, the FNS primarily based its decision not on the Instruction, but rather on an independent evaluation of the seriousness of Nguyen's violations, the two prior warnings directed to him, and the failure of anyone at his store ever to refuse an improper sale.

REVERSED.

Notes and Questions

1. *The duty to publish.* The Supreme Court touched indirectly on the APA publication requirement in *Morton v. Ruiz,* 415 U.S. 199 (1974), also discussed in § 6.2.1 N.6. In that case the Bureau of Indian Affairs (BIA) instituted a practice of paying welfare benefits only to Indians who lived *on* reservations. The issue was whether Indians who live *near* reservations should also receive benefits, as they had in the past. The Court concluded that, although the latter would normally be entitled to benefits, the BIA could impose restrictions in order to deal with a budgetary shortfall. In order to invoke that option, however, the agency would have to limit benefits through a "legislative rule," i.e., a rule that had the force of law. Such a rule, the Court noted, would have to be published in the *Federal Register.* The Court found support for this publication obligation both in § 552(a)(1) of the APA and in the BIA's own regulations. In this instance, however, the agency had published its restriction only in an internal manual, so the Indians who lived near reservations could not be refused benefits on that basis.

Although frequently cited, *Ruiz* has had only limited impact on the law, in part because the Court did not probe very far into the interpretive problems surrounding § 552(a)(1), which are discussed in the *Nguyen* case and the following note. Is the holding consistent with *Nguyen?*

2. *Nonlegislative rules.* The *Nguyen* case is concerned with interpretive rules and policy statements, which lack the force of law. (These categories are discussed more fully in § 6.1.4.) Questions concerning agencies' responsibility to publish such pronouncements have caused a great deal of confusion. One clause of the APA provides for publication in the *Federal Register* of "statements of general policy or interpretations of general applicability formulated and adopted by the agency." 5 U.S.C. § 552(a)(1)(D). But another clause directs agencies to make available for public inspection and copying "those statements of policy and interpretations which have been adopted by the agency and are not published in the Federal Register." *Id.* § 552(a)(2)(B). As the *Nguyen* opinion recognizes, courts have had difficulty determining what pronouncements fall within the first of these clauses as opposed to the second.

In *New York v. Lyng,* 829 F.2d 346, 354 (2d Cir.1987), the Secretary of Agriculture declared in an interpretive ruling that a state's payment of a "restaurant allowance" to welfare recipients who could not prepare meals at home (due to disability, lack of kitchen facilities, etc.) was "income" that reduced their eligibility for food stamps. The court upheld the Secretary on the merits and also rejected a claim that the Secretary should have published his interpretation. The court concluded that

> "the requirement for publication attaches only to matters which if not published would adversely affect a member of the public." ... We adopt this reading of the statute because it comports with the stated purpose of providing guidance to the public ... and reconciles the broad language of this provision with the impracticability of publishing all interpretative rulings. Because the food stamp program is administered by the State and City of New York, which are, of course, aware of the ruling, and because no argument has been presented that any recipient might be adversely affected by its non-publication, the ruling does not come within the publication requirement of § 552.

As support for its "impracticability" argument, the court cited to Professor Davis' treatise, which says:

> Probably a requirement that *all* interpretative rules be published cannot be responsibly imposed by a court, unless the court considers such questions as whether the requirement of publication extends to (1) a written memorandum from the agency head to the staff about how to interpret something, (2) such a memorandum to one staff member, (3) an informal ruling in a particular case that is buried in the file, (4) such a ruling that is occasionally regarded as a precedent, (5) such a ruling that is the foundation for all later decisions on the subject, (6) an opinion in a formal adjudication that may or may not become a precedent, (7) an adjudicative opinion that is explicitly written for the purpose of formulating a "rule" to guide future decisions, or (8) an opinion rejecting the old "rule" and establishing a new "rule." The list could be eighty-eight instead of eight.

1 Kenneth Culp Davis, ADMINISTRATIVE LAW TREATISE § 5:11 at 342 (2d ed.1978). Should the analysis in *Nguyen* be preferred over that of *Lyng* or the *Powderly* case mentioned in the *Nguyen* opinion?

Under any of these cases, of course, an agency has only a limited incentive to publish its interpretive rules and policy statements. Indeed, it appears that agencies publish such nonlegislative rules only sporadically and haphazardly. *See* Randy S. Springer, Note, "Gatekeeping and the *Federal Register*: An Analysis of the Publication Requirement of Section 552(a)(1)(D) of the Administrative Procedure Act," 41 Admin.L.Rev. 533 (1989).

3. *Filing of rules.* Federal law and virtually all state APAs provide for the filing of rules in a designated, centrally located depository that is open to the public and independent of the issuing agency. *See* 44 U.S.C. § 1507; 1961 MSAPA § 4(a); 1981 MSAPA § 3–114(a). These statutes typically provide that an unfiled rule is wholly ineffective. *See, e.g., People v. Cull,* 176 N.E.2d 495 (N.Y.1961) (rule imposing speed limit was unenforceable because traffic commission had neglected to file it with secretary of state, although public was apprised of limit through signs on highway). What is the argument in

favor of such a requirement? Under § 3–115(a) of the 1981 MSAPA, rules generally cannot be effective prior to their publication *and* indexing *and* filing. What is the argument for requiring all three as a condition of a rule's effectiveness?

4. *Delayed effectiveness.* How does one measure the thirty days' minimum notice period required by APA § 553(d)? That question divided the court in *Rowell v. Andrus,* 631 F.2d 699 (10th Cir.1980). The Interior Department adopted an increase in the amounts to be paid by oil and gas lease owners from fifty cents per acre to a dollar per acre. The rule appeared in the Federal Register on January 5, 1977, with a stated effective date of February 1. The plaintiffs, applicants for leases who wanted to be charged the lower rate, argued that the agency had violated § 553(d). The dissent said that plaintiffs were in no position to claim any unfair surprise, because the agency had proposed the increase nine months earlier, plaintiffs had undoubtedly heard about it then, and the final rule was identical to the proposed rule. The majority, however, said that the notice of proposed rulemaking could not serve as the required publication for purposes of § 553(d); the increase could not go into effect until thirty days after a separate publication of the final rule at the time of its adoption. Which view is preferable?

5. *Remedy.* The court in *Rowell* went on to say that the Interior Department's breach of § 553(d) did not mean that the price increase on lease payments had to be vacated. Rather, the rule would simply go into effect thirty days after its publication. Does this holding leave agencies with an adequate incentive to comply with § 553(d)? Is it justifiable?

6. *Exemptions from the deferred effectiveness requirements.* The federal APA allows an agency to make a rule effective immediately "for good cause found and published with the rule." Analogously, § 3–115(b)(2)(iv) of the 1981 MSAPA contains a catch-all emergency provision stating that a rule may be made effective after filing at an earlier date than usual if the agency makes a finding that the earlier date is *"necessary* because of *imminent peril* to the public health, safety, or welfare." (Emphasis supplied). This phrase comes from § 4(b)(2) of the 1961 MSAPA and is found in APAs of many states. Note that the state language is worded more stringently than its federal counterpart. These provisions are discussed in greater detail in § 6.1.1.

Both the federal APA, § 553(d)(1), and the 1981 MSAPA, § 3–115(b)(2)(ii), provide that an agency need not delay the effective date of newly adopted rules if they grant an exemption or relieve a restriction. Since such rules confer benefits rather than impose burdens on regulated persons, those persons usually do not need and do not want a delayed effective date. They want the rules to be effective as soon as possible. Finally, the federal APA allows interpretive rules and general statements of policy to be immediately effective. § 553(d)(2).

7. *Problem.* Certain genetic abnormalities, which can be identified through genetic testing, are associated with increased risks of heart disease, colon cancer, multiple sclerosis, and other diseases. Insurers that obtain the results of genetic testing sometimes use that information as a reason to decline coverage of affected individuals or to charge them a higher rate. This

practice has been condemned as discriminatory, although the insurance industry has contended that such underwriting decisions are not based on stereotypes but on scientifically valid methods of identifying high-risk individuals whom an insurer should not have to treat in just the same way as everyone else.

Section 3 of the state of Madison's recently enacted Fair Insurance Act prohibits insurance companies from selling policies or setting rates on an unfairly discriminatory basis. It is enforced by the Madison Insurance Department (MID). An insurer that is found to have violated the Act or a regulation promulgated thereunder may be required to refund premiums to the extent of the discriminatory overcharge.

Shortly after the Act went into effect, the MID proposed a rule, to be designated Regulation 49, that would prohibit insurance companies from declining coverage or setting rates for life or health insurance on the basis of an individual's genetic history. At the same time, the Department sent a bulletin (Bulletin 320) to its regional offices, apprising them of this proposed rule. The bulletin commented that, even without a regulation, the use of genetic history in underwriting decisions appeared to violate § 3 of the Act and could be grounds for immediate enforcement action.

The Monroe County regional office of MID learned that an insurance carrier in its region, the Reputable Insurance Company, was making underwriting decisions using information from genetic testing. The office advised the company on January 15 that this practice violated § 3 and that any increased premiums attributable to such discrimination would have to be refunded. When Martin, the president of Reputable, went to see Ethel, the regional MID director, to discuss this accusation, she told him that her office was relying squarely on "Department policy" but would give him no further information.

As Reputable began preparing for litigation, Regulation 49 was published (without change) as a final rule on April 20. The rule said it was "effective immediately." The accompanying statement did not explain why immediate effectiveness was imposed.

Reputable filed suit to challenge the commission's actions. (Assume that this suit would not be dismissed on jurisdiction grounds such as exhaustion or ripeness.) Then Martin learned for the first time about Bulletin 320. He was all the more perturbed when he found out that none of the other four MID regional offices had interpreted Bulletin 320 as equating the use of genetic history for underwriting purposes with discrimination. Until Regulation 49 was finalized, the other regional offices had taken the position that the legality of this practice depended on the circumstances.

In its court action, Reputable contends that, because Bulletin 320 was never published, the company cannot be required to refund any premiums it charged prior to the effective date of Regulation 49. Reputable also contends that Regulation 49 is unlawful because it provided for immediate effectiveness instead of allowing a preparation period. The plaintiff asks the court to vacate Regulation 49, or at least to postpone its effective date until thirty days after the court has resolved the questions about the legality of genetic history underwriting and the agency's abusive conduct in regard to secret directives. How should the court respond, if Madison follows (i) federal law, or (ii) the 1981 MSAPA?

§ 5.8 REGULATORY ANALYSIS

A regulatory analysis is an intensive, formal examination by an agency of the merits of a proposed rule. It is intended to involve a more detailed and systematic assessment than is inherent in the ordinary process of notice-and-comment rulemaking. The most common variety of regulatory analysis utilizes the methods of economics to evaluate whether the benefits of a proposed rule compare favorably with its costs. A regulatory analysis that has this focus is also frequently known as a cost-benefit analysis or CBA (some writers prefer "benefit-cost analysis").

At their best, regulatory analyses can aid careful consideration of the desirability of particular rules by structuring agency consideration of their costs and benefits, their advantages and disadvantages, and the various alternatives available. In addition, regulatory analyses can help to focus public attention on, and public discussion of, proposed rules in a manner that can improve the ultimate agency decisionmaking process. An issue explored in this section is whether existing regulatory analysis schemes are designed to fulfill these objectives effectively. For detailed discussions of the policy issues presented by regulatory analysis, see Thomas O. McGarity, REINVENTING RATIONALITY (1991); Richard H. Pildes & Cass R. Sunstein, "Reinventing the Regulatory State," 62 U.Chi.L.Rev. 1 (1995); Project, "The Impact of Cost–Benefit Analysis on Federal Administrative Law," 42 Admin.L.Rev. 545 (1990).

At the federal level, a series of presidential executive orders have mandated that executive-branch agencies engage in cost-benefit analysis. These presidential directives had roots in the Nixon, Ford, and Carter administrations, but they first reached full-blown form with Executive Order 12291, 46 Fed.Reg. 13193 (1981), which was issued by President Reagan and retained by President Bush. That order was later supplanted by Executive Order 12866, 58 Fed.Reg. 51735 (1993), adopted by President Clinton. The orders have been implemented by the Office of Information and Regulatory Affairs (OIRA), a branch of the Office of Management and Budget (OMB). (The role of the executive orders in facilitating supervision of the agencies by OIRA, and ultimately by the President, is the subject of § 7.8. The present section deals primarily with the impact of regulatory analysis requirements within the agencies themselves.) Following are some of the key provisions of the Clinton order:

EXECUTIVE ORDER 12866
REGULATORY PLANNING AND REVIEW
58 Fed.Reg. 51735 (1993).

[B]y the authority vested in me as President by the Constitution and laws of the United States of America, it is hereby ordered as follows:

Sec. 1. Statement of Regulatory Philosophy and Principles.

(a) *The Regulatory Philosophy.* Federal agencies should promulgate only such regulations as are required by law, are necessary to interpret the law, or are made necessary by compelling public need, such as material failures of private markets to protect or improve the health and safety of the public, the environment, or the well-being of the American people. In deciding whether and how to regulate, agencies should assess all costs and benefits of available regulatory alternatives, including the alternative of not regulating.

Costs and benefits shall be understood to include both quantifiable measures (to the fullest extent that these can be usefully estimated) and qualitative measures of costs and benefits that are difficult to quantify, but nevertheless essential to consider. Further, in choosing among alternative regulatory approaches, agencies should select those approaches that maximize net benefits (including potential economic, environmental, public health and safety, and other advantages; distributive impacts; and equity), unless a statute requires another regulatory approach. . . .

(b) *The Principles of Regulation:* [A]gencies should adhere to the following principles, to the extent permitted by law and where applicable . . .

> (6) Each agency shall assess both the costs and the benefits of the intended regulation and, recognizing that some costs and benefits are difficult to quantify, propose or adopt a regulation only upon a reasoned determination that the benefits of the intended regulation justify its costs.

Sec. 3. Definitions.

(f) "Significant regulatory action" means any regulatory action that is likely to result in a rule that may (1) Have an annual effect on the economy of $100 million or more or adversely affect in a material way the economy, a sector of the economy, productivity, competition, jobs, the environment, public health or safety, or State, local, or tribal governments or communities. . . .

Sec. 6. Centralized Review of Regulations. . . .

[(a)(3)(C)] For those matters identified as, or determined by the Administrator of OIRA to be, a significant regulatory action within the scope of section 3(f)(1), the agency shall . . . provide to OIRA the following . . . information, developed as part of the agency's decision-making process (unless prohibited by law):

> (i) An assessment, including the underlying analysis, of benefits anticipated from the regulatory action . . . together with, to the extent feasible, a quantification of those benefits;

> (ii) An assessment, including the underlying analysis, of costs anticipated from the regulatory action . . . together with, to the extent feasible, a quantification of those costs; and

(iii) An assessment, including the underlying analysis, of costs and benefits of potentially effective and reasonably feasible alternatives to the planned regulation, identified by the agencies or the public ... and an explanation why the planned regulatory action is preferable to the identified potential alternatives. ...

SEC. 9.   AGENCY AUTHORITY.

Nothing in this order shall be construed as displacing the agencies' authority or responsibilities, as authorized by law....

SEC. 10.   JUDICIAL REVIEW.

Nothing in this Executive order shall affect any otherwise available judicial review of agency action. This Executive order is intended only to improve the internal management of the Federal Government and does not create any right or benefit, substantive or procedural, enforceable at law or equity by a party against the United States, its agencies or instrumentalities, its officers or employees, or any other person....

Notes and Questions

1. *Legislative developments.* Since the election of the 104th Congress, with its turnover in party control, the legislative branch has displayed an active interest in adopting regulatory analysis requirements of its own. The Unfunded Mandates Reform Act and the Small Business Regulatory Enforcement Act, discussed in NN. 8–9 below, were products of this burst of activity. Other measures, which did not pass, were considered under the banner of what came to be known as "regulatory reform." In the early weeks of the session, the House of Representatives passed one such bill as part of the "Contract with America." H.R. 1022, 104th Cong. (1995). In the Senate, similar bills made front-page news during the summer of 1995, as proposals for extensive requirements for cost-benefit and other types of regulatory analysis were heatedly debated in the Senate. The most prominent bill was S. 343, 104th Cong. (1995), sponsored by Senator Robert Dole. It failed because its sponsors lacked the sixty votes they needed in order to force an end to debate. Less ambitious legislation along similar lines has been introduced in the current Congress. *See* S. 981, 105th Cong. (1997).

Meanwhile, during the past decade or so, nearly half the states have amended their APAs (or in a few instances have used executive orders) to require regulatory analyses in rulemaking. *See* Richard Whisnant & Diane DeWitt Cherry, "Economic Analysis of Rules: Devolution, Evolution, and Realism," 31 Wake Forest L.Rev. 693, 694 n.2 (1996) (compiling provisions). According to these authors, "[t]he states' experience with economic analysis is problematic and unique for three main reasons: the lack of resources typically devoted to analysis of rules at the state level, the absence of staff expertise to conduct additional benefit-cost analysis, and the minimal state judicial expertise to review these analyses." *Id.* at 696–97.

2. *The merits of CBA.* The drive towards cost-benefit analysis is spurred by a widespread feeling that agencies too often take actions that are not cost-justified. Judge (now Justice) Breyer illustrates the problem:

Tunnel vision, a classic administrative disease, arises when an agency ... effectively carries single-minded pursuit of a single goal too far, to the point where it brings about more harm than good. ... The regulating agency considers a substance that poses serious risks, at least through long exposure to high doses. It then promulgates standards so stringent—insisting, for example, upon rigidly strict site cleanup requirements—that the regulatory action ultimately imposes high costs without achieving significant additional safety benefits. A former EPA administrator put the problem succinctly when he noted that about 95 percent of the toxic material could be removed from waste sites within a few months, but years are spent trying to remove the last little bit. Removing that last little bit can involve limited technological choice, high costs, devotion of considerable agency resources, large legal fees, and endless argument.

Stephen Breyer, BREAKING THE VICIOUS CIRCLE: TOWARD EFFECTIVE RISK REGULATION 11 (1993).

Yet cost-benefit analysis requirements have been criticized on the ground that they exceed the practical capacity of the administrative process:

[I]s it really possible to determine in advance all of the material consequences of all possible alternative means to all reasonable intermediate goals that would further some given ultimate end, and to assess these various consequences in terms of some common standards of "costs" and "benefits"? The theory of cost-benefit analysis, taken to its extreme, would require such a herculean undertaking in order to arrive at a truly rational result. However, it commonly is noted that, at least as a practical matter, cost-benefit analysis must take for granted some reasonably limited set of preconceived ends and means, and their selection will depend on choices that themselves are not founded on any cost-benefit analysis.

Moreover, assuming a limited range of preconceived ends and means, will it actually be possible to measure with accuracy the benefits as well as the costs of the consequences of different possible agency actions? One must establish some common denominator in terms of which to assess or assign weights to various outcomes. However, the outcomes may have significantly differing characteristics and thus may not be readily susceptible to reduction to a common standard of measurement. Also, it frequently is observed that cost-benefit analysis may be systematically skewed by the particular difficulties of predicting and assigning values to the benefits, as opposed to the costs, of rules. Benefits, such as cleaner air or water, may be more difficult to predict and measure simply because of limits in our scientific understanding, for instance of the effects on human health and the environment of varying degrees of improvement in air or water quality. Also, benefits are especially difficult to state in quantifiable terms since they commonly are diffuse and long-term.

Thomas O. Sargentich, "The Reform of the American Administrative Process: The Contemporary Debate," 1984 Wis.L.Rev. 385, 416–17. *See also* McGarity, *supra*, at 124–64.

Professor Weidenbaum's perspective on the use of CBA in administrative rulemaking is more sympathetic:

> The motive for incorporating benefit-cost analysis into public decision making is to lead to a more efficient allocation of government resources by subjecting the public sector to the same type of quantitative constraints as those in the private sector. In making an investment decision, for example, business executives compare the total costs to be incurred with the total revenues expected to accrue. If the expected costs exceed the revenues, the investment is usually not considered worthwhile....

> The government agency decision maker, however, usually does not face such constraints. If the costs to society of an action by an agency exceed the benefits, that situation has no immediate adverse impact on the agency, as would be the case if the private business executive makes a bad investment decision.... In requiring agencies to perform benefit-cost analysis, the aim is to make the government's decision-making process more effective, eliminating those regulatory actions for which net benefits are negative. This result is not ensured by benefit-cost analysis, as political and other important but non-quantifiable considerations may dominate and result in actions which are not economically efficient, but which are desired on grounds of equity or income distribution. Yet benefit-cost analysis can provide valuable information for government decision makers.

Murray L. Weidenbaum, BUSINESS AND GOVERNMENT IN THE GLOBAL MARKETPLACE 215 (5th ed. 1995).

Pildes and Sunstein, *supra*, at 72–73, see merit on both sides of the argument:

> [Despite its limitations,] CBA could still help discipline and systematize important aspects of the policy-making process. It forces more focused and precise thinking about the potential consequences of policy. Pragmatically, there is even more to be said for retaining some role for CBA. Perhaps this way of proceeding offers a less than full description of what is really at stake; but if the alternative is a totally intuitive, ad hoc process, even the rough tools of CBA might be preferable. Moreover, a completely open-textured and undisciplined regulatory process would be an invitation to allow interest-group power and sensationalist anecdotes, rather than deliberation, to determine regulatory priorities and approaches. ... CBA should continue to be a part of the regulatory process, but a part whose relation to the whole is understood in a particular way.

> First, ... CBA should be modified to allow disclosure of and publicity for disaggregated cost and benefit data [i.e., identification of who would benefit from the proposed rule and who would pay]. Second, ... policymakers should view CBA as a tool to inform thoughtful decision making, ... but also examine the possibility that it fails to capture the relevant values at issue. There is nothing exotic about this suggestion. Few people suppose that CBA can tell us whether to devote limited research funds to AIDS, global climate change, heart disease, or breast cancer. Few people suppose that an analysis of endangered

species cases, or of antidiscrimination policies, should turn exclusively on CBA. ... Where expert and lay assessments appear at odds, lay perspectives should be identified and explored to the extent feasible. If lay assessments rest on factual misinformation, or on cognitive distortions in the way inferences are drawn from the known facts, they need not be credited. But to the extent that they reflect different valuations of risk, such as concern for how equitably distributed a risk is, or whether the processes by which the risk is imposed and managed are fair, they are the kind of citizen preferences, backed up by legitimate reasons and values, that democracies should take seriously.

3. *Cost-benefit decisional criteria.* Notice that E.O. 12866 not only requires agencies to study costs and benefits, but also provides, with many qualifications, that agency action must be guided by cost-benefit considerations. § 2(b)(6). The Reagan order was much firmer in its language. It provided, for example, that "[r]egulatory action shall not be undertaken unless the potential benefits to society for the regulation outweigh the potential costs to society;" and "[a]mong alternative approaches to any given regulatory objective, the alternative involving the least net cost to society shall be chosen." E.O. 12291, §§ 2(b), 2(d). Was the Reagan version too confining? Or is the Clinton version too open-ended? How far should cost-benefit analysis be used as a decisional criterion, not just as a source of background information?

4. *Legal constraints.* Notice that E.O. 12866 indicates repeatedly that it applies only "to the extent permitted by law." §§ 1(b), 9. E.O. 12291 had contained similar disclaimers. Thus, if a statute directs an agency to issue a rule that even the agency itself would not deem cost-justified, the agency must follow the statute. A famous example of such a statute is the controversial Delaney Clause, under which the FDA was required to ban foods that were carcinogenic to any degree, no matter how infinitesimal. 21 U.S.C. § 348(c)(3)(A). The FDA itself found this mandate excessive but was bound by it until Congress repealed it in 1996. *See Public Citizen v. Young,* 831 F.2d 1108 (D.C.Cir.1987) (statute clearly prohibits FDA from carving out a "de minimis" exception to Delaney Clause). *See also American Textile Mfrs. Inst. v. Donovan,* 452 U.S. 490, 509 (1981) (by statute, OSHA must require employers to use all feasible means to reduce risks of inhaling cotton dust, regardless of what cost-benefit analysis may imply).

However, some of the 1995 regulatory reform bills in Congress would have overcome these statutory boundaries through the use of so-called "supermandates." For example, H.R. 1022, discussed in N.1, would have required that "major rules" (similar to "significant regulatory actions" in E.O. 12866) be cost-justified; this provision was to "supplement and, to the extent there is a conflict, supersede the decision criteria for rulemaking otherwise applicable under the statute pursuant to which the rule is promulgated." § 202(b)(1). Should that approach to regulatory reform be commended as an effort to get Congress to take a stand on an important regulatory policy issue instead of evading the subject? Or would this approach have created too many problems? Would it have led to an increase or a decrease in political accountability? *See* William W. Buzbee, "Regulatory Reform or Statutory Muddle: The 'Legislative Mirage' of Single–Statute Regulatory Reform," 5 NYU Envir.L.J. 298 (1996).

5. *Triggering regulatory analysis.* Some states require regulatory analyses for all rules. *E.g.,* N.Y. State APA Law § 202–a; W.Va. Code § 29A–3–5. Usually, however, such analyses are required only under limited circumstances. One justification for these limitations is that the preparation of careful, technically proficient regulatory analyses can be burdensome and expensive. At the federal level, estimates of the dollar cost of a CBA typically range between $100,000 to several times that sum, depending on the particular rule. *See, e.g.,* McGarity, *supra,* at 139; Whisnant & Cherry, *supra,* at 720. Nor is money the only source of concern:

> If the regulatory analysis requirement were not limited, opponents of proposed rules could request the issuance of these time-consuming and expensive statements simply to harass agencies, or to delay their rule making without any compensating public benefit. Moreover, if agencies were required to issue such an analysis [upon request] in every instance of rule making, ... agencies would be likely to compile those statements in a haphazard way, to divert resources to that task from more essential functions, or to de-emphasize policy making by rule in favor of increased law making by ad hoc adjudicatory orders that could subsequently be relied upon as precedent.

Arthur Earl Bonfield, STATE ADMINISTRATIVE RULE MAKING 214 (1986).

A variety of approaches have been used to determine what rules will be subjected to analysis. E.O. 12866 requires a formal regulatory analysis only for "significant regulatory actions" (see the definition in § 3(f)). Compare the approach taken by 1981 MSAPA § 3–105(a). That section requires an agency to prepare a regulatory analysis only if requested to do so. Brackets in the Model Act offer states alternatives as to who should be eligible to make the request: e.g., the administrative rules review committee of the legislature, the governor, a political subdivision, another agency, and any group of 300 or more private persons. Is the "by request" mechanism preferable to the "significant regulatory action" filtering device found in the Executive Order? Which entities on the MSAPA list have the strongest claims to be eligible to trigger the regulatory analysis requirement?

Some state APAs use a dollar-cost criterion like the federal one (often as an alternative to a "by request" criterion). In some of these states the amount of estimated economic impact that will trigger a duty to prepare a regulatory analysis runs into the millions of dollars. *See, e.g.,* N.C. Gen.Stat. § 150B–21.4(b1) (five million dollars in a year). At the other end of the spectrum is Missouri's threshold for analysis: a "fiscal note" is required if the rule is expected to impose aggregate costs of at least $500 on private persons or businesses. Mo.Ann.Stat. § 536.205. In the only reported case on this requirement, which was enacted in 1978, the court set aside a rule because no fiscal note had been filed. *Missouri Hospital Ass'n v. Air Conservation Comm'n,* 874 S.W.2d 380 (Mo.App.1994). The opinion observed that most Missouri rules lack fiscal notes, as agencies regularly find that the $500 threshold has not been met. The court called this pattern "disconcerting." If it is, what should be done about it?

6. *Judicial review of analysis requirements.* On both the federal and state levels, judicial review of agencies' compliance with CBA obligations is

usually quite limited. See, for example, § 10 of E.O. 12866, which replicates almost identical language from E.O. 12291. The courts have respected this intention: they have consistently declined to review agencies' compliance with the two orders. *Michigan v. Thomas,* 805 F.2d 176, 187 (6th Cir.1986). In this context, unreviewability means that the agency's failure to perform the analysis in the prescribed manner will not, standing alone, cause a court to set aside the rule. It does not mean, however, that a court must ignore the conclusions that an agency reached while conducting a regulatory analysis. Normally, the agency's analysis and data will be added to the rulemaking record, and on appeal the court can take account of this material as it decides whether the rule is reasonable on the merits. *Id.*

Controversy over reviewability of CBA requirements was a key issue in the 1995 regulatory reform debate in Congress. A major factor contributing to the defeat of Senator Dole's bill was the objection by environmentalists and other public interest groups to provisions of the bill that would have allowed court challenges to allegedly insufficient cost-benefit analyses. Opponents argued that these provisions would open up too many opportunities for challengers to attack rules in court, and that agencies would respond by spending too much time polishing their CBAs so that they would stand up in court. Yet, even though similar concerns have been expressed about judicial review of agencies' compliance with APA § 553, no one argues that agencies' compliance with notice-and-comment obligations should be entirely unreviewable. Is there a valid distinction between the two situations, or was this argument just a political ploy? For several perspectives on this debate, see Symposium, *Fiftieth Anniversary of the Administrative Procedure Act,* 48 Admin.L.Rev. 307, 350–69 (1996).

7. *State-level judicial review.* Although § 3–105(f) of the 1981 MSAPA limits judicial review of regulatory analyses, it does so to a lesser extent than does E.O. 12866. It instructs courts to uphold a rule if the agency made a "good faith effort to comply" with regulatory analysis requirements. The Comment to this provision of the 1981 MSAPA says: "To ascertain 'good faith' for this purpose, . . . a court should only determine if the analysis was actually issued, and if on its face it actually addresses in some manner all of the points specified in subsections (b)-(c). If so, the sufficiency or accuracy of its contents are not subject to judicial review." Does § 3–105(f) limit judicial review sufficiently? Too much?

In a number of states with regulatory analysis requirements in their APAs, the statute does not explicitly limit the judicial role in reviewing the contents of those analyses. Nevertheless, some courts seem disinclined to police statutory CBA requirements very aggressively. *See Northeast Ohio Regional Sewer Dist. v. Shank,* 567 N.E.2d 993 (Ohio 1991); *Methodist Hospitals of Dallas v. Texas Industrial Accident Board,* 798 S.W.2d 651 (Tex.App.1990). In *Methodist Hospitals,* the Board issued a rule setting the amounts that hospitals would receive for treating workers' compensation patients. By statute, it was required to file a "public benefit-cost note showing [on a yearly basis] (A) the public benefits to be expected as a result of adoption of the proposed rule; and (B) the probable economic cost to persons who are required to comply with the rule." The Board's note stated that "[f]or each year . . . the public benefit anticipated . . . will be provision of a uniform standard for fair and reasonable fees . . . that should result in:

(1) improved delivery and quality of health facility goods and services to claimants; and (2) reduced premiums for employers.... " The description of costs was that "public health facilities should experience impact on revenue resulting from [the rate ceiling, the facility's payment ratio, and administrative costs]." Rejecting the argument that the Board should have assigned monetary amounts to these propositions, the court held that the Board had substantially complied with the statute. Do you agree?

8. *Specialized regulatory analyses.* Even prior to the Reagan executive order prescribing broad use of CBA, Congress had provided for more specialized forms of regulatory analysis of agency rules. Since 1969 the National Environmental Policy Act (NEPA) has instructed all agencies to prepare a detailed environmental impact statement in connection with "major Federal actions significantly affecting the quality of the human environment." *See* 42 U.S.C. §§ 4321–61. The purpose is to force agencies to become more sensitive to the (frequently unintended) environmental consequences of their actions.

Similarly, the Regulatory Flexibility Act (RFA), 5 U.S.C. §§ 601 et seq., first adopted in 1980, requires agencies to consider and to embody in an analysis the impact of proposed rules on "small entities"—primarily small businesses, although "small (not-for-profit) organizations" and "small governmental jurisdictions" are also included. The requirement sweeps broadly and is not limited to "significant" rules. This Act attempts to correct for a perceived tendency among agencies to overlook the implications of their actions for the small business community. *See* Paul R. Verkuil, "A Critical Guide to the Regulatory Flexibility Act," 1982 Duke L.J. 213. Until recently, the RFA specifically forbade judicial review of the obligations it imposed. Thus, courts refused to hear claims arising under that Act, much as they have declined to hear claims arising under E.O. 12866. *See Small Refiner Lead Phase–Down Task Force v. USEPA,* 705 F.2d 506, 537–39 (D.C.Cir. 1983) (court cannot review compliance with RFA, but can consider material in the analysis in reviewing a rule under the arbitrary and capricious test).

In 1996, responding to criticism that the RFA was not fulfilling its goals, Congress adopted legislation to strengthen it. *See* Small Business Regulatory Enforcement Act of 1996 (SBREFA), Pub.L.No. 104–121. One change wrought by SBREFA was to permit judicial review of alleged RFA violations. Courts can now redress such violations in about the same manner as they have previously redressed violations of the environmental impact statement requirements of NEPA. *See Associated Fisheries of Maine v. Daley,* 127 F.3d 104 (1st Cir.1997) (reviewing agency's compliance with RFA for good faith and reasonableness). "These changes were long sought by the small business community, which came to believe, as the [new] Act's sponsors noted, that many agencies gave the RFA lip service at best. The question is whether judicial review will improve compliance, and thus serve the purposes of the Act, more than it will complicate and slow the regulatory process." Thomas O. Sargentich, "The Small Business Regulatory Enforcement Act," 49 Admin.L.Rev. 123, 128 (1997). Was this change in the law desirable?

9. *Unfunded mandates.* Certain provisions of the Unfunded Mandates Reform Act of 1995, Pub.L. No. 104–4, have been described as "stealth regulatory reform," because they slipped through Congress virtually unno-

ticed. The most prominent purpose of the Act as a whole was to discourage agencies and future Congresses from thrusting new duties onto state and local governments without providing resources to pay for the execution of these duties. Also included in the Act, however, was a provision requiring that any agency rule that imposes costs of $100 million on state or local governments, *or on the private sector*, must be accompanied by a cost-benefit statement. 2 U.S.C. § 1532(a). The statement must include a quantitative and qualitative assessment of the costs and benefits of the regulation. The agency must then select the "least costly, most cost-effective or least burdensome alternative that achieves the objectives of the rule" or explain why it did not do so. *Id.* § 1535.

Judicial remedies for breach of the Unfunded Mandates Act are a hybrid of the approaches described above. A court can require administrators to prepare the statement required by that Act if they have failed to do so, but the court cannot overturn the rule on the basis of the agency's failure to prepare the statement or the inadequacy of a statement the agency did prepare. The agency's obligation to choose the least burdensome regulatory alternative (or explain why it did not) is entirely unreviewable. *Id.* § 1571. Under these circumstances, how much impact do you expect the Act will have? *See* Daniel E. Troy, "The Unfunded Mandates Reform Act of 1995," 49 Admin.L.Rev. 139, 145–47 (1997).

10. *Specialized analyses by executive order.* Last—and perhaps least— are several executive orders directing agencies to write regulatory analyses in specialized areas. One order, issued by President Reagan, instructs agencies to assess the impact of any proposed rule on federalism values; other orders have required assessment of impacts on trade, property rights, the family, etc. The proliferation of such requirements led the ABA to adopt a resolution in 1992 that "urge[d] the President and Congress to exercise restraint in the overall number of required rulemaking impact analyses.... " According to the supporting report:

> [A] study conducted ... during a three-month period revealed that of the 717 rules issued, none contained a "Takings" impact statement ..., or a "Trade" impact statement ..., and only three had either a "Family" or "Federalism" impact statement.... Even supporters of rulemaking review concede that some of the current required reviews are not, and should not, be taken seriously. Retention of these requirements may demean the importance of other reviews [and] have the effect of stymieing appropriate and necessary rulemaking.

11. *Problem.* Recall the Madison Insurance Department (MID), the agency involved in the genetic testing problem in § 5.7 N.7. MID implements a variety of statutes that are designed to maintain the financial reliability of insurance companies in the state. It also enforces consumer protection legislation, such as the Fair Insurance Act involved in the earlier problem.

Although the Madison APA contains no provisions on regulatory analysis, a state senator has introduced a bill to require the MID to incorporate cost-benefit analysis into its rulemaking process. The bill provides that (i) the agency must perform a regulatory analysis, applying the standards in 1981 MSAPA § 3–105(b)-(c), if a proposed rule is expected to have an impact of at least $100,000 on the state's economy; (ii) the agency may not issue a rule unless it finds, pursuant to such a regulatory analysis, that the benefits of the rule will be commensurate with its costs; and (iii) a reviewing court shall set aside an MID rule if the agency was required by this legislation to prepare a cost-benefit analysis to accompany the rule but failed to do so; however, if the agency did prepare the analysis, a court may not set aside the rule on the ground that the analysis did not meet the standards prescribed in MSAPA § 3–105(b)–(c).

As an aide to the senator, you have been asked for your comments on the bill. Which, if any, of these provisions should be adopted? Would you recommend any revisions?

§ 5.9   NEGOTIATED RULEMAKING

ACUS, A GUIDE TO FEDERAL AGENCY RULEMAKING
145–49 (2d ed.1991).

In [the Negotiated Rulemaking Act of 1990 (NRA), now codified at 5 U.S.C. §§ 561–70,] Congress endorsed the use by agencies of an alternative procedure known as "negotiated rulemaking." This procedure, sometimes called "regulatory negotiation" or "reg-neg," has been used by several agencies to bring interested parties into the rule drafting process at an early stage, under circumstances that foster cooperative efforts to achieve solutions to regulatory problems. Where successful, negotiated rulemaking can lead to better, more acceptable rules, based on a clearer understanding of the concerns of all affected interests. Negotiated rules may be easier to enforce and less likely to be challenged in litigation.

[In the ordinary rulemaking process, any] agency contacts with regulated parties or the general public while the agency is considering or drafting a proposed rule are usually informal and unstructured. Typically, there is no opportunity for interchange of views among potentially affected parties, even where an agency chooses to conduct a hearing.

The dynamics of the rulemaking process tend to encourage interested parties to take extreme positions in their written and oral statements—in pre-proposal contacts as well as in comments on any published proposed rule. They may choose to withhold information that they view as damaging. A party may appear to put equal weight on every argument, giving the agency little clue as to the relative importance it places on the various issues. There is usually little willingness to recognize the legitimate viewpoints of others. The adversarial atmosphere often contributes to the expense and delay associated with regulatory proceedings as parties try to position themselves for the expected litigation. What is lacking is an opportunity for the parties to exchange views and to focus on finding constructive, creative solutions to problems.

In negotiated rulemaking, the agency, with the assistance of one or more neutral advisers known as "convenors," assembles a committee of representatives of all affected interests to negotiate a proposed rule. The goal of the process is to reach consensus on a text that all parties can accept. The agency is represented at the table by an official who is sufficiently senior to be able to speak authoritatively on behalf of the agency. Negotiating sessions, however, are led not by the agency representative, but by a neutral mediator or facilitator skilled in assisting in the resolution of multi-party disputes.

Negotiated rulemaking is clearly not suitable for all agency rulemaking. The Negotiated Rulemaking Act sets forth [in § 563(a)] several criteria to be considered when an agency determines whether to use reg-neg. These include (1) whether there are a limited number of identifiable interests—usually not more than 25, including any relevant government agencies—that will be significantly affected by the rule; (2) whether a balanced committee can be convened that can adequately represent the various interests and negotiate in good faith to reach a consensus on a proposed rule; (3) whether the negotiation process will not unreasonably delay issuance of the rule; (4) whether the agency has adequate resources to support the negotiating committee; and (5) whether the agency—to the maximum extent consistent with its legal obligations—will use a committee consensus as the basis for a proposed rule. . . .

In addition, there should be a number of diverse issues that participants can rank according to their own priorities, so that there will be room for compromise on some of the issues as an agreement is sought. However, it is essential that the issues to be negotiated not require compromise of principles so fundamental to the parties that meaningful negotiations are impossible. Parties must indicate a willingness to negotiate in good faith, and no single interest should be able to dominate the negotiations.

The goal of the committee is to reach consensus on a draft rule. The word "consensus" is usually understood in this context to mean that each interest represented, including the agency, concurs in the result, unless all members of the committee agree at the outset to a different meaning. Negotiators try to reach a consensus through a process of evaluating their own priorities and making tradeoffs to achieve an acceptable outcome on the issues of greatest importance to them. . . .

If a consensus is achieved by the committee, the agency ordinarily would publish the draft rule based on that consensus in a notice of proposed rulemaking—and the agency would have committed itself in advance to doing so. Such a commitment is not an abdication of the agency's statutory responsibility, for there would not be a consensus without the agency's concurrence in the committee's proposed rule. Even negotiations that result in less than full consensus on a draft rule can still be very useful to the agency by narrowing the issues in dispute, identifying information necessary to resolve issues, ranking priorities, and finding potentially acceptable solutions.

Negotiated rulemaking should be viewed as a supplement to the rulemaking provisions of the Administrative Procedure Act. This means that the negotiation sessions generally take place prior to issuance of the notice and the opportunity for the public to comment on a proposed rule that are required by the Act. In some instances, negotiations may be appropriate at a later stage of the proceeding.

The Negotiated Rulemaking Act was intended to clarify agency authority to use the process. The Act establishes basic public notice requirements, including provision of an opportunity for members of the public who believe they are inadequately represented on a negotiating committee to apply for membership or better representation. . . .

WILLIAM FUNK, "WHEN SMOKE GETS IN YOUR EYES: REGULATORY NEGOTIATION AND THE PUBLIC INTEREST—EPA's WOODSTOVE STANDARDS"

18 Envtl.L. 55 (1987).

Regulatory negotiation is a recent development in administrative law. Philip Harter provided its first real description and justification in ["Negotiating Regulations: A Cure for Malaise," 71 Geo.L.J. 1 (1982)]. . . .

Since Harter's article, several agencies, including especially the Environmental Protection Agency (EPA), have experimented with negotiating proposed regulations according to Harter's formula, as reflected in the recommendations of the Administrative Conference of the United States. Assessments of those experiments have been uniformly positive, even where the regulatory negotiation failed to result in a proposed or final regulation. One of the most recent experiments resulted in an EPA proposed rule to establish emission limitations for residential woodstoves under the Clean Air Act.

It is the thesis of this Article that this proposed rule is not authorized by the Clean Air Act, and that the process of developing the rule by regulatory negotiation directly contributed to this unlawful proposal. Moreover, this Article concludes that the nature of regulatory negotiation has the tendency to obscure, if not pervert, the public interest to the benefit of private interests, and that the regulatory negotiation of the woodstove emission limitation is a case study of such a perversion.

. . . Under section 111 [of the Clean Air Act, the principal provision on which the woodstove standard purportedly rests], a "stationary source" is "any building, structure, facility, or installation which emits or may emit any air pollutant." . . . After the effective date of any standard of performance under this section, it is unlawful for "any owner or operator of any new source to operate such source in violation" of that standard. . . .

The prohibitions in the regulations run primarily to the manufacturers and retailers of woodstoves, not to the [residential] operators of the stoves. . . . There is some difficulty in fitting the proposed rule . . . to the statutory scheme. . . . [The] terms "building, structure, facility, or installation" [in section 111] are clearly not the terms one would choose to use to indicate a consumer product a person buys at a store, brings home, and uses there. . . . [Compounding the doubtful legality of the woodstove rule is] the fact that section 111 only applies to "owners or operators" of sources; there is no mention of manufacturers or importers of sources, unlike every other statutory scheme governing consumer products. . . .

[Particularly questionable] is the portion of the proposed rule which requires any woodstove sold meeting the applicable emission limits to have affixed to the stove a removable label that shows its estimated emissions, efficiency, and heat output data. This label . . . has nothing to do with pollution control but is an informative label that will enable consumers to make more informed choices concerning woodstove purchases. Nothing in section 111 would authorize such a label. . . .

In the absence of a regulatory negotiation, it is highly likely that a number of commenters would have objected to the particular method of regulating woodstoves under section 111, if not to the basic concept of their regulation under section 111. Unable to rely on their "inside" ability to achieve a regulation that would meet their substantive objections, commenters would have an interest in raising legal objections to the rule. The negotiation process, however, not only mutes legal objections, it does bring the parties in interest "inside" the substantive rulemaking process. In the case of woodstoves, for example, it meant that manufacturers and environmentalists could negotiate which woodstoves would be regulated at what level according to what timetable.

. . . The Regulatory Impact Analysis . . . states unambiguously that "the stringency of the [standard] in terms of the maximum grams of emissions per hour was negotiated." In other words, the maximum emission rate is not something derived by scientific method, but rather derived through the relative power of the negotiating parties.

This is not to say that the scientific information or statistical methods described in the preamble to the proposed rule were irrelevant in the negotiations. To the contrary, data and statistical methods may provide negotiating power to one side or the other. But other matters, such as concessions or agreements on other features of the proposed rule, may also provide negotiating power to one side or the other. Knowing that the numerical limits were "negotiated," rather than determined solely on the basis of the data and methodology described in the preamble, we are left not knowing *what* role the data and methodology played, if any. . . .

The concept of regulatory negotiation stands [a rulemaking agency's traditional] role on its head, first, by reducing the agency to the level of a mere participant in the formulation of the rule, and second, by essentially denying that the agency has any responsibility beyond giving effect to the consensus achieved by the group. [While] the agency technically has the final decision, this power becomes theoretical at best where the agency has already agreed beforehand along with all the other participants to seek consensus in good faith, to support the consensus result, and in particular to publish as a proposed rule the rule developed by that consensus....

This fundamental change in the role of the agency in the rulemaking process is mirrored by the fundamental change in the underlying theoretical justification for the eventual rule. As Harter admits: "[U]nder the traditional ... process, the legitimacy of the rule rests on a resolution of complex factual materials and rational extrapolation from those facts, guided by the criteria of the statute. Under regulatory negotiation, however, the regulation's legitimacy would lie in the overall agreement of the parties." Stated another way, the parties to the rule are happy with it; therefore, it matters not whether the rule is rational or lawful. Discretion delegated to the agency by Congress is effectively exercised by the group of interested parties, constrained only by the need to obtain consensus. The law no longer directs or even necessarily constrains the outcome but has become merely a factor in the give-and-take necessary to achieve consensus. ...

Reliance on the absence of disagreement as evidence of legitimacy for a regulation puts a premium on assuring that the negotiating group adequately represents all affected interests. There are, however, both practical and theoretical limitations on the number of interests that may be represented and the quality of representation each interest may obtain. Where the interest is strong enough to make itself known and felt, little difficulty arises—either that interest will be represented in the negotiation or the negotiation in the end will not likely be successful. More problematic is where the interest is not well defined, organized, or strong. ... For example, in the woodstove negotiation, the Consumer Federation of America (CFA) was supposed to represent the interests of the consumer, but consumers, as the CFA would be the first to admit, are hardly a homogenous entity. The CFA may have represented the interests associated with the mentality of a *Consumers Reports* reader, but it did not appear to lobby on behalf of poor, rural folk for whom the rule will provide little benefit and perhaps significant burden. Moreover, the fact that these people do not comment on the proposed rule or challenge a final rule in court hardly establishes that the rule is fair and wise as to them.

... However, it is not the purpose of this Article to conclude that regulatory negotiation is necessarily bad and should be shot dead in its tracks. To the contrary, the practical benefits of regulatory negotiation cannot be gainsaid, and if they have not received much attention here, it is only because there are ample other sources. It is of no small moment when the professional defenders of the environment, the affected industry, and government entities can achieve consensus on how to deal with a particular source of pollution. Rather, it is the purpose of this Article to demonstrate that regulatory negotiation ... fundamentally alters the dynamics of traditional administrative rulemaking from a search for the public interest, however imperfect that search may be, to a search for a consensus among private parties representing particular interests.

Only after one recognizes this fundamental change can one fully assess the advantages and disadvantages of regulatory negotiation as an alternative to traditional administrative rulemaking. Up to now, the debate over regulatory negotiation has revolved around its feasibility and methods to improve its "success" rate. Now, however, the debate should include the appropriateness of private interests determining the public values at stake in the rulemaking. In some cases the issues to be decided in the negotiation may be so bounded that any threat to public values disappears. In other cases the negotiation may claim as its subject matter issues which properly should be decided only by an agency.

Notes and Questions

1. *Legal context.* Obviously, the theory and practice of negotiated rulemaking draw directly upon the philosophy and techniques of the alternative dispute resolution movement. (Recall the Administrative Dispute Resolution Act, discussed in § 4.1.3., which applies ADR techniques to agency *adjudication.*) As Funk mentions, the Administrative Conference provided much of the initial impetus for the development of negotiated rulemaking. The ACUS *Negotiated Rulemaking Sourcebook* (1995) remains the most complete collection of research materials on reg-neg. Although regulatory negotiation was generally viewed as permissible even without specific authorizing legislation, Congress enacted the NRA in 1990 in order to encourage use of the technique and to standardize its procedures. At first the NRA was adopted on a temporary basis, but in 1996 Congress renewed it to continue indefinitely.

2. *Reg-neg in the states.* Many states have enacted legislation similar to the NRA or have experimented more informally with regulatory negotiation. *See* ACUS *Sourcebook* at 369–74. If anything, reg-neg may come more naturally to state agencies than federal agencies, because in some ways it is less of a departure from the way states have always developed rules:

> Most states have far fewer resources for the administrative process than the federal government. Accordingly, administrative litigation before state agencies has not reached the level of complexity that it has before federal agencies. Rather, a measure of informal negotiation between affected interests is a regular feature of the state process. Such negotiations are not very visible though. In addition, a number of states have adopted various procedures to permit legislative ... advice on specific proposed agency rules. Participation by the legislative branch in the rulemaking process also facilitates negotiation among affected interests of the kind commonly conducted in the legislative arena.

Henry H. Perritt, Jr., "Negotiated Rulemaking and Administrative Law," 38 Admin.L.Rev. 471, 474 (1986).

3. *Candidates for reg-neg.* Although success with negotiated rulemaking can serve to expedite the regulatory process by avoiding a court appeal, negotiations sometimes fail—in which case the net effect of the effort may be greater delay. Therefore, as the above ACUS reading emphasizes, an agency

must exercise great care in its selection of issues that it will attempt to resolve through negotiation. Consider this example: In 1987 the Federal Aviation Administration convened an advisory committee to negotiate issues of how airlines should accommodate passengers with disabilities. Among the matters on the agenda were: making aircraft restrooms more accessible to passengers who used wheelchairs; setting training requirements for airline employees on how to treat disabled passengers; and determining whether exit row seating, which normally is subject to special restrictions because of safety concerns, would be available to passengers who were blind. The negotiations were partly successful, but not entirely so. Why do you suppose that was? *See* "Despite Impasse, Parties Praise DOT's Non-discrimination Reg-neg," 2 ADR Rep. (BNA) 117 (1988).

4. *Criticisms.* Funk's article is accurate in its initial observation that participants in regulatory negotiation usually come away satisfied with the process. Nevertheless, he criticizes the process for subjecting rulemaking to inordinate influence by well organized interest groups, to the detriment of the overall public interest and the rule of law. How valid is the contrast, in this regard, between negotiated rulemaking and the ordinary process of notice and comment rulemaking? Isn't the latter also somewhat political? To the extent that negotiated rulemaking is particularly vulnerable to the tendencies Funk identifies, are these vices an acceptable price to pay for the virtues of reg-neg, as summarized in the ACUS excerpt? For a continuation of this debate, see Symposium, 46 Duke L.J. 1255 (1997); Jody Freeman, "Collaborative Governance in the Administrative State," 45 UCLA L.Rev. 1 (1997).

5. *Judicial review.* One of the chief attractions of a successfully negotiated rule, from an agency's point of view, is that affected interests usually do not seek judicial review of it. Indeed, most negotiated rules (including the woodstove rule) have not been challenged in court. Occasionally, however, the process misfires and an appeal occurs. The NRA provides that "[a] rule which is the product of negotiated rulemaking and is subject to judicial review shall not be accorded any greater deference by a court than a rule which is the product of other rulemaking procedures." § 570. Does this mean that the agency must demonstrate to a court that it has made the same legal determinations, performed the same studies, and engaged in the same reasoning as if it had not used negotiated rulemaking? Or would that expectation make regulatory negotiation unworkable or meaningless? *See generally* Patricia M. Wald, "ADR and the Courts: An Update," 46 Duke L.J. 1445, 1466–68 (1997); Philip J. Harter, "The Role of the Courts in Regulatory Negotiation—A Response to Judge Wald," 11 Colum.J.Envtl.L. 51 (1986); Patricia M. Wald, "Negotiation of Environmental Disputes: A New Role for the Courts?," 10 Colum.J.Envtl.L. 1 (1985).

6. *"Reneging" in reg-neg.* Suppose an agency proposes a rule to the public that departs from the consensus reached earlier by a negotiated rulemaking committee. Has the agency negotiated in bad faith, and is there anything that the disappointed negotiator can do about it? According to Chief Judge Posner, the answers are "no" and "no." *USA Group Loan Services, Inc. v. Riley*, 82 F.3d 708, 714–15 (7th Cir.1996):

During the negotiations, an official of the Department of Education promised the servicers that the Department would abide by any consensus reached by them unless there were compelling reasons to depart. The propriety of such a promise may be questioned. It sounds like an abdication of regulatory authority to the regulated, the full burgeoning of the interest-group state, and the final confirmation of the "capture" theory of administrative regulation. . . .

We have doubts about the propriety of the official's promise to abide by a consensus of the regulated industry, but we have no doubt that the Negotiated Rulemaking Act did not make the promise enforceable. . . . The practical effect of enforcing it would be to make the Act extinguish notice and comment rulemaking in all cases in which it was preceded by negotiated rulemaking; the comments would be irrelevant if the agency were already bound by promises that it had made to the industry. . . . The Act simply creates a consultative process in advance of the more formal arms' length procedure of notice and comment rulemaking.

Do you agree with the court's "doubts about the propriety" of an agency's pledging that it will be strongly inclined to adopt whatever deal the negotiating committee endorses? Is that an "abdication of regulatory authority to the regulated"? On the other hand, even if an agency must remain open to changing the consensus agreement if it receives comments that demonstrate a need for revision, shouldn't the department at least have *proposed* the agreement in its notice of proposed rulemaking? If the courts are not going to forbid "bad faith" such as that of the department here, does an agency have any good reasons to adhere to an agreement it reaches during regulatory negotiation?

What about the opposite situation, in which a *private party* withdraws support for the consensus agreement and begins actively opposing it? Typically, private participants in a regulatory negotiation sign a pledge at the outset that they will support the consensus agreement (if the agency adheres to it) before the agency and in any court proceeding. The pledge is probably not legally enforceable, but a desire to maintain good relations with other groups may provide an informal deterrent to breach of the promise. Moreover, in the event of a judicial appeal, the other parties can inform the court that most signatories support the consensus agreement, and a court may well take account of that information. For example, EPA used negotiated rulemaking to develop guidelines for removal of asbestos from old school buildings. When asbestos manufacturers sought judicial review of the rule, school associations and others who had helped write the rule intervened in support of the agency. The court upheld the rule, finding it "highly ironic that industry representatives assail EPA for supplying inadequate guidance to school officials when their counsel have assured us that those officials are now thoroughly satisfied with the regulatory guidance provided by EPA." *Safe Buildings Alliance v. EPA,* 846 F.2d 79, 82 (D.C.Cir.1988).

7. *Problem.* Under § 18 of the Federal Insecticide, Fungicide and Rodenticide Act (FIFRA), the EPA Administrator has authority to grant "emergency" exemptions from pesticide restrictions. An exemption allows farmers in a given area to make short-term use of a pesticide that is still undergoing testing for safety. Eligibility for an exemption turns in part on

whether farmers will suffer "significant economic loss" if relief is denied. In the mid–1980's, EPA and congressional committees became concerned that the agency's program for implementing this authority needed overhauling; grants of exemptions were increasing rapidly, threatening the integrity of the regulatory regime. The agency convened a negotiating committee to draft new rules. Four environmental groups, four state organizations, four agricultural user groups, two manufacturers, the Department of Agriculture, and EPA were represented. After four months the participants arrived at a consensus agreement, and EPA published it as a proposed rule, inviting comments.

The American Farm Bureau Federation, one of the signatories to the consensus agreement, filed comments proposing a change in the proposal. The proposed rule stated that "significant economic loss" must be determined only in terms of decreased crop yield. Thus, for example, no exemption could be granted to resist an infestation that merely caused harmless spotting on apples. The Federation argued that significant economic loss should be determined in terms of overall profitability; this test would allow a different result in the apples example, because consumers might refuse to buy the fruit. The Federation contended that the agency's proposal would be ineffective, unfairly restrictive, and contrary to congressional intent.

EPA adopted its proposed rule without material change. In its statement of basis and purpose, the agency said in relevant part: "While the Federation's argument has some logical appeal in the abstract, the negotiating committee decided to use a crop-yield definition of economic loss. We believe it is in the public interest to adhere to that agreement, which enjoys broad support from affected interests. The committee concluded that the proposal will allow farmers to sustain reasonable profit margins, and we do not disagree." How should the court respond to this line of argument? (In real life, only the events described in the first paragraph above actually occurred; EPA adopted the committee's proposal as a final rule without controversy. 51 Fed.Reg. 1896 (1986).)

Chapter 6

RULES AS PART OF THE AGENCY POLICYMAKING PROCESS

Chapter 5 outlined the basic procedures used in rulemaking. It focused primarily on the notice and comment models prescribed in the federal and state APAs (supplemented in some instances by additional procedures, such as those prescribed in regulatory analysis statutes and executive orders). Important as it is, however, notice and comment rulemaking does not exist in a vacuum. Rather, it constitutes only one element in the overall enterprise of agency policymaking.

As they carry out their policymaking responsibilities, agencies have a number of procedural tools at their disposal, and many choices to make. Sometimes they can elect to adopt a rule without resorting to the procedural steps explained in the preceding chapter. Sometimes they can avoid rulemaking procedure by enunciating a new policy through case-by-case adjudication, in the manner of a common law court. Sometimes they can decline to launch a new policymaking initiative at all, if they prefer to devote their attention to other priorities. And sometimes they can decide to soften an existing policy by granting waivers from an otherwise applicable regulation. Although each of these choices involves significant elements of discretion, all are bounded by legal obligations, which are explored in this chapter.

§ 6.1 EXEMPTIONS FROM RULEMAKING PROCEDURE

§ 6.1.1 GOOD CAUSE EXEMPTIONS

Federal and state APAs contain exemptions providing that notice and comment proceedings may be omitted in particular circumstances for "good cause." These exemptions provide some flexibility so that the need to observe usual rulemaking procedures can, in appropriate situations, be accommodated with the equally important need to conduct government administration in an expeditious, effective, and economical manner.

Read federal APA § 553(b)(B) and the almost identical provision contained in 1981 MSAPA § 3–108. They exempt rules from usual notice and comment procedures when it would be "unnecessary, impracticable, or contrary to the public interest" for the agency to follow them. The agency must make an explicit finding at the time of issuance that good cause exists and must give reasons to support that finding. Numerous court decisions have declared that the good cause exemptions from notice-and-comment procedure must be "narrowly construed and reluctantly countenanced." *See, e.g., Action on Smoking and Health v. CAB,* 713 F.2d 795, 800 (D.C.Cir.1983); *American Fed'n of Gov't Employees v. Block,* 655 F.2d 1153, 1156 (D.C.Cir.1981).

Despite this clear message in the judicial case law, however, agencies do rely on the exemption with some frequency. A scholar who examined every issue of the *Federal Register* published during a six-month period found that agencies expressly invoked the exemption in twenty-five percent of the rules they issued. In other instances, he said, agencies appeared to rely on it by implication, so that the true figure might be closer to thirty-three percent. Juan J. Lavilla, "The Good Cause Exemption to Notice and Comment Rulemaking Requirements Under the Administrative Procedure Act," 3 Admin.L.J. 317, 338–39 & n.86 (1989). "Although this figure would seem to be excessive," he added, "an examination of the actual cases where the clause is invoked does not reveal general misuse." *Id.* at 339–40.

A separate provision in the APA, 5 U.S.C. § 553(d)(3), provides that for "good cause" an agency may dispense with the normal requirement that a rule may not become effective until thirty days after its issuance. The two exemptions are commonly invoked simultaneously, because an agency that is in a hurry to move forward with a rule often wishes to avoid both a comment period and a delay in effectiveness.

Notes and Questions

1. *"Unnecessary" rulemaking procedures.* When are usual rulemaking procedures "unnecessary" within the meaning of the federal APA and the 1981 MSAPA good cause exemptions? The legislative history of the federal act indicates that the exemption should apply when comment is "unnecessary so far as the public is concerned, as would be the case if a minor or merely technical amendment in which the public is not particularly interested were involved." *APA Legislative History,* S.Doc.No. 79–248, at 200 (1946) (Senate report); *id.* at 248 (House report). An example would be a rule that makes a "technical correction" by reinstating a rule that was earlier dropped by mistake in a recodification of an agency's regulations. *United States v. Sutton,* 795 F.2d 1040, 1053–54 (Temp.Emer.Ct.App.1986). *Sutton* is one of the very few cases upholding the invocation of this exemption. Why do you suppose there are so few? Another example is a repeal of Coast Guard regulations that had become meaningless because of the destruction of the bridge to which they referred. 52 Fed.Reg. 670 (1987).

Public comment is also considered "unnecessary" when the agency has absolutely no discretion about the contents of its rule, as where its task is merely to make a mathematical calculation or ascertain an objective fact. Since nothing the public might say could affect the rule, the agency has good cause to forego a comment period.

A third situation in which the exemption has been invoked grew out of the EPA's approval, without notice and comment proceedings, of implementation plans tendered by state governments under the Clean Air Act. Two circuits held that APA public procedures were "unnecessary," because EPA was acting under a congressional deadline and the details of the plans had all been aired during proceedings at the state level. *Duquesne Light Co. v. EPA,* 481 F.2d 1 (3d Cir.1973), *vacated on other grounds,* 427 U.S. 902 (1976); *Appalachian Power Co. v. EPA,,* 477 F.2d 495 (4th Cir.1973). Do you agree with this analysis? What if there had been no statutory deadline? *Cf.* Ellen R. Jordan, "The Administrative Procedure Act's 'Good Cause' Exemption," 36 Admin.L.Rev. 113, 132–33 (1984) (questioning these cases' reasoning).

2. *Direct final rules.* The Administrative Conference of the United States has recommended that when an agency plans to rely on the "unnecessary" prong of the good cause exemption, it should issue its rule using "direct final rulemaking." *See* ACUS Recommendation 95–4, 60 Fed.Reg. 43110 (1995); Ronald M. Levin, "Direct Final Rulemaking," 64 Geo. Wash.L.Rev. 1 (1995). Direct final rulemaking is a streamlined variation on the normal § 553 procedure. Agencies use it for issuing rules that they consider totally noncontroversial. Under this procedure, the agency publishes the rule and announces that if no adverse comment is received within a specified time period, the rule will become effective as of a specified later date. But if even a single adverse comment is received, the agency withdraws the rule and republishes it as a proposed rule under the normal notice-and-comment procedure. For example, the Agriculture Department used this technique to authorize importation of meat products from the Czech Republic (rather than from "Czechoslovakia," as under the prior rule) and to update its technical standards for scales used for weighing grain. *See id.* at 7. Would it be going too far to say that when an agency manages to issue a rule through this technique, the rule should automatically be deemed to have satisfied the "good cause" exemption? Why is the use of the "direct final rule" device better than simply adopting the rule in reliance on the "unnecessary" exemption?

3. *Urgent rules.* Little if any distinction is drawn between the remaining two criteria in the good cause exemption, which address situations in which usual rulemaking procedures would be "impracticable" or "contrary to the public interest." Both terms are construed as coming into play when an agency has an overriding need to take immediate action. Rules that are designed to meet a serious health or safety problem, or some other risk of irreparable harm, often qualify for exemption on this basis. *See, e.g., Hawaii Helicopter Operators Ass'n v. FAA,* 51 F.3d 212, 214 (9th Cir.1995) (safety rule designed to counteract growing number of helicopter accidents); *Northern Arapahoe Tribe v. Hodel,* 808 F.2d 741, 750–52 (10th Cir.1987) (urgent need for hunting regulations where season had begun and herds could dwindle to extinction). Yet, pursuant to the policy of narrow construction of the exemption, courts sometimes refuse to accept an agency's assertion of urgency at face value. *See Action on Smoking and Health v. CAB,* 713 F.2d

795, 801–02 (D.C.Cir.1983) (fact that existing rule is confusing and difficult to enforce does not furnish good cause to replace it without prior notice).

Another line of cases has found good cause on the basis of a statutory deadline for the issuance of rules. *See, e.g., Sepulveda v. Block,* 782 F.2d 363, 366 (2d Cir.1986) (statute effective immediately, amid indications that Congress was dissatisfied with slow pace of implementation of prior statute). This rationale is unlikely to succeed, however, if the court believes that the agency itself was dilatory and brought the deadline pressure on itself. *Council of Southern Mountains, Inc. v. Donovan,* 653 F.2d 573, 581 (D.C.Cir. 1981).

Still another situation in which notice and comment procedure can be "impracticable" or "contrary to the public interest" is where the usual procedures would undermine the objectives of the statutory scheme the agency is trying to enforce. For example, when the government imposed wage and price controls in the early 1970's, it acted without a comment period, because advance notice of an impending price freeze would have caused merchants to raise their prices before the controls took effect, thus worsening the inflationary spiral that the controls were designed to alleviate. *DeRieux v. Five Smiths, Inc.,* 499 F.2d 1321, 1332 (Temp.Emer.Ct.App.1974) (upholding agency).

4. *State law.* Section 3(b) of the 1961 MSAPA, adopted in many states, provides:

> If an agency finds that an imminent peril to the public health, safety, or welfare requires adoption of a rule upon fewer than 20 days' notice and states in writing its reasons for that finding, it may proceed without prior notice or hearing or upon any abbreviated notice and hearing that it finds practicable, to adopt an emergency rule.

Is the § 3(b) "imminent peril" test different from the "impracticable, unnecessary, or contrary to the public interest" language of federal APA and 1981 MSAPA § 3–108(a)? If so, which is preferable? Suppose a governor signs legislation on June 8 to reduce general assistance (welfare) benefits in the next fiscal year. Without following rulemaking procedure, the commissioner of income maintenance immediately promulgates an emergency regulation to implement this law, explaining that the "State Budget ... is predicated on realizing savings from the above mentioned changes beginning on July 1," and the lack of timely regulations might therefore "imperil[] the integrity of the ... State Budget." Does this rationale pass the federal test? The 1961 MSAPA test? *See Melton v. Rowe,* 619 A.2d 483 (Conn.Super.1992).

5. *Interim-final rules.* Agencies that adopt a rule in reliance on the "impracticable" or "public interest" prongs of the good cause exemption usually request comments on the rule *after* it becomes effective. Such rules are often called "interim-final" rules, because they are both interim (they will be reconsidered and perhaps revised or replaced in light of the comments received) and final (they go into effect immediately). The Administrative Conference has recommended that the interim-final technique be used in connection with all rules expedited under the "impracticable" or "public interest" tests. ACUS Recommendation 95–4, *supra.* Does this recommendation go too far? After all, if a rule was lawfully issued under the good cause

exemption in the first place, anyone who disagrees with it could file a petition explaining her objection and asking the agency to change it (*see* § 6.3). Why isn't that sufficient? *See* Michael R. Asimow, "Interim–Final Rules," 1994–95 A.C.U.S. 477, 496–99. Incidentally, ACUS did not recommend that the interim-final approach be used when the agency invokes the "unnecessary" prong of the good cause exemption. Why not?

In a survey of numerous interim-final rules, it was found that nearly half remained unrevised after three years' time. *Id.* at 500. In that regard, consider § 3(b) of the 1961 MSAPA, which provides that rules issued on the basis of its good cause exemption "may be effective for a period of not longer than 120 days [renewable once for a period not exceeding ____ days]," although the subsequent adoption of an identical rule through the usual notice-and-comment procedures is not precluded. Should a 120–day limit on the shelf life of an interim-final rule be adopted at the federal level? *See id.* at 492, 503–04. Another response to the same concerns is 1981 MSAPA § 3–108(c). Under that section, after an agency has adopted a rule using the good cause exemption, the governor or a legislative committee may request the agency to hold a rulemaking proceeding, and the rule will cease to be effective 180 days after that request. Is this a better solution?

Finally, suppose an agency adopts an interim-final rule, and then, upon receiving and considering public comments, adopts a similar rule to last indefinitely. Later a court finds that the interim-final rule failed to qualify under the APA's good cause exemption because the agency failed to demonstrate exigent circumstances. In this situation, some cases have invalidated not only the interim-final rule, but also the final one. *See, e.g., New Jersey v. USEPA*, 626 F.2d 1038, 1049–50 (D.C.Cir.1980). These cases have expressed mistrust of the post-promulgation comment process, because of doubts "that persons would bother to submit their views or that the [agency] would seriously consider their suggestions after the regulations are a *fait accompli.*" *Kelly v. U.S. Department of Interior*, 339 F.Supp. 1095, 1101 (E.D.Cal. 1972). *But see Advocates for Highway & Auto Safety v. FHA*, 28 F.3d 1288, 1291–93 (D.C.Cir.1994). The *Advocates* case upheld such a final rule, noting that the agency had invited and taken seriously the post-adoption comments it received on the interim-final rule. The ACUS recommendation encourages courts to follow the *Advocates* approach. Should they?

6. *Immediate effectiveness.* As we saw in § 5.7, the federal APA provides that an agency usually must allow regulated parties thirty days' preparation time before a final rule goes into effect, but the agency may shorten or eliminate that waiting period if it can establish "good cause" for doing so. 5 U.S.C. § 553(d)(3). Like the § 553(b)(B) good cause exemption, this provision is intended to accommodate situations in which the government has urgent reasons to act quickly. Again, however, courts sometimes respond skeptically to government pleas of urgency.

An example of this skepticism is *United States v. Gavrilovic,* 551 F.2d 1099 (8th Cir.1977), in which the Drug Enforcement Agency issued a rule classifying mecloqualone as a Schedule I drug (the most strictly controlled category) and made the rule immediately effective, citing the dangers of the drug and the congressional desire for preventive controls. Defendants, who were manufacturing the drug in a warehouse disguised as a T-shirt company, were arrested 21 days later. Ultimately, the court overturned their conviction, because the DEA had not shown good cause for making the regulation effective in fewer than 30 days. The court said that the government's haste in promulgating the rule had been directly motivated by a desire to suppress the activities of these defendants. Yet, the court continued, the government did not need the Schedule I classification for that purpose: these defendants were not registered as drug manufacturers, so their operations could have been civilly enjoined immediately. The court said that the government's burden of justification under § 553(d)(3) is heavy when its rule creates criminal liability for previously lawful conduct. Was *Gavrilovic* correctly decided?

Despite the similarity in wording between § 553(b)(B) and § 553(d)(3), the two APA provisions to which the good cause exemptions are attached serve somewhat different purposes. Therefore, in unusual cases, an agency can have good cause to dispense with one safeguard but not the other. *See, e.g., Riverbend Farms, Inc. v. Madigan*, 958 F.2d 1479 (9th Cir.1992). That case concerned rules that limited the volume of oranges that producers could sell. Riverbend exceeded its quota and the agency sought to penalize it. Because of the volatility of the market, which fluctuated from week to week, the agency could not have waited 30 days for its rules to be effective. Consequently, the court decided, it had good cause to make the rule effective immediately. However, the agency could at least have given interested parties a few days' notice of proposed restrictions and accepted written comment on them; thus, it failed to establish good cause under § 553(b)(B). In the future, the agency would have to allow at least a minimal notice and comment opportunity.

Could the converse situation also exist, in which an agency has good cause to avoid soliciting comments on a rule but must still allow the thirty-day preparation period?

7. *Problem.* In 1982 a child was born in Bloomington, Indiana, with Down's syndrome, as well as a blockage in his digestive tract. His parents refused to consent to surgery to correct the blockage, and the child, who came to be known as "Baby Doe," died a few days later. The incident gave rise to nationwide controversy about the ethics of withholding life-sustaining medical treatment from newborn infants with severe physical or mental defects.

About a year later, the Secretary of Health and Human Services (HHS) promulgated an interim-final rule to address the issues in the Baby Doe incident. Hospitals were directed to post conspicuous notices declaring that discriminatory denial of food or care to handicapped infants violated federal law (a reference to the Rehabilitation Act of 1973). The notices invited anyone with knowledge of such discrimination to call a toll-free "hotline" at HHS to report the violation. Hospitals were also directed to provide access to their records and facilities to officials investigating alleged discrimination of the "Baby Doe" variety. Access would have to be provided outside of normal business hours if HHS officials deemed such access necessary to protect the life or health of a handicapped infant.

Explaining her failure to allow prior notice and comment on the rule, the Secretary noted that investigators already had authority to obtain access to hospital records and facilities. The extension of this authority to compulsory access outside of normal business hours was a "minor technical change and necessary to meet emergency situations." More generally, she said, "[a]ll modifications made by the interim final rule are necessary to protect life from imminent harm. Any delay would leave lives at risk." The regulation was set to go into effect in fifteen days, which the Secretary estimated was the minimum time needed to set up the hotline apparatus.

After the comment period, the Secretary issued a final rule that was essentially the same as the previous rule. Was the interim-final rule procedurally valid? How about the final rule? *See American Academy of Pediatrics v. Heckler,* 561 F.Supp. 395 (D.D.C.1983).

§ 6.1.2 EXEMPTED SUBJECT MATTER

Both federal and state APAs provide categorical exemptions from the usual notice-and-comment requirements for rules relating to certain governmental functions. Unlike the good cause exemptions, discussed in the preceding section, the categorical exemptions are not based upon an evaluation of the particular circumstances surrounding an individual rulemaking. Instead, they represent a generalized judgment that *all* rules falling into the defined categories should be exempt, regardless of individual circumstances.

The policy of narrow construction of rulemaking exemptions also applies to these provisions, at least at the federal level. Indeed, that policy is bolstered by indications in the legislative history of the APA that these exemptions apply only " 'to the extent' that the excepted subject matter is clearly and directly involved." *APA Legislative History,* S.Doc.No. 79–248, at 257 (1946) (House committee report). Moreover, these exemptions are inapplicable to the extent other law requires an agency to follow usual rulemaking procedures for any of the rules within the excepted categories. Even so, many observers believe that some of the exemptions are still too broad and should be repealed or substantially narrowed by legislative action.

Notes and Questions

1. *Proprietary matters.* Federal APA § 553(a)(2) excludes rules relating to "public property, loans, grants, benefits, or contracts" from all of the provisions of § 553, including notice and comment procedure as well as the requirements for deferred effective date and the right to petition. This broad exemption covers rulemaking involving hundreds of billions of dollars each year and affects a vast number of business concerns as well as recipients of government benefits.

Consider some of the activities that can potentially come within its sweep: the sale or lease of public lands or of mineral, timber, or grazing rights in such lands; the use of national forests and national parks; loans to local government for urban mass transportation systems, small business loans, disaster loans, and student loans; grants-in-aid programs; pensions, social security old age and disability payments, and such welfare programs as food stamps; and government contracts for the procurement of land, goods, or services, and for construction of any kind. The exemption means that, in all of these areas, affected people have no right under the APA to influence the contents of agency rules. It also means that agencies covered by the exemption may become out of touch with public needs and desires.

The exemption is apparently an outgrowth of the right-privilege distinction, which in recent decades has been rejected in due process law. *See* § 2.2. Does that distinction nevertheless have a place in the rulemaking context? Even if it is obsolete, might some of the categories listed in the exemption be justified simply in order to allow agencies necessary flexibility in their decisionmaking in the areas in question? The Administrative Conference found none of these rationales convincing and recommended that the proprietary matters exemption should be repealed. *See* ACUS Recommendation 69–8, 38 Fed.Reg. 19782 (1969). This recommendation was based on Arthur Earl Bonfield, "Public Participation in Federal Rulemaking Relating to Public Property, Loans, Grants, Benefits, or Contracts," 118 U.Pa.L.Rev. 540 (1970).

2. *Waiver of exemptions.* In its recommendation opposing the proprietary matters exemption, ACUS called on agencies to utilize rulemaking procedures in these areas without awaiting a legislative command to do so. Numerous agencies have followed this advice by issuing regulations waiving any reliance on the exemption.

When an agency adopts a procedural rule that commits it to follow § 553 procedure, despite a statutory exemption, it is required to conform to its own rule. *See Alcaraz v. Block,* 746 F.2d 593, 611 (9th Cir.1984); *Rodway v. USDA,* 514 F.2d 809, 813–14 (D.C.Cir.1975). Should a similar requirement apply to an agency that has not formally adopted such a rule but does routinely provide notice and comment in exempt situations? *See Malek–Marzban v. INS,* 653 F.2d 113, 116 (4th Cir.1981) (no).

3. *Proprietary matters in state law.* Although the 1981 MSAPA does not contain an exemption with the broad scope of federal APA § 553(a)(2), it does exempt certain categories of rules from rulemaking requirements (other than the right to petition). *See* § 3–116(3)–(5). For example, a rule that "establishes specific prices to be charged for particular goods or services sold by an agency" or that concerns "care of agency owned or operated facilities" is exempted. If, as ACUS concluded, the proprietary matters exemption in the federal APA should be abandoned, are these MSAPA exemptions likewise unjustified?

4. *Agency management and personnel.* Under federal APA § 553(a)(2), rules "relating to agency management or personnel" are excepted from all rulemaking requirements. Although this exemption is codified in the same sentence of the APA as the proprietary matters exemption, ACUS did *not* call for its repeal. Nevertheless, the scope of the exemption is uncertain. The legislative history of the APA contains indications that the exemption should not apply to rules that have a substantial effect on persons outside of the national government. Indeed, some case law reflects that assumption. *See, e.g., Joseph v. U.S. Civil Service Comm'n,* 554 F.2d 1140, 1153 n. 23 (D.C.Cir.1977) (rules authorizing federal employees to participate in District of Columbia elections, despite Hatch Act restrictions on political activity, were void for lack of notice and comment).

On the other hand, the same court reached a contrasting result in *Stewart v. Smith,* 673 F.2d 485, 496–500 (D.C.Cir.1982). That case involved a rule by which the Bureau of Prisons announced that it would refuse to consider persons over thirty-four years of age for employment within correctional facilities. (According to the court, a statutory exception to the age discrimination laws permitted such a policy.) The court held, 2–1, that § 553 procedures were not required, because of the agency management and personnel exemption. Do you agree with the procedural holding?

In practice, the effect of the federal APA personnel exemption has been reduced somewhat by other statutes. The Federal Civil Service Reform Act of 1978, for example, requires the Office of Personnel Management to follow notice and comment procedures in formulating government-wide personnel rules unless they are "temporary in nature and . . . necessary to be implemented expeditiously as the result of an emergency." 5 U.S.C. §§ 1103(b)(3), 1105.

Section 3–116(1) of the 1981 MSAPA explicitly adopts the *Joseph* analysis: it excepts from usual rulemaking procedures rules "concerning only the internal management of an agency which [do] not directly and substantially affect the procedural or substantive rights or duties of any segment of the public." A similarly worded exemption is found in § 1(7)(A) of the 1961 MSAPA and in the acts of many states.

Under the federal APA or the 1981 MSAPA, would a rule describing the performance criteria for agency employees engaged in law enforcement be exempt from the usual rulemaking procedures? How about a rule prescribing the office hours of an agency?

5. *Military and foreign affairs functions.* Federal APA § 553(a)(1) exempts a rule from all rulemaking procedures "to the extent there is involved . . . a military or foreign affairs function of the United States." Like the proprietary matters exemption, this provision seems much broader than necessary. The Administrative Conference has proposed that Congress should narrow it. *See* ACUS Recommendation 73–5, 39 Fed.Reg. 4847 (1974); Arthur Earl Bonfield, "Military and Foreign Affairs Function Rulemaking Under the APA," 71 Mich.L.Rev. 221 (1972). Again, nonstatutory developments have made the exemption less influential than it might be. The Department of Defense has established a general policy favoring notice and comment procedures in the development of rules having a substantial and direct effect on the public, unless a "significant and legitimate interest" of the DOD or the public requires the omission of those procedures. *See* 32 C.F.R. § 296.3.

Meanwhile, agencies and courts have had to work out the boundaries of the existing exemption. Some applications are relatively straightforward, as with regulations implementing international trade agreements. *See International Brotherhood of Teamsters v. Pena,* 17 F.3d 1478 (D.C.Cir.1994); *American Ass'n of Exporters & Importers v. United States,* 751 F.2d 1239, 1249 (Fed.Cir.1985). In *Independent Guard Ass'n v. O'Leary,* 57 F.3d 766 (9th Cir.1995), amended, 69 F.3d 1038 (9th Cir.1995), however, the court held that the exemption did *not* apply to a rule governing drug abuse by armed guards at a site at which the Department of Energy researched, produced, and tested nuclear explosive devices for the military. Wackenhut, a private contractor, hired and supervised the guards. The rule provided for random drug testing and permanent disqualification from duty for any employee who had ever used hallucinogens. The court said that DOE, although a "civilian" agency, does perform some "military functions" to which the rulemaking exemption could apply. Nevertheless:

> The legislative history and relevant case law direct that exceptions to the APA be narrowly construed, and that the exception can be invoked only where the activities being regulated directly involve a military function. If the Secretary's position were adopted, and contractor support activities held to be within the scope of the military function exception, maintenance staff, custodial help, food service workers and even window washers could find their undoubtedly necessary support tasks swept within the exception's ambit, and DOE regulations affecting their employment exempt from notice and comment. Neither the statute, nor common sense, requires such a result.

> We do not mean to imply that the military function exception can never apply to a contractor's services. Indeed, at argument IGAN conceded that contractor employees could perform a military function within the meaning of the APA. For example, if they were making military weapons, they might well be performing such a function. The record shows that the guards employed and supervised by Wackenhut were performing duties similar to those performed by civilian security guards everywhere. They were no more performing a "military function" than civilian contract guards employed to guard judges are performing a "judicial function." The exemption should not be stretched to encompass civilian support services.

6. *Problem.* Suppose that the rule in *Independent Guard Ass'n* had barred civilian guards from using hallucinogens while serving on duty, or within twenty-four hours of such service. Would it be exempted from notice and comment obligations by the military function exemption? By the agency management and personnel exemption?

§ 6.1.3 PROCEDURAL RULES

"Rules of agency organization, procedure, or practice" are exempted from usual notice and comment procedures by federal APA § 553(b)(A). There is no similar exemption for such rules in the MSAPAs or in state APAs. A constant problem in the law is to distinguish "procedure" from "substance." Nevertheless, such a distinction must be drawn under this exemption.

UNITED STATES DEPARTMENT OF LABOR v. KAST METALS CORP.
744 F.2d 1145 (5th Cir.1984).

[Before inspecting a factory for unsafe working conditions, OSHA must secure a warrant. Recall *Marshall v. Barlow's, Inc.,* discussed in § 4.1.2. Under prior practice, OSHA selected businesses for inspection by a random method. Without notice and comment, OSHA adopted a new instruction to staff to select businesses with the highest accident rates.

Instruction CPL 2.25B. Applying that formula, OSHA selected Kast Metals for inspection. OSHA secured a warrant, but Kast denied entry to the inspectors and moved to quash the warrant, arguing that CPL 2.25B was invalidly adopted. The District Court agreed because it found that CPL 2.25B had a substantial impact on regulated persons.

The Court of Appeals (Goldberg, J.) first held that CPL 2.25B was a rule as defined in APA § 551(4), rather than an investigatory action that was outside the definition of a "rule."]

The APA expressly exempts "rules of agency organization, procedure, or practice" from the requirements of notice and comment rulemaking. 5 U.S.C. § 553(b)(A). This exemption, as well as others specified proximately in the Act, is a consequence of Congress's belief that "certain administrative pronouncements [do] not require public participation in their formulation." In exempting procedural rules, Congress has placed a premium on efficiency by avoiding the often cumbersome and time-consuming mechanisms of public input. This judgment prevailed despite the widely-shared recognition that administrative agencies need direct lines to the public voice because of their distance from the elective process.

It is beyond dispute that CPL 2.25B is, on the surface, a procedural rule.... Whereas substantive or "legislative" rules affect individual rights and obligations and are binding on the courts, nonlegislative rules do not have the force of law. At least initially, courts "will honor [an agency's] characterization if it reasonably describes what the agency in fact has done."

The plan's stated purpose was to "describe[ ] the steps to be followed and the criteria to be applied in selecting workplace establishments for programmed inspection" pursuant to the OSH Act. Moreover, the plan does not purport or seem to create new law; instead, it contained an OSHA policy of "simplified ... scheduling procedures in order to ease the administrative burden." The Secretary used CPL 2.25B to concentrate OSHA's inspection resources in industries with the highest potential for safety and health violations. The plan is procedural on its face.

This conclusion, however, does not end our inquiry. As noted earlier, the distinction between a rule of procedure and one of substance is not black and white...].

Inevitably, in determining whether the APA requires notice and comment rulemaking, the interests of agency efficiency and public input are in tension. The exemption from informal rulemaking requirements for procedural rules reflects the congressional judgment that such rules, because they do not directly guide public conduct, do not merit the administrative burdens of public input proceedings. In applying this exemption, then, courts have been less concerned with the formal appellation of a rule—whether it is "procedural" or "substantive"—than with its effect on those within its regulatory scope.

In *Brown Express [Inc. v. United States,* 607 F.2d 695 (5th Cir. 1979)], we recognized that a seemingly procedural rule does not have its apparent nature cast in stone for purposes of APA rulemaking requirements:

> "[W]hen a proposed regulation of general applicability has a *substantial impact* on the regulated industry, or an important class of the members or the products of that industry, notice and opportunity for comment should first be provided." The exemption of section 553(b)(A) from the duty to provide notice by publication [and a forum for public comment] does not extend to those procedural rules that depart from existing practice and have a substantial impact on those regulated.

In essence, the substantial impact test is the primary means by which courts look beyond the label "procedural" to determine whether a rule is of the type Congress thought appropriate for public participation. An agency rule that modifies substantive rights and interests can only be nominally procedural and the exemption for such rules of agency procedure cannot apply. Kast urges that, having found CPL 2.25B to be a procedural rule, we should nevertheless not give effect to the APA's procedural rules exemption from informal rulemaking requirements because the rule has substantial impact on those regulated. We disagree.

OSHA's inspection plan casts not the stone of substantial impact. . . . CPL 2.25B has no cognizable impact, substantial or otherwise, on any right or interest of Kast. While the company has an "interest . . . in being free from *unreasonable* intrusions onto its property by agents of the government," this interest does not extend to freedom from *any* OSHA inspection. The government still must satisfy a federal magistrate, as it did in this case, "that the inspection is reasonable under the Constitution, is authorized by statute, and is pursuant to an administrative plan containing specific neutral criteria." *Marshall v. Barlow's, Inc.*
. . .

Moreover, the rights and obligations of an employer within OSHA's jurisdiction exist independently of a plan whose sole purpose is the funnelling of agency inspection resources. If Kast's argument is that another directive might have spared it an inspection, or given rise to one at another time, we find no merit therein. Adherence to the safety and health standards promulgated by OSHA under 29 U.S.C. § 655, should not turn on the agency's ability or inclination to play watchdog. No inspection plan creates in an employer the right to be free of citation; the relevant standards of employer conduct originate not in CPL 2.25B but elsewhere. . . .

In our case . . . appellee asserts no defeated expectations as a result of CPL 2.25B. . . . Although the plan departed from a previous inspection formula, change alone is insufficient to satisfy the twin prongs of departure and substantial impact found in *Brown Express.* . . .

The substantive effect of CPL 2.25B is purely derivative: the source of the employers' woes is the OSH Act itself as well as in the legislative rules promulgated in its shadow, which alone are responsible for having shaped employer conduct.... Because the district court should have honored the inspection warrant, we reverse the judgment below and remand with instructions to dismiss appellee's motion to quash.

Notes and Questions

1. *Substance and procedure—rationale.* State APAs do not exempt procedural rules from notice and comment procedures. Why does the federal APA do so? Does the *Kast Metals* case answer this question?

2. *Substance v. procedure—the substantial impact test.* In the *Kast Metals* case, the court acknowledged that the rule "on the surface" was "procedural," since it told agency staff how to select businesses for inspection and did not tell the businesses to do anything. Why did not the opinion stop there? Would *any* rule that tells staff what to do be "procedural" rather than "substantive"? What if the rule told agency inspectors to cite all factories as unsafe which used two-prong rather than three-prong electrical outlets, and there was no other rule relating to electrical outlets?

In *Kast Metals* the court claims it is following the holding in the *Brown Express* case that a rule is not "procedural" if it "departs from existing practice" and has a "substantial impact on the regulated industry...." Did not CPL 2.25B clearly "depart from existing practice" and have a "substantial impact"? CPL 2.25B meant that dangerous factories, like those of Kast Metals Corporation, were more likely to be inspected and to become subject to penalties than under the prior practice of random selection. That seems quite "substantial." Or did the court mean something different by its "substantial impact" test?

3. *Alternative criteria.* The District of Columbia Circuit has sought, with mixed success, to develop an alternative to the substantial impact test. In *American Hospital Ass'n v. Bowen*, 834 F.2d 1037, 1047 (D.C.Cir.1987), the court said that its cases had "gradually shifted focus from asking whether a given procedure has a 'substantial impact' on parties to inquiring more broadly whether the agency action also encodes a substantive value judgment or puts a stamp of approval or disapproval on a given type of behavior. The gradual move away from looking solely into the substantiality of impact reflects a candid recognition that even unambiguously procedural measures affect parties to some degree."

However, the court's alternative formula has not proved easy to administer. In *Air Transport Ass'n v. Department of Transp.*, 900 F.2d 369 (D.C.Cir.1990), *remanded*, 498 U.S. 1077 (1991), *vacated as moot*, 933 F.2d 1043 (D.C.Cir.1991), the court held that the FAA should have used notice and comment before promulgating a new set of practice rules providing for discovery, adversary hearings, administrative appeals, etc., in civil penalty actions. The court said that these rules " 'encode[d] a substantive value judgment' on the appropriate balance between a defendant's rights to adjudicatory procedures and the agency's interest in efficient prosecution." *Id.* at 376 (emphasis omitted).

This reasoning attracted much criticism, *see, e.g.,* Jeffrey S. Lubbers & Nancy G. Miller, "The APA Procedural Rule Exemption: Looking for a Way to Clear the Air," 6 Admin.L.J.Am.U. 481, 489–90 (1992), and the court expressly disavowed it in *JEM Broadcasting Co. v. FCC,* 22 F.3d 320 (D.C.Cir.1994). There, the FCC anticipated a flood of applications for some new FM stations. To streamline the application process, it adopted, without notice and comment, a rule to the effect that incomplete applications would be rejected without any opportunity for corrections. Appellant JEM fell victim to this rule and complained that it was procedurally invalid. According to JEM, the rule "encoded the substantive value judgment that applications containing minor errors should be sacrificed to promote efficient application processing." The court rejected this argument, stating that the rule was procedural because it "did not change the *substantive standards* by which the FCC evaluates license applications...." In applying the procedural rule exemption, the court said, the issue " 'is one of degree,' and our task is to identify which substantive effects are 'sufficiently grave so that notice and comment are needed to safeguard the policies underlying the APA.' " How far removed is the D.C. Circuit's ultimate stance from that of *Kast Metals?*

4. *Problem.* Refer back to the *Baby Doe* problem in § 6.1.1 N.7. Should the § 553 challenge to the regulation in that case have been rejected on the basis of the procedural rule exemption?

§ 6.1.4 NONLEGISLATIVE RULES

§ 6.1.4a Legislative and nonlegislative rules

Legislative rules are rules issued by an agency pursuant to an express or implied grant of authority to issue rules with the force of law. Because they can directly alter the rights and obligations of citizens, they are often considered to be the most important type of agency rules, and most of the cases examined in the preceding chapter concerned the procedural requirements that must accompany their issuance.

Also vital to the administrative process, however, are nonlegislative rules, also known as guidance documents. These are agency rules that do not have the force of law, as they are not based upon delegated authority to issue such rules. (That is, either the agency did not possess such authority or chose not to use it.) Agencies issue large numbers of guidance documents, and many are of great practical importance:

> Members of the public who live and do business in the shadow of regulation need to learn what the agency thinks the law means and how discretion may be exercised. Increasing the level of people's understanding about what the law requires of them is a good thing for society; it reduces the number of unintentional law violations, and it reduces the transaction costs incurred in planning private transactions. Agency staff members also require authoritative information about these subjects in order to apply the law consistently, fairly, and efficiently.

Michael Asimow, "California Underground Regulations," 44 Admin.L.Rev. 43, 43 (1992). Indeed, many agencies generate dozens or hundreds of pages of nonlegislative rules for every page of legislative rules they promulgate. Moreover, according to some scholars, the tendency for agencies to rely on guidance documents as instruments of policy development is now on the increase, because of the recent growth in procedural hurdles that agencies must surmount when they attempt to promulgate legislative rules. *See* § 5.1 N.1. Agencies' widespread use of guidance documents is a reality that administrative law must accommodate, but it also creates risks of abuses. Some of the legal system's efforts to curb such abuses are explored in this section.

The preeminent characteristic of a legislative rule, inherent in its having "the force of law," is that it is binding and enforceable in the same way as other species of effective law. So, for example, the United States Supreme Court has noted that a "regulation ... made by ... [a] commission in pursuance of constitutional statutory authority ... has the same force as though prescribed in terms by the statute." *Atchison, T. & S.F. Ry. Co. v. Scarlett,* 300 U.S. 471, 474 (1937). Violation of a valid legislative rule, therefore, is often a basis for imposing civil and criminal sanctions. The binding nature of legislative rules does not appear to be required by due process; instead, it appears to be a product of federal and state administrative law. *Board of Curators of Univ. of Mo. v. Horowitz,* 435 U.S. 78, 92 n. 8 (1978); 1981 MSAPA § 5–116(c)(8)(ii).

More particularly, valid legislative rules are binding on *private persons;* as we have seen in cases such as *Heckler v. Campbell,* excerpted in § 3.2, they can extinguish citizens' right to be heard on the issues that they address. At the same time, legislative rules are also binding on the *issuing agency,* which must adhere to them until such time as they may be revoked or invalidated by a court. *United States v. Nixon,* 418 U.S. 683, 694–96 (1974); *Tew v. City of Topeka Police & Fire Civil Service Comm'n,* 697 P.2d 1279, 1282–83 (Kan.1985). Consequently, an agency may not violate its own legislative rules, although it may be able to waive them if it has authority to do so. *See* § 6.4. Finally, legislative rules are sometimes said to be "binding on the courts." That notion, however, is somewhat less helpful to understanding, because the circumstances under which courts may invalidate administrative rules are governed by a complex body of doctrines that cannot be captured very well in a short phrase. *See* Chapter 9.

Legislative rules are sometimes known as "substantive rules," but that usage can be misleading, because it undesirably implies a contrast with "procedural rules." Actually, procedural rules are often legislative rules, having the force of law, and, therefore, binding the issuing agency. *See Service v. Dulles,* 354 U.S. 363, 388 (1957), and *Vitarelli v. Seaton,* 359 U.S. 535 (1959) (holding agencies bound by procedural rules they had previously adopted).

In contrast, nonlegislative rules are not automatically binding on agencies or citizens. *See Vietnam Veterans of America v. Secretary of Navy,* 843 F.2d 528, 536–38 (D.C.Cir.1988); Byron Swift, "Interpretive Rules and the Legal Opinions of Government Attorneys," 33 Ad.L.Rev. 425, 434–38 (1981). To be sure, nonlegislative rules can sometimes have *some* constraining effects on subsequent agency action, such as where the elements of an estoppel are present, or where the agency's failure to explain why it did not adhere to the rule renders the action arbitrary and capricious. But these constraining effects result from the agency's misuse of its discretion, not from a belief that the nonlegislative rule is "law." (In the states, however, the law seems to be less clear-cut on this point. *See* § 6.1.4c N.7.)

Nonlegislative rules are commonly subdivided into "interpretive rules" and "general statements of policy." Federal APA §§ 553(b)(A) and 553(d)(2) exempt both those two categories of rules from the usual notice and comment and delayed effectiveness procedures. (Actually, the APA uses the word "interpretative," not "interpretive," but both terms are in common usage.) Most of the federal case law on nonlegislative rules has grown out of efforts to determine whether a given rule should have been issued using notice and comment procedures. This has proved a difficult task in practice. Meanwhile, most state APAs do not exempt interpretive rules and policy statements from rulemaking procedural requirements; state law thus offers some revealing contrasts with the federal model.

§ 6.1.4b   Policy statements

MADA–LUNA v. FITZPATRICK
813 F.2d 1006 (9th Cir.1987).

[Petitioner Mada–Luna was a Mexican national who had been a legal permanent resident of the U.S. He was subject to deportation because of a narcotics conviction. He applied for "deferred action" status that would delay his deportation. He had served as an undercover agent for the federal government, his wife and children were U.S. citizens, and he had been kidnapped and threatened with death by Mexican drug traffickers.

The Immigration and Naturalization Service (INS) adopted an Operations Instruction to its staff in 1978. It provided that "[i]n every case where the district director determines that adverse action would be unconscionable or result in undue hardship because of the existence of appealing humanitarian factors, he shall recommend consideration for deferred action category." In any such decision, "consideration should include but not be limited to" age, years present in the United States, physical or mental condition, "family situation in the United States— effect of expulsion," and criminal activities. In 1981, INS adopted a new version of the Instruction, which said that the district director "may, in his discretion, recommend consideration of deferred action, an act [that is] in no way an entitlement, in appropriate cases." This instruction also listed several factors that, "among others, should be considered." The agency did not employ notice and comment procedures in 1978 or 1981 and did not publish either version in the *Federal Register*.

The INS district director denied deferred action status under the 1981 Instruction. Mada–Luna would have had a better chance under the

1978 version, so he contends that the 1981 version was invalidly adopted and the 1978 version invalidly repealed. The INS contends that both versions were "general statements of policy."]

FLETCHER, J.: The APA does not define the term "general statements of policy" as it is used in § 553. However, it is defined in the Attorney General's Memorandum on the APA, which was issued in 1947, just after the APA's enactment, as "statements issued by an agency to advise the public prospectively of the manner in which the agency proposes to exercise a discretionary power." When agencies have been delegated discretionary authority over a given area, such as the Attorney General and the INS in the field of immigration, such policy statements serve a dual purpose. Besides informing the public concerning the agency's future plans and priorities for exercising its discretionary power, they serve to "educate" and provide direction to the agency's personnel in the field, who are required to implement its policies and exercise its discretionary power in specific cases. Bonfield, *Some Tentative Thoughts on Public Participation in the Making of Interpretative Rules and General Statements of Policy Under the APA,* 23 Admin.L.Rev. 101, 115 (1970–71) ("It may be that 'general statements of policy' are rules directed primarily at the staff of an agency describing how it will conduct agency discretionary functions, while other rules are directed primarily at the public in an effort to impose obligations on them.").

When a federal agency issues a directive concerning the future exercise of its discretionary power, for purposes of APA section 553, its directive will constitute either a substantive rule, for which notice-and-comment procedures are required, or a general statement of policy, for which they are not. The critical factor to determine whether a directive announcing a new policy constitutes a rule or a general statement of policy is "the extent to which the challenged [directive] leaves the agency, or its implementing official, free to exercise discretion to follow, or not to follow, the [announced] policy in an individual case." To the extent that the directive merely provides *guidance* to agency officials in exercising their discretionary powers while preserving their flexibility and their opportunity to make "individualized determination[s]," it constitutes a general statement of policy.

In such cases, Congress has determined that notice-and-comment rulemaking would be of limited utility, *see* 5 U.S.C. §§ 553(b)(A), 553(d)(2), and parties can challenge the policy determinations made by the agency only if and when the directive has been applied specifically to them. In contrast, to the extent that the directive "narrowly limits administrative discretion" or establishes a *"binding norm"* that "so fills out the statutory scheme that upon application one need only determine whether a given case is within the rule's criterion," it effectively replaces agency discretion with a new "binding rule of substantive law." In these cases, notice-and-comment rulemaking proceedings are required, as they would be for any other substantive rule, and they will represent the only opportunity for parties to challenge the policy determinations upon which the new rule is based. Pacific Gas & Elec. Co. v. FPC, 506 F.2d 33, 38 (D.C.Cir.1974).

Thus, for the 1978 and 1981 Operating Instructions to qualify under section 553's "general statement of policy" exception, they must satisfy two requirements. First, they must operate only prospectively. Second, they must not establish a "binding norm" or be "finally determinative of the issues or rights to which [they are] addressed," but must instead leave INS officials "free to consider the individual facts in the various cases that arise." . . .

. . . Mada apparently assumes that the 1978 Instruction cannot constitute a general statement of policy under section 553 because the INS's replacement of the 1978 Operating Instruction with the 1981 Instruction diminishes the likelihood that he and other similarly situated aliens will be granted deferred action status, and eliminates their opportunity to obtain judicial review. In essence, Mada suggests that if the repeal of an agency directive will cause a "substantial impact" to the rights of a specific class it cannot be exempt from section 553's notice-and-comment requirements. However, we have expressly "rejected the argument that, for the purposes of imposing notice-and-comment requirements on [an] agency for a particular rule, [courts should] look to the 'substantial impact' of the rule."

We have concluded that " '[s]imply because agency action has substantial impact does not mean it is subject to notice and comment if it is otherwise expressly exempt under the APA.' " Rivera v. Becerra, 714 F.2d [887, 890–91 (9th Cir.1983)] (citing the Supreme Court's admonition in *Vermont Yankee* that courts should not impose procedural requirements upon agencies beyond those expressly provided in the APA). . . .

In determining whether particular regulations or directives qualify for one of section 553's exemptions from notice-and-comment requirements, we have focused upon the effect of the regulation or directive upon *agency decisionmaking*, not the public at large.[11] . . .

Applying [our] two requirements to the 1978 Operating Instruction, we conclude that it constituted a general statement of policy, and thus could be validly repealed and superseded without notice-and-comment proceedings. The 1978 Instruction operated only prospectively, and did not establish a "binding norm" that would limit the district director's discretion. The Instruction expressly authorizes the district director 'to consider [any] individual facts' that he may feel appropriate in addition to the five enumerated factors in the instruction. It requires him to evaluate whether departing or excluding an individual petitioning for

---

11. Because many general statements of policy have a substantial impact, *see Jean,* 711 F.2d at 1480, broad application of the "substantial impact" test could well obliterate much of the "general statement of policy" exception to the APA's notice-and-comment procedures. We conclude that Congress could not have intended such a result, given the structure of section 553 and its use of classifications like "general statement of policy," which focus upon the effect a directive has upon agency decisionmaking, rather than the effect on the public at large.

deferred action status 'would be *unconscionable* or result in *undue hardship* because of the existence of *appealing humanitarian factors*"; these terms allow for great agency latitude and discretion, and cannot be viewed as establishing a 'binding norm.' " ...

We conclude that the 1981 Operating Instruction presents even a clearer case of a general statement of policy. Like the 1978 Operating Instruction, it operates only prospectively. Moreover, the wording and structure of the amended Instruction emphasizes the broad and unfettered discretion of the district director in making deferred action determinations. None of the factors listed in the 1981 Instruction establishes a "binding norm": they require the district director to evaluate the "sympathetic" appeal of the deferred action applicant and to surmise the possible internal agency reaction and publicity that would result from his deportation and exclusion. The Instruction leaves the district director "free to consider the individual facts" in each case.

Notes and Questions

1. *Criticism of nonlegislative rules.* Agencies are frequently accused of circumventing normal rulemaking procedures by using guidance documents in an inflexible or coercive way. Too often, it is argued, agency staff turn a deaf ear to criticisms of a policy statement, and citizens feel obliged to comply with the statement because they lack the resources or nerve to resist. In this fashion, guidance documents are said to become, in practical effect, as binding on private parties as a legislative rule is. Professor Anthony has summarized the objections that this recurrent situation provokes:

> In such cases, affected persons and the public generally will not have been accorded a regularized notice of the agencies' actions or an assured opportunity to participate in their development. Citizens or lawyers in Pocatello, or even in Washington, sometimes do not have ready access to the guidances or manuals that agencies are using to bind them. And when they do, they can be confused about the legal import of documents like these, and frustrated at their inability to escape the practical obligations or standards the documents impose. Often, in order to win a needed approval, they must accept the conditions demanded by the nonlegislative rule, and thereby as a practical matter surrender the opportunity to obtain court review of the offending conditions. The agencies, for their part, might not have issued these pronouncements so freely if legislative rulemaking procedures had had to be followed.

Robert A. Anthony, "Interpretive Rules, Policy Statements, Guidances, Manuals, and the Like—Should Federal Agencies Use Them to Bind the Public?," 41 Duke L.J. 1311, 1372 (1992).

The American Bar Association and the Administrative Conference have adopted recommendations to address some of these concerns. In a 1993 resolution, the ABA stated:

> When an agency proposes to apply a nonlegislative rule in an enforcement or other proceeding, it should provide affected private parties an opportunity to challenge the wisdom or legality of the rule, either in the instant proceeding or in a separate proceeding established for that

purpose. The agency should not allow the fact that a rule has already been published or made available to the public to foreclose consideration of the positions advanced by the affected private parties.

Summary of Actions of ABA House of Delegates, August 1993, at 23–24; *see also* ACUS Recommendation 92–2, 57 Fed.Reg. 30103 (1992).

2. *Support for nonlegislative rules.* The literature also contains vigorous defenses of agencies' use of guidance documents. According to Professor Strauss, Anthony's argument does not adequately take into account the competing equities of people who *want* the guidance that nonlegislative rules provide:

> Professor Anthony sees in a potential *complainant* about the policy judgments entailed in [the Nuclear Regulatory Commission's] technical specifications for nuclear power plants, a party bound in practical effect by those guidelines.... But ... [f]rom the perspective of an applicant whose chief interest is to build a plant that will meet NRC standards, receiving such guidance from the agency where possible is strongly preferable to being left to speculate about the details of agency policies and to pay for case-by-case demonstration that it has met those policies' demands. The NRC *may* leave these issues to determination first in negotiations with uninstructed staff and then in the adjudicatory licensing proceedings in which the applicant bears the burden of showing that its design will satisfy safety requirements. Do we wish to encourage it to do so?

Peter L. Strauss, "The Rulemaking Continuum," 41 Duke L.J. 1463, 1481–82 (1992).

The experience of California suggests what would happen if the exemption for nonlegislative rules were eliminated. Although state APAs generally require pre-adoption procedure for nonlegislative rules, with only very limited exemptions, agencies in most states are permitted to ignore the requirement with impunity. In California, however, the requirement is vigorously enforced. As a practical reality, then, "underground regulations," meaning guidance documents adopted without full compliance with the APA rulemaking formalities, are considered invalid. Michael Asimow, "California Underground Regulations," 44 Admin.L.Rev. 43, 44–45 (1992).

Asimow's study showed that the California system had numerous negative consequences for agencies in that state. Because of the costs and delays of rulemaking procedure, most agencies stopped issuing guidance documents entirely. In many cases, agencies found it quicker and cheaper to go to the legislature and change the statute than to adopt guidance documents through rulemaking. Other agencies relied on techniques of dubious validity to provide interpretive guidance (such as announcing "tentative" policy positions but never finalizing them, or sending out identical letters to numerous regulated parties but never generalizing them). Other agencies simply defied the law, adopting guidance documents without advance procedures, and gambling that they wouldn't be challenged. Indeed, the study points out that a conservative estimate suggests that 100,000 to 200,000 underground regulations are currently being enforced by California state agencies. *Id.* at 56–61.

You will recall that, according to some scholars, increases in the procedural burdens associated with rulemaking have caused agencies to issue fewer rules. *See* § 5.1 N.1. Asimow's study maintains that this chilling effect is particularly powerful in the case of guidance documents:

> The reason for this assumption is that nonlegislative rules are different from other bureaucratic outputs in one critical respect: normally the regulatory program can function without them. Legislative rules are usually necessary to set a regulatory program in motion, particularly if the agency's statute is not self-executing. Similarly, an agency must adjudicate the cases on its docket and respond to complaints. But nonlegislative rules can be dispensed with because an agency is not usually required to issue them. Their primary function is to diminish uncertainty, but the agency is not required to diminish uncertainty.
>
> The costs of uncertainty are largely borne by the members of the public, not by agency officials. For that reason, public uncertainty is an externality that agency utility-maximizers need not take into account. Thus an agency may well choose to muddle through without producing any guidance documents, or it may find some informal way to communicate the information. ... [S]ince the production of nonlegislative rules can usually be deferred until additional resources become available, such rules must often be losers in the unending internal struggle for resources.

Asimow, *supra*, at 64–65.

3. *Policy statements v. legislative rules.* According to the court in *Mada-Luna*, policy statements differ from legislative rules in that they must be prospective and nonbinding. Why should it matter whether a purported policy statement is "prospective"? Suppose an INS district director issues a statement summarizing the criteria that she has informally used for several months when acting on deferred action petitions. She states that she plans to continue using those criteria unless someone persuades her to do otherwise. Could that declaration be a policy statement? *See McLouth Steel Products Corp. v. Thomas,* 838 F.2d 1317, 1320 (D.C.Cir.1988).

Next consider the court's distinction between rules that "establish a binding norm" and rules that leave officials "free to consider the individual facts in the various cases that arise." The rationale for the distinction appears to be as follows: When an agency makes a discretionary decision that is guided by a policy statement (i.e. a rule that leaves the agency free to consider particular facts), an individual can later argue that the agency should disregard the policy statement and treat his case differently. However, if a discretionary decision is dictated by a legislative rule, the agency has not left itself free to consider individual circumstances. In the latter situation, therefore, the individual should have a chance to influence the rule at the time it is adopted, since it will be binding at the time it is applied.

Yet, is it feasible for a court to determine whether the agency has, in fact, left itself free to consider individual circumstances? *See generally* Michael Asimow, "Nonlegislative Rulemaking and Regulatory Reform," 1985 Duke L.J. 381, 389–93 (reviewing the case law). Some courts put weight on whether the agency itself characterizes its pronouncement as a legislative rule or a policy statement. *See, e.g., American Hospital Ass'n v. Bowen,* 834

F.2d 1037, 1056 (D.C.Cir.1987). Yet the case law also contains assertions that the courts' deference to an agency's label "is not overwhelming," and that the words of the statement itself carry greater weight. *Brock v. Cathedral Bluffs Shale Oil Co.,* 796 F.2d 533, 537 (D.C.Cir.1986) (Scalia, J.). Under this approach, a statement that declares that "the Commission *will*" take action in specified circumstances is likely to be classified as a legislative rule, *American Bus Ass'n v. United States,* 627 F.2d 525 (D.C.Cir.1980), while a statement that is written in permissive terms, like the 1981 Instruction in *Mada-Luna,* is more likely to be regarded as nonlegislative. Did the court properly classify the 1978 Instruction?

Consider also *Pacific Gas & Electric Co. v. FPC,* a frequently quoted decision about the policy statement exception that is cited in the principal case. The "statement of policy" in that case invited natural gas pipeline companies to include in their regularly filed "tariff sheets" a new approach to rationing gas supplies in the event of a shortage. Under this new approach, pipelines would no longer reduce supplies to all customers on a pro rata basis, as in the past; instead, they would make reductions on the basis of need (low priority customers, such as utilities that could readily convert to substitute fuels, would lose all their gas supplies before higher priority customers, such as homeowners, would lose anything). The Commission also said that "exceptions to those priorities may be permitted" if the agency were to find "extraordinary circumstances after a hearing" in an individual case. The court focused on an assertion in the statement that the agency would follow the proposed priorities "subject to the rights of intervenors to hearing and adjudication of any claim of preference, discrimination, unjustness or unreasonableness of the provisions contained in the proposed tariff sheets.... " On the basis of this language, the court held that the pronouncement, which had been issued without notice and comment, was valid as a policy statement. Do you agree?

4. *Substantial impact.* The court in *Mada-Luna* rejects the substantial impact test as a basis for applying the nonlegislative rules exemption, in part because of the lessons of *Vermont Yankee.* On the other hand, *Brown Express* and *Kast Metals* do rely on substantial impact in applying the procedural rule exemption. Are the latter cases erroneous?

Both the American Bar Association and the Administrative Conference have recommended that agencies should, as a matter of practice, provide an opportunity for public participation in the adoption of guidance documents that are expected to have a substantial impact. Thus, in the 1993 resolution cited in N.1, the ABA recommended:

> Before an agency adopts a nonlegislative rule that is likely to have significant impact on the public, the agency should provide an opportunity for members of the public to comment on the proposed rule and to recommend alternative policies or interpretations, provided that it is practical do to so. When nonlegislative rules are adopted without prior public participation, the agency should afford members of the public an opportunity for post-adoption comment and give notice of this opportunity.

See also ACUS Recommendation 76–5, 41 Fed.Reg. 56769 (1976). If, as these organizations maintain, notice and comment for rules that will have substantial impact is desirable, should § 553(b)(A) be amended to require it? *See* Asimow, "Nonlegislative Rulemaking and Regulatory Reform," *supra,* at 399–401, 417–21. Under that standard, would the result in *Mada-Luna* change?

5. *Binding effects in practice.* Members of the public sometimes complain that an agency policy statement has been *applied* against them in a binding fashion. Recall the *Flagstaff* case in § 4.4.2 N.3, in which the FCC was reversed for relying on "established policies" (embodied in a policy statement) instead of meeting the challengers' arguments head-on. A similar case is *McLouth Steel Products, supra.* McLouth, which produced sludge as a byproduct at its steel factory, petitioned the EPA to exclude the sludge from regulation as a hazardous waste. EPA refused after using a mathematical model to predict the extent to which lead and cadmium in the sludge would contaminate the nearby groundwater. The model had been adopted without notice and comment. The court agreed with McLouth that EPA was invalidly treating the model as a legislative rule. The notice announcing the model sounded as though the agency had made up its mind; and, more significantly, when McLouth and another steel company raised objections to the model in their petitions for individual relief, EPA brushed the objections aside by saying that questions about the model were no longer open for consideration. The court thus instructed EPA either to subject the model to § 553 proceedings or "reconsider McLouth's delisting petition with full recognition that [the] issues are open."

Compare *Panhandle Producers & Royalty Owners Ass'n v. Economic Regulatory Admin. (ERA),* 847 F.2d 1168 (5th Cir.1988). Domestic producers of natural gas challenged an ERA order authorizing imports of gas from Canada. The order had been based on a guideline in which the Secretary of Energy had prescribed a presumption favoring such imports. Plaintiffs alleged that the guideline was invalid because it had not been issued through rulemaking procedures. The court rejected this argument, finding that the ERA had not treated the guideline as "establishing a 'binding precedent,'" and, therefore, had not given it the force of a legislative rule. Yet, although ERA had responded fully to each of the producers' *new* arguments, it had not reexamined from scratch *all* of the principles underlying the policy statement, including those it had previously confronted in earlier cases. Is *Panhandle* reconcilable with the ABA recommendation quoted in N.1? With the statement in *Pacific Gas* (cited in *Mada-Luna*) that an agency must be "prepared to support the policy just as if the policy statement had never been issued"? *See* Ronald M. Levin, "Nonlegislative Rules and the Administrative Open Mind," 41 Duke L.J. 1497, 1500–02 (1992).

6. *Self-binding effect.* Is an administrative pronouncement that binds only the agency, not members of the public, exempt from notice and comment obligations? In *Community Nutrition Institute v. Young,* 818 F.2d 943 (D.C.Cir.1987), the Food and Drug Administration (FDA) adopted an "action level" stating that the agency would take no enforcement action against corn producers whose products contained less than 20 parts per billion (ppb) of aflatoxin, a carcinogen that occurs naturally in corn. In a suit brought by consumer groups, which considered the rule too lenient, the court held that the action level was a legislative rule and should have been adopted through notice and comment. The court acknowledged that the rule

was not binding on food producers; in an enforcement proceeding, the FDA would have to prove a violation of the underlying statute, instead of merely proving a violation of the action level. However, the court continued, "we are convinced that FDA has bound *itself*. As FDA conceded at oral argument, it would be daunting indeed to try to convince a court that the agency could appropriately prosecute a producer for shipping corn with *less* than 20 ppb aflatoxin." *Id.* at 948 (emphasis added). Judge Starr dissented, contending that the rule could not be legislative, because it would not have the force of law in any future proceeding.

Responding to the *CNI* decision, Congress declared in 1997 that FDA guidance documents are nonbinding—but that the agency must obtain public input on such documents either before or after promulgation. 21 U.S.C. § 371(h)(1). This law clarifies the FDA's specific situation, but do you agree with the court's more general conclusion that constraining effects *within the agency* can trigger § 553? Commentators have criticized the court's holding: "[I]f regularity of agency action, centralized control of agency personnel, and imposition of public, agency-wide policy are desired—and they *are* desired by most critics of unchanneled agency discretion—then a rule that essentially penalizes an agency for restricting the discretion of its own personnel would appear to be counter-productive." Richard M. Thomas, "Prosecutorial Discretion and Agency Self–Regulation," 44 Admin.L.Rev. 131, 155 (1992); *see also* Strauss, *supra,* at 1483–85. *See generally* Lars Noah, "The FDA's New Policy on Guidelines: Having Your Cake and Eating It Too," 47 Cath. U.L.Rev. 113 (1997).

7. *Supreme Court perspective.* The Supreme Court offered its only application of the policy statement exemption in *Lincoln v. Vigil,* 508 U.S. 182 (1993). The Indian Health Service provided direct clinical services to handicapped Indian children in a pilot program in Albuquerque. Then the IHS closed the pilot program in order to replace it with a nationwide treatment program. A court of appeals held that the termination of the program was invalid because the Service had failed to follow rulemaking procedures. A unanimous Court disagreed, stating: "Whatever else may be considered a 'general statemen[t] of policy,' the term surely includes an announcement like the one before us, that an agency will discontinue a discretionary allocation of unrestricted funds from a lump-sum appropriation." The Court also pointed out that the decision merely "affect[ed] the availability of services in a particular geographic area" and did not do "anything to modify eligibility standards for Service care, . . . any more than the Service's initiation of the pilot program in 1978 altered the criteria for assistance to Indians in South Dakota."

Vigil has so far had little influence, and scholarly reaction to it has been decidedly negative. *See, e.g.,* Robert A. Anthony, "The Supreme Court and the APA: Sometimes They Just Don't Get It," 10 Admin.L.J.Am.U. 1, 14–16 (1996). Is its poor reputation deserved? In any event, could the § 553(b)(A) exemption for "rules of agency organization, procedure, or practice" justify the IHS's decision to proceed without notice and comment in this case, as the Court also suggested?

8. *State internal document exemption.* Although the 1981 MSAPA contains no general exemption for policy statements, it does contain some

narrow exemptions that exclude from usual rulemaking requirements many pronouncements that would also be policy statements under federal APA § 553(b)(A). For example, § 3–116(2) exempts "criteria or guidelines to be used by the staff of an agency" in performing certain functions, such as the "defense, prosecution, or settlement of cases," but only if disclosure of those criteria or guidelines would facilitate the disregard of requirements imposed by law, enable law violators to avoid detection, or might give persons contracting with the state an unfair competitive advantage. Would the INS Operations Instructions in *Mada–Luna* be exempt from notice and comment under MSAPA § 3–116(2)?

9. *Problem.* The Federal Communications Act permits the FCC to assess monetary penalties for violations of that Act, such as sending false distress communications or failing to maintain a current license. The FCC issued, without notice and comment, what it termed a "policy statement" setting forth a schedule of base penalties for computing such sanctions. For example, the base penalty for a false distress signal was $20,000 for broadcasters and $80,000 for common carriers (including telephone companies). The schedule also provided for upward adjustments from the base figure in cases of "substantial economic gain," downward adjustments for "voluntary disclosure of violations," etc. The explanation accompanying the penalty schedule added that the FCC reserved discretion to depart from the schedule in particular cases.

An association of telephone companies petitioned for reconsideration, questioning why the base penalties for them were higher than for broadcasters. The Commission declined to revise the schedule, observing that the association's concerns would be more appropriately addressed in the context of specific cases.

Later the association challenged the penalty schedule in court, arguing that the FCC should have complied with § 553 procedures before issuing the schedule. The evidence before the court indicated that the FCC had made use of the schedule in 300 cases since its promulgation and had followed the figures listed in the schedule in 295 of those cases. In the other five cases, the FCC had imposed more lenient fines than the schedule prescribed, but the agency's brief written opinions in those cases were unclear as to whether these departures had involved downward adjustments pursuant to the guidelines themselves, or instead had involved completely independent decisions.

Should the plaintiff's challenge under § 553 succeed? *See United States Telephone Ass'n v. FCC,* 28 F.3d 1232 (D.C.Cir.1994).

§ 6.1.4c   Interpretive rules

HOCTOR v. UNITED STATES DEPARTMENT OF AGRICULTURE
82 F.3d 165 (7th Cir.1996).

Posner, C.J.:

[The Animal Welfare Act authorizes the Department of Agriculture (USDA) to adopt rules "to govern the humane handling, care, treatment, and transportation of animals by dealers." Using notice and comment procedure, USDA adopted a rule entitled "Structural Strength" requiring that the facility housing animals "must be constructed of such material and of such strength as appropriate for the animals involved." 9 C.F.R. § 3.125(a). USDA later adopted an internal memorandum addressed to its inspectors, in which it said that all dangerous animals must be inside a perimeter fence at least 8 feet high.

Hoctor dealt in exotic cats, including three lions, two tigers, and seven ligers (a liger is a cross between a male lion and a female tiger), six cougars, and two snow leopards (but no tigons). The pens were surrounded by a "containment fence" and the entire property by a "perimeter fence" 6 feet high. Hoctor was penalized by USDA because the perimeter fence was only 6 rather than 8 feet high. It would cost him many thousands of dollars to replace the fence. The issue is whether the internal memorandum is a valid interpretive rule.]

A rule promulgated by an agency that is subject to the APA is invalid unless the agency first issues a public notice of proposed rulemaking, describing the substance of the proposed rule, and gives the public an opportunity to submit written comments; and if after receiving the comments it decides to promulgate the rule it must set forth the basis and purpose of the rule in a public statement. These procedural requirements do not apply, however, to "interpretative rules, general statements of policy, or rules of agency organization, procedure, or practice." § 553(b)(A).

Distinguishing between a "legislative" rule, to which the notice and comment provisions of the Act apply, and an interpretive rule, to which these provisions do not apply, is often very difficult—and often very important to regulated firms, the public, and the agency. Notice and comment rulemaking is time-consuming, facilitates the marshaling of opposition to a proposed rule, and may result in the creation of a very long record that may in turn provide a basis for a judicial challenge to the rule if the agency decides to promulgate it. There are no formalities attendant upon the promulgation of an interpretive rule, but this is tolerable because such a rule is "only" an interpretation. Every governmental agency that enforces a less than crystalline statute must interpret the statute, and it does the public a favor if it announces the interpretation in advance of enforcement, whether the announcement takes the form of a rule or of a policy statement, which the Administrative Procedure Act assimilates to an interpretive rule. It would be no favor to the public to discourage the announcement of agencies' interpretations by burdening the interpretive process with cumbersome formalities. . . .

We may assume, though we need not decide, that USDA has the statutory authority to require dealers in dangerous animals to enclose their compounds with eight foot-high fences. . . .

The only ground on which the Department defends sanctioning Hoctor for not having a high enough fence is that requiring an eight-foot-high perimeter fence for dangerous animals is an interpretation of the Department's own structural-strength regulation, and "provided an agency's interpretation of its own regulations does not violate the Constitution or a federal statute, it must be given 'controlling weight unless it is plainly erroneous or inconsistent with the regulation.'" The "provided" clause does not announce a demanding standard of judicial review, although the absence of any reference in the housing regulation to fences or height must give us pause. The regulation appears only to require that pens and other animal housing be sturdy enough in design and construction, and sufficiently well maintained, to prevent the animals from breaking through the enclosure—not that any enclosure, whether a pen or a perimeter fence, be high enough to prevent the animals from escaping by jumping over the enclosure. . . .

Our doubts about the scope of the regulation that the eight-foot rule is said to be "interpreting" might seem irrelevant, since even if a rule requiring an eight-foot perimeter fence could not be based on the regulation, it could be based on the statute itself, which in requiring the Department to establish minimum standards for the housing of animals presumably authorizes it to promulgate standards for secure containment. But if the eight-foot rule were deemed one of those minimum standards that the Department is required by statute to create, it could not possibly be thought an interpretive rule. For what would it be interpreting? When Congress authorizes an agency to create standards, it is delegating legislative authority, rather than itself setting forth a standard which the agency might then particularize through interpretation. Put differently, when a statute does not impose a duty on the persons subject to it but instead authorizes (or requires—it makes no difference) an agency to impose a duty, the formulation of that duty becomes a legislative task entrusted to the agency. Provided that a rule promulgated pursuant to such a delegation is intended to bind, and not merely to be a tentative statement of the agency's view, which would make it just a policy statement, and not a rule at all, the rule would be the clearest possible example of a legislative rule, as to which the notice and comment procedure not here followed is mandatory, as distinct from an interpretive rule; for there would be nothing to interpret. . . . That is why the Department must argue that its eight-foot rule is an interpretation of the structural-strength regulation—itself a standard, and therefore interpretable—in order to avoid reversal.

Even if, despite the doubts that we expressed earlier, the eight-foot rule is consistent with, even in some sense authorized by, the structural-strength regulation, it would not necessarily follow that it is an interpretive rule. It is that only if it can be derived from the regulation by a process reasonably described as interpretation. Supposing that the regulation imposes a general duty of secure containment, the question is, then, Can a requirement that the duty be implemented by erecting an eight-foot-high perimeter fence be thought an interpretation of that general duty?

"Interpretation" in the narrow sense is the ascertainment of meaning. It is obvious that eight feet is not part of the meaning of secure containment. But "interpretation" is often used in a much broader sense. A process of "interpretation" has transformed the Constitution into a body of law undreamt of by the framers. To skeptics the Miranda rule is as remote from the text of the Fifth Amendment as the eight-foot rule is from the text of 9 C.F.R. § 3.125(a). But our task in this case is not to plumb the mysteries of legal theory; it is merely to give effect to a distinction that the Administrative Procedure Act makes, and we can do this by referring to the purpose of the distinction. The purpose is to separate the cases in which notice and comment rulemaking is required from the cases in which it is not required. As we noted at the outset, unless a statute or regulation is of crystalline transparency, the agency enforcing it cannot avoid interpreting it, and the agency would be stymied in its enforcement duties if every time it brought a case on a new theory it had to pause for a bout, possibly lasting several years, of notice and comment rulemaking. Besides being unavoidably continuous, statutory interpretation normally proceeds without the aid of elaborate factual inquiries. When it is an executive or administrative agency that is doing the interpreting it brings to the task a greater knowledge of the regulated activity than the judicial or legislative branches have, and this knowledge is to some extent a substitute for formal fact-gathering.

At the other extreme from what might be called normal or routine interpretation is the making of reasonable but arbitrary (not in the "arbitrary or capricious" sense) rules that are consistent with the statute or regulation under which the rules are promulgated but not derived from it, because they represent an arbitrary choice among methods of implementation. A rule that turns on a number is likely to be arbitrary in this sense. There is no way to reason to an eight-foot perimeter-fence rule as opposed to a seven-and-a-half foot fence or a nine-foot fence or a ten-foot fence. None of these candidates for a rule is uniquely appropriate to, and in that sense derivable from, the duty of secure containment. This point becomes even clearer if we note that the eight-foot rule actually has another component—the fence must be at least three feet from any animal's pen. Why three feet? Why not four? Or two?

The reason courts refuse to create statutes of limitations is precisely the difficulty of reasoning to a number by the methods of reasoning used by courts. One cannot extract from the concept of a tort that a tort suit should be barred unless brought within one, or two, or three, or five years. The choice is arbitrary and courts are uncomfortable with making arbitrary choices. They see this as a legislative function. Legislators have the democratic legitimacy to make choices among value judgments, choices based on hunch or guesswork or even the toss of a coin, and other arbitrary choices. When agencies base rules on arbitrary choices they are legislating, and so these rules are legislative or substantive and require notice and comment rulemaking, a procedure that is analogous to the procedure employed by legislatures in making statutes. The notice of proposed rulemaking corresponds to the bill and the reception of written comments to the hearing on the bill.

The common sense of requiring notice and comment rulemaking for legislative rules is well illustrated by the facts of this case. There is no process of cloistered, appellate-court type reasoning by which the Department of Agriculture could have excogitated the eight-foot rule from the structural-strength regulation. The rule is arbitrary in the sense that it could well be different without significant impairment of any regulatory purpose. But this does not make the rule a matter of indifference to the people subject to it. There are thousands of animal dealers, and some unknown fraction of these face the prospect of having to tear down their existing fences and build new, higher ones at great cost. The concerns of these dealers are legitimate and since, as we are stressing, the rule could well be otherwise, the agency was obliged to listen to them before settling on a final rule and to provide some justification for that rule, though not so tight or logical a justification as a court would be expected to offer for a new judge-made rule. Notice and comment is the procedure by which the persons affected by legislative rules are enabled to communicate their concerns in a comprehensive and systematic fashion to the legislating agency. The Department's lawyer speculated that if the notice and comment route had been followed in this case the Department would have received thousands of comments. The greater the public interest in a rule, the greater reason to allow the public to participate in its formation.

We are not saying that an interpretive rule can never have a numerical component. *See, e.g., American Mining Congress v. Mine Safety & Health Administration,* [1108, 995 F.2d 1106, 1113 (D.C.Cir. 1993)]. There is merely an empirical relation between interpretation and generality on the one hand, and legislation and specificity on the other. Especially in scientific and other technical areas, where quantitative criteria are common, a rule that translates a general norm into a number may be justifiable as interpretation. . . . Even in a nontechnical area the use of a number as a rule of thumb to guide the application of a general norm will often be legitimately interpretive. Had the Department of Agriculture said in the internal memorandum that it could not imagine a case in which a perimeter fence for dangerous animals that was lower than eight feet would provide secure containment, and would therefore presume, subject to rebuttal, that a lower fence was insecure, it would have been on stronger ground. For it would have been tying the rule to the animating standard, that of secure containment, rather than making it stand free of the standard, self-contained, unbending, arbitrary. To switch metaphors, the "flatter" a rule is, the harder it is to conceive of it as merely spelling out what is in some sense latent in a statute or regulation, and the eight-foot rule in its present form is as flat as they come. At argument the Department's lawyer tried to loosen up the rule, implying that the Department might have bent it if Hoctor proposed to dig a moat or to electrify his six-foot fence. But an agency's lawyer is not authorized to amend its rules in order to make them more palatable to the reviewing court.

The Department's position might seem further undermined by the fact that it has used the notice and comment procedure to promulgate rules prescribing perimeter fences for dogs and monkeys. Why it proceeded differently for dangerous animals is unexplained. But we attach no weight to the Department's inconsistency, not only because it would be unwise to penalize the Department for having at least partially complied with the requirements of the APA, but also because there is nothing in the Act to forbid an agency to use the notice and comment procedure in cases in which it is not required to do so. We are mindful that the court in United States v. Picciotto, 875 F.2d 345, 348 (D.C.Cir. 1989), thought that the fact that an agency had used notice and comment rulemaking in a setting similar to the case before the court was evidence that the agency "intended" to promulgate a legislative rule in that case, only without bothering with notice and comment. The inference is strained, and in any event we think the agency's "intent," though a frequently cited factor, is rather a makeweight. What the agency intends is to promulgate a rule. It is for the courts to say whether it is the kind of rule that is valid only if promulgated after notice and comment. It is that kind of rule if, as in the present case, it cannot be derived by interpretation. The order under review, based as it was on a rule that is invalid because not promulgated in accordance with the required procedure, is therefore

VACATED.

Notes and Questions

1. *Required or prohibited legislative rulemaking.* Judge Posner says that if the USDA internal memorandum were considered to be based directly on the Animal Welfare Act, it "could not possibly be thought an *interpretive* rule." This is true, he explains, because the statute itself does not impose a duty on dealers to keep their animals secured; instead, it authorizes the agency to impose such a duty. *See* 7 U.S.C. § 2143(a)(1) (*"The Secretary shall promulgate standards* to govern the humane handling ... of animals ... by dealers....") (emphasis added). The court is certainly right on this point. Among the various situations in which a court can assume that an agency must have intended to use its legislative rulemaking authority, the "clearest case is where, in the absence of a legislative rule by the agency, the legislative basis for agency enforcement would be inadequate." *American Mining Congress v. MSHA,* 995 F.2d 1106, 1109 (D.C.Cir.1993).

Conversely, a rule is plainly *not* legislative, but rather interpretive, if the agency has no legislative rulemaking authority at all with respect to the subject area of the rule. For example, the EEOC has no authority to promulgate legislative rules to define the scope of the antidiscrimination laws, so its guidelines on that subject are all interpretive. *General Electric Co. v. Gilbert,* 429 U.S. 125, 141 (1976). The statute quoted in the preceding paragraph delegates *specific* authority to adopt legislative rules. For matters not covered by such a provision, however, Congress has also given USDA a *general* rulemaking authority, which simply empowers the Secretary to "promulgate such rules, regulations, and orders as he may deem necessary in order to effectuate the purposes" of the Animal Welfare Act. 7 U.S.C.

§ 2151. Similar language is found in the enabling statutes of many, probably most, administrative agencies. Whether a general rulemaking provision empowers an agency to make legislative rules (as opposed to merely guidance documents), and how far the power extends, are issues of statutory interpretation. Usually, but not always, ambiguities are resolved in favor of legislative rulemaking power, because the courts tend to believe that such power is an essential tool in carrying out a regulatory program. *See* § 5.1 N.2.

In situations in which the overall nature of an agency's authority does not determine whether a given rule must have been legislative or interpretive, the court's task of making the classification becomes harder, as the following notes illustrate. The difficulty is amplified by the fact that a rule is *not* necessarily interpretive merely because it ascribes a meaning to a statutory term. Sometimes an agency uses a legislative rule to do just that. A famous example is *Chevron U.S.A. Inc. v. NRDC,* 467 U.S. 837 (1984), excerpted in § 9.2, in which the EPA used a legislative rule to define "stationary source" in the Clean Air Act to mean an entire factory rather than an individual piece of equipment.

2. *Intent standard.* Sometimes courts classify a rule as interpretive or legislative on the basis of whether the agency *intended* to exercise its delegated authority to make law, as opposed to interpreting existing text. *See, e.g. Orengo Caraballo v. Reich,* 11 F.3d 186, 195 (D.C.Cir.1993); *General Motors Corp. v. Ruckelshaus,* 742 F.2d 1561, 1565 (D.C.Cir.1984) (en banc). In *Hoctor,* Judge Posner refers to this test as a "makeweight," but how clear is it that the agency's intentions were irrelevant to his analysis? In any event, is an intent standard an administrable and attractive approach to deciding whether a rule is interpretive? *See* Michael Asimow, "Nonlegislative Rulemaking and Regulatory Reform," 1985 Duke L.J. 381, 393–97. Did the USDA intend to use its legislative rulemaking authority in *Hoctor?*

In applying an intent standard, courts sometimes give particular weight to the agency's own characterization of the rule as legislative or interpretive. *See, e.g., Chrysler Corp. v. Brown,* 441 U.S. 281, 312–16 (1979), excerpted in § 8.1. Is such emphasis warranted? *See* Asimow, "Nonlegislative Rulemaking," *supra,* at 389–90.

3. *"Interpretation" v. "arbitrary choice."* In *Hoctor,* Judge Posner suggests that he can resolve his case without regard to the agency's intentions. He rejects the argument that the USDA's eight-foot fence standard is an interpretive rule construing the "structural strength" regulation, because the standard is an arbitrary (legislative-type) choice that *cannot* be derived from the regulation through "a process reasonably described as interpretation." Many other cases employ similar reasoning to distinguish interpretive from legislative rules. *See, e.g., Paralyzed Veterans of America v. D.C. Arena L.P.,* 117 F.3d 579, 588 (D.C.Cir.1997) ("the distinction ... likely turns on how tightly the agency's interpretation is drawn linguistically from the actual language of the statute"); *United Technologies Corp. v. EPA,* 821 F.2d 714, 719–20 (D.C.Cir.1987) (interpretive rule must be "based on specific statutory provisions" rather than on "an agency's power to exercise its judgment as to how best to implement a general statutory mandate").

If one requirement of a valid interpretive rule is that it can be "derived by interpretation," however, some cases do not seem to enforce the requirement very stringently. In *Shalala v. Guernsey Memorial Hospital*, 514 U.S. 87 (1995), an informal Medicare guideline provided that, for reimbursement purposes, losses that hospitals incurred when they refinanced their debts should be "amortized" (spread over a period of many years), instead of being recognized in full in the year the transaction occurred. The guideline purported to implement (i) a statute that simply said that the Medicare program should bear its fair share of costs, and (ii) a regulation authorizing reimbursement of costs that are "appropriate and helpful in . . . maintaining the operation of patient care facilities." The Court found that, although these provisions said nothing about the timing of loss recognition, the guideline was a valid interpretive rule. *Id.* at 97–99. Similarly, in *American Mining Congress, supra*, the Mine Safety and Health Administration issued a "program policy letter" stating that if the chest x-ray of a miner measured 1/0 or higher (the fourth most severe of twelve possible ratings), it would be regarded as a "diagnosis" of black lung disease that would trigger reporting obligations. The court held that the letter was a valid interpretive rule that construed the term "diagnosis" in an existing legislative regulation. Notice that Judge Posner cites *American Mining* with approval. Can holdings such as *Guernsey* and *American Mining* be reconciled with the main rationale of the *Hoctor* opinion?

4. *Inconsistency with the interpreted provision.* In *Guernsey, supra,* the Supreme Court did not try to limit interpretive rules to any particular mode of reasoning, but the Court did indicate that the Medicare guideline would have been invalid if it had been inconsistent with the regulation that it purported to interpret. A similar analysis underlay the holding in *National Family Planning & Reproductive Health Ass'n v. Sullivan*, 979 F.2d 227 (D.C.Cir.1992). After the Supreme Court had upheld the "gag rule" by which the Department of Health and Human Services had forbidden personnel in federally funded clinics to give abortion counseling to their patients, *Rust v. Sullivan*, 500 U.S. 173 (1991), the Department decided to modify that ban. On instructions from President Bush, the Department issued directives providing that the gag rule would no longer apply to doctors, but only to other clinic personnel. The directives had not been preceded by notice and comment, and the court held that they were not exempt as interpretive rules. According to the court, "It is a maxim of administrative law that: 'If a second rule repudiates or is irreconcilable with [a prior legislative rule], the second rule must be an amendment of the first; and, of course, an amendment to a legislative rule must itself be legislative.' "

Why would a court in a case like *National Family Planning* hold the challenged rule procedurally invalid, instead of simply holding that it was invalid on the merits by virtue of being inconsistent with the legal text it was supposed to be interpreting? *Cf. Fertilizer Institute v. EPA*, 935 F.2d 1303, 1308 (D.C.Cir.1991) (holding that an EPA pronouncement was within the interpretive rule exemption but untenable on the merits, and stating: "Simply because an agency may fail to interpret a statute correctly does not mean that the agency has not in fact interpreted it.").

5. *Lack of binding effect.* Some courts, when faced with claims that a so-called interpretive rule is really a legislative rule, manage to avoid having to compare the substance of the challenged pronouncement with that of the provision being interpreted. Taking a more purely procedural approach, they

simply ask whether the agency intended the rule to establish a binding norm. In effect, this sort of reasoning equates the test for an interpretive rule with that for a policy statement. *See Alaska v. United States Dep't of Transp.,* 868 F.2d 441 (D.C.Cir.1989); *Community Nutrition Inst. v. Young,* 818 F.2d 943 (D.C.Cir.1987). For example, in *New York City Employees' Retirement System v. SEC,* 45 F.3d 7 (2d Cir.1995), shareholders of Cracker Barrel Old Country Store, Inc., asked the company to send all shareholders, as part of a proxy solicitation, a proposal that the company should cease discriminating in employment on the basis of sexual orientation. The company rejected this request. In a "no-action letter" to the complainants, the SEC declined to intervene. The letter stated that, under SEC regulations, companies need not circulate shareholders' proposals relating to "ordinary business operations." This was a reversal of a prior SEC position, under which issues of social concern were not considered ordinary business operations. The court concluded that the no-action letter was a "rule," because it announced a broadly applicable Commission view on securities law. Nevertheless, it was only an interpretive rule and did not have to be issued through notice and comment. The court explained that a no-action letter is binding on no one.

These cases are far outnumbered by decisions stating, or at least assuming, that the exemptions for interpretive rules and policy statements are sharply distinct. *Syncor International Corp. v. Shalala,* 127 F.3d 90, 94 (D.C.Cir.1997); *Paralyzed Veterans, supra.* How different is the test applied in cases like *Cracker Barrel* from the "intent" standard discussed above?

6. *Rationales for the exemption.* Why does the APA provide an exemption for interpretive rules? Some of the reasons are utilitarian. As Judge Posner explains, notice and comment procedure is costly to the agency and very time consuming. "[T]he agency would be stymied in its enforcement duties if every time it brought a case on a new theory it had to pause for a bout, possibly lasting several years, of notice and comment rulemaking." And, as he points out, an agency "does the public a favor if it announces the interpretation in advance of enforcement.... It would be no favor to the public to discourage the announcement of agencies' interpretations by burdening the interpretive process with cumbersome formalities." But what about the countervailing interest in procedural fairness for individuals who could be disadvantaged by an interpretive rule? What does Judge Posner mean when he says that the absence of procedural formalities for an interpretive rule "is tolerable because such a rule is 'only' an interpretation"?

He himself suggests one possible reason for not requiring notice and comment: when an agency is "interpreting," it "brings to the task a greater knowledge of the regulated activity than the judicial or legislative branches have, and this knowledge is to some extent a substitute for formal fact-gathering." Is this argument persuasive? Does it satisfactorily distinguish interpretive rules from other matters about which the agency does have a duty to solicit public comment?

The legislative history of the APA suggests a different rationale: interpretive rules do not require notice and comment because they are "subject to plenary judicial review." *APA Legislative History,* S.Doc.No. 79–248, at 18

(1946) (Senate committee print). That argument has been criticized on the ground that modern courts do, in fact, often defer to administrative constructions expressed in interpretive rules. *See, e.g.,* Kevin W. Saunders, "Interpretative Rules With Legislative Effect: An Analysis and a Proposal for Public Participation," 1986 Duke L.J. 346, 353–58. In *Hoctor,* the court quotes the widely followed maxim that an agency's reading of its own regulation is entitled to "controlling weight unless it is plainly erroneous or inconsistent with the regulation." Judicial deference to agencies' interpretations of statutes is also commonplace, although the case law is neither simple nor uniform. *See* §§ 9.2–.3. In that light, how satisfactory is the Senate committee report's argument?

Still another rationale for the exemption is that an interpretive rule does not require notice and comment because it is not a definitive resolution of anyone's interests; the agency has expressed its opinion, but no one is foreclosed from contesting that view later. Is this reasoning persuasive?

7. *State law.* The 1961 MSAPA contained no exception for interpretive rules, but, as previously noted, most state agencies have ignored the requirement that they employ notice and comment procedures before adopting such rules. Section 3–109 of the 1981 MSAPA contains an exception for interpretive rules that is much narrower than federal APA § 553(b)(A). For one thing, it requires an initial determination of whether the agency has been delegated authority to issue rules with the binding force of law. If the agency has that authority, the exception becomes unavailable: the agency *must* follow the MSAPA rulemaking procedures, even though the agency intends the rule to be wholly interpretive rather than legislative. Only if the agency lacks delegated lawmaking power is it free to omit notice and comment for that rule. The MSAPA thus avoids the fact-intensive inquiry into agencies' intentions that has bedeviled the federal courts in administering § 553(b)(A). Would Congress do well to emulate this approach? Or does the MSAPA approach seem likely to create other and perhaps larger problems?

Notice also that, under the MSAPA, when an agency that lacks legislative rulemaking power does exercise the option to issue an interpretive rule without following the usual rulemaking procedures, there is a significant price-tag: on judicial review, a court must determine wholly de novo the validity of that interpretive rule. § 3–109(b). Is this prohibition of the usual judicial deference to such a rule an appropriate response to the agency's failure to use notice and comment in promulgating the rule? For evaluations of 1981 MSAPA § 3–109, see Asimow, "Nonlegislative Rulemaking," *supra,* at 410–15; Arthur Earl Bonfield, STATE ADMINISTRATIVE RULE MAKING § 6.9.2 (1986).

State law may also diverge from federal law on the issue of whether an interpretive rule is binding on an agency. *See Realty Group, Inc. v. Department of Revenue,* 702 P.2d 1075, 1079 n. 3 (Or.1985) (agency bound to follow an interpretive rule until it amends or rescinds that rule). Under the 1981 MSAPA, nonlegislative rules arguably are binding on the issuing agency, because the Act provides that an agency may not violate its own rules and the Act's definition of "rule" includes nonlegislative rules. *See* §§ 5–116(c)(8)(ii), 1–102(10). How can these authorities be reconciled with the defining characteristic of a nonlegislative rule, i.e., that it lacks the force of law?

8. *California revisited.* Recall the troubling findings about the consequences of California's APA, which has for many years been construed as not exempting nonlegislative rules from rulemaking procedures. *See* § 6.1.4b N.2. That longstanding construction was challenged in *Tidewater Marine Western, Inc. v. Bradshaw,* 927 P.2d 296 (Cal.1996). Tidewater and Zapata were maritime firms that transported people and cargo to and from offshore oil drilling platforms. They sought an injunction to prevent the Division of Labor Standards Enforcement from requiring them to pay their employees extra compensation for overtime work. The case required an interpretation of certain legislative regulations that applied the state's labor laws to workers "in this state." A DLSE operations manual maintained that the regulations did cover Californians working in the state's territorial waters, but the plaintiff firms argued that the manual provision was invalid because it had not been adopted through rulemaking procedures.

California's APA says that its rulemaking procedures apply to "the exercise of any quasi-legislative power conferred by statute." It was argued in *Tidewater* that this provision should not be read as referring to interpretive rules, because an agency does not adopt such rules pursuant to delegated lawmaking power, and they do not have the force of law. The court, although acknowledging that the application of mandatory rulemaking procedures to interpretive rules raises "serious [policy] concerns," concluded that the language of the APA did not adequately support the thesis that interpretive rules are exempt. Therefore, the court said, the manual provision was void, and did not warrant any judicial deference. Nevertheless, the court reached the merits and agreed with the DLSE that Tidewater and Zapata had to pay extra for overtime.

Should the court have held that interpretive rules may be issued without rulemaking procedure? Given its holding that they may not, does the remedy of withholding deference provide an adequate sanction to keep agencies from violating the APA? The court declined to follow earlier cases that had gone further—rejecting the actual interpretation contained in an interpretive rule because the agency had adopted the rule without observing APA procedures. Would that have been a better remedy? Or was even the milder *Tidewater* remedy too strict?

9. *Problem.* The Madison Nonpublic Schools Act provides that "the courses of study at any nonpublic school shall be of the same standard as provided by the general school laws of the state." By its terms the Act applies to "any primary-or secondary-level school in the state other than a public school," and the Madison Supreme Court has construed the Act to apply to home schools. The Madison Board of Education has legislative rulemaking authority to implement the Act.

Without prior notice or a comment period, the Board recently adopted a set of "Home School Compliance Guidelines." The document had the stated aim of advising parents who engage in home-schooling about their legal obligations under the Nonpublic Schools Act. According to the guidelines, every home school must provide instruction in classes on social studies and science, during a school year lasting at least 180 days. The Board said that it inferred the 180–day requirement from the fact that, under Madison's school aid statute, a public school district that holds fewer than 180 days of classes forfeits some of its state aid. (Madison provides no financial aid to home schools.)

The Board then mailed a copy of the guidelines to all known home school families in Madison. The mailing instructed them to complete and return the attached information forms, in order to confirm that they were in compliance with the stated "legal requirements." One recipient of this mailing was Irene. She has little confidence in the public schools of Madison, so she is educating her three school-age children at home, in cooperation with a private school at which the children take a few classes. She has now filed suit to challenge the guidelines as having been adopted unlawfully. The Board contends that they are valid interpretive rules.

(a) Assuming that Madison follows federal law on rulemaking procedure, how should the litigation be resolved?

(b) Now assume that the Board plainly has no legislative rulemaking authority in regard to nonpublic schools. How should Irene's suit be resolved if Madison follows federal law? What if Madison has enacted 1981 MSAPA § 3–109 instead? *Cf. Clonlara, Inc. v. State Board of Education,* 501 N.W.2d 88 (Mich.1993).

§ 6.2 REQUIRED RULEMAKING

§ 6.2.1 FEDERAL LAW

Reread § 5.1, which suggested some advantages and disadvantages of adjudication and rulemaking as agency lawmaking modalities. Although the decision to make law by rule rather than by order or vice versa has significant consequences, courts have generally been reluctant to interfere with an agency's choice of lawmaking procedures. That is particularly true in the federal courts. *See generally* Arthur Earl Bonfield, "State Administrative Policy Formulation and the Choice of Lawmaking Methodology," 42 Admin.L.Rev. 121 (1990); Russell L. Weaver, *"Chenery II:* A Forty-year Retrospective," 40 Admin.L.Rev. 161 (1988).

NLRB v. WYMAN–GORDON CO.
394 U.S. 759 (1969).

[The NLRB held an election to allow Wyman–Gordon's employees to choose an exclusive bargaining representative or to choose not to be represented by a union at all. The Board ordered the company to furnish the competing unions a list of the names and addresses of its employees for electioneering purposes. In issuing that order, the NLRB cited its earlier adjudicatory decision in *Excelsior Underwear, Inc.,* 156 N.L.R.B. 1236 (1966). There the Board had initiated the practice of list disclosure, saying that "we now establish a requirement that will be applied in all election cases," and "[f]ailure to comply with this requirement shall be grounds for setting aside the election whenever proper objections are filed." However, the Board had declined to apply its new requirement to the companies involved in the *Excelsior* case itself. Instead, it had stated that the requirement would apply "only in those elections that are directed, or consented to, subsequent to 30 days from the date of [the] Decision."]

JUSTICE FORTAS announced the judgment of the Court and delivered an opinion in which THE CHIEF JUSTICE, JUSTICE STEWART, and JUSTICE WHITE join.

. . . The Board asks us to hold that it has discretion to promulgate new rules in adjudicatory proceedings, without complying with the requirements of the Administrative Procedure Act.

The rule-making provisions of that Act, which the Board would avoid, were designed to assure fairness and mature consideration of rules of general application. They may not be avoided by the process of making rules in the course of adjudicatory proceedings. There is no warrant in law for the Board to replace the statutory scheme with a rule-making procedure of its own invention. Apart from the fact that the device fashioned by the Board does not comply with statutory command, it obviously falls short of the substance of the requirements of the Administrative Procedure Act. The "rule" created in *Excelsior* was not published in the Federal Register, which is the statutory and accepted means of giving notice of a rule as adopted; only selected organizations were given notice of the "hearing," whereas notice in the Federal Register would have been general in character; under the Administrative Procedure Act, the terms or substance of the rule would have to be stated in the notice of hearing, and all interested parties would have an opportunity to participate in the rule making.

The Solicitor General does not deny that the Board ignored the rule-making provisions of the [APA in *Excelsior*].[3] But he appears to argue that *Excelsior's* command is a valid substantive regulation, binding upon this respondent as such, because the Board promulgated it in the *Excelsior* proceeding, in which the requirements for valid adjudication had been met. This argument misses the point. There is no question that, in an adjudicatory hearing, the Board could validly decide the issue whether the employer must furnish a list of employees to the union. But that is not what the Board did in *Excelsior*. The Board did not even apply the rule it made to the parties in the adjudicatory proceeding, the only entities that could properly be subject to the order in that case. Instead, the Board purported to make a rule: *i.e.*, to exercise its quasi-legislative power.

Adjudicated cases may and do, of course, serve as vehicles for the formulation of agency policies, which are applied and announced therein. They generally provide a guide to action that the agency may be expected to take in future cases. Subject to the qualified role of *stare*

---

3. The Board has never utilized the Act's rule-making procedures. It has been criticized for contravening the Act in this manner. See, *e.g.*, 1 K. Davis, Administrative Law Treatise § 6.13 (Supp.1965); Peck, The Atrophied Rule–Making Powers of the National Labor Relations Board, 70 Yale L.J. 729 (1961).

decisis in the administrative process, they may serve as precedents. But this is far from saying, as the Solicitor General suggests, that commands, decisions, or policies announced in adjudication are "rules" in the sense that they must, without more, be obeyed by the affected public.

In the present case, however, the respondent itself was specifically directed by the Board to submit a list of the names and addresses of its employees for use by the unions in connection with the election. This direction, which was part of the order directing that an election be held, is unquestionably valid. Even though the direction to furnish the list was followed by citation to *"Excelsior Underwear Inc.,* 156 NLRB No. 111," it is an order in the present case that the respondent was required to obey. Absent this direction by the Board, the respondent was under no compulsion to furnish the list because no statute and no validly adopted rule required it to do so.

Because the Board in an adjudicatory proceeding directed the respondent itself to furnish the list, the decision of the Court of Appeals for the First Circuit must be reversed. . . .

MR. JUSTICE BLACK, with whom MR. JUSTICE BRENNAN and MR. JUSTICE MARSHALL join, concurring in the result. . . .

Most administrative agencies, like the Labor Board here, are granted two functions by the legislation creating them: (1) the power under certain conditions to make rules having the effect of laws, that is, generally speaking, quasi-legislative power; and (2) the power to hear and adjudicate particular controversies, that is quasi-judicial power. The line between these two functions is not always a clear one and in fact the two functions merge at many points. For example, in exercising its quasi-judicial function an agency must frequently decide controversies on the basis of new doctrines, not theretofore applied to a specific problem, though drawn to be sure from broader principles reflecting the purposes of the statutes involved and from the rules invoked in dealing with related problems. If the agency decision reached under the adjudicatory power becomes a precedent, it guides future conduct in much the same way as though it were a new rule promulgated under the rule-making power, and both an adjudicatory order and a formal "rule" are alike subject to judicial review. Congress gave the Labor Board both of these separate but almost inseparably related powers. No language in the National Labor Relations Act requires that the grant or the exercise of one power was intended to exclude the Board's use of the other.

Nor does any language in the Administrative Procedure Act require such a conclusion. . . .

Thus, although it is true that the adjudicatory approach frees an administrative agency from the procedural requirements specified for rule making, the Act permits this to be done whenever the action involved can satisfy the definition of "adjudication" and then imposes separate procedural requirements that must be met in adjudication. Under these circumstances, so long as the matter involved can be dealt with in a way satisfying the definition of either "rule making" or "adjudication" under the Administrative Procedure Act, that Act should be read as conferring upon the Board the authority to decide, within its informed discretion, whether to proceed by rule making or adjudication. . . .

In the present case there is no dispute that all the procedural safeguards required for "adjudication" were fully satisfied in connection with the Board's *Excelsior* decision, and it seems plain to me that that decision did constitute "adjudication" within the meaning of the Administrative Procedure Act, even though the requirement was to be prospectively applied. See *Great Northern R. Co. v. Sunburst Co.,* 287 U.S. 358 (1932). The Board did not abstractly decide out of the blue to announce a brand new rule of law to govern labor activities in the future, but rather established the procedure as a direct consequence of the proper exercise of its adjudicatory powers. . . .

A controversy arose between the Excelsior Company and its employees as to the bargaining agent the employees desired to act for them. The Board's power to provide the procedures for the election was invoked. Undoubtedly the Board proceeding for determination of whether to confirm or set aside that election was "agency process for the formulation of an order" and thus was "adjudication" within the meaning of the Administrative Procedure Act. . . .

Apart from the fact that the decisions whether to accept a "new" requirement urged by one party and, if so, whether to apply it retroactively to the other party are inherent parts of the adjudicatory process, I think the opposing theory accepted by the Court of Appeals and by the prevailing opinion today is a highly impractical one. In effect, it would require an agency like the Labor Board to proceed by adjudication only when it could decide, *prior* to adjudicating a particular case, that any new practice to be adopted would be applied retroactively. Obviously, this decision cannot properly be made until all the issues relevant to adoption of the practice are fully considered in connection with the final decision of that case. If the Board were to decide, after careful evaluation of all the arguments presented to it in the adjudicatory proceeding, that it might be fairer to apply the practice only prospectively, it would be faced with the unpleasant choice of either starting all over again to evaluate the merits of the question, this time in a "rule-making" proceeding, or overriding the considerations of fairness and applying its order retroactively anyway, in order to preserve the validity of the new practice and avoid duplication of effort. I see no good reason to impose any such inflexible requirement on the administrative agencies.

For all of the foregoing reasons I would hold that the Board acted well within its discretion in choosing to proceed as it did.

JUSTICE DOUGLAS, dissenting.

I am willing to assume that, if the Board decided to treat each case on its special facts and perform its adjudicatory function in the conventional way, we should have no difficulty in affirming its action. The difficulty is that it chose a different course in the *Excelsior* case and, having done so, it should be bound to follow the [rulemaking] procedures prescribed in the Act. . . .

The Committee reports make plain that the Act "provides quite different procedures for the 'legislative' and 'judicial' functions of administrative agencies." . . .

The rule-making procedure performs important functions. It gives notice to an entire segment of society of those controls or regimentation that is forthcoming. It gives an opportunity for persons affected to be heard. . . . Failure to make full use of rule-making power is attributable at least in part "to administrative inertia and reluctance to take a clear stand."

Rule making is no cure-all; but it does force important issues into full public display and in that sense makes for more responsible administrative action.

I would hold the agencies governed by the rule-making procedure strictly to its requirements and not allow them to play fast and loose as the National Labor Relations Board apparently likes to do.

As stated by the Court of Appeals, the procedure used in the *Excelsior* case plainly flouted the Act:

"Recognizing the problem to be one affecting more than just the parties before it, the Board chose to solicit the assistance of selected amici curiae, and, ultimately, to establish a rule which not only did not apply to the parties before it, but did not take effect for thirty days. In so doing we consider that the Board, to put it bluntly, designed its own rulemaking procedure, adopting such part of the Congressional mandate as it chose, and rejecting the rest." . . .

JUSTICE HARLAN, dissenting.

The language of the Administrative Procedure Act does not support the Government's claim that an agency is "adjudicating" when it announces a rule which it refuses to apply in the dispute before it. The Act makes it clear that an agency "adjudicates" only when its procedures result in the "formulation of an *order*." 5 U.S.C. § 551(7). (Emphasis supplied.) An "order" is defined to include "the whole or a *part* of a final disposition . . . of an agency *in a matter other than rule making*. . . . " 5 U.S.C. § 551(6). (Emphasis supplied.) This definition makes it apparent that an agency is not adjudicating when it is making a rule, which the Act defines as "an agency statement of general or particular applicability and *future effect*. . . . " 5 U.S.C. § 551(4). (Emphasis supplied.) Since the Labor Board's *Excelsior* rule was to be effective only 30 days after its promulgation, it clearly falls within the rule-making requirements of the Act.

Nor can I agree that the natural interpretation of the statute should be rejected because it requires the agency to choose between giving its rules immediate effect or initiating a separate rule-making proceeding. An agency chooses to apply a rule prospectively only because it represents such a departure from pre-existing understandings that it would be unfair to impose the rule upon the parties in pending matters. But it is precisely in these situations, in which established patterns of conduct are revolutionized, that rule-making procedures perform the vital functions that my Brother DOUGLAS describes so well in a dissenting opinion with which I basically agree.

Given the fact that the Labor Board has promulgated a rule in violation of the governing statute, I believe that there is no alternative but to affirm the judgment of the Court of Appeals in this case. . . .

NLRB v. BELL AEROSPACE CO.
416 U.S. 267 (1974).

MR. JUSTICE POWELL delivered the opinion of the Court.

[Among the issues in this case is] whether the Board must proceed by rulemaking rather than by adjudication in determining whether certain buyers are "managerial employees." . . .

[The United Auto Workers petitioned the NLRB to hold] a representation election to determine whether the union would be certified as the bargaining representative of the buyers in the purchasing and procurement department at [Bell Aerospace's New York] plant. The company opposed the petition on the ground that the buyers were "managerial employees" and thus were not covered by the Act. . . .

[The Supreme Court upheld the Court of Appeals' decision that the Board had applied the wrong legal standard when it held that these buyers were covered by the Act. As a result, the Supreme Court remanded the case to the NLRB.]

[T]he present question is whether on remand the Board must invoke its rulemaking procedures if it determines, in light of our opinion, that these buyers are not "managerial employees" under the Act. The Court of Appeals thought that rulemaking was required because *any* Board finding that the company's buyers are not "managerial" would be contrary to its prior decisions and would presumably be in the nature of a general rule designed "to fit all cases at all times."

A similar issue was presented to this Court in its second decision in *SEC v. Chenery Corp.*, 332 U.S. 194 (1947) *(Chenery II)*. There, the respondent corporation argued that in an adjudicative proceeding the Commission could not apply a general standard that it had formulated for the first time in that proceeding. Rather, the Commission was required to resort instead to its rulemaking procedures if it desired to promulgate a new standard that would govern future conduct. In rejecting this contention, the Court first noted that the Commission had a statutory duty to decide the issue at hand in light of the proper standards and that this duty remained "regardless of whether those standards previously had been spelled out in a general rule or regulation." The Court continued:

The function of filling in the interstices of the [Public Utility Holding Company] Act should be performed, as much as possible, through this quasi-legislative promulgation of rules to be applied in the future. But any rigid requirement to that effect would make the administrative process inflexible and incapable of dealing with many of the specialized problems which arise.... Not every principle essential to the effective administration of a statute can or should be cast immediately into the mold of a general rule. Some principles must await their own development, while others must be adjusted to meet particular, unforeseeable situations. *In performing its important functions in these respects, therefore, an administrative agency must be equipped to act either by general rule or by individual order. To insist upon one form of action to the exclusion of the other is to exalt form over necessity.*

In other words, problems may arise in a case which the administrative agency could not reasonably foresee, problems which must be solved despite the absence of a relevant general rule. Or the agency may not have had sufficient experience with a particular problem to warrant rigidifying its tentative judgment into a hard and fast rule. *Or the problem may be so specialized and varying in nature as to be impossible of capture within the boundaries of a general rule.* In those situations, the agency must retain power to deal with the problems on a case-to-case basis if the administrative process is to be effective. There is thus a very definite place for the case-by-case evolution of statutory standards. (Emphasis added.)

The Court concluded that "the choice made between proceeding by general rule or by individual, *ad hoc* litigation is one that lies primarily in the informed discretion of the administrative agency." ...

The views expressed in *Chenery II* and *Wyman-Gordon* make plain that the Board is not precluded from announcing new principles in an adjudicative proceeding and that the choice between rulemaking and adjudication lies in the first instance within the Board's discretion. Although there may be situations where the Board's reliance on adjudication would amount to an abuse of discretion or a violation of the Act, nothing in the present case would justify such a conclusion. Indeed, there is ample indication that adjudication is especially appropriate in the instant context. As the Court of Appeals noted, "[t]here must be tens of thousands of manufacturing, wholesale and retail units which employ buyers, and hundreds of thousands of the latter." Moreover, duties of buyers vary widely depending on the company or industry. It is doubtful whether any generalized standard could be framed which would have more than marginal utility. The Board thus has reason to proceed with caution, developing its standards in a case-by-case manner with attention to the specific character of the buyers' authority and duties in each company. The Board's judgment that adjudication best serves this purpose is entitled to great weight.

The possible reliance of industry on the Board's past decisions with respect to buyers does not require a different result. It has not been shown that the adverse consequences ensuing from such reliance are so substantial that the Board should be precluded from reconsidering the issue in an adjudicative proceeding. Furthermore, this is not a case in which some new liability is sought to be imposed on individuals for past actions which were taken in good-faith reliance on Board pronouncements. Nor are fines or damages involved here. In any event, concern about such consequences is largely speculative, for the Board has not yet finally determined whether these buyers are "managerial."

It is true, of course, that rulemaking would provide the Board with a forum for soliciting the informed views of those affected in industry and labor before embarking on a new course. But surely the Board has discretion to decide that the adjudicative procedures in this case may also produce the relevant information necessary to mature and fair consideration of the issues. Those most immediately affected, the buyers and the company in the particular case, are accorded a full opportunity to be heard before the Board makes its determination....

[Four Justices dissented on labor law grounds. All concurred in the portion of the opinion reprinted here.]

Notes and Questions

1. *Purely prospective adjudication.* Did the Board act unlawfully in *Excelsior*? Can you reconcile the *Wyman-Gordon* plurality's apparent belief that it did with the Court's ultimate decision to uphold the Board's order against Wyman–Gordon? How significantly did the Court limit the Board's ability to engage in lawmaking by adjudication?

2. *Willingness to reconsider.* If the Board's lawmaking by adjudication in *Wyman-Gordon* was valid, or at least not open to judicial correction, under what circumstances would that device be impermissible? In *Mercy Hospitals of Sacramento, Inc. v. Local 250, Hospital & Institutional Workers Union,* 217 N.L.R.B. 765 (1975), the Board announced a policy that registered nurses at nonprofit hospitals may always be represented by a separate bargaining unit. A hospital challenged that policy and sought a larger bargaining unit in *NLRB v. St. Francis Hospital,* 601 F.2d 404, 414–17 (9th Cir.1979), but the Board refused to receive evidence to support this position. The Ninth Circuit reversed:

> The key question raised herein is whether the *per se* policy established in the Board's *Mercy* decision ... is consistent with the congressional directive.... Further, one may question the fairness of a policy that is applied without a chance for an effected [sic] party to demonstrate that its situation does not fall within the scope of the policy or otherwise to argue why the policy should not be applied in its case. This is especially so herein because the Board ... has, on more than one occasion, placed registered nurses in the same bargaining unit as other health care professionals, as the Hospital argued it should do in this case....

... Because we find the Hospital's proffered evidence as to the appropriateness of an all-professional unit to be definitely relevant and because we do not believe that the Board's *Mercy* decision can or should control this case, we find the refusal to receive the Hospital's evidence herein to be arbitrary and capricious.

What was wrong with the Board's adjudicative lawmaking in this case? How was the case different from *Wyman-Gordon*? Would the result have been different if the Board had used § 553 rulemaking? *Cf. American Hospital Ass'n v. NLRB,* 499 U.S. 606 (1991), discussed in § 3.2 N.3.

3. *Bell Aerospace.* At the time of *Bell Aerospace,* the NLRB was still avoiding the rulemaking procedures of the APA, and was still being criticized as a result. *See, e.g.,* Merton C. Bernstein, "The NLRB's Adjudication–Rule Making Dilemma Under the Administrative Procedure Act," 79 Yale L.J. 571 (1970). Echoing this criticism, the court of appeals decision in *Bell Aerospace,* written by Judge Henry Friendly, had argued: "The Board was prescribing a new policy, not just with respect to 25 buyers in Wheatfield, N.Y., but in substance ... 'to fit all cases at all times.' ... Yet the Board did not even attempt to inform industry and labor organizations ... of its proposed new policy and to invite comment thereon, as it has sometimes done in the past.... [T]he argument for rule-making is especially strong when the Board is proposing to reverse a long-standing and oft-repeated policy on which industry and labor have relied.... [W]hen the Board has so long been committed to a position, it should be particularly sure that it has all available information before adopting another, in a setting where nothing stands in the way of a rule-making proceeding except the Board's congenital disinclination to follow [that] procedure...." *Bell Aerospace Co. v. NLRB,* 475 F.2d 485, 496–97 (2d Cir.1973). In this light, is the Supreme Court's ruling persuasive?

4. *Reliance and retroactivity. Bell Aerospace* alludes to three situations in which reliance interests might require a "different result." They are situations in which: (1) the adverse consequences of retrospective adjudicative lawmaking would be substantial to parties who had relied on past decisions of the agency; (2) new liability is sought to be imposed retrospectively by adjudication on individuals for past actions which were taken in good-faith reliance on agency pronouncements; or (3) fines or damages are involved. In current federal practice, the "different result" that courts would prescribe under such circumstances would generally not be a directive to engage in rulemaking proceedings. Instead, the court would probably hold on the merits that the agency order was arbitrary and capricious in its application to that particular case, so that the complaining litigant would not have to comply with it. *See, e.g., Pfaff v. HUD,* 88 F.3d 739, 747–50 (9th Cir.1996); *Stoller v. CFTC,* 834 F.2d 262, 265 (2d Cir.1987). If otherwise valid, however, the precedent itself would stand, and the agency would be free to enforce it in the future against parties who did have timely notice of it. *McDonald v. Watt,* 653 F.2d 1035, 1041–46 (5th Cir.1981).

According to a leading case, the question of whether a new case-law rule announced in an agency adjudication is unfairly retroactive, so as to constitute an abuse of discretion, entails balancing at least five factors: "(1) whether the particular case is one of first impression; (2) whether the new rule represents an abrupt departure from well established practice or merely attempts to fill a void in an unsettled area of the law; (3) the extent to which the party against whom the new law is applied relied on the prior law; (4) the degree of the burden which a retroactive order imposes on a party; and (5) the statutory interest in applying the new rule to the case at hand despite the reliance of a party on the old standard." *Retail, Wholesale & Dept. Store Clerks Union v. NLRB*, 466 F.2d 380, 390 (D.C.Cir.1972).

In *Retail Union*, certain workers who had been on strike against Coca-Cola Bottling Works, Inc., were ineligible for reinstatement when the strike ended but were eligible for jobs that opened up later. The NLRB found that the employer had committed an unfair labor practice by failing to rehire them. The Board also required the employer to pay back wages to these employees. The company appealed, arguing that its refusal to rehire had been permissible under the Board's case law at the time it occurred. *After* Coca-Cola's refusal, the Board had overruled that case law. Its finding against Coca-Cola was based on the newly announced precedent. Applying the above factors to these circumstances, the court decided that the NLRB's back pay order was an abuse of discretion and, therefore, should be set aside. For subsequent applications of the same test, see *United Food Workers v. NLRB*, 1 F.3d 24 (D.C.Cir.1993); *Clark-Cowlitz Joint Operating Agency v. FERC*, 826 F.2d 1074 (D.C.Cir.1987).

Is the *Retail Union* remedy for unfairly retroactive agency lawmaking better or worse than the approach of the lower court in *Bell Aerospace*, i.e., holding that the agency must institute rulemaking proceedings if it wants to consider overruling its prior case law?

5. *Abuse of discretion.* According to *Bell Aerospace*, "there may be situations where the Board's reliance on adjudication would amount to an abuse of discretion . . . ." Among the few federal cases to find that an agency has abused its discretion in this sense is *Ford Motor Co. v. FTC*, 673 F.2d 1008 (9th Cir.1981). In that case the Federal Trade Commission issued a cease and desist order against Francis Ford, a retail automobile dealer. The Commission found the repossession practices used by Francis Ford against its defaulting purchasers to be a violation of Section 5 of the FTC Act. The court of appeals vacated the order, stating:

> In the present case, the FTC, by its order, has established a rule that would require a secured creditor to credit the debtor with the "best possible" value of the repossessed vehicle, and forbid the creditor from charging the debtor with overhead and lost profits. . . . [T]he precise issue therefore is whether this adjudication changes existing law, and has widespread application. It does, and the matter should be addressed by rulemaking.

> The FTC admits that industry practice has been to do what Francis Ford does—credit the debtor with the wholesale value and charge the debtor for indirect expenses. . . .

> By all accounts this adjudication is the first agency action against a dealer for violating ORS 79.5040 by doing what Francis Ford does. Although the U.C.C. counterpart of ORS 79.5040 is enacted in 49 states, nearly word for word, we have been cited to no case which has interpreted the provision to require a secured creditor to credit the debtor for the

"best possible price" and not charge him for overhead and lost profits....

Ultimately, however, we are persuaded to set aside this order because the rule of the case made below will have general application. It will not apply just to Francis Ford. Credit practices similar to those of Francis Ford are widespread in the car dealership industry; and the U.C.C. section the FTC wishes us to interpret exists in 49 states....

Id. at 1009–10.

Is *Ford Motor Co.* distinguishable from *Bell Aerospace*? *See* Richard K. Berg, "Re-examining Policy Procedures: The Choice Between Rulemaking and Adjudication," 38 Admin.L.Rev. 149, 155–58 (1986); "*Ford Motor Co. v. FTC:* No Rule without a Rulemaking?," Regulation, Sept./Oct. 1981, at 13.

The Ninth Circuit mentioned in passing that the FTC had appended to its decision a "Synopsis of Determination" that it planned to send to other car dealers. The Commission wanted to be able to take advantage of § 5(m)(1)(B) of the FTC Act, 15 U.S.C. § 45(m)(1)(B). According to that provision, after the Commission has held a practice to be unfair or deceptive under the FTC Act and issued a cease and desist order (other than a consent decree) against one violator, it can go to court to obtain a civil penalty from any other persons who engage in the same practice with "actual knowledge" that it is unfair or deceptive. These latter persons are entitled to judicial review of whether the practice is indeed unfair or deceptive; but the statute does not provide that they may ask the Commission for further consideration of that question. Thus, the synopsis in *Ford Motor Co.* was designed to ensure that potential targets of civil penalty actions would have "actual knowledge" of the FTC's decision.

Does § 5(m)(1)(B) shed any light on the propriety of the Ninth Circuit's decision? Also, in light of judicial doctrine on the legitimate uses of adjudication for lawmaking purposes, is the § 5(m)(1)(B) procedure itself fair? *See United States v. Hopkins Dodge, Inc.,* 849 F.2d 311, 313 n. 8 (8th Cir.1988) (§ 5(m) complies with due process because "there is no reason why the F.T.C. should be required to determine over and over again the illegality of a 'practice' ... if the defendant charged with engaging in it knows that it has been found illegal by the Commission, and is given an opportunity to litigate the facts regarding whether or not he has engaged in the proscribed practice"). Do you agree? *Compare* Berg, *supra,* at 176 (questioning fairness of the procedure), *with* David O. Bickart, "Civil Penalties Under Section 5(m) of the Federal Trade Commission Act," 44 U.Chi.L.Rev. 761 (1977) (supporting statute).

The *Ford Motor Co.* case was the subject of a study conducted by the ABA Section of Administrative Law. The Section prepared the following resolution, which was adopted by the ABA's House of Delegates.

RESOLVED, That the American Bar Association approves the following principles respecting the choice between rulemaking and adjudication in administrative agency proceedings:

1. An agency is generally free to announce new policy through an adjudicative proceeding.

2. When rulemaking is feasible and practicable, an agency which has been granted broad rulemaking authority ordinarily should use rulemaking rather than adjudication for large-scale changes, such as proscribing established industry-wide practices not previously thought to be unlawful.

3. An agency should not be empowered to treat its adjudicatory decisions precisely as if they were rules. In particular, it is inappropriate to empower an agency or court to treat third-party departures from holdings in agency adjudications as, *ipso facto,* violations of law. Where the precedent of a prior adjudication is sought to be applied in a subsequent adjudication, a party should have a meaningful opportunity to persuade the agency that the principle involved should be modified or held inapplicable to his situation.

Is the resolution simply a restatement of current federal law? Or does it go beyond current federal law in certain respects? If so, how? For an explanation of the study and resolution, see Berg, *supra.*

6. *Benefit programs.* A few other federal cases assert that an agency must execute specified lawmaking by rule rather than by order, despite the absence of a statute explicitly requiring that approach. The most salient such case is *Morton v. Ruiz,* 415 U.S. 199, 231–35 (1974), also discussed at § 5.7 N.1. The issue was whether welfare benefits should be paid to those Indians who live near but not on reservations. According to *Ruiz,* if the Bureau of Indian Affairs did not have sufficient funds to pay all eligible beneficiaries, "it would be incumbent upon [the agency] to develop an eligibility standard to deal with this problem.... But in such a case the agency must, at a minimum, let the standard be generally known so as to assure that it is being applied consistently and so as to avoid both the reality and the appearance of arbitrary denial of benefits to potential beneficiaries.... No matter how rational or consistent with congressional intent a particular decision might be, the determination of eligibility cannot be made on an ad hoc basis by the dispenser of the funds."

Ruiz was decided a few months before *Bell Aerospace,* which did not even cite it. Thus, most commentators have regarded *Ruiz* as a "sport" decision that cannot be reconciled with the main body of federal law on required rulemaking. Do you agree?

§ 6.2.2 STATE LAW

Most states appear to follow the principle that agencies generally have discretion to make their law either by order or by rule. This discretion appears to be limited only by a specific statute or agency rule to the contrary, and by a general unreasonableness or abuse of discretion standard. *See* Arthur Earl Bonfield, "State Administrative Policy Formation and the Choice of Lawmaking Methodology," 42 Admin.L.Rev. 121, 140–41 (1990).

A number of states, however, appear to be in the vanguard of a developing movement in the contrary direction. Several state cases have relied upon a principle of statutory construction as a means of requiring agencies to elaborate their law by rule rather than by order. A few additional state courts have relied upon the demands of due process or an abuse of discretion standard for this purpose. And other states have resorted to the enactment of specific statutes to impose such a requirement. So far, however, fewer than a dozen states have used these mechanisms to impose on their agencies a general requirement that they make their law primarily by rules.

MEGDAL v. OREGON STATE BOARD OF DENTAL EXAMINERS

605 P.2d 273 (Ore.1980).

LINDE, JUSTICE.

Petitioner, a dentist licensed both in Oregon and in California and maintaining offices in both states, seeks review of an order of the State Board of Dental Examiners which revoked his Oregon license on the ground of "unprofessional conduct."

The conduct which the board found unprofessional under the statute was that petitioner obtained malpractice insurance coverage for other dentists employed by him in his California practice by a misrepresentation that they were employed in Oregon.... The issue, in sum, is whether the board may revoke a dentist's license under an unparticularized rubric of "unprofessional conduct" upon an administrative finding that he practiced a fraud on an insurance company.

Petitioner objects that before revoking a license for unprofessional conduct other than the kinds specified in the statute itself the board must first adopt rules indicating the forbidden conduct, because the phrase "unprofessional conduct" alone is too vague a standard to be applied directly from case to case.... We allowed review in order to reexamine the role of broadly stated standards in laws governing disciplinary actions against occupational licensees. For the reasons that follow, we conclude that the board's order must be reversed....

There is no lack of suggestion that a prior specification of grounds should be a prerequisite of due process in administrative as well as penal deprivations. *See, e.g.,* Davis, Administrative Law of the Seventies 28, 224 (1976); Note, Due Process Limitations on Occupational Licensing, 59 Va.L.Rev. 1097, 1104–1106 (1973). At least one modern court has held that the grounds to revoke a pharmacist's license for "grossly unprofessional conduct" must be limited to those further spelled out in the statute or in rules, because "revocation of licenses and permits for conduct not specifically defined or prohibited by the statute, would render the statute unconstitutional on grounds of vagueness in violation of the Due Process Clause of the Fourteenth Amendment." *Pennsylvania State Board of Pharmacy v. Cohen,* 292 A.2d 277, 282 (1972). To support this conclusion the court took the step of tacking together the two propositions that an individual's exclusion from an occupation requires due process and that penal statutes must give adequate notice of the forbidden or required conduct....

Perhaps federal "due process" law will move toward the step anticipated by the Pennsylvania court. But, there has been no clear signal
from the United States Supreme Court that the standards for occupational licensing decisions must meet those for penal laws. The Court's
later holdings sustaining the adequacy of phrases such as "conduct
unbecoming an officer and a gentleman" for military punishment, *Par-
ker v. Levy,* 417 U.S. 733 (1974), and a string of epithets for disciplinary
discharge of civil service employees, *Arnett v. Kennedy,* 416 U.S. 134
(1974), can be distinguished as dealing with special relationships. Nonetheless, the gravity of the losses there permitted to be inflicted under
vague standards leaves the crucial step assumed by the Pennsylvania
court in doubt. Again, the factors from which *Mathews v. Eldridge,* 424
U.S. 319 (1976), directs us to derive the requirements of due process—
the private interest affected, the chances of error and of its reduction by
better procedures, and the countervailing governmental interests—clearly affirm a licensee's right to the kind of adjudicatory procedures of
notice, hearing, and findings based on evidence that, in this state, are
provided him under the administrative procedure act; but nothing indicates whether this due process calculus extends also to restricting
adverse action to the enforcement of previously specified norms. For the
moment, at least, support for finding such a requirement in federal due
process appears primarily in *Soglin v. Kauffman,* 418 F.2d 163 (7th
Cir.1969), which applied the requirement to standards for expelling
university students for "misconduct," and in decisions involving criteria
for the bestowing of benefits.

In sum, the most that can be said about "due process" as a possible
premise for petitioner's constitutional attack on the phrase "unprofessional conduct" is that the state of the federal law is inconclusive and
the attack perhaps only premature. . . .

Since 1939 the statute has authorized the board to "make and
enforce rules . . . for regulating the practice of dentistry." The statute
does not expressly state that the expanded grounds for disciplinary
action under the rubric "unprofessional conduct" were to be created by
board rules. But there are reasons to believe that this is the legislative
policy. One is that the legislature should not be assumed to be insensitive to the importance of fair notice of grounds that may lead to loss of
one's profession or occupation, whether or not this is a constitutional
requirement. More concretely, the legislature made this policy explicit in
many similar licensing statutes even if not in this one. Repeatedly the
legislature has specified that the several boards are to exercise their
control over professional standards by adopting codes or rules. . . .

Sometimes such differences in statutory drafting represent deliberate differences in policy. We see no reason to believe that this was the
case here. The difference of the potential impact, when one occupation is
given fair notice of obligatory standards of propriety by prior rulemaking
and another occupation is given no such prior notice, is too pronounced
to be attributed to the legislature without some showing that it was
intended. Thus we doubt that the stylistic differences among 30–odd

statutes separately enacted over many years mean that some of the boards are to develop professional standards by rulemaking and others by ad hoc determinations, insofar as they are authorized to add to the express statutory grounds for discipline at all. Rather, we infer from statutes such as those cited above that when a licensing statute contains both a broad standard of "unprofessional conduct" that is not fully defined in the statute itself and also authority to make rules for the conduct of the regulated occupation, the legislative purpose is to provide for the further specification of the standard by rules, unless a different understanding is shown. . . .

When a board lays down a new rule of proscribed or required conduct under delegated authority to do so, this is reviewable to determine whether the rule remains within the intended scope and purpose of the delegated authority. . . .

Doubts are sometimes expressed whether rules can encompass the variety of acts that should be recognized as "unprofessional," or "unethical," or "unbecoming," or otherwise improper. An attempt to "catalogue all the types of professional misconduct" might well seem infeasible. . . . But rules need not imitate a detailed criminal code to serve the two purposes of giving notice of censurable conduct and confining disciplinary administration to the announced standards. Nor is the only alternative to include some form of catchall clause that is as general as the standard it purports to elucidate. The resources of rulemaking are not so limited.

For instance, as this case illustrates, an important question is what relationships are covered by the term "unprofessional conduct" and thus within the range of professional discipline. It might be agreed that the term covers conduct in the course of rendering the professional service on the one hand, and on the other that it excludes the licensee's purely private affairs unrelated to any relevant professional qualification or performance. But between these two poles, there may be questions how far "unprofessional conduct" extends to financial arrangements or to mixing professional with other relationships. There may be disagreement whether the term should extend beyond conduct toward the patient or other recipient of the regulated service so as to cover relationships with employees or suppliers, with other professionals, or perhaps with the regulating agency itself. As stated above, in many licensing statutes the legislature does not itself provide explicit or implicit answers to these and similar questions; it delegates this task, within the limits of each statute's objectives, to the licensing agencies. . . . Thus, when the statute itself offers no further definition, the legislative delegation to the agency calls for such questions to be resolved in principle by rules rather than being confronted and disputed for the first time in charging a particular respondent directly under a conclusory term such as "unprofessional conduct." . . .

We conclude that petitioner is entitled to relief. His license has been revoked under a statutory standard of "unprofessional conduct," that was broadened beyond its original list of specifications, which the statute means the board to particularize by rules. Although his original attack was couched in constitutional terms, its target was the same lack of comprehensible and channeling criteria that the rules are meant to provide. No such rule having been made to proscribe the kind of conduct charged against petitioner, there was no legal ground on which to revoke his license. . . .

Notes and Questions

1. *Due process.* A number of federal and state cases hold that in some circumstances due process requires agencies to structure their discretionary powers with agency-created standards. *See, e.g., Holmes v. New York City Housing Authority,* 398 F.2d 262, 265 (2d Cir.1968) (distribution of public housing units); *Hornsby v. Allen,* 326 F.2d 605, 610 (5th Cir.1964) (issuance of liquor licenses). While these cases require agencies to create such standards in order to ensure that they do not exercise their discretionary powers in a wholly arbitrary manner, they do not appear to require those standards to be created by rule rather than by a system of precedents created in individual cases.

Although the court in *Megdal* concluded that due process does not limit the discretion of agencies exercising authority in a nonpenal context to make law by retrospective order rather than by prospective rule, the *Pennsylvania State Board of Pharmacy* case discussed in *Megdal,* and a few other cases, have come to the opposite conclusion. For example, *Elizondo v. State Department of Revenue,* 570 P.2d 518, 521 (Colo.1977), held that due process required the issuance of rules "to guide hearing officers in their decisions regarding requests for probationary [driver's] licenses" in order to assure advance notice to the public and to avoid arbitrary agency decisionmaking. The court apparently assumed that case-by-case decisionmaking would not adequately secure those results.

Similarly, *White v. Roughton,* 530 F.2d 750 (7th Cir.1976), held invalid the denial or termination of benefits under a local general relief welfare program. No written standards governed the eligibility for such aid, which appeared to be determined wholly on the basis of the "unwritten personal standards" of administrators. In these circumstances the court held that the lack of "written standards and *regulations*" was a denial of due process. Id. at 754 (emphasis supplied).

Note that *Soglin v. Kauffman,* 418 F.2d 163, 168 (7th Cir.1969), discussed in *Megdal,* also appeared to require the agency to create discretion-limiting standards by *rule.* But *Soglin* may be distinguished from *Elizondo* and *White* on the ground that the student disciplinary proceedings involved in *Soglin* were viewed as *penal,* thereby justifying a due process requirement of rulemaking in that case on a ground not available on the facts of the other two cases.

In view of these authorities, was the *Megdal* court's approach to the due process clause too restrictive?

2. *Megdal principle.* Was the court in *Megdal* justified in construing the relevant enabling act to require the Board of Dental Examiners to

elaborate *by rule* the meaning of the term "unprofessional conduct"? After all, that act did not explicitly indicate any such intention, and the enabling acts of some other agencies did. Do policy considerations justify that outcome?

Professor Bonfield has argued that *Megdal* stands for the following proposition: "In the absence of clear evidence to the contrary, the legislature is presumed to intend an agency that has been delegated express authority to issue rules and express or implied authority to decide individual cases, subject to a vague statutory standard, to elaborate that statutory standard by rule rather than by order, as soon as feasible and to the extent practicable." Bonfield, *supra,* at 161. Is that broad reading of the case defensible as an assumption about probable legislative intent? Is it defensible on policy grounds?

Finally, assuming that the courts adopt a presumption that the legislature intends that an agency develop law through rules, how far should it reach? Suppose the Oregon Dental Board promulgates a rule defining "unprofessional conduct" to include "making misrepresentations in one's professional or business activities." If Willy, another dentist in Oregon, were accused of conduct identical to Megdal's, would that rule support revocation of his license?

3. *Subsequent developments in Oregon.* In *Trebesch v. Employment Division,* 710 P.2d 136, 139–40 (Ore.1985), the Oregon Supreme Court read the *Megdal* principle more narrowly than it might have. It construed *Megdal* to mean that in situations where the legislature has not expressly indicated its specific intentions with respect to mandatory agency rulemaking, courts must determine those intentions by analyzing a number of factors. These factors included the character of the statutory term in dispute, the specific breadth and type of tasks assigned to the agency, and the structure used by the agency to execute its tasks. In this instance, the question was whether the Division had to use rulemaking to determine what individuals were "actively seeking work" and thus eligible for unemployment benefits. Applying the first two factors, the court found that the statute was amenable to rulemaking and that the agency's tasks included a responsibility to ensure that the statute was applied uniformly throughout the state. However, applying the third factor, the court was unsure whether the agency head had the authority to elaborate on the meaning of "actively seeking work" in adjudicative proceedings. If he did possess that authority, the court would allow him to use it to achieve the necessary uniformity; if he lacked such authority, he would have to use rulemaking in order to fulfill the uniformity goal.

It has been argued that the approach of *Trebesch* appears to "substitute a full-scale, particularized inquiry producing indeterminate and inconsistent results, for a broad rule of construction based on *Megdal* that would be easier to apply and that would yield relatively predictable and consistent results." Bonfield, *supra,* at 164. Since *Trebesch,* indeed, Oregon cases have proved somewhat unpredictable, sometimes inferring a legislative intention to require rulemaking and sometimes not. *Id.* Is Bonfield's criticism of the case persuasive?

4. *Other state cases.* Cases in other states have also required agencies to elaborate the major contours of their law by rule, despite the absence of an express statutory requirement. Some of these cases have followed the lead of the *Wyman-Gordon* dissenters (*see* § 6.2.1), holding particular agency action invalid because that action was deemed to be a rule *de facto* but had been issued without observance of ordinary rulemaking procedures. *See, e.g., CBS Inc. v. Comptroller of the Treasury,* 575 A.2d 324, 330 (Md.1990); *In re Hibbing Taconite Co.,* 431 N.W.2d 885, 894–95 (Minn.App.1988); *Metromedia v. Director, Division of Taxation,* 478 A.2d 742 (N.J.1984); Bonfield, *supra,* at 152–53. In other state cases, particular agency adjudicatory actions have been held invalid because they made legal or policy decisions that, in the court's view, should have been made by rule instead. *See Aluli v. Lewin,* 828 P.2d 802 (Hawaii 1992); *Matter of Bessemer Mountain,* 856 P.2d 450 (Wyo. 1993). The latter cases have reached this result by relying primarily on policy considerations, as opposed to a *Megdal*-like presumption about the legislature's expectations.

In *Bessemer*, for example, the Environmental Quality Council designated Bessemer Mountain, the site of unique fossil remains, as a "very rare or uncommon" area with "particular historical, archaeological ... or scenic value." The result of the designation was to put the mountain off limits to mining.

The court held that "the EQC cannot classify lands within the state as 'very rare or uncommon' without first establishing by regulation the criteria and factors which will set the standard for that classification. We are satisfied that, in the absence of such a regulatory standard, the phrase 'very rare or uncommon' is too amorphous to permit judicial review of the action of the EQC. Consequently, any such classification inherently is arbitrary and capricious." 856 P.2d at 453. By way of illustrating the amorphousness of the statutory criteria and the consequent difficulties facing a reviewing court, the decision quoted from the hearing in the proceedings below:

> When asked what the words "rare and uncommon" meant, one of the people at the hearing said, "You asked the right person, because I tried to write a law that defined scenic this year.... I finally threw up my hands and decided that scenic probably is in the eye of the behold-er.... " We perceive fundamental truth in that statement, and we simply add that the same comment very clearly applies to "very rare or uncommon." What might appear to be "very rare or uncommon" to one person, such as an area like Bessemer Mountain, might seem simply ordinary to another.

Id. at 452. Are you persuaded that the absence of regulations should have been fatal to the EQC's determination? *Bessemer* is criticized in Michael Gregory Weisz, Casenote, 29 Land & Water L.Rev. 615 (1994).

5. *1981 MSAPA.* Section 2–104(3) of the 1981 MSAPA provides that "as soon as feasible, and to the extent practicable, [each agency must] adopt rules, in addition to those otherwise required ... embodying appropriate standards, principles, and procedural safeguards, that the agency will apply to the law it administers." According to the reporter for that Act, "[t]his model statutory provision embodies a clear legislative determination that the values of *prompt* elaboration of agency law by rule and *detailed* elaboration

of agency law by rule are to be preferred over the competing general values of agency convenience or agency preference for ad hoc law making in the course of adjudications. As a result, the MSAPA provision would fundamentally change existing law in most states...." Bonfield, *supra,* at 145. Iowa adopted the same language in 1998. *See* Iowa Code § 17A.3(1)(c). Is so large a shift towards rulemaking desirable?

Another scholar has criticized the section on the ground that, "[a]lthough [the] reasons for preferring rulemaking over adjudication are persuasive, we should be skeptical about entrusting to judges the task of invalidating otherwise proper adjudications on the ground that, in their opinion, the agency failed to issue a rule with the 'precision and detail' that was 'capable of being accomplished successfully under the circumstances.' " Carl A. Auerbach, "Bonfield on State Administrative Rulemaking: A Critique," 71 Minn. L.Rev. 543, 549 (1987). Bonfield acknowledges that the words "as soon as feasible and to the extent practicable" in § 2–104(3) are vague, but he points out that the same may be said about many general requirements imposed in administrative law, such as the directive in most APAs that courts must overturn agency action that is "arbitrary," "capricious," or "an abuse of discretion." He notes that the benefits of that generally worded directive are commonly thought to outweigh its costs (including the costs stemming from the ambiguity of the relevant language), and the authors of the 1981 MSAPA made the same judgment about that Act's preference for mandatory lawmaking through rules. Bonfield, *supra,* at 145–46. Who has the better of this argument?

6. *Mandatory codification of case law.* Section 2–104(4) of the 1981 MSAPA also requires agencies, "as soon as feasible and to the extent practicable, [to] adopt rules to supersede principles of law or policy lawfully declared by the agency as the basis for its decisions in particular cases." Is this a sound idea? One scholar (later turned jurist) expressed concern about the vagueness of the provision and also foresaw a dilemma as far as "the perceived fairness of agency lawmaking" was concerned: "If the subsequent rulemakings regularly endorse the holdings of earlier adjudications, they will rightly be regarded as charades. But if, on the other hand, they often reverse (for the future) those holdings—which have been the basis for particularized commands or even penalties in the past—then the adjudicatory process is bound to fall into deserved disrepute." Antonin Scalia, "Back to Basics: Making Law without Making Rules," Regulation, July/Aug. 1981, at 25, 28. Do you agree?

The official Comment to § 2–104(4) states that "[i]f an agency breaches, in particular circumstances, its duty ... to issue ... a rule displacing a line of its precedent, the agency may not subsequently rely on that line of precedent. Instead, it would have to readjudicate wholly *de novo,* and free of prior precedent, whatever principles of law might apply to those circumstances." Does this appear to be an effective and desirable remedy? *Cf.* 1981 MSAPA § 5–116(c)(8)(iii). An alternative approach is that of the Washington APA, which *encourages* agencies to codify their precedents as rules but does not purport to make that expectation legally enforceable. Wash.Rev.Code § 34.05.220(4). What good would a statute like that do?

7. *The Florida rulemaking counter-revolution.* In 1991, Florida adopted a version of the 1981 MSAPA required-rulemaking standard. By statute, "rulemaking is not a matter of agency discretion." Agencies are required to use rulemaking as a means for making statements of general applicability and future effect to the extent that it is "feasible and practicable" to do so. Agencies bear the burden of showing that rulemaking is not feasible or practicable. Fla.Stat.Ann. § 120.54(1)(a).

This so-called "presumptive rulemaking" statute was applied to invalidate a policy maintained by the Florida agency responsible for foster parent placements. The policy was that foster parents must be heterosexual and married to each other. As a result, the agency disqualified a lesbian couple. The court noted that it need not reach the constitutional questions presented by the case because the policies violated the APA. "The homosexual and unmarried couple policies are of general applicability. By applying those policies and not following the rulemaking procedures prescribed in [the APA], HRS exceeded its delegated authority." *Matthews v. Weinberg*, 645 So.2d 487, 489 (Fla.App.1994).

Unsurprisingly, the effect of the presumptive rulemaking provision was an immediate and substantial increase in the number of agency rules. That development sparked a sharp reaction. The governor claimed that presumptive rulemaking resulted in a "proliferation of overly-precise rules [and] overwhelming red tape and deprives agency decision-makers of the ability to exercise good judgment and common sense." In 1996, the legislature sharply revised the rulemaking structure, although it did not repeal the presumptive rulemaking provision.

Among the changes enacted in 1996 was one provision (discussed in § 6.4 N.6) that made waivers or variances from existing rules *mandatory* under certain broadly defined circumstances. Another provision (discussed in § 7.3 N.4) limited agency rulemaking power to situations in which an agency is implementing a specific provision of law; agencies may no longer adopt rules that merely are deemed reasonably related to the purposes of the underlying legislation. A third provision revised the APA's regulatory analysis requirements and enabled private parties to enforce them more easily. A fourth provision abolished the presumption of validity normally accorded to agency rules—it shifted the burden of proof to agencies when their proposed rules are challenged in hearings before the Florida central panel.

This description of events is taken from Jim Rossi, "The 1996 Revised Florida Administrative Procedure Act: A Rulemaking Revolution or Counter–Revolution?," 49 Admin.L.Rev. 345 (1997). To what extent, if at all, does the Florida rulemaking counter-revolution cast doubt on the desirability of required rulemaking provisions such as those of the 1981 MSAPA?

8. *Problem.* Madison University (MU) student disciplinary rules (adopted after appropriate notice and comment procedures) provide that a student can be suspended or expelled for "conduct inappropriate for a student." A Student Discipline Board (SDB), consisting of both faculty and students, administers the student disciplinary rules.

Mark, an MU student, received 185 tickets for illegal parking in MU parking lots. After providing notice and a trial-type hearing, the SDB suspended Mark from school for six months, holding that such flagrant disregard of the MU parking rules was "conduct inappropriate for a student." In its opinion the Board stated: "Suspension is clearly not an excessive sanction for a student who has committed over 150 parking infractions." The SDB had never before treated a parking or traffic violation as a violation of the student disciplinary rules.

(a) Should the SDB's decision be reversed because of insufficient prior rulemaking? Assume that MU is (i) a federal government institution; or, alternatively, (ii) a state university in a state that has adopted the 1981 MSAPA.

(b) Suppose that, a year after Mark's case, Belinda accumulated 175 parking tickets and was brought before the SDB. By this time a new group of faculty and students had rotated onto the Board. The SDB suspended Belinda, stating in its decision that "to distinguish between 175 and 185 tickets would be artificial, so we must follow the precedent set in Mark's case." Should the SDB's decision in Belinda's case be reversed?

§ 6.3   RULEMAKING PETITIONS AND AGENCY AGENDA–SETTING

Section 553(e) of the federal APA, § 6 of the 1961 MSAPA, and § 3–117 of the 1981 MSAPA all authorize members of the public to petition an agency for the issuance, amendment, or repeal of a rule. The worthwhile objectives of these provisions have resulted in their widespread incorporation in state APAs.

Perhaps the most important purpose of the petition for rulemaking is to force an agency to re-examine the status quo. A petition might request that the agency undertake additional regulation, or that the agency repeal or modify existing rules that are not working properly or have become obsolete. Such petitions bring to the agency's attention situations requiring prompt action and thus help to insure more responsive government.

Another important purpose of petitions for rulemaking is to supply a means for focused public input when an agency has adopted a rule without advance notice and comment under one of the § 553 exemptions. *See Guardian Federal Savings and Loan Ass'n v. FSLIC*, 589 F.2d 658, 668 (D.C.Cir.1978). Similarly, even when an agency has provided advance notice and comment, some members of the public who did not know about the proposed rule, or who did not participate in the process, may be dissatisfied with the final rule and wish to persuade the agency to modify it. The right to file a rulemaking petition may help them.

Both MSAPAs require a statement of reasons upon denial of a rulemaking petition. Federal APA § 553(e) does not require any such statement, but § 555(e) of that Act requires a brief statement of the grounds for denial of any application or petition filed with an agency. *See Auer v. Robbins*, 519 U.S. 452, ___ (1997) (proper remedy for allegedly obsolete regulations is "a petition to the agency for rulemaking, § 553(e), denial of which must be justified by a statement of reasons,

§ 555(e), and can be appealed to the courts"). The requirement of an explanatory statement is important, because it forces agencies to consider carefully their precise reasons for any such denial, thereby discouraging automatic or impulsive dismissals of rulemaking petitions. The required written statement also facilitates judicial review.

From the government's point of view, rulemaking petitions give rise to concerns about the extent to which an agency will be able to determine its own priorities and workload, notwithstanding pressures from outsiders. This concern surfaces not only when the agency is asked to commence a proceeding, but also when outside parties seek to hasten the completion of a proceeding that the agency has already begun. This section examines a number of contexts in which the law seeks to reconcile these competing private and governmental interests.

WWHT, INC. v. FCC
656 F.2d 807 (D.C.Cir.1981).

EDWARDS, J.:

[Several broadcasters of subscription television (STV) programs asked the FCC to issue a rule that would require cable television operators to carry scrambled signals of STV shows. The Commission refused, citing the following reasons (among others): There was no evidence that mandatory carriage on cable was essential to the survival of STV stations. Carriage of scrambled signals would impose greater burdens on cable operators than regular broadcast signals do. And only a fraction of cable customers would purchase STV, yet all would bear the costs of providing it.]

This case raises the questions of whether, and under what circumstances, a reviewing court may require an agency to institute rulemaking proceedings after the agency has denied a petition for rulemaking....

... Although the legislative history accompanying section 4(d) [of the original APA, now § 553(e),] makes it plain that an agency must receive and respond to petitions for rulemaking, it is equally clear from the legislative history that Congress did not intend to compel an agency to undertake rulemaking merely because a petition has been filed.... In its report on the APA, the Senate Judiciary Committee emphasized that

> [t]he mere filing of a petition does not require an agency to grant it, or to hold a hearing, or engage in any other public rule making proceedings. The refusal of an agency to grant the petition or to hold rule making proceedings, therefore, would not per se be subject to judicial reversal. However, the facts or considerations brought to the attention of an agency by such a petition might be such as to require the agency to act to prevent the rule from continuing or becoming vulnerable upon judicial review....

... While we agree that judicial intrusion into an agency's exercise of discretion in the discharge of its essentially legislative rulemaking functions should be severely circumscribed, we reject the suggestion that agency denials of requests for rulemaking are exempt from judicial review. [*See* § 10.5 N.5, for a discussion of the relevant case law, which has remained consistent with the court's position.] ...

The most comprehensive statement by this court as to the availability and scope of review of an agency's decision to deny a petition for rulemaking can be found in the thoughtful opinion by Judge McGowan in *Natural Resources Defense Council, Inc. v. SEC,* 606 F.2d 1031 (D.C.Cir.1979).... [W]ith respect to an agency decision *not* to promulgate a certain rule, the court stated:

> An agency's discretionary decision *not* to regulate a given activity is inevitably based, in large measure, on factors not inherently susceptible to judicial resolution—*e.g.,* internal management considerations as to budget and personnel; evaluations of its own competence; weighing of competing policies within a broad statutory framework. Further, even if an agency considers a particular problem worthy of regulation, it may determine for reasons lying within its special expertise that the time for action has not yet arrived.... The circumstances in the regulated industry may be evolving in a way that could vitiate the need for regulation, or the agency may still be developing the expertise necessary for effective regulation.

... In determining the scope of review in this case, we follow the lead of *NRDC.* In particular, we adhere to Judge McGowan's suggestion that, where the proposed rule pertains to a matter of policy within the agency's expertise and discretion, the scope of review should "perforce be a narrow one, limited to ensuring that the Commission has adequately explained the facts and policy concerns it relied on and to satisfy ourselves that those facts have some basis in the record." We also recognize that where the agency decides not to proceed with rulemaking, the "record" for purposes of review need only include the petition for rulemaking, comments pro and con where deemed appropriate, and the agency's explanation of its decision to reject the petition....

It is only in the rarest and most compelling of circumstances that this court has acted to overturn an agency judgment not to institute rulemaking.

In *Geller v. FCC,* 610 F.2d 973 (D.C.Cir.1979), [the] regulations at issue had been promulgated initially to reflect a "consensus agreement" reached by parties affected by the Commission's cable television policies in their efforts to facilitate the passage of new copyright legislation. After the new copyright legislation was passed in 1976, petitioner had requested the Commission to re-examine the regulations to determine their continuing validity. The Commission refused.... The court reversed the Commission's order, [ruling] that an agency "cannot sidestep a re-examination of particular regulations when abnormal circumstances make that course imperative." The rule that emerges from *Geller,* then, is a limited one: that an agency may be forced by a reviewing court to institute rulemaking proceedings if a significant factual predicate of a prior decision on the subject (either to promulgate or not to promulgate specific rules) has been removed.

This court found equally compelling the circumstances in *NAACP v. FPC,* 520 F.2d 432 (D.C.Cir.1975), *aff'd,* 425 U.S. 662 (1976).... In *NAACP,* this court vacated the Commission's order dismissing petitioner's request for rulemaking on the ground that the Commission was mistaken in concluding that it lacked jurisdiction to promulgate regulations concerning employment discrimination by its regulatees....

It is significant that in [*NAACP* the court did not] compel the agency to actually institute rulemaking proceedings. Rather, [the] agency was required on remand to *reconsider* its denial of the petition, in light of the correct interpretation of the law as enunciated by the court....

For us to seriously indulge petitioners' claims in this case would be to ignore the institutional disruption that would be visited on the Commission by our second-guessing its "expert" determination not to pursue a particular program or policy at a given time. It would also require us to ignore the plain fact that the policy determinations made by the Commission in this case—as to the relative merits of mandatory cable carriage of STV signals—raise issues that are not well-suited for determination by this court. These considerations lead us to conclude that our review of the Commission's actions should be *extremely narrow,* consistent with the views heretofore expressed. The Commission's substantive determinations are essentially legislative in this case and are thus committed to the discretion of the agency.

Nevertheless, as we have already held, the Commission is required to give some explanation for its actions. Such an explanation enables a reviewing court to satisfy itself that the agency's action was neither arbitrary, nor capricious, nor an abuse of discretion, nor otherwise contrary to statutory, procedural or constitutional requirements.

Having considered the record in this case, we are satisfied that the orders of the Commission must be affirmed. The Commission adequately explained the facts and policy concerns it relied on, and there is nothing to indicate that the opinions of the Commission are unlawful, arbitrary, capricious or wholly irrational. Therefore, the judgment of the Commission not to proceed with rulemaking at this time must be left undisturbed.

Notes and Questions

1. *"Extremely narrow" judicial review.* Why *should* judicial review of an agency's refusal to commence a rulemaking proceeding be "narrower" than for other decisions? *See* William V. Luneburg, "Petitioning Federal Agencies for Rulemaking: An Overview of Administrative and Judicial Practice and Some Recommendations for Improvement," 1988 Wis.L.Rev. 1, 48–50 (questioning the validity of that distinction). Do the court's reasons for the distinction justify exceptional deference in the circumstances of *WWHT* itself?

2. *State case. Community Action Research Group v. Iowa State Commerce Comm'n*, 275 N.W.2d 217 (Iowa 1979), involved a petition for rulemaking under a state APA and came to a result like that of the *WWHT* case. A citizens group asked the commission to adopt a rule prohibiting utilities from passing on to the ratepaying public their costs of constructing a plutonium breeder reactor "or any other project which conflicts with our international efforts to control nuclear proliferation." The commission conceded that the President and other administration officials had determined that construction of the reactor should be deferred indefinitely because it was a "potential security risk." Nevertheless, the commission, noting that the Senate was supporting the project, concluded that "this important national issue has not yet been resolved at the federal level," and thus adoption of the proposed rule would be "inappropriate."

The Iowa APA provides that, within sixty days of receiving a rulemaking petition, "the agency either shall deny the petition in writing on the merits, ... or initiate rule-making proceedings ... or issue a rule...." The court upheld the agency, holding that this provision "requires only that an agency give fair consideration to the propriety of issuing the proposed rule. It does not require the agency to take a stand on the substantive issues that might prompt the proposal of a rule." Do you agree that the commission rejected the rule "on the merits," even though it did not resolve the environmental issue tendered by the appellants? Hasn't the court construed the phrase "on the merits" out of the statute?

3. *Deadline for response.* Even if courts cannot or will not supervise the petitioning process very closely, an APA can impose constraints on the process at the agency level. Section 3–117 of the 1981 MSAPA requires that an agency act on a petition within sixty days, either to deny the petition, to initiate rulemaking proceedings, or to adopt a rule. The 1961 MSAPA provision, adopted by many states, requires such an agency response within thirty days. Federal APA § 553(e), however, contains no time limit provision. As a result, petitions are often filed with a federal agency and never heard of again. Should the federal act be amended to provide that an agency must respond to a rulemaking petition within a specified number of days? *See* Luneburg, *supra,* at 16–17.

4. *Agency procedures for dealing with petitions.* Note that 1981 MSAPA § 3–117 requires an agency to adopt rules prescribing the form of petitions and the procedure for their submission, consideration, and disposition. Federal APA § 553(e) contains no such requirement. However, the Administrative Conference has recommended procedural guidelines. ACUS Recommendation 86–6, 51 Fed.Reg. 46988 (1986); *see* Luneburg, *supra,* at 20–35, 55–63. Consider one possible procedural reform: Some agencies routinely solicit public comment on rulemaking petitions, while others do not. Should all agencies adopt that procedure? *See id.* at 30–31. *See also Wisconsin Electric Power Co. v. Costle,* 715 F.2d 323, 328–29 (7th Cir.1983) (declining on *Vermont Yankee* grounds to impose such an obligation).

5. *Reexamination of existing rules.* Even without a formal proposal from outsiders, an agency can conduct internal reviews of its rules to determine which ones should be changed or abandoned. As one scholar has

explained, such self-examination has not been common in the past, but may be more prevalent in the future:

> I will offer three explanations concerning why agencies have not favored rule review, and I will argue that this tendency has changed. The first explanation is that agencies have made a rational allocation of their scarce resources. [A study I conducted in the mid–1980's with Professor Thomas McGarity] found that OSHA has sufficient resources to pursue actively about 15 to 20 rulemaking efforts at any given moment. Since it takes OSHA four to eight years to develop a rule, we estimated that OSHA could take on only two to five new projects in any single year. In light of this constraint, OSHA can argue that protection of workers from unregulated hazards is a more pressing problem than fine-tuning existing rules. The problem with this explanation is that many agencies do not appear to have a formal, organized, priority-setting process that weighs the relative merits of new projects.... Thus, it is not clear how carefully agencies make allocation decisions. The bureaucratic culture of an agency is a second explanation. Staff members who are dedicated to the proactive mission of an agency will be more interested in solving new problems than in refining existing regulations. Employees may also avoid rule review because it involves the unpleasant task of finding out the mistakes that were made when the rule was established....

> [Thirdly,] agencies have favored new rules in response to political pressure, but this situation has changed. With Republican presidents, congressional Democrats sought to expose the failure of agencies to address pressing problems, such as unsafe meat, dirty air, or dangerous cars. Such oversight stymied the most aggressive attempts by Presidents Reagan and Bush to deregulate. Now that Congress is controlled by Republicans, the effort is to expose regulatory excesses by the Democrat in the White House. The administration has responded by giving rule review a high priority....

Sidney A. Shapiro, "Agency Priority Setting and the Review of Existing Agency Rules," 48 Admin.L.Rev. 370, 372 (1996).

One element of the increasing attention to review of existing rules has been a debate over whether, and to what extent, agencies should engage in an across-the-board, systematic review process (often called a "lookback" process). Section 5 of Executive Order 12866, the presidential oversight order discussed in § 5.8 and § 7.8, called upon agencies to develop a program for periodic review of their "significant" rules (generally, rules with an annual effect on the economy of at least $100 million). Several regulatory reform bills pending in Congress in 1995 would have made such a process mandatory, with enforceable deadlines. Is a mandatory process for systematic examination by agencies of their existing regulations a good idea? If so, should it encompass all of an agency's rules, all of its "major" or "significant" rules, or only the rules that the agency chooses for serious consideration? Or could the desire for more frequent or intensive reviews be addressed satisfactorily through measures that would simply strengthen the petitioning process? *See generally* ACUS Recommendation 95–3, 60 Fed.Reg. 43109 (1995); Neil R. Eisner & Judith S. Kaleta, "Federal Agency Review of Existing Regulations," 48 Admin.L.Rev. 139 (1996).

6. *Delay in completing rulemaking proceedings.* Even after an agency has launched a rulemaking proceeding, it may stir controversy by not issuing a final rule as quickly as proponents had expected or hoped. Congress has frequently responded to apparent foot-dragging on agencies' part by enacting deadlines for the completion of particular proceedings. Such deadlines have been widely criticized as ineffective and counterproductive. *See* ACUS Recommendation 78–3, 43 Fed.Reg. 27509 (1978); Alden F. Abbott, "The Case Against Federal Statutory and Judicial Deadlines: A Cost–Benefit Analysis," 39 Admin.L.Rev. 171 (1987). Declaring that Congress has imposed far more deadlines on EPA than the agency could possibly meet, one scholar says that this device provokes a "deadline-litigation syndrome" that "transfers responsibility for setting agency priority from top administrators to interest groups.... It is hard to imagine a worse way to apportion agency resources." R. Shep Melnick, "Administrative Law and Bureaucratic Reality," 44 Admin.L.Rev. 245, 249–50 (1992).

However, when Congress prescribes such a deadline, should a court enforce it in a suit brought by a would-be beneficiary of the proposed rule? Often courts decline to do so, if they are persuaded that the agency is proceeding in good faith. *See, e.g., National Congress of Hispanic American Citizens v. Usery,* 554 F.2d 1196 (D.C.Cir.1977); Abbott, *supra,* at 178. Professor Pierce, although highly critical of Congress for imposing deadlines without providing agencies the resources with which to meet them, disagrees with these judicial decisions. "A court cannot deviate from [such] clear commands without doing violence to the principle of legislative supremacy. That principle is too valuable to sacrifice even when adherence to the principle is certain to produce a plethora of unintended adverse effects.... When the legislative branch is the sole source of a problem, the courts should leave its solution solely to the legislative branch." Richard J. Pierce, Jr., "Judicial Review of Agency Actions in a Period of Diminishing Agency Resources," 49 Admin.L.Rev. 61, 77–84, 93 (1997). Do you agree? For a reply, see Patricia M. Wald, "Judicial Review in the Time of Cholera," 49 Admin.L.Rev. 659, 663–64 (1997).

Even in the absence of a statutory deadline, private citizens sometimes seek the courts' aid in inducing agencies to conclude a protracted proceeding. *See* APA § 706(1) (reviewing court shall "compel agency action unlawfully withheld or unreasonably delayed"). Judicial relief in this sort of suit is highly discretionary. According to *In re International Chemical Workers Union,* 958 F.2d 1144, 1149–50 (D.C.Cir.1992), a court must consider four factors in determining whether an agency's delay was unreasonable:

> First, the "court should ascertain the length of time that has elapsed since the agency came under a legal duty to act." ... Second, "the reasonableness of the delay must be judged 'in the context of the statute' which authorizes the agency's action." ... Third, the court must examine the consequences of the agency's delay.... Finally, the court should give due consideration in the balance to "any plea of administrative error, administrative convenience, practical difficulty in carrying out a legislative mandate, or need to prioritize in the face of limited resources."

In this case the Occupational Safety and Health Administration had spent six years postponing action on a proposed new standard for occupational exposure to cadmium. The court held the delay unreasonable and imposed a five-month deadline on the agency for the issuance of such a rule. In doing so, the court relied upon the availability of compelling evidence concerning the toxicity of cadmium and the agency's numerous failures to meet past deadlines it had announced for that action. "There is a point when the court must 'let the agency know, in no uncertain terms, that enough is enough,' . . . and we believe that point has been reached." *See generally* Neil R. Eisner, "Agency Delay in Informal Rulemaking," 3 Admin.L.J. 7 (1989).

7. *Lapse of rulemaking proceedings.* In some states, statutes place an outside limit on the rulemaking period. *See* California Gov't Code § 11346.4(b), which provides that the effective period of a notice of proposed rulemaking is one year. If the agency cannot finish in a year, it must start over. The 1981 MSAPA prescribes a six-month period. § 3–106(b). The official Comment to that section explains: "On occasion, an agency has published notice of proposed adoption of a rule, encountered a furor which prevented further action at that time on the proposed rule, waited a year or two until people forgot about the proposed rule because they assumed it was dead, and then suddenly adopted the proposed rule." A time limit thus prevents an agency from using undue delay "as a means of defusing or circumventing widespread public opposition to its action." Is such a time limit a good idea?

8. *Problem.* In the Horse Protection Act, Congress sought to curtail the practice of deliberately injuring show horses to improve their performance in the ring. This practice, called soring, may involve fastening chains or similar equipment on a horse's front limbs. As a result of wearing chains, the horse suffers intense pain as its forefeet touch the ground. This pain causes it to adopt a high-stepping gait that is highly prized in show horses.

The Act contains a statement of findings declaring that "(1) the soring of horses is cruel and inhumane; [and] (2) horses shown or exhibited which are sore, where such soreness improves the performance of such horse, compete unfairly with horses which are not sore. . . . " The Act accordingly prohibits the "showing or exhibiting, in any horse show or horse exhibition, of any horse which is sore;" imposes criminal penalties for violations of this ban; and empowers the Secretary of Agriculture to issue rules to carry out the provisions of the Act.

Initially, the Secretary promulgated regulations forbidding the training of horses through the use of chains that weighed more than ten ounces. In the statement of basis and purpose accompanying these regulations, the Secretary stated that he had commissioned a study by veterinary medicine researchers at a prominent university to evaluate the effectiveness of these measures.

The university study was completed three years later. It suggested that training chains weighing eight to ten ounces caused horses to suffer lesions, bleeding, and inflammation. The Horse Defense Alliance submitted a letter highlighting these findings and asking that the regulations be strengthened. The HDA was dismayed when, several months later, the Secretary wrote back to state: "I have reviewed your letter and the referenced studies. I have also consulted informally with industry representatives, who doubt that the allowable weight of action devices can be lowered while retaining the desired gait. As presently advised I believe that the most effective method of enforcing the Act is to continue the current regulations."

On review, should the court sustain the Secretary's decision? If it does not, what relief should it prescribe? *See American Horse Protection Ass'n v. Lyng,* 812 F.2d 1 (D.C.Cir.1987).

§ 6.4 WAIVERS OF RULES

Rules apply across the board. They may work fairly and well in the generality of cases, but they sometimes produce harsh or unanticipated consequences when applied in particular situations. Agencies often entertain requests for waivers in cases in which the applicants can demonstrate that the rule does not work appropriately in their cases. But are waivers consistent with the rule of law? Isn't there a danger of favoritism or that too many waivers will completely undermine a rule?

WAIT RADIO v. FCC
418 F.2d 1153 (D.C.Cir.1969)

Before DANAHER, LEVENTHAL and ROBINSON, Circuit Judges.

LEVENTHAL, J.:

WAIT Radio brings this appeal to protest a decision by the Federal Communications Commission rejecting as unacceptable its application for authority to operate its station on an unlimited time basis. We think the Commission erred by not giving adequate reasons for denying and refusing to hold a hearing on appellant's request for waiver of certain FCC rules and we remand for further consideration.

WAIT operates a Chicago AM radio station on a frequency of 820 kHz, one of the so-called clear channels. Under FCC "clear channel" rules certain AM frequencies are designated as clear channels that can be used at night only by specified stations that broadcast a signal to "white areas," sparsely populated regions that have no local radio service.... As a result, WAIT operates on a sunrise to sunset basis.

WAIT filed an application requesting a waiver of the clear channel rules. Its proposal included plans for constructing a directionalized antenna that would beam its signal away from "white" areas that were being served by [two clear channel stations in] Fort Worth/Dallas, Texas. WAIT's application asserted that by confining its signal, its ... beam would not interfere with ... the signal from the Texas stations except in regions that receive primary groundwave service from at least one other station, and its ostensible violation of Commission rules would not conflict with the policy underlying the "clear channel" rules.

In support of its waiver request WAIT further alleged that its programming of "good" music and forum discussions on matters of public interest is a unique AM service in the Chicago area.... The application further alleged that the present fluctuating broadcast schedule, dependent on the actual time of sunrise and sunset, and no evening service, is a disadvantage. WAIT makes particular reference to its distinctive adult audience, able during the evening hours to listen to, and understand, serious social, political and educational programs....

The Commission rejected WAIT's request ... and ordered that the application be returned as unacceptable. WAIT appeals....

We hold that the Commission must state its basis for decision with greater care and clarity than was manifested in its disposition of WAIT's claims, and remand for a clearer statement of reasons.

1. Two strands of doctrine apply to the judicial review of administrative determinations. First is the principle that an agency or commission must articulate with clarity and precision its findings and the reasons for its decisions. The importance of this requirement is inherent in the doctrine of judicial review....

Of course busy agency staffs are not expected to dot "i's" and cross "t's." Our decisions recognize the presumption of regularity. We adhere to "salutary principles of judicial restraint." ...

2. The tension between these principles is heightened when a court undertakes to review administrative action on an application for waiver. Presumptions of regularity apply with special vigor when a Commission acts in reliance on an established and tested agency rule. An applicant for waiver faces a high hurdle even at the starting gate. "When an applicant seeks a waiver of a rule, it must plead with particularity the facts and circumstances which warrant such action." Yet an application for waiver has an appropriate place in the discharge by an administrative agency of its assigned responsibilities. The agency's discretion to proceed in difficult areas through general rules is intimately linked to the existence of a safety valve procedure for consideration of an application for exemption based on special circumstances.

The salutary presumptions do not obviate the need for serious consideration of meritorious applications for waiver, and a system where regulations are maintained inflexibly without any procedure for waiver poses legal difficulties. The Commission is charged with administration in the "public interest." That an agency may discharge its responsibilities by promulgating rules of general application which, in the overall perspective, establish the "public interest" for a broad range of situations, does not relieve it of an obligation to seek out the "public interest" in particular, individualized cases. A general rule implies that a commission need not re-study the entire problem de novo and reconsider policy every time it receives an application for waiver of the rule. On the other hand, a general rule, deemed valid because its overall objectives are in the public interest, may not be in the "public interest" if extended to an applicant who proposes a new service that will not undermine the policy, served by the rule, that has been adjudged in the public interest. An agency need not sift pleadings and documents to identify such applications, but allegations such as those made by petitioners, stated with clarity and accompanied by supporting data, are not subject to perfunctory treatment, but must be given a "hard look."[9]

3.   These principles are not easily reduced to a quantifiable formula for deciding when an agency disposing of a waiver application has crossed the line from the tolerably terse to the intolerably mute. There are strong indications that the boundary has been transgressed in the case before us. The Commission's order suggested, and perhaps even required, that WAIT's waiver application may not be entertained because it failed to proceed broadside against the clear channel policy.... This approach is without merit. The very essence of waiver is the assumed validity of the general rule, and also the applicant's violation unless waiver is granted. And as already noted, provision for waiver may have a pivotal importance in sustaining the system of administration by general rule.

The somewhat perfunctory treatment in the Commission's opinion is capped by the startling statement ... that the application is subject to dismissal out of hand because it revealed that in the absence of waiver there would be a violation of the Commission's rules.[12]

4.   The court's insistence on the agency's observance of its obligation to give meaningful consideration to waiver applications emphatically does not contemplate that an agency must or should tolerate evisceration of a rule by waivers. On the contrary a rule is more likely to be undercut if it does not in some way take into account considerations of hardship, equity, or more effective implementation of overall policy, considerations that an agency cannot realistically ignore, at least on a continuing basis. The limited safety valve permits a more rigorous adherence to an effective regulation.

Sound administrative procedure contemplates waivers, or exceptions granted only pursuant to a relevant standard—expressed at least in decisions accompanied by published opinions, especially during a period when an approach is in formation, but best expressed in a rule that obviates discriminatory approaches. The agency may not act out of unbridled discretion or whim in granting waivers any more than in any other aspect of its regulatory function. The process viewed as a whole leads to a general rule, and limited waivers or exceptions granted pursuant to an appropriate general standard. This combination of a general rule and limitations is the very stuff of the rule of law, and with diligent effort and attention to essentials administrative agencies may maintain the fundamentals of principled regulation without sacrifice of administrative flexibility and feasibility.

9.   The agency is not bound to process in depth what are only generalized pleas, a requirement that would condemn it to divert resources of time and personnel to hollow claims. The applicant for waiver must articulate a specific pleading, and adduce concrete support, preferably documentary. Even when an application complies with these rigorous requirements, the agency is not required to author an essay for the disposition of each application. It suffices, in the usual case, that we can discern the "why and wherefore."

12.   ... It is manifest error to deny a waiver on the ground that there would be a violation in the absence of the waiver sought.

5. We have identified deficiencies in the FCC's opinion rejecting the application for waiver. We have examined the significance of the waiver procedure and pointed out that it is not necessarily a step-child, but may be an important member of the family of administrative procedures, one that helps the family stay together. . . .

We think the pleading filed by WAIT, supported by data sufficient to overcome the initial hurdle, was entitled to reflective consideration. . . . We do not rule on substantive contentions, but remand for further consideration.

So ordered.

[A dissenting opinion by DANAHER, J., is omitted. On remand, the FCC again denied a waiver, writing a longer opinion, and the court affirmed. *WAIT Radio v. FCC*, 459 F.2d 1203 (D.C.Cir.1972).]

Notes and Questions

1. *Hospitality to administrative waivers.* There is a substantial scholarly literature on waivers. In general, academic opinion accords with Judge Leventhal's position, endorsing waivers as a necessary corrective to the rigidity of rules. A recent comment by Professor Rossi is representative:

> What some commentators have called administrative "equity" provides one adjudicative-type alternative to rulemaking that is not necessarily inconsistent with the democratic and Rule of Law ideals of the administrative state. Administrative equity, like the traditional forms of equity in private law, eschews the ability of rules to provide universal justice. Published regulations applied absent discretion provide predictability, stability, uniformity, and control, while equity, on the form of agency waivers or exceptions, provides a more particularized determination.

> As a general matter most commentators prefer rulemaking as a legalistic methodology for agency policymaking; however, equitable adjustments in the implementation of regulations promulgated by rule provide an important "safety valve" in the administrative process ... Administrative equity in the form of waivers or exceptions has become a fairly commonplace regulatory mechanism in federal agencies. If appropriately constrained—and constraints are certainly needed—equitable-type mechanisms can serve as an important regulatory tool in pursuing the democratic goals of the administrative state.

Jim Rossi, "Making Policy Through the Waiver of Regulations at the Federal Energy Regulatory Commission," 47 Admin. L. Rev. 255, 277–78 (1995). For essays developing this theme in comprehensive detail, see Peter H. Schuck, "When the Exception Becomes the Rule," 1984 Duke L.J. 163; Alfred C. Aman, Jr., "Administrative Equity: An Analysis of Exceptions To Administrative Rules," 1982 Duke L.J. 277.

2. *Are waivers essential?* A broad reading of *WAIT Radio* and the above scholarly literature might suggest that *every* significant rule must leave room for some sort of meaningful opportunity to apply for a waiver. We saw in § 3.2 that the Supreme Court seemed to throw cold water on that proposition in *FCC v. WNCN Listeners Guild*, 450 U.S. 582 (1981), and

arguably in *Heckler v. Campbell,* 461 U.S. 458 (1983). There the Court upheld regulations in the face of objections that they lacked waiver provisions. In those situations, however, the issue arose only incidentally, because the cases did not involve actual requests for waivers.

In *KCST–TV, Inc. v. FCC,* 699 F.2d 1185 (D.C.Cir.1983), the majority cited *WAIT Radio* for the proposition that an agency "must take a 'hard look' at meritorious applications for waiver," but then-Judge Scalia disagreed. He argued that if this statement were applied broadly, it

> would mean, in effect, that there could be no rules but only case-by-case adjudication. What *is* true, and what in my view *WAIT* represents, is the proposition that a rule *which otherwise might be impermissibly broad* can be saved by the "safety valve" of waiver or exemption procedures. That does not preclude the possibility that an agency may craft a rule which—either because it is quite precise or because the subject is not one as to which precision is required . . .—does not need for its validity the availability of exemption. Moreover, I know of nothing which prevents an agency from making one of its rules inflexible, leaving the courts (if they consider it invalid in that form) only the power to strike it down and require a more precise rule, but not the power to mandate the agency's administrative choice between a regime governed entirely by rule and one in which adjudicatory waiver determinations must be made.

Id. at 1200 (Scalia, J., dissenting). Did Justice Scalia read *WAIT Radio* properly?

In any event, some agencies have steadfastly refused to grant any waivers from certain of their rules, and the courts have acquiesced in this refusal. A well-known example is the Federal Aviation Administration's rule that prohibits any large commercial airliner from taking off under the command of a pilot aged 60 or more. The rule has been in force since 1959, and the FAA has never waived it, although pilots have filed numerous petitions seeking individual exemptions. Repeated court challenges to this policy have occasionally resulted in remands for fuller explanation, but in the end the FAA has always prevailed. As one judge has noted: "Pilots with tens of thousands of hours of flight time and flawless records, and who pass every physical test with flying colors, suddenly find themselves grounded on their sixtieth birthdays, even though [they] are still deemed qualified to pilot planes with thirty passengers or less." *Baker v. FAA,* 917 F.2d 318, 323 (7th Cir.1990) (Will, J., dissenting).

The FAA's long-held position is that after age 60, physical abilities decline and the risk of sudden incapacitation in flight increases; and that, although some pilots in their sixties remain fully qualified, no medical test is reliable enough to distinguish them from more dangerous ones. Despite doubts about the medical evidence, the majority in *Baker,* like other courts before it, deferred to the expert agency, observing that "safety is the dominant and controlling consideration." *Id.* at 319. Should courts demand that the FAA devise a more flexible policy?

3. *Duty to explain waiver denials.* Some courts, without embracing any explicit theory about the proper role of waivers in the administrative process, have come to the aid of waiver applicants by invoking the general

principle that agencies must give reasoned explanations for their actions. *See, e.g., Dickson v. Secretary of Defense,* 68 F.3d 1396 (D.C.Cir.1995); *Matlovich v. Secretary of the Air Force,* 591 F.2d 852 (D.C.Cir.1978). In *Dickson* three veterans who had received unfavorable discharges from the Army twenty or more years earlier applied to have their discharges upgraded. According to the applications, their offenses had been alcohol-related; the Army's alcohol abuse policies had changed and would now justify a more favorable discharge. Although the three-year statute of limitations for such applications had long since expired, the Army Board for Correction of Records could have waived the time bar "in the interest of justice," but it refused to do so.

The court reversed, noting that the Board had not spelled out its reasons for finding that waivers were not "in the interest of justice." For example, it had not clarified whether the denials were based solely on inadequacy of the applicants' reasons for delay, or whether the underlying merits of their claims had also been a factor. Even though judicial review of waiver determinations would ultimately be entitled to "great deference," the court said, the Board did have to "meet the ordinary requirements of the APA as to explanation of its reasoning." The court added: "Review of waivers helps ensure that a second tier of 'secret law' does not impugn the equality of the principal law.... " 68 F.3d at 1404–07.

A dissenter charged that the majority's "heavy-handed judicial supervision" was incompatible with the "maximum deference" that courts should display towards waiver determinations. He wrote:

> Judicial review of agency action has, as its core concern, the notion that agencies should treat the subjects of their authority equally.... We, thus, force agencies to carefully explain deviations in course whether adopted in a regulatory or adjudicatory mode. On the other hand, we recognize that rules can have a harsh impact in unusual situations. When an agency waives its rules in a particular case, we will not typically hold the agency to a very exacting standard of explanation, recognizing that if we do we may make it practically impossible for the agency to grant any waivers....
>
> To be sure, we will not typically accept an agency decision that is unaccompanied by an explanation adequate to permit us to understand the agency's reasoning. But a decision to grant or not to grant a waiver, which is subject to such deferential review, is in a different category....

Id. at 1408 (Silberman, J., dissenting). Who had the better of this exchange? Wasn't the Board's decision sufficiently self-explanatory to meet a "great deference" standard?

4. *Structured waiver programs.* Agencies are not always reluctant to entertain requests for waivers. In fact, some rely heavily on waiver programs as a tool of regulatory policy. The exceptions process at the Department of Energy in the 1970's and 1980's is an example. *See* Aman, *supra;* Schuck, *supra.* A current example is the Environmental Protection Agency's Excellence and Leadership Program (Project XL), under which EPA gives regulated entities, within limits, the flexibility to devise their own strategies to comply with pollution regulations, instead of doing it the agency's way. *See*

Marshall J. Breger, "Regulatory Flexibility and the Administrative State," 32 Tulsa L.J. 325, 331–33 (1996).

5. *Potential dangers of waivers.* As a species of deregulation, waiver programs can give rise to charges that the agency is enforcing its mandate too leniently. For instance, in *Chemical Manufacturers Ass'n v. Natural Resources Defense Council, Inc.,* 470 U.S. 116 (1985), the Court split 5–4 on the legality of a program through which EPA granted variances from its toxic pollutant regulations under the Clean Water Act. A company could qualify for a variance if it could show that its operations involved "fundamentally different factors" from those which EPA had considered when it wrote its regulations on treatment of effluent discharges. The dissent argued that this system was contrary to the congressional plan. Congress had intended the Act to incorporate a "technology-forcing" approach that would require all companies in an industrial category to adopt technologies used by the best-performing companies in that category. Thus, the agency's willingness to grant variances to companies on the basis of their exceptional characteristics, rather than with reference to the best performer, would inevitably lead to a lower level of environmental protection. *See id.* at 156–58 (Marshall, J., dissenting). The majority, however, saw the variance program as a useful method of fine-tuning regulations that had by necessity been written imprecisely at the outset. The Court even suggested that the underlying regulations would have been too rigid if a variance program had not been available to supply an element of flexibility. *Id.* at 129–30, 133 n.25. *See generally* William Funk, "The Exception That Approves the Rule: FDF Variances Under the Clean Water Act," 13 B.C.Env.Aff.L.Rev. 1 (1985).

Another potential problem with waivers is that an agency might grant them on the basis of favoritism or other impermissible considerations. Because the exceptions process is usually less visible than the rule-writing process, it triggers particular concerns about the need to ensure agency accountability. *See* Breger, *supra,* at 339–44, 347–49. Some states *prohibit* waivers unless the agency has enunciated rules to channel its discretion in awarding them. *See* N.C.Gen.Stat. § 150B–19; N.H.Rev.Stat.Ann. § 541–A–22; Vt.Stat.Ann. tit. 3, § 845.

6. *Florida provision.* A recently adopted Florida statute *requires* that agencies grant waivers or variances when (1) the person subject to a rule demonstrates that the purpose of the underlying statute will be or has been achieved by other means; and (2) application of a rule would create a substantial hardship or would violate principles of fairness.

On receiving a waiver request, the agency must provide an opportunity for comment by interested persons, and grant or deny the petition within 90 days. If it fails to act within this time period, the petition is deemed granted. A decision granting or denying a waiver must include a statement of reasons and must be supported by competent substantial evidence. Fla.Stat.Ann. § 120.542.

Prior to this legislation, Florida law had been widely interpreted as prohibiting waivers or variances, except by agencies that had previously provided for such action in published rules. The proponents of the waiver statute favored it as "part of a political compromise to introduce flexibility into the regulatory process without sacrificing the apparent values of Florida's presumptive rulemaking mechanism." Jim Rossi, "The 1996 Revised Florida Administrative Procedure Act: A Rulemaking Revolution or Counter–Revolution?," 49 Admin.L.Rev. 345, 356 (1997). Would you give the legislature high marks for promoting flexibility in the regulatory process? Should other states emulate the Florida example?

7. *Iowa alternative.* Another approach to statutory reform of waiver policies is a proposal developed by the Iowa State Bar Association (and drafted by Professor Arthur Bonfield). Under this draft legislation, an agency "shall" waive one of its rules upon a showing that application of the rule to the petitioner "would not serve any of the purposes of the rule." In addition, according to the proposed statute, an agency "may" grant a waiver if (a) application of the rule to the petitioner would cause undue hardship, (b) the waiver would be consistent with the public interest, and (c) the waiver would not prejudice the substantial rights of any other person. Is this plan preferable to the Florida provision?

8. *Problem.* According to a 1937 regulation of the Federal Highway Administration (FHWA), drivers of commercial trucks operating in interstate commerce must possess at least 20/40 vision in each eye (measured with or without corrective lenses). For many years, however, drivers who have the required vision in only one eye have qualified for commercial licenses under state law. Such licenses allow them to drive in *intrastate* commerce. By 1992, legal and societal efforts to curb discrimination against the disabled were burgeoning, and members of Congress were suggesting that the FHWA regulation was obsolete. The FHWA decided to conduct a study to determine whether to amend its safety regulation.

The agency said that preliminary, but inconclusive, studies indicated that the accident records of these "monocular" drivers are no worse than those of drivers with normal sight, presumably because the monocular drivers have learned to adapt their driving practices to take account of their disability. Thus, the agency announced that it would waive the regulation for certain monocular truck drivers, so that they could serve as subjects in a controlled experiment that would compare their safety experience with the experience of drivers who were already qualified under federal law. The program was open only to drivers who were licensed under state law and had maintained accident-free records for three years. This experiment, the FHWA said, would serve the public interest in furthering the employment of qualified drivers with impaired vision.

The Highway Safety League, a public interest group composed of insurance companies and law enforcement associations, challenged the waiver program in court, arguing that by statute any waiver must be "consistent with public safety" and the FHWA had not made a determination as to whether drivers participating in the experiment would pose risks to other cars on the road. In fact, the agency's own statement indicated uncertainty on that point. The court agreed and remanded the rule. After further deliberation, the agency reaffirmed its commitment to the waiver program, concluding that initial experience with it had been satisfactory and strengthened the belief that the participation of monocular drivers in the study was "consistent with public safety."

At this point, Bert, a monocular truck driver with a record of 22 accident-free years on the road, applied for a waiver of the safety regulation. He stated that he had not known about the experimental program until after the deadline for applying to join it had expired. The deputy administrator of FHWA refused his request in a brief letter, stating that "if we were to grant your request for a waiver, it could set a precedent and we might have to allow it for everyone, making it impossible for us to enforce the regulation during this transition period." Bert has filed for review in court, arguing that the denial of his waiver request was unlawful.

Questions: (a) Do you agree with the court's ruling in the suit brought by the Highway Safety League? (b) How should the court respond to Bert's suit? Would the result change if FHWA's enabling statute contained a provision like the Florida waiver statute? What if the Iowa waiver proposal were applicable instead? *Cf. Rauenhorst v. United States Department of Transportation*, 95 F.3d 715 (8th Cir.1996); *Advocates for Highway and Auto Safety v. FHWA*, 28 F.3d 1288 (D.C.Cir.1994).

Part II

NONJUDICIAL CONTROL OF AGENCY ACTION

In this Part we examine mechanisms, other than agency procedures and judicial review, for ensuring that administrative action is consistent with legal requirements and with the current political will of the community. The primary focus, therefore, will be on mechanisms calculated to ensure that the political branches of government—the legislature and the chief executive—control agency action. Because effective control of administrative action by the political process in the community requires widespread access to information about the policies and activities of agencies, this Part also examines the right of the public to obtain such information.

Chapter 7

CONTROL OF AGENCIES BY THE POLITICAL BRANCHES OF GOVERNMENT

§ 7.1 INTRODUCTION

An examination of the role of political bodies in controlling agency action requires consideration of two fundamental constitutional principles: *separation of powers* and *checks and balances*. The founders created three distinct branches of government, each authorized to exercise its own specialized powers. They also believed that each branch must be protected against encroachment by the others, and each must be in a position to curb arbitrary or unwise actions by the others.

Administrative agencies, which are barely mentioned in the federal Constitution, have often been regarded as posing threats to the constitutional structure. They typically possess delegated authority to make rules, to adjudicate individual cases, to engage in law enforcement, and to conduct other activities related to those functions. Yet these are the functions normally entrusted to the three branches of government that the Constitution establishes in express and detailed terms. The legitimacy of such delegations has long been contested, because most agency heads are appointed rather than elected and, therefore, are not directly responsible to the voters. Furthermore, the modern administrative agency seems to defy the principle of separation of powers, since a single entity exercises rulemaking, adjudication, and law enforcement functions. Nevertheless, most people today concede that this combination of functions within a single administrative unit is legitimate and a practical necessity in modern government. *See* Peter L. Strauss, "The Place of Agencies in Government: Separation of Powers and the Fourth Branch," 84 Colum.L.Rev. 573 (1984).

The notion of separated but mutually interacting powers plays out in several ways in administrative law. It gives rise to claims that some of the functions exercised by agencies may not be entrusted to them, because those functions more properly belong to other branches of government. It also has led to the creation of mechanisms by which the political branches can, on a continuing basis, supervise the processes of administration in order to assure the legality of agency action and its consistency with the wishes of the people.

On the other hand, some of the actions that the named branches of government take in order to supervise agency action may themselves offend separation of powers principles. A given branch might, in the name of agency oversight, attempt to perform a task that more properly belongs elsewhere, or might attempt to restrain other branches from carrying out their constitutionally assigned functions. The legal system has to resolve these interbranch conflicts. Sometimes the controversy focuses on the language of the Constitution. At other times, it may involve an appeal to the general design of our tripartite governmental structure—for the "separation of powers doctrine" shapes the relationships among branches even where no specific constitutional provision is at issue.

In state agencies, the problems of separation of powers and checks and balances may differ from the situation under federal law. First, some state agencies are directly created by state constitutions, giving such agencies a status equivalent to the legislature and governor. Second, some state officials are directly elected by the voters, which provides a form of direct accountability. When an agency has constitutional status, or when agency heads are elected, the normal legislative and executive checks on agency action may not be applicable or may apply in a different way.

In this chapter, we first consider how far the legislature may go in vesting agencies with legislative and adjudicative powers. We then inquire into the means by which the legislature and chief executive may control the exercises of agency authority, and also into the circumstances in which such efforts at control exceed permissible bounds.

§ 7.2 DELEGATION OF LEGISLATIVE POWER TO AGENCIES

§ 7.2.1 THE NONDELEGATION DOCTRINE AND FEDERAL AGENCIES

Article I of the federal Constitution vests legislative power in Congress and authorizes Congress to enact laws that are necessary and proper means of implementing its powers. Despite the necessary and proper clause, however, the *non-delegation doctrine* maintains that Congress' power to delegate its legislative authority is limited.

The non-delegation doctrine invokes both separation of powers and checks and balances arguments. The separation of powers argument is that the Constitution assigned all legislative power to the legislature; therefore Congress cannot transfer any part of that power to executive-branch agencies. The checks and balances argument recognizes that delegation to agencies may be inevitable, but insists that the legislature impose adequate limits on the *discretion* of such agencies. It remains a source of continuing controversy whether there really is a delegation doctrine today and, if there is, whether courts can and should enforce it by invalidating improper delegations.

§ 7.2.1a   From *Field* to the New Deal

Field v. Clark, 143 U.S. 649 (1892), sounded themes of both separation of powers and checks and balances. A statute empowered the President to raise tariffs and suspend trade with foreign countries "for such time as he shall deem just." The President was to take this action if he deemed the tariffs imposed by such countries on American goods to be unequal and unreasonable. (Of course, Congress ordinarily reserves to itself decisions on the imposition of import tariffs. Why would Congress have delegated such an important power to the President?)

The Supreme Court stated the nondelegation doctrine broadly. "That Congress cannot delegate legislative power to the President is a principle universally recognized as vital to the integrity and maintenance of the system of government ordained by the constitution." (What makes this "principle" so "vital"?)

Nevertheless, the Court upheld the delegation:

As the suspension was absolutely required when the President ascertained the existence of a particular fact, it cannot be said that in ascertaining that fact and in issuing his proclamation, in obedience to the legislative will, he exercised the function of making laws. Legislative power was exercised when Congress declared that the suspension should take effect upon a named contingency. What the President was required to do was simply in execution of the act of Congress. It was not the making of law. He was the mere agent of the law-making department to ascertain and declare the event upon which its expressed will was to take effect. It was a part of the law itself as it left the hands of Congress that [favorable tariff provisions] should be suspended, in a given contingency, and in [such cases] certain duties should be imposed.

143 U.S. at 693.

Of course, the power given to the President in the *Field* case was far more significant than a mere power to "ascertain the fact" of whether a "given contingency" had occurred. It was indeed "the making of law." A decision about whether foreign tariffs are unequal and unreasonable, and thus justify retaliation, calls for subtle judgment and entails deeply political as well as economic calculations.

From the time of the *Field* case until the early 1930's, the Supreme Court continued to assert that a non-delegation doctrine existed. Yet it upheld every delegation in a line of cases that involved steadily more sweeping delegations. In those cases, the Court applied the non-delegation doctrine by attempting to ascertain whether Congress had established an "intelligible principle" or a "primary standard" to guide the delegate in making the decision. *See, e.g., J.W. Hampton Jr. & Co. v. United States,* 276 U.S. 394 (1928) ("if Congress shall lay down by legislative act an intelligible principle to which the person or body authorized to [regulate] is directed to conform, such legislative action is not a forbidden delegation of legislative power"). During this period the Court upheld delegations to the Federal Trade Commission to prohibit "unfair methods of competition" and to the predecessor of the Federal Communications Commission to regulate the airwaves as the "public convenience, interest or necessity requires." *FTC v. Gratz,* 253 U.S. 421 (1920); *Federal Radio Comm'n v. Nelson Bros. Bond & Mortgage Co.,* 289 U.S. 266 (1933).

Do general and vague standards like "unfair methods of competition" and "public convenience, interest or necessity" really furnish any guidance to anyone? Why should the presence in a statute of an intelligible principle or a primary standard validate a statute under attack on delegation grounds?

In 1935, the Supreme Court twice held statutes unconstitutional under the delegation doctrine. Both provisions were contained in the National Industrial Recovery Act (NIRA) of 1933, an early New Deal measure passed in the depths of the Great Depression. These cases were the first and the last Supreme Court decisions to overturn statutes as invalid legislative delegations to administrative agencies. They must be viewed in light of the extreme judicial activism of the early 1930's, an attitude which also resulted in the invalidation of numerous New Deal laws on other grounds, including a lack of congressional power to enact the particular statute.

The NIRA contained various legislative findings about the economic emergency and declared congressional policy that there should be cooperation among trade groups, including labor and management, to revive the economy, relieve unemployment, increase production and consumption, and conserve natural resources. Thus the Act apparently contained a wealth of "standards" and "intelligible principles" to guide the delegate.

The first delegation case arose under § 9 of the NIRA, a provision that allowed the President to ban from interstate commerce the shipment of oil that had been produced in violation of a state agency's order (so-called "hot oil"). The background of this provision was that new oil discoveries in Texas led to massive overproduction. Each producer pumped as fast as possible lest other producers deplete the pool first. The result was a drastic fall in the price of oil, a massive waste of a nonrenewable resource, and complete disorganization of the oil industry.

Texas set up a state agency to control the amount that each producer could pump, but the interstate nature of the oil business meant that state regulation couldn't work without national help. The language and legislative history of § 9 indicated that it was intended to provide that help by making interstate shipment of "hot oil" a federal crime when the President deemed such a ban desirable.

In *Panama Refining Co. v. Ryan*, 293 U.S. 388 (1935), the Supreme Court invalidated this delegation. It declared:

> In every case in which the question has been raised, the Court has recognized that there are limits of delegation which there is no constitutional authority to transcend. We think that section 9(c) goes beyond those limits. As to the transportation of oil production in excess of state permission, the Congress has declared no policy, has established no standard, has laid down no rule. There is no requirement, no definition of circumstances and conditions in which the transportation is to be allowed or prohibited.

293 U.S. at 430. Only Justice Cardozo dissented, pointing out that the statute defined the precise act which the President was to perform and, in context, made abundantly clear the circumstances in which it should be performed. Was *Panama* consistent with *Field v. Clark?*

The second decision invalidated a much more important and vastly more sweeping delegation. The background of § 3 of NIRA was the catastrophic depression engulfing the American economy. Unemployment exceeded 25%, wages and prices plummeted, banks and businesses of every sort failed. The NIRA was an attempt to reverse the terrifying downward spiral of the Depression and start the economy moving upward again. Section 3 empowered the President to adopt "codes of fair competition" for any industry. The codes would prescribe maximum and minimum prices to be charged, wages, hours and working conditions of labor, levels of production, and many other competitive practices which previously were determined by the market. Violations of a code were a criminal offense.

In *A.L.A. Schechter Poultry Corp. v. United States*, 295 U.S. 495 (1935), the Supreme Court invalidated § 3 under the non-delegation doctrine. It also held that § 3 exceeded Congress' power to regulate interstate commerce, a rationale that was totally repudiated by later decisions.

Schechter arose under the poultry code. In addition to setting poultry prices, the code required retailers to take all the chickens offered to them by wholesalers; they could no longer pick and choose. Schechter Poultry, a wholesaler in New York, was convicted of a crime because it permitted retailers to reject chickens.

The Supreme Court held unanimously that the delegation to the President to adopt "codes of fair competition" was invalid because the NIRA lacked an adequate standard to govern the drafting of codes. The Court objected to the lack of any procedure for adopting the codes, and questioned the involvement of dominant private producers in proposing and writing a code that would bind their competitors. It distinguished the earlier cases which had upheld delegations to various agencies, including the Federal Trade Commission, to prevent "unfair methods of competition" or to act in the "public interest." In these situations, unlike the NIRA, Congress created agencies to enforce the law in accordance with defined and fair procedures.

Moreover, as Justice Cardozo pointed out in his concurring opinion, the statutes involved in the earlier precedents were different from the NIRA because they focused on practices which generally would be considered oppressive or unfair, or upon economically unsound practices in specific industries. The NIRA went much further. It extended to the entire economy and entailed a "roving commission" to achieve positive reform of industrial practice. "The extension becomes as wide as the field of industrial regulation. If that conception shall prevail, anything that Congress may do within the limits of the commerce clause for the betterment of business may be done by the President upon the recommendation of a trade association by calling it a code. This is delegation running riot. No such plenitude of power is susceptible of transfer. The statute, however, aims at nothing less, as one can learn both from its terms and from the administrative practice under it." *Id.* at 553. How can one explain Justice Cardozo's dissent in *Panama* in light of his concurrence in *Schechter?*

§ 7.2.1b From the New Deal to the Present

Following the *Schechter* and *Panama* decisions, the Supreme Court returned to its pre–1930's practice of giving lip service to the delegation doctrine, while upholding ever more sweeping and vague delegations of legislative authority to administrative agencies. For example, in *Yakus v. United States,* 321 U.S. 414 (1944), the Court upheld (with a single dissent) a delegation in the Emergency Price Control Act of 1942 to the Price Administrator to fix maximum prices. Like the NIRA, the 1942 Act was designed to deal comprehensively with an economic emergency—in this case, the inflationary spiral generated by World War II. The standard for fixing prices was that such prices had to be "generally fair and equitable." The Administrator had to ascertain and give due consideration to the prices prevailing in October, 1941, and was required to furnish a statement of the considerations involved in setting particular prices.

Yakus was convicted of selling beef for a price in excess of a ceiling set by the Administrator. In responding to the claim that the statute was an unlawful delegation, the Supreme Court stated:

> The Constitution as a continuously operative charter of government does not demand the impossible or the impracticable.... The essentials of the legislative function are the determination of the legislative policy and its formulation and promulgation as a defined and binding rule of conduct—here the rule, with penal sanctions, that prices shall not be greater than those fixed by maximum price regulations which conform to standards and will tend to further the policy which Congress has established.... It is no objection that the determination of facts and the inferences to be drawn from them in

the light of the statutory standards and declaration of policy call for the exercise of judgment, and for the formulation of subsidiary administrative policy within the prescribed statutory framework. . . .

Congress is not confined to that method of executing its policy which involves the least possible delegation of discretion to administrative officers. . . . It is free to avoid the rigidity of such a system, which might well result in serious hardship, and to choose instead the flexibility attainable by the use of less restrictive standards. . . . Only if we could say that there is an absence of standards for the guidance of the Administrator's action, so that it would be impossible in a proper proceeding to ascertain whether the will of Congress has been obeyed, would we be justified in overriding its choice of means for effecting its declared purpose of preventing inflation.

Id. at 424–26.

The Court quickly distinguished *Schechter* on the ground that the NIRA had failed to provide standards for the codes of fair competition and because the delegation to write the codes was to individuals in the industries to be regulated. *Panama Refining* was not mentioned. Although cases like *Yakus* (and there have been many) suggest that the Supreme Court is unwilling to invalidate a statute on the basis of unlawful delegation, the *Schechter* and *Panama* cases have never been overruled.

§ 7.2.1c Revival of the Delegation Doctrine

Is the delegation doctrine dead? Consider the following two cases. *Amalgamated Meat Cutters* is an often-cited opinion by Judge Leventhal for a special three-judge court. In the second case, *Industrial Union Department,* we focus primarily on a concurring opinion by Justice Rehnquist.

AMALGAMATED MEAT CUTTERS AND BUTCHER WORKMEN v. CONNALLY
337 F.Supp. 737 (D.D.C.1971).

[The Economic Stabilization Act of 1970 (Act) empowered the President "to issue such orders and regulations as he may deem appropriate to stabilize prices, rents, wages, and salaries." To restrain inflation during the Vietnam war, President Nixon used that authority to freeze prices, rents, wages, and salaries for ninety days. He adopted rules imposing wage and price controls after the freeze expired. Violators were subject to criminal fines. Plaintiff Union argued that the Act "vests unbridled legislative power in the President."]

The Government cites numerous authorities but relies most heavily on *Yakus.* . . . [which] carries forward the doctrine [of *J.W. Hampton*] . . . that there is no forbidden delegation of legislative power "if Congress shall lay down by legislative act an intelligible principle" to which the official or agency must conform.

Concepts of control and accountability define the constitutional requirement. The principle permitting a delegation of legislative power, if there has been a sufficient demarcation of the field to permit a judgment whether the agency has kept within the legislative will, establishes a principle of accountability under which compatibility with the legislative design may be ascertained not only by Congress but by the courts and the public. That principle was conjoined in *Yakus* with a recognition that the burden is on the party who assails the legislature's choice of means for effecting its purpose, a burden that is met "only if we could say that there is an absence of standards for the guidance of the Administrator's action, so that it would be impossible in a proper proceeding to ascertain whether the will of Congress has been obeyed. . . . "

[The Act supplied sufficient standards. It did not permit the President to set prices and wages below their level on May 25, 1970. It precluded the President from singling out a particular sector of the economy in which to impose controls, absent a finding that wages or prices in that sector had increased disproportionately. Moreover, the legislative history set forth Congress' purpose—the same purpose as the 1942 act sustained in *Yakus*. Standards can be articulated in legislative history rather than in express statutory language.]

We see no merit in the contention that the Act is constitutionally defective because the timing of the imposition of controls was delegated to the President. . . . Viewing the President as a physician in charge, Congress could advise but not mandate his diagnosis. It sought in the national interest to have the right remedy available on a standby basis, if the President should wish to adopt that prescription, following his further reflection and taking into account future developments and experience. . . .

[The court emphasized the connection between domestic inflation and international trade.] The consequence for international trade, liquidity and monetary relationships enhances the range of power Congress can permissibly delegate to the President.

It is also material, though not dispositive, to note the limited time frame established by Congress for the stabilization authority delegated to the President. [The 1970 Act had a six month lifespan.] Two subsequent extensions provided even shorter durations.

[The court concluded that Congress had provided sufficient standards for wage-price controls after the freeze expired—broad fairness and the removal of "gross inequities."] Another feature that blunts the "blank check" rhetoric is the requirement that any action taken by the Executive under the law, subsequent to the freeze, must be in accordance with further standards as developed by the Executive. This requirement, inherent in the Rule of Law and implicit in the Act, means that however broad the discretion of the Executive at the outset, the standards once developed limit the latitude of subsequent executive action. . . . [T]here is an on-going requirement of intelligible administrative policy that is corollary to and implementing of the legislature's ultimate standard and objective....

The safeguarding of meaningful judicial review is one of the primary functions of the doctrine prohibiting undue delegation of legislative powers.... The Government concedes and we agree that the Executive's actions under the 1970 Act are not immune from judicial review.... Challenges may be made under the provisions for judicial review in the [APA].

By the same token actions under this 1970 Act are subject to the administrative procedure provisions of the APA. [However, neither the rulemaking nor adjudication sections of the APA would be applicable, since the President could utilize the good-cause exemptions from rule-making and no statute required the agency to provide adjudicatory hearings. The court suggested that the ongoing administration of the program could be challenged for failure to provide meaningful opportunity for interested persons to present objections or for courts to discharge their judicial review function.]

We end this section of the opinion with broad closing references to precedent.... We do not understand *Yakus* to rest in a crucial sense on the exercise of the war power.... [T]here have not been any Supreme Court rulings holding statutes unconstitutional for excessive delegation of legislative power since *Panama Refining* and *Schechter*.... These cases express a principle that has validity—reserved for the extreme instance.... Both cited cases dealt with delegation of a power to make federal crimes of acts that never had been such before and to devise novel rules of law in a field in which there had been no settled law or custom. They are without vigor in a case like [this] where the delegation is in a context of historical experience with anti-inflation legislation....

INDUSTRIAL UNION DEPARTMENT, AFL–CIO v. AMERICAN PETROLEUM INSTITUTE
448 U.S. 607 (1980).

[The Occupational Safety and Health Act delegates authority to the Secretary of Labor to adopt safety and health standards for the work-place. Under § 3(8), the standards must be "reasonably necessary or appropriate to provide safe or healthful ... places of employment." In setting standards for toxic materials, § 6(b)(5) of the Act directs the Secretary "to set the standard which most adequately assures, to the extent feasible ... that no employee will suffer material impairment of health...."

The Occupational Safety and Health Administration (OSHA), which discharges the Secretary's responsibilities under this Act, construed the statute to require it to set standards at the safest possible level which is technologically feasible and which would not cause material economic impairment of the industry.

This case involves the standard for benzene, an industrial chemical which in high concentration causes leukemia and other illnesses. OSHA set the standard for benzene at 1 part per million, although OSHA did not find, and research did not establish, that there is danger to the health of workers at levels of concentration below 10 parts per million.

In the enabling act Congress never specified whether it wanted OSHA to balance costs to industry against benefits to workers or whether it wanted OSHA to set standards at the safest possible level without consideration of costs. A four-justice plurality, in an opinion written by STEVENS, J., overturned the benzene standard. Interpreting § 6(b)(5), the plurality held that OSHA must find, before promulgating a standard, that it is necessary and appropriate to remedy a *significant risk* of material health impairment:]

In the absence of a clear mandate in the Act, it is unreasonable to assume that Congress intended to give the Secretary the unprecedented power over American industry that would result from the Government's view of §§ 3(8) and 6(b)(5), coupled with OSHA's cancer policy. Expert testimony that a substance is probably a human carcinogen—either because it has caused cancer in animals or because individuals have contracted cancer following extremely high exposures—would justify the conclusion that the substance poses some risk of serious harm no matter how minute the exposure and no matter how many experts testified that they regarded the risk as insignificant. That conclusion would in turn justify pervasive regulation limited only by the constraint of feasibility. In light of the fact that there are literally thousands of substances used in the workplace that have been identified as carcinogens or suspect carcinogens, the Government's theory would give OSHA power to impose enormous costs that might produce little, if any, discernible benefit.

If the Government was correct in arguing that neither § 3(8) nor § 6(b)(5) requires that the risk from a toxic substance be quantified sufficiently to enable the Secretary to characterize it as significant in an understandable way, the statute would make such a "sweeping delegation of legislative power" that it might be unconstitutional under the Court's reasoning in *Schechter Poultry* and *Panama Refining*. A construction of the statute that avoids this kind of open-ended grant should certainly be favored.

[REHNQUIST, J., concurred in the judgment, arguing that § 6(b)(5) was invalid under the delegation doctrine:]

[I]n my opinion decisions such as *Panama Refining* suffer from none of the excesses of judicial policymaking that plagued some of the other decisions of that era. The many later decisions that have upheld congressional delegations of authority to the Executive Branch have done so largely on the theory that Congress may wish to exercise its authority in a particular field, but because the field is sufficiently technical, the ground to be covered sufficiently large, and the Members of Congress themselves not necessarily expert in the area in which they choose to legislate, the most that may be asked under the separation-of-powers doctrine is that Congress lay down the general policy and standards that animate the law, leaving the agency to refine those standards, "fill in the blanks," or apply the standards to particular cases. These decisions, to my mind, simply illustrate the above-quoted principle stated more than 50 years ago by Mr. Chief Justice Taft that delegations of legislative authority must be judged "according to common sense and the inherent necessities of the governmental co-ordination."

Viewing the legislation at issue here in light of these principles, I believe that it fails to pass muster. Read literally, the relevant portion of § 6(b)(5) is completely precatory, admonishing the Secretary to adopt the most protective standard if he can, but excusing him from that duty if he cannot. In the case of a hazardous substance for which a "safe" level is either unknown or impractical, the language of § 6(b)(5) gives the Secretary absolutely no indication where on the continuum of relative safety he should draw his line. Especially in light of the importance of the interests at stake, I have no doubt that the provision at issue, standing alone, would violate the doctrine against uncanalized delegations of legislative power. For me the remaining question, then, is whether additional standards are ascertainable from the legislative history or statutory context of § 6(b)(5) or, if not, whether such a standardless delegation was justifiable in light of the "inherent necessities" of the situation.

One of the primary sources looked to by this Court in adding gloss to an otherwise broad grant of legislative authority is the legislative history of the statute in question.... I believe that the legislative history demonstrates that the feasibility requirement, as employed in § 6(b)(5), is a legislative mirage, appearing to some Members but not to others, and assuming any form desired by the beholder.... [and] there is little or nothing in the remaining provisions of the Occupational Safety and Health Act to provide specificity to the feasibility criterion in § 6(b)(5)....

In some cases where broad delegations of power have been examined, this Court has upheld those delegations because of the delegatee's residual authority over particular subjects of regulation. In *United States v. Curtiss–Wright Export Corp.,* 299 U.S. 304, 307 (1936), this Court upheld a statute authorizing the President to prohibit the sale of arms to certain countries if he found that such a prohibition would "contribute to the reestablishment of peace." This Court reasoned that, in the area of foreign affairs, Congress "must often accord to the President a degree of discretion and freedom from statutory restriction which would not be admissible were domestic affairs alone involved...." In the present cases, however, neither the Executive Branch in general nor the Secretary in particular enjoys any independent authority over the subject matter at issue.

Finally, as indicated earlier, in some cases this Court has abided by a rule of necessity, upholding broad delegations of authority where it would be "unreasonable and impracticable to compel Congress to prescribe detailed rules" regarding a particular policy or situation. But no need for such an evasive standard as "feasibility" is apparent in the present cases. In drafting § 6(b)(5), Congress was faced with a clear, if difficult, choice between balancing statistical lives and industrial resources or authorizing the Secretary to elevate human life above all concerns save massive dislocation in an affected industry.... That Congress chose, intentionally or unintentionally, to pass this difficult choice on to the Secretary is evident from the spectral quality of the standard it selected....

As formulated and enforced by this Court, the nondelegation doctrine serves three important functions. First, and most abstractly, it ensures to the extent consistent with orderly governmental administration that important choices of social policy are made by Congress, the branch of our Government most responsive to the popular will.... Second, the doctrine guarantees that, to the extent Congress finds it necessary to delegate authority, it provides the recipient of that authority with an "intelligible principle" to guide the exercise of the delegated discretion.... Third, and derivative of the second, the doctrine ensures that courts charged with reviewing the exercise of delegated legislative discretion will be able to test that exercise against ascertainable standards.

I believe the legislation at issue here fails on all three counts. The decision whether the law of diminishing returns should have any place in the regulation of toxic substances is quintessentially one of legislative policy. For Congress to pass that decision on to the Secretary in the manner it did violates, in my mind, John Locke's caveat—reflected in the cases cited earlier in this opinion—that legislatures are to make laws. Nor, as I think the prior discussion amply demonstrates, do the provisions at issue or their legislative history provide the Secretary with any guidance that might lead him to his somewhat tentative conclusion that he must eliminate exposure to benzene as far as technologically and economically possible. Finally, I would suggest that the standard of "feasibility" renders meaningful judicial review impossible.

We ought not to shy away from our judicial duty to invalidate unconstitutional delegations of legislative authority solely out of concern that we should thereby reinvigorate discredited constitutional doctrines of the pre-New Deal era. If the nondelegation doctrine has fallen into the same desuetude as have substantive due process and restrictive interpretations of the Commerce Clause, it is, as one writer has phrased it, "a case of death by association." J.H. Ely, Democracy and Distrust: A Theory of Judicial Review 133 (1980)....

If we are ever to reshoulder the burden of ensuring that Congress itself make the critical policy decisions, these are surely the cases in which to do it. It is difficult to imagine a more obvious example of Congress simply avoiding a choice which was both fundamental for purposes of the statute and yet politically so divisive that the necessary decision or compromise was difficult, if not impossible, to hammer out in the legislative forge. Far from detracting from the substantive authority of Congress, a declaration that the first sentence of § 6(b)(5) of the

Occupational Safety and Health Act constitutes an invalid delegation to the Secretary of Labor would preserve the authority of Congress. If Congress wishes to legislate in an area which it has not previously sought to enter, it will in today's political world undoubtedly run into opposition no matter how the legislation is formulated. But that is the very essence of legislative authority under our system. It is the hard choices, and not the filling in of the blanks, which must be made by the elected representatives of the people. When fundamental policy decisions underlying important legislation about to be enacted are to be made, the buck stops with Congress and the President insofar as he exercises his constitutional role in the legislative process.

[The concurring opinion of POWELL, J., argued that a cost-benefit balancing was required before OSHA could set a standard. MARSHALL, J., dissented (joined by BRENNAN, WHITE, and BLACKMUN, JJ.). Marshall argued that Congress had intended precisely what OSHA had done. As to delegation, he wrote:]

. . . While my brother Rehnquist eloquently argues that there remains a place for [the delegation] doctrine in our jurisprudence, I am frankly puzzled as to why the issue is thought to be of any relevance here. The non-delegation doctrine is designed to assure that the most fundamental decisions will be made by Congress, the elected representatives of the people, rather than by administrators. Some minimal definiteness is therefore required in order for Congress to delegate its authority to administrative agencies. Congress has been sufficiently definite here. The word "feasible" has a reasonably plain meaning, and its interpretation can be informed by other contexts in which Congress has used it. . . . In short Congress has made the "critical policy decision" in this case. . . .

The plurality's apparent suggestion . . . that the nondelegation doctrine might be violated if the Secretary were permitted to regulate definite but nonquantifiable risks is plainly wrong. Such a statute would be quite definite and would thus raise no constitutional question under *Schechter Poultry*. . . .

Notes and Questions

1. *Subsequent case.* In a subsequent case involving the same issue, the Supreme Court held that OSHA was not required to balance costs and benefits when it set standards. This time Justice Rehnquist dissented on delegation grounds and was joined by Chief Justice Burger. *American Textile Mfrs. Inst., Inc. v. Donovan,* 452 U.S. 490 (1981).

2. *Standards.* What are the purposes of the standards requirement, according to Justice Rehnquist in *Industrial Union?* Where, aside from the language of the statute, may such standards be found? What sources are identified in *Amalgamated Meat Cutters?*

Courts have often required more precise standards in a legislative delegation when the statute threatens a fundamental right such as freedom of speech. *See Shuttlesworth v. Birmingham,* 394 U.S. 147 (1969), holding unconstitutional a delegation to issue a parade permit "unless in its judgment the public welfare, peace, safety, health, decency, good order, morals or convenience require that it be refused." Distinguishing cases in which vague standards like this have been upheld in cases involving economic interests, *Shuttlesworth* insisted that "narrow, objective, and definite standards [are necessary] to guide the licensing authority" in the First Amendment area.

3. *Safeguards.* Note the reliance of the *Amalgamated Meat Cutters* opinion on the safeguards provided by an agency's adoption of its own discretion-limiting standards, by administrative procedure, and by judicial review. Recall the importance of "checks and balances" in our constitutional system. Can the presence of safeguards serve a checking function and serve as a substitute for meaningful legislative standards? Davis argues:

> Five principal steps should be taken to alter the non-delegation doctrine and to move toward a system of judicial protection against unnecessary and uncontrolled discretionary power:
>
> (a) the purpose of the non-delegation doctrine should no longer be either to prevent delegation or to require meaningful statutory standards; the purpose should be the much deeper one of protecting against unnecessary and uncontrolled discretionary power;
>
> (b) the exclusive focus on standards should be shifted to an emphasis more on safeguards than on standards;
>
> (c) when legislative bodies have failed to provide standards, the courts should not hold the delegation unlawful but should require that the administrators must as rapidly as feasible supply the standards;
>
> (d) the non-delegation doctrine should gradually grow into a broad requirement extending beyond the subject of delegation—that officers with discretionary power must do about as much as feasible to structure their discretion through appropriate safeguards and to confine and guide their discretion through standards, principles, and rules;
>
> (e) the protection should reach not merely delegated power but also such undelegated power as that of selective enforcement....
>
> Safeguards are usually more important than standards, although both may be important. The criterion for determining the validity of a delegation should be the totality of the protection against arbitrariness, not just the one strand having to do with statutory standards.
>
> For instance, a delegation *without standards* of power to make rules in accordance with proper rule-making procedure and a delegation *without standards* of power to work out policy through case-to-case adjudication based on trial-type hearings should normally be sustained, whenever the general legislative purpose is discernible. The risk of arbitrary or unjust action is much greater from informal discretionary action, but even there the protection from safeguards is likely to be more effective than protection from standards. For instance, if one administrator in exercising discretionary power without hearings uses a system of open findings, open reasons, and open precedents, but another who is also acting without hearings never states findings or reasons and

never uses precedents as a guide, the delegation to the first administrator is much more deserving of judicial support than the delegation to the second.... What is needed is not simply a substitution of a requirement of safeguards for a requirement of standards but a consideration of both safeguards and standards in order to determine whether the total protection against arbitrary power is adequate....

When an administrator is making a discretionary determination affecting a private party, standards which have been adopted through administrative rule-making are just as effective in confining and guiding the discretionary determination as would be standards stated in the statute. They are not only as effective but in one important aspect they are better. The weakness of a judicial requirement of *statutory* standards is that legislators are often unable or unwilling to supply them. The strength of a judicial requirement of *administrative* standards is that, with the right kind of judicial prodding, the administrators can be expected to supply them....

Kenneth C. Davis, "A New Approach to Delegation," 36 U.Chi.L.Rev. 713, 725–32 (1969).

4. *Arguments for reviving delegation doctrine.* There is a body of academic opinion in favor of reviving the delegation doctrine. One of the most articulate commentators is David Schoenbrod. Schoenbrod believes that courts should invalidate statutes that state only the *goals* that Congress wishes to achieve (like providing safe and healthful workplaces or cleaning up the air) but leave to agencies the hard decisions about *means*. In POWER WITHOUT RESPONSIBILITY 82, 93 (1993), Schoenbrod writes:

> Statutes that purport to give lawmaking power to an agency actually entail a sharing of lawmaking power among several groups, including the agency, the most powerful members of the legislative committees with jurisdiction over the agency, their counterparts in the White House, and concentrated interests [such as a regulated industry]. Concurrently, political benefits accrue to legislators and the president. First, they can claim credit for the promised benefits of a regulatory program, yet shift blame for the disappointments and costs of the program to the agency. Second, with delegation they increase their opportunities to obtain campaign contributions and other favors from concentrated interests.

> [The ways] in which legislators can use delegation to maximize their credit and minimize their blame help to explain why delegation systematically produces the delay, complexity, and confusion that the Clean Air Act illustrates. As former EPA Administrator Lee Thomas put it, "Everybody is accountable and nobody is accountable under the way [Congress] is setting it up, but [the legislators] have got a designated whipping boy."

Similarly, *see* Peter Aranson, et.al., "A Theory of Legislative Delegation," 68 Cornell L.Rev. 1 (1982), which argues that the delegation doctrine should be revived in order to block the enactment of laws dictated by special interests.

While still a law professor, Justice Scalia wrote the following analysis of Rehnquist's *Industrial Union* opinion:

> There are several problems with revivification of the unconstitutional delegation doctrine.... [especially] the difficulty of enunciating how much delegation is too much. The relevant factors are simply too multifarious.... A doctrine so vague, it may be said, is no doctrine at all, but merely an invitation to judicial policy making in the guise of constitutional law. This fear is indeed the reason for the alleged demise of the doctrine—because its use in 1935 paralleled the Court's now discredited use of the due process clause to impose its own notions of acceptable social legislation. But surely vague constitutional doctrines are not automatically unacceptable.... And the risk of vagueness here is much less than elsewhere. Decisions under the due process clause ... are an absolute impediment to governmental action. A decision based on the unconstitutional delegation doctrine is not; it merely requires the action to be taken in a different fashion....

> [I]n modern circumstances the unconstitutional delegation doctrine, far from permitting an increase in judicial power, actually reduces it. For now that judicial review of agency action is virtually routine, it is the courts, rather than the agencies, that can ultimately determine the content of standardless legislation. In other words, to a large extent judicial invocation of the unconstitutional delegation doctrine is a self-denying ordinance—forbidding the transfer of legislative power not to the agencies, but to the courts themselves. The benzene case is illustrative. In giving content to a law which in fact says no more than that OSHA should ensure "safe places of employment" (whatever that means) and should maximize protection against toxic materials "to the extent feasible" (whatever that means), it was the plurality of the Court, rather than OSHA, that ended up doing legislator's work.

> So even with all its Frankenstein-like warts, knobs, and (concededly) dangers, the unconstitutional delegation doctrine is worth hewing from the ice. The alternative appears to be continuation of the widely felt trend toward government by bureaucracy or (what is no better) government by courts....

Antonin Scalia, "A Note on the Benzene Case," Regulation, July/August 1980, at 27–28.

In *Mistretta v. United States,* 488 U.S. 361 (1989), Scalia (in a lone dissent) argued that Congress had violated the non-delegation rule when it created the Sentencing Commission. The Commission was an independent agency within the judicial branch empowered to issue binding guidelines for sentencing in federal criminal cases. The Commission engaged only in research and rulemaking, not law enforcement or adjudication. Scalia argued that a delegation of "naked" lawmaking power, not ancillary to other functions, was constitutionally invalid.

> By reason of today's decision, I anticipate that Congress will find delegation of its lawmaking powers much more attractive in the future. If rulemaking can be entirely unrelated to the exercise of judicial or executive powers, I foresee all manner of "expert" bodies, insulated from the political process, to which Congress will delegate various

portions of its lawmaking responsibility.... This is an undemocratic precedent that we set—not because of the scope of the delegated power, but because its recipient is not one of the three Branches of Government. The only governmental power the Commission possesses is the power to make law; and it is not the Congress.

Is Justice Scalia on sound ground in suggesting that Congress may not delegate lawmaking authority to a body empowered *only* to engage in rulemaking, even if Congress provides adequate standards to guide and limit that delegation?

5. *Arguments against reviving delegation doctrine.* Richard Stewart opposes any effort to revive the delegation doctrine:

> [A]ny large-scale enforcement of the nondelegation doctrine would clearly be unwise. Detailed legislative specification of policy under contemporary conditions would be neither feasible nor desirable in many cases and the judges are ill-equipped to distinguish contrary cases....

> ... [T]here appear to be serious institutional constraints on Congress' ability to specify regulatory policy in meaningful detail. Legislative majorities typically represent coalitions of interests that must not only compromise among themselves but also with opponents. Individual politicians often find far more to be lost than gained in taking a readily identifiable stand on a controversial issue of social or economic policy. Detailed legislative specification of policy would require intensive and continuous investigation, decision, and revision of specialized and complex issues. Such a task would require resources that Congress has in most instances, been unable or unwilling to muster....

> Finally there are serious problems in relying upon the judiciary to enforce the nondelegation doctrine. A court may not properly insist on a greater legislative specification of policy than the subject matter admits of. But how is the judge to decide the degree of policy specification that is possible? ... Such judgments are necessarily quite subjective, and a doctrine that made them determinative of an administrative program's legitimacy could cripple the program by exposing it to continuing threats of invalidation and encouraging the utmost recalcitrance by those opposed to its effectuation. Given such subjective standards, and the controversial character of decisions on whether to invalidate legislative delegations, such decisions will almost inevitably appear partisan, and might often be so.

Richard B. Stewart, "The Reformation of American Administrative Law," 88 Harv.L.Rev. 1667, 1695–97 (1975).

In attacking the views of Aranson, Schoenbrod and other theorists, Jerry Mashaw points out that private special interests seeking to redistribute wealth to themselves might prefer a narrow delegation that answers the hard questions in ways favorable to themselves. "No one has been able to demonstrate any systematic relationship between improving accountability, or enhancing the public welfare, or respecting the rule of law, and the specificity of legislation.... If that is the case, then surely the Supreme Court has been wise to leave the choice of statutory generality to the legislature itself.'' Jerry L. Mashaw, GREED, CHAOS AND GOVERNANCE 147–48 (1997).

Mashaw argues that broad delegations of power actually *promote* democratic values:

> Strangely enough, it may make sense to imagine the delegation of political authority to administrators as a device for improving the responsiveness of government to the desires of the general electorate. This argument can be made even if we accept many of the insights of the political and economic literature that premises its predictions of congressional and voter behavior on a direct linkage between benefits transferred to constituents and the election or reelection of representatives. All we need do is not forget there are also presidential elections. . . .

> The voter's vision of presidential electoral politics is arguably quite different from the [cynical way the voters are assumed to choose representatives in Congress]. . . . Citizens vote for a president based almost wholly on a perception of the difference that one or another candidate might make to general governmental policies. If this description of voting in national elections is reasonably plausible, then the utilization of vague delegations to administrative agencies takes on significance as a device for facilitating responsiveness to voter preferences expressed in presidential elections. The high transactions costs of legislating specifically suggests that legislative activity directed to the modification of administration mandates will be infrequent. Agencies will thus persist with their statutory empowering provisions relatively intact over substantial periods of time.

> . . . Indeed one can reasonably expect that a president will be able to affect policy in a four-year term only because being elected president entails acquiring the power to exercise, direct, or influence policy discretion. The group of executive officers we commonly call ''the administration'' matters only because of the relative malleability of the directives that administrators have in their charge. If congressional statutes were truly specific with respect to the actions that administrators were to take, presidential politics would be a mere beauty contest.

Id. at 152–53.

§ 7.2.2 THE NON–DELEGATION DOCTRINE AND STATE AGENCIES

The delegation doctrine has much greater practical significance at the state level than at the federal level. Consider why many state courts have not given up on the delegation doctrine; the extent to which the delegation doctrine is any more likely to achieve its objectives at the state level than the federal level; and whether federal courts should emulate state courts.

THYGESEN v. CALLAHAN

385 N.E.2d 699 (Ill.1979).

Moran, J.:

[This case involved a challenge, on grounds of undue delegation, to § 19.3 of the Illinois currency exchange act, which provided:]

> "The Director [of Financial Institutions] shall, by rules adopted in accordance with the Illinois Administrative Procedure Act, formulate and issue, within 120 days from the effective date of this amendatory Act, schedules of maximum rates which can be charged for check cashing and writing of money orders by community currency exchanges and ambulatory currency exchanges. Such rates may vary according to such circumstances and conditions as the Director determines to be appropriate. The schedule so established may be modified by the Director from time to time by the same procedure." . . .

For this court's most recent and comprehensive pronouncement on the delegation of power to administrative agencies, we defer to *Stofer v. Motor Vehicle Casualty Co.*, 369 N.E.2d 875 (1977). In *Stofer,* the court reaffirmed its adherence to the guiding principle that intelligible standards or guidelines must accompany legislative delegations of power. This court, thus, implicitly recognized both the constitutional dimensions of the principle (Ill. Const.1970, art. IV, sec. 1) and the practical functions which standards continue to serve. Intelligible standards help guide the administrative agency in the application of the statutes involved and, thereby, safeguard against the unwarranted or unintended extension of legislative delegation. They tend to insure that the legislature does not abdicate to the agency the legislature's primary responsibility to determine, from among the policy alternatives, those objectives the legislation is meant to achieve. Moreover, intelligible standards are indispensable to a meaningful judicial review of any action ultimately taken by the administrative agency. . . .

In an attempt to endow the requisite of intelligible standards with a conceptual foundation, the *Stofer* court declared that a legislative delegation is valid if it sufficiently identifies:

> (1) The *persons* and *activities* potentially subject to regulations;

> (2) the *harm* sought to be prevented; and

> (3) the general *means* intended to be available to the administrator to prevent the identified harm.

In *Stofer,* the legislature had delegated to the Director of Insurance the power to promulgate a standard policy as a means of ensuring uniformity in the insurance of identical risks. The legislation clearly satisfied the first prong of the test by specifying that the regulation was to apply to fire and lightning insurance issued in Illinois. As to the second prong, the court noted that the legislature had articulated its intention to prevent a chaotic proliferation of disparate fire insurance policies. In discussing the general *means* intended to be available to the Director to prevent the identified harm (the third prong), the court cautioned:

> "[H]ad the legislature left the Director completely free to promulgate a 'reasonable' uniform fire insurance policy, we would have serious doubts as to the constitutionality of such uncabined discretion. We find, however, that the legislature has provided substantial additional standards defining the harm sought to be prevented and thereby limit[ed] the Director's discretion."

The court then referred to a related statutory provision which delegated to the Director the power to order the discontinuation of any policy which contained "inconsistent, ambiguous or misleading clauses, or [any] exceptions or conditions that will unreasonably or deceptively affect the risks that are purported to be assumed by the policy.... " The court, reasoning that the delegated authority to promulgate a reasonable uniform policy necessarily incorporated the above-quoted limitation, held that the Director's discretion was limited sufficiently to withstand constitutional scrutiny.

Here, as in *Stofer,* the legislature clearly satisfied the first prong of the test. Those subject to regulation under § 19.3 of the currency exchange act are community and ambulatory currency exchanges, and the regulation is limited to the activities of cashing checks and issuing money orders. In contrast to *Stofer,* the legislature made no attempt to identify the "harm sought to be prevented" in delegating to defendant the power to set maximum rates and did not sufficiently identify the "means ... intended to be available ... to prevent the identified harm." Section 19.3 is devoid of any reference to the harm to be remedied. The currency exchange act contains no other provision which indicates, explicitly or implicitly, general purposes which the legislature might have intended to foster with respect to setting rates for cashing checks and issuing money orders.

The legislature's failure to convey, within the Act, the harm which it sought to remedy by the setting of maximum rates, is compounded by its failure to set forth any meaningful standards to guide defendant in setting the maximum rates. The only provision cited by defendant which in any way guides defendant's discretion in setting maximum rates is an omnibus provision which states:

> "The Director may make and enforce such *reasonable,* relevant regulations, directions, orders, decisions and findings as may be necessary for the execution and enforcement of this Act *and the purposes sought to be attained herein.*"

As we have already discussed, the Act fails to identify any purposes which the legislature might have sought to attain by providing for the establishment of maximum check-cashing and money-order rates. Defendant refers to various provisions in the Act that, he contends, limit his discretion to the promulgation of maximum rates which promote economic benefit and stability to both the currency exchange and the public. The provisions cited by defendant, however, apply to regulatory matters, such as the issuance of licenses and the appointment of advisory board members, which are totally unrelated to the promulgation of maximum check-cashing and money-order rates. We find that the only statutory limitation on defendant's discretion in establishing maximum rates is that the rates be *reasonable*. This court, in *Stofer,* rightfully expressed serious doubt as to the constitutionality of such "uncabined discretion." Here, where the legislature has not only failed to provide any additional standards to guide defendant's discretion, but has failed to communicate to defendant the harm it intended to prevent, it is clear that the legislature has unlawfully delegated its power to set such maximum rates.

Notes and Questions

1. *Delegation in the states.* Many state supreme courts still insist that a delegation of authority to an agency may not be upheld absent adequate statutory standards. *See generally* Gary J. Greco, "Standards or Safeguards: A Survey of the Delegation Doctrine in the States," 8 Admin.L.J.Am.J. 567 (1994). This survey lists 18 states that at least purport to insist on adequate legislative standards; 24 states that require only a general guiding rule and consider the combination of standards and safeguards together; and 6 states that require no standards but only procedural safeguards. In which category does Illinois fall, based on *Thygesen?* Is *Thygesen* a wise application of the delegation doctrine?

2. *Relevance of procedural safeguards.* The Illinois statute involved in *Thygesen* provided that the agency had to comply with the rulemaking procedures of the state APA in its ratemaking for check cashing services. However, the court seemed indifferent to the presence of these procedural safeguards. Numerous other states have taken the presence of procedural safeguards into account in applying the delegation doctrine. In a case involving a delegation challenge to a building code, the Oregon Supreme Court said:

> It is now apparent that the requirement of expressed standards has, in most instances, been little more than a judicial fetish for legislative language, the recitation of which provides no additional safeguards to persons affected by the exercise of the delegated authority. Thus, we have learned that it is of little or no significance in the administration of a delegated power that the statute which generated it stated the permissible limits of its exercise in terms of such abstractions as "public convenience, interest or necessity" or "unjust or unreasonable," or "for the public health, safety, and morals" and similar phrases accepted as satisfying the standards requirement.
>
> As pointed out in Davis on Administrative Law, the important consideration is not whether the statute delegating the power expresses *standards,* but whether the procedure established for the exercise of the power furnishes adequate *safeguards* to those who are affected by the administrative action.... We believe that the appeals procedure provid-

ed a sufficient safeguard to persons wishing to contest administrative action in the enforcement of the code.

Warren v. Marion County, 353 P.2d 257 (Or.1960). Similarly, see *Barry & Barry, Inc. v. Dep't of Motor Vehicles*, 500 P.2d 540, 543 (Wash.1972).

However, this approach was squarely rejected by the Florida Supreme Court. That court overturned a delegation of authority to an agency to identify the areas in the state in which development should be regulated to protect "environmental, historical, natural, or archeological resources of regional or statewide importance." Because the statute transferred the fundamental policy decision to the agency of which areas were to be protected, it was invalid in spite of Florida's extensive system of procedural safeguards. *Askew v. Cross Key Waterways*, 372 So.2d 913 (Fla.1978).

3. *Delegation of authority to private persons.* Legislatures sometimes delegate governmental authority to private persons or entities. Such delegations raise serious issues, because private delegatees are not subject to direct political controls nor to administrative procedure laws. Moreover, they often have a severe conflict of interest.

On one occasion, the U. S. Supreme Court invalidated a federal statute providing that maximum hours and minimum wages agreed upon by a majority of affected miners and mine-operators would be binding upon the rest of them. *Carter v. Carter Coal Co.*, 298 U.S. 238 (1936). The Court in *Carter* stressed the peculiar dangers inherent in a delegation of governmental authority to private parties: Such a delegation "is not even delegation to an official or an official body, presumptively disinterested, but to private persons whose interests may be and often are adverse to the interests of others in the same business." *Id.* at 311.

Since 1936 the federal courts have upheld a number of delegations of governmental authority to private delegatees. *See* Ira P. Robbins, "The Impact of the Delegation Doctrine on Prison Privatization," 35 U.C.L.A.L.Rev. 911, 919 n. 44, 922–25 (1988). For instance, the Court of Appeals upheld a federal statute authorizing a private securities dealer association to issue rules and discipline its members for violation of those rules. Both the rules and the disciplinary proceedings were subject to Securities and Exchange Commission (SEC) review. *Todd & Co., Inc. v. SEC*, 557 F.2d 1008, 1012 (3d Cir.1977).

In contrast to federal cases, a significant number of state cases have overturned delegations to private persons or entities. For example, *Texas Boll Weevil Eradication Foundation v. Lewellen*, 952 S.W.2d 454 (Tex.1997), invalidated a legislative scheme whereby a private foundation was empowered to establish boll weevil eradication zones and conduct elections of cotton farmers within each zone. If a majority of cotton farmers in a zone voted favorably, the foundation assessed each farmer a fixed amount (whether or not they agreed and whether or not their crop was infested) and spent the money on projects to eradicate the dreaded weevil. Farmers who failed to pay the assessment were guilty of a misdemeanor and their crop was destroyed whether or not infested with weevils.

The court noted: "We believe it axiomatic that courts should subject private delegations to a more searching scrutiny than their public counterparts." The court employed a multi-factor test in making its determination. Factors that suggested invalidity of the delegation included: the foundation was subject to only minimal control by a state agency; the foundation not only made rules, it also had power to apply them to particular farmers; the foundation board members (themselves cotton farmers) had a pecuniary interest in the foundation's activity; the foundation's rules were backed up by the criminal law; the delegation of authority was not limited by cost or duration; there was no guarantee that the board members would have any special training or experience; and the legislature provided few statutory standards to guide the Foundation.

Could the Texas legislature redraft the boll weevil eradication program to pass constitutional muster without turning it into just another agency-run regulatory scheme?

In *Hillman v. Northern Wasco County People's Utility District,* 323 P.2d 664 (Or.1958), the court invalidated a statute that adopted an electrical code of a private organization of electricians, including future amendments to the code, and made violations of that code unlawful. Similarly, several cases concerned private accrediting agencies. Only persons who graduated from professional schools certified by the private agencies could practice the profession (such as dentistry or pharmacy). These statutes also were held invalid private delegations. *Garces v. Department of Registration and Education,* 254 N.E.2d 622 (Ill.1969); *Gumbhir v. Kansas State Bd. of Pharmacy,* 618 P.2d 837 (Kan.1980).

May a state delegate to a private entity the authority to run a prison? Consider the importance of these distinctions: i) delegation to such an entity of purely management functions as opposed to a delegation of lawmaking or law-applying functions; ii) delegations of authority to private entities over property rights as opposed to delegations of authority over liberty rights. *See* Robbins, *supra,* at 929–52.

4. *Incorporation by reference of future federal law.* All states operate programs that are funded in part by the national government. Typically, these programs require that the states abide by federal rules, even though those rules are constantly changing. As a result, many state statutes incorporate federal statutes and regulations by reference or authorize state agencies to adopt federal law by reference in their rules. The same problem arises where a state tax statute mirrors a federal tax statute; the state statute provides that the state tax law automatically changes when the federal law changes. Should statutes that incorporate *future* changes in federal law be treated as an unlawful delegation of power to the federal government?

This issue arose in *Oklahoma City v. State ex rel Oklahoma Dep't of Labor,* 918 P.2d 26 (Okla.1995), which involved the state's version of the federal Davis–Bacon Act. These Acts require governmental units to pay prevailing wages on construction projects. The Oklahoma statute delegated determination of local prevailing wages to the federal Labor Department. The Court said:

> The current Act leaves an important determination to the unrestricted and standardless discretion of unelected bureaucrats. Worse, it delegates to an administrative arm of the federal government. As a result, the federal agency which actually determines the prevailing wage is less

answerable to the will of the people of Oklahoma than is the Labor Commissioner who holds elected offices. *Id.* at 30.

In contrast, however, *McFaddin v. Jackson*, 738 S.W.2d 176 (Tenn. 1987), upheld a state inheritance tax law that incorporated future changes in the federal estate tax.

One commentator wrote:

The state adoption of federal law issue should be addressed in terms of the governmental policies being sought, and the substantive area being regulated. In matters where uniform regulation among the states and the federal government is desirable in order to implement a consistent national and local policy, to further identical state and federal goals, and to combat one "evil" which impacts on both the national and local level equally, and where the area being regulated involves matters which are highly technical, requires a level of expertise beyond that available to the states, requires a commitment of resources greater than what can be allocated by the states, and requires constant revision and quick response to new developments, state adoption of federal law should be encouraged. This is especially true if the state adoption of federal law would not create additional significant burdens on regulated persons, and if the efficiency of the regulatory process would be improved by state adoption.

Arnold Rochvarg, "State Adoption of Federal Law—Legislative Abdication or Reasoned Policymaking," 36 Admin.L.Rev. 277, 298–98 (1984). Under Rochvarg's analysis, was *Oklahoma City* correctly decided? How about *McFaddin?*

5. *Problem.* The Madison state constitution requires that the annual state budget be balanced. Because the state encountered unexpected budget deficits in recent years, the legislature passed a statute requiring the Budget Commission, an executive agency, to make such cuts in the current year's appropriations as are necessary to bring the budget into balance.

Because of a shortfall in tax revenues, the Commission had to cut state spending by $600,000,000. Therefore, it cut various spending items, including one for the construction of housing for homeless families. Children who would have received this housing sue to restore the appropriation. Assuming they have standing and that the case is otherwise justiciable, is the Commission's action valid? *See Chiles v. Children A, B, C, D, E, and F*, 589 So.2d 260 (Fla.1991).

§ 7.3 NARROWLY DEFINING AN AGENCY'S AUTHORITY TO AVOID CONSTITUTIONAL QUESTIONS

Agencies have no authority other than that conferred on them by statute (or, in some cases, by the executive or by the state constitution). Agency action is illegal ("ultra vires") if it is not authorized. The determination as to whether particular agency action is ultra vires necessarily involves a process of statutory interpretation, a process discussed in detail in § 9.2. This section considers a technique sometimes employed by courts to avoid a difficult constitutional question either under separation of powers or the bill of rights—invalidating agency action as ultra vires by narrowly construing the authorizing statute.

KENT v. DULLES
357 U.S. 116 (1958).

[The Secretary of State refused to issue a passport to Rockwell Kent on the basis of § 51.135 of the Department of State regulations, which provided that passports would not be issued to members of the Communist party or to persons who engage in activities which support the Communist movement. A statute enacted in 1856 and codified in 1926 authorized the Secretary to grant and issue passports "under such rules as the President shall designate." Another statute, adopted in 1952, prohibits citizens from entering or leaving the U.S. without a valid passport.]

DOUGLAS, J.:

Freedom to travel is, indeed, an important aspect of the citizen's "liberty." We need not decide the extent to which it can be curtailed. We are first concerned with the extent, if any, to which Congress has authorized its curtailment.

The difficulty is that while the power of the Secretary of State over the issuance of passports is expressed in broad terms, it was apparently long exercised quite narrowly. So far as material here, the cases of refusal of passports generally fell into two categories. First, questions pertinent to the citizenship of the applicant and his allegiance to the United States had to be resolved by the Secretary, for the command of Congress was that "No passport shall be granted or issued to or verified for any other persons than those owing allegiance, whether citizens or not, to the United States." Second, was the question whether the applicant was participating in illegal conduct, trying to escape the toils of the law, promoting passport frauds, or otherwise engaging in conduct which would violate the laws of the United States. . . .

The grounds for refusal asserted here do not relate to citizenship or allegiance on the one hand or to criminal or unlawful conduct on the other. Yet, so far as relevant here, those two are the only ones which it could fairly be argued were adopted by Congress in light of prior administrative practice. . . .

Since we start with an exercise by an American citizen of an activity included in constitutional protection, we will not readily infer that Congress gave the Secretary of State unbridled discretion to grant or withhold it. If we were dealing with political questions entrusted to the Chief Executive by the Constitution we would have a different case. But there is more involved here. In part, of course, the issuance of the passport carries some implication of intention to extend the bearer diplomatic protection, though it does no more than "request all whom it may concern to permit safely and freely to pass, and in case of need to give all lawful aid and protection" to this citizen of the United States. But that function of the passport is subordinate. Its crucial function today is control over exit. And, as we have seen, the right of exit is a personal right included within the word "liberty" as used in the Fifth Amendment. If that "liberty" is to be regulated, it must be pursuant to the law-making functions of the Congress. And if that power is delegated, the standards must be adequate to pass scrutiny by the accepted tests. Where activities or enjoyment, natural and often necessary to the well-being of an American citizen, such as travel, are involved, we will construe narrowly all delegated powers that curtail or dilute them. . . .

Thus we do not reach the question of constitutionality. We only conclude that [the Act of 1856 does] not delegate . . . the . . . authority exercised here.

Notes and Questions

1. *The dissent.* Four justices dissented, arguing that the legislative history of the relevant statutes and prior administrative practice establish that the Secretary was authorized to prohibit travel for reasons relating to national security. They furnished numerous examples of this practice. Why did the majority not respond to these arguments?

2. *Avoiding constitutional questions. Kent v. Dulles* is one of many cases that construe statutory delegations narrowly to avoid serious constitutional questions. Why not decide constitutional questions directly instead of avoiding them by narrow statutory construction?

3. *A different approach to ultra vires. Rust v. Sullivan,* 500 U.S. 173 (1991), departs from the tradition of construing delegations narrowly to avoid constitutional questions. *Rust* involved a challenge to the validity of rules issued by HHS to implement a provision of the Public Health and Human Services Act. The statute provided that federal funds appropriated for family-planning services could not "be used in programs where abortion is a method of family planning." The rules prohibited family-planning projects receiving funds under that Act from engaging in referrals, counseling, or any other activities relating to abortion. Furthermore, the rules required all such family-planning projects to be physically separated from facilities where abortion counseling took place.

In a 5–4 decision, the Supreme Court held that the rules were authorized by the statute, finding that "the regulations . . . do not raise the sort of 'grave and doubtful constitutional questions' that would lead us to assume Congress did not intend to authorize their issuance."

Justice Blackmun's dissent stated:

> Casting aside established principles of statutory construction and administrative jurisprudence, the majority in these cases today unnecessarily passes upon important questions of constitutional law. In so doing, the court, for the first time, upholds viewpoint-based suppression of speech solely because it is imposed on those dependent upon the Government for economic support. Under essentially the same rationale, the majority upholds direct regulation of dialogue between a pregnant

woman and her physician when that regulation has both the purpose and the effect of manipulating her decision as to the continuance of her pregnancy. I conclude that the Secretary's regulation of referral, advocacy, and counseling activities exceeds his statutory authority.... The majority does not dispute that "[f]ederal statutes are to be so construed as to avoid serious doubt of their constitutionality." Nor does the majority deny that this principle is fully applicable to cases such as the instant one, in which a plausible but constitutionally suspect statutory interpretation is embodied in an administrative regulation. Rather, in its zeal to address the constitutional issues, the majority sidesteps this established canon of construction with the feeble excuse that the challenged Regulations "do not raise the sort of 'grave and doubtful constitutional questions,' ... that would lead us to assume Congress did not intend to authorize their issuance.... "

Thus, this is not a situation in which "the intention of Congress is revealed too distinctly to permit us to ignore it because of mere misgivings as to power." Indeed, it would appear that our duty to avoid passing unnecessarily upon important constitutional questions is strongest where, as here, the language of the statute is decidedly ambiguous. It is both logical and eminently prudent to assume that when Congress intends to press the limits of constitutionality in its enactments, it will express that intent in explicit and unambiguous terms.

BOREALI v. AXELROD

517 N.E.2d 1350 (N.Y.1987).

Titone, J.:

We hold that the Public Health Council overstepped the boundaries of its lawfully delegated authority when it promulgated a comprehensive code to govern tobacco smoking in areas that are open to the public....

More than two decades ago, the Surgeon General of the United States began warning the American public that tobacco smoking poses a serious health hazard. Within the past five years, there has been mounting evidence that even nonsmokers face a risk of lung cancer as a result of their exposure to tobacco smoke in the environment. As a consequence, smoking in the workplace and other indoor settings has become a cause for serious concern among health professionals.

This growing concern about the deleterious effects of tobacco smoking led our State Legislature to enact a bill in 1975 restricting smoking in certain designated areas, specifically, libraries, museums, theaters and public transportation facilities. [Subsequent efforts] ... to adopt more expansive restrictions on smoking in public places were, however, unsuccessful. In fact, it is undisputed that while some 40 bills on the subject have been introduced in the Legislature since 1975, none have passed both houses.

In late 1986 the Public Health Council (PHC) took action of its own. Purportedly acting pursuant to the broad grant of authority contained in its enabling statute, the PHC published proposed rules, held public hearings and, in February of 1987, promulgated the final set of regulations prohibiting smoking in a wide variety of indoor areas that are open to the public, including schools, hospitals, auditoriums, food markets, stores, banks, taxicabs and limousines. Under these rules, restaurants with seating capacities of more than 50 people are required to provide contiguous nonsmoking areas sufficient to meet customer demand. Further, employers are required to provide smoke-free work areas for nonsmoking employees and to keep common areas free of smoke, with certain limited exceptions for cafeterias and lounges. Affected businesses are permitted to prohibit all smoking on the premises if they so choose. Expressly excluded from the regulations' coverage are restaurants with seating capacities of less than 50, conventions, trade shows, bars, private homes, private automobiles, private social functions, hotel and motel rooms and retail tobacco stores. Additional "waivers" of the regulations' restrictions may be obtained from the Commissioner upon a showing of financial hardship. Implementation of these regulations, which were to become effective May 7, 1987, has been suspended during the pendency of this litigation. . . .

Section 225(5)(a) of the Public Health Law authorizes the PHC to "deal with any matters affecting the . . . public health." At the heart of the present case is the question whether, . . . assuming the propriety of the Legislature's grant of authority, the agency exceeded the permissible scope of its mandate by using it as a basis for engaging in inherently legislative activities. While the separation of powers doctrine gives the Legislature considerable leeway in delegating its regulatory powers, enactments conferring authority on administrative agencies in broad or general terms must be interpreted in light of the limitations that the Constitution imposes (N.Y. Const., art. III, § 1).

However facially broad, a legislative grant of authority must be construed, whenever possible, so that it is no broader than that which the separation of powers doctrine permits. . . . Here, we cannot say that the broad enabling statute in issue is itself an unconstitutional delegation of legislative authority. However, we do conclude that the agency stretched that statute beyond its constitutionally valid reach when it used the statute as a basis for drafting a code embodying its own assessment of what public policy ought to be. . . .

A number of coalescing circumstances that are present in this case persuade us that the difficult-to-define line between administrative rule-making and legislative policy-making has been transgressed. While none of these circumstances, standing alone, is sufficient to warrant the conclusion that the PHC has usurped the Legislature's prerogative, all of these circumstances, when viewed in combination, paint a portrait of an agency that has improperly assumed for itself "[t]he open-ended discretion to choose ends" which characterizes the elected Legislature's role in our system of government.

First, while generally acting to further the laudable goal of protecting nonsmokers from the harmful effects of "passive smoking," the PHC has, in reality, constructed a regulatory scheme laden with exceptions based solely upon economic and social concerns. The exemptions the PHC has carved out for bars, convention centers, small restaurants, and the like, as well as the provision it has made for "waivers" based on financial hardship, have no foundation in considerations of public health. Rather, they demonstrate the agency's own effort to weigh the goal of promoting health against its social cost and to reach a suitable compromise. . . .

Striking the proper balance among health concerns, cost and privacy interests, however, is a uniquely legislative function. While it is true that many regulatory decisions involve weighing economic and social concerns against the specific values that the regulatory agency is mandated to promote, the agency in this case has not been authorized to structure its decision making in a "cost-benefit" model and, in fact, has not been given any legislative guidelines at all for determining how the competing concerns of public health and economic cost are to be weighed. Thus, to the extent that the agency has built a regulatory scheme on its own conclusions about the appropriate balance of trade-offs between health and cost to particular industries in the private sector, it was "acting solely on [its] own ideas of sound public policy" and was therefore operating outside of its proper sphere of authority. This conclusion is particularly compelling here, where the focus is on administratively created exemptions rather than on rules that promote the legislatively expressed goals, since exemptions ordinarily run counter to such goals and, consequently, cannot be justified as simple implementations of legislative values. . . .

The second, and related, consideration is that in adopting the antismoking regulations challenged here the PHC did not merely fill in the details of broad legislation describing the over-all policies to be implemented. Instead, the PHC wrote on a clean slate, creating its own comprehensive set of rules without benefit of legislative guidance. Viewed in that light, the agency's actions were a far cry from the "interstitial" rule making that typifies administrative regulatory activity. . . .

A third indicator that the PHC exceeded the scope of the authority properly delegated to it by the Legislature is the fact that the agency acted in an area in which the Legislature had repeatedly tried—and failed—to reach agreement in the face of substantial public debate and vigorous lobbying by a variety of interested factions. While we have often been reluctant to ascribe persuasive significance to legislative inaction, our usual hesitancy in this area has no place here. Unlike the cases in which we have been asked to consider the Legislature's failure to act as some indirect proof of its actual intentions, in this case it is appropriate for us to consider the significance of legislative inaction as evidence that the Legislature has so far been unable to reach agreement on the goals and methods that should govern in resolving a society-wide health problem. Here, the repeated failures by the Legislature to arrive at such an agreement do not automatically entitle an administrative agency to take it upon itself to fill the vacuum and impose a solution of its own. Manifestly, it is the province of the people's elected representatives, rather than appointed administrators, to resolve difficult social problems by making choices among competing ends.

Finally, although indoor smoking is unquestionably a health issue, no special expertise or technical competence in the field of health was involved in the development of the antismoking regulations challenged here. Faced with mounting evidence about the hazards to bystanders of indoor smoking, the PHC drafted a simple code describing the locales in which smoking would be prohibited and providing exemptions for various special interest groups. . . .

In summary, we conclude that while Public Health Law § 225(5)(a) is a valid delegation of regulatory authority, it cannot be construed to encompass the policy-making activity at issue here without running afoul of the constitutional separation of powers doctrine. . . .

BELLACOSA, J. (dissenting):

I would reverse and uphold the Public Health Council (PHC) regulation, adopted to preserve and improve the public health, prohibiting smoking indoors in some public places and in designated portions of workplaces.

The Legislature declared its intent that there be a PHC in this State and empowered it to adopt a Sanitary Code for the preservation and improvement of the public health. The Legislature also wisely refrained from enacting a rigid formula for the exercise of the PHC's critical agenda of concerns because that calls for expert attention. That legislative forbearance represents both a sound administrative law principle and, at the threshold, a constitutional one as well. . . . It was prescient and sound governance as well to grant flexibility to the objective expert entity so it could in these exceptional instances prescribe demonstrably needed administrative regulation for the public health, free from the sometimes paralyzing polemics associated with the legislative process. . . .

It is painfully ironic that the PHC, as the legislatively designated body of experts for a vast litany of public health concerns is declared for the first time and against a long line of precedents to lack expertise in this instance. . . .

Along the way to its decision, the majority somewhat hesitantly deals with a legislative history aspect of the case. It concludes that the law passed by the Legislature and on the books for 75 years is nullified or neutralized by the inability of the Legislature to broaden its existing narrow ban. The functional consequence of the negatively implied repeal of the broader authorization, imputed by the majority to these recent failed legislative efforts, will be welcomed by opponents of all kinds of existing laws from now on, because the majority's rule dramatically changes the use of legislative history and of the principles of ordinary statutory construction. . . .

No decision of this court and no relevant administrative law princi-ple have been found where general rule-making power was nullified by a court because exceptions to the rule were also promulgated by the regulating entity in response to ancillary social, economic or even policy factors. The majority argument in this respect seems to assert that the PHC was too reasonable and too forthright, and that what it perhaps should have done was create an absolute ban on indoor smoking express-ly and pristinely premised on public health concerns. Life and govern-ment are not so neatly categorized. Surely, if the greater power exists, the lesser, as responsibly exercised here, should not be forbidden! ...

Finally, there should be great concern about another and broader precedential regression lurking behind the diaphanous analysis of the majority's holding.... The majority's invocation of the nondelegation doctrine sounds a discordant note which can summon no good in future administrative law disputes. This doctrine was last used to invalidate an act of Congress in 1935.

Notes and Questions

1. *Comparing Boreali and Kent.* In *Kent*, the Supreme Court construed a federal agency enabling act narrowly because of concerns that a broader construction might violate constitutional provisions. In *Boreali*, the New York Court of Appeals construed a state agency enabling act narrowly because of concerns that a broader construction might violate the delegation doctrine. Recall also Justice Stevens' plurality opinion in *Industrial Union* in § 7.2.1; that opinion gave a narrowing construction to the OSHA statute to avoid a delegation problem. Is a court more justified in narrowly construing a statute to avoid a problem under the bill of rights than to avoid a problem under separation of powers?

2. *Lawyering skills or predictable results?* Would you have advised the parties who challenged these rules that there was a good chance that the Court of Appeals would declare them ultra vires? Which of the arguments made by the majority opinion are most persuasive? Which by the dissent?

Consider, for example, the use of legislative history by the majority opinion. Was it persuasive? Contrast the use of legislative history in the *Boreali* opinions with the use of administrative practice in the *Kent* opinions. May any useful generalizations concerning the construction of agency en-abling acts be drawn from the use of such materials as legislative history and administrative practice in these two cases?

3. *An agency's proper sphere of authority.* The *Boreali* majority states that the circumstances :

> paint a portrait of an agency that has improperly assumed for itself "[t]he open-ended discretion to choose ends" which characterizes the elected Legislature's role in our system of Government.

> Striking the proper balance between health concerns, cost and privacy interests, is a uniquely legislative function.... Thus to the extent that the agency has built a regulatory scheme on its own conclusions about the appropriate balance of tradeoffs between health and cost to particu-lar industries in the private sector, it was "acting solely on [its] own

ideas of sound public policy" and was therefore operating outside of its proper sphere of authority.

Do you agree with the distinction drawn by the majority between the sorts of questions appropriate for the legislature as opposed to those appropriate for an agency?

4. *A statutory approach to narrow construction.* A Florida statute enacted in 1996 is intended to reduce the number of new and existing rules adopted by state agencies. Fla. Stat. Ann. § 120.536(1). In effect, it extends the technique of *Kent v. Dulles* to its logical conclusion (or logical extreme) by mandating that *all* delegations to rulemaking agencies be restrictively construed. It provides:

> A grant of rulemaking authority is necessary but not sufficient to allow an agency to adopt a rule; a specific law to be implemented is also required. An agency may adopt only rules that implement, interpret, or make specific the particular powers and duties granted by the enabling statute. No agency shall have the authority to adopt a rule only because it is reasonably related to the purpose of the enabling legislation and is not arbitrary and capricious, nor shall an agency have the authority to implement statutory provisions setting forth general legislative intent or policy. Statutory language granting rulemaking authority or generally describing the powers and functions of an agency shall be construed to extend no further than the particular powers and duties conferred by the same statute.

The Florida Medical Board is empowered by statute to license physicians. It adopts a rule providing that to receive a license, a physician must have taken a course on drug addiction in medical school. The Board adopted this rule under a statute providing that it could adopt rules "as may be necessary to protect the health, safety, and welfare of the public." Is this rule ultra vires? *See* Jim Rossi, "The 1996 Revised Florida Administrative Procedure Act: A Rulemaking Revolution or Counter–Revolution?" 49 Admin.L.Rev. 345, 358–61 (1997).

5. *Problem.* Public hysteria about the uncontrolled spread of AIDS caused Congress to enact a statute giving the Director of the Public Health Service the power to adopt rules to contain the epidemic. The rules are to be "appropriate and necessary" in light of the AIDS public health emergency. The statute provides that violation of the rules is a criminal offense.

The Director adopted a rule requiring every federal government employee, and every applicant for a federal government job, to take a blood test. If the employee or applicant is HIV positive, the individual must be discharged from government employment (or the person's application for employment must be rejected).

Before adopting the rule, the Director gave public notice of the proposal and invited comments. Research studies, on which the Director relied, indicate that at least one million Americans are HIV positive. The research study indicates that AIDS can be spread through sexual contact and through contact with contaminated blood or needles, but not through other forms of contact.

A union of government employees opposed to the rule has consulted you. Assuming that the rule is judicially reviewable, what arguments can you make that would invalidate the rule and what are the prospects that these arguments will be accepted?

§ 7.4 DELEGATION OF ADJUDICATORY POWER TO AGENCIES

§ 7.4.1 GENERALLY

This section examines the legitimacy of legislative delegations of adjudicatory power to agencies—the power to determine the rights or duties of particular persons based on their individual circumstances. The materials pertaining to legislative delegations are equally applicable here. The presence of standards and safeguards seems relevant to the propriety of adjudicatory as well as legislative delegations. Indeed, some of the cases considered in the prior section involve delegations of adjudicatory authority.

The federal judicial power was vested in Article III judges—judges with life tenure and protection against salary reduction—to ensure unbiased consideration of cases and to ensure that the other branches could not deprive the judiciary of its essential functions. A delegation of adjudicatory power to agencies transfers to them authority that appears to belong exclusively to the judicial branch. This section considers whether such delegations run afoul of the requirements of Article III of the United States Constitution or comparable provisions in state constitutions. Before considering the principal case, it will be helpful to summarize two of the leading federal cases on adjudicatory delegation.

In *Northern Pipeline Constr. Co. v. Marathon Pipe Line Co.,* 458 U.S. 50 (1982), the Supreme Court invalidated a statute that assigned the trial of all the issues in a bankruptcy case, including breach of contract issues, to bankruptcy judges. The bankruptcy judges were not appointed according to the requirements of Article III and, therefore, lacked life tenure and salary protection. Writing for a plurality of four, Justice Brennan held that such contract cases involve "private rights" and, consequently, must be decided by Article III judges. Justices Rehnquist and O'Connor concurred in the result but on a narrower ground limited to contract disputes.

Crowell v. Benson, 285 U.S. 22 (1932), was decided during the brief period in which a majority of the Supreme Court was hostile to administrative delegations. Recall the *Schechter* and *Panama Refining* cases, § 7.2.1. *Crowell* concerned a federal workers' compensation statute that provided benefits based on strict liability if an "employee" was injured while working on "navigable waters." The statute empowered an administrative agency to conduct the necessary adjudications. Despite the fact that the statute at issue in *Crowell* displaced a common law cause of action and affected a pre-existing relationship based on a common law employment contract, the Supreme Court upheld the delegation to the agency to try such cases.

However, because "private rights" were involved (i.e. tort liability of employer to employee), the Court held that Article III judges must have *independent power* to decide all issues of law and "jurisdictional fact" on review of the agency's decision. Jurisdictional facts were those on which the agency's jurisdiction depended—in *Crowell,* whether an employment relationship existed and whether the injury occurred on navigable waters.

COMMODITY FUTURES TRADING COMMISSION v. SCHOR
478 U.S. 833 (1986).

[The Commodity Exchange Act (CEA) created the Commodity Futures Trading Commission (CFTC) as an independent agency to regulate trading in commodity futures. CEA empowered the CFTC to award reparations (damages) to customers from their brokers for violations of the Act or regulations. CFTC regulations provided that in such cases brokers could submit counterclaims against their customers. The brokers could also choose to assert their counterclaims in court.

Schor incurred heavy commodity trading losses in his account with Conti. His account reflected a large debit balance (*i.e.* an amount owed to Conti). Schor commenced a reparation proceeding against Conti before the CFTC, and Conti counterclaimed for the amount of the debit balance (essentially a claim for contract damages). The CFTC held for Conti on both claim and counterclaim. Schor contends that the delegation to the CFTC to try the counterclaim violates Article III.]

O'CONNOR, J.:

Article III, § 1 directs that the "judicial Power of the United States shall be vested in one supreme Court and in such inferior Courts as the Congress may from time to time ordain and establish," and provides that these federal courts shall be staffed by judges who hold office during good behavior, and whose compensation shall not be diminished during tenure in office. Schor claims that these provisions prohibit Congress from authorizing the initial adjudication of common law counterclaims by the CFTC, an administrative agency whose adjudicatory officers do not enjoy the tenure and salary protections embodied in Article III.

Although our precedents in this area do not admit of easy synthesis, they do establish that the resolution of claims such as Schor's cannot turn on conclusory reference to the language of Article III. Rather, the constitutionality of a given congressional delegation of adjudicative functions to a non-Article III body must be assessed by reference to the purposes underlying the requirements of Article III. This inquiry, in turn, is guided by the principle that "practical attention to substance rather than doctrinaire reliance on formal categories should inform application of Article III."

Article III, § 1 serves both to protect the role of the independent judiciary within the constitutional scheme of tripartite government, and to safeguard litigants' right to have claims decided before judges who are free from potential domination by other branches of government.... Article III, § 1 safeguards the role of the Judicial Branch in our tripartite system by barring congressional attempts to transfer jurisdiction [to non-Article III tribunals] for the purpose of emasculating constitutional courts, and thereby preventing the encroachment or aggrandizement of one branch at the expense of the other....

In determining the extent to which a given congressional decision to authorize the adjudication of Article III business in a non-Article III tribunal impermissibly threatens the institutional integrity of the Judicial Branch, the Court has declined to adopt formalistic and unbending rules.

Although such rules might lend a greater degree of coherence to this area of the law, they might also unduly constrict Congress' ability to take needed and innovative action pursuant to its Article I powers. Thus, in reviewing Article III challenges, we have weighed a number of factors, none of which has been deemed determinative, with an eye to the practical effect that the congressional action will have on the constitutionally assigned role of the federal judiciary.

Among the factors upon which we have focused are the extent to which the "essential attributes of judicial power" are reserved to Article III courts, and, conversely, the extent to which the non-Article III forum exercises the range of jurisdiction and powers normally vested only in Article III courts, the origins and importance of the right to be adjudicated, and the concerns that drove Congress to depart from the requirements of Article III.

An examination of the relative allocation of powers between the CFTC and Article III courts in light of the considerations given prominence in our precedents demonstrates that the congressional scheme does not impermissibly intrude on the province of the judiciary. The CFTC's adjudicatory powers depart from the traditional agency model in just one respect: the CFTC's jurisdiction over common law counterclaims. While wholesale importation of concepts of pendent or ancillary jurisdiction into the agency context may create greater constitutional difficulties, we decline to endorse an absolute prohibition on such jurisdiction out of fear of where some hypothetical "slippery slope" may deposit us....

[T]here is little practical reason to find that this single deviation from the agency model is fatal to the congressional scheme. Aside from its authorization of counterclaim jurisdiction, the CEA leaves far more of the "essential attributes of judicial power" to Article III courts than did that portion of the Bankruptcy Act found unconstitutional in *Northern Pipeline*.

The CEA scheme in fact hews closely to the agency model approved by the Court in *Crowell v. Benson*. The CFTC, like the agency in

Crowell, deals only with a "particularized area of law," whereas the jurisdiction of the bankruptcy courts found unconstitutional in *Northern Pipeline* extended to broadly "all civil proceedings arising under title 11 or arising in or *related to* cases under title 11."

CFTC orders, like those of the agency in *Crowell,* but unlike those of the bankruptcy courts under the 1978 Act, are enforceable only by order of the District Court. CFTC orders are also reviewed under the same "weight of the evidence" standard sustained in *Crowell,* rather than the more deferential standard found lacking in *Northern Pipeline.* The legal rulings of the CFTC, like the legal determinations of the agency in *Crowell,* are subject to *de novo* review. Finally, the CFTC, unlike the bankruptcy courts under the 1978 Act, does not exercise "all ordinary powers of district courts," and thus may not, for instance, preside over jury trials or issue writs of habeas corpus.

Of course, the nature of the claim has significance in our Article III analysis quite apart from the method prescribed for its adjudication. The counterclaim asserted in this case is a "private" right for which state law provides the rule of decision. It is therefore a claim of the kind assumed to be at the "core" of matters normally reserved to Article III courts. Yet this conclusion does not end our inquiry; just as this Court has rejected any attempt to make determinative for Article III purposes the distinction between public rights and private rights, there is no reason inherent in separation of powers principles to accord the state law character of a claim talismanic power in Article III inquiries.

We have explained that "the public rights doctrine reflects simply a pragmatic understanding that when Congress selects a quasi-judicial method of resolving matters that 'could be conclusively determined by the Executive and Legislative Branches,' the danger of encroaching on the judicial powers" is less than when private rights, which are normally within the purview of the judiciary, are relegated as an initial matter to administrative adjudication.... Accordingly, where private, common law rights are at stake, our examination of the congressional attempt to control the manner in which those rights are adjudicated has been searching. See, *e.g., Northern Pipeline.*

In this case, however, "[l]ooking beyond form to the substance of what" Congress has done, we are persuaded that the congressional authorization of limited CFTC jurisdiction over a narrow class of common law claims as an incident to the CFTC's primary, and unchallenged, adjudicative function does not create a substantial threat to the separation of powers....

When Congress authorized the CFTC to adjudicate counterclaims, its primary focus was on making effective a specific and limited federal regulatory scheme, not on allocating jurisdiction among federal tribunals. Congress intended to create an inexpensive and expeditious alternative forum through which customers could enforce the provisions of the CEA against professional brokers. Its decision to endow the CFTC with jurisdiction over such reparations claims is readily understandable given the perception that the CFTC was relatively immune from political pressures, and the obvious expertise that the Commission possesses in applying the CEA and its own regulations. This reparations scheme itself is of unquestioned constitutional validity. *Crowell v. Benson.*

It was only to ensure the effectiveness of this scheme that Congress authorized the CFTC to assert jurisdiction over common law counterclaims.... [T]he CFTC's assertion of counterclaim jurisdiction is limited to that which is necessary to make the reparations procedure workable. The CFTC adjudication of common law counterclaims is incidental to, and completely dependent upon, adjudication of reparations claims created by federal law, and in actual fact is limited to claims arising out of the same transaction or occurrence as the reparations claim.

In such circumstances, the magnitude of any intrusion on the Judicial Branch can only be termed *de minimis.* Conversely, were we to hold that the Legislative Branch may not permit such limited cognizance of common law counterclaims at the election of the parties, it is clear that we would "defeat the obvious purpose of the legislation to furnish a prompt, continuous, expert and inexpensive method for dealing with a class of questions of fact which are peculiarly suited to examination and determination by an administrative agency specially assigned to that task." *Crowell v. Benson....* [T]he separation of powers question presented in this case is whether Congress impermissibly undermined, without appreciable expansion of its own power, the role of the Judicial Branch. In any case, we have looked to a number of factors in evaluating the extent to which the congressional scheme endangers separation of powers principles under the circumstances presented, but have found no genuine threat to those principles to be present in this case....

[BRENNAN and MARSHALL, JJ. dissented, arguing that the delegation to CFTC to adjudicate state-law counterclaims offended both the system of checks and balances and the right of litigants to impartial adjudication by life-tenured judges. They found the case indistinguishable from *Northern Pipeline.*]

Notes and Questions

1. *Public and private rights.* In *Northern Pipeline,* the court defined "public rights" as matters arising between the government and private persons. "Private rights" were defined as the liability of one private person to another. According to the plurality opinion in *Northern Pipeline,* Congress could not delegate authority to a non-Article III tribunal to decide questions of private right. The concurring opinion in that case argued that Congress could not delegate authority to decide typical state law contract issues. Recall, however, that *Crowell v. Benson* upheld a delegation to an agency of authority to adjudicate a dispute between two private persons over a statutory form of tort liability—but only if a reviewing court had power to independently review questions of law and jurisdictional fact.

Courts are concerned that without some check on the legislature's ability to delegate adjudicatory power to agencies, potentially all such power could be transferred, leaving the courts with nothing to do and the public without the protection of a life-tenured judiciary. Given the validity of this concern, does the public rights/private rights distinction make any sense?

Common law principles that settle private rights have the same purpose as statutory principles that settle public rights—to maximize public welfare. It is difficult to see why the distinction is relevant to the question of whether a legislature has authority to vest adjudicatory power in agencies. Should not judicial independence be a *greater* concern in cases involving *public rights* where government is one of the litigants, than in cases involving private rights where the government is not involved?

If adequate judicial review by an Article III court is provided (whether the case involves public rights or private rights), is there really any problem with a delegation of adjudicatory power to an agency? *See* Richard H. Fallon, "Of Legislative Courts, Administrative Agencies, and Article III," 101 Harv. L.Rev. 915 (1988).

2. *After Schor.* After *CFTC v. Schor,* when, if ever, would a delegation of adjudicatory power to a federal agency violate the mandate of the Constitution that the judicial power be vested in Article III courts? Note the reliance in *Schor* on Congress' reasons for making the delegation and on safeguards such as judicial review. Is there any fundamental difference, after *Schor,* between federal law concerning the delegation of legislative powers and federal law concerning the delegation of adjudicatory powers?

3. *Crowell v. Benson today.* Both *Northern Pipeline* and *Schor* rely on *Crowell v. Benson,* discussed above. As noted, *Crowell* upheld a delegation to an agency of authority to adjudicate a workers' compensation claim arising under a federal statute. However, *Crowell* also required a de novo judicial trial of the issues of "jurisdictional fact" arising in the case.

Although never formally overruled, *Crowell's* "jurisdictional fact" holding is considered to be a relic of a bygone era. *See, e.g., Estep v. United States,* 327 U.S. 114, 142 (1946) (Frankfurter, J. concurring) (in view of the criticism of *Crowell* and "the attritions of that case through later decisions, one had supposed that the [jurisdictional fact] doctrine had earned a deserved repose"). In *Northern Pipeline,* Justice Brennan noted that *Crowell's* precise holding, with respect to de novo trials of "jurisdictional" or "constitutional" facts, had been undermined by later cases.

4. *State cases and adjudication of private rights.* A number of state decisions have insisted that adjudication of private rights cannot be vested in administrative agencies. Thus, the New Mexico Supreme Court invalidated a workers' compensation law on the basis that it unlawfully delegated adjudicatory power to an agency.

> This is not to say that the legislature, in the exercise of its police powers, may not confer "quasi-judicial" power on administrative boards for the protection of the rights and interest of the public in general whose orders are not to be overruled if supported by substantial evidence. For instance, boards regulating common carriers, transportation, telephone rates, Barber Boards, Medical Boards, Boards of Registration, Tax Boards, Division of Liquor Control, etc. . . . But nowhere does this power extend to a determination of rights and liabilities between individuals.

State ex rel. Hovey Concrete Products Co. v. Mechem, 316 P.2d 1069 (N.M. 1957).

Similarly, in *Wright v. Central DuPage Hospital Association,* 347 N.E.2d 736 (Ill.1976), the court invalidated a scheme for adjudication of medical malpractice disputes by a panel of a judge, a doctor, and an attorney. The court stated that the scheme violated the Illinois Constitution because it vested essentially judicial functions in nonjudicial personnel, and because it impaired plaintiff's constitutionally protected interests in trial by jury.

Finally, *In re Opinion of the Justices,* 179 A. 344 (N.H.1935), advised that the adjudication of negligence cases arising out of auto accidents could not be transferred to an agency. The court concluded that "the function of trying and deciding litigation is strictly and exclusively for the judiciary when it is between private parties, neither of whom seeks to come under the protection of a public interest and to have it upheld and maintained for his benefit. The function cannot be executive unless executive activity may embrace litigation in general. If the proposed jurisdiction might be bestowed, the limits of executive authority would be almost without bounds and indefinite encroachment on judicial power would be possible."

5. *Jury trials.* The Seventh Amendment to the United States Constitution provides: "In Suits at common law, where the value in controversy shall exceed twenty dollars, the right of trial by jury shall be preserved.... "

Congress can avoid jury trials by removing certain kinds of adjudications from courts to agencies. *Atlas Roofing Co. v. Occupational Safety and Health Rev. Comm'n,* 430 U.S. 442 (1977), involved the validity of a statute authorizing OSHRC to impose civil money penalties, which could range up to $10,000 per violation, on employers who maintained an unsafe workplace. If an employer did not pay a penalty, the government could collect it by an action in federal district court.

In *Atlas,* the Supreme Court rejected a Seventh Amendment attack on the enabling statute, holding that the imposition of the penalty was a means of enforcing a "public right" rather than a "private right." The Court stated that "Congress is not required by the Seventh Amendment to choke the already crowded federal courts with new types of litigation or prevented from committing some new types of litigation to administrative agencies with special competence in the relevant field. This is the case even if the Seventh Amendment would have required a jury where the adjudication of those rights is assigned to a federal court of law instead of an administrative agency."

In a footnote, the Court pointed out that decisions of the Commission were reviewable by the federal court of appeals (both as to legal questions and as to whether there was substantial evidence to support its fact findings). "Thus these cases do not present the question whether Congress may commit the adjudication of fines for [the] violation [of these public rights] to an administrative agency without any sort of intervention by a court at any stage of the proceedings." *Atlas* was followed under a state constitution in *National Velour Corp. v. Durfee,* 637 A.2d 375 (R.I.1994) (no right to jury trial when environmental agency imposes $205,000 civil penalty).

Compare *Tull v. United States,* 481 U.S. 412 (1987), to the *Atlas Roofing* case. In *Tull,* a *court* awarded injunctive relief and monetary penalties to the government in a suit under the Clean Water Act. It was held that the defendant had a right to a jury trial on the question of whether civil penalties should be imposed (but not on the issue of the amount of the penalties). Thus the right to a jury trial may turn on whether the agency sets the penalty *(Atlas Roofing)* or whether a court sets the penalty *(Tull).*

§ 7.4.2 DELEGATION OF AUTHORITY TO PENALIZE OR FINE

Although delegations of adjudicatory authority to agencies have become generally accepted, questions remain with respect to whether agencies can impose the same remedies that courts can impose.

McHUGH v. SANTA MONICA RENT CONTROL BD.
777 P.2d 91 (Cal.1989).

Lucas, C.J.:

[The Santa Monica Rent Control ordinance allows the Board to set maximum rents. It also provides for administrative adjudication of excess rent claims and imposition of treble damages. It allows a tenant to deduct excess rent and treble damages from future rent payments. McHugh argued that these provisions were an unlawful delegation of adjudicatory power. The court agreed with cases from nine other states upholding administrative adjudication of restitutionary and compensatory damages. These cases set out the following guidelines:]

An administrative agency may constitutionally hold hearings, determine facts, apply the law to those facts, and order relief—including certain types of monetary relief—so long as (i) such activities are authorized by statute or legislation and are *reasonably necessary* to effectuate the administrative agency's *primary, legitimate regulatory purposes* [substantive limitations] and (ii) *the "essential" judicial power* (i.e., the power to make enforceable, binding judgments) *remains ultimately in the courts through review of agency determinations* [procedural limitations or the "principle of check"]. . . .

Practical considerations . . . militate against a less accommodating view of the judicial powers doctrine. If nonconstitutional administrative agencies were barred from adjudicating all money claims between private individuals who are subject to administrative regulation, such agencies would be precluded from exercising powers routinely employed, and not previously challenged. . . .

We too will carefully apply the [substantive limitations] "reasonable necessity/legitimate regulatory purpose" requirements in order to guard against unjustified delegation of authority to decide disputes that otherwise belong in the courts. Specifically, we will inquire whether the challenged remedial power is authorized by legislation, and reasonably necessary to accomplish the administrative agency's regulatory purposes. Furthermore, we will closely scrutinize the agency's asserted regulatory purposes in order to ascertain whether the challenged remedial power is merely incidental to a proper, primary regulatory purpose, or whether it is in reality an attempt to transfer determination of traditional common law claims from the courts to a specialized agency whose primary purpose is the processing of such claims.

Thus, for example, we would not approve the Board's adjudication of a landlord's common law counterclaims (extraneous to the Board's regulatory functions) against a tenant. Such adjudication would (i) not reasonably effectuate the Board's regulatory purposes—ensuring enforcement of rent levels—and (ii) it would shift the Board's primary purpose from one of ensuring the enforcement of rent levels, to adjudicating a broad range of landlord-tenant disputes traditionally resolved in the courts. Finally, we will continue to apply the [procedural limitations] "principle of check" in order to reserve to the courts the "true" judicial power....

[In this case] ... the Board held hearings, heard testimony, and determined that plaintiff charged excess rents of $1,068 to tenant Plevka, and $600.50 to tenant Smith. We conclude that such actions, although judicial in nature, are both authorized by the Charter Amendment and reasonably necessary to accomplish the administrative agency's primary, legitimate regulatory purposes, *i.e.*, setting and regulating maximum rents in the local housing market. The Board's legitimate regulatory authority, and hence its incidental remedial authority, is circumscribed. It may not, and does not, hear and adjudicate all manner of disputes between landlords and tenants. Its authority ... extends only so far as necessary to set and regulate rents. Incidental to that legitimate primary purpose—and "in order to produce an efficient and effective administrative enforcement of the public interest" the Board may review the rents actually charged, and order necessary adjustments to assure compliance with its price control regulations.

The trial court erred therefore in concluding that the Board exercised judicial powers in violation of the Constitution by adjudicating (subject to judicial review) tenants' claims for excess rents, and ordering restitution of the excess amounts. We conclude, however, that the administrative orders in this case violated the "principle of check."

The Board authorized tenant Plevka to "withhold his entire month's rent in the first month following the Board's decision ... and the remaining monies in the months thereafter. The withheld amounts shall not form the basis for an unlawful detainer proceeding based upon nonpayment of rent.... " [Consequently, the agency order is effectively self-executing because it has immediate practical and legal effect. Before the landlord could seek judicial review, the tenant would have already withheld the rent and the landlord could not bring an unlawful detainer action because of the unpaid rent.]

An administrative order of this nature is unlike any other of which we are aware. And, in our view, for the reasons set out above it represents an unwarranted intrusion into the power of the courts to "check" administrative adjudications. We thus conclude that the rent withholding order in this case violated the judicial powers provision of our Constitution. . . .

In addition to the "restitutive" excess rent amounts, the Board assessed treble damages against portions of both tenants' excess rents. Tenant Plevka was awarded an extra $1,632, and tenant Smith was awarded an extra $941.

We emphasize at the outset the limited question posed here. We do not consider the constitutional propriety of administrative imposition of penalties, nor do we consider the propriety of relatively minor "punitive damages" under statutory schemes that expressly authorize such damages, and set a cap on such awards. We consider only the authority of the rent control board to impose *treble damages*.

Applying the "substantive limitations" prong of the test ... we conclude treble damages, although authorized by the Charter Amendment, may not constitutionally be imposed by the Board. First, we note that administrative agencies regularly exercise a range of powers designed to induce compliance with their regulatory authority (e.g., imposition of fines or penalties, awards of costs and attorney fees), and there is no reason to believe that such options would be insufficient here. (Indeed, we observe that after the award in this case, the Charter Amendment was revised to delete the Board's power to award such damages.) Most significantly, however, we believe that the power to award treble damages in the present context poses a risk of producing arbitrary, disproportionate results that magnify, beyond acceptable risks, the possibility of arbitrariness inherent in any scheme of administrative adjudication.

Accordingly, we [hold that] imposition of treble damages ... violates the judicial powers clause, and enjoin future imposition of treble damages under that provision. [The court also rejected claims that administrative adjudication of monetary penalties violated the right to a jury trial in the California constitution. It followed cases from other states holding that constitutional rights to a jury do not apply to otherwise proper administrative adjudicatory schemes.]

Notes and Questions

1. *Criminal and civil penalties.* Only the judiciary may impose a sentence of imprisonment. *Wong Wing v. United States,* 163 U.S. 228 (1896), indicated that a person may be temporarily detained by an agency pending proceedings to decide whether exclusion or expulsion as an illegal alien is appropriate, and that an alien may be administratively excluded or expelled from the country. However, an illegal alien may not be sentenced to prison without the protection of a judicial trial. Similarly, an agency cannot impose a criminal fine, because of constitutional restrictions applicable to the criminal process.

However, a legislature can delegate to an agency the power to adopt rules, the violation of which will be crimes to be punished by a court. In these situations, the legislature has made the decision that violations of the rules will be criminal and the statute establishes the penalty. *See, e.g., United States v. Grimaud*, 220 U.S. 506 (1911) (criminal conviction for violation of agency's grazing rules). *But see State v. Broom*, 439 So.2d 357 (La.1983), holding that agencies cannot define criminal offenses.

Although an agency cannot itself dispense criminal penalties, both federal and state courts permit agencies to impose civil monetary penalties. At the federal level, recall *Atlas Roofing*, § 7.4.1. At the state level, *Waukegan v. Pollution Control Bd.*, 311 N.E.2d 146 (Ill.1974) is typical of many cases in allowing a state environmental agency to impose a civil penalty against a polluter. *McHugh* also recognizes that agencies can impose civil penalties.

Some states permit the legislature to delegate authority to impose fixed penalties but not variable penalties. *See, e.g., County Council for Montgomery County v. Investors Funding Corp.*, 312 A.2d 225, 246 (Md.1973); *Tite v. State Tax Commission*, 57 P.2d 734, 740 (Utah 1936). Is there a possibility that an agency with authority to determine the level of a monetary penalty will abuse that discretion? Is that any more of a problem than giving an agency authority to suspend or revoke a license?

2. *Agency imposition of damage awards and other remedies. McHugh* is typical of many cases that uphold delegations to agencies of authority to award damages to a non-governmental litigant. For instance, in *Jackson v. Concord Co.*, 253 A.2d 793, 800 (N.J.1969), a state civil rights agency ordered reimbursement for out-of-pocket loss suffered in a racial discrimination case. The New Jersey Supreme Court stated that "at this advanced date in the development of administrative law, we see no constitutional objection to legislative authorization to an administrative agency to award, as incidental relief in connection with a subject delegable to it, money damages, ultimate judicial review thereof being available."

However, *McHugh* drew the line at allowing an agency to award treble damages to a tenant. Why is an award of treble damages different from the restitutionary damage award that the court upheld? Why is an award of treble damages different from a civil money penalty?

Courts are often reluctant to allow agencies to impose court-like remedies that have not been clearly authorized by statute. Recall cases like *Boreali*, § 7.3, which construe statutes narrowly to avoid delegation issues. Thus *Iron Workers Local No. 67 v. Hart*, 191 N.W.2d 758 (Iowa 1971) held that a state civil rights commission lacked power to award compensatory damages to a business that had been harmed by a union that objected to the business' hiring practices. The court said that the Commission's power to award damages to employees could not, by analogy, support a right to grant common law damages to victims other than employees.

Similarly, California cases have denied agencies power to impose various remedies routinely available from courts because the legislature failed to clearly authorize such remedies. These decisions concede that such remedies would clearly promote the regulatory system the agency administers. *AFL-CIO v. Unemployment Insurance Appeals Board*, 920 P.2d 1314 (Cal.1996) (agency cannot award prejudgment interest on a grant of unemployment benefits despite long delays before employee receives award); *Peralta Community Coll. Dist. v. FEHC*, 801 P.2d 357 (Cal.1990) (agency cannot award damages for emotional distress in sexual harassment case); *Dyna-Med, Inc. v. FEHC*, 743 P.2d 1323 (Cal.1987) (agency cannot award punitive damages for violation of employment discrimination law).

Why do courts narrowly construe statutes providing for agency-level remedies?

3. *Enforcement of agency orders.* Typically agencies must go to court to enforce their orders. *McHugh* illustrates this principle; it invalidated rent withholding as a remedy because it is self-executing.

A failure to obey an enforcement order issued by a court is punishable as contempt. Historically, only courts, not agencies, were given contempt powers. *See ICC v. Brimson,* 154 U.S. 447, 485 (1894); *Wright v. Plaza Ford,* 395 A.2d 1259, 1265 (N.J.Super.1978). It was generally believed that such powers could not be conferred upon agencies. Should this principle be reconsidered?

Would you favor a statute which made it a crime to violate a lawful agency order? If criminalizing the violation of agency orders is a desirable and efficient method for their enforcement, why don't statutes ordinarily provide criminal sanctions for violation of lawful agency orders?

4. *Problem.* A recent state statute transferred adjudication of all moving traffic violations and parking tickets to a newly formed Traffic Agency. The purpose of the statute was to lessen congestion in the criminal courts and to assure expedited treatment of such offenses.

If the Traffic Agency finds that a violation has been proved by a preponderance of the evidence, it may impose penalties of up to $1000 per violation. Your client Ralph is charged with speeding. Can he object to trial of his case before the Traffic Agency? *See Van Harken v. City of Chicago,* 103 F.3d 1346 (7th Cir.1997); *Rosenthal v. Hartnett,* 326 N.E.2d 811 (N.Y.1975). What if the Traffic Agency were a federal agency created to adjudicate cases involving alleged moving traffic violations and parking tickets on federal lands?

§ 7.5   RATIONALE FOR LEGISLATIVE AND EXECUTIVE REVIEW OF AGENCY ACTION

ARTHUR EARL BONFIELD, STATE ADMINISTRATIVE RULE MAKING

456–60 (1986).

Through judicial review of agency rules, courts can help to ensure that [rules] are legal in all respects.... But courts are not the proper bodies to protect us against legal agency rules that are simply unwise or unpopular, because courts are not broadly representative institutions that are directly responsible to the people.... On the other hand, gubernatorial and legislative review of agency rules can provide a direct and effective check on unwise or unpopular agency rules. The governor and the legislature are directly elected, have broad constituencies, and therefore have great legitimacy to decide finally, on behalf of all the people, issues of everyday public policy....

Judicial review of agency rule making should also be supplemented by an effective scheme of gubernatorial and legislative review of rule making because such a scheme will make that agency law-making process more realistically approximate the representative legislative process it was intended to replace....

A related reason to supplement judicial review of agency rules with an effective scheme of external review directly involving the governor and legislature has to do with the right of those institutions to preserve the effectiveness of their law-making function. Agencies should be directly accountable to those authorizing their rule-making actions. Ordinarily, both the governor and the legislature approve laws delegating rule-making authority to agencies. Consequently, both the governor and the legislature should be able to satisfy themselves that their will is being executed in a manner consistent with their wishes and, if it is not, should be able to take suitable action to ensure conformity with their wishes....

Furthermore, ... [o]nly institutions with direct political legitimacy like the governor and the legislature can coordinate potentially divergent, conflicting, or inconsistent rules of several agencies purely on policy grounds. The courts cannot perform that function because their intervention is limited entirely to resolving matters of legality rather than matters of policy....

Gubernatorial and legislative review of rules can also check unlawful agency rule making. While the courts can perform that function, as will be seen, they can often do so only in an untimely fashion, at an unacceptable cost, or in a relatively ineffective way....

Another reason why judicial review of agency rule making should be supplemented by a scheme for gubernatorial and legislative review of that agency function is that the agencies themselves will often benefit from systematic review of their rules by the governor and legislature. In practice, that external review will provide them with an additional means by which to discover deficiencies in their rules before they become effective or are invalidated by the courts.

§ 7.6 LEGISLATIVE CONTROLS

§ 7.6.1 THE LEGISLATIVE VETO

The most direct means by which a legislature may control agency action is by specifying its desires in the agency's enabling act at the outset. However, for reasons explored in § 7.2, legislatures have frequently been unable or unwilling to be very specific in their statutes delegating authority to agencies. Instead, they have typically vested agencies with broad discretion under open-ended statutory delegations of authority. When a legislature finds an exercise of that authority unacceptable, it can respond by narrowing the agency's enabling act or by overturning the specific agency action deemed objectionable.

However, enactment of a statute to overcome agency action is difficult, in part because it requires the concurrence of both houses of the legislature and the chief executive (or, if the latter vetoes the legislature's action, an override of that veto by a supermajority of both houses). That is why many legislatures have turned to the "legislative veto."

The term "legislative veto" describes a mechanism that allows legislators to invalidate or suspend agency action by less cumbersome means than the enactment of a statute. For example, it might provide for disapproval of an agency rule solely by a resolution passed by one or two houses of the legislature, or by a legislative committee, without any participation by the chief executive.

The legislative veto device made its first appearance in a smattering of laws passed at both the federal and state levels in the 1930's. It became particularly popular in the 1970's, as legislatures stepped up their search for responses to the burgeoning administrative state and what they regarded as "overregulation." For a survey of state provisions, see L. Harold Levinson, "The Decline of the Legislative Veto: Federal/State Comparisons and Interactions," 17 Publius: The Journal of Federalism 115, 115–20 (1987). In recent years, however, the use of the legislative veto has withered in the face of constitutional challenges, exemplified most notably by the decision that follows.

IMMIGRATION AND NATURALIZATION SERVICE [INS] v. CHADHA
462 U.S. 919 (1983).

[Section 244(a)(1) of the Immigration and Nationality Act provides that the Attorney General shall have discretion to "suspend" the deportation of an otherwise deportable alien who meets certain statutory standards, one of which is that deportation would cause "extreme hardship." The Attorney General delegated this power to the INS.

Chadha was an East Indian who had been born in Kenya and held a British passport; he had been admitted on a student visa but had overstayed the expiration date. Following an on-the-record hearing, an immigration judge held that Chadha was deportable but ordered that deportation be suspended because Chadha met the "extreme hardship" requirements of the statute.

Section 244(c)(1) provides that the Attorney General must report all suspensions of deportation to Congress; and § 244(c)(2) provides that if, during the legislative session in which the suspension is reported or the next session, either the House or the Senate passes a resolution "stating in substance that it does not favor the suspension of such deportation," the effect will be to "veto" the suspension.

Chadha's suspension was reported to Congress and remained outstanding for a year and a half. At almost the last possible moment, a resolution was introduced in the House to veto deportation suspensions of six aliens, including that of Chadha. The sponsor of the resolution stated that, in the Judiciary Committee's view, those aliens had not met the statutory requirement of undue hardship, but there was no debate and no recorded vote. Because the resolution passed, Chadha was ordered to be deported. He questions the constitutionality of the legislative veto provision in § 244(c)(2).

The Court first held that the provision for legislative veto was "severable" from the provision for suspension of deportation. Consequently, if the veto were invalidated, the INS decision suspending Chadha's deportation would remain in effect.

Burger, C.J.:]

We turn now to the question whether action of one House of Congress under § 244(c)(2) violates strictures of the Constitution. We begin, of course, with the presumption that the challenged statute is valid....

By the same token, the fact that a given law or procedure is efficient, convenient, and useful in facilitating functions of government, standing alone, will not save it if it is contrary to the Constitution. Convenience and efficiency are not the primary objectives—or the hallmarks—of democratic government and our inquiry is sharpened rather than blunted by the fact that Congressional veto provisions are appearing with increasing frequency in statutes which delegate authority to executive and independent agencies....

Justice White undertakes to make a case for the proposition that the one-House veto is a useful "political invention," and we need not challenge that assertion. We can even concede this utilitarian argument although the long range political wisdom of this "invention" is arguable.... But policy arguments supporting even useful "political inventions" are subject to the demands of the Constitution which defines powers and, with respect to this subject, sets out just how those powers are to be exercised.

Explicit and unambiguous provisions of the Constitution prescribe and define the respective functions of the Congress and of the Executive in the legislative process. Since the precise terms of those familiar provisions are critical to the resolution of this case, we set them out verbatim. Art. I provides:

> "All legislative Powers herein granted shall be vested in a Congress of the United States, which shall consist of a Senate *and* a House of Representatives." Art. I, § 1.

> "Every Bill which shall have passed the House of Representatives and the Senate, *shall,* before it becomes a Law, be presented to the President of the United States; ..." Art. I, § 7, cl. 2.

"Every Order, Resolution, or Vote to which the Concurrence of the Senate and House of Representatives may be necessary (except on a question of Adjournment) *shall be* presented to the President of the United States; and before the Same shall take Effect, *shall be* approved by him, or being disapproved by him, shall be repassed by two thirds of the Senate and House of Representatives, according to the Rules and Limitations prescribed in the Case of a Bill." Art. I, § 7, cl. 3.

These provisions of Art. I are integral parts of the constitutional design for the separation of powers.... [T]he purposes underlying the Presentment Clauses, Art. I, § 7, cls. 2, 3, and the bicameral requirement of Art. I, § 1 and § 7, cl. 2, guide our resolution of the important question presented in this case....

The records of the Constitutional Convention reveal that the requirement that all legislation be presented to the President before becoming law was uniformly accepted by the Framers. Presentment to the President and the Presidential veto were considered so imperative that the draftsmen took special pains to assure that these requirements could not be circumvented. During the final debate on Art. I, § 7, cl. 2, James Madison expressed concern that it might easily be evaded by the simple expedient of calling a proposed law a "resolution" or "vote" rather than a "bill." As a consequence, Art. I, § 7, cl. 3, was added.

The decision to provide the President with a limited and qualified power to nullify proposed legislation by veto was based on the profound conviction of the Framers that the powers conferred on Congress were the powers to be most carefully circumscribed. It is beyond doubt that lawmaking was a power to be shared by both Houses and the President. In The Federalist No. 73 (H. Lodge ed. 1888), Hamilton focused on the President's role in making laws:

> "If even no propensity had ever discovered itself in the legislative body to invade the rights of the Executive, the rules of just reasoning and theoretic propriety would of themselves teach us that the one ought not to be left to the mercy of the other, but ought to possess a constitutional and effectual power of self-defense." *Id.*, at 457–458....

The President's role in the lawmaking process also reflects the Framers' careful efforts to check whatever propensity a particular Congress might have to enact oppressive, improvident, or ill-considered measures....

The bicameral requirement of Art. I, §§ 1, 7 was of scarcely less concern to the Framers than was the Presidential veto and indeed the two concepts are interdependent. By providing that no law could take effect without the concurrence of the prescribed majority of the Members of both Houses, the Framers reemphasized their belief, already remarked upon in connection with the Presentment Clauses, that legislation should not be enacted unless it has been carefully and fully considered by the Nation's elected officials....

We see therefore that the Framers were acutely conscious that the bicameral requirement and the Presentment Clauses would serve essential constitutional functions. The President's participation in the legislative process was to protect the Executive Branch from Congress and to protect the whole people from improvident laws. The division of the Congress into two distinctive bodies assures that the legislative power would be exercised only after opportunity for full study and debate in separate settings. The President's unilateral veto power, in turn, was limited by the power of two thirds of both Houses of Congress to overrule a veto thereby precluding final arbitrary action of one person. It emerges clearly that the prescription for legislative action in Art. I, §§ 1, 7 represents the Framers' decision that the legislative power of the Federal government be exercised in accord with a single, finely wrought and exhaustively considered, procedure....

When any Branch acts, it is presumptively exercising the power the Constitution has delegated to it. See *J W Hampton Jr. & Co. v. United States*, 276 U.S. 394, 406 (1928). When the Executive acts, it presumptively acts in an executive or administrative capacity as defined in Art. II. And when, as here, one House of Congress purports to act, it is presumptively acting within its assigned sphere.

Beginning with this presumption, we must nevertheless establish that the challenged action under § 244(c)(2) is of the kind to which the procedural requirements of Art. I, § 7 apply. Not every action taken by either House is subject to the bicameralism and presentment requirements of Art. I. Whether actions taken by either House are, in law and fact, an exercise of legislative power depends not on their form but upon "whether they contain matter which is properly to be regarded as legislative in its character and effect."

Examination of the action taken here by one House pursuant to § 244(c)(2) reveals that it was essentially legislative in purpose and effect. In purporting to exercise power defined in Art. I, § 8, cl. 4 to "establish an uniform Rule of Naturalization," the House took action that had the purpose and effect of altering the legal rights, duties and relations of persons, including the Attorney General, Executive Branch officials and Chadha, all outside the legislative branch....

The legislative character of the one-House veto in this case is confirmed by the character of the Congressional action it supplants. Neither the House of Representatives nor the Senate contends that, absent the veto provision in § 244(c)(2), either of them, or both of them acting together, could effectively require the Attorney General to deport an alien once the Attorney General, in the exercise of legislatively delegated authority,[16] had determined the alien should remain in the

---

✳16. Congress protests that affirming the Court of Appeals in these cases will sanction "lawmaking by the Attorney General.... Why is the Attorney General exempt from submitting his proposed changes in

the law to the full bicameral process?" To be sure, some administrative agency action—rulemaking, for example—may resemble "lawmaking." See 5 U.S.C. § 551(4), which defines an agency's "rule"

United States. Without the challenged provision in § 244(c)(2), this could have been achieved, if at all, only by legislation requiring deportation. . . .

The nature of the decision implemented by the one-House veto in this case further manifests its legislative character. After long experience with the clumsy, time consuming private bill procedure, Congress made a deliberate choice to delegate to the Executive Branch, and specifically to the Attorney General, the authority to allow deportable aliens to remain in this country in certain specified circumstances. It is not disputed that this choice to delegate authority is precisely the kind of decision that can be implemented only in accordance with the procedures set out in Art. I. Disagreement with the Attorney General's decision on Chadha's deportation—that is, Congress' decision to deport Chadha—no less than Congress' original choice to delegate to the Attorney General the authority to make that decision, involves determinations of policy that Congress can implement in only one way; bicameral passage followed by presentment to the President. Congress must abide by its delegation of authority until that delegation is legislatively altered or revoked. . . .

. . . There are but four provisions in the Constitution, explicit and unambiguous, by which one House may act alone with the unreviewable force of law, not subject to the President's veto: [initiation of impeachments by the House; and impeachment trials, approval of presidential appointments, and ratification of treaties by the Senate]. These carefully defined exceptions from presentment and bicameralism underscore the difference between the legislative functions of Congress and other unilat-

---

as "the whole or part of an agency statement of general or particular applicability and future effect designed to implement, interpret, or prescribe *law* or policy. . . . " This Court has referred to agency activity as being "quasi-legislative" in character. Clearly, however, "[i]n the framework of our Constitution, the President's power to see that the laws are faithfully executed refutes the idea that he is to be a lawmaker."

When the Attorney General performs his duties pursuant to § 244, he does not exercise "legislative" power. The bicameral process is not necessary as a check on the Executive's administration of the laws because his administrative activity cannot reach beyond the limits of the statute that created it—a statute duly enacted pursuant to Art. I, §§ 1, 7. The constitutionality of the Attorney General's execution of the authority delegated to him by § 244 involves only a question of delegation doctrine. The courts, when a case or controversy arises, can always "ascertain whether the will of Congress has been obeyed," and can enforce adherence to statutory standards.

It is clear, therefore, that the Attorney General acts in his presumptively Art. II capacity when he administers the Immigration and Nationality Act. Executive action under legislatively delegated authority that might resemble "legislative" action in some respects is not subject to the approval of both Houses of Congress and the President for the reason that the Constitution does not so require. That kind of Executive action is always subject to check by the terms of the legislation that authorized it; and if that authority is exceeded it is open to judicial review as well as the power of Congress to modify or revoke the authority entirely. A one-House veto is clearly legislative in both character and effect and is not so checked; the need for the check provided by Art. I, §§ 1, 7, is therefore clear. Congress' authority to delegate portions of its power to administrative agencies provides no support for the argument that Congress can constitutionally control administration of the laws by way of a congressional veto.

eral but important and binding one-House acts provided for in the Constitution. . . .

Since it is clear that the action by the House under § 244(c)(2) was not within any of the express constitutional exceptions authorizing one House to act alone, and equally clear that it was an exercise of legislative power, that action was subject to the standards prescribed in Article I. . . .

The veto authorized by § 244(c)(2) doubtless has been in many respects a convenient shortcut; the "sharing" with the Executive by Congress of its authority over aliens in this manner is, on its face, an appealing compromise. In purely practical terms, it is obviously easier for action to be taken by one House without submission to the President; but it is crystal clear from the records of the Convention, contemporaneous writings and debates, that the Framers ranked other values higher than efficiency. The records of the Convention and debates in the States preceding ratification underscore the common desire to define and limit the exercise of the newly created federal powers affecting the states and the people. There is unmistakable expression of a determination that legislation by the national Congress be a step-by-step, deliberate and deliberative process.

The choices we discern as having been made in the Constitutional Convention impose burdens on governmental processes that often seem clumsy, inefficient, even unworkable, but those hard choices were consciously made by men who had lived under a form of government that permitted arbitrary governmental acts to go unchecked. There is no support in the Constitution or decisions of this Court for the proposition that the cumbersomeness and delays often encountered in complying with explicit Constitutional standards may be avoided, either by the Congress or by the President. . . .

We hold that the Congressional veto provision in § 244(c)(2) is severable from the Act and that it is unconstitutional.

POWELL, J., concurring in the judgment.

The Court's decision, based on the Presentment Clauses, Art. I, § 7, cls. 2 and 3, apparently will invalidate every use of the legislative veto. The breadth of this holding gives one pause. Congress has included the veto in literally hundreds of statutes, dating back to the 1930s. Congress clearly views this procedure as essential to controlling the delegation of power to administrative agencies. One reasonably may disagree with Congress' assessment of the veto's utility, but the respect due its judgment as a coordinate branch of Government cautions that our holding should be no more extensive than necessary to decide this case. In my view, the case may be decided on a narrower ground. When Congress finds that a particular person does not satisfy the statutory criteria for permanent residence in this country it has assumed a judicial function in violation of the principle of separation of powers. Accordingly, I concur only in the judgment. . . .

Functionally, the [separation of powers] doctrine may be violated in two ways. One branch may interfere impermissibly with the other's performance of its constitutionally assigned function. Alternatively, the doctrine may be violated when one branch assumes a function that more properly is entrusted to another. This case presents the latter situation. . . .

On its face, the House's action appears clearly adjudicatory. The House did not enact a general rule; rather it made its own determination that six specific persons did not comply with certain statutory criteria. It thus undertook the type of decision that traditionally has been left to other branches. Even if the House did not make a *de novo* determination, but simply reviewed the Immigration and Naturalization Service's findings, it still assumed a function ordinarily entrusted to the federal courts. See 5 U.S.C. § 704 (providing generally for judicial review of final agency action). Where, as here, Congress has exercised a power "that cannot possibly be regarded as merely in aid of the legislative function of Congress," the decisions of this Court have held that Congress impermissibly assumed a function that the Constitution entrusted to another branch.

The impropriety of the House's assumption of this function is confirmed by the fact that its action raises the very danger the Framers sought to avoid—the exercise of unchecked power. In deciding whether Chadha deserves to be deported, Congress is not subject to any internal constraints that prevent it from arbitrarily depriving him of the right to remain in this country. Unlike the judiciary or an administrative agency, Congress is not bound by established substantive rules. Nor is it subject to the procedural safeguards, such as the right to counsel and a hearing before an impartial tribunal, that are present when a court or an agency adjudicates individual rights. The only effective constraint on Congress' power is political, but Congress is most accountable politically when it prescribes rules of general applicability. When it decides rights of specific persons, those rights are subject to "the tyranny of a shifting majority."

. . . In my view, when Congress undertook to apply its rules to Chadha, it exceeded the scope of its constitutionally prescribed authority. I would not reach the broader question whether legislative vetoes are invalid under the Presentment Clauses.

WHITE, J., dissenting.

Today the Court not only invalidates § 244(c)(2) of the Immigration and Nationality Act, but also sounds the death knell for nearly 200 other statutory provisions in which Congress has reserved a "legislative veto." For this reason, the Court's decision is of surpassing importance. And it is for this reason that the Court would have been well-advised to decide the case, if possible, on the narrower grounds of separation of powers, leaving for full consideration the constitutionality of other congressional review statutes operating on such varied matters as war powers and agency rulemaking, some of which concern the independent regulatory agencies.

The prominence of the legislative veto mechanism in our contemporary political system and its importance to Congress can hardly be overstated. It has become a central means by which Congress secures the accountability of executive and independent agencies. Without the legislative veto, Congress is faced with a Hobson's choice: either to refrain from delegating the necessary authority, leaving itself with a hopeless task of writing laws with the requisite specificity to cover endless special circumstances across the entire policy landscape, or in the alternative, to abdicate its lawmaking function to the executive branch and independent agencies. To choose the former leaves major national problems unresolved; to opt for the latter risks unaccountable policymaking by those not elected to fill that role. Accordingly, over the past five decades, the legislative veto has been placed in nearly 200 statutes. The device is known in every field of governmental concern: reorganization, budgets, foreign affairs, war powers, and regulation of trade, safety, energy, the environment and the economy. . . .

Even this brief review suffices to demonstrate that the legislative veto is more than "efficient, convenient, and useful." It is an important if not indispensable political invention that allows the President and Congress to resolve major constitutional and policy differences, assures the accountability of independent regulatory agencies, and preserves Congress' control over lawmaking. Perhaps there are other means of accommodation and accountability, but the increasing reliance of Congress upon the legislative veto suggests that the alternatives to which Congress must now turn are not entirely satisfactory.

The history of the legislative veto also makes clear that it has not been a sword with which Congress has struck out to aggrandize itself at the expense of the other branches—the concerns of Madison and Hamilton. Rather, the veto has been a means of defense, a reservation of ultimate authority necessary if Congress is to fulfill its designated role under Article I as the nation's lawmaker. While the President has often objected to particular legislative vetoes, generally those left in the hands of congressional committees, the Executive has more often agreed to legislative review as the price for a broad delegation of authority. To be sure, the President may have preferred unrestricted power, but that could be precisely why Congress thought it essential to retain a check on the exercise of delegated authority. . . .

The Court holds that the disapproval of a suspension of deportation by the resolution of one House of Congress is an exercise of legislative power without compliance with the prerequisites for lawmaking set forth in Art. I of the Constitution. Specifically, the Court maintains that the provisions of § 244(c)(2) are inconsistent with the requirement of bicameral approval, implicit in Art. I, § 1, and the requirement that all bills and resolutions that require the concurrence of both Houses be presented to the President, Art. I, § 7, cl. 2 and 3.

I do not dispute the Court's truismatic exposition of these clauses. There is no question that a bill does not become a law until it is approved by both the House and the Senate, and presented to the President. Similarly, I would not hesitate to strike an action of Congress in the form of a concurrent resolution which constituted an exercise of original lawmaking authority. I agree with the Court that the President's qualified veto power is a critical element in the distribution of powers under the Constitution, widely endorsed among the Framers, and intended to serve the President as a defense against legislative encroachment and to check the "passing of bad laws through haste, inadvertence, or design." The Federalist No. 73, at 458 (A. Hamilton). The records of the Convention reveal that it is the first purpose which figured most prominently but I acknowledge the vitality of the second. *Id.,* at 443. I also agree that the bicameral approval required by Art. I, §§ 1, 7 "was of scarcely less concern to the Framers than was the Presidential veto," and that the need to divide and disperse legislative power figures significantly in our scheme of Government. All of this ... is entirely unexceptionable.

It does not, however, answer the constitutional question before us. The power to exercise a legislative veto is not the power to write new law without bicameral approval or presidential consideration. The veto must be authorized by statute and may only negative what an Executive department or independent agency has proposed. On its face, the legislative veto no more allows one House of Congress to make law than does the presidential veto confer such power upon the President. Accordingly, the Court properly recognizes that it "must establish that the challenged action under § 244(c)(2) is of the kind to which the procedural requirements of Art. I, § 7 apply" and admits that "not every action taken by either House is subject to the bicameralism and presentation requirements of Art. I." ...

It is long-settled that Congress may "exercise its best judgment in the selection of measures, to carry into execution the constitutional powers of the government," and "avail itself of experience, to exercise its reason, and to accommodate its legislation to circumstances." *McCulloch v. Maryland,* 4 Wheat. 316, 415–416, 420 (1819).

The Court heeded this counsel in approving the modern administrative state. The Court's holding today that all legislative-type action must be enacted through the lawmaking process ignores that legislative authority is routinely delegated to the Executive branch, to the independent regulatory agencies, and to private individuals and groups....

This Court's decisions sanctioning such delegations make clear that Article I does not require all action with the effect of legislation to be passed as a law....

If Congress may delegate lawmaking power to independent and executive agencies, it is most difficult to understand Article I as forbidding Congress from also reserving a check on legislative power for itself. Absent the veto, the agencies receiving delegations of legislative or quasi-legislative power may issue regulations having the force of law without bicameral approval and without the President's signature. It is thus not apparent why the reservation of a veto over the exercise of that legislative power must be subject to a more exacting test. In both cases, it is enough that the initial statutory authorizations comply with the Article I requirements.

Nor are there strict limits on the agents that may receive such delegations of legislative authority so that it might be said that the legislature can delegate authority to others but not to itself. While most authority to issue rules and regulations is given to the executive branch and the independent regulatory agencies, statutory delegations to private persons have also passed this Court's scrutiny. . . . [T]he Court's decision today suggests that Congress may place a "veto" power over suspensions of deportation in private hands or in the hands of an independent agency, but is forbidden from reserving such authority for itself. Perhaps this odd result could be justified on other constitutional grounds, such as the separation of powers, but certainly it cannot be defended as consistent with the Court's view of the Article I presentment and bicameralism commands. . . .

The Court also takes no account of perhaps the most relevant consideration: However resolutions of disapproval under § 244(c)(2) are formally characterized, in reality, a departure from the status quo occurs only upon the concurrence of opinion among the House, Senate, and President. Reservations of legislative authority to be exercised by Congress should be upheld if the exercise of such reserved authority is consistent with the distribution of and limits upon legislative power that Article I provides. . . .

The central concern of the presentation and bicameralism requirements of Article I is that when a departure from the legal status quo is undertaken, it is done with the approval of the President and both Houses of Congress—or, in the event of a presidential veto, a two-thirds majority in both Houses. This interest is fully satisfied by the operation of § 244(c)(2). The President's approval is found in the Attorney General's action in recommending to Congress that the deportation order for a given alien be suspended. The House and the Senate indicate their approval of the Executive's action by not passing a resolution of disapproval within the statutory period. Thus, a change in the legal status quo—the deportability of the alien—is consummated only with the approval of each of the three relevant actors. The disagreement of any one of the three maintains the alien's pre-existing status. . . .

It is true that the purpose of separating the authority of government is to prevent unnecessary and dangerous concentration of power in one branch. For that reason, the Framers saw fit to divide and balance the powers of government so that each branch would be checked by the others. Virtually every part of our constitutional system bears the mark of this judgment.

But the history of the separation of powers doctrine is also a history of accommodation and practicality. . . . This is the teaching of *Nixon v. Administrator of General Services*, 433 U.S. 425 (1977), which, in rejecting a separation of powers objection to a law requiring that the Administrator take custody of certain presidential papers, set forth a framework for evaluating such claims:

> [I]n determining whether the Act disrupts the proper balance between the coordinate branches, the proper inquiry focuses on the extent to which it prevents the Executive Branch from accomplishing its constitutionally assigned functions. Only where the potential for disruption is present must we then determine whether that impact is justified by an overriding need to promote objectives within the constitutional authority of Congress.

Section 244(c)(2) survives this test. The legislative veto provision does not "prevent the Executive Branch from accomplishing its constitutionally assigned functions." ...

A legislative check on an inherently executive function, for example that of initiating prosecutions, poses an entirely different question. But the legislative veto device here—and in many other settings—is far from an instance of legislative tyranny over the Executive. It is a necessary check on the unavoidably expanding power of the agencies, both executive and independent, as they engage in exercising authority delegated by Congress.

I regret that I am in disagreement with my colleagues on the fundamental questions that this case presents. But even more I regret the destructive scope of the Court's holding. It reflects a profoundly different conception of the Constitution than that held by the Courts which sanctioned the modern administrative state. Today's decision strikes down in one fell swoop provisions in more laws enacted by Congress than the Court has cumulatively invalidated in its history. I fear it will now be more difficult "to insure that the fundamental policy decisions in our society will be made not by an appointed official but by the body immediately responsible to the people."

[Justice Rehnquist dissented, arguing that the suspension and veto provisions were not severable. Justice White agreed.]

Notes and Questions

1. *"Legislative" acts.* The majority holds that the House's veto of the Attorney General's decision to suspend deportation was "legislative"—and invalid because of a failure to satisfy the bicameralism and presentment provisions of the United States Constitution. Do you agree that the House's action was "legislative"? Why is a decision as to whether Chadha may stay in the United States "legislative" if a house of Congress makes it, but not if the Attorney General does?

2. *Legislative veto versus delegation.* Assuming the House's action in Chadha's case was "legislative," should the House's failure to comply with the bicameralism and presentment safeguards have been fatal to the constitutionality of that action? Notice the dissent's argument that, if Congress may delegate the decision on Chadha's fate to an administrative agency, it should also be able to delegate that decision to a subunit of itself. Does the

majority have a persuasive reply? Why isn't the fact that the Immigration and Naturalization Act was enacted through the Article I, § 7 process a sufficient answer to the constitutional challenge in this case?

3. *Legislative vetoes of agency adjudications.* The statute at issue in *Chadha* was somewhat exceptional. At the time of the Supreme Court's decision, legislative veto schemes were usually regarded as a tool by which legislatures could supervise administrative *rulemaking,* as opposed to agency decisions about individuals such as Mr. Chadha. Indeed, Justice Powell's concurrence focuses on the adjudicative nature of the matter at hand, arguing that the House had no business overturning an agency order of that kind. Was he right? If the procedure was, indeed, unconstitutional for the reasons Powell identifies, would the addition of bicameralism and presentment guarantees have cured the problem?

4. *Extension of Chadha to rulemaking.* The Court obviously intended its *Chadha* opinion to apply to both adjudication and rulemaking situations. Only a few weeks after *Chadha,* without even pausing to write an opinion, the Court affirmed two lower court decisions that had struck down legislative veto provisions in a rulemaking context. In one of these cases, Congress had empowered the Federal Trade Commission to adopt consumer protection rules, subject to a two-house veto provision. In other words, any such rule was to be ineffective if both houses of Congress disapproved it through a concurrent resolution (a resolution that is not submitted to the President for his approval or veto). In 1981 the FTC adopted a rule covering used car warranties, but Congress vetoed it. The court of appeals held that the legislative veto provision was invalid and, as noted, the Supreme Court summarily affirmed. *Consumers Union v. FTC,* 691 F.2d 575 (D.C.Cir.1982), *aff'd sub nom. United States Senate v. FTC,* 463 U.S. 1216 (1983). In a companion case, the Court struck down a one-house legislative veto provision pertaining to FERC gas pricing rules. *Process Gas Consumers Group v. Consumer Energy Council,* 463 U.S. 1216 (1983).

5. *Policy issues.* Justice White's dissent argues that the legislative veto is a desirable political invention that "allows the President and Congress to resolve major constitutional and policy differences, assures accountability of independent regulatory agencies, and preserves Congress' control over lawmaking." Others have portrayed the practical consequences of this "invention" in much less flattering terms. A prominent study of several federal regulatory programs in which agency rules were subject to legislative veto found that the device led to a number of problems:

> [T]he practices observed here violate the ideal of equal access to the rulemaking process.... Those groups having greater resources or prior influence with congressional committees have an additional chance to affect agency action not available to those without such resources or influence....

> [T]he review process was necessarily an attempt by Congress to second-guess the agency without the benefit of all the facts the agency had developed.... As a result of Congress' heavy workload, even the committee members were not normally as familiar with a rule under review as agency personnel, or as a reviewing court would be....

... Most of the effective review occurred at the committee or subcommittee level, often focusing on the concerns of a single chairman or member.... [T]he power of review was really exercised by congressional committees and their staffs, [which] inevitably are bodies of relatively narrow composition compared to Congress as a whole.

... Since the veto provides an easier method for altering agency policy, it reduces the incentive of the oversight committees to sponsor legislation. Because the veto is negative, and because it reduces pressure on committees to report legislation affirmatively resolving policy disputes with agencies, it increases substantially the chance that no policy will be formed by Congress or by the agency.

Harold H. Bruff & Ernest Gellhorn, "Congressional Control of Administrative Regulation: A Study of Legislative Vetoes," 90 Harv.L.Rev. 1369, 1414–18, 1423 (1977). How many of these difficulties were attributable to the veto device itself, and how many would be inherent in any vigorous legislative oversight scheme?

6. *Reality check.* The practical effect of the *Chadha* decision has been less dramatic than the Justices seemed to expect. The legislative veto has not disappeared. Indeed, in the thirteen years following *Chadha,* about four hundred new legislative vetoes have been enacted into law, usually in the form of provisions requiring agencies to obtain the approval of appropriations committees for various actions. Because these measures have made Congress more willing to grant particular kinds of authority, Presidents have acquiesced in them, despite their seeming unconstitutionality. Louis Fisher, CONSTITUTIONAL CONFLICTS BETWEEN CONGRESS AND THE PRESIDENT 156–59 (1996). Even where it does not use the legislative veto itself, Congress has found other, equally effective means of challenging agency actions that it finds undesirable and has remained a vigilant counterforce to the executive. Jessica Korn, THE POWER OF SEPARATION: AMERICAN CONSTITUTIONALISM AND THE MYTH OF THE LEGISLATIVE VETO 116–21 (1996).

7. *State legislative vetoes.* Many state legislatures have adopted legislative veto provisions, often authorizing a single legislative committee to exercise disapproval authority over agency regulations. Courts in at least a dozen states have held such provisions unconstitutional, in line with *Chadha. See, e.g., Missouri Coalition for the Environment v. Joint Committee on Administrative Rules,* 948 S.W.2d 125 (Mo.1997); *State v. A.L.I.V.E. Voluntary,* 606 P.2d 769 (Alaska 1980); Kenneth D. Dean, "Legislative Veto of Administrative Rules in Missouri: A Constitutional Virus," 57 Mo.L.Rev. 1157, 1169–84 (1992) (compiling case law). However, some states, including Connecticut, Iowa, and South Dakota, have explicit provisions for legislative veto in their constitutions. And one state supreme court, relying heavily on Justice White's analysis, has squarely upheld a two-house legislative veto scheme for administrative rules. *Mead v. Arnell,* 791 P.2d 410 (Idaho 1990); *see* Phillip M. Barber, *"Mead v. Arnell:* The Legislative Veto and Too Much Separation of Powers," 27 Idaho L.Rev. 157 (1991).

Professor Devlin has argued that creative methods of facilitating legislative control over administration may be more defensible at the state level than at the federal level:

Congress is in session for the bulk of each year and is endowed with a large and professional staff. It thus enjoys a substantial institutional capacity to gather information on a continuous basis and to deal with emergencies as they arise. In marked contrast, many state legislatures meet for only short and intermittent sessions, and the legislators themselves are often only part-time politicians with other livelihoods that require attention. State legislative staffs are smaller and less regimented than their federal counterparts. [These factors] tend to make state legislators far less able than members of Congress to exercise influence through informal oversight mechanisms, such as hearings or direct contact with administrators.

[Moreover,] states today do not operate in a legal vacuum, but rather are subject to the restraining influence of paramount federal law. This pervasive background of federal law is especially salient in the area of individual rights, providing a "floor" beneath which protection of individual liberties may not fall. In particular, the Federal Bill of Rights and, to a lesser extent, the Federal Civil Rights and Voting Rights statutes, provide a potentially significant degree of protection against anti-democratic or oppressive acts by state authorities.... [And] all of these rights can be vindicated in the federal courts, a system that is by design independent of any control by state authorities.

... [T]he unique position of states as actors within a federal system may, rightly understood, free state courts construing state constitutions to concentrate somewhat less on remote and hypothetical concerns about the prevention of oppression, in order to concentrate more on the other concerns that underlie distribution of powers analysis—concerns such as maintaining efficiency, preserving accountability, and preventing any branch from abdicating its responsibilities.

John Devlin, "Toward a State Constitutional Analysis of Allocation of Powers: Legislators and Legislative Appointees Performing Administrative Functions," 66 Temp.L.Rev. 1205, 1228–35 (1993). Does it follow that states should uphold the legislative veto?

8. *Legislative vetoes in limited contexts.* Perhaps, even if a jurisdiction has held the legislative veto to be constitutionally impermissible as a general matter, it could find that some contexts in which the device has been used are sufficiently distinguishable from the norm that the veto should be upheld there. For example, the New Jersey supreme court unanimously struck down a statute authorizing the legislature to disapprove any agency rule by concurrent resolution (without presentation to the governor). The court said that this system enabled the legislature to interfere with executive functions and allowed it, in effect, to amend or repeal statutes without the governor's participation. *General Assembly v. Byrne,* 448 A.2d 438 (N.J.1982). In a companion case, however, the court upheld a statute that authorized the legislature to veto, by concurrent resolution, any specific building project or lease agreement proposed by the state Building Authority. *Enourato v. New Jersey Building Authority,* 448 A.2d 449 (N.J.1982). The court reasoned that this arrangement ensured that every new state government building would have a legislative imprimatur, so that the legislature would be more likely to continue appropriating money to pay for the building over time. Further-

more, the system had minimal impact on executive functions, because it was limited to disapproval of discrete buildings or leases; and it did not substantially detract from the powers of the chief executive, because the governor, too, had been given power to veto specific projects that he did not favor. Are the court's distinctions valid? *See* Peter L. Strauss, "Was There a Baby in the Bathwater? A Comment on the Supreme Court's Legislative Veto Decision," 1983 Duke L.J. 789, 812–16.

Notice that *Enourato* exemplifies what is sometimes known as a "functionalist" approach to separation of powers problems. It is a relatively flexible approach that asks whether a given structural arrangement intrudes *too far* on the functions of any branch of government, or concentrates *too much* power in any branch. It thus contrasts with the so-called "formalist" approach, under which certain functions are deemed to belong exclusively to particular branches of government, so that *any* misallocation of tasks to the "wrong" branch is deemed unconstitutional. The White and Burger opinions in *Chadha* are regarded, respectively, as examples of functionalist and formalist reasoning. *See* Peter L. Strauss, "Formal and Functional Approaches to Separation-of-Powers Questions—A Foolish Inconsistency?," 72 Cornell L.Rev. 488 (1987). Does the functionalist approach, as exemplified by *Enourato,* open up too much leeway for result-oriented judicial manipulation? Or is the formalist approach too rigid?

9. *Doctrinal evolution.* Post-*Chadha* cases from the Supreme Court have reinforced the constitutional constraints on Congress's ability to control administrative actions, but the Court's doctrinal analysis has changed. Instead of relying squarely on textual provisions, such as the bicameralism and presentment clauses involved in *Chadha,* the Court has used the separation of powers doctrine in its nontextual aspect. *See* § 7.1. Remember how Justice Powell relied on that doctrine in his separate opinion in *Chadha.*

The first of these later cases was *Bowsher v. Synar,* 478 U.S. 714 (1986), more fully discussed in § 7.7.2b N.3. There the Court found implicit in the Constitution a "command ... that Congress play no direct role in the execution of the laws." *Id.* at 736. Therefore, Congress may not remove an officer who is engaged in executive functions, *even if it complies with the bicameralism and presentment clauses of the Constitution.* Even the possibility of such removal disqualifies an officer from wielding executive power. In *Bowsher* itself, this meant that the Comptroller General (who headed a congressional support agency and by statute could have been removed by Congress) could not perform the "executive" task of determining how much spending would have to be cut from the federal budget in order to meet the deficit reduction targets of the Gramm–Rudman–Hollings balanced budget legislation.

In *Metropolitan Washington Airports Authority (MWAA) v. Citizens for the Abatement Of Aircraft Noise, Inc.,* 501 U.S. 252 (1991), a federal statute provided for a regional airport authority (MWAA) that was controlled by a Review Board composed of nine members of Congress. The Board was authorized to veto any decisions made by MWAA. The Court held that the structure of this Board was unconstitutional. In effect, the Board was an agent of Congress. Thus, if the Board's actions were deemed to be legislative,

Chadha required that they be exercised in conformity with the bicameralism and presentment requirements. On the other hand, if the Board's actions were considered to be executive, the separation of powers doctrine as interpreted in *Bowsher* would not permit their exercise at all.

The implication of *MWAA* seems to be that the Court has become less interested in classifying a congressional action as "legislative" or "executive." Instead, the Court will simply ask whether Congress has sought to take legally binding action through a means other than the full enactment process. If it has, the action violates separation of powers principles and is unconstitutional. Is that proposition more persuasive than the reasoning of *Chadha*? Does it tie Congress's hands too tightly?

§ 7.6.2 ALTERNATIVES TO THE LEGISLATIVE VETO

1. *Congressional Review Act.* A variation on the legislative veto, which applies throughout the federal government, was enacted as part of the Contract with America Advancement Act of 1996, P.L. 104–121, Title II, to be codified at 5 U.S.C. § 801–08. Familiarly known as the Congressional Review Act (CRA), this statute requires that virtually all rules of general applicability, adopted by virtually all agencies (including independent agencies), be submitted to Congress and to the General Accounting Office (GAO) before they take effect. The rule must be accompanied by a report containing various items of information about the rule.

The CRA distinguishes between major and non-major rules. A major rule is one determined to be economically significant by OIRA under Executive Order 12866; there are about 75–100 major rules each year. *See* § 5.8. A non-major rule may take effect whenever the agency determines, but a major rule cannot take effect for at least 60 calendar days after it is submitted to Congress (or, in some situations, a longer period).

In case of either major or non-major rules, Congress can veto the rule by enacting a joint resolution of disapproval. A joint resolution is like a statute; it must be approved by both houses and signed by the President (or repassed by two-thirds of each house if the President vetoes it). The statute provides for a fast-track system of congressional consideration of disapproval resolutions, although Congress is not bound by the fast tracking system and can proceed more slowly if it wishes. On the other hand, where Congress does not enact a disapproval resolution, courts are instructed not to draw any inferences about Congress' attitude toward the rule.

The statute's definition of rule is not limited to those rules that can be adopted only after notice and comment rulemaking. The definition includes interpretive rules, policy statements, and a vast array of other documents issued by an agency. As a result of this broad coverage, Congress received over 75 rules per week for review during the first year in which the Act was in effect. Supporters of the law have argued that its wide scope is necessary, because many non-major rules embody questionable decisions; moreover, agencies must not be allowed to shield new policies from congressional scrutiny by burying them in supposedly nonbinding documents such as policy statements. However, a resolution of the American Bar Association, adopted in August 1997, has recommended that the process should apply only to major rules and other limited classes of high-impact rules (although other rules could be included on an individual basis at the request of a congressional committee).

Does the new legislative veto meet the constitutional requirements set forth in *Chadha*? Should its scope be limited in the manner suggested by the ABA? More generally, is the CRA a wise enhancement of legislative oversight of the agencies? Or is it just another costly hurdle that agencies must jump over to adopt rules, and a tempting backdoor route by which special interests may thwart unwelcome rules? *See generally* Daniel Cohen & Peter L. Strauss, "Congressional Review of Agency Regulations," 49 Admin.L.Rev. 95 (1997); Pantelis Michalopoulos, "Holding Back Time to Hold Back Rules," Legal Times of Wash., May 13, 1996, at 25.

2. *Effects of CRA disapproval.* It is likely that rules will frequently go into effect before Congress has decided whether or not to pass a resolution of disapproval. Even the 60 day waiting period provided for major rules will usually not provide enough time for Congress to complete consideration of a resolution of disapproval and have it signed by the President. The CRA provides that, in such cases, if a resolution of disapproval is eventually enacted, the rule must be treated as if it had never taken effect. *Id.* § 801(f). This provision may lead to problems: "Assume that the Commerce Department's National Marine Fisheries Service issues a final rulemaking that, for conservation purposes, requires fishermen to cut a four foot hole in the middle of their nets. If the enactment of a joint resolution after this rule takes effect returns the law to its prior state, while raising questions about the department's continuing authority to regulate nets for conservation reasons, a great many fishermen are going to have to pay the cost of replacing their nets." Cohen & Strauss, *supra,* at 109. Should § 801(f) be dropped from the Act, or is there some other way to fix this problem?

The CRA further provides that, if a rule is disapproved, the agency may not re-issue the rule in substantially the same form unless Congress enacts legislation allowing it to do so. 5 U.S.C. § 801(b)(2). This provision may also create significant difficulties, because it could place an entire rule off limits, even though Congress might object to only a small part of it. Moreover, a resolution of disapproval is a simple "no;" it does not explain to the agency how the rule might be successfully redrafted. Courts will have to decide whether a later rule is sufficiently different from the disapproved earlier rule to pass muster. The ABA resolution mentioned in N.1 proposes that § 801(b)(2) be replaced by a requirement that, when an agency proposes a substitute rule, it must explain how the new rule meets the objections raised against the old rule. Does this alternative go to the opposite extreme, by giving agencies too much latitude to readopt a similar (or even identical) rule to the one that Congress has already repudiated?

3. *Suspensive veto.* May a state adopt a statute that authorizes a legislative committee to suspend an agency rule for a limited period of time? Such a statute was at issue in *Martinez v. Department of Industry, Labor, & Human Relations [DILHR]*, 478 N.W.2d 582, 585–87 (Wis. 1992). It allowed the legislature's Joint Committee for Review of Administrative Rules (JCRAR) to suspend a rule for any of the following reasons: (1) absence of statutory authority; (2) an emergency relating to public health, safety or welfare; (3) failure to comply with legislative intent; (4) conflict with state law; (5) changed circumstances; or (6) arbitrariness and capriciousness, or imposition of an undue hardship. The committee was required, immediately after imposing any suspensive action, to introduce a bill in each house to repeal the suspended rule. If neither of those bills was enacted as a law, the rule would go into effect, and the committee could not suspend it again.

In *Martinez,* DILHR adopted a regulation allowing employers to pay a "sub-minimum wage" to short-term workers. The JCRAR suspended it for failing to comply with statutory intent and imposing an undue hardship on workers. However, DILHR regarded the suspension as unconstitutional and instructed employers that they could pay the sub-minimum wage anyway. Eventually DILHR raised the wage level, but twelve migrant workers, who had been paid at the lower rate, filed suit against the agency. They claimed that the JCRAR suspension had been lawful and that DILHR should therefore require employers to pay back wages to any employee who had been subjected to the sub-minimum wage that the agency had illegally prescribed.

In rejecting this challenge, the Wisconsin Supreme Court noted that it interpreted the separation of powers principles of the Wisconsin state constitution liberally, because those principles are only implied, unlike the constitutions of many other states, which contain express separation of powers provisions. Consequently, in Wisconsin, a sharing of powers between the legislative and executive branches is not inappropriate unless it demonstrably disturbs "the balance between the three branches of government," interferes with "their respective independence and integrity," or causes a "concentration of unchecked power in the hands of any one branch." The court concluded that the JCRAR authority to suspend an agency rule did not cause any of these evils. The legislative and executive branches "share inherent interests in the legislative creation and oversight of administrative agencies," so that this was not a situation where "one branch interferes with a constitutionally guaranteed 'exclusive zone' of authority vested in another branch." Furthermore, the court said, "legislative power may be delegated . . . so long as adequate standards for conducting the allocated power are in place," and the statute vesting the JCRAR with authority to suspend agency rules contained "sufficient procedural safeguards . . . to prevent unauthorized decisions by the committee."

The court also said that the JCRAR temporary suspensive power did not violate the bicameralism or presentment provisions of the state constitution, because "only the formal bicameral enactment process coupled with executive action can make permanent a rule suspension." The court was convinced that the "full involvement of both houses of the legislature and the governor are critical elements [of the statutory scheme] and these elements distinguish Wisconsin from the [otherwise similar] statutory schemes" found to be unconstitutional in other states. It stressed that this statute was "carefully designed so that the people of this state, through their elected representatives, will continue to exercise a significant check on the activities of nonelected bureaucrats ... [and that it] provides a legislative check ... which prevents potential agency overreaching."

Another state supreme court has endorsed a suspensive veto in dictum, *Opinion of the Justices,* 431 A.2d 783, 789 (N.H.1981), but a third has held such a statute unconstitutional. *Legislative Research Commission v. Brown,* 664 S.W.2d 907, 917–19 (Ky.1984). *See also* Philip P. Frickey, "The Constitutionality of Legislative Committee Suspension of Administrative Rules: The Case of Minnesota," 70 Minn.L.Rev. 1237 (1986) (arguing against the validity of Minnesota's suspensive veto, which has since been repealed). Was *Martinez* correctly decided?

4. *Grounds for objection.* Notice that the suspensive veto statute in *Martinez* provided a limited list of grounds on which the legislative committee was authorized to object to an agency rule. This is a fairly common feature among legislative review statutes of various kinds. Some provide that a veto or suspension is permitted only if the review committee believes that a rule is unauthorized by statute. *See* Idaho Code § 67–5218. Section 3–204(d) of the 1981 MSAPA, discussed more fully in the next note, instructs the legislature's review committee to object to a rule only if it is beyond the agency's procedural or substantive authority. In other states, however, the grounds for objection are essentially unrestricted. *See* N.H. Rev.Stat.Ann. § 541–A:13(IV)(c) (committee may object to rule as being not "in the public interest").

Supporting the MSAPA approach, Bonfield argues that the ARRC should not be authorized to object to a rule on pure policy grounds, because "such a committee power would divest the agencies of the very discretion that they were authorized to exercise by statute. It would also deny the public the benefit of the agencies' expertise on policy matters within their lawful authority. Finally, a power of this kind would permit the administrative rules review committee to impugn otherwise legal action taken by agencies pursuant to authorizations by the legislature as a whole, and would thereby allow that committee to undercut actions of its principal." *See* Arthur Earl Bonfield, STATE ADMINISTRATIVE RULE MAKING 521 (1986). Another scholar agrees, adding that pure policy review would give too much influence to well-connected interest groups. Carl A. Auerbach, "Bonfield on State Administrative Rulemaking: A Critique," 71 Minn.L.Rev. 543, 568 (1987).

The effectiveness of such limits has been questioned. " 'It would doubtless be unrealistic to assume that a group of state legislators would be content to make judgments about the *legal* power of administrative agencies, and ignore the *political* implications of administrative policies as these are revealed in actual application in specific instances. Legislative review of administrative rule-making is almost certain, in the United States, to be *political* review.' " *State ex rel. Barker v. Manchin,* 279 S.E.2d 622, 632 n. 5 (W.Va.1981) (quoting political scientist Glendon Schubert). Yet, even assuming that legislators' compliance with statutory grounds for objections will be imperfect, are such limitations desirable in principle, and, therefore, perhaps worth a try? Which issue is a legislator better qualified to address: the consistency of a rule with statutory intent, or the political acceptability of the rule? *See* Harold H. Bruff & Ernest Gellhorn, "Congressional Control of Administrative Regulation: A Study of Legislative Vetoes," 90 Harv.L.Rev. 1369, 1429–30 (1977).

Finally, if a statute does prescribe specific grounds on which the review committee may intervene, should the courts entertain allegations that the committee has overstepped those limits? In *Mead v. Arnell,* 791 P.2d 410 (Idaho 1990), after upholding the constitutionality of the legislative veto, the court held that a *particular* use of the device had been unlawful. The veto was supposed to be employed only if the challenged rule exceeded the agency's statutory authority; but the legislature had not expressly found this to be the case, and, indeed, had apparently objected to the rule because of perceived procedural and factual errors in the agency's decision. Such judicial review of the merits of a legislative veto has, however, been extremely rare.

5. *Burden-shifting.* Section 3–204(d) of the 1981 MSAPA contains a provision for legislative review of agency rules. This provision, a compromise between the views of proponents and opponents of the legislative veto, assigns a reviewing role to an "administrative rules review committee" (ARRC), consisting of three members from each of the two houses of the legislature (§ 3–203). The committee may object to all or a portion of a rule that it considers to be "beyond the procedural or substantive authority delegated to the adopting agency." The committee must file a concise statement of its reasons for objecting, and the agency may then respond in writing. But if the committee does not withdraw its objection, the burden will be on the agency to establish the validity of the rule in any subsequent judicial review proceedings. (Normally, the challenger bears the burden of showing that the rule is *not* valid. § 5–116(a)(1).) Among states that have provisions similar to § 3–204(d) are Iowa, Minnesota, Montana, New Hampshire, North Dakota, and Vermont.

The official Comment to § 3–204(d) suggests that this device is not a legislative veto because it only authorizes the ARRC to "alter one aspect of the procedure by which *the legality of the rule will be finally determined by the courts.*" In light of the fact that legislatures regularly allocate the burden of persuasion in civil litigation, the Comment argues that the shift in the burden of persuasion authorized by that provision is legitimate. Furthermore, it is "logical to shift to the agency the burden of demonstrating the validity of a rule in subsequent litigation when a more politically accountable and independent body [like the ARRC] objects thereto." The Comment also argues that the mere existence of § 3–204(d) will make agencies act more responsibly than otherwise, and that the actual use of that provision by the ARRC will induce agencies to withdraw or modify rules of "doubtful or clear illegality," thereby saving members of the public "the cost of complying with those rules or contesting them in the courts." Finally, the shift in burden of persuasion that occurs after the filing of an objection under this provision "will result in the invalidation of many rules of doubtful legality." For a fuller explication of the case for § 3–204(d), see Bonfield, *supra,* at § 8.3.3.

Are the above arguments for § 3–204(d) persuasive? Is it constitutional? Desirable?

6. *Rulemaking as proposing.* Until recently, the West Virginia APA provided that agencies had no power to promulgate rules at all; rather, their rules had the status of *proposals,* which would not take effect unless the legislature affirmatively adopted them (adhering to bicameralism and presentment requirements). In a federal context, eminent scholars have given serious attention to this structure for legislative involvement in the rulemaking process. *See* Stephen Breyer, "The Legislative Veto After *Chadha,*" 72 Geo.L.J. 785 (1984) (outlining how such a system could be constructed, but taking no position on its desirability): Paul R. Verkuil, "Comment: Rulemaking Ossification—A Modest Proposal," 47 Admin.L.Rev. 453, 457–58 (1995) (proposing a system of this kind for "major" rules only). Nevertheless, West Virginia's highest court held the state's APA provision unconstitutional. *State ex rel. Meadows v. Hechler,* 462 S.E.2d 586 (W.Va.1995). Is this case correct? After all, the legislature doesn't have to empower an agency to use rulemaking to address a given regulatory problem. *See* § 5.1 N.2. Why is an APA provision as described above materially different? Would it be valid if it provided that a rule cannot go into effect unless approved by a concurrent (two-house) resolution, without presentment to the governor? *See Blank v. Department of Corrections,* 564 N.W.2d 130 (Mich.App.1997) (no).

§ 7.6.3   OTHER LEGISLATIVE CONTROLS

Aside from amendment or repeal of substantive legislation and the various forms of legislative veto, what other mechanisms are available to Congress or a state legislature to control administrative agencies?

a. *Oversight committees.* In recent decades, most states have adopted formal continuing legislative oversight mechanisms to review the legality and desirability of agency rules. *See generally* Arthur Earl Bonfield, STATE ADMINISTRATIVE RULE MAKING § 8.3.1 (1986); L. Harold Levinson, "Legislative and Executive Veto of Rules of Administrative Agencies: Models and Alternatives," 24 Wm. & Mary L.Rev. 79 (1982). These oversight functions are normally performed by special standing joint legislative committees. *See, e.g.,* 1981 MSAPA §§ 3–203 to–204, establishing an Administrative Rules Review Committee (ARRC) to review state agency rules. Committees of this kind are typically authorized to hold public hearings on proposed or adopted agency rules, to give advice to agencies concerning such rules, and to submit bills to the legislature to overcome by statute rules that the agency declines to withdraw on its own.

In Congress, responsibility of oversight of federal agencies is much more diffused. The *authorization* committees of Congress are responsible for considering legislation in a particular area—such as commerce or energy or labor. These committees also supervise the agencies that implement previously enacted legislation in those particular areas. In addition, the Government Affairs Committees of both houses of Congress conduct oversight over a variety of government business, including many issues that involve administrative agencies.

Moreover, an agency's budget request is annually scrutinized by the appropriations committees of each house. Specialized subcommittees of the appropriations committees are expert in the work of each agency. Their investigations of the manner in which the agency is spending money can touch upon virtually everything the agency does. Finally, senatorial hearings to consider the confirmation of politically appointed personnel (such as agency heads) often focus on policy issues and involve scrutiny of an agency's performance. This would be especially likely to occur if the individual is seeking reappointment to the job or is being promoted from the staff level to the agency head level.

b. *Investigations and hearings.* The many standing committees of Congress and state legislatures constantly investigate the manner in which agencies spend money as well as discharge their responsibilities. Thus they hold hearings, request agencies to furnish written reports or studies, and write committee reports. Inadequate legislative staffing and less professionalism in some state legislatures appears to make this form of oversight less effective in some states than at the federal level.

Some legislative committee hearings draw the attention of print or broadcast media and generate a great deal of publicity. At times, the proceedings become quite adversary, and committee members seem more interested in scoring political points than in obtaining information. Preparing for legislative committee hearings, and actually testifying, often consumes a large fraction of the time of an agency head. *See* Richard J. Lazarus, "The Neglected Question of Congressional Oversight of EPA: *Quis Custodiet Ipsos Custodes* (Who Shall Watch the Watchers Themselves)?," 54 L. & Contemp.Prob. 205 (1991).

In connection with a legislative investigation, an agency may be requested to furnish information or documents; if these are not forthcoming, the legislative committee or investigative agency sometimes exercises its subpoena power to obtain documents that the agency prefers not to disclose. The extent to which an agency can withhold documents from the legislature, upon a claim of executive privilege, remains unsettled, in part because most of these conflicts are resolved through negotiation. *See generally* Neal Devins, "Congressional–Executive Information Disputes: A Modest Proposal—Do Nothing," 48 Admin.L.Rev. 109 (1996); Peter M. Shane, "Legal Disagreement and Negotiation in a Government of Laws: The Case of Executive Privilege Claims Against Congress," 71 Minn.L.Rev. 461 (1987).

In addition to committee investigations, legislative investigative agencies may be employed for oversight purposes. The federal General Accounting Office (GAO), headed by the Comptroller General, is an example of such a legislative agency. The GAO is concerned primarily with the efficiency of federal government operation and with the manner in which government funds are used. Much of its time is spent in studying executive branch activities and evaluating particular programs. The GAO can launch an investigation on its own initiative or at the request of a member of Congress or a committee.

A few states have also created an office of ombudsman that is authorized to receive and investigate citizen complaints about any state agency or aspect of the state administrative process, and to make a report and recommendation to the legislature and/or governor on such complaints. The office of ombudsman may have various names, such as Ombudsman, Citizens' Aide, or Public Counsel, and is usually located in the legislative branch. *See, e.g.,* Hawaii Rev.Stat. § 96–2; Iowa Code ch. 601G; Neb.Rev.Stat. §§ 81–8, 240–254. The most potent oversight weapon of this body is usually publicity for its investigations and recommendations. Proposals for an congressional office of constituent assistance have been offered over the years, but most members of Congress believe that contacts made by their own offices (discussed below) are an adequate or even superior alternative. Thus, ombudsman offices at the federal level tend to be situated within the agencies themselves. *See* David R. Anderson & Diane M. Stockton, "Federal Ombudsmen: An Underused Resource," 5 Admin.L.J. 275 (1991).

c. *Funding measures.* Congress and state legislatures appropriate funds for every unit of government—usually every year, although in some states it occurs every other year. Consequently, the appropriations mechanism provides a convenient way to achieve legislative objectives without altering the statutes which furnish authority to agencies. For example, measures appropriating money to an agency sometimes contain provisions cutting the amount spent on one agency function while increasing another—thus altering an agency's priorities. Similarly, an activity can be deliberately underfunded, thus preventing effective enforcement. Indeed, appropriation measures sometimes bar an agency from spending any money in carrying out a particular program or enforcing a particular regulation. *See* Neal Devins, "Regulation of Government Agencies Through Limitation Riders," 1987 Duke L.J. 456.

Often, legislative action in the appropriation process falls short of the enactment of binding legislation. Instead, a committee report (or even a statement in committee or on the floor) will contain an admonition to the agency about how it should conduct its business. While not binding, such statements are likely to influence the persons responsible for spending the appropriated funds. *See* Jessica Korn, THE POWER OF SEPARATION: AMERICAN CONSTITUTIONALISM AND THE MYTH OF THE LEGISLATIVE VETO 40 (1996).

d. *Direct contacts.* Individual members of Congress and state legislatures consider that their responsibilities include making direct contacts with units of government that are causing problems for their constituents. *See generally* John R. Johannes, TO SERVE THE PEOPLE: CONGRESS AND CONSTITUENCY SERVICE (1984); Ronald M. Levin, "Congressional Ethics and Constituent Advocacy in an Age of Mistrust," 95 Mich.L.Rev. 1, 16–31 (1996). For example, at the federal level, legislative staff members frequently contact the Department of Veterans Affairs or the Social Security Administration on behalf of constituents. For the most part, these contacts are relatively harmless requests by staff for "status reports" about pending matters, or attempts to cut through red tape for a constituent who is inexperienced in dealing with bureaucracy. Responding to such requests, however, can consume a considerable portion of agency resources. When these contacts turn into efforts to influence the outcome of a pending matter, such as an adjudication or a grantmaking decision, serious questions of propriety can arise, especially if the participation is off-the-record. *See* § 3.2.5.

§ 7.7 EXECUTIVE CONTROL: PERSONNEL DECISIONS

Presidents and governors indirectly control agency action by exercising their authority to appoint and discharge officials who execute the laws. This section considers the scope of this authority, as well as the extent to which Congress or a state legislature may limit, or even share in, the exercise of appointment and removal powers.

§ 7.7.1 APPOINTMENT OF OFFICERS

BUCKLEY v. VALEO
424 U.S. 1 (1976).

[Under legislation adopted in 1974, the Federal Election Commission] consists of eight members. The Secretary of the Senate and the Clerk of the House of Representatives are *ex officio* members of the Commission without the right to vote. Two members are appointed by the President pro tempore of the Senate "upon the recommendations of the majority leader of the Senate and the minority leader of the Senate." Two more are to be appointed by the Speaker of the House of Representatives, likewise upon the recommendations of its respective majority and minority leaders. The remaining two members are appointed by the President. . . .

Appellants urge that since Congress has given the Commission wide-ranging rulemaking and enforcement powers with respect to the substantive provisions of the Act, Congress is precluded under the principle of separation of powers from vesting in itself the authority to appoint those who will exercise such authority. Their argument is based on the language of Art. II, § 2, cl. 2, of the Constitution, which provides in pertinent part as follows:

> [The President] shall nominate, and by and with the Advice and Consent of the Senate, shall appoint ... all other Officers of the United States, whose Appointments are not herein otherwise provided for, and which shall be established by Law: but the Congress may by Law vest the Appointment of such inferior Officers, as they think proper, in the President alone, in the Courts of Law, or in the Heads of Departments."

... We think ... that any appointee exercising significant authority pursuant to the laws of the United States is an "Officer of the United States," and must, therefore, be appointed in the manner prescribed by § 2, cl. 2, of that Article.... [S]urely the Commissioners before us are at the very least such "inferior Officers" within the meaning of that Clause.[162] ... While the second part of the Clause authorizes Congress to vest the appointment of the officers described in that part in "the Courts of Law, or in the Heads of Departments," neither the Speaker of the House nor the President *pro tempore* of the Senate comes within this language.

The phrase "Heads of Departments," used as it is in conjunction with the phrase "Courts of Law," suggests that the Departments referred to are themselves in the Executive Branch or at least have some connection with that branch. While the Clause expressly authorizes Congress to vest the appointment of certain officers in the "Courts of Law," the absence of similar language to include Congress must mean that neither Congress nor its officers were included within the language "Heads of Departments" in this part of cl. 2.

Thus with respect to four of the six voting members of the Commission, neither the President, the head of any department, nor the Judiciary has any voice in their selection....

We are ... told by appellees and amici that Congress had good reason for not vesting in a Commission composed wholly of Presidential appointees the authority to administer the Act, since the administration of the Act would undoubtedly have a bearing on any incumbent President's campaign for re-election. While one cannot dispute the basis for this sentiment as a practical matter, it would seem that those who sought to challenge incumbent Congressmen might have equally good reason to fear a Commission which was unduly responsive to Members of Congress whom they were seeking to unseat. But such fears, however

---

162. "Officers of the United States" does not include all employees of the United States, but there is no claim made that the Commissioners are employees of the United States rather than officers. Employees are lesser functionaries subordinate to officers of the United States....

rational, do not by themselves warrant a distortion of the Framers' work.

Appellee Commission and amici finally contend ... that whatever shortcomings the provisions for the appointment of members of the Commission might have under Art. II, Congress had ample authority under the Necessary and Proper Clause of Art. I to effectuate this result. We do not agree.... Congress could not, merely because it concluded that such a measure was "necessary and proper" to the discharge of its substantive legislative authority, pass a bill of attainder or ex post facto law contrary to the prohibitions contained in § 9 of Art. I. No more may it vest in itself, or in its officers, the authority to appoint officers of the United States when the Appointments Clause by clear implication prohibits it from doing so.

... [T]he Commission's powers fall generally into three categories: functions relating to the flow of necessary information—receipt, dissemination, and investigation; functions with respect to the Commission's task of fleshing out the statute—rulemaking and advisory opinions; and functions necessary to ensure compliance with the statute and rules—informal procedures, administrative determinations and hearings, and civil suits.

Insofar as the powers confided in the Commission are essentially of an investigative and informative nature, falling in the same general category as those powers which Congress might delegate to one of its own committees, there can be no question that the Commission as presently constituted may exercise them....

But when we go beyond this type of authority to the more substantial powers exercised by the Commission, we reach a different result. The Commission's enforcement power, exemplified by its discretionary power to seek judicial relief, is authority that cannot possibly be regarded as merely in aid of the legislative function of Congress. A lawsuit is the ultimate remedy for a breach of the law, and it is to the President, and not to the Congress, that the Constitution entrusts the responsibility to "take Care that the Laws be faithfully executed." Art. II, § 3.

We hold that these provisions of the Act, vesting in the Commission primary responsibility for conducting civil litigation in the courts of the United States for vindicating public rights, violate Art. II, § 2, cl. 2, of the Constitution. Such functions may be discharged only by persons who are "Officers of the United States" within the language of that section.

All aspects of the Act are brought within the Commission's broad administrative powers: rulemaking, advisory opinions, and determinations of eligibility for funds and even for federal elective office itself. These functions, exercised free from day-to-day supervision of either Congress or the Executive Branch, are more legislative and judicial in nature than are the Commission's enforcement powers, and are of kinds usually performed by independent regulatory agencies or by some department in the Executive Branch under the direction of an Act of Congress. Congress viewed these broad powers as essential to effective and impartial administration of the entire substantive framework of the Act. Yet each of these functions also represents the performance of a significant governmental duty exercised pursuant to a public law. While the President may not insist that such functions be delegated to an appointee of his removable at will, *Humphrey's Executor v. United States,* 295 U.S. 602 (1935), none of them operates merely in aid of congressional authority to legislate or is sufficiently removed from the administration and enforcement of public law to allow it to be performed by the present Commission. These administrative functions may therefore be exercised only by persons who are "Officers of the United States."

Notes and Questions

1. *Buckley.* The Federal Election Commission makes numerous decisions that can profoundly affect the competition between the two major political parties in the United States. Isn't it extreme to read the Constitution as requiring that *all* members of the Commission must be chosen by the President—who of course will always be a Republican or a Democrat? Should the Court have read the Necessary and Proper Clause more generously, to avoid this anomaly?

2. *Principal versus inferior officers.* Notice the Court's distinction in *Buckley* between principal officers, who must be selected by the President with the advice and consent of the Senate, and inferior officers, whom Congress may allow to be appointed by "the President alone, [by] the Courts of Law, or [by] the Heads of Departments." The Court has had difficulty distinguishing between the two categories.

In *Morrison v. Olson,* 487 U.S. 654 (1988), the Court upheld the statute that allows a special court to appoint an independent counsel to investigate and prosecute possible violations of federal law by high ranking executive officials. Chief Justice Rehnquist, writing for seven Justices, admitted that the line between principal and inferior officers was far from clear. Nevertheless, the Court said, the independent counsel was clearly an inferior officer. She was subject to removal by a higher executive branch officer, even though she possessed a degree of independent discretion in the exercise of the powers of her office. Further, her duties were limited to the investigation of certain federal crimes; she could only act within the scope of the jurisdiction conferred by the special court; and her position was temporary, in that she was "appointed essentially to accomplish a specific task, and when that task is over the office is terminated." *Id.* at 671–72.

Justice Scalia, in dissent, contended that the independent counsel was not an inferior officer and, therefore, had to be appointed by the President. *Id.* at 715–23. He denied that the job was as limited in power or duration as the majority maintained. More fundamentally, he argued that the status of being an inferior officer should depend primarily on whether one is subordinate to some other official. Because the independent counsel could be removed under only very limited circumstances, she was "*independent* of, not *subordinate* to, the President and the Attorney General," according to Scalia. Who had the better of this argument?

Moving beyond this point of disagreement with the dissent, the majority opinion addressed the appellees' contention that the Appointments Clause should not be construed to allow *judicial* officials to appoint a prosecutor, whose functions were basically *executive*. *Id.* at 673–77. Quoting from an earlier case, the Court acknowledged that " 'incongruous' interbranch appointments" were prohibited by the Constitution. But there was nothing incongruous about the appointment of the independent counsel by a special court, because judicial appointments of prosecutors had a long history. "Indeed, in light of judicial experience with prosecutors in criminal cases, it could be said that courts are especially well qualified to appoint prosecutors. This is not a case in which judges are given power to appoint an officer in an area in which they have no special knowledge or expertise, as in, for example, a statute authorizing the courts to appoint officials in the Department of Agriculture or the Federal Energy Regulatory Commission." *Id.* at 676 n.13. Besides, the Court added, "Congress of course was concerned when it created the office of independent counsel with the conflicts of interest that could arise in situations when the Executive Branch is called upon to investigate its own high-ranking officers. If it were to remove the appointing authority from the Executive Branch, the most logical place to put it was in the Judicial Branch." *Id.* at 677. (Other aspects of *Morrison* are addressed in § 7.7.2.)

3. *More inferiority complexities.* In *Edmond v. United States,* 117 S.Ct. 1573 (1997), the Court held that members of the Coast Guard Court of Criminal Appeals, a tribunal that hears appeals in court-martial cases, were inferior rather than principal officers. Thus, they could be appointed by the Secretary of Transportation. Justice Scalia, writing for the Court, observed that some of the factors relied on in *Morrison* were absent here, because these military judges did not have the kind of case-specific jurisdiction or limited tenure that an independent counsel had. Nevertheless:

> Generally speaking, the term 'inferior officer' connotes a relationship with some higher ranking officer or officers below the President: whether one is an 'inferior' officer depends on whether he has a superior.... [I]n the context of a clause designed to preserve political accountability relative to important government assignments, we think it evident that 'inferior officers' are officers whose work is directed and supervised at some level by others who were appointed by presidential nomination with the advice and consent of the Senate.

Id. at 1580–81. That test was satisfied in this instance, because the Judge Advocate General (a subordinate of the Secretary of Transportation) exercised administrative oversight over the Coast Guard court and had authority to remove its judges without cause; moreover, decisions of the Coast Guard court were reviewable on the merits by the Court of Appeals for the Armed Forces. Justice Souter concurred separately, arguing that, although the supervision under which the Coast Guard judges worked did not conclusively show that they were "inferior officers," the issue was close enough to justify the Court's deferring to the judgment of the political branches.

In light of the holding in *Edmond,* could Congress authorize someone other than the President, such as the Chief Justice, to appoint United States district judges? It has been argued that this would be constitutional. *See*

Burke Shartel, "Federal Judges—Appointment, Supervision, and Removal—Some Possibilities Under the Constitution," 28 Mich.L.Rev. 485 (1930). *But see Edmond,* 117 S.Ct. at 1582–83 (Souter, J., concurring).

4. *Courts of law and department heads.* The ground rules for determining who can appoint "inferior officers" remain somewhat indeterminate. In *Freytag v. Commissioner,* 501 U.S. 868 (1991), a statute created the Tax Court as an independent Article I legislative court with both regular judges and special trial judges. The statute provided that the special trial judges (comparable to magistrate judges in the Article III district courts) would be appointed by the chief judge of the court. The taxpayers in *Freytag* contended that this appointment scheme was inconsistent with the requirements of the Constitution. The Supreme Court unanimously disagreed, but the Justices were sharply divided as to their reasons for this conclusion.

In an opinion for five members of the Court, Justice Blackmun asserted that the Tax Court exercised judicial power and thus was one of the "Courts of Law" mentioned in the Appointments Clause. At the same time, he rejected the argument that the Tax Court could be considered a "department" within the meaning of the clause, because that term referred only to "executive divisions like the Cabinet-level departments." Blackmun refused to read the term "department" broadly, because the Appointments Clause "reflects our Framers' conclusion that widely distributed appointment power subverts democratic government. Given the inexorable presence of the administrative state, a holding that every organ in the Executive Branch is a department would multiply indefinitely the number of actors eligible to appoint." *Id.* at 885.

The Court added, however, that the term "Department" might not be "strictly limit[ed]" to Cabinet departments: "We do not address here any question involving an appointment of an inferior officer by the head of one of the principal agencies, such as the Federal Trade Commission, the Securities Exchange Commission, the Federal Energy Regulatory Commission, the Central Intelligence Agency, or the Federal Reserve Bank of St. Louis." *Id.* at 887 n.4.

Four concurring Justices, in an opinion by Justice Scalia, rejected the basis for the majority's holding, noting that the Appointments Clause "refers to '*the* Courts of Law.' . . . The definite article 'the' obviously narrows the class of eligible 'Courts of Law' to those Courts of Law envisioned by the Constitution. Those are Article III courts, and the Tax Court is not one of them." *Id.* at 902 (concurrence). However, Scalia maintained that the appointment of special trial judges was valid "because the Tax Court is a 'Department' and the Chief Judge is its head." *Id.* at 901. He saw no reason to limit the phrase 'the Heads of Departments' in the Appointments Clause to Cabinet officials. *Id.* at 915–22. According to Scalia, the Clause was not intended to prevent diffusion of appointment authority within the executive branch, as the majority supposed; instead, its purpose was to keep appointments out of the hands of Congress, so that legislators could not appoint their friends to various government jobs. *Id.* at 904. Which analysis is more persuasive, the majority's or the concurrence's?

5. *Employees.* Notice footnote 162 of *Buckley,* which explains that mere "employees" of an agency (who do not exercise "significant authority pursu-

ant to the laws of the United States") need not be hired pursuant to the Appointments Clause at all. Obviously, neither the President, the courts, nor the department heads should have to be involved in hiring every desk clerk or field inspector who works for the federal government. Could Congress appoint such civil servants itself? Perhaps not—the Appointments Clause would not be an obstacle, but the separation of powers doctrine might be. *See Springer v. Government of Philippine Islands,* 277 U.S. 189, 202 (1928) (construing the Philippine Organic Act, assumed to be based on the U.S. Constitution): "Legislative power, as distinguished from executive power, is the authority to make laws, but not to enforce them or appoint the agents charged with the duty of such enforcement. The latter are executive functions." Do you think this case would be followed today?

6. *State appointments.* State governors appoint most executive branch officers, some with and some without legislative confirmation. Other state executive branch officials are elected by the voters rather than appointed. In some instances, the governor must share the appointment power with the legislature or other governmental officials. *See* 31 Council of State Governments, THE BOOK OF THE STATES 35–39 (1996–97).

These differences among states are partly a result of the wide variety of state constitutional provisions on this subject. "Some [state constitutions] vest a general power to make administrative appointments in the governor ..., while others leave it to the legislature to decide the method by which officials will be appointed—including, in some cases, reserving that power to itself.... [I]n other states the text is, on its face, remarkably unclear...." John Devlin, "Toward a State Constitutional Analysis of Allocation of Powers: Legislators and Legislative Appointees Performing Administrative Functions," 66 Temp.L.Rev. 1205, 1237–38 (1993). (Devlin's article is an invaluable analysis of numerous state-level appointments issues.)

In states in which the constitution does not expressly limit the appointment power to the governor, the courts have resorted to general separation of powers principles in order to sort out the respective prerogatives of the governmental branches. *See id.* at 1242–50. Some state courts have ruled that appointments are inherently executive and, therefore, may only be made by the governor. *See, e.g., Opinion of the Justices,* 309 N.E.2d 476 (Mass.1974) (holding that neither the legislature nor the judiciary could constitutionally appoint members of a commission with responsibility for setting government-wide policies for electronic data transmissions and telecommunications). Prominent in these cases is the suggestion that, if powers are to remain *separated,* officials who enact the laws should play no role in selecting the personnel who will implement them.

In *Parcell v. State,* 620 P.2d 834 (Kan.1980), however, the court adopted a more flexible approach. The facts in *Parcell* were very similar to those of *Buckley.* Six members of the state Governmental Ethics Commission were appointed by legislative party leaders and five by the governor, although the governor was entitled to appoint its chairperson. The commission's membership had to be balanced with regard to political party affiliation. The commission had rulemaking and report-collecting responsibilities, but could not initiate enforcement actions on its own. Parcell, a political candidate who was under investigation for failing to file campaign reports with the commission, challenged the constitutionality of the agency's composition.

The court endorsed a balancing test consisting of four criteria: (1) the nature of the powers being exercised by the agency; (2) the degree of control being exercised by the legislature; (3) whether the legislature's objective was to cooperate with the executive branch, as opposed to establishing its superiority in an executive domain; and (4) the practical results of this blending of legislative and executive powers. *Id.* at 836. Applying this standard, the court upheld the commission's structure, calling it "a cooperative venture rather than the usurpation of power by the legislative branch from the executive branch." The goal of the underlying legislation was to increase public trust in elected officials, and the appointment scheme " 'gives the Commission needed independence should it be called upon to investigate those officials who appointed some of its members.' " *Id.* at 837.

The court in *State Board of Ethics for Elected Officials v. Green,* 566 So.2d 623 (La.1990), reached a similar result, although the board in that case did have the responsibility for filing suit against suspected violators of the campaign finance disclosure laws. Two members of this board were appointed by the Senate, two by the House, and the fifth had to be a retired or former judge appointed by the governor. The court upheld the scheme because "the appointees are not subject to such significant legislative control that the Legislature can be deemed to be performing executive functions." (Would this structure satisfy the *Parcell* test?)

But a third state supreme court refused to follow *Parcell* and *Green,* noting that its case law has "rejected the notion of a 'blending' of powers in favor of a more strict separation of powers." *Spradlin v. Arkansas Ethics Commission,* 858 S.W.2d 684 (Ark.1993). One member of the election commission had to be appointed by the chief justice of the state. The court held this scheme unconstitutional, because the commission "is not related to the administration of justice and is not part of the judicial department of government." The commission did not act in a judicial capacity, because it could not enter binding orders, as a court does; it could only issue warnings or report findings to law enforcement authorities. Was the case correctly decided?

7. *Legislators as appointees.* Constitutional limits on legislatures' ability to place their own members in administrative positions tend to be particularly strict. The Incompatibility Clause of the federal Constitution provides: "No Senator or Representative shall, during the Time for which he was elected, be appointed to any civil Office under the Authority of the United States.... ," art. I, § 6, cl.2. Most state constitutions contain similar clauses, although they vary in their stringency. *See* Devlin, *supra,* at 1239–40.

Even when an incompatibility clause does not apply, many state court decisions rely on the separation of powers doctrine to bar legislators from holding executive branch jobs. For example, in *State ex rel. Wallace v. Bone,* 286 S.E.2d 79 (N.C.1982), the North Carolina Supreme Court held unconstitutional a state statute providing that two members of the State Environmental Management Commission would be appointed by the Speaker of the House from among its membership and two members would be appointed by the President of the Senate from among its membership. The Court noted that the duties of the Commission were administrative or executive in character and had no relation to the function of the legislative branch. *Accord: Book v. State Office Building Commission,* 149 N.E.2d 273 (Ind. 1958); *Greer v. State,* 212 S.E.2d 836 (Ga.1975). Recall that in the *MWAA* case, § 7.6.1 N.9, the U.S. Supreme Court reached a similar holding on separation of powers grounds, even though it might well have relied on the federal Incompatibility Clause instead.

State decisions do not fall easily into any single pattern, however. *See generally* Devlin, *supra,* at 1250–64. In *State ex rel. Schneider v. Bennett,* 547 P.2d 786 (Kan.1976), the court used the same four-factor test as in *Parcell* to analyze the functions of the Kansas State Finance Council. The court held that the legislature could not authorize the Council, which had several legislator members, to supervise the day-to-day operations of the Department of Administration. Such supervision amounted to a legislative usurpation of executive power. However, the court did allow the Council to authorize expenditures from the state emergency fund, because this was "a cooperative effort between the executive department and the legislative department . . . to insure prompt state action in the event of a major disaster." There was no usurpation of executive power because the Council, of which the governor was also a member, could act only by unanimous vote. Other state courts have used the same analysis to sustain other "cooperative" arrangements between the political branches. *See, e.g., J.F. Ahern Co. v. Wisconsin State Building Commission,* 336 N.W.2d 679 (Wis.Ct.App.1983); *State ex rel. McLeod v. Edwards,* 236 S.E.2d 406 (S.C.1977).

Consider *Alexander v. State ex rel. Allain,* 441 So.2d 1329 (Miss.1983). The court invalidated several functions of the Commission on Budget and Accounting, an entity composed of the governor and several legislators. Among these functions was to prepare an executive budget for enactment by the legislature. The court said that, although the governor does submit a budget proposal, and the legislature ultimately adopts a budget, the "constitutional imperative that the powers of government be divided into separate and distinct departments . . . renders unconstitutional the organization of any commission or agency on which both legislators and members of the executive branch serve as voting members." *Id.* at 1340. Was this holding sound?

8. *Qualifications.* Legislatures regularly prescribe the qualifications that executive appointees to various agencies must meet. Years ago Justice Brandeis listed some of the many congressional specifications for various offices: for example, in some cases Congress has required that certain offices may be held only by residents of a particular state, by persons who speak a certain language, by persons who have passed an examination, or (at one time) by persons who show "habitual temperance in the use of intoxicating liquors." *Myers v. United States,* 272 U.S. 52, 265–74 (1926) (dissent). More common today are requirements that the membership of multimember commissions must be balanced as between political parties.

Such specifications are generally upheld at both the federal and state levels. In exceptional cases, however, they have been held unconstitutional for infringing too far on the chief executive's appointment discretion. *See*

Wittler v. Baumgartner, 144 N.W.2d 62, 71–72 (Neb.1966) (legislature invalidly defined qualifications for directors of public power authority so narrowly that, in some instances, only one individual could possibly qualify). At the federal level, Congress has provided that, in appointing a new Comptroller General, the President must select from a list of three names submitted by the Speaker of the House and President pro tem of the Senate. 31 U.S.C. § 703(a)(2). The Court noted but did not pass on the constitutionality of this requirement in *Bowsher v. Synar,* 478 U.S. 714, 728 n. 6 (1986). Is it valid?

9. *Problem.* A recently enacted Madison statute, S.B. 234, provides that the Chief Justice of the Madison Supreme Court shall appoint the Director of the state's Office of Administrative Hearings (OAH). That Office is situated for organizational purposes within the state Department of Administration, but it enjoys substantial autonomy in its operations, with little oversight from the Secretary of Administration.

The Director of OAH serves as the chief administrative law judge of the state. Like other ALJs, he hears testimony, applies rules of evidence, and writes findings of fact in contested cases. These cases might come from any of Madison's administrative agencies. The Director also is responsible for administrative tasks within OAH, such as designating particular ALJs to preside over specific types of cases, hiring hearing officers for certain assignments, and resolving disciplinary complaints against ALJs (including, potentially, removing an ALJ for just cause).

Implementing the new statute, Madison's Chief Justice, Anna, has appointed Gunther to be the Director of OAH. Stuart, a respondent in a license revocation proceeding pending before Gunther, has filed a court action, claiming that Gunther was appointed illegally. He relies on § 8 of the Madison constitution, which states that "The Governor shall nominate and by and with the advice and consent of the Senate appoint all officers whose appointments are not otherwise provided for." In the alternative, Stuart alleges that S.B. 234 violates § 1 of the constitution, which provides that "[t]he legislative, executive, and judicial powers of the State government shall be forever separate and distinct from each other," as well as § 3: "The executive power of the State shall be vested in the Governor."

How should Stuart's claims be resolved? If Madison followed federal law principles instead of the constitutional provisions quoted here, would the result change? *Cf. State ex rel. Martin v. Melott,* 359 S.E.2d 783 (N.C.1987).

§ 7.7.2   REMOVAL OF OFFICERS

§ 7.7.2a   The Rise of the Independent Agency

Except in its provisions on impeachment, the federal Constitution does not expressly speak to the question of removing administrative officials from office. The subject was debated in the first Congress, in the context of legislation that created the position of Secretary of State. Apparently, the sense of Congress in 1789 was that the President could remove the Secretary of State whether Congress gave him removal power or not.

The 1867 Tenure of Office Act challenged the view that the principal officers of government had to serve at the President's pleasure. This statute forbade presidential removal of designated cabinet members without the consent of the Senate. President Andrew Johnson dismissed the Secretary of War, in violation of the Tenure of Office Act. That action led to the President's impeachment by the House; but a Senate vote to convict him failed by a single vote.

The constitutional issues surrounding the Tenure of Office Act did not reach the Supreme Court until *Myers v. United States,* 272 U.S. 52 (1926). The issue arose in connection with a suit for back pay by a postmaster in Oregon whom President Wilson had discharged without cause. The discharge violated a statute (passed a few years after the Tenure of Office Act) that required the consent of the Senate for the appointment and also for the suspension or removal of a postmaster.

Chief Justice Taft (who had earlier been President) wrote for the Court that Congress could not limit the President's removal power over any officer of the United States whom the President had appointed. Consequently, both the Tenure of Office Act (which had long since been repealed) and the statute relating to postmasters were invalid. In part, this holding was grounded on the notion that the power to remove is an incident of the power to appoint. *Id.* at 119. More significantly, the Court emphasized the President's constitutional duty to take care that the laws "be faithfully executed:"

> The ordinary duties of officers prescribed by statute come under the general administrative control of the President by virtue of the general grant to him of the executive power, and he may properly supervise and guide their construction of the statutes under which they act in order to secure that unitary and uniform execution of the laws which Article II of the Constitution evidently contemplated in vesting general executive power in the President alone. Laws are often passed with specific provision for the adoption of regulations by a department or bureau head to make the law workable and effective. The ability and judgment manifested by the official thus empowered, as well as his energy and stimulation of his subordinates, are subjects which the President must consider and supervise in his administrative control. Finding such officers to be negligent and inefficient, the President should have the power to remove them. Of course there may be duties so peculiarly and specifically committed to the discretion of a particular officer as to raise a question whether the President may overrule or revise the officer's interpretation of his statutory duty in a particular instance. Then there may be duties of a quasi-judicial character imposed on executive officers and members of executive tribunals whose decisions after hearing affect interests of individuals, the discharge of which the President can not in a particular case properly influence or control. But even in such a case he may consider the decision after its rendition as a reason for removing the officer, on the ground that the discretion regularly entrusted to that officer by statute has not been on the whole intelligently or wisely exercised. Otherwise he

does not discharge his own constitutional duty of seeing that the laws be faithfully executed.

Id. at 135. Less than a decade later, however, the Court was suggesting that some of the language in *Myers* had been too broad.

HUMPHREY'S EXECUTOR v. UNITED STATES
295 U.S. 602 (1935).

[The Federal Trade Commission Act provided that a commissioner could be removed only for "inefficiency, neglect of duty, or malfeasance in office." Despite this limitation, President Roosevelt wrote to request the resignation of the chairman of the FTC, William Humphrey, who had been appointed by President Hoover. Instead of invoking one of the statutory grounds, Roosevelt's letter said: "I do not feel that your mind and my mind go along together on either the policies or the administering of the Federal Trade Commission, and, frankly, I think it is best for the people of the country that I should have a full confidence." The chairman refused to resign, but Roosevelt discharged him. After Humphrey's death, his estate sued to recover his salary.]

The commission is to be non-partisan; and it must, from the very nature of its duties, act with entire impartiality. It is charged with the enforcement of no policy except the policy of the law.... Like the Interstate Commerce Commission, its members are called upon to exercise the trained judgment of a body of experts "appointed by law and informed by experience." ...

The office of a postmaster is so essentially unlike the office now involved that the decision in the *Myers* case cannot be accepted as controlling our decision here. A postmaster is an executive officer restricted to the performance of executive functions. He is charged with no duty at all related to either the legislative or judicial power....

The Federal Trade Commission is an administrative body created by Congress to carry into effect legislative policies embodied in the statute in accordance with the legislative standard therein prescribed, and to perform other specified duties as a legislative or as a judicial aid. Such a body cannot in any proper sense be characterized as an arm or an eye of the executive. Its duties are performed without executive leave and, in the contemplation of the statute, must be free from executive control. In administering the provisions of the statute in respect of "unfair methods of competition"—that is to say in filling in and administering the details embodied by that general standard—the commission acts in part quasi-legislatively and in part quasi-judicially....

We think it plain under the Constitution that illimitable power of removal is not possessed by the President in respect of officers of the character of those just named. The authority of Congress, in creating quasi-legislative or quasi-judicial agencies, to require them to act in discharge of their duties independently of executive control cannot well be doubted; and that authority includes, as an appropriate incident, power to fix the period during which they shall continue in office, and to forbid their removal except for cause in the meantime. For it is quite evident that one who holds his office only during the pleasure of another, cannot be depended upon to maintain an attitude of independence against the latter's will.

Notes and Questions

1. *Independent agencies.* The *Humphrey's Executor* decision fostered the development of the so-called "independent agencies." The Federal Reserve Board, the Nuclear Regulatory Commission, the Securities and Exchange Commission, and the Federal Communications Commission are familiar examples of agencies that are considered independent and thus not subject to direct presidential control. Theoretically, at least, Congress creates an independent agency in the hope of lessening political influence over its decisions; the idea is that, free of direct executive control, the agency can perform its administrative functions impartially and regulate purely in the public interest.

The most fundamental characteristic of an independent agency is that its head or heads may not be removed by the President, except for "good cause." In that respect such agencies differ from "executive" agencies, whose top officers serve at the pleasure of the President. Independent agencies are usually constituted as multi-member boards or commissions. (But not all of them: for example, the Social Security Administration was reorganized in 1994 as an "independent agency within the executive branch," headed by a single Commissioner.) Statutory requirements of staggered terms and party balance among the members of these agencies are intended to bolster their independence. The executive branch agencies, on the other hand, are typically Cabinet departments, headed by a Secretary. (But not all of them: for example, the EPA is an executive branch agency, but not a Cabinet department.)

2. *Supreme Court analysis.* Do you agree with *Myers* that the separation of powers doctrine should guarantee the President the right to discharge some administrative officers, even if Congress has legislated to the contrary? If so, how persuasively did *Humphrey's Executor* delimit the circumstances in which Congress may prescribe "independence"? Can one effectively distinguish between the "purely executive" administrative functions performed by Myers and the "quasi-legislative" and "quasi-adjudicative" functions performed by Humphrey? Indeed, why should Congress be allowed to set up *any* "independent agencies" that are outside the direct control of the President? *See generally* Peter M. Shane, "Independent Policymaking and Presidential Power: A Constitutional Analysis," 57 Geo. Wash.L.Rev. 596 (1989); Peter L. Strauss, "The Place of Agencies in Government: Separation of Powers and the Fourth Branch," 84 Colum.L.Rev. 573, 611–16 (1984).

3. *Removal of adjudicators.* In *Wiener v. United States,* 357 U.S. 349 (1958), the Court invalidated President Eisenhower's removal of a member of the War Claims Commission. Congress had established the commission, with a three year life span, to resolve claims concerning injuries to person or property during World War II. The statute said nothing about the circum-

stances under which a commissioner could be removed. The Court held, however, that because the Commission had been created to "adjudicate according to law," the philosophy of *Humphrey's Executor* precluded the President from removing its members simply because he wanted his own appointees to serve instead.

Does it make sense for the Court to have implied a right of tenure where Congress did not see fit to specify one? Can the logic of *Wiener* be extended to justify tenure for members of agencies that perform a wider range of functions than the War Claims Commission did, such as the FCC and SEC?

4. *The significance of independence.* An emerging body of scholarship suggests that the distinction between independent and executive agencies is ultimately not very important, because the similarities between the two types of entities outweigh the differences. *See, e.g.,* Susan Bartlett Foote, "Independent Agencies Under Attack: A Skeptical View of the Importance of the Debate," 1988 Duke L.J. 223, 232–37; Glen O. Robinson, "Independent Agencies: Form and Substance in Executive Prerogative," 1988 Duke L.J. 238, 241–50; Strauss, *supra,* at 583–96. This is particularly true of their routine operations. Both kinds of agencies function in about the same way (carrying out rulemaking, adjudication, and law enforcement) and are subject identically to the APA and to judicial review. Indeed, most of the principles of law discussed in this book apply identically to independent and executive agencies. In addition, all agencies are staffed (below the top levels) by civil service employees, who are protected against discharge except for cause (and thus often resist new initiatives).

To be sure, independent agencies do appear to have somewhat more autonomy from presidential control than executive branch agencies have. In addition to their protection from removal without cause, the heads of independent agencies typically appoint the agency staff on their own authority; in executive agencies, the White House often plays a larger role in staffing decisions. Moreover, independent agencies tend to have somewhat greater authority to conduct their own litigation than executive branch agencies. The White House has to date exempted the independent agencies from formal participation in executive oversight of rulemaking proceedings (*see* § 7.8). They also can face less scrutiny of their communications with Congress, such as through advance submission of draft statutes or testimony. *See* Strauss, *supra,* at 589–90.

But even this distinction can be exaggerated. As a practical matter, both independent and executive agencies usually work closely with the President and his staff in formulating policy and in mediating inter-agency disputes. All agencies submit budgetary requests each year to the Office of Management and Budget, and all are treated alike in the President's budget as submitted to Congress. In any event, because agency heads frequently choose not to serve their full terms, a newly elected President usually does not have to wait for very long before he can appoint a majority of any given commission. In addition, the President usually has power to choose which of the several agency heads of multi-member independent agencies will be the chair. The chair, who makes a great many important practical decisions for the agency, is likely to be a person with whom the President has a good working relationship. In short, the de facto independence of an agency from presidential control depends much more on political factors than on whether the agency is formally independent. *Id.* at 583–596. According to Foote, *supra,* at 237:

> Does the structure of administrative agencies matter? My answer is a resounding "it depends." Independence is one factor among many in the complex political environment in which regulatory policy is made. When Congress is strong, it can impose its imprint on the structure of the administrative state through the creation of independent agencies. When the balance of power shifts, however, formal structures cannot prevent pressure, even domination, by the executive branch. There are many other critical factors that influence regulatory outcomes, including powerful business interests and the public at large.... Separation of powers may be of greater importance to constitutional theorists than to regulators.

§ 7.7.2b   Removal Issues in the Modern Era

Humphrey's Executor has always been a controversial decision. During the 1980's, criticism of the case became particularly prominent. Proponents of the so-called "unitary executive" theory maintained that all agencies that perform functions of an executive nature should be under the effective control of the President. *See FTC v. American Cellular, Inc.,* 810 F.2d 1511 (9th Cir.1987) (rejecting an attempt to litigate anew the constitutionality of the FTC's independent status); Geoffrey P. Miller, "Independent Agencies," 1986 Sup.Ct.Rev. 41. Acting in an atypical context, the Supreme Court responded to this debate in the following case.

MORRISON v. OLSON
487 U.S. 654 (1988).

[The 1978 Ethics in Government Act created a special court (the Special Division) that was authorized, in response to a request by the Attorney General, to appoint an independent counsel to investigate and prosecute possible violations of federal law by certain high ranking government officials. The Act provided that the Attorney General could remove the independent counsel, but only for "good cause." Pursuant to the procedures outlined in the Act, the Special Division appointed Morrison an independent counsel to investigate Assistant Attorney General Olson's alleged obstruction of a congressional inquiry. Olson moved to quash certain subpoenas issued by a grand jury at Morrison's request. He argued that the Act creating the office of independent counsel was unconstitutional and, therefore, that Morrison had no authority to proceed. The district court held that the Act was valid. The court of appeals reversed, holding that the Act violated the Appointments Clause and the principle of separation of powers. In an opinion joined by seven members of the Supreme Court, REHNQUIST, C.J., first rejected the Appointments Clause challenge, *see* § 7.7.1 N.2, and then continued:]

We now turn to consider whether the Act is invalid under the constitutional principle of separation of powers. Two related issues must be addressed. The first is whether the provision of the Act restricting the Attorney General's power to remove the independent counsel to only those instances in which he can show "good cause," taken by itself, impermissibly interferes with the President's exercise of his constitutionally appointed functions. The second is whether, taken as a whole, the Act violates the separation of powers by reducing the President's ability to control the prosecutorial powers wielded by the independent counsel. . . .

Unlike both *Bowsher [v. Synar,* 478 U.S. 714 (1986),] and *Myers,* this case does not involve an attempt by Congress itself to gain a role in the removal of executive officials other than its established powers of impeachment and conviction. The Act instead puts the removal power squarely in the hands of the Executive Branch; an independent counsel may be removed from office "only by the personal action of the Attorney General, and only for good cause." There is no requirement of congressional approval of the Attorney General's removal decision, though the decision is subject to judicial review. In our view, the removal provisions of the Act make this case more analogous to *Humphrey's Executor v. United States,* 295 U.S. 602 (1935), and *Wiener v. United States,* 357 U.S. 349 (1958), than to *Myers* or *Bowsher*. . . .

Appellees contend that *Humphrey's Executor* and *Wiener* are distinguishable from this case because they did not involve officials who performed a "core executive function." They argue that our decision in *Humphrey's Executor* rests on a distinction between "purely executive" officials and officials who exercise "quasi-legislative" and "quasi-judicial" powers. In their view, when a "purely executive" official is involved, the governing precedent is *Myers,* not *Humphrey's Executor.* And, under *Myers,* the President must have absolute discretion to discharge "purely" executive officials at will.

We undoubtedly did rely on the terms "quasi-legislative" and "quasi-judicial" to distinguish the officials involved in *Humphrey's Executor* and *Wiener* from those in *Myers,* but our present considered view is that the determination of whether the Constitution allows Congress to impose a "good cause"-type restriction on the President's power to remove an official cannot be made to turn on whether or not that official is classified as "purely executive." The analysis contained in our removal cases is designed not to define rigid categories of those officials who may or may not be removed at will by the President,[28] but to ensure that Congress does not interfere with the President's exercise of the "executive power" and his constitutionally appointed duty to "take care that the laws be faithfully executed" under Article II. *Myers* was undoubtedly correct in its holding, and in its broader suggestion that there are some "purely executive" officials who must be removable by the President at

28. . . . [I]t is hard to dispute that the powers of the FTC at the time of *Humphrey's Executor* would at the present time be considered "executive," at least in some degree.

will if he is to be able to accomplish his constitutional role. But as the Court noted in *Wiener,*

> The assumption was short-lived that the *Myers* case recognized the President's inherent constitutional power to remove officials no matter what the relation of the executive to the discharge of their duties and no matter what restrictions Congress may have imposed regarding the nature of their tenure.

At the other end of the spectrum from *Myers,* the characterization of the agencies in *Humphrey's Executor* and *Wiener* as "quasi-legislative" or "quasi-judicial" in large part reflected our judgment that it was not essential to the President's proper execution of his Article II powers that these agencies be headed up by individuals who were removable at will.[30] We do not mean to suggest that an analysis of the functions served by the officials at issue is irrelevant. But the real question is whether the removal restrictions are of such a nature that they impede the President's ability to perform his constitutional duty, and the functions of the officials in question must be analyzed in that light.

Considering for the moment the "good cause" removal provision in isolation from the other parts of the Act at issue in this case, we cannot say that the imposition of a "good cause" standard for removal by itself unduly trammels on executive authority. There is no real dispute that the functions performed by the independent counsel are "executive" in the sense that they are law enforcement functions that typically have been undertaken by officials within the Executive Branch. As we noted above, however, the independent counsel is an inferior officer under the Appointments Clause, with limited jurisdiction and tenure and lacking policymaking or significant administrative authority. Although the counsel exercises no small amount of discretion and judgment in deciding how to carry out her duties under the Act, we simply do not see how the President's need to control the exercise of that discretion is so central to the functioning of the Executive Branch as to require as a matter of constitutional law that the counsel be terminable at will by the President.[31]

Nor do we think that the "good cause" removal provision at issue here impermissibly burdens the President's power to control or supervise the independent counsel, as an executive official, in the execution of

---

30. The terms also may be used to describe the circumstances in which Congress might be more inclined to find that a degree of independence from the Executive, such as that afforded by a "good cause" removal standard, is necessary to the proper functioning of the agency or official. It is not difficult to imagine situations in which Congress might desire that an official performing "quasi-judicial" functions, for example, would be free of executive or political control.

31. We note by way of comparison that various federal agencies whose officers are covered by "good cause" removal restrictions exercise civil enforcement powers that are analogous to the prosecutorial powers wielded by an independent counsel. See, *e.g.,* 15 U.S.C. § 45(m) (giving the FTC the authority to bring civil actions to recover civil penalties for the violations of rules respecting unfair competition); 15 U.S.C. §§ 2061, 2071, 2076(b)(7)(A) (giving the Consumer Product Safety Commission the authority to obtain injunctions and apply for seizure of hazardous products).

her duties under the Act. This is not a case in which the power to remove an executive official has been completely stripped from the President, thus providing no means for the President to ensure the "faithful execution" of the laws. Rather, because the independent counsel may be terminated for "good cause," the Executive, through the Attorney General, retains ample authority to assure that the counsel is competently performing her statutory responsibilities in a manner that comports with the provisions of the Act.[32] Although we need not decide in this case exactly what is encompassed within the term "good cause" under the Act, the legislative history of the removal provision also makes clear that the Attorney General may remove an independent counsel for "misconduct." Here, as with the provision of the Act conferring the appointment authority of the independent counsel on the special court, the congressional determination to limit the removal power of the Attorney General was essential, in the view of Congress, to establish the necessary independence of the office. We do not think that this limitation as it presently stands sufficiently deprives the President of control over the independent counsel to interfere impermissibly with his constitutional obligation to ensure the faithful execution of the laws.

The final question to be addressed is whether the Act, taken as a whole, violates the principle of separation of powers by unduly interfering with the role of the Executive Branch. Time and again we have reaffirmed the importance in our constitutional scheme of the separation of governmental powers into the three coordinate branches. . . . On the other hand, we have never held that the Constitution requires that the three Branches of Government "operate with absolute independence." . . . In the often-quoted words of Justice Jackson,

> "While the Constitution diffuses power the better to secure liberty, it also contemplates that practice will integrate the dispersed powers into a workable government. It enjoins upon its branches separateness but interdependence, autonomy but reciprocity." *Youngstown Sheet & Tube Co. v. Sawyer,* 343 U.S. 579, 635 (1952) (concurring opinion).

We observe first that this case does not involve an attempt by Congress to increase its own powers at the expense of the Executive Branch. Unlike some of our previous cases, most recently *Bowsher v. Synar,* this case simply does not pose a "dange[r] of congressional usurpation of Executive Branch functions." Indeed, with the exception of the power of impeachment—which applies to all officers of the United States—Congress retained for itself no powers of control or supervision over an independent counsel. . . .

Similarly, we do not think that the Act works any *judicial* usurpation of properly executive functions. . . .

---

32. Indeed, during the hearings on the 1982 amendments to the Act, a Justice Department official testified that the "good cause" standard contained in the amendments "would make the special prosecutor no more independent than officers of the many so-called independent agencies in the executive branch."

Finally, we do not think that the Act "impermissibly undermine[s]" the powers of the Executive Branch, or "disrupts the proper balance between the coordinate branches [by] prevent[ing] the Executive Branch from accomplishing its constitutionally assigned functions." It is undeniable that the Act reduces the amount of control or supervision that the Attorney General and, through him, the President exercises over the investigation and prosecution of a certain class of alleged criminal activity. The Attorney General is not allowed to appoint the individual of his choice; he does not determine the counsel's jurisdiction; and his power to remove a counsel is limited. Nonetheless, the Act does give the Attorney General several means of supervising or controlling the prosecutorial powers that may be wielded by an independent counsel. Most importantly, the Attorney General retains the power to remove the counsel for "good cause," a power that we have already concluded provides the Executive with substantial ability to ensure that the laws are "faithfully executed" by an independent counsel. No independent counsel may be appointed without a specific request by the Attorney General, and the Attorney General's decision not to request appointment if he finds "no reasonable grounds to believe that further investigation is warranted" is committed to his unreviewable discretion. The Act thus gives the Executive a degree of control over the power to initiate an investigation by the independent counsel. In addition, the jurisdiction of the independent counsel is defined with reference to the facts submitted by the Attorney General, and once a counsel is appointed, the Act requires that the counsel abide by Justice Department policy unless it is not "possible" to do so. Notwithstanding the fact that the counsel is to some degree "independent" and free from Executive supervision to a greater extent than other federal prosecutors, in our view these features of the Act give the Executive Branch sufficient control over the independent counsel to ensure that the President is able to perform his constitutionally assigned duties.

In sum, we conclude today that ... the Act does not violate the separation of powers principle by impermissibly interfering with the functions of the Executive Branch. The decision of the Court of Appeals is therefore

Reversed.

SCALIA, J., dissenting.

[Justice Scalia emphasized that in separation of powers disputes between Congress and the President, neither can be presumed to be correct. Then he stressed that Article II, § 1, Cl. 1 of the Constitution vests the executive power in *the President*. His dissent continued:]

As I described at the outset of this opinion, this does not mean *some of* the executive power, but *all of* the executive power. It seems to me, therefore, that the decision of the Court of Appeals invalidating the present statute must be upheld on fundamental separation-of-powers principles if the following two questions are answered affirmatively: (1) Is the conduct of a criminal prosecution (and of an investigation to decide whether to prosecute) the exercise of purely executive power? (2) Does the statute deprive the President of the United States of exclusive control over the exercise of that power? Surprising to say, the Court appears to concede an affirmative answer to both questions, but seeks to avoid the inevitable conclusion that since the statute vests some purely executive power in a person who is not the President of the United States it is void.

The Court concedes that "[t]here is no real dispute that the functions performed by the independent counsel are 'executive'." . . . Governmental investigation and prosecution of crimes is a quintessentially executive function.

As for the second question, whether the statute before us deprives the President of exclusive control over that quintessentially executive activity: The Court does not, and could not possibly, assert that it does not. That is indeed the whole object of the statute. Instead, the Court points out that the President, through his Attorney General, has at least *some* control. That concession is alone enough to invalidate the statute, but I cannot refrain from pointing out that the Court greatly exaggerates the extent of that "some" presidential control. "Most importan[t]" among these controls, the Court asserts, is the Attorney General's "power to remove the counsel for 'good cause.' " This is somewhat like referring to shackles as an effective means of locomotion. As we recognized in *Humphrey's Executor v. United States,* 295 U.S. 602 (1935)— indeed, what *Humphrey's Executor* was all about—limiting removal power to "good cause" is an impediment to, not an effective grant of, presidential control. . . . Congress, of course, operated under no such illusion when it enacted this statute, describing the "good cause" limitation as "protecting the independent counsel's ability to act independently of the President's direct control" since it permits removal only for "misconduct."

Moving on to the presumably "less important" controls that the President retains, the Court notes that no independent counsel may be appointed without a specific request from the Attorney General. As I have discussed above, the condition that renders such a request mandatory (inability to find "no reasonable grounds to believe" that further investigation is warranted) is so insubstantial that the Attorney General's discretion is severely confined. And once the referral is made, it is for the Special Division to determine the scope and duration of the investigation. And in any event, the limited power over referral is irrelevant to the question whether, *once appointed,* the independent counsel exercises executive power free from the President's control. Finally, the Court points out that the Act directs the independent counsel to abide by general Justice Department policy, except when not "possible." The exception alone shows this to be an empty promise. . . . Almost all investigative and prosecutorial decisions—including the ultimate decision whether, after a technical violation of the law has been found, prosecution is warranted—involve the balancing of innumerable legal and practical considerations. [This balancing] is the very essence of prosecutorial discretion. To take this away is to remove the core of the prosecutorial function, and not merely "some" presidential control.

As I have said, however, it is ultimately irrelevant *how much* the statute reduces presidential control.... We should say here that the President's constitutionally assigned duties include *complete* control over investigation and prosecution of violations of the law, and that the inexorable command of Article II is clear and definite: the executive power must be vested in the President of the United States....

The Court has, nonetheless, replaced the clear constitutional prescription that the executive power belongs to the President with a "balancing test." What are the standards to determine how the balance is to be struck, that is, how much removal of presidential power is too much? Once we depart from the text of the Constitution, just where short of that do we stop? The most amazing feature of the Court's opinion is that it does not even purport to give an answer....

In my view, moreover, even as an ad hoc, standardless judgment the Court's conclusion must be wrong.... Perhaps the boldness of the President himself will not be affected—though I am not even sure of that. (How much easier it is for Congress, instead of accepting the political damage attendant to the commencement of impeachment proceedings against the President on trivial grounds—or, for that matter, how easy it is for one of the President's political foes outside of Congress—simply to trigger a debilitating criminal investigation of the Chief Executive under this law.) But as for the President's high-level assistants, who typically have no political base of support, it is as utterly unrealistic to think that they will not be intimidated by this prospect, and that their advice to him and their advocacy of his interests before a hostile Congress will not be affected, as it would be to think that the Members of Congress and their staffs would be unaffected by replacing the Speech or Debate Clause with a similar provision. It deeply wounds the President, by substantially reducing the President's ability to protect himself and his staff. That is the whole object of the law, of course, and I cannot imagine why the Court believes it does not succeed.

Besides weakening the Presidency by reducing the zeal of his staff, it must also be obvious that the institution of the independent counsel enfeebles him more directly in his constant confrontations with Congress, by eroding his public support. Nothing is so politically effective as the ability to charge that one's opponent and his associates are not merely wrongheaded, naive, ineffective, but, in all probability, "crooks." And nothing so effectively gives an appearance of validity to such charges as a Justice Department investigation and, even better, prosecution. The present statute provides ample means for that sort of attack, assuring that massive and lengthy investigations will occur, not merely when the Justice Department in the application of its usual standards believes they are called for, but whenever it cannot be said that there are "no reasonable grounds to believe" they are called for. The statute's highly visible procedures assure, moreover, that unlike most investigations these will be widely known and prominently displayed....

Since our 1935 decision in *Humphrey's Executor v. United States,* ... it has been established that the line of permissible restriction upon removal of principal officers lies at the point at which the powers exercised by those officers are no longer purely executive. Thus, removal restrictions have been generally regarded as lawful for so-called "independent regulatory agencies," such as the Federal Trade Commission, the Interstate Commerce Commission, and the Consumer Products Safety Commission, which engage substantially in what has been called the "quasi-legislative activity" of rulemaking, and for members of Article I courts, such as the Court of Military Appeals, who engage in the "quasi-judicial" function of adjudication. It has often been observed, correctly in my view, that the line between "purely executive" functions and "quasi-legislative" or "quasi-judicial" functions is not a clear one or even a rational one. But at least it permitted the identification of certain officers, and certain agencies, whose functions were entirely within the control of the President. Congress had to be aware of that restriction in its legislation. Today, however, *Humphrey's Executor* is swept into the dustbin of repudiated constitutional principles. "[O]ur present considered view," the Court says, "is that the determination of whether the Constitution allows Congress to impose a 'good cause'-type restriction on the President's power to remove an official cannot be made to turn on whether or not that official is classified as 'purely executive.'" What *Humphrey's Executor* (and presumably *Myers*) really means, we are now told, is not that there are any "rigid categories of those officials who may or may not be removed at will by the President," but simply that Congress cannot "interfere with the President's exercise of the 'executive power' and his constitutionally appointed duty to 'take care that the laws be faithfully executed.'"

... There are now no lines. If the removal of a prosecutor, the virtual embodiment of the power to "take care that the laws be faithfully executed," can be restricted, what officer's removal cannot? This is an open invitation for Congress to experiment. What about a special Assistant Secretary of State, with responsibility for one very narrow area of foreign policy, who would not only have to be confirmed by the Senate but could also be removed only pursuant to certain carefully designed restrictions? Could this possibly render the President "[un]able to accomplish his constitutional role"? Or a special Assistant Secretary of Defense for Procurement? The possibilities are endless, and the Court does not understand what the separation of powers, what "[a]mbition ... counteract[ing] ambition," Federalist No. 51 (Madison), is all about, if it does not expect Congress to try them....

Only someone who has worked in the field of law enforcement can fully appreciate the vast power and the immense discretion that are placed in the hands of a prosecutor with respect to the objects of his investigation.... Under our system of government, the primary check against prosecutorial abuse is a political one. The prosecutors who exercise this awesome discretion are selected and can be removed by a President, whom the people have trusted enough to elect. Moreover, when crimes are not investigated and prosecuted fairly, nonselectively, with a reasonable sense of proportion, the President pays the cost in political damage to his administration.... The President is directly dependent on the people, and since there is only *one* President, *he* is responsible. The people know whom to blame, whereas "one of the weightiest objections to a plurality in the executive ... is that it tends to conceal faults and destroy responsibility." [Federalist No. 70 (Hamilton).] ...

That is the system of justice the rest of us are entitled to, but what of that select class consisting of present or former high-level Executive Branch officials? ... An independent counsel is selected, and the scope of his or her authority prescribed, by a panel of judges. What if they are politically partisan, as judges have been known to be, and select a prosecutor antagonistic to the administration, or even to the particular individual who has been selected for this special treatment? There is no remedy for that, not even a political one....

[A]n additional advantage of the unitary Executive [is] that it can achieve a more uniform application of the law. Perhaps that is not always achieved, but the mechanism to achieve it is there. The mini-Executive that is the independent counsel, however, operating in an area where so little is law and so much is discretion, is intentionally cut off from the unifying influence of the Justice Department, and from the perspective that multiple responsibilities provide. What would normally be regarded as a technical violation (there are no rules defining such things), may in his or her small world assume the proportions of an indictable offense. What would normally be regarded as an investigation that has reached the level of pursuing such picayune matters that it should be concluded, may to him or her be an investigation that ought to go on for another year. How frightening it must be to have your own independent counsel and staff appointed, with nothing else to do but to investigate you until investigation is no longer worthwhile—with whether it is worthwhile not depending upon what such judgments usually hinge on, competing responsibilities. And to have that counsel and staff decide, with no basis for comparison, whether what you have done is bad enough, willful enough, and provable enough, to warrant an indictment. How admirable the constitutional system that provides the means to avoid such a distortion. And how unfortunate the judicial decision that has permitted it.

... Today's decision on the basic issue of fragmentation of executive power is ungoverned by rule, and hence ungoverned by law. It extends into the very heart of our most significant constitutional function the "totality of the circumstances" mode of analysis that this Court has in recent years become fond of. Taking all things into account, we conclude that the power taken away from the President here is not really *too* much. The next time executive power is assigned to someone other than the President we may conclude, taking all things into account, that it *is* too much. . . . This is not analysis; it is ad hoc judgment. . . . I prefer to rely upon the judgment of the wise men who constructed our system, and of the people who approved it, and of two centuries of history that have shown it to be sound. Like it or not, that judgment says, quite plainly, that "[t]he executive Power shall be vested in a President of the United States."

Notes and Questions

1. *Morrison.* Does the Court's analysis in *Morrison* satisfactorily explain its holding on the removal issue? How can one tell whether a removal restriction "impede[s] the President's ability to perform his constitutional duty"? And does *Morrison* constitute, as Justice Scalia charges, an invitation to Congress to experiment with giving tenure to numerous other officers, such as assistant secretaries in the State or Defense Department? If you find the Court's reasoning unconvincing, could the result be justified on a stronger basis? (Consider, as one possibility, the somewhat different separation of powers test articulated in *Nixon v. Administrator of General Services,* 433 U.S. 425, 433 (1977), quoted in Justice White's dissent in *Chadha.*)

For commentary on separation of powers in the wake of *Morrison,* see, e.g., Stephen L. Carter, "The Independent Counsel Mess," 102 Harv.L.Rev. 105 (1988); and symposia at 38 Am.U.L.Rev. 255 (1989); 57 Geo.Wash.L.Rev. 401 (1989); and 1988 Duke L.J. 215.

2. *Independent counsels reconsidered.* Public dissatisfaction with the independent counsel statute has burgeoned since the time of *Morrison.* Illustrative of the newly emergent doubts about the Ethics in Government Act are these views:

> [T]he independent counsel statute . . . has evolved into an engine of perpetual muckraking through past lives in pursuit of the pettiest of peccadilloes—a destructive and costly diversion from the business of the nation, taking an intolerable toll on the president and his appointees.

> There is, of course, a risk that doing away with it might enable officials to cover up wrongdoing. That's why I have previously defended the statute, and then proposed fine-tuning it or replacing it with a quasi-independent office of public prosecutions. But I have learned that there are worse things than the risk of a cover-up. And we have found them. . . .

> It has become ever more apparent that one-case, court-appointed independent counsel, with few institutional constraints and no competing prosecutorial responsibilities, have a natural tendency to be overly zealous and overly exhaustive in trying to build criminal cases from the messy raw material of political life. . . .

> Beyond that, the Clinton years have dramatized two specific problems not widely appreciated before.

> First, although the purpose of the independent counsel statute is to police criminal abuses of the powers of high office, it has become a fount of prosecutorial scrutiny of what officials did *before taking office.* . . . Even if independent counsel were all models of fairness and restraint, the statute would give them powerful incentives to dig harder and

deeper into the past for any hints of possible wrongdoing than we should want any prosecutor digging.

Second, it has become painfully obvious that the choice of a prosecutor to probe the president cannot be depoliticized by handing the job to judges. Indeed, it has become *more* politicized.... [T]he statute is clearly a failure to the extent that its purpose was to create a public perception of nonpartisan professionalism.

Nor is the statute necessary for those rare occasions when such grave allegations are raised against the president that his own subordinates cannot be trusted to resolve them.

Public opinion could still force appointment of a special prosecutor the old-fashioned way—by the attorney general.

Stuart Taylor Jr., "Repeal the Independent Counsel Law," Legal Times of Wash., May 20, 1996, at 25. Others who share Taylor's disillusionment with the present independent counsel system favor revision of the statute, not repeal. *See, e.g.,* Abner J. Mikva, "The Damage Starr Does," Legal Times of Wash., Feb. 2, 1998, at 25. In some quarters, however, support for the current system remains unabated:

What the independent counsel legislation has done is to remove the threat of another Saturday Night Massacre [when President Nixon fired Special Prosecutor Archibald Cox;] attempt to take such special prosecution out of politics, as humanly as possible[;] and seek to assure the public that criminal investigations of the president and high executive branch officials will not be burdened with conflicts of interest, and will be objectively and independently conducted. No matter how competent and honest an attorney general may be, history has shown that the public has little confidence in Justice Department prosecutors investigating their boss, the president, even though, in fact, these prosecutors would carry out such investigations with skill and integrity....

[T]he statute gives the independent counsel no more authority or power than the attorney general has. He is only a federal prosecutor.

Indeed, under the statute, his accountability is even heavier than is true for the attorney general. Congress has retained oversight authority over the independent counsel and can summon him for public hearings at any time to examine his conduct. The attorney general can fire him for good cause. The special division of the court that appointed him must audit him....

[A] fly on the wall of an independent counsel conference room ... would observe overcautiousness and restraint rather than the buccaneering conduct of [critics'] imagination.

The very real concern ... about independent counsel investigations involving heavy costs in money and time and having a tendency to expand is not an independent counsel abuse. Anyone familiar with major federal prosecutions knows that such costs are the usual consequences of a federal prosecutor or prosecution task force investigating complex white-collar matters involving thousands of documents and powerful, influential suspects or targets.

Sam Dash, "Why We Have the Independent Counsel Law," Wash. Post, Jan. 9, 1998, at A21.

Does hindsight indicate that the independent counsel statute does "impede the President's ability to perform his constitutional duty," and thus should have been declared unconstitutional after all, on the basis of the *Morrison* Court's own standard?

3. *Legislative removal.* While *Humphrey's Executor, Wiener,* and *Morrison* declare that Congress may limit the President's power to remove some agency officials, it does not follow that Congress may retain for itself the power to remove officials engaged in administrative functions. Indeed, Congress lacks that power, according to *Bowsher v. Synar,* 478 U.S. 714 (1986), which is discussed in *Morrison.* There the Court struck down part of the Gramm–Rudman Act, a budget-balancing measure enacted in 1985. The Act provided for an automatic reduction in appropriations for nearly all federal spending programs if the projected budget deficit for a particular year exceeded a certain level. But who would be responsible for making the complex and difficult estimate of the size of the projected deficit? The Act assigned this determination to the Comptroller General, who heads the Government Accounting Office. Under the 1921 law which created that post, the Comptroller General may be removed by a joint congressional resolution (which the President could veto) for inefficiency, neglect of duty, or malfeasance. However, Congress had never exercised this power or even threatened to do so.

The Court held that the Comptroller General's duties were clearly "executive" in nature: "Interpreting a law enacted by Congress to implement the legislative mandate is the very essence of 'execution' of the law." Since Congress had reserved the right to remove the Comptroller General (by a route other than impeachment) and he performed executive functions under this Act, Congress had in effect retained control over the execution of the law. Such control was unacceptable, because of "the command of the Constitution that the Congress play no direct role in the execution of the laws."

In a concurring opinion, Justice Stevens, joined by Justice Marshall, argued that the flaw in the Gramm–Rudman Act was that the Comptroller General was an agent of Congress. That officer was part of the legislative branch not only because the authority to remove him was vested in Congress, but also, and much more importantly, because most of his other duties were intended to aid Congress in the process of passing laws and appropriating money. But, the concurrence continued, when Congress seeks to make policy that will bind the nation, it must do so by following Article I legislative procedures, as *Chadha* had held. The same must be true when Congress delegates power to one of its own agents rather than to the Executive or an independent agency.

Justice White's dissent argued that the carefully limited and never used congressional power to remove the Comptroller was of no practical significance. There was no genuine likelihood that the Comptroller General would be subservient to Congress. Justice Blackmun's dissent argued that the Court should strike down the removal power by stating that it would refuse to uphold a removal and save the Gramm–Rudman Act.

Notice how *Bowsher* applied a strict rule against Congress's controlling executive functions through the possibility of removal, despite the minimal nature of the threat in this case. Two years later *Morrison* displayed a much more flexible mode of analysis, looking to a variety of factors in order to decide whether, in the particular circumstances, a statute intruded unduly on the President's ability to carry out his duties. Does this change in analytical method from "formalism" to "functionalism" suggest that the Court would not adhere to *Bowsher* if a similar question arose again—or does *Morrison* offer a credible explanation for the discrepancy in analytical styles?

Of course, *Bowsher* only denies Congress a *formal* role in discharging agency officials. On an informal level, members of Congress can exert enormous influence on an administration's decisions about whether particular agency officials will stay or go. It has even been suggested that "congressional pressure is responsible for more firings and reassignments of executive branch personnel than presidential actions." *See* Louis Fisher, CONSTITUTIONAL CONFLICTS BETWEEN CONGRESS AND THE PRESIDENT 83–86 (4th ed. 1997).

4. *More functionalism.* If anyone suspected that the Court's "functionalist" approach in *Morrison* was merely a response to the unique circumstances of the independent counsel law, the later decision in *Mistretta v. United States,* 488 U.S. 361 (1989), cast doubt on that assumption. Once again the Court displayed a flexible, permissive stance toward an administrative structure that did not fit easily into the traditional allocation of powers among the branches of government. The case involved a challenge to the constitutionality of the United States Sentencing Commission, an agency that was responsible for promulgating sentencing guidelines for federal criminal cases. The Court called the agency a "peculiar institution," because Congress had designated it an "independent commission in the judicial branch," and several seats on the Commission were reserved for federal judges. Nevertheless, the Court rejected the challenge, reasoning that the Commission's structure did not *unduly* strengthen or weaken the judicial branch. Justice Scalia was again the only dissenter.

5. *State constitutions.* "State constitutional provisions relating to the power of the governor to remove public officials vary dramatically from state to state." Thomas C. Marks, Jr. & John F. Cooper, STATE CONSTITUTIONAL LAW 65 (1988). Most state constitutions, unlike the federal one, explicitly vest removal authority in the chief executive. In many states, however, this authority is less than absolute. The provision may limit removal to "for cause" situations, or may authorize the legislature to impose similar constraints.

Even where a constitution provides that the governor may "remove any officer appointed by him for incompetency, neglect of duty or malfeasance in office," some courts have in effect treated the removal power as plenary. They have said that the governor need not give reasons for his decision, nor allow any kind of hearing before he acts; nor will the courts review the decision. *State ex rel. Duran v. Anaya,* 698 P.2d 882 (N.M.1985); *Wilcox v. People ex rel. Lipe,* 90 Ill. 186 (1878). In Illinois, *Wilcox* was regarded as authoritative for almost a century. *See Adams v. Walker,* 492 F.2d 1003 (7th

Cir.1974). In *Lunding v. Walker*, 359 N.E.2d 96 (Ill.1976), however, the court limited *Wilcox,* concluding that the constitutional provision should be read to harmonize with *Myers* and *Humphrey's Executor*. Thus, the governor's removal of a member of the State Board of Elections for failing to file a financial disclosure statement, as required by the governor's executive order, was judicially reviewable. The court based this conclusion on the independent nature of the election board and noted that it might still follow *Wilcox* in a case involving a "purely executive officer directly responsible to the Governor." Can you justify *Wilcox? Lunding?*

6. *Inferring tenure.* Even where a legislature has the power to confer removal protection on a government official, the relevant statute may leave room for debate as to whether the legislature intended to do so. Both federal and state courts have often had to resolve such debates. Many cases recite the maxim that "[i]n the absence of specific provision to the contrary, the power of removal from office is incident to the power of appointment." *Keim v. United States,* 177 U.S. 290, 293 (1900). But that is only a starting point.

Where the term of office is unspecified, courts are strongly inclined to find that the officer serves at the pleasure of the appointing authority. Otherwise, the individual would be able, by avoiding misconduct, to remain in office for life—a conclusion that the courts have understandably been reluctant to reach. *Shurtleff v. United States,* 189 U.S. 311 (1903) (upholding removal without cause, even though the statute expressly specified grounds for removal!); *Kalaris v. Donovan,* 697 F.2d 376 (D.C.Cir.1983). In *Kalaris* the court held that members of the Benefits Review Board, a workers' compensation tribunal within the Department of Labor, could be removed by the Secretary of Labor without a showing of cause. Despite the purely judicial nature of the Board's functions, the court held that the *Wiener* case, discussed in § 7.7.2a N.3, was not controlling, in part because of the indefinite duration of the Board members' terms.

Where an officer has been appointed for a specific number of years, results vary more widely. Sometimes, if the agency has a structure and functions resembling those of a typical independent agency, courts have little trouble inferring a legislative intention that its members should be removable only for cause. *See, e.g., FEC v. NRA Political Victory Fund,* 6 F.3d 821, 826 (D.C.Cir.1993), *cert. dismissed,* 513 U.S. 88 (1994) (FEC); *SEC v. Blinder, Robinson & Co.,* 855 F.2d 677 (10th Cir.1988) (SEC). But there are contrary holdings as well. *See, e.g., Parsons v. United States,* 167 U.S. 324, 338–39 (1897) (President may freely remove U.S. Attorneys before their four year terms expire).

Among the states, Pennsylvania has the most extensive case law on this issue. In *Watson v. Pennsylvania Turnpike Commission,* 125 A.2d 354, 357 (Pa.1956), the court held that a statute fixing the term of an officer deprived the governor of the authority to remove the officer at will. *Watson* has been read to mean that, in such a situation, "[i]t is presumed that the creators of the office intended the occupant to serve out the term unless good cause could be shown as to why he should be removed." Marks & Cooper, *supra,* at 66; *accord Partain v. Maddox,* 182 S.E.2d 450, 456 (Ga.1971). However, in *Schluraff v. Rzymek,* 208 A.2d 239 (Pa.1965), a plurality of the court limited *Watson* to situations in which members of an agency serve *staggered terms.*

If they have fixed terms that by law can expire concurrently, they serve at the pleasure of the appointing authority. Thus, a member of a local real estate assessment board was properly removed without cause by the county commissioners in the second year of his four year term. Interestingly, a majority of the seven justices in *Schluraff* found the plurality's distinction unconvincing. One concurring justice would have overruled *Watson,* so that agency members would be freely removable even if they had been appointed to staggered terms; three dissenters would have followed *Watson.* With which of these three positions do you agree?

In the end, it is difficult to generalize about the removal power of governors over administrative officers. Consequently, the constitution, statutes, and case law of each state must be examined to determine the exact scope of this power.

7. *Problem.* The Publius River Port Authority (PRPA) was established to construct and operate bridges spanning the Publius River; to construct and maintain facilities for transporting passengers across the river; and to improve and develop the ports on each bank. The river runs between the states of Madison and Hamilton. The governor of each state appoints four commissioners to the PRPA, which was created by an interstate compact between the two states. Such compacts must be approved by Congress, and their terms are interpreted and applied according to federal law.

The compact provides that Madison's representatives on the PRPA "are appointed by the Governor of Madison for terms of five years," subject to confirmation by the Madison Senate. Three years ago, Marjorie, the governor of Madison, appointed Jane to serve on the PRPA. Last week, the recently elected governor, Alex, told Jane that he was disappointed about her vote for a new chairperson of the PRPA. He asked for Jane's resignation. She refused and was notified the next day that Alex intended to remove her from office.

(a) Jane has filed suit to enjoin Alex from removing her. How should the case be resolved?

(b) Now assume that the Publius River runs entirely within the boundaries of Madison, and the PRPA is exclusively a creature of Madison state law. Should the result in Jane's suit change? *Cf. Pievsky v. Ridge,* 98 F.3d 730 (3d Cir.1996).

§ 7.8 EXECUTIVE OVERSIGHT

Exercise of the power to appoint and remove officials is by no means the only tool by which Presidents and governors exert influence over administrative action. Agencies normally maintain a significant working relationship with the chief executive. The President or governor typically coordinates agencies' activities, defends them against political opposition, and prevails upon them to pursue the policies of "the administration."

In the last two decades, sporadic instances of White House intervention into administrative affairs have been eclipsed by the growth of a structured system for presidential review of agency rulemaking. As discussed earlier in § 5.8, the Office of Information and Regulatory Affairs (OIRA), a division of the Office of Management and Budget (OMB), regularly conducts oversight of significant rulemaking proceedings on behalf of the White House. This function received a broad charter when President Reagan issued Executive Order 12291, 46 Fed. Reg. 13193 (1981). A related directive, Executive Order 12498, 50 Fed.Reg. 1036 (1985), created a "regulatory planning" process, under which agencies would submit their anticipated rulemaking initiatives to OIRA each year for approval. President Clinton, upon taking office, promulgated a revised version of both directives in Executive Order 12866, 58 Fed.Reg. 51735 (1993).

Meanwhile, a few states have also developed executive oversight programs, some following the federal model and others displaying a quite different emphasis.

At this point you should review the provisions of E.O. 12866 reprinted in § 5.8. Following are additional provisions of the order, which bear more directly on OIRA's role.

EXECUTIVE ORDER 12866
REGULATORY PLANNING AND REVIEW
58 Fed.Reg. 51735 (1993).

Sec. 2. *Organization.*

(a) *The Agencies.* Because Federal agencies are the repositories of significant substantive expertise and experience, they are responsible for developing regulations and assuring that the regulations are consistent with applicable law, the President's priorities, and the principles set forth in this Executive order.

(b) *The Office of Management and Budget.* Coordinated review of agency rulemaking is necessary to ensure that regulations are consistent with applicable law, the President's priorities, and the principles set forth in this Executive order, and that decisions made by one agency do not conflict with the policies or actions taken or planned by another agency. The Office of Management and Budget (OMB) shall carry out that review function....

(c) *The Vice President.* The Vice President is the principal advisor to the President on, and shall coordinate the development and presentation of recommendations concerning, regulatory policy, planning, and review, as set forth in this Executive order....

Sec. 3. *Definitions.*

(b) "Agency," unless otherwise indicated, means any authority of the United States that is an "agency" ... other than those considered to be independent regulatory agencies....

Sec. 4. *Planning Mechanism.* ... [T]o the extent permitted by law:

(a) *Agencies' Policy Meeting.* Early in each year's planning cycle, the Vice President shall convene a meeting of the [President's policy advisors] and the heads of agencies to seek a common understanding of priorities and to coordinate regulatory efforts to be accomplished in the upcoming year.

(c) *The Regulatory Plan.* For purposes of this subsection, the term "agency" or "agencies" shall also include those considered to be independent regulatory agencies. . . .

(1) . . . [E]ach agency shall prepare a Regulatory Plan (Plan) of the most important significant regulatory actions that the agency reasonably expects to issue in proposed or final form in that fiscal year or thereafter. The Plan shall be approved personally by the agency head. . . .

(5) If the Administrator of OIRA believes that a planned regulatory action of an agency may be inconsistent with the President's priorities or the principles set forth in this Executive order or may be in conflict with any policy or action taken or planned by another agency, the Administrator of OIRA shall promptly notify, in writing, the affected agencies, the [President's policy advisors], and the Vice President. . . .

Sec. 6. *Centralized Review of Regulations.*

(a) *Agency Responsibilities.*

. . . [(3)(E)] After [a proposed rule] has been published in the Federal Register or otherwise issued to the public, the agency shall:
. . .

(i) Make available to the public the [agency's regulatory analysis];

(ii) Identify for the public, in a complete, clear, and simple manner, the substantive changes between the draft submitted to OIRA for review and the action subsequently announced; and

(iii) Identify for the public those changes in the regulatory action that were made at the suggestion or recommendation of OIRA.

(b) *OIRA Responsibilities.* The Administrator of OIRA shall provide meaningful guidance and oversight so that each agency's regulatory actions are consistent with applicable law, the President's priorities, and the principles set forth in this Executive order and do not conflict with the policies or actions of another agency. . . .

(1) OIRA may review only actions identified by the agency or by OIRA as significant regulatory actions. . . .

(2) [In most cases OIRA must complete its review within 90 calendar days after it receives the agency's regulatory analysis.]

(3) For each regulatory action that the Administrator of OIRA returns to an agency for further consideration of some or all of its

provisions, the Administrator of OIRA shall provide the issuing agency a written explanation for such return . . .

(4) [I]n order to ensure greater openness, accessibility, and accountability in the regulatory review process, OIRA shall be governed by the following disclosure requirements: . . .

(A) Only the Administrator of OIRA (or a particular designee) shall receive oral communications initiated by persons not employed by the executive branch of the Federal Government regarding the substance of a regulatory action under OIRA review;

(B) All substantive communications between OIRA personnel and persons not employed by the executive branch of the Federal Government regarding a regulatory action under review shall be governed by the following guidelines: (i) A representative from the issuing agency shall be invited to any meeting between OIRA personnel and such person(s); (ii) OIRA shall forward to the issuing agency, within 10 working days of receipt of the communication(s), all written communications, regardless of format, between OIRA personnel and any person who is not employed by the executive branch of the Federal Government. . . .

(D) After [a proposed rule] has been published in the Federal Register or otherwise issued to the public, or after the agency has announced its decision not to publish or issue the [proposed rule], OIRA shall make available to the public all documents exchanged between OIRA and the agency during the review by OIRA. . . .

Sec. 7. *Resolution of Conflicts.* To the extent permitted by law, disagreements or conflicts between or among agency heads or between OMB and any agency that cannot be resolved by the Administrator of OIRA shall be resolved by the President, or by the Vice President acting at the request of the President, with the relevant agency head (and, as appropriate, other interested government officials). . . .

At the end of this review process, the President, or the Vice President acting at the request of the President, shall notify the affected agency and the Administrator of OIRA of the President's decision with respect to the matter.

Sec. 9. *Agency Authority.* Nothing in this order shall be construed as displacing the agencies' authority or responsibilities, as authorized by law.

Notes and Questions

1. *Case law background.* Supreme Court guidance regarding the proper relationship between the President and the federal agencies has been sparse. An early case that defined some of the outer boundaries of that relationship

was *Kendall v. United States ex rel. Stokes,* 37 U.S. (12 Pet.) 524, 610–12 (1838). Congress had passed a special law to resolve a dispute between the postmaster general and a contract carrier for the Post Office. The law directed the postmaster to pay the amount owed to the carrier, as calculated by the solicitor of the treasury. The postmaster refused to pay, claiming that the President had instructed him not to comply. The Court upheld a writ of mandamus against the postmaster:

> There are certain political duties imposed upon many officers in the executive department, the discharge of which is under the direction of the President. But it would be an alarming doctrine, that congress cannot impose upon any executive officer any duty they may think proper, which is not repugnant to any rights secured and protected by the constitution; and in such cases, the duty and responsibility grow out of and are subject to the control of the law, and not to the direction of the President. And this is emphatically the case, where the duty enjoined is of a mere ministerial character....

> It was urged at the bar, that the postmaster general was alone subject to the direction and control of the President, with respect to the execution of the duty imposed upon him by this law, and this right of the President is claimed, as growing out of the obligation imposed upon him by the constitution, to take care that the laws be faithfully executed. This is a doctrine that cannot receive the sanction of this court.... To contend that the obligation imposed on the President to see the laws faithfully executed, implies a power to forbid their execution, is a novel construction of the constitution, and entirely inadmissible....

Another important historical milestone was *Youngstown Sheet & Tube Co. v. Sawyer,* 343 U.S. 579 (1952). President Truman used an executive order to direct the Secretary of Commerce to take control of the nation's steel mills for the purpose of preventing a strike during the Korean War. The Supreme Court held this seizure invalid.

Justice Black's opinion for the Court took a straightforward approach to the separation of powers issue. It argued that the President's seizure was not authorized by statute and could not be justified by his independent constitutional powers as commander-in-chief. "Nor," Black continued, "can the seizure order be sustained because of the several constitutional provisions that grant executive power to the President. In the framework of our Constitution, the President's power to see that the laws are faithfully executed refutes the idea that he is to be a lawmaker. The Constitution ... is neither silent nor equivocal about who shall make laws which the President is to execute. The first section of the first article says that 'All legislative Powers herein granted shall be vested in a Congress of the United States....'" *Id.* at 585–88.

The well known concurring opinion of Justice Jackson in the *Youngstown* case took a more flexible view of the President's power. Justice Jackson sketched three situations. In the first, where "the President acts pursuant to an express or implied authorization of Congress, his authority is at its maximum." In the second, the President acts in the absence of statutes supporting or prohibiting his action. Here the President "can only rely on his own independent constitutional powers," and, therefore, he has less authority than in the first situation; "but there is a zone of twilight in which he and Congress may have concurrent authority, or in which its distribution is uncertain. Therefore, congressional inertia, indifference or quiescence may sometimes, at least as a practical matter, enable, if not invite, measures on independent presidential responsibility. In this area, any actual test of power is likely to depend on the imperatives of events and contemporary imponderables rather than on abstract theories of law." In the third situation, the President takes action that is "incompatible with the expressed or implied will of Congress." In this situation "his power is at its lowest ebb, for then he can rely only upon his own constitutional powers minus any constitutional powers of Congress over the matter." *Id.* at 634–38.

Jackson concluded that the *Youngstown* situation fit into the third category and was impermissible. Congress had specified conditions under which the President could seize private property; those conditions had not been met. By implication, Congress had forbidden seizures under other circumstances. In essence, a majority of the Court apparently believed that, in the event of a conflict between Congress and the President concerning matters over which they each have constitutional competence to act, the conflict should be resolved in favor of Congress.

2. *From rivalry to cooperation.* The initial years of the formal oversight program, during the Reagan and Bush administrations, were stormy ones. Relations between OIRA and the agencies were often marked by mutual suspicion. Moreover, countless academic and journalistic critiques accused OIRA of interfering with legitimate rulemaking initiatives. *See, e.g.,* Alan B. Morrison, "OMB Interference with Agency Rulemaking: The Wrong Way to Write a Regulation," 99 Harv.L.Rev. 1059 (1986). *But see* Christopher C. DeMuth & Douglas H. Ginsburg, "White House Review of Agency Rulemaking," 99 Harv.L.Rev. 1075 (1986) (a defense by two of the program's administrators). For appraisals of the program during this period, see Harold H. Bruff, "Presidential Management of Agency Rulemaking," 57 Geo. Wash.L.Rev. 533 (1989); Symposium, "Presidential Oversight of Regulatory Decisionmaking," 36 Am.U.L.Rev. 443 (1987).

Rivalry between agencies and presidential reviewers continued during the Bush years. A particular target of complaint was the Council on Competitiveness, which was established within Vice President Quayle's office to supervise OIRA's functions. It operated with a strong deregulatory emphasis and few regularized procedures. *See, e.g.,* Peter M. Shane, "Political Accountability in a System of Checks and Balances: The Case of Presidential Review of Rulemaking," 48 Ark.L.Rev. 161, 165–73 (1995); Symposium, "The Council on Competitiveness: Executive Oversight of Agency Rulemaking," 7 Ad.L.J.Am.U. 297 (1993).

In contrast, implementation of E.O. 12866 during the Clinton years has been strikingly uncontroversial. The public has witnessed few if any public struggles between OIRA and rulemaking agencies during this period. Is the changed atmosphere simply a function of differences in the ideological commitments of these three administrations, or are there other explanations? Consider this question throughout the following materials. For helpful comparisons between the two executive orders, see Shane, *supra,* at 174–92;

Richard H. Pildes & Cass R. Sunstein, "Reinventing the Regulatory State," 62 U.Chi.L.Rev. 1, 16–33 (1995).

3. *Merits of executive oversight.* Recall the strong endorsement of presidential oversight of rulemaking in *Sierra Club v. Costle,* § 5.5.2, and the reasons given for that endorsement. Of course, the court's vote of confidence preceded any experience under E.O. 12291. Moreover, it pertained to the actions of the President personally, as opposed to a review office acting on his behalf. Do the court's arguments also support the OIRA oversight program? According to some observers, they do:

> [T]here are strong reasons for creating and maintaining an executive office entrusted with the job of coordinating modern regulation, promoting sensible priority setting, and ensuring conformity with the President's basic mission. In view of the wide array of regulatory programs administered by modern government, the absence of such an office would probably guarantee duplication, parochial perspectives, and inefficiency. A number of separate agencies and programs deal with environmental and other risks, and it is therefore important to share information, to reduce inconsistency, and to devote scarce resources to places where they will do the most good.

Pildes & Sunstein, *supra,* at 16.

Does OIRA's actual track record measure up to these aspirations? Published appraisals of experience under the Clinton process have not yet appeared, but events during the Reagan–Bush era have sometimes been judged harshly:

> Presidential overseers have had little or no scientific or technical expertise; they have been, for the most part, economists, often with only a few years of experience. Nevertheless, White House oversight is said to improve the quality of regulation because it provides a broad and general perspective that counteracts the more narrow perspective of the experts in the agencies. If this had been the OMB's role, regulatory policy might have been improved, but OMB failed to provide a generalist perspective for two reasons. First, it was not selective in what was reviewed. Because overseers tended to look at everything, rather than focus on what was important, they often missed important issues, and wound up fighting with the agency over unimportant details. This tendency resulted from the overseers' lack of expertise and experience and from their distrust of the agencies they were reviewing. Second, the administration's ideological beliefs usually prevailed over an agency's policy analysis. While "[t]here are literally hundreds of cases of OMB intervention into agency rulemakings to urge less stringent regulations," there are "at most a handful of cases of OMB urging the agencies to regulate more stringently." Indeed, in OMB "[t]here [was] a strong sense among most agency analysts that a good analysis will not save a decision with which OMB disagrees and a poor analysis will not slow down a decision with which OMB agrees."

Sidney A. Shapiro, "Political Oversight and the Deterioration of Regulatory Policy," 46 Admin.L.Rev. 1, 24 (1994). The Clinton order has ameliorated at least one of these problems, by limiting the number of rules that OIRA reviews. *See* E.O. 12866, §§ 3(f), 6(a)(3)(A), 6(b)(1). The more basic question about OIRA's qualifications is more difficult to evaluate. According to Richard Pierce, however, that office's oversight at least compares favorably with judicial review of whether a major rule displays "reasoned decisionmaking":

> OIRA has significant advantages over courts in performing this review function.... OIRA is staffed by an interdisciplinary team of social and natural scientists. Its reviewers know how to read and interpret conflicting studies and analyses. By contrast, generalist judges and their bright young law clerks typically know virtually nothing about the disciplines relevant to the policy disputes resolved in a major rulemaking.... OIRA also can devote more resources to the review process than can a federal court.... [I]t seems unlikely that any judge ever gets very far into the 10,000 to 250,000 page record of a major rulemaking. Judges necessarily rely on the briefs of the parties and the selected excerpts from the record submitted by the parties as their near exclusive basis for obtaining a picture of the rulemaking. The lawyers that represent petitioners in rulemaking review proceedings are experts at distorting that picture....
>
> OIRA's flexibility advantage inheres in its ability to engage in expeditious, two-way communications with a rulemaking agency.... OIRA typically communicates its questions and concerns within a week or two of receiving an agency's proposed final rule, and the agency often responds to OIRA's satisfaction within a week or two thereafter.... The OIRA review process always is completed in a small fraction of the time required for completion of the process of judicial application of the duty to engage in reasoned decisionmaking.
>
> Finally, OIRA is more politically accountable than a reviewing court. [R]ulemaking is, and should be, a political process.... Moreover, the president will be held politically accountable for the results of the OIRA review process.... By contrast, no one can be held politically accountable for analogous judicial decisions [although judges often] exercise significant power to veto policy decisions based on each judge's political and ideological perspective.

Richard J. Pierce, Jr., "Seven Ways to Deossify Agency Rulemaking," 47 Admin.L.Rev. 59, 70–71 (1995).

Pierce's emphasis on the President's political accountability, as a justification for centralized review of rulemaking, recalls Bonfield's similar argument in favor of gubernatorial review at the state level. *See* § 7.5. Is this a strong rationale? Consider these views:

> The connection between presidential control of administration and accountability is [often considered] self-evident. Of course, if one simply defines "accountability" as the vesting of ultimate decisional authority in a person who is elected, not appointed, it is, indeed, self-evident that the President is elected, and bureaucrats are not.... But no adequate analysis can rest entirely on that observation....
>
> ... There is no evidence that the President, at any given moment, embodies that set of policy predilections across a wide set of issues that is held by a contemporaneous majority—or, more accurately, by contem-

poraneous *majorities* of Americans. Indeed, one of the most remarkable features of the Reagan Presidency was the dissonance between his strong electoral mandates and the public's apparent rejection of his policy positions on a variety of highly significant issues. This emphatically is true with respect to environmental regulation. Throughout the [Reagan–Bush] era, consistent and overwhelming majorities of Americans subscribed to the view that the quantity of U.S. environmental regulation was appropriate or too low....

There is one most obvious reason why the President would mirror public opinion polls quite imperfectly—the President is a single person.... A President whose every view tracked the majority in the latest relevant opinion poll would presumably be so conspicuously lacking in any internal compass as to call into question at least the President's capacity for leadership, not to mention his mental health....

Moreover, the President's incentives to follow the polls in any close way are not as strong as is often assumed. After all, despite common academic references to a presidential candidate's unique "national constituency," any candidate is subject to election only twice....

If bureaucratic accountability to elected politicians is to be used as a structural mechanism aimed at achieving direct responsiveness to public opinion, it would probably make more sense to intensify the influence that Congress—especially the House—has over the agencies. Members of Congress are eligible for reelection indefinitely; a common observation of the House is that its members are in a constant election campaign.... [A] tight concentration of power over bureaucratic decision making [through the Presidency] would seem to impede, rather than advance, the cause of accountability.... It is precisely the large size and relative openness of Congress that makes it realistic to hope that all interests relevant to a policy decision will find some effective legislative representation and voice. If ultimate policy making power were lodged in a single individual, such an arrangement necessarily would increase the chances that one interest or set of interests will have disproportionate access and influence....

    ... Administrative decision making in the public interest requires an extension to the executive branch of a policy dialogue that is vigorous, thorough, and reasoned.... [I]t is thus important not to tighten the reins on subordinates, but to provide incentives for subordinates to speak freely and for the President actually to listen to diverse voices despite the predictable dominance of his own.... If the country wants decision making attentive to [what Madison called] "the permanent and aggregate interests of the community," thoughtfully determined, then decision making structures should maximize opportunities for transcending partisanship and ideology. Tightly hierarchical structures do not.

Shane, *supra,* at 196–206.

    4. *Legality of executive oversight.* Like its predecessor orders, E.O. 12866 repeatedly declares that its prescriptions apply only "to the extent permitted by law." But to what "extent" is a presidential review program "permitted"? Congress has not explicitly authorized presidential review, but

this program has been widely assumed to fall, at the very least, within the second, "zone of twilight" category that Justice Jackson identified in *Youngstown* as the proper mode of analysis for actions that Congress has neither authorized nor prohibited. According to commentators who support the program, its legality is rooted in the President's constitutional duty to "take Care that the Laws be faithfully executed," and also in a less well known clause of the Constitution under which the President may "require the Opinion, in writing, of the principal Officer in each of the executive Departments, upon any Subject relating to the Duties of their respective Offices." Art. II, § 2, cl. 1. *See* Peter L. Strauss, "The Place of Agencies in Government: Separation of Powers and the Fourth Branch," 84 Colum.L.Rev. 573, 653–62 (1984).

On the other hand, could it be argued that Congress has implicitly directed the President *not* to involve himself in the agencies' rulemaking? If so, OIRA's operations would presumably fall into the third, and most disfavored, of Justice Jackson's three categories. This thesis would be supportable if regulatory legislation were interpreted as implying that an agency head should make his or her decision without White House participation. Such a suggestion was made in the early years of the Reagan oversight program. *See* Morton Rosenberg, "Beyond the Limits of Executive Power: Presidential Control of Agency Rulemaking Under Executive Order 12,291," 80 Mich.L.Rev. 193 (1981). In subsequent years, however, wholesale attacks on the validity of OIRA review have ebbed.

Nevertheless, *particular* exercises of OIRA's authority can still pose legal problems. For example, during the Reagan–Bush years, critics sometimes claimed that OIRA was violating the law by forcing agencies to delay their issuance of regulations, notwithstanding applicable statutory deadlines. *See Environmental Defense Fund, Inc. v. Thomas,* 627 F.Supp. 566 (D.D.C. 1986) (ordering immediate promulgation of rule despite OMB's "interference"). This specific problem has been addressed by the Clinton order, which contains deadlines by which OIRA itself must act. The order states that the agency may proceed with issuance of a rule if OIRA does not raise an objection by the deadline. §§ 6(b)(2), 8. On the other hand, when OIRA does return a rule for further consideration by the agency, the potential for delays remains.

More generally, *Kendall* has commonly been read to mean that if a matter is entrusted to an agency official, the President cannot lawfully require the official to act at variance with the statutory mandate. Notice, however, that in *Kendall* the postmaster's duty was considered ministerial. What if an agency head has been given discretion—can the President (or, perhaps, the President's designee) order the agency head to exercise it in a particular way? Could the President fire the agency head because of her failure to comply with his directive? Consider the reasoning of *Sierra Club v. Costle,* 657 F.2d 298 (D.C.Cir.1981), excerpted in § 5.5.2, and *Myers v. United States,* 272 U.S. 52 (1926), quoted in § 7.7.2a. *See generally* Peter L. Strauss, "Presidential Rulemaking," 72 Chi.-Kent L.Rev. 965 (1997).

5. *Where the buck stops.* What happens if White House officials and the rulemaking agency reach an impasse? This issue arose even before the promulgation of E.O. 12291: "[A] well-publicized example of staff abuse

occurred during the Carter administration when the Chairman of the Council of Economic Advisors (CEA) ordered the Assistant Secretary for Occupational Safety and Health to change a standard for protecting workers from exposure to cotton dust. When the Secretary of Labor demanded to meet with the president on the matter, the President overruled the CEA Chairman." Thomas O. McGarity, "Presidential Control of Regulatory Agency Decisionmaking," 36 Am.U.L.Rev. 443, 455 (1987).

The same author cites an incident involving Vice President Bush, to whom President Reagan had delegated a degree of supervisory authority under E.O. 12291. OSHA proposed a rule to require labeling for hazardous substances in the workplace. OMB's assessment of the rule's likely benefits differed from OSHA's. The issue reached the Vice President, who ultimately sided with OSHA. Thomas O. McGarity, REINVENTING RATIONALITY: THE ROLE OF REGULATORY ANALYSIS IN THE FEDERAL BUREAU-CRACY 100 (1991). As two commentators have remarked, "the fact that [Bush] endorsed OSHA's regulatory approach is perhaps less revealing than the fact that he believed it to be his decision whether OSHA would prevail." Pildes & Sunstein, *supra,* at 24 n.95.

Against this background, consider the conflict resolution role assigned to the President and Vice President in E.O. 12866, particularly in §§ 2(c) and 7. In practice, the supervisory role devolves mainly on the Vice President. In fact, the order has been described as having vested an unprecedented degree of responsibility in the Vice President, making him a virtual "chief operating officer of the Executive Branch." *See* John F. Cooney, "Regulatory Review in the Clinton Administration," Admin.L. News, Fall 1993, at 1. As between the Vice President and the rulemaking agency, does the order make clear who has the last word? To the extent the order is ambiguous, who *should* have the last word?

6. *Independent agencies.* Both E.O. 12291 and E.O. 12866 exempted independent agencies' rulemaking proceedings from OIRA review (although the Clinton order includes the independent agencies in its provisions for government-wide planning of rulemaking initiatives). The Justice Department has maintained that the President does have authority to prescribe OIRA review of rulemaking by independent agencies, but the White House has chosen to avoid the controversy that such an extension of the oversight program would be likely to engender.

ACUS recommended that, "[a]s a matter of principle, presidential review of rulemaking should apply to independent regulatory agencies to the same extent as it applies to the rulemaking of Executive Branch departments and other agencies." ACUS Recommendation 88–9, 54 Fed.Reg. 5207 (1989). The American Bar Association has taken the same position. Defending this view, two scholars write:

> From the standpoint of sound regulatory policy, fashioned in a process of informal rulemaking, we believe that there is no meaningful difference between the "independent" agencies and those agencies to which the two executive orders are currently applicable. The two categories of agencies engage in regulatory activities that are, from a functional standpoint, indistinguishable. Indeed, often those activities concern the same or similar subject areas; consider the overlapping work of the

Department of Justice and the Federal Trade Commission. The same considerations that justify a coordinating presidential role with respect to "executive" agencies apply with full force to those characterized as "independent."

Peter L. Strauss & Cass R. Sunstein, "The Role of the President and OMB in Informal Rulemaking," 38 Admin.L.Rev. 181, 205 (1986). Wouldn't such an extension defeat the congressional goal of keeping the independent agencies' actions apolitical and free of presidential influence? *See* Bruff, *supra,* at 590–93.

7. *Disclosure issues.* Particularly disturbing to many observers of presidential review during the Reagan and Bush years was the secrecy of various aspects of the process. Under congressional pressure, OIRA agreed to institute certain procedural reforms in 1986, but this commitment was undercut during the Bush years by the creation of the Council on Competitiveness, which played a key role in the oversight process but did not consider itself bound by that agreement. Against this background, one of the most important aspects of the Clinton order was the administration's adoption of various "sunshine" principles.

First, during the E.O. 12291 period, OIRA and the Competitiveness Council were persistently accused of serving as "conduits" for the views of private interests. Allegedly they served as a back channel by which communications from business groups could reach the agency without being disclosed on the public record. Thus, the presidential review process was thought to be aggravating the problem of secretive private influence on the rulemaking process. Whatever the scope of this behavior may have been, the Clinton order instituted formal constraints on "conduit communications," so as to minimize the problem in the future. *See* E.O. 12866, §§ 6(b)(4)(A)–(B).

Second, OIRA and the Competitiveness Council themselves were accused of harboring skeptical (if not downright hostile) attitudes toward the regulatory programs that rulemaking agencies were charged with implementing. Thus, supporters of those programs insisted that communications from the presidential reviewers should also be on the public record. Responding to this critique, E.O. 12866 now provides for disclosure, at the end of a rulemaking proceeding, of "all documents exchanged between OIRA and the agency during the review." § 6(b)(4)(D). However, most contacts between OIRA and the agencies occur at meetings or on the telephone, and the order does not guarantee disclosure of *oral* communications. Should agencies be required to summarize these conversations for the public record? Recall, in this connection, the tolerant attitude of the court in *Sierra Club v. Costle* toward the possibility of undisclosed presidential contacts. *See* § 5.5.2, and also N.5 following that case. This issue is discussed in the OIRA context in Bruff, *supra,* at 587–89.

A third reform in E.O. 12866 is also aimed at making OIRA more accountable. Under § 6(a)(3)(E), an agency must identify the "substantive changes made between the draft submitted to OIRA for review and the action subsequently announced," (clause (ii)). Moreover, the agency must identify which of these changes were made at the suggestion or recommendation of OIRA (clause (iii)). However, a January 1998 report by the General Accounting Office charges that agencies have not complied very faithfully with clause (iii). Is that a serious problem? If the actual changes made following OIRA review are disclosed, pursuant to clause (ii), how important is it that the agency disclose which ones were OIRA's idea? Indeed, if a change emerges as the result of mutual discussion between OIRA staff and the agency staff, is the disclosure mandated by clause (iii) even meaningful? (For background on these disclosure requirements, see Margaret Gilhooley, "Executive Oversight of Administrative Rulemaking: Disclosing the Impact," 25 Ind.L.Rev. 299 (1991).)

8. *State executive review.* At the state level, executive review takes a variety of forms. Some schemes are based on the federal model. In Arizona, Governor Bruce Babbitt established a review program by executive order in 1981. The order created a five member council to review all proposed rules issued by agencies whose heads were appointed by the governor. These agencies would submit an analysis of all proposed rules, including a cost-benefit analysis and an economic impact statement, to the council *prior* to the usual notice and comment period. The council then would review the rules and determine if their benefits outweighed their costs, if the rules were clearly and understandably written, and if they served the public interest. *See* Jonathan Rose, "Executive Oversight of Rulemaking in Arizona: The Governor's Regulatory Review Council—The First Three Years," 1985 Ariz. St.L.J. 425. The system has since been revised. Now, as in most other oversight schemes, the council reviews rules prior to *final* adoption. Ariz. Rev.Stat.Ann. § 41–1051 et. seq. Virginia and Pennsylvania also have review programs modeled on OIRA's functions. *See* Va. Code Ann. § 9–6.14:9.1 (rules are submitted for review to governor, who may suggest changes or order brief suspension, but may not cancel the rule); Pa. Exec. Order 1996–1. In other states, gubernatorial review is integrated with the functions of the legislature's rules review committee. *See* Md. Code Ann., State Gov't § 10–111.1; Wash.Rev. Code Ann. § 34.05.640(3).

9. *Executive review in California.* In California, the Office of Administrative Law (OAL), an executive-branch agency, must approve virtually all administrative rules. *See* Cal.Govt. Code §§ 11349 et seq. Created in 1979, OAL functions as a surrogate for judicial review. It decides whether a rule is "necessary" based on substantial evidence in the rulemaking record. It also decides whether a rule meets tests of legality ("consistency") and whether the agency complied with APA procedural requirements. It serves as the state's English teacher—deciding whether the meaning of the rule will be easily understood by those persons directly affected by it. And it asks whether the rule is duplicative of other statutes or rules and whether the agency has cited to the relevant authorities under which the rule is issued.

If OAL disapproves a rule, the agency can resubmit it within 120 days. However, if a resubmitted rule comes after 120 days, or its substantive provisions have been significantly changed, the agency must begin the rulemaking process anew. There is an opportunity for an appeal to the governor, but this is seldom attempted and seldom successful.

Like their federal counterparts, OAL and the agencies had an antagonistic and hostile relationship until the early 1990's. Now, however, OAL is viewed as constructive and useful, by both agency staff and members of the public. It seems to function fairly smoothly. Leadership changes at OAL and agencies' growing familiarity with OAL's ways are among the reasons for this changed atmosphere.

Notice, however, the differences between OAL and OIRA. The latter's function is openly political. It is designed to improve inter-agency coordination, to analyze whether the benefits of a regulation justify its costs, and to make certain that regulations are consistent with the President's priorities. In contrast, OAL's function is not explicitly political and is not intended to further any particular method of analysis. It does not receive political input from the governor. Instead, it is designed to serve a judicial-review type of function and to improve the drafting of rules. Given the availability of judicial review, is this layer of executive review needed or appropriate? If it is, should OIRA's role be changed to make it more like OAL's?

10. *Gubernatorial vetoes.* In some states, rules may not take effect without the governor's approval. *See* Hawaii Rev.Stat. § 91–3(c); Neb.Rev. Stat. § 84–908; Okla.Stat. tit. 75, §§ 303.1(E), 308.1. In these states the governor may decline to approve a rule for any reason. In Wyoming, each rule requires the governor's approval, which must be denied unless the rule is authorized, consistent with the legislative purpose, and procedurally valid. The law is unclear as to whether the governor may withhold approval for other reasons as well. *See* Wyo.Stat. § 16–3–103(d); Barton R. Voigt, Comment, "Wyoming's Administrative Regulation Review Act," 14 Land & Water L.Rev. 189 (1979). In a few other states, a rule may go into effect without gubernatorial involvement, but the governor may rescind the rule by disapproving it within a short period following its promulgation. *See* Ind. Code § 4–22–2–34; Iowa Code § 17.4(6); La.Rev.Stat.Ann. § 49:970.

1981 MSAPA § 3–202 follows the lead of these states by empowering the governor to rescind or suspend any rule or to summarily terminate any pending rulemaking proceeding, to the extent the agency involved would itself have had such authority. Before rescinding or suspending a rule, the governor must follow MSAPA rulemaking procedures, but he or she may terminate a pending rulemaking proceeding without observing any procedural formalities. The official Comment accompanying the section says that these powers "will facilitate ultimate coordination of all rulemaking and provide a direct and easily usable political check on the rulemaking process." The absence of a time limit on the governor's authority to rescind a rule "is justified because this state wide, directly elected official is closer to and more representative of the people than the unelected agency."

A commentator has argued, however, that § 3–202 "is too broad and lacks sufficient safeguards.... [T]he governor's power to veto existing agency rules enables each successive governor to unilaterally terminate past policies.... The governor's power is limited only by minimal procedural requirements [and] is not subject to effective public, judicial, or legislative control. Although the governor is politically accountable to the general public, the veto of any specific agency rule is unlikely to be a significant political issue." David S. Neslin, Comment, "Quis Custodiet Ipsos Custodes?: Gubernatorial and Legislative Review of Agency Rulemaking Under the 1981 Model Act," 57 Wash.L.Rev. 669, 683–84 (1982). The reporter for the Act replies that § 3–202 does require the governor to follow MSAPA rulemaking procedures; and, in any event, "when the governor vetoes a statute, we find it entirely satisfactory to hold the chief executive responsible for such action at the polls. The same should be true of gubernatorial rescissions or suspensions of rules." Another restraining factor is that "a governor must maintain an effective and close working relationship with state agencies." Arthur Earl Bonfield, STATE ADMINISTRATIVE RULE MAKING 478–81 (1986). Who has the better of this argument?

11. *Problem.* Recently the Department of Pollution Control (DPC), an executive branch agency in the state of Madison, announced rules designed to regulate municipal incinerators, which are a significant source of air pollution. Soon afterwards, a local newspaper published an article purporting to give the inside story as to why some of the restrictions that DPC had tentatively endorsed in its notice of proposed rulemaking were eliminated from the final version of the rules. Among the details in the story were the following:

One of these abandoned proposals was a ban on burning lead-acid automobile batteries in city incinerators. According to the newspaper, Bonita, a policy analyst with the Madison Office of Information and Regulatory Affairs (MOIRA), questioned the proposed ban in a face-to-face meeting with Chad, the deputy secretary of DPC. Bonita suggested that a partial ban would be adequate, because the burning of vehicle batteries is already regulated under other environmental laws. Chad then decided that the partial ban would be too complicated to administer, so DPC simply dropped the battery provision from its rules. However, the agency in no way disclosed that MOIRA had played a role in influencing this particular aspect of the rules.

That negotiation proceeded in a cooperative fashion, but another aspect of the negotiations between MOIRA and DPC went less smoothly. Bonita challenged the agency's proposed requirement that cities must develop programs to recycle old newspapers, in order to minimize the quantity of newsprint that would be burned in municipal incinerators. When Chad resisted dropping the recycling requirement, Bonita insisted: "I have it straight from the governor that this change is imperative. We're really hearing from the mayors on this. They say the kind of recycling you would require is just too expensive and wouldn't have much effect on pollution anyway. So, we aren't just asking you to drop this—we're telling you." Chad reluctantly replied, "All right—but only because the governor says we have to do this." The agency disclosed nothing about MOIRA's influence on this decision, either.

The Alliance for a Clean Environment intends to petition the agency to reconsider its omission of the vehicle battery and recycling requirements. As counsel to the Alliance, you are asked whether the group can fairly argue that, if the newspaper's story is true, MOIRA or DPC violated its legal obligations. Assuming that MOIRA conducts its oversight activities pursuant to a state executive order that is substantially identical to federal E.O. 12866, and that Madison's judicial case law is the same as federal law, were any actions by either of these government entities impermissible? As a matter of policy, *should* any of their actions have been prohibited? Would your assessment of the legality of the participants' conduct change if the only pertinent restrictions on MOIRA's oversight activities were found in the MSAPA? *Cf. New York v. Reilly,* 969 F.2d 1147 (D.C.Cir.1992).

Chapter 8

FREEDOM OF INFORMATION AND OTHER OPEN GOVERNMENT LAWS

This chapter addresses statutes that relate in various ways to the issue of governmental openness. It asks whether government functions and documents should be open to public scrutiny. It also considers whether such openness might be viewed as a political check on agency action, like the legislative and executive controls discussed in chapter 7.

The chapter concentrates on freedom of information legislation and also considers open meeting laws and the Federal Advisory Committee Act.

§ 8.1 FREEDOM OF INFORMATION

The federal Freedom of Information Act (often referred to as FOIA) was passed in 1966. It was amended and vastly strengthened in 1974, at a time when mistrust of government was rampant. In 1996 it was amended again to take account of electronic records. The Act consists of three parts, all found in § 552 of the APA:

(i) Under APA § 552(a)(1) (parts of which were in the original 1946 APA), an agency must *publish* certain important information, such as a statement of its organization and procedure and substantive rules of general applicability. The latter category includes statements of general policy and interpretations of general applicability. As earlier discussed in § 5.7, if such material is not published, a person without actual and timely knowledge of the terms thereof cannot be adversely affected by it. For a similar provision, see 1981 MSAPA § 2–101.

(ii) Under APA § 552(a)(2), agencies must *make available* (but not necessarily publish) specified additional material. This includes final opinions, staff manuals, instructions to staff that affect the public, and policy statements and interpretations of particular (rather than general) applicability. This requirement is discussed in the *Sears, Roebuck* case which follows.

Material covered by § 552(a)(2) must be indexed, and, for records created after November 1, 1996, must be placed in a computer database. Material covered by this provision may not be used adversely to a person unless these requirements are met or the person had actual and timely knowledge of its contents. *See Smith v. NTSB*, 981 F.2d 1326 (D.C.Cir. 1993) (decision suspending pilot's license set aside because agency failed to make publicly available a staff instruction setting the penalties for such violations). For a similar provision, see 1981 MSAPA § 2–102.

(iii) Most important, under APA § 552(a)(3), an agency must furnish *any reasonably described record requested by any person for any reason*. This truly revolutionary provision is what people generally mean when they discuss the Freedom of Information Act.

If an agency refuses to furnish the record (or fails to act within the very short time frame described in § 552(a)(6)), the requester is entitled to go to federal district court to compel disclosure. A requester who substantially prevails in court can often recover attorney's fees.

The agency has the burden to justify non-disclosure on the basis of one of the nine exemptions to the Act's disclosure requirements contained in § 552(b). To satisfy its burden, the agency must claim and justify exemptions for each document (or part of a document) through a detailed index and itemization. The court decides the matter de novo (i.e. without deferring to the agency's judgment).

Comparable provisions have been adopted in every state. *See* Burt A. Braverman & Wesley R. Heppler, "A Practical Review of State Open Records Laws," 49 Geo.Wash.L.Rev. 720 (1981); Henry P. Tseng & Donald B. Pederson, "Acquisition of State Administrative Rules and Regulations—Update 1983," 35 Admin.L.Rev. 349 (1983).

Many states also recognize a common law right to inspect state and local documents. Traditionally, this right was really a form of civil discovery; it was available only to persons who needed the document for litigation purposes, and it covered only records that were legally required to be kept. *See* Thomas H. Moore, Comment, "You Can't Always Get What You Want: A Look at North Carolina's Public Records Law," 72 N.C.L. Rev. 1527, 1529–43 (1994). But in some states any public purpose was a sufficient interest to demand documents. And in some states the common law right of inspection survives the adoption of a Freedom of Information law. *See Irval Realty Inc. v. Board of Public Util. Comm'rs*, 294 A.2d 425 (N.J.1972) (common law right applies to information exempt under state information law).

There is a sharp difference of opinion about whether the benefits of laws like FOIA or similar state acts outweigh the costs. Bonfield is a proponent of a strong FOIA but also points out the need for some limits:

A broad right of public access to governmental information confirms the idea that the people are sovereign and facilitates control by the principals (the people) over their agent (the government). Easily accessible information about government operations enables members of the general public to discover the actual norms guiding governmental behavior, to monitor the government's compliance with law, to evaluate the quality of its performance, and to object in a more effective way to improper or unacceptable governmental behavior.... Broad public access to information about government operations also deters official misconduct and induces greater care by officials in their dealings with the general public and in their handling of its affairs.... [T]he sunlight of public access to information about governmental operations kills or retards the growth of mould in government....

On the other hand ... a broad public right of access to governmental information must have limits and can be overdone ... At some point, the costs of such a right exceed its benefits.... As a result, any broad public right of access must be limited to accommodate in a reasonable way other important public interests that, at some point, compete and conflict with that right. Of course a completely fair balance between the important public right of access and the other potentially conflicting important public interests in effective, efficient, and economical government administration, and personal privacy, is hard to achieve.

Arthur E. Bonfield, "Chairman's Message," 40 Admin.L.Rev. iii (Win. 1988).

At the federal level, FOIA's costs have proved to be far in excess of what FOIA's drafters ever imagined. The federal government is estimated to receive more than 300,000 requests for information under FOIA each year, of which about 90% are granted administratively. Many requests appear to involve efforts by one business to obtain information about another business for private gain. Many agencies are hopelessly backlogged with FOIA requests and cannot possibly comply with FOIA's time requirements. A single request can be enormously time consuming; one company's request to the Navy was estimated to include several million documents which would span 10,000 linear feet. Thomas M. Susman, "Introduction to the Issues, Problems, and Relevant Law," 34 Admin.L.Rev. 117, 118 (1982). Recent amendments allow agencies to place burdensome demands on a slow track, so that a single such request will not stall numerous requests that could be handled more quickly.

It is difficult to estimate the cost to government, but estimates range between about $50 million and $250 million per year or more. A large number of agency employees, who would otherwise be engaged in carrying out agency programs, are instead employed to respond to FOIA requests—searching for documents, redacting (deleting) material from records that should not become public in full (sometimes word-by-word review is needed), making copies, or reviewing disclosure decisions by other employees. This work is laborious and unpopular.

Thousands of FOIA cases have been filed in the already swamped federal courts; the cases often receive priority (28 U.S.C. § 1657) and require the judge to conduct painstaking in camera review of a mass of documents. The U.S. Supreme Court has decided over two dozen FOIA cases, and the Arkansas Supreme Court has decided over three dozen FOIA cases. John Watkins, "The Arkansas Freedom of Information Act: Time for a Change," 44 Ark.L.Rev. 535 (1991).

> FOIA ... is the Taj Mahal of the Doctrine of Unanticipated Consequences, the Sistine Chapel of Cost Benefit Analysis Ignored ... The foregoing defects [of excessive costs and burdens on government and the courts] ... might not be defects in the best of all possible worlds. They are foolish extravagances only because we do not have an unlimited amount of federal money to spend, an unlimited number of agency employees to assign, an unlimited number of judges to hear and decide cases. We must, alas, set some priorities— and unless the world is mad the usual FOIA request should not be high on the list.

Antonin Scalia, "The Freedom of Information Act Has No Clothes," Regulation, March/April 1982, at 15, 17–18.

To alleviate the burden on courts of resolving FOIA cases, Connecticut, Minnesota, and New York route disputes between a requestor and an agency to an independent agency for decision. *See* Margaret Westin, "The Minnesota Government Data Practices Act," 22 Wm. Mitchell L.Rev,. 839 (1996). The independent agency's decision is judicially reviewable, but at least a reviewing court does not consider the case de novo, as it must do under federal law and the law of most states.

In evaluating FOIA, it is necessary to take account of its nine exemptions. If FOIA is too costly, one policy alternative is to broaden the existing exemptions or create new ones. Or are these exemptions already too broad? The following discussion considers two of the exceptions in the federal act: § 552(b)(5), discussed in *Sears, Roebuck,* and § 552(b)(4), discussed in *Chrysler.*

§ 8.1.1 PROTECTING DELIBERATION: § 552(b)(5)

NLRB v. SEARS, ROEBUCK & CO.
421 U.S. 132 (1975).

WHITE, J.:

The National Labor Relations Board (the Board) and its General Counsel seek to set aside an order of the United States District Court directing disclosure to respondent, Sears, Roebuck & Co. (Sears), pursuant to the Freedom of Information Act, 5 U.S.C. § 552 (Act), of certain memoranda, known as "Advice Memoranda" and "Appeals Memoranda," and related documents generated by the Office of the General Counsel in the course of deciding whether or not to permit the filing with the Board of unfair labor practice complaints....

[When an employer or union believes that an unfair labor practice has occurred, it files a "charge" with a regional director of the NLRB.

The regional director then decides whether or not to issue a "complaint" and thus set the Board's adjudicatory process into motion. If the director refuses to issue a complaint and the charging party disagrees with that decision, the charging party can appeal the regional director's decision to the office of the General Counsel which makes the ultimate decision whether or not a complaint should issue. This decision is embodied in a General Counsel's "appeal memorandum."

In some situations, a regional director either seeks or is required to seek advice from the Office of General Counsel before making a decision whether or not to issue a complaint. The advice is furnished in a document called an "advice memorandum."

Sears requested that the General Counsel disclose to it under FOIA all advice memos and appeal memos issued within the previous five years concerning the propriety of withdrawals by employers or unions from multi-employer bargaining units, but the General Counsel declined to provide this material.]

As the Act is structured, virtually every document generated by an agency is available to the public in one form or another, unless it falls within one of the Act's nine exemptions. Certain documents described in 5 U.S.C. § 552(a)(1) such as "rules of procedure" must be published in the Federal Register; others, including "final opinions ... made in the adjudication of cases," "statements of policy and interpretations which have been adopted by the agency," and "instructions to staff that affect a member of the public," described in 5 U.S.C. § 552(a)(2), must be indexed and made available to a member of the public on demand. Finally, and more comprehensively, all "identifiable records" must be made available to a member of the public on demand. 5 U.S.C. § 552(a)(3). The Act expressly states, however, that the disclosure obligation "does not apply" to those documents described in the nine enumerated exempt categories listed in § 552(b).

Sears claims, and the courts below ruled, that the memoranda sought are expressions of legal and policy decisions already adopted by the agency and constitute "final opinions" and "instructions to staff that affect a member of the public," both categories being expressly disclosable under § 552(a)(2) of the Act, pursuant to its purposes to prevent the creation of "secret law." In any event, Sears claims, the memoranda are nonexempt "identifiable records" which must be disclosed under § 552(a)(3). The General Counsel, on the other hand, claims that the memoranda sought here are not final opinions under § 552(a)(2) and that even if they are "identifiable records" otherwise disclosable under § 552(a)(3), they are exempt under § 552(b), principally as "intra-agency" communications under § 552(b)(5) (Exemption 5), made in the course of formulating agency decisions on legal and policy matters....

It is clear, and the General Counsel concedes, that Appeals and Advice Memoranda are at the least "identifiable records" which must be disclosed on demand, unless they fall within one of the Act's exempt categories. It is also clear that, if the memoranda do fall within one of the Act's exempt categories, our inquiry is at an end, for the Act "does not apply" to such documents. Thus our inquiry, strictly speaking, must be into the scope of the exemptions which the General Counsel claims to be applicable—principally Exemption 5 relating to "intra-agency memorandums." The General Counsel also concedes, however, and we hold for the reasons set forth below, that Exemption 5 does not apply to any document which falls within the meaning of the phrase "final opinion ... made in the adjudication of cases." 5 U.S.C. § 522(a)(2)(A). The General Counsel argues, therefore, as he must, that no Advice or Appeals Memorandum is a final opinion made in the adjudication of a case and that all are "intra-agency" memoranda within the coverage of Exemption 5....

A

The parties are in apparent agreement that Exemption 5 withholds from a member of the public documents which a private party could not discover in litigation with the agency. Since virtually any document not privileged may be discovered by the appropriate litigant, if it is relevant to his litigation, and since the Act clearly intended to give any member of the public as much right to disclosure as one with a special interest therein, it is reasonable to construe Exemption 5 to exempt those documents, and only those documents, normally privileged in the civil discovery context. The privileges claimed by petitioners to be relevant to this case are (i) the "generally ... recognized" privilege for "confidential intra-agency advisory opinions....," disclosure of which "would be injurious to the consultative functions of government ..." (sometimes referred to as "executive privilege"), and (ii) the attorney-client and attorney work-product privileges generally available to all litigants.

(I)

That Congress had the Government's executive privilege specifically in mind in adopting Exemption 5 is clear.... The cases uniformly rest the privilege on the policy of protecting the "decision making processes of government agencies," and focus on documents "reflecting advisory opinions, recommendations and deliberations comprising part of a process by which governmental decisions and policies are formulated." ... [T]he "frank discussion of legal or policy matters" in writing might be inhibited if the discussion were made public; and that the "decisions" and "policies formulated" would be the poorer as a result. As a lower court has pointed out, "there are enough incentives as it is for playing it safe and listing with the wind," and as we have said in an analogous context, "[h]uman experience teaches that those who expect public dissemination of their remarks may well temper candor with a concern for appearances ... to the *detriment of the decisionmaking process*." *United States v. Nixon*, 418 U.S. 683, 705 (1974).

Manifestly, the ultimate purpose of this long-recognized privilege is to prevent injury to the quality of agency decisions. The quality of a particular agency decision will clearly be affected by the communications received by the decisionmaker on the subject of the decision prior to the time the decision is made. However, it is difficult to see how the quality of a decision will be affected by communications with respect to the decision occurring after the decision is finally reached; and therefore equally difficult to see how the quality of the decision will be affected by forced disclosure of such communications, as long as prior communications and the ingredients of the decisionmaking process are not disclosed. Accordingly, the lower courts have uniformly drawn a distinction between predecisional communications, which are privileged, and communications made after the decision and designed to explain it, which are not.[19] This distinction is supported not only by the lesser injury to the decisionmaking process flowing from disclosure of postdecisional communications, but also, in the case of those communications which explain the decision, by the increased public interest in knowing the basis for agency policy already adopted. The public is only marginally concerned with reasons supporting a policy which an agency has rejected, or with reasons which might have supplied, but did not supply, the basis for a policy which was actually adopted on a different ground. In contrast, the public is vitally concerned with the reasons which did supply the basis for an agency policy actually adopted. These reasons, if expressed within the agency, constitute the "working law" of the agency and have been held by the lower courts to be outside the protection of Exemption 5. Exemption 5, properly construed, calls for "disclosure of all 'opinions and interpretations' which embody the agency's effective law and policy, and the withholding of all papers which reflect the agency's group thinking in the process of working out its policy and determining what its law shall be."

This conclusion is powerfully supported by the other provisions of the Act. The affirmative portion of the Act, expressly requiring indexing of "final opinions," "statements of policy and interpretations which have been adopted by the agency," and "instructions to staff that affect a member of the public," 5 U.S.C. § 552(a)(2), represents a strong congressional aversion to "secret [agency] law," and represents an affirmative congressional purpose to require disclosure of documents which have "the force and effect of law." We should be reluctant, therefore, to construe Exemption 5 to apply to the documents described in 5 U.S.C. § 552(a)(2); and with respect at least to "final opinions," which not only invariably explain agency action already taken or an agency decision already made, but also constitute "final dispositions" of matters by an agency, Exemption 5 can never apply.

19. We are aware that the line between predecisional documents and postdecisional documents may not always be a bright one. Indeed, even the prototype of the postdecisional document—the "final opinion"—serves the dual function of explaining the decision just made and providing guides for decisions of similar or analogous cases arising in the future. In its latter function, the opinion is predecisional; and the manner in which it is written may, therefore, affect decisions in later cases. For present purposes it is sufficient to note that final opinions are *primarily* postdecisional—looking back on and explaining, as they do, a decision already reached or a policy already adopted—and that their disclosure poses a negligible risk of denying to agency decisionmakers the uninhibited advice which is so important to agency decisions.

(II)

It is equally clear that Congress had the attorney's work-product privilege specifically in mind when it adopted Exemption 5 and that such a privilege had been recognized in the civil discovery context by the prior case law. The case law clearly makes the attorney's work-product rule of *Hickman v. Taylor*, 329 U.S. 495 (1947), applicable to Government attorneys in litigation. Whatever the outer boundaries of the attorney's work-product rule are, the rule clearly applies to memoranda prepared by an attorney in contemplation of litigation which set forth the attorney's theory of the case and his litigation strategy.

B

Applying these principles to the memoranda sought by Sears, it becomes clear that Exemption 5 does not apply to those Appeals and Advice Memoranda which conclude that no complaint should be filed and which have the effect of finally denying relief to the charging party; but that Exemption 5 does protect from disclosure those Appeals and Advice Memoranda which direct the filing of a complaint and the commencement of litigation before the Board.

(I)

Under the procedures employed by the General Counsel, Advice and Appeals Memoranda are communicated to the Regional Director *after* the General Counsel, through his Advice and Appeals Branches, has decided whether or not to issue a complaint; and represent an explanation to the Regional Director of a legal or policy decision already adopted by the General Counsel. In the case of decisions *not* to file a complaint, the memoranda effect as "final" a "disposition" as an administrative decision can—representing, as it does, an unreviewable rejection of the charge filed by the private party. Disclosure of these memoranda would not intrude on predecisional processes, and protecting them would not improve the quality of agency decisions, since when the memoranda are communicated to the Regional Director, the General Counsel has already reached his decision and the Regional Director who receives them has no decision to make—he is bound to dismiss the charge. Moreover, the General Counsel's decisions not to file complaints together with the Advice and Appeals Memoranda explaining them, are precisely the kind of agency law in which the public is so vitally interested and which Congress sought to prevent the agency from keeping secret.

For essentially the same reasons, these memoranda are "final opinions" made in the "adjudication of cases" which must be indexed pursuant to 5 U.S.C. § 552(a)(2)(A). The decision to dismiss a charge is a decision in a "case" and constitutes an "adjudication": an "adjudication" is defined under the Administrative Procedure Act, of which 5 U.S.C. § 552 is a part, as "agency process for the formulation of an order," 5 U.S.C. § 551(7); an "order" is defined as "the whole or a part of a *final disposition,* whether affirmative [or] negative ... of an agency in a matter ...," 5 U.S.C. § 551(6); and the dismissal of a charge, as noted above, is a "final disposition." Since an Advice or Appeals Memorandum explains the reasons for the "final disposition" it plainly qualifies as an "opinion"; and falls within 5 U.S.C. § 552(a)(2)(A)....

(II)

Advice and Appeals Memoranda which direct the filing of a complaint, on the other hand, fall within the coverage of Exemption 5. The filing of a complaint does not finally dispose even of the General Counsel's responsibility with respect to the case. The case will be litigated before and decided by the Board; and the General Counsel will have the responsibility of advocating the position of the charging party before the Board. The Memoranda will inexorably contain the General Counsel's theory of the case and may communicate to the Regional Director some litigation strategy or settlement advice. Since the Memoranda will also have been prepared in contemplation of the upcoming litigation, they fall squarely within Exemption 5's protection of an attorney's work product. At the same time, the public's interest in disclosure is substantially reduced by the fact that the basis for the General Counsel's legal decision will come out in the course of litigation before the Board; and that the "law" with respect to these cases will ultimately be made not by the General Counsel but by the Board or the courts.

We recognize that an Advice or Appeals Memorandum directing the filing of a complaint—although representing only a decision that a legal issue is sufficiently in doubt to warrant determination by another body—has many of the characteristics of the documents described in 5 U.S.C. § 552(a)(2). Although not a "final opinion" in the "adjudication" of a "case" because it does not effect a "final disposition," the memorandum does explain a decision already reached by the General Counsel which has real operative effect—it permits litigation before the Board; and we have indicated a reluctance to construe Exemption 5 to protect such documents. We do so in this case only because the decisionmaker—the General Counsel—must become a litigating party to the case with respect to which he has made his decision. The attorney's work-product policies which Congress clearly incorporated into Exemption 5 thus come into play and lead us to hold that the Advice and Appeals Memoranda directing the filing of a complaint are exempt whether or not they are, as the District Court held, "instructions to staff that affect a member of the public."

C

Petitioners assert that the District Court erred in holding that documents incorporated by reference in nonexempt Advice and Appeals Memoranda lose any exemption they might previously have held as "intra-agency" memoranda. We disagree.

The probability that an agency employee will be inhibited from freely advising a decisionmaker for fear that his advice, *if adopted,* will become public is slight. First, when adopted, the reasoning becomes that of the agency and becomes *its* responsibility to defend. Second, agency employees will generally be encouraged rather than discouraged by public knowledge that their policy suggestions have been adopted by the agency. Moreover, the public interest in knowing the reasons for a policy actually adopted by an agency supports the District Court's decision below. Thus, we hold that, if an agency chooses *expressly* to adopt or incorporate by reference an intra-agency memorandum previously covered by Exemption 5 in what would otherwise be a final opinion, that memorandum may be withheld only on the ground that it falls within the coverage of some exemption other than Exemption 5.

Petitioners also assert that the District Court's order erroneously requires it to produce or create explanatory material in those instances in which an Appeals Memorandum refers to the "circumstances of the case." We agree. The Act does not compel agencies to write opinions in cases in which they would not otherwise be required to do so. It only requires disclosure of certain documents which the law requires the agency to prepare or which the agency has decided for its own reasons to create. Thus, insofar as the order of the court below requires the agency to create explanatory material, it is baseless. Nor is the agency required to identify, after the fact, those pre-existing documents which contain the "circumstances of the case" to which the opinion may have referred, and which are not identified by the party seeking disclosure. . . .

Notes and Questions

1. *FOIA Exemption 5—deliberative documents.* As explained by *Sears,* under Exemption (5) a document that would be normally privileged from discovery in civil litigation is exempt from FOIA disclosure. The most important such privilege, for FOIA purposes, is the government's right to withhold records that would expose its deliberative processes. What is the rationale for the deliberative process privilege? Does the privilege diminish the value of FOIA as a political check on agencies?

Courts often distinguish between factual and non-factual material. The notion is that disclosure of factual material in agency memoranda would not have a detrimental effect on the decision-making process. *See Petroleum Information Corp. v. Dep't of Interior,* 976 F.2d 1429 (D.C.Cir.1992). Is this always true? The New York statute explicitly provides that its deliberative process exemption neither applies to "statistical or factual tabulations or data" nor to "instructions to staff that affect the public." Public Officers Law § 87(g).

A provision comparable to the deliberative process exemption exists in about one-third of state open records laws. Many states exempt preliminary drafts of government reports. Braverman & Heppler, *supra,* at 743–45. However, in many states these exemptions are significantly narrower than FOIA Exemption (5). A California catchall exemption requires the agency to establish that the public interest in withholding the records clearly outweighs the public interest in disclosure. *See Times Mirror Co. v. Superior Court,* 813 P.2d 240 (Cal.1991) (denying disclosure of governor's appointment schedules for five years in order to preserve his ability to hold candid discussions). Similarly, the Michigan statute requires a showing that the public interest in encouraging frank communications within agencies outweighs the public interest in disclosure. *See Milford v. Gilb,* 384 N.W.2d 786 (Mich.App.1985). Do these narrower exemptions better serve the objective of using FOIA as a political check on agency action?

Another important privilege is the attorney work-product privilege. In *Kent Corp. v. NLRB,* 530 F.2d 612, 622–24 (5th Cir.1976), Kent sought disclosure of "final investigative reports" prepared by NLRB regional board attorneys (for cases in which the regional director refused to issue a complaint). These reports contained both legal theories and analyses of factual materials. The court held that both the legal and the factual portions of these reports fell under the work-product privilege and thus were exempt from FOIA disclosure. The work-product privilege "is based on the public policy of preserving the independence of lawyers through the avoidance of unwarranted intrusion into their private files and mental processes ... and since the litigants before the Labor Board are legion, the evil of harassment ... is correspondingly multiplied. The function of deciding controversies might soon be overwhelmed by the duty of answering questions about them."

2. *The Sears holdings.* In *Sears,* certain of the NLRB general counsel's appeals or advice memos were found to be exempt from disclosure. Others were not exempt from disclosure and were treated as "final opinions." Under § 552(a)(2), the non-exempt memos must be routinely made available (as distinguished from being furnished on specific request) and indexed. How did the Court distinguish between exempt and non-exempt memoranda?

Sears holds that Exemption 5 does not apply to the documents described in § 552(a)(2)—documents which embody the agency's effective law and policy. Is there something especially odious about "secret law"? Does that suggest a greater justification for § 552(a)(1) and (2) than for § 552(a)(3)?

3. *FOIA as discovery.* Why did Sears want the documents? Why did the NLRB want to keep them confidential?

Sears had filed a charge with a regional director who refused to issue a complaint after receiving an advice memorandum from the General Counsel. Sears was in the process of preparing an appeal to the General Counsel of that refusal. The Court observed:

> Sears' rights under the Act are neither increased nor decreased by reason of the fact that it claims an interest in the Advice and Appeals Memoranda greater than that shared by the average member of the public. The Act is fundamentally designed to inform the public about agency action and not to benefit private litigants.

421 U.S. at 143 n.10. The *Sears* case is a good example of one of the most important functions of FOIA—and one of its most controversial. It is used as a technique for discovery in pending administrative or judicial litigation. *See generally* Edward A. Tomlinson, "Use of the Freedom of Information Act for Discovery Purposes," 43 Md.L.Rev. 119 (1984).

A litigator might well prefer to conduct discovery through a FOIA request because discovery practice may be much less useful. Agency rules may provide only for very limited discovery or none at all. *See* § 4.1.2.

Discovery may not be available in connection with judicial review in appellate courts of agency rules. When discovery is available, it is provided only at defined times (i.e. after a complaint is filed) and is controlled by an adjudicator (an ALJ or a judge if the case is in court). Under conventional discovery rules, a party can resist production of irrelevant or excessively burdensome materials. But when documents are demanded under FOIA, there are no such limits. Unless an exemption applies, all of the requested documents must be promptly disclosed.

On the other hand, the regular discovery process offers litigants some advantages over FOIA. For example, a person making a FOIA request must ordinarily pay the costs of search and duplication. See APA § 552(a)(4)(A). No such costs are imposed in discovery. Discovery offers processes such as depositions and interrogatories that are unavailable under FOIA. Finally, discovery privileges might be less protective to the government than the FOIA exemptions. For example, although the deliberative process privilege involved in *Sears, Roebuck* is also applicable to a request for documents in discovery, a court may require disclosure of the documents upon a showing of special need. *See, e.g., United States v. Nixon,* 418 U.S. 683 (1974) (documents and tapes protected by executive privilege must be disclosed because needed in prosecution of criminal case).

Should FOIA be amended to preclude requests by persons engaged in litigation with the agency, thus remitting such persons to conventional discovery? Or is such a litigant the person with the strongest claim for FOIA disclosure? ACUS recommended that a party in litigation against the government be required to notify government counsel of any FOIA requests relevant to the proceeding. But it did not recommend closing FOIA to parties in litigation. *See* ACUS Recommendation 83–4, 48 Fed.Reg. 57463 (1983).

4. *Related exemptions.* A state secret exemption is spelled out in exemption (1) of FOIA. Exemption (1) leaves substantial discretion to the executive branch in making classification decisions. Nevertheless, exemption (1) does permit the court to conduct an in camera review of the propriety of the decision to classify a document.

FOIA Exemption (7) protects the government's interest in the confidentiality of law enforcement files and manuals. For example, a document that could reasonably be expected to disclose the identity of a confidential source is protected. Similarly, material that would disclose law enforcement techniques or guidelines is exempt if disclosure might facilitate circumvention of the law. *See also* 1981 MSAPA §§ 3–116(2) and 2–101(g)(1).

FOIA exemption (5) also includes a privilege for presidential communications. This privilege covers not only communications with the President but also those authored by, or solicited and received by, members of the White House staff with significant responsibility for formulating advice to be given to the President. The presidential privilege is obviously similar to the deliberative process privilege involved in *Sears,* but it is much broader. Unlike the deliberative process privilege, the presidential privilege covers factual materials and is not limited to predecisional materials. *See In re Sealed Case,* 116 F.3d 550 (D.C.Cir.1997), which involved a grand jury subpoena to White House staff members. According to *Sealed Case,* in order to secure such documents, the grand jury must demonstrate that it has an important need for the information and it is unavailable from other sources. Similarly, *United States v. Nixon*, 418 U.S. 683 (1974), recognized that the presidential privilege had to give way in the face of need for information contained in President Nixon's tapes to be used in a criminal case.

§ 8.1.2   CONFIDENTIAL PRIVATE INFORMATION: § 552(b)(4)

CHRYSLER CORP. v. BROWN
441 U.S. 281 (1979).

[Chrysler was required to comply with Executive Orders 11246 and 11275, which prohibited government contractors from engaging in employment discrimination on the basis of race or sex. Under regulations adopted by the Office of Federal Contract Compliance Programs (OFCCP), Chrysler must file with the Defense Logistics Agency (DLA) detailed reports on its affirmative action plans and composition of its workforce.

OFCCP regulations provide that such reports shall be made available for public inspection and copying "if it is determined that the requested inspection or copying furthers the public interest and does not impede any of the functions of OFCCP or the Compliance Agencies except in the case of records, disclosure of which is prohibited by law." OFCCP proposed to furnish Chrysler's affirmative action plan to someone who requested it. Chrysler sought to enjoin this release in the district court, asserting that exemption (4) of FOIA *prevented* disclosure of the material (a so-called "reverse FOIA" suit). That court granted the injunction but the court of appeals reversed, holding that Chrysler had no right to prevent the release.]

REHNQUIST, J.:

The expanding range of federal regulatory activity and growth in the Government sector of the economy have increased federal agencies' demands for information about the activities of private individuals and corporations. These developments have paralleled a related concern about secrecy in Government and abuse of power. The Freedom of Information Act (hereinafter FOIA) was a response to this concern, but it has also had a largely unforeseen tendency to exacerbate the uneasiness of those who comply with governmental demands for information. For under the FOIA third parties have been able to obtain Government files containing information submitted by corporations and individuals who thought that the information would be held in confidence....

II

Chrysler contends that the nine exemptions in general, and Exemption 4 in particular, reflect a sensitivity to the privacy interests of private individuals and nongovernmental entities. That contention may be conceded without inexorably requiring the conclusion that the exemptions impose affirmative duties on an agency to withhold information sought....

That the FOIA is exclusively a disclosure statute is, perhaps, demonstrated most convincingly by examining its provision for judicial relief. Subsection (a)(4)(B) gives federal district courts "jurisdiction to enjoin the agency from withholding agency records and to order the production of any agency records improperly withheld from the complainant." That provision does not give the authority to bar disclosure, and thus fortifies our belief that Chrysler, and courts which have shared its view, have incorrectly interpreted the exemption provisions of the FOIA. The Act is an attempt to meet the demand for open government while preserving workable confidentiality in governmental decisionmaking. Congress appreciated that, with the expanding sphere of governmental regulation and enterprise, much of the information within Government files has been submitted by private entities seeking Government contracts or responding to unconditional reporting obligations imposed by law. There was sentiment that Government agencies should have the latitude, in certain circumstances, to afford the confidentiality desired by these submitters. But the congressional concern was with the *agency's* need or preference for confidentiality; the FOIA by itself protects the submitters' interest in confidentiality only to the extent that this interest is endorsed by the agency collecting the information.

Enlarged access to governmental information undoubtedly cuts against the privacy concerns of nongovernmental entities, and as a matter of policy some balancing and accommodation may well be desirable. We simply hold here that Congress did not design the FOIA exemptions to be mandatory bars to disclosure....

III

Chrysler contends, however, that even if its suit for injunctive relief cannot be based on the FOIA, such an action can be premised on the Trade Secrets Act, 18 U.S.C. § 1905. The Act provides:

> Whoever, being an officer or employee of the United States ... makes known in any manner or to any extent *not authorized by law* any information coming to him in the course of his employment or official duties or by reason of any examination or investigation made by, or return, report or record made to or filed with, such department or agency or officer or employee thereof, which information concerns or relates to the trade secrets, processes, operations, style of work, or apparatus, or to the identity, confidential statistical data, amount or source of any income, profits, losses, or expenditures of any person, firm, partnership, corporation, or association; or permits any income return or copy thereof or any book containing any abstract or particulars thereof to be seen or examined by any person except as provided by law; shall be fined not more than $1,000, or imprisoned not more than one year, or both; and shall be removed from office or employment.

There are necessarily two parts to Chrysler's argument: that § 1905 is applicable to the type of disclosure threatened in this case, and that it affords Chrysler a private right of action to obtain injunctive relief.

A

The Court of Appeals held that § 1905 was not applicable to the agency disclosure at issue here because such disclosure was "authorized by law" within the meaning of the Act. The court found the source of that authorization to be the OFCCP regulations that DLA relied on in deciding to disclose information on the Hamtramck and Newark plants. Chrysler contends here that these agency regulations are not "law" within the meaning of § 1905.

It has been established in a variety of contexts that properly promulgated, substantive agency regulations have the "force and effect of law." This doctrine is so well established that agency regulations implementing federal statutes have been held to pre-empt state law under the Supremacy Clause. It would therefore take a clear showing of contrary legislative intent before the phrase "authorized by law" in § 1905 could be held to have a narrower ambit than the traditional understanding. . . .

In order for a regulation to have the "force and effect of law," it must have certain substantive characteristics and be the product of certain procedural requisites. The central distinction among agency regulations found in the APA is that between "substantive rules" on the one hand and "interpretative rules, general statements of policy, or rules of agency organization, procedure, or practice" on the other. . . . We described a substantive rule—or a "legislative-type rule"—as one "affecting individual rights and obligations." This characteristic is an important touchstone for distinguishing those rules that may be "binding" or have the "force of law."

That an agency regulation is "substantive," however, does not by itself give it the "force and effect of law." The legislative power of the United States is vested in the Congress, and the exercise of quasi-legislative authority by governmental departments and agencies must be rooted in a grant of such power by the Congress. . . . The regulations relied on by the respondents in this case as providing "authorization by law" within the meaning of § 1905 certainly affect individual rights and obligations. . . .

But in order for such regulations to have the "force and effect of law," it is necessary to establish a nexus between the regulations and some delegation of the requisite legislative authority by Congress. . . . The pertinent inquiry is whether under any of the arguable *statutory* grants of authority the OFCCP disclosure regulations relied on by the respondents are reasonably within the contemplation of that grant of authority. We think that it is clear that when it enacted these statutes, Congress was not concerned with public disclosure of trade secrets or confidential business information. [Rather, they are housekeeping statutes, civil rights laws, etc.]

There is also a procedural defect in the OFCCP disclosure regulations which precludes courts from affording them the force and effect of law. That defect is a lack of strict compliance with the APA. . . .

Certainly regulations subject to the APA cannot be afforded the "force and effect of law" if not promulgated pursuant to the statutory procedural minimum found in that Act. . . . [When he adopted the rules in question, the Secretary declared that they were interpretive rules, general statements of policy, or rules of procedure, so that notice and comment was not required.] We need not decide whether these regulations are properly characterized as "interpretative rules." It is enough that such regulations are not properly promulgated as substantive rules, and therefore not the product of procedures which Congress prescribed as necessary prerequisites to giving a regulation the binding force of law. An interpretative regulation or general statement of policy cannot be the "authorization by law" required by § 1905.

This disposition best comports with both the purposes underlying the APA and sound administrative practice. Here important interests are in conflict: the public's access to information in the Government's files and concerns about personal privacy and business confidentiality. The OFCCP's regulations attempt to strike a balance. In enacting the APA, Congress made a judgment that notions of fairness and informed administrative decisionmaking require that agency decisions be made only after affording interested persons notice and an opportunity to comment. With the consideration that is the necessary and intended consequence of such procedures, OFCCP might have decided that a different accommodation was more appropriate.

B

We reject, however, Chrysler's contention that the Trade Secrets Act affords a private right of action to enjoin disclosure in violation of the statute. In *Cort v. Ash,* 422 U.S. 66 (1975), we noted that this Court has rarely implied a private right of action under a criminal statute, and where it has done so "there was at least a statutory basis for inferring that a civil cause of action of some sort lay in favor of someone." Nothing in § 1905 prompts such an inference. Nor are other pertinent circumstances outlined in *Cort* present here. As our review of the legislative history of § 1905—or lack of same—might suggest, there is no indication of legislative intent to create a private right of action. Most importantly, a private right of action under § 1905 is not "necessary to make effective the congressional purpose," for we find that review of DLA's decision to disclose Chrysler's employment data is available under the APA.

IV

While Chrysler may not avail itself of any violations of the provisions of § 1905 in a separate cause of action, any such violations may have a dispositive effect on the outcome of judicial review of agency action pursuant to the APA. . . .

[O]ur discussion in Part III demonstrates that § 1905 and any "authoriz[ation] by law" contemplated by that section place substantive limits on agency action. Therefore, we conclude that DLA's decision to disclose the Chrysler reports is reviewable agency action and Chrysler is a person "adversely affected or aggrieved".... For the reasons previously stated, we believe any disclosure that violates § 1905 is "not in accordance with law" within the meaning of 5 U.S.C. § 706(2)(A).... The District Court in this case concluded that disclosure of some of Chrysler's documents was barred by § 1905, but the Court of Appeals did not reach the issue. We shall therefore vacate the Court of Appeals' judgment and remand for further proceedings consistent with this opinion in order that the Court of Appeals may consider whether the contemplated disclosures would violate the prohibition of § 1905.

Vacated and remanded.

[MARSHALL, J., concurred, pointing out that the Court had not ruled on the validity of the executive orders.]

Notes and Questions

1. *The (4) exemption.* Unlike the *Chrysler* situation, in many cases an agency *refuses* to furnish information previously submitted to it because the information falls under exemption (4): it is "trade secrets and commercial or financial information obtained from a person and privileged or confidential." The difficult problem is to decide what information should be treated as "confidential," given that the submitters of the material would like all of it kept confidential.

The key variable in applying exemption (4) is whether the information in question was provided to the government voluntarily or under compulsion. If it was submitted voluntarily and the government discloses it under FOIA, it is likely that in the future no such information would be provided to the government. If, however, the information was submitted under compulsion, disclosure would not dry up the future flow of the information, but it might still affect the reliability and accuracy of the information.

For that reason, the courts have developed a double test. If the information is submitted to the government *voluntarily*, it falls under exemption (4) if "it is of a kind that would customarily not be released to the public by the person from whom it was obtained." If the information is submitted to the government *under compulsion* (like the information involved in *Chrysler*), it falls under exemption (4) if disclosure would cause substantial harm to the competitive position of the person from whom the information was obtained. *Critical Mass Energy Project v. NRC*, 975 F.2d 871 (D.C.Cir.1992).

Approximately one-third of the states have a comparable exemption in their information statutes (and most of the others protect confidential information under other statutes). Braverman & Heppler, *supra*, at 741–43.

2. *Disclosure of confidential material.* Agency disclosure of materials submitted to it by outsiders poses severe practical problems. There is a vast amount of technical or financial information which government obtains through its regulatory, procurement, licensing, and law enforcement activity. The submitters of much of that material have a vital stake in keeping it confidential. And there is no doubt that a high percentage of FOIA requesters are actually commercial firms trying to find out information about their competitors.

Although the *Chrysler* decision might seem to have provided adequate protection, it was not sufficient standing alone. For a time, one problem that remained was that, when an agency proposed to disclose business information, the submitter was not necessarily informed in time to be able to raise an objection or take legal action. Although many agencies did notify submitters as a matter of course when such material was requested, not all did. Apparently some information that might be covered by § 1905 was released inadvertently by low-level personnel who did not appreciate its confidentiality. (Many submitters would stamp their material "confidential" to alert agency personnel to such claims.) As one commentator noted:

> Suzuki Motor Company has been an effective collector of Toyota's submissions to the U.S. government in 1981, though neither firm would enjoy access to the other's data in Japan. A food processor which saves tens of thousands of dollars of its filtration costs because of its innovations may never enjoy the ... advantages, because its blueprints were photocopied last week at a regional office of the EPA and mailed to its larger competitor for ten cents per copy. And the small inventor with the archetypal better mousetrap finds that contracting or proposing to contract with the government opens detailed design data to larger competitors, who can enter the market more quickly and dispose of both mice and the innovator.

> The FOIA was meant by all its sponsors to keep agencies accountable for their workings and official conduct. By 1982, the quarter of a billion dollar cost of the Act was subsidizing Swedish ball bearing makers in their searches at [the] FTC, French aviation firms at [the] DOT, and competitive searches throughout the government.

James O'Reilly, "Regaining a Confidence: Protection of Business Confidential Data through Reform of the Freedom of Information Act," 34 Admin.L.Rev. 263, 263–64 (1982). Eventually this problem was ameliorated through a presidential executive order. Now, when agencies receive a FOIA request for potentially exempt commercial information, they must notify the submitter and give the latter an opportunity to present objections to disclosure. Exec. Order 12600, 52 Fed.Reg. 23781 (1987).

3. *Reverse FOIA and Trade Secrets. Chrysler* refused to interpret FOIA as *prohibiting* disclosure of information—thus the "reverse-FOIA" theory perished. Instead, it seized on the Trade Secrets Act, § 1905, as a judicially enforceable tool to prohibit agency disclosures of confidential material. The Trade Secrets Act is traceable to legislation originally enacted in 1864, largely to prevent leaks of information by corrupt internal revenue agents. The section reads more like an attempt to deter and punish crooked or indiscreet government employees than as an attempt to limit agency discretion to disclose documents.

From the point of view of information submitters who wish to prevent disclosure, § 1905 has some flaws. In addition to the practical problems mentioned in the previous note, the agency can adopt a rule permitting it to disclose the information. Why did OFCCP's rule not permit it to disclose the reports at issue in *Chrysler*? As an information submitter trying to prevent disclosure, would you prefer to proceed under FOIA or under § 1905?

4. *Privacy exemption—judicial weighing?* Consider also FOIA exemption (6), which prevents disclosure of material (such as personnel or medical files) that would constitute a clearly unwarranted invasion of personal privacy. This exemption requires a court to balance the public's interest in disclosure against the private interest in preserving privacy. See *Department of Defense v. FLRA*, 510 U.S. 487 (1994), which concerned a request by a union to obtain the home addresses of non-member federal employees.

The Court upheld the government's refusal to supply the information under exemption (6), despite the Union's claim that the information was needed for collective bargaining purposes. The Court emphasized that the particular needs of the requestor to obtain the information would not be considered. The public's interest in disclosure of this particular information was slight, since it would tell the public nothing about what the Government is up to. In contrast, the invasion of the privacy interest of the federal employees is quite substantial.

Should this sort of weighing be employed when the government seeks to take advantage of other FOIA exemptions, such as exemptions (4) and (5)?

5. *Problem.* Gloria is a psychology professor at Madison State Univ. (MSU) who is doing research on the effect on parents of having been subjected to physical abuse in childhood. The work has no commercial application, but it requires substantial outside funding. As a result Gloria applied to the National Institute of Mental Health (NIMH), a federal agency that makes research grants to scholars, and received a $400,000 grant for the current year.

Gloria's application set forth the methodology for her research and the results she hoped to achieve. NIMH submits each application to a committee of professors that writes candid appraisals. The committee recommends which applications should be granted or denied and creates a priority list for granted applications in case funds are not sufficient for all of them. However, John, NIMH's director, makes the ultimate decision on each application. He writes a detailed report on his reasons for each decision. NIMH promised its applicants that all of the above material would remain confidential.

Bob, a psychology professor at Adams State University, filed a FOIA request to receive Gloria's application, the minutes of the committee's deliberation, and John's report.

(a) Assume that NIMH refuses to disclose any of the information and Bob brings a FOIA action to compel its disclosure. What part of the material, if any, is exempt from disclosure?

(b) Assume that NIMH proposes to disclose all of the information. Gloria seeks judicial review of this decision. Can she prevent the disclosure? See *Washington Research Project v. HEW*, 504 F.2d 238 (D.C.Cir.1974).

§ 8.2 THE SUNSHINE AND ADVISORY COMMITTEE ACTS

§ 8.2.1 SUNSHINE ACTS

All fifty states have statutes requiring that most state or local agency meetings (as well as meetings of the legislature) be held in public.

See Teresa Pupillo, Note, "The Changing Weather Forecast: Government in the Sunshine in the 1990s—An Analysis of State Sunshine Laws," 71 Wash.U.L.Q. 1165 (1993). In 1976, the federal government followed suit by enacting the Sunshine Act, 5 U.S.C. § 552b. Like typical state laws, the federal Sunshine Act requires the meetings of the heads of multi-member agencies to be held in public unless the meeting falls under one of ten exemptions in the statute. It requires advance public notice of such meetings, certification by the chief legal officer of the agency that a meeting can be closed to the public, and the making of a transcript of all closed meetings.

a. *Costs and benefits of Sunshine laws*: The primary benefit of open meeting laws is that they can serve as a political check on agency action. One court summarized the purposes of the federal Act:

> Congress enacted the Sunshine Act to open the deliberations of multi-member federal agencies to public view. It believed that increased openness would enhance citizen confidence in government, encourage higher quality work by government officials, stimulate well-informed public debate about government programs and policies, and promote cooperation between citizens and government. In short, it sought to make government more fully accountable to the people.

Common Cause v. NRC, 674 F.2d 921, 928 (D.C.Cir.1982).

However, numerous scholars and agency officials have pointed out the very real costs of Sunshine laws. Note that Sunshine laws contain no exemption parallel to FOIA exemption (5). As a result, pre-decisional communications between agency members, occurring in meetings, must be open to the public. The public's presence inevitably has a chilling effect on collective deliberations. Some observers contend that agency members *never* engage in candid deliberation and debate in public meetings.

> Among the reasons given for the inhibiting effect of public meetings on collective decisionmaking are the following: concern that providing initial deliberative views publicly, without sufficient thought and information, may harm the public interest by irresponsibly introducing uncertainty or confusion to industry or the general public; a desire on the part of members to speak with a uniform voice on matters of particular importance or to develop negotiating strategies which might be thwarted if debated publicly; reluctance of an agency member to embarrass another agency member or to embarrass himself, through inadvertent, argumentative, or exaggerated statements; concern that an agency member's statements may be used against the agency in subsequent litigation, or misinterpreted or misunderstood by the public or the press, as for example, when the agency member is testing a position by "playing devil's advocate" or

merely "thinking out loud"; and concerns that a member's statements may affect financial markets.

Special Committee of the Administrative Conference, "Report and Recommendation by the Special Committee to Review the Government in the Sunshine Act," 49 Admin.L.Rev. 421, 422 (1997).

In addition to chilling discussion, the Special Committee noted, the open meeting requirement results in fewer meetings of agency heads, decisions made through written approvals without discussion (so-called "notation voting"), or time-consuming seriatim one-on-one meetings between the agency head and the various members. The Act is also circumvented by having staff members representing their bosses engage in deliberative meetings; the agency heads then rubber-stamp the staff decision in an open meeting without further discussion. *Id.* at 423–24. Yet multi-member agencies exist so that members with diverse viewpoints can discuss and decide policy issues in a collegial manner; this goal is thwarted by the various techniques used to avoid open meeting laws.

Short of repealing sunshine laws (which is politically impossible), the solution to this problem is far from obvious. The Special Committee recommended that Congress enact a pilot program allowing agencies to conduct deliberations in executive session if they agreed to memorialize the discussion through a detailed memorandum which would be made available to the public within five days. In addition, agencies would have to agree to hold regular public meetings, to vote in public, and avoid notation voting.

In interpreting sunshine acts, the main difficulties center on the definition of "meeting," the requirement that agencies publish agendas of their meetings in advance, the application of the exemptions, and the sanctions for violation of the acts.

b. *Definition of meeting.* If "meeting" is defined too broadly, the Act would prevent informal discussions between members of the agency; but if it is defined too narrowly, the members can easily circumvent it by making collegial decisions in secret, then rubberstamping them in brief public sessions.

In *Moberg v. Indep. School Dist. No. 281,* 336 N.W.2d 510, 517–18 (Minn.1983), the Court considered a series of informal discussions between members of a school board who were seeking to break a deadlock over an important policy issue. It said:

> We therefore hold that "meetings" subject to the requirements of the Open Meeting Law are those gatherings of a quorum or more members of the governing body, or a quorum of a committee ... at which members discuss, decide, or receive information as a group on issues relating to the official business of that governing body. Although "chance or social gatherings" are exempt from the requirements of the statute ... a quorum may not, as a group, discuss or receive information on official business in any setting under the guise of a private social gathering. The statute does not apply to letters or telephone conversations between fewer than a quorum.

Appellants correctly point out that this rule may be circumvented by serial face-to-face or telephone conversations between board members to marshall their votes on an issue before it is initially raised at a public hearing. It does not follow that two-or three-person conversations should be prohibited, however, because officials who are determined to act furtively will hold such discussions anyway, or might simply use an outsider as an intermediary. There is a way to illegally circumvent any rule the court might fashion, and therefore it is important that the rule not be so restrictive as to lose the public benefit of personal discussion between public officials while gaining little assurance of openness. Of course, serial meetings in groups of less than a quorum for the purposes of avoiding public hearings or fashioning agreement on an issue may also be found to be a violation of the statute depending upon the facts of the individual case.

However, in *FCC v. ITT World Communications, Inc.*, 466 U.S. 463 (1984), the Supreme Court defined "meeting" more narrowly under the Sunshine Act to exclude gatherings of an agency to receive information. The *ITT* case involved a committee of FCC members who engaged in consultation with their foreign counterparts. The FCC committee was itself treated as an "agency" because it had power to approve certain applications. But its consultations were not "meetings" because they did not concern such approvals. According to the Court, a "meeting" occurs only when the agency deliberates on matters within its formal delegated authority, whereas the meetings in question were background discussions and exchanges of views with non-agency members. "Informal background discussions that clarify issues and expose varying views" are not "meetings," because Congress thought that keeping such discussions private was necessary for the effective conduct of agency business.

Which definition of "meeting" better serves the objective of using open meeting statutes as a political check on agencies?

c. *Advance publication of agendas.* In order for open meeting statutes to be a meaningful political check on government, members of the public must be able to attend the meetings. This requires reasonable advance publication of the time and place of the meeting and the agenda. Yet an overly rigid application of this rule would prevent agencies from dealing with important new business that demands immediate attention. Thus the Texas Supreme Court held that a Board of Education violated the act when it merely notified the public that it would consider "personnel" and "litigation" matters. The public was entitled to a more specific agenda, in this case that the Board was going to consider the appointment of a new school superintendent and a major desegregation lawsuit—even though it was legally entitled to go into closed session on these matters. *Cox Enterprises v. Board of Trustees of Austin Independent School Dist.*, 706 S.W.2d 956 (Tex.1986).

d. *Exemptions.* The exemptions to the federal act closely parallel the FOIA exemptions, except, as already mentioned, for the absence of a deliberative communication exemption. Generally speaking, if an agency could resist a FOIA demand, it could close a meeting which considers the same sort of information. Where a meeting or part of a meeting falls within an exemption, it can be closed, but the rest of the meeting, dealing with non-exempt matters, must be kept open.

There are several exemptions in the Sunshine Act not found in FOIA. One is for information, premature disclosure of which would "be likely to significantly frustrate implementation of a proposed agency action." § 552b(c)(9)(B). This exemption has been held to be very narrow—relating only to matters like a pending embargo. Premature disclosure of an embargo would cause the goods to be exported before the agency had time to act. *Common Cause v. NRC, supra* (discussions about agency budget must be public).

Another Sunshine exception not found in FOIA concerns discussions of the agency's participation in pending civil litigation or its discussions concerning the initiation, conduct, or disposition of formal, on-the-record agency adjudication. Thus the agency can close a meeting where it discusses how to decide an appeal from an ALJ adjudicatory decision. But it must hold open meetings at which it makes decisions about rulemaking.

For treatment of exemptions to state open meeting laws, see John Peterson, Note, "When Open–Meeting Laws Confront State Legislatures: How Privacy Survives in the Capitol," 10 Nova L.J. 106, 110–14 (1985). In some states, there is a much broader exemption. In Nebraska, for example, a meeting can be closed if "clearly necessary for the protection of the public interest or for the prevention of needless injury to the reputation of an individual." For a strict construction, see *Grein v. Board of Educ.*, 343 N.W.2d 718 (Neb.1984).

e. *Sanctions for Sunshine violations*: Like FOIA, the Sunshine Act allows any person to seek judicial enforcement and allows the award of attorney's fees to a substantially prevailing party. Under the federal act, a court cannot invalidate agency action simply because a closed meeting should have been open. However, many state laws give courts discretion to invalidate the action taken at an improperly closed meeting.

A court must exercise such discretion sparingly, however, since the possibility of invalidation of such action leaves the finality of government action in limbo, perhaps for many years, while litigation wends its way through the courts. Moreover, invalidation might be extremely detrimental to the public interest if the result is to abrogate agency rules protective of health or safety. Some states also provide for civil money penalties, contempt citations, or even criminal penalties against members of an agency that violate open meeting laws.

§ 8.2.2 FEDERAL ADVISORY COMMITTEE ACT (FACA)

FACA, enacted in 1972, is located in 5 U.S.C. App. 2. A recent article provides background on this statute:

[FACA's enactment should not] suggest that agencies began to receive advice from nongovernmental entities only in 1972. Much to the contrary, the FACA was designed to formalize and routinize what was already an age-old institution. . . .

[T]here is a common understanding that the great growth of advisory committees occurred after World War II, generally in response to the increased government regulation occasioned by the New Deal and perhaps by increased government and industry cooperation during the war. This increase in outside advice naturally inspired some concerns. Initially the concerns involved antitrust problems that might arise from collusion within advisory groups composed of business members, which prompted the Justice Department to issue its Guidelines in 1950. . . .

And yet, while the institution to which FACA's passage gave discipline and organization has a long heritage, advisory committees before and since the Act have until recently been largely "Beltway" phenomena—established by and for agency officials inside Washington and with Washington-oriented memberships. Lately, however, advisory committees have been and are being established throughout the country. As a result, field-level agency personnel, as well as potential committee members in various regions, have of necessity become familiar with FACA, thereby raising the important if uncelebrated Act's general visibility and, with that visibility, urgent questions about how it is (and should be) interpreted, applied, and administered.

Steven B. Croley & William F. Funk, "The Federal Advisory Committee Act and Good Government," 14 Yale J. on Reg. 452, 453, 458–59 (1997).

FACA requires that the membership of an advisory committee "be fairly balanced in terms of the points of view represented and the functions to be performed . . ." The document setting up the committee must "contain appropriate provisions to assure that the advice and recommendations of the advisory committee will not be inappropriately influenced by the appointing authority or by any special interest . . ."

FACA requires that a detailed charter of each advisory committee be filed with the agency. Notice of committee meetings must be published in advance in the Federal Register, and the meetings must be open to the public (except under the same exemptions that apply to the Sunshine Act). All of the Committee's records and documents must be open to the public (except under the same exceptions that apply to FOIA). Detailed minutes must be kept. A designated agency employee must be present at every such meeting and must approve the agenda. There are detailed record-keeping requirements.

An "advisory committee" covered by FACA includes every "committee . . . or other similar group . . . established or utilized" by the President or an agency to obtain advice. This definition is broad enough to cover any meeting of two or more persons with agency staff. It could, in theory, apply "any time the President seeks the views of the NAACP before nominating commissioners to the Equal Employment Opportunity Commission, or asks the leaders of an American Legion Post he is visiting for the organization's opinion on some aspect of military policy" or asks the Republican National Committee for advice about picking the cabinet. *Public Citizen v. Department of Justice*, 491 U.S. 440, 453 (1989).

Giving the word "utilized" a narrow meaning to avoid these extreme outcomes, *Public Citizen* held that the ABA's Standing Committee on the Federal Judiciary was not covered by FACA even though it advises the President and the Attorney General about the qualifications of potential nominees for federal judgeships. Drawing on the legislative history of FACA, the Court (by a 6–3 majority) held that the only committees that are covered by FACA are those established directly or indirectly by the President, an agency, or a quasi-public entity. Clearly, this definition leaves out the Committee in question, which was created by the ABA.

The Court also pointed out that a contrary construction of FACA would raise grave constitutional issues. It might very well infringe on the President's power to nominate federal judges and violate the separation of powers. For an argument that FACA indeed violates the separation of powers by interfering with the President's ability to get advice, see Jay S. Bybee, "Advising the President: Separation of Powers and the Federal Advisory Committee Act," 104 Yale L.J. 51 (1994).

FACA does not apply to "any committee which is composed wholly of full-time officers or employees of the Federal Government." The President's Task Force on National Health Care Reform consisted of high level federal employees and was chaired by Hillary Rodham Clinton. Was Mrs. Clinton a full-time officer or employee of the Government? In *Association of American Physicians and Surgeons v. Clinton*, 997 F.2d 898 (D.C.Cir.1993), the Court held that she was. As a result, the Task Force was not required to comply with FACA and open its meetings to the public.

The court had to stretch to classify Mrs. Clinton as a federal officer or employee, since she does not get paid and was never formally appointed to any position. The theory was that in a different statute Congress had recognized that the First Lady acts as the functional equivalent of assistant to the President. Once more, the subtext of the decision was that serious constitutional problems would be raised if the Task Force were made subject to FACA, in light of its close proximity to the President and the President's need for confidential advice. A dissenter disagreed with the statutory interpretation treating Mrs. Clinton as a federal officer or employee; he would have reached the same ultimate result by ruling that FACA cannot constitutionally be applied to the Task Force.

The court in the *Clinton* case also wrestled with whether FACA applied to the Working Group that advised the Task Force. The Working Group consisted of about 300 federal employees from the executive branch and a number of private consultants who attended working group meetings. The court remanded the case to the lower court to determine whether the private consultants or part-time federal employees required the Working Group to be classified as an advisory committee that would be regulated by FACA. The court described a continuum. At one end, a formal group consisting of a limited number of private citizens (whether or not described as consultants) are brought together to advise the government. FACA would apply to this group. At the other end of the continuum is an unstructured arrangement in which the government seeks advice from a collection of individuals who do not interact with each other. Such an arrangement would not trigger FACA.

Recently, President Clinton issued an executive order requiring all agencies to reduce the number of its advisory committees by one-third and which placed ceilings on the number of committees which each agency could maintain. Exec. Order 12838, 58 Fed.Reg. 8207 (1993). Does this make sense?

> [T]he Administration should view the FACA as a useful tool for promoting its goals of reducing regulatory costs while promoting consensus-oriented decisionmaking. Unfortunately, the White House so far has sent mixed signals about how advisory committees fit within its vision of reinvented government ... [T]he White House should ... ensure through executive oversight that advisory committees are dissolved when they are no longer useful. But oversight can be achieved through more productive means than advisory-committee ceilings, for often creation of an advisory committee provides citizens with cost-effective access to their government.... Simply put, the number of committees that any given agency "should" have cannot be determined in the abstract. Rather, whether an agency should establish a committee depends upon whether the advice or recommendations the committee would generate would be worth the agency's trouble.

Croley & Funk, *supra*, at 532–33.

Part III

JUDICIAL REVIEW

In Part III, we examine judicial review of agency action—the role of the courts as a check upon improper administration. We first consider the scope of judicial review—the doctrines that mark out the boundaries between judicial and administrative authority (Chapter 9). Part III then turns to limitations on the availability of judicial review (Chapter 10) and doctrines concerning the persons who can seek judicial review and the timing of such review (Chapter 11).

Chapter 9

SCOPE OF JUDICIAL REVIEW

The doctrines that fix the scope of judicial review define the court's checking power over the actions of administrative agencies. If the line is placed in a way that favors agencies too much, the vital principle of judicial check will be sacrificed. But if it is placed in a way that favors courts too much, agencies will be unable to carry out their regulatory roles and judges will expend excessive resources on the reviewing function.

Broadly speaking, the choices about the appropriate scope of judicial review can be reduced to two: either a court has or does not have the power to substitute its judgment for the rational judgment of agency decisionmakers. Thus the basic question is which of two rational views should prevail—that of agency heads or judges.

In reviewing an agency's *fact findings*, or *policy choices*, courts cannot substitute their judgment for that of the agency. With respect to the *legality* of agency action, courts are much likelier to assert the power to substitute their judgment for that of the agency.

However, these generalizations are only a starting point. They are not totally clear-cut, especially as they are applied by federal courts. On legal issues, federal courts have imposed limitations on their own powers through the so-called *Chevron* doctrine. And on policy issues, the courts often overturn an agency's decision by claiming that the agency did not analyze its position carefully enough, even though the policy may not be inherently unreasonable.

As you consider the material that follows, keep in mind the relationship between the scope of judicial review and the law relating to delegation of power to the agency. After all, a delegation of discretion to an agency suggests that the agency, not a court, has primary responsibility for resolution of matters falling within the zone of the discretionary authority. On the other hand, when the legislature settles a matter by a statutory provision, thereby withholding discretion from the agency, the court can substitute its judgment for the agency's. Typically, the legislature delegates authority to the agency to *find the facts* and establish *policy*. Sometimes the legislature delegates power to *interpret* the meaning of words in the statute. Of course, all this leaves the initial question to be determined: did the legislature delegate discretion to decide a particular matter?

§ 9.1   SCOPE OF REVIEW OF AGENCY FINDINGS OF BASIC FACT

An agency's findings of basic fact determine what happened and why, or who did what to whom, with what state of mind. Many formulas describe the scope of a reviewing court's power to overturn an agency's findings of basic fact. These formulas might be arrayed as follows, starting with those that provide for the largest judicial powers and finishing with the smallest:

i. *Trial de novo*. The court rehears the evidence and redecides the case. *See* APA § 706(2)(F). A court with power to rehear the case is not engaged in judicial review; instead the court decides the case as if the agency proceeding had never occurred. There are a number of examples in state and federal administrative law of de novo judicial trials on specific issues of fact determined initially by an agency. They will be discussed in § 9.1.2.

ii. *Independent judgment on the evidence*. The court decides the case on the record made by the agency but need not give any deference to agency fact findings. This formula is infrequently employed in federal administrative law (except with reference to a few constitutionally sensitive issues) but is sometimes employed in the states, especially in California. Independent judgment will be discussed in § 9.1.2.

iii. *Clearly erroneous*. The court reverses if it "is left with the definite and firm conviction that a mistake has been committed." *United States v. U.S. Gypsum Co.*, 333 U.S. 364, 395 (1948). Sometimes this test is referred to as the "manifest weight of the evidence" test. It is the standard used by a federal court of appeals to review the decision of a trial judge when there is no jury. Fed.R.Civ.P. 52(a). It was used in the 1961 Model State APA, § 15(g)(5), and in a substantial number of states, as in the *DeFries* case excerpted below.

iv. *Substantial evidence*. The court cannot reverse if a *reasonable person* could have reached the same conclusion as the agency. This is the standard used by a federal court of appeals in reviewing the findings of a jury (or by a trial court in taking a matter from the jury). *See Allentown Mack Sales & Serv. Co. v. NLRB*, 118 S.Ct. 818 (1998), in which the Supreme Court explicitly equated the substantial evidence test with the court's power to review a jury verdict. It is a prominent standard in federal administrative law, APA § 706(2)(E), and is discussed in the *Universal Camera* below. It is used in many states and is the standard set forth under 1981 MSAPA, § 5–116(c)(7).

The substantial evidence test of APA § 706(2)(E) is applicable only to judicial review of agency factfinding occurring in formal adjudication or formal rulemaking. Agency factfinding in informal adjudication is reviewed under § 706(2)(A), which authorizes a reviewing court to reverse the agency only if its findings are arbitrary, capricious, or an abuse of discretion. Because that test also boils down to an assessment of the reasonableness of agency action, the scrutiny it calls for probably does not differ significantly from the substantial evidence test. That similarity will be discussed in § 9.5 N.5.

v. *Some evidence.* The court cannot reverse if there is some evidence in support of the agency's conclusion. Sometimes this is called the "scintilla" test. It was employed in judicial review of the determinations of selective service boards. *Estep v. United States,* 327 U.S. 114 (1946). When states use the "some evidence" test, they obviously intend to greatly restrict judicial power to second-guess an agency's fact findings. For example, "some evidence" is the test used by the Ohio Supreme Court in reviewing workers' compensation decisions. *State ex rel. Jeffrey Mining Div. v. Industrial Comm'n,* 564 N.E.2d 437 (Ohio 1990).

vi. *Facts not reviewable at all.* A statute may preclude any judicial review of an agency's factual determinations. Some statutes take this approach even though they do allow review of an agency's procedures and its determinations of law. The issue of preclusion of review is treated in § 10.4.

You should ask whether these gradations (especially numbers ii. to v.) make any practical difference: is a reviewing court likely to reverse agency fact findings which it strongly believes are wrong, regardless of what formula is employed?

§ 9.1.1 THE SUBSTANTIAL EVIDENCE AND CLEARLY ERRONEOUS TESTS

UNIVERSAL CAMERA CORP. v. NLRB
340 U.S. 474 (1951).

[The NLRB decided that Universal had discharged an employee (Chairman) in reprisal for his testimony at a previous NLRB hearing. Universal contended that Chairman had been discharged for insubordination, which had occurred about two months after he gave the testimony. The NLRB's hearing examiner believed the company's witnesses, but the NLRB reversed and reinstated Chairman with back pay.

In an opinion by Judge Learned Hand, the Second Circuit affirmed the Board, finding that there was substantial evidence in support of the Board's findings. The court decided that it should attach no importance to the agency's rejection of the hearing examiner's findings.]

FRANKFURTER, J.:

The essential issue raised by this case ... is the effect of the Administrative Procedure Act and ... the Taft–Hartley Act on the duty of Courts of Appeals when called upon to review orders of the National Labor Relations Board.

I

.... The Wagner Act provided: "The findings of the Board as to the facts, if supported by evidence, shall be conclusive." This Court read "evidence" to mean "substantial evidence," and we said that "[s]ubstantial evidence is more than a mere scintilla. It means such relevant evidence as a reasonable mind might accept as adequate to support a conclusion." Accordingly, it "must do more than create a suspicion of the existence of the fact to be established.... [I]t must be enough to justify, if the trial were to a jury, a refusal to direct a verdict when the conclusion sought to be drawn from it is one of fact for the jury."

The very smoothness of the "substantial evidence" formula as the standard for reviewing the evidentiary validity of the Board's findings established its currency. But the inevitably variant applications of the standard to conflicting evidence soon brought contrariety of views and in due course bred criticism. Even though the whole record may have been canvassed in order to determine whether the evidentiary foundation of a determination by the Board was "substantial," the phrasing of this Court's process of review readily lent itself to the notion that it was enough that the evidence supporting the Board's result was "substantial" when considered by itself....

Criticism of so contracted a reviewing power reinforced dissatisfaction felt in various quarters with the Board's administration of the Wagner Act in the years preceding the war....

[T]he legislative history of [the APA] hardly speaks with that clarity of purpose which Congress supposedly furnishes courts in order to enable them to enforce its true will. On the one hand, the sponsors of the legislation indicated that they were reaffirming the prevailing "substantial evidence" test. But with equal clarity they expressed disapproval of the manner in which the courts were applying their own standard. The committee reports of both houses refer to the practice of agencies to rely upon "suspicion, surmise, implications, or plainly incredible evidence," and indicate that courts are to exact higher standards "in the exercise of their independent judgment" and on consideration of "the whole record."

Similar dissatisfaction with too restricted application of the "substantial evidence" test is reflected in the legislative history of the Taft–Hartley Act. The bill as reported to the House provided that the "findings of the Board as to the facts shall be conclusive unless it is made to appear to the satisfaction of the court either (1) that the findings of fact are against the manifest weight of the evidence, or (2) the findings of fact are not supported by substantial evidence." The bill left the House with this provision. Early committee prints in the Senate provided for review by "weight of the evidence" or "clearly erroneous" standards. But, as the Senate Committee Report relates, "it was finally decided to conform the statute to the corresponding section of the Administrative Procedure Act where the substantial evidence test prevails. In order to clarify any ambiguity in that statute, however, the committee inserted the words "questions of fact, if supported by substantial evidence *on the record considered as a whole....*'"...

It is fair to say that in all this Congress expressed a mood. And it expressed its mood not merely by oratory but by legislation. As legislation that mood must be respected, even though it can only serve as a standard for judgment and not as a body of rigid rules assuring sameness of application....

Whether or not it was ever permissible for courts to determine the substantiality of evidence supporting a Labor Board decision merely on the basis of evidence which in and of itself justified it, without taking into account contradictory evidence or evidence from which conflicting inferences could be drawn, the new legislation definitely precludes such a theory of review and bars its practice. The substantiality of evidence must take into account whatever in the record fairly detracts from its weight. This is clearly the significance of the requirement in both statutes that courts consider the whole record. Committee reports and the adoption in the Administrative Procedure Act of the minority views of the Attorney General's Committee demonstrate that to enjoin such a duty on the reviewing court was one of the important purposes of the movement which eventuated in that enactment.

To be sure, the requirement for canvassing "the whole record" in order to ascertain substantiality does not furnish a calculus of value by which a reviewing court can assess the evidence. Nor was it intended to negative the function of the Labor Board as one of those agencies presumably equipped or informed by experience to deal with a specialized field of knowledge, whose findings within that field carry the authority of an expertness which courts do not possess and therefore must respect. Nor does it mean that even as to matters not requiring expertise a court may displace the Board's choice between two fairly conflicting views, even though the court would justifiably have made a different choice had the matter been before it de novo. Congress has merely made it clear that a reviewing court is not barred from setting aside a Board decision when it cannot conscientiously find that the evidence supporting that decision is substantial, when viewed in the light that the record in its entirety furnishes, including the body of evidence opposed to the Board's view.

There remains then the question whether enactment of these two statutes has altered the scope of review other than to require that substantiality be determined in the light of all that the record relevantly presents. A formula for judicial review of administrative action may afford grounds for certitude but cannot assure certainty of application. Some scope for judicial discretion in applying the formula can be avoided only by falsifying the actual process of judging or by using the formula as an instrument of futile casuistry.... To find the change so elusive that it cannot be precisely defined does not mean it may be ignored. We should fail in our duty to effectuate the will of Congress if we denied recognition to expressed Congressional disapproval of the finality accorded to Labor Board findings by some decisions of this and lower courts, or even of the atmosphere which may have favored those decisions.

We conclude, therefore, that the Administrative Procedure Act and the Taft–Hartley Act direct that courts must now assume more responsibility for the reasonableness and fairness of Labor Board decisions than some courts have shown in the past. Reviewing courts must be influenced by a feeling that they are not to abdicate the conventional judicial function. Congress has imposed on them responsibility for assuring that the Board keeps within reasonable grounds. That responsibility is not less real because it is limited to enforcing the requirement that evidence appear substantial when viewed, on the record as a whole, by courts invested with the authority and enjoying the prestige of the Courts of Appeals. The Board's findings are entitled to respect; but they must nonetheless be set aside when the record before a Court of Appeals clearly precludes the Board's decision from being justified by a fair estimate of the worth of the testimony of witnesses or its informed judgment on matters within its special competence or both....

Our power to review the correctness of application of the present standard ought seldom to be called into action. Whether on the record as a whole there is substantial evidence to support agency findings is a question which Congress has placed in the keeping of the Courts of Appeals. This Court will intervene only in what ought to be the rare instance when the standard appears to have been misapprehended or grossly misapplied.

II.

... The decision of the Court of Appeals is assailed on two grounds. It is said (1) that the court erred in holding that it was barred from taking into account the report of the examiner on questions of fact insofar as that report was rejected by the Board, and (2) that the Board's order was not supported by substantial evidence on the record considered as a whole, even apart from the validity of the court's refusal to consider the rejected portions of the examiner's report.

The latter contention is easily met.... [I]t is clear from the court's opinion in this case that it in fact did consider the "record as a whole," and did not deem itself merely the judicial echo of the Board's conclusion. The testimony of the company's witnesses was inconsistent, and there was clear evidence that the complaining employee had been discharged by an officer who was at one time influenced against him because of his appearance at the Board hearing. On such a record we could not say that it would be error to grant enforcement.

The first contention, however, raises serious questions to which we now turn.

III.

The Court of Appeals deemed itself bound by the Board's rejection of the examiner's findings because the court considered these findings not "as unassailable as a master's." They are not. Section 10(c) of the

Labor Management Relations Act provides that "If upon the preponderance of the testimony taken the Board shall be of the opinion that any person named in the complaint has engaged in or is engaging in any such unfair labor practice, then the Board shall state its findings of fact. . . ." The responsibility for decision thus placed on the Board is wholly inconsistent with the notion that it has power to reverse an examiner's findings only when they are "clearly erroneous." Such a limitation would make so drastic a departure from prior administrative practice that explicitness would be required. . . .

We are aware that to give the examiner's findings less finality than a master's and yet entitle them to consideration in striking the account, is to introduce another and an unruly factor into the judgmatical process of review. But we ought not to fashion an exclusionary rule merely to reduce the number of imponderables to be considered by reviewing courts.

The Taft–Hartley Act provides that "The findings of the Board with respect to questions of fact if supported by substantial evidence on the record considered as a whole shall be conclusive." Surely an examiner's report is as much a part of the record as the complaint or the testimony. According to the Administrative Procedure Act, "All decisions (including initial, recommended, or tentative decisions) shall become a part of the record. . . ." [§ 557(c)]. . . .

It is therefore difficult to escape the conclusion that the plain language of the statutes directs a reviewing court to determine the substantiality of evidence on the record including the examiner's report. . . . Nothing in the statutes suggests that the Labor Board should not be influenced by the examiner's opportunity to observe the witnesses he hears and sees and the Board does not. Nothing suggests that reviewing courts should not give to the examiner's report such probative force as it intrinsically commands. To the contrary, § 11 of the Administrative Procedure Act contains detailed provisions designed to maintain high standards of independence and competence in examiners. Section 10(c) of the Labor Management Relations Act requires that examiners "shall issue . . . a proposed report, together with a recommended order." Both statutes thus evince a purpose to increase the importance of the role of examiners in the administrative process. High standards of public administration counsel that we attribute to the Labor Board's examiners both due regard for the responsibility which Congress imposes on them and the competence to discharge it. . . .

We do not require that the examiner's findings be given more weight than in reason and in the light of judicial experience they deserve. The "substantial evidence" standard is not modified in any way when the Board and its examiner disagree. We intend only to recognize that evidence supporting a conclusion may be less substantial when an impartial, experienced examiner who has observed the witnesses and lived with the case has drawn conclusions different from the Board's than when he has reached the same conclusion. The findings of the examiner are to be considered along with the consistency and inherent probability of testimony. The significance of his report, of course, depends largely on the importance of credibility in the particular case. To give it this significance does not seem to us materially more difficult than to heed the other factors which in sum determine whether evidence is "substantial." . . .

We therefore remand the cause to the Court of Appeals. On reconsideration of the record it should accord the findings of the trial examiner the relevance that they reasonably command in answering the comprehensive question whether the evidence supporting the Board's order is substantial. But the court need not limit its reexamination of the case to the effect of that report on its decision. We leave it free to grant or deny enforcement as it thinks the principles expressed in this opinion dictate.

Judgment vacated and cause remanded.

BLACK and DOUGLAS, JJ., concur with parts I and II of this opinion but as to part III agree with the opinion of the court below.

DEFRIES v. ASSOCIATION OF OWNERS, 999 WILDER

555 P.2d 855 (Hawaii 1976).

RICHARDSON, C.J.:

Claimant-appellant appeals from an order of the Labor and Industrial Relations Appeals Board denying workers' compensation benefits for a partially disabled right knee.

It is undisputed that claimant stumbled and fractured the big toe of his right foot on August 30, 1970, in the course of his employment as a security guard. The factual issue presently in dispute is whether or not the same stumble also aggravated or accelerated an osteoarthritic condition in claimant's right knee.

At the appeals board hearing, claimant testified that, while running after a suspicious person, he failed to notice a step up to a higher floor level so that he struck his foot against the face of the step, fracturing his toe and also striking his knees on the floor, although his hands helped break the impact of the fall. The employer does not dispute that claimant stumbled and fractured his toe, but does question whether claimant's knees struck the ground. It is undisputed that claimant then weighed approximately 285 pounds and was 63 years old.

The Employer's Report of Industrial Injury and two Physician's Reports to the Division of Workmen's Compensation, all filed during the latter months of 1970, refer only to the fracture of the right big toe and make no mention of impact or injury to the right knee. However, one of the physician's reports does make reference to "[claimant's] fall."

At the appeals board hearing, claimant stated that his right knee did not hurt until about a week after the accident; that the pain then felt "very minor"; that he couldn't remember whether or not he mentioned such pain to the doctor then treating the fractured toe; that the knee thereafter bothered him off and on, perhaps once a month; and that he treated it at home with a heating pad and ointment. He further testified that on July 21, 1972, approximately two years later, while in the continued employ of appellee, his right knee seemed to lock as he was stepping down from his work stool and he was forced to limp because of the pain. It is undisputed that on the next day, July 22, 1972, claimant obtained treatment for the knee from Dr. Shimamura, the same doctor who had treated the broken toe. At the hearing claimant stated that, at this July 22, 1972 office visit, as far as he could remember, he did not mention the 1970 accident to the doctor. He explained that he assumed Dr. Shimamura already knew that he had struck his knees in the 1970 stumble and fall. In a letter in evidence at the hearing, Dr. Shimamura wrote that the first time claimant told him that the injury to the right knee was related to the 1970 stumble was on September 8, 1972. . . .

Dr. Richard Dodge, who had been treating claimant since October 1972, was called as an expert witness for the employer. With respect to claimant's testimony that he had not noticed pain in the right knee until about a week after the stumble, Dr. Dodge testified that it was "not the usual case" for pain to be so slow in manifesting itself; that the week's delay before pain was noticed "raises questions in my mind"; that it "would be possible, but it would be very strange for him to go a week after a fall" without any pain or mention of pain to his doctor. However, other testimony by Dr. Dodge is more favorable:

"Q [Chairman of Appeals Board] I know anything's possible but based on medical probability, what is your opinion? Probability, now.

"A [Dr. Dodge] . . . My opinion is that it [injury to the knee in the 1970 stumble] couldn't have been very severe, but it could have happened. If he did have a fall it could have happened and he could have gone on and treated it at home until it became severe enough to seek medical help in 1972. . . ."

Even though claimant did see Dr. Shimamura a number of times during 1970–1972 for other ailments, Dr. Dodge still saw nothing unusual about failure to mention minor knee pain to Dr. Shimamura during that period. . . .

A letter from the employer's medical expert, Dr. Luke, concludes on the basis of a single examination:

"Based on the facts known about this case as rendered by the patient and based on this examination, it is my opinion that the patient's right knee problem has nothing to do either by way of injury or by way of aggravation in so far as the accident of 1970 is concerned. It is only by retrospect and hindsight that the patient is trying to establish a causal relationship for purposes of putting in an industrial claim. . . . "

THE APPEALS BOARD DECISION

Although the Director of the Department of Labor and Industrial Relations had determined after an administrative hearing that claimant's right knee injury was compensable, the appeals board reversed: It is clear from the board's written decision that its primary reason for reversing the director was its conclusion that claimant's testimony was not credible.

In its decision, the board noted that claimant had limped decidedly at the hearing and had testified that his limp had been even worse on the day he first consulted Dr. Dodge in 1972; and yet, the board noted, Dr. Dodge had not recorded claimant's limping in his 1972 medical records, even though Dr. Dodge testified that he thought he "surely would have" made a note in 1972 of limping so obvious as the limping at the hearing. No one disputes that claimant was suffering from objectively manifested osteoarthritis by the time of his first consultation with Dr. Dodge in 1972, but the board evidently believed that claimant's testimony, by reason of deliberate exaggeration or confused memory, inaccurately described the extent of the 1972 limp. From this the board apparently drew the inference that claimant's testimony on material issues was less credible.

The board's decision also noted that claimant had emphatically, and inaccurately, denied having filed any workers' compensation claim prior to 1970; yet the board found the record to show that claimant had filed a claim for his left knee in 1962. The board found it difficult to believe that the claimant, after prior experience with a claim involving a knee, would fail to claim or mention an injury to his other knee in 1970, "particularly in light of his testimony that his right knee bothered him to the extent that he subjected himself to heat treatments at home."

The board found that, in general, conflicts between claimant's testimony and evidence in the record "cast a very dark shadow on his credibility." The board concluded that in light of claimant's "general course of conduct" and the "evident lack of credibility" in his testimony, no connection existed between the 1970 stumble and claimant's right knee injury.

STANDARD OF REVIEW ON APPEAL

... [A]ppeals from the Labor and Industrial Relations Appeals Board are governed by Hawaii's Administrative Procedure Act, which provides in pertinent part that:

> "[T]he court may ... reverse ... the decision and order [of an administrative body] if ... the administrative findings, conclusions, ... or orders are: ... (5) *Clearly erroneous* in view of the reliable, probative, and substantial evidence on the whole record...."

Under the clearly erroneous standard, this court will reverse findings by the appeals board if this court is left with the definite and firm conviction that a mistake has been made.

The clearly erroneous standard gives the reviewing court greater leeway to reverse a lower court's findings than the substantial evidence test applicable to review of jury verdicts (including jury verdicts in criminal cases) and administrative fact-finding under the *federal* Administrative Procedures Act. Under the clearly erroneous standard, the reviewing court *will reverse*

"[i]f the findings [by the lower court] ... are against the clear weight of the evidence or [if] the appellate court otherwise reaches a definite and firm conviction that a mistake has been made, ... *even though there is evidence* [supporting the findings] *that, by itself, would be substantial.*" 9 Wright & Miller, Federal Practice and Procedure: Civil § 2585 (emphasis added)

BURDEN OF PROOF

In reviewing the decision by the appeals board, this court must also take into consideration the burden of proof imposed upon the employer by HRS § 386–85:

"Presumptions. In any proceeding for the enforcement of a claim for compensation ... it shall be presumed, in the absence of substantial evidence to the contrary;

"(1) That the claim is for a covered work injury."

This section has been construed in numerous Hawaii cases. The cases have liberally construed the statutory language in order to effectuate the humanitarian purposes of the workers' compensation act. In general, it has been found that the workers' compensation act "cast[s] a heavy burden on the employer". The "substantial evidence" burden imposed on employers by § 386–85 entails not only a burden of going forward with the evidence but also a burden of ultimate persuasion.... "Substantial evidence" as used in § 386–85 means a high quantum of evidence. This is evident from *Akamine v. Hawaiian Packing*, in which this court, after rigorously examining the extensive testimony offered by two medical experts on behalf of the employer, concluded that the experts' testimony was insufficiently relevant and probative in "net weight" to qualify as "substantial evidence" under the statute. However, the court in *Akamine* did not rely solely on the "substantial evidence" requirement of § 386–85 in reaching its results. *Akamine* further holds that the broad humanitarian purpose of the workers' compensation statute *read as a whole* requires that all reasonable doubts be resolved in favor of the claimant:

"[I]f there is *reasonable doubt* as to whether an injury is work-connected, the humanitarian nature of the statute demands that doubt be *resolved in favor of the claimant.*"

· · ·

APPLICATION OF LEGAL STANDARDS TO THE FACTS OF THIS CASE

This court concludes that the decision of the appeals board was clearly erroneous. We hold that, taking the evidence as a whole and giving due consideration to the opportunity of the appeals board to judge the demeanor and credibility of witnesses, there was insufficient evidence, giving the claimant the benefit of every reasonable doubt, including the factual, for the board to conclude that the 1970 stumble neither aggravated nor accelerated the arthritic condition in claimant's right knee.

The board's conclusion that claimant's testimony lacked credibility is of course entitled to weight on appeal. If this had been a case where there existed no objective corroboration of claimant's story, then the board's finding of a lack of credibility, coupled with expert medical testimony favoring the employer, would permit the board to conclude that the claim was invalid. In this case, however, even assuming arguendo that portions of claimant's testimony were confused or fabricated, there is objective corroboration of the claim itself. . . . Given the undisputed facts in this case and the opinion by two medical experts that injury to the knee may have been caused by the stumble, the rule that reasonable doubts be resolved in claimant's favor forces the conclusion that the claim in this case is valid.

The judgment of the appeals board is reversed, and the case is remanded to the board for determination of the amount of compensation to be awarded.

KIDWELL, J., dissenting, with whom KOBAYASHI, J., joins.

I respectfully dissent.

This case presents the troublesome question of the weight which should be given to a finding of the Labor and Industrial Relations Appeals Board that a claimant's testimony as to the occurrence of an injury is incredible in light of the attendant circumstantial evidence. The majority imposes on the board the obligation to resolve all reasonable doubts in the claimant's favor and concludes that the circumstantial evidence indicating fabrication of the claim was insufficient to overcome the claimant's testimony. I agree that this court may review the sufficiency of the evidence upon which the board relied in rejecting the claimant's testimony. However, I cannot concur in the majority's conclusion that the decision of the board was "clearly erroneous". . . .

Notes and Questions

1. *Substantial evidence v. clearly erroneous.* If Hawaii used the standard of substantial evidence on the whole record rather than the clearly erroneous test, do you think the court would have reversed the appeals board? How about substantial evidence with a mood of more rigorous review, as described by Justice Frankfurter in *Universal Camera?*

2. *Rationales for substantial evidence test.* The substantial evidence test is designed to limit an appellate court's power to reverse agency fact findings. The court's power is the same when it reviews factual determinations made by a jury. Should a jury be entitled to greater latitude than an agency?

Why shouldn't a court which believes that agency findings are clearly erroneous (but supported by substantial evidence) be permitted to overturn the agency decision? Some possible explanations might be:

i.   Agencies specialize and develop expertise in the areas they regulate. Their fact-finding process reflects that expertise, and thus their findings should receive only limited judicial scrutiny.

ii.   When it creates a regulatory program, the legislature usually delegates to an agency all of the powers necessary to execute the legislative scheme, including the power to adjudicate and to find facts. Because fact-finding is an essential element of the delegated power, the legislature intends a court to respect those findings, absent a very serious error by the agency.

iii.   The narrowness of the reviewing power discourages disappointed litigants from appealing, thus conserving the resources of both courts and agencies.

iv.   Courts are likely to have a different political orientation than agencies. An agency is expected to carry out the objective set by the legislature and to reflect the views of the executive who appointed its members. A reasonableness scope of review limits the ability of a court to impose its values in place of the agency's values.

3.   *Is there a difference between the tests?* Compare these views:

a.   Frank E. Cooper, "Administrative Law: The 'Substantial Evidence' Rule," 44 A.B.A.J. 945, 947 (1958)* (Cooper was a draftsman of the 1961 Model State APA which adopted the clearly erroneous test):

Many judges find it most difficult to distinguish between the "substantial evidence" and "clear error" tests. Attempts to differentiate between the two tests produce confusion for Bench and Bar alike.... The cases studied [188 federal court of appeals cases between 1951 and 1958] vindicate the rule-of-thumb test commonly employed by practicing attorneys, *viz.* if the appellant can convince the appellate court that the administrative finding of facts is obviously just plain wrong, and if the appellant can at the same time arouse the court with a zealous desire to correct the error, the court can always find means to do so, whatever labels must be applied.

Cooper's study indicated that the Fifth Circuit reversed 16 of 30 NLRB cases (53%) while the Second Circuit reversed 3 out of 24 (12%). What might account for this divergence?

b.   Louis L. Jaffe, JUDICIAL CONTROL OF ADMINISTRATIVE ACTION 603 (1965):

But the abuse of the "whole record" test is not a sufficient reason for disowning it. If the distinction between substantial evidence and weight of evidence is subtle and difficult, it is nevertheless an old one, long used in jury trials. It has never been easy to verbalize or to apply. Its sound administration has depended on the intelligence and self-discipline of

---

* Reprinted with permission from the *ABA Journal*, The Lawyer's Magazine, pub-   lished by the American Bar Association (1958).

the judges, and the answer must be the same for review of administrative findings.

4. *Burden of proof and scope of review.* The issues relating to burden of proof are discussed in § 4.2. In general, a party that is the proponent of an issue has the burden of persuading the trier of fact by a preponderance of the evidence. *DeFries* indicates that in some situations the burden of persuasion is heavier than a preponderance of the evidence. Indeed, the court's discussion suggests that the employer's burden to show that an injury is not work-related is about the same as the prosecution's burden in a criminal case of proving guilt beyond a reasonable doubt.

Consider the relationship between burden of persuasion at the hearing and scope of judicial review and note that *these need not be the same.* In a criminal case tried to a jury, for example, the prosecution must prove its case beyond a reasonable doubt; but an appellate court must affirm if a reasonable juror could have found the defendant guilty beyond a reasonable doubt. That is not at all the same as allowing the appellate court to reverse if its examination of the record indicates to it that the prosecution failed to prove guilt beyond a reasonable doubt.

How did the burden of persuasion affect the result in *DeFries?*

5. *Disagreement between agency and ALJ.* In *Universal Camera,* the NLRB overturned fact findings made by its hearing examiner (hearing examiners are now called ALJs). The dispute concerned the credibility of witnesses which the examiner had heard and the Board had not.

Both the Second Circuit and the Supreme Court rejected the analogy between a hearing officer and a master appointed by a trial court to take testimony. A trial court cannot reverse a master's findings unless it finds them clearly erroneous. Fed.R.Civ.P. 53(e)(2); agency heads have more power to reverse an examiner's findings than that. Why is the relationship between a court and a master different from that between an agency and its ALJ? Consider the relevance of APA § 557(b) (third sentence) and 1981 MSAPA § 4–216(d).

Judge Hand's first opinion in *Universal Camera* stated that a reviewing court has no middle ground between disregarding an agency's reversal of its examiner and making the examiner's findings as unassailable as those of a master. 179 F.2d 749, 753 (2d Cir.1950). Did the Supreme Court identify a middle ground? Where is that ground located?

On remand, Judge Hand went to the opposite extreme: he ruled "an examiner's findings on veracity must not be overruled without a very substantial preponderance in the testimony as recorded." 190 F.2d 429, 430 (2d Cir.1951). The Supreme Court later disapproved this approach, since it appeared to equate the relationship between ALJs and agency heads with that of masters and trial courts. *FCC v. Allentown Broadcasting Corp.,* 349 U.S. 358 (1955).

Under *Universal Camera,* if agency heads reverse an ALJ's credibility findings, this disagreement is treated by courts reviewing the agency heads' decision under the substantial evidence test as a *minus factor.* According to one formula, the reviewing court requires the agency heads "to fully articulate [their] reasons" for disagreeing with an ALJ on credibility questions;

the court then decides "with heightened scrutiny" whether the heads' decision is supportable. *Aylett v. Sec'y of Housing & Urban Development*, 54 F.3d 1560 (10th Cir.1995) (reversing HUD's decision that housing discrimination took place, where ALJ believed the landlord).

The *Universal Camera* rule applies most clearly to disagreements between ALJs and agency heads about the credibility of witnesses—and especially to that subset of credibility determinations that depend on assessment of the demeanor of a witness. As to other factual issues, should the agency heads be free to substitute their judgment without the disagreement being treated as a minus factor? For example, imagine an antitrust case before the FTC in which the ALJ makes detailed fact findings about the relevant market. Could the agency heads make different fact findings on this subject without running into a *Universal Camera* problem?

Not all states follow *Universal Camera*. In Wisconsin, for example, the agency heads must explain their disagreement with the ALJ's credibility findings; the court must reverse if the disagreement is unexplained. *Pieper Electric, Inc. v. Labor & Ind. Rev. Comm'n*, 346 N.W.2d 464 (Wis.App.1984).

Under the Florida and Montana APAs, an agency cannot reject or modify an ALJ's findings of fact if the findings are based on "competent substantial evidence." Interpreting this statute, a Florida court reviewing a medical board decision stated that the board could override the ALJ's findings only where the issue requires "special knowledge and expertise in the practice of medicine." The issue was whether a doctor had prescribed inappropriate amounts of an opiate to patients in pain. The ALJ thought not; the medical board reversed. The court reversed the board decision, stating that "the circumstances of this case do not present a unique question that is not susceptible to ordinary methods of proof, resolution of which falls within the special expertise of the board to the point that the board may overturn the findings of the hearing officer when those findings are based upon competent substantial evidence in the record." *Johnston v. Dept. of Prof. Reg..*, 456 So.2d 939 (Fla.App.1984). Is this a sounder approach to the problem than the *Universal Camera* approach? Does it appropriately enhance the status of the ALJ in the adjudicatory process? Does it enhance the status of the ALJ too much?

Traditionally, in California, reviewing courts ignored the fact findings of ALJs. Agency heads were free to substitute their own findings about witness credibility, even though they never heard or saw the witness. However, a recent amendment to the APA changed this rule:

> If the factual basis for the decision includes a determination based substantially on the credibility of a witness, the statement shall identify any specific evidence of the observed demeanor, manner, or attitude of the witness that supports the determination, and on judicial review the court shall give great weight to the determination to the extent the determination identifies the observed demeanor, manner, or attitude of the witness that supports it. Cal. Gov't Code § 11425.50(b) (West Supp.1997).

Does this provision codify *Universal Camera*? The statutory comment indicates that this was the intent. Or does the provision go even further than *Universal Camera* in enhancing the status of ALJs vis-à-vis agency heads?

6. *Supreme Court review of court of appeals.* In *Universal Camera,* the Court noted that it would seldom overturn a court of appeals decision applying the substantial evidence test. However, in *Allentown Mack Sales & Service, Inc. v. NLRB,* 118 S.Ct. 818 (1998), the Court did exactly that.

The issue in *Allentown Mack* was whether an employer had a "reasonable doubt, based on objective considerations, that the Union continued to enjoy the support of a majority of the bargaining unit employees." Only an employer that entertains such a doubt is permitted to conduct a poll of its employees to find out whether they in fact continue to support the union. The NLRB held that various statements made by employees to the employer were insufficient to raise a reasonable doubt. But the Court concluded: "Giving fair weight to Allentown's circumstantial evidence, we think it quite impossible for a rational factfinder to avoid the conclusion that Allentown had reasonable good-faith grounds to doubt—to be *uncertain about*—the union's retention of majority support." Four justices dissented.

One possible reason for the Court's departure from its normal practice of leaving substantial evidence cases to the courts of appeals is that it wanted to make a more general point. Apparently the NLRB had applied a different (and much more demanding) standard for deciding "reasonable doubt" than the words of that test suggested. This undisclosed standard violated the norm of reasoned decisionmaking. This aspect of the case is discussed further in § 9.4.

Should *Universal Camera* be interpreted to mean that the Supreme Court will display *deference* toward a lower court's application of the substantial evidence test? Or only that the Court will seldom *review* such applications but will apply the same test as the lower court in cases that it does review? *Allentown Mack* is an example of the latter approach, but other cases follow the former one. *See FTC v. Standard Oil Co.,* 355 U.S. 396, 400–01 (1958).

In some states, the supreme court reviews agency factfindings as if the lower court decision had not occurred. *See, e.g., Jackson County Public Hospital v. Public Employment Rel. Bd.,* 280 N.W.2d 426, 429 (Iowa 1979). Another alternative is to give less scrutiny to lower court decisions that agree with agency decisions, but more scrutiny to lower court decisions that disagree with agency decisions. *Clowes v. Terminix Int'l,* 538 A.2d 794, 801 (N.J.1988). Should state supreme courts follow the *Standard Oil* model and defer to lower court decisions applying the substantial evidence test?

7. *Problem.* Madison law prohibits discrimination by any business establishment on the basis of race, religion, gender, or "affectional preference." Ted was a homosexual member of City Health Club. On April 2, Joe (a staff member of the Club) overheard Ted making a date with another male Club member. As Ted was leaving the Club, Mark (the manager) asked Ted to come into the office and discuss his conduct. Ted told him to drop dead and left the Club. That day, Mark terminated Ted's membership. Mark's letter stated that termination occurred because Ted's conduct had offended a member of the staff and because he had refused to discuss the matter with management.

Ted complained to the Civil Rights Commission (CRC), which enforces the anti-discrimination law. Gloria, the CRC's ALJ, found that Ted had been terminated because his conduct had offended a staff member and because of his refusal to discuss it, not because of his affectional preference. Consequently, she denied relief.

Ted appealed the decision to the full CRC, which reversed. Its opinion stated that Ted had been terminated because he was a homosexual, not because of his conduct. It found that the Club was trying to rid itself of homosexual members. It also found that Joe had not been offended, and that Ted's conduct could not be the basis for terminating him, whether Joe was offended or not. Thus it awarded Ted compensatory and punitive damages, as well as attorney's fees, as permitted by the statute.

Should a court reverse this decision, assuming the state subscribes to (i) the substantial evidence on the whole record test? (ii) The clearly erroneous test?

Suppose the CRC had agreed with Gloria, and Ted sought judicial review. What result? *See Blanding v. Sports & Health Club, Inc.,* 373 N.W.2d 784 (Minn.App.1985).

§ 9.1.2 INDEPENDENT JUDGMENT AND DE NOVO REVIEW

§ 9.1.2a Federal Decisions

As just discussed, the prevailing test for judicial review of basic facts in both federal and state courts is a reasonableness test (substantial evidence on the whole record), although many states use the clearly erroneous test. This subchapter explores instances in which a much broader scope of basic fact review is employed. An odd collection of Supreme Court decisions of the 1920's and 1930's call for the substitution of judicial judgment for agency judgment on the basis of the record made before the agency or even for a judicial trial de novo.

i. *Constitutional facts.* The earliest such case is *Ohio Valley Water Co. v. Ben Avon Borough,* 253 U.S. 287 (1920), involving judicial review of a state agency's valuation of the property of a utility company. That value was critical, since the company was constitutionally entitled to rates which yield a fair return on its assets. The Supreme Court held that due process entitled a utility to a judicial trial de novo on the valuation issue.

In *St. Joseph Stock Yards Co. v. United States,* 298 U.S. 38 (1936), a decision involving ratemaking for a stockyard, the Court reaffirmed the *Ben Avon* decision. It held that a stockyard was entitled to a trial de novo on the valuation issue and implied that the right might extend to alleged administrative denial of any constitutional right. However, the *St. Joseph* case modified *Ben Avon* in several significant respects. First, it required that a reviewing court give presumptive weight to the fact findings of the agency; these findings should be sustained unless a complaining party makes a convincing showing that they are wrong. The Court also precluded the company from introducing evidence in court that could have been introduced at the agency hearing.

These cases have never been overruled and they are still followed in a minority of the states. *See* Leslie A. Glick, "Independent Judicial

Review of Administrative Rate–Making: The Rise and Demise of the Ben Avon Doctrine," 40 Ford.L.Rev. 305, 313 (1971). However, the Supreme Court has never extended the *Ben Avon* and *St. Joseph* cases and has failed to apply them even in cases which raised the issue of whether administrative orders had confiscated a plaintiff's property. *See, e.g., Railroad Comm'n v. Rowan & Nichols Oil Co.,* 310 U.S. 573 (1940), 311 U.S. 570 (1941) (rejecting claims that a court should independently examine a state oil proration order).

Moreover, the very issue on which the *Ben Avon* and *St. Joseph* cases turned—valuation of a utility's property by a ratemaking agency—need no longer be judicially reviewed in detail. Any method of valuation is permitted, provided that the final result of the ratemaking process is reasonable in the sense that the rates cover the utility's costs. *FPC v. Hope Natural Gas Co.,* 320 U.S. 591 (1944).

ii. *Jurisdictional facts.* Traditionally, a person claiming to be a citizen and seeking *admission* to the United States has no right to judicial review of an administrative finding of non-citizenship. *United States v. Ju Toy,* 198 U.S. 253 (1905). Thus it was surprising when, shortly after the *Ben Avon* case, the Supreme Court held that individuals in the United States whose *deportation* had been ordered, but who maintained they were citizens, were entitled to a judicial trial de novo on the citizenship issue. *Ng Fung Ho v. White,* 259 U.S. 276 (1922). Citizenship was stated to be an essential "jurisdictional fact," and deportation of a citizen based on agency action "deprives him of liberty.... It may result also in loss of both property and life; or of all that makes life worth living. Against the danger of such deprivation without the sanction afforded by judicial proceedings, the Fifth Amendment affords protection in its guarantee of due process of law." *Id.* at 284–85. The *Ng Fung Ho* principle is still followed today; persons facing deportation (but not persons seeking admission) are entitled to a de novo judicial trial on the citizenship issue. Indeed, Congress has codified the principle, so the Court has not recently had to decide whether the Constitution also requires it. *Agosto v. INS,* 436 U.S. 748 (1978).

The other major "jurisdictional fact" case is *Crowell v. Benson,* 285 U.S. 22 (1932). *Crowell* involved judicial review of a commissioner's decision awarding compensation under the Longshoremen's and Harbor Workers' Act (a federal statute providing benefits for persons injured in the course of employment on navigable waters). That Act provided for judicial review of such decisions in district court.

The Court upheld the administrative scheme against most constitutional objections. It drew a distinction between "public rights" and "private rights." Public rights, roughly speaking, are disputes between the government and private individuals arising out of the performance of legislative or executive functions; "private rights" are disputes between individuals, like the employee-employer dispute at issue in *Crowell.* In matters of public right, Article III allows Congress to provide for settlement of disputes in legislative courts or in agencies.

Even in disputes concerning private rights, the Court noted, Congress could provide for hearings before an agency rather than a court, with appropriate provision for judicial review. It found that the judicial review provisions in the Longshoremen's Act were, for the most part, acceptable; the Act was construed to allow a reviewing court to redetermine questions of law and fact (but if a fact finding was "supported by evidence" it would be final).

However, the Court drew a distinction between most factual disputes (such as whether an injury occurred) and those that are "jurisdictional" in the sense that their existence is a condition precedent to the operation of the statutory scheme. In *Crowell*, the issues of "jurisdictional fact" were whether an employment relationship existed and whether the injury occurred on navigable waters. The Court held that, under article III of the Constitution, an employer was entitled to a judicial trial de novo at which a court would independently determine jurisdictional facts on a new record. Note that the distinction between jurisdictional and other facts necessary to support an agency decision may be illusory because the existence of every fact necessary to support such a decision may be deemed to be a prerequisite to the agency action and therefore jurisdictional.

Crowell has never been squarely overruled, but the courts have never extended it to any other "jurisdictional" facts under the Longshoremen's Act or any other statute. Indeed, it is now largely ignored even in cases arising under that Act. *Associated Indem. Corp. v. Shea,* 455 F.2d 913, 914 n. 2 (5th Cir.1972). *Crowell's* jurisdictional fact doctrine has seldom been followed in state courts. Although *Crowell's* distinction between public rights and private rights was endorsed by the plurality opinion of the United States Supreme Court in *Northern Pipeline Const. Co. v. Marathon Pipe Line Co.,* 458 U.S. 50 (1982) (discussed in § 7.4), the Court observed in a footnote that *Crowell's* jurisdictional/nonjurisdictional fact distinction is no longer followed. *Id.* at 82 n.34.

iii. *Summary.* It is interesting to note that the Court has never extended *Ben Avon* or *St. Joseph*—but also has not overruled them. Similarly, it has allowed *Crowell v. Benson* to continue in limbo, never following it but never overruling it, until its public right-private right distinction (but not its jurisdictional-nonjurisdictional fact distinction) was employed in *Northern Pipeline.*

One explanation for the shadowy existence of these cases might be that they can prove useful in the event the Supreme Court wishes to protect federal court jurisdiction against Congressional incursion. For example, suppose Congress seeks to make administrative fact-findings final or to prevent judicial review in sensitive constitutional cases such as school prayer or abortion. Consider the relevance of the dictum in *Crowell v. Benson:*

[T]he question [is] whether . . . Congress may substitute for constitutional courts, in which the judicial power of the United States is vested, an administrative agency ... for the final determination of the existence of the facts upon which the enforcement of the constitutional rights of the citizen depend.... [Allowing Congress] ... [to] completely oust the courts of all determinations of fact ... would be to sap the judicial power as it exists under the Federal Constitution, and to establish a government of a bureaucratic character alien to our system, wherever fundamental rights depend, as not infrequently they do depend, upon the facts and finality as to facts becomes in effect finality in law.... In cases brought to enforce constitutional rights, the judicial power of the United States necessarily extends to the independent determination of all questions, both of fact and law, necessary to the performance of that supreme function.

285 U.S. at 56–57, 60.

It is also worth noting that the Court has historically employed independent judgment in judicially reviewing the findings of lower courts in certain sensitive constitutional areas. The *Ng Fung Ho* case (concerning citizenship in deportation cases) is still followed. *See Miller v. Fenton*, 474 U.S. 104 (1985) (habeas review of confession issue); *Bose Corp. v. Consumers Union*, 466 U.S. 485 (1984) (first amendment limitations on defamation liability); *Bekiaris v. Board of Educ.*, 493 P.2d 480 (Cal.1972) (whether probationary teacher was dismissed because of exercising First Amendment rights).

It seems clear that the precise holdings of *Ben Avon*, *St. Joseph*, and *Crowell* are discredited, but the idea that, in cases requiring enhanced judicial protection, a court should engage in independent judgment of the facts is by no means dead. And, as we shall see, that idea remains very much alive in some state courts.

iv. *De novo trials*. In certain unusual situations, Congress requires that an administrative decision be reviewed by a de novo trial. One such example is an administrative disqualification of a food retailer from the food stamp program. It is reviewed by a trial de novo in either state or federal court. *See Warren v. United States*, 932 F.2d 582 (6th Cir.1991) (court makes its own findings based on preponderance of the evidence and is not limited to matters in the administrative record).

Another instance of de novo review involves judicial review of a school board decision under the Individuals with Disabilities Education Act (IDEA). IDEA calls for appropriate educational placements for disabled children. In IDEA cases, the court receives the record of the administrative proceeding, takes additional evidence at the request of a party, and basing its decision on the preponderance of the evidence, grants appropriate relief. *See Ojai Unified School Dist. v. Jackson*, 4 F.3d 1467 (9th Cir.1993). Why would Congress call for this sort of judicial review in food stamp and IDEA cases?

§ 9.1.2b   State Decisions

State statutes requiring de novo trials for review of particular administrative decisions are not uncommon. *See, e.g., Weeks v. Personnel*

Bd. of Review, 373 A.2d 176 (R.I.1977) (review of decision to discharge police officer), which cites cases from other states. Texas provides the best example of de novo judicial review. Apparently Texas legislators distrust administrative agencies, because de novo trials of matters already determined by administrative decisions are common. At such trials, the previous agency decision is treated as a complete nullity. *See* Janine Oldemeyer Hill, Note, "The Future of Judicial Review Under the Administrative Procedure and Texas Register Act," 57 Tex.L.Rev. 253, 271–73 (1979) (listing thirty statutes which grant de novo review, sometimes including jury trials).

California provides the leading example of judicial review of agency fact-findings without trial de novo but under an independent judgment standard. Cal.Code Civ.Proc. § 1094.5 (West 1988) provides for judicial review (through mandamus in the Superior Court) of agency decisions resulting from a trial-type agency hearing. However, the writ actually resembles certiorari rather than mandamus, since it calls for the court to review the evidence in the trial record. *See* § 10.1.2.

In general, § 1094.5 provides that the agency has abused its discretion if its fact findings are not supported by "substantial evidence in the light of the whole record." However, "in cases in which the court is authorized by law to exercise its independent judgment on the evidence, abuse of discretion is established if the court determines that the findings are not supported by the weight of the evidence." When the independent judgment test is employed, the court can permit introduction of evidence which could not reasonably have been produced before the agency or evidence which was improperly excluded. Thus independent judgment review can turn into a partial trial de novo.

The independent judgment test of § 1094.5 was originally (but is no longer) grounded in state constitutional law; it has been maintained and steadily expanded through judicial discretion. It applies to decisions of local and state agencies (other than those created by the California constitution). It applies only if the decision "substantially affects a vested, fundamental right." Note the ambiguity in this phrase: does it mean "vested *and* fundamental" or "vested *or* fundamental"? And how does one distinguish vested from non-vested rights, not to mention fundamental from non-fundamental ones?

In *Bixby v. Pierno,* 481 P.2d 242 (Cal.1971), the California Supreme Court announced its continued adherence to the independent judgment test. It reviewed the tortured history of the standard, making clear its close kinship with *Ben Avon, St. Joseph,* and *Crowell,* and offered an articulate defense of the test:

> Since the 1930's the courts have redefined their role in the protection of individual and minority rights. The courts have realized that in the area of economic due process the will of the majority as expressed by the Legislature and its delegated administrative agencies must be permitted to meet contemporary crucial problems.... Courts have explained that powerful economic forces can

obtain substantial representation in the halls of the Legislature and in the departments of the executive branch and thus do not impel the same kind of judicial protection as do the minorities: the unpopular religions, the racial subgroups, the criminal defendants, the politically weak and underrepresented.

By carefully scrutinizing administrative decisions which substantially affect vested, fundamental rights, the courts of California have undertaken to protect such rights, and particularly the right to practice one's trade or profession, from untoward intrusions by the massive apparatus of government. If the decision of an administrative agency will substantially affect such a right, the trial court not only examines the administrative record for errors of law but also exercises its independent judgment upon the evidence disclosed in a limited trial de novo. . . .

Although we recognize that the California rule yields no fixed formula and guarantees no predictably exact ruling in each case, it performs a precious function in the protection of the rights of the individual. Too often the independent thinker or crusader is subjected to the retaliation of the professional or trade group; the centripetal pressure toward conformity will often destroy the advocate of reform. The unpopular protestant may well provoke an aroused zeal of scrutiny by the licensing body that finds trivial grounds for license revocation. Restricted to the narrow ground of review of the evidence and denied the power of an independent analysis, the court might well be unable to save the unpopular professional or practitioner. Before his license is revoked, such an individual, who walks in the shadow of the governmental monoliths, deserves the protection of a full and independent judicial hearing.

481 P.2d at 250–51, 254.

FRINK v. PROD

643 P.2d 476 (Cal.1982).

BROUSSARD, J.:

Helene Frink petitioned for writ of mandate to vacate an administrative decision denying benefits under the aid to the totally disabled program (ATD). The Social Welfare Department's ALJ rejected her application on the grounds that her disability was not "permanent." The director of the Department adopted this decision. The superior court judgment states that while "the weight of the evidence was in petitioner's favor, there was substantial evidence in the administrative record to support the respondent's decision." Relief was denied. On this appeal, petitioner contends that the trial court should have exercised its independent judgment on the evidence rather than apply the substantial evidence rule. . . .

In administrative mandamus actions to review decisions *terminating* welfare assistance, the trial court exercises its independent judgment on the evidence. However, administrative determinations of *applications* for welfare benefits traditionally have been reviewed under the substantial evidence rule.... [It] is apparent that in accordance with section 1094.5, subdivision (c), it is for the courts to establish the appropriate standard of review in determining whether there has been an abuse of discretion....

In *Bixby v. Pierno,* it was concluded that the "courts must decide on a case-by-case basis whether an administrative decision or class of decisions substantially affects fundamental vested rights and thus requires independent judgment review.... In determining whether the right is fundamental the courts do not alone weigh the economic aspect of it, but the effect of it in human terms and the importance of it to the individual in the life situation. This approach finds its application in such an instance as the opportunity to continue the practice of one's trade or profession—a right which induced this court's statement in 1939: "it necessarily follows that the court to which the application for mandate is made to secure the restoration of a professional license must exercise an independent judgment on the facts.... ""

The court also pointed out that "in determining whether the right is sufficiently basic and fundamental to justify independent judgment review, the courts have considered the degree to which that right is 'vested,' that is, already possessed by the individual." In cases involving applications for a license, the courts have largely deferred to the administrative expertise of the agency. Courts are relatively ill-equipped to determine whether an individual would be qualified, for example, to practice a particular profession or trade. In a case involving the agency's initial determination whether an individual qualifies to enter a profession or trade the courts uphold the agency decision unless it lacks substantial evidentiary support or infringes upon the applicant's statutory or constitutional rights. Once the agency has initially exercised its expertise and determined that an individual fulfills the requirements to practice his profession, the agency's subsequent revocation of the license calls for an independent judgment review of the facts underlying any such administrative decision....

Weighing the importance and effect of the right and the degree to which it is possessed, it is apparent that the right of the needy disabled to public assistance is of such significance as to require independent judgment review.... The right of the needy applicant to welfare benefits is as fundamental as the right of a recipient to continued benefits. Because need is a condition of benefits, erroneous denial of aid in either case deprives the eligible person "of the very means for his survival and his situation becomes immediately desperate.... "

Evaluating the degree to which the right is vested, it is apparent that the right to welfare benefits is not based on expertise, competence, learning, or purchase or ownership claim. Determination of qualification for public assistance does not involve the "delicate task" of evaluating competence to engage in a broad field of endeavor as is true in most licensing cases. . . .

While the degree to which the right is vested may not be overwhelming, the degree of fundamentalness is. Weighing them together as required by *Bixby,* we conclude the independent judgment standard should be applied to decisions denying applications for welfare benefits. . . . The judgment is reversed with directions to enter judgment for petitioner.

[NEWMAN, J., joined by RICHARDSON and KAUS, JJ., dissented.]

Notes and Questions

1. *California's independent judgment test.* Recall the rationales for the substantial evidence test set forth in N.2 following *Universal Camera.* Based on these arguments and those developed in *Bixby,* is California's independent judgment test wise policy? Even if it is, is the independent judgment test needed in a case like *Frink?*

2. *Vested, fundamental rights.* After *Frink,* when should a trial court use the substantial evidence test and when should it use the independent judgment test? Is the vagueness of the California test acceptable?

3. *Universal Camera in California?* Recall the recent amendment to California's APA quoted in N.5 following *Universal Camera.* This statute requires reviewing courts to give great weight to properly labelled credibility findings of ALJs. What effect will this statute have in independent judgment cases? Would it change the result in *Frink?*

4. *Problem.* Recall the problem about Ted's membership termination by City Health Club in § 9.1.1 N.7. Suppose it arose in California. Would the court have power to exercise independent judgment if the CRC had found in Ted's favor? The Club's favor? Suppose the case was before a health club licensing board which revoked City's license because of repeated incidents of affectional discrimination?

§ 9.2 SCOPE OF REVIEW OF ISSUES OF LEGAL INTERPRETATION

In the course of its work, an agency constantly interprets and reinterprets the meaning of the words in legal texts like statutes or its own prior rules or decisions. For example, an agency might engage in the process of legal interpretation in rendering an adjudicative decision, in engaging in legislative or interpretive rulemaking, or in giving advice to the public.

A court might take three approaches when reviewing such interpretations. Under the traditional view (sometimes called "substitution of judgment," "rightness" or "independent judgment"), a court decides the interpretive issue for itself. Both federal and state APAs appear to authorize this approach. *See* APA § 706 (first paragraph and (2)(B), (C)) and 1981 MSAPA § 5–116(c)(2), (4). When substituting judgment on questions of law, courts usually grant at least some "weight" (sometimes referred to as "deference" or "weak deference") to the agency's interpretation. The *Connecticut Medical Society* case which follows illustrates the substitution of judgment-weak deference approach.

A second approach also employs substitution of judgment, but the court gives no deference to the agency's view. The agency view about questions of statutory interpretation receives no more weight than the court gives to the view of the private litigants.

A third approach (sometimes referred to as the "reasonableness" or "strong deference" approach) requires courts to treat interpretive issues the same as they treat agency findings of basic fact under the substantial evidence test. Under this approach, a court must accept an agency's interpretation of an ambiguous statute or other text if the interpretation is "reasonable;" it cannot substitute its own preferred interpretation for that of the agency. The *Chevron* case illustrates the reasonableness-strong deference approach. The reasonableness approach gives agencies much greater interpretive power than does the substitution of judgment-weak deference approach.

As you might expect, the first and third approaches shade into one another. A court which purports to employ the substitution of judgment approach, but which grants some degree of deference to the agency's interpretation, may really be using the "reasonableness" approach. If a court employing the "reasonableness" approach conducts an intensive examination of the statute's history and policy to assess whether the statute is "ambiguous" or whether the agency's interpretation of an ambiguous statute is "reasonable," it may really be using the substitution of judgment-weak deference approach.

CONNECTICUT STATE MEDICAL SOCIETY v. CONNECTICUT BOARD OF EXAMINERS IN PODIATRY

546 A.2d 830 (Conn.1988)

HULL, J.:

[The Podiatry Board issued a declaratory ruling that the ankle is part of the foot so that podiatrists could treat ankle ailments. It noted that "podiatrists in Connecticut have conservatively treated minor sprains, strains and fractures of the foot or ankle for many years without any regulatory or reimbursement questions being raised." The Medical Society sought judicial review, claiming that the ruling was contrary to § 20.50, Ct. Gen'l Statutes, which provides: "Podiatry is defined to be the diagnosis, prevention, and treatment of foot ailments ..." Relying on the dictionary definition of "foot," the trial court overturned the Podiatry Board's ruling.]

STANDARD OF REVIEW ...

[The Board claims] that the court substituted its judgment for that of the agency as to the weight of the evidence on questions of fact ...

[and] that the court erred in failing to afford "special deference" to the board's factual findings, and to time-tested agency interpretations.

The standard of judicial review of administrative agency rulings is well established. [The Connecticut APA] permits modification or reversal of an agency's decision "if substantial rights of the appellant have been prejudiced because the administrative findings, inferences, conclusions, or decisions are: (1) In violation of constitutional or statutory provisions; (2) in excess of the statutory authority of the agency; (3) made upon unlawful procedure; (4) affected by other error of law; (5) clearly erroneous in view of the reliable, probative, and substantial evidence on the whole record; or (6) arbitrary or capricious or characterized by abuse of discretion or clearly unwarranted exercise of discretion.' "The trial court may not retry the case or substitute its judgment for that of the agency on the weight of the evidence or questions of fact. Rather, an agency's factual and discretionary determinations are to be accorded considerable weight by the courts.

On the other hand, it is the function of the courts to expound and apply governing principles of law. This case presents a question of law turning upon the interpretation of a statute. Both the board and the trial court had to construe § 20–50 to determine the permissible scope of podiatry practice in Connecticut. In our view, this is purely a question of law, requiring that the intent of the legislature be discerned. Such a question invokes a broader standard of review than is ordinarily involved in deciding whether, in light of the evidence, the agency has acted unreasonably, arbitrarily, illegally or in abuse of its discretion.

Ordinarily, we give great deference to the construction given a statute by the agency charged with its enforcement. We agree with the trial court, however, that, in this case, the board's interpretation of § 20–50 is not entitled to any special deference. Ordinarily, the construction and interpretation of a statute is a question of law for the courts where the administrative decision is not entitled to special deference, particularly where, as here, the statute has not previously been subjected to judicial scrutiny or time-tested agency interpretations . . .

The podiatrists . . . claim that "a practical construction placed on legislation over many years" will be accorded special deference by a reviewing court. We have accorded deference to such a time-tested agency interpretation of a statute, but only when the agency has consistently followed its construction over a long period of time, the statutory language is ambiguous, and the agency's interpretation is reasonable. The defendants rely on the fact that podiatrists have long performed the procedures in question in this case. We disagree that such practices constitute time-tested agency interpretation of the statute. Further, we do not consider the board's knowledge of and acquiescence in certain podiatric practices to rise to the level of statutory construction entitled to judicial deference. . . .

The board's contention that the issue presented was a mixed question of law and fact is also without merit. Interpretation of the statute should effect the intent of the legislature and not expand the law's meaning to accommodate unauthorized practices simply because they have been performed in the past ...

INTERPRETATION OF THE TERM "FOOT"

[The Court affirmed the trial court. It relied partly on dictionary definitions of "foot" such as the one in Webster's Third New International Dictionary:] "[t]he terminal part of the vertebrate leg upon which an individual stands consisting in most bipeds (as man) and in many quadrupeds (as the cat) of all the structures (as heel, arches, and digits) below the ankle joint."

... The podiatrists argue [that the legislature delegated to the Board the ability to define the scope of podiatric practice].... We are unconvinced that the assertions of the [State Health Commissioner, made to the legislature in 1935 when the statute was revised,] are entitled to the weight the podiatrists urge us to accord them. While relevant to our inquiry, [excerpts from legislative proceedings] are by no means conclusive in determining legislative intent. ... As to occurrences at legislative public hearings, these are not admissible as a means of interpreting a legislative act and may not be considered. ... Further, our examination of the statutory scheme as it now exists belies such a conclusion.

[The Court ruled that the purpose of § 20–50 was both to] authorize the practice of podiatry and to define its limits ... The provisions limiting the scope of podiatry and, thus, tempering the expansion, however, are the predominant theme of the statutes. This is in marked contrast to chapter 370 of the General Statutes, entitled "Medicine and Surgery," wherein the scope of practice of medicine and surgery is not defined. ... We conclude, therefore, that it was not the intention of the legislature to empower the board to define the scope of podiatry practice in Connecticut.

The podiatrists rely heavily on *Finoia v. Winchester Repeating Arms Co.*, 34 A.2d 636 (1943), in which we interpreted "hands" as used in a workers' compensation statute in its common anatomical sense as including the wrist and not the forearm ... We can see no basis, however, for translating that statement into a declaration that the legislature intended the foot to include the ankle within the meaning of the podiatry statutes ...

There is no error.

CHEVRON U.S.A., INC. v. NATURAL RESOURCES DEFENSE COUNCIL
467 U.S. 837 (1984).

[The Clean Air Act required states that had not met EPA's air quality standards to prohibit the construction of a "new or modified major stationary source" of air pollution without obtaining a permit. No such permit can be issued without meeting stringent conditions.

An EPA legislative regulation allows states to treat an entire plant as a single "stationary source." Under this approach, if a plant contains several pollution-emitting devices, it may install or modify one piece of equipment without meeting the permit requirements if the alteration will not increase the total emissions from the plant. For example, a plant might install a new process which increases pollution if, at the same time, it alters or abandons other equipment which produces an equal or greater amount of pollution. This approach is often referred to as the "bubble" concept, since it treats a single plant as if it were encased in a "bubble."

The issue is whether the statutory term "stationary source" means each major source of pollution within a plant or whether it can refer to an entire plant (the view EPA took in the "bubble" regulation). The Court of Appeals found that the statute and legislative history were inconclusive, but it decided that EPA's interpretation was contrary to Congressional purpose in improving air quality in non-attainment areas. Thus it invalidated the "bubble" regulation.]

STEVENS, J:

... When a court reviews an agency's construction of the statute which it administers, it is confronted with two questions. First, always, is the question whether Congress has directly spoken to the precise question at issue. If the intent of Congress is clear, that is the end of the matter; for the court, as well as the agency, must give effect to the unambiguously expressed intent of Congress.[9] If, however, the court determines Congress has not directly addressed the precise question at issue, the court does not simply impose its own construction on the statute, as would be necessary in the absence of an administrative interpretation. Rather, if the statute is silent or ambiguous with respect to the specific issue, the question for the court is whether the agency's answer is based on a permissible construction of the statute.[11]

"The power of an administrative agency to administer a congressionally created ... program necessarily requires the formulation of policy and the making of rules to fill any gap left, implicitly or explicitly, by Congress." If Congress has explicitly left a gap for the agency to fill, there is an express delegation of authority to the agency to elucidate a specific provision of the statute by regulation. Such legislative regulations are given controlling weight unless they are arbitrary, capricious, or manifestly contrary to the statute. Sometimes the legislative delegation to an agency on a particular question is implicit rather than explicit. In such a case, a court may not substitute its own construction of a

9. The judiciary is the final authority on issues of statutory construction and must reject administrative constructions which are contrary to clear congressional intent. If a court, employing traditional tools of statutory construction, ascertains that Congress had an intention on the precise question at issue, that intention is the law and must be given effect.

11. The court need not conclude that the agency construction was the only one it permissibly could have adopted to uphold the construction, or even the reading the court would have reached if the question initially had arisen in a judicial proceeding.

statutory provision for a reasonable interpretation made by the administrator of an agency.

We have long recognized that considerable weight should be accorded to an executive department's construction of a statutory scheme it is entrusted to administer, and the principle of deference to administrative interpretations

> has been consistently followed by this Court whenever decision as to the meaning or reach of a statute has involved reconciling conflicting policies, and a full understanding of the force of the statutory policy in the given situation has depended upon more than ordinary knowledge respecting the matters subjected to agency regulations ... If this choice represents a reasonable accommodation of conflicting policies that were committed to the agency's care by the statute, we should not disturb it unless it appears from the statute or its legislative history that the accommodation is not one that Congress would have sanctioned.

In light of these well-settled principles it is clear that the Court of Appeals misconceived the nature of its role in reviewing the regulations at issue. Once it determined, after its own examination of the legislation, that Congress did not actually have an intent regarding the applicability of the bubble concept to the permit program, the question before it was not whether in its view the concept is "inappropriate" in the general context of a program designed to improve air quality, but whether the Administrator's view that it is appropriate in the context of this particular program is a reasonable one. Based on the examination of the legislation and its history which follows, we agree with the Court of Appeals that Congress did not have a specific intention on the applicability of the bubble concept in these cases, and conclude that the EPA's use of that concept here is a reasonable policy choice for the agency to make.
. . .

The legislative history ... does not contain any specific comment on the "bubble concept" or the question whether a plantwide definition of a stationary source is permissible under the permit program. It does, however, plainly disclose that in the permit program Congress sought to accommodate the conflict between the economic interest in permitting capital improvements to continue and the environmental interest in improving air quality. . . .

[T]he plantwide definition [of stationary source] is fully consistent with one of those concerns—the allowance of reasonable economic growth—and, whether or not we believe it most effectively implements the other, we must recognize that the EPA has advanced a reasonable explanation for its conclusion that the regulations serve the environmental objectives as well. Indeed, its reasoning is supported by the public record developed in the rulemaking process, as well as by certain private studies. . . .

In [this case,] the Administrator's interpretation represents a reasonable accommodation of manifestly competing interests and is entitled to deference: the regulatory scheme is technical and complex, the agency considered the matter in a detailed and reasoned fashion, and the decision involves reconciling conflicting policies. Congress intended to accommodate both interests, but did not do so itself on the level of specificity presented by this case. Perhaps that body consciously desired the Administrator to strike the balance at this level, thinking that those with great expertise and charged with responsibility for administering the provision would be in a better position to do so; perhaps it simply did not consider the question at this level; and perhaps Congress was unable to forge a coalition on either side of the question, and those on each side decided to take their chances with the scheme devised by the agency. For judicial purposes, it matters not which of these things occurred.

Judges are not experts in the field, and are not part of either political branch of the Government. Courts must, in some cases, reconcile competing political interests, but not on the basis of the judges' personal policy preferences. In contrast, an agency to which Congress has delegated policy-making responsibilities may, within the limits of that delegation, properly rely upon the incumbent administration's views of wise policy to inform its judgments. While agencies are not directly accountable to the people, the Chief Executive is, and it is entirely appropriate for this political branch of the Government to make such policy choices—resolving the competing interests which Congress itself either inadvertently did not resolve, or intentionally left to be resolved by the agency charged with the administration of the statute in light of everyday realities.

When a challenge to an agency construction of a statutory provision, fairly conceptualized, really centers on the wisdom of the agency's policy, rather than whether it is a reasonable choice within a gap left open by Congress, the challenge must fail. In such a case, federal judges—who have no constituency—have a duty to respect legitimate policy choices made by those who do. The responsibilities for assessing the wisdom of such policy choices and resolving the struggle between competing views of the public interest are not judicial ones: "Our Constitution vests such responsibilities in the political branches."

We hold that the EPA's definition of the term "source" is a permissible construction of the statute which seeks to accommodate progress in reducing air pollution with economic growth. "The Regulations which the Administrator has adopted provide what the agency could allowably view as . . . [an] effective reconciliation of these twofold ends. . . ."

The judgment of the Court of Appeals is reversed.

REHNQUIST, O'CONNOR and MARSHALL, JJ. did not participate.

Notes and Questions

1. *Reasonableness or substitution of judgment?* The *Connecticut State Medical Society* decision probably represents the dominant view among state courts. A minority of the states follow a strong deference approach like that

in *Chevron,* while others grant little or no deference to agency interpretations.

An example of the latter approach is *State ex rel. Celebrezze v. National Lime & Stone Co.,* 627 N.E.2d 538 (Ohio 1994). That case involved a regulation of the state's Environmental Protection Agency requiring a permit for the "installation" of new equipment. The agency interpreted the regulation so that "installation" included "replacement" of one machine with a new machine. The court overturned this interpretation, saying:

> Keeping in mind the purposes of the [air pollution statute], we must strive to reach a balance between promoting and enhancing clean air and protecting and encouraging economic growth and opportunities for the people of this state. This requires that business entities not be subjected to an interminable task of dealing with excessive regulation or requirements not explicitly covered by statute or rule. Therefore, any uncertainty with regard to the interpretation of [the air pollution statute] and rules promulgated thereunder should be construed in favor of the person or entity (manufacturer or otherwise) affected by the law.

2. *The weight of an agency's interpretation. Connecticut Medical* is a typical substitution of judgment-weak deference approach to reviewing an agency's legal interpretation. A number of factors are commonly mentioned as bearing on whether weak deference will be accorded and, if so, how much. These factors can best be thought of as principles of statutory construction. A checklist of several such factors follows. Each factor has significant case law support. Yet, because this is *weak* deference, judges do feel fairly free to override any of these principles if other considerations persuade them that the agency's construction is incorrect. Thus, courts give weight to these factors in much the same way as they often give weight to a precedent from a court of another state or from a lower court. *See* Thomas W. Merrill, "Judicial Deference to Executive Precedent," 101 Yale L.J. 969 (1992).

a. *Factors indicating that an agency has a comparative interpretive advantage over a court.*

i. *Comparative competence.* Because of its expertise and experience, an agency might be better suited than a court to interpret text that deals with technically complex matters (such as air pollution, nuclear power, or banking). Similarly, an agency may be immersed in administering a particular statute and thus have an intimate knowledge of the administrative consequences arising from particular interpretations. On the other hand, a court might be better suited for interpretive jobs that require facility in dealing with non-technical issues or with common law or constitutional concepts.

ii. *Interpretation of rules.* Greater deference is owed to an agency's interpretation of its own rules or precedents than to its interpretation of a statute, since an agency is likely to be intimately familiar with the rules or precedents it authored and sensitive to the practical implications of possible interpretations.

b. *Factors indicating that a particular agency interpretation is probably correct.*

i. *Procedure in adopting interpretation.* The procedures employed in adopting the interpretation are important. For example, an interpretation contained in a rule adopted by the agency head after full-fledged notice and comment procedure should be entitled to greater weight than one adopted by a single staff member without any public input or without review by superior levels within the agency. Similarly, an interpretation adopted by an agency head in the course of adversary adjudication (including a declaratory order proceeding as in *Connecticut Medical*) is entitled to greater weight than an interpretation adopted without the use of adversary procedure.

ii. *Thoroughness of consideration.* A carefully considered, persuasively written interpretation is entitled to more weight than one which appears to have been arrived at with relatively little deliberation or without much explanation.

iii. *Contemporaneous construction.* Greater deference is due to an interpretation made contemporaneously with enactment of the statute, particularly if the agency members or staff participated in drafting the legislation.

iv. *Long-standing construction.* An interpretation maintained for a long time (or "time-tested" as in the *Connecticut Medical* case) is entitled to more deference than one recently adopted (and much more than one adopted while the case is pending).

v. *Consistency.* Greater deference is owed to a consistently maintained interpretation, less to one that contradicts an earlier view.

vi. *Reliance.* Greater deference is owed to an interpretation on which the public has relied.

vii. *Reenactment.* Greater deference is owed to an interpretation if it can be shown that the legislature endorsed it. If the legislature reenacts a statute, with knowledge of a prior agency interpretation, this is strong evidence in favor of that interpretation. Usually, however, it cannot be shown that legislators knew about the interpretation so that the mere fact of statutory reenactment is uninformative.

How do these factors point in *Connecticut Medical?* In *Chevron?* Would the *Connecticut Medical* case have been decided differently by a court that followed the "strong deference" approach of *Chevron?*

3. *The Chevron two-step. Chevron* is the leading federal authority for the strong deference approach. It has been cited thousands of times by lower courts. Nevertheless, many questions remain about just what *Chevron* means and how far the Court intended it to go.

The *Chevron* opinion requires a two step process. In step one, the court decides whether the statute being interpreted has a clear meaning ("whether Congress has directly spoken to the precise question at issue"). If the agency's interpretation conflicts with this clear meaning, it is invalid. But if the statute is ambiguous in relevant respects ("Congress has not directly addressed the precise question at issue"), the court proceeds to step two and asks whether the agency interpretation is "permissible" or "reasonable."

The *Chevron* formula rests on the understanding that Congress frequently delegates interpretive power to agencies. The "permissibility" or "reasonableness" inquiry in step two reflects the idea that agency action taken pursuant to a delegation must be reviewed deferentially. The step two inquiry is closely related to, or perhaps identical to, the "arbitrary and capricious" standard that courts apply to agency discretionary decisions. *See* Ronald M. Levin, "The Anatomy of *Chevron:* Step Two Reconsidered," 72 Chi.-Kent L. Rev. 1253, 1266–69 (1997). The arbitrary and capricious standard is explained more fully in §§ 9.4 and 9.5.

What makes the *Chevron* test an especially "strong" deference principle is the Court's willingness to *presume,* at step one, that Congress intended to delegate discretion to the agency to resolve any given issue, unless the statute "clearly" indicates otherwise. Statutory ambiguity may reflect a deliberate delegation, or may have resulted from inadvertence, the Court says, but "[f]or judicial purposes, it matters not which of these things occurred."

In practice, therefore, controversies under *Chevron* usually center around a litigant's effort to persuade a reviewing court that Congress "directly addressed the precise question at issue." The litigant might show, for example, that the statute "clearly" rules out an option that the agency chose, or that the agency failed to consider a factor that Congress "clearly" directed the agency to take into account.

4. *Does Chevron apply to agency interpretations regardless of format?* Note that the EPA's bubble interpretation in *Chevron* was part of a legislative rule. *Chevron* strong deference also applies to legal interpretations contained in the opinions of agency heads in formal adjudication.

But does *Chevron* apply to *every* interpretation, regardless of the *format* in which it appears? For example, should it apply to an interpretation that is announced in an interpretive rule adopted without notice and comment procedure? Present law fails to answer this question definitively. *See* Robert A. Anthony, "Which Agency Interpretations Should Bind Citizens and Courts?," 7 Yale J. on Reg. 1 (1990) (*Chevron* should not apply to interpretive rules). Similarly, it is unclear whether *Chevron* applies to an interpretation rendered in the course of informal adjudication. *See Pension Benefit Guaranty Corp. v. LTV Corp.*, 496 U.S. 633 (1990), which applies *Chevron* in the informal adjudication context but does not discuss the appropriateness of doing so.

In *Martin v. Occupational Safety and Health Review Comm'n*, 499 U.S. 144 (1991), the Court suggested that *Chevron* does not apply to an interpretive rule.

> The Secretary regularly employs less formal means of interpreting regulations.... These include the promulgation of interpretive rules, and the publication of agency enforcement guidelines. Although not entitled to the same deference as norms that derive from the exercise of the Secretary's delegated lawmaking powers, these informal interpretations are still entitled to some weight on judicial review. *See Skidmore v. Swift & Co..*, 323 U.S. 134, 140 (1944) [a leading weak deference case]. A reviewing court may certainly consult them to determine whether the Secretary has consistently applied the interpretation embodied in the

citation, a factor bearing on the reasonableness of the Secretary's position.

5. *Exceptions to Chevron*. Are there agency interpretations even in legislative regulations or formal adjudication to which *Chevron* does not apply? For example:

a. *Constitutional issues*. The Court does not grant *Chevron* deference when an interpretation raises serious constitutional questions. In such cases, the Court decides the issue itself. *Miller v. Johnson*, 515 U.S. 900 (1995). Yet the Court has not been consistent in this view. It applied *Chevron* in order to uphold the validity of a regulation that banned personnel in federally funded family planning centers from discussing abortion with clients, despite the presence of a significant constitutional issue. *Rust v. Sullivan*, 500 U.S. 173 (1991).

b. *Departures from Supreme Court precedent*. Logically, under *Chevron*, an agency should be able to discard one reasonable interpretation of an ambiguous statute and substitute a new one, so long as it explains the change in position. But what if the first interpretation was affirmed by the Supreme Court? See *Lechmere, Inc. v. NLRB*, 502 U.S. 527 (1992) (agency not free to alter statutory interpretation previously affirmed by the Supreme Court—statute is no longer ambiguous). What if the first interpretation was affirmed by a federal court of appeals? Recall the material on "acquiescence" in § 4.4.1.

c. *Private rights of action*. *Chevron* does not apply to an agency's interpretation that limits a private right of action conferred by statute on one private party against another private party. Congress did not delegate to the agency power to affect this judicial remedy. *Adams Fruit Co. v. Barrett*, 494 U.S. 638 (1990). Or is that so clear? *See* Richard J. Pierce, Jr., "Agency Authority to Define the Scope of Private Rights of Action," 48 Admin.L.Rev. 1 (1996) (criticizing *Adams Fruit*).

d. *Limits on jurisdiction*. Suppose the agency's legal interpretation is one that expands its jurisdiction. Must the courts give it strong deference? The argument against giving it deference is that the courts, not the agencies, should decide the limits of an agency's power. See *Mississippi Power & Light Co. v. Mississippi ex rel. Moore*, 487 U.S. 354 (1988) (Brennan, J. dissenting). The argument in favor of giving it deference is that almost any issue of statutory interpretation can be phrased in terms of agency jurisdiction; hence the distinction between jurisdictional and non-jurisdictional issues is unintelligible. See *Mississippi Power & Light* (Scalia, J. concurring in the judgment).

e. *Broad procedural statutes*. Recall *Chemical Waste Management, Inc. v. EPA*, § 3.1.1 N.3. That case applied *Chevron* to uphold EPA's interpretation of the term "public hearing." EPA interpreted the term to mean "public hearing not on the record" so that the APA formal adjudication provisions became inapplicable. Is this an appropriate use of *Chevron*? Or should courts retain power to decide the meaning of procedural language where the effect of the interpretation is to render statutes like the APA inapplicable to agency proceedings?

6. *Commentary on Chevron.* Commentary on *Chevron* has been prolific. Compare these views:

a.   1 Kenneth C. Davis & Richard J. Pierce, Jr., ADMINISTRATIVE LAW TREATISE 112–14 (3d ed.1994):

> The *Chevron* Court's reconceptualization of the process of statutory construction is an enormous improvement over the inconsistent and wooden characterizations of the process that dominated judicial decisionmaking in the pre-*Chevron* era.... Understanding *Chevron* requires acceptance of a reality courts have often denied. Many questions concerning the meaning to be given statutes cannot be characterized as issues of law. If Congress has resolved a policy dispute in the process of enacting a statute, an agency or court can, and must, adopt Congress' resolution.... This is the situation governed by *Chevron* step one....

> Congress cannot, and does not, resolve all policy disputes when it enacts a statute, however. For a variety of reasons ... Congress leaves many policy issues open. When Congress drafts a statute that does not resolve a policy dispute that later arises under the statute, some institution must resolve that dispute. The institution called upon to perform this task is not engaged in statutory interpretation.... It is not resolving an issue of "law." Rather, it is resolving an issue of policy. That is the situation governed by *Chevron* step two.... In other words, policy disputes within the scope of authority Congress has delegated an agency are to be resolved by agencies rather than courts.

> ... The *Chevron* Court's reasoning in support of this institutional allocation of responsibility is based on political accountability, a value central to the concept of democratic government....

b.   Merrill, *supra,* at 993:

> Unfortunately, evidence is mounting that the Court picked the wrong framework [for structuring the choice between independent judgment and deference].... Theory and practice diverge in many ways: the failure to apply *Chevron* in at least half the cases in which, by its own terms, it should govern; the continuing use of traditional factors of deference which *Chevron* appears to render irrelevant; the creation of numerous exceptions to *Chevron* that do not seem to cohere with the decision's rationale.... The Court's persistent refusal to abide by the narrow strictures of *Chevron* suggests that there must be something wrong with either *Chevron's* implicit theory of deference, or its practical implications, or both.

c.   Cass R. Sunstein, "Law and Administration After Chevron," 90 Colum.L.Rev. 2071, 2074–75 (1990):

> The *Chevron* principle means that in the face of ambiguity, agency interpretations will prevail so long as they are "reasonable." This principle is quite jarring to those who recall the suggestion, found in *Marbury v. Madison* and repeated time and again in American public law, that it is for judges, and no one else, to "say what the law is." ... *Chevron* promises to be a pillar in administrative law for many years to come. It has become a kind of *Marbury*, or counter-*Marbury*, for the administrative state.

d. Cynthia R. Farina, "Statutory Interpretation and the Balance of Power in the Administrative State," 89 Colum.L.Rev. 452, 487–88 (1989):

> A crucial aspect of the capacity for external control upon which the permissibility of delegating regulatory power hinged was judicial policing of the terms of the statute.... The constitutional accommodation ultimately reached in the nondelegation cases implied that principal power to say what the statute means must rest *outside* the agency, in the courts. Hence, a key assumption of *Chevron's* "judicial usurpation" argument—that Congress may give agencies primary responsibility not only for making policy within the limits of their organic statutes, but also for defining those limits whenever the text and surrounding legislative materials are ambiguous—is fundamentally incongruous with the constitutional course by which the Court came to reconcile agencies and separation of powers.

7. *Strong deference to interpretations of regulations.* A well-established line of federal strong deference cases (many of which pre-date *Chevron*) involve interpretations by agencies of their *own* legislative regulations.

> Our task is not to decide which among several competing interpretations [of a regulation] best serves the regulatory purpose. Rather, the agency's interpretation must be given "controlling weight unless it is plainly erroneous or inconsistent with the regulation." ... In other words, we must defer to the Secretary's interpretation unless an "alternative reading is compelled by the regulation's plain language or by other indications of the Secretary's intent at the time of the regulation's promulgation." *Thomas Jefferson Univ. v. Shalala*, 512 U.S. 504 (1994).

Do the arguments in favor of *Chevron* strong deference apply to an agency's interpretation of its own regulation? If strong deference is given to an agency's interpretation of its own regulation, does this encourage the agency to adopt vague regulations?

8. *Legislative history and statutory interpretation.* Both commentators and judges have debated the appropriateness of consulting legislative history in construing statutes. Note the dismissive approach taken in *Connecticut Medical* toward the use of material from legislative hearings. Recall that in *Chevron*, the Court made clear that legislative history is relevant in determining at step 1 whether a statute is ambiguous.

Justice Scalia has been the Court's most tenacious opponent of reliance on legislative history. For example:

> The meaning of terms on the statute books ought to be determined, not on the basis of which meaning can be shown to have been understood by a larger handful of the members of Congress; but rather on the basis of which meaning is (1) most in accord with context and ordinary usage, and thus most likely to have been understood by the *whole* Congress which voted on the words of the statute (not to mention the citizens subject to it), and (2) most compatible with the surrounding body of law into which the provision must be integrated—a compatibility which, by a benign fiction, we assume Congress always has in mind. *Green v. Bock Laundry Machine Co.*, 490 U.S. 504, 528 (1989) (concurring opinion).

However, most of the other justices are willing to consult legislative history to ascertain the meaning of a statutory text, including the determination of whether a statute is ambiguous under *Chevron* step 1. Justice Breyer has written:

> Using legislative history to help interpret unclear statutory language seems natural. Legislative history helps a court understand the context and purpose of a statute. Outside the law we often turn to context and purpose to clarify ambiguity. Consider, for example, a sign that says "no animals in the park." The meaning of even so simple a sign depends heavily on context and purpose.... Is this not true of words in statutes as well? Should one not look to the background of a statute, the terms of the debate over its enactment, the factual assumptions the legislators made, the conventions they thought applicable, and their expressed objectives in an effort to understand the statute's relevant context, conventions, and purposes?

Stephen G. Breyer, "On the Uses of Legislative History in Interpreting Statutes," 65 S.Cal.L.Rev. 845, 848 (1992):

9. *Problem.* Six years ago, Madison enacted a statute relating to cleanup of oil spills. Section 201 of the Act requires any person responsible for an oil spill to pay "damages for injury to natural resources" to the Madison Environmental Quality Agency (MEQA). Section 203 provides: "Damages recovered under § 201 can be spent only on restoration of the resource. The measure of damages under § 201 shall not be limited by the amount needed to restore the resource."

MEQA has power to adopt regulations to implement the statute and also has power to adjudicate the amount of any damages to be paid under § 201. The Report of the Senate Environmental Affairs Committee stated: "Section 201 is intended to provide funds to MEQA to restore any resources destroyed by a spill and also to encourage oil companies to take appropriate precautions to prevent spills."

Last year, Petrol Oil Co.'s tanker went aground and sank off a remote part of the Madison coast. The resulting oil spill killed 300 fur seals and destroyed their breeding area. MEQA, which had adopted no regulations under § 201, conducted an adjudicatory proceeding to determine Petrol's liability for damages. The Sierra Club intervened in the proceeding. The Petrol case was the first to apply § 201.

MEQA's decision construed § 201 so that the amount of damages would be the market value of the natural resource destroyed, or the cost of restoring the resource, whichever is less. The seals were worth $15 each (the value of their fur) for a total of $4500. The oil soaked beach area is worth $3000. As a result, MEQA assessed damages of $7500. The cost of restoring the breeding area and bringing back the colony of seals is $30,000,000.

Sierra Club seeks judicial review of this decision. How should the court rule? *See Ohio v. Dep't of the Interior*, 880 F.2d 432 (D.C.Cir.1989).

§ 9.3　SCOPE OF REVIEW OF APPLICATION OF LAW TO FACTS

Once an agency has found the basic facts (§ 9.1) and interpreted the governing law (§ 9.2), it must *apply* that law to the facts. Sometimes the application of law to facts is referred to as a "mixed question of law and fact," an "ultimate fact," or an "inference" from the facts. Should the court use a "reasonableness" or a "substitution of judgment" standard in reviewing the agency's application of law to facts?

McPHERSON v. EMPLOYMENT DIVISION

591 P.2d 1381 (Or.1979).

LINDE, J.

Petitioner, Marlynn McPherson, seeks review of a decision of the Employment Division denying her unemployment compensation on the ground that she left her employment voluntarily and without good cause.... A referee denied her claim upon findings of fact and conclusions of law that will be discussed below. The Employment Appeals Board affirmed the referee's decision.

The issue is whether the Division misconstrued the unemployment compensation law in concluding that McPherson did not have "good cause" to leave her employment. That question in turn involves a question of the scope of judicial review of the Division's determinations of "good cause." This court has not previously had occasion to address these questions. For the reasons that follow, we reverse and remand petitioner's claim to the Division.

The statute and the facts. Since its initial enactment in 1935, the unemployment law has been a program designed to provide a source of substitute income from a public fund for any eligible unemployed person unless the person is disqualified for one of the reasons provided in the statute.... ORS 657.176 provides: ...

> (c) [If] the individual voluntarily left work without good cause the individual shall be disqualified from the receipt of benefits....

Throughout her employment [with the City of Salem] two male coworkers with whom [McPherson] was required to work complained to her and to others that they did not approve of a female worker in the maintenance position, and that she lacked the strength to do the job. They did not give McPherson information or other assistance that she needed to develop her job skills. She filed a union grievance over additional difficulties with one of the men after she declined to date him, which was later settled by an apology. McPherson repeatedly brought the matter to the attention of her supervisor and the employer's affirmative action officer. The supervisor told her to ignore the men's remarks; he also said that he was satisfied with her work and progress and recommended her periodically for pay raises. However, claimant decided that she would not be able to obtain technical work experience on the job beyond attending courses or seminars and reading manuals. She gave notice in February, 1977, and quit the following month.

In summary, it is undisputed that claimant left work voluntarily and that she did so because of the "sexist" behavior of male employees with whom she was assigned to work and who objected to her doing "men's work." The issue before us is not whether we would reach the same decision on the facts that the Employment Division did. The purpose of our review is to determine whether the Division reached its conclusion denying claimant unemployment benefits under a misapprehension of the scope of "good cause." Before examining that question, we must clarify the appropriate scope of review.

Scope of review. At the outset, it should be recalled that the scope of judicial review of an administrative decision does not follow simply from the nature of the decision and of the disputed issue. The rules governing judicial review can be and generally are provided by law. In [this case the APA provides]: ...

The court shall reverse or remand the order only if it finds:

(a) The order to be unlawful in substance or procedure ... [or]

(d) The order is not supported by substantial evidence in the whole record.

The statute thus requires a party challenging an agency determination to specify, and the court to decide, whether the asserted agency error is one of fact, lacking support in the evidence, or a misapplication of the relevant substantive or procedural law. Of course the challenge may involve several grounds, but it remains necessary to identify which is which....

The identification of errors of fact and errors of law for scope of review [purposes], when an agency applies a broad statutory term to a particular situation, is one of the most problematic issues in administrative law. Agency decisions interpreting a legal term in applying it to particular facts are sometimes said to pose a "mixed question of law and fact."

The Court of Appeals has so characterized determinations of "good cause" under the unemployment compensation law. When such a determination is reviewed, [the APA] calls for separating the elements of the mixture that are "facts" from those that interpret the law....

"Facts," it has been said, are those elements entering into the decision that describe phenomena and events without reference to their significance under the law in question, or to put it another way, as they might be described by a lay person unaware of the disputed legal issue. In that sense, the claimant's reasons for quitting her employment and the events that led up to them are questions of fact. The meaning of the words "good cause" ... on the other hand, is plainly a question of law. But that is not the end of the inquiry into the scope of judicial review, for this question of law in turn leads to the question how far section

657.176 entrusts to the agency the determination of what kind of reasons are "good cause" to leave employment and what kind of reasons are not.

In prior cases under the unemployment compensation law, this court has faced the problem of reviewing agency determinations whether various relationships between providers of services and those who pay for them constituted "employment" within the coverage of the act. *Baker v. Cameron*, 401 P.2d 691 (1965), concluded that "if the facts are not disputed, the question of whether one is an 'employee' or the contractor of another is a question of law," although the views of the agency on the issue "should be given some consideration." This stops well short of the position taken in *NLRB v. Hearst Publications*, 322 U.S. 111 (1944), that a specialized agency's view of an employment relationship within the meaning of its governing statute should be accepted if it has "a reasonable basis in law." Judicial respect for an agency's interpretation of a legal term, though it is a question of law, is often explained on a theory of agency "expertise." That may apply where statutory terms are drawn from a technical vocabulary which takes its meaning from a particular science, industry, trade, or occupation in which the agency has genuine expertise, but an agency's administration of a specialized program does not mean that its political head or changing personnel either need or acquire expertise in that sense. As this court said about applying the *Hearst Publications* formula to the Public Utility Commissioner's interpretation of a term in a highway use tax law, the agency's special experience calls for deference to "the degree to which the problem involves knowledge peculiar to the industry, business, etc.," knowledge which was not shown to be involved in interpreting the term at issue.

Distinct from such agency "expertise" in giving meaning to a technical or specialized terminology is the question how far the statutory term entrusts to the agency some range of choice in carrying out the legislative policy. We do not regard the Employment Division as the kind of "expert agency" that has special knowledge of the meaning of such statutory terms as "employment," "direction or control," "independently established business," and the like. In those phrases, the legislature refers to relationships that meet certain definable legal tests, though applying the tests to the facts of any given arrangement may sometimes be a close question.

But the phrase "good cause" is not that kind of a statutory term. Like standards such as "fair" or "unfair," "undue" or "unreasonable," or "public convenience and necessity," "good cause" in its own terms calls for completing a value judgment that the legislature itself has only indicated: evaluating what are "good" reasons for giving up one's employment and what are not. Judicial review of such evaluations, though a "question of law," requires a court to determine how much the legislature has itself decided and how much it has left to be resolved by the agency. For an agency decision is not "unlawful in substance," if the agency's elaboration of a standard like "good cause" is within the range of its responsibility for effectuating a broadly stated statutory policy.

Review under ORS 657.176. The history of Oregon's unemployment compensation law shows that some range of agency responsibility for defining "good cause" was intended.... [T]he responsibility to which we refer has been placed in the administrator, now the Assistant Director of Employment.... He is directed to "determine all questions of general policy and promulgate rules and regulations and be responsible for the administration of this chapter." If, for instance, the Division were to issue interpretative rules describing one or more characteristics of "good cause" independently of the decision of a concrete case, the assistant director is the "agency" authorized to do so....

In prior cases, the Court of Appeals appears to have decided the question of "good cause" without always distinguishing whether the result followed because the statute itself imposed a test or rule to be applied to the facts found by the agency or only permitted the Division to adopt that test or rule. *Fajardo v. Morgan,* 516 P.2d 495 (1973), clearly intended a binding statutory interpretation both in holding that wage discrimination based on sex is "good cause" to quit because it is an unlawful employment practice, and also in adopting the "objective" test that "good cause" must be one that would "reasonably motivate in a similar situation the average able-bodied and qualified worker to give up his or her employment.... "

The decision closest to the present case, *McCain v. Employment Division,* 522 P.2d 1208 (1974), is perhaps somewhat ambiguous.... The Court stated that it "agreed" with the referee and the Board that this display [of provocative pictures and sexist cartoons] was not good cause for claimant to quit. That alone does not show ... whether the court regarded the matter to be within the range of judgment entrusted to the agency. However, the *McCain* opinion continued by stating that "good cause" would exist "only if this 'sexist' attitude produced some actual discrimination" or "undue harassment," and that "offensive character habits of fellow workers, however, distasteful" will not constitute good cause. This could certainly convey to the agency that its decision was not only permitted by the statute but compelled by it. If *McCain* conveyed that impression, it certainly would affect the agency's view of the law governing the present case, in which "good cause" is also claimed to have resulted from "sexist attitudes."

Application to the present case. We therefore turn to the agency's decision to examine on what view of the governing law it was based.... Since the referee thus based his decision entirely on the quoted opinion in *McCain,* he apparently assumed that his conclusions were not merely permitted but compelled as a matter of law. As stated above, this assumption takes an improperly narrow view of the Division's own responsibility to define "good cause" within the overall policy and provisions of the Unemployment Compensation Law. But there is little in the record or briefs to show what criteria of "good cause" the Division might develop in the absence of that misconception. . . .

The law does not extend its benefits to a worker who has a job and voluntarily gives it up without "good cause." But it also does not impose upon the employee the one-dimensional motivation of Adam Smith's "economic man." The workplace is the setting of much of the worker's daily life. The statute does not demand as a matter of law that he or she sacrifice all other than economic objectives and, for instance, endure racial, ethnic, or sexual slurs or personal abuse, for fear that abandoning an oppressive situation will disqualify the worker from unemployment benefits. . . .

How far "good cause" encompasses such non-economic values also is left to the agency in the first instance.

Conclusion. As stated above, there are implications in the referee's "Conclusions and Reasons," adopted by the Employment Appeals Board, that the agency assumed its decision to be compelled as a matter of law by the statute. . . . We cannot discern what criteria of "good cause" the agency might have applied on its own in the absence of that assumption. This does not mean that on the present record the Court of Appeals or this court might not have reached the same result. That, however, is not our assignment but the Division's, subject only to review whether its assessment of the kind of reasons that are "good cause" to leave employment is "unlawful in substance." For these reasons, the case must be remanded to the Division for reconsideration by the assistant director's authorized representative in the light of this opinion.

Reversed and remanded.

TONGUE, J., dissenting [dissent omitted].

Notes and Questions

1. *Fact or law?* Should a court review an agency's application of law to facts (such as whether Ms. McPherson had "good cause" to quit) as a question of *fact* or a question of *discretion* or a question of *law?* In considering whether the "voluntariness" of a confession was a question of fact or law, the Supreme Court said:

> [T]he appropriate methodology for distinguishing questions of fact from questions of law has been, to say the least, elusive. . . . [T]he Court has yet to arrive at "a rule or principle that will unerringly distinguish a factual finding from a legal conclusion." Perhaps much of the difficulty in this area stems from the practical truth that the decision to label an issue a "question of law," a "question of fact," or a "mixed question of law and fact" is sometimes as much a matter of allocation as it is of analysis. At least in those instances in which Congress has not spoken and in which the issue falls somewhere between a pristine legal standard and a simple historical fact, the fact/law distinction at times has turned on a determination that, as a matter of the sound administration of justice, one judicial actor is better positioned than another to decide the issue in question. *Miller v. Fenton*, 474 U.S. 104, 113–14 (1985).

Courts often treat issues of application of law to fact as questions of law or of fact depending on how they want to review the issue. If a court decides to substitute judgment, it identifies the issue as one of law, while if it decides that the agency's application is acceptable, it identifies the issue as one of fact or discretion. Of course, application issues involve law, fact, and discretion—which is the reason they are often referred to as "mixed questions of law and fact."

2. *Delegation of power to apply law to fact.* If a court followed *Chevron* (§ 9.2) with respect to interpretation questions, it would presumably apply a reasonableness standard to application questions, on the theory that the legislature meant to delegate to the agency the power both to interpret and apply the law. On the other hand, if a court followed California's independent judgment rule (§ 9.1.2), the court would presumably exercise substitution of judgment on application questions.

If, as in Oregon, a court follows the substantial evidence test as to questions of fact, but the substitution of judgment-weak deference test as to questions of law, the court must decide whether any given application question falls on the law side or the fact side of the line. *McPherson* penetrates more deeply than most decisions in approaching that question: To the extent that the legislature meant to *delegate* the power to apply the law to the facts, the court must uphold a reasonable application. But delegations of authority are usually not blank checks. They normally have boundaries, and if the challenger demonstrates that the agency's view is outside the range of possibilities that the statute leaves open, the court can find an error of law and reverse. For example, the court cites the *Fajardo* case for the propositions that wage discrimination is "good cause" and that the test of "good cause" is an objective one. The opinion makes clear that the Employment Division would not be free to decide otherwise. Thus, when a challenger argues that the agency overstepped the delegation in this fashion, the court should review that aspect of the agency's decision as a question of law, using the appropriate methodology (such as "weak deference").

McPherson indicates that agencies *sometimes* have delegated power to *apply* vague statutory phrases (like "good cause") to the facts. On the other hand, *McPherson* says that other application issues (such as whether a person is an "employee") present questions of law. *McPherson* contrasts an Oregon case, *Baker v. Cameron*, 401 P.2d 691 (1965), with *NLRB v. Hearst Publications, Inc.*, 322 U.S. 111 (1944).

Baker concerned the issue of whether aluminum siding salesmen were "employees" or "independent contractors" for purposes of the unemployment compensation law. The Oregon statute defined a person as an "employee" by using the common law tort test for drawing this distinction. The Court treated the issue as one of law and substituted its judgment, although it gave "some consideration" to the agency's decision because of its "expertise."

Hearst is the leading federal case calling for reasonableness review of application questions. In *Hearst,* the issue was whether newsboys were "employees," as the NLRB held they were, so that they were entitled to be represented by a union. The Supreme Court first decided (using "substitution of judgment") that the NLRB correctly held that the common law tort definition of "employee" should not be used because it would defeat the purposes of the Act. Instead, the proper legal test was whether all the conditions of the relationship (such as inequality of bargaining power) required the protection of a union.

However, when it came to applying this test to the actual facts of the case, the Court switched to "reasonableness" review and upheld the Board's determination. Explicitly using delegation analysis, the Court explained:

> That task has been assigned primarily to the agency created by Congress to administer the Act. Determination of "where all the conditions of the relation require protection" involves inquiries for the Board charged with this duty. Everyday experience in the administration of the statute gives it familiarity with the circumstances and backgrounds of employment relationships in various industries, with the abilities and needs of the workers for self-organization and collective action, and with the adaptability of collective bargaining for the peaceful settlement of their disputes with their employers. The experience thus acquired must be brought frequently to bear on the question who is an employee under the Act. Resolving that question, like determining whether unfair labor practices have been committed, "belongs to the usual administrative routine" of the Board.
>
>   ... Undoubtedly questions of statutory interpretation, especially when arising in the first instance in judicial proceedings, are for the courts to resolve, giving appropriate weight to the judgment of those whose special duty is to administer the questioned statute. But where the question is one of specific application of a broad statutory term in a proceeding in which the agency administering the statute must determine it initially, the reviewing court's function is limited.... [T]he Board's determination that specified persons are "employees" under this Act is to be accepted if it has "warrant in the record" and a reasonable basis in law. 322 U.S. at 130–31.

3. *MSAPA view*. The 1981 MSAPA seems to be ambivalent on the issue of the appropriate scope of review of application questions. The statute provides that the court should grant relief if "the agency has erroneously interpreted or applied the law." 5–116(c)(4). However, the comment to that provision states:

> Paragraph (c)(4) includes two distinct matters—interpretation and application of the law. With regard to the agency's *interpretation* of the law, courts generally give little deference to the agency.... By contrast, with regard to the agency's *application* of the law to specific situations, the enabling statute normally confers some discretion upon the agency. Accordingly, a court should find reversible error in the agency's application of the law only if the agency has improperly exercised its discretion, within the framework of paragraph (c)(8) [which allows reversal "if the agency action is outside the range of discretion delegated to the agency" or is "unreasonable, arbitrary or capricious"].

4. *Undisputed facts*. In *McPherson*, the court quoted *Baker v. Cameron's* conclusion that "if the facts are not disputed, the question of whether one is an 'employee' or the contractor of another is an issue of law." But what if the facts *are* disputed?

It seems strange to treat the same application question as an issue of fact if the facts are disputed or as an issue of law if the facts are not disputed. Suppose the case has two highly disputed issues: i) does A's boss supervise the details of A's work? ii) is A an employee or an independent contractor? Under the *Baker* approach (which is followed in many states but has been rejected by the U. S. Supreme Court), issue ii) will be treated as a question of fact because issue i) is disputed. But if issue i) is not disputed, issue ii) will be treated as a question of law. Does this make sense? Does it encourage parties to stipulate or not stipulate factual issues so as to manipulate the scope of review of application issues?

5. *Interpretation by the agency.* The *McPherson* opinion calls on the agency to adopt rules clarifying the meaning of "good cause" in the context of sexual harassment. Suppose the agency adopts a rule identical to *McCain*: sexual harassment will not be treated as good cause to quit unless it produces actual discrimination. A hostile work environment will not be considered as good cause. Would the Oregon Supreme Court uphold this rule?

6. *Problem.* Dr. Sherman specialized in the treatment of obesity. He believed that the best treatment for obesity was the use of a combination of amphetamine and barbiturate drugs in conjunction with diet. He routinely prescribed the same drugs for every patient. Patients were told to call if they had any adverse reaction to the drugs and to return in two weeks.

Dr. Sherman testified that he had studied the problem of obesity extensively, had served 48,000 patients, and had never been sued for malpractice. He testified that none of the drugs he prescribed could adversely affect any medical condition.

Several other doctors testified that the method of treatment used by Dr. Sherman was a fraud, that it could not help patients, was likely to produce addiction, and could adversely affect other medical conditions.

The State Medical Board revoked Dr. Sherman's license to practice medicine on the ground that this method of treatment was a "fraud and deceit in the practice of medicine" (one of the statutory grounds for discipline of physicians). What is the scope of judicial review of the Board's finding that Dr. Sherman's method of treatment was a "fraud and deceit in the practice of medicine"? *See Sherman v. Board of Regents,* 266 N.Y.S.2d 39 (N.Y.A.D.1966), *aff'd,* 225 N.E.2d 559 (N.Y.1967).

§ 9.4 JUDICIAL REVIEW OF DISCRETIONARY DETERMINATIONS IN ADJUDICATION

A great variety of administrative action is judicially reviewed under § 706(2)(A) of the APA and corresponding provisions in state law: "arbitrary, capricious, an abuse of discretion, or otherwise not in accordance with law." This review standard is referred to as the "arbitrary and capricious" test.

Courts use the arbitrary and capricious test in reviewing the discretionary element of all kinds of agency actions, including administrative rules (as in *Motor Vehicle,* reprinted in § 9.5), informal adjudications (as in *Overton Park*, discussed in N.2 of this section), and formal adjudications (as in *Salameda*, which follows). As noted at the beginning of § 9.1, the arbitrary-capricious standard is often applied to review of factfinding in informal adjudication. Finally, that standard seems equivalent to the "reasonableness" standard applied to agency legal interpretations under *Chevron* step 2.

SALAMEDA v. IMMIGRATION AND NATURALIZATION SERVICE
70 F.3d 447 (7th Cir.1995).

POSNER, C.J.:

Daniel Salameda and his wife Angelita came to the United States from the Philippines in 1982. Salameda had a student visa; his wife was admitted as the spouse of, and their two-year-old child, Lancelot, as the child of, a nonimmigrant student. The visa was for one year, and two days after it expired Salameda went to an office of the Immigration and Naturalization Service in an effort to renew it. ... The only result of Salameda's effort to renew his visa was to precipitate deportation proceedings against him and his wife. The proceedings dragged on in the usual manner until 1991, when the Salamedas appeared at a hearing before an immigration judge at which they conceded deportability but requested suspension of deportation under § 244(a)(1) of the Immigration and Nationality Act, 8 U.S.C. § 1254(a)(1). The immigration judge turned down their request and the Board of Immigration Appeals affirmed.

To invoke the discretion of the Attorney General (delegated to the Board of Immigration Appeals) to suspend deportation under section 244(a)(1), the alien must prove that ... his deportation would "result in extreme hardship to the alien or to his spouse, parent, or child, who is a citizen of the United States or an alien lawfully admitted for permanent residence." It is up to the Board to decide what shall count as "extreme hardship." Judicial review is limited to making sure that the Board has considered in a rational fashion the issues tendered by the alien's application.

The proceedings of the Immigration and Naturalization Service are notorious for delay, and the opinions rendered by its judicial officers, including the members of the Board of Immigration Appeals, often flunk minimum standards of adjudicative rationality. The lodgment of this troubled Service in the Department of *Justice* of a nation that was built by immigrants and continues to be enriched by a flow of immigration is an irony that should not escape notice. We imagine that Congress is more to blame than the Department or even the INS itself. The agency is absurdly understaffed. In 1994, when it decided the Salamedas' appeal from the decision by the immigration judge to deport them, the Board of Immigration Appeals had an effective membership of only four—to handle the more than 14,000 appeals lodged with the Board that year.

There is no doubt that the Salamedas will experience hardship as a result of being deported to the Philippines with uncertain prospects of ever being readmitted to the United States. Besides Lancelot, now 15 years old, who has lived in the United States since he was 2, the Salamedas have a child born in the United States (hence a U.S. citizen) who is now almost 7. It is hardly to be supposed that the Salamedas would leave their children in the United States. Of course, as the INS's counsel reminded us at argument, it is the Salamedas' "fault" that their children face the prospect of deportation to an alien land. [Yet] these aliens cannot be expected to live in a state of suspended animation until their status is resolved; here that would have required the Salamedas to postpone conceiving a second child for thirteen years. The Board traditionally considers long residence in the United States a source of extreme hardship to the deportee.

The remaining element of hardship in this case concerns the extensive round of community and charitable activities in which both adult Salamedas engage in their home town of Rockford, Illinois. One might wonder how the termination of these activities could constitute a hardship to the aliens, as distinct from a hardship to their communities. The answer is that these activities are evidence of a high degree of integration of the aliens into the community, increasing the wrench to them of being expelled from it. A number of decisions by federal courts of appeals hold (none to the contrary) that the Board, in considering whether "extreme hardship" has been shown, *must* consider the alien's "community assistance." As an original matter, bearing in mind the lack of any statutory definition of extreme hardship and the deference ... that judges owe to administrative interpretations of open-ended regulatory statutes, we might be inclined to doubt the soundness of these decisions. ... But because the government acknowledges in its brief the Board's obligation to consider community assistance in deciding whether extreme hardship has been shown, this is hardly the right case in which to create an intercircuit conflict on the issue.

The Board itself may have decided, in the exercise of its discretion to interpret the vague statutory term "extreme hardship," that community assistance should be considered. This would bolster the judicial interpretations that we have been discussing, but it would also have independent significance for our review of the order of deportation. An agency may not abandon an interpretation without an explanation, not here attempted. Agencies do not have the same freedom as courts to change direction without acknowledging and justifying the change. [I]t may be significant that in this case the immigration judge considered the factor and the Board said that he had considered all the factors that are legally relevant to a judgment of extreme hardship. The Board did not say or hint that the administrative law judge had wasted his time in considering the Salamedas' contribution to their community. [I]n light of the holdings of the other circuits and the Board's apparent acquiescence in the immigration judge's adoption of that position and the government's acknowledgment that it is the Board's position, we think it is the law of this case that community assistance must be considered. The government's lawyer may be wrong but we think she probably knows the Board's collective mind better than we do.

Whether the impact on the children of expulsion to the Philippines plus the termination of the Salamedas' volunteer activities sums to extreme hardship may be doubted, depending on the force of "extreme" or, what is the same issue really, the typicality of the Salamedas' plight. But that is not the issue for us. . . .

The issue that we decide today is not one of statutory interpretation. It is whether the INS's judicial officers addressed in a rational manner the questions that the aliens tendered for consideration. They did not. The two opinions, that of the immigration judge and that of the Board of Immigration Appeals, are incomprehensible at the critical junctures—the issue of hardship to the children and the issue of community service. With regard to the first, the immigration judge stated flatly that the statute precluded his considering the hardship to Lancelot. . . . For this reason the Salamedas' lawyer asked that Lancelot be named a party to the deportation proceeding, but the INS refused. . . . [T]he only motivation we can think of for the INS's refusing to include such an alien, at the parents' request, in the pending proceeding is—since Lancelot has no greater right than his parents to remain in the United States—to prevent the hardship to him from being considered. This strikes us as an ignoble ploy. Since Lancelot will have to follow his parents into exile, having no legal right to remain in the United States, he is constructively deported and should therefore, one might suppose, be entitled to ask—or more realistically his parents' lawyer should be entitled to ask on his behalf—for suspension. . . . For all that appears, Lancelot has no competence in any language other than English. The extent to which this or other aspects of his upbringing would impair his chances of adjusting to Philippine society is an element of potential hardship that the Immigration and Naturalization Service is not free to disregard without any explanation.

It would be curious if the fact that a family member was not the formal target of the deportation order had the effect of depriving that person of the right to request suspension of deportation. Maybe that is how the statute ought to be read, but we think the Board has an obligation to consider this novel interpretive question, rather than ignore it, as the Board did.

We do not of course suggest that Lancelot has the right of a citizen or that the Board can be ordered to institute deportation proceedings against Lancelot. . . . All we are suggesting is that he may be entitled to have the hardship to him considered as if he had been a formal party to the proceeding.

As for community service, the Board seems to have considered this irrelevant as a matter of law. [T]he Board has without explanation changed the standard that its lawyer acknowledges as the position of the

Board—that the Board *itself* seems to have acknowledged when it said the immigration judge had touched all the bases.

We may seem awfully picky in remanding a case in which the showing of extreme hardship is as marginal as it is here, and awfully unforgiving of the resource constraints that prevent the judicial officers of the immigration service from doing a competent job. But the government has not argued harmless error, and understaffing is not a defense to a violation of principles of administrative law admitted to bind the Immigration and Naturalization Service. (It would be pretty weird if an agency could get a reduced standard of judicial review of its decisions simply by asking Congress for a reduced appropriation!) The richest nation in the world, which happens to be a nation of immigrants, can afford to staff its immigration service. . . .

EASTERBROOK, Circuit Judge, dissenting.

Congress has starved the immigration bureaucracy of funds, so the process of deportation takes unconscionably long. During the delay, in this case 13 years and counting, aliens must try to live normal lives, and the passing milestones (marriage, children, employment, religious and civic activities) create new arguments for remaining here. The longer the delay, the more people join the queue, because delay itself gives them what they principally desire—the opportunity to remain in the United States. A short-handed INS is hard pressed to keep up with the flow of new cases, let alone address the evolving circumstances in ongoing ones. It is inevitable that in the process some arguments will be dealt with in passing, or not at all, and that judges disposed to question any of the Board's decisions won't want for opportunity. But should we seek to use that opportunity?

Any adjudicatory system—even one flush with resources—must decide which cases require the greatest investment. Some cases are close, some lopsided. Courts know this and respond accordingly. We dispense with oral argument in simple cases and issue curt orders; even our published opinions make short work of (or ignore) arguments we deem legally unfounded or factually unsupported. Any approach that lavished on simple cases the resources required to decide hard ones would do a disservice to the litigants in the hard cases, who would receive less attention, without providing benefits (which is to say, more accurate decisions) for the litigants in the easy cases. See Jerry L. Mashaw, *Bureaucratic Justice* 187–90 (1983).

This is an easy case. Have the Salamedas demonstrated (it is their burden) not only that deportation would "result in extreme hardship to the alien or to his spouse, parent, or child, who is a citizen of the United States or an alien lawfully admitted for permanent residence" but also that a favorable exercise of discretion is warranted? See 8 U.S.C. § 1254(a)(1). The BIA decided adversely to them on the first question and did not reach the second. What else could the Board have done?

The Salamedas do not think that they and their children will flourish in the Philippines as they do in the United States. This is "hardship." But what is "extreme" about it? Differences in economic circumstances, and the wrenching experience of moving to a different nation, are staples of immigration cases; they explain why the alien wants to stay in the United States. The Philippines are more advanced than many a country to which we deport people; 90 percent of the population is literate. Insurrection has abated; people are not dragooned into the military; there is no serious religious oppression; the political system is reasonably open. The Salamedas, who have advanced degrees, are more able to make a transition than most. They have children accustomed to the United States, but that is normal rather than extreme. Normal and extreme are legal antipodes. Unless the word "extreme" has lost all meaning, this is a routine case.

The BIA is entitled to be hard-nosed, to take "extreme" literally. *INS v. Jong Ha Wang*, 450 U.S. 139, 145 (1981) (observing that "a narrow interpretation is consistent with the 'extreme hardship' language, which itself indicates the exceptional nature of the suspension remedy"). ... "Extreme hardship" presents an exceptionally high hurdle for the Salamedas, one they did not surmount. The Board wrote that their "hardship did not exceed that imposed on most aliens who had resided in the United States for some time." That finding is unimpeachable.

I asked: "What else could the Board have done?" The majority thinks that it could and should have discussed two legal issues: first, whether parents are entitled to have the hardship to a non-citizen child considered; second, whether an interruption by deportation of service the aliens are providing *to their community* counts as "extreme hardship" *to the aliens*. Administrative agencies must deal with the arguments presented to them—must deal with these arguments rationally, and in line with their precedents, even though not in depth. But they need deal only with arguments presented. The Salamedas did not make these arguments until arriving in this court.

Counsel did not propound either of the arguments that my colleagues chastise the Board for ignoring. The brief [to the Board] does not mention Lancelot, does not contend that he should have been made a respondent or that hardship to him is relevant, and does not argue that the discontinuation of service to the community would be extreme hardship to the Salamedas. The Salamedas did not make these arguments to the immigration judge either. Although it deemed the Salamedas' brief so skimpy as to render the appeal "amenable to summary dismissal", the Board did not give them the immediate heave-ho but mulled over the questions fairly presented by the record without the aid of counsel. The thanks it gets from the majority—exemplifying the maxim that no good deed goes unpunished—will dissuade the Board from showing similar kindness in the future.

According to the majority, "the issue that we decide today is ... whether the INS's judicial officers addressed in a rational manner the questions that the aliens tendered for consideration. They did not."

Given the nature of the Salamedas' administrative brief, my colleagues' characterization of "the issue" is untenable.

At all events, would consideration of these questions have made a difference? [L]et us suppose the immigration judge had permitted Lancelot to join the proceedings, where he could have argued that deportation would expose him to "extreme hardship." What hardship would that be? Lancelot may today be an average Midwestern teenager, with American attitudes, and may not be fluent in either of the major languages in the Philippines ([F]ilipino and English). He will lose touch with his friends, and his economic opportunities may be straitened. Still, the BIA understands "extreme hardship" to mean something, well, extreme:

> it is only when other factors such as advanced age, severe illness, family ties, etc. combine with economic detriment to make deportation extremely hard on the alien or the citizen or permanent resident members of his family that Congress has authorized suspension of the deportation order.

In re Anderson, 16 I. & N. Dec. 596, 598 (1978). . . . Lancelot's claim is as ordinary as his parents', and making him a party could do nothing but produce a formal order of deportation against him, which would impede his return to this country later in life. 8 U.S.C. §§ 1182(a)(6), 1326. My colleagues think that the immigration judge acted ignobly in keeping Lancelot out of the case; I think that the judge did Lancelot a favor. Protecting minors from bad lawyers is an important task for a Department of *Justice*.

Anderson plays a role in the Salamedas' second legal argument, too. They cite it for the proposition that an interruption in an alien's service to the community can be "extreme hardship" to the alien. The BIA said about the Salamedas:

> As a final note, the [Salamedas'] community service is a very positive factor with respect to the exercise of discretion but, having failed to establish statutory eligibility under section 244 of the Act, we do not reach that question.

This implies, though it does not quite say, that community service is not a way to establish "extreme hardship" *to the alien*. According to the Salamedas, this approach conflicts with *Anderson*; and, because agencies may not change stands without explanation, the Salamedas believe that the Board's decision in their case is defective. The minor premise in this syllogism is correct—agencies must stick with established norms unless they justify the adoption of new ones—but the major premise is wrong. *Anderson* did not establish a norm about community service.

An alien sought relief from deportation on the ground that his economic position would deteriorate. In an effort to persuade the Board that financial hardship could satisfy the statutory criterion, Anderson relied on a passage from a committee report in the House of Representatives. This passage mentions community service; the Board quoted from the passage; ever since, litigants have been arguing that the language of the House Report represents the Board's own position. But Anderson did not make a community-service claim, so the Board did not discuss the subject. What is more, the [House] proposal to change the law failed, and with that failure the significance of the Committee Report evaporated. This report does not elucidate the statute on the books, and [in *Anderson*] the Board gave it the significance that failure earned it.

No administrative opinion has held that an end of service to the community can produce extreme hardship to the alien. The BIA did not have to explain a change of position, for it has not changed positions. I therefore do not understand what the majority can mean in saying that "it is the law of this case that community assistance must be considered." The Board said (well, strongly implied) the opposite. The immigration judge mentioned the Salamedas' community service, and the BIA said that he had considered all relevant facts, but this is distinct from saying that all facts the immigration judge mentioned are relevant. ... Similarly, I do not follow my colleagues' assertion that "by deeming community service irrelevant to deciding whether the alien has shown extreme hardship, the Board has without explanation changed the standard that its lawyer acknowledges as the position of the Board". ... Counsel must conform to the agency's view, not the other way 'round. *Motor Vehicle Manufacturers Ass'n v. State Farm Mutual Automobile Insurance Co.* [§ 9.5]; ... *SEC v. Chenery Corp.*, 332 U.S. 194, 196 (1947). In the event of disparity it is the lawyer's views that must be discarded. No other case treats a disagreement between agency and counsel as a flaw in the agency's decision. [Judge Easterbrook also strongly disputed the majority's claim that other circuits had held that the Board must consider community assistance in deciding whether an alien would suffer "extreme hardship" from deportation.]

... Deciding 14,000 cases a year, the Board is bound to commit some howlers. Our own output of 1,800 or so decisions per year likewise contains a healthy portion of incorrect legal assertions, suppressed but questionable assumptions, and incomplete analyses. The inevitability of error in a large population of decisions does not justify reversing *this* one, however—not unless the Board must lavish scarce time and energy on non-issues in simple cases.

Notes and Questions

1. *Salameda—the sequel.* In 1996, as part of the Illegal Immigration Reform and Immigrant Responsibility Act, P.L. 104–208, Congress toughened the standard for suspension of deportation. The standard became "exceptional and extremely unusual hardship" and an alien must have resided in the U. S. for ten years before applying for relief. Most significantly, Congress prohibited judicial review of such determinations by the INS. *See* William C. B. Underwood, Note, "Unreviewable Discretionary Justice: The New Extreme Hardship in Cancellation of Deportation Cases," 72 Ind.L.J. 885 (1997).

2. *Overton Park.* A leading federal case on the scope of review of discretionary agency action is *Citizens to Preserve Overton Park, Inc. v. Volpe,* 401 U.S. 402 (1971). *Overton Park* involved review of a decision by the Secretary of Transportation to grant funds to build an interstate highway through a park. A statute prohibited the use of parks for highways unless "there is no feasible and prudent alternative" route. The Secretary did not explain why there was no feasible and prudent alternative route.

The Court interpreted the statute to mean that the Secretary could not approve a parkland route unless each alternative route was unsound from an engineering point of view (i.e., not "feasible") or would present "unique problems" (i.e., not "prudent"). The Court then proceeded to discuss how the district court should review the Secretary's application of this test (assuming that he had indeed applied it, a question that was left to be explored on remand, *see* § 3.3.1 N.6).

The Court noted that the "substantial evidence" standard was not applicable. It applies only to formal rulemaking or formal adjudication, and the decision in *Overton Park* was neither. Although a hearing was required, it was merely a public hearing for the purpose of informing the community about the project and eliciting its views. Such a hearing "is not designed to produce a record that is to be the basis of agency action—the basic requirement for substantial evidence review." Therefore, the district court would have to apply the arbitrary and capricious test instead. The Court elaborated:

> ... [T]he reviewing court [must] engage in a substantial inquiry. Certainly, the Secretary's decision is entitled to a presumption of regularity. But that presumption is not to shield his action from a thorough, probing, in-depth review.
>
> The court is first required to decide whether the Secretary acted within the scope of his authority. This determination naturally begins with a delineation of the scope of the Secretary's authority and discretion. As has been shown, Congress has specified only a small range of choices that the Secretary can make....
>
> Section 706(2)(A) [further] requires a finding that the actual choice made was not "arbitrary, capricious, an abuse of discretion.... " To make this finding the court must consider whether the decision was based on a consideration of the relevant factors and whether there has been a clear error of judgment. Although this inquiry into the facts is to be searching and careful, the ultimate standard of review is a narrow one. The court is not empowered to substitute its judgment for that of the agency. *Id.* at 415–16.

3. *Chalking in the boundary lines.* As explained by *Overton Park,* a court's inquiry under the arbitrary-capricious test begins with issues of legal *interpretation:* what are the boundaries of the agency's discretionary power? This inquiry would require an application of *Chevron* or one of its less deferential state-law counterparts, discussed in § 9.2.

In cases involving discretionary action, the questions of legal interpretation include determination of which factors a statute requires the agency to consider and which ones it should not consider. If the agency failed to consider a relevant factor, or took account of a factor it should not have considered, its action should be set aside as arbitrary and capricious.

In *Salameda*, the interpretive issue was whether an applicant's community assistance should be treated as a relevant factor in determining "extreme hardship." Since the INS had failed to clarify its view on this issue, the agency's interpretation received little deference and the court followed the views of other circuits. However, because the term "extreme hardship" is so vague, it seems clear that Congress intended to delegate substantial interpretive authority to the INS. Under most circumstances, *Chevron* would have left little room for the court to reject the agency's interpretation of this term. Indeed, the court itself hinted that it would have deferred to a clearly articulated Board position that community assistance was irrelevant to the "extreme hardship" issue.

In *Pension Benefit Guaranty Corp. v. LTV Corp.*, 496 U.S. 633 (1990), the Supreme Court limited the "relevant factor" approach. It overturned a lower court decision which required the agency to consider as relevant factors the policies expressed in various federal labor and bankruptcy statutes. The Court said:

> To begin with, there are numerous federal statutes that could be said to embody countless policies. If agency action may be disturbed whenever a reviewing court is able to point to an arguably relevant statutory policy that was not explicitly considered, then a very large number of agency decisions might be open to judicial invalidation. ... [In addition], because the PBGC can claim no expertise in the labor and bankruptcy areas, it may be ill-equipped to undertake the difficult task of discerning and applying the "policies and goals" of these fields.

4. *Exercise of discretionary power.* After resolving issues of legal interpretation, a court reviewing an agency's exercise of discretionary power under the "arbitrary, capricious" standard must satisfy itself that the factual underpinnings of the agency action find support in the record. We discuss the standard for judicial review of an agency's factual determinations in § 9.5. Finally, the court reviews the exercise of discretion itself.

In suspension of deportation cases, if the INS finds that the alien would suffer extreme hardship, it then must decide whether to exercise discretion to suspend deportation. Similarly, an agency that finds that a licensee committed misconduct has to decide what penalty to impose—anything from revoking the license to putting a warning letter in the file. Government makes an almost infinite number of these sorts of discretionary calls. As *Overton Park* explains, such decisions are judicially reviewable for "clear error of judgment" (unless the action is "committed to agency discretion," as discussed in § 10.3). Recall the language in *Overton Park*: "Although this inquiry into the facts is to be searching and careful, the ultimate standard of review is a narrow one. The court is not empowered to substitute its judgment for that of the agency."

In *Butz v. Glover Livestock Co.*, 411 U.S. 182 (1973), the agency found that a licensee had negligently weighed livestock. It imposed a twenty-day suspension, even though in the past it had never suspended a license except in cases of intentional and flagrant violations. The Court of Appeals reversed the suspension because of this disparate treatment, but the Supreme Court reversed.

The Court held that the decision below "was an impermissible intrusion into the administrative domain." The agency's choice of sanction is not to be overturned unless found to be "unwarranted in law or without justification in fact." The Court held that there is no legal requirement that licensees be treated uniformly or that license suspension can occur only in cases of intentional or flagrant violation. Since the licensee had been warned about short-weighting in the past, there was sufficient factual justification for the sanction. "The fashioning of an appropriate and reasonable remedy is for the Secretary, not the court."

5. *Other abuses of discretion.* Modern arbitrary and capricious review extends well beyond the "clear error of judgment" test articulated in *Overton Park.* A "Restatement of Scope-of-Review Doctrine" formulated by the ABA Section of Administrative Law, 38 Admin.L.Rev. 235 (1986), contains a checklist of the kinds of agency errors that can constitute an abuse of discretion:

> i. The action rests upon a policy judgment that is so unacceptable as to render the action arbitrary.

> ii. The action rests upon reasoning that is so illogical as to render the action arbitrary.

> iii. The asserted or necessary factual premises of the action do not withstand scrutiny under [the relevant standard of review].

> iv. The action is, without good reason, inconsistent with prior agency policies or precedents.

> v. The agency arbitrarily failed to adopt an alternative solution to the problem addressed in the action.

> vi. The action fails in other respects to rest upon reasoned decisionmaking.

See Ronald M. Levin, "Scope-of-Review Doctrine Restated: An Administrative Law Section Report," 38 Admin.L.Rev. 239, 253–60 (1986). The first of these criteria corresponds to the "clear error of judgment" test, *id.* at 253, while the others have more to do with the agency's reasoning process. In the end, however, as *Overton Park* makes clear, arbitrary and capricious review is supposed to be for reasonableness, not rightness.

Does this array of potential challenges under the arbitrary and capricious test give a court too much power to interfere with legitimate agency discretion? What light do the opinions in *Salameda* shed on this question? In 1998, Iowa adopted a lengthy statutory list of review standards, based roughly on the ABA restatement. *See* Iowa Code § 17A.19(8).

6. *Reasoned decisionmaking—the Chenery rule.* Under the rule in the second *Chenery* case, a court cannot affirm an agency decision on some ground other than the one relied on by the agency in the decision under review. As a result, so-called post-hoc rationalizations for agency decisions are disallowed. *SEC v. Chenery Corp.,* 332 U.S. 194 (1947), discussed in § 4.3 N.6.

In a recent decision, the Supreme Court applied this principle to the NLRB. The agency found that an employer did not have reasonable doubt, based on objective considerations, that a union continued to enjoy majority support; as a result, the agency found that the employer's poll of its employees was an unfair labor practice. The Court held (by a 5–4 vote) that this finding was not supported by substantial evidence on the whole record, because several employees had told the employer that numerous fellow employees no longer supported the union. *Allentown Mack Sales & Service, Inc. v. NLRB*, 118 S.Ct. 818 (1998), also discussed in § 9.1 N.6.

Apparently, the NLRB applied the "reasonable doubt" standard in a non-obvious manner. It required direct evidence that a majority of employees had repudiated the union before it allowed a poll to be taken. Thus the standard actually being applied by the agency (requiring direct evidence of a majority repudiation) was different from the standard it seemed to be applying (requiring only reasonable doubt that the union enjoyed majority support). The Court's criticism of the Board was caustic:

> Reasoned decisionmaking, in which the rule announced is the rule applied, promotes sound results, and unreasoned decisionmaking the opposite. The evil of a decision that applies a standard other than the one it enunciates spreads in both directions, preventing both consistent application of the law by subordinate agency personnel (notably administrative law judges), and effective review by the courts. . . .

> . . . If revision of the Board's standard of proof can be achieved thus subtly and obliquely, it becomes a much more complicated enterprise for a court of appeals to determine whether substantial evidence supports the conclusion that the required standard has or has not been met. . . . An agency should not be able to impede judicial review, and indeed even political oversight, by disguising its policymaking as factfinding. . . .

> The Board can, of course, forthrightly and explicitly adopt counterfactual evidentiary presumptions (which are in effect substantive rules of law) as a way of furthering particular legal or policy goals. . . . That is not the sort of Board action at issue here, however, but rather the Board's allegedly systematic undervaluation of certain evidence, or allegedly systematic exaggeration of what the evidence must prove. . . . When the Board purports to be engaged in simple factfinding, unconstrained by substantive presumptions or evidentiary rules of exclusion, it is not free to prescribe what inferences from the evidence it will accept and reject, but must draw all those inferences that the evidence fairly demands.

Id. at 827–29.

7. *Closed or open record?* A recurring judicial review issue concerns the contents of the record that a court considers in reviewing informal agency action. *See generally* Gordon G. Young, "Judicial Review of Informal Agency Action on the Fiftieth Anniversary of the APA: The Alleged Demise and Actual Status of *Overton Park*'s Requirement of Judicial Review 'On the Record,'" 10 Admin.L.J.Am.U. 179 (1996).

Under one approach, a court is limited to the materials considered by the agency (the "closed record" approach). Under a second approach, that record can be supplemented by additional evidence in the form of testimony or affidavits (the "open record" approach). Federal law opts firmly for the closed record. In *IMS, P.C. v. Alvarez*, 129 F.3d 618 (D.C.Cir.1997), the court summarized federal practice as follows:

> It is a widely accepted principle of administrative law that the courts base their review of an agency's actions on the materials that were before the agency at the time its decision was made. ... [citing *Overton Park* and *Camp v. Pitts*, 411 U.S. 138 (1973), which stated]: "in applying the [arbitrary and capricious] standard, the focal point for judicial review should be the administrative record already in existence, not some new record made initially in the reviewing court." It is not necessary that the agency hold a formal hearing in compiling its record, for "the APA specifically contemplates judicial review on the basis of the agency record compiled in the course of informal agency action in which a hearing has not occurred."

There are some narrow exceptions to the federal closed record rule, but the court in *IMS, P.C.* found them inapplicable: "IMS has not demonstrated that the agency failed to examine all relevant factors or to adequately explain its grounds for decision, or that the agency acted in bad faith or engaged in improper behavior in reaching its decision." Some cases recognize an additional exception to the closed record requirement: the court can take evidence to help it understand technical material in the record. *Ass'n of Pacific Fisheries v. EPA*, 615 F.2d 794, 811–12 (9th Cir.1980).

The *IMS* case mentioned that an exception to the closed record requirement occurs where an agency fails to explain its decision sufficiently for the court to review the decision. As explained in § 4.3, however, courts ordinarily remand such cases to the agency to provide the needed explanation, rather than conducting a trial to ascertain why the agency acted as it did. *Camp v. Pitts, supra.*

Some states follow an open record approach. *See*, for example, *Borden* in § 9.5, which calls for an open record approach in the review of regulations. Also, 1981 MSAPA § 5–114(a)(3) permits a court to consider new evidence regarding "any material fact that was not required by any provision of law to be determined exclusively on an agency record of a type reasonably suitable for judicial review." Thus, according to the accompanying comment, the open record approach applies to all MSAPA proceedings except formal adjudication and "conference" adjudication. Similarly, 1981 MSAPA 3–112(c) provides for an open record in judicial review of rulemaking, although § 3–110(b) limits the open record approach by prohibiting the agency from adding new reasons for a rule at the time the rule is judicially reviewed.

What are the arguments in favor of the closed and open record approaches?

In favor of the closed record approach is judicial economy. An open record approach insures lengthy trials in which either side is free to bring in new expert witnesses or economic analyses to buttress its position. In addition, an open record encourages private parties to engage in strategic behavior called "sandbagging"—that is, holding back evidence until the judicial review stage so that the agency never gets to pass on that evidence. A recent California decision, which opted for the closed record approach in review of rules, made an additional argument founded on the respective role of courts and agencies:

> Were we to hold that courts could freely consider extra-record evidence in these circumstances, we would in effect transform the highly deferential substantial evidence standard of review ... into a de novo standard, and under that standard the issue would be not whether the administrative decision was rational in light of the evidence before the agency but whether it was the wisest decision given all the available scientific data. The propriety or impropriety of a particular legislative decision is a matter for the Legislature and the administrative agencies to which it has lawfully delegated quasi-legislative authority; such matters are not appropriate for the judiciary....

> [If parties could introduce scientific testimony in court that was not produced before the agency, this] would seriously undermine the finality of quasi-legislative administrative decisions. Any individual dissatisfied with a regulation could hire an expert who is likewise dissatisfied to prepare a report or give testimony explaining the grounds for his disagreement, introduce this evidence in a traditional mandamus proceeding, and, if he can persuade the court that the report raises a question regarding the wisdom of the regulation, obtain an order reopening the rulemaking proceedings....

Western States Petroleum Ass'n v. Superior Court, 888 P.2d 1268 (Cal.1995). However, the *Western States* case struck a compromise: the record is closed in rulemaking cases but open in cases reviewing "informal or ministerial" agency actions (since the latter often fail to produce an adequate record at the agency level).

There are good arguments for using an open record methodology, particularly at the state level and particularly in the sort of "informal or ministerial" cases described in *Western States*. Because informal decisions (like the highway routing decision at issue in *Overton Park*) are often made after years of bureaucratic consideration and politicking, the agency's file may be a complete mess. Indeed, it might contain truckloads of disorganized documents. Thus it may be extremely difficult to get this material into manageable form so that it can be treated as the record for judicial review.

Also, parties who have an interest in a particular matter may not have known about the agency proceeding and thus may have failed to furnish timely input. Even if they knew about it, they may not have participated or retained counsel to help them participate effectively. Thus it may seem unfair to prevent them from introducing relevant evidence at the time of judicial review.

Moreover, the closed record approach requires both the agency and private parties to place into the record every conceivable piece of relevant information in their possession, lest they be prevented from relying on it at the judicial review stage. This could increase costs and cause serious delays at the agency level. Yet building a massive record may be unnecessary, because the agency action may never be judicially reviewed or particular arguments may never be raised in court. Thus an open record may simplify and speed up the agency decisionmaking process.

8. *Resource constraints.* The two *Salameda* opinions forthrightly confront the fundamental question of whether courts should make allowances when agencies simply lack the resources necessary to do their assigned job. In a case like *Salameda*, should a court allow the INS to cut corners by not requiring a reasoned explanation of a discretionary decision? After all, four BIA members had to deal with a caseload of over 14,000 new appeals per year! The result was an ever-lengthening queue of cases, sloppy and rushed decisionmaking, and a twelve-year delay in *Salameda.* In that case, Posner remarked that "understaffing is not a defense to a violation of administrative law." Should it be? *See* Richard J. Pierce, "Judicial Review of Agency Actions in a Period of Diminishing Agency Resources," 49 Admin.L.Rev. 61 (1997).

9. *Problem.* A local school board discharged two tenured high school teachers for misconduct. Both had taught in the district for thirty years.

At Alice's hearing, testimony by her ex-husband revealed that Alice had, over a period of years, taken home for her own use $35 of school supplies (paper, pens, tape, etc.). She admitted that it was true.

Bob was discharged for insubordination. The evidence showed that parents had complained to the principal and the school board about Bob's use of the book "Catcher in the Rye" in English class in 1995. They objected to the "explicit street language" used in the book. After a discussion with the principal, Bob agreed not to use the book again. However, in 1997, Bob assigned "Catcher in the Rye." When summoned to a conference with the principal to discuss this, Bob walked out and refused to discuss it any further.

Alice and Bob seek judicial review. They question only the Board's choice to discharge them instead of imposing some lesser sanction such as a reprimand in their file. How should the court rule? *See Pell v. Board of Educ.,* 313 N.E.2d 321 (N.Y.1974); *Harris v. Mechanicville Central Sch. Dist.,* 380 N.E.2d 213 (N.Y.1978).

§ 9.5 JUDICIAL REVIEW OF DISCRETIONARY DECISIONS IN RULEMAKING

In exercising their delegated rulemaking power, agencies necessarily make policy. As we observed in § 9.4, courts use the "arbitrary and capricious" test to review these policy choices. Whether courts should engage in penetrating "hard look" review of these choices, or whether they should engage in more deferential "soft look" review, is itself an important policy issue.

MOTOR VEHICLE MANUFACTURERS ASS'N v. STATE FARM MUTUAL AUTOMOBILE INS. CO.
463 U.S. 29 (1983).

[This case concerned the issue of whether the National Highway Traffic Safety Administration (NHTSA) should require "passive restraints," meaning either airbags or automatic seatbelts. The need for regulation arose out of the fact that relatively few people buckle up on their own. A passive restraint requirement would be very costly for auto manufacturers but would have enormous safety benefits: if everyone actually wore seatbelts or were protected by passive restraints, there would be 12,000 fewer traffic deaths and 100,000 fewer serious injuries each year.

This issue was the subject of 60 rulemaking notices; a passive restraint requirement was imposed, amended, rescinded, and reimposed. At one point, NHTSA required an "ignition interlock," which prevented cars from starting until seatbelts were attached; this was unpopular and was banned by statute. Eventually, NHTSA adopted Motor Vehicle Safety Standard 208 in 1977. The Standard required cars produced after 1982 to be equipped with passive restraints.

In 1981, pursuant to a deregulatory initiative of the Reagan administration, NHTSA delayed the effective date of the 1977 standard. After a notice and comment proceeding, NHTSA rescinded the standard.

NHTSA explained that it could not find that the standard would produce significant safety benefits. The industry had decided that virtually all cars would be produced with *automatic detachable belts* (rather than airbags). Once this type of belt is unbuckled, it loses its automatic feature until it is rebuckled. Thus, Standard 208 might not significantly increase usage of restraints at all.

Since the standard would cost $1 billion to implement, NHTSA did not believe it reasonable to impose such costs on manufacturers and consumers without more adequate assurance of sufficient safety benefits. In addition, NHTSA concluded that automatic restraints might have an adverse effect on the public's attitude toward safety, "poisoning popular sentiment toward efforts to improve occupant restraint systems in the future." Insurance companies challenged the rescission, which the D.C. Circuit held arbitrary and capricious.]

WHITE, J.: . . . .

III

Unlike the Court of Appeals, we do not find the appropriate scope of judicial review to be the "most troublesome question" in the case. [The statute indicates] that motor vehicle safety standards are to be promulgated under the informal rulemaking procedures of § 553 of the [APA]. The agency's action in promulgating such standards therefore may be set aside if found to be "arbitrary, capricious, an abuse of discretion, or otherwise not in accordance with law." § 706(2)(A). *Citizens to Preserve Overton Park v. Volpe,* 401 U.S. 402 (1971). We believe that the rescission or modification of an occupant protection standard is subject to the same test. . . .

Petitioner [MVMA] disagrees, contending that the rescission of an agency rule should be judged by the same standard a court would use to judge an agency's refusal to promulgate a rule in the first place—a standard Petitioner believes considerably narrower than the traditional arbitrary and capricious test. [*See* § 6.3.] We reject this view. The Motor Vehicle Safety Act expressly equates orders "revoking" and "establishing" safety standards; neither that Act nor the APA suggests that revocations are to be treated as refusals to promulgate standards. Petitioner's view would render meaningless Congress' authorization for judicial review of orders revoking safety rules. Moreover, the revocation of an extant regulation is substantially different than a failure to act. Revocation constitutes a reversal of the agency's former views as to the proper course. "A settled course of behavior embodies the agency's informed judgment that, by pursuing that course, it will carry out the policies committed to it by Congress. There is, then, at least a presumption that those policies will be carried out best if the settled rule is adhered to." Accordingly, an agency changing its course by rescinding a rule is obligated to supply a reasoned analysis for the change beyond that which may be required when an agency does not act in the first instance.

In so holding, we fully recognize that "regulatory agencies do not establish rules of conduct to last forever," and that an agency must be given ample latitude to "adapt their rules and policies to the demands of changing circumstances." But the forces of change do not always or necessarily point in the direction of deregulation. In the abstract, there is no more reason to presume that changing circumstances require the rescission of prior action, instead of a revision in or even the extension of current regulation. If Congress established a presumption from which judicial review should start, that presumption—contrary to petitioners' views—is not *against* safety regulation, but *against* changes in current policy that are not justified by the rulemaking record. While the removal of a regulation may not entail the monetary expenditures and other costs of enacting a new standard, and accordingly, it may be easier for an agency to justify a deregulatory action, the direction in which an agency chooses to move does not alter the standard of judicial review established by law. . . .

[U]nder [the arbitrary and capricious] standard, a reviewing court may not set aside an agency rule that is rational, based on consideration of the relevant factors and within the scope of the authority delegated to the agency by the statute. We do not disagree with this formulation.[9] The scope of review under the "arbitrary and capricious" standard is narrow and a court is not to substitute its judgment for that of the agency. Nevertheless, the agency must examine the relevant data and articulate a satisfactory explanation for its action including a "rational connection between the facts found and the choice made." *Burlington Truck Lines v. United States,* 371 U.S. 156 (1962). In reviewing that

---

9. The Department of Transportation suggests that the arbitrary and capricious standard requires no more than the minimum rationality a statute must bear in order to withstand analysis under the Due Process Clause. We do not view as equivalent the presumption of constitutionality afforded legislation drafted by Congress and the presumption of regularity afforded an agency in fulfilling its statutory mandate.

explanation, we must "consider whether the decision was based on a consideration of the relevant factors and whether there has been a clear error of judgment." *Citizens to Preserve Overton Park v. Volpe, supra.*

Normally, an agency rule would be arbitrary and capricious if the agency has relied on factors which Congress has not intended it to consider, entirely failed to consider an important aspect of the problem, offered an explanation for its decision that runs counter to the evidence before the agency, or is so implausible that it could not be ascribed to a difference in view or the product of agency expertise. The reviewing court should not attempt itself to make up for such deficiencies: "We may not supply a reasoned basis for the agency's action that the agency itself has not given." *SEC v. Chenery Corp.*, 332 U.S. 194 (1947). We will, however, "uphold a decision of less than ideal clarity if the agency's path may reasonably be discerned." For purposes of this case, it is also relevant that Congress required a record of the rulemaking proceedings to be compiled and submitted to a reviewing court, 15 U.S.C. § 1394, and intended that agency findings under the Motor Vehicle Safety Act would be supported by "substantial evidence on the record considered as a whole" [citing committee reports]. . . .

V

The ultimate question before us is whether NHTSA's rescission of the passive restraint requirement of Standard 208 was arbitrary and capricious. We conclude, as did the Court of Appeals, that it was. We also conclude, but for somewhat different reasons, that further consideration of the issue by the agency is therefore required. We deal separately with the rescission as it applies to airbags and as it applies to seatbelts.

A

The first and most obvious reason for finding the rescission arbitrary and capricious is that NHTSA apparently gave no consideration whatever to modifying the Standard to require that airbag technology be utilized. Standard 208 sought to achieve automatic crash protection by requiring automobile manufacturers to install either of two passive restraint devices: airbags or automatic seatbelts. . . . The agency has now determined that the detachable automatic belts will not attain anticipated safety benefits because so many individuals will detach the mechanism. . . . Given the effectiveness ascribed to airbag technology by the agency, the mandate of the Safety Act to achieve traffic safety would suggest that the logical response to the faults of detachable seatbelts would be to require the installation of airbags. At the very least this alternative way of achieving the objectives of the Act should have been addressed and adequate reasons given for its abandonment. But the agency not only did not require compliance through airbags, it did not even consider the possibility in its 1981 rulemaking. Not one sentence of its rulemaking statement discusses the airbags-only option. Because, as the Court of Appeals stated, "NHTSA's . . . analysis of airbags was nonexistent," what we said in *Burlington Truck Lines v. United States,* is apropos here:

There are no findings and no analysis here to justify the choice made, no indication of the basis on which the [agency] exercised its expert discretion. We are not prepared to and the [APA] will not permit us to accept such ... practice.... Expert discretion is the lifeblood of the administrative process, but "unless we make the requirements for administrative action strict and demanding, *expertise,* the strength of modern government, can become a monster which rules with no practical limits on its discretion."

We have frequently reiterated that an agency must cogently explain why it has exercised its discretion in a given manner, and we reaffirm this principle again today.

The automobile industry has opted for the passive belt over the airbag, but surely it is not enough that the regulated industry has eschewed a given safety device. For nearly a decade, the automobile industry waged the regulatory equivalent of war against the airbag and lost—the inflatable restraint was proven sufficiently effective. Now the automobile industry has decided to employ a seatbelt system which will not meet the safety objectives of Standard 208. This hardly constitutes cause to revoke the standard itself. Indeed, the Motor Vehicle Safety Act was necessary because the industry was not sufficiently responsive to safety concerns. The Act intended that safety standards not depend on current technology and could be "technology-forcing" in the sense of inducing the development of superior safety design....

... [P]etitioners recite a number of difficulties that they believe would be posed by a mandatory airbag standard.... But these are not the agency's reasons for rejecting a mandatory airbag standard. Not having discussed the possibility, the agency submitted no reasons at all. The short—and sufficient—answer to petitioners' submission is that the courts may not accept appellate counsel's *post hoc* rationalizations for agency action. It is well-established that an agency's action must be upheld, if at all, on the basis articulated by the agency itself.

Petitioners also invoke our decision in *Vermont Yankee* as though it were a talisman under which any agency decision is by definition unimpeachable. Specifically, it is submitted that to require an agency to consider an airbags-only alternative is, in essence, to dictate to the agency the procedures it is to follow. Petitioners both misread *Vermont Yankee* and misconstrue the nature of the remand that is in order. In *Vermont Yankee,* we held that a court may not impose additional procedural requirements upon an agency. We do not require today any specific procedures which NHTSA must follow. Nor do we broadly require an agency to consider all policy alternatives in reaching decision. It is true that a rulemaking "cannot be found wanting simply because the agency failed to include every alternative device and thought conceivable by the mind of man ... regardless of how uncommon or unknown that alternative may have been.... " But the airbag is more than a policy alternative to the passive restraint standard; it is a technological alternative within the ambit of the existing standard. We hold only that given the judgment made in 1977 that airbags are an effective and cost-beneficial life-saving technology, the mandatory passive-restraint rule may not be abandoned without any consideration whatsoever of an airbags-only requirement.

B

Although the issue is closer, we also find that the agency was too quick to dismiss the safety benefits of automatic seatbelts. NHTSA's critical finding was that, in light of the industry's plans to install readily detachable passive belts, it could not reliably predict "even a 5 percentage point increase as the minimum level of expected usage increase." The Court of Appeals rejected this finding because there is "not one iota" of evidence that Modified Standard 208 will fail to increase nationwide seatbelt use by at least 13 percentage points, the level of increased usage necessary for the standard to justify its cost. Given the lack of probative evidence, the court held that "only a well-justified refusal to seek more evidence could render rescission non-arbitrary."

Petitioners object to this conclusion. In their view, "substantial uncertainty" that a regulation will accomplish its intended purpose is sufficient reason, without more, to rescind a regulation. We agree with petitioners that just as an agency reasonably may decline to issue a safety standard if it is uncertain about its efficacy, an agency may also revoke a standard on the basis of serious uncertainties if supported by the record and reasonably explained. Rescission of the passive restraint requirement would not be arbitrary and capricious simply because there was no evidence in direct support of the agency's conclusion. It is not infrequent that the available data does not settle a regulatory issue and the agency must then exercise its judgment in moving from the facts and probabilities on the record to a policy conclusion. Recognizing that policymaking in a complex society must account for uncertainty, however, does not imply that it is sufficient for an agency to merely recite the terms "substantial uncertainty" as a justification for its actions. The agency must explain the evidence which is available, and must offer a "rational connection between the facts found and the choice made." Generally, one aspect of that explanation would be a justification for rescinding the regulation before engaging in a search for further evidence.

In this case, the agency's explanation for rescission of the passive restraint requirement is *not* sufficient to enable us to conclude that the rescission was the product of reasoned decisionmaking. To reach this conclusion, we do not upset the agency's view of the facts, but we do appreciate the limitations of this record in supporting the agency's decision. We start with the accepted ground that if used, seatbelts unquestionably would save many thousands of lives and would prevent tens of thousands of crippling injuries. Unlike recent regulatory decisions we have reviewed, *Industrial Union Department v. American Petroleum Institute*, 448 U.S. 607 (1980), the safety benefits of wearing seatbelts are not in doubt and it is not challenged that were those benefits to accrue, the monetary costs of implementing the standard would be easily justified. We move next to the fact that there is no direct evidence in support of the agency's finding that detachable automatic belts cannot be predicted to yield a substantial increase in usage. The empirical evidence on the record, consisting of surveys of drivers of automobiles equipped with passive belts, reveals more than a doubling of the usage rate experienced with manual belts. Much of the agency's rulemaking statement—and much of the controversy in this case— centers on the conclusions that should be drawn from these studies. The agency maintained that the doubling of seatbelt usage in these studies could not be extrapolated to an across-the-board mandatory standard because the passive seatbelts were guarded by ignition interlocks and purchasers of the tested cars are somewhat atypical. Respondents insist these studies demonstrate that Modified Standard 208 will substantially increase seatbelt usage. We believe that it is within the agency's discretion to pass upon the generalizability of these field studies. This is precisely the type of issue which rests within the expertise of NHTSA, and upon which a reviewing court must be most hesitant to intrude.

But accepting the agency's view of the field tests on passive restraints indicates only that there is no reliable real-world experience that usage rates will substantially increase. To be sure, NHTSA opines that "it cannot reliably predict even a 5 percentage point increase as the minimum level of increased usage." But this and other statements that passive belts will not yield substantial increases in seatbelt usage apparently take no account of the critical difference between detachable automatic belts and current manual belts. A detached passive belt does require an affirmative act to reconnect it, but—unlike a manual seat belt—the passive belt, once reattached, will continue to function automatically unless again disconnected. Thus, inertia—a factor which the agency's own studies have found significant in explaining the current low usage rates for seatbelts—works in *favor* of, not *against,* use of the protective device. Since 20 to 50% of motorists currently wear seatbelts on some occasions, there would seem to be grounds to believe that seatbelt use by occasional users will be substantially increased by the detachable passive belts. Whether this is in fact the case is a matter for the agency to decide, but it must bring its expertise to bear on the question.

The agency is correct to look at the costs as well as the benefits of Standard 208. The agency's conclusion that the incremental costs of the requirements were no longer reasonable was predicated on its prediction that the safety benefits of the regulation might be minimal. Specifically, the agency's fears that the public may resent paying more for the automatic belt systems is expressly dependent on the assumption that detachable automatic belts will not produce more than "negligible safety benefits." When the agency reexamines its findings as to the likely increase in seatbelt usage, it must also reconsider its judgment of the reasonableness of the monetary and other costs associated with the Standard. In reaching its judgment, NHTSA should bear in mind that

Congress intended safety to be the preeminent factor under the Motor Vehicle Safety Act....

The agency also failed to articulate a basis for not requiring nondetachable belts under Standard 208. It is argued that the concern of the agency with the easy detachability of the currently favored design would be readily solved by a continuous passive belt, which allows the occupant to "spool out" the belt and create the necessary slack for easy extrication from the vehicle ... By failing to analyze the continuous seatbelts in its own right, the agency has failed to offer the rational connection between facts and judgment required to pass muster under the arbitrary and capricious standard....

VI

"An agency's view of what is in the public interest may change, either with or without a change in circumstances. But an agency changing its course must supply a reasoned analysis.... " *Greater Boston Television Corp. v. FCC*, 444 F.2d 841, 852 [(D.C.Cir.1970)].... [T]he agency has failed to supply the requisite "reasoned analysis" in this case. Accordingly, we vacate the judgment of the Court of Appeals and remand the case to that court with directions to remand the matter to the NHTSA for further consideration consistent with this opinion.

[REHNQUIST, J., joined by BURGER, C.J. and POWELL and O'CONNOR, JJ., joined most of the Court's opinion but dissented from Part V.B. They argued that NHTSA had adequately explained its decision to reject the automatic seatbelt alternative. It was reasonable for NHTSA to accept studies indicating that such belts would not save enough lives to be worth the cost.]

The agency's changed view of the standard seems to be related to the election of a new President of a different political party. It is readily apparent that the responsible members of one administration may consider public resistance and uncertainties to be more important than do their counterparts in a previous administration. A change in administration brought about by the people casting their votes is a perfectly reasonable basis for an executive agency's reappraisal of the costs and benefits of its programs and regulations. As long as the agency remains within the bounds established by Congress,* it is entitled to assess administrative records and evaluate priorities in light of the philosophy of the administration.

BORDEN, INC. v. COMMISSIONER
OF PUBLIC HEALTH
448 N.E.2d 367 (Mass.1983).

[General Laws c. 94B provides that the Commissioner of Public Health can ban any hazardous substance if public health cannot be

---

* Of course, a new administration may not refuse to enforce laws of which it does not approve, or to ignore statutory standards in carrying out its regulatory functions. But in this case, as the Court correctly concludes, Congress has not required the agency to require passive restraints.

protected through adequate labelling. After notice and comment procedure, the Commissioner banned urea-formaldehyde foamed-in-place insulation (UFFI), finding that it emitted gases hazardous to particularly sensitive people (such as asthmatics). Manufacturers of UFFI challenged the regulation in the trial court, which held an evidentiary hearing at which both sides presented evidence about the toxicity of UFFI. The trial court invalidated the regulation.]

NOLAN, J.:

... We take this opportunity to set forth, once again, the guiding principles for judicial review of agency regulations. We begin by noting that an agency's power to make regulations is delegated by the Legislature. Acting upon this delegation, an agency may, unless specifically prohibited, properly base its regulatory decisions on the same kinds of "legislative facts" on which the Legislature could rely in its enactment of a statute. A regulation is essentially an expression of public policy. The issue on review is not whether the regulation was supported by substantial evidence in the record before the agency. Indeed, "[f]acts represented in material submitted to an agency, unless stipulated as admitted, may not be relied on in a judicial challenge to an administrative regulation." Rather, the person challenging the regulation must prove in the judicial proceeding that the regulation is illegal, arbitrary, or capricious.[8] Because the agency proceeding is not an adjudicatory one, a plaintiff may not meet its burden "by arguing that the record does not affirmatively show facts which support the regulation." "If the question is fairly debatable, courts cannot substitute their judgment for that of the Legislature."

A plaintiff must prove "the absence of any conceivable ground upon which [the rule] may be upheld."[9] This is so because a properly promulgated regulation has the force of law and must be accorded all the deference due to a statute. "Thus, [a court] must apply all rational presumptions in favor of the validity of the administrative action and not declare it void unless its provisions cannot by any reasonable construction be interpreted in harmony with the legislative mandate." This deference is necessary to maintain the separation between the powers of the Legislature and administrative agencies and the powers of the

---

8. The plaintiffs contend that the court's function is "to determine whether there is any rational basis upon which the regulation can be sustained." We agree. However, we do not agree with the plaintiffs' contentions that in making this determination the court must view the regulations in light of the factors and standards required or deemed relevant under the Federal Administrative Procedure Act. While some of these factors are helpful, others are neither necessary nor appropriate under this State's Administrative Procedure Act. Cf. *Grocery Mfrs. of America, Inc. v. Department of Pub. Health,* 393 N.E.2d 881 (1979) (State agency need not make findings of

legislative facts in the record of regulatory proceeding although Federal agency would be so required). The United States Supreme Court itself did not rely on these factors when it recently upheld the validity of State legislation banning the use of plastic, non-refillable milk containers. *Minnesota v. Clover Leaf Creamery Co.,* 449 U.S. 456 (1981)....

9. This is consistent with the fact that an agency is not, barring a specific statutory mandate, obliged to provide a statement of the reasons which support its adoption of a regulation.

judiciary. "A court may not substitute its judgment for that of the Legislature if the regulation comports with the power delegated." This deference also precludes the possibility that a plaintiff may frustrate administrative policy merely by amassing facts, statistics, and testimony before a judge, all of which may have little or nothing to do with the legislative facts which the administrative agency relied upon in making its regulation. "[R]espect for the legislative process means that it is not the province of the court to sit and weigh conflicting evidence supporting or opposing a legislative enactment." ... There are no requirements in G.L. c. 94B that the commissioner conduct any specific tests or determine that any specific number of people are or will be affected by a particular substance in making his finding concerning [whether it is a "hazardous substance."]. Nor is there any indication that the commissioner must hold an adjudicatory hearing before making his finding. The commissioner may act only with respect to those substances concerning which he makes certain findings, but his power to make those findings is limited only in that he must not exercise it illegally, arbitrarily, or capriciously.

The judge found that "[f]ormaldehyde ... at some level of concentration, becomes an irritant.... [F]urther ... as this abrasive level of exposure is increased, the exposure level becomes toxic." We accept this finding. Since formaldehyde meets the definition of hazardous substance, we conclude that formaldehyde is properly regulated under G.L. c. 94B. The crux of the issue before us, then, is—as it was before the judge— whether the presence of formaldehyde in UFFI justifies the ban of the latter product. The ban would be justified if the commissioner could rationally find that UFFI could not "be labeled adequately to protect the public health and safety, or [that UFFI] present[ed] an imminent danger to the public health and safety."

We have in the past sustained regulations on the ground that there was a conceivable basis for the agency decision.... In this case, we need not go so far. We have examined relevant portions of the trial transcript, and we conclude that there was evidence presented there which warranted the commissioner's action.

We briefly summarize portions of that evidence. At trial, Dr. Richard Gammage, a chemist, testified that tests conducted at the Oak Ridge National Laboratory on panels of wood foamed internally with UFFI and maintained under conditions which would approximate those of a corner room in a normal house indicated that UFFI emitted formaldehyde into the "room" in levels of concentration which ranged from .03 to about .25 or .3 parts per million.... Dr. Andrew Ulsamer, Director of the Division of Health Effects at the CPSC, testified that his opinion, based on his review of the National Academy of Sciences report, was that "there are health effects of formaldehyde at relatively low levels, and if one considers the various sensitive populations that may be involved, that there may indeed not be a population threshold at any measurable level of formaldehyde within the general population." He further testified that persons who suffer from asthma, chronic obstructive pulmonary diseases such as emphysema or chronic bronchitis, and persons who are allergic to formaldehyde, would suffer health effects at exposure to levels less than .1 parts per million. He estimated these groups to compose about ten per cent of the population. . . .

Thus, there was evidence before the judge indicating that UFFI would potentially in some conditions emit formaldehyde into houses at levels above which at least a significant portion of the population would experience adverse health effects. In light of this evidence, we cannot say that the commissioner acted arbitrarily or capriciously in banning UFFI. That the commissioner was unable to determine the amount of formaldehyde that UFFI contributed to the indoor environment, that he did not know how many people in the Commonwealth had been affected by UFFI, that he had not compared the levels of formaldehyde in UFFI and non-UFFI houses, that he had not caused epidemiological studies to be made to determine the incidence of symptoms allegedly caused by UFFI, that experts called by the plaintiff at trial offered evidence contrary to the commissioner's, and that the commissioner's experts significantly qualified their testimony on cross-examination does not obviate the fact that he had a rational and certainly conceivable basis for his decision. . . .

Conclusion. We conclude that the judge erred in holding that the commissioner's regulations were illegal, arbitrary, and capricious. Accordingly, we reverse the judgments of the Superior Court and remand the case with directions to grant declaratory relief consistent with this decision.

Notes and Questions

1. *Hard look review.* Traditionally, judicial review of an agency's policy decisions under the arbitrary-capricious standard was extremely deferential, perhaps close to the "minimum rationality" test for the validity of *statutes* under substantive due process. "[W]here the regulation is within the scope of authority legally delegated, the presumption of the existence of facts justifying its specific exercise attaches alike to statutes, to municipal ordinances, and to orders of administrative bodies." *Pacific States Box & Basket Co. v. White,* 296 U.S. 176, 186 (1935). *Borden* is an example of a state court decision that employs minimum rationality analysis in reviewing rules. As note 9 of *Motor Vehicle* points out, federal courts now reject this approach.

Today, the phrase "hard look" often is used to describe the review function, particularly in federal courts. *Motor Vehicle* is the leading example. Few state courts engage in hard look review, although Washington broke new ground in adopting it by statute. A "legislative note" to a 1995 Washington statute states that while "a court should not substitute its judgment for that of an administrative agency, the court should determine whether the agency decisionmaking was rigorous and deliberative; whether the agency reached its result through a process of reason; and whether the agency took a hard look at the rule before its adoption." Note to RCW § 34.05.328.

What is meant by hard look review? *See* Mark Seidenfeld, "Demystifying Deossification: Rethinking Recent Proposals to Modify Judicial Review of Notice and Comment Rulemaking," 75 Texas L. Rev. 483, 491–92 (1997):

> Essentially, under the hard look test, the reviewing court scrutinizes the agency's reasoning to make certain that the agency carefully deliberated about the issues raised by its decision. . . . Courts require that agencies offer detailed explanations for their actions. The agency's explanation must address all factors relevant to the agency's decision. A court may reverse a decision if the agency fails to consider plausible alternative measures and explain why it rejected these for the regulatory path it chose. If an agency route veers from the road laid down by its precedents, it must justify the detour in light of changed external circumstances or a changed view of its regulatory role that the agency can support under its authorizing statute. The agency must allow broad participation in its regulatory process and not disregard the views of any participants. In addition to these procedural requirements, courts have, on occasion, invoked a rigorous substantive standard by remanding decisions that the judges believed the agency failed to justify adequately in light of information in the administrative record.

Which elements of hard look review did the Supreme Court employ in *Motor Vehicle*? Do you see an inconsistency between hard look review and the principle of *Vermont Yankee*? See § 5.4.3 N.4.

2. *The merits of hard look review.* Is hard look review appropriate? Some argue that it allows unelected and inexpert judges to substitute their own judgments and values for those of an expert agency, even though the agency was legislatively designated to make the choice. But others argue that it is a necessary corrective to bureaucratic tendencies to build empires, be captured by the regulated industry, or act unreasonably, maliciously, politically, carelessly, or inconsistently. Compare these views:

a. A. Shep Melnick, "Administrative Law and Bureaucratic Reality," 44 Admin.L.Rev. 245, 245–46, 258 (1992):

> [One view about judicial review] is that without "searching and thorough" judicial review, bureaucrats would be running wild, issuing arbitrary and capricious orders with utter abandon. Another view is that without such judicial review agencies would be in the hip pocket of "special interests," captured, we are always told, "by the very interests they are supposed to control." It is bad enough that these two views are incompatible. What is worse is that usually they are both wrong . . .

> [Recent studies] show that judicial intervention has had an unfortunate effect on policymaking. Judicial review has subjected agencies to debilitating delay and uncertainty. Courts have heaped new tasks on agencies while decreasing their ability to perform any of them. They have forced agencies to substitute trivial pursuits for important ones. And they have discouraged administrators from taking responsibility for their actions and for educating the public.

> What is to be done? Most obviously, judges should remember a key part of the Hippocratic oath: First, do no harm. In administrative law that translates into the command, defer! defer!

b. Stephen Breyer, "Judicial Review of Questions of Law and Policy," 38 Admin.L.Rev. 363, 388, 391 (1986):

One might ask with the "airbags" case in mind whether the judiciary is institutionally well suited for strict policy scrutiny. To what extent can a group of men and women, typically trained as lawyers rather than as administrators or regulators, operating with limited access to information and under the constraints of adversary legal process, be counted upon to supervise the vast realm of substantive agency policymaking?

First, to what extent are judges likely to sympathetically understand the problems the agency faces in setting technical standards in complex areas? In the "airbags" case, for example, the Supreme Court faulted NHTSA for not having more studies or more accurate studies. But was the Court fully aware of how difficult it is for an agency seeking to set standards to obtain accurate, relevant, unbiased information? Where is the agency to look? ...

Moreover, strict judicial review creates one incentive that from a substantive perspective may be perverse. The stricter the review and the more clearly and convincingly the agency must explain the need for change, the more reluctant the agency will be to change the status quo.

c. Merrick B. Garland, "Deregulation and Judicial Review," 98 Harv. L.Rev. 507, 587–88 (1985):

Under the emerging model [of hard look judicial review as exemplified by the "airbags" case] courts ensure not only that fidelity to congressional purpose marks the outer bounds of agency discretion, but also that it animates the exercise of that discretion. ... Agencies may still function as quasi-legislatures, but the courts now seem intent on reminding them that quasi-legislatures do not possess the same authority that real ones do. ... Vindicating congressional intent may protect not only the autonomy of regulated parties, but also the interests of statutory beneficiaries—by ensuring not only that the agency not *exceed* its congressional authorized power, but also that it *use* that power as Congress intended.

d. Thomas O. McGarity, "Some Thoughts on 'Deossifying' the Rulemaking Process," 41 Duke L.J. 1385, 1412, 1419–20, 1426 (1992):

Many observers have concluded that substantive judicial review has had a profound impact on the way agencies make rules. Fully aware of the consequences of a judicial remand, the agencies are constantly "looking over their shoulders" at the reviewing courts in preparing supporting documents, in writing preambles, in responding to public comments, and in assembling the rulemaking "record." Because they can never know what issues dissatisfied litigants will raise on appeal, they must attempt to prepare responses to all contentions that may prove credible to an appellate court, no matter how ridiculous they may appear to agency staff. Having gone to the considerable effort of a successful rulemaking, the agencies are understandably reluctant to change their rules to adapt to experience with the rules or changed circumstances. ...

The predictable result of stringent "hard look" judicial review of complex rulemaking is ossification. Because the agencies perceive that the reviewing courts are inconsistent in the degree to which they are deferential, they are constrained to prepare for the worst-case scenario on judicial review. This can be extremely resource-intensive and time-consuming. Moreover, since the criteria for substantive judicial review are the same for repealing old rules as for promulgating new rules, the agencies are equally chary of revisiting old rules, even in the name of flexibility. . . .

The net result of all of the aforementioned procedural, analytical, and substantive requirements is a rulemaking process that creeps along, even when under the pressure of statutory deadlines. In the absence of deadlines, the process barely moves at all. Given all of the barriers to writing a rule in the first place, few agencies are anxious to revisit the process in light of changed conditions or new information. Knowing that mistakes or miscalculations in rules will be very difficult to remedy, agencies are also reluctant to write innovative or flexible rules in the first instance. Consequently, an important policymaking tool has become extraordinarily cumbersome. Like formal rulemaking, section 553 informal rulemaking may soon become a little-used relic, invoked only when no less burdensome alternatives for making and communicating agency policy are legally available.

e.　Seidenfeld, "Demystifying Deossification," *supra*, at 523–24:

Critics of hard look review are on solid ground in concluding that aggressive judicial review of agency reasoning has contributed to ossification of the rulemaking process. Their assertion, however, that merely easing the standard of review will deossify this process is more tenuous. . . .

[I]ncreasing overall deference to agency rulemaking will forfeit many of the benefits of hard look review. A better approach to reforming judicial review would be to specify operational modifications to how courts perform hard look review. In particular, courts should look for signals from interested parties, the regulators themselves, and Congress about what issues raised by a challenge to a rulemaking are significant. Also, courts should hesitate to remand a rule for further development of data by the agency. If courts modified hard look review according to these criteria, they might increase the flexibility of the rulemaking process without encouraging sloppy or nondeliberative agency decision-making.

In short, what are the costs and benefits of hard look review? What are the costs and benefits of the minimum rationality approach taken in *Borden?* Is hard look review consistent with the "strong deference" to agency interpretations mandated by *Chevron?*

3. *Soft look and predictive facts.* When it rescinded Standard 208, NHTSA concluded that seat belt usage would not increase much even if automatic seat belts were mandatory. This was a prediction—nobody could know for sure. NHTSA argued that courts must accept an agency's prediction, particularly when it relied on agency expertise. Similarly, in *Borden,*

the Commissioner predicted that UFFI emissions would cause health problems for sensitive individuals.

This is an important issue, because most health, safety, and environmental regulations rely on predictions, computer modeling, extrapolations, and other techniques by which government tries to minimize risks in the face of economic or scientific uncertainty. For example, suppose high dosage of a chemical induces cancer in rats. Can an agency conclude that much lower doses will induce cancer in some humans and thus ban or restrict exposure to the chemical?

In *Baltimore Gas & Elec. Co. v. NRDC,* 462 U.S. 87 (1983), the Supreme Court upheld a rule adopted by the Nuclear Regulatory Commission which was premised on a conclusion that permanent storage of nuclear waste would have no significant environmental impact. This was a newer version of the rule considered in the *Vermont Yankee* case. As in *Vermont Yankee,* the Court of Appeals had invalidated the rule. The Supreme Court said:

> [A] reviewing court must remember that the Commission is making predictions, within its area of special expertise, at the frontiers of science. When examining this kind of scientific determination, as opposed to simple findings of fact, a reviewing court must generally be at its most deferential. *Id.* at 103.

This sounds like soft look review. Does it call for review as deferential as *Borden?* How did the majority in *State Farm* respond to NHTSA's argument that the Court must defer to its predictions of seatbelt usage?

Perhaps doubts about the judiciary's ability to cope with scientific issues have been carried too far. In the *Benzene* case, discussed in § 7.2, Justice Stevens remarked, "Some risks are plainly acceptable and others are plainly unacceptable. If, for example, the odds are one in a billion that a person will die from cancer by taking a drink of chlorinated water, the risk clearly could not be considered significant. On the other hand, if the odds are one in a thousand that regular inhalation of gasoline vapors that are two percent benzene will be fatal, a reasonable person might well consider the risk significant and take appropriate steps to decrease or eliminate it." *Industrial Union Dep't, AFL–CIO v. American Petroleum Institute,* 448 U.S. 607, 655 (1980). That seems reasonable enough, doesn't it? *See* McGarity, *supra,* at 1402 n.74.

4. *Judicial remedy.* In *Motor Vehicle,* the Court ordered the lower court to remand the case to NHTSA "for further consideration." This approach left the suspension of Standard 208 in effect and, at least in theory, permits NHTSA to supply the missing analysis and readopt the rescission. Another possible remedy is to vacate the rule, which would require the agency to start over. Which remedy to employ (remanding or vacating) appears to be within the discretion of the reviewing court. The courts consider such factors as the extent to which vacating the rule would cause disruption or disappoint reliance interests.

In *Checkosky v. SEC,* 23 F.3d 452 (D.C.Cir.1994), the court split sharply over whether the court has the power to remand agency action without vacating it. The dissenting judge claimed that remanding is contrary to the APA which requires the court—in the absence of any contrary statute—to vacate the agency's action. ... Section 706(2)(A) provides that a "reviewing court" faced with an arbitrary and capricious agency decision "shall"—*not may*—"hold unlawful and set aside" the agency action. Setting aside means vacating; no other meaning is apparent.

For a critique of that view, see Ronald M. Levin, " 'Vacation' at Sea: Judicial Remands and the APA," Admin. & Reg.L. News, Spring 1996, at 4.

5. *Substantial evidence v. arbitrary and capricious.* Recall that the legislative history of the Motor Vehicle Safety Act (construed in *Motor Vehicle*) said that the findings of the agency must be supported by "substantial evidence on the record considered as a whole." However, the statute itself called only for arbitrary and capricious review and the Court makes nothing of the difference. Yet it would be hard to imagine more searching review than the *Motor Vehicle* decision, regardless of what test was employed.

In a number of other statutes, Congress has explicitly called for substantial evidence judicial review of legislative rules. For example, occupational safety and health standards adopted by OSHA must be supported by substantial evidence. 29 U.S.C. § 655(f).

The substantial evidence test ordinarily applies to formal adjudication or formal rulemaking—proceedings at which evidence is taken in a trial-type setting and the decision-maker considers only material in the record. This is not true of many decisions reviewed under the arbitrary and capricious test; often there has been no hearing (formal or informal) or any opportunity to examine and rebut materials considered by the decision-maker. Yet all of those materials constitute the record for purposes of judicial review.

Probably, judicial review of rules under a substantial evidence standard is no different than under an arbitrary and capricious standard. Both standards call for reasonableness review and both require that there be a sufficient factual basis in the record (however that record is assembled) for the result reached by the agency. *See Association of Data Processing Service Orgs. v. Board of Governors, Fed. Reserve Sys.,* 745 F.2d 677, 680–86 (D.C.Cir.1984); Matthew J. McGrath, Note, "Convergence of the Substantial Evidence and Arbitrary and Capricious Standards of Review During Informal Rulemaking," 54 Geo.Wash.L.Rev. 541 (1986).

However, there is a conflicting view: when Congress deliberately calls for substantial evidence review, it intends more rigorous judicial scrutiny than would occur under the arbitrary and capricious test. For example, in a case reviewing health standards set by OSHA for hazardous workplace chemicals, the Eleventh Circuit said:

Under this [substantial evidence] test, we must take a harder look at OSHA's action than we would if we were reviewing the action under the more deferential arbitrary and capricious standard applicable to agencies governed by the [APA]. ... The substantial evidence test applies to review of policy decisions as well as factual determinations, even though policy decisions are not so susceptible to verification or refutation by the record. In setting an element of the standard, OSHA must demonstrate substantial evidence for all matters of determinable fact and, on matters having no possible basis in determinable fact, must explain the relevant considerations on which it relied and its reasons for rejecting alternate views. OSHA's policy decisions must be: (1) consistent with the language and purpose of the OSH Act, and (2) reasonable under the rulemaking record. *AFL–CIO v. OSHA*, 965 F.2d 962 (11th Cir.1992).

6. *State law review of discretionary action. Borden* represents the traditional, extremely deferential approach taken by many states in the review of agency rules. It requires that a rule be upheld if there was a conceivable basis for the agency's decision, with the burden on the challenger to demonstrate the lack of any such basis. Under this model, the agency is not required to explain the rule at the time it was adopted. In meeting the challenge, the agency is not limited to the evidence that it considered at the time it adopted the rule.

However, many states have moved much closer to the federal model, although few have embraced true hard look review. For example, *Liberty Homes, Inc. v. Dep't of Industry*, 401 N.W.2d 805 (Wis.1987), involved a rule similar to the one reviewed in *Borden*: it prohibited concentrations of formaldehyde over .4 ppm in mobile homes. The court noted that it would not presume the presence of facts supporting the rule. Instead, it would apply the arbitrary and capricious test by asking whether, based on facts in the record, the agency could reasonably have concluded that the rule would effectuate the legitimate governmental objective it is directed to implement. The record consisted both of materials considered by the agency and additional materials introduced by either side in the trial court. Thus the court exercised review for rationality, but not necessarily hard look review. Ultimately, it upheld the rule.

The *Liberty Homes* court rejected the contention that its task in reviewing a regulation was the same as in reviewing a statute. It noted:

> Although agency rules have the full force and effect of legislative enactments, these rules do not receive the active scrutiny by the legislature that bills receive. A rule does not require approval by a majority of both houses of the legislature and the governor. To the contrary the process for legislative review of agency rules provides for final approval of the rule by legislative inaction. The process of agency rulemaking though admittedly a very public process, is nevertheless a delegated process. For these reasons we believe that the courts should not presume conceivable facts to sustain agency rulemaking. The court must look at the record to determine whether the rule is reasonably related to a legitimate governmental objective.

The 1961 MSAPA, § 15(g)(6), allowed a court to reverse if administrative decisions were "arbitrary or capricious or characterized by abuse of discretion or clearly unwarranted exercise of discretion." This section, especially the last clause, appeared to call for a fairly hard look. However, it applied only to review of "contested cases"—essentially adjudication.

The 1981 MSAPA covers judicial review of all "agency action." Sec. 5–116(c) reflects serious misgivings on the part of its drafters about hard look review of discretionary action. It provides some specific bases for judicial reversal (*see* §§ (c)(7) and (c)(8)(i), (ii), (iii)). It then *brackets* the language "otherwise unreasonable, arbitrary or capricious." The effect of bracketing the language is to offer states the option of omitting the language. The drafters explain:

> Without the bracketed language, this paragraph provides a more limited judicial role than the 1961 Model Act. The intent of this limitation is to discourage reviewing courts from substituting their judgment for that of the agency as to the wisdom or desirability of the agency action under review.

See Donald W. Brodie & Hans A. Linde, "State Court Review of Administrative Action: Prescribing the Scope of Review," 1977 Ariz.St.L.J. 537, 553–60 (describing omission of "accordion-like" epithets arbitrary, capricious and abuse from Florida APA). Did the drafters of 1981 MSAPA opt for the *State Farm* model, the *Borden* model, or something in between?

7. *Problem.* By statute, OSHA must set reasonably necessary and feasible standards for exposure of workers to toxic chemicals at a level that assures that no employee will suffer material impairment of health. The statute also provides that OSHA standards must be sustained if supported by substantial evidence in the record considered as a whole.

Ethylene oxide (EtO) is a hazardous chemical used to sterilize hospital instruments. In 1971, OSHA adopted a standard that workers must not be exposed to more than 50 parts per million (ppm) of EtO averaged over a workday. Since 1971, there has been increasing (though inconclusive) evidence that EtO causes cancer and spontaneous abortion. Last year, after a lengthy notice and comment proceeding, OSHA found that any exposure to EtO presented a significant health risk; it set an exposure limit of 1 ppm averaged over a workday. Compliance with this standard will cost hospitals many millions of dollars over the next few years. A standard of 5 ppm would save the industry 85% of those costs.

OSHA relied on several studies in support of the standard. According to the Hogstedt study, there were 3 deaths from leukemia at a Swedish hospital out of 230 workers (all exposed to significant EtO) when only 0.2 deaths would normally be expected in a similar group. The Bushy Run study indicated that rats exposed to 100 ppm of EtO every day for a year developed various cancers; rats exposed to 60 ppm developed fewer cancers. However, the rats also developed a severe viral ailment during the study. The Hemminki study indicated that nurses exposed to EtO while pregnant reported on questionnaires that they had a higher rate of spontaneous abortion than a control group. However, the nurses studied knew the purpose of the questionnaire was to test the effects of EtO on pregnant women.

The level of 1 ppm was set by extrapolating the results of the Bushy Run study to humans by making a series of mathematical assumptions. OSHA found that there would be between 12 and 23 additional cancer deaths even at a level of 1 ppm, but it found that it was not technically or economically feasible to set a zero tolerance.

At the same time it originally proposed the 1 ppm limit for exposure to EtO averaged over a workday, OSHA also proposed a short-term exposure limit (STEL)—that no single exposure to EtO could exceed 10 ppm, no matter how brief. The Office of Management and Budget objected to the STEL (on the grounds of excessive cost and lack of benefit), and OSHA decided not to adopt any STEL. Its stated reason was that the 1 ppm limit offered sufficient protection, especially because it would induce hospitals to lower short-term exposures so as to meet the eight-hour average.

Industry groups seek review of the 1 ppm standard. Public interest groups seek review of the decision not to adopt a STEL. What should the court decide? *See Public Citizen Health Research Group v. Tyson,* 796 F.2d 1479 (D.C.Cir.1986).

Chapter 10

REMEDIES AND REVIEWABILITY
OF AGENCY DECISIONS

The previous chapter made clear the indispensable role of judicial review in controlling illegal or unwarranted agency action—but it also demonstrated that limitations on the scope of review restrain courts from substituting their judgment for the judgment of agencies.

The next two chapters concern additional limitations on judicial review. Chapter 10 begins with a treatment of judicial procedure: jurisdiction to review agency action and the availability of and limitations on judicial remedies. It then considers two additional remedies: damage actions against an official or against an agency and recovery of attorney fees from an agency. It concludes with doctrines which make agency action unreviewable: preclusion of review and commitment to agency discretion. Chapter 11 considers problems of standing—whether a particular plaintiff can challenge agency action—and timing—whether judicial review is premature.

Of course, quite apart from these legalistic limits on review, judicial review may be useless for practical reasons. Judicial review means hiring lawyers, and a great deal must be at stake to justify the costs of paying counsel in what may well be a losing enterprise. Moreover, obtaining judicial relief is likely to take a long time; litigants must take their turn in an ever-lengthening queue. Besides, the harm from the agency's action may already be done and it may be irremediable. Once a person is out of business or a product has been banned, it may be impossible ever to start up again, regardless of what a court might say. Even if review is successful, the remedy may be a remand to the agency which may take the same action for different reasons, thus starting the process anew. Also, quite often, it may be imprudent to antagonize an agency with which a litigant must continue to live and be regulated by. In short, it is often better to accept an unfavorable result and move on than undergo years of costly struggle and uncertainty.

As you consider judicial review from the point of view of a private client who feels wronged by agency action, the many limitations on review may seem frustratingly technical. However, there is another side to this coin, for judicial interference with agencies has significant systemic costs as well as benefits. Judicial review, particularly of complex agency action or of legislative rules, can consume enormous resources, particularly the time and energy of judges that could be used for other matters. It can greatly congest appellate dockets, thus exacerbating an already serious problem. And the public interest is not always served by the substitution of a less-informed judicial view for a better-informed agency view.

Consider also the balance of resources: we often think of an ordinary person (say a taxpayer, welfare recipient, or professional licensee) up against a huge, unfeeling bureaucracy. But sometimes the balance is quite different. The private party may be a Fortune 500 corporation with virtually unlimited resources that can be deployed to prevent or at least delay unfavorable agency action. Judicial review can be a very costly process for the agency as well as its opponent and it can take a long time; during that time, the private litigant may be able to continue polluting or selling a product that harms the public. Or, during the review process, plans to build a highway, a dam, a shopping mall or a nuclear power plant can be sidetracked indefinitely or even killed by delays and rising construction costs during the appeal period. Perhaps the projects should not be built, but the decision should not be a function of whether tenacious opponents can litigate them to death.

Indeed, an agency may be hopelessly overloaded with regulatory chores and operating under severe budget constraints which prevent it from hiring sufficient staff, or sufficiently skillful and experienced staff, to discharge its responsibilities. Thus, rather than defend a completely justified action in court, it may feel compelled to settle the case unfavorably or give up entirely. Beware of accepting claims that more judicial review is always a good thing and should be encouraged without reservation.

§ 10.1 JUDICIAL REMEDIES

In order to seek the assistance of a court in reviewing agency action, counsel must confront the basics:

(i) the chosen court must have jurisdiction to hear the case, and

(ii) plaintiff must plead a recognized cause of action and seek a recognized remedy that provides the needed relief.

We consider these hurdles in turn.

§ 10.1.1 JUDICIAL JURISDICTION

a. *Explicit statutory review procedure.* The statute that creates an agency often explicitly lays out the road to judicial review of its actions—what court has jurisdiction, who can seek review, time limits for seeking review, and so on. Ordinarily, when a statute prescribes a review procedure, that procedure is exclusive, and no other route can be pursued.

The clear trend at the federal level is to lodge responsibility for statutory review of rules and final orders in appellate, not in trial courts. In most states, however, judicial review typically begins at the trial court level. *See* 1961 MSAPA § 7, 15(b). The 1981 MSAPA, § 5–104, gives states a choice in this regard—Alternative A provides for venue in a trial court while Alternative B provides for venue in an appellate court.

Unfortunately, statutes are not always clear about where a particular agency action should be reviewed, and courts have had to struggle with numerous disputes about whether an appeal was filed in the proper court. In construing ambiguous review statutes, courts often prefer appellate court, not trial court, review unless there is a need for additional evidence to be taken, in which case a trial court is preferred.

There are some persuasive reasons for preferring appellate court review. Judicial review is, after all, an appellate function; appellate judges may be better at it than trial judges, who are accustomed to deciding matters de novo. In general, appellate judges are likely to be more experienced and, on the whole, better qualified than trial judges, to decide issues with important public policy dimensions. The waiting line may be shorter at the appellate than at the trial court level. More important, the matter may well be appealed anyway; why not save the cost and delay of an unnecessary trial court proceeding?

On the other hand, if the class of matters produces a great many appeals, involving relatively small amounts of money and seldom raising significant legal questions, it may be better to place them in trial, rather than appellate courts. This conserves the scarce time of appellate court judges (remember, cases at the appellate level are typically considered by panels of three or five judges, whereas trial court judges work alone). In addition, it may be more convenient for litigants to go to court in their home town than in the state capital or some other distant city. Thus social security disability and retirement cases are reviewed in federal district court. There are a vast number of these cases, and the decision to place them in trial courts seems sensible.

If the particular review function requires a court to receive testimony, a trial court is more appropriate than an appellate court. For example, § 9.1 noted that some action is reviewed de novo; if that entails a retrial, a trial court is the best place to do it. Also, review of administrative rules or orders sometimes occurs in the context of a judicial enforcement action against a private party who has violated the rule or order; enforcement actions typically occur in a trial court.

Sometimes, in the course of reviewing a case, an appellate court finds that the record is inadequate and that additional evidence must be taken. In some circumstances, the appellate court can take the evidence itself. *See* 1981 MSAPA § 5–114(a). That provision allows an appellate court to take evidence, assisted by a referee, master, or trial court judge, with respect to facts which would not appear in the record—such as improper qualification, bias or motives of the decisionmakers, or unlawfulness of the agency procedure.

More often, however, an appellate court will not receive the additional evidence itself but will remand to the agency (or in some circumstances to a trial court) to amplify the record. *See, e.g.,* 28 U.S.C. § 2347(b) and (c) (applicable to review of orders of the FCC, FMC, ICC, NRC and several other agencies); 1981 MSAPA § 5–114(b). Thus, the possibility that additional evidence might be needed does not, in itself, require that a trial court conduct judicial review.

b. *Administrative procedure statutes.* Many states have adopted statutes specifically conferring jurisdiction on particular courts to review some or all agency actions. For example, New York law (Civil Practice Law and Rules Art. 78) provides for a proceeding against a body or officer to take the place of certiorari, mandamus, and prohibition; it is commenced in a trial court and, if it entails review of formal adjudication, is transferred to an appellate court. California Code of Civ.Proc. § 1094.5, considered in § 9.1.2, also lodges responsibility for review of all agency adjudication in trial courts.

The 1961 MSAPA provided for judicial review of "contested cases" by filing a petition in a trial court. It also provided for review of the validity or applicability of a rule by an action for declaratory judgment in a trial court. However, it provided no guidance on review of other kinds of agency action (such as informal adjudication) and it did not cover local agencies. The 1981 MSAPA is more comprehensive. It states: "This Act establishes the exclusive means of judicial review of agency action ..." § 5–101. Review is obtained by filing a petition in the appropriate court. § 5–104. However, the 1981 MSAPA covers only state, not local agencies. § 1–102(1). Thus even where the 1961 or 1981 MSAPA has been adopted, counsel must still resort to other law to obtain judicial review of local action.

c. *No explicit statutory review procedure.* If there is no explicit statute concerning judicial review of particular agency action or of agency action in general, a private litigant must file a civil action against the agency or the official who invaded the person's legal rights. The ordinary rules about jurisdiction and venue are applicable to such cases.

Federal district courts have jurisdiction to conduct judicial review of agency action under:

> i. 28 U.S.C. § 1331, which covers actions "arising under the Constitution, laws, or treaties of the United States." For most purposes, this section is adequate to provide for jurisdiction to review the actions of any federal agency or official in a federal district court.

> ii. 28 U.S.C. § 1361, which gives district courts jurisdiction of "any action in the nature of mandamus to compel an officer or employee of the United States or any agency thereof to perform a duty owed to the plaintiff."

iii. 28 U.S.C. § 1343(3) which provides jurisdiction to hear cases under 42 U.S.C. § 1983 and other federal civil rights statutes. Section 1983 actions provide a remedy against *state* officials who have subjected persons to deprivation of constitutional rights. We consider section 1983 actions in § 10.2.

In years past, section 1331 was unavailable unless the "amount in controversy" exceeded $10,000; sometimes it was difficult to decide whether various kinds of intangible claims met that test. The $10,000 limit was deleted in 1976 with respect to judicial review of federal agency action; it was deleted with respect to all federal question cases in 1980. Whether plaintiff should proceed under § 1361 for mandamus is a distinct question postponed to later discussion.

In prior years, the doctrine of sovereign immunity sometimes barred the courthouse door. This doctrine immunized the United States from being sued without its consent. Consequently, a litigant seeking non-statutory judicial review of agency action had to sue a federal official instead of the agency itself. Such actions were permitted only if the official acted under an unconstitutional statute or was acting outside the powers conferred by statute. *See, e.g., Larson v. Domestic & Foreign Commerce Corp.,* 337 U.S. 682 (1949).

The confusion and serious injustices resulting from the doctrine of sovereign immunity led Congress to abolish it in 1976. *See* APA §§ 702 (all material after the first sentence) and 703 (middle sentence). Note, however, that the 1976 waiver of sovereign immunity applies only to actions "seeking relief other than money damages." We consider the narrower waiver of immunity in suits for money damages in § 10.2.

In an action seeking judicial review of federal agency action under section 1331, the plaintiff may choose to sue in any judicial district where a defendant resides, or the cause of action arose, or any real property involved in the action is situated, or the plaintiff resides (if no real property is involved). 28 U.S.C. § 1391(e). The defendant is the United States, the agency by its official title, or the appropriate officer. APA § 703; Fed.R.Civ.Proc. 25(d)(2).

Once federal jurisdiction under section 1331 is established, the federal APA comes into play. Sections 701 to 706 establish the parameters for judicial review: what action is reviewable, who can seek review, when can it be sought, what are the court's powers, what is the scope of review. The APA does not itself provide for federal jurisdiction; it provides the ground rules for review once jurisdiction is otherwise established. *Califano v. Sanders,* 430 U.S. 99 (1977).

d. *Removal to federal court. City of Chicago v. International College of Surgeons,* 118 S.Ct. 523 (1997), concerned a typical local land use dispute—whether an owner can demolish a building designated as a historic landmark. The owner lost before the Chicago Landmarks Commission and sought judicial review in an Illinois trial court. It argued that the Commission's decision was not supported by the evidence in the record. It also raised a series of statutory arguments as well as federal constitutional claims. The City then removed the case to federal court. By a 7–2 majority, the Supreme Court held that removal was proper.

The Court reasoned that removal is proper if a case could have been filed in federal court in the first place. This case could have been filed in federal court because the constitutional claims create a federal question; the state law claims, including review of the factual conclusions, can be performed by the federal court under its power to hear supplemental state claims. The fact that the court would be called upon to exercise an appellate function (reviewing the agency's findings of fact under a deferential review standard) makes no difference.

Normally, government defendants would not seek to remove a case to federal court; they would typically perceive a "home court" advantage if cases are heard in the state court system. However, the *City of Chicago* case at least implies that the owner of the building could have *initially* sought judicial review of the local agency's action in the federal court rather than the state court. That might be quite an attractive option for those private parties who can articulate substantial constitutional claims in addition to state administrative law claims. They might well feel that they would get a better shake in the federal than in the state courts.

The majority opinion in *City of Chicago* suggests that federal courts have discretion to refuse to hear cases originating in state or local administrative agencies under the flexible provisions of the supplemental jurisdiction statute. 28 U.S.C. § 1367(c). Alternatively, such cases might be dismissed or stayed under one of a series of abstention doctrines. How these protective doctrines will be applied remains to be seen. Thus it is unclear whether *City of Chicago* will result in shifting a large number of judicial review cases from state to federal courts.

Contrary to what might be expected, the two dissenters in *City of Chicago* were not conservative justices seeking to exclude cases from the federal courts. Instead, the dissent was written by Justice Ginsburg, with Justice Stevens concurring. They argued that Congress could not possibly have intended to permit removal in such cases. In addition, the dissent argued:

> Just last term, two Members of today's majority recognized the vital interest States have in developing and elaborating state administrative law, for that law regulates the citizen's contact with state and local government at every turn, for example, in gaining life-sustaining public benefits, obtaining a license or, as in this case, receiving a permit. Last Term's lead opinion observed:
>
> > In the states there is an ongoing process by which state courts and state agencies work to elaborate an administrative law designed to reflect the State's own rules and traditions concerning the respective scope of judicial review and administrative discretion. ... [T]he elaboration of administrative law ... is one of the primary responsibilities of the state judiciary. ... *Idaho v. Coeur d'Alene Tribe of Idaho,* [117 S.Ct. 2028] (1997).

Today's decision jeopardizes the "strong interest" courts of the State have in controlling the actions of local as well as state agencies. State court superintendence can now be displaced or dislodged in any case against a local agency in which the parties are of diverse citizenship and in any case in which a Fourteenth Amendment plea can be made.

Id. at 539–40 (Ginsburg, J., concurring).

§ 10.1.2 CAUSE OF ACTION AND REMEDY

If the party seeking review proceeds under a statute specific to the agency, that statute establishes the ground rules for judicial review and may set forth some or all of the available remedies. If an administrative procedure statute is applicable, that statute too will set forth at least some of the parameters of judicial review. Generally, such statutes are vague about available remedies and they must be understood in light of existing procedural and remedial law. *See* APA § 703; 1981 MSAPA § 5–117(b).

If there is no statute specific to the agency or no applicable administrative procedure statute, a plaintiff must state a claim for relief in a trial court under other state or federal law. This subchapter is concerned largely with non-monetary relief—an order that an agency should do something, or not do something, as opposed to an order for the payment of money. The problems of seeking monetary damages are addressed in § 10.2.

As so often occurs in the law, the problem of cause of action and remedy are inextricably mixed. Therefore, it is convenient to consider substance and procedure together by examining the remedies which a plaintiff might seek in an action for judicial review.

§ 10.1.2a Injunction and Declaratory Judgment

Generally the most useful remedies, and those least encumbered by technicalities, are injunction and declaratory judgment. For all practical purposes, these are the same—it does not matter whether plaintiff seeks a *declaration* that agency action is illegal or an *injunction* ordering the agency to take action or refrain from taking action. One caution, however: if the plaintiff seeks a mandatory injunction (*i.e.* ordering the agency to do something as opposed to stop doing something), the court may treat the action as one for *mandamus*—which brings in its wake a series of complexities that are treated below.

Injunction as an administrative remedy has long been recognized in federal court. For example, in the famous case of *American School of Magnetic Healing v. McAnnulty*, 187 U.S. 94 (1902), the plaintiff sought relief from an order by the post office cutting off its mail because of fraud. Previous Supreme Court decisions had ruled that common law writs like mandamus and certiorari were not available in federal court (see below). No problem: the Supreme Court held that plaintiff could obtain an injunction requiring the post office to deliver its mail, assum-

ing that plaintiff sufficiently established that the fraud order was erroneous.

Both injunction and declaratory judgment are equitable remedies
and thus *discretionary*. If a court believes that an injunction or declaration against the government would cause harm to the public that
outweighs the benefit to the plaintiff, or the remedies are for some other
reason inappropriate, it can refuse to grant relief.

In many states, a plaintiff must pursue other remedies at law if they
are available, such as the "extraordinary" or "prerogative" writs of
mandamus, certiorari or prohibition (discussed below). In those states,
injunction and declaratory judgment are unavailable whenever the prerogative writs might be used. This sometimes results in "Catch 22"
situations in which cases are dismissed because litigants sought the
wrong remedy. The better approach, of course, is to freely permit
amendment of the pleadings so that a plaintiff is not penalized for
selecting the wrong cause of action.

In federal courts, the extraordinary writs (perhaps fortunately) were
generally unavailable; thus injunction and declaratory judgment became
the remedies of choice, as they remain today. Thus the flexible "equity"
tradition prevailed, not the typically inflexible traditions associated with
prerogative writs.

§ 10.1.2b Mandamus

American courts inherited the prerogative writs from English jurisprudence; each writ developed separately in the English courts to enable
the judges to look into and correct a particular injustice and each had its
own peculiar limitations. The writs became generally available in the
United States to review administrative action, but courts often preserved
the rigid body of rules relating to each writ. Sometimes they have done
so even though a statute purports to dispense with the writs in favor of a
new administrative review petition.

The various rules relating to prerogative writs became the subject of
extensive litigation in every state. As a result, each state has its own
body of statutes and confusing case law relating to these writs; precedents from one state, or from the federal system, are largely worthless
elsewhere.

The usual use of mandamus in administrative law is to compel
("mandate") action which an agency refuses to take—for example, to
issue a license, grant a zoning variance, pay a claim, hold a hearing.
However, in some states the writ is used much more broadly. In
California, for instance, mandamus is used to review rules and formal
adjudication as well.

In many states, a mandamus plaintiff must show that the defendant
owes a "clear legal duty" to plaintiff and that the desired action is
"ministerial" rather than "discretionary." The law of mandamus is
haunted by the need to distinguish ministerial and discretionary acts. In

addition, mandamus is available only if a plaintiff has no other adequate remedy. In some states, as in Illinois, the writ will correct abuse of discretion. Even if the other requirements are met, a court can decline to issue the writ in its discretion (if, for example, the harm to government outweighs the benefit to plaintiff).

A court which wants to dispel rather than create confusion should not jump to the conclusion that a duty is "discretionary" or that it is "unclear" and thus dismiss the case out of hand. Instead, the court should interpret the relevant law—whether it is clear or unclear—to establish the precise scope of agency discretion. *See, e.g., 13th Regional Corp. v. U.S. Dept. of Interior,* 654 F.2d 758 (D.C.Cir.1980) (construing statute to find the duty to make a study was ministerial—but denying mandamus on the equitable ground of plaintiff's laches). In § 9.4, this process was called "chalking in the boundary line" of discretion. This process may reveal that the action taken is not within the scope of delegated authority or that the agency took account of an improper factor (or failed to consider an appropriate factor). If discretionary action thus turns out to be legally improper, plaintiff should be entitled to mandamus.

After deciding that action is within the scope of discretion, the court should then ask whether there has been an abuse of discretion. In other words, it should apply the arbitrary and capricious analysis discussed in § 9.4. However, many states refuse to review for abuse of discretion in mandamus cases.

A typical mandamus case comes to court without a formal evidentiary record. The court has discretion to receive additional evidence from either side in order to assemble an adequate record for its decision (or, in many states, a jury's decision). Often, the court must reconsider agency findings of fact (as well as conclusions of law or discretion). State law varies as to whether the courts simply accept agency factual conclusions, apply the substantial evidence test, or retry the facts for themselves.

Mandamus in the federal courts began auspiciously with *Marbury v. Madison,* 5 U.S. (1 Cranch) 137 (1803). In *Marbury,* the Supreme Court held that mandamus would lie to require Madison to issue Marbury his judicial commission (but only in an inferior court—not by an original action in the Supreme Court). Soon thereafter, the Court held that federal courts outside the District of Columbia could not issue mandamus. *McIntire v. Wood,* 11 U.S. (7 Cranch) 504 (1813); *Kendall v. United States ex rel. Stokes,* 37 U.S. (12 Pet.) 524 (1838).

Federal courts outside the District evaded this limitation by issuing injunctions which were prohibitory in form but mandatory in effect, as in *American School of Magnetic Healing v. McAnnulty,* discussed above (enjoining local postmaster from refusing to deliver plaintiff's mail). The equity tradition made it possible to provide flexible and adequate relief, even if it was affirmative in character. However, other courts held that the mandamus tradition prevailed even though plaintiff sought an injunction instead of mandamus.

The inability of federal courts outside the District to issue mandamus changed in 1962 with the enactment of 28 U.S.C. § 1361, which provides: "The district courts shall have original jurisdiction of any action in the nature of mandamus to compel an officer or employee of the United States or any agency thereof to perform a duty owed to the plaintiff." Thus plaintiffs often seek mandamus in federal district court. Unfortunately, many courts still feel compelled to wander into the ministerial/discretionary swamp or to search for a "clear duty." Sometimes, the federal courts in § 1361 cases have refused to decide questions of law about the scope of discretion.

So far, the Supreme Court has not had occasion to decide whether mandamus under § 1361 (or, for that matter, mandatory injunctions) are still inhibited by restrictive mandamus tradition. See, however, *American Cetacean Soc. v. Baldrige,* 768 F.2d 426, 433–34 (D.C.Cir. 1985), *rev'd on other grounds,* 478 U.S. 221 (1986), treating an action for mandamus the same as one for injunction and declaratory judgment and reviewing the decision under the APA.

Generally, counsel are well advised not to sue under § 1361 but to seek an injunction and declaratory judgment under § 1331 instead. It should not matter whether the desired relief is affirmative or negative. After all, § 706(1) of the APA clearly provides that a court can "compel agency action unlawfully withheld." Under these circumstances, there seems little to be gained by suing under § 1361—and quite a bit to be lost.

§ 10.1.2c Certiorari

At common law, certiorari was a writ directed to an inferior tribunal (which could be a court or an administrative body) which required that the latter certify a copy of the record and convey it to the reviewing court. Review lay only for absence of jurisdiction or for an error of law that appeared on the face of the record.

Certiorari is designed to provide judicial review of action of a *judicial* character based upon a hearing on the record. Indeed certiorari was the model for judicial review of adjudication spelled out in the 1961 and 1981 MSAPA's. Despite a proliferation of state statutes providing for judicial review, certiorari remains important in many states, particularly in reviewing decisions of local agencies or school boards.

Traditionally, certiorari could be used to review only "judicial" action, meaning functions that had been historically performed by judges (or at least action taken after a trial-type hearing). It was not available to review action of a "legislative" or "administrative" nature. Needless to say, these categories are difficult to distinguish and the lawbooks contain a large body of formalistic decisions struggling with the distinction. *See* 3 Kenneth Culp Davis, ADMINISTRATIVE LAW TREATISE § 24.02 (1958) (later editions of this treatise do not pursue the subject); Louis L. Jaffe, JUDICIAL CONTROL OF ADMINISTRATIVE ACTION 169–73 (1965).

The scope of review available in a certiorari action varies from state to state. Generally, the court reviews the case strictly on the record; it does not receive additional evidence. At the other extreme, some states cling to the historically narrow scope of review: lack of jurisdiction or errors of law on the face of the record and no review of factual determinations. Most states are probably in between: in addition to errors of law, a court considers whether the agency action was arbitrary and capricious or completely lacking in factual support in the record. *See Yerardi's Moody Street Restaurant v. Board of Selectmen,* 473 N.E.2d 1154 (Mass.App.1985).

In an early decision, the Supreme Court held that *federal* courts could not grant certiorari to review a fraud order by the post office. *Degge v. Hitchcock,* 229 U.S. 162 (1913). As a result, injunction and declaratory judgment emerged to fill the gap—remedies happily free of the ancient restrictions on certiorari.

§ 10.1.2d Other Writs

A few other common law writs have utility as forms of judicial review of administrative action. Prohibition lies to prevent an inferior judicial body (including an agency) from initiating a case over which it lacks jurisdiction. Quo warranto is used to test the right to an office. Habeas corpus has been used to review orders relating to the confinement of aliens or mentally ill persons. It has also been used to review decisions which interfere with the liberty of a member of the military (such as a refusal to discharge the member).

§ 10.2 DAMAGE ACTIONS AS A FORM OF JUDICIAL REVIEW

The discussion of remedies in § 10.1 concentrated on non-monetary remedies, such as statutory forms of judicial review and non-statutory writs such as mandamus, injunction or declaratory judgment. This subchapter, which considers damage actions against officials or against government as a form of relief, could be entitled "public torts."

Tort actions are an important administrative law remedy. It may be that a private individual has already been harmed by a government official; damages are the only remedy that would make any difference. In addition, there are certain kinds of illegal government action (such as negligent infliction of economic or physical harm) that are inevitable byproducts of government activity but could not be prevented by any form of prospective relief. Again, money damages are the only effective remedy. In other situations, damages are a plausible alternative to trial-type hearings required by procedural due process: perhaps it is better to pay damages to the victims of government errors than to require government always to provide hearings before it acts. Finally, the existence of a tort remedy may serve as a potent deterrent against illegal government action.

The subject of common law and constitutional torts committed by government officials has grown enormously in recent years. Complex statutes govern many aspects of the problem. Courses in torts and civil rights cover much of the ground. Therefore, this chapter is intended largely as a survey which will omit many important details. It will, however, highlight some particularly contentious issues, focussing on damage remedies as a form of review of agency action.

§ 10.2.1   TORT LIABILITY OF GOVERNMENT

Historically, the doctrine of sovereign immunity protected government from liability unless it consented to be sued. But government has often consented to be sued for money damages.

§ 10.2.1a   The Federal Tort Claims Act

In 1946 Congress abolished the federal government's traditional immunity from tort liability. The Federal Tort Claims Act, 28 U.S.C. §§ 1346(b) and 2671–80 ("FTCA") makes government liable for the wrongful acts of its employees committed within the scope of their employment. Broadly speaking, the federal government is vicariously liable in tort if a private employer would be liable under state law.

However, some special rules distinguish the government from other employers.

i.   *Intentional torts.* Under a 1974 amendment to the FTCA, the government is liable for injuries arising out of assault, battery, false imprisonment, false arrest, abuse of process, or malicious prosecution, if these torts were committed by federal investigative or law enforcement officers. § 2680(h). The government is liable for other intentional torts such as trespass or conversion, but not for defamation, misrepresentation, or interference with contract rights.

ii.   *Discretionary functions.* The most important FTCA exemption immunizes the government from damages for any claim "based upon the exercise or performance or the failure to exercise or perform a discretionary function or duty on the part of a federal agency or an employee of the Government, whether or not the discretion involved be abused." § 2680(a). Although the Supreme Court has addressed the discretionary function exception on several occasions, it remains difficult to apply to concrete situations.

High-level policy judgments about how to implement a regulatory program fall within the discretionary function exception. The more difficult problem is whether actions taken in carrying out regulatory programs are discretionary functions. The key issue is whether the action in question involves the "permissible exercise of policy judgment." *Berkovitz v. United States,* 486 U.S. 531 (1988). If the action in question is not permissible under a statute or regulation, obviously it involved no choice and could not be a discretionary function. Even if the action did involve some judgment, it would not be a discretionary function unless the judgment involved the application of policy. The

Berkovitz case makes clear that government can be liable even though the action in question arises out of a regulatory program (in that case, the licensing of polio vaccine).

§ 10.2.1b   State and Local Government Liability

In considering the liability of state and local government for damages, it is necessary to separate the question of liability in state court from the question of liability in federal court.

Looking first to state courts: Traditionally, state government was completely immune from tort liability. Local government was immune from actions for damages arising out of "governmental" functions but liable for claims arising out of "proprietary" functions. Sometimes the governmental/proprietary distinction was changed into a discretionary/ministerial distinction (similar to that in the FTCA). Although it is easy to classify many functions as either "governmental" or "proprietary" (it is "governmental" to fight fires, "proprietary" to operate a bus company), the distinction gave rise to a vast and confusing body of case law. The governmental/proprietary distinction was rejected by the United States Supreme Court in construing the discretionary function exception of the FTCA. *Indian Towing Co. v. United States,* 350 U.S. 61 (1955).

For the most part, state legislatures refused to consent to suit, despite the enormous injustice caused by governmental tort immunity. However, pioneering state supreme court decisions abolished governmental immunity in many states. *See Muskopf v. Corning Hospital Dist.,* 359 P.2d 457 (Cal.1961). This forced legislatures to act. In the great majority of states (around 40), state and local government is now vicariously liable for most torts committed by government employees. In some states, there is a cap on liability (apparently to limit exposure of the state to judgments in excess of insurance policies) and there may be exemptions (such as one for discretionary functions) comparable to those in FTCA. As under the FTCA, courts and legislatures struggle to define the circumstances in which government is different from the private sector and thus to carve out some remaining sphere of immunity. *See, e.g., Commonwealth of Kentucky, Dep't of Banking & Securities v. Brown,* 605 S.W.2d 497 (Ky.1980) (state not liable for negligence of bank examiners in failing to detect bank fraud, since bank auditing has no private sector counterpart).

Looking now to damage actions against a state government entity in *federal court*: the eleventh amendment deprives federal courts of jurisdiction over suits against a state (whether by citizens of that state or of a different state). The eleventh amendment does not provide immunity to local government entities—only to states. *Mt. Healthy City School Dist. v. Doyle,* 429 U.S. 274 (1977).

The eleventh amendment does not preclude *injunctive* relief against a state *official* whose authority is based upon an unconstitutional statute (or whose action is otherwise contrary to federal law), even though the effect is to prevent the official from carrying out state law. *Ex parte Young,* 209 U.S. 123 (1908). Nor does it preclude, in most cases, actions against officials in their *individual* capacity (discussed below).

The eleventh amendment can be overridden by later constitutional amendments. Thus, a statute passed under the authority of the fourteenth amendment can impose damage liability on states if Congress explicitly makes states liable. *Atascadero State Hospital v. Scanlon,* 473 U.S. 234 (1985) (state not liable for damages under Rehabilitation Act of 1973, authorizing suits by handicapped victims of discrimination, because Congress did not explicitly authorize actions against states). The *Atascadero* case also held that a state does not waive the protection of the eleventh amendment by consenting to actions against itself in state court or by accepting funds under a federal statute that imposes obligations on states.

The eleventh amendment does not bar *prospective* relief against a state, even if compliance will be expensive. *See, e.g., Edelman v. Jordan,* 415 U.S. 651 (1974) (dictum approving orders that increase future welfare payments). Nor does it preclude an award of attorneys' fees against a state, provided that the state is otherwise liable for damages or other relief. *Kentucky v. Graham,* 473 U.S. 159 (1985).

§ 10.2.2   TORT LIABILITY OF OFFICIALS

Officials may commit common law torts or constitutional torts (meaning actions that violate the constitution but are not otherwise tortious). If a federal official acting within the scope of employment is charged with a common law tort, the action against the individual must be dismissed; the action proceeds against the United States under the FTCA. 28 U.S.C. § 2679(b)(1), (d)(1) (the Westfall Act, enacted in 1988). However, if the official is charged with a constitutional tort, or if the official acted outside the scope of employment, the Westfall Act does not apply and the tort action against the official can proceed. *Id.* § 2679(b)(2). State law on this issue varies greatly but in many states any tort action brought against a state official is dismissed and the state is substituted as the defendant.

§ 10.2.2a   Bases of Liability

State and local officials can be held personally liable for constitutional torts in federal court actions. Under 42 U.S.C. § 1983 (enacted in 1871):

> Every person who, under color of any statute, ordinance, regulation, custom, or usage, of any State or Territory, subjects, or causes to be subjected, any citizen of the United States or other person within the jurisdiction thereof to the deprivation of any rights, privileges, or immunities secured by the Constitution and laws, shall be liable to the party injured in an action at law, suit in equity, or other proper proceeding for redress.

Section 1983 makes state or local government officials liable for actions that violate rights protected under the federal constitution or federal statutes. It applies to officials of state and local government and to local government entities (but not state government entities). A prevailing party under § 1983 is entitled in an appropriate case to compensatory damages, to injunctive relief, to punitive damages from individual (but not governmental) defendants, and to reasonable attorneys fees. 42 U.S.C. § 1988.

No statute makes *federal officials* personally liable for constitutional or statutory violations, but the Supreme Court has filled the gap. In *Bivens v. Six Unknown Agents of the Federal Bureau of Narcotics,* 403 U.S. 388 (1971), the Court held that the fourth amendment itself gives rise to a right of action against federal law enforcement officials for damages from an unlawful search and seizure.

The process of spelling out which provisions of the Constitution give rise to implied rights of action has continued since the *Bivens* decision. The Court has vacillated considerably, holding that *Bivens* does not apply in cases where there are "special factors counseling hesitation." For example, social security disability recipients were denied a *Bivens* remedy, despite allegations of due process violations, because of the extensive statutory treatment of the rights of disability recipients. Thus the Court inferred that Congress did not wish the courts to administer a damage remedy in disability cases. *Schweiker v. Chilicky,* 487 U.S. 412 (1988).

§ 10.2.2b Immunity From Liability

The most difficult problems arising in damage actions against officials for constitutional torts concern *immunity.* At common law an official carrying out a statute was subject to strict liability if he made a mistake. *Miller v. Horton,* 26 N.E. 100 (Mass.1891) (official who mistakenly destroyed a horse suspected of disease is liable in tort without regard to good faith or reasonableness).

This view has long been rejected. Courts have worked out elaborate doctrines of both qualified immunity and absolute immunity, in light of two mutually dependent rationales:

> (1) the injustice, particularly in the absence of bad faith, of subjecting to liability an officer, who is required by the legal obligations of his position, to exercise discretion, and (2) the danger that the threat of such liability would deter his willingness to execute his office with the decisiveness and the judgment required by the public good.

Scheuer v. Rhodes, 416 U.S. 232 (1974).

The leading federal authority on immunity of officials from constitutional tort liability is *Butz v. Economou,* 438 U.S. 478 (1978). That case involved an action for constitutional tort (under *Bivens*) by a regulated party against various officials of the Department of Agriculture (USDA).

Economou, a regulated commodity broker, complained that USDA had revoked his license without due process and in retaliation for his exercise of first amendment rights.

The case has three important holdings:

(i) Agency prosecutors and adjudicators, including ALJs, are entitled to absolute immunity from damage suits, like judges and criminal prosecutors.

(ii) Other law enforcement officials (including the heads of agencies) have only qualified immunity from damage suits.

(iii) The rules of qualified immunity are the same in actions against state officials under § 1983 and against federal officials under *Bivens*.

In addition, the *Butz* decision recognized that officials charged with common law torts, and acting within the scope of their authority, would enjoy absolute immunity. This reflected prior law. *Barr v. Matteo*, 360 U.S. 564 (1959) (agency head who issued defamatory press release within the scope of his employment had absolute immunity). Today, this holding is less important because of the Westfall Act: common law tort actions against officials are dismissed and the United States is substituted as a defendant. At that point, the various defenses under the FTCA come into play.

The president and presidential aides enjoy absolute immunity from damage actions; the immunity of aides extends only to highly sensitive activity. *Nixon v. Fitzgerald*, 457 U.S. 731 (1982); *Harlow v. Fitzgerald*, 457 U.S. 800 (1982). Members of Congress enjoy immunity for actions in a legislative capacity under the Speech and Debate Clause (Art. I, § 6) and state legislators have comparable immunity. *Tenney v. Brandhove*, 341 U.S. 367 (1951). Legislative immunity probably extends to agency officials engaged in rulemaking. *Redwood Village Partnership, Inc. v. Graham*, 26 F.3d 839 (8th Cir.1994). *But see Walter v. Torres*, 917 F.2d 1379 (5th Cir.1990).

An official entitled to qualified immunity is liable only if his conduct is not "objectively reasonable." Conduct is not immune if it violated "clearly established" constitutional limitations of which the official reasonably should have been aware. This test is objective; it does not matter whether the official actually was aware of the limitation or acted "maliciously." *Harlow v. Fitzgerald, supra; Davis v. Scherer*, 468 U.S. 183 (1984). An objective test makes it easier to resolve cases quickly on summary judgment, since the defendant's "malice" or knowledge of constitutional law is not in issue.

Problem: The Commission on Pornography was appointed to study the impact of pornography on society and to recommend legal means by which the spread of pornography could be contained. The Commission concluded that erotic photographs in nationally circulated magazines provoke assaults against women. Since such photographs are not "obscene" and thus are protected by the first amendment, they cannot legally be suppressed. The Commission singled out several magazines, including *Penthouse,* for special criticism. Its report recommended that local citizens institute boycotts against "pornographers" who sell these magazines and it named several retail chains as "pornographers" and thus possible boycott targets.

Mercury Stores was on the list of possible targets. It ignored the report and continued to sell *Penthouse.* As a result it was subjected to picketing and boycotts in several states which caused it considerable damage. Mercury has asked for advice about suing the government or the Commission members for damages. Analyze the prospects for litigation if

(a) The Commission was appointed by the President of the United States;

(b) The Commission was appointed by a state governor.

Cf. Playboy Enterprises, Inc. v. Meese, 639 F.Supp. 581 (D.D.C.1986).

§ 10.3　RECOVERY OF FEES

Like all litigation, administrative adjudication is time consuming and costly. A client must take account of those costs in deciding whether it is worthwhile to challenge an adverse agency decision; many times the costs of litigation simply make it impracticable to proceed.

The cost of litigation is a particularly severe problem for public interest plaintiffs. Typically, public interest groups (such as environmental, civil rights, or consumer protection organizations) are underfunded. Even if great numbers of citizens agree with them, the free rider effect makes it difficult and costly to obtain voluntary contributions (free riders refuse to contribute since they can receive the benefits provided by the group whether they contribute or not). Yet to challenge agency action, such a group must be prepared for long and costly years of litigation against skilled, determined and well-funded adversaries.

For these reasons, a vitally important remedial issue is whether a prevailing party can obtain an award of attorney's fees (as well as other costs such as the fees charged by expert witnesses). There are now a large number of statutory provisions which authorize a court to require the losing party to pay the winner's fees. If such a statute is applicable, it may be feasible to pursue litigation against the government which otherwise would be too costly. In addition, fee-shifting statutes may change agency behavior; the possibility of a substantial fee award, which probably must be absorbed from the agency's existing budget, may make the agency more cautious in taking action. This subchapter explores a range of issues arising under fee shifting statutes.

Notes and Questions

1. *The American rule.* In *Wilderness Society v. Morton,* 495 F.2d 1026 (D.C.Cir.1974), the court held that public interest environmental groups were entitled to an award of attorney's fees for their efforts (4500 hours of

lawyers' time) in halting the trans-Alaska pipeline. The rationale was that they had served as a private attorney general in vindicating important Congressional policies protective of the environment.

This decision was reversed by the Supreme Court in *Alyeska Pipeline Service Co. v. Wilderness Society*, 421 U.S. 240 (1975). Under the "American rule" each party in litigation bears its own attorneys' fees, absent a statute providing for fees or some other exception (such as creation of a common fund in a class action). There is no exception for suits brought by a private attorney general vindicating an important public interest.

However, not all states follow the *Alyeska* case. *See Serrano v. Priest,* 569 P.2d 1303 (Cal.1977) (public interest law firms win $800,000 attorney fee award under private attorney general theory in case relating to constitutionality of public school financing). *Serrano* was codified by Cal.Code of Civ.Proc. § 1021.5:

> Upon motion, a court may award attorneys' fees to a successful party against one or more opposing parties in any action which has resulted in the enforcement of an important right affecting the public interest if:
>
> (a) a significant benefit, whether pecuniary or nonpecuniary, has been conferred on the general public or a large class of persons,
>
> (b) the necessity and financial burden of private enforcement are such as to make the award appropriate, and
>
> (c) such fees should not in the interest of justice be paid out of the recovery, if any. . . .

2. *Statutes providing for fees.* Numerous federal statutes authorize a court to require one side to pay the other's fees. Numerous civil rights statutes contain fee shifting provisions. For example, the Civil Rights Attorney's Fees Awards Act, 42 U.S.C. § 1988, provides that a prevailing plaintiff in a § 1983 action is entitled to recover attorneys' fees unless special circumstances render an award unjust. However, this statute is not reciprocal: a prevailing defendant gets a fee award only if the plaintiff's action was frivolous. *Hughes v. Rowe,* 449 U.S. 5 (1980).

Like a number of other environmental statutes, § 304 of the Clean Air Act provides for attorneys' fees if the trial court determines that an award is "appropriate." How should the court decide when it is "appropriate" to make the loser pay the winner's fees?

In *Western States Petroleum Ass'n v. EPA*, 87 F.3d 280, 286 (9th Cir.1996), a group of plaintiffs consisting of five air pollution dischargers and two trade associations, petitioned for judicial review of an EPA regulation. The court decided that an award of attorney's fees would not be "appropriate."

> An award of attorneys' fees is "appropriate" where petitioners have: (1) attained some success on the merits; and (2) contributed substantially to the goals of the Clean Air Act in doing so. Because we reverse the EPA's Washington decision as an unexplained departure from precedent, petitioners have attained sufficient success on the merits to be eligible for attorneys' fees.

The second question—whether petitioners have contributed substantially to the goals of the Clean Air Act—is more difficult.... [T]he legislative history indicates that Congress neither intended to subsidize all litigation under the Clean Air Act nor contemplated that § 307(f) would benefit financially able parties who, out of their own substantial economic interests, would have litigated anyway. For this reason, we hold that petitioners are ineligible for a fee award under § 307(f).

Moreover, petitioners do not assert, nor do we find, that their litigation of this case has served the public interest in assisting in the interpretation and implementation of the Clean Air Act.... The issue under the Act has been relatively narrow and concerns only the anomalousness of the EPA's Washington decision. Petitioners do not identify any other Title V programs that this litigation will affect. We are simply confronted with an anomalous decision which the agency should correct. Because petitioners, who are financially able to and would have litigated regardless of any potential for a fee award, have not contributed substantially to the goals of the Clean Air Act, for this further reason we do not find an award of attorneys' fees to be appropriate.

3. *Reasonable attorneys' fees.* Generally, attorney's fees are calculated by the "lodestar method," which requires a court to multiply the hours spent on a case by a reasonable hourly rate. Upward modifications are permitted only in exceptional cases. No modification is appropriate simply because of counsel's superior skill or the excellent results obtained. *Pennsylvania v. Delaware Valley Citizens' Council for Clean Air*, 478 U.S. 546 (1986). This case also held that counsel in a long-running environmental dispute could be compensated for a variety of services in addition to participation in adjudication and judicial review. In particular, the prevailing party was compensated for participation in the rulemaking process and in monitoring compliance with a consent decree.

In *City of Burlington v. Dague*, 505 U.S. 557 (1992), the Court held that the lodestar amount could not be increased because the attorneys were retained on a contingent fee basis, even though the lodestar is an hourly rate which attorneys charge when they expect to be paid whether they win or lose.

In calculating the lodestar, good record keeping pays off. *See City of Riverside v. Rivera,* 477 U.S. 561 (1986), arising under § 1988. On the merits, the *Riverside* case involved an action by Hispanics against the police who broke up a party and arrested them without a warrant. The jury awarded them damages of $33,350. After a lengthy struggle over the fee issue, the Supreme Court upheld attorneys' fees of $245,456 (based on 1,946.75 hours spent by attorneys at $125 per hour and 84.5 hours spent by law clerks at $25 per hour). This was more than seven times the damages in the case! However, the decision was 5–4 and Justice Powell's concurrence in the judgment was reluctant. On the other hand, "when a plaintiff recovers only nominal damages because of his failure to prove an essential element of his claim for monetary relief, the only reasonable fee is usually no fee at all." *Farrar v. Hobby,* 506 U.S. 103, 116 (1992).

Note that the $245,456 figure in *Riverside* covers only the cost of litigating the merits—not the cost of litigating the fee issue. Considering that the fee issue went to the Supreme Court twice (and also included two Ninth Circuit and one district court decision), the attorneys' fees arising out of the attorney fee issue may well exceed the fees arising from the merits.

4. *Equal Access to Justice Act.* Under the Equal Access to Justice Act (EAJA), enacted in 1980 and expanded several times, Congress departed substantially from the American rule. In litigation at the agency level or in court, EAJA provides that a prevailing party (other than the United States) is entitled to attorneys' fees and other expenses unless the government's position was "substantially justified" or special circumstances make an award unjust. Similarly, fees can be awarded whenever the demand by an agency in an adversary adjudication or a civil action brought by the United States is "substantially in excess of the decision of the adjudicative officer and is unreasonable when compared with such decision."

Should EAJA be amended to make it a two-way rather than a one-way street? In other words, should an agency be able to collect its attorney's fees and costs from the private party if the latter's litigating position was not substantially justified?

EAJA consists of two related statutes: Under 5 U.S.C. § 504, an agency shall award fees and expenses to a prevailing party unless an ALJ finds that the agency's position was substantially justified. The person seeking fees can appeal the agency's decision in court but the government cannot. Section 504 covers the costs of a formal agency adjudication (other than ratemaking or granting a license) in which the government is represented by counsel. It excludes cases to which the APA does not apply, such as deportation. *Ardestani v. INS,* 502 U.S. 129 (1991).

Under 28 U.S.C. § 2412(d) a court shall award to a prevailing party fees and expenses incurred in any civil action (except a tort action) brought by or against the United States, *including judicial review of agency action,* unless the court finds that the government's position was substantially justified. Section 2412(d) permits an award of costs incurred at both the agency and judicial levels.

Both §§ 504 and 2412(d) permit awards only to parties who need assistance in litigating against the government: broadly speaking, awards can be made only to an individual whose net worth did not exceed $2 million or to a business whose net worth did not exceed $7 million and which had not more than 500 employees. However, tax exempt charitable organizations (such as most public interest law firms) qualify regardless of their net worth. Small local government units also qualify. Should an award also be available to a trade association that has a $3.3 million budget and 36 employees, if its members include multi-billion dollar corporations? *See Texas Food Industry Ass'n v. Department of Agriculture,* 81 F.3d 578 (5th Cir.1996) (answering yes by 2–1 vote).

The amount which can be paid under these sections includes the cost of expert witnesses, the costs of necessary studies or tests, and reasonable attorney fees. However, attorney fees cannot exceed $125 per hour unless it is determined that an increase in the cost of living or a special factor (such as limited availability of qualified attorneys for the proceedings involved) justifies a higher fee. The $125 per hour figure is far below the amount currently charged by big city law firms. The exception for "limited availability" applies only to attorneys with some distinctive knowledge or specialized skill, such as a specialty like patent law or knowledge of foreign law or language. *Pierce v. Underwood,* 487 U.S. 552 (1988).

Under both sections 504 and 2812, the government has the burden to show that its "position" was "substantially justified." Recent amendments to EAJA make clear that the government's "position" covers both its litigating position and also the original action, or failure to act, on which the adjudication was based. "Substantially justified" means that the government's position had a "reasonable basis in both law and fact." *Pierce v. Underwood, supra.*

Could the government's position be "substantially justified" if it lost the case because its action was found not to be supported by substantial evidence or to be arbitrary and capricious? *See Sotelo–Aquije v. Slattery,* 62 F.3d 54, 58 (2d Cir.1995). That case holds that "substantial justification" and "substantial evidence" are not congruent; a decision could lack substantial evidence yet still be substantially justified. However, a merits decision based on lack of substantial evidence places a high hurdle in front of the government when it seeks to show that its position was substantially justified.

The states have embraced the EAJA model; by 1995, 30 states had adopted similar provisions. Susan M. Olson, "How Much Access to Justice From State 'Equal Access to Justice Acts?'" 71 Chi.-Kent L. Rev. 547 (1995). A similar provision applies to fees incurred in tax litigation by or against the IRS if the government's position was "unreasonable." Recovery is limited to $25,000. Int.Rev.Code § 7430.

5. *Problem.* Assume the state of Monroe adopts provisions identical to EAJA and to Calif.Code of Civ.Proc. § 1021.5 (quoted in N.1).

The Monroe Civil Rights Act prohibits discrimination by landlords on the basis of race and sex. Your clients Mary and Bernice, who are lesbians, sought to rent an apartment from Ruth. Ruth refused to rent to them, stating that she did not feel they were financially responsible. However, Mary and Bernice believe that Ruth decided not to rent to them because Ruth disapproves of homosexuality. They both have good jobs and believe there was no basis to question their financial responsibility. However, Mary went through bankruptcy three years ago.

After an adjudicatory hearing, the Monroe Civil Rights Commission (MCRC) ruled i) Ruth's reason for refusing to rent the apartment was that she believed that Mary was not financially responsible because of Mary's bankruptcy; ii) the Civil Rights Act does not apply to discrimination on the basis of sexual orientation.

On judicial review, a superior court judge ruled i) substantial evidence supported MCRC's ruling that Ruth's decision was based on financial responsibility; ii) the Civil Rights Act does apply to discrimination on the basis of sexual orientation.

Your fees in representing Mary and Bernice before the Commission total $15,000 (60 hours at $250 per hour). Your fees in representing them on judicial review total $10,000 (40 hours at $250 per hour). These fees were paid by the Monroe Gay Rights Action League. How much, if any, of these fees can MCRC be compelled to pay?

§ 10.4   PRECLUSION OF JUDICIAL REVIEW

Although there is a presumption that administrative action is subject to judicial review, that presumption can be rebutted. The legislature can preclude judicial review, thus rendering administrative action partially or completely unreviewable. *See* APA § 701(a)(1): "This chapter applies ... except to the extent that—(1) statutes preclude judicial review ..." Compare 1981 MSAPA 5–102(a) and 1–103(b) (to diminish any right created by MSAPA, another statute must expressly so provide). What happens if judicial review seems inconsistent with a statutory scheme, but the legislature did not explicitly preclude judicial review?

BOWEN v. MICHIGAN ACADEMY OF FAMILY PHYSICIANS
476 U.S. 667 (1986).

[A regulation adopted by the Secretary of Health and Human Services, under Part B of the Medicare program, provided for lower payments to allopathic family physicians than other physicians. The issue before the Court was whether the Medicare Act precluded judicial review of this regulation. The Secretary pointed out that the judicial review provision of the Act, § 1395ff, provided for appeals from adverse *eligibility* determinations under both Part A (basic Medicare) and Part B (optional coverage), but it authorized judicial review of *amount* determinations under Part A only. The government read this provision to imply that courts could not review amounts paid under Part B.]

STEVENS, J.:

. . . . We begin with the strong presumption that Congress intends judicial review of administrative action. From the beginning "our cases [have established] that judicial review of a final agency action by an aggrieved person will not be cut off unless there is persuasive reason to believe that such was the purpose of Congress." *Abbott Laboratories v. Gardner,* 387 U.S. 136 (1967). In *Marbury v. Madison,* 5 U.S. 137, (1803), a case itself involving review of executive action, Chief Justice Marshall insisted that "[t]he very essence of civil liberty certainly consists in the right of every individual to claim the protection of the laws." . . .

Committees of both Houses of Congress have endorsed this view in undertaking the comprehensive rethinking of the place of administrative agencies in a regime of separate and divided powers that culminated in the passage of the Administrative Procedure Act (APA). . . . The Committee on the Judiciary of the House of Representatives agreed that Congress ordinarily intends that there be judicial review, and emphasized the clarity with which a contrary intent must be expressed:

"The statutes of Congress are not merely advisory when they relate to administrative agencies, any more than in other cases. To preclude judicial review under this bill a statute, if not specific in withholding such review, must upon its face give clear and convincing evidence of an intent to withhold it. The mere failure to provide specially by statute for judicial review is certainly no evidence of intent to withhold review." . . . .

This standard has been invoked time and again when considering whether the Secretary has discharged "the heavy burden of overcoming the strong presumption that Congress did not mean to prohibit all judicial review of his decision," *Dunlop v. Bachowski,* 421 U.S. 560 (1975).[3]

Subject to constitutional constraints, Congress can, of course, make exceptions to the historic practice whereby courts review agency action. The presumption of judicial review is, after all, a presumption, and "like all presumptions used in interpreting statutes, may be overcome by," *inter alia,* "specific language or specific legislative history that is a reliable indicator of congressional intent," or a specific congressional intent to preclude judicial review that is "fairly discernible in the detail of the legislative scheme." *Block v. Community Nutrition Institute,* 467 U.S. 340 (1984).

In this case, the Government asserts that [a] statutory provision remove[s] the Secretary's regulation from review under the grant of general federal-question jurisdiction found in 28 U.S.C. § 1331. The Government contends that 42 U.S.C. § 1395ff(b), which authorizes "Appeal by individuals," impliedly forecloses administrative or judicial review of any action taken under Part B of the Medicare program by failing to authorize such review while simultaneously authorizing administrative and judicial review of "any determination . . . as to . . . the amount of benefits under part A." . . . Section 1395ff on its face is an explicit authorization of judicial review, not a bar. As a general matter, "[t]he mere fact that some acts are made reviewable should not suffice to support an implication of exclusion as to others. The right to review is too important to be excluded on such slender and indeterminate evidence of legislative intent." *Abbott Laboratories v. Gardner.*

In the Medicare program, however, the situation is somewhat more complex. Under Part B of that program . . . the Secretary contracts with private health insurance carriers to provide benefits for which individuals voluntarily remit premiums. This optional coverage, which is federally subsidized, supplements the mandatory institutional health benefits

---

3. . . . Of course, this Court has "never applied the 'clear and convincing evidence' standard in the strict evidentiary sense;" nevertheless, the standard serves as "a useful reminder to courts that, where substantial doubt about the congressional intent exists, the general presumption favoring judicial review of administrative action is controlling."

A strong presumption finds support in a wealth of scholarly literature. See, *e.g.,* 2 K. Davis, Administrative Law § 9:6, p. 240 (1979) (praising "the case law since 1974" for being "strongly on the side of reviewability"). . . .

(such as coverage for hospital expenses) provided by Part A. Subject to an amount in controversy requirement, individuals aggrieved by delayed or insufficient payment with respect to benefits payable under Part B are afforded an "opportunity for a fair hearing by the *carrier.*" In comparison, and subject to a like amount in controversy requirement, a similarly aggrieved individual under Part A is entitled "to a hearing thereon by the *Secretary* . . . and to judicial review."

"In the context of the statute's precisely drawn provisions," we held in *United States v. Erika, Inc.,* 456 U.S. 201 (1982), that the failure "to authorize further review for determinations of the amount of Part B awards . . . provides persuasive evidence that Congress deliberately intended to foreclose further review of such claims." Not limiting our consideration to the statutory text, we investigated the legislative history which "confirm[ed] this view," and disclosed a purpose to "avoid overloading the courts with trivial matters," "a consequence which would 'unduly ta[x]' " the federal court system with "little real value" to be derived by participants in the program.

Respondents' federal-court challenge to the validity of the Secretary's regulation is not foreclosed by § 1395ff as we construed that provision in *Erika.* The reticulated statutory scheme, which carefully details the forum and limits of review of "any determination of the amount of benefits under part A" and of the "amount of payment" of benefits under Part B simply does not speak to challenges mounted against the *method* by which such amounts are to be determined rather than the *determinations* themselves. As the Secretary has made clear, "the legality, constitutional or otherwise, of any provision of the Act or regulations relevant to the Medicare Program" is not considered in a "fair hearing" held by a carrier to resolve a grievance related to a determination of the amount of a Part B award. As a result, an attack on the validity of a regulation is not the kind of administrative action that we described in *Erika* as an "amount determination" which decides "the amount of the Medicare payment to be made on a particular claim" and with respect to which the Act impliedly denies judicial review. . . .

In light of Congress' express provision for carrier review of millions of what it characterized as "trivial" claims, it is implausible to think it intended that there be *no* forum to adjudicate statutory and constitutional challenges to regulations promulgated by the Secretary. The Government nevertheless maintains that this is precisely what Congress intended to accomplish. . . . [W]e will not indulge the Government's assumption that Congress contemplated review by carriers of "trivial" monetary claims, but intended no review at all of substantial statutory and constitutional challenges to the Secretary's administration of Part B of the Medicare program. This is an extreme position, and one we would be most reluctant to adopt without a showing of "clear and convincing evidence," to overcome the "strong presumption that Congress did not mean to prohibit all judicial review" of executive action. We ordinarily presume that Congress intends the executive to obey its statutory commands and, accordingly, that it expects the courts to grant relief when an executive agency violates such a command. That presumption has not been surmounted here.[12]

Notes and Questions

1. *The APA and the presumption of reviewability.* In *Michigan Academy,* the Court relied on legislative history for the proposition that the APA broadened the right to judicial review. However, other legislative history indicates that Congress intended no change in the pre–1946 law of judicial review. *See* ATTORNEY GENERAL'S MANUAL ON THE APA 94 (1947). Regardless of Congressional intent in 1946, the APA has dramatically broadened the right to judicial review—not only as to reviewability but also as to standing and ripeness.

In *United States v. Erika, Inc.,* 456 U.S. 201 (1982), the Court interpreted the same provisions that were at issue in *Michigan Academy.* It held that Congress *impliedly* precluded judicial review of a Medicare carrier's determination that it would pay only a certain amount for kidney dialysis supplies used in Medicare Part B. Is *Michigan Academy* distinguishable from *Erika?*

2. *Interpreting preclusive statutes.* Courts frequently construe apparently preclusive statutory language to permit some form of review. Thus a statute providing that certain agency action "shall be final" is often read to permit review of the action on some grounds or by some means. *See, e.g., Shaughnessy v. Pedreiro,* 349 U.S. 48 (1955) ("shall be final" means final in administrative branch and is not intended to preclude judicial review). One commentator discerns some general patterns in these holdings:

> [T]he Court has been developing what might be considered a "common law of preclusion." A critical reading of recent case law . . . indicates that the Court tends to allow some issues to be precluded more readily than other issues. At the top of the scale, . . . the presumption against preclusion of constitutional grievances against an agency is practically irrebuttable. The Court also has proved less willing to find preclusion in cases involving administrative rules than in cases involving agency adjudication, and less willing to foreclose legal challenges than factual ones, especially where the legal issues are not within the administering agency's expertise. At the bottom of the hierarchy are issues of fact and application of law to fact, which the Court allows to be precluded more readily than any others.
>
> In most of these cases, the Court also found technical grounds for reading the statutes to support these results; thus the Court's lawmaking was peripheral and somewhat covert. Yet these holdings clearly have been informed by practical judgments about the relative importance of

---

12. Our disposition avoids the "serious constitutional question" that would arise if we construed § 1395(ff) to deny a judicial forum for constitutional claims arising under Part B of the Medicare program. *Johnson v. Robison,* 415 U.S. 361 (1974). *See Yakus v. United States,* 321 U.S. 414 (1944); *St. Joseph Stock Yards Co. v. United States,* 298 U.S. 38, 84 (1936) (Brandeis, J., concurring); Gunther, Congressional Power to Curtail Federal Court Jurisdiction: An Opinionated Guide to the Ongoing Debate, 36 Stanford L.Rev. 895, 921, n. 113 (1984) ("[A]ll agree that Congress cannot bar all remedies for enforcing federal constitutional rights"). Cf. Hart, The Power of Congress to Limit the Jurisdiction of Federal Courts: An Exercise in Dialectic, 66 Harv. L.Rev. 1362, 1378–1379 (1953)....

judicial review of various kinds of issues. One would have been astonished if the Court had adopted any of the opposite distinctions—for example, if it had made factual contentions reviewable in a situation in which legal issues were unreviewable.

Ronald M. Levin, "Understanding Unreviewability in Administrative Law," 74 Minn.L.Rev. 689, 739–40 (1990).

McNary v. Haitian Refugee Center, 498 U.S. 479 (1991), concerned an amnesty program for alien farmworkers. A class action raised statutory and constitutional challenges to the manner in which the INS handled applications for amnesty. For example, INS allegedly failed to supply translators and to record its interviews with applicants. A statute precluded judicial review "of a determination respecting an application" except in the context of a subsequent deportation order. The Court held that the district court had jurisdiction to hear the class action. The preclusion statute applied only to direct review of *individual* denials of amnesty, not to collateral challenges to unlawful practices used by the INS in processing applications *in general*. The Court observed that, as a practical matter, judicial review of individual deportation orders would be virtually useless as a means of testing the legality of the application procedures used by the INS. Does this holding follow logically from *Michigan Academy*? Notice that the challenged practices were not expressed in INS regulations.

3. *Preclusion of constitutional claims.* The final footnote of *Michigan Academy* highlights a famous unresolved constitutional question: the power of Congress to deprive federal courts of jurisdiction over constitutional issues (such as abortion or school prayer). As in *Michigan Academy,* the Court generally construes preclusion statutes to permit review of constitutional issues, thus avoiding the problem. In *Webster v. Doe,* 486 U.S. 592 (1988), the Court held that the National Security Act had the effect of rendering the CIA's decision to discharge the plaintiff basically unreviewable, but did not prevent review of his constitutional claims: "Where Congress intends to preclude judicial review of constitutional claims its intent to do so must be clear." However, Justice Scalia's dissent argued strongly that Congress had foreclosed review of all of the plaintiff's claims, including those based on the Constitution.

We cannot do justice to this debate here. *See, e.g.,* Laurence H. Tribe, AMERICAN CONSTITUTIONAL LAW §§ 3–5 (2d ed.1988). The consensus of commentators is that Congress can deprive the federal courts of the power to review some disputes (such as claims for Medicare benefits), but cannot deny litigants a federal forum for the assertion of constitutional claims. Scalia's dissent in *Webster v. Doe* takes strong issue with the latter assertion.

4. *Time limits.* A number of modern environmental statutes provide for pre-enforcement review of rules during a short period such as 60 days— but they preclude review of the rules in subsequent enforcement actions against polluters who violate the rules. *See* § 11.2.3 N.5; Paul R. Verkuil, "Congressional Limitations on Judicial Review of Rules," 57 Tul.L.Rev. 733 (1983). Should this be allowed? What if the subject of the enforcement action did not even know about the rule in time to seek review of it?

The prototype for these statutes is *Yakus v. United States,* 321 U.S. 414 (1944), which involved regulations setting maximum prices for goods during wartime. The only way the regulations could be challenged was by an action brought in the Emergency Court of Appeals within 60 days after the regulation was promulgated. The statute provided that persons who were criminally prosecuted for violating a price regulation could not question its validity.

Yakus was criminally charged with violating a regulation which set a ceiling price for meat. He had not challenged the regulation within 60 days of its adoption. Over a strong dissent by Justice Rutledge, the Court held that he could not challenge the regulation in his criminal trial. However, the majority reserved the question of whether Congress could preclude a *constitutional* challenge to the regulation. Should *Yakus* be treated as a precedent applicable only in a wartime emergency? Justice Powell has suggested that possibility. *See Adamo Wrecking Co. v. United States,* 434 U.S. 275, 289–91 (1978) (concurring opinion).

Some due process constraints on the use of time limits to preclude review do exist. In the context of a criminal enforcement action, Congress apparently cannot totally preclude judicial review of prior administrative action—even for nonconstitutional errors. *United States v. Mendoza–Lopez,* 481 U.S. 828 (1987). That case involved a prosecution of an alien for illegal entry into the country, following an earlier deportation for a prior illegal entry. A second illegal entry, after a prior deportation, is a felony; thus the earlier deportation was an element of the crime. The Court held that due process requires that the prior deportation be judicially reviewable, *either* at the time it occurred or in the criminal trial relating to the second illegal entry.

Should *Mendoza–Lopez* be read to mean that Congress *can* preclude review at the time of an enforcement proceeding if review was available at the time of the earlier administrative action? Should it apply only to criminal cases?

5. *State law.* The states vary considerably in their approach to preclusion of judicial review. Some states allow preclusion without any exceptions. *See Neyland v. Board of Educ.,* 487 A.2d 181 (Conn.1985); *Mason v. Thetford School Board,* 457 A.2d 647 (Vt.1983).

Some states allow only limited preclusion. *See, e.g., New York City Dep't of Envir. Protec. v. N. Y. City Civil Serv. Comm'n,* 579 N.E.2d 1385 (N.Y.1991) (statute can preclude review but not of claims that agency acted illegally, unconstitutionally, or in excess of jurisdiction).

At the other extreme, some states do not permit any preclusion of review. *See Salk v. Weinraub,* 390 N.E.2d 995 (Ind.1979) (statute cannot preclude review of local decision to approve urban renewal). In some states, constitutional provisions guarantee a right of judicial review of all quasi-judicial agency action affecting private rights; such provisions would invalidate a preclusion statute. *See State ex rel. Missouri Power & Light Co. v. Riley,* 546 S.W.2d 792 (Mo.App.1977); *McAvoy v. H.B. Sherman Co.,* 258 N.W.2d 414 (Mich.1977).

6. *Problem.* Monroe state employees are entitled to a pension if they are compelled to retire because of a permanent work-related disability. The Monroe Personnel Agency (MPA) adjudicates questions arising under the

disability retirement program. The applicable statute provides that MPA decisions "are final and conclusive and are not subject to judicial review."

Joan claims that she is unable to continue working in her state job as a data analyst because of injuries to her wrists arising out of the repetitive motions of typing on a computer keyboard. Dr. Bruce, a physician in general practice appointed by MPA to examine Joan, filed a written report concluding that Joan's wrist injury was mild and would not prevent her from working as a data analyst (with some slight changes in the placement of her keyboard). He also stated that the injury would clear up by itself. Consequently, he concluded that Joan did not qualify for a pension.

Joan's lawyer requested Dr. Bruce to appear at the hearing but he declined to do so, saying he was too busy. MPA has subpoena power, but the ALJ refused to issue a subpoena because it was agency practice to rely on written physician reports.

At the hearing, Joan presented testimony of two doctors who specialized in repetitive motion injuries. Both concluded that Joan's injury was disabling and permanent. Joan's counsel moved to exclude Dr. Bruce's report, but the ALJ denied the motion. The ALJ's decision rejected Joan's claim because he decided that Dr. Bruce's report was more persuasive than the testimony of Joan's physicians. MPA adopted the ALJ's decision.

Is MPA's decision judicially reviewable? *See Lindahl v. OPM,* 470 U.S. 768 (1985); *Czerkies v. U.S. Dep't of Labor,* 73 F.3d 1435 (7th Cir.1996); *New York City Dep't of Envir. Protec. v. N.Y. City CSC, supra.* Assume Monroe has adopted the 1981 MSAPA.

§ 10.5   COMMITMENT TO AGENCY DISCRETION

Chapter 9.4 considered the scope of judicial review of an agency's exercise of discretion in adjudication. You should review that material now. This subchapter considers agency action which is unreviewable because it is "committed to agency discretion by law." APA § 701(a)(2). Thus the federal APA contemplates two kinds of agency discretion—that which is reviewable under APA § 706(2)(A) ("arbitrary, capricious, an abuse of discretion, or otherwise not in accordance with law") and that which is not reviewable at all.

HECKLER v. CHANEY
470 U.S. 821 (1985).

[Chaney was a prisoner sentenced to death by lethal injection under Texas law. He wrote to the Food and Drug Administration (FDA), alleging that the use of drugs for capital punishment violated the Food, Drug, and Cosmetic Act (FDCA), because such use had not been approved as "safe and effective." He petitioned the FDA to take enforcement action to prevent the violation. The FDA Commissioner refused to do so. He disagreed with Chaney's construction of the law, and also relied on his discretion not to enforce the Act in cases where there is no serious danger to the public health or a blatant scheme to defraud. The lower court held that the FDA's refusal to take enforcement action was reviewable and an abuse of discretion.]

REHNQUIST, J.:

... [T]his case turns on the important question of the extent to which determinations by the FDA *not to exercise* its enforcement authority over the use of drugs in interstate commerce may be judicially reviewed. That decision in turn involves the construction of two separate but necessarily interrelated statutes, the APA and the FDCA.

The APA's comprehensive provisions for judicial review of "agency actions" are contained in 5 U.S.C. §§ 701–706. Any person "adversely affected or aggrieved" by agency action, see § 702, including a "failure to act," is entitled to "judicial review thereof," as long as the action is a "final agency action for which there is no other adequate remedy in a court," see § 704. The standards to be applied on review are governed by the provisions of § 706. But before any review at all may be had, a party must first clear the hurdle of § 701(a). That section provides that the chapter on judicial review "applies, according to the provisions thereof, except to the extent that—(1) statutes preclude judicial review; or (2) agency action is committed to agency discretion by law." Petitioner urges that the decision of the FDA to refuse enforcement is an action "committed to agency discretion by law" under § 701(a)(2).[2]

This Court has not had occasion to interpret this second exception in § 701(a) in any great detail. On its face, the section does not obviously lend itself to any particular construction; indeed, one might wonder what difference exists between § 701(a)(1) and § 701(a)(2). The former section seems easy in application; it requires construction of the substantive statute involved to determine whether Congress intended to preclude judicial review of certain decisions... But one could read the language "committed to agency discretion *by law*" in § (a)(2) to require a similar inquiry. In addition, commentators have pointed out that construction of § (a)(2) is further complicated by the tension between a literal reading of § (a)(2), which exempts from judicial review those decisions committed to agency "discretion," and the primary scope of review prescribed by § 706(2)(A)—whether the agency's action was "arbitrary, capricious, or an *abuse of discretion*." How is it, they ask, that an action committed to agency discretion can be unreviewable and yet courts still can review agency actions for abuse of that discretion? ... [W]e think there is a proper construction of § (a)(2) which satisfies each of these concerns.

This Court first discussed § (a)(2) in *Citizens to Preserve Overton Park v. Volpe*. That case dealt with the Secretary of Transportation's approval of the building of an interstate highway through a park in Memphis, Tennessee. The relevant federal statute provided that the Secretary "shall not approve" any program or project using public

---

2. ... Respondents have not challenged the statement that all they sought were certain enforcement actions, and this case therefore does not involve the question of agency discretion not to invoke rulemaking proceedings.

parkland unless the Secretary first determined that no feasible alternatives were available.... After setting out the language of § 701(a), the Court stated:

> Similarly, the Secretary's decision here does not fall within the exception for action "committed to agency discretion." This is a very narrow exception.... The legislative history of the Administrative Procedure Act indicates that it is applicable in those rare instances where "statutes are drawn in such broad terms that in a given case there is no law to apply."

The above quote answers several of the questions raised by the language of § 701(a), although it raises others. First, it clearly separates the exception provided by § (a)(1) from the § (a)(2) exception. The former applies when Congress has expressed an intent to preclude judicial review. The latter applies in different circumstances; even where Congress has not affirmatively precluded review, review is not to be had if the statute is drawn so that a court would have no meaningful standard against which to judge the agency's exercise of discretion. In such a case, the statute ("law") can be taken to have "committed" the decisionmaking to the agency's judgment absolutely. This construction avoids conflict with the "abuse of discretion" standard of review in § 706—if no judicially manageable standards are available for judging how and when an agency should exercise its discretion then it is impossible to evaluate agency action for "abuse of discretion." In addition, this construction satisfies the principle of statutory construction [that every statutory clause should be given some effect], by identifying a separate class of cases to which § 701(a)(2) applies.

To this point our analysis does not differ significantly from that of the Court of Appeals. That court purported to apply the "no law to apply" standard of *Overton Park*. We disagree, however, with that court's insistence that the "narrow construction" of § (a)(2) required application of a presumption of reviewability even to an agency's decision not to undertake certain enforcement actions. Here we think the Court of Appeals broke with tradition, case law, and sound reasoning.

Overton Park did not involve an agency's refusal to take requested enforcement action. It involved an affirmative act of approval under a statute that set clear guidelines for determining when such approval should be given. Refusals to take enforcement steps generally involve precisely the opposite situation, and in that situation we think the presumption is that judicial review is not available. This Court has recognized on several occasions over many years that an agency's decision not to prosecute or enforce, whether through civil or criminal process, is a decision generally committed to an agency's absolute discretion. This recognition of the existence of discretion is attributable in no small part to the general unsuitability for judicial review of agency decisions to refuse enforcement.

The reasons for this general unsuitability are many. First, an agency decision not to enforce often involves a complicated balancing of a number of factors which are peculiarly within its expertise. Thus, the agency must not only assess whether a violation has occurred, but whether agency resources are best spent on this violation or another, whether the agency is likely to succeed if it acts, whether the particular enforcement action requested best fits the agency's overall policies, and indeed, whether the agency has enough resources to undertake the action at all. An agency generally cannot act against each technical violation of the statute it is charged with enforcing. The agency is far better equipped than the courts to deal with the many variables involved in the proper ordering of its priorities. Similar concerns animate the principles of administrative law that courts generally will defer to an agency's construction of the statute it is charged with implementing, and to the procedures it adopts for implementing that statute.

In addition to these administrative concerns, we note that when an agency refuses to act it generally does not exercise its *coercive* power over an individual's liberty or property rights, and thus does not infringe upon areas that courts often are called upon to protect. Similarly, when an agency *does* act to enforce, that action itself provides a focus for judicial review, inasmuch as the agency must have exercised its power in some manner. The action at least can be reviewed to determine whether the agency exceeded its statutory powers. Finally, we recognize that an agency's refusal to institute proceedings shares to some extent the characteristics of the decision of a prosecutor in the Executive Branch not to indict—a decision which has long been regarded as the special province of the Executive Branch, inasmuch as it is the executive who is charged by the Constitution to "take care that the Laws be faithfully executed." U.S. Const., Art. II, § 3.

We of course only list the above concerns to facilitate understanding of our conclusion that an agency's decision not to take enforcement action should be presumed immune from judicial review under § 701(a)(2). For good reasons, such a decision has traditionally been "committed to agency discretion," and we believe that the Congress enacting the APA did not intend to alter that tradition. In so stating, we emphasize that the decision is only presumptively unreviewable; the presumption may be rebutted where the substantive statute has provided guidelines for the agency to follow in exercising its enforcement powers. Thus, in establishing this presumption in the APA, Congress did not set agencies free to disregard legislative direction in the statutory scheme that the agency administers. Congress may limit an agency's exercise of enforcement power if it wishes, either by setting substantive

4. We do not have in this case a refusal by the agency to institute proceedings based solely on the belief that it lacks jurisdiction. Nor do we have a situation where it could justifiably be found that the agency has "consciously and expressly adopted a general policy" that is so extreme as to amount to an abdication of its statutory responsibilities. See, *e.g., Adams v. Richardson,* 480 F.2d 1159 (1973) (en banc). Although we express no opinion on whether such decisions would be unreviewable under § 701(a)(2), we note that in those situations the statute conferring authority on the agency might indicate that such decisions were not "committed to agency discretion."

priorities, or by otherwise circumscribing an agency's power to discriminate among issues or cases it will pursue....

[The Court referred to *Dunlop v. Bachowski,* 421 U.S. 560 (1975), also discussed in § 4.3 N.5. The statute in that case had provided that the Secretary of Labor "shall" sue to set aside a union election "if he finds probable cause to believe that a violation ... has occurred." Thus, the] statute being administered quite clearly withdrew discretion from the agency and provided guidelines for exercise of its enforcement power. [In contrast, the FDCA's] general provision for enforcement, § 372, provides only that "the [Commissioner] is *authorized* to conduct examinations and investigations.... "

[The Court of Appeals placed considerable weight on an FDA policy statement that seemed to constrain enforcement discretion. However,] the statement was attached to a rule that was never adopted. Whatever force such a statement might have, and leaving to one side the problem of whether an agency's rules might under certain circumstances provide courts with adequate guidelines for informed judicial review of decisions not to enforce, we do not think the language of the agency's "policy statement" can plausibly be read to override the agency's express assertion of unreviewable discretion contained in [a separate] rule.

... The FDA's decision not to take the enforcement actions requested by respondents is therefore not subject to judicial review under the APA. The general exception to reviewability provided by § 701(a)(2) for action "committed to agency discretion" remains a narrow one, see *Overton Park,* but within that exception are included agency refusals to institute investigative or enforcement proceedings, unless Congress has indicated otherwise. In so holding, we essentially leave to Congress, and not to the courts, the decision as to whether an agency's refusal to institute proceedings should be judicially reviewable. No colorable claim is made in this case that the agency's refusal to institute proceedings violated any constitutional rights of respondents, and we do not address the issue that would be raised in such a case. Cf. *Johnson v. Robison,* 415 U.S. 361 (1974); *Yick Wo v. Hopkins,* 118 U.S. 356 (1886).

The fact that the drugs involved in this case are ultimately to be used in imposing the death penalty must not lead this Court or other courts to import profound differences of opinion over the meaning of the Eighth Amendment to the United States Constitution into the domain of administrative law.

Reversed.

JUSTICE MARSHALL, concurring in the judgment.

I write separately to argue for a different basis of decision: that refusals to enforce, like other agency actions, are reviewable in the absence of a "clear and convincing" congressional intent to the contrary, but that such refusals warrant deference when, as in this case, there is nothing to suggest that an agency with enforcement discretion has abused that discretion.... [Justice Brennan concurred in the majority opinion but wrote briefly to point out the numerous issues left open in that opinion.]

Notes and Questions

1. *The expanding circle.* Although the *Overton Park* decision stated that the APA § 701(a)(2) exception was "very narrow," the Supreme Court has steadily expanded the circle. In each case, the Court offered a series of pragmatic arguments that supported its decision to deny review. In addition to non-enforcement decisions, found unreviewable in *Chaney*, the Court has held that the following decisions are committed to agency discretion:

· The President's decision to accept or reject a list of military base closings proposed to him by the Defense Base Closure and Realignment Commission. *Dalton v. Specter*, 512 U.S. 1247 (1994).

· An agency's decision not to continue to fund a health program out of its lump sum appropriation. *Lincoln v. Vigil*, 508 U.S. 182 (1993).

· An agency's refusal to reconsider its own decision. *ICC v. Brotherhood of Locomotive Engineers*, 482 U.S. 270 (1987).

· The CIA director's decision to terminate an employee. The director, who gave no reasons, acted under a statute providing that "The [CIA] Director may, in his discretion, terminate the employment of any officer or employee of the Agency whenever he shall deem such termination necessary or advisable in the interests of the United States ..." *Webster v. Doe*, 486 U.S. 592 (1988), also discussed in § 10.4.

2. *No law to apply.* In *Overton Park*, the Court stated that action was committed to agency discretion only when "statutes are drawn in such broad terms that in a given case there is no law to apply." In *Chaney* the Court expresses the same idea, stating that action is unreviewable if a "statute is drawn so that a court would have no meaningful standard against which to judge the agency's exercise of discretion."

The Court has continued to invoke this test. In *Webster v. Doe,* Chief Justice Rehnquist emphasized the word "deem" in the statute.

> This standard fairly exudes deference to the Director, and appears to us to foreclose the application of any meaningful judicial standard of review. Short of permitting cross-examination of the Director concerning his views of the Nation's security and whether the discharged employee was inimical to those interests, we see no basis on which a reviewing court could properly assess an Agency termination decision.

However, it is apparent that the question of whether agency action is committed to agency discretion is largely a policy question, not simply a matter of whether there is "law to apply." As it did in *Chaney,* the Court typically offers pragmatic and policy reasons for its conclusion. In *Webster v. Doe,* for example, Rehnquist relied on the entire structure of the Act and the peculiar need for protecting intelligence sources and assuring the reliability and trustworthiness of CIA employees. Recall, however, that the Court also held that the CIA's decision was reviewable on *constitutional* grounds and it remanded to the lower court for that purpose.

Justice Scalia's concurring opinion in *Webster* aptly describes the inadequacy of the "law to apply" test. He wrote:

> The key to understanding the "committed to agency discretion *by law*" provision of § 701(a)(2) lies in contrasting it with the "*statutes* preclude judicial review" provision of § 701(a)(1). Why "statutes" for preclusion, but the much more general term "law" for commission to agency discretion? The answer is, as we implied in *Chaney,* that the latter was intended to refer to "the 'common law' of judicial review of agency action"—a body of jurisprudence that had marked out, with more or less precision, certain issues and certain areas that were beyond the range of judicial review. That jurisprudence included principles ranging from the "political question" doctrine, to sovereign immunity . . ., to official immunity, to prudential limitations upon the courts' equitable powers, to what can be described no more precisely than a traditional respect for the functions of the other branches. . . .

> All this law, shaped over the course of centuries and still developing in its application to new contexts, cannot possibly be contained within the phrase "no law to apply." It is not surprising, then, that although the Court recites the test it does not really apply it. . . . It is not really true "that a court would have no meaningful standard against which to judge the agency's exercise of discretion . . ." The standard set forth in § 102(c) . . . "necessary or advisable in the interests of the United States," at least excludes dismissal out of personal vindictiveness, or because the Director wants to give the job to his cousin. Why, on the Court's theory, is respondent not entitled to assert the presence of such excesses, under the "abuse of discretion" standard of § 706?

For further criticism of *Overton Park*'s "no law to apply" test, see Ronald M. Levin, "Understanding Unreviewability in Administrative Law," 74 Minn. L.Rev. 689 (1990). Should the presence or absence of "law to apply" be abandoned as a factor bearing on reviewability?

3. *Affirmative v. negative.* While the *Chaney* decision agreed with *Overton Park* that the exception in § 701(a)(2) was "very narrow" in cases of affirmative agency action, it held that an agency decision *not* to enforce the law is presumed to be unreviewable. What reasons does Justice Rehnquist give for this presumption? Are they persuasive?

The majority opinion mentions numerous possible exceptions to the presumption. How many can you list? Why did Justice Rehnquist take such care to mention the issues he was *not* deciding?

In *Chaney,* the Court holds that Congress imposed no limits on the FDA's enforcement discretion. Is this delegation of power invalid? How would Rehnquist reconcile his concurring opinion in the *Benzene* case, § 7.2.1c, with his conclusion in *Chaney* that there was no law to apply and, therefore, the agency's inaction was unreviewable?

4. *Agency inaction and rights of initiation.* Note that plaintiffs who complain of agency *inaction* are likely to be the persons who are beneficiaries of the statutory scheme. Suppose your clients ask EPA to take action against a particular environmental hazard, but the agency does nothing. Will a court

compel the agency to take action if it finds the agency's inaction to be arbitrary and capricious? What other remedies should your clients consider?

How about:

(i) considering the various loopholes left by the *Chaney* decision? For example, did the legislature really give the agency discretion to refuse to regulate?

(ii) did the agency's non-enforcement decision contain an erroneous legal interpretation? It is unclear whether courts will decide legal issues that arise in connection with attempted review of an agency non-enforcement decision. *See Crowley Caribbean Transport, Inc. v. Pena*, 37 F.3d 671 (D.C.Cir.1994), holding that the court will not carve out for review a legal issue buried in an *individualized* enforcement decision. However, earlier cases provide review of issues of legal interpretation raised by an agency's *general* enforcement policy, even though these arise in conjunction with a non-enforcement decision. *Edison Elec. Inst. v. USEPA*, 996 F.2d 326 (D.C.Cir.1993). Outside the D.C. Circuit, courts seem readier to review claims of legal error affecting a non-enforcement error, even if the *Crowley* test is not met. *See Montana Air Chapter No. 29 v. FLRA*, 898 F.2d 753, 756–57 (9th Cir.1990). Is this just a straightforward application of the *Chaney* law to apply test?

(iii) construing the statute to provide a private right of action in court against the person creating the health hazard? The implication of private rights of action is discussed in § 11.2.5.

(iv) petitioning the agency to adopt a legislative rule on the subject or a policy statement that would structure its discretion? *See* § 6.3.

(v) engaging in political action—either through grass roots activism or lobbying the legislature to take corrective action?

5. *Refusal to make a rule.* Recall the *State Farm* case (§ 9.5), in which the Court invalidated NHTSA's rescission of its safety standard. What if NHTSA had refused to adopt any seatbelt rule in the first place? Could a court review that decision? The Court reserved this question in note 2 in *Chaney*.

Recently the Court stated in dictum that an agency's denial of a petition for rulemaking is appealable to the courts. *Auer v. Robbins*, 519 U.S. 452, ___, 117 S.Ct. 905, 910 (1997). This would seem to imply reviewability, a position that post-*Chaney* cases in the lower courts have already endorsed. *See, e.g., Brown v. Secretary of HHS*, 46 F.3d 102, 110 n. 14 (1st Cir.1995); *American Horse Protection Ass'n v. Lyng*, 812 F.2d 1 (D.C.Cir.1987). But the Court did not explain why such a denial is different from a refusal to take enforcement action. Doesn't an agency's decision about whether to launch a rulemaking proceeding implicate resource allocation choices that are "peculiarly within its expertise," just as the Court says non-enforcement decisions do? *See* § 6.3. Is a court more likely to have "law to apply" to the agency's decision not to proceed with rulemaking? Does the reasoning of *Michigan Academy*, § 10.4, shed light on this issue? *See generally American Horse Protection, supra*; Levin, *supra*, at 762–69.

6. *State law.* How would *Chaney* be decided under the 1981 MSAPA? *See* §§ 1–102(2), 5–102(a), 5–116(c)(8). In an action for mandamus?

7. *Problem.* The Farmers Home Administration (FmHA) is a federal agency that makes loans to farmers. Section 19 of FmHA's statute provides: "At the request of the borrower, the Secretary of Agriculture may permit the deferral of principal and interest payments on any outstanding loan, and may forego foreclosure of any such loan, for such period as the Secretary deems necessary, upon a showing by the borrower that due to circumstances beyond the borrower's control, the borrower is temporarily unable to continue making such payments when due without impairing the standard of living of the borrower."

The House Report accompanying the bill which contained § 19 said: "The purpose of this legislation is to broaden FmHA's authority to cope with today's problems and be of greater service to farmers and the rural community."

Mary failed to make payments of principal or interest on her $250,000 FmHA loan because of a disastrous drought which wiped out her crop. The FmHA foreclosed the loan and sold her farm; Mary appeals from the judgment of foreclosure. Mary did not request FmHA to defer payments or to forego foreclosure because she did not know about § 19 until after foreclosure was completed.

FmHA has never used its authority under § 19 to defer payments or forego foreclosure because it believes that the program is permissive, not mandatory. It has never notified any borrowers about its authority under § 19.

Should the court affirm the judgment of foreclosure and, if not, what relief should it grant?

Suppose FmHA did occasionally exercise its § 19 authority—but declined to do so in Mary's case, despite a timely request on her part. Would that decision be reviewable? *See United States v. Markgraf,* 736 F.2d 1179 (7th Cir.1984).

Chapter 11

STANDING TO SEEK JUDICIAL REVIEW AND THE TIMING OF JUDICIAL REVIEW

This chapter considers several important obstacles to seeking judicial review. First, it addresses the issue of standing—can a particular plaintiff seek review? Second, it considers timing issues—has the plaintiff sought review prematurely?

§ 11.1   STANDING TO SEEK REVIEW

In the history of administrative law, few issues have remained as contentious and as unsettled as the question of whether a particular individual or entity can seek the aid of a court to review the legality of government action.

In part, standing to sue in federal court is a constitutional doctrine, one of several access restrictions encompassed under the nebulous term "justiciability." Under Article III, a federal court can only entertain "cases" or "controversies." The case or controversy requirement is not satisfied unless the person seeking judicial assistance has a sufficient stake in the dispute. In part, the standing doctrine is also statutory; statutes (including the APA) often define who has standing to seek review. Finally, standing has a "prudential" component, meaning that in some circumstances the courts rely on principles of institutional self-restraint to deny standing to someone who otherwise has it. In reading the materials which follow, try to separate these three strands of standing doctrine.

Ask yourself also whether, as a matter of policy, a particular plaintiff who wishes to challenge agency action should be permitted to do so. And consider whether a particular standing decision is really a surrogate for a decision on the merits—are judges voting to grant or deny standing because they wish to decide, or to avoid, the underlying legal questions in the case?

§ 11.1.1 STANDING TO SEEK REVIEW IN THE FEDERAL COURTS: HISTORICAL INTRODUCTION

A person seeking judicial review is usually the *object* of government action, meaning that the action in question requires the person to do or not do something. Normally, that person's standing to seek review is unquestioned. Thus a person can seek judicial review of an agency rule or order that requires that person to pay money, charge a specific rate, or cease and desist from a business practice.

However, standing is in issue when a person is harmed indirectly by government action that directly involves someone else. That person often claims that the action is unlawful because he or she was the intended *beneficiary* of a law that the government action violated. For example, suppose the government gives A a license to open a bank. B, an existing bank in the same town, believes that A's license was granted unlawfully. However, B may lack standing to seek judicial review because the impact on B of the licensing order is indirect. B suffers harm from unwanted competition, but the agency has not required B to do or not do anything.

The traditional rule denying standing to B flowed logically from the "legal interest" approach to standing. That test required an analysis of whether B would have a *common law* right to prevent A from opening the bank and competing with B. Since under our free market system there is no such right in tort, property, or contract law, B would have no standing to seek judicial review of the licensing decision.

Thus, in *Tennessee Electric Power Co. v. TVA,* 306 U.S. 118 (1939), the Court held that private power companies lacked standing to enjoin the Tennessee Valley Authority (a federal agency) from competing with them on the ground that the Constitution does not allow the federal government to enter the power business. Politically, this narrow approach to standing served the interests of Supreme Court justices who wanted to prevent judicial challenges of New Deal legislation.

Statutory standing was an exception to the "legal interest" test. In *FCC v. Sanders Brothers Radio Station,* 309 U.S. 470 (1940), the FCC granted a license to a radio station that would compete with one operated by Sanders. The Communications Act provided that anyone "aggrieved or whose interests were adversely affected" by a licensing decision of the FCC could seek review. Since Sanders was "aggrieved," it had standing to challenge the FCC's order. The Court made clear that Congress could confer such standing in order to promote the public's interest in a correct interpretation and application of federal law, even though Sanders' own economic injury was irrelevant to the FCC's decision. In effect, the statute deputized Sanders to serve as a "private attorney general."

Some cases also recognized statutory standing where Congress had evidenced a specific intention to benefit the plaintiff's class. *See Hardin v. Kentucky Utilities Co.,* 390 U.S. 1 (1968) (competitor of TVA has standing to challenge its actions because Congress enacted a statute protecting such competitors).

As enacted in 1946, § 10(a) of the federal APA (now the first sentence of § 702) provided: "A person suffering legal wrong because of agency action, or adversely affected or aggrieved by agency action within the meaning of a relevant statute, is entitled to judicial review thereof." In his authoritative Manual on the APA, the Attorney General argued that § 10(a) merely codified but did not change the pre-existing law of standing. ATTORNEY GENERAL'S MANUAL ON THE ADMINISTRATIVE PROCEDURE ACT 96 (1947).

Between 1946 and 1970, the issue of whether the APA changed prior law remained unresolved. Nevertheless, the lower courts pushed the available precedents to the limit by granting standing to beneficiaries of statutory schemes including consumers, users of polluted rivers, or welfare recipients. For example, under the same statute construed in *Sanders Brothers,* the Court of Appeals held that television viewers had standing in a case involving TV licensing.

In *United Church of Christ v. FCC,* 359 F.2d 994 (D.C.Cir.1966), television viewers in Jackson, Mississippi, challenged renewal of the license of WLBT. The basis of the challenge was that WLBT failed to serve the interests of black viewers in Jackson, and that it was guilty of overt racism in its programming. The court of appeals (in a famous decision written by Judge Warren Burger) held that the viewers had standing both to intervene as parties before the FCC and to seek judicial review to "vindicate the broad public interest relating to a licensee's performance of the public trust inherent in every license." In the past, the court noted, it had relied on the agency to protect the interest of viewers, but it could no longer indulge in that comfortable assumption.

§ 11.1.2   INJURY IN FACT AND ZONE OF INTEREST TESTS

ASSOCIATION OF DATA PROCESSING SERVICE ORGS. v. CAMP
397 U.S. 150 (1970).

[Petitioners, who sold data processing services, challenged a ruling by the Comptroller of the Currency that national banks could provide data processing services. This ruling was alleged to have violated the National Bank Act. The lower courts dismissed for lack of standing. The Court surveyed prior law and disapproved cases such as *Tennessee Electric Power.*]

DOUGLAS, J.:

.... Generalizations about standing to sue are largely worthless as such. One generalization is, however, necessary and that is that the question of standing in the federal courts is to be considered in the framework of Article III which restricts judicial power to "cases" and "controversies." As we recently stated in *Flast v. Cohen,* 392 U.S. 83: "[I]n terms of Article III limitations on federal court jurisdiction, the question of standing is related only to whether the dispute sought to be adjudicated will be presented in an adversary context and in a form historically viewed as capable of judicial resolution." *Flast* was a *taxpayer's* suit. The present is a *competitor's* suit. And while the two have the same Article III starting point, they do not necessarily track one another.

(1)The first question is whether the plaintiff alleges that the challenged action has caused him injury in fact, economic or otherwise. There can be no doubt but that petitioners have satisfied this test. The petitioners not only allege that competition by national banks in the business of providing data processing services might entail some future loss of profits for the petitioners, they also allege that respondent American National Bank & Trust Company was performing or preparing to perform such services for two customers for whom petitioner Data Systems, Inc., had previously agreed or negotiated to perform such services. . . .

(2)[The second] question [is] whether the interest sought to be protected by the complainant is arguably within the zone of interests to be protected or regulated by the statute or constitutional guarantee in question. Thus the Administrative Procedure Act grants standing to a person "aggrieved by agency action within the meaning of a relevant statute." § 702. That interest, at times, may reflect "aesthetic, conservational, and recreational" as well as economic values. *United Church of Christ v. FCC* . . . A person or a family may have a spiritual stake in First Amendment values sufficient to give standing to raise issues concerning the Establishment Clause and the Free Exercise Clause. We mention these noneconomic values to emphasize that standing may stem from them as well as from the economic injury on which petitioners rely here. Certainly he who is "likely to be financially" injured, *FCC v. Sanders Bros. Radio Station*, may be a reliable private attorney general to litigate the issues of the public interest in the present case. . . .

[Section] 4 of the Bank Service Corporation Act of 1962 . . . provides: "No bank service corporation may engage in any activity other than the performance of bank services for banks. . . . " We think . . . that § 4 arguably brings a competitor within the zone of interests protected by it.

(3)That leaves the remaining question, whether judicial review of the Comptroller's action has been precluded. We do not think it has been. . . . We find no evidence that Congress in either the Bank Service Corporation Act or the National Bank Act sought to preclude judicial review of administrative rulings by the Comptroller as to the legitimate scope of activities available to national banks under those statutes. Both Acts are clearly "relevant" statutes within the meaning of § 702. The Acts do not in terms protect a specified group. But their general policy is apparent; and those whose interests are directly affected by a broad or narrow interpretation of the Acts are easily identifiable. It is clear that petitioners, as competitors of national banks which are engaging in data processing services, are within that class of "aggrieved" persons who, under § 702, are entitled to judicial review of "agency action."

Whether anything in the Bank Service Corporation Act or the National Bank Act gives petitioners a "legal interest" that protects them against violations of those Acts, and whether the actions of respondents did in fact violate either of those Acts, are questions which go to the merits and remain to be decided below.

We hold that petitioners have standing to sue and that the case should be remanded for a hearing on the merits.

[In a case decided the same day as *Data Processing,* the Court held that tenant cotton farmers had standing to challenge a regulation which would allow them, for the first time, to pledge federal subsidy payments to their landlords as security for the payment of rent. The farmers met the "injury in fact" test by alleging that the regulation would allow landlords to demand such assignments, thus increasing their dependency on the landlords. The "zone of interests" test was met because the statute provides that "the Secretary shall provide adequate safeguards to protect the interests of tenants ..." *Barlow v. Collins,* 397 U.S. 159 (1970).

JUSTICE BRENNAN, joined by JUSTICE WHITE, concurred in the result of both cases, but disagreed with their reasoning:]

.... My view is that the inquiry in the Court's first step [injury in fact] is the only one that need be made to determine standing. I had thought we discarded the notion of any additional requirement when we discussed standing solely in terms of its constitutional content in *Flast v. Cohen.* By requiring a second, non-constitutional step [zone of interest] the Court comes very close to perpetuating the discredited requirement that conditioned standing on a showing by the plaintiff that the challenged governmental action invaded one of his legally protected interests....

Before the plaintiff is allowed to argue the merits, it is true that a canvass of relevant statutory materials must be made in cases challenging agency action. But the canvass is made, not to determine *standing,* but to determine an aspect of *reviewability;* that is, whether Congress meant to deny or to allow judicial review of the agency action at the instance of the plaintiff. The Court in the present cases examines the statutory materials for just this purpose but only after making the same examination during the second step of its standing inquiry....

I submit that in making such examination of statutory materials an element in the determination of standing, the Court not only performs a useless and unnecessary exercise but also encourages badly reasoned decisions, which may well deny justice in this complex field. When agency action is challenged, standing, reviewability, and the merits pose discrete, and often complicated, issues which can best be resolved by recognizing and treating them as such.... Where, as in the instant cases, there is no express grant of review, reviewability has ordinarily been inferred from evidence that Congress intended the plaintiff's class to be a beneficiary of the statute under which the plaintiff raises his claim.... [S]light indicia that the plaintiff's class is a beneficiary will suffice to support the inference....

[A]n approach that treats separately the distinct issues of standing, reviewability, and the merits, and decides each on the basis of its own criteria, assures that these often complex questions will be squarely faced, thus contributing to better reasoned decisions and to greater confidence that justice has in fact been done. The Court's approach does too little to guard against the possibility that judges will use standing to slam the courthouse door against plaintiffs who are entitled to full consideration of their claims on the merits. The Court's approach must trouble all concerned with the function of the judicial process in today's world.

Notes and Questions

1. *Standing and the APA.* What is the relationship between the two prongs in the *Data Processing* case (injury in fact and zone of interest) and APA § 702? Based on *Data Processing,* how should each phrase in the first sentence of § 702 be construed?

Under § 7 of 1961 MSAPA, which is the law of many states, "the validity or applicability of a rule may be determined in an action for declaratory judgment ... if it is alleged that the rule, or its threatened application, interferes with or impairs ... the legal rights or privileges of the plaintiff." How would *Data Processing* have been decided if § 7 applied?

Read 1981 MSAPA § 5–106(a). Does it change the rule in 1961 MSAPA § 7? Does it adopt the legal interest test? The injury in fact test? The zone of interest test?

2. *Applying the zone of interests test.* The zone of interest test received only cursory consideration in *Data Processing,* and it was applied in undemanding fashion in *National Credit Union Adm'n v. First National Bank & Trust Co.,* 118 S.Ct. 927 (1998) *(NCUA).* The statute at issue in *NCUA* provided that "credit union membership shall be limited to groups having a *common bond* of occupation or association," and the issue was whether a credit union could sign up members from several different employers. Each group of employees would have a "common bond" with their co-workers, but would not have a common bond with employees from other companies. Banks which disliked competition from credit unions asserted that a credit union could sign up employees of only a single company.

In a 5–4 decision, the Court held that the banks had standing because the "common bond" provision was intended to limit the market that a credit union could serve. The banks wanted to limit the credit unions from entering additional markets. That link provided "some indication" that the interests of banks were "arguably within the zone of interests protected" by the statute.

The dissent maintained that the "common bond" provision had nothing to do with preventing competition or protecting banks. Instead, it was intended to safeguard the soundness of credit unions by preventing them from over-expanding. The dissent argued that the majority's view would "eviscerate" the zone test by allowing any party who suffered injury in fact to meet the zone of interest test. The dissent argued:

> I read our decisions as establishing that there must at least be some indication in the statute, beyond the mere fact that its enforcement has the effect of incidentally benefiting the plaintiff, from which one can draw an inference that the plaintiff's injury arguably falls within the zone of interests sought to be protected by the statute. . . . This, then, is a case where "the plaintiff's interests are so marginally related to or inconsistent with the purposes implicit in the statute that it cannot reasonably be assumed that Congress intended to permit the suit." [*Clarke v. Securities Industry Ass'n*, 479 U.S. 388, 399 (1987)].

Id. at 947 (O'Connor, J., dissenting).

A few years before *NCUA*, the Supreme Court had shown that the zone test is not always toothless in *Air Courier Conference of America v. American Postal Workers Union*, 498 U.S. 517 (1991). That case involved the Private Express Statute (PES), which gives the U.S. Postal Service (USPS) a monopoly over carrying the mail. In 1979, USPS suspended the PES restrictions in order to allow private courier services to deliver overnight mail. Postal employees challenged the legality of the USPS decision. The employees met the injury in fact test since the decision could result in the loss of postal jobs, but they flunked the zone of interest test. The Court used an example drawn from *Lujan v. National Wildlife Federation*, 497 U.S. 871 (1990), to show that the injury in fact test and the zone of interest test are separate:

> The failure of an agency to comply with a statutory provision requiring 'on the record' hearings would assuredly have an adverse effect upon the company that has the contract to record and transcribe the agency's proceedings; but since the provision was obviously enacted to protect the interests of the parties to the proceedings and not those of the reporters, that company would not be 'adversely affected within the meaning' of the statute.

The PES was first enacted in 1792 when there were no postal employees. It was reconsidered in 1845. Both in 1792 and 1845, the purpose of the PES was to protect the postal service from competition, not to protect the jobs of postal workers. The right of postal workers to unionize was recognized in a 1970 statute (the Postal Reorganization Act or PRA), but that had nothing to do with the PES.

> To adopt petitioners' contention would require us to hold that the "relevant statute" in this case is the PRA, with all of its various provisions united only by the fact that they deal with USPS. But to accept this level of generality in defining the "relevant statute" could deprive the zone-of-interests test of virtually all meaning.
>
> . . . [N]one of the provisions of the PES has any integral relationship with the labor-management provisions of the PRA. When it enacted the PRA, Congress made no substantive changes to PES. . . . None of the documents constituting the PRA legislative history suggests that those concerned with postal reforms saw any connection between the

PES and the provisions of the PRA dealing with labor-management relations . . .

Are *NCUA* and *Air Courier* distinguishable? The dissent in *NCUA* argued that they were not.

3. *Merits of the zone of interest test.* Unlike the injury in fact test, which is rooted in Article III, the zone of interests test is "prudential," meaning that Congress could abolish it. In *Bennett v. Spear*, 520 U.S. 154 (1997), the Court considered the relationship between the zone of interest tests and the citizen suit provision of the Endangered Species Act, which allows "any citizen" to sue to enjoin certain violations of the Act. It held that Congress could have and did dispense with the zone of interest test in litigation under the Act. Thus Congress, if it wished to do so, could abolish the zone test in cases arising under the APA as well.

The zone of interest test supposedly excludes plaintiffs "whose suits are more likely to frustrate than to further statutory objectives." *Clarke v. Securities Industry Ass'n*, cited in N.2. However, the zone test achieves this goal at a substantial cost. The test requires courts to analyze difficult statutory materials at the threshold of litigation to ascertain whether Congress meant to place a particular plaintiff within the zone of interests protected or regulated by the statute (or other integrally related statutes) in question. And the test can be hard to apply, as the 5–4 division in *NCUA* attests. (Reconsider this point after you have read the following section. As between the zone test and the injury in fact test, which is probably easier for courts to administer?)

Why not follow Justice Brennan's suggestion in his concurring opinion in *Data Processing*: assume that a plaintiff who has been injured in fact has standing unless statutory materials indicate that Congress intended to preclude that plaintiff from seeking judicial review? *Cf. Block v. Community Nutrition Institute*, 467 U.S. 340 (1984) (Congress impliedly intended to preclude review by consumers of milk marketing orders). Or is that not a fair reading of Brennan's opinion? How different is his concept of reviewability from the zone test?

Many states have rejected the zone of interest test. See *Greer v. Illinois Housing Dev. Auth.*, 524 N.E.2d 561 (Ill.1988) (zone test would "unnecessarily confuse and complicate the law"). But other states have accepted it. *See Sun–Brite Car Wash, Inc. v. Board of Zoning Appeals of North Hempstead*, 508 N.E.2d 130 (N.Y.1987), in which a car wash challenged the grant of a zoning variance that permitted construction of another car wash across the street. The Court held that this sort of injury was not among the interests served by the zoning law. Arguably 1981 MSAPA § 5–106(a)(5)(ii) accepts the zone test as well.

4. *Standing of agencies.* In state administrative law, a recurring issue is whether a government official or an agency that is displeased with the decision of another agency can seek judicial review of that decision. In general, if the plaintiff agency is viewed as a subordinate to the decision-maker, it cannot seek review. *See, e.g., Mortensen v. Pyramid Sav. & Loan Ass'n,* 191 N.W.2d 730 (Wis.1971) (savings and loan commissioner cannot appeal decision of savings and loan review board).

However, if the plaintiff is a separate agency or governmental unit whose legal mission is jeopardized by the decision, it can seek judicial review. *See, e.g., Bradford Central School Dist. v. Ambach,* 436 N.E.2d 1256 (N.Y. 1982) (school board can seek review of decision by state education commissioner certifying a teacher). *See generally* Frederick Davis, "Standing of a Public Official to Challenge Agency Decisions: A Unique Problem of State Administrative Law," 16 Admin.L.Rev. 163 (1964).

When a statute creates a separate administrative court, both the government and the private litigant can seek judicial review of such court's decisions. *See, e.g. Missouri Health Facilities Rev. Committee v. Administrative Hearing Comm'n,* 700 S.W.2d 445 (Mo.1985). Similarly, the Commissioner of Internal Revenue can obtain judicial review of decisions of the United States Tax Court, and OSHA can seek review of decisions by the Occupational Safety and Health Review Commission.

What is the objection to allowing government officials who disagree with agency decisions to appeal them? Could this be a valuable check on the tendency of agencies to be captured by the interests they regulate? Or would it entangle a court excessively in conflicts within the executive branch of government? *See generally Director, Office of Workers' Compensation Programs v. Newport News Shipbuilding & Dry Dock Co.,* 514 U.S. 122 (1995); *Carsten v. Psychology Examining Committee,* 614 P.2d 276 (Cal.1980).

5. *Problem*: The shortnose sucker is a small deep-water fish that is considered an endangered species. It is found only in Lost Lake, a body of water formed by High Dam and controlled by the Bureau of Reclamation. To protect the sucker, the Secretary of the Interior adopted a rule under the Endangered Species Act prohibiting withdrawal of water stored in Lost Lake if it would diminish the lake's depth below 12 feet.

Ted's farm is downstream from High Dam. In dry years, Ted relies on irrigation water released by the Bureau from Lost Lake. Ted challenges the rule in District Court, alleging that the rule would prevent releases of water and thus his individual allocation of water would be decreased. Ted claims that the rulemaking record shows that the rule was not based on the "best scientific and commercial data available" as required by the statute. Ted believes that the evidence in the record shows that the sucker can survive in water much shallower than 12 feet.

Although Ted's claim arises under the Endangered Species Act, the citizen suit provision of that Act (*see* N.3) does not apply to this claim. Thus, he sues under the APA. Does Ted have standing? *See Bennett v. Spear,* 520 U.S. 154 (1997).

§ 11.1.3 IMMINENT INJURY, CAUSATION, REMEDIABILITY— THE PUBLIC ACTION

LUJAN v. DEFENDERS OF WILDLIFE
504 U.S. 555 (1992).

Scalia, J.:

[The Endangered Species Act (ESA) requires federal agencies to consult with the Secretary of the Interior to ensure that any action funded by the agency is not likely to jeopardize the continued existence or habitat of an endangered or threatened species. Plaintiff, an environmental organization, challenges a rule promulgated by the Secretary. The rule provides that there is no obligation to consult as to actions outside the United States. Under the rule, therefore, the Agency for International Development (AID) need not consult with the Secretary regarding the funding of projects that would threaten the Asian elephant and Asian leopard in Sri Lanka and the Nile crocodile in Egypt. The only issue is whether plaintiff has standing to seek review of the rule.]

II

While the Constitution of the United States divides all power conferred upon the Federal Government into "legislative Powers," "[t]he executive Power," and "[t]he judicial Power," it does not attempt to define those terms. To be sure, it limits the jurisdiction of federal courts to "Cases" and "Controversies," but an executive inquiry can bear the name "case" (the Hoffa case) and a legislative dispute can bear the name "controversy" (the Smoot–Hawley controversy). Obviously, then, the Constitution's central mechanism of separation of powers depends largely upon common understanding of what activities are appropriate to legislatures, to executives, and to courts ... One of those landmarks, setting apart the "Cases" and "Controversies" that are of the justiciable sort referred to in Article III ... is the doctrine of standing. Though some of its elements express merely prudential considerations that are part of judicial self-government, the core component of standing is an essential and unchanging part of the case-or-controversy requirement of Article III.

Over the years, our cases have established that the irreducible constitutional minimum of standing contains three elements. First, the plaintiff must have suffered an "injury in fact"—an invasion of a legally-protected interest which is (a) concrete and particularized,[1] and (b) "actual or imminent, not 'conjectural' or 'hypothetical.' Second, there must be a causal connection between the injury and the conduct complained of—the injury has to be "fairly ... trace[able] to the challenged action of the defendant, and not ... th[e] result [of] the independent action of some third party not before the court." Third, it must be "likely," as opposed to merely "speculative," that the injury will be "redressed by a favorable decision."

The party invoking federal jurisdiction bears the burden of establishing these elements. Since they are not mere pleading requirements but rather an indispensable part of the plaintiff's case, each element must be supported in the same way as any other matter on which the plaintiff bears the burden of proof, i.e., with the manner and degree of evidence required at the successive stages of the litigation. At the pleading stage, general factual allegations of injury resulting from the

---

1. By particularized, we mean that the injury must affect the plaintiff in a personal and individual way.

defendant's conduct may suffice, for on a motion to dismiss we "presum[e] that general allegations embrace those specific facts that are necessary to support the claim." In response to a summary judgment motion, however, the plaintiff can no longer rest on such "mere allegations," but must "set forth" by affidavit or other evidence "specific facts," which for purposes of the summary judgment motion will be taken to be true. And at the final stage, those facts (if controverted) must be "supported adequately by the evidence adduced at trial."

When the suit is one challenging the legality of government action or inaction, the nature and extent of facts that must be averred (at the summary judgment stage) or proved (at the trial stage) in order to establish standing depends considerably upon whether the plaintiff is himself an object of the action (or foregone action) at issue. If he is, there is ordinarily little question that the action or inaction has caused him injury, and that a judgment preventing or requiring the action will redress it. When, however, as in this case, a plaintiff's asserted injury arises from the government's allegedly unlawful regulation (or lack of regulation) of someone else, much more is needed. In that circumstance, causation and redressability ordinarily hinge on the response of the regulated (or regulable) third party to the government action or inaction—and perhaps on the response of others as well. The existence of one or more of the essential elements of standing "depends on the unfettered choices made by independent actors not before the courts and whose exercise of broad and legitimate discretion the courts cannot presume either to control or to predict," and it becomes the burden of the plaintiff to adduce facts showing that those choices have been or will be made in such manner as to produce causation and permit redressability of injury. . . .

III

We think the Court of Appeals failed to apply the foregoing principles in denying the Secretary's motion for summary judgment. Respondents had not made the requisite demonstration of (at least) injury and redressability.

A

Respondents' claim to injury is that the lack of consultation with respect to certain funded activities abroad "increas[es] the rate of extinction of endangered and threatened species." Of course, the desire to use or observe an animal species, even for purely aesthetic purposes, is undeniably a cognizable interest for purpose of standing. *See, e.g., Sierra Club v. Morton,* 405 U.S. 727 (1972). "But the 'injury in fact' test requires more than an injury to a cognizable interest. It requires that the party seeking review be himself among the injured . . ." *Id.* . . . To survive the Secretary's summary judgment motion, respondents had to submit affidavits or other evidence showing, through specific facts, not only that listed species were in fact being threatened by funded activities abroad, but also that one or more of respondents' members would thereby be "directly" affected apart from their 'special interest' in th[e] subject."

With respect to this aspect of the case, the Court of Appeals focused on the affidavits of two Defenders' members—Joyce Kelly and Amy Skilbred.... Ms. Skilbred averred that she traveled to Sri Lanka in 1981 and "observed.th[e] habitat" of "endangered species such as the Asian elephant and the leopard" at what is now the site of the Mahaweli Project funded by the Agency for International Development (AID), although she "was unable to see any of the endangered species;" "this development project," she continued, "will seriously reduce endangered, threatened, and endemic species habitat including areas that I visited [which] may severely shorten the future of these species;" that threat, she concluded, harmed her because she "intend[s] to return to Sri Lanka in the future and hope[s] to be more fortunate in spotting at least the endangered elephant and leopard." When Ms. Skilbred was asked at a subsequent deposition if and when she had any plans to return to Sri Lanka, she reiterated that "I intend to go back to Sri Lanka," but confessed that she had no current plans: "I don't know [when]. There is a civil war going on right now. I don't know. Not next year, I will say. In the future." [Ms. Kelly furnished similar allegations concerning her plans to observe the Nile crocodile]

We shall assume for the sake of argument that these affidavits contain facts showing that certain agency-funded projects threaten listed species—though that is questionable. They plainly contain no facts, however, showing how damage to the species will produce "imminent" injury to Mss. Kelly and Skilbred. That the women "had visited" the areas of the projects before the projects commenced proves nothing ... And the affiants' profession of an "inten[t]" to return to the places they had visited before—where they will presumably, this time, be deprived of the opportunity to observe animals of the endangered species—is simply not enough. Such "some day" intentions—without any description of concrete plans, or indeed even any specification of when the some day will be—do not support a finding of the "actual or imminent" injury that our cases require.

Besides relying upon the Kelly and Skilbred affidavits, respondents propose a series of novel standing theories. The first, inelegantly styled "ecosystem nexus," proposes that any person who uses *any part* of a "contiguous ecosystem" adversely affected by a funded activity has standing even if the activity is located a great distance away. This approach, as the Court of Appeals correctly observed, is inconsistent with our opinion in *Lujan v. National Wildlife Federation*, which held that a plaintiff claiming injury from environmental damage must use the area affected by the challenged activity and not an area roughly "in the vicinity" of it. 497 U.S. 871, 887–889 (1990) ...

Respondents' other theories are called, alas, the "animal nexus" approach, whereby anyone who has an interest in studying or seeing the endangered animals anywhere on the globe has standing; and the "vocational nexus" approach, under which anyone with a professional interest in such animals can sue. Under these theories, anyone who goes to see Asian elephants in the Bronx Zoo, and anyone who is a keeper of Asian elephants in the Bronx Zoo, has standing to sue because the Director of AID did not consult with the Secretary regarding the AID-funded project in Sri Lanka. This is beyond all reason. Standing is not "an ingenious academic exercise in the conceivable," but as we have said requires, at the summary judgment stage, a factual showing of perceptible harm. It is clear that the person who observes or works with a particular animal threatened by a federal decision is facing perceptible harm, since the very subject of his interest will no longer exist. It is even plausible—though it goes to the outermost limit of plausibility—to think that a person who observes or works with animals of a particular species in the very area of the world where that species is threatened by a federal decision is facing such harm, since some animals that might have been the subject of his interest will no longer exist . . . It goes beyond the limit, however, and into pure speculation and fantasy, to say that anyone who observes or works with an endangered species, anywhere in the world, is appreciably harmed by a single project affecting some portion of that species with which he has no more specific connection . . .

B

Besides failing to show injury, respondents failed to demonstrate redressability. [Even if plaintiffs prevailed, so that funding agencies had to consult the Secretary about the impact of foreign projects on endangered species, it was unclear whether the agencies would follow the Secretary's advice; therefore, a judgment against the Secretary would not necessarily redress the harm to endangered species. The Court declined to clear up this legal uncertainty by deciding the substantive issue—whether funding agencies must follow the Secretary's advice—because the holding would not be binding on the funding agencies, who were not parties to the case.

Moreover, the funding agencies typically supply only a small fraction of the total cost for a foreign project; if that fraction were eliminated, it is unclear whether the projects would be stopped and the danger to the animals thus eliminated. Only three justices concurred with Scalia with respect to part III B, so it does not represent an opinion of the Court.]

IV

The Court of Appeals found that respondents had standing for an additional reason: because they had suffered a "procedural injury." The so-called "citizen-suit" provision of the ESA provides, in pertinent part, that "any person may commence a civil suit on his own behalf (A) to enjoin any person, including the United States and any other governmental instrumentality or agency . . . who is alleged to be in violation of any provision of this chapter." The court held that, because [the ESA] requires interagency consultation, the citizen-suit provision creates a "procedural right" to consultation in all "persons"—so that *anyone* can file suit in federal court to challenge the Secretary's . . . failure to follow the assertedly correct consultative procedure, notwithstanding their inability to allege any discrete injury flowing from that failure.

To understand the remarkable nature of this holding one must be clear about what it does *not* rest upon: This is not a case where plaintiffs are seeking to enforce a procedural requirement the disregard of which could impair a separate concrete interest of theirs (e.g., the procedural requirement for a hearing prior to denial of their license application, or the procedural requirement for an environmental impact statement before a federal facility is constructed next door to them).[7] Nor is it simply a case where concrete injury has been suffered by many persons, as in mass fraud or mass tort situations. Nor, finally, is it the unusual case in which Congress has created a concrete private interest in the outcome of a suit against a private party for the government's benefit, by providing a cash bounty for the victorious plaintiff. Rather, the court held that the injury-in-fact requirement had been satisfied by congressional conferral upon all persons of an abstract, self-contained, noninstrumental "right" to have the Executive observe the procedures required by law. We reject this view.

We have consistently held that a plaintiff raising only a generally available grievance about government—claiming only harm to his and every citizen's interest in proper application of the Constitution and laws, and seeking relief that no more directly and tangibly benefits him than it does the public at large—does not state an Article III case or controversy....

To be sure, our generalized-grievance cases have typically involved Government violation of procedures assertedly ordained by the Constitution rather than the Congress. But there is absolutely no basis for making the Article III inquiry turn on the source of the asserted right. Whether the courts were to act on their own, or at the invitation of Congress, in ignoring the concrete injury requirement described in our cases, they would be discarding a principle fundamental to the separate and distinct constitutional role of the Third Branch—one of the essential elements that identifies those "Cases" and "Controversies" that are the business of the courts rather than of the political branches....

If the concrete injury requirement has the separation-of-powers significance we have always said, the answer must be obvious: To permit Congress to convert the undifferentiated public interest in executive officers' compliance with the law into an "individual right" vindicable in the courts is to permit Congress to transfer from the President to the courts the Chief Executive's most important constitutional duty, to

---

7. There is this much truth to the assertion that "procedural rights" are special: The person who has been accorded a procedural right to protect his concrete interests can assert that right without meeting all the normal standards for redressability and immediacy. Thus, under our case-law, one living adjacent to the site for proposed construction of a federally licensed dam has standing to challenge the licensing agency's failure to prepare an Environmental Impact Statement, even though he cannot establish with any certainty that the Statement will cause the license to be withheld or altered, and even though the dam will not be completed for many years....

"take Care that the Laws be faithfully executed," Art. II, § 3. It would enable the courts, with the permission of Congress, "to assume a position of authority over the governmental acts of another and co-equal department," and to become "virtually continuing monitors of the wisdom and soundness of Executive action." We have always rejected that vision of our role. . . .

Nothing in this contradicts the principle that "[t]he . . . injury required by Art. III may exist solely by virtue of 'statutes creating legal rights, the invasion of which creates standing.' " *Linda R.S. v. Richard D.*, 410 U.S. 614 (1973). Both of the cases used by *Linda R. S.* as an illustration of that principle involved Congress's elevating to the status of legally cognizable injuries concrete, de facto injuries that were previously inadequate in law (namely, injury to an individual's personal interest in living in a racially integrated community and injury to a company's interest in marketing its product free from competition). As we said in *Sierra Club*, "[Statutory] broadening [of] the categories of injury that may be alleged in support of standing is a different matter from abandoning the requirement that the party seeking review must himself have suffered an injury." . . . [It] is clear that in suits against the government, at least, the concrete injury requirement must remain. . . .

KENNEDY, J. with whom SOUTER, J. joins, concurring in part and concurring in the judgment.

. . . I also join Part IV of the Court's opinion with the following observations. As government programs and policies become more complex and far-reaching, we must be sensitive to the articulation of new rights of action that do not have clear analogs in our common-law tradition. . . . In my view, Congress has the power to define injuries and articulate chains of causation that will give rise to a case or controversy where none existed before, and I do not read the Court's opinion to suggest a contrary view. In exercising this power, however, Congress must at the very least identify the injury it seeks to vindicate and relate the injury to the class of persons entitled to bring suit. The citizen-suit provision of ESA does not meet these minimal requirements, because while the statute purports to confer a right on "any person . . . to enjoin . . . the United States and any other governmental instrumentality or agency . . . who is alleged to be in violation of any provision of this chapter," it does not of its own force establish that there is an injury in "any person" by virtue of any "violation." . . .

STEVENS, J., concurring in the judgment. [Stevens disagreed with the majority's views on standing but concurred in reversal since the consultation requirement in ESA does not apply to activities in foreign countries.]

BLACKMUN, J., with whom O'CONNOR, J., joins, dissenting. [Respondents raised genuine issues of fact, sufficient to survive summary judgment, as to injury in fact and remediability.] I question the Court's breadth of language in rejecting standing for "procedural" injuries. I fear the Court seeks to impose fresh limitations on the constitutional authority of Congress to allow citizen-suits in the federal courts for injuries deemed "procedural" in nature ... In conclusion, I cannot join the Court on what amounts to a slash-and-burn expedition through the law of environmental standing. In my view, "[t]he very essence of civil liberty certainly consists in the right of every individual to claim the protection of the laws, whenever he receives an injury." *Marbury v. Madison....*

Notes and Questions

1. *Injury in fact.* The Court agrees that the type of aesthetic or environmental injury claimed by Kelly and Skilbred could meet the injury in fact requirement. Why did they fail to pass the test? Must they have an airline ticket to Sri Lanka or Egypt in hand when they file suit?

2. *Associations as plaintiffs.* The plaintiff in this case was the environmental organization Defenders of Wildlife. Defenders paid the attorneys and made the strategic decisions. As an association, Defenders would have standing only if it had one or more members who could have sued on their own. Since neither Kelly nor Skilbred had the requisite standing, Defenders also lacked standing.

The ability of associations to seek review on behalf of their members is very important. Only established organizations can overcome the free rider problem: that people are unwilling to pay for something they can get for free. Similarly, only established organizations can overcome the problem of transaction costs: it is very expensive to assemble a new group to fund a lawsuit.

Under *Hunt v. Washington State Apple Advertising Comm'n*, 432 U.S. 333 (1977), an association has standing to sue on behalf of its members when a) one or more of its members would otherwise have standing to sue in their own right, b) the interests the association seeks to protect are germane to the organization's purpose, and (c) neither the claim nor the relief requested requires the participation of individual members in the lawsuit. In practice, the latter two requirements are usually easy to meet, so the organization can normally bring suit if it can identify one of its members who has standing.

Most states follow the federal lead on this issue. See, e.g., *Dental Society of New York v. Carey*, 462 N.E.2d 362 (1984) (dental trade association has standing to challenge Medicaid reimbursement schedule). However, in Oregon, the concept of associational standing was rejected. The state supreme court decided that a union could not sue on behalf of some of its members who would have had standing. *Local 290, Plumbers and Pipefitters v. Oregon Dep't of Environmental Quality*, 919 P.2d 1168 (1996). The Oregon APA, like the federal Act and the 1961 and 1981 MSAPAs, provides standing to persons who are "aggrieved" or "adversely affected," but it says nothing about associational standing. The court did not look beyond the language of the statute and did not refer to policy considerations or to federal cases or the law of other states.

3. *The public action.* To meet the Article III injury in fact requirement, the injury in question must be immediate rather than speculative, particularized to the plaintiff rather than generalized to many citizens, and concrete

rather than ideological. These rules are relatively recent judicial innovations with little historical grounding.

The leading federal authority for denying standing in such cases is *Sierra Club v. Morton,* 405 U.S. 727 (1972). In that case the Sierra Club sought to enjoin a ski development in Mineral King, a pristine area of the Sierras. It based its standing solely on its historic interest in the conservation of the Sierras and other wilderness areas. The Court held that Sierra Club lacked standing because it had failed to allege that it or its members had suffered any injury. A historic commitment to conservation is not enough.

In dissent, Justice Douglas argued that standing should be granted to an "inanimate object about to be despoiled, defaced, or invaded by roads and bulldozers and where injury is the subject of public outrage." *Id.* at 741. Sierra Club then amended its complaint to allege that its members camped in Mineral King. The defendants' motion to dismiss the amended complaint was denied. Ultimately the developer abandoned the project.

Many states permit "public actions." For example, *Common Cause v. Board of Supervisors,* 777 P.2d 610 (Cal.1989), allowed a public interest group to sue a county for failing to implement a state voter registration mandate. The Court stated: "Where the question is one of public right and the object of the mandamus is to procure the enforcement of a public duty, the relator need not show that he has any legal or special interest in the result, since it is sufficient that he is interested as a citizen in having the laws executed and the duty in question enforced ... The question in this case involves a public right to voter outreach programs, and plaintiffs have standing as citizens to seek its vindication."

Which makes better sense—the California rule allowing well-funded, determined public interest groups to sue or the federal rule denying such groups the right to sue unless an identified member demonstrably meets the injury in fact test? What is wrong with granting standing to "ideological" plaintiffs? Is the problem that such plaintiffs may do a poor job of presenting their case, thus depriving the federal courts of the sharp adversary clash necessary to decide difficult issues? Or would the federal courts be flooded with cases if it allowed outraged citizens to sue? Or is the concern that such cases inevitably present difficult remedial problems? Or is the real explanation based on separation of powers doctrine? If so, what *is* the separation of powers problem?

4. *Causation and remediability.* To establish standing under Article III, a plaintiff that has been "injured in fact" must also establish that the injury is "fairly traceable" to the conduct complained of (the causation requirement) and also that it is "likely" that the injury will be redressed by a favorable decision (the remediability requirement). These requirements often pose difficulty when the plaintiff is a beneficiary of the statutory scheme, rather than an "object" of regulation.

The causation and remediability requirements overlap. For example, in Part III.B of *Defenders of Wildlife,* the plurality could have said that the Secretary's failure to require consultation by the funding agencies was not the cause of plaintiff's injury (causation) or that requiring consultation would not remedy the plaintiff's injury (remediability).

Do you agree that plaintiff should have to supply evidence regarding the possibility that AID might proceed with funding the projects over the Secretary of the Interior's opposition? Or that Sri Lanka or Egypt might go through with the projects even if AID did not fund them?

Numerous cases have applied the causation and remediability tests to deny standing to plaintiffs in public actions. For example, in *Steel Co. v. Citizens for a Better Environment*, 118 S.Ct. 1003 (1998), the defendant admittedly failed to file required reports concerning its release of toxic chemicals between 1988 and 1995. However, before plaintiff (an environmental organization) filed suit under a citizen suit provision in the statute, the defendant filed all of the reports. Plaintiff's alleged injury in fact concerned harm to its members occurring between 1988 and 1995 arising from unavailability of information that should have been disclosed in the reports. Plaintiff sought to compel defendant to pay civil penalties to the United States and to open its records to plaintiff. Plaintiff also sought to recover its own costs.

The Court first held that federal courts must *always* resolve questions of Article III standing before reaching any other issues, such as whether the statute permits a citizen suit arising out of past statutory violations. This holding required the Court to disapprove lower court cases espousing a doctrine of "hypothetical jurisdiction." Under that doctrine, courts could dismiss a case on statutory grounds and thus avoid reaching and deciding questions of Article III jurisdiction. By holding that difficult Article III questions must always be decided before easy statutory questions, the *Steel Co.* decision makes life harder for the federal courts.

In *Steel Co.*, the Court held that none of the environmental injuries in fact claimed by the organization's members could be redressed by the payment of civil penalties to the Treasury or by any of the other relief sought by the plaintiff. Consequently, the plaintiff lacked standing.

Questions of causation and remediability have also arisen in cases involving state or local laws that inhibit the construction of low income housing. For example, *Warth v. Seldin*, 422 U.S. 490 (1975), held that poor people who wanted to live in Penfield had no standing to challenge Penfield's zoning laws which prohibited the construction of low-income housing. The Court held that even if the zoning laws were struck down, builders still might not construct housing which the plaintiffs could afford. The zoning laws did not necessarily cause the injury; striking them down would not necessarily redress that injury. Causation requirements have emerged in state standing cases as well. *See, e.g., Fox v. Wisconsin Dept. of Health & Soc. Serv.*, 334 N.W.2d 532 (Wis.1983).

Yet the causation and remediability barriers can be overcome. In *Village of Arlington Heights v. Metropolitan Housing Dev. Corp.*, 429 U.S. 252 (1977), a builder and a buyer of low income housing were granted standing to attack exclusionary zoning laws. They demonstrated that the challenged law had prevented construction of a specific low income housing project which the builder was prepared to build and in which the buyer could have afforded to purchase a home.

Does 1981 MSAPA § 5–106(a)(5)(iii) adopt the causation and remediability tests? To the extent it does, do you agree with the decision to incorporate those doctrines into state law?

5. *Procedural injuries.* In note 7, the Court distinguishes "procedural injuries" from the claims made by plaintiffs in the *Defenders* case. For example, suppose an agency fails to prepare a required environmental impact statement (EIS) before building a dam. An EIS is an elaborate document that studies the costs and benefits of a proposed agency action that might adversely affect the environment. An EIS compels the agency to at least consider the environmental aspects of proposed action, but it does not require the agency to desist from the project regardless of environmental damage.

A person who can establish injury in fact from construction of the dam has standing to challenge the agency's failure to prepare an EIS. But observe that, pursuant to note 7, this constitutes a relaxation of the usual causation and remediability requirements. In many (perhaps most) cases, an agency that prepares a proper EIS goes ahead and constructs the project anyway. *See* Christopher L. Burt, Comment, "Procedural Injury Standing After *Lujan v. Defenders of Wildlife*," 62 U.Chi.L.Rev. 275 (1995); *Florida Audubon Soc. v. Bentsen*, 94 F.3d 658 (D.C.Cir.1996) (plaintiff in EIS case must meet Article III standards with respect to the environmental injury that will occur if the project is built, but need only show that omission of EIS "may" cause agency to overlook environmental risks of project). Is this discrepancy justified?

6. *Citizen suit provisions.* The most important holding in *Defenders of Wildlife* is the invalidity of the citizen suit provision of the ESA. A large number of environmental and other statutes have citizen suit provisions; the *Defenders* decision casts doubt on the validity of each of those provisions.

Note the majority's separation of powers rationales: In addition to the theme of judicial restraint (which it routinely invokes when it rejects the standing of plaintiffs who fail one of the Article III tests), the Court asserts that the citizen suit provision amounts to legislative interference with the President's duty to "take care" that the laws be faithfully executed. Thus the decision prevents Congress from constraining the president's discretion through judicial review. Does this approach strengthen the separation of powers? Or weaken it? See Cass R. Sunstein, "What's Standing After *Lujan*? Of Citizen Suits, 'Injuries,' and Article III," 91 Mich.L.Rev. 163 (1992).

The Kennedy–Souter concurrence (which provided two critical votes for the result) does not go as far as the majority opinion. In light of the concurrence, suppose Congress redrafted the ESA to provide that every citizen of the United States has an interest in the survival of an endangered species anywhere in the world on the theories of "ecosystem nexus" or "animal nexus" rejected by the majority. With the addition of that provision, would a citizen suit provision be constitutional? If so, why did Justices Kennedy and Souter regard the actual case as different?

How about providing a $100 bounty for any citizen who brings a successful suit under the ESA. Would the prospect of recovering the bounty be sufficient to support standing?

Several states have adopted statutes allowing any citizen to sue to prevent unreasonable damage to natural resources. *See* Andrew J. Piela, Comment, "A Tale of Two Statutes . . .," 21 B.C.Env.Aff.L.Rev. 401 (1994), summarizing experience under the Connecticut and Minnesota statutes. The Comment concludes that the Minnesota statute has worked well in opening the door to judicial review of all sorts of generalized environmental claims.

7. *Taxpayer actions.* In almost every state, taxpayers have standing to challenge the legality of action taken by the legislature or the executive branch (at either the state or local level) which they allege involves an unlawful expenditure of public funds. See, e.g., *District of Columbia Common Cause v. District of Columbia,* 858 F.2d 1 (D.C.Cir.1988) (D.C. taxpayer has standing to challenge unlawful expenditure by D.C. municipal government— federal rules not applicable to the District's courts). Typically the remedy sought is injunctive, and in some states a prevailing plaintiff is entitled to attorney's fees. Apparently the result has not been an unmanageable flood of litigation. *See generally* Susan L. Parsons, Comment, "Taxpayers' Suits: Standing Barriers and Pecuniary Restraints," 59 Temp.L.Q. 951 (1986).

In contrast to experience at the state level, at the federal level recognition of taxpayer actions has been extremely grudging. A federal taxpayer ordinarily lacks standing to challenge the expenditure of federal funds unless it can be demonstrated that a victory on the merits will reduce the amount of taxes the taxpayer is required to pay. However, in *Flast v. Cohen,* 392 U.S. 83 (1968), the Court allowed a taxpayer standing to challenge as facially unconstitutional a government expenditure program benefiting religious schools. But it designed its test so narrowly that only plaintiffs challenging establishment clause violations could qualify.

8. *Third party standing.* An important prudential limitation on standing is the rule that a plaintiff cannot assert the rights of third parties—only its own rights. This is often referred to as the *jus tertii* rule. *See* 1981 MSAPA § 5–106(a)(5)(i).

The courts have frequently made exceptions to the *jus tertii* rule. For example, a plaintiff can assert the rights of third parties when the latter are legally or practically disabled from suing or when there is a protected relationship (such as doctor-patient or vendor-purchaser) between the plaintiff and the third party. *See generally* Laurence H. Tribe, AMERICAN CONSTITUTIONAL LAW 134–42 (2d ed.1988).

9. *Congressional standing.* In *Raines v. Byrd,* 117 S.Ct. 2312 (1997), several Congressmen challenged the Line Item Veto Act, which allows the President to veto particular appropriations without vetoing the whole bill. The Congressmen claimed that the Act injured them because it altered the legal and practical effect of their votes, divested them of their constitutional role in the repeal of legislation, and altered the constitutional balance of power between the legislative and executive branches. The Court held the Congressmen lacked standing. "The institutional injury they allege is wholly abstract and widely dispersed . . . and their attempt to litigate this dispute at this time and in this form is contrary to historical experience."

In *Raines,* the Court distinguished an earlier case, *Coleman v. Miller,* 307 U.S. 433 (1939). In *Coleman,* a group of Kansas legislators had been granted standing to challenge the state's approval of a constitutional amendment where their votes against the amendment would have been sufficient to defeat it but had not been counted. In contrast, in *Raines* the Congressmen did not allege that their votes for or against any particular bill had not been counted.

10. *Problem.* The Madison Arts Fund (MAF) makes grants to an array of local arts organizations. According to MAF's regulations, between 15% and 25% of the annual grants should go to theatrical organizations, and the grants should be distributed equitably throughout the state. The regulations also provide that MAF grants should be used primarily, though not exclusively, to help new organizations get started as opposed to providing an annual subsidy.

For each of the last four years, MAF granted $200,000 to Dinner Theater Company in the city of Elm to offset Dinner's annual deficit. Dinner stages musicals and light comedy in a dinner theater format. Mort, the director of MAF, used to be a donor to and director of Dinner.

For several years, Ellen has been trying to start another theater company in the same city—the Elm Actors Theater (EAT)—to produce new plays. EAT has not raised enough funds to produce any plays. Her troupe of actors are willing to work for free or for very low salaries. Ellen has applied three times for an MAF grant which would be used to match contributions from the community. Each time, MAF rejected her application, stating that Elm cannot support two theater companies.

Ellen believes that the grants to Dinner are an abuse of MAF's discretion. She points to Mort's pre-existing relationship to Dinner and to the fact that Dinner has been treated with undue favoritism; its three grants were to offset operating expenses rather than to aid in development, and its cultural contribution is minimal.

As a lover of avant garde theater, Nate has volunteered to litigate pro bono on EAT's behalf. Should the plaintiff be Nate or EAT? What are the prospects for this lawsuit? Assume Madison has adopted 1981 MSAPA.

§ 11.2   TIMING OF JUDICIAL REVIEW

§ 11.2.1   INTRODUCTION

This subchapter addresses issues of timing: when can a litigant engage a court in a dispute which involves an administrative agency? Often, the question of whether judicial review can be obtained immediately—or only after protracted administrative proceedings—is critically important.

The four parts of the subchapter concern four different timing doctrines. Each of them can be viewed as a separate hurdle over which a litigant must jump before securing judicial involvement. The four doctrines are closely related and sometimes overlap. They are often confused with one another in discussion and in judicial decisions. In principle, however, each of the four doctrines serves different functions, draws upon different bodies of precedent, and should be carefully distinguished. Thus a preliminary sketch of the doctrines, and how they differ from each other, may be helpful.

a. *The final order rule.* Litigants are sometimes dissatisfied with decisions taken by the agency during the administrative process. For example, an agency might exclude certain evidence at a hearing or refuse to take immediate action to remove a dangerous pesticide from the market. However, as a general rule, courts review only "final orders." This means that ordinarily—but not always—a litigant must complete the entire administrative process before a court will review decisions which the agency took along the way.

b. *Ripeness.* A private party may be threatened by agency action which has not yet occurred. For example, an agency might adopt a new rule or policy—but not yet actually have enforced or otherwise applied it against the plaintiff. In many cases, but by no means always, such disputes are not yet "ripe" for review. This means that a court will await a concrete application of the agency action to the plaintiff before reviewing its legality.

c. *Exhaustion of remedies.* A private party may have an administrative remedy available which has not yet been employed. It is possible that this remedy might be successful; the party's position might prevail and the problem would be solved. Nevertheless, the party wants to skip the administrative remedy and go immediately to court. By the general rule—but not always—a court will not hear the case until the party has first exhausted all administrative remedies.

d. *Primary jurisdiction.* In many situations, *both* a trial court *and* an agency have jurisdiction to deal with a particular problem. If the doctrine of "primary jurisdiction" applies, the trial court refrains from acting so that the matter can be brought to the agency. Thus the courts become involved only by judicially reviewing the agency decision, as opposed to conducting the original trial. In other cases, the court may reject jurisdiction in favor of agency jurisdiction over only a single issue; after the agency adjudicates that issue, the court tries the remaining issues.

Primary jurisdiction differs significantly from the three timing doctrines mentioned above. These doctrines (final order, ripeness, exhaustion) all concern the issue of when a court may *review* agency action. The primary jurisdiction doctrine comes into play in controversies in which the agency might not be initially involved at all—the question is whether a dispute in court between *other* litigants should be dumped into the agency's lap.

This introduction has crudely sketched the four timing doctrines as if they were simple, absolute rules. Nothing could be further from the truth. Each of the four doctrines is riddled with exceptions and qualifications. Many cases are judicially reviewed in the absence of a final order, or before an administrative policy has been applied to the plaintiff, or despite a plaintiff's failure to exhaust administrative remedies. Similarly, the courts frequently retain jurisdiction, holding the doctrine of primary jurisdiction inapplicable.

As you study the material which follows, try to identify the policy reasons for denying someone immediate judicial review (or an immediate judicial trial). Then identify the circumstances in which exceptions are appropriate: when those policy reasons are inapplicable or are outweighed by considerations of hardship.

§ 11.2.2   THE FINAL ORDER RULE

FTC v. STANDARD OIL CO. OF CALIFORNIA
449 U.S. 232 (1980).

[In 1973, the FTC issued a complaint against major oil companies (including Socal), averring that it had "reason to believe" that they were engaging in unfair methods of competition. Socal moved to dismiss the complaint on the ground that the FTC did not have "reason to believe" that it had violated the Act, but the FTC denied the motion. Adjudication before an ALJ of the Commission's charges began and was still pending when, in 1975, Socal filed a complaint in the district court seeking review of whether the FTC had "reason to believe" it was violating the Act. Socal argued that political pressure arising from gasoline shortages in 1973 had induced the FTC to issue a complaint against the major oil companies despite insufficient investigation.

The issue was whether issuance of the FTC complaint before administrative adjudication concludes is "final agency action" subject to judicial review. The district court dismissed the complaint but the Ninth Circuit reversed. It held that the district court could inquire whether the Commission *in fact* had made the determination that it had "reason to believe" Socal was violating the Act.

The Supreme Court held that issuance of the complaint was reviewable only if it was "final agency action" or otherwise was "directly reviewable" under § 704 of the APA. It concluded that it was neither.]

POWELL, J.:

A

The Commission's issuance of its complaint was not "final agency action." The Court observed in *Abbott Laboratories v. Gardner,* 387 U.S. 136, 149 (1967) [discussed in § 11.2.3] that "[t]he cases dealing with judicial review of administrative actions have interpreted the 'finality' element in a pragmatic way." In *Abbott Laboratories,* for example, the publication of certain regulations by the Commissioner of Food and Drugs was held to be final agency action subject to judicial review in an action for declaratory judgment brought prior to any Government action for enforcement....

By its terms, the Commission's averment of "reason to believe" that Socal was violating the Act is not a definitive statement of position. It represents a threshold determination that further inquiry is warranted and that a complaint should initiate proceedings. To be sure, the issuance of the complaint is definitive on the question whether the

Commission avers reason to believe that the respondent to the complaint is violating the Act. But the extent to which the respondent may challenge the complaint and its charges proves that the averment of reason to believe is not "definitive" in a comparable manner to the regulations in *Abbott Laboratories* and the cases it discussed. . . .

Serving only to initiate the proceedings, the issuance of the complaint averring reason to believe has no legal force comparable to that of the regulation at issue in *Abbott Laboratories,* nor any comparable effect upon Socal's daily business. The regulations in *Abbott Laboratories* forced manufacturers to "risk serious criminal and civil penalties" for noncompliance, or "change all their labels, advertisements, and promotional materials; destroy stocks of printed matter; and invest heavily in new printing type and new supplies." Socal does not contend that the issuance of the complaint had any such legal or practical effect, except to impose upon Socal the burden of responding to the charges made against it. Although this burden certainly is substantial, it is different in kind and legal effect from the burdens attending what heretofore has been considered to be final agency action.

In contrast to the complaint's lack of legal or practical effect upon Socal, the effect of the judicial review sought by Socal is likely to be interference with the proper functioning of the agency and a burden for the courts. Judicial intervention into the agency process denies the agency an opportunity to correct its own mistakes and to apply its expertise. *Weinberger v. Salfi,* 422 U.S. 749, 765 (1975). Intervention also leads to piecemeal review which at the least is inefficient and upon completion of the agency process might prove to have been unnecessary. *McGee v. United States,* 402 U.S. 479, 484 (1971) [discussed in § 11.2.4]; *McKart v. United States,* 395 U.S. 185, 195 (1969). Furthermore, unlike the review in *Abbott Laboratories,* judicial review to determine whether the Commission decided that it had the requisite reason to believe would delay resolution of the ultimate question whether the Act was violated. Finally, every respondent to a Commission complaint could make the claim that Socal had made. Judicial review of the averments in the Commission's complaints should not be a means of turning prosecutor into defendant before adjudication concludes.

In sum, the Commission's issuance of a complaint averring reason to believe that Socal was violating the Act is not a definitive ruling or regulation. It had no legal force or practical effect upon Socal's daily business other than the disruptions that accompany any major litigation. And immediate judicial review would serve neither efficiency nor enforcement of the Act. These pragmatic considerations counsel against the conclusion that the issuance of the complaint was "final agency action."

B

Socal relies, however, upon different considerations than these in contending that the issuance of the complaint is "final agency action."

Socal first contends that it exhausted its administrative remedies by moving in the adjudicatory proceedings for dismissal of the complaint.

By thus affording the Commission an opportunity to decide upon the matter, Socal contends that it has satisfied the interests underlying the doctrine of administrative exhaustion. The Court of Appeals agreed. We think, however, that Socal and the Court of Appeals have mistaken exhaustion for finality. By requesting the Commission to withdraw its complaint and by awaiting the Commission's refusal to do so, Socal may well have exhausted its administrative remedy as to the averment of reason to believe. But the Commission's refusal to reconsider its issuance of the complaint does not render the complaint a "definitive" action. The Commission's refusal does not augment the complaint's legal force or practical effect upon Socal. Nor does the refusal diminish the concerns for efficiency and enforcement of the Act.

Socal also contends that it will be irreparably harmed unless the issuance of the complaint is judicially reviewed immediately. Socal argues that the expense and disruption of defending itself in protracted adjudicatory proceedings constitutes irreparable harm. As indicated above, we do not doubt that the burden of defending this proceeding will be substantial. But "the expense and annoyance of litigation is 'part of the social burden of living under government.' " ...

Socal further contends that its challenge to the Commission's averment of reason to believe can never be reviewed unless it is reviewed before the Commission's adjudication concludes. As stated by the Court of Appeals, the alleged unlawfulness in the issuance of the complaint "is likely to become insulated from any review" if deferred until appellate review of a cease-and-desist order. Socal also suggests that the unlawfulness will be "insulated" because the reviewing court will lack an adequate record and it will address only the question whether substantial evidence supported the cease-and-desist order.[11]

We are not persuaded by this speculation. The Act expressly authorizes a court of appeals to order that the Commission take additional evidence. Thus, a record which would be inadequate for review of alleged unlawfulness in the issuance of a complaint can be made adequate. We also note that the APA specifically provides that a "preliminary, procedural, or intermediate agency action or ruling not directly reviewable is subject to review on the review of the final agency action," 5 U.S.C. § 704, and that the APA also empowers a court of appeals to "hold unlawful and set aside agency action ... found to be ... without observance of procedure required by law." 5 U.S.C. § 706. Thus, assuming that the issuance of the complaint is not "committed to agency discretion by law," a court of appeals reviewing a cease-and-desist order has the power to review alleged unlawfulness in the issuance of a

11. The Court of Appeals additionally suggested that the complaint would be "insulated" from review because the alleged unlawfulness would be moot if Socal prevailed in the adjudication. These concerns do not support a conclusion that the issuance of a complaint averring reason to believe is "final agency action." To the contrary, one of the principal reasons to await the termination of agency proceedings is "to obviate all occasion for judicial review." Thus, the possibility that Socal's challenge may be mooted in adjudication warrants the requirement that Socal pursue adjudication, not shortcut it.

complaint. We need not decide what action a court of appeals should take if it finds a cease-and-desist order to be supported by substantial evidence but the complaint to have been issued without the requisite reason to believe. It suffices to hold that the possibility does not affect the application of the finality rule. . . .

Because the Commission's issuance of a complaint averring reason to believe that Socal has violated the Act is not "final agency action" under § [704] of the APA, it is not judicially reviewable before administrative adjudication concludes.[14] . . .

JUSTICE STEVENS concurred in the judgment.

Notes and Questions

1. *The final order rule.* Judicial review statutes frequently authorize the courts to review only "final orders." Even when the adjective "final" does not appear, the statute is construed as if it did. *See, e.g., Carolina Power & Light Co. v. U.S. Dep't of Labor,* 43 F.3d 912 (4th Cir.1995) (statute providing for review of orders means final orders).

The final order doctrine is embodied in both federal and state APA's. Read and compare § 704 of the federal APA and MSAPA §§ 5–102 and 5–103. The FTC's determination that it had "reason to believe" that Socal was violating the law was not a final order under either federal law or under MSAPA § 5–102(b).

In *Bennett v. Spear,* 520 U.S. 154 (1997), the Court summarized earlier cases defining final orders under § 704 of the APA:

> As a general matter, two conditions must be satisfied for agency action to be "final": First, the action must mark the "consummation" of the agency's decisionmaking process—it must not be of a merely tentative or interlocutory character. And second, the action must be one by which "rights or obligations have been determined," or from which "legal consequences will flow."

Is this definition consistent with 1981 MSAPA § 5–102?

In *Socal* the Court indicated that the "reason to believe" determination would be reviewable when a court reviews a final FTC cease and desist order against the company, citing APA § 704 (second sentence). It even suggests that, if necessary, additional evidence could be taken to indicate that the FTC's determination was in bad faith. What arguments would the FTC make against review of the "reason to believe" determination at the time of review of the final order in the case?

2. *When is a non-final order final?* Note that MSAPA § 5–103 allows immediate review of a non-final order where "postponement of judicial

---

14. By this holding, we do not encourage the issuance of complaints by the Commission without a conscientious compliance with the "reason to believe" obligation in 15 U.S.C. § 45(b). The adjudicatory proceedings which follow the issuance of a complaint may last for months or years. They result in substantial expense to the respondent and may divert management personnel from their administrative and productive duties to the corporation. Without a well-grounded reason to believe that unlawful conduct has occurred, the Commission does not serve the public interest by subjecting business enterprises to these burdens.

review would result in an inadequate remedy or irreparable harm disproportionate to the public benefit derived from postponement." *Socal* indicates that the first sentence of § 704 contains a similar implicit exception. Why did the oil company believe that the FTC's "reason to believe" determination should be treated as final?

An example of review of non-final orders arose in several cases involving the pesticide DDT. By statute, EPA must cancel the registration of a pesticide (and thus prevent its sale) if it is unsafe. After EPA issues a "notice of cancellation," a lengthy administrative investigatory and adjudicatory process ensues before the pesticide is finally banned. In the case of an "imminent hazard to health and safety," however, EPA can suspend registration and thereby remove the product from the market immediately.

Despite having information indicating that DDT posed an imminent health hazard, EPA took no action on a request to suspend DDT's registration. Instead, it issued a notice of cancellation for some uses of DDT while continuing to study other uses. The court of appeals held that EPA's failure to take action on the petition to suspend was immediately reviewable. If DDT posed an "imminent" health hazard, the public would suffer irreparable injury during the lengthy cancellation process, because DDT would remain on the market. On two different occasions, the court remanded the matter to EPA to suspend DDT's registration or explain why it had not done so. *Environmental Defense Fund, Inc. v. Hardin*, 428 F.2d 1093 (D.C.Cir. 1970); *Environmental Defense Fund, Inc. v. Ruckelshaus*, 439 F.2d 584 (D.C.Cir.1971) *(EDF II)*.

If EPA had *granted* the suspension, would the manufacturer be eligible for immediate review of that action, as opposed to having to wait until EPA's final decision on permanent cancellation of DDT's registration? *Compare Nor–Am Agricultural Products, Inc. v. Hardin*, 435 F.2d 1151 (7th Cir.1970) (en banc) (no), *with EDF II, supra*, at 589–92 (yes).

3. *Catch 22*. The State of Massachusetts wanted to challenge the methodology used in the 1990 census, which cost it a House seat. The underlying question was how to count federal employees living abroad. The State argued that the methodology was arbitrary and capricious under the APA, but it was defeated by a combination of administrative law doctrines. *Franklin v. Massachusetts*, 505 U.S. 788 (1992). By statute, the Secretary of Commerce conducts the census and reports the results to the President, who transmits a statement to Congress allocating the number of seats for each state.

The Court held that the Secretary of Commerce's action was not "final," and thus not reviewable under the APA, because it was subject to review and revision by the President before it would have any direct and immediate effect on anyone. And the President's decision was not reviewable under the APA because the President is not an "agency." The APA is vague on whether the President falls within the definition of "agency" in § 551(1). The Court held that if Congress wants the President to be covered by broad procedural statutes like the APA, it must say so explicitly.

The Court followed *Franklin* in *Dalton v. Specter*, 511 U.S. 462 (1994), when it refused to review action taken by the Secretary of Defense and the President under the Base Closing Act. The Secretary recommends which bases to close; the President has discretion either to accept or reject the Secretary's report (but can't pick and choose). Once more, the Court held that the Secretary's report was not "final" and the President is not an "agency."

But the Court distinguished these cases in *Bennett v. Spear*, quoted in N.1. In *Bennett*, ranchers sought review of a Biological Opinion issued by the Fish and Wildlife Service. The Opinion recommended that the Bureau of Reclamation—a separate agency—take certain steps to preserve an endangered species of fish. The Court held that the Opinion was a final order because the Opinion "alters the legal regime." In effect the Opinion provides a permit authorizing the Bureau to take action that may harm an endangered species without concern for the penalties that might otherwise apply.

4. *Petitions for reconsideration.* A party to adjudication that disagrees with an agency decision often petitions the agency to reconsider that decision. Normally, a pending petition for reconsideration renders the agency's decision non-final. The party cannot seek judicial review until the reconsideration petition has been resolved. The time period for seeking judicial review of the underlying order starts running at the time the reconsideration petition is denied. *ICC v. Brotherhood of Locomotive Engineers*, 482 U.S. 270 (1987).

5. *Exhaustion, finality, and ripeness.* Did Socal exhaust its remedies? What is the difference between the rule that the courts review only "final orders" and that a litigant must "exhaust its administrative remedies?" Between the "final order" rule and the "ripeness" doctrine?

6. *Witchhunts and judicial review.* Socal claimed that the FTC's decision to prosecute was politically motivated (it occurred during a period of extreme public resentment of big oil companies) and was not based upon an adequate investigation. This claim was not at all implausible. What can a victim do if an agency prosecutes it for reasons relating to politics or public relations? Is immediate judicial review of the agency's decision to issue a complaint a good remedy? Do you think that footnote 14 of the *Socal* opinion will help?

7. *The final order rule and administrative delay.* Despite the final order rule, a court can review an agency's failure to act on a matter before it. *See* APA §§ 555(b), 706(1). However, a court asked to remedy agency footdragging faces a dilemma: an order to expedite one matter may delay other matters or force the agency to decide a matter before it is prepared to do so. After all, an agency has broad discretion with respect to the deployment of its limited resources in carrying out all of its assigned tasks. Thus a court should hesitate before imposing its own timing priorities. *See* § 6.3 N.6.

In *Heckler v. Day*, 467 U.S. 104 (1984), a group of Vermont applicants for Social Security disability benefits brought a class action to force a speed-up in claims processing. In fact, administration of the disability program is characterized by agonizing delays. Recall *Mathews v. Eldridge*, § 2.3.

The trial court ordered that the state agency complete its reconsideration of negative initial decisions within 90 days and that Social Security schedule hearings before ALJs within 90 days. In a 5–4 decision, the

Supreme Court set the decision aside. While Congress was concerned about sluggish administration of the disability program, it had repeatedly rejected mandatory deadline schemes. Congress was concerned that deadlines might jeopardize the quality and uniformity of decisions. The Supreme Court deferred to that Congressional judgment. Moreover, the Court observed, it made no sense to have rigid deadlines in Vermont but not in other states, since Social Security might simply shift resources from other states to Vermont.

8. *Problem*. Madison has adopted 1981 MSAPA. By statute, the Madison Insurance Commission (MIC) has power to seek an injunction in court against unfair insurance practices. It also has power to conduct administrative adjudication against insurance companies leading to a cease and desist order. MIC believes that Security Insurance Co. has a practice of systematically denying undisputed health insurance benefit claims.

Recently, MIC sought an injunction against Security. There was a six-day trial before a judge who refused to issue the injunction on the grounds that Security had proved that it had no such practice. MIC did not appeal this decision.

MIC has since issued an administrative complaint against Security. MIC's ALJ has rejected Security's argument that the administrative case is barred by collateral estoppel. The MIC agency heads refused to review this ruling. Security predicts that the ALJ hearing will take two months and will cost it one million dollars in attorneys fees.

Security seeks immediate judicial review under the APA of the ALJ's ruling. Should the court hear the case? *See R.R. Donnelley & Sons v. FTC*, 931 F.2d 430 (7th Cir.1991); *Town of Huntington v. New York State Division of Human Rights*, 624 N.E.2d 678 (N.Y.1993).

§ 11.2.3   RIPENESS

ABBOTT LABORATORIES v. GARDNER
387 U.S. 136 (1967).

[This case involves the labelling of prescription drugs which are sold under both a trade (or "proprietary" name) and at a lower price under a generic (or "established") name. In 1962, Congress amended the Federal Food, Drug and Cosmetic Act to require makers of drugs with trade names to print the generic names on labels and other printed material. The purpose of the law was to bring to the attention of doctors and patients the fact that many drugs sold under familiar trade names are identical to drugs sold under generic names at lower prices.

The Food and Drug Administration (FDA), exercising legislative rulemaking authority, adopted a rule requiring that the generic name appear on labels and other material *every time* the trade name is used. The manufacturers of 90% of the nation's prescription drugs brought the present case as a class action, seeking declaratory and injunctive relief against the rule. They argued that the "every time" rule exceeded FDA's authority. The court of appeals held that i) pre-enforcement review of

FDA rules was precluded by statute, and ii) the regulation was not ripe for review. In effect, this meant that the manufacturers would be unable to challenge the rules until such time as the government brought suit to force them to comply. The Supreme Court first held that Congress had not precluded pre-enforcement review of FDA regulations.]

HARLAN, J.: . . .

A further inquiry must, however, be made. The injunctive and declaratory judgment remedies are discretionary, and courts traditionally have been reluctant to apply them to administrative determinations unless these arise in the context of a controversy "ripe" for judicial resolution. Without undertaking to survey the intricacies of the ripeness doctrine it is fair to say that its basic rationale is to prevent the courts, through avoidance of premature adjudication, from entangling themselves in abstract disagreements over administrative policies, and also to protect the agencies from judicial interference until an administrative decision has been formalized and its effects felt in a concrete way by the challenging parties. The problem is best seen in a twofold aspect, requiring us to evaluate both the fitness of the issues for judicial decision and the hardship to the parties of withholding court consideration.

As to the former factor, we believe the issues presented are appropriate for judicial resolution at this time. First, all parties agree that the issue tendered is a purely legal one: whether the statute was properly construed by the Commissioner to require the established name of the drug to be used *every time* the proprietary name is employed. Both sides moved for summary judgment in the District Court, and no claim is made here that further administrative proceedings are contemplated. It is suggested that the justification for this rule might vary with different circumstances, and that the expertise of the Commissioner is relevant to passing upon the validity of the regulation. This of course is true, but the suggestion overlooks the fact that both sides have approached this case as one purely of congressional intent, and that the Government made no effort to justify the regulation in factual terms.

Second, the regulations in issue we find to be "final agency action" within the meaning of § [704 of the APA], as construed in judicial decisions. . . .

The regulation challenged here, promulgated in a formal manner after announcement in the Federal Register and consideration of comments by interested parties is quite clearly definitive. There is no hint that this regulation is informal, see *Helco Products Co. v. McNutt*, 137 F.2d 681, or only the ruling of a subordinate official, or tentative. It was made effective upon publication, and the Assistant General Counsel for Food and Drugs stated in the District Court that compliance was expected. . . .

[The regulations] have the status of law and violations of them carry heavy criminal and civil sanctions. . . . Moreover, the agency does have direct authority to enforce this regulation in the context of passing upon applications for clearance of new drugs, or certification of certain antibiotics.

This is also a case in which the impact of the regulations upon the petitioners is sufficiently direct and immediate as to render the issue appropriate for judicial review at this stage. These regulations purport to give an authoritative interpretation of a statutory provision that has a direct effect on the day-to-day business of all prescription drug companies; its promulgation puts petitioners in a dilemma that it was the very purpose of the Declaratory Judgment Act to ameliorate. As the District Court found on the basis of uncontested allegations, "Either they must comply with the every time requirement and incur the costs of changing over their promotional material and labeling or they must follow their present course and risk prosecution." The regulations are clear-cut, and were made effective immediately upon publication; as noted earlier the agency's counsel represented to the District Court that immediate compliance with their terms was expected. If petitioners wish to comply they must change all their labels, advertisements, and promotional materials; they must destroy stocks of printed matter; and they must invest heavily in new printing type and new supplies. The alternative to compliance—continued use of material which they believe in good faith meets the statutory requirements, but which clearly does not meet the regulation of the Commissioner—may be even more costly. That course would risk serious criminal and civil penalties for the unlawful distribution of "misbranded" drugs.

It is relevant at this juncture to recognize that petitioners deal in a sensitive industry, in which public confidence in their drug products is especially important. To require them to challenge these regulations only as a defense to an action brought by the Government might harm them severely and unnecessarily. Where the legal issue presented is fit for judicial resolution, and where a regulation requires an immediate and significant change in the plaintiffs' conduct of their affairs with serious penalties attached to noncompliance, access to the courts under the Administrative Procedure Act and the Declaratory Judgment Act must be permitted, absent a statutory bar or some other unusual circumstance, neither of which appears here. . . .

The Government further contends that the threat of criminal sanctions for noncompliance with a judicially untested regulation is unrealistic; the Solicitor General has represented that if court enforcement becomes necessary, "the Department of Justice will proceed only civilly for an injunction . . . or by condemnation." We cannot accept this argument as a sufficient answer to petitioners' petition. This action at its inception was properly brought and this subsequent representation of the Department of Justice should not suffice to defeat it.

Finally, the Government urges that to permit resort to the courts in this type of case may delay or impede effective enforcement of the Act. We fully recognize the important public interest served by assuring prompt and unimpeded administration of the Pure Food, Drug, and

Cosmetic Act, but we do not find the Government's argument convincing. First, in this particular case, a pre-enforcement challenge by nearly all prescription drug manufacturers is calculated to speed enforcement. If the Government prevails, a large part of the industry is bound by the decree; if the Government loses, it can more quickly revise its regulation.

The Government contends, however, that if the Court allows this consolidated suit, then nothing will prevent a multiplicity of suits in various jurisdictions challenging other regulations. The short answer to this contention is that the courts are well equipped to deal with such eventualities. The venue transfer provision, 28 U.S.C. § 1404(a), may be invoked by the Government to consolidate separate actions. Or, actions in all but one jurisdiction might be stayed pending the conclusion of one proceeding. A court may even in its discretion dismiss a declaratory judgment or injunctive suit if the same issue is pending in litigation elsewhere. . . .

Further, the declaratory judgment and injunctive remedies are equitable in nature, and other equitable defenses may be interposed. If a multiplicity of suits are undertaken in order to harass the Government or to delay enforcement, relief can be denied on this ground alone. The defense of laches could be asserted if the Government is prejudiced by a delay. . . .

In addition to all these safeguards against what the Government fears, it is important to note that the institution of this type of action does not by itself stay the effectiveness of the challenged regulation. There is nothing in the record to indicate that petitioners have sought to stay enforcement of the "every time" regulation pending judicial review. See 5 U.S.C. § 705. If the agency believes that a suit of this type will significantly impede enforcement or will harm the public interest, it need not postpone enforcement of the regulation and may oppose any motion for a judicial stay on the part of those challenging the regulation. It is scarcely to be doubted that a court would refuse to postpone the effective date of an agency action if the Government could show, as it made no effort to do here, that delay would be detrimental to the public health or safety. . . .

Reversed and remanded.

[On the same day as the *Abbott Laboratories* decision, the Court decided *Toilet Goods Ass'n v. Gardner,* 387 U.S. 158 (1967), holding that a different FDA rule was *not* ripe for pre-enforcement review. The rule in *Toilet Goods* provided that if a maker of color additives refused to permit FDA inspectors free access to its facility and formulae, FDA could immediately suspend certification service to the maker. Without FDA certification the additives could not be sold.

Although the regulation was "final" and its validity presented a legal issue, the Court held that the case was not ripe for immediate review. The rule provided that the FDA "may" order an inspection and, if it is refused, "may" suspend certification. Thus, postponing review would help the Court to know about FDA's enforcement problems and the adequacy of safeguards to protect trade secrets. "We believe that judicial appraisal of these factors is likely to stand on a much surer footing in the context of a specific application of this regulation than could be the case in the framework of the generalized challenge made here."

Moreover, the Court was not impressed by the degree of hardship encountered by the additive makers. It was not comparable to that in the *Abbott* case

> where the impact of the administrative action could be said to be felt immediately by those subject to it in conducting their day to day affairs.... This is not a situation in which primary conduct is affected—when contracts must be negotiated, ingredients tested or substituted, or special records compiled.... Moreover, no irremediable adverse consequences flow from requiring a later challenge to this regulation by a manufacturer who refuses to allow this type of inspection.... [R]efusal to allow an inspector here would at most lead only to suspension of certification services to the particular party, a determination that can then be promptly challenged through an administrative procedure, which in turn is reviewable by a court. Such review will provide an adequate forum for testing the regulation in a concrete situation.

Justice Fortas dissented from *Abbott Laboratories* and concurred in *Toilet Goods*. He contended that both cases were not ripe for review "at this stage, under these facts and in this gross, shotgun fashion."]

The Court, by today's decisions, has opened Pandora's box. Federal injunctions will now threaten programs of vast importance to the public welfare. The Court's holding here strikes at programs for the public health. The dangerous precedent goes even further. It is cold comfort—it is little more than delusion—to read in the Court's opinion that "It is scarcely to be doubted that a court would refuse to postpone the effective date of an agency action if the Government could show ... that delay would be detrimental to the public health or safety." Experience dictates, on the contrary, that it can hardly be hoped that some federal judge somewhere will not be moved as the Court is here, by the cries of anguish and distress of those regulated, to grant a disruptive injunction.... I believe that this approach improperly and unwisely gives individual federal district judges a roving commission to halt the regulatory process, and to do so on the basis of abstractions and generalities instead of concrete fact situations, and that it impermissibly broadens the license of the courts to intervene in administrative action by means of a threshold suit for injunction rather than by the method provided by statute....

As to the "every time" rule, the Court says that this confronts the manufacturer with a "real dilemma." But the fact of the matter is that the dilemma is no more than citizens face in connection with countless statutes and with the rules of the SEC, FTC, FCC, ICC, and other regulatory agencies. This has not heretofore been regarded as a basis for injunctive relief unless Congress has so provided. The overriding fact here is—or should be—that the public interest in avoiding the delay in implementing Congress' program far outweighs the private interest; and that the private interest which has so impressed the Court is no more than that which exists in respect of most regulatory statutes or agency rules. Somehow, the Court has concluded that the damage to petitioners if they have to engage in the required redesign and reprint of their labels and printed materials without threshold review outweighs the damage to the public of deferring during the tedious months and years of litigation a cure for the possible danger and asserted deceit of peddling plain medicine under fancy trademarks and for fancy prices which, rightly or wrongly, impelled the Congress to enact this legislation. I submit that a much stronger showing is necessary than the expense and trouble of compliance and the risk of defiance. Actually, if the Court refused to permit this shotgun assault, experience and reasonably sophisticated common sense show that there would be orderly compliance without the disaster so dramatically predicted by the industry, reasonable adjustments by the agency in real hardship cases, and where extreme intransigence involving substantial violations occurred, enforcement actions in which legality of the regulation would be tested in specific, concrete situations. I respectfully submit that this would be the correct and appropriate result. Our refusal to respond to the vastly overdrawn cries of distress would reflect not only healthy skepticism, but our regard for a proper relationship between the courts on the one hand and Congress and the administrative agencies on the other. It would represent a reasonable solicitude for the purposes and programs of the Congress. And it would reflect appropriate modesty as to the competence of the courts. The courts cannot properly—and should not—attempt to judge in the abstract and generally whether this regulation is within the statutory scheme. Judgment as to the "every time" regulation should be made only in light of specific situations, and it may differ depending upon whether the FDA seeks to enforce it as to doctors' circulars, pamphlets for patients, labels, etc. . . .

Notes and Questions

1. *The Abbott Labs equation.* Justice Harlan's opinion in *Abbott Labs* dominates the law of ripeness. Its statement of the rationale for the ripeness doctrine and its balancing test have been repeated and applied in countless federal and state decisions. What is balanced against what under the *Abbott Labs* test? How does the ripeness doctrine relate to the final order rule? Do you agree that *Abbott Labs* and *Toilet Goods* should have been decided differently?

In practice, the *Abbott Labs* balance is normally struck in favor of immediate reviewability of legislative rules—but there are occasional exceptions. An example is the rule that the National Highway Traffic Safety Administration issued after remand in the *Motor Vehicle* case, § 9.5. The new rule required auto manufacturers to install passive restraints in their vehicles, but with the proviso that this obligation would be rescinded if, by 1989, states accounting for two-thirds of the nation's population had enacted strict mandatory seat belt usage laws. State Farm and other insurance interests sued again, but their challenge to this provision failed on ripeness grounds. *State Farm Mutual Auto. Ins. Co. v. Dole,* 802 F.2d 474 (D.C.Cir. 1986). The court predicted (accurately, as it turned out) that the conditions of the proviso would probably never be satisfied. By declining review, the court was able to advance the judicial interest in "avoiding adjudication of speculative controversies" (which was said to bear upon the "fitness" of the issues for review, in *Abbott Labs* terms), while exposing the petitioners to little risk of "hardship" as a realistic matter.

2. *Justice Fortas and predictions of doom.* Before Justice Fortas was appointed to the Supreme Court, he had been a partner in a leading Washington D.C. law firm. He had ample experience in challenging administrative regulations and in using the courts to obstruct enforcement of unwelcome rules. Thus his dissenting remarks about the risks of broadening pre-enforcement review of rules deserve careful consideration.

For several decades, the professional consensus was that *Abbott Labs* was rightly decided. Pre-enforcement review of regulations seemed to function well in clearing away legal doubts about the validity of regulations, thus allowing administration to proceed, or in immediately exposing legal problems which could be promptly corrected by the agency or by Congress.

Recently, some scholars have questioned *Abbott Labs* and the strong presumption of pre-enforcement reviewability articulated in that case. They have identified pre-enforcement review as one of the causes of ossification of the rulemaking process.

Mashaw claims that pre-enforcement review often encourages regulated parties to litigate instead of comply with rules, since there is virtually no penalty (other than paying attorney fees) for launching a challenge. Pre-enforcement review requires courts to review a whole laundry-list of objections to the rules rather than the precise problems that emerge when regulated entities actually attempt to comply. Early review requires the agencies to anticipate every possible legal issue that anyone might raise, which produces massive rulemaking records and lengthy statements of basis and purpose. Mashaw continues:

> A period of attempted compliance, experimentation, and negotiation between the agency and affected parties, induced by the unavailability of immediate review, might well produce better rules, swifter compliance, and less litigation. Moving back toward the older regime of rulemaking review primarily at the time of enforcement thus has much to recommend it, for unnecessary judicial review simultaneously stultifies the policy process while imperiling judicial *and* administrative legitimacy.

Jerry L. Mashaw, "Improving the Environment of Agency Rulemaking: An Essay on Management, Games, and Accountability," 57 L. & Contemp. Prob. 185, 236 (1994).

Seidenfeld takes issue with Mashaw's analysis. He contends that pre-enforcement review compels agencies to do a better job in writing their rules. He also argues that dispensing with pre-enforcement review would cut beneficiaries of a regulatory program (as opposed to regulated parties) out of the judicial review loop, since beneficiaries could not get into court to argue that a regulation was too weak. He also believes that in a regime of high penalties for non-compliance and uncertainty about the validity of a rule, regulated parties would have to comply even with rules they reasonably believe are invalid and which might well turn out to be invalid. Mark Seidenfeld, "Playing Games with the Timing of Judicial Review: An Evaluation of Proposals to Restrict Pre–Enforcement Review of Agency Rules," 58 Ohio St.L.J. 85 (1997). Both Mashaw and Seidenfeld rely heavily on game theory to make their points.

✦3. *Ripeness and non-legislative rules.* Under *Abbott Labs* and *Toilet Goods*, most (but not all) legislative regulations are deemed ripe for pre-enforcement review. But how about interpretive rules and policy statements? Why are non-legislative rules less likely to be treated as ripe for immediate review than legislative rules? *See, e.g., Pacific Legal Foundation v. California Coastal Comm'n,* 655 P.2d 306 (Cal.1982) (guidelines were not ripe for review because they would be clarified by application in particular cases and because they imposed no great hardship except uncertainty in planning).

In some cases, however, interpretive rules and policy statements have been held ripe for review. *See Better Government Ass'n v. Department of State,* 780 F.2d 86 (D.C.Cir.1986), involving guidelines adopted by the Justice Department which listed factors that agencies should consider in granting fee waivers to document requesters under the Freedom of Information Act. Other agencies routinely followed the guidelines. Upon a showing of hardship by the plaintiffs (public interest groups who constantly requested documents and had to pay the fees), the court held that the guidelines were ripe for immediate review.

An important factor that can militate against ripeness in the context of informal administrative actions is the concept of "finality." In this situation, as the discussion in *Abbott Labs* indicates, the concern is not so much with avoiding interruption of a pending proceeding, as in *Socal,* as with ascertaining whether the agency has reached a firm or "definitive" position at all. In *National Automatic Laundry and Cleaning Council v. Shultz,* 443 F.2d 689 (D.C.Cir.1971), the court provided some guidance on this point. There the D.C. Circuit allowed review of a *letter* in which the Administrator of the Wage–Hour Division of the Department of Labor had declared that employees at coin-operated laundries were protected by the Fair Labor Standards Act. The court recognized that the threat of judicial review might deter agencies from dispensing advice. This case, however, involved the relatively rare situation of an interpretive ruling signed by the Administrator himself. The court continued:

> Even the head of an agency, it may be contended, operates on more than one level of deliberativeness. And it may be urged that a ruling made without that kind of assurance of deliberativeness that is presented by a hearing, or a structured controversy, may be the kind of ruling that is more truly subject to reconsideration. Certainly we know that the head of an agency may make tentative rulings and may reconsider rulings previously made....
>
> We think the sound course is to accept the ruling of a board or commission, or the head of an agency, as presumptively final. If it does not indicate on its face that it is only tentative, it would be likely to be

accepted as authoritative.... [However,] a court might decline to entertain a litigation if it was presented ... with an affidavit of the agency head advising the court that the ruling in question was only tentative and outlining the method of seeking reconsideration.

Id. at 701. Despite these guidelines, however, efforts to decide whether an informal pronouncement is "final" can lead to difficult line-drawing problems. *See, e.g., Aulenback, Inc. v. Federal Highway Admin.,* 103 F.3d 156, 165–67 (D.C.Cir.1997) (enforcement manual might not be followed and was thus nonfinal); *Her Majesty The Queen in Right of Ontario v. U.S. EPA,* 912 F.2d 1525 (D.C.Cir.1990) (letter by assistant administrator appeared to speak for agency, so its interpretation of statute was susceptible of review).

4. *Undermining Abbott Labs?* A few recent U.S. Supreme Court cases can be read to indicate that a majority of the justices want to set limits on pre-enforcement review of rules under *Abbott Labs.*

a. *Reno v. Catholic Social Services, Inc.,* 509 U.S. 43 (1993). This case involved review of rules adopted by the Immigration and Naturalization Service under a statute that allowed certain undocumented aliens to apply for permanent residence. The statute required that aliens be continuously present in the U.S. after 1986, with the exception of "brief, casual, and innocent absences." But the challenged regulation provided that *any* absence from the U.S. would break the chain of continuous presence unless the alien first sought permission from the INS.

This regulation created a major problem for undocumented aliens who wanted to apply for permanent residence. They had been absent from the U.S. for brief periods but, needless to say, they didn't seek INS permission. Now, if they applied for permanent residence, they would be ineligible under the regulation, yet by applying they would admit they were undocumented and thus would risk deportation. And the time limit for applying for permanent residence status had run out; the aliens hoped that this litigation would result in a judicially-ordered extension of the deadline. This predicament sounds much like the dilemma that confronted Abbott Labs and persuaded the Court to allow pre-enforcement review.

The Court refused to entertain a challenge to the INS regulation before it was applied to particular aliens, since the regulation did not impose any penalty for violating its restriction but merely limited access to a benefit created by statute. As a result, aliens generally had to await judicial review of the regulation until their applications were formally denied *and* they were ordered deported. This case has triggered concern because of its seeming assumption that the ripeness rule applies differently in cases of benefit-conferring statutes as opposed to regulatory statutes.

The Court did, however, leave a loophole. For aliens whose applications had been rejected immediately by the INS and never processed ("front-desked"), there had been no INS formal procedure regarding that alien. Thus there would have been no formal order rejecting the application and no opportunity to challenge the regulation. So front-desked aliens were permitted to seek pre-enforcement review of the regulation.

b. *Thunder Basin Coal Co. v. Reich,* 510 U.S. 200 (1994). This case held that Congress intended to *preclude* pre-enforcement review of regulations under the Mine Safety Act. The regulation put coal companies in a bind: they could a) allow union officials to conduct safety inspections of their non-union mines (thus giving the union access to information and a toe-hold with the workers) or b) refuse to allow the inspections and take the risk of being subjected to severe penalties (which mounted up on a day-to-day basis) for flouting the regulation. This is just the sort of dilemma that persuaded the Court to allow pre-enforcement review in *Abbott Labs*.

However, in *Thunder Basin,* the Court held that Congress intended that the issue of validity of the regulation be raised only in connection with an agency enforcement action. The evidence for this conclusion was that the statute provided an elaborate post-enforcement administrative procedure which could address petitioner's claims of invalidity of the regulation, plus indications in the legislative history that Congress was concerned that delays in safety inspections put miners at risk.

5. *Ripeness and short time limits on judicial review*. Recall that Congress frequently imposes relatively short statutes of limitation on challenging newly adopted rules. § 10.4 N.4. A typical statute says: "A petition for judicial review shall be filed within sixty days from the date of such action [adoption of a rule] or after such date if the petition is based solely on grounds arising after the sixtieth day."

Because of *Abbott Labs*, Congress assumes that most rules will be challenged before they are enforced; a short statute of limitations assures that the challenges will be brought and cleared up quickly. Moreover, the short limitation period protects the reliance interests of those who intend to comply with the rule, because they can be certain that the rule is valid once the limitation period has passed.

However, the short time period may seriously disadvantage many potential challengers who either didn't know about the rule when it was adopted or who never imagined that it would apply to them. Indeed, the challenger might not even have been in existence when the rule was adopted. When the agency finally applies the rule to the challenger in an enforcement action or by rejecting its application, it is too late to mount a challenge to the rule. Some cases do allow a challenge to a rule when it is actually applied to the petitioner, on the theory that the limitation provision was intended only to preclude pre-enforcement judicial review of the statute, not an as-applied challenge. *See, e.g., Functional Music, Inc. v. FCC*, 274 F.2d 543 (D.C.Cir. 1958).

The harsh effect of a short statute is illustrated by *JEM Broadcasting Co. v. FCC*, 22 F.3d 320 (D.C.Cir.1994). In that case, JEM filed a defective application for a TV license. The FCC had previously adopted a rule, without notice and comment, stating that defective applications would be rejected with no opportunity for correction. By the time JEM was affected by this rule, the 60–day period for challenging the rule had run out. JEM was not permitted to raise the question of whether the rule was validly adopted, even though it had never imagined within the 60 days that it would be affected by the rule since it had never planned to file a defective application. The *Functional Music* case was distinguished because it involved a substantive, rather than a procedural, challenge.

What if a rule is not yet ripe for review by any potential challenger within the limitations period? Does this mean that the rule can never be challenged since the time period will have run out before the rule becomes ripe for review? Generally the courts have held the time periods must be applied with the ripeness doctrine in mind. The time period begins running from the time the rule becomes ripe for review. *See, e.g., Louisiana Environmental Action Network v. Browner*, 87 F.3d 1379, 1385 (D.C.Cir.1996). In *JEM Broadcasting*, however, the court held that the procedural challenge to the rule (based on lack of notice and comment) was ripe when the rule was adopted and that JEM would have had standing, as a potential license applicant, to challenge it at that time. Consequently the 60–day period began running immediately.

6. *Ripeness under state law.* Read 1981 MSAPA §§ 5–102, 5–103. If *Abbott Labs* and *Toilet Goods* arose under state law, would the rules be subject to pre-enforcement judicial review? How about the Justice Department guidelines in *Better Government Ass'n?* *See* Carl A. Auerbach, "Bonfield on State Administrative Law: A Critique," 71 Minn.L.Rev. 543, 571–73 (1987) (criticizing Act for vagueness on issue of whether non-legislative rules are immediately reviewable).

7. *Judicial stays.* A reviewing court has discretion to grant a stay of the agency action while it completes the review process. Often the court does so by granting a preliminary injunction against the agency action in question. See APA § 705; 1981 MSAPA § 5–111. Whether a stay is granted may be the most critical timing issue of all. If the court refuses a stay, the damage to the petitioner may be irreparable; even if the petitioner ultimately wins on the merits, it may be too late to rectify the harm. However, if the court does stay the agency action, a law enforcement program may be sidetracked for years, with great damage to the public interest.

The decision about whether to grant a stay requires a court to take a "peek" at the merits, in order to make an intelligent assessment of the request for a stay. *Cronin v. USDA*, 919 F.2d 439 (7th Cir.1990), suggests that whenever possible the court should resolve both the stay request and the merits all at once rather than doing so in two separate proceedings.

MSAPA § 5–111 sets forth the factors that a court should consider in deciding whether to grant a stay when an agency has already refused to grant a stay because of concern about the public health, safety or welfare:

 i) the likelihood the applicant will prevail on the merits;

 ii) whether the applicant will suffer irreparable injury;

 iii) whether relief will substantially harm other parties to the proceeding; and

 iv) whether the threat to the public health, safety, or welfare relied on by the agency is not sufficiently serious to justify the agency's refusal to grant a stay.

Federal law calls for a similar balance. See *Cuomo v. NRC*, 772 F.2d 972 (D.C.Cir.1985), refusing to grant a stay of NRC's decision to permit low power testing of the Shoreham Nuclear Power Station.

Note the discussion of judicial stays in both the Harlan and Fortas opinions in *Abbott Labs*. Harlan argues that pre-enforcement review of regulations won't harm the public interest because courts would refuse to grant a stay. Fortas counters that some court, somewhere, undoubtedly would grant a stay despite harm to the public interest.

Should a court grant a stay of the "every time" regulation in *Abbott Labs?* Of the Justice Department guidelines in *Better Government Ass'n?*

8. *Problem.* The "Superfund" Act provides for cleaning up toxic waste dumps. Without notice and comment, EPA adopted a policy statement called the Hazardous Ranking System (HRS). EPA intended HRS to serve as a guideline (to itself and to the public) in setting toxic waste cleanup priorities, but it was not to be binding on anyone. HRS is a methodology for setting priorities as to which sites are most dangerous and should be cleaned up first. HRS took account of many factors, such as the toxicity of the particular hazardous substance that might be released, the likelihood of release into the environment, and the threatened population or other sensitive environment. While HRS enabled the calculation of a danger "score" for a particular site, it did not set any cleanup priorities or single out any sites.

Zolt Chemicals anticipates that the HRS methodology would place its toxic waste dump high on a cleanup priority list. Can Zolt Chemicals get immediate judicial review of HRS? *See Eagle–Picher Industries v. U.S. EPA,* 759 F.2d 905 (D.C.Cir.1985). If so, should the court grant a stay?

§ 11.2.4   EXHAUSTION OF ADMINISTRATIVE REMEDIES

McCARTHY v. MADIGAN
503 U.S. 140 (1992).

[While a federal prisoner, McCarthy filed a damages action under the *Bivens* case, § 10.2.2, alleging that respondent prison officials had violated his Eighth Amendment rights by their deliberate indifference to his medical condition. The lower courts dismissed his complaint on the ground that he had failed to exhaust the Bureau of Prisons' administrative remedy procedure.]

BLACKMUN, J.:

. . . Under the "Administrative Remedy Procedure for Inmates" at federal correctional institutions, a prisoner may "seek formal review of a complaint which relates to any aspect of his imprisonment." When an inmate files a complaint or appeal, the responsible officials are directed to acknowledge the filing with a "signed receipt" which is returned to the inmate, to "[c]onduct an investigation," and to "[r]espond to and sign all complaints or appeals." The general grievance regulations do not provide for any kind of hearing or for the granting of any particular type of relief.

To promote efficient dispute resolution, the procedure includes rapid filing and response timetables. An inmate first seeks informal resolution of his claim by consulting prison personnel. If this informal effort fails, the prisoner "may file a formal written complaint on the appropriate form, within 15 calendar days of the date on which the basis of the complaint occurred." Should the warden fail to respond to the inmate's satisfaction within 15 days, the inmate has 20 days to appeal to the Bureau's Regional Director, who has 30 days to respond. If the inmate still remains unsatisfied, he has 30 days to make a final appeal to the Bureau's General Counsel, who has another 30 days to respond. If the inmate can demonstrate a "valid reason for delay," he "shall be allowed" an extension of any of these time periods for filing. . . .

II

The doctrine of exhaustion of administrative remedies is one among related doctrines—including abstention, finality, and ripeness—that govern the timing of federal court decisionmaking. Of "paramount importance" to any exhaustion inquiry is congressional intent. Where Congress specifically mandates, exhaustion is required. But where Congress has not clearly required exhaustion, sound judicial discretion governs. Nevertheless, even in this field of judicial discretion, appropriate deference to Congress' power to prescribe the basic procedural scheme under which a claim may be heard in a federal court requires fashioning of exhaustion principles in a manner consistent with congressional intent and any applicable statutory scheme.

A

This Court long has acknowledged the general rule that parties exhaust prescribed administrative remedies before seeking relief from the federal courts. See, e.g., *Myers v. Bethlehem Shipbuilding Corp.*, 303 U.S. 41 (1938). Exhaustion is required because it serves the twin purposes of protecting administrative agency authority and promoting judicial efficiency.

As to the first of these purposes, the exhaustion doctrine recognizes the notion, grounded in deference to Congress' delegation of authority to coordinate branches of government, that agencies, not the courts, ought to have primary responsibility for the programs that Congress has charged them to administer. Exhaustion concerns apply with particular force when the action under review involves exercise of the agency's discretionary power or when the agency proceedings in question allow the agency to apply its special expertise. The exhaustion doctrine also acknowledges the commonsense notion of dispute resolution that an agency ought to have an opportunity to correct its own mistakes with respect to the programs it administers before it is haled into federal court. Correlatively, exhaustion principles apply with special force when "frequent and deliberate flouting of administrative processes" could weaken an agency's effectiveness by encouraging disregard of its procedures.

As to the second of the purposes, exhaustion promotes judicial efficiency in at least two ways. When an agency has the opportunity to correct its own errors, a judicial controversy may well be mooted, or at least piecemeal appeals may be avoided. And even where a controversy survives administrative review, exhaustion of the administrative procedure may produce a useful record for subsequent judicial consideration, especially in a complex or technical factual context.

B

Notwithstanding these substantial institutional interests, federal courts are vested with a "virtually unflagging obligation" to exercise the jurisdiction given them.... Accordingly, this Court has declined to require exhaustion in some circumstances even where administrative and judicial interests would counsel otherwise. In determining whether exhaustion is required, federal courts must balance the interest of the individual in retaining prompt access to a federal judicial forum against countervailing institutional interests favoring exhaustion. "[A]dministrative remedies need not be pursued if the litigant's interests in immediate judicial review outweigh the government's interests in the efficiency or administrative autonomy that the exhaustion doctrine is designed to further." Application of this balancing principle is "intensely practical," because attention is directed to both the nature of the claim presented and the characteristics of the particular administrative procedure provided.

C

This Court's precedents have recognized at least three broad sets of circumstances in which the interests of the individual weigh heavily against requiring administrative exhaustion. First, requiring resort to the administrative remedy may occasion undue prejudice to subsequent assertion of a court action. Such prejudice may result, for example, from an unreasonable or indefinite timeframe for administrative action. Even where the administrative decisionmaking schedule is otherwise reasonable and definite, a particular plaintiff may suffer irreparable harm if unable to secure immediate judicial consideration of his claim. By the same token, exhaustion principles apply with less force when an individual's failure to exhaust may preclude a defense to criminal liability.

Second, an administrative remedy may be inadequate "because of some doubt as to whether the agency was empowered to grant effective relief." For example, an agency, as a preliminary matter, may be unable to consider whether to grant relief because it lacks institutional competence to resolve the particular type of issue presented, such as the constitutionality of a statute. In a similar vein, exhaustion has not been required where the challenge is to the adequacy of the agency procedure itself, such that "the question of the adequacy of the administrative remedy ... [is] for all practical purposes identical with the merits of [the plaintiff's] lawsuit." Alternatively, an agency may be competent to adjudicate the issue presented, but still lack authority to grant the type of relief requested.

Third, an administrative remedy may be inadequate where the administrative body is shown to be biased or has otherwise predetermined the issue before it.

III

In light of these general principles, we conclude that petitioner McCarthy need not have exhausted his constitutional claim for money damages. As a preliminary matter, we find that Congress has not meaningfully addressed the appropriateness of requiring exhaustion in this context. Although respondents' interests are significant, we are left with a firm conviction that, given the type of claim McCarthy raises and the particular characteristics of the Bureau's general grievance procedure, McCarthy's individual interests outweigh countervailing institutional interests favoring exhaustion....

B

Because Congress has not *required* exhaustion of a federal prisoner's *Bivens* claim, we turn to an evaluation of the individual and institutional interests at stake in this case. The general grievance procedure heavily burdens the individual interests of the petitioning inmate in two ways. First, the procedure imposes short, successive filing deadlines that create a high risk of forfeiture of a claim for failure to comply. Second, the administrative "remedy" does not authorize an award of monetary damages—the only relief requested by McCarthy in this action. The combination of these features means that the prisoner seeking only money damages has everything to lose and nothing to gain from being required to exhaust his claim under the internal grievance procedure ...

As a practical matter, the filing deadlines, of course, may pose little difficulty for the knowledgeable inmate accustomed to grievances and court actions. But they are a likely trap for the inexperienced and unwary inmate, ordinarily indigent and unrepresented by counsel, with a substantial claim.... All in all, these deadlines require a good deal of an inmate at the peril of forfeiting his claim for money damages. The "first" of "the principles that necessarily frame our analysis of prisoners' constitutional claims" is that "federal courts must take cognizance of the valid constitutional claims of prison inmates." Because a prisoner ordinarily is divested of the privilege to vote, the right to file a court action might be said to be his remaining most "fundamental political right, because preservative of all rights." The rapid filing deadlines counsel strongly against exhaustion as a prerequisite to the filing of a federal court action.[8]

As we have noted, the grievance procedure does not include any mention of the award of monetary relief. Respondents argue that this should not matter, because "in most cases there are other things that the inmate wants." This may be true in some instances. But we cannot presume, as a general matter, that when a litigant has deliberately foregone any claim for injunctive relief and has singled out discrete past

---

8. Petitioner concedes that if his complaint contained a prayer for injunctive relief, exhaustion principles would apply differently. Were injunctive relief sought, the grievance procedure probably would be capable of producing the type of corrective action desired. Additionally, because of the continuing nature of conduct subject to injunctive relief, the short filing deadlines would pose less difficulty because the limitations period would be triggered anew by ongoing conduct.

wrongs, specifically requesting monetary compensation only, that he is likely interested in "other things." The Bureau, in any case, is always free to offer an inmate administrative relief in return for withdrawal of his lawsuit. We conclude that the absence of any monetary remedy in the grievance procedure also weighs heavily against imposing an exhaustion requirement . . .

We do not find the interests of the Bureau of Prisons to weigh heavily in favor of exhaustion in view of the remedial scheme and particular claim presented here. To be sure, the Bureau has a substantial interest in encouraging internal resolution of grievances and in preventing the undermining of its authority by unnecessary resort by prisoners to the federal courts. But other institutional concerns relevant to exhaustion analysis appear to weigh in hardly at all. The Bureau's alleged failure to render medical care implicates only tangentially its authority to carry out the control and management of the federal prisons. Furthermore, the Bureau does not bring to bear any special expertise on the type of issue presented for resolution here.

The interests of judicial economy do not stand to be advanced substantially by the general grievance procedure. No formal factfindings are made. The paperwork generated by the grievance process might assist a court somewhat in ascertaining the facts underlying a prisoner's claim more quickly than if it has only a prisoner's complaint to review. But the grievance procedure does not create a formal factual record of the type that can be relied on conclusively by a court for disposition of a prisoner's claim on the pleadings or at summary judgment without the aid of affidavits.

C

In conclusion, we are struck by the absence of supporting material in the regulations, the record, or the briefs that the general grievance procedure here was crafted with any thought toward the principles of exhaustion of claims for money damages. The Attorney General's professed concern for internal dispute resolution has not translated itself into a more effective grievance procedure that might encourage the filing of an administrative complaint as opposed to a court action. Congress, of course, is free to design or require an appropriate administrative procedure for a prisoner to exhaust his claim for money damages. Even without further action by Congress, we do not foreclose the possibility that the Bureau itself may adopt an appropriate administrative procedure consistent with congressional intent.

REVERSED.

REHNQUIST, C.J., with whom SCALIA, J. and THOMAS, J. join, concurring in the judgment.

I agree with the Court's holding that a federal prisoner need not exhaust the procedures promulgated by the Federal Bureau of Prisons. My view, however, is based entirely on the fact that the grievance procedure at issue does not provide for any award of monetary damages.

As a result, in cases such as this one where prisoners seek monetary relief, the Bureau's administrative remedy furnishes no effective remedy at all, and it is therefore improper to impose an exhaustion requirement.

Because I would base the decision on this ground, I do not join the Court's extensive discussion of the general principles of exhaustion, nor do I agree with the implication that those general principles apply without modification in the context of a *Bivens* claim. In particular, I disagree with the Court's reliance on the grievance procedure's filing deadlines as a basis for excusing exhaustion. As the majority observes, we have previously refused to require exhaustion of administrative remedies where the administrative process subjects plaintiffs to unreasonable delay or to an indefinite timeframe for decision. This principle rests on our belief that when a plaintiff might have to wait seemingly forever for an agency decision, agency procedures are "inadequate" and therefore need not be exhausted.

But the Court makes strange use of this principle in holding that filing deadlines imposed by agency procedures may provide a basis for finding that those procedures need not be exhausted. Whereas before we have held that procedures without "reasonable time limit[s]" may be inadequate because they make a plaintiff wait too long, today the majority concludes that strict filing deadlines might also contribute to a finding of inadequacy because they make a plaintiff move too quickly. But surely the second proposition does not follow from the first. In fact, short filing deadlines will almost always promote quick decisionmaking by an agency, the very result that we have advocated repeatedly in the cases cited above. So long as there is an escape clause, as there is here, and the time limit is within a zone of reasonableness, as I believe it is here, the length of the period should not be a factor in deciding the adequacy of the remedy.

NEW JERSEY CIVIL SERVICE ASS'N (NJCSA) v. STATE
443 A.2d 1070 (N.J.1982).

SCHREIBER, J.

At issue in this case is whether state employees who formerly functioned as hearing officers in the Division of Motor Vehicles are entitled to appointment as administrative law judges under the act creating the Office of Administrative Law.... Prior to 1978 many contested cases before state agencies were initially heard by a hearing officer or an examiner who was an employee of the agency responsible for rendering a decision. Some hearing officers were part-time employees who were paid on a per diem basis; others were full-time state employees who performed other duties for their agencies in addition to holding hearings. The use of agency employees to adjudicate claims against an agency encouraged an institutional bias that undermined the fairness and impartiality desired in administrative adjudication.

To rectify this condition the Legislature amended the APA in 1978 to create an independent Office of Administrative Law (OAL), staffed by a corps of independent examiners known as administrative law judges. The major purpose of this legislation was "to bring impartiality and objectivity to agency hearings and ultimately to achieve higher levels of fairness in administrative adjudications." Except for [three agencies], state agencies can no longer use their own employees to preside over contested cases. Instead, that function is performed by administrative law judges, who are directly responsible to the Director of the Office of Administrative Law. . . .

[The State Agency Transfer Act provides that when the powers of one state agency are transferred, the employees of the agency are transferred as well. However, the Attorney General advised the Director of OAL that the Transfer Act did not require that hearing officers were entitled to appointment as ALJs under the APA amendments. As a result, hearing officers were invited to apply for appointment as ALJs. Of the 45 ALJs, about half were formerly hearing officers. Former hearing officers who were not appointed as ALJs sought judicial review.]

I

. . . We have declined to review mere "opinions" or "conclusions" of administrative officers on which no official action was based.

Certainly the Attorney General's Opinion expressing the view that hearing officers are not entitled to appointment as administrative law judges was not a final agency action subject to review. However, the Director of OAL has followed the Attorney General's advice and has not appointed any of the individual appellants as administrative law judges. The appellants' action may thus fairly be considered an appeal from the implicit refusal of the Director to appoint them as administrative law judges.

Such a construction does not conflict with the Court's reluctance to render opinions in the abstract. Our principal aim in avoiding premature review of administrative determinations has been to protect the Court from becoming entangled in abstract disagreements over administrative policies, and also to refrain from judicial interference until an administrative decision has been formed and its effects felt in a concrete way by the challenging parties. In this case, although administrative policy has not been formally expressed, three years have passed since the Director of the Office of Administrative Law received the Attorney General's opinion. The Director's failure to appoint any of the individual appellants as an administrative law judge is tantamount to final agency action. The effect of that action is directly felt by appellants. In considering their claim we do not intrude into agency policymaking.

Similar considerations prompt us to excuse the failure to exhaust available administrative remedies. Rather than pursue their rights as classified civil service employees to present their claim to the Civil Service Commission, the individual appellants went directly to the Appellate Division in apparent violation of R. 2:2–3(a). The rule provides that "[u]nless the interest of justice requires otherwise, review ... shall not be maintainable so long as there is available a right of review before any administrative agency or office."

The exhaustion of administrative remedies is not an absolute prerequisite to seeking appellate review, however. Exceptions are made when the administrative remedies would be futile, when irreparable harm would result, when jurisdiction of the agency is doubtful, or when an overriding public interest calls for a prompt judicial decision. We have frequently held that in a case involving only legal questions, the doctrine of exhaustion of administrative remedies does not apply. As Justice Jacobs has explained, in determining when the exhaustion requirement may be waived,

> we are not particularly concerned with the label or description placed on the issue but are concerned with underlying considerations such as the relative delay and expense, the necessity for taking evidence and making factual determinations thereon, the nature of the agency and the extent of judgment, discretion and expertise involved, and such other pertinent factors ... as may fairly serve to aid in determining whether, on balance, the interests of justice dictate the extraordinary course of bypassing the administrative remedies made available by the Legislature. [*Roadway Express, Inc. v. Kingsley,* 179 A.2d 729 (1962).]

In this case, there are no facts in dispute. We need consider only the law and legislative history. Nor does resolution of the disputed issue call for the exercise of special administrative expertise. In these circumstances, putting appellants to the additional expense and delay of bringing their case in the appropriate administrative forum is unjustified.... [On the merits, the court rejected the appellant's legal argument, stating that the Legislature intended "to create a corps of independent professionals, who were not simply hearing officers under a different title, but had greatly expanded duties. There is nothing in the Office of Administrative Law act that suggests that former hearing officers were to be imported en masse into the new office."]

Notes and Questions

1. *Exhaustion of remedies or exhaustion of litigants? McCarthy* is exceptional. Most litigants are required to exhaust all available administrative remedies before going to court, even though the remedies seem slow, costly, frustrating, and useless. A good example is *Portela-Gonzalez v. Secretary of the Navy,* 109 F.3d 74 (1st Cir.1997). Portela–Gonzalez was fired from her civilian job at a Naval Exchange in Puerto Rico. She had held this job for 30 years. She had placed some articles of clothing on layaway for herself; when the store slashed prices during the post-Christmas lull, she cancelled the layaway and bought them on sale, saving herself $154. The Navy claimed that this violated the regulations.

She filed a grievance and appealed her discharge through three levels— the Officer in Charge of the Exchange, the Commanding Officer of the base, and the Commanding Officer of the Naval Support Service. Although there was one more level to which she could appeal (the Deputy Assistant Secretary of the Navy, Equal Employment Opportunity Office), she skipped this appeal and filed suit. The court held that the case should be dismissed because of a failure to exhaust remedies.

It noted that, like *McCarthy*, this was not a case of exhaustion explicitly required by statute; as a result, the court has more discretion to relax the exhaustion requirement. Portela–Gonzalez argued that the futility exception should apply, because she would have gotten nowhere if she had taken the final step. The court noted:

> Reliance on the exception in a given case must be anchored in demonstrable reality. A pessimistic prediction or a hunch that further administrative proceedings will prove unproductive is not enough to sidetrack the exhaustion rule.... [C]laimants who seek safe harbor under the futility exception "must show that it is certain that their claim will be denied on appeal, not merely that they doubt an appeal will result in a different decision."

> Portela cannot surmount this hurdle. The claim of futility is merely a self-serving pronouncement in the circumstances of this case. The evidence is uncontradicted that the Deputy Assistant Secretary is an impartial official who has reversed termination decisions affecting Navy Exchange personnel in the past. Though the prognosis for Portela's unused administrative appeal may have been poor and her expectations modest, neither courts nor litigants are allowed to equate pessimism with futility. Because there is nothing in the record to suggest that Portela's lack of success at the previous levels of review necessarily signified that the final level of review would be an empty gesture, her failure to exhaust an available administrative remedy cannot be overlooked on the ground of futility.

The lower court ruled that to minimize waste of resources, it would excuse the failure to exhaust remedies and decide the case on the merits, but the court of appeals disagreed.

> Were we to adopt the lower court's reasoning, the resulting exception would swallow the exhaustion rule in a single gulp. Once an aggrieved party has brought suit, forcing her to retreat to any unused administrative appeal potentially wastes resources. The Supreme Court ... explained that a "primary purpose" of the exhaustion doctrine is "the avoidance of premature interruption of the administrative process." Consequently, it is generally inefficient to permit a party to seek judicial recourse without first exhausting her administrative remedies. Following this train of thought, the Court has concluded that, by and large, concerns regarding efficiency militate in favor of, rather than against, strict application of the exhaustion doctrine.

> This view is steeped in real-world wisdom. Insisting on exhaustion forces parties to take administrative proceedings seriously, allows administrative agencies an opportunity to correct their own errors, and potentially avoids the need for judicial involvement altogether. Furthermore, disregarding available administrative processes thrusts parties prematurely into overcrowded courts and weakens an agency's effectiveness by encouraging end-runs around it.

2. *Factors in the judicial balance.* Assuming a court has discretion whether to excuse a failure to exhaust, some factors that it might consider include:

    i.   The nature and severity of harm to plaintiff from delayed review;

    ii.   The need for agency expertise in resolving the issue;

    iii.   The nature of the issue involved (issues of law, constitutional issue, jurisdictional issue, application of law to fact);

    iv.   The adequacy of the remedy in light of plaintiff's particular claim;

    v.   The extent to which the claim appears to be serious rather than a tactic for delaying the agency process;

    vi.   The apparent clarity or doubt as to the resolution of the merits of plaintiff's claim;

    vii.   The extent to which exhaustion would be futile because an adverse decision is certain.

    viii.   The extent to which petitioner had a valid excuse for its failure to exhaust.

Because the exhaustion issue is decided through an ad hoc application of numerous factors, the results are difficult to predict, the exhaustion issue is litigated constantly, and litigants are encouraged to try for premature review. Would you favor a more determinate rule? If so, what would it be? Always require exhaustion? Never require it?

3. *Exhaustion of remedies and issues of law or jurisdiction.* Under federal law, a party must exhaust remedies even though the dispute concerns a question of law or of the agency's jurisdiction or its authority. In the leading case, *Myers v. Bethlehem Shipbuilding Corp.*, 303 U.S. 41 (1938), the employer in an NLRB proceeding argued that it was not operating in interstate commerce and, therefore, that the agency had no jurisdiction over it as a matter of law. Accordingly, it sought judicial intervention to stop the Board from holding a hearing. The Court said:

> The contention is at war with the long-settled rule of judicial administration that no one is entitled to judicial relief for a supposed or threatened injury until the prescribed administrative remedy has been exhausted. That rule has been repeatedly acted on in cases where, as here, the contention is made that the administrative body lacked power over the subject matter.

As the *NJCSA* case shows, New Jersey law differs sharply from federal law. New Jersey courts, and those of many other states, allow courts to rule on questions of law or jurisdiction before the party has exhausted administrative remedies. *See Ward v. Keenan*, 70 A.2d 77 (N.J.1949) (no exhaustion required if agency jurisdiction challenged on persuasive grounds); *On-Line Financial Serv. v. Dep't of Human Rts.*, 592 N.E.2d 509 (Ill.App.1992) (no exhaustion required on claim that agency action against petitioner was untimely); *Watergate II Apartments v. Buffalo Sewer Authority*, 385 N.E.2d 560 (N.Y.1978) (no exhaustion required on claim that agency action is wholly beyond its power because of a prior agreement between the parties).

What is the rationale for making an exception from the exhaustion requirement in cases of legal or jurisdictional disputes? Is such an exception in "the interests of justice" as held in *NJCSA*?

4. *Model Act provisions.* Study carefully the two provisions on exhaustion in the 1981 MSAPA: §§ 5–107, 5–112. Why were two different exhaustion sections needed? Is § 5–107 consistent with *McCarthy?* With *NJCSA?*

5. *Exhaustion of remedies under the APA.* What is meant by the last sentence of APA § 704? It provides:

> Except as otherwise expressly required by statute, agency action otherwise final is final for the purposes of this section whether or not there has been presented or determined an application for a declaratory order, for any form of reconsideration, or, unless the agency otherwise requires by rule and provides that the action meanwhile is inoperative, for an appeal to superior agency authority.

In *Darby v. Cisneros*, 509 U.S. 137 (1993), the Court held that, although the last sentence of § 704 is written in terms of finality, it must also be intended as an exception to the exhaustion rule. In *Darby*, HUD rules provided that a party could appeal an ALJ decision to the Secretary of Housing, but did not require such an appeal or provide for a stay of the ALJ's decision during the course of the appeal. As a result, the Court held that Darby could seek judicial review of an adverse ALJ decision without bothering to appeal to the Secretary.

Presumably, HUD will immediately amend its rules to require persons like Darby to appeal an ALJ decision to the Secretary and to provide a stay of the ALJ's decision pending appeal. After such an amendment, litigants like Darby will have to appeal unfavorable ALJ decisions to the Secretary before seeking judicial review.

After such an amendment occurs, could litigants like Darby still take advantage of the exceptions to the exhaustion rule recognized in *McCarthy v. Madigan?* Recall the distinction drawn in *McCarthy* between exhaustion that is jurisdictional because required by statute and exhaustion that is imposed by judicial discretion. If the last sentence of § 704 is treated as a form of exhaustion required by statute, it could be argued that courts have no discretion to excuse a failure to exhaust, for example on the grounds that the remedy in question would be futile. *See Volvo GM v. United States Dep't of Labor*, 118 F.3d 205 (4th Cir.1997), holding that the court lacks authority to excuse a failure to exhaust remedies in a case brought under the APA.

6. *Exhaustion and constitutional issues.* One of the more puzzling applications of the exhaustion requirement concerns constitutional issues. The general rule is that an agency lacks authority to determine the constitutionality of statutes. *See* Glenn Justin Hovemann, Comment, "When Constitutional Issues Arise in Agency Adjudications: A Suggested Approach," 65 Ore.L.Rev. 413 (1986). Indeed, the California Constitution prohibits an agency from invalidating its own statute on constitutional grounds. Art. III, § 3.5.

As a result, a party who launches an on-the-face challenge of the constitutionality of a statute or regulations is not required to exhaust remedies since there is no effective administrative remedy in such cases.

This principle applies both to substantive attacks (such as that the statute or regulation violates the first amendment) or procedural attacks (such as that the statute or regulation violates procedural due process). *See, e.g., Rafeedie v. INS*, 880 F.2d 506 (D.C.Cir.1989) (no exhaustion required in case of due process attack on summary deportation procedure); *Giffin v. Chronister*, 616 A.2d 1070 (Pa. Cmnwlth. 1992) (same—combination of functions in a licensing scheme). Note the language in *McCarthy* on this point (¶ IIC of the opinion).

However, exhaustion is often required in several situations that involve constitutional claims. First, if a statute requires exhaustion (as opposed to the situation in which exhaustion is discretionary), a court is likely to insist that even on-the-face constitutional claims be first presented to the agency. *See, e.g., Massieu v. Reno*, 91 F.3d 416 (3d Cir.1996). Even in this situation, exhaustion might not be required if the constitutional issue is wholly collateral to the issue on the merits and could not be effectively reviewed at the time the merits are reviewed. *Mathews v. Eldridge*, § 2.3 (excusing exhaustion as to the issue of whether due process requires a pre-termination hearing in disability cases).

Second, exhaustion may be required if the case presents both constitutional and non-constitutional issues, since the party may win on the non-constitutional issue and thus allow the court to avoid dealing with the constitutional issue.

Third, exhaustion is usually required if the constitutional challenge is to the statute or regulation or other agency action *as applied* to the plaintiff as opposed to an *on-the-face* attack. In these situations, the facts of the particular case are usually needed to decide the constitutional question and the agency decision will assist the court by assembling a factual record. *See* Hovemann, *supra,* 65 Ore.L.Rev. at 420 n.31, 443–49; Bernard Schwartz, ADMINISTRATIVE LAW § 8.40 at 557–59 (3d ed.1991). Note, however, that *McCarthy* is a case involving an as-applied constitutional challenge—and the Court excused exhaustion of remedies.

Remember that in non-statutory exhaustion cases, the court often applies a balancing test in deciding whether to excuse exhaustion. Especially where the plaintiff suffers serious injury from delay, the court may well decide to resolve serious constitutional issues without exhaustion, even though the plaintiff's challenge is as-applied or there are non-constitutional issues in the case. *See, e.g., Andrade v. Lauer*, 729 F.2d 1475 (D.C.Cir.1984) (deciding serious constitutional issue but not unrelated legal issue).

7. *Too late to exhaust—exhaustion as preclusion.* Normally, a party who is unable to secure judicial review because of a failure to exhaust remedies can go back to the agency and avail itself of the remedy. However, in some situations, this is not possible. For example, a party might have failed to raise a particular claim before the ALJ who heard the case or before the agency heads on an administrative appeal. Courts generally refuse to consider that issue on judicial review because the party has waived it. This doctrine is sometimes referred to as the "exact issue" rule.

The leading case on the exact issue rule is *United States v. L.A. Tucker Truck Lines*, 344 U.S. 33, 37 (1952): "Simple fairness to those who are engaged in the tasks of administration, and to litigants, requires as a general rule that courts should not topple over administrative decisions unless the administrative body not only has erred but has erred against objection made at the time appropriate under its practice." Yet the exact issue rule is not absolute. *See* 1981 MSAPA § 5–112, which provides for exceptions to the exact issue principle. Federal case law also provides various exceptions such as for futility or inability to raise the issue. *See, e.g., California Dept. of Education v. Bennett,* 843 F.2d 333, 339 (9th Cir.1988); *Washington Ass'n for Television & Children v. FCC,* 712 F.2d 677 (D.C.Cir.1983).

An even more serious problem arises when the appellant has not pursued an administrative remedy that is no longer available, such as a failure to appeal an ALJ's decision to the agency heads within the time period for such appeals. If a court requires exhaustion of the administrative remedy in such cases, it has wholly precluded judicial review. See, e.g., *McGee v. United States,* 402 U.S. 479 (1971), which involved attempted judicial review of a draft board classification. The only means by which a registrant could obtain review was by refusing to be inducted into the armed forces. In a criminal case for refusing induction, the court would consider an erroneous classification by the draft board as a defense. In *McGee,* however, the registrant had failed to appeal his classification to the state appeal board. As a result of his failure to exhaust remedies, he was not permitted to question his classification in the criminal trial.

8. *Actions under § 1983.* In *Patsy v. Florida Board of Regents,* 457 U.S. 496 (1982), the Court considered whether exhaustion of state remedies was required before bringing a civil rights suit in federal court under § 1983. Ms. Patsy was employed by a public university in Florida and alleged that she had been discriminated against in promotions because of her age and sex. Patsy did not take advantage of the remedies provided by Florida for race and sex discrimination (a grievance procedure within the university). The Supreme Court held that a § 1983 plaintiff is never required to exhaust state remedies, no matter how adequate or easily exhausted those remedies might be. Does this mean that Ms. Patsy was not even required to complain to her boss about the alleged discrimination before filing suit? Is this wise policy? Why might Patsy prefer to avoid the state remedies and go directly to court?

9. *Problem*: Our client Ann has applied to receive payments of $400 per month under the state's Aid for the Totally Disabled Program (ATD) which is administered by the Welfare Board. She desperately needs the money and is facing eviction from her apartment and a cutoff of utility services. Until recently, Ann received money from her mother but that source of funds has ended because her mother lost her job.

Recipients of ATD must be totally disabled (meaning unable to work) and also must meet severe tests based on financial need. Regulations of the Welfare Board provide that a recipient of ATD who has worked for any compensation whatever during the last six months is disqualified from receiving ATD.

Two years ago, Ann (who lives alone) had a baby who was born with severe handicaps, including Down's Syndrome. Under the county's program of In–Home Supportive Services (IHSS), Ann has been receiving $200 per month to care for her baby.

Sheila, who is Ann's social worker, has determined that Ann is unable to work because of disabling psychiatric problems including paralyzing anxieties and depression. However, Sheila recommended that Ann's application for ATD be rejected because the IHSS payments are compensation for work within the meaning of the regulation. On March 2, Ann received a notice from the Welfare Board rejecting her application, and stating that she could request a fair hearing with regard to her application on April 20. A decision in that hearing could be expected about 6 weeks later. In the event Ann is dissatisfied with the decision, she can file an appeal with the head of the Welfare Board.

You wish to seek immediate judicial review of the issues raised by the notice. You intend to question the Board's application of its regulation to Ann's situation and, if the regulation is found to be applicable, to question whether it is consistent with statute and with the state and federal constitutions. If that fails, you want to urge that the agency should waive its usual rules in the case of the IHSS payment. You also hope to obtain a court order requiring that Ann receive ATD payments pending her hearing or at least an order requiring her to receive a hearing within 5 days.

Will the court dismiss some or all of Ann's claims under the doctrine of exhaustion of remedies? Assume the state follows i) New Jersey law, ii) the 1981 MSAPA, or iii) federal law. See *Uzwil v. Robins,* 519 N.Y.S.2d 866 (N.Y.A.D.1987).

Should you request a Welfare Board fair hearing on April 6 even if you plan to go to court immediately? Assuming the court case is pending on April 6, should you attend that hearing and put on your case? If you do go through the agency hearing and lose at that level, should you appeal to the Welfare Board?

§ 11.2.5   PRIMARY JURISDICTION

FARMERS INSURANCE EXCHANGE
v. SUPERIOR COURT
826 P.2d 730 (Cal.1992).

Lucas, C.J.:

[The California Attorney General (sometimes referred to as The People) sued Farmers to require it to offer good driver discounts to its auto insurance customers. Count 1 was based on Insurance Code § 1861.02 which was enacted by the voters as an initiative and requires insurers to offer good driver discounts. However, the Court held that the Insurance Code vests enforcement of § 1861.02 exclusively in the Insurance Commissioner. Consequently, it upheld the lower court's decision which dismissed count 1.

The second count was based on the Unfair Practices Act, Business & Professions Code § 17000, which provides remedies in cases of illegal business practices. The Attorney General has power to enforce § 17000 through an injunction action and an action for civil penalties. Farmers argued that the second count should be dismissed under the doctrine of primary jurisdiction.]

III. THE PRIMARY JURISDICTION DOCTRINE

A. *Development of the Doctrine*

The judicially created doctrine of "primary jurisdiction" (also referred to as the doctrine of "prior resort" or "preliminary jurisdiction") originated in *Texas & Pac. Ry. v. Abilene Cotton Oil Co..*, 204 U.S. 426 (1907) (hereafter *Abilene*), and as explained below, most of the development of the doctrine has occurred in the federal courts.

In *Abilene*, a shipper sued a railroad in state court under the common law to recover alleged unreasonable amounts charged for transporting interstate freight.... Under the Commerce Act, Congress granted the ICC power to hear such complaints by shippers, and to order reparations to those injured. Despite provisions of the Commerce Act allowing a litigant to elect between administrative enforcement of statutory rights and judicial enforcement of common law rights, the high court declined to allow the common law suit in the first instance. Instead, it ruled that in order to promote uniformity and consistency of rate regulations, the shipper "must ... primarily invoke redress through the Interstate Commerce Commission.... " The Court explained that "if, without previous action by the Commission, power might be exerted by courts and juries generally to determine the reasonableness of an established rate, it would follow that unless all courts reached an identical conclusion a uniform standard of rates in the future would be impossible, as the standard would fluctuate and vary, depending on the divergent conclusions reached as to reasonableness by the various courts called upon to consider the subject as an original question.... "

The doctrine of *Abilene* was refined and clarified in *Great Northern Ry. v. Merchants Elevator Co.*, 259 U.S. 285 (1922). In *Merchants*, another case in which a shipper attempted to press suit against a railway to recover asserted overcharges, Justice Brandeis, speaking for the court, allowed the state court suit to proceed because the issue presented in that case—i.e., the proper interpretation of a tariff—was one of law and neither involved disputed facts, nor required the exercise of expertise possessed by the ICC. The court explained, "Preliminary resort to the Commission [is necessary when] ... the enquiry is essentially one of fact and of discretion in technical matters; and uniformity can be secured only if its determination is left to the Commission. Moreover, that determination is reached ordinarily upon voluminous and conflicting evidence, for the adequate appreciation of which acquaintance with many intricate facts of transportation is indispensable; and such acquaintance is commonly to be found only in a body of experts. But what construction shall be given to a railroad tariff presents ordinarily a question of law which does not differ in character from those presented when the construction of any other document is in dispute."

In a third railroad shipping case, *United States v. Western Pac. R. Co.*, 352 U.S. 59 (1956), the shipper (the United States government) filed suit in the Court of Claims to recover alleged overcharges. The issue presented was similar to that in *Merchants*, i.e., the construction of a railroad tariff. Specifically, the question posed was whether shipments of steel bomb cases filled with napalm gel should be classified as "incendiary bombs" (subject to a high first-class tariff rate) or merely "gasoline in steel drums" (subject to a lower, fifth-class rate).

The high court considered the factors articulated in *Abilene* and *Merchants* ... The court asserted that the term "incendiary bomb," as used in the tariff regulations, posed a question of construction that "involves factors 'the adequate appreciation of which' presupposes an 'acquaintance with many intricate facts of transportation'" possessed by the ICC. Accordingly, the court concluded, "in the circumstances here presented the question of tariff construction, as well as that of the reasonableness of the tariff as applied, was within the exclusive primary jurisdiction of the Interstate Commerce Commission."

A more recent high court case illustrates both procedural and substantive aspects of the primary jurisdiction doctrine. In *Nader v. Allegheny Airlines*, 426 U.S. 290 (1976), the plaintiff filed a common law tort action for fraudulent misrepresentation against an airline that sold him a confirmed ticket on an overbooked flight, causing the plaintiff to miss his flight.... The high court [allowed the fraud case to proceed and declined to apply the primary jurisdiction doctrine]. It noted that under the administrative scheme at issue, individual consumers were "not even entitled" to initiate proceedings before the Board. The fact that the plaintiff in the case before it had no authority to bring an administrative action, however, did not resolve the court's primary jurisdiction inquiry.... It concluded the proposed misrepresentation action posed no challenge to uniformity of regulation and that "the standards to be applied in an action for fraudulent misrepresentation are within the conventional competence of the courts, and the judgment of a technically expert body is not likely to be helpful in the application of these standards to the facts of this case...."

B.　*The Primary Jurisdiction and Exhaustion Doctrines Compared*

Petitioners assert throughout their briefs that the People should be required to "exhaust" their administrative remedies before pursuing their civil action in this case, [but] the applicable principle in this case is the primary jurisdiction doctrine, not the exhaustion doctrine.

Petitioners' mischaracterization is understandable because courts have often confused the two closely related concepts. "Both are essentially doctrines of comity between courts and agencies. They are two sides of the timing coin: Each determines whether an action may be brought in a court or whether an agency proceeding, or further agency proceeding, is necessary." B. Schwartz, Administrative Law § 8.23 (1984).

In *Western Pacific*, the high court explained: "Exhaustion applies where a claim is cognizable in the first instance by an administrative agency alone; judicial interference is withheld until the administrative process has run its course. Primary jurisdiction, on the other hand, applies where a claim is originally cognizable in the courts, and comes into play whenever enforcement of the claim requires the resolution of issues which, under a regulatory scheme, have been placed within the special competence of an administrative body; in such a case the judicial process is suspended pending referral of such issues to the administrative body for its views." [Unlike the People's first count, its claim under § 17000] is originally cognizable in the courts, and thus it triggers application of the primary jurisdiction doctrine.

C. Policy Considerations Underlying the Primary Jurisdiction and Exhaustion Doctrines

The policy reasons behind the two doctrines are similar and overlapping. The exhaustion doctrine is principally grounded on concerns favoring administrative autonomy (i.e., courts should not interfere with an agency determination until the agency has reached a final decision) and judicial efficiency (i.e., overworked courts should decline to intervene in an administrative dispute unless absolutely necessary). As explained above, the primary jurisdiction doctrine advances two related policies: it enhances court decisionmaking and efficiency by allowing courts to take advantage of administrative expertise, and it helps assure uniform application of regulatory laws.

No rigid formula exists for applying the primary jurisdiction doctrine. Instead, resolution generally hinges on a court's determination of the extent to which the policies noted above are implicated in a given case.[9] This discretionary approach leaves courts with considerable flexibility to avoid application of the doctrine in appropriate situations, as required by the interests of justice. . . .

VI. APPLICATION OF THE PRIMARY JURISDICTION DOCTRINE IN THIS CASE

First . . . the Insurance Commissioner has at his disposal a "pervasive and self-contained system of administrative procedure" to deal with the precise questions involved herein.

Second, and more important, based on the allegations in the People's complaint, there is good reason to require that these administrative procedures be invoked here. As we explain below, we conclude that considerations of judicial economy, and concerns for uniformity in application of the complex insurance regulations here involved, strongly militate in favor of a stay to await action by the Insurance Commissioner in the present case . . . [C]ourts have observed that questions involving insurance rate making pose issues for which specialized agency fact-finding and expertise is needed in order to both resolve complex factual questions and provide a record for subsequent judicial review. . . .

The People assert the claims at issue here "involve relatively simple factual determinations which do not require the detailed examination of experts within the Department of Insurance. . . . " [On the contrary] the

---

9. Although this approach focuses on the benefits to be gained by courts (e.g., efficiency and uniform application of regulatory laws) and agencies (e.g., autonomy) under the primary jurisdiction doctrine, courts have also appropriately considered the alleged "inadequacy" of administrative remedies, and other factors affecting litigants, in determining whether the interests of justice militate against application of the doctrine in a particular case.

resolution of these questions mandates exercise of expertise presumably possessed by the Insurance Commissioner, and poses a risk of inconsistent application of the regulatory statutes if courts are forced to rule on such matters without benefit of the views of the agency charged with regulating the insurance industry. . . .

The determination of whether a given Good Driver Discount policy comports with the "20 percent discount" provision of the statute also calls for exercise of administrative expertise preliminary to judicial review. Inevitably, analysis of the People's claim will require "a searching inquiry into the factual complexities of [automobile] insurance rate-making and the conditions of that market during the turbulent time here involved." To address the People's claim, one must inquire into the insurer's ratemaking process in order to determine what the rate would be for a given driver without the discount. Thereafter one must discern whether the rate offered on a given Good Driver Discount policy is 20 percent below what the insured would otherwise have been charged. . . .

VII. CONCLUSION

We conclude, based on the complaint as it stands, that a paramount need for specialized agency review militates in favor of imposing a requirement of prior resort to the administrative process, and . . . we reject any suggestion that the interests of justice militate against application of a prior resort requirement in this case.

Accordingly, the judgment of the Court of Appeal is reversed with directions to issue a writ of mandate directing the superior court to stay judicial proceedings in this case and retain the matter on the court's docket pending proceedings before the Insurance Commissioner, and to closely monitor the progress of the administrative proceedings to ensure against unreasonable delay of the People's civil action.

MOSK, J., dissented. . . .

Notes and Questions

1. *Primary jurisdiction and exclusive jurisdiction.* The issue presented in final order, ripeness, and exhaustion of remedy cases is the timing of judicial review of agency action. In primary jurisdiction cases, the issue is not the timing of judicial *review* of agency action. Instead, these cases present the problem of concurrent *trial* jurisdiction.

In some situations, the legislature *precludes* judicial jurisdiction, making the agency's jurisdiction exclusive. The *Farmers* court so held as to the People's first count. Where preclusion has not occurred, so that *both* a court and an agency have *concurrent* jurisdiction to try a case (as in the second count in *Farmers*), the question is: who goes first? If the court decides that the agency should go first, it has applied the doctrine of primary jurisdiction.

Most primary jurisdiction cases involve disputes between two private parties (such as the various U. S. Supreme Court cases discussed in *Farmers*). Some, like *Farmers*, are law enforcement cases brought by a state or federal attorney general. In neither situation is the case brought by or against the regulatory agency that controls the particular industry. When the case is brought by or against the regulatory agency, the problem is generally one of finality or exhaustion of remedies, not primary jurisdiction.

Primary jurisdiction cases are of two different kinds. If a court finds that the agency should go first, and the agency proceeding will dispose of *all* the issues in the case, the court dismisses the action. The matter returns to court only upon judicial review of the agency action. This is primary jurisdiction of the whole case. If the court finds that the agency cannot dispose of the entire case, the court stays the action, sends the parties to the agency, and retains jurisdiction to try the remaining issues after the agency is finished. *Reiter v. Cooper,* 507 U.S. 258 (1993). This is primary jurisdiction of an *issue or issues*. Note the concluding paragraph of the court's opinion in *Farmers*.

In a case of primary jurisdiction over issues, could a court simply ask the agency to express its views by filing an amicus brief instead of sending the case to the agency?

2. *Rationale for primary jurisdiction.* Why should a court, which has jurisdiction over a matter, decide that the entire case, or some of the issues, should be tried by an agency? There needs to be some persuasive reason for the court not to exercise its statutory jurisdiction. The cases discussed in *Farmers* indicate that there may be three reasons for doing so:

    i.   A need for uniform results;

    ii.   A need for the agency's expertise;

    iii.   The possibility that agency approval of a challenged practice may immunize that practice from judicial challenge, or at least alter the legal status of the practice.

On which of these rationales did the court rely in *Farmers*?

Note that the People in *Farmers* sought civil penalties under § 17000. The Insurance Commissioner did not have power to award that remedy. Courts sometimes identify the lack of remedy as a factor suggesting that primary jurisdiction should not apply. How did the court get around the problem in *Farmers*?

3. *Primary jurisdiction and the administration of justice.* Why did the Attorney General resist having the case sent to the Insurance Commissioner? Why did Farmers want the case to be sent there?

National Communications Ass'n v. AT&T, 46 F.3d 220, 225 (2d Cir. 1995), involved a dispute between AT&T and a relatively small wholesaler of long distance time. The dispute concerned the interpretation of AT&T's tariff. The court refused to send the case to the FCC under the primary jurisdiction doctrine. It said:

Agency decisionmaking often takes a long time and the delay imposes enormous costs on individuals, society and the legal system. Delay in agency decisionmaking is often due to 1) large workload, 2) difficult issues, 3) inadequate funding and staffing, 4) poor organizational structure and management, 5) time-consuming decisionmaking procedures, 6) judicial review, 7) OMB review, and 8) intentional delay. Davis & Pierce, Admin. L. Treatise § 12.1 (3d ed.1994).

The parties estimated that the delay resulting from sending the case back to the FCC would be from two to five years. "Since the district court can conclude this matter far more expeditiously, a potential delay of even two years more than outweighs any benefit that might be achieved by having the FCC resolve this relatively simple factual dispute."

4. *Criminal cases*. Should the doctrine of primary jurisdiction apply in a *criminal* case when the defendant argues that agency expertise is needed to resolve technical issues? *Compare United States v. General Dynamics Corp.,* 828 F.2d 1356 (9th Cir.1987) (primary jurisdiction should not apply in a criminal case for defrauding the government on a defense contract) *with United States v. Yellow Freight Sys., Inc.,* 762 F.2d 737 (9th Cir.1985) (case remanded to ICC to resolve tariff construction issues). Does referral of some issues in a criminal case to an administrative agency undermine the right to jury trial or the right to a speedy trial? Is there some way by which an agency can furnish input into a criminal trial without actually sending the case to the agency?

5. *Private rights of action*. The primary jurisdiction doctrine comes into play when both a court and an agency have jurisdiction to hear the case.

Many statutes provide for administrative or criminal remedies but are unclear about whether private parties have a civil remedy to enforce the statute. The issue then becomes whether the court should imply a "private right of action" into the statute. The court declined to imply a private right of action with respect to the first count in *Farmers Insurance*. Even if a private right of action does exist, the court must decide whether the agency has primary jurisdiction of the claim.

The problem of whether a statute gives rise to an implied private right of action by a victim against the party who caused the harm is difficult and recurrent. In *Cort v. Ash,* 422 U.S. 66 (1975), the Court set forth a four-factor test to analyze whether Congress intended to create a private right of action.

    i. Is the plaintiff one of the class for whose special benefit the statute was enacted?

    ii. Is there evidence of legislative intent to create such a remedy or deny it?

    iii. Is it consistent with the underlying purposes of the legislative scheme to imply such a remedy?

    iv. Is the cause of action one traditionally relegated to state law, so that it would be inappropriate to infer a cause of action based solely on federal law?

More recent federal cases display great reluctance to infer private rights of action from federal statutes, absent some indication that Congress intended that this remedy exist. *See* Richard Fallon et.al., *Hart & Wechsler's The Federal Courts and the Federal System* 829–46 (4th ed.1996).

6. *Problem*. Madison has legal casino gambling and heavily regulates the casino industry. A statute provides that the Casino Control Commission (CCC) shall have exclusive jurisdiction over all matters delegated to it. It provides that the CCC shall regulate the industry so as to create and

preserve public confidence and trust in the credibility and integrity of the regulatory process and of casino operations.

Casinos must receive a license from CCC. The agency is empowered to suspend or revoke casino licenses, or assess civil penalties against casinos, for violation of CCC regulations. The statute also provides that the CCC can order restitution of any money unlawfully obtained by a casino. All adjudicatory matters (licensing, penalties, and restitution) are initiated by the CCC director. CCC's regulations prohibit casinos from allowing persons to gamble while intoxicated.

Leonard lost over $1,000,000 in one night playing blackjack at Dusty's Casino. He was served 12 free drinks during this period and was visibly very intoxicated. Leonard files suit in Madison superior court seeking to recover $1,000,000 from Dusty's and to recover an additional $3,000,000 in punitive damages. Dusty's moves to dismiss the action because the CCC has either exclusive jurisdiction or primary jurisdiction over the claim. *See Greate Bay Hotel & Casino v. Tose*, 34 F.3d 1227 (3d Cir.1994). How should the court rule on this motion?

Appendix A

UNITED STATES CONSTITUTION (SELECTED PROVISIONS)

Article I

Section 1. All legislative Powers herein granted shall be vested in a Congress of the United States, which shall consist of a Senate and House of Representatives.

Section 7. [1] All Bills for raising Revenue shall originate in the House of Representatives; but the Senate may propose or concur with Amendments as on other Bills.

[2] Every Bill which shall have passed the House of Representatives and the Senate, shall, before it become a Law, be presented to the President of the United States; If he approve he shall sign it, but if not he shall return it, with his Objections to that House in which it shall have originated, who shall enter the Objections at large on their Journal, and proceed to reconsider it. If after such Reconsideration two thirds of that House shall agree to pass the Bill, it shall be sent, together with the Objections, to the other House, by which it shall likewise be reconsidered, and if approved by two thirds of that House, it shall become a Law. But in all such Cases the Votes of both Houses shall be determined by yeas and Nays, and the Names of the Persons voting for and against the Bill shall be entered on the Journal of each House respectively. If any Bill shall not be returned by the President within ten Days (Sundays excepted) after it shall have been presented to him, the Same shall be a Law, in like Manner as if he had signed it, unless the Congress by their Adjournment prevent its Return, in which Case it shall not be a Law.

[3] Every Order, Resolution, or Vote to Which the Concurrence of the Senate and House of Representatives may be necessary (except on a question of Adjournment) shall be presented to the President of the United States; and before the Same shall take Effect, shall be approved by him, or being disapproved by him, shall be repassed by two thirds of the Senate and House of Representatives, according to the Rules and Limitations prescribed in the Case of a Bill.

Section 8. The Congress shall have Power . . .

[18]   To make all Laws which shall be necessary and proper for carrying into Execution the foregoing Powers, and all other Powers vested by this Constitution in the Government of the United States, or in any Department or Officer thereof.

Section 9. [3] No Bill of Attainder or ex post facto law shall be passed.

[7]   No Money shall be drawn from the Treasury, but in Consequence of Appropriations made by Law; and a regular Statement and Account of the Receipts and Expenditures of all public Money shall be published from time to time.

Article II

Section 1. [1] The executive Power shall be vested in a President of the United States of America....

Section 2. [1] The President shall be Commander in Chief of the Army and Navy of the United States; ... he may require the Opinion, in writing, of the principal Officer in each of the executive Departments, upon any Subject relating to the Duties of their respective Offices....

[2]   He shall have Power, by and with the Advice and Consent of the Senate, to make Treaties, provided two thirds of the Senators present concur; and he shall nominate, and by and with the Advice and Consent of the Senate, shall appoint Ambassadors, other public Ministers and Consuls, Judges of the supreme Court, and all other Officers of the United States, whose Appointments are not herein otherwise provided for, and which shall be established by Law; but the Congress may by Law vest the Appointment of such inferior Officers, as they think proper, in the President alone, in the Courts of Law, or in the Heads of Departments....

Section 3. He shall from time to time give to the Congress Information of the State of the Union, and recommend to their Consideration such Measures as he shall judge necessary and expedient; ... he shall take Care that the Laws be faithfully executed, and shall Commission all the Officers of the United States.

Section 4. The President, Vice President and all civil Officers of the United States, shall be removed from Office on Impeachment for, and Conviction of, Treason, Bribery, or other high Crimes and Misdemeanors.

Article III

Section 1. The judicial Power of the United States, shall be vested in one supreme Court, and in such inferior Courts as the Congress may from time to time ordain and establish....

Section 2. [1] The judicial Power shall extend to all Cases, in Law and Equity, arising under this Constitution, the Laws of the United States, and Treaties made, or which shall be made, under their Authority;—to all Cases affecting Ambassadors, other public Ministers and

Consuls;—to all Cases of admiralty and maritime Jurisdiction;—to Controversies to which the United States shall be a Party;—to Controversies between two or more States;—between a State and Citizens of another State;—between Citizens of different States;—between Citizens of the same State claiming Lands under the Grants of different States, and between a State, or the Citizens thereof, and foreign States, Citizens or Subjects.

Amendment I [1791]

Congress shall make no law respecting an establishment of religion, or prohibiting the free exercise thereof; or abridging the freedom of speech, or of the press; or the right of the people peaceably to assemble, and to petition the Government for a redress of grievances.

Amendment IV [1791]

The right of the people to be secure in their persons, houses, papers, and effects, against unreasonable searches and seizures, shall not be violated, and no Warrants shall issue, but upon probable cause, supported by Oath or affirmation, and particularly describing the place to be searched, and the persons or things to be seized.

Amendment V [1791]

No person shall be held to answer for a capital, or otherwise infamous crime, unless on a presentment or indictment of a Grand Jury, except in cases arising in the land or naval forces, or in the Militia, when in actual service in time of War or public danger; nor shall any person be subject for the same offence to be twice put in jeopardy of life or limb; nor shall be compelled in any criminal case to be a witness against himself, nor be deprived of life, liberty, or property, without due process of law; nor shall private property be taken for public use, without just compensation.

Amendment VII [1791]

In Suits at common law, where the value in controversy shall exceed twenty dollars, the right of trial by jury shall be preserved, and no fact tried by a jury, shall be otherwise re-examined in any Court of the United States, than according to the rules of the common law.

Amendment XIV [1868]

Section 1. All persons born or naturalized in the United States, and subject to the jurisdiction thereof, are citizens of the United States and of the State wherein they reside. No State shall make or enforce any law which shall abridge the privileges or immunities of citizens of the United States; nor shall any State deprive any person of life, liberty, or property, without due process of law; nor deny to any person within its jurisdiction the equal protection of the laws.

Appendix B

FEDERAL ADMINISTRATIVE PROCEDURE ACT UNITED STATES CODE, TITLE 5

Table of Sections

Sec.
551.   Definitions.
552.   Public information; agency rules, opinions, orders, records, and proceedings [Freedom of Information Act—excerpts only].
552a.   Records maintained on individuals [Privacy Act omitted.]
552b.   Open meetings [Sunshine Act omitted.]
553.   Rule making.
554.   Adjudications.
555.   Ancillary matters.
556.   Hearings; presiding employees; powers and duties; burden of proof; evidence; record as basis of decision.
557.   Initial decisions; conclusiveness; review by agency; submissions by parties; contents of decisions; record.
558.   Imposition of sanctions; determination of applications for licenses; suspension, revocation, and expiration of licenses.
559.   Effect on other laws; effect of subsequent statute.
561–70. [Negotiated Rulemaking Act omitted.]
571–83. [Administrative Dispute Resolution Act omitted.]
601–12. [Regulatory Flexibility Act omitted.]
701.   Application; definitions.
702.   Right of review.
703.   Form and venue of proceeding.
704.   Actions reviewable.
705.   Relief pending review.
706.   Scope of review.
801–08. [Congressional Review Act omitted.]
3105.   Appointment of administrative law judges.
7521.   Actions against administrative law judges.
5372.   Administrative law judges.
3344.   Details; administrative law judges.
1305.   Administrative law judges.

CHAPTER 5—ADMINISTRATIVE PROCEDURE

§ 551. Definitions

For the purpose of this subchapter—

(1) "agency" means each authority of the Government of the United States, whether or not it is within or subject to review by another agency, but does not include—

    (A) the Congress;

    (B) the courts of the United States;

    (C) the governments of the territories or possessions of the United States;

    (D) the government of the District of Columbia;

or except as to the requirements of section 552 of this title—

    (E) agencies composed of representatives of the parties or of representatives of organizations of the parties to the disputes determined by them;

    (F) courts martial and military commissions;

    (G) military authority exercised in the field in time of war or in occupied territory; or

    (H) functions conferred by sections 1738, 1739, 1743, and 1744 of title 12; chapter 2 of title 41; subchapter II of chapter 471 of title 49; or sections 1884, 1891–1902, and former section 1641(b)(2), of title 50, appendix;

(2) "person" includes an individual, partnership, corporation, association, or public or private organization other than an agency;

(3) "party" includes a person or agency named or admitted as a party, or properly seeking and entitled as of right to be admitted as a party, in an agency proceeding, and a person or agency admitted by an agency as a party for limited purposes;

(4) "rule" means the whole or a part of an agency statement of general or particular applicability and future effect designed to implement, interpret, or prescribe law or policy or describing the organization, procedure, or practice requirements of an agency and includes the approval or prescription for the future of rates, wages, corporate or financial structures or reorganizations thereof, prices, facilities, appliances, services or allowances therefor or of valuations, costs, or accounting, or practices bearing on any of the foregoing;

(5) "rule making" means agency process for formulating, amending, or repealing a rule;

(6) "order" means the whole or a part of a final disposition, whether affirmative, negative, injunctive, or declaratory in form, of an agency in a matter other than rule making but including licensing;

(7) "adjudication" means agency process for the formulation of an order;

(8) "license" includes the whole or a part of an agency permit, certificate, approval, registration, charter, membership, statutory exemption or other form of permission;

(9) "licensing" includes agency process respecting the grant, renewal, denial, revocation, suspension, annulment, withdrawal, limitation, amendment, modification, or conditioning of a license;

(10) "sanction" includes the whole or a part of an agency—

(A) prohibition, requirement, limitation, or other condition affecting the freedom of a person;

(B) withholding of relief;

(C) imposition of penalty or fine;

(D) destruction, taking, seizure, or withholding of property;

(E) assessment of damages, reimbursement, restitution, compensation, costs, charges, or fees;

(F) requirement, revocation, or suspension of a license; or

(G) taking other compulsory or restrictive action;

(11) "relief" includes the whole or a part of an agency—

(A) grant of money, assistance, license, authority, exemption, exception, privilege, or remedy;

(B) recognition of a claim, right, immunity, privilege, exemption, or exception; or

(C) taking of other action on the application or petition of, and beneficial to, a person;

(12) "agency proceeding" means an agency process as defined by paragraphs (5), (7), and (9) of this section;

(13) "agency action" includes the whole or a part of an agency rule, order, license, sanction, relief, or the equivalent or denial thereof, or failure to act; and

(14) "ex parte communication" means an oral or written communication not on the public record with respect to which reasonable prior notice to all parties is not given, but it shall not include requests for status reports on any matter or proceeding covered by this subchapter.

§ 552. Public information; agency rules, opinions, orders, records, and proceedings [Freedom of Information Act—excerpts only]

(a) Each agency shall make available to the public information as follows:

(1) Each agency shall separately state and currently publish in the Federal Register for the guidance of the public—

(A) descriptions of its central and field organization and the established places at which, the employees (and in the case of a uniformed service, the members) from whom, and the methods whereby, the public may obtain information, make submittals or requests, or obtain decisions;

(B) statements of the general course and method by which its functions are channeled and determined, including the nature and requirements of all formal and informal procedures available;

(C) rules of procedure, descriptions of forms available or the places at which forms may be obtained, and instructions as to the scope and contents of all papers, reports, or examinations;

(D) substantive rules of general applicability adopted as authorized by law, and statements of general policy or interpretations of general applicability formulated and adopted by the agency; and

(E) each amendment, revision, or repeal of the foregoing.

Except to the extent that a person has actual and timely notice of the terms thereof, a person may not in any manner be required to resort to, or be adversely affected by, a matter required to be published in the Federal Register and not so published. For the purpose of this paragraph, matter reasonably available to the class of persons affected thereby is deemed published in the Federal Register when incorporated by reference therein with the approval of the Director of the Federal Register.

(2) Each agency, in accordance with published rules, shall make available for public inspection and copying—

(A) final opinions, including concurring and dissenting opinions, as well as orders, made in the adjudication of cases;

(B) those statements of policy and interpretations which have been adopted by the agency and are not published in the Federal Register;

(C) administrative staff manuals and instructions to staff that affect a member of the public;

(D) copies of all records, regardless of form or format, which have been released to any person under paragraph (3) and which, because of the nature of their subject matter, the agency determines have become or are likely to become the subject of subsequent requests for substantially the same records; and

(E) a general index of the records referred to under subparagraph (D);

unless the materials are promptly published and copies offered for sale. For records created on or after November 1, 1996, within one year after such date, each agency shall make such records available, including by computer telecommunications or, if computer telecommunications means have not been established by the agency, by other electronic means. To the extent required to prevent a clearly unwarranted invasion of personal privacy, an agency may delete identifying details when it makes available or publishes an opinion, statement of policy, interpretation, staff manual, instruction, or copies of records referred to in subparagraph (D). However, in each case the justification for the deletion shall be explained fully in writing, and the extent of such deletion shall be indicated on the portion of the record which is made available or published, unless including that indication would harm an interest protected by the exemption in subsection (b) under which the deletion was made. Each agency shall also maintain and make available for public inspection and copying current indexes providing identifying information for the public as to any matter issued, adopted, or promulgated after July 4, 1967, and required by this paragraph to be made available or published.... A final order, opinion, statement of policy, interpretation, or staff manual or instruction that affects a member of the public may be relied on, used, or cited as precedent by an agency against a party other than an agency only if—

(i) it has been indexed and either made available or published as provided by this paragraph; or

(ii) the party has actual and timely notice of the terms thereof.

(3)(A) Except with respect to the records made available under paragraphs (1) and (2) of this subsection, each agency, upon any request for records which (i) reasonably describes such records and (ii) is made in accordance with published rules stating the time, place, fees (if any), and procedures to be followed, shall make the records promptly available to any person.

(B) In making any record available to a person under this paragraph, an agency shall provide the record in any form or format requested by the person if the record is readily reproducible by the agency in that form or format. Each agency shall make reasonable efforts to maintain its records in forms or formats that are reproducible for purposes of this section....

(4)(A)(i) In order to carry out the provisions of this section, each agency shall promulgate regulations, pursuant to notice and receipt of public comment, specifying the schedule of fees applicable to the processing of requests under this section ...

(B) On complaint, the district court of the United States in the district in which the complainant resides, or has his principal place of business, or in which the agency records are situated, or in the District of Columbia, has jurisdiction to enjoin the agency from withholding agency records and to order the production of any agency records improperly withheld from the complainant. In such a case the court shall determine the matter de novo, and may examine the contents of such agency records in camera to determine whether such records or any part thereof shall be withheld under any of the exemptions set forth in subsection (b) of this section, and the burden is on the agency to sustain its action. In addition to any other matters to which a court accords substantial weight, a court shall accord substantial weight to an affidavit of an agency concerning the agency's determination as to technical feasibility under paragraph (2)(C) and subsection (b) and reproducibility under paragraph (3)(B)....

(E) The court may assess against the United States reasonable attorney fees and other litigation costs reasonably incurred in any case under this section in which the complainant has substantially prevailed....

(b) This section does not apply to matters that are—

(1)(A) specifically authorized under criteria established by an Executive order to be kept secret in the interest of national defense or foreign policy and (B) are in fact properly classified pursuant to such Executive order;

(2) related solely to the internal personnel rules and practices of an agency;

(3) specifically exempted from disclosure by statute (other than section 552b of this title), provided that such statute (A) requires that the matters be withheld from the public in such a manner as to leave no discretion on the issue, or (B) establishes particular criteria for withholding or refers to particular types of matters to be withheld;

(4) trade secrets and commercial or financial information obtained from a person and privileged or confidential;

(5) inter-agency or intra-agency memorandums or letters which would not be available by law to a party other than an agency in litigation with the agency;

(6) personnel and medical files and similar files the disclosure of which would constitute a clearly unwarranted invasion of personal privacy;

(7) records or information compiled for law enforcement purposes, but only to the extent that the production of such law enforcement records or information (A) could reasonably be expected to interfere with enforcement proceedings, (B) would deprive a person of a right to a fair trial or an impartial adjudication, (C) could reasonably be expected to constitute an unwarranted invasion of personal privacy, (D) could reasonably be expected to disclose the identity of a confidential source, including a State, local, or foreign agency or authority or any private institution which furnished information on a confidential basis, and, in the case of a record or information compiled by criminal law enforcement authority in the course of a criminal investigation or by an agency conducting a lawful national security intelligence investigation, information furnished by a confidential source, (E) would disclose techniques and procedures for law enforcement investigations or prosecutions, or would disclose guidelines for law enforcement investigations or prosecutions if such disclosure could reasonably be expected to risk

circumvention of the law, or (F) could reasonably be expected to endanger the life or physical safety of any individual;

(8) contained in or related to examination, operating, or condition reports prepared by, on behalf of, or for the use of an agency responsible for the regulation or supervision of financial institutions; or

(9) geological and geophysical information and data, including maps, concerning wells.

Any reasonably segregable portion of a record shall be provided to any person requesting such record after deletion of the portions which are exempt under this subsection. The amount of information deleted shall be indicated on the released portion of the record, unless including that indication would harm an interest protected by the exemption in this subsection under which the deletion is made. If technically feasible, the amount of the information deleted shall be indicated at the place in the record where such deletion is made. . . .

(d) This section does not authorize withholding of information or limit the availability of records to the public, except as specifically stated in this section. This section is not authority to withhold information from Congress. . . .

§ 552a. Records maintained on individuals

[This section, known as the Privacy Act, is omitted.]

§ 552b. Open meetings

[This section, known as the Government in the Sunshine Act, is omitted.]

§ 553. Rule making

(a) This section applies, according to the provisions thereof, except to the extent that there is involved—

(1) a military or foreign affairs function of the United States; or

(2) a matter relating to agency management or personnel or to public property, loans, grants, benefits, or contracts.

(b) General notice of proposed rule making shall be published in the Federal Register, unless persons subject thereto are named and either personally served or otherwise have actual notice thereof in accordance with law. The notice shall include—

(1) a statement of the time, place, and nature of public rule making proceedings;

(2) reference to the legal authority under which the rule is proposed; and

(3) either the terms or substance of the proposed rule or a description of the subjects and issues involved.

Except when notice or hearing is required by statute, this subsection does not apply—

(A) to interpretative rules, general statements of policy, or rules of agency organization, procedure, or practice; or

(B) when the agency for good cause finds (and incorporates the finding and a brief statement of reasons therefor in the rules issued) that notice and public procedure thereon are impracticable, unnecessary, or contrary to the public interest.

(c) After notice required by this section, the agency shall give interested persons an opportunity to participate in the rule making through submission of written data, views, or arguments with or without opportunity for oral presentation. After consideration of the relevant matter presented, the agency shall incorporate in the rules adopted a concise general statement of their basis and purpose. When rules are required by statute to be made on the record after opportunity for an agency hearing, sections 556 and 557 of this title apply instead of this subsection.

(d) The required publication or service of a substantive rule shall be made not less than 30 days before its effective date, except—

(1) a substantive rule which grants or recognizes an exemption or relieves a restriction;

(2) interpretative rules and statements of policy; or

(3) as otherwise provided by the agency for good cause found and published with the rule.

(e) Each agency shall give an interested person the right to petition for the issuance, amendment, or repeal of a rule.

§ 554. Adjudications

(a) This section applies, according to the provisions thereof, in every case of adjudication required by statute to be determined on the record after opportunity for an agency hearing, except to the extent that there is involved—

(1) a matter subject to a subsequent trial of the law and the facts de novo in a court;

(2) the selection or tenure of an employee, except a[n] administrative law judge appointed under section 3105 of this title;

(3) proceedings in which decisions rest solely on inspections, tests, or elections;

(4) the conduct of military or foreign affairs functions;

(5) cases in which an agency is acting as an agent for a court; or

(6) the certification of worker representatives.

(b) Persons entitled to notice of an agency hearing shall be timely informed of—

(1) the time, place, and nature of the hearing;

(2) the legal authority and jurisdiction under which the hearing is to be held; and

(3) the matters of fact and law asserted.

When private persons are the moving parties, other parties to the proceeding shall give prompt notice of issues controverted in fact or law; and in other instances agencies may by rule require responsive pleading. In fixing the time and place for hearings, due regard shall be had for the convenience and necessity of the parties or their representatives.

(c) The agency shall give all interested parties opportunity for—

(1) the submission and consideration of facts, arguments, offers of settlement, or proposals of adjustment when time, the nature of the proceeding, and the public interest permit; and

(2) to the extent that the parties are unable so to determine a controversy by consent, hearing and decision on notice and in accordance with sections 556 and 557 of this title.

(d) The employee who presides at the reception of evidence pursuant to section 556 of this title shall make the recommended decision or initial decision required by section 557 of this title, unless he becomes unavailable to the agency. Except to the extent required for the disposition of ex parte matters as authorized by law, such an employee may not—

(1) consult a person or party on a fact in issue, unless on notice and opportunity for all parties to participate; or

(2) be responsible to or subject to the supervision or direction of an employee or agent engaged in the performance of investigative or prosecuting functions for an agency.

An employee or agent engaged in the performance of investigative or prosecuting functions for an agency in a case may not, in that or a factually related case, participate or advise in the decision, recommended decision, or agency review pursuant to section 557 of this title, except as witness or counsel in public proceedings. This subsection does not apply—

(A) in determining applications for initial licenses;

(B) to proceedings involving the validity or application of rates, facilities, or practices of public utilities or carriers; or

(C) to the agency or a member or members of the body comprising the agency.

(e) The agency, with like effect as in the case of other orders, and in its sound discretion, may issue a declaratory order to terminate a controversy or remove uncertainty.

§ 555. Ancillary matters

(a) This section applies, according to the provisions thereof, except as otherwise provided by this subchapter.

(b) A person compelled to appear in person before an agency or representative thereof is entitled to be accompanied, represented, and advised by counsel or, if permitted by the agency, by other qualified representative. A party is entitled to appear in person or by or with counsel or other duly qualified representative in an agency proceeding. So far as the orderly conduct of public business permits, an interested person may appear before an agency or its responsible employees for the presentation, adjustment, or determination of an issue, request, or controversy in a proceeding, whether interlocutory, summary, or otherwise, or in connection with an agency function. With due regard for the convenience and necessity of the parties or their representatives and within a reasonable time, each agency shall proceed to conclude a matter presented to it. This subsection does not grant or deny a person who is not a lawyer the right to appear for or represent others before an agency or in an agency proceeding.

(c) Process, requirement of a report, inspection, or other investigative act or demand may not be issued, made, or enforced except as authorized by law. A person compelled to submit data or evidence is entitled to retain or, on payment of lawfully prescribed costs, procure a copy or transcript thereof, except that in a non-public investigatory proceeding the witness may for good cause be limited to inspection of the official transcript of his testimony.

(d) Agency subpenas authorized by law shall be issued to a party on request and, when required by rules of procedure, on a statement or showing of general relevance and reasonable scope of the evidence sought. On contest, the court shall sustain the subpena or similar process or demand to the extent that it is found to be in accordance with law. In a proceeding for enforcement, the court shall issue an order requiring the appearance of the witness or the production of the evidence or data within a reasonable time under penalty of punishment for contempt in case of contumacious failure to comply.

(e) Prompt notice shall be given of the denial in whole or in part of a written application, petition, or other request of an interested person made in connection with any agency proceeding. Except in affirming a prior denial or when the denial is self-explanatory, the notice shall be accompanied by a brief statement of the grounds for denial.

§ 556. Hearings; presiding employees; powers and duties; burden of proof; evidence; record as basis of decision

(a) This section applies, according to the provisions thereof, to hearings required by section 553 or 554 of this title to be conducted in accordance with this section.

(b) There shall preside at the taking of evidence—

(1) the agency;

(2) one or more members of the body which comprises the agency; or

(3) one or more administrative law judges appointed under section 3105 of this title.

This subchapter does not supersede the conduct of specified classes of proceedings, in whole or in part, by or before boards or other employees specially provided for by or designated under statute. The functions of presiding employees and of employees participating in decisions in accordance with section 557 of this title shall be conducted in an impartial manner. A presiding or participating employee may at any time disqualify himself. On the filing in good faith of a timely and sufficient affidavit of personal bias or other disqualification of a presiding or participating employee, the agency shall determine the matter as a part of the record and decision in the case.

(c) Subject to published rules of the agency and within its powers, employees presiding at hearings may—

(1) administer oaths and affirmations;

(2) issue subpenas authorized by law;

(3) rule on offers of proof and receive relevant evidence;

(4) take depositions or have depositions taken when the ends of justice would be served;

(5) regulate the course of the hearing;

(6) hold conferences for the settlement or simplification of the issues by consent of the parties or by the use of alternative means of dispute resolution as provided in subchapter IV of this chapter;

(7) inform the parties as to the availability of one or more alternative means of dispute resolution, and encourage use of such methods;

(8) require the attendance at any conference held pursuant to paragraph (6) of at least one representative of each party who has authority to negotiate concerning resolution of issues in controversy;

(9) dispose of procedural requests or similar matters;

(10) make or recommend decisions in accordance with section 557 of this title; and

(11) take other action authorized by agency rule consistent with this subchapter.

(d) Except as otherwise provided by statute, the proponent of a rule or order has the burden of proof. Any oral or documentary evidence may be received, but the agency as a matter of policy shall provide for the exclusion of irrelevant, immaterial, or unduly repetitious evidence. A sanction may not be imposed or rule or order issued except on consideration of the whole record or those parts thereof cited by a party and supported by and in accordance with the reliable, probative, and substantial evidence. The agency may, to the extent consistent with the interests of justice and the policy of the underlying statutes administered by the agency, consider a violation of section 557(d) of this title sufficient grounds for a decision adverse to a party who has knowingly committed such violation or knowingly caused such violation to occur. A party is entitled to present his case or defense by oral or documentary evidence, to submit rebuttal evidence, and to conduct such cross-examination as may be required for a full and true disclosure of the facts. In rule making or determining claims for money or benefits or applications for initial licenses an agency may, when a party will not be prejudiced thereby, adopt procedures for the submission of all or part of the evidence in written form.

(e) The transcript of testimony and exhibits, together with all papers and requests filed in the proceeding, constitutes the exclusive record for decision in accordance with section 557 of this title and, on payment of lawfully prescribed costs, shall be made available to the parties. When an agency decision rests on official notice of a material fact not appearing in the evidence in the record, a party is entitled, on timely request, to an opportunity to show the contrary.

§ 557. Initial decisions; conclusiveness; review by agency; submissions by parties; contents of decisions; record

(a) This section applies, according to the provisions thereof, when a hearing is required to be conducted in accordance with section 556 of this title.

(b) When the agency did not preside at the reception of the evidence, the presiding employee or, in cases not subject to section 554(d) of this title, an employee qualified to preside at hearings pursuant to section 556 of this title, shall initially decide the case unless the agency requires, either in specific cases or by general rule, the entire record to be certified to it for decision. When the presiding employee makes an initial decision, that decision then becomes the decision of the agency without further proceedings unless there is an appeal to, or review on motion of, the agency within time provided by rule. On appeal from or review of the initial decision, the agency has all the powers which it would have in making the initial decision except as it may limit the issues on notice or by rule. When the agency makes the decision without having presided at the reception of the evidence, the presiding employee or an employee qualified to preside at hearings pursuant to section 556 of this title shall first recommend a decision, except that in rule making or determining applications for initial licenses—

(1) instead thereof the agency may issue a tentative decision or one of its responsible employees may recommend a decision; or

(2) this procedure may be omitted in a case in which the agency finds on the record that due and timely execution of its functions imperatively and unavoidably so requires.

(c) Before a recommended, initial, or tentative decision, or a decision on agency review of the decision of subordinate employees, the parties are entitled to a reasonable opportunity to submit for the consideration of the employees participating in the decisions—

(1) proposed findings and conclusions; or

(2) exceptions to the decisions or recommended decisions of subordinate employees or to tentative agency decisions; and

(3) supporting reasons for the exceptions or proposed findings or conclusions.

The record shall show the ruling on each finding, conclusion, or exception presented. All decisions, including initial, recommended, and tentative decisions, are a part of the record and shall include a statement of—

(A) findings and conclusions, and the reasons or basis therefor, on all the material issues of fact, law, or discretion presented on the record; and

(B) the appropriate rule, order, sanction, relief, or denial thereof.

(d)(1) In any agency proceeding which is subject to subsection (a) of this section, except to the extent required for the disposition of ex parte matters as authorized by law—

(A) no interested person outside the agency shall make or knowingly cause to be made to any member of the body comprising the agency, administrative law judge, or other employee who is or may reasonably be expected to be involved in the decisional process of the proceeding, an ex parte communication relevant to the merits of the proceeding;

(B) no member of the body comprising the agency, administrative law judge, or other employee who is or may reasonably be expected to be involved in the decisional process of the proceeding, shall make or knowingly cause to be made to any interested person outside the agency an ex parte communication relevant to the merits of the proceeding;

(C) a member of the body comprising the agency, administrative law judge, or other employee who is or may reasonably be expected to be involved in the decisional process of such proceeding who receives, or who makes or knowingly causes to be made, a communication prohibited by this subsection shall place on the public record of the proceeding:

(i) all such written communications;

(ii) memoranda stating the substance of all such oral communications; and

(iii) all written responses, and memoranda stating the substance of all oral responses, to the materials described in clauses (i) and (ii) of this subparagraph;

(D) upon receipt of a communication knowingly made or knowingly caused to be made by a party in violation of this subsection, the agency, administrative law judge, or other employee presiding at the hearing may, to the extent consistent with the interests of justice and the policy of the underlying statutes, require the party to show cause why his claim or interest in the proceeding should not be dismissed, denied, disregarded, or otherwise adversely affected on account of such violation; and

(E) the prohibitions of this subsection shall apply beginning at such time as the agency may designate, but in no case shall they begin to apply later than the time at which a proceeding is noticed for hearing unless the person responsible for the communication has knowledge that it will be noticed, in which case the prohibitions shall apply beginning at the time of his acquisition of such knowledge.

(2) This subsection does not constitute authority to withhold information from Congress.

§ 558. Imposition of sanctions; determination of applications for licenses; suspension, revocation, and expiration of licenses

(a) This section applies, according to the provisions thereof, to the exercise of a power or authority.

(b) A sanction may not be imposed or a substantive rule or order issued except within jurisdiction delegated to the agency and as authorized by law.

(c) When application is made for a license required by law, the agency, with due regard for the rights and privileges of all the interested parties or adversely affected persons and within a reasonable time, shall set and complete proceedings required to be conducted in accordance with sections 556 and 557 of this title or other proceedings required by law and shall make its decision. Except in cases of willfulness or those in which public health, interest, or safety requires otherwise, the withdrawal, suspension, revocation, or annulment of a license is lawful only if, before the institution of agency proceedings therefor, the licensee has been given—

(1) notice by the agency in writing of the facts or conduct which may warrant the action; and

(2) opportunity to demonstrate or achieve compliance with all lawful requirements.

When the licensee has made timely and sufficient application for a renewal or a new license in accordance with agency rules, a license with reference to an activity of a continuing nature does not expire until the application has been finally determined by the agency.

§ 559. Effect on other laws; effect of subsequent statute

This [Act does] not limit or repeal additional requirements imposed by statute or otherwise recognized by law. Except as otherwise required by law, requirements or privileges relating to evidence or procedure apply equally to agencies and persons. Each agency is granted the authority necessary to comply with the requirements of this subchapter through the issuance of rules or otherwise. Subsequent statute may not be held to supersede or modify this [Act], except to the extent that it does so expressly.

Subchapter III—Negotiated Rulemaking Procedure

[This subchapter, known as the Negotiated Rulemaking Act, is omitted.]

Subchapter IV—Alternative Means of Dispute Resolution in the Administrative Process

[This subchapter, known as the Administrative Dispute Resolution Act, is omitted.]

CHAPTER 6—THE ANALYSIS OF REGULATORY FUNCTIONS

[This chapter, known as the Regulatory Flexibility Act, is omitted.]

CHAPTER 7—JUDICIAL REVIEW

§ 701. Application; definitions

(a) This chapter applies, according to the provisions thereof, except to the extent that—

(1) statutes preclude judicial review; or

(2) agency action is committed to agency discretion by law.

(b) For the purpose of this chapter—

(1) "agency" means each authority of the Government of the United States, whether or not it is within or subject to review by another agency, but does not include—

(A) the Congress;

(B) the courts of the United States;

(C) the governments of the territories or possessions of the United States;

(D) the government of the District of Columbia;

(E) agencies composed of representatives of the parties or of representatives of organizations of the parties to the disputes determined by them;

(F) courts martial and military commissions;

(G) military authority exercised in the field in time of war or in occupied territory; or

(H) functions conferred by sections 1738, 1739, 1743, and 1744 of title 12; chapter 2 of title 41; subchapter II of chapter 471 of title 49; or sections 1884, 1891–1902, and former section 1641(b)(2), of title 50, appendix; and

(2) "person", "rule", "order", "license", "sanction", "relief", and "agency action" have the meanings given them by section 551 of this title.

§ 702. Right of review

A person suffering legal wrong because of agency action, or adversely affected or aggrieved by agency action within the meaning of a relevant statute, is entitled to judicial review thereof. An action in a court of the United States seeking relief other than money damages and stating a claim that an agency or an officer or employee thereof acted or failed to act in an official capacity or under color of legal authority shall not be dismissed nor relief therein be denied on the ground that it is against the United States or that the United States is an indispensable party. The United States may be named as a defendant in any such action, and a judgment or decree may be entered against the United States: *Provided,* That any mandatory or injunctive decree shall specify the Federal officer or officers (by name or by title), and their successors in office, personally responsible for compliance. Nothing herein (1) affects other limitations on judicial review or the power or duty of the court to dismiss any action or deny relief on any other appropriate legal or equitable ground; or (2) confers authority to grant relief if any other statute that grants consent to suit expressly or impliedly forbids the relief which is sought.

§ 703. Form and venue of proceeding

The form of proceeding for judicial review is the special statutory review proceeding relevant to the subject matter in a court specified by statute or, in the absence or inadequacy thereof, any applicable form of legal action, including actions for declaratory judgments or writs of prohibitory or mandatory injunction or habeas corpus, in a court of competent jurisdiction. If no special statutory review proceeding is applicable, the action for judicial review may be brought against the United States, the agency by its official title, or the appropriate officer. Except to the extent that prior, adequate, and exclusive opportunity for judicial review is provided by law, agency action is subject to judicial review in civil or criminal proceedings for judicial enforcement.

§ 704. Actions reviewable

Agency action made reviewable by statute and final agency action for which there is no adequate remedy in a court are subject to judicial review. A preliminary, procedural, or intermediate agency action or ruling not directly reviewable is subject to review on the review of the final agency action. Except as otherwise expressly required by statute, agency action otherwise final is final for the purposes of this section whether or not there has been presented or determined an application for a declaratory order, for any form of reconsideration, or, unless the agency otherwise requires by rule and provides that the action meanwhile is inoperative, for an appeal to superior agency authority.

§ 705.   Relief pending review

When an agency finds that justice so requires, it may postpone the effective date of action taken by it, pending judicial review. On such conditions as may be required and to the extent necessary to prevent irreparable injury, the reviewing court, including the court to which a case may be taken on appeal from or on application for certiorari or other writ to a reviewing court, may issue all necessary and appropriate process to postpone the effective date of an agency action or to preserve status or rights pending conclusion of the review proceedings.

§ 706.   Scope of review

To the extent necessary to decision and when presented, the reviewing court shall decide all relevant questions of law, interpret constitutional and statutory provisions, and determine the meaning or applicability of the terms of an agency action. The reviewing court shall—

(1) compel agency action unlawfully withheld or unreasonably delayed; and

(2) hold unlawful and set aside agency action, findings, and conclusions found to be—

(A) arbitrary, capricious, an abuse of discretion, or otherwise not in accordance with law;

(B) contrary to constitutional right, power, privilege, or immunity;

(C) in excess of statutory jurisdiction, authority, or limitations, or short of statutory right;

(D) without observance of procedure required by law;

(E) unsupported by substantial evidence in a case subject to sections 556 and 557 of this title or otherwise reviewed on the record of an agency hearing provided by statute; or

(F) unwarranted by the facts to the extent that the facts are subject to trial de novo by the reviewing court.

In making the foregoing determinations, the court shall review the whole record or those parts of it cited by a party, and due account shall be taken of the rule of prejudicial error.

CHAPTER 8—CONGRESSIONAL REVIEW
OF AGENCY RULEMAKING

[This chapter, known as the Congressional Review Act, is omitted.]

[ADMINISTRATIVE LAW JUDGES]

§ 3105. Appointment of administrative law judges

Each agency shall appoint as many administrative law judges as are necessary for proceedings required to be conducted in accordance with sections 556 and 557 of this title. Administrative law judges shall be assigned to cases in rotation so far as practicable, and may not perform duties inconsistent with their duties and responsibilities as administrative law judges.

§ 7521. Actions against administrative law judges

(a) An action may be taken against an administrative law judge appointed under section 3105 of this title by the agency in which the administrative law judge is employed only for good cause established and determined by the Merit Systems Protection Board on the record after opportunity for hearing before the Board.... [Actions covered include removal, suspension, and reduction in grade or pay.]

§ 5372. Administrative law judges

Administrative law judges appointed under section 3105 of this title are entitled to pay prescribed by the Office of Personnel Management independently of agency recommendations or ratings and in accordance with subchapter III of this chapter and chapter 51 of this title.

§ 3344. Details; administrative law judges

An agency as defined by section 551 of this title which occasionally or temporarily is insufficiently staffed with administrative law judges appointed under section 3105 of this title may use administrative law judges selected by the Office of Personnel Management from and with the consent of other agencies.

§ 1305. Administrative law judges

For the purpose of sections 3105, 3344, 4301(2)(D), and 5372 of this title and the provisions of section 5335(a)(B) of this title that relate to administrative law judges, the Office of Personnel Management may, and for the purpose of section 7521 of this title, the Merit Systems Protection Board may investigate, require reports by agencies, issue reports, including an annual report to Congress, prescribe regulations, appoint advisory committees as necessary, recommend legislation, subpena witnesses and records, and pay witness fees as established for the courts of the United States.

Appendix C

MODEL STATE ADMINISTRATIVE PROCEDURE ACT (1981)

Uniform Law Commissioners

Table of Sections

ARTICLE I. GENERAL PROVISIONS

Sec.
1–101. [Short Title.]
1–102. [Definitions.]
1–103. [Applicability and Relation to Other Law.]
1–104. [Suspension of Act's Provisions When Necessary to Avoid Loss of Federal Funds or Services.]
1–105. [Waiver.]
1–106. [Informal Settlements.]
1–107. [Conversion of Proceedings.]
1–108. [Effective Date.]
1–109. [Severability.]

ARTICLE II. PUBLIC ACCESS TO AGENCY LAW AND POLICY

2–101. [Administrative Rules Editor; Publication, Compilation, Indexing, and Public Inspection of Rules.]
2–102. [Public Inspection and Indexing of Agency Orders.]
2–103. [Declaratory Orders.]
2–104. [Required Rule Making.]
2–105. [Model Rules of Procedure.]

ARTICLE III. RULE MAKING

Chapter I. Adoption and Effectiveness of Rules

3–101. [Advice on Possible Rules before Notice of Proposed Rule Adoption.]
3–102. [Public Rule-making Docket.]
3–103. [Notice of Proposed Rule Adoption.]
3–104. [Public Participation.]
3–105. [Regulatory Analysis.]
3–106. [Time and Manner of Rule Adoption.]

Sec.

3–107. [Variance between Adopted Rule and Published Notice of Proposed Rule
            Adoption.]
3–108. [General Exemption from Public Rule-making Procedures.]
3–109. [Exemption for Certain Rules.]
3–110. [Concise Explanatory Statement.]
3–111. [Contents, Style, and Form of Rule.]
3–112. [Agency Rule-making Record.]
3–113. [Invalidity of Rules Not Adopted According to Chapter; Time Limita-
            tion.]
3–114. [Filing of Rules.]
3–115. [Effective Date of Rules.]
3–116. [Special Provision for Certain Classes of Rules.]
3–117. [Petition for Adoption of Rules.]

Chapter II.   Review of Agency Rules

3–201. [Review by Agency.]
3–202. [Review by Governor; Administrative Rules Counsel.]
3–203. [Administrative Rules Review Committee.]
3–204. [Review by Administrative Rules Review Committee.]

ARTICLE IV.   ADJUDICATIVE PROCEEDINGS

Chapter I.   Availability of Adjudicative Proceedings; Applications; Licenses

4–101. [Adjudicative Proceedings; When Required; Exceptions.]
4–102. [Adjudicative Proceedings; Commencement.]
4–103. [Decision Not to Conduct Adjudicative Proceeding.]
4–104. [Agency Action on Applications.]
4–105. [Agency Action Against Licensees.]

Chapter II.   Formal Adjudicative Hearing

4–201. [Applicability.]
4–202. [Presiding Officer, Disqualification, Substitution.]
4–203. [Representation.]
4–204. [Pre-hearing Conference—Availability, Notice.]
4–205. [Pre-hearing Conference—Procedure and Pre-hearing Order.]
4–206. [Notice of Hearing.]
4–207. [Pleadings, Briefs, Motions, Service.]
4–208. [Default.]
4–209. [Intervention.]
4–210. [Subpoenas, Discovery and Protective Orders.]
4–211. [Procedure at Hearing.]
4–212. [Evidence, Official Notice.]
4–213. [Ex parte Communications.]
4–214. [Separation of Functions.]
4–215. [Final Order, Initial Order.]
4–216. [Review of Initial Order; Exceptions to Reviewability.]
4–217. [Stay.]
4–218. [Reconsideration.]
4–219. [Review by Superior Agency.]
4–220. [Effectiveness of Orders.]
4–221. [Agency Record.]

Chapter III. Office of Administrative Hearings

Sec.
4–301. [Office of Administrative Hearings—Creation, Powers, Duties.]

Chapter IV. Conference Adjudicative Hearing

4–401. [Conference Adjudicative Hearing—Applicability.]
4–402. [Conference Adjudicative Hearing—Procedures.]
4–403. [Conference Adjudicative Hearing—Proposed Proof.]

Chapter V. Emergency and Summary Adjudicative Proceedings

4–501. [Emergency Adjudicative Proceedings.]
4–502. [Summary Adjudicative Proceedings—Applicability.]
4–503. [Summary Adjudicative Proceedings—Procedures.]
4–504. [Administrative Review of Summary Adjudicative Proceedings—Applicability.]
4–505. [Administrative Review of Summary Adjudicative Proceedings—Procedures.]
4–506. [Agency Record of Summary Adjudicative Proceedings and Administrative Review.]

ARTICLE V. JUDICIAL REVIEW AND CIVIL ENFORCEMENT

Chapter I. Judicial Review

5–101. [Relationship Between this Act and Other Law on Judicial Review and Other Judicial Remedies.]
5–102. [Final Agency Action Reviewable.]
5–103. [Non-final Agency Action Reviewable.]
5–104. [Jurisdiction, Venue.]
5–105. [Form of Action.]
5–106. [Standing.]
5–107. [Exhaustion of Administrative Remedies.]
5–108. [Time for Filing Petition for Review.]
5–109. [Petition for Review—Filing and Contents.]
5–110. [Petition for Review—Service and Notification.]
5–111. [Stay and Other Temporary Remedies Pending Final Disposition.]
5–112. [Limitation on New Issues.]
5–113. [Judicial Review of Facts Confined to Record for Judicial Review and Additional Evidence Taken Pursuant to Act.]
5–114. [New Evidence Taken by Court or Agency Before Final Disposition.]
5–115. [Agency Record for Judicial Review—Contents, Preparation, Transmittal, Cost.]
5–116. [Scope of Review; Grounds for Invalidity.]
5–117. [Type of Relief.]
5–118. [Review by Higher Court.]

Chapter II. Civil Enforcement

5–201. [Petition by Agency for Civil Enforcement of Rule or Order.]
5–202. [Petition by Qualified Person for Civil Enforcement of Agency's Order.]
5–203. [Defenses; Limitation on New Issues and New Evidence.]
5–204. [Incorporation of Certain Provisions on Judicial Review.]
5–205. [Review by Higher Court.]

ARTICLE I

GENERAL PROVISIONS

§ 1–101. [Short Title]

This Act may be cited as the [state] Administrative Procedure Act.

§ 1–102. [Definitions]

As used in this Act:

(1) "Agency" means a board, commission, department, officer, or other administrative unit of this State, including the agency head, and one or more members of the agency head or agency employees or other persons directly or indirectly purporting to act on behalf or under the authority of the agency head. The term does not include the [legislature] or the courts [, or the governor] [, or the governor in the exercise of powers derived directly and exclusively from the constitution of this State]. The term does not include a political subdivision of the state or any of the administrative units of a political subdivision, but it does include a board, commission, department, officer, or other administrative unit created or appointed by joint or concerted action of an agency and one or more political subdivisions of the state or any of their units. To the extent it purports to exercise authority subject to any provision of this Act, an administrative unit otherwise qualifying as an "agency" must be treated as a separate agency even if the unit is located within or subordinate to another agency.

(2) "Agency action" means:

(i) the whole or a part of a rule or an order;

(ii) the failure to issue a rule or an order; or

(iii) an agency's performance of, or failure to perform, any other duty, function, or activity, discretionary or otherwise.

(3) "Agency head" means an individual or body of individuals in whom the ultimate legal authority of the agency is vested by any provision of law.

(4) "License" means a franchise, permit, certification, approval, registration, charter, or similar form of authorization required by law.

(5) "Order" means an agency action of particular applicability that determines the legal rights, duties, privileges, immunities, or other legal interests of one or more specific persons. [The term does not include an "executive order" issued by the governor pursuant to Section 1–104 or 3–202.]

(6) "Party to agency proceedings," or "party" in context so indicating, means:

(i) a person to whom the agency action is specifically directed; or

(ii) a person named as a party to an agency proceeding or allowed to intervene or participate as a party in the proceeding.

(7) "Party to judicial review or civil enforcement proceedings," or "party" in context so indicating, means:

(i) a person who files a petition for judicial review or civil enforcement; or

(ii) a person named as a party in a proceeding for judicial review or civil enforcement or allowed to participate as a party in the proceeding.

(8) "Person" means an individual, partnership, corporation, association, governmental subdivision or unit thereof, or public or private organization or entity of any character, and includes another agency.

(9) "Provision of law" means the whole or a part of the federal or state constitution, or of any federal or state (i) statute, (ii) rule of court, (iii) executive order, or (iv) rule of an administrative agency.

(10) "Rule" means the whole or a part of an agency statement of general applicability that implements, interprets, or prescribes (i) law or policy, or (ii) the organization, procedure, or practice requirements of an agency. The term includes the amendment, repeal, or suspension of an existing rule.

(11) "Rule making" means the process for formulation and adoption of a rule.

§ 1–103. [Applicability and Relation to Other Law]

(a) This Act applies to all agencies and all proceedings not expressly exempted.

(b) This Act creates only procedural rights and imposes only procedural duties. They are in addition to those created and imposed by other statutes. To the extent that any other statute would diminish a right created or duty imposed by this Act, the other statute is superseded by this Act, unless the other statute expressly provides otherwise.

(c) An agency may grant procedural rights to persons in addition to those conferred by this Act so long as rights conferred upon other persons by any provision of law are not substantially prejudiced.

§ 1–104. [Suspension of Act's Provisions When Necessary to Avoid Loss of Federal Funds or Services]

(a) To the extent necessary to avoid a denial of funds or services from the United States which would otherwise be available to the state, the [governor by executive order] [attorney general by rule] [may] [shall] suspend, in whole or in part, one or more provisions of this Act. The [governor by executive order] [attorney general by rule] shall declare the termination of a suspension as soon as it is no longer necessary to prevent the loss of funds or services from the United States.

[(b) An executive order issued under subsection (a) is subject to the requirements applicable to the adoption and effectiveness of a rule.]

(c) If any provision of this Act is suspended pursuant to this section, the [governor] [attorney general] shall promptly report the suspension to the [legislature]. The report must include recommendations concerning any desirable legislation that may be necessary to conform this Act to federal law.]

§ 1–105.   [Waiver]

Except to the extent precluded by another provision of law, a person may waive any right conferred upon that person by this Act.

§ 1–106.   [Informal Settlements]

Except to the extent precluded by another provision of law, informal settlement of matters that may make unnecessary more elaborate proceedings under this Act is encouraged. Agencies shall establish by rule specific procedures to facilitate informal settlement of matters. This section does not require any party or other person to settle a matter pursuant to informal procedures.

§ 1–107.   [Conversion of Proceedings]

(a) At any point in an agency proceeding the presiding officer or other agency official responsible for the proceeding:

(1) may convert the proceeding to another type of agency proceeding provided for by this Act if the conversion is appropriate, is in the public interest, and does not substantially prejudice the rights of any party; and

(2) if required by any provision of law, shall convert the proceeding to another type of agency proceeding provided for by this Act.

(b) A conversion of a proceeding of one type to a proceeding of another type may be effected only upon notice to all parties to the original proceeding.

(c) If the presiding officer or other agency official responsible for the original proceeding would not have authority over the new proceeding to which it is to be converted, that officer or official, in accordance with agency rules, shall secure the appointment of a successor to preside over or be responsible for the new proceeding.

(d) To the extent feasible and consistent with the rights of parties and the requirements of this Act pertaining to the new proceeding, the record of the original agency proceeding must be used in the new agency proceeding.

(e) After a proceeding is converted from one type to another, the presiding officer or other agency official responsible for the new proceeding shall:

(1) give such additional notice to parties or other persons as is necessary to satisfy the requirements of this Act pertaining to those proceedings;

(2) dispose of the matters involved without further proceedings if sufficient proceedings have already been held to satisfy the requirements of this Act pertaining to the new proceedings; and

(3) conduct or cause to be conducted any additional proceedings necessary to satisfy the requirements of this Act pertaining to those proceedings.

(f) Each agency shall adopt rules to govern the conversion of one type of proceeding to another. Those rules must include an enumeration of the factors to be considered in determining whether and under what circumstances one type of proceeding will be converted to another.

§ 1–108. [Effective Date]

This Act takes effect on [date] and does not govern proceedings pending on that date. This Act governs all agency proceedings, and all proceedings for judicial review or civil enforcement of agency action, commenced after that date. This Act also governs agency proceedings conducted on a remand from a court or another agency after the effective date of this Act.

§ 1–109. [Severability]

If any provision of this Act or the application thereof to any person or circumstance is held invalid, the invalidity does not affect other provisions or applications of the Act which can be given effect without the invalid provision or application, and for this purpose the provisions of this Act are severable.

ARTICLE II
PUBLIC ACCESS TO AGENCY LAW AND POLICY

§ 2–101. [Administrative Rules Editor; Publication, Compilation, Indexing, and Public Inspection of Rules]

(a) There is created, within the executive branch, an [administrative rules editor]. The governor shall appoint the [administrative rules editor] who shall serve at the pleasure of the governor.

(b) Subject to the provisions of this Act, the [administrative rules editor] shall prescribe a uniform numbering system, form, and style for all proposed and adopted rules caused to be published by that office [, and shall have the same editing authority with respect to the publication of rules as the [reviser of statutes] has with respect to the publication of statutes].

(c) The [administrative rules editor] shall cause the [administrative bulletin] to be published in pamphlet form [once each week]. For purposes of calculating adherence to time requirements imposed by this Act, an issue of the [administrative bulletin] is deemed published on the later of the date indicated in that issue or the date of its mailing. The [administrative bulletin] must contain:

(1) notices of proposed rule adoption prepared so that the text of the proposed rule shows the text of any existing rule proposed to be changed and the change proposed;

(2) newly filed adopted rules prepared so that the text of the newly filed adopted rule shows the text of any existing rule being changed and the change being made;

(3) any other notices and materials designated by [law] [the administrative rules editor] for publication therein; and

(4) an index to its contents by subject.

(d) The [administrative rules editor] shall cause the [administrative code] to be compiled, indexed by subject, and published [in loose-leaf form]. All of the effective rules of each agency must be published and indexed in that publication. The [administrative rules editor] shall also cause [loose-leaf] supplements to the [administrative code] to be published at least every [3 months]. [The loose-leaf supplements must be in a form suitable for insertion in the appropriate places in the permanent [administrative code] compilation.]

(e) The [administrative rules editor] may omit from the [administrative bulletin or code] any proposed or filed adopted rule the publication of which would be unduly cumbersome, expensive, or otherwise inexpedient, if:

(1) knowledge of the rule is likely to be important to only a small class of persons;

(2) on application to the issuing agency, the proposed or adopted rule in printed or processed form is made available at no more than its cost of reproduction; and

(3) the [administrative bulletin or code] contains a notice stating in detail the specific subject matter of the omitted proposed or adopted rule and how a copy of the omitted material may be obtained.

(f) The [administrative bulletin and administrative code] must be furnished to [designated officials] without charge and to all subscribers at a cost to be determined by the [administrative rules editor]. Each agency shall also make available for public inspection and copying those portions of the [administrative bulletin and administrative code] containing all rules adopted or used by the agency in the discharge of its functions, and the index to those rules.

(g) Except as otherwise required by a provision of law, subsections (c) through (f) do not apply to rules governed by Section 3–116, and the following provisions apply instead:

(1) Each agency shall maintain an official, current, and dated compilation that is indexed by subject, containing all of its rules within the scope of Section 3–116. Each addition to, change in, or deletion from the official compilation must also be dated, indexed, and a record thereof kept. Except for those portions containing rules governed by Section 3–116(2), the compilation must be made available for public inspection and copying. Certified copies of the full compilation must also be furnished to the [secretary of state, the administrative rules counsel, and members of the administrative rules review committee], and be kept current by the agency at least every [30] days.

(2) A rule subject to the requirements of this subsection may not be relied on by an agency to the detriment of any person who does not have actual, timely knowledge of the contents of the rule until the requirements of paragraph (1) are satisfied. The burden of proving that knowledge is on the agency. This provision is also inapplicable to the extent necessary to avoid imminent peril to the public health, safety, or welfare.

§ 2–102.   [Public Inspection and Indexing of Agency Orders]

(a) In addition to other requirements imposed by any provision of law, each agency shall make all written final orders available for public inspection and copying and index them by name and subject. An agency shall delete from those orders identifying details to the extent required by any provision of law [or necessary to prevent a clearly unwarranted invasion of privacy or release of trade secrets]. In each case the justification for the deletion must be explained in writing and attached to the order.

(b) A written final order may not be relied on as precedent by an agency to the detriment of any person until it has been made available for public inspection and indexed in the manner described in subsection (a). This provision is inapplicable to any person who has actual timely knowledge of the order. The burden of proving that knowledge is on the agency.

§ 2–103.   [Declaratory Orders]

(a) Any person may petition an agency for a declaratory order as to the applicability to specified circumstances of a statute, rule, or order within the primary jurisdiction of the agency. An agency shall issue a declaratory order in response to a petition for that order unless the agency determines that issuance of the order under the circumstances would be contrary to a rule adopted in accordance with subsection (b). However, an agency may not issue a declaratory order that would substantially prejudice the rights of a person who would be a necessary party and who does not consent in writing to the determination of the matter by a declaratory order proceeding.

(b) Each agency shall issue rules that provide for: (i) the form, contents, and filing of petitions for declaratory orders; (ii) the procedural rights of persons in relation to the petitions and (iii) the disposition of the petitions. Those rules must describe the classes of circumstances in which the agency will not issue a declaratory order and must be consistent with the public interest and with the general policy of this Act to facilitate and encourage agency issuance of reliable advice.

(c) Within [15] days after receipt of a petition for a declaratory order, an agency shall give notice of the petition to all persons to whom notice is required by any provision of law and may give notice to any other persons.

(d) Persons who qualify under Section 4–209(a)(2) and (3) and file timely petitions for intervention according to agency rules may intervene in proceedings for declaratory orders. Other provisions of Article IV apply to agency proceedings for declaratory orders only to the extent an agency so provides by rule or order.

(e) Within [30] days after receipt of a petition for a declaratory order an agency, in writing, shall:

(1) issue an order declaring the applicability of the statute, rule, or order in question to the specified circumstances;

(2) set the matter for specified proceedings;

(3) agree to issue a declaratory order by a specified time; or

(4) decline to issue a declaratory order, stating the reasons for its action.

(f) A copy of all orders issued in response to a petition for a declaratory order must be mailed promptly to petitioner and any other parties.

(g) A declaratory order has the same status and binding effect as any other order issued in an agency adjudicative proceeding. A declaratory order must contain the names of all parties to the proceeding on which it is based, the particular facts on which it is based, and the reasons for its conclusion.

(h) If an agency has not issued a declaratory order within [60] days after receipt of a petition therefor, the petition is deemed to have been denied.

§ 2–104. [Required Rule Making]

In addition to other rule-making requirements imposed by law, each agency shall:

(1) adopt as a rule a description of the organization of the agency which states the general course and method of its operations

and where and how the public may obtain information or make submissions or requests;

(2) adopt rules of practice setting forth the nature and requirements of all formal and informal procedures available to the public, including a description of all forms and instructions that are to be used by the public in dealing with the agency; [and]

(3) as soon as feasible and to the extent practicable, adopt rules, in addition to those otherwise required by this Act, embodying appropriate standards, principles, and procedural safeguards that the agency will apply to the law it administers [; and] [.]

[(4) as soon as feasible and to the extent practicable, adopt rules to supersede principles of law or policy lawfully declared by the agency as the basis for its decisions in particular cases.]

§ 2–105. [Model Rules of Procedure]

In accordance with the rule-making requirements of this Act, the [attorney general] shall adopt model rules of procedure appropriate for use by as many agencies as possible. The model rules must deal with all general functions and duties performed in common by several agencies. Each agency shall adopt as much of the model rules as is practicable under its circumstances. To the extent an agency adopts the model rules, it shall do so in accordance with the rule-making requirements of this Act. Any agency adopting a rule of procedure that differs from the model rules shall include in the rule a finding stating the reasons why the relevant portions of the model rules were impracticable under the circumstances.

ARTICLE III

RULE MAKING

Adoption and Effectiveness of Rules

§ 3–101. [Advice on Possible Rules before Notice of Proposed Rule Adoption]

(a) In addition to seeking information by other methods, an agency, before publication of a notice of proposed rule adoption under Section 3–103, may solicit comments from the public on a subject matter of possible rule making under active consideration within the agency by causing notice to be published in the [administrative bulletin] of the subject matter and indicating where, when, and how persons may comment.

(b) Each agency may also appoint committees to comment, before publication of a notice of proposed rule adoption under Section 3–103, on the subject matter of a possible rule making under active consideration within the agency. The membership of those committees must be published at least [annually] in the [administrative bulletin].

§ 3–102. [Public Rule-making Docket]

(a) Each agency shall maintain a current, public rule-making docket.

(b) The rule-making docket [must] [may] contain a listing of the precise subject matter of each possible rule currently under active consideration within the agency for proposal under Section 3–103, the name and address of agency personnel with whom persons may communicate with respect to the matter, and an indication of the present status within the agency of that possible rule.

(c) The rule-making docket must list each pending rule-making proceeding. A rule-making proceeding is pending from the time it is commenced, by publication of a notice of proposed rule adoption, to the time it is terminated, by publication of a notice of termination or the rule becoming effective. For each rule-making proceeding, the docket must indicate:

(1) the subject matter of the proposed rule;

(2) a citation to all published notices relating to the proceeding;

(3) where written submissions on the proposed rule may be inspected;

(4) the time during which written submissions may be made;

(5) the names of persons who have made written requests for an opportunity to make oral presentations on the proposed rule, where those requests may be inspected, and where and when oral presentations may be made;

(6) whether a written request for the issuance of a regulatory analysis of the proposed rule has been filed, whether that analysis has been issued, and where the written request and analysis may be inspected;

(7) the current status of the proposed rule and any agency determinations with respect thereto;

(8) any known timetable for agency decisions or other action in the proceeding;

(9) the date of the rule's adoption;

(10) the date of the rule's filing, indexing, and publication; and

(11) when the rule will become effective.

§ 3–103. [Notice of Proposed Rule Adoption]

(a) At least [30] days before the adoption of a rule an agency shall cause notice of its contemplated action to be published in the [administrative bulletin]. The notice of proposed rule adoption must include:

(1) a short explanation of the purpose of the proposed rule;

(2) the specific legal authority authorizing the proposed rule;

(3) subject to Section 2–101(e), the text of the proposed rule;

(4) where, when, and how persons may present their views on the proposed rule; and

(5) where, when, and how persons may demand an oral proceeding on the proposed rule if the notice does not already provide for one.

(b) Within [3] days after its publication in the [administrative bulletin], the agency shall cause a copy of the notice of proposed rule adoption to be mailed to each person who has made a timely request to the agency for a mailed copy of the notice. An agency may charge persons for the actual cost of providing them with mailed copies.

§ 3–104. [Public Participation]

(a) For at least [30] days after publication of the notice of proposed rule adoption, an agency shall afford persons the opportunity to submit in writing, argument, data, and views on the proposed rule.

(b)(1) An agency shall schedule an oral proceeding on a proposed rule if, within [20] days after the published notice of proposed rule adoption, a written request for an oral proceeding is submitted by [the administrative rules review committee,] [the administrative rules counsel,] a political subdivision, an agency, or [25] persons. At that proceeding, persons may present oral argument, data, and views on the proposed rule.

(2) An oral proceeding on a proposed rule, if required, may not be held earlier than [20] days after notice of its location and time is published in the [administrative bulletin].

(3) The agency, a member of the agency, or another presiding officer designated by the agency, shall preside at a required oral proceeding on a proposed rule. If the agency does not preside, the presiding official shall prepare a memorandum for consideration by the agency summarizing the contents of the presentations made at the oral proceeding. Oral proceedings must be open to the public and be recorded by stenographic or other means.

(4) Each agency shall issue rules for the conduct of oral rulemaking proceedings. Those rules may include provisions calculated to prevent undue repetition in the oral proceedings.

§ 3–105. [Regulatory Analysis]

(a) An agency shall issue a regulatory analysis of a proposed rule if, within [20] days after the published notice of proposed rule adoption, a written request for the analysis is filed in the office of the [secretary of state] by [the administrative rules review committee, the governor, a political subdivision, an agency, or [300] persons signing the request]. The [secretary of state] shall immediately forward to the agency a certified copy of the filed request.

(b) Except to the extent that the written request expressly waives one or more of the following, the regulatory analysis must contain:

(1) a description of the classes of persons who probably will be affected by the proposed rule, including classes that will bear the costs of the proposed rule and classes that will benefit from the proposed rule;

(2) a description of the probable quantitative and qualitative impact of the proposed rule, economic or otherwise, upon affected classes of persons;

(3) the probable costs to the agency and to any other agency of the implementation and enforcement of the proposed rule and any anticipated effect on state revenues;

(4) a comparison of the probable costs and benefits of the proposed rule to the probable costs and benefits of inaction;

(5) a determination of whether there are less costly methods or less intrusive methods for achieving the purpose of the proposed rule; and

(6) a description of any alternative methods for achieving the purpose of the proposed rule that were seriously considered by the agency and the reasons why they were rejected in favor of the proposed rule.

(c) Each regulatory analysis must include qualification of the data to the extent practicable and must take account of both short-term and long-term consequences.

(d) A concise summary of the regulatory analysis must be published in the [administrative bulletin] at least [10] days before the earliest of:

(1) the end of the period during which persons may make written submissions on the proposed rule;

(2) the end of the period during which an oral proceeding may be requested; or

(3) the date of any required oral proceeding on the proposed rule.

(e) The published summary of the regulatory analysis must also indicate where persons may obtain copies of the full text of the regulatory analysis and where, when, and how persons may present their views on the proposed rule and demand an oral proceeding thereon if one is not already provided.

(f) If the agency has made a good faith effort to comply with the requirements of subsections (a) through (c), the rule may not be invalidated on the ground that the contents of the regulatory analysis are insufficient or inaccurate.

§ 3–106. [Time and Manner of Rule Adoption]

(a) An agency may not adopt a rule until the period for making written submissions and oral presentations has expired.

(b) Within [180] days after the later of (i) the publication of the notice of proposed rule adoption, or (ii) the end of oral proceedings thereon, an agency shall adopt a rule pursuant to the rule-making proceeding or terminate the proceeding by publication of a notice to that effect in the [administrative bulletin].

(c) Before the adoption of a rule, an agency shall consider the written submissions, oral submissions or any memorandum summarizing oral submissions, and any regulatory analysis, provided for by this Chapter.

(d) Within the scope of its delegated authority, an agency may use its own experience, technical competence, specialized knowledge, and judgment in the adoption of a rule.

§ 3–107. [Variance between Adopted Rule and Published Notice of Proposed Rule Adoption]

(a) An agency may not adopt a rule that is substantially different from the proposed rule contained in the published notice of proposed rule adoption. However, an agency may terminate a rule-making proceeding and commence a new rule-making proceeding for the purpose of adopting a substantially different rule.

(b) In determining whether an adopted rule is substantially different from the published proposed rule upon which it is required to be based, the following must be considered:

(1) the extent to which all persons affected by the adopted rule should have understood that the published proposed rule would affect their interests;

(2) the extent to which the subject matter of the adopted rule or the issues determined by that rule are different from the subject matter or issues involved in the published proposed rule; and

(3) the extent to which the effects of the adopted rule differ from the effects of the published proposed rule had it been adopted instead.

§ 3–108. [General Exemption from Public Rule-making Procedures]

(a) To the extent an agency for good cause finds that any requirements of Sections 3–103 through 3–107 are unnecessary, impracticable, or contrary to the public interest in the process of adopting a particular rule, those requirements do not apply. The agency shall incorporate the required finding and a brief statement of its supporting reasons in each rule adopted in reliance upon this subsection.

(b) In an action contesting a rule adopted under subsection (a), the burden is upon the agency to demonstrate that any omitted requirements of Sections 3–103 through 3–107 were impracticable, unnecessary, or contrary to the public interest in the particular circumstances involved.

(c) Within [2] years after the effective date of a rule adopted under subsection (a), the [administrative rules review committee or the governor] may request the agency to hold a rule-making proceeding thereon according to the requirements of Sections 3–103 through 3–107. The request must be in writing and filed in the office of the [secretary of state]. The [secretary of state] shall immediately forward to the agency and to the [administrative rules editor] a certified copy of the request. Notice of the filing of the request must be published in the next issue of the [administrative bulletin]. The rule in question ceases to be effective [180] days after the request is filed. However, an agency, after the filing of the request, may subsequently adopt an identical rule in a rule-making proceeding conducted pursuant to the requirements of Sections 3–103 through 3–107.

§ 3–109.   [Exemption for Certain Rules]

(a) An agency need not follow the provisions of Sections 3–103 through 3–108 in the adoption of a rule that only defines the meaning of a statute or other provision of law or precedent if the agency does not possess delegated authority to bind the courts to any extent with its definition. A rule adopted under this subsection must include a statement that it was adopted under this subsection when it is published in the [administrative bulletin], and there must be an indication to that effect adjacent to the rule when it is published in the [administrative code].

(b) A reviewing court shall determine wholly de novo the validity of a rule within the scope of subsection (a) that is adopted without complying with the provisions of Sections 3–103 through 3–108.

§ 3–110.   [Concise Explanatory Statement]

(a) At the time it adopts a rule, an agency shall issue a concise explanatory statement containing:

(1) its reasons for adopting the rule; and

(2) an indication of any change between the text of the proposed rule contained in the published notice of proposed rule adoption and the text of the rule as finally adopted, with the reasons for any change.

(b) Only the reasons contained in the concise explanatory statement may be used by any party as justifications for the adoption of the rule in any proceeding in which its validity is at issue.

§ 3–111.   [Contents, Style, and Form of Rule]

(a) Each rule adopted by an agency must contain the text of the rule and:

(1) the date the agency adopted the rule;

(2) a concise statement of the purpose of the rule;

(3) a reference to all rules repealed, amended, or suspended by the rule;

(4) a reference to the specific statutory or other authority authorizing adoption of the rule;

(5) any findings required by any provision of law as a prerequisite to adoption or effectiveness of the rule; and

(6) the effective date of the rule if other than that specified in Section 3–115(a).

[(b) To the extent feasible, each rule should be written in clear and concise language understandable to persons who may be affected by it.]

(c) An agency may incorporate, by reference in its rules and without publishing the incorporated matter in full, all or any part of a code, standard, rule, or regulation that has been adopted by an agency of the United States or of this state, another state, or by a nationally recognized organization or association, if incorporation of its text in agency rules would be unduly cumbersome, expensive, or otherwise inexpedient. The reference in the agency rules must fully identify the incorporated matter by location, date, and otherwise, [and must state that the rule does not include any later amendments or editions of the incorporated matter]. An agency may incorporate by reference such matter in its rules only if the agency, organization, or association originally issuing that matter makes copies of it readily available to the public. The rules must state where copies of the incorporated matter are available at cost from the agency issuing the rule, and where copies are available from the agency of the United States, this State, another state, or the organization or association originally issuing that matter.

(d) In preparing its rules pursuant to this Chapter, each agency shall follow the uniform numbering system, form, and style prescribed by the [administrative rules editor].

§ 3–112. [Agency Rule-making Record]

(a) An agency shall maintain an official rule-making record for each rule it (i) proposes by publication in the [administrative bulletin] of a notice of proposed rule adoption, or (ii) adopts. The record and materials incorporated by reference must be available for public inspection.

(b) The agency rule-making record must contain:

(1) copies of all publications in the [administrative bulletin] with respect to the rule or the proceeding upon which the rule is based;

(2) copies of any portions of the agency's public rule-making docket containing entries relating to the rule or the proceeding upon which the rule is based;

(3) all written petitions, requests, submissions, and comments received by the agency and all other written materials considered by

the agency in connection with the formulation, proposal, or adoption of the rule or the proceeding upon which the rule is based;

(4) any official transcript of oral presentations made in the proceeding upon which the rule is based or, if not transcribed, any tape recording or stenographic record of those presentations, and any memorandum prepared by a presiding official summarizing the contents of those presentations;

(5) a copy of any regulatory analysis prepared for the proceeding upon which the rule is based;

(6) a copy of the rule and explanatory statement filed in the office of the [secretary of state];

(7) all petitions for exceptions to, amendments of, or repeal or suspension of, the rule;

(8) a copy of any request filed pursuant to Section 3–108(c);

[(9) a copy of any objection to the rule filed by the [administrative rules review committee] pursuant to Section 3–204(d) and the agency's response;] and

(10) a copy of any filed executive order with respect to the rule.

(c) Upon judicial review, the record required by this section constitutes the official agency rule-making record with respect to a rule. Except as provided in Section 3–110(b) or otherwise required by a provision of law, the agency rule-making record need not constitute the exclusive basis for agency action on that rule or for judicial review thereof.

§ 3–113. [Invalidity of Rules Not Adopted According to Chapter; Time Limitation]

(a) A rule adopted after [date] is invalid unless adopted in substantial compliance with the provisions of Sections 3–102 through 3–108 and Sections 3–110 through 3–112. However, inadvertent failure to mail a notice of proposed rule adoption to any person as required by Section 3–103(b) does not invalidate a rule.

(b) An action to contest the validity of a rule on the grounds of its noncompliance with any provision of Sections 3–102 through 3–108 or Sections 3–110 through 3–112 must be commenced within [2] years after the effective date of the rule.

§ 3–114. [Filing of Rules]

(a) An agency shall file in the office of the [secretary of state] each rule it adopts and all rules existing on the effective date of this Act that have not previously been filed. The filing must be done as soon after adoption of the rule as is practicable. At the time of filing, each rule adopted after the effective date of this Act must have attached to it the explanatory statement required by Section 3–110. The [secretary of state] shall affix to each rule and statement a certification of the time and date of filing and keep a permanent register open to public inspection of all filed rules and attached explanatory statements. In filing a rule, each agency shall use a standard form prescribed by the [secretary of state].

(b) The [secretary of state] shall transmit to the [administrative rules editor], [administrative rules counsel], and to the members of the [administrative rules review committee] a certified copy of each filed rule as soon after its filing as is practicable.

§ 3–115. [Effective Date of Rules]

(a) Except to the extent subsection (b) or (c) provides otherwise, each rule adopted after the effective date of this Act becomes effective [30] days after the later of (i) its filing in the office of the [secretary of state] or (ii) its publication and indexing in the [administrative bulletin].

(b)(1) A rule becomes effective on a date later than that established by subsection (a) if a later date is required by another statute or specified in the rule.

(2) A rule may become effective immediately upon its filing or on any subsequent date earlier than that established by subsection (a) if the agency establishes such an effective date and finds that:

(i) it is required by constitution, statute, or court order;

(ii) the rule only confers a benefit or removes a restriction on the public or some segment thereof;

(iii) the rule only delays the effective date of another rule that is not yet effective; or

(iv) the earlier effective date is necessary because of imminent peril to the public health, safety, or welfare.

(3) The finding and a brief statement of the reasons therefor required by paragraph (2) must be made a part of the rule. In any action contesting the effective date of a rule made effective under paragraph (2), the burden is on the agency to justify its finding.

(4) Each agency shall make a reasonable effort to make known to persons who may be affected by it a rule made effective before publication and indexing under this subsection.

(c) This section does not relieve an agency from compliance with any provision of law requiring that some or all of its rules be approved by other designated officials or bodies before they become effective.

§ 3–116. [Special Provision for Certain Classes of Rules]

Except to the extent otherwise provided by any provision of law, Sections 3–102 through 3–115 are inapplicable to:

(1) a rule concerning only the internal management of an agency which does not directly and substantially affect the procedural or substantive rights or duties of any segment of the public;

(2) a rule that establishes criteria or guidelines to be used by the staff of an agency in performing audits, investigations, or inspections, settling commercial disputes, negotiating commercial arrangements, or in the defense, prosecution, or settlement of cases, if disclosure of the criteria or guidelines would:

    (i) enable law violators to avoid detection;

    (ii) facilitate disregard of requirements imposed by law; or

    (iii) give a clearly improper advantage to persons who are in an adverse position to the state;

(3) a rule that only establishes specific prices to be charged for particular goods or services sold by an agency;

(4) a rule concerning only the physical servicing, maintenance, or care of agency owned or operated facilities or property;

(5) a rule relating only to the use of a particular facility or property owned, operated, or maintained by the state or any of its subdivisions, if the substance of the rule is adequately indicated by means of signs or signals to persons who use the facility or property;

(6) a rule concerning only inmates of a correctional or detention facility, students enrolled in an educational institution, or patients admitted to a hospital, if adopted by that facility, institution, or hospital;

(7) a form whose contents or substantive requirements are prescribed by rule or statute, and instructions for the execution or use of the form;

(8) an agency budget; [or]

(9) an opinion of the attorney general[; or] [.]

(10) [the terms of a collective bargaining agreement.]

§ 3–117. [Petition for Adoption of Rule]

Any person may petition an agency requesting the adoption of a rule. Each agency shall prescribe by rule the form of the petition and the procedure for its submission, consideration, and disposition. Within [60] days after submission of a petition, the agency shall either (i) deny the petition in writing, stating its reasons therefor, (ii) initiate rule-making proceedings in accordance with this Chapter, or (iii) if otherwise lawful, adopt a rule.

Review of Agency Rules

§ 3–201. [Review by Agency]

At least [annually], each agency shall review all of its rules to determine whether any new rule should be adopted. In conducting that review, each agency shall prepare a written report summarizing its findings, its supporting reasons, and any proposed course of action. For each rule, the [annual] report must include, at least once every [7] years, a concise statement of:

(1) the rule's effectiveness in achieving its objectives, including a summary of any available data supporting the conclusions reached;

(2) criticisms of the rule received during the previous [7] years, including a summary of any petitions for waiver of the rule tendered to the agency or granted by it; and

(3) alternative solutions to the criticisms and the reasons they were rejected or the changes made in the rule in response to those criticisms and the reasons for the changes. A copy of the [annual] report must be sent to the [administrative rules review committee and the administrative rules counsel] and be available for public inspection.

§ 3-202. [Review by Governor; Administrative Rules Counsel]

(a) To the extent the agency itself would have authority, the governor may rescind or suspend all or a severable portion of a rule of an agency. In exercising this authority, the governor shall act by an executive order that is subject to the provisions of this Act applicable to the adoption and effectiveness of a rule.

(b) The governor may summarily terminate any pending rule-making proceeding by an executive order to that effect, stating therein the reasons for the action. The executive order must be filed in the office of the [secretary of state], which shall promptly forward a certified copy to the agency and the [administrative rules editor]. An executive order terminating a rule-making proceeding becomes effective on [the date it is filed] and must be published in the next issue of the [administrative bulletin].

(c) There is created, within the office of the governor, an [administrative rules counsel] to advise the governor in the execution of the authority vested under this Article. The governor shall appoint the [administrative rules counsel] who shall serve at the pleasure of the governor.

§ 3-203. [Administrative Rules Review Committee]

There is created the ["administrative rules review committee"] of the [legislature]. The committee must be [bipartisan] and composed of [3] senators appointed by the [president of the senate] and [3] representatives appointed by the [speaker of the house]. Committee members must be appointed within [30] days after the convening of a regular legislative session. The term of office is [2] years while a member of the [legislature] and begins on the date of appointment to the committee. While a member of the [legislature], a member of the committee whose term has expired shall serve until a successor is appointed. A vacancy on the committee may be filled at any time by the original appointing authority for the remainder of the term. The committee shall choose a chairman from its membership for a [2]–year term and may employ staff it considers advisable.

§ 3–204. [Review by Administrative Rules Review Committee]

(a) The [administrative rules review committee] shall selectively review possible, proposed, or adopted rules and prescribe appropriate committee procedures for that purpose. The committee may receive and investigate complaints from members of the public with respect to possible, proposed, or adopted rules and hold public proceedings on those complaints.

(b) Committee meetings must be open to the public. Subject to procedures established by the committee, persons may present oral argument, data, or views at those meetings. The committee may require a representative of an agency whose possible, proposed, or adopted rule is under examination to attend a committee meeting and answer relevant questions. The committee may also communicate to the agency its comments on any possible, proposed, or adopted rule and require the agency to respond to them in writing. Unless impracticable, in advance of each committee meeting, notice of the time and place of the meeting and the specific subject matter to be considered must be published in the [administrative bulletin].

(c) The committee may recommend enactment of a statute to improve the operation of an agency. The committee may also recommend that a particular rule be superseded in whole or in part by statute. The [speaker of the house and the president of the senate] shall refer those recommendations to the appropriate standing committees. This subsection does not preclude any committee of the legislature from reviewing a rule on its own motion or recommending that it be superseded in whole or in part by statute.

[(d)(1) If the committee objects to all or some portion of a rule because the committee considers it to be beyond the procedural or substantive authority delegated to the adopting agency, the committee may file that objection in the office of the [secretary of state]. The filed objection must contain a concise statement of the committee's reasons for its action.

(2) The [secretary of state] shall affix to each objection a certification of the date and time of its filing and as soon thereafter as practicable shall transmit a certified copy thereof to the agency issuing the rule in question, the [administrative rules editor, and the administrative rules counsel]. The [secretary of state] shall also maintain a permanent register open to public inspection of all objections by the committee.

(3) The [administrative rules editor] shall publish and index an objection filed pursuant to this subsection in the next issue of the [administrative bulletin] and indicate its existence adjacent to the rule in question when that rule is published in the [administrative code]. In case of a filed objection by the committee to a rule that is

subject to the requirements of Section 2–101(g), the agency shall indicate the existence of that objection adjacent to the rule in the official compilation referred to in that subsection.

(4) Within [14] days after the filing of an objection by the committee to a rule, the issuing agency shall respond in writing to the committee. After receipt of the response, the committee may withdraw or modify its objection.

[(5) After the filing of an objection by the committee that is not subsequently withdrawn, the burden is upon the agency in any proceeding for judicial review or for enforcement of the rule to establish that the whole or portion of the rule objected to is within the procedural and substantive authority delegated to the agency.]

(6) The failure of the [administrative rules review committee] to object to a rule is not an implied legislative authorization of its procedural or substantive validity.]

(e) The committee may recommend to an agency that it adopt a rule. [The committee may also require an agency to publish notice of the committee's recommendation as a proposed rule of the agency and to allow public participation thereon, according to the provisions of Sections 3–103 through 3–104. An agency is not required to adopt the proposed rule.]

(f) The committee shall file an annual report with the [presiding officer] of each house and the governor.

ARTICLE IV
ADJUDICATIVE PROCEEDINGS
CHAPTER I. AVAILABILITY OF ADJUDICATIVE PROCEEDINGS; APPLICATIONS; LICENSES

§ 4–101. [Adjudicative Proceedings; When Required; Exceptions]

(a) An agency shall conduct an adjudicative proceeding as the process for formulating and issuing an order, unless the order is a decision:

(1) to issue or not to issue a complaint, summons, or similar accusation;

(2) to initiate or not to initiate an investigation, prosecution, or other proceeding before the agency, another agency, or a court; or

(3) under Section 4–103, not to conduct an adjudicative proceeding.

(b) This Article applies to rule-making proceedings only to the extent that another statute expressly so requires.

§ 4–102. [Adjudicative Proceedings; Commencement]

(a) An agency may commence an adjudicative proceeding at any time with respect to a matter within the agency's jurisdiction.

(b) An agency shall commence an adjudicative proceeding upon the application of any person, unless:

(1) the agency lacks jurisdiction of the subject matter;

(2) resolution of the matter requires the agency to exercise discretion within the scope of Section 4–101(a);

(3) a statute vests the agency with discretion to conduct or not to conduct an adjudicative proceeding before issuing an order to resolve the matter and, in the exercise of that discretion, the agency has determined not to conduct an adjudicative proceeding;

(4) resolution of the matter does not require the agency to issue an order that determines the applicant's legal rights, duties, privileges, immunities, or other legal interests;

(5) the matter was not timely submitted to the agency; or

(6) the matter was not submitted in a form substantially complying with any applicable provision of law.

(c) An application for an agency to issue an order includes an application for the agency to conduct appropriate adjudicative proceedings, whether or not the applicant expressly requests those proceedings.

(d) An adjudicative proceeding commences when the agency or a presiding officer:

(1) notifies a party that a pre-hearing conference, hearing, or other stage of an adjudicative proceeding will be conducted; or

(2) begins to take action on a matter that appropriately may be determined by an adjudicative proceeding, unless this action is:

(i) an investigation for the purpose of determining whether an adjudicative proceeding should be conducted; or

(ii) a decision which, under Section 4–101(a), the agency may make without conducting an adjudicative proceeding.

§ 4–103. [Decision Not to Conduct Adjudicative Proceeding]

If an agency decides not to conduct an adjudicative proceeding in response to an application, the agency shall furnish the applicant a copy of its decision in writing, with a brief statement of the agency's reasons and of any administrative review available to the applicant.

§ 4–104. [Agency Action on Applications]

(a) Except to the extent that the time limits in this subsection are inconsistent with limits established by another statute for any stage of the proceedings, an agency shall process an application for an order, other than a declaratory order, as follows:

(1) Within [30] days after receipt of the application, the agency shall examine the application, notify the applicant of any apparent errors or omissions, request any additional information the agency wishes to obtain and is permitted by law to require, and notify the

applicant of the name, official title, mailing address and telephone number of an agency member or employee who may be contacted regarding the application.

(2) Except in situations governed by paragraph (3), within [90] days after receipt of the application or of the response to a timely request made by the agency pursuant to paragraph (1), the agency shall:

(i) approve or deny the application, in whole or in part, on the basis of emergency or summary adjudicative proceedings, if those proceedings are available under this Act for disposition of the matter;

(ii) commence a formal adjudicative hearing or a conference adjudicative hearing in accordance with this Act; or

(iii) dispose of the application in accordance with Section 4–103.

(3) If the application pertains to subject matter that is not available when the application is filed but may be available in the future, including an application for housing or employment at a time no vacancy exists, the agency may proceed to make a determination of eligibility within the time provided in paragraph (2). If the agency determines that the applicant is eligible, the agency shall maintain the application on the agency's list of eligible applicants as provided by law and, upon request, shall notify the applicant of the status of the application.

(b) If a timely and sufficient application has been made for renewal of a license with reference to any activity of a continuing nature, the existing license does not expire until the agency has taken final action upon the application for renewal or, if the agency's action is unfavorable, until the last day for seeking judicial review of the agency's action or a later date fixed by the reviewing court.

§ 4–105.   [Agency Action Against Licensees]

An agency may not revoke, suspend, modify, annul, withdraw, or amend a license unless the agency first gives notice and an opportunity for an appropriate adjudicative proceeding in accordance with this Act or other statute. This section does not preclude an agency from (i) taking immediate action to protect the public interest in accordance with Section 4–501 or (ii) adopting rules, otherwise within the scope of its authority, pertaining to a class of licensees, including rules affecting the existing licenses of a class of licensees.

Formal Adjudicative Hearing

§ 4–201.   [Applicability]

An adjudicative proceeding is governed by this chapter, except as otherwise provided by:

(1) a statute other than this Act;

(2) a rule that adopts the procedures for the conference adjudicative hearing or summary adjudicative proceeding in accordance with the standards provided in this Act for those proceedings;

(3) Section 4–501 pertaining to emergency adjudicative proceedings; or

(4) Section 2–103 pertaining to declaratory proceedings.

§ 4–202.   [Presiding Officer, Disqualification, Substitution]

(a) The agency head, one or more members of the agency head, one or more administrative law judges assigned by the office of administrative hearings in accordance with Section 4–301 [, or, unless prohibited by law, one or more other persons designated by the agency head], in the discretion of the agency head, may be the presiding officer.

(b) Any person serving or designated to serve alone or with others as presiding officer is subject to disqualification for bias, prejudice, interest, or any other cause provided in this Act or for which a judge is or may be disqualified.

(c) Any party may petition for the disqualification of a person promptly after receipt of notice indicating that the person will preside or promptly upon discovering facts establishing grounds for disqualification, whichever is later.

(d) A person whose disqualification is requested shall determine whether to grant the petition, stating facts and reasons for the determination.

(e) If a substitute is required for a person who is disqualified or becomes unavailable for any other reason, the substitute must be appointed by:

(1) the governor, if the disqualified or unavailable person is an elected official; or

(2) the appointing authority, if the disqualified or unavailable person is an appointed official.

(f) Any action taken by a duly-appointed substitute for a disqualified or unavailable person is as effective as if taken by the latter.

§ 4–203.   [Representation]

(a) Any party may participate in the hearing in person or, if the party is a corporation or other artificial person, by a duly authorized representative.

(b) Whether or not participating in person, any party may be advised and represented at the party's own expense by counsel or, if permitted by law, other representative.

§ 4–204. [Pre-hearing Conference—Availability, Notice]

The presiding officer designated to conduct the hearing may determine, subject to the agency's rules, whether a pre-hearing conference will be conducted. If the conference is conducted:

(1) The presiding officer shall promptly notify the agency of the determination that a pre-hearing conference will be conducted. The agency shall assign or request the office of administrative hearings to assign a presiding officer for the pre-hearing conference, exercising the same discretion as is provided by Section 4–202 concerning the selection of a presiding officer for a hearing.

(2) The presiding officer for the pre-hearing conference shall set the time and place of the conference and give reasonable written notice to all parties and to all persons who have filed written petitions to intervene in the matter. The agency shall give notice to other persons entitled to notice under any provision of law.

(3) The notice must include:

(i) the names and mailing addresses of all parties and other persons to whom notice is being given by the presiding officer;

(ii) the name, official title, mailing address, and telephone number of any counsel or employee who has been designated to appear for the agency;

(iii) the official file or other reference number, the name of the proceeding, and a general description of the subject matter;

(iv) a statement of the time, place, and nature of the pre-hearing conference;

(v) a statement of the legal authority and jurisdiction under which the pre-hearing conference and the hearing are to be held;

(vi) the name, official title, mailing address and telephone number of the presiding officer for the pre-hearing conference;

(vii) a statement that at the pre-hearing conference the proceeding, without further notice, may be converted into a conference adjudicative hearing or a summary adjudicative proceeding for disposition of the matter as provided by this Act; and

(viii) a statement that a party who fails to attend or participate in a pre-hearing conference, hearing, or other stage of an adjudicative proceeding may be held in default under this Act.

(4) The notice may include any other matters that the presiding officer considers desirable to expedite the proceedings.

§ 4–205. [Pre-hearing Conference—Procedure and Pre-hearing Order]

(a) The presiding officer may conduct all or part of the pre-hearing conference by telephone, television, or other electronic means if each participant in the conference has an opportunity to participate in, to hear, and, if technically feasible, to see the entire proceeding while it is taking place.

(b) The presiding officer shall conduct the pre-hearing conference, as may be appropriate, to deal with such matters as conversion of the proceeding to another type, exploration of settlement possibilities, preparation of stipulations, clarification of issues, rulings on identity and limitation of the number of witnesses, objections to proffers of evidence, determination of the extent to which direct evidence, rebuttal evidence, or cross-examination will be presented in written form, and the extent to which telephone, television, or other electronic means will be used as a substitute for proceedings in person, order of presentation of evidence and cross-examination, rulings regarding issuance of subpoenas, discovery orders and protective orders, and such other matters as will promote the orderly and prompt conduct of the hearing. The presiding officer shall issue a pre-hearing order incorporating the matters determined at the pre-hearing conference.

(c) If a pre-hearing conference is not held, the presiding officer for the hearing may issue a pre-hearing order, based on the pleadings, to regulate the conduct of the proceedings.

§ 4–206. [Notice of Hearing]

(a) The presiding officer for the hearing shall set the time and place of the hearing and give reasonable written notice to all parties and to all persons who have filed written petitions to intervene in the matter.

(b) The notice must include a copy of any pre-hearing order rendered in the matter.

(c) To the extent not included in a pre-hearing order accompanying it, the notice must include:

(1) the names and mailing addresses of all parties and other persons to whom notice is being given by the presiding officer;

(2) the name, official title, mailing address and telephone number of any counsel or employee who has been designated to appear for the agency;

(3) the official file or other reference number, the name of the proceeding, and a general description of the subject matter;

(4) a statement of the time, place, and nature of the hearing;

(5) a statement of the legal authority and jurisdiction under which the hearing is to be held;

(6) the name, official title, mailing address, and telephone number of the presiding officer;

(7) a statement of the issues involved and, to the extent known to the presiding officer, of the matters asserted by the parties; and

(8) a statement that a party who fails to attend or participate in a pre-hearing conference, hearing, or other stage of an adjudicative proceeding may be held in default under this Act.

(d) The notice may include any other matters the presiding officer considers desirable to expedite the proceedings.

(e) The agency shall give notice to persons entitled to notice under any provision of law who have not been given notice by the presiding officer. Notice under this subsection may include all types of information provided in subsections (a) through (d) or may consist of a brief statement indicating the subject matter, parties, time, place, and nature of the hearing, manner in which copies of the notice to the parties may be inspected and copied, and name and telephone number of the presiding officer.

§ 4–207. [Pleadings, Briefs, Motions, Service]

(a) The presiding officer, at appropriate stages of the proceedings, shall give all parties full opportunity to file pleadings, motions, objections and offers of settlement.

(b) The presiding officer, at appropriate stages of the proceedings, may give all parties full opportunity to file briefs, proposed findings of fact and conclusions of law, and proposed initial or final orders.

(c) A party shall serve copies of any filed item on all parties, by mail or any other means prescribed by agency rule.

§ 4–208. [Default]

(a) If a party fails to attend or participate in a pre-hearing conference, hearing, or other stage of an adjudicative proceeding, the presiding officer may serve upon all parties written notice of a proposed default order, including a statement of the grounds.

(b) Within [7] days after service of a proposed default order, the party against whom it was issued may file a written motion requesting that the proposed default order be vacated and stating the grounds relied upon. During the time within which a party may file a written motion under this subsection, the presiding officer may adjourn the proceedings or conduct them without the participation of the party against whom a proposed default order was issued, having due regard for the interests of justice and the orderly and prompt conduct of the proceedings.

(c) The presiding officer shall either issue or vacate the default order promptly after expiration of the time within which the party may file a written motion under subsection (b).

(d) After issuing a default order, the presiding officer shall conduct any further proceedings necessary to complete the adjudication without the participation of the party in default and shall determine all issues in the adjudication, including those affecting the defaulting party.

§ 4–209.   [Intervention]

(a) The presiding officer shall grant a petition for intervention if:

(1) the petition is submitted in writing to the presiding officer, with copies mailed to all parties named in the presiding officer's notice of the hearing, at least [3] days before the hearing;

(2) the petition states facts demonstrating that the petitioner's legal rights, duties, privileges, immunities, or other legal interests may be substantially affected by the proceeding or that the petitioner qualifies as an intervener under any provision of law; and

(3) the presiding officer determines that the interests of justice and the orderly and prompt conduct of the proceedings will not be impaired by allowing the intervention.

(b) The presiding officer may grant a petition for intervention at any time, upon determining that the intervention sought is in the interests of justice and will not impair the orderly and prompt conduct of the proceedings.

(c) If a petitioner qualifies for intervention, the presiding officer may impose conditions upon the intervener's participation in the proceedings, either at the time that intervention is granted or at any subsequent time. Conditions may include:

(1) limiting the intervener's participation to designated issues in which the intervener has a particular interest demonstrated by the petition;

(2) limiting the intervener's use of discovery, cross-examination, and other procedures so as to promote the orderly and prompt conduct of the proceedings; and

(3) requiring 2 or more interveners to combine their presentations of evidence and argument, cross-examination, discovery, and other participation in the proceedings. . . .

§ 4–210.   [Subpoenas, Discovery and Protective Orders]

(a) The presiding officer [at the request of any party shall, and upon the presiding officer's own motion,] may issue subpoenas, discovery orders and protective orders, in accordance with the rules of civil procedure.

(b) Subpoenas and orders issued under this section may be enforced pursuant to the provisions of this Act on civil enforcement of agency action.

§ 4–211.   [Procedure at Hearing]

At a hearing:

(1) The presiding officer shall regulate the course of the proceedings in conformity with any pre-hearing order.

(2) To the extent necessary for full disclosure of all relevant facts and issues, the presiding officer shall afford to all parties the opportunity to respond, present evidence and argument, conduct cross-examination, and submit rebuttal evidence, except as restricted by a limited grant of intervention or by the pre-hearing order.

(3) The presiding officer may give nonparties an opportunity to present oral or written statements. If the presiding officer proposes to consider a statement by a nonparty, the presiding officer shall give all parties an opportunity to challenge or rebut it and, on motion of any party, the presiding officer shall require the statement to be given under oath or affirmation.

(4) The presiding officer may conduct all or part of the hearing by telephone, television, or other electronic means, if each participant in the hearing has an opportunity to participate in, to hear, and, if technically feasible, to see the entire proceeding while it is taking place.

(5) The presiding officer shall cause the hearing to be recorded at the agency's expense. The agency is not required, at its expense, to prepare a transcript, unless required to do so by a provision of law. Any party, at the party's expense, may cause a reporter approved by the agency to prepare a transcript from the agency's record, or cause additional recordings to be made during the hearing if the making of the additional recordings does not cause distraction or disruption.

(6) The hearing is open to public observation, except for the parts that the presiding officer states to be closed pursuant to a provision of law expressly authorizing closure. To the extent that a hearing is conducted by telephone, television, or other electronic means, and is not closed, the availability of public observation is satisfied by giving members of the public an opportunity, at reasonable times, to hear or inspect the agency's record, and to inspect any transcript obtained by the agency.

§ 4–212. [Evidence, Official Notice]

(a) Upon proper objection, the presiding officer shall exclude evidence that is irrelevant, immaterial, unduly repetitious, or excludable on constitutional or statutory grounds or on the basis of evidentiary privilege recognized in the courts of this state. In the absence of proper objection, the presiding officer may exclude objectionable evidence. Evidence may not be excluded solely because it is hearsay.

(b) All testimony of parties and witnesses must be made under oath or affirmation.

(c) Statements presented by nonparties in accordance with Section 4–211(3) may be received as evidence.

(d) Any part of the evidence may be received in written form if doing so will expedite the hearing without substantial prejudice to the interests of any party.

(e) Documentary evidence may be received in the form of a copy or excerpt. Upon request, parties must be given an opportunity to compare the copy with the original if available.

(f) Official notice may be taken of (i) any fact that could be judicially noticed in the courts of this State, (ii) the record of other proceedings before the agency, (iii) technical or scientific matters within the agency's specialized knowledge, and (iv) codes or standards that have been adopted by an agency of the United States, of this State or of another state, or by a nationally recognized organization or association. Parties must be notified before or during the hearing, or before the issuance of any initial or final order that is based in whole or in part on facts or material noticed, of the specific facts or material noticed and the source thereof, including any staff memoranda and data, and be afforded an opportunity to contest and rebut the facts or material so noticed.

§ 4–213.   [Ex parte Communications]

(a) Except as provided in subsection (b) or unless required for the disposition of ex parte matters specifically authorized by statute, a presiding officer serving in an adjudicative proceeding may not communicate, directly or indirectly, regarding any issue in the proceeding, while the proceeding is pending, with any party, with any person who has a direct or indirect interest in the outcome of the proceeding, or with any person who presided at a previous stage of the proceeding, without notice and opportunity for all parties to participate in the communication.

(b) A member of a multi-member panel of presiding officers may communicate with other members of the panel regarding a matter pending before the panel, and any presiding officer may receive aid from staff assistants if the assistants do not (i) receive ex parte communications of a type that the presiding officer would be prohibited from receiving or (ii) furnish, augment, diminish, or modify the evidence in the record.

(c) Unless required for the disposition of ex parte matters specifically authorized by statute, no party to an adjudicative proceeding, and no person who has a direct or indirect interest in the outcome of the proceeding or who presided at a previous stage of the proceeding, may communicate, directly or indirectly, in connection with any issue in that proceeding, while the proceeding is pending, with any person serving as presiding officer, without notice and opportunity for all parties to participate in the communication.

(d) If, before serving as presiding officer in an adjudicative proceeding, a person receives an ex parte communication of a type that could not properly be received while serving, the person, promptly after starting to serve, shall disclose the communication in the manner prescribed in subsection (e).

(e) A presiding officer who receives an ex parte communication in violation of this section shall place on the record of the pending matter all written communications received, all written responses to the communications, and a memorandum stating the substance of all oral communications received, all responses made, and the identity of each person from whom the presiding officer received an ex parte communication, and shall advise all parties that these matters have been placed on the record. Any party desiring to rebut the ex parte communication must be allowed to do so, upon requesting the opportunity for rebuttal within [10] days after notice of the communication.

(f) If necessary to eliminate the effect of an ex parte communication received in violation of this section, a presiding officer who receives the communication may be disqualified and the portions of the record pertaining to the communication may be sealed by protective order.

(g) The agency shall, and any party may, report any willful violation of this section to appropriate authorities for any disciplinary proceedings provided by law. In addition, each agency by rule may provide for appropriate sanctions, including default, for any violations of this section.

§ 4–214. [Separation of Functions]

(a) A person who has served as investigator, prosecutor or advocate in an adjudicative proceeding or in its pre-adjudicative stage may not serve as presiding officer or assist or advise a presiding officer in the same proceeding.

(b) A person who is subject to the authority, direction, or discretion of one who has served as investigator, prosecutor, or advocate in an adjudicative proceeding or in its pre-adjudicative stage may not serve as presiding officer or assist or advise a presiding officer in the same proceeding.

(c) A person who has participated in a determination of probable cause or other equivalent preliminary determination in an adjudicative proceeding may serve as presiding officer or assist or advise a presiding officer in the same proceeding, unless a party demonstrates grounds for disqualification in accordance with Section 4–202.

(d) A person may serve as presiding officer at successive stages of the same adjudicative proceeding, unless a party demonstrates grounds for disqualification in accordance with Section 4–202.

§ 4–215. [Final Order, Initial Order]

(a) If the presiding officer is the agency head, the presiding officer shall render a final order.

(b) If the presiding officer is not the agency head, the presiding officer shall render an initial order, which becomes a final order unless reviewed in accordance with Section 4–216.

(c) A final order or initial order must include, separately stated, findings of fact, conclusions of law, and policy reasons for the decision if it is an exercise of the agency's discretion, for all aspects of the order, including the remedy prescribed and, if applicable, the action taken on a petition for stay of effectiveness. Findings of fact, if set forth in language that is no more than mere repetition or paraphrase of the relevant provision of law, must be accompanied by a concise and explicit statement of the underlying facts of record to support the findings. If a party has submitted proposed findings of fact, the order must include a ruling on the proposed findings. The order must also include a statement of the available procedures and time limits for seeking reconsideration or other administrative relief. An initial order must include a statement of any circumstances under which the initial order, without further notice, may become a final order.

(d) Findings of fact must be based exclusively upon the evidence of record in the adjudicative proceeding and on matters officially noticed in that proceeding. Findings must be based upon the kind of evidence on which reasonably prudent persons are accustomed to rely in the conduct of their serious affairs and may be based upon such evidence even if it would be inadmissible in a civil trial. The presiding officer's experience, technical competence, and specialized knowledge may be utilized in evaluating evidence.

(e) If a person serving or designated to serve as presiding officer becomes unavailable, for any reason, before rendition of the final order or initial order, a substitute presiding officer must be appointed as provided in Section 4–202. The substitute presiding officer shall use any existing record and may conduct any further proceedings appropriate in the interests of justice.

(f) The presiding officer may allow the parties a designated amount of time after conclusion of the hearing for the submission of proposed findings.

(g) A final order or initial order pursuant to this section must be rendered in writing within [90] days after conclusion of the hearing or after submission of proposed findings in accordance with subsection (f) unless this period is waived or extended with the written consent of all parties or for good cause shown.

(h) The presiding officer shall cause copies of the final order or initial order to be delivered to each party and to the agency head.

§ 4–216. [Review of Initial Order; Exceptions to Reviewability]

(a) The agency head, upon its own motion may, and upon appeal by any party shall, review an initial order, except to the extent that:

(1) a provision of law precludes or limits agency review of the initial order; or

(2) the agency head, in the exercise of discretion conferred by a provision of law,

(i) determines to review some but not all issues, or not to exercise any review,

(ii) delegates its authority to review the initial order to one or more persons, or

(iii) authorizes one or more persons to review the initial order, subject to further review by the agency head. . . .

(b) A petition for appeal from an initial order must be filed with the agency head, or with any person designated for this purpose by rule of the agency, within [10] days after rendition of the initial order. If the agency head on its own motion decides to review an initial order, the agency head shall give written notice of its intention to review the initial order within [10] days after its rendition. The [10]-day period for a party to file a petition for appeal or for the agency head to give notice of its intention to review an initial order on the agency head's own motion is tolled by the submission of a timely petition for reconsideration of the initial order pursuant to Section 4–218, and a new [10]-day period starts to run upon disposition of the petition for reconsideration. If an initial order is subject both to a timely petition for reconsideration and to a petition for appeal or to review by the agency head on its own motion, the petition for reconsideration must be disposed of first, unless the agency head determines that action on the petition for reconsideration has been unreasonably delayed.

(c) The petition for appeal must state its basis. If the agency head on its own motion gives notice of its intent to review an initial order, the agency head shall identify the issues that it intends to review.

(d) The presiding officer for the review of an initial order shall exercise all the decision-making power that the presiding officer would have had to render a final order had the presiding officer presided over the hearing, except to the extent that the issues subject to review are limited by a provision of law or by the presiding officer upon notice to all parties.

(e) The presiding officer shall afford each party an opportunity to present briefs and may afford each party an opportunity to present oral argument.

(f) Before rendering a final order, the presiding officer may cause a transcript to be prepared, at the agency's expense, of such portions of the proceeding under review as the presiding officer considers necessary.

(g) The presiding officer may render a final order disposing of the proceeding or may remand the matter for further proceedings with instructions to the person who rendered the initial order. Upon remanding a matter, the presiding officer may order such temporary relief as is authorized and appropriate.

(h) A final order or an order remanding the matter for further proceedings must be rendered in writing within [60] days after receipt of briefs and oral argument unless that period is waived or extended with the written consent of all parties or for good cause shown.

(i) A final order or an order remanding the matter for further proceedings under this section must identify any difference between this order and the initial order and must include, or incorporate by express reference to the initial order, all the matters required by Section 4–215(c).

(j) The presiding officer shall cause copies of the final order or order remanding the matter for further proceedings to be delivered to each party and to the agency head.

§ 4–217. [Stay]

A party may submit to the presiding officer a petition for stay of effectiveness of an initial or final order within [7] days after its rendition unless otherwise provided by statute or stated in the initial or final order. The presiding officer may take action on the petition for stay, either before or after the effective date of the initial or final order.

§ 4–218. [Reconsideration]

Unless otherwise provided by statute or rule:

(1) Any party, within [10] days after rendition of an initial or final order, may file a petition for reconsideration, stating the specific grounds upon which relief is requested. The filing of the petition is not a prerequisite for seeking administrative or judicial review.

(2) The petition must be disposed of by the same person or persons who rendered the initial or final order, if available.

(3) The presiding officer shall render a written order denying the petition, granting the petition and dissolving or modifying the initial or final order, or granting the petition and setting the matter for further proceedings. The petition may be granted, in whole or in part, only if the presiding officer states, in the written order, findings of fact, conclusions of law, and policy reasons for the decision if it is an exercise of the agency's discretion, to justify the order. The petition is deemed to have been denied if the presiding officer does not dispose of it within [20] days after the filing of the petition.

§ 4–219. [Review by Superior Agency]

If, pursuant to statute, an agency may review the final order of another agency, the review is deemed to be a continuous proceeding as if before a single agency. The final order of the first agency is treated as an initial order and the second agency functions as though it were reviewing an initial order in accordance with Section 4–216.

§ 4–220. [Effectiveness of Orders]

(a) Unless a later date is stated in a final order or a stay is granted, a final order is effective [10] days after rendition, but:

(1) a party may not be required to comply with a final order unless the party has been served with or has actual knowledge of the final order;

(2) a nonparty may not be required to comply with a final order unless the agency has made the final order available for public inspection and copying or the nonparty has actual knowledge of the final order.

(b) Unless a later date is stated in an initial order or a stay is granted, the time when an initial order becomes a final order in accordance with Section 4–215 is determined as follows:

(1) when the initial order is rendered, if administrative review is unavailable;

(2) when the agency head renders an order stating, after a petition for appeal has been filed, that review will not be exercised, if discretion is available to make a determination to this effect; or

(3) [10] days after rendition of the initial order, if no party has filed a petition for appeal and the agency head has not given written notice of its intention to exercise review.

(c) Unless a later date is stated in an initial order or a stay is granted, an initial order that becomes a final order in accordance with subsection (b) and Section 4–215 is effective [10] days after becoming a final order, but:

(1) a party may not be required to comply with the final order unless the party has been served with or has actual knowledge of the initial order or of an order stating that review will not be exercised; and

(2) a nonparty may not be required to comply with the final order unless the agency has made the initial order available for public inspection and copying or the nonparty has actual knowledge of the initial order or of an order stating that review will not be exercised.

(d) This section does not preclude an agency from taking immediate action to protect the public interest in accordance with Section 4–501.

§ 4–221. [Agency Record]

(a) An agency shall maintain an official record of each adjudicative proceeding under this Chapter.

(b) The agency record consists only of:

(1) notices of all proceedings;

(2) any pre-hearing order;

(3) any motions, pleadings, briefs, petitions, requests, and intermediate rulings;

(4) evidence received or considered;

(5) a statement of matters officially noticed;

(6) proffers of proof and objections and rulings thereon;

(7) proposed findings, requested orders, and exceptions;

(8) the record prepared for the presiding officer at the hearing, together with any transcript of all or part of the hearing considered before final disposition of the proceeding;

(9) any final order, initial order, or order on reconsideration;

(10) staff memoranda or data submitted to the presiding officer, unless prepared and submitted by personal assistants and not inconsistent with Section 4–213(b); and

(11) matters placed on the record after an ex parte communication.

(c) Except to the extent that this Act or another statute provides otherwise, the agency record constitutes the exclusive basis for agency action in adjudicative proceedings under this Chapter and for judicial review thereof.

Office of Administrative Hearings

§ 4–301. [Office of Administrative Hearings—Creation, Powers, Duties]

(a) There is created the office of administrative hearings within the [Department of _____], to be headed by a director appointed by the governor and confirmed by the senate.

(b) The office shall employ administrative law judges as necessary to conduct proceedings required by this Act or other provision of law. [Only a person admitted to practice law in [this State] [a jurisdiction in the United States] may be employed as an administrative law judge.]

(c) If the office cannot furnish one of its administrative law judges in response to an agency request, the director shall designate in writing a fulltime employee of an agency other than the requesting agency to serve as administrative law judge for the proceeding, but only with the consent of the employing agency. The designee must possess the same qualifications required of administrative law judges employed by the office.

(d) The director may furnish administrative law judges on a contract basis to any governmental entity to conduct any proceeding not subject to this Act.

(e) The office may adopt rules:

(1) to establish further qualifications for administrative law judges, procedures by which candidates will be considered for employment, and the manner in which public notice of vacancies in the staff of the office will be given;

(2) to establish procedures for agencies to request and for the director to assign administrative law judges; however, an agency may neither select nor reject any individual administrative law judge for any proceeding except in accordance with this Act;

(3) to establish procedures and adopt forms, consistent with this Act, the model rules of procedure, and other provisions of law, to govern administrative law judges;

(4) to establish standards and procedures for the evaluation, training, promotion, and discipline of administrative law judges; and

(5) to facilitate the performance of the responsibilities conferred upon the office by this Act.

(f) The director may:

(1) maintain a staff of reporters and other personnel; and

(2) implement the provisions of this section and rules adopted under its authority.

Conference Adjudicative Hearing

§ 4–401. [Conference Adjudicative Hearing—Applicability]

A conference adjudicative hearing may be used if its use in the circumstances does not violate any provision of law and the matter is entirely within one or more categories for which the agency by rule has adopted this chapter [; however, those categories may include only the following:

(1) a matter in which there is no disputed issue of material fact; or

(2) a matter in which there is a disputed issue of material fact, if the matter involves only:

(i) a monetary amount of not more than [$1,000];

(ii) a disciplinary sanction against a prisoner;

(iii) a disciplinary sanction against a student which does not involve expulsion from an academic institution or suspension for more than [10] days;

(iv) a disciplinary sanction against a public employee which does not involve discharge from employment or suspension for more than [10] days;

(v) a disciplinary sanction against a licensee which does not involve revocation, suspension, annulment, withdrawal, or amendment of a license; or

(vi) . . . .]

§ 4–402. [Conference Adjudicative Hearing—Procedures]

The procedures of this Act pertaining to formal adjudicative hearings apply to a conference adjudicative hearing, except to the following extent:

(1) If a matter is initiated as a conference adjudicative hearing, no pre-hearing conference may be held.

(2) The provisions of Section 4–210 do not apply to conference adjudicative hearings insofar as those provisions authorize the issuance and enforcement of subpoenas and discovery orders, but do apply to conference adjudicative hearings insofar as those provisions authorize the presiding officer to issue protective orders at the request of any party or upon the presiding officer's motion.

(3) Paragraphs (1), (2) and (3) of Section 4–211 do not apply; but,

(i) the presiding officer shall regulate the course of the proceedings,

(ii) only the parties may testify and present written exhibits, and

(iii) the parties may offer comments on the issues.

§ 4–403. [Conference Adjudicative Hearing—Proposed Proof]

(a) If the presiding officer has reason to believe that material facts are in dispute, the presiding officer may require any party to state the identity of the witnesses or other sources through whom the party would propose to present proof if the proceeding were converted to a formal adjudicative hearing, but if disclosure of any fact, allegation, or source is privileged or expressly prohibited by any provision of law, the presiding officer may require the party to indicate that confidential facts, allegations, or sources are involved, but not to disclose the confidential facts, allegations, or sources.

(b) If a party has reason to believe that essential facts must be obtained in order to permit an adequate presentation of the case, the party may inform the presiding officer regarding the general nature of the facts and the sources from whom the party would propose to obtain those facts if the proceeding were converted to a formal adjudicative hearing.

Emergency and Summary Adjudicative Proceedings

§ 4–501. [Emergency Adjudicative Proceedings]

(a) An agency may use emergency adjudicative proceedings in a situation involving an immediate danger to the public health, safety, or welfare requiring immediate agency action.

(b) The agency may take only such action as is necessary to prevent or avoid the immediate danger to the public health, safety, or welfare that justifies use of emergency adjudication.

(c) The agency shall render an order, including a brief statement of findings of fact, conclusions of law, and policy reasons for the decision if it is an exercise of the agency's discretion, to justify the determination of an immediate danger and the agency's decision to take the specific action.

(d) The agency shall give such notice as is practicable to persons who are required to comply with the order. The order is effective when rendered.

(e) After issuing an order pursuant to this section, the agency shall proceed as quickly as feasible to complete any proceedings that would be required if the matter did not involve an immediate danger.

(f) The agency record consists of any documents regarding the matter that were considered or prepared by the agency. The agency shall maintain these documents as its official record.

(g) Unless otherwise required by a provision of law, the agency record need not constitute the exclusive basis for agency action in emergency adjudicative proceedings or for judicial review thereof.

§ 4–502.   [Summary Adjudicative Proceedings—Applicability]

An agency may use summary adjudicative proceedings if:

(1) the use of those proceedings in the circumstances does not violate any provision of law;

(2) the protection of the public interest does not require the agency to give notice and an opportunity to participate to persons other than the parties; and

(3) the matter is entirely within one or more categories for which the agency by rule has adopted this section and Sections 4–503 to 4–506 [; however, those categories may include only the following:

(i) a monetary amount of not more than [$100];

(ii) a reprimand, warning, disciplinary report, or other purely verbal sanction without continuing impact against a prisoner, student, public employee, or licensee;

(iii) the denial of an application after the applicant has abandoned the application;

(iv) the denial of an application for admission to an educational institution or for employment by an agency;

(v) the denial, in whole or in part, of an application if the applicant has an opportunity for administrative review in accordance with Section 4–504;

(vi) a matter that is resolved on the sole basis of inspections, examinations, or tests;

(vii) the acquisition, leasing, or disposal of property or the procurement of goods or services by contract;

(viii) any matter having only trivial potential impact upon the affected parties; and

(ix) . . . .]

§ 4–503.   [Summary Adjudicative Proceedings—Procedures]

(a) The agency head, one or more members of the agency head, one or more administrative law judges assigned by the office of administrative hearings in accordance with Section 4–301 [, or, unless prohibited by law, one or more other persons designated by the agency head], in the discretion of the agency head, may be the presiding officer. Unless prohibited by law, a person exercising authority over the matter is the presiding officer.

(b) If the proceeding involves a monetary matter or a reprimand, warning, disciplinary report, or other sanction:

(1) the presiding officer, before taking action, shall give each party an opportunity to be informed of the agency's view of the matter and to explain the party's view of the matter; and

(2) the presiding officer, at the time any unfavorable action is taken, shall give each party a brief statement of findings of fact, conclusions of law, and policy reasons for the decision if it is an exercise of the agency's discretion, to justify the action, and a notice of any available administrative review.

(c) An order rendered in a proceeding that involves a monetary matter must be in writing. An order in any other summary adjudicative proceeding may be oral or written.

(d) The agency, by reasonable means, shall furnish to each party notification of the order in a summary adjudicative proceeding. Notification must include at least a statement of the agency's action and a notice of any available administrative review.

§ 4–504.   [Administrative Review of Summary Adjudicative Proceedings—Applicability]

Unless prohibited by any provision of law, an agency, on its own motion, may conduct administrative review of an order resulting from summary adjudicative proceedings, and shall conduct this review upon the written or oral request of a party if the agency receives the request within [10] days after furnishing notification under Section 4–503(d).

§ 4–505.   [Administrative Review of Summary Adjudicative Proceedings—Procedures]

Unless otherwise provided by statute [or rule]:

(1) An agency need not furnish notification of the pendency of administrative review to any person who did not request the review, but the agency may not take any action on review less favorable to any party than the original order without giving that party notice and an opportunity to explain that party's view of the matter.

(2) The reviewing officer, in the discretion of the agency head, may be any person who could have presided at the summary adjudicative proceeding, but the reviewing officer must be one who is authorized to grant appropriate relief upon review.

(3) The reviewing officer shall give each party an opportunity to explain the party's view of the matter unless the party's view is apparent from the written materials in the file submitted to the reviewing officer. The reviewing officer shall make any inquiries necessary to ascertain whether the proceeding must be converted to a conference adjudicative hearing or a formal adjudicative hearing.

(4) The reviewing officer may render an order disposing of the proceeding in any manner that was available to the presiding officer at the summary adjudicative proceeding or the reviewing officer may remand the matter for further proceedings, with or without conversion to a conference adjudicative hearing or a formal adjudicative hearing.

(5) If the order under review is or should have been in writing, the order on review must be in writing, including a brief statement of findings of fact, conclusions of law, and policy reasons for the decision if it is an exercise of the agency's discretion, to justify the order, and a notice of any further available administrative review.

(6) A request for administrative review is deemed to have been denied if the reviewing officer does not dispose of the matter or remand it for further proceedings within [20] days after the request is submitted.

§ 4–506. [Agency Record of Summary Adjudicative Proceedings and Administrative Review]

(a) The agency record consists of any documents regarding the matter that were considered or prepared by the presiding officer for the summary adjudicative proceeding or by the reviewing officer for any review. The agency shall maintain these documents as its official record.

(b) Unless otherwise required by a provision of law, the agency record need not constitute the exclusive basis for agency action in summary adjudicative proceedings or for judicial review thereof.

ARTICLE V
JUDICIAL REVIEW AND CIVIL ENFORCEMENT
CHAPTER I. JUDICIAL REVIEW

§ 5–101. [Relationship Between this Act and Other Law on Judicial Review and Other Judicial Remedies]

This Act establishes the exclusive means of judicial review of agency action, but:

(1) The provisions of this Act for judicial review do not apply to litigation in which the sole issue is a claim for money damages or compensation and the agency whose action is at issue does not have statutory authority to determine the claim.

(2) Ancillary procedural matters, including intervention, class actions, consolidation, joinder, severance, transfer, protective orders, and

other relief from disclosure of privileged or confidential material, are governed, to the extent not inconsistent with this Act, by other applicable law.

(3) If the relief available under other sections of this Act is not equal or substantially equivalent to the relief otherwise available under law, the relief otherwise available and the related procedures supersede and supplement this Act to the extent necessary for their effectuation. The applicable provisions of this Act and other law must be combined to govern a single proceeding or, if the court orders, 2 or more separate proceedings, with or without transfer to other courts, but no type of relief may be sought in a combined proceeding after expiration of the time limit for doing so.

§ 5–102.   [Final Agency Action Reviewable]

(a) A person who qualifies under this Act regarding (i) standing (Section 5–106), (ii) exhaustion of administrative remedies (Section 5–107), and (iii) time for filing the petition for review (Section 5–108), and other applicable provisions of law regarding bond, compliance, and other pre-conditions is entitled to judicial review of final agency action, whether or not the person has sought judicial review of any related non-final agency action.

(b) For purposes of this section and Section 5–103:

(1) "Final agency action" means the whole or a part of any agency action other than non-final agency action;

(2) "Non-final agency action" means the whole or a part of an agency determination, investigation, proceeding, hearing, conference, or other process that the agency intends or is reasonably believed to intend to be preliminary, preparatory, procedural, or intermediate with regard to subsequent agency action of that agency or another agency.

§ 5–103.   [Non-final Agency Action Reviewable]

A person is entitled to judicial review of non-final agency action only if:

(1) it appears likely that the person will qualify under Section 5–102 for judicial review of the related final agency action; and

(2) postponement of judicial review would result in an inadequate remedy or irreparable harm disproportionate to the public benefit derived from postponement.

[Alternative A.]

§ 5–104.   [Jurisdiction, Venue]

(a) The [trial court of general jurisdiction] shall conduct judicial review.

(b) Venue is in the [district] [that includes the state capital] [where the petitioner resides or maintains a principal place of business] unless otherwise provided by law.

[*Alternative B.*]

§ 5–104. [Jurisdiction, Venue]

(a) The [appellate court] shall conduct judicial review.

(b) Venue is in the [district] [that includes the state capital] [where the petitioner resides or maintains a principal place of business] unless otherwise provided by law.

(c) If evidence is to be adduced in the reviewing court in accordance with Section 5–114(a), the court shall appoint a [referee, master, trial court judge] for this purpose, having due regard for the convenience of the parties.

§ 5–105. [Form of Action]

Judicial review is initiated by filing a petition for review in [the appropriate] court. A petition may seek any type of relief available under Sections 5–101(3) and 5–117.

§ 5–106. [Standing]

(a) The following persons have standing to obtain judicial review of final or non-final agency action:

(1) a person to whom the agency action is specifically directed;

(2) a person who was a party to the agency proceedings that led to the agency action;

(3) if the challenged agency action is a rule, a person subject to that rule;

(4) a person eligible for standing under another provision of law; or

(5) a person otherwise aggrieved or adversely affected by the agency action. For purposes of this paragraph, no person has standing as one otherwise aggrieved or adversely affected unless:

(i) the agency action has prejudiced or is likely to prejudice that person;

(ii) that person's asserted interests are among those that the agency was required to consider when it engaged in the agency action challenged; and

(iii) a judgment in favor of that person would substantially eliminate or redress the prejudice to that person caused or likely to be caused by the agency action.

[(b) A standing committee of the legislature which is required to exercise general and continuing oversight over administrative agencies and procedures may petition for judicial review of any rule or intervene in any litigation arising from agency action.]

§ 5–107. [Exhaustion of Administrative Remedies]

A person may file a petition for judicial review under this Act only after exhausting all administrative remedies available within the agency whose action is being challenged and within any other agency authorized to exercise administrative review, but:

(1) a petitioner for judicial review of a rule need not have participated in the rule-making proceeding upon which that rule is based, or have petitioned for its amendment or repeal;

(2) a petitioner for judicial review need not exhaust administrative remedies to the extent that this Act or any other statute states that exhaustion is not required; or

(3) the court may relieve a petitioner of the requirement to exhaust any or all administrative remedies, to the extent that the administrative remedies are inadequate, or requiring their exhaustion would result in irreparable harm disproportionate to the public benefit derived from requiring exhaustion.

§ 5–108. [Time for Filing Petition for Review]

Subject to other requirements of this Act or of another statute:

(1) A petition for judicial review of a rule may be filed at any time, except as limited by Section 3–113(b).

(2) A petition for judicial review of an order is not timely unless filed within [30] days after rendition of the order, but the time is extended during the pendency of the petitioner's timely attempts to exhaust administrative remedies, if the attempts are not clearly frivolous or repetitious.

(3) A petition for judicial review of agency action other than a rule or order is not timely unless filed within [30] days after the agency action, but the time is extended:

(i) during the pendency of the petitioner's timely attempts to exhaust administrative remedies, if the attempts are not clearly frivolous or repetitious; and

(ii) during any period that the petitioner did not know and was under no duty to discover, or did not know and was under a duty to discover but could not reasonably have discovered, that the agency had taken the action or that the agency action had a sufficient effect to confer standing upon the petitioner to obtain judicial review under this Act.

§ 5–109. [Petition for Review—Filing and Contents]

(a) A petition for review must be filed with the clerk of the court.

(b) A petition for review must set forth:

(1) the name and mailing address of the petitioner;

(2) the name and mailing address of the agency whose action is at issue;

(3) identification of the agency action at issue, together with a duplicate copy, summary, or brief description of the agency action;

(4) identification of persons who were parties in any adjudicative proceedings that led to the agency action;

(5) facts to demonstrate that the petitioner is entitled to obtain judicial review;

(6) the petitioner's reasons for believing that relief should be granted; and

(7) a request for relief, specifying the type and extent of relief requested.

§ 5–110. [Petition for Review—Service and Notification]

(a) A petitioner for judicial review shall serve a copy of the petition upon the agency in the manner provided by [statute] [the rules of civil procedure].

(b) The petitioner shall use means provided by [statute] [the rules of civil procedure] to give notice of the petition for review to all other parties in any adjudicative proceedings that led to the agency action.

§ 5–111. [Stay and Other Temporary Remedies Pending Final Disposition]

(a) Unless precluded by law, the agency may grant a stay on appropriate terms or other temporary remedies during the pendency of judicial review.

(b) A party may file a motion in the reviewing court, during the pendency of judicial review, seeking interlocutory review of the agency's action on an application for stay or other temporary remedies.

(c) If the agency has found that its action on an application for stay or other temporary remedies is justified to protect against a substantial threat to the public health, safety, or welfare, the court may not grant relief unless it finds that:

(1) the applicant is likely to prevail when the court finally disposes of the matter;

(2) without relief the applicant will suffer irreparable injury;

(3) the grant of relief to the applicant will not substantially harm other parties to the proceedings; and

(4) the threat to the public health, safety, or welfare relied on by the agency is not sufficiently serious to justify the agency's action in the circumstances.

(d) If subsection (c) does not apply, the court shall grant relief if it finds, in its independent judgment, that the agency's action on the application for stay or other temporary remedies was unreasonable in the circumstances.

(e) If the court determines that relief should be granted from the agency's action on an application for stay or other temporary remedies, the court may remand the matter to the agency with directions to deny a stay, to grant a stay on appropriate terms, or to grant other temporary remedies, or the court may issue an order denying a stay, granting a stay on appropriate terms, or granting other temporary remedies.

§ 5–112. [Limitation on New Issues]

A person may obtain judicial review of an issue that was not raised before the agency, only to the extent that:

(1) the agency did not have jurisdiction to grant an adequate remedy based on a determination of the issue;

(2) the person did not know and was under no duty to discover, or did not know and was under a duty to discover but could not reasonably have discovered, facts giving rise to the issue;

(3) the agency action subject to judicial review is a rule and the person has not been a party in adjudicative proceedings which provided an adequate opportunity to raise the issue;

(4) the agency action subject to judicial review is an order and the person was not notified of the adjudicative proceeding in substantial compliance with this Act; or

(5) the interests of justice would be served by judicial resolution of an issue arising from:

(i) a change in controlling law occurring after the agency action; or

(ii) agency action occurring after the person exhausted the last feasible opportunity for seeking relief from the agency.

§ 5–113. [Judicial Review of Facts Confined to Record for Judicial Review and Additional Evidence Taken Pursuant to Act]

Judicial review of disputed issues of fact must be confined to the agency record for judicial review as defined in this Act, supplemented by additional evidence taken pursuant to this Act.

§ 5–114. [New Evidence Taken by Court or Agency Before Final Disposition]

(a) The court [(if Alternative B of Section 5–104 is adopted), assisted by a referee, master, trial court judge as provided in Section 5–104(c),] may receive evidence, in addition to that contained in the agency record for judicial review, only if it relates to the validity of the agency action at the time it was taken and is needed to decide disputed issues regarding:

(1) improper constitution as a decision-making body, or improper motive or grounds for disqualification, of those taking the agency action;

(2) unlawfulness of procedure or of decision-making process; or

(3) any material fact that was not required by any provision of law to be determined exclusively on an agency record of a type reasonably suitable for judicial review.

(b) The court may remand a matter to the agency, before final disposition of a petition for review, with directions that the agency conduct fact-finding and other proceedings the court considers necessary and that the agency take such further action on the basis thereof as the court directs, if:

(1) the agency was required by this Act or any other provision of law to base its action exclusively on a record of a type reasonably suitable for judicial review, but the agency failed to prepare or preserve an adequate record;

(2) the court finds that (i) new evidence has become available that relates to the validity of the agency action at the time it was taken, that one or more of the parties did not know and was under no duty to discover, or did not know and was under a duty to discover but could not reasonably have discovered, until after the agency action, and (ii) the interests of justice would be served by remand to the agency;

(3) the agency improperly excluded or omitted evidence from the record; or

(4) a relevant provision of law changed after the agency action and the court determines that the new provision may control the outcome.

§ 5–115. [Agency Record for Judicial Review—Contents, Preparation, Transmittal, Cost]

(a) Within [_____] days after service of the petition, or within further time allowed by the court or by other provision of law, the agency shall transmit to the court the original or a certified copy of the agency record for judicial review of the agency action, consisting of any agency documents expressing the agency action, other documents identified by the agency as having been considered by it before its action and used as a basis for its action, and any other material described in this Act as the agency record for the type of agency action at issue, subject to the provisions of this section.

(b) If part of the record has been preserved without a transcript, the agency shall prepare a transcript for inclusion in the record transmitted to the court, except for portions that the parties stipulate to omit in accordance with subsection (d).

(c) The agency shall charge the petitioner with the reasonable cost of preparing any necessary copies and transcripts for transmittal to the court. [A failure by the petitioner to pay any of this cost to the agency does not relieve the agency from the responsibility for timely preparation of the record and transmittal to the court.]

(d) By stipulation of all parties to the review proceedings, the record may be shortened, summarized, or organized.

(e) The court may tax the cost of preparing transcripts and copies for the record:

(1) against a party who unreasonably refuses to stipulate to shorten, summarize, or organize the record;

(2) as provided by Section 5–117; or

(3) in accordance with any other provision of law.

(f) Additions to the record pursuant to Section 5–114 must be made as ordered by the court.

(g) The court may require or permit subsequent corrections or additions to the record.

§ 5–116. [Scope of Review; Grounds for Invalidity]

(a) Except to the extent that this Act or another statute provides otherwise:

(1) The burden of demonstrating the invalidity of agency action is on the party asserting invalidity; and

(2) The validity of agency action must be determined in accordance with the standards of review provided in this section, as applied to the agency action at the time it was taken.

(b) The court shall make a separate and distinct ruling on each material issue on which the court's decision is based.

(c) The court shall grant relief only if it determines that a person seeking judicial relief has been substantially prejudiced by any one or more of the following:

(1) The agency action, or the statute or rule on which the agency action is based, is unconstitutional on its face or as applied.

(2) The agency has acted beyond the jurisdiction conferred by any provision of law.

(3) The agency has not decided all issues requiring resolution.

(4) The agency has erroneously interpreted or applied the law.

(5) The agency has engaged in an unlawful procedure or decision-making process, or has failed to follow prescribed procedure.

(6) The persons taking the agency action were improperly constituted as a decision-making body, motivated by an improper purpose, or subject to disqualification.

(7) The agency action is based on a determination of fact, made or implied by the agency, that is not supported by evidence that is substantial when viewed in light of the whole record before the court, which includes the agency record for judicial review, supplemented by any additional evidence received by the court under this Act.

(8) The agency action is:

(i) outside the range of discretion delegated to the agency by any provision of law;

(ii) agency action, other than a rule, that is inconsistent with a rule of the agency; [or]

(iii) agency action, other than a rule, that is inconsistent with the agency's prior practice unless the agency justifies the inconsistency by stating facts and reasons to demonstrate a fair and rational basis for the inconsistency;

(iv) [otherwise unreasonable, arbitrary or capricious.]

§ 5–117. [Type of Relief]

(a) The court may award damages or compensation only to the extent expressly authorized by another provision of law.

(b) The court may grant other appropriate relief, whether mandatory, injunctive, or declaratory; preliminary or final; temporary or permanent; equitable or legal. In granting relief, the court may order agency action required by law, order agency exercise of discretion required by law, set aside or modify agency action, enjoin or stay the effectiveness of agency action, remand the matter for further proceedings, render a declaratory judgment, or take any other action that is authorized and appropriate.

(c) The court may also grant necessary ancillary relief to redress the effects of official action wrongfully taken or withheld, but the court may award attorney's fees or witness fees only to the extent expressly authorized by other law.

(d) If the court sets aside or modifies agency action or remands the matter to the agency for further proceedings, the court may make any interlocutory order it finds necessary to preserve the interests of the parties and the public pending further proceedings or agency action.

[§ 5–118. [Review by Higher Court]

Decisions on petitions for review of agency action are reviewable by the [appellate court] as in other civil cases.]

Civil Enforcement

§ 5–201. [Petition by Agency for Civil Enforcement of Rule or Order]

(a) In addition to other remedies provided by law, an agency may seek enforcement of its rule or order by filing a petition for civil enforcement in the [trial court of general jurisdiction.]

(b) The petition must name, as defendants, each alleged violator against whom the agency seeks to obtain civil enforcement.

(c) Venue is determined as in other civil cases.

(d) A petition for civil enforcement filed by an agency may request, and the court may grant, declaratory relief, temporary or permanent injunctive relief, any other civil remedy provided by law, or any combination of the foregoing.

§ 5–202. [Petition by Qualified Person for Civil Enforcement of Agency's Order]

(a) Any person who would qualify under this Act as having standing to obtain judicial review of an agency's failure to enforce its order may file a petition for civil enforcement of that order, but the action may not be commenced:

(1) until at least [60] days after the petitioner has given notice of the alleged violation and of the petitioner's intent to seek civil enforcement to the head of the agency concerned, to the attorney general, and to each alleged violator against whom the petitioner seeks civil enforcement;

(2) if the agency has filed and is diligently prosecuting a petition for civil enforcement of the same order against the same defendant; or

(3) if a petition for review of the same order has been filed and is pending in court.

(b) The petition must name, as defendants, the agency whose order is sought to be enforced and each alleged violator against whom the petitioner seeks civil enforcement.

(c) The agency whose order is sought to be enforced may move to dismiss on the grounds that the petition fails to qualify under this section or that enforcement would be contrary to the policy of the agency. The court shall grant the motion to dismiss unless the petitioner demonstrates that (i) the petition qualifies under this section and (ii) the agency's failure to enforce its order is based on an exercise of discretion that is improper on one or more of the grounds provided in Section 5–116(c)(8).

(d) Except to the extent expressly authorized by law, a petition for civil enforcement filed under this section may not request, and the court may not grant any monetary payment apart from taxable costs.

§ 5–203. [Defenses; Limitation on New Issues and New Evidence]

A defendant may assert, in a proceeding for civil enforcement:

(1) that the rule or order sought to be enforced is invalid on any of the grounds stated in Section 5–116. If that defense is raised, the

court may consider issues and receive evidence only within the limitations provided by Sections 5–112, 5–113, and 5–114; and

(2) any of the following defenses on which the court, to the extent necessary for the determination of the matter, may consider new issues or take new evidence:

(i) the rule or order does not apply to the party;

(ii) the party has not violated the rule or order;

(iii) the party has violated the rule or order but has subsequently complied, but a party who establishes this defense is not necessarily relieved from any action provided by law for past violations; or

(iv) any other defense allowed by law.

§ 5–204. [Incorporation of Certain Provisions on Judicial Review]

Proceedings for civil enforcement are governed by the following provisions of this Act on judicial review, as modified where necessary to adapt them to those proceedings:

(1) Section 5–101(2) (ancillary procedural matters); and

(2) Section 5–115 (agency record for judicial review—contents, preparation, transmittal, cost.)

§ 5–205. [Review by Higher Court]

Decisions on petitions for civil enforcement are reviewable by the [appellate court] as in other civil cases.

†

Index

References are to pages

ADJUDICATION
Generally, 8, 18, 83 et seq.
Alternative dispute resolution, 180 et seq.
Bias, 123 et seq., 284
Bias, pecuniary, 128, 131
Bias, prejudgment, 129, 131
Bias, ALJs, 153 et seq.
Burden of proof, 187, 544, 547
Closed or open hearing, 188
Comparative hearings, 91
Conference hearings, 99
Criminal sanctions, 437
Declaratory orders, 216
Defined, 8
Difference, agency and judicial, 8
Discovery, 179
Emergency hearings, 99
Estoppel, 210 et seq.
Evidence, 185 et seq.
Ex parte contact, 90, 132 et seq.
Examining decision-makers' mental process
    (Morgan IV), 115, 140
Exclusive record, 84, 116, 122
Factual dispute, absence of, 107
Findings of fact, 196 et seq.
Forcing hearing where agency refuses to
    prosecute, 167
Hearings, due process, 18 et seq.
Hearings, statutory—federal, 83 et seq.
Hearings, statutory—state, 93 et seq.
Independence of adjudicatory agencies, 476
Informal adjudication, 90, 147, 150
Institutionalized v. judicial decisions, 109 et
    seq., 149 et seq.
Intermediate reports, 113
Intervention, 167 et seq.
Investigation, see **INVESTIGATION**
Legislative pressure, 142 et seq.
Legislative v. adjudicative facts, 77 et seq.,
    191 et seq.
Morgan I rule, 110 et seq.
Necessity, principle of, 122, 128, 131
Notice, 163 et seq.
Nuclear industry, 85 et seq.
Official notice, 104, 189 et seq.
On the record requirement, 84 et seq.
Penalties and fines, 435 et seq.
Preclusion of hearing through rule, 100 et
    seq.

ADJUDICATION—Cont'd
Prejudicial error, 167
President, 140
Prospective only, 358 et seq., 365
Reasons, statement of, 196 et seq.
Remedies, 435 et seq.
Res judicata, 203 et seq.
Separation of functions-agency head excep-
    tion, 122
Separation of functions—federal view, 117
    et seq.
Separation of functions—state view, 120
Stare decisis, 208
Statute of limitations, 165
Summary judgment, 106
Summary proceedings, 99
Vermont Yankee rule, 91, 199, 261

ADMINISTRATIVE AGENCIES
Generally, 1

ADMINISTRATIVE CONFERENCE
Generally, 11

ADMINISTRATIVE LAW
Generally, 1
Reasons to study, 2
State, importance of, 3

ADMINISTRATIVE LAW JUDGES
Generally, 8, 89, 149 et seq.
Administrative court, 160 et seq.
Administrative judges and, 150
Bias, 153
Central panels, 150, 158 et seq.
Disagreement between ALJ and agency
    heads on fact findings, 539, 547
Immunity from suit, 626
Obligation to bring out evidence, 188
Selection and appointment, 151 et seq.
Separation of functions, 121

**ADMINISTRATIVE   PROCEDURE   ACT,
    FEDERAL**
Generally, 3
Administrative law judges—federal, 151 et
    seq.
Alternative dispute resolution, 181, 314 et
    seq.
Bias, 131
Burden of proof, 187

ADMINISTRATIVE PROCEDURE ACT, FEDERAL—Cont'd
Comment, rulemaking, 245 et seq.
Commitment to agency discretion, 638 et seq.
Declaratory orders, 216
Evidence, 185
Ex parte contact, 132 et seq., 146
Exhaustion of remedies, 696
Explanation, in rulemaking, 286 et seq.
Federal, history, 4
Final order rule, 669 et seq.
Findings of fact, 196 et seq.
Hearing, right to 83 et seq.
Importance of, 3
Intervention, 168 et seq.
Judicial review, 615
Notice, adjudication, 166
Notice, rulemaking, 235 et seq.
Official notice, 189 et seq.
On the record requirement, 84 et seq.
Preclusion of judicial review, 632
Reasons, statement of, 196 et seq.
Regulatory analysis, state, 310
Rules, definition of, 223 et seq.
Rulemaking procedure. See **RULEMAKING**
Rulemaking exceptions. See **RULEMAKING EXCEPTIONS**
Separation of functions, 121
Standing to seek judicial review, 649 et seq. See **STANDING TO SEEK JUDICIAL REVIEW**
Substantial evidence on the whole record, 535 et seq.

ADMINISTRATIVE PROCEDURE ACT, STATE
Administrative law judges—state, 150
Bias, 130, 131
Counsel, right to, 71
Declaratory orders, 216
Effective date of rules, 302
Evidence, 185
Ex parte contact, 139, 140
Exhaustion of remedies, 696
Final order rule, 672
Findings of fact, 196 et seq.
Hearing, right to, 98 et seq.
Legislative veto, burden shifting, 460
Model Act (1961), 5, 83, 93, 97, 614
Model Act (1981), 5, 83, 93, 98, 614
Nonlegislative rules, 356
Notice, 166
Open hearing, 188
Oral argument, 117
Rule, definition, 225
Rulemaking procedure, 239, 240, 252, 262, 263, 264, 276, 385
Rulemaking, required, 376
Rulemaking, petition, 378, 382
Separation of functions, 121
Standing to seek judicial review, 665
Stays pending judicial review, 685

ADMINISTRATIVE PROCEDURE ACT, STATE—Cont'd
Veto of rules, governor's, 505

ADMINISTRATIVE PROCESS
Adjudication, 8
Criteria to evaluate, 10
Cost, 19
Defined, 5
Discretion, 11, 19
Executive controls, 9
Investigation, 8, 170 et seq.
Judicial review, 9
Legislative controls, 9, 142 et seq.
Legitimacy, theories of, 12
Licensing, 6
Ratemaking, 9
Research and publicity, 5
Rulemaking, 6, 218 et seq.

ADVISORY COMMITTEES
Generally, 529
Federal Advisory Committee Act, history, 529 et seq.
Federal Advisory Committee Act, requirements, 530 et seq.
Rulemaking, consultation with, 239

ALASKA
Obligation to explain decision, 200

ALTERNATE DISPUTE RESOLUTION
Adjudication, 180 et seq.
Rulemaking, 314 et seq.

ARIZONA
Executive rule review, 504

ARKANSAS
Appointments power, 471
Equitable estoppel, 211

ATTORNEY'S FEES, RECOVERY OF
Generally, 627
American rule, 627
Equal Access to Justice Act, 630
Public interest attorney's fees, 627
Reasonable fees, 629
State law, 630
When appropriate standard, 628

CALIFORNIA
Administrative law judge fact findings, 548
Attorney's fees, recovery of, 628
Bias of ALJs, 123 et seq.
Closed record, judicial review of rules, 591
Delegation of adjudicative power, 435 et seq.
Due process, 41
Freedom of information exception, 516
Hearing, land use cases, 167
Investigation, failure to pay minimum wage, 170 et seq.
Judicial review statute, 554, 614
Nonlegislative rules, 342, 357
Office of Administrative Law, 504

CALIFORNIA—Cont'd
Official notice, 189 et seq.
Primary jurisdiction doctrine, 699
Remedies, authority to impose, 435, 438
Rulemaking, requirement of explanation, 286
Rulemaking, time limits, 385
Scope of review, independent judgment test, 553 et seq.
Standing, public actions, 663
Subpoenas, duty to notify subject, 175

COLORADO
Rulemaking, required, 373

COMMITMENT TO AGENCY DISCRETION
Generally, 638
No law to apply test, 640 et seq., 643
Enforcement action, failure to take, 638 et. seq.
Prosecutorial discretion, unreviewability, 641
Rights of initiation, 644
CONGRESS
Congressional standing to seek review, 666
See **LEGISLATIVE CONTROL OVER AGENCY ACTION**

CONNECTICUT
Question of law, scope of review, 558 et seq.
Res judicata, 207
Rulemaking, notice, 239
Standing in environmental cases, 666

COST BENEFIT ANALYSIS
Generally, 10
Due process, 52 et seq.
Regulatory analysis, 304 et seq., 493 et seq.

DAMAGE ACTIONS
Generally, 621
Bivens rule, 625, 686
Due process, alternative to, 69
Eleventh Amendment, 623
Federal Tort Claims Act, 622 et seq.
Federal Tort Claims Act, discretionary functions, 622
Immunity of officials, 625 et seq.
Qualified immunity, 626
Section 1983, violation of federal constitution or statute, 624 et seq.
Section 1983, exhaustion of remedies, 698
State and local government liability, 623

DELAY BY AGENCIES
Deadlines for rulemaking, 384
Licensing, 165
Review despite lack of final order, 674
Rulemaking, 384

DELEGATION TO AGENCIES
Generally, 12, 397, 428
Adjudicatory power, 428 et seq.
Criminal sanctions, 437
Federal rules, history, 397 et seq.
Federal rule, revival, 402 et seq., 410 et seq.

DELEGATION TO AGENCIES—Cont'd
Foreign affairs, 406
Incorporation by reference of federal law, 418
Jury trial, right to, 434
Narrow definition of agency's authority, 419 et seq.
National Industrial Recovery Act, 399
Penalties or fines, 435 et seq.
Price control, 401 et seq.
Private persons, delegation to, 417
Public v. private rights, 428 et seq.
Purposes, nondelegation doctrine, 407
Remedies, 435 et seq.
Safeguards, importance in analyzing delegation, 409, 416, 428
Scope of judicial review, role of delegation, 546, 563, 566, 576
Standards, importance in analyzing delegation, 408
State law, 414

DISCOVERY
Adjudication, 179
Freedom of Information as, 517

DISCRETION
Generally, 11, 19, 31
Abuse of discretion, 367, 578 et seq., 586, 588, 592
Arbitrary, capricious standard, 578 et seq., 586, 588, 592
Commitment to agency discretion, see **COMMITMENT TO AGENCY DISCRETION**
Discretionary function exception, Federal Tort Claims Act, 622
Due process, 41, 72
Findings and reasons, 200
Hard look review, 592 et seq.
Scope of review, abuse of discretion, 578 et seq.

DUE PROCESS
Generally, 18, 30,
Administrative Procedure Acts and, 87, 92
Adjudication-rulemaking distinction, 73 et seq.
Bitter with the sweet, 44
Confrontation, right of, 71, 187
Contracts and contract remedies, 41, 45, 69
Costs of, 19, 44
Counsel, right to, 70
De minimis deprivations, 46
Deprivation, meaning of, 42, 70
Elements of hearing, 25, 64 et seq.
Emergencies, 61, 99
Findings of fact, 27, 196 et seq.
Goldberg opinion, issues determined, 29
Government jobs, 33 et seq., 42 et seq., 61, 100, 117, 118
Investigatory hearings, 51
Legislative v. adjudicative facts, 77 et seq., 191 et seq.

DUE PROCESS—Cont'd

Liberty, meaning of, 33 et seq., 35, 39, 46 et seq.

Licenses as property, 45

Mass justice, 31

Notice, 163 et seq.

Paper hearings, 72

Prisoners, due process rights of, 47 et seq., 686

Property, meaning of, 33 et seq., 37, 39, 42

Purposes of due process, 30

Rulemaking, required, 373

Right-privilege doctrine, 38, 330

Separation of functions, 119

Students, rights of, 46, 64 et seq., 70, 71, 95 et seq., 108

State constitutional law, 41

Stigma as deprivation of liberty, 50

Substantive v. procedural, 40

Suspension, 62

Timing of hearings, 22 et seq., 51 et seq.

Torts and tort remedies, 64 et seq.

Welfare hearings, 22 et seq., 52 et seq., 73

EMPLOYMENT DISCRIMINATION

Attorney's fees, recovery of, 628

Federal contractors, executive order, 519 et seq.

Judicial review of fact findings, 549

Res judicata, 203 et seq.

Sexual harassment, scope of review, 571 et seq.

ENVIRONMENTAL PROTECTION

Attorney's fees, recovery of, 628

Ex parte contact, 140, 267

Final order rule, 673

Good cause exception from rulemaking, 327

Hard look review, 260

Legal interpretation, scope of review, 560 et seq., 570

Legislative influence on rulemaking, 271

Policy statement exception to rulemaking, 345

Presidential influence on rulemaking, 270

Reasons, statement of, 196

Regulatory negotiation, 316

Right to hearing, 89

Rulemaking, addition to the record, 243

Rulemaking, application to guideline, 227

Rulemaking, disclosure of methodology, 242

Separation of functions, 123

ESTOPPEL

Generally, 210

Advice-giving, reliability of, 215

Fair notice, 215

Federal law, 212

Prerequisites for estoppel, 214

Rationale in administrative law, 210 et seq.

Substitutes for estoppel, 215

EXECUTIVE CONTROLS OVER AGENCY ACTION

Generally, 9, 15, 439, 464 et seq.

EXECUTIVE CONTROLS OVER AGENCY ACTION—Cont'd

Appointment power, limited to president, 464 et seq.

Appointment power, states, 470

Disclosure of contacts with OMB, 503

Implied tenure, 491

Inferior officers, 467, 468, 469

Independent agencies, 473 et seq. See **INDEPENDENT AGENCIES**

Independent counsel, 478 et seq.

Judiciary, appointment of officials, 467, 469, 473

Legislature, precluded from making appointments, 464 et seq., 471

Merits of executive oversight, 498 et seq.

President's power vis-à-vis agencies, 495 et seq.

Regulatory analysis, 493 et seq.

Removal of officers, power of Congress to limit, 473 et seq.

States, power of governors, 490

States, executive oversight, 504

Veto of rules, governors, 505

EXECUTIVE ORDERS

Generally, 304 et seq.

Advisory committees, 531

Employment discrimination, 519 et seq.

Regulatory analysis, 304 et. seq., 493 et seq.

Specialized executive orders, 313

EXHAUSTION OF ADMINISTRATIVE REMEDIES

Generally

Administrative Procedure Act exception, 696

Constitutional issues, 696

Exceptions, 687 et seq.

Factors, 695

Futility exception, 694

New Jersey rule, 198, 691

Preclusion, relation to exhaustion, 697

Primary jurisdiction, relation to exhaustion, 701

Questions of law, 695

Rationale, 687 et seq.

Section 1983 and exhaustion, 698

EX PARTE CONTACT

Adjudication, 132 et seq.

Administrative Procedure Act, federal, 132 et seq., 146

Administrative Procedure Act, state, 139

Endangered Species, 90

Environmental cases, 90, 267

Interested persons, 139

President, application to, 140

Ratemaking, in, 141

Office of Management & Budget, regulatory analysis 278, 503

Remedies for violation, 140

Rulemaking, 264 et seq., 275

EX PARTE CONTACT—Cont'd
Staff members, contact with, 141

FEDERAL COMMUNICATIONS COMMISSION
Ex parte contacts in rulemaking, 264 et seq., 275
Intervention, 168
Refusal to reconsider precedent, 210, 345
Rulemaking, petition, 379
Rules, waiver, 106, 386, 390
Standing to seek review, 168
Sunshine Act, 528

FEDERAL TRADE COMMISSION
Bias in rulemaking, 279
Cease and desist orders, 367
Delegation of power, 399
Hybrid rulemaking, 254
Independent agency, 475
Legislative pressure, 142
Rulemaking authority, 222
Rulemaking, required, 367

FINAL ORDER RULE
Generally, 667
Delay and final order rule, 674
Defined, 672
Exceptions, 672
President, decisions reviewable by, 673
Rationale, 670
Timing rules, relation of final order rule to, 668, 670, 674

FLORIDA
Adjudicatory hearings, 95 et seq.
Administrative law judge fact findings, 548
Delegation, rulemaking, 417
Narrow construction of rulemaking authority, 427
Rulemaking, required, 377
Waiver of rules, 392

FOOD AND DRUG ADMINISTRATION
Summary judgment, 106

FREEDOM OF INFORMATION ACT (FOIA)
Generally, 507 et seq.
Confidential private information, exemption (4), 519 et seq.
Costs, 509
Deliberative documents, exemption (5), 510 et seq.
Discovery, FOIA used for, 517
Final opinions, publicity and indexing, 508, 513 et seq.
History, 507
Law enforcement, exemption (7), 518
Merits of Act, 508
Personal privacy, invasion of, exemption (6), 535
Presidential communication privilege, 518
Reverse FOIA action, 519 et seq.
Rules, publication of, see **PUBLIC RECORDS**

FREEDOM OF INFORMATION ACT (FOIA)
—Cont'd
State freedom of information laws, 508, 510, 516, 523
State secret, exemption (1), 518
Trade Secrets Act, 520
Work product privilege, 514, 517

GOVERNMENT JOBS
Civil service, 42 et seq., 100
Evidence at hearing, 182
Morgan I, application of, 117
Pre-termination hearing, 61
Right to hearing on non-renewal, 33 et seq.
Separation of functions, 118
Suspension, 62

GOVERNORS
See **EXECUTIVE CONTROL OVER AGENCY ACTION**
Veto of rules, 505

HAWAII
Clearly erroneous scope of review, 541 et seq.

HEARING, RIGHT TO ADJUDICATORY
See **ADJUDICATION, DUE PROCESS**
Administrative Procedure Act, federal, 83 et.seq.
Administrative Procedure Act, state, 93 et seq.
Deferring to agency's view, 90
Due process, relation of APA, 92
External source rule, 84 et seq.
Informal adjudication, 90
On the record, meaning, 89, 90

IDAHO
Legislative veto, 453, 460

ILLINOIS
Delegation, rulemaking power, 414, 416
Delegation, adjudicatory, 434
Exhaustion of administrative remedies, question of law, 695
Penalties, authority to impose, 438
Removal, governor's power, 490

IMMIGRATION AND NATURALIZATION
Burden of proof, 187
Confrontation, 187
Discretionary decision, scope of review, 579 et seq.
Due process, 92
Estoppel, 211, 215
Findings, 202
Legislative veto, 441
Jurisdictional facts, judicial review, 551
Official notice, 193
Passports, authority to deny, 420
Policy statements, 338
Res judicata, 205

INDEPENDENT AGENCIES
Generally, 10, 473 et seq.

INDEPENDENT AGENCIES—Cont'd
Adjudicatory agencies, 476
Development of, 476
Importance of, 477
Independent counsel, restriction on President's removal power, 478
Regulatory analysis and, 502
Validity, 473 et seq.

INDEPENDENT COUNSEL
Generally, 478 et seq.

INDIANA
Rulemaking, notice, 241

INVESTIGATION
Generally, 8, 170
Congressional, 462
Constitutional limits on investigation, 170 et seq.
Defenses to subpoena, 174 et seq.
Discovery, 179
Exclusionary rule, 178
Fifth amendment privileges, 172, 176
Judicial enforcement requirement, 174
Physical searches, 177
Privileges, 176
Publicity, 178

IOWA
Damages, authority to impose, 438
Rulemaking, notice, 241
Rulemaking, petition, 382
Waiver of rules, 393

JUDICIAL REMEDIES
Generally, 612
Attorney's fees, see **ATTORNEY'S FEES**
Certiorari, 620
Damage actions, see **DAMAGE ACTIONS**
Declaratory judgment, 617 et seq.
Federal civil rights, 615
Federal jurisdiction, 614
Initiation, rights of, 644, 705
Injunction, 617 et seq.
Mandamus, 614, 618
Model Act (1961), 614
Model Act (1981), 614
New evidence, 613
Preclusion, see **PRECLUSION OF JUDICIAL REVIEW**
Private rights of action, 645, 705
Removal, state to federal court, 615
Sovereign immunity, 615
Time limits on seeking review, 636
Venue, appellate or trial court, 612

JUDICIAL REVIEW
Generally, 9, 15
Closed or open record, 589
Consistency, requirement of, 210
Exhaustion of administrative remedies, see **EXHAUSTION OF ADMINISTRATIVE REMEDIES**
Ex parte contact in rulemaking and, 264 et seq.

JUDICIAL REVIEW—Cont'd
Jurisdictional fact, issues of, 433
Narrow delegation of agency's authority, 419 et seq.
Nonlegislative rules, 356
Petitions for rulemaking, 379, 645
Post hoc rationalizations, 201, 293, 588
Preclusion of review, see **PRECLUSION OF JUDICIAL REVIEW**
Regulatory analysis, 311
Remedies, 606, see **JUDICIAL REMEDIES**
Resources, 611
Scope of judicial review, see **SCOPE OF JUDICIAL REVIEW**
Standing to seek judicial review, see **STANDING TO SEEK JUDICIAL REVIEW**
Timing of judicial review, 667. See **FINAL ORDER RULE, EXHAUSTION OF ADMINISTRATIVE REMEDIES, RIPENESS, PRIMARY JURISDICTION, STAYS PENDING JUDICIAL REVIEW**
Venue, appellate or trial court, 612
Vermont Yankee rule, impact on judicial review, 260
Waiver of rules, refusal to grant, 386 et seq.

JURY TRIAL
Right to, 434

KANSAS
Application of *Morgan I* rule, 115
Appointments power, 470, 472

LABOR RELATIONS
Administrative law judge, disagreement with agency heads, 547
Application of law to fact, scope of review, 573, 576
Bias, 123
Ex parte contact, 132
Evidence at discharge hearing, 182
Evidence, refusal to take, 365
Factual determinations, scope of review, 536 et seq.
Freedom of information, and, 510, 517, 525
General Counsel Memoranda, 510 et seq.
Investigation, failure to pay minimum wage, 170
Reasoned decision, requirement, 589
Rulemaking, adjudication disguised as, 358
Rulemaking, choice of adjudication or, 363
Rulemaking, required, 367
Substantial evidence test, 536 et seq.
Work product privilege, 517

LEGISLATIVE CONTROLS OVER AGENCY ACTION
Generally, 9, 15, 439
Adjudication, legislative pressure 142 et seq.
Administrative Rules Review Committee, 459

LEGISLATIVE CONTROLS OVER AGENCY ACTION—Cont'd
Appointment of officials, 464 et seq.
Congressional Review Act, 456
Constituent service, 148, 464
Funding and appropriations, 463
Investigations, 462
Legislative veto, 440 et seq.
Legislative veto, alternatives to, 456 et seq.
Model Act approach, 459
Ombudsman, 463
Oversight committees, 461
Removal of officials, 489 et seq.

LICENSING
Generally, 6
Application of law to fact, scope of review, 578
Bias, 128, 131
Clearance system, 7
Delay, 165
Findings of fact, 196
Importance of, 6
Intermediate report, disclosure of, 114
Legislative pressure, 149
Official notice, 189 et seq.
Permit systems, 7, 169
Scope of review, question of law, 558 et seq.
Statute of limitations, 165
Suspension of license, 62, 165

LOUISIANA
Appointments power, 471

MAINE
Administrative court, 161

MARYLAND
Adjudicatory hearings, 94 et seq.

MASSACHUSETTS
Appointments power, 470
Open record, judicial review of rules, 599 et seq.
Soft look review of rules, 599 et seq.

MICHIGAN
Freedom of information, exceptions, 517
Rulemaking authority, 461

MINNESOTA
Standing in environmental cases, 666
Sunshine Act, definition of meeting, 527

MISSISSIPPI
Appointments power, legislators, 472

MISSOURI
Administrative Hearing Commission, 161
Legislative veto, 453
Regulatory analysis, 310

MORGAN CASES
Morgan I, 110, 114, 251, 262
Morgan II, 113, 251

MORGAN CASES—Cont'd
Morgan IV, 115, 116

NATIONAL LABOR RELATIONS BOARD
See **LABOR RELATIONS**

NATIONAL ENVIRONMENTAL POLICY ACT
Generally, 312
Standing to seek judicial review, 665

NATIONAL INDUSTRIAL RECOVERY ACT
Generally, 399

NEBRASKA
Appointments, qualifications, 473
Sunshine Act, 529

NEW HAMPSHIRE
Delegation, adjudicatory, 434
Legislative veto, 459

NEW JERSEY
Exhaustion of administrative remedies, 198, 691
Damages, authority to impose, 438
Intermediate report, disclosure of, 114
Legislative veto, 454
Right to hearing, 78

NEW MEXICO
Delegation, adjudicatory, 433

NEW YORK
Application of law to fact, judicial review, 578
Discretionary decisions, scope of review, 592
Exhaustion of remedies, questions of law, 695
Investigative subpoenas, 175
Judicial review statute, 614
Notice rules, 163
Res judicata, 205
Residuum rule, 183
Rulemaking, narrow construction of delegated authority, 422
Warrant for physical searches, 177

NORTH CAROLINA
Appointments power, legislators, 471

NUCLEAR REGULATORY COMMISSION
Hearing, right to, 85 et seq.
Intervention, 167
Judicial review of scientific decision, 260
Morgan I, application, 116
Rulemaking, disclosure of data, 242
Rulemaking, ability of court to add procedures, 254 et seq.
Sunshine Act, 526

OCCUPATIONAL SAFETY AND HEALTH ACT
Generally, 404
Conflict with OMB, 501

OCCUPATIONAL SAFETY AND HEALTH ACT—Cont'd

Delegation of legislative power, 404 et seq., 408

Hybrid rulemaking, 253

Instructions to staff, rulemaking exception, 332

Interpretation, 404, 408

Procedural exception to rulemaking, 332

Rulemaking, delays, 384

Scope of review, rules, 609

Warrant requirement, 177

OFFICE OF MANAGEMENT AND BUDGET

Disclosure of contacts, 503

President control of rulemaking, 492 et seq.

Rivalry with agencies, 497

Rulemaking, role in process, 304

OHIO

Legal interpretation, scope of review, 564

OKLAHOMA

Delegation, to federal government, 418

OREGON

Application of law to fact, scope of review, 571

Associational standing, rejected, 662

Delegation, rulemaking, 416

Delegation, private parties, 418

Nonlegislative rules, binding effect, 356

Required rulemaking, 370 et seq.

Residuum rule, 183

PENNSYLVANIA

Governor's power of removal, 491

Rulemaking, notice, 241

Separation of functions, 120

PRECLUSION OF JUDICIAL REVIEW

Generally, 632

Administrative Procedure Act provision, 632

Constitutional claims, preclusion of, 635, 636

Constitutionality of preclusion, 30, 633 et seq.

Interpretation of preclusion statutes, 635

Presumption of reviewability, 632 et seq., 635

Standing to seek review, relation of preclusion, 650

State law, 637

Time limits, 636

PRESIDENT

See **EXECUTIVE CONTROL OVER AGENCY ACTION**

Agency, president not treated as, 673

Ex parte contacts in adjudication, 140

Ex parte contacts in rulemaking, 267 et seq.

First lady, as federal officer, 531

Immunity from suit, 626

Powers, in twilight zone, 496, 501

PRESIDENT—Cont'd

Regulatory analysis, 492 et seq.

PRIMARY JURISDICTION

Generally, 699

Criminal cases, and 705

Exclusive jurisdiction, relationship to 703

Exhaustion and primary jurisdiction, relation of, 701

History, 700 et seq.

Private rights of action, 645, 705

Rationale, 699 et seq.

Retaining jurisdiction, 704

PUBLIC RECORDS

Federal Register Act, 294

Failure to publish rule, effect, 296 et seq.

Rules, publication of, 294 et seq.

RATEMAKING

Generally, 9

Ex parte contact, 141

Official notice, 195

Rulemaking or adjudication, 247 et seq.

REASONS, STATEMENT OF

Adjudication, 196

Administrative Procedure Act, 196

Discretion, exercise of, 200

Rulemaking, 286 et seq.

Waivers, refusal to grant, 386 et seq.

REGULATORY ANALYSIS

Generally, 304

Disclosure of contacts, 278, 503

Presidential control, 493 et seq.

Rulemaking, in, 304 et seq.

REGULATORY FLEXIBILITY ACT

Generally, 312

RES JUDICATA

Generally, 203

Civil rights, 204

Criminal cases, 207

Non-mutual collateral estoppel, 205

Non-acquiescence, 206

Opportunity to litigate, 207

Preclusion against government, 205

RIPENESS

Generally, 675

Abbott Labs equation, 680

Abbott Labs, commentary, 681

Nonlegislative rules, 682

Stays, 685

Time limits for seeking review, relationship of ripeness, 684

Undermining *Abbott Labs*, 683

RULES

Generally, 6

Authority to adopt, 222

Definition, 223

Force of law, 521

Importance of, 6, 218 et seq.

Nonlegislative rules, 227, 336 et seq., 521

RULES—Cont'd
Nonlegislative rules, publication requirement, 296 et seq.
Nonlegislative rules, ripeness for review, 682
Precluding hearings through rules, 100 et seq.
Regulations, same as rules, 6
Re-examination of existing rules, 382
Retroactivity of rules, 229 et seq., 366
Waiver of rules, 106, 386 et seq.

RULEMAKING
Generally, 6, 218 et seq.
Adjudication, rulemaking v., 218 et seq.
Agenda setting, 336 et seq.
Basis and purpose, concise general statement, 286 et seq.
Bias, 279 et seq.
Comments by public, written or oral, 245
Comments by public, required response, 291
Deadlines, 384
Delay, 384
Definition of rules, 223
Disclosure of agency's information, 241 et seq.
Due process, 73 et seq.
Effective date, delayed, 296 et seq.
Ex parte communications, 264 et seq.
Exceptions to rulemaking procedure. See **RULEMAKING, PROCEDURAL EXCEPTIONS**
Federal Register Act, 284
Findings of fact, 286 et seq.
Formal rulemaking, 89, 110, 244, 247 et seq.
Good cause exception, 323 et seq.
Hybrid rulemaking, 253 et seq., 284
Importance of, 6
Legislative pressure, 271 et seq.
Legislative v. nonlegislative rules, 336, 352
Military and foreign affairs exception, 331
Morgan I rule, 262 et seq.
Negotiated rulemaking, 314 et seq.
Nonlegislative rules, 336 et seq.
Notice, 235 et seq.
Ossification, 221, 307
Participation by the poor, 246
Petitions, 378 et seq.
Policy statements, 338 et seq.
Political process, 273
Prejudicial error, 243
President, role of, 267 et seq.
Procedural exception, 332 et. seq.
Proprietary exception, 329
Publication of rules, 294 et seq.
Reasonable time to comment, 239
Reasons, statement of, 286 et seq.
Reasons, waiver requests, 386 et seq.
Regulatory analysis, 304 et seq.
Required rulemaking. See **RULEMAKING, REQUIRED**

RULEMAKING—Cont'd
Vermont Yankee rule, 253 et seq.

RULEMAKING, PROCEDURAL EXCEPTIONS
Generally, 323 et seq.
Agency management and personnel, 330
Contrary to the public interest, 325 et seq.
Effective date, 327
Good cause, 323 et seq.
Impracticable, 325 et seq.
Interim-final rules, 326
Internal documents, 347
Interpretive rules, 347 et seq.
Military and foreign affairs, 331
Nonlegislative rules, 336 et seq.
Nonlegislative rules, criticism of, 341
Procedural rules, 332 et. seq.
Policy statements, 338 et seq.
Policy statements, tentative v. binding effect, 343 et seq.
Proprietary matters, 329
Public property, loans, grants, benefits, or contracts, 329
Substantial impact test, 344
Unnecessary, 324
Urgency, 325 et seq.
Waiver of exemptions, 330

RULEMAKING, REQUIRED
Generally, 358
Abuse of discretion, 367
Chenery II rule, 363
Federal law, 363 et seq.
Model Act provision, 376
Retroactivity of rules, 366
State law, 369 et seq.

SCOPE OF JUDICIAL REVIEW
Generally, 534 et seq.
Application of law to fact, 571 et seq.
Arbitrary and capricious standard, 578 et seq.
Chevron rule, 90, 560 et seq., 565
Chevron rule, applications, 566
Chevron rule, commentary, 568
Clearly erroneous rule, 535, 541 et seq.
Constitutional fact, issues of, 550
Deference, weak, 564 et seq.
Deference, strong, 565 et seq., 569
Delegation to decide issue, 546, 563, 566, 576
Discretionary decisions in adjudication, scope of review, 578 et seq.
Discretionary decisions in rulemaking, scope of review, 592 et seq.
Findings of fact, variations, 535
Hard look review, 592 et seq.
Hard look review, commentary, 603 et seq.
Independent judgment, California rule, 553 et seq.
Jurisdictional fact, issues of, 433, 551
Legal interpretation, variations, 557 et seq.
Legislative history, 569
Narrowly defining agency's authority, 419

SCOPE OF JUDICIAL REVIEW—Cont'd
Penalties, judicial review of, 587
Predictive facts, review of, 605
Regulations, legal interpretations of, 569
Relevant factors, 587
Remedy, suspension or vacation of rule, 606 et seq.
States, review of rules, 608
Substantial evidence rule, 186, 535 et seq.
Substantial evidence and clearly erroneous, compared, 546
Substantial evidence and arbitrary-capricious, 607
Supreme Court review of lower court decisions, 549
Whole record, substantial evidence on the, 538

SEPARATION OF FUNCTIONS
Generally, 117
ALJ rule, 121
Agency head exception, 122
Command influence, 122
Due process, 119
Exceptions, federal, 122
Federal rules, 117 et seq.
State rules, 120

SEPARATION OF POWERS
Generally, 396 et seq.
Appointments power. See **EXECUTIVE CONTROL OVER AGENCY ACTION**
Checks and balances, 396 et seq.
Delegation of legislative power, see **DELEGATION**
Delegation of adjudicative power, see **DELEGATION**
Functionalist approach, 490
Independent agencies. See **INDEPENDENT AGENCIES**
Independent counsel, restriction on Presidential removal power, 478 et seq.
Legislative veto, 440 et seq.
Legislative veto, alternatives to, 456 et seq.
President's power vis-à-vis agencies, 495
Removal power. See **EXECUTIVE CONTROL OVER AGENCY ACTION**
Standing to seek judicial review, relationship of, 655 et seq., 665

SOCIAL SECURITY
Bias of ALJs, 153 et seq.
Disability, determination through rules, 100 et seq.
Hearings, disability cases, 52 et seq.
Non-acquiescence, 206
Nonlegislative rules, 354
Retroactive rules, 230 et. seq.

SOUTH CAROLINA
Finality of ALJ decisions, 162

SOVEREIGN IMMUNITY
Federal, abolished, 615

SOVEREIGN IMMUNITY—Cont'd
Federal Tort Claims Act, 622

STANDING TO SEEK JUDICIAL REVIEW
Generally, 647
Administrative Procedure Act provision, 649 et seq.
Associational standing, 662
Causation, 655 et seq.
Citizen suit provisions, 659 et seq., 665
Congressional standing, 666
Generalized grievances, 660 et seq.
History of standing doctrine, 648
Imminence of injury, 655 et seq.
Injury in fact test, 649 et seq.
Intervention, relation to standing, 168 et seq.
Merits, resolve standing question first, 664
Procedural injuries, 665
Public actions, 655 et seq.
Remediability, 655 et seq.
Standing of agencies, 654
Taxpayer suits, 666
Third party standing, 666
Zone of interest test, 649 et seq., 652 et seq.

STARE DECISIS
Generally, 208
Consistency, duty to explain, 208 et seq.

STAYS PENDING JUDICIAL REVIEW
Generally, 685
Rationale, 205
Reconsideration of precedents, 210
Standards for granting judicial stay, 685

STUDENTS, RIGHTS OF
Academic decision, 71
Admission to law school, right to hearing, 95 et seq.
Corporal punishment, 64 et seq.
Fifth amendment privilege, 176
Hearing, if no factual issues, 108
Right to counsel, 70
Rulemaking, required, 371, 373
Suspension from school, 46

SUNSHINE ACT
Generally, 525 et seq.
Agendas, publication of, 528
Costs and benefits, 526
Exemptions, 528
Meeting, definition of, 527
Sanctions for violation, 529

TENNESSEE
Delegation, federal government, 419

TEXAS
Delegation, private parties, 417
De novo trials, judicial review, 554
Ex parte contacts, 139
Regulatory analysis, 311

Sunshine Act, 528

UNFUNDED MANDATES REFORM ACT
Generally, 312

UTAH
Requirement of findings, 199

WASHINGTON
Appearance of bias, 130
Bias in rulemaking, 284
Rule, definition of, 225
Rulemaking, required, 376

WELFARE
Generally, 20
AFDC, 20, 72
Disability, 52
Effect of *Goldberg* decision, 31
Hearings, 22 et seq., 52 et seq.
Judicial review, California, 555 et seq.
Judicial review, Medicare decisions, 632 et seq.
Policy statement, exception to rulemaking, 346

WELFARE—Cont'd
Rulemaking, required, 369, 373
SSI, 20

WEST VIRGINIA
Legislative veto, 460
Rulemaking power, 461

WISCONSIN
Administrative law judge fact findings, 548
Suspensory legislative veto, 458
Scope of review of rules, 608

WORKERS' COMPENSATION
Burden of proof, 544
Clearly erroneous test, 541
Delegation, adjudicatory, 428, 433
Findings of fact, 199
Judicial review, findings of fact, 541
Judicial review, jurisdictional facts, 551
Tenure of adjudicators, 491

WYOMING
Governor's power to veto rules, 505
Rulemaking, required, 375

0–314–07206–3

90000